LINCOLN ARCHAEOLOGICAL STUDIES No. 10
GENERAL EDITORS: MICHAEL J JONES AND ALAN VINCE

# The City by the Pool

## Assessing the archaeology of the city of Lincoln

by
Michael J Jones, David Stocker and Alan Vince
with the assistance of John Herridge

edited by
David Stocker

CITY OF **Lincoln** COUNCIL

ENGLISH HERITAGE

Oxbow Books

*Lincoln Archaeological Studies are published by*
Oxbow Books, Park End Place, Oxford OX1 1HN

© *English Heritage, City of Lincoln Council and the Authors, 2003*

ISBN 1 84217 107 0


A CIP record for this book is available from the British Library



*This book is published with the aid of a grant
from English Heritage.*



*This book is available direct from*

Oxbow Books, Park End Place, Oxford OX1 1HN
(Phone 01865-241249; Fax 01865-794449)

*and*

The David Brown Book Company
PO Box 511, Oakville, CT 06779, USA
(Phone 860-945-9329; Fax 860-945-9468)

*or from our website*

www.oxbowbooks.com



*Printed in Great Britain at
The Short Run Press
Exeter*

# Contents

# Acknowledgements

Some form of 'archaeological assessment' of Lincoln was originally intended as part of English Heritage's efforts to generate coverage of such assessments nationally. This effort has been led by Roger Thomas and his assistance behind the scenes of this project is gratefully acknowledged. The idea of combining the synthetic element of the Lincoln Post-Excavation Programme with an attempt to explore new models for urban assessment was Chris Scull's and his help and support has been of the greatest value throughout our work. Graham Fairclough hosted the project within his team in English Heritage and, in addition to his wise advice throughout and his help with the preparation of Appendix 1, his valuable comments on Chapters 1 and 2 are gratefully acknowledged. Similarly valuable assistance has been given at various times by several other members of English Heritage staff, notably Peter Beacham, Andrew Brown, Martin Cherry, Glyn Coppack, Paul Everson, Jon Last, Alison Peach and Dave Went.

An early draft of this study was reviewed for English Heritage by Steve Roskams of the University of York. He provided incisive and detailed, yet supportive comments, which caused the whole enterprise to be re-thought from first principles. His help at that stage is gratefully acknowledged.

This unique study has been made possible by the vision of Keith Laidler, the City of Lincoln's Director of Planning, who made his department its home. Within the City of Lincoln Council our principal debt is to John Herridge, who was a member of the team drawn together to produce the *Assessment* and who made a significant written contribution to this book and to the GIS and data-base on the CD Rom known as LARA. Even this understates his contribution because it fell to John to make the computer system work and to provide information for the other authors. Most of all, perhaps, he produced the extraordinary survey of the industrial archaeology of Lincoln in 1999, which converted the original UAD into a platform suitable for a holistic assessment, and which supports Chapter 11. Arthur Ward, Head of Heritage at the City Council, also played a key role in the development of the project and undertook much of the administration associated with it. It could not have been brought to a conclusion so quickly without his cheerful assistance and hard work.

The post-excavation analysis of the 1972–87 excavations was a team effort that, from 1988, produced the excavation archive, drafts and publications on which the archaeological accounts in this volume have been based. During this time the composition of the team has changed and clearly some have contributed more or less than others, in time if nothing else. Even so, we feel it would be impossible to distinguish between the contributions made and the team is therefore listed in alphabetical order: Jeremy Ashbee, Lucy Bown, Prince Chitwood, Jane Cowgill, Maggi Darling, Lisa Donel, Mickey Doré, Pam Graves, Chris Guy, Rick Kemp, Caroline Kemp, Jen Mann, Paul Miles, Judy O'Neill, Helen Palmer-Brown, Barbara Precious, Kate Steane, Jane Young.

The work on the documentary history of later periods in Lincoln's history has benefited greatly through help from Christopher Johnson of Lincolnshire County Council Archives Office. His unrivalled knowledge of the documentary sources has been most valuable to us, as it has been to all historians working on the City. Paul Bischoff of the University of Oklahoma has generously shared his conclusions on the social and economic structure of the later medieval city and Alan Vince and David Stocker are grateful for the speed and care with which he has addressed our enquiries. Those familiar with previous work at Lincoln will recognise that the authors owe a heavy debt to the many colleagues, past and present, who have been responsible for recording and/or analysing the sites: Mark Blackburn, John Clipson, Christina Colyer, Barbara Crawford, Brian Gilmour, Lauren Gilmour, Christopher Guy, Robert Jones, John Magilton, Terry O'Connor, Dominic Perring, Richard Reece, David Roffe, Sally Scott and Richard Whinney, are among those who made major contributions. Many other specialists have provided reports on various artefacts and environmental samples that have also contributed to this volume: they are acknowledged in the appropriate place. Neil Faulkner, Mark Corney, John Wacher and Simon Esmonde Cleary have all made suggestions on individual points of interpretation in the sections on the Roman period.

The realisation of the GIS, with its linked data-base, which we eventually christened 'LARA' and which forms the core of the Lincoln Assessment, was developed by Dominic Powlesland, and his vision and help throughout the project is gratefully acknowledged. He

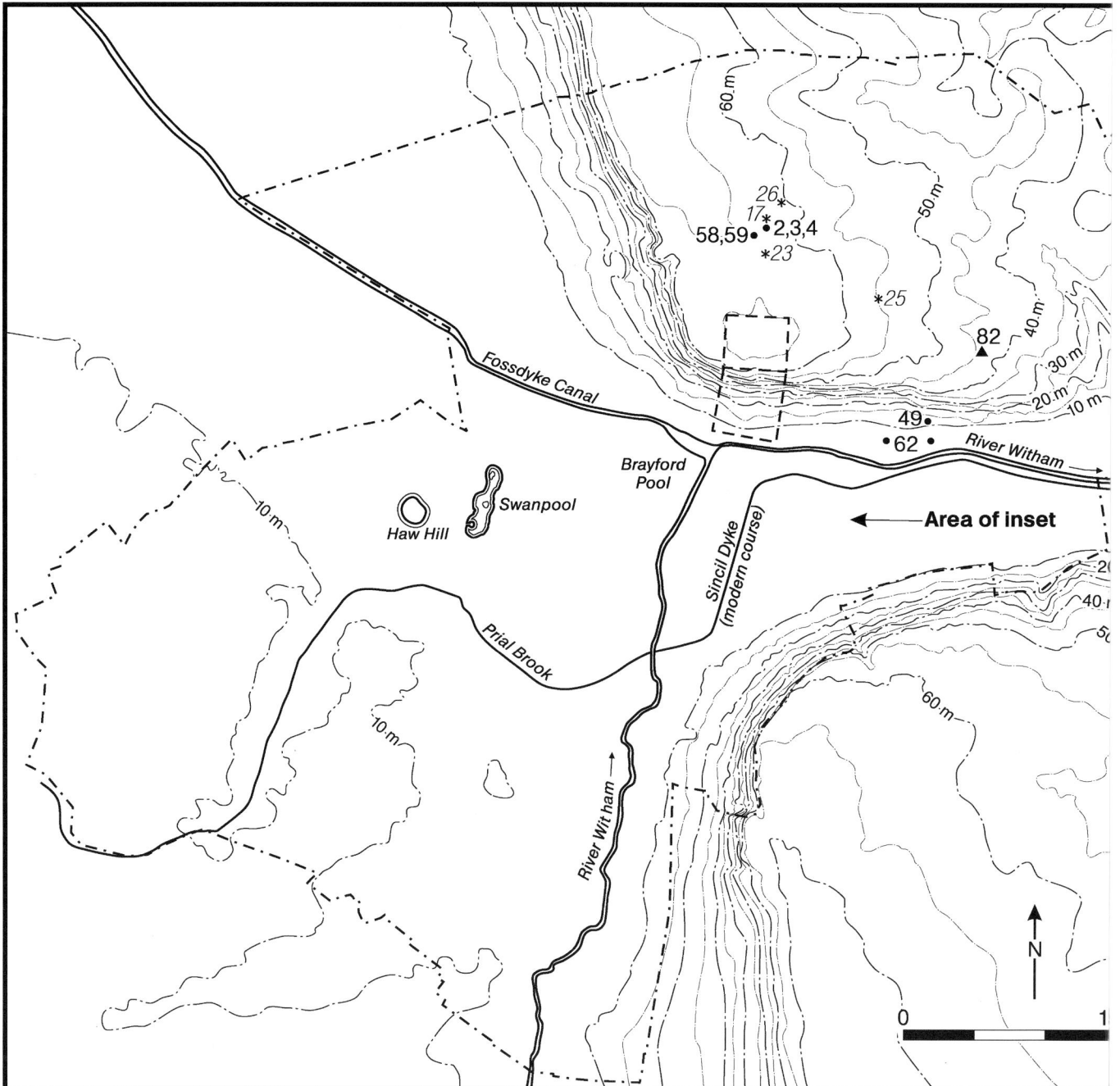

**• Excavation site Codes**

| | | | | |
|---|---|---|---|---|
| 1: BE 73 | 21: EB 66 | 41: LIN 73b | 61: P 70 | 81: WC 87 |
| 2: BGA 95 | 22: EB 80 | 42: LIN 73c | 62: PS 94 | ▲ 82: WEB 92 |
| 3: BGB 95 | 23: EBS 70 | 43: LIN 73e | 63: RLB 97 | ◆ 83: WEBA 93 |
| 4: BGC 96 | 24: F 72 | 44: LIN 73f | 64: SB 85 | 84: WF 89 |
| 5: BN 89 | 25: GC 90 | 45: LKG 91 | 65: SES 97 | 85: WN 87 |
| 6: BR 85 | 26: GL91 | 46: LKGA 92 | 66: SESA 97 | 86: WNW 88 |
| 7: BWE 82 | 27: GLA 94 | 47: LT 72 | 67: SH 74 | 87: WO 89 |
| 8: BWN 75 | 28: GLB 94 | 48: M 82 | 68: SLG 89 | 88: WP 71 |
| 9: CAS 91 | 29: H 83 | 49: MA 83 | 69: SM 76 | 89: WS 82 |
| 10: CAT 86 | 30: HG 72 | 50: MCH 84 | 70: SMG 82 | 90: WW 89 |
| 11: CFC 94 | 31: HSG 97 | 51: MGC 00 | 71: SP 72 | 91: Z 86 |
| 12: CL 85 | 32: KP 92 | 52: MH 77 | 72: SPM 83 | 92: ZE 87 |
| 13: CP 56 | 33: L 86 | 53: MW 79 | 73: SW 82 | 93: ZEA 95 |
| 14: CS 73 | 34: LA 85 | 54: MWS 83 | 74: TC 93 | 94: ZEB 95 |
| 15: CWG 82 | 35: LBP 72 | 55: NEB 96 | 75: TCA 94 | 95: ZWB 94 |
| 16: CWG 86 | 36: LC 84 | 56: NH 92 | 76: TG 89 | |
| 17: CY 89 | 37: LG 89 | 57: NHA 93 | 77: VC 93 | |
| 18: DM 72 | 38: LG 90 | 58: NP 93 | 78: W 73 | ▲ Symbols denote |
| 19: DT 74 | 39: LH 84 | 59: NPB 94 | 79: WB 76 | ◆ locations of linear |
| 20: DT 78 | 40: LIN 73a | ◇ 60: NSS 97 | 80: WB 80 | ◇ watching briefs |

**∗ Observation num[...]**

*1: ON 1a*
*2: ON 10*
*3: ON 11*
*4: ON 27*
*5: ON 57*
*6: ON 77*
*7: ON 83*
*8: ON 101*
*9: ON 105*
*10: ON 128*
*11: ON 204*
*12: ON 208*
*13: ON 217*
*14: ON 232*

**Key**

Lincoln City Counc[...]
Local Authority bou[...]

Lines of Roman Cit[...]

*Fig. 1.1. Locations of major archaeological excavations and interventions in the city since 1945, against the modern [...] ways and street network (sources, Vince and Jones 1990 and others – drawn by Dave Watt, copyright English Herita[...]*

# Summaries

## English

This book integrates the results of two major programmes of work. It is the first attempt to write a complete archaeology of Lincoln from prehistory to 1945, based on more than a hundred publicly-funded excavations and building surveys undertaken between c.1945 and c.2000, and it is also the next step forward in the city's heritage management following completion of an Urban Archaeological Database in 1999. Combining these two strands of work has allowed us to produce the first-ever public statement about the character of the whole of the city's archaeology, and to present this characterisation to the wider community and to the general public in an accessible manner. It provides the fullest synthesis available of what we know about Lincoln's long past as a major city and regional capital, and it gives us the foundation for many directions of future research. One important and innovative function, envisaged from the outset, is as the archaeological framework for the City Council's continuing discussion with its citizens about how Lincoln's heritage should be managed in future. The volume includes a Geographic Information System (GIS) and a relational data-base known as LARA (the Lincoln Archaeological Research Assessment), supplied as a CD-Rom and intended to be used in conjunction with the volume.

The city revealed by this work, by standing back from the detail of excavations (now being presented in other volumes in this series), is markedly different from the one we thought we knew. We have suggested, for the first time, the presence of a major ritual causeway of the late Bronze and Iron Age, and outlined the extent to which ritual monuments also contributed to the character of Roman Lincoln. We have hypothesised a Middle Saxon ecclesiastical and market site, at what later became Monks Abbey, and we have shown for the first time that High Medieval Lincoln consisted of a ring of markets laid out around a reserved enclosure housing the religious and secular aristocracy. We have also produced, again for the first time, a credible sequence for the topographical development of the settlement in the valley floor, which (as well as defining a new topography) relocates Lincoln's docklands and casts some doubt on the city's image as a major port. Our researches have revealed unexpected evidence for an urban concentration of early Dissenting communities, and finally, bringing the story up to date, we have noted that the archaeology suggests that industrial Lincoln was an entirely new city, but one which was not inaugurated until the 1840s – a century later than the date usually given. Although Lincoln's development has been punctuated by periods of extraordinary economic expansion (in the 4th century, the 9th–12th centuries and between 1850 and 1900), nevertheless the 'City by the Pool' was a major religious centre long before the Roman invasion, and from bronze-age shamans to early Baptists, people have always been attracted here for spiritual as well as mundane purposes.

## German

Dieses Buch integriert die Ergebnisse zweier größerer Arbeitsprogramme. Es handelt sich um den ersten Versuch, die Archäologie der Stadt Lincoln von der Vorgeschichte bis 1945 umfassend darzustellen, und bildet seit der Fertigstellung einer städtischen archäologischen Datenbank (*Urban Archaeological Database*) 1999 einen weiteren Schritt in der boden- und baudenkmalpflegerischen Tätigkeit der Stadt. Die Erkenntnisse basieren auf über hundert mit öffentlichen Geldern finanzierten Ausgrabungen und Bauaufnahmen, die *ca.* 1945 – 2000 durchgeführt wurden. Die Kombination dieser beiden Arbeitsprogramme hat es uns zum allerersten Male ermöglicht, ein Bild der Archäologie der gesamten Stadt zu entwerfen und dieses Bild der Fachwelt und der Öffentlichkeit zugänglich zu machen. Das Werk bietet die bisher vollständigste Synthese dessen, was wir über die lange Geschichte Lincolns als einer bedeutenden Stadt und regionalen Metropole wissen, und bietet eine Grundlage für vielfältige künftige Forschungen. Eine wichtige und innovative Funktion, die von Anfang an geplant war, ist die Rolle des Werkes als eine Diskussionsgrundlage für den fortgeführten Dialog der Stadtverwaltung mit ihren Bürgern darüber, wie das archäologische Erbe Lincolns in Zukunft verwaltet werden soll. Dem Band auf CD-Rom beigefügt ist ein *Geographic Information System* (GIS) und eine relationale Datenbank bekannt als LARA (*Lincoln Archaeological*

*Research Assessment*), deren Benutzung in Kombination mit dem gedruckten Werk gedacht ist.

Das Bild der Stadt, das sich im Abstand vom Detail der einzelnen Ausgrabungen (vorgelegt in anderen Bänden dieser Serie) ergeben hat, unterscheidet sich in bemerkenswerter Weise von dem, was wir zu kennen glaubten. Es zeichnet sich zum ersten Male ein größeres rituelles Erdwerk der späten Bronzezeit und der Eisenzeit ab. Zudem waren wir in der Lage zu umreißen, welche Rolle Ritualbauten im römerzeitlichen Lincoln spielten. Wir stellen die Hypothese auf, daß Monks Abbey in Lincoln einen mittelsächsischen Vorläufer in Form einer Kirche und eines Marktes besaß, und wir können zum ersten Male zeigen, daß das hochmittelalterliche Lincoln aus einem Ring von Märkten bestand, der sich um ein umfriedetes Gelände zog, das der kirchlichen und säkularen Aristokratie vorbehalten war. Zudem konnten wir, wiederum zum ersten Male, eine glaubwürdige Sequenz für die topographische Entwicklung der Besiedelung der Talsohle erstellen, die nicht nur eine neue Topographie definiert, sondern auch das Hafenviertel verlegt und die Rolle Lincolns als einen bedeutenden Hafen in Frage stellt. Unsere Forschungen haben unerwartete Nachweise für eine städtische Konzentration von frühen Gemeinden sogenannter *Dissenters* erbracht und schließlich, im industriellen Zeitalter angelangt, haben wir feststellen können, daß die Archäologie darauf hinweist, daß das industrielle Lincoln eine völlig neue Stadt bildete, die jedoch nicht vor den 1840ern gegründet wurde – ein Jahrhundert später, als üblicherweise angegeben wird. Obwohl die Entwicklung Lincolns von Perioden außerordentlicher wirtschaftlicher Ausdehnung durchsetzt war (im 4. Jahrhundert, dem 9. bis 12. Jahrhundert und zwischen 1850 und 1900), war die „Stadt am See" trotzdem ein wichtiges religiöses Zentrum lange vor der römischen Eroberung. Von bronzezeitlichen Schamanen bis zu frühen Baptisten wurden zu allen Zeiten Menschen mit spirituellen und profanen Beweggründen von diesem Ort angezogen.

## French

Cet ouvrage intègre les résultats de deux programmes de travail majeurs. Il s'agit du premier essai de synthèse archéologique sur Lincoln, de la préhistoire jusqu'à 1945, synthèse fondée sur plus d'une centaine de fouilles et d'analyses du bâti subventionnées par des fonds publics et entreprises entre environ 1945 et 2000. Il s'agit aussi d'une étape supplémentaire dans la gestion du patrimoine de la ville après l'achèvement en 1999 d'une base de données archéologiques. L'association de ces deux programmes a permis de produire le premier bilan jamais publié sur Lincoln et de le présenter à la communauté scientifique et au grand public d'une manière accessible. Il fournit la synthèse la plus complète de ce que nous savons du long passé historique de Lincoln en tant que grande ville et capitale régionale et il pose les bases de nombreuses pistes de recherche pour l'avenir.

L'une des fonctions majeures et novatrices de ce travail, envisagée dès l'origine, est de fournir un cadre permettant la poursuite du dialogue entre la municipalité de Lincoln et les citoyens en matière de gestion du patrimoine. Le volume comporte un Système d'Information Géographique et une base de données dénommée LARA (Lincoln Archaeological Research Assessment), fournis sous la forme d'un CD-Rom et destinés à être utilisés en association avec cet ouvrage.

La ville révélée par ce travail, qui ne fait pas état du détail des fouilles en cours de publication dans d'autres volumes de la même collection, est nettement différente de celle que nous pensions connaître. Pour la première fois est suggérée l'existence d'un important passage à fonction rituelle, à la fin de l'Age du Bronze et à l'Age du Fer, de même qu'est souligné le poids des monuments religieux dans la formation urbaine à l'époque romaine. A l'époque saxonne moyenne, le site qui devint plus tard celui de Monks Abbey devait avoir une fonction ecclésiastique et commerciale, tandis qu'au Moyen Age central Lincoln consistait en un ensemble de marchés entourant un enclos réunissant les habitations ecclésiastiques et aristocratiques. C'est également la première fois qu'est élaborée une chronologie plausible pour le développement de l'habitat dans la vallée, ce qui aboutit à une nouvelle topographie, notamment pour la localisation des installations portuaires de Lincoln dont l'importance en tant que port est à minimiser. L'enquête a aussi livré des informations insoupçonnées sur la forte concentration des communautés religieux minoritaires (« Dissenters ») à l'époque moderne et, pour finir, les données archéologiques montrent que la ville fut largement transformée à l'époque industrielle mais seulement à partir des années 1840, soit un siècle après la date traditionnellement admise. Bien que le développement de Lincoln ait été marqué par des périodes de forte expansion économique (au 4e siècle, entre le 9e et le 12e siècle et pendant les années 1850–1900), la ville fut un centre religieux d'importance majeure bien avant la conquête romaine et des chamans de l'Age du Bronze jusqu'aux premiers baptistes les hommes y ont été attirés pour des raisons spirituelles autant que pratiques.

# 1. Introduction

## Michael J Jones and David Stocker

'... it is impossible that everything removable should of a sudden be put in any book. Every age sees something more than another, and every year almost some monuments are digg'd up out of the earth some where or other that was not discovered before, so that it is impossible that such a book as it should be perfect ...' (de la Pryme 1870, 60)

Archaeological remains in Lincoln, especially of the Roman period, have always been the subject of interest, both scholarly and popular. This should come as no surprise. The historical importance of the city and the very visible survival of its larger structures, notably the Cathedral and Castle, as well as Roman and medieval defensive walls and gates, have meant that the citizens have always conducted their lives against the backdrop of the past (Plate 5.1). We might think that intense interest in the city's past is a recent phenomenon, but we can now suggest that it might be traced back to the very origins of the city. The foundation of the Roman fortress here, in the mid 1st century, can now be seen as the conquerors' response to the prehistoric significance of the place, and for each generation it has been the same. Bede set his account of Paulinus' conversion of the men of Lindsey against a Roman backdrop, Henry of Huntingdon's Anglo-Norman bishops parade through the same Roman remains and, in the 13th century, the plot of the *Lay of Havelock the Dane* was dependent on the antiquity of Lincoln Castle. John Leland and Celia Fiennes, who visited in the 1540s and in 1697 respectively, were struck by the abundance of ancient buildings, amongst which the people lived, and Daniel Defoe's famous conclusion (published in 1724–6) was that Lincoln:

'is an ancient, ragged, decay'd and still decaying city; it is so full of the ruins of monasteries and religious houses, that in short, the very barns, stables, out-houses, and as they shew'd, some of the very hogstyes, were built churchfashion' (1925–6)

We live in a country whose contemporary self-image is so intimately linked with its history that T S Eliot's poem about national salvation, *Little Gidding*, concludes that '... History is now and in England' (canto V). Yet even in such a country, Lincoln's past has always been very much part of the present, in the imagination as well as in the round of daily life.

From our perspective, in the 21st century, it sometimes seems that the development of interest in the city's past began during the Enlightenment, but through studies like the one which follows we can see that Lincoln citizens have always responded to the setting bequeathed to them by previous generations. That is not to say, of course, that earlier generations of citizens have always cherished the city's history and its monuments. The same Enlightenment, which saw early antiquarians like William Stukeley write about the city at length, also saw the demolition of much of the surviving Roman city wall and the wholesale removal of Roman and medieval gatehouses in the name of progress. Although Stukeley sketched the Roman north gate to the Upper City in 1722, its companion on the east side of the Upper City, also partly Roman in its fabric, was demolished in the following decade to give carts better access. The story of Lincolnians' relationship with their archaeological monuments is not straight-forward, then, and it is certainly not the case that recognition has ensured survival (although, as in the case of William Stukeley, it might have prompted 'emergency recording'). Even so, in order for such treasures to stand any chance of survival in the modern world, it is an essential first step that they be recognised and that their significance is understood.

This is the fundamental aim of the *Lincoln Assessment*. It is an attempt to 'sum-up' existing knowledge of the city's archaeology and to make it accessible for professional townscape managers as well as for the academic and general public alike. But that is not to say that this account is definitive. The Lincolnshire antiquarian Abraham de la Pryme (1671–1704), who is quoted above, knew that all interpretations of the past are provisional and will vary both according to the material we have to hand, and to our individual perspectives. Provision has been made for this volume to be revisited regularly over the coming years and revised in the light of new discoveries and changing academic and social priorities – and that is how it should be.

This *Assessment* is primarily concerned, of course, with archaeology rather than with documentary history. The relationship between these two topics is complex and frequently problematic. Fortunately the distinction which posits that history deals with the past as it has been recorded in written sources, whilst archaeology deals with the past in so far as it is legible through material remains, is widely held – and it is the position adopted here. It is important to appreciate, then, that the *Assessment* is not a complete history of Lincoln, rather it is an account of Lincoln's past told through the interpretation of material remains. We can only produce this account, of course, because the documentary history of Lincoln has already been so marvellously dealt with by earlier generations of scholars. Pre-eminent amongst these is Sir Francis Hill, whose four-volume history of the city (1948, 1956, 1966, 1974) represents the most extraordinary achievement; one which allows us to set our conclusions based on the material remains against a persuasive and complete narrative. Hill was not working in isolation. Lincoln (and Lincolnshire) has been fortunate in attracting the interest of a whole 'school' of historical scholarship based in the County Archives Office and its prede-cessors. The first 'professor' of this school was the redoubtable Canon Foster (1866–1935), whose energy underpinned both the Diocesan Archives and the Lincoln Record Society and who brought-on the remarkable group of female scholars, Dorothy Owen (née Williamson – 1920–2002), Joan Varley (1904–2002) and, particularly, Kathleen Major (1906–2000). Neither Sir Francis Hill nor this *Assessment* could have managed without Miss Major's exemplary completion of Canon Foster's edition of the Cathedral cartulary, the *Registrum Antiquissimum* (ed. Foster 1931, 1933, 1935; ed. Major and Foster 1937; ed. Major 1940, 1950, 1953, 1958, 1968, 1973), which in its 2980 items depicts the development of the medieval city in the most extraordinary detail.

We have relied heavily on other historians as well; Prof. Paul Bischoff, of the University of Oklahoma, undertook crucial work on the city's medieval econ-omy in the 1970s, explaining for the first time the collapse of the city's cloth trade in the late 13th and early 14th centuries and describing the economic catastrophe which ensued (Bischoff 1975). In the 1980s the major contribution to the documentary history of the city was the completion of the *English Place-Names Society* volume (Cameron 1985). To archaeologists, place-names are, of course, of the greatest help and importance, and the late Ken Cameron's detailed and painstaking account has been an invaluable source for the medieval and post-medieval parts of this *Assessment*. More recently, Jim Johnston has begun to publish his analytical accounts of 17th-century Lincoln

inventories, which (as Maurice Barley – himself a Lincolnian – showed us a generation ago) represent another important source of information for those interested in material culture (ed. Johnston 1991).

Whilst strides were made with the documentary history of the city in the central part of the 20th century, progress with understanding the city's material past had been slow, to say the least. Although many significant finds were made during the re-development of the city in the late 18th and 19th centuries, they had often been poorly recorded and important artefacts were frequently lost. Some notable collections were gathered, including that of Edward Trollope, which was later donated to the British Museum, and that compiled by the Cathedral clergy, which was donated to the City Council in 1906 to form the core of the City and County Museum (Smith 1909a; 1909b; 1929). Even so, there was still no comprehensive or scholarly published account of the city's antiquities.

The establishment of the Museum in 1906 set a positive ambition for the new century and provided both a home for the public collections and a base for their study, and finally the first coherent essay on the Roman period in Lincoln was produced by F T Baker in 1938. Baker's energetic researches also attracted the interest of scholars of international standing and he contributed much detail to Ian Richmond's 1946 account of the Roman city (produced for the Royal Archaeological Institute's summer meeting in Lincoln in that year). Moreover, in an adjacent paper Richmond was able to compare the four British *coloniae*, noting that 'Roman Lincoln offers a glimpse of flourishing Roman urban culture in imported purity such has not yet emerged anywhere else on British provincial soil'. Such comments illustrate, nicely, the imperial outlook of archaeologists of the period and have set the tone for much writing on Roman Lincoln since.

Even so, Richmond's 1946 essay has yet to be surpassed – although, as Richmond himself would surely have expected, some of his conjectures have been superseded by subsequent discoveries. The Royal Archaeological Institute met in Lincoln in the atmos-phere of enthusiasm surrounding the newly-formed (1945) Lincoln Archaeological Research Committee. Over the subsequent quarter-century, its various excavation directors – Graham Webster, Hugh Thomp-son, Dennis Petch and Ben Whitwell – achieved a number of goals; the most notable being a definition of the defensive sequence of the fortress and upper *colonia* (Webster 1949; Thompson 1956; Petch 1960; Thompson and Whitwell 1973; Jones 1980). There was also important work on the possible source of the aqueduct (Thompson 1955), on a public fountain in the Lower City (Thompson 1956), on the public baths, and the pottery kilns in the Swanpool area.

Much of this work on the Roman period in the city was, frankly, at the expense of the archaeology of later periods. As was the case in towns across the country, excavations in Lincoln tended to dismiss the medieval

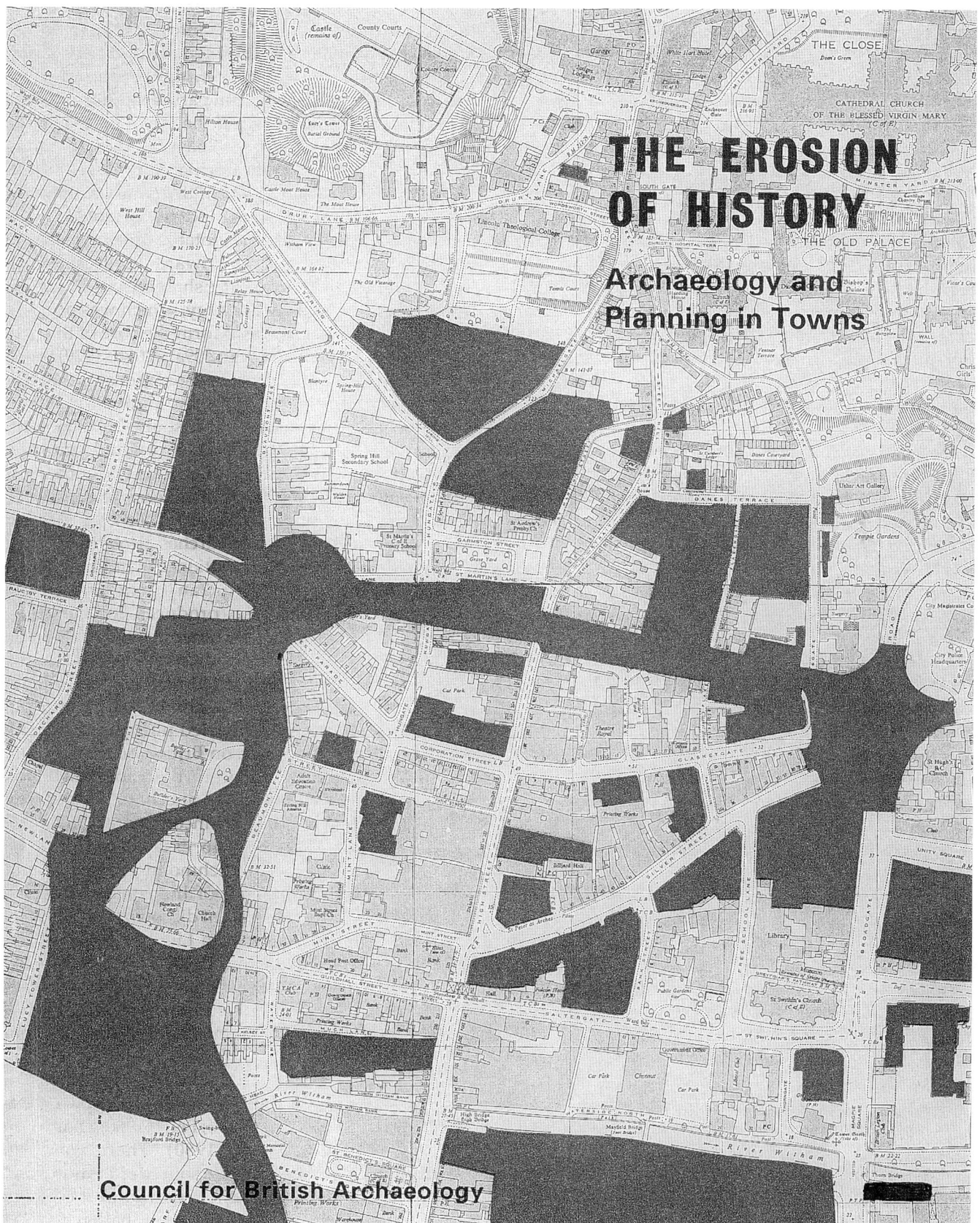

*Fig. 1.2. The scale of development proposed in central Lincoln in 1971. At that time it was presumed that the archaeology of the shaded areas would be destroyed, and this loss was thought so dramatic that the map was used on the cover of the influential report on 'rescue' archaeology in towns nationally,* The Erosion of History *(ed. Heighway 1972) (copyright, Council for British Archaeology).*

and later urban layers as 'overburden'. It is even difficult (though not impossible), for example, to ascertain where the huge masonry walls of the medieval upper east gate lay, even though the site was largely excavated in 1959–66. Although the Cathedral had attracted many generations of scholars to work on its fabric, and there had been a major excavation in the choir in the 1880s directed by the indefatigable Precentor, Edmund Venables (Venables 1885–6), forensic research of a recognisably modern kind was not undertaken until the remarkable archaeologist and architectural historian John Bilson became interested in the Anglo-Norman church between 1909 and 1911 (Bilson 1911). But very few discoveries of the medieval period came from the redevelopment work in the city more widely in the first half of the 20th century and the first excavation to make a systematic exploration of medieval deposits did not come until Graham Webster's work on the east side of Flaxengate in 1945–8 (Coppack 1973).

It was hoped, however, that the formation of an archaeological 'unit' in 1970 in response to sweeping urban development schemes would raise the standard of archaeological work and the rate of recovery of information, particularly about the medieval city. The 'unit' was initially established under Ms Christina Colyer with a constrained brief to undertake work on the western defences of the Lower City at The Park and West Parade (ed. Jones 1999), but in the autumn of 1972 the Lincoln Archaeological Trust was established under the chairmanship of Sir Francis Hill and with considerable financial support from Central Government and a much wider remit. Its brief, much influenced by the Winchester Research Unit, was to capitalise on archaeological opportunities afforded by redevelopment in all parts of the city – which was becoming intensive in the early 1970s (Fig. 1.2). It was a sign of the times that the unit had a chronological ceiling of '*c*.1800'. Perhaps this was because industrial archaeology was already established in the city through the energy and commitment of Catherine Wilson and the Industrial Archaeology Committee of the Society for Lincolnshire History and Archaeology (founded before the parent body in 1965–6). It may also reflect the fact, however, that in 1970, industrial archaeology was still not thought to be a fit topic for professional research. The fact that much industrial archaeology was considered to be beyond the new Trust's brief meant that only modest recording has been undertaken, whilst Lincoln's impressive and

**1) The Archaeology of Lincoln Series, published by the Council for British Archaeology in London and York.**

Volume VI/1   M Blackburn, C Colyer and M Dolley, *Early Medieval Coins from Lincoln and its Shire c.770–1100*, 1983.

Volume VI/2   J E Mann and R Reece, *Roman coins from Lincoln 1970–1979*, 1983.

Volume VII/1   M J Jones *et al.*, *The Defences of the Upper Roman Enclosure*, 1980.

Volume VII/2   M J Jones (ed.), *The Defences of the Lower City. Exacavations at The Park and West Parade 1970–2 and a Discussion of other sites excavated up to 1994*, 1999.

Volume IX/1   D Perring, *Early Medieval Occupation at Flaxengate Lincoln*, 1981.

Volume XI/1   R H Jones, *Medieval Houses at Flaxengate Lincoln*, 1980.

Volume XII/1   D Stocker *et al.*, *St Mary's Guildhall, Lincoln. The Survey and Excavation of a Medieval Building Complex*, 1991.

Volume XIII/1   B J J Gilmour and D A Stocker, *St Mark's Church and Cemetery*, 1986.

Volume XIV/1   J E Mann, *Early Medieval Finds from Flaxengate I: Objects of antler, bone, stone, horn, ivory, amber, and jet*, 1982.

Volume XV/1   J E Mann, *Clay Tobacco Pipes from Excavations in Lincoln 1970–74*, 1977.

Volume XVI/1   M J Darling, *A Group of Late Roman Pottery from Lincoln*, 1977.

Volume XVI/2, M J Darling *et al.*, *Roman Pottery from the Upper Defences*, 1984.

Volume XVII/1 L Adams, *Medieval Pottery from Broadgate East Lincoln 1973*, 1977.

Volume XVII/2 L Adams Gilmour *et al.*, *Early Medieval Pottery from Flaxengate, Lincoln*, 1988.

Volume XVII/3 P Miles, J Young and J Wacher, *A Late Saxon Kiln Site at Silver Street, Lincoln*, 1989.

Volume XVIII/1T O'Connor with M Wilkinson, *Animal Bones from Flaxengate, Lincoln c. 870–1500*, 1982.

**2) The Lincoln Archaeological Studies Series, published by Oxbow Books in Oxford**

No. 1   A G Vince (ed.), *Pre-Viking Lindsey*, 1993.

No. 2   K Steane *et al.*, *The Archaeology of Wigford and the Brayford Pool*, 2001.

No. 3   K Steane *et al.*, *The Archaeology of the Upper City and Adjacent Suburbs*, 2003.

No. 4   K Steane *et al.*, *The Archaeology of the Lower City and Adjacent Suburbs*, forthcoming.

No. 5   K M Dobney, S D Jaques and B G Irving, *Of Butchers and Breeds. Report on vertebrate remains from various sites in the City of Lincoln*, 1996

No. 6   M Darling and B Precious, *Corpus of Roman Pottery from Lincoln*, forthcoming.

No. 7   J Young and A Vince *et al.*, *Corpus of Anglo-Saxon and Medieval Pottery from Lincoln*, forthcoming.

No. 8   J Price *et al.*, *Corpus of Roman Glass from Lincoln*, forthcoming.

No. 9   J E Mann *et al.*, *Finds from the Well at St Paul-in-the-Bail*, forthcoming.

No. 10 M J Jones, D Stocker and A G Vince, *The City by the Pool, Assessing the Archaeology of The City of Lincoln*, 2003.

*Figure 1.3. Publications in* The Archaeology of Lincoln *and* Lincoln Archaeological Studies Series.

singular industrial heritage was largely erased between *c.*1960 and 2000.

Meanwhile, of course, the city's Roman past was receiving greater attention than ever (e.g. Wacher 1975) and there has been a constant flow of articles and books by Michael Jones since the late 1970s, summarised in a popular book based partly on work undertaken for this *Assessment* (2002). Roman Lincoln is now one of the most intensively studied cities of the period in Britain, but improvements in our understanding of the Anglo-Saxon, medieval and later periods have been equally dramatic. The significance of the Danish settlement and the urban revival of the 10th and 11th centuries have been realised, and studied, and work has been undertaken on several churches, friaries and major secular buildings and sites. But ironically perhaps, the single most important contribution to the archaeology of buildings of the later medieval period in the city came not from the large professional archaeological 'unit', but from the efforts of a group of amateurs and professionals meeting under the auspices of the Lincoln Civic Trust and with the inspiration and guidance of Kathleen Major and Stanley Jones. This was the *Survey of Ancient Houses* (S R Jones *et al.*, 1984, 1987, 1992, 1996), a remarkable enterprise which sought to match the incomparable documentation for the houses in the Upper City with a complete survey of surviving fabrics. Although published and distributed modestly, this is a study of international significance and is in no way inferior to the impressive studies of domestic architecture in French cities like Cluny (Garrigou Grandchamp *et al.* 1997).

The new archaeological unit dug 67 large sites between 1972 and 1987 (eds. Vince and Jones 1990), and has investigated another 10 or so subsequently. These major excavations have been supplemented by several hundred small-scale investigations and watching briefs. The site codes for these sites are given in brackets throughout the following text and the locations of the major sites are planned against the modern city street plan in Fig. 1.1. The large excavations of the 1970s and 1980s cast a long shadow. Although most of the individual sites have now been published, either in the *Archaeology of Lincoln* series or in its successor, *Lincoln Archaeological Studies* (Fig. 1.3), no attempt had been made to collect the enormous wealth of new information – the fruit of this 'golden age' of excavation and building survey – together. This volume is an attempt to do just this, by bringing together the work of the various groups and individuals involved in past work. It is offered both in grateful recognition of all the hard work already undertaken and – as past scholars would have wished – as a new starting-point for future work by coming generations of students of Lincoln's archaeology.

# 2. Urban archaeological assessment in Lincoln – introducing 'LARA'.
# The scope and content of the present volume

## David Stocker

When it was founded in 1984, English Heritage saw the need to consolidate the gains made during thirty years of state-funded urban excavation. Accordingly, as an important priority, it commissioned a series of pilot studies aimed at exploring the management of urban archaeology in England. These studies (at York – Ove Arup 1991; Durham – Lowther *et al.* 1993 and Cirencester – Darvill and Gerrard 1994) were not conducted in a vacuum. With the introduction of a Planning Policy Guidance Note by Central Government in November 1990 (PPG 16), it became imperative that urban archaeological research was fed directly into the planning process to inform decision-making by planning authorities. English Heritage conceived this as a three-stage process (English Heritage 1992). First, it was argued, the enormous quantity of data from previous excavations, finds and other work had to be regularised and made easily accessible. Then that data needed professional 'assessment' to make it comprehensible and to set the results within a proper research framework. And finally it was thought that a 'strategy' phase would be required to ensure that the archaeological research framework was properly embedded in the planning policy for the city in question. This strategy phase was always intended to be intimately connected with the generation of strategic plans and with approval by elected members – at the time a role played the Local Plan consultation and approval process.

Of the three pilots, the York and Durham studies attempted to accommodate all three stages in single projects. They contained both a collection and organisation of data, an archaeological 'assessment' of that data, and proposals directing future archaeological research within the existing planning system. On the other hand, the Cirencester project was much the most theoretically driven of the three pilots, and the publication focused more exclusively on the 'assessment' stage. The data on which that study was based had been collected in an earlier Urban Archaeological Database (UAD) project, and furthermore it was argued that the management of urban archaeology required innovative designation systems beyond the scope of the Local Plan system. The Cirencester study concluded that a system of urban 'monuments' could be defined, based on ideas which had been developed (but not implemented) for English Heritage's newly-devised Monument Protection Programme, and it looked forward to a time when some new form of designation would be applied to such monuments. The Cirencester report is a remarkable piece of theoretical research, still standing alone in the field after ten years, and it represents a bold attempt to propose archaeological priorities to the planners.

By contrast the York Assessment put the emphasis less on the definition of 'monuments' and more on the formulation of research questions. In a piece of thinking, which was developed and elaborated in Martin Carver's influential book, *Arguments in Stone* (1993), the York study toyed with a theoretical position that (in its most extreme form) stated that it was only worth excavating or preserving urban sites where both a worthwhile research agenda and the survival of suitable deposits had been documented in advance. The City of York has subsequently paid great attention to the construction of a city-wide 'deposit model' (which attempts to document deposit quality), although a unified research agenda has not yet been forthcoming.

The current *Assessment* has adopted some of the ideas brought forward at Cirencester, but crucially, instead of trying to identify monuments on which some form of designation will be imposed, it was intended from the outset at Lincoln to insert archaeological research priorities directly into the planning process. In this respect our work in Lincoln is responding to the challenge Carver issued, to use the inherent value and interest of research questions to drive the management of urban archaeological deposits and structures.

In the current environment, rightly, heritage management lays great stress on the definition of *everyone's* heritage and on the professional's responsibility to inform all citizens of the heritage within which they live (English Heritage 2000). All our experience tells us that, once people are told about it, the historic environment surrounding them is apprcciated by everyone. Furthermore, once people know why their communities look the way they do, it is argued, they will press for conservation, regeneration and re-development schemes which incorporate and respect the identity of their historic buildings and archaeology. As we write, such thinking (about informing the electorate and gaining its consent for development control decisions) is at the heart of changes being incorporated into local planning systems. The Lincoln *Assessment* has been produced with these changes in mind – it is intended to be an easy-to-use information system, which not only makes technical information accessible to the general public, but which also provides a basic platform on which other planning functions, such as development control and strategic planning can be constructed.

It was fortunate that the new GIS (Geographical Information Systems) technology began to filter into local authority planning departments just at the time that English Heritage began its ambitious urban archaeology programmes, in pursuit of the policies set out in its 1992 statement. GIS held out the possibility of being able to map and interrogate spatially the com-plexities of archaeological data in urban contexts, and Lincoln was amongst the first local authorities to be grant aided by English Heritage to generate such a GIS-based UAD. The Lincoln UAD (based in the City Council's Planning Department) uses a programme called G-Sys which connects the complex data-bases generated by urban excavations to detailed mapping systems. It is based around the summary reports of about 50 excavations undertaken in Lincoln since the Second World War, but it also has incidental infor-mation from many casual observations and watching briefs. Although, like the original brief of the Lincoln unit, the UAD originally stopped at *c.*1750, an im-portant enhancement – produced by John Herridge of the City Council (Herridge 1999) – now extends its range up to at least 1945. The Lincoln UAD, like all of its contemporaries, was envisaged as a method of feeding archaeological information into the planning process. At the last count it permits non-specialists to access 11,823 items of information ranging from excavation contexts to antiquarian notes.

Such a large body of information, however, required considerable processing, by professionals, before it could be translated into planning strategy and con-ditions on individual applications. By 2000, as well as the UAD being complete, the preparation of draft reports on many of the excavated sites dug between 1972 and 1987 was well in hand (Steane *et al.* 2001; Steane *et al.* 2003). These reports on individual sites are prefaced with brief introductions setting them in context within the city, and, more than anything else, they pointed to the need for a comprehensive treatment of all the archaeology of the city. There was a wide-spread feeling, amongst both Lincoln City Council staff, English Heritage officers and the academic mentor – Steve Roskams of York University – that the complex

meanings of these excavated sites could only be recovered when discussed within an holistic overview of the development of the city. In 2000, therefore, the two strands of UAD and site reports were combined. In order to both complete the account of the exca-vations undertaken between 1972 and 1987 and to provide the next step in integrating the archaeological research agenda into planning policy, an assessment of the archaeological knowledge of the entire city was required. This step would not only allow the excavation reports to be seen in their spatial and temporal context, but it would also provide the first ever articulation of a complete archaeological research agenda for the city.

Now known as LARA (Lincoln Archaeological Research Assessment), the particular assessment structure developed to accommodate these ambitions is straightforward and the theoretical framework underpinning it was discussed and established in a series of seminars between 2000 and 2002. A copy of the final version of the paper arising from these seminars is included here as Appendix I. First the various phases of activity in the city's history have been divided into chronological blocks which we have called 'Eras' (Fig. 2.1). These Eras are not just con-ventional historical or convenient period divisions, they are an analytical tool to shape understanding and perception; a preliminary (and slightly crude) attempt to divide up the city's material culture into coherent groups. They can be seen as the temporal equivalent of character areas in *Historic Landscape Characterisation* methodologies, that emphasise general similarities rather than promoting differences. The Era structure creates a measure of homogeneity that can support synthesis, overall judgements, predictive modelling and planning decisions (Fairclough 2002; Fairclough *et al.* 2002).

Within each Era it is considered that the material culture of the city is markedly different in character both from what went before and what came after. So we have a brief Era of Roman military occupation (no more than 60 years long), which was clearly different from the Prehistoric Era which went before, but is also quite distinct in many ways – for example in terms of

| Era No | Era Name | Era dates |
|---|---|---|
| *Era 5)* | *The Prehistoric Era* | – from the Mesolithic period to *c.* AD43. |
| *Era 6)* | *The Roman Military Era* | – from *c.* AD43 to *c.* AD90. |
| *Era 7)* | *The Roman* Colonia *Era* | – from *c.* AD90 to the early 5th century. |
| *Era 8)* | *The Anglo-Saxon Era* | – from the early 5th century to the late 9th century. |
| *Era 9)* | *The High Medieval Era* | – from the late 9th century to *c.*1350. |
| *Era 10)* | *The Early Modern Era* | – from *c.*1350 to *c.*1750. |
| *Era 11)* | *The Industrial Era* | – from *c.*1750 to 1945. |

*Fig. 2.1. List of 'Eras' into which Lincoln's material culture has been divided for the purposes of this Assessment.*

buildings and pottery types – from the *Colonia* Era that came after. Essentially, the remainder of the Roman period, from the end of the military occupation to the end of the Roman rule forms a continuum in terms of material culture, although many important and interesting variations are visible, for example between the 4th century and those which went before. As in so many English cities, the early and middle Saxon periods in Lincoln were marked by a completely contrasting style of material culture, which lasted from the end of the Roman period until the 're-foundation' of the city in the late 9th century (the Early Medieval Era); whilst from the 9th until the 13th century, Lincoln enjoyed a more or less continuous period of homogenous material culture, based on economic prosperity. In some towns, this 'High Medieval Era' would have extended to the Dissolution of the Monasteries, or even later, but in Lincoln the period of great civic expansion, huge population pressures, market-bustle and pan-European contacts came to dramatic end with the catastrophic collapse of the cloth trade at the end of the 13th century (on which see Bischoff 1975). Only a generation or two after 1300, Lincoln had been reduced from a major international city with regular contacts across Europe to a moderately-sized market town with contacts across Lindsey and Kesteven – and this change is dramatically reflected in all aspects of its material culture. It is a change that has also been noted by several other writers on English urban history (e.g. ed. Palliser 2000, 14–5, 741, 744). Moreover, the city of the late 14th century was much more similar in size and material culture to the city of the late 17th century than it had been to the city of the 13th century. Consequently, in this *Assessment*, the 'Early Modern Era' starts in the decades following 1300 and extends right through to the middle of the 18th century. Then, following the re-establishment of trading links with the remainder of England in the later 18th century, and the rest of the world in the later 19th century, Lincoln changed its character again. The new city of the later Victorian and Edwardian period (for it was a new city) was based on heavy engineering and the workers in Ruston's or Clayton's or Robey's in the late 19th century would not have recognised the life-styles or the material culture of their great-grandfathers of *c.*1750. It is not for us to state that the 'Industrial Era' in Lincoln has yet come to an end – that issue remains in the hands of the current generation of Lincoln citizens. But we might well question whether, at the turn of the millennium, our material culture and the ways of life expressed by townscape have any similarities at all with those known by our grandparents. The date chosen as the terminal date for this *Assessment*, 1945, is an arbitrary one, reflecting current historical perceptions, but it (or one close to it – *c.*1960 perhaps?) may eventually come to be seen as a marked shift in material culture, similar to others marking Era boundaries here.

Within this basic chronological framework, the consideration of each Era in the *Assessment* that follows is divided into two quite distinct parts. First the known archaeology of the Era is described and discussed. These discussions will be recognised by archaeologists as an attempt to draw out chronological and thematic history from the material evidence; a 'synthesis' in fact – the manufacture of a new narrative from diverse evidence. They make full use of results of the excavations over the past 30 years and also call on information derived from all the other data stored and organised on the UAD.

The second part of our consideration of each Era, the core of the LARA methodology, is more novel and fundamental to its objective of being a serious management tool. These sections aim to provide a 'research agenda' for future work in the Era. Furthermore they attempt to accomplish that goal spatially, and in a manner applicable both to individual planning decisions and to strategic planning more generally. Consequently, within each of the seven Eras, the city has been divided up geographically into what we have called RAZs – Research Agenda Zones. There are about 550 of these (listed in Appendix II) and, based on the archaeological discussion in the first part of the section, they attempt to define which archaeological questions in each Era should be addressed in future research or development work in any, and every, part of the city. Each entry contains a brief summary of the known archaeological significance of the zone, an account of the research questions which should be addressed in future work within that zone, and an attempt to describe or justify the boundary of the zone.

LARA is primarily a simple interactive and updateable GIS database, installed at Lincoln City Council's Planning Department, and copies of the 2002 version are contained on the CD-Rom in the back pocket here. The practical result of the system is that, wherever the cursor is placed on the base map of the District Council area, the programme will automatically access all seven archaeological summaries and research agendas for that point. Consequently, if the reader wants to explore the arguments raised in the letterpress in this volume further, by placing the cursor at the appropriate place on the LARA base map, a limited amount of extra data and a discussion of the research agenda for the item will automatically appear. In this printed account, the RAZs for each Era have been given a brief introduction (part 'b' of each Era discussion below), which aims to chart the main research themes explored in the RAZ texts themselves. But to fully grasp the complexity of the discussion and the way in which the research themes interact, this volume needs to be read alongside the GIS database on CD-Rom.

Current wisdom accepts that different scholars will interpret the past according to personal perspectives, which reflect *inter alia* the approaches of their own generation. We have returned to an outlook not dissimilar from that espoused by Abraham de la Pryme (above p. 1). It is no longer considered to be a desirable or realistic aim for any individual to produce a definitive account of an archaeological complex which will last for all time, but part of LARA's purpose is to consider the known patterns in Lincoln's archaeology to date, and to explain what further questions we now think need asking as a consequence. The archaeology of Lincoln, like the archaeology of any other place, is not a single artefact on which all will be agreed if only it can be uncovered. It is more of a debate between the present generation and its predecessors, the product of which can support a dialogue – or argument – with future generations. The present generation arranges the evidence it has inherited in such a way that it forms a satisfactory narrative for today's society, but the past is always throwing up new scraps of information which need to be accommodated. Our dealings with the past are like an eternal game of dominoes between the present and the past: you can never know which tiles will prove significant in the next round.

It is precisely because we know that our current view of what was significant in the past will change in the future, that we have already agreed that the 'master' copy of LARA, held at the City Council, will be revisited once every five years by the City Archaeologist, as part of the Local Planning cycle. Not only will alterations be made both to the basic data and, more importantly, to the research agenda, through this bureaucratic mechanism, but all research, from whatever quarter (local, national or international; youthful, amateur or specialist), can now be easily built into an overall picture. New information is coming in all the time, some of it answering old questions proposed here, but much of it setting new questions for future generations to address. That is how it should be. Just as we no longer investigate the questions asked by our grandfathers about their past, we must make sure that future generations are not constrained forever by the archaeological preoccupations we hold today.

# 3. Instructions for the use of LARA on CD-Rom

## Alan Vince

## Introduction

As we have already seen, one of the novelties of the Lincoln *Assessment* is the attempt we have made to document our understanding of the City's archaeology both chronologically and geographically. The end result of this process is LARA, an attempt to organise both our current research understanding and our future research directions in a way which can be accessed geographically, via a Geographic Information System (GIS). The master copy of this GIS system is held at the City of Lincoln Council, Planning Department, but, thanks to the co-operation of the owner, Dominic Powlesland, we have developed the CD-Rom contained in the back of this volume. This CD-Rom replicates many of the functions of the GIS system known as G-SYS, on which the master copy at Lincoln runs. The GIS capacity of the CD-Rom is tailored to operate exclusively with the maps and relational data-base supplied on the disc, giving (perhaps for the first time in an archaeological application) a report which can be accessed geographically, simply by moving the cursor across the map of the City.

We have tried to integrate the CD-Rom into the argument of the *Assessment* by providing a thematic discussion and summary of the material on the CD-Rom relevant to each Era in the 'part b' Introductions to the research agendas, which are placed after the Archaeological Account within each Era. Using these Introductions, LARA provides a commentary and discussion on the preceding Archaeological Account and, most importantly, a prospectus for future work. Many of the sites and issues mentioned in the Archaeological Accounts are dealt with in greater depth and from different perspectives in LARA. Alternatively LARA can be used independently of the *Assessment* volume to provide a group of seven, or more, discussions and research agendas for any given point on the map, within the City Council's area.

## Operating System Requirements

The CD is designed to be read using any CD drive that supports the ISO Mode 1 format. However, the G-SYS LARA software is only designed to run on a PC with at least 64Mb Ram and a Windows Operating System (*Windows 98* or later).

## Installing the CD-Rom

When the CD is inserted into the CD drive, *Windows* may automatically start the installation program (**Autoinst.exe**, which can be found in the top directory/folder of the CD). If not, then start this program manually using the 'run' or 'install' option on the 'start' or 'explorer' menu.

If any other programs are running, the setup routine will identify them and pause whilst you close them down. The program will then ask for a directory in which to install the LARA software and help files. These take up about 20Mb.

Depending on the software present on the computer, you may be asked to reboot the computer after the installation is finished.

It is also possible that the software will fail to install, or will install but not run. This is almost certain to be because the libraries required to manipulate the LARA database, which is in *Access 97* format, need to be installed or updated. Programs to install these libraries can be found on the CD in the **/ms_ data_comp_upgrades** directory. These are **Sr2bof97.exe**, which installs the *Microsoft Office* SR-2b software, **mdac_ typ2_7.exe**, which installs *Microsoft Data Access* Ver.2.7 libraries, and **Jet40Sp3_ comp.exe**, which installs the Jet 4.0 database libraries. If your system already has these packages or later versions loaded you will be asked if you wish to overwrite them (say "no").

*LARA reads its data from the installation CD, which*

*must therefore be in the CD drive from which the software was installed in order to operate.*

## Removing the software

Since the installation program adds files to the *Windows* system directories and alters the *Windows* Registry it cannot be completely removed simply by deleting the **c:/program files/LARA** directory and its sub-directories. Instead, run the **Autoinst.exe** program on the CD-Rom again. The program will recognise that LARA is already installed and give two options, *repair* (useful if one or more components has been removed or damaged) or *remove.* The second option will remove the LARA software and undo the changes to the Windows Registry. The software can be installed, removed and reinstalled at will. It can also be used on any number of computers.

## Using LARA

On loading, LARA will load the background map and the Era overlaps. Depending on the specifications of the PC, this may take some time. The Status Bar at the bottom of the map window indicates progress. Do not click the mouse until the following message is displayed: *All Data Loaded Click Left to Open Control Panel.* A single mouse click anywhere in the map window will then bring up the control panel.

The control panel has, at the top, ten buttons, whose functions are explained by 'tool tips', visible if the mouse cursor is hovering over the button, and by text in a message box at the bottom of the panel. Counting from the top left the first four tool buttons control the maps themselves. In sequence they are: 'zoom in', 'zoom out', 'create a box to zoom into' and 'move the maps within the screen'. To perform any of these operations, first click the tool button on the control panel and then place the cursor at the desired point on the map and click. Please note that, like all GIS systems, LARA has to be instructed in which mode to operate (using the tool buttons) *before* a particular operation is specified by the cursor. Remember to *re-select* the tool button before each subsequent operation.

The next three tool buttons perform operations on the RAZ maps and database. In the top row, the final button (marked with an 'i' – tool tip: *zoom to an object in the active list*) gives access to all of the RAZ texts and mapped locations by clicking on the appropriate RAZ text code in the drop-down window. Please note that all of the RAZ texts 'in play' are listed, so it is recommended that (to avoid scrolling through a long list) irrelevant Era maps should be deleted before this function is used. The second button (marked with an 'eye') provides direct access to a particular RAZ text through its RAZ number. This function is replicated by a type-in box located near the bottom of the control panel. Use this box by entering a RAZ code, high-

lighting it within the drop-down list and clicking on the entry. The third button (marked with a question mark and arrow) permits direct access to the RAZ texts and their mapped locations by simply clicking the cursor at any point on the map. Performing this operation will bring up the list of RAZ entries relevant to that particular point on the map. Clicking on the individual entry will then extract the RAZ text from the database.

To go directly from the *Assessment* text to a RAZ account, use the 'eye' button or the type-in box at the base of the control panel. To locate the RAZ on the map as well as obtaining its text, either zoom to the general map area and click, or enter via the 'i' button.

The final three tool buttons perform operations on the summary layer of the Lincoln Urban Archaeological Database (UAD) which we have prepared specially to accompany LARA on this disc. Please note that only a summary of the UAD entry is available here. The complete entries are to be found on the master copy of the UAD at the City's Heritage Team (address below).

To locate an excavation or an observation held on the UAD, click the button marked with a 'target' and then to point on the map to be interrogated and click. A single click on the drop-down list of UAD entries for the location will reveal the summary of the UAD information for that entry.

The two remaining buttons permit searches of the UAD summaries by drawing a line around the data points to be interrogated.

Towards the bottom of the control panel is a window providing an alternative way into the UAD data summaries. The complete list of UAD entries can be scrolled through here using the 'arrow up' and 'arrow down' keys on the keyboard. Simply highlight the code on the left (the site code – complete list given on Fig. 1.1) or right (recognition event – RE -number). Clicking on the headers of the columns will permit sorting the list of sites. A second click will reverse the sort. A single mouse click on the required UAD entry will then flash the location of the site on the map. A double click will zoom in to show the site trench outline (if the trench was large enough to be plotted).

Various features can be turned on and off on the control panel by mouse clicks in the boxes provided. The diameter of the search zone can be enlarged or reduced from its default value of 100m using the *Set Search Buffer* button. We hope the various other functions on the control panel are self-explanatory. Please note that, as with all such systems, the user will find it worthwhile to familiarise themselves with its parameters before using to it to address specific questions.

An illustrated help file, documenting the various features of the software, is installed in the **c:/program files/LARA** directory during installation. It is present in three formats: *Word* 2000, *Acrobat* PDF and HTML. It cannot be opened directly from the LARA package so open the version of the file you want in one window and open LARA in another. This file will guide you through the features of the LARA package. *A print-out of the help file kept beside your keyboard whilst using LARA will be very helpful.*

A website with copies of the latest version of the help files, bug reports and any downloadable upgrades to the data or software can be found at http://www.postex.demon.co.uk/lara.

## Data Structures

The RAZ text data fields have the following structure:

- *Identifier (RAZ Number).* This consists of two or three numbers separated by points. The first number indicates the Era and the second and (optional) third simply identify the zone. In several cases the zones are not contiguous and there are therefore two or more areas on a map with the same identifier. The zones may overlap so that a single point can be in two or more zones.
- *Description.* The Research Agenda for the zone.
- *Boundaries.* A statement describing and possibly justifying the boundaries of the zone.

The Site List data has the following structure:

- *Identifier.* This is the Recognition Event number by which this site or observation is known in the Lincoln UAD, for example *RE1370*.
- *Site Code.* This is the code by which the site is referred to in the *Assessment*, for example *DM 72*. In some instances a single site code refers to two or more Recognition Events (for example where the site consisted of several separate trenches or area excavations).
- *Site Name.* This is the name by which the site is referred to in this volume, for example *Dickinson's Mill 1972*. In several cases alternative names may be present in the archaeological literature.
- *Grid Square.*
- *Grid Eastings.*
- *Grid Northings.*

Both of these data-sets are partial copies of data housed in the Lincoln UAD and LARA and were extracted from that database in April 2003. Both data-sets are subject to constant modification and further information is available from the Heritage Team, Directorate of Development and Environmental Services, City of Lincoln Council, City Hall, Lincoln, LN1 1DF (Telephone 01522 881188). The data provided here should

only be used to inform formal applications for development following discussion with the Directorate of Development and Environmental Services at the address above.

## Technical content of the CD-Rom

The CD-Rom contains the following:
**/ASCII data** – Copies of the RAZ text and site lists in comma-separated ASCII format.
**/Data** – Copies of the seven Era maps and their associated indices in G-Sys format, the RAZ text and UAD data in *Access* 97 format, and the background map in TIF format.
**/Help** – The help files in *Word*, PDF and HTML formats.
**/MS_data_comp_upgrades** – Executable files to update Microsoft components required by the LARA software.

## A note on the base map and on registration of the LARA overlays

For copyright reasons, the version of LARA used on this CD-Rom sits over a digitised version of the latest editions of the Ordnance Survey 'County Series' map, some of which were published in 1930 and some in 1938. In the period between the two publications, however, some areas of the city had changed and, consequently, there are sudden dislocations along original sheet boundaries. Furthermore, the 'master' version of LARA uses the most recent Ordnance Survey 'Landline' data-set, used by the City Council. Improvements in accuracy of mapping and the introduction of the National Grid since 1945 have meant that data mapped against the 'Landline' map of Lincoln can no longer be mapped directly onto the 'County Series' map without extensive 'rubber-sheeting'. As LARA was originally produced as overlays on the 'Landline' data-set, a direct result is that the RAZ and UAD data on the CD-Rom is sometimes up to 2.5m out of registration with the base map. As the version of LARA presented on this CD-Rom is not intended for use within such fine tolerances, we have not attempted to correct the registration errors. It is almost always clear where RAZ boundaries should run, and anyway, every RAZ text contains a statement about its boundary line. In cases where this uncertainty proves critical, however, we suggest that the user consults the master version at the City's Heritage Team (address above).

# 4. Geological and topographical background

## Michael J Jones and David Stocker

The City of Lincoln lies in the north-eastern corner of the English Midlands (Fig. 4.1), some 50km north-east of Nottingham, almost as far north as Sheffield and further north than Chester. Lincolnshire has always been disputed territory, sometimes considered a part of Northern England (it was part of the kingdom of Northumbria in the 7th century, for example), and sometimes a part of the South (since the 10th century the diocese has been within the province of Canterbury). Yet Lincolnshire, which still looks towards Lincoln as its provincial capital, has always been a place apart from both the North and the Midlands. The Anglo-Saxon kingdom of Lindsey, indeed, derived its -ey place-name from its island status. It was surrounded by water on all four sides, by the North Sea, the Rivers Trent and Witham and, along its south-western boundary, extensive marshes.

The City of Lincoln itself stands at the main entrance to the island of Lindsey from the south. The point at which the crossing point of the river Witham is narrowest – where admission could be controlled and administered. This is the point where the Jurassic limestone ridge known as the Lincoln Edge, extending northwards out of the plateau-land of Kesteven and Northamptonshire, was pierced by a glacial gap. Here the river Witham itself turns sharply eastwards to flow through the gap (Fig. 4.2), which is between one and two kilometres wide, with steep scarps rising to a height above sea level of about 60m on either side. The limestone of the ridge has been extensively studied by geologists (it was first described by William Bedford 1839; 1843) but, increasingly, studies have stressed the geological complexity of this range of hills (Swinnerton and Kent 1949; Fenton 1980; Ashton 1980; Worssam 1999). It forms the greater part of the Inferior Oolite Group, which extends from Kettering in the south-west towards the Humber. Where it outcropped on either side of the Lincoln Gap (Fig. 4.3), the stone was found eminently suitable for both building and sculpture, and it gave a distinctive physical character to the built environment of the Roman and medieval town. The Lincoln strata provided stones of several different types, which (in

so far as they were used for Roman fabric and for 10th- and 11th-century sculpture) have been distinguished by Fenton and by Worssam (*Ibid.*). Such stones have been exploited since at least the Roman period and they continue in use today, providing stone for the Cathedral repairs and ballast for the building industry.

Immediately beneath the limestone is a thick bed of Liassic clay, which also outcrops on the two hillsides north and south of the gap. Between the limestone and the clay beneath is a marked spring-line, which continues north and south of the city for many miles. Many of the springs along this line are still active and they have played an important part in the development of the city throughout the period of its occupation. Since at least the Roman period the Liassic clay has been used for the making of pottery and bricks and Lincoln became an important centre of pottery manufacture between the 2nd and 4th, and the 10th and the 14th centuries. Roman bricks and tiles are frequently found in the city's excavations, although no firm evidence that they were produced any closer than Heighington (5 km south-east) has yet been discovered. Throughout much of the medieval period, however, tile production sites exploiting the local clays are documented, and one was excavated on the site of St Mark's Station in Wigford in 1987 (Z 87). By the 18th century Lincoln had developed a substantial brick industry and in the 19th century there were at least two major brick-work complexes within the city boundary and a third just outside it.

The valley floor in the gap between the two escarpments contains a variety of quaternary deposits, including layers of sands and gravels, and to the south of the walled city in particular, the terraces formed by these gravels have been of great importance, offering hard land for both settlement and permanent grazing. The sands and gravels have also been exploited by Lincoln citizens for construction work, from the Roman period onwards – most notably in the 19th century, when large quantities were taken for ballast by the railways. This part of the city is drained by a small

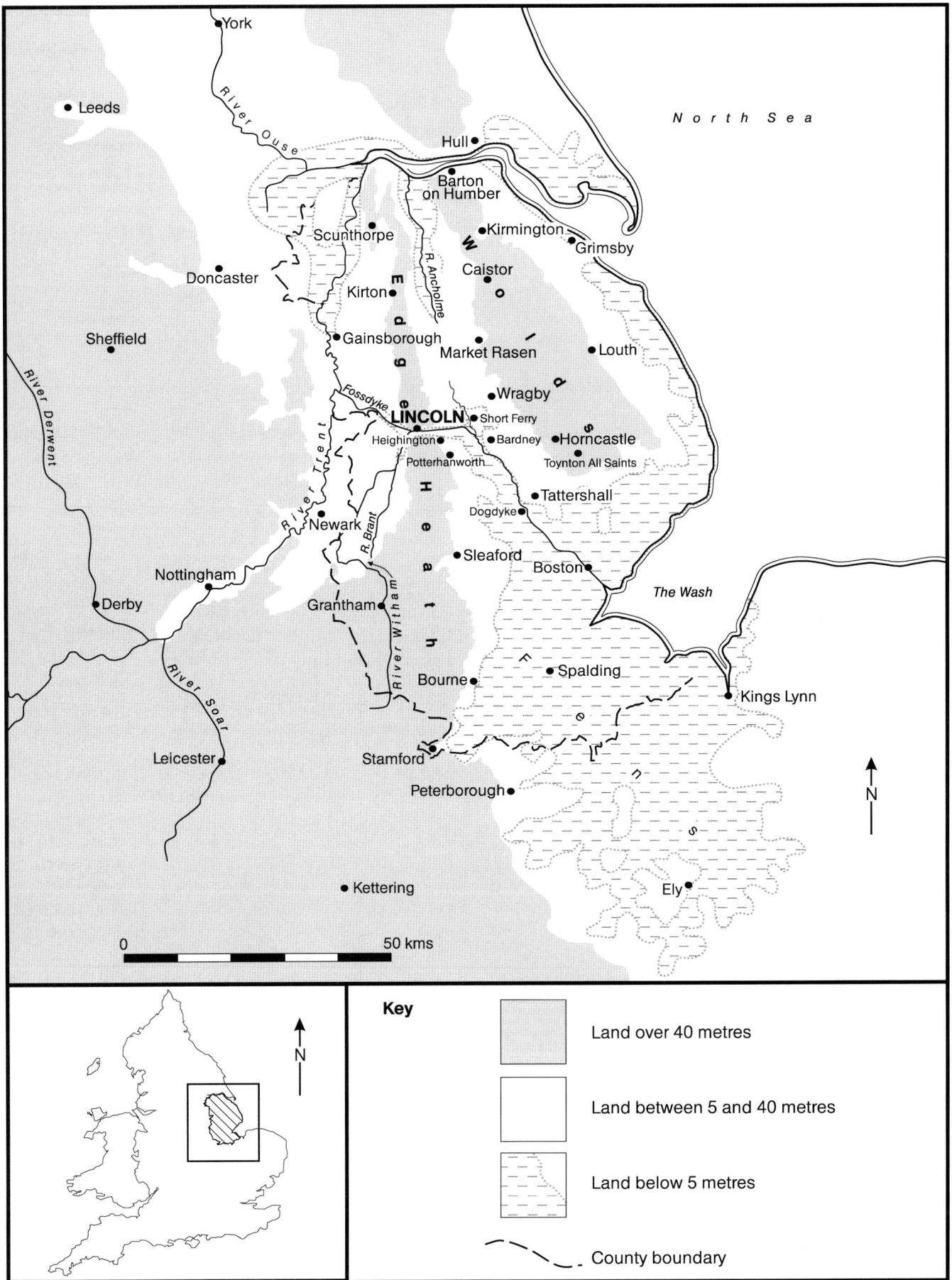

*Fig. 4.1. Lincoln, Lincolnshire, major settlements of the East Midlands and smaller places mentioned in the text (drawn by Dave Watt, copyright English Heritage).*

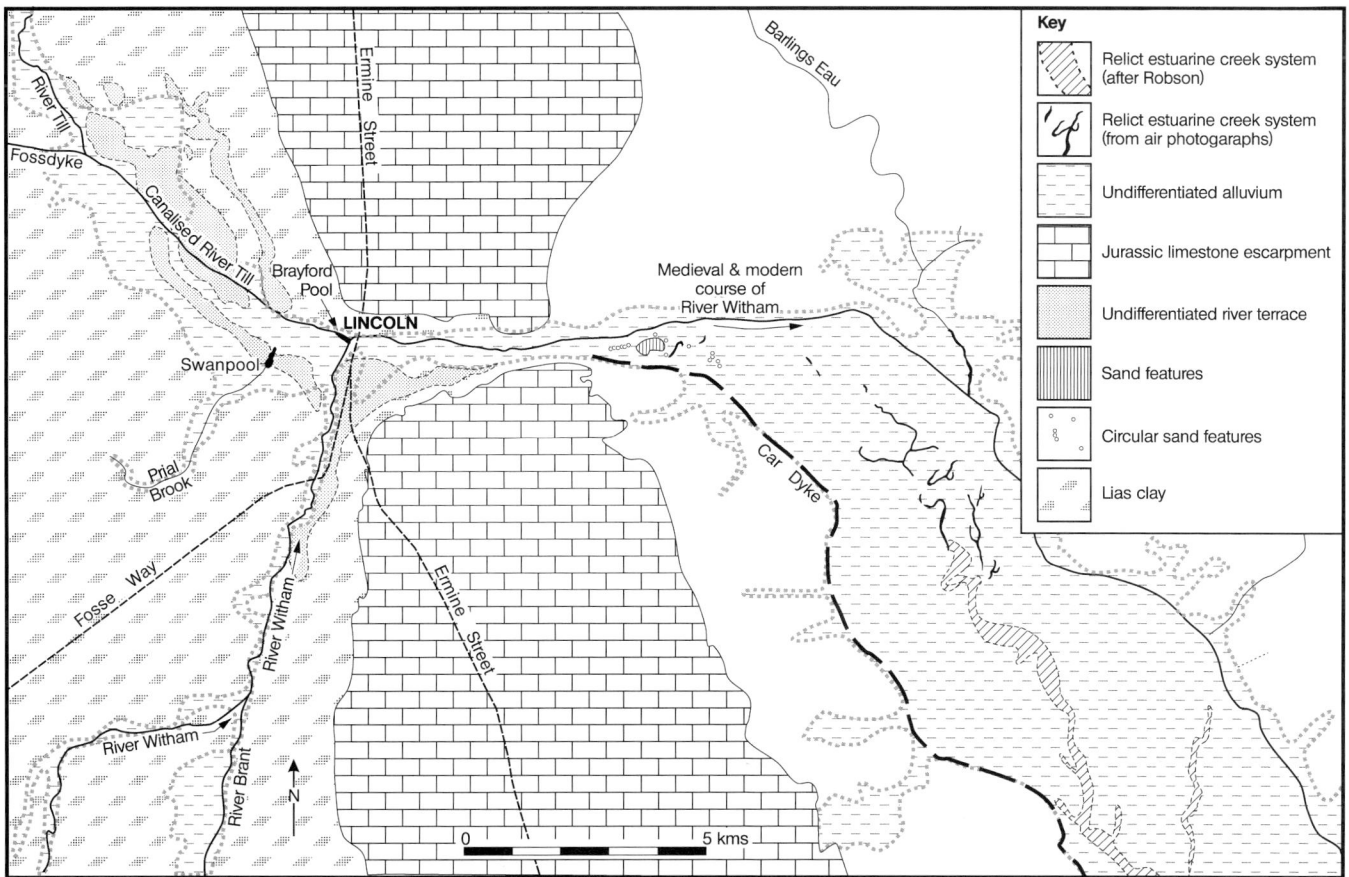

*Fig. 4.2. Selected solid and drift geology in the Lincoln area. Riverine deposits are based on Wilkinson 1986–7 fig.20. Other information is from the British Geological Survey. Swanpool is shown in its modern location (drawn by Dave Watt, copyright English Heritage).*

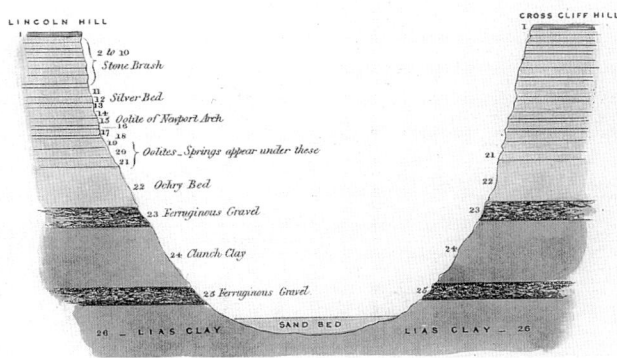

*Fig. 4.3. Simplified section north–south through the Witham Valley at the Lincoln gap. Not to scale (Bedford 1843 plate 2) (Plate 1.2).*

river, the Prial Brook, which flows north-eastwards in what are now a series of man-made drains and lakes, but which was once a shallow valley. The brook originally emptied into the carr-land south of the area of open water called Swanpool, and via the Swanpool into the Brayford, but since the Lincoln Drainage

scheme of 1813–15, it has been carried eastwards across the contours, in a man-made channel, to join the Witham above the city. The original courses of Prial Brook are shown on Armstrong's map of 1779, and that map also shows the Swanpool occupying a much larger area of carr-land than it has done since the early 19th century.

The valley floor also contains a depth of alluvial deposits, derived from the Witham and its predecessors, which have flowed northwards towards the gap and met the river Till as it cut east. At the Witham gap, indeed, the river was joined by the main channel of the Trent in the Late Last Glacial period (from about 15–10,000 BC), when that river's route took it towards the Wash rather than the Humber (Swinnerton and Kent 1949, 105; Wymer 1999, 115, table 10). The eastern part of the valley along which the Trent had flowed is now occupied by the river Till. The lower reaches of the Till, above Lincoln, were subsequently straightened to form the eastern section of the Fossdyke, and we have little evidence for its original main channel. The junction of the two rivers, the Witham and the Till, formed a natural expanse of slow-moving water, known today in its much reduced form as the Brayford

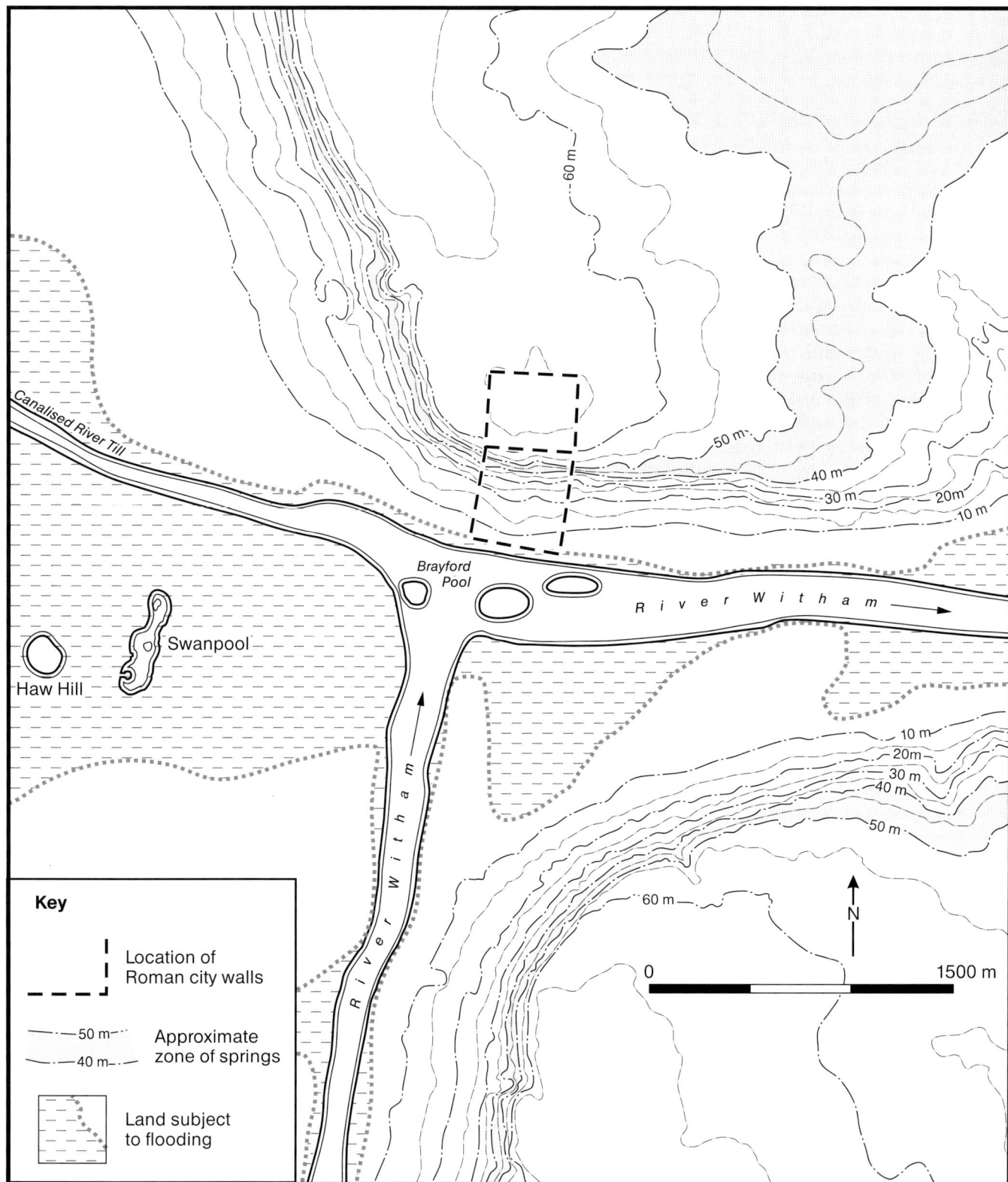

*Fig. 4.4. Provisional map attempting to reconstruct the known islands, main river courses and areas subject to winter flooding in the Lincoln Gap in the later prehistoric period. Swanpool is shown in its modern location (drawn by Dave Watt, copyright English Heritage).*

Pool. The existence of sediments overlying "Fen Clay", which appear to have been deposited here in the 1st or 2nd millennium BC, may suggest tidal influence in the pool, possibly connected with rising sea levels (Waller 1994). This deposit was first noted in excavations on the east side of the pool at Brayford Wharf East in 1982 (BWE 82 – Wilkinson 1986–7) and again in 1998 (Rackham 1998). The evidence of the molluscs and diatoms from the same sites indicated a slow-moving body of water, with only occasional hints of marine influence. Sea levels were falling throughout the later Bronze Age and Iron Age and the valley floor seems to have reverted to an area of river channels and marshes, subject to seasonal flooding between the gravel terraces. In the winter months the water would expand to occupy much of the valley floor, shrinking in summer to create a landscape of river channels, meres and pools. The Swanpool, south-west of the city, is now the only such pool to have survived, but the *Cuckoo Pool*, which was nearly as large but at least partly outside the modern City boundary, survived long enough to be mapped on Armstrong's map and probably formed the core of the Skellingthorpe decoy. We have documentary evidence that there were several more such pools, seasonal or otherwise, in the Middle Ages and they were very probably present at much earlier dates. Without a detailed micro-topographical study of the valley floor beneath the peat it is impossible to document exactly where the hard ground was at any particular period (especially in the prehistoric period). Nevertheless, using the very limited information we have to hand, and some guesswork, we have arrived at a map (Fig. 4.4) which attempts to indicate where the hard land was located throughout later prehistory. This map is highly provisional, but it has proved useful for developing our understanding of the early city.

Levels of water in this part of the valley after the Iron Age continued to fluctuate, and this may also have been linked to changing sea levels. But this *Assessment* has suggested the presence of artificial barriers across the valley at the point where the hard land creates the narrowest crossing point in the area later known as Stamp End – about 1 km east of the Roman city. Any such barriers may also have influenced river levels upstream. Provided it could be controlled, the water offered opportunities for travel and transport, fishing, and settlement – in some cases on sand-islands and on reclaimed land. But the river system, it must be said, remained unstable. Only in recent years have flood alleviation schemes been implemented to offer assurances to those who reside below the ten-metre contour – and that means most of the lower part of town (Plate 5.4).

In stark contrast to conditions by the pool, the Upper City, site of the legionary fortress and Cathedral, sits on the Jurassic limestone, close to its western scarp, overlooking the valley of the Trent to the west and the Witham gap to the south. The tabular bedrock, some of which was quarried during the Roman and the medieval and later periods, only occurs at depth. Its upper 1.5m is laminated, and covered by a subsoil known as 'corn brash'. This layer of small rubble mixed with a light-coloured clay is, on average, about 1m thick and, sometimes, mixed with or sealed by an orange or brown, blown sand. This sand can also fill solution-

holes and other surface geological features, with a resulting confusion for excavators who might otherwise interpret them as structural features. Webster's 'Iron Age rock-cut postholes' are almost certainly solution-holes of this type, as he himself later accepted (Webster 1949, 60–62). An investigation of the lower parts of the limestone sequence was achieved during 1984 when the well shaft at St. Paul-in-the-Bail (SP 84) was emptied (Fig. 4.5). The shaft had been cut through a deposit of the Upper Lincolnshire Limestone about 8m thick beneath the 'corn brash'. The limestone overlay a band some 3m thick of the sandy, ferruginous, Lower Lincolnshire Limestone (sometimes known as the Northamptonshire Ironstone). The Liassic clay, into the upper surface of which the well's sump had been cut, was found at a depth of about 15m. Across the remainder of the Upper City, archaeological deposits are not deep – being frequently encountered less than 1m below modern ground surfaces – and although deposits at St Paul's were some 3 to 4m in depth, they are frequently less.

Between the river basin and the hilltop is the lower walled city, on the northern scarp of the gap. Here, below the limestone outcrop at the top of the cliff, the

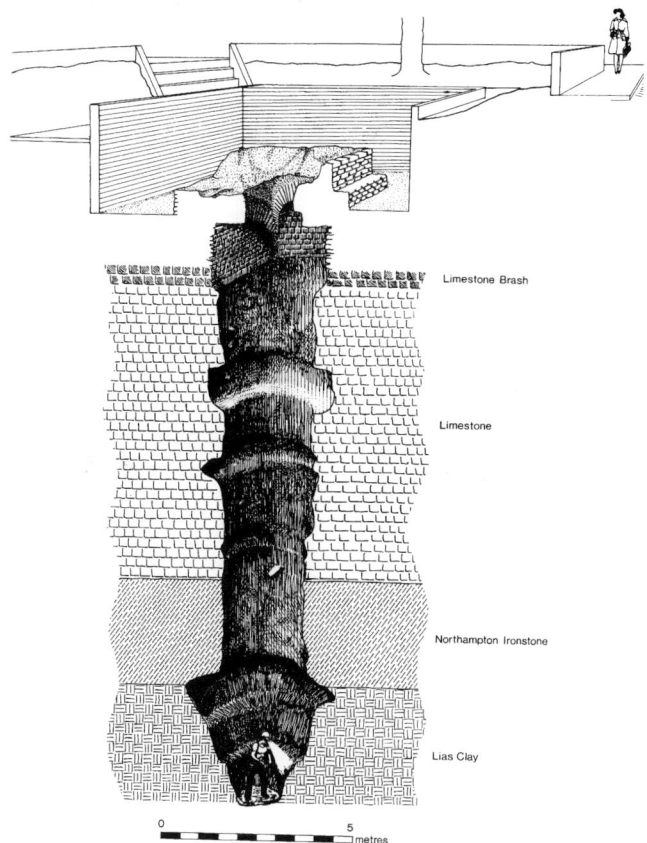

*Fig. 4.5. Section through the Limestone cap on the north side of the Lincoln Gap, as revealed in excavations at the well at St Paul-in-the-Bail in 1984 (SP 84) (drawn by Tig Sutton, copyright City of Lincoln Archaeology Unit).*

Liassic clay subsoils give way nearer the river to sandy terraces. The clay occurs on the steeper part of the slope, and any settlement here required both substantial terracing and management of the springs. The sandy terraces on the more gentle slopes below, by contrast, drained well and were ideally suited to occupation above the river. This underlying geology means, in practice, that archaeological deposits on the steeper hillside can either be very deeply buried, right at the surface, or even completely removed by later terracing. On the lower part of the hillside, for two or three hundred metres north of the river, archaeological deposits are much more uniform and they average 4 or 5m in depth.

Clay and sand are also to be found at various heights in the area that subsequently became the 'great suburb' of Wigford. In Wigford, and close to the waterside, however, the micro-topography is more complicated, and several definite sand and gravel terraces have now been identified amongst the alluvium. The northern terrace, found in excavations at Nos. 181–3 High Street (HG 72) and in boreholes at No. 190 High Street, probably represents a long-standing island in the river, as made-up ground over alluvium was found both south and north of it. Finds of natural sand and gravel at the bases of archaeological sequences further south, however, are more likely to represent a peninsula of hard ground extending northwards into the alluvium from the foot of the southern cliff (SMG 82 and sites further south). We now believe that the island at the northern end of what is now Wigford was not connected with the mainland to north and south by causeways and bridges until the Roman period, and it was not until the 2nd century AD that substantial dumps of earth were deposited to make the ground alongside the causeway suitable for settlement (chapters 6 and 7 below). To the east, a second island in the river, known as Thorngate, was present and occupied by the 12th century, but little progress has been made in identifying it archaeologically and its boundaries have yet to be accurately defined. A third sand-island, immediately to the south-west of the Lower City has recently been identified through work by James Rackham (1998) and it is thought likely that the pronounced 'upland', still visible in the topography, and known as Haw Hill (south-west of Swanpool), represents yet another sand-island of this type (Hockley 1992).

All three topographical areas of the ancient city, then, had disadvantages from the point of view of settlement. In the south, the Wigford (valley floor) area was liable to flooding; on the hilltop, in the Upper City, there was a shortage of water, and on the hillside in the Lower City (in addition to the steep slope) there were problems of drainage of surface water from springs. However, in the Lower City also, along the northern side of the riverbank and above the limit of seasonal flooding, but below the zone of land-slips and springs, there was a zone of free-draining subsoil on a gentle south-facing slope which was ideal for settlement. It is no surprise that it is this zone, not more than 200 metres north to south, which has produced some of Lincoln's most impressive archaeology.

# 5. Settlement in the Lincoln area in the Prehistoric Era

## A. Archaeological Account

### Michael J Jones and David Stocker

Until the 1970s, the foundation of a settlement at Lincoln was thought to be a characteristically Roman action, one impelled by the strategic value of its geographical position for military control. Hence Frere could write, in his classic work on Roman Britain, 'to Rome we owe the choice of such sites as... Lincoln ...' (1967, 3) . This was a reasonable deduction at the time of writing of the first edition, as excavations in the city had produced no definite evidence for pre-Roman occupation, but the work undertaken over the last thirty years (and not brought forward until the present publication) now casts some uncertainty on Frere's unequivocal position.

It was only with the expansion of rescue archaeology, and the adoption of a more comprehensive approach to the city's past from 1972, that investigation of a site over 200m south of the walled city (at 181–3 High Street) brought to light the first traces of late iron-age occupation (HG 72). Given its location and depth, buried beneath c.3m of later deposits, it was not surprising that such evidence had been so long in coming. The discovery also took place against an increasing awareness of the iron-age background of much of Romano-British settlement (e.g. Cunliffe 1991), including that of Lincolnshire itself, for which our knowledge has continued to grow (e.g. May 1976; 1984; 1988; 1994; 1996).

It is now clear, however, that the site of what ultimately became the city of Lincoln was of importance to the region from a much earlier date (Fig. 5.1). The Witham gap through the limestone hills could not fail to be a nodal site – a site where different societies would locate key events and activities, even if those activities merely reflected attempts to cross the river itself. Neolithic and bronze-age flint implements of various types have been found within the city boundary, and their distribution calls for some comment (Fig. 5.2). Stone tools known and collected by the 1970s showed no great concentrations in the Lincoln area (Cummins and Moore 1973; May 1976, 53–7; Moore 1979), although most came from the east side of the city in or close to the valley. The most recent study indicates little change in the pattern (McKerrell Clough, and Cummins 1988). Analysis of the material from the area of the city suggests that the distribution pattern of finds made since c.1970, all in secondary contexts, may merely reflect the locations of investigations, although it is notable that they have been found only in the areas where we have deduced solid ground using other criteria. That is, they have all been made in the lower part of town close to the river. A recent exception is represented by the finding of a cluster of 138 knapped flints of mesolithic to early bronze-age date close to the Roaring Meg spring, 1km north-east of the Upper City, which may indicate small-scale domestic occupation for the later part of this period (Bonner 1999). It may be relevant, however, that the Roaring Meg spring has been identified here as a potential ritual site in the Roman period (RAZ 7.17).

At present, we can provide little context for these early finds from within the city boundary. It has long been presumed that the Witham gap lies across the path of the long-distance route-way known as the Jurassic Way, which is thought to have followed the cliff edge throughout its length in the county (Grimes 1951). The very existence of the Jurassic Way as a long-distance route (at least in Northamptonshire) is open to serious doubt (Taylor 1979, 32–7), but even the sternest critics of such proposed long-distance trackways agree that, in places where they follow prominent ridges, such route-ways are likely to be of great antiquity. But, even though such a ridge-way is very likely to have existed somewhere along the top

*Fig. 5.3. Bronze-age collared urn (City and County Museum – cat. 295.16) found 'in a sandpit' in 1914 in Canwick parish – perhaps on the site of the City Council's new refuse destructor, which was under construction in that year. This site was considerably further west than the other known barrows at Canwick and would be close to the southern terminal of the proposed early causeway at Stamp End. Conceivably, then, it could represent an offering at the causeway rather than a barrow as such (photo and copyright, Lincolnshire County Council, Lincolnshire Museums Service).*

stream of Canwick (Wilkinson 1986–7, 55; SMR). Indeed, we now have evidence that many locations in the river valley floor between Lincoln and Tattershall were regarded as appropriate sites for the burial of the dead and at least five such barrow cemeteries have been noted in these reaches (Stocker and Everson 2003). At a somewhat later date, in the late Bronze Age, valley crossings near all of these five barrow groups may have been marked with elaborate timber causeways (Field and Parker-Pearson 2003; Stocker and Everson 2003). At these points, then, it seems the early bronze-age barrow cemeteries, like that now known from Canwick, were accompanied by late bronze-age causeways as the water levels in the peat-choked river rose. We should suspect, therefore, that there may also have been a late bronze-age causeway across the valley close to Lincoln. In fact there is independent evidence for such a causeway, whose

southern terminal was probably some 1km to the west of the barrows plotted from air photography, and it will be discussed in its place below.

Wilkinson (1986–7, 55) noted that the sand islands in the river course would have been attractive to settlement from as early as the Mesolithic period. The closest known occupation site in the near vicinity of Lincoln, not just of the Bronze Age, but of the whole prehistoric period up to the late Iron Age, may have been between Lincoln and Washingborough (5km east – Fig. 5.1). Here a pool had formed during the course of the inundations to which the Witham valley was subjected in the late Bronze Age, and into this pool, according to the excavators, was washed a mixed assemblage of animal bones, pottery, worked and unworked wood and a single harness fitting (Coles *et al.* 1979). The excavators concluded that the pottery, in particular, should indicate that there was a settlement of late bronze-age date, not far up-stream, which could have been the origin of this material. More recently, finds of pottery of similar date, made during field-walking somewhat further to the east, have been interpreted in the same way and have been used to add further scale to this proposed settlement (Elsdon 1994).

Evidence for bronze-age settlement on the limestone heath land around the later city is more equivocal. The significance of the late bronze-age hoard of palstaves, axes and spearheads found to the north, in Nettleham parish, in 1860 (Davey 1973, nos. 263–71) is unclear. Although such finds have often been given utilitarian explanations, in the context of contemporary bronze-working markets, they are increasingly seen as votive offerings (Bradley 1998, passim, esp. 97–154; Pryor 2001b) and may bear no relationship to settlement patterns at all. Within Bradley's analysis, the Nettleham hoard looks most like a 'dry land' offering of a type which, although common in the early and middle Bronze Ages, was being superseded by votive offerings of swords made in rivers by the date of the artefacts it contains.

Although we have relatively little to say about the city area in earlier periods, from the late Bronze Age onwards (from perhaps *c.*1000 – *c.*700BC), the status of the river valley at Lincoln as a place of great significance is more clearly revealed. Furthermore it seems certain that it owed that prominence to its topography. The narrowest point of the Witham valley does not lie where the Roman road would later cross the river (in the Wigford suburb), but about 1km to the east, in the vicinity of the modern Stamp End lock and further east still, where the gravel terraces come down close to the river (Figs. 4.4 and 5.2). We now know from work on the early Roman period (Steane *et al.* 2001, 308–11) that the Wigford causeway across the valley floor was partly man-made and, before its existence, the narrowing of the valley in the vicinity of Stamp End would have made a more obvious crossing point. It has been precisely here, in the stretch

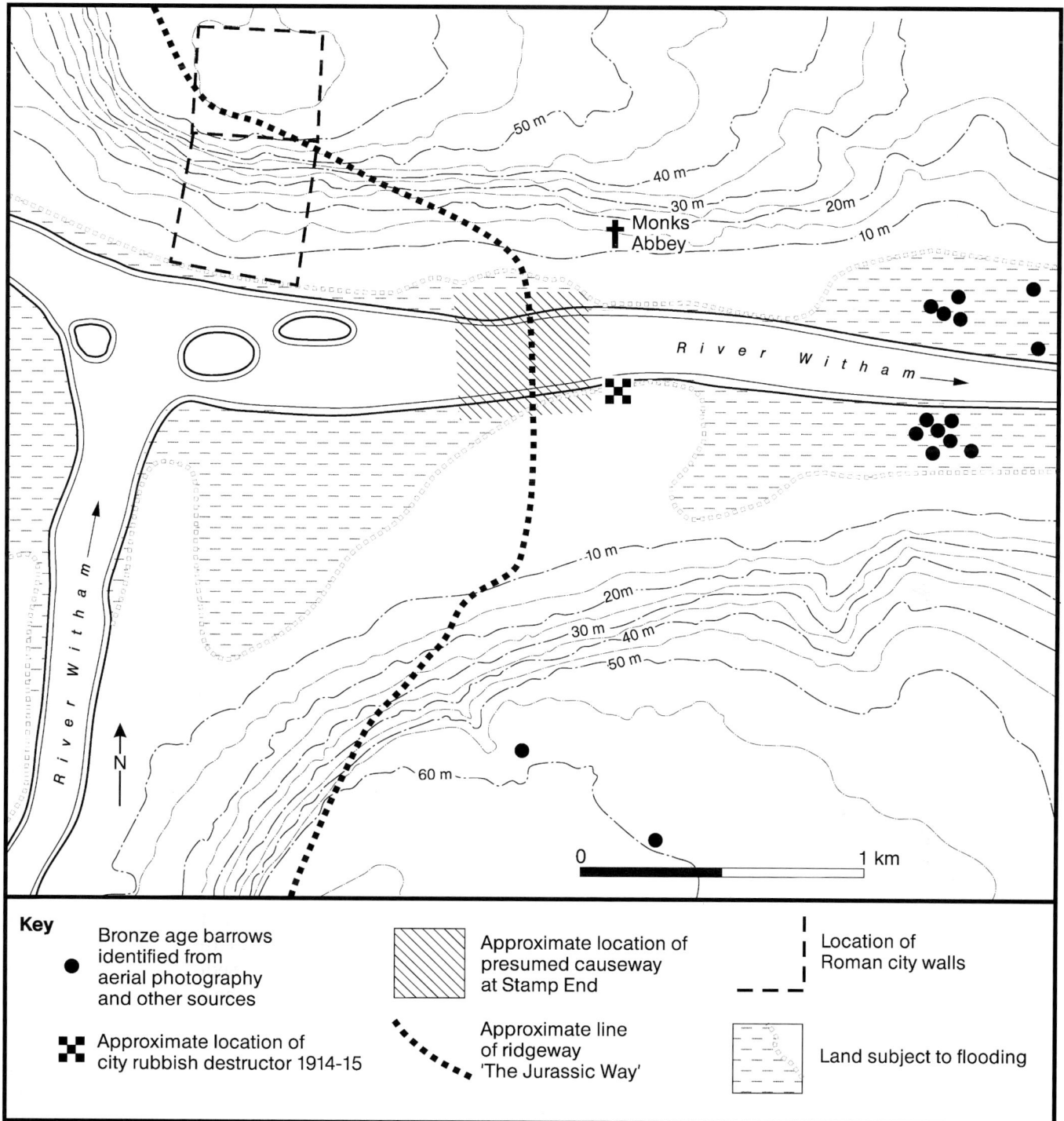

*Fig. 5.4. Known and suspected barrows in the valley floor east of Lincoln, based on data from the NMP and the Lincolnshire SMR (drawn by Dave Watt, copyright English Heritage).*

of river below the Stamp End lock, that more than 24 finds of high quality metalwork have been made (Davey 1971; 1973; White 1979a; 1979b; 1979c; Stocker and Everson 2003). Of these artefacts, 20 are of late bronze-age and iron-age date (Fig. 5.5). The greatest number of finds was recovered in the summer of 1826 when the lock at Stamp End was being reconstructed to allow it to take passenger steamers. Five of the

bronze-age finds are swords, the remainder axes and spearheads, but as a group they form part of an easily recognisable pattern of votive 'offerings' similar to those made at the other known and presumed causeways in the central part of the Witham valley and in similar contexts elsewhere (Fitzpatrick 1984; Bradley 1998).

The distribution of later bronze-age metalwork in

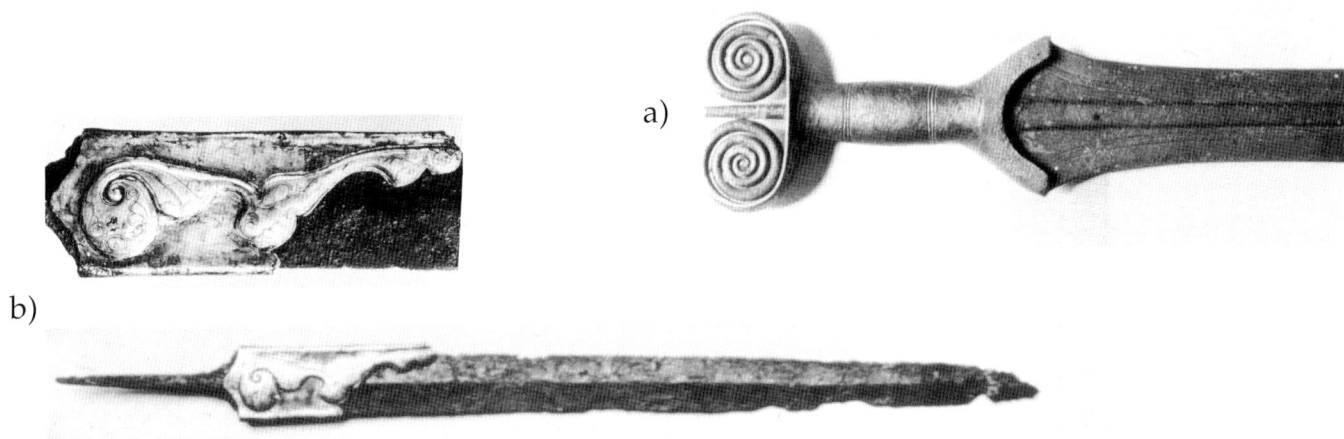

a)

b)

*Fig. 5.5. a) 'Antennae-hilted' sword of late bronze-age date found in the reach below Stamp End in 1826 and now in the museum of His Grace the Duke of Northumberland at Alnwick Castle, Northumberland (cat. 235) (photo and copyright, Lincolnshire County Council, Lincolnshire Museums Service). b) Iron sword of the 2nd century BC with scabbard decorated in bronze relief. It was also found in 1826 in the reach below Stamp End and is now in the museum of His Grace the Duke of Northumberland at Alnwick Castle, Northumberland (cat. 276) (photo and copyright, Lincolnshire County Council, Lincolnshire Museums Service).*

Lincolnshire as a whole is notable and most of it comes from the Witham between Lincoln and Tattershall. The finds from Stamp End represent only a small percentage of the total of at least 150 metalwork finds made between Lincoln and Tattershall in the last 200 years (Davey 1971; 1973; May 1976, 114–9; White 1979a; 1979b; 1979c). In 1981 Naomi Field undertook important excavations close to the find-site of some of the richest of these discoveries, at Fiskerton (5km east) (Field nd.; 1986; Field and Parker Pearson 2003) (Fig. 5.6). These investigations clearly demonstrated both that the finds were votive in intention, and that they were associated with an iron-age timber causeway, much like the late bronze-age example excavated at Flag Fen near Peterborough by Francis Pryor (1991, 112–20; 2001a). The recent discovery of log-boats and further metal objects near to the earlier Fiskerton site was not therefore completely unexpected, while a currency bar from the same site – probably of the 1st century BC in date – extends the use of the site right to the end of the Iron Age.

A more recent study (Stocker and Everson 2003) has demonstrated that the pattern of structures and finds most clearly seen at Fiskerton is probably also present at all of the nine medieval causeways in the Witham valley and its tributaries between Lincoln and Tattershall. The sequence of monuments at these locations mostly starts with a barrow cemetery of early or middle bronze-age date, which was frequently buried beneath the advancing peat, as water levels in the Witham valley rose during the late Bronze Age. During this inundation stage it seems likely that a series of causeways was laid out across the developing fen. Although Fiskerton is the only causeway to have

been found through excavation, the pattern of bronze-age, iron-age and later finds at each of the other eight medieval or earlier causeway sites suggests that similar structures may have been laid out at these locations also. At Stamp End, also the site of a documented medieval causeway (p. 235 below), the same pattern of bronze- and iron-age votive depositions occurs – so we may confidently predict that there will have been a timber causeway structure here from the late Bronze Age into the Roman period and later. Such longevity seems to be confirmed by the finding, not just of late bronze-age metalwork in the vicinity of the putative causeway but also six items of iron-age date, including, probably, the famous Witham Shield (Fig. 5.7) (Stocker and Everson 2003).

It is unlikely that any of the Witham causeways were continuous across the main channel of the river itself, as the power of the main stream in flood would probably make such an arrangement impractical. Nevertheless, the causeways may have extended from the dry land (i.e. from above the 5m contour) across the valley floor right up to the sides of the main stream. At the other causeways it is thought that the terminals of the causeways against the main channel of the river may have served as the mooring points for ferries – and we can guess that such an arrangement existed at Stamp End as well.

The work of the Fenland Survey (Lane *et al.* 1993; Hall and Coles 1994; Waller 1994) has followed Simmons' research (1979; 1980; 1985) on the iron-age coastline, which at high tide lay considerably inland of its present line. This implies that, as the Bronze Age gave way to the Iron Age, the putative 'causeway' at Stamp End will have formed a further barrier in the

*Fig. 5.6. The iron-age 'causeway' excavated by N Field south-east of Fiskerton church in 1981. This view of the excavations looks east, with the North Delph bank and River Witham to the right (photo and copyright, N. Field & Lindsey Archaeological Services).*

*Fig. 5.7 (right). The 'Witham Shield'. This magnificent object was dredged from the Witham in August 1826 (White 1979a, 4). The shield is first recorded in the ownership of Rev H Waldo-Sibthorpe (Meyrick 1831, 97). Its find-site is sometimes given as Washingborough parish, although the precise location of the find was not recorded. However, in August 1826, major works were undertaken in the river at, and immediately downstream of, the Stamp End lock. This work was sponsored by the Witham Navigation Company, in which the Sibthorpe family were both major shareholders and riparian owners (Hill 1974, 100, 113, etc.). Humphrey Sibthorpe was indeed rector of Washingborough at the time, but his 'property', near to which Meyrick said the find was made, was in Canwick parish (not Washingborough) and the Sibthorpes owned the land south of Stamp End – where the work in 1826 was being done (Mills, Mills and Trott 2001) (photo and copyright, The British Museum).*

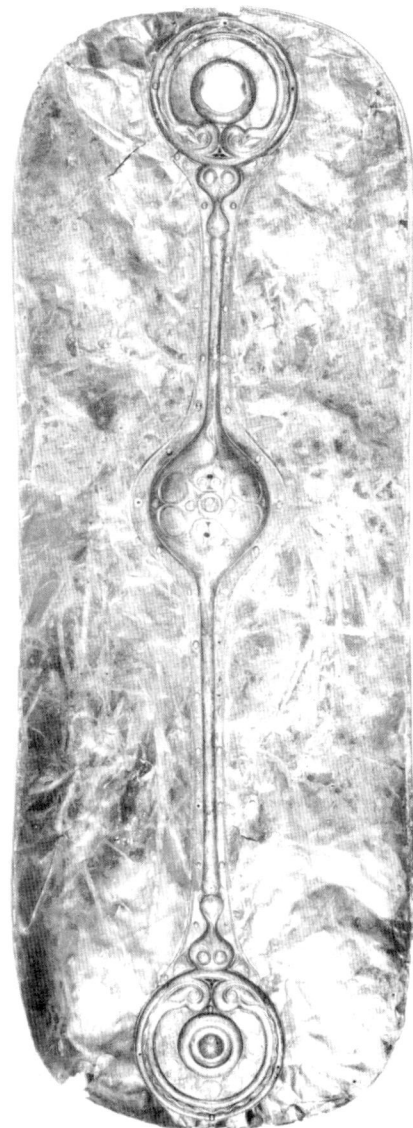

flow of the Witham, and the flat basin at the junction of the rivers Witham and Till (always prone to flooding) will have become more and more a landscape of pools and meres in the centre of an extensive wetland. Research into the nature of the early Brayford by Mr R Carey (unpublished) seems to indicate that the Till flowed along the southern side of the Pool – then considerably larger than now – up to its junction with the Witham. More recent research based on analysis of boreholes in the area of the developing Lincoln University campus has identified the former course of the Till as it entered Brayford Pool to the south of the present Fossdyke (Rackham 1999). Based partly on work by the Soil Survey and on aerial photographs, Wilkinson explained the wider geographical background of these features by identifying an estuarine creek system of late prehistoric date with only occasional tidal influence (1986–7), and his conclusions have informed Figs. 4.2 and 4.4. Numerous studies have suggested that such 'liminal' landscapes of pools and meres provided the ideal locations for the deposition of metalwork. Such environments were frequently thought to be interfaces between the gods and man, portals at which communication between the natural and the super-natural became possible. It is easy to see, then, that the existence of an extensive area of water, and pools, and containing some sand-islands, gave a very special character to the site of what was to become Lincoln.

Environmental sampling of the buried peats on the south side of the existing Pool, undertaken in 1994 in connection with the development of the first phase of the University, has produced more concrete information on the early landscape (Fig. 5.8). Although detailed study of the samples has not yet been possible, the results available to date from the Environmental Archaeology Unit at the University of York are of some interest (Carrott *et al.* 1994). The peat samples were particularly rich in plant and invertebrate remains, indicating a natural wetland with developing reed swamp, fen carr and incipient raised bog. Two of the samples from adjacent contexts, both containing much oak and alder pollen, were subjected to dating by radiocarbon assay, and produced dates in the late Neolithic and Bronze Ages (4850±50 BP (2850BC) and 3100±60 BP (1150BC) – not yet calibrated). Earlier peat layers were noted in this area, suggesting that sedimentation may have begun as early as the Mesolithic period, at a time when even the sandy areas as low as 1m OD may have been habitable (Rackham 1999). There was almost no indication in these peat deposits of any human activity, but given the character of the area as a potentially 'reserved' and 'sacred' place, bronze- and iron-age 'settlement' of a conventional type may not be expected.

It is precisely because we would not expect ordinary domestic settlement in the area of Brayford Pool that the discovery of an iron-age 'house' and its related structures at at 181–3 High Street (HG72) is now seen as such an important event. The extensive iron-age and early Roman pottery assemblages from the site have already been published (Darling 1988), and an updated brief account appears in the site reports volume in this series (Steane *et al.* 2001). These deposits lie about 200m south of the present river line, and over 100m east of the present Brayford Pool. Two phases of features, including an eaves-drip gully partly defining a circular or sub-circular 'building', 5–7m in diameter, and a rectilinear timber structure represented by post-holes, probably belong to the period between 100 BC and the Roman Conquest (Fig. 5.9). A north–south ditch to the east was possibly as late as the Conquest period itself. These structural remains resemble those found at other late iron-age

sites in the region, notably Dragonby, Colsterworth and Ancaster (May 1996, 599–601).

The remains at 181–3 High Street were found on a sand terrace at an elevation of about 4.8m OD. Lower ground, evidently permanently waterlogged at this date, was identified at sites to north (SB 85) and south (SM 76), while the open water to the west lay less than 100m away (and 70m or more east of its present line) (Fig. 5.10). This site, then, was very probably an island in the Iron Age. Other areas of higher ground within the wetland have been provisionally identified as islands in the late Iron Age (Rackham 1999) and it is likely that Haw Hill, still further to the south-west, owes its origin to a similar natural feature. Given that we now suspect that the island was located in the centre of a complex of pools and meres with a clear ritualistic significance to the iron-age peoples of the area, however, we must now question whether this occupation was domestic in character. No evidence was found in these early phases for the character of occupation here, but given what we now know of the island's topographical and ritual context, comparisons between this early structure and, for example, the round-houses at Dragonby may be less relevant than was once thought. Certainly, in the later Roman period, when there is more evidence for the character of occupation on the site, the artefact assemblage clearly indicates a specialised, if not a ritual, use (p. 104 below).

The native-style pottery from the excavations at 181–3 High Street included much shell-tempered ware, and types dated as far back as the 1st century BC (notably a burnished and decorated jar) (Darling 1988). A large proportion of the material came from residual deposits and could post-date the Conquest, and locally-made pottery may have continued in use by the Roman army. Darling also discussed the problem of whether the material was used by natives or incoming Romans. No definite non-ceramic artefacts can be attributed definitely to the pre-Conquest occupation, although several of those discovered were possibly pre-Roman in origin (Mann 1988). The admittedly small collection of the animal bones from the early deposits is probably not statistically valid but, if representative, did reinforce the view that natives occupied the site in the earliest phases, based partly on the range of species represented and evidence of butchery techniques (Scott 1988).

The island at 181–3 High Street, of course, was some way west of the proposed causeway, perhaps too far west for it to be linked, and it may have been accessed only by boat. But there must have been a major trackway leading northwards from the northern terminal of the Stamp End causeway towards the hilltop. The hillside itself across which it passed was then, as it still is today, the site of an active spring line. Although our understanding of the natural topography of the area of the later Lower City is not very detailed, it seems likely that these springs issued into the streams which rushed down the steeper parts

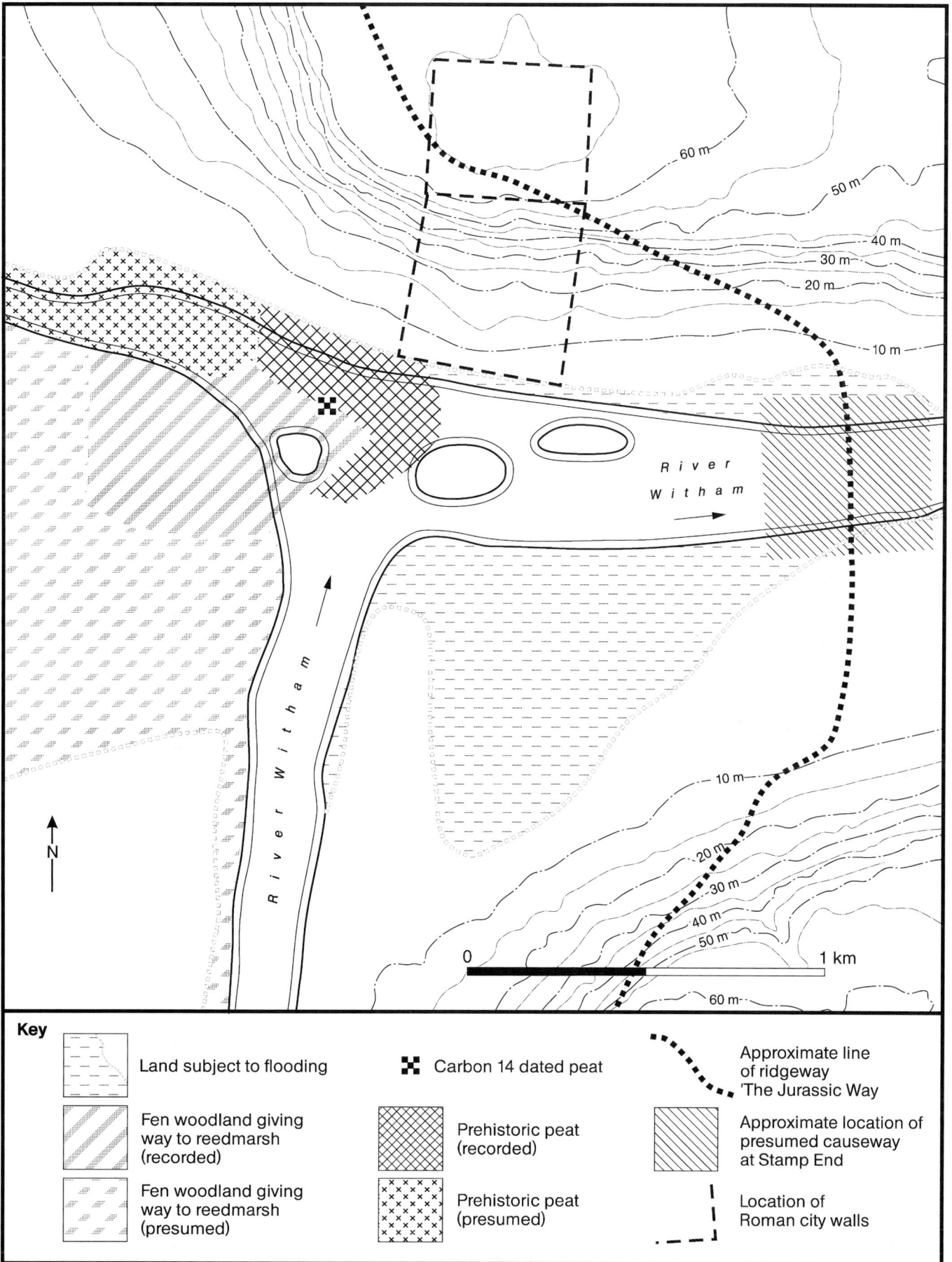

**Key**

| | | |
|---|---|---|
| Land subject to flooding | Carbon 14 dated peat | Approximate line of ridgeway 'The Jurassic Way |
| Fen woodland giving way to reedmarsh (recorded) | Prehistoric peat (recorded) | Approximate location of presumed causeway at Stamp End |
| Fen woodland giving way to reedmarsh (presumed) | Prehistoric peat (presumed) | Location of Roman city walls |

*Fig. 5.8. The Lincoln pool in the later prehistoric period, with current assessment of paleoecology (Carrott et al. 1994; Rackham 1999)(drawn by Dave Watt, copyright English Heritage).*

*Fig. 5.9. The remains of the circular, or sub-circular, late iron-age structure (No. 11) excavated at 181–3 High Street (HG 72) in 1972, looking south. The curving line of the gully is clearly visible. The scale is 2m long. The building was located on a sand island in the slow-moving river and may have had some ritual function. (photo and copyright, City of Lincoln Archaeology Unit).*

of the hill side and may have formed pools on the ledge or terrace which can still be appreciated in the modern topography, approximately between Clasketgate–West Parade and Saltergate–Guildhall Street. Given what we have said about the apparent sacred significance of the pools behind the Stamp End causeway, it is likely that these pools of unadulterated fresh water (the river water above Stamp End would occasionally be brackish) will also have been of some interest, both practical and ritual, to prehistoric peoples.

Other than the site at 181–3 High Street, no structures of definite iron-age date have been found in the city itself, but a number of features of this date are known or suspected in the neighbourhood (Fig. 5.10). North–south ditches found on the site of the football stadium at Sincil Bank in 1994 had been sealed by alluvium, but probably of the late Roman period rather than of the prehistoric. They are probably associated with the Roman urban settlement (Trimble 1994a). Above hill, a mile to the NW, however, shelly pottery of the early 1st century AD was found at Burton Cliff in pits revealed during the construction of the Lincoln Relief Road in 1984 (Field 1985, 72). It is likely to indicate a settlement site of the late Iron Age. A collection of native type pottery of the Conquest period, including both beakers and bowls, has also been recovered from the Lawn site, to the west of the uphill fortress (Darling 1988, 46–50, fig. 9). It would be unwise to claim this as being pre-Roman, since its use may have been associated with the presence of the army. A line of what were either postholes or geological solution-holes was also found at the site, but these do not necessarily indicate pre-Roman occupation. A pit containing bone fragments,

found on the site of St Paul-in-the-Bail, the site of the Roman legionary headquarters and the subsequent civic *forum*, was initially associated with the early churches (Jones M J 1994; Steane *et al.* 2003). The stratigraphy was unclear, but the radicarbon date subsequently obtained for the bone in this feature was 370 Cal BC – Cal AD 220, with a medial date of 43BC. In retrospect therefore, it is quite possible that this was a pit of late iron-age date.

Although it may be easy to dismiss the pottery evidence for late iron-age occupation on the hilltop, it must be said that some form of activity here prior to the Roman period should be expected, if only on topographical grounds. The butt-ends of the cliff at the Lincoln gap are amongst the most spectacular landforms in the county and both cliff tops, but especially the northern, are prominent from the east as well as being visible for many miles across the Trent valley. Although it is the most dramatic example, Lincoln is one of three sites in early Romano-British Lincolnshire which share a similar 'gap' location, the other two being Ancaster and Kirmington. Both of these other sites seem, superficially, to have had a similar development in the Roman period to Lincoln – at both sites a substantial Roman settlement developed in the valley floor, despite drainage problems. At both Kirmington and Ancaster however, a pre-Roman iron-age phase of great importance and interest is evident. At each place, on the crest of one of the hills dominating the settlement in valley floor, there is a highly specialised enclosure.

These two sites have conventionally been called 'hillforts', but such a description does not fit their form comfortably. The enclosure in Honington parish (above Ancaster) has two ditches and possibly three banks and is an irregular parallelogram about 150m × 100m (Fig. 5.11). It has been the site of many important finds of Roman coins and other Roman material. More significantly for our purposes, late iron-age harness fragments and weaponry have been found here (Stukeley 1724, 81; ed. Gough 1806, II, 359). Similarly, while no late iron-age coins are reported from the site, such coins have been found in the settlement which preceded the town of Ancaster in the valley below (May 1984, 21). The hilltop enclosure at Kirmington (called Yarburgh Camp) is a similar sub-rectangular earthwork to that at Honington (measuring *c.*90m × 70m), but it has only a single ditch. Like Honington, Yarburgh Camp can be dated to the later prehistoric period, although it has so far produced few finds – in contrast to the nearby settlement at Kirmington (May 1976, 143; 1984, 21; Albone and Field 2000, 45–6; Leahy forthcoming). These are clearly not settlement sites of any recognised type, nor do they have similar characteristics to hill-forts in southern and western Britain. Their dramatic locations and the character of the finds which they have produced point strongly towards their being 'reserved' enclosures, perhaps converted, after the Roman invasion, into temple precincts.

Was there any similar iron-age enclosure in the very

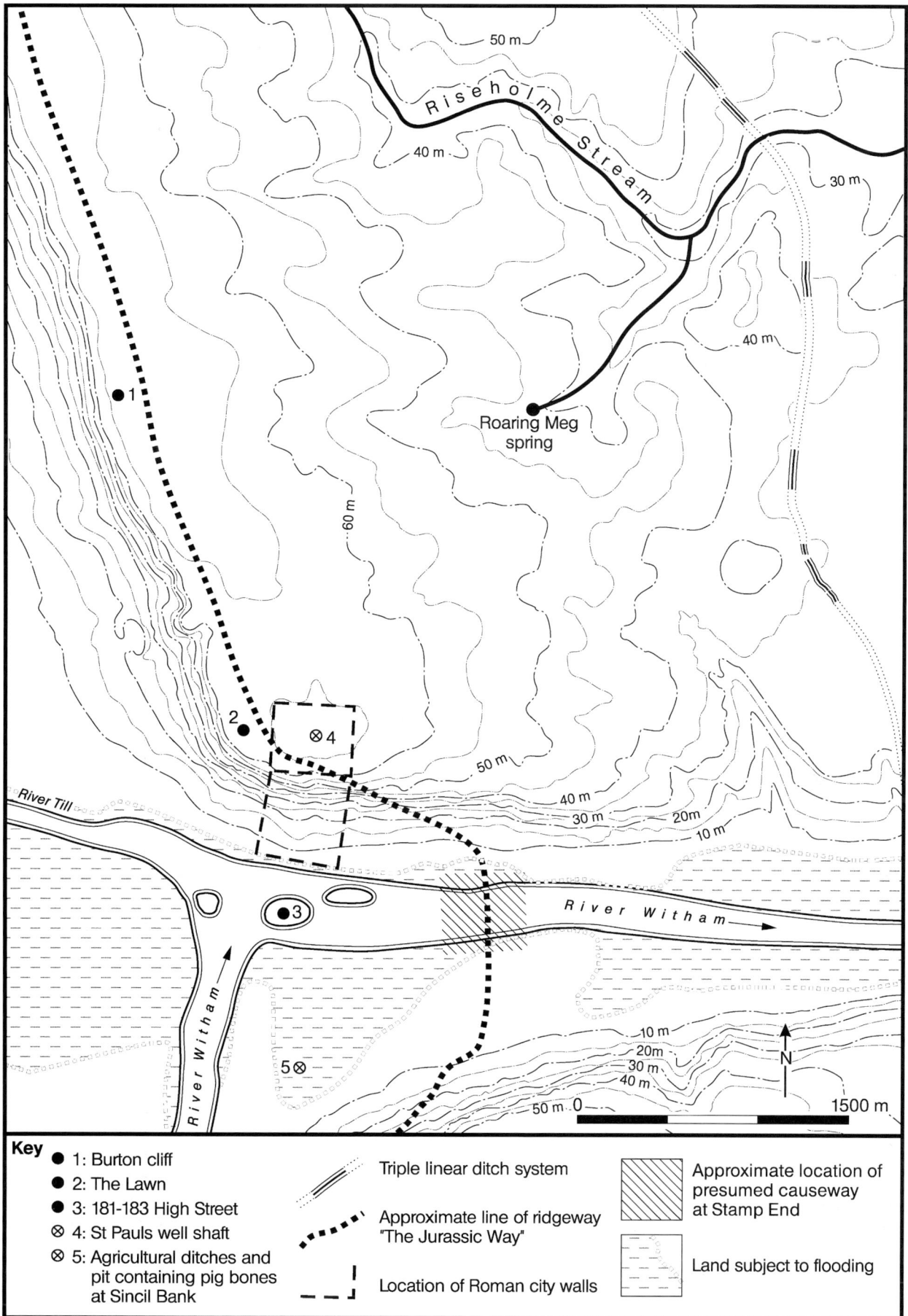

*Fig. 5.10. Known and suspected late iron-age features around Lincoln. (sources, Everson 1979 and Lincolnshire SMR – drawn by Dave Watt, copyright English Heritage).*

_Fig. 5.11. The so called 'hill-fort' at Honington, above the gap in the limestone ridge at Ancaster, Kesteven, from the north-west. Rich finds from the site suggest that it was occupied during the Iron Age and that occupation continued into the Roman period. Was there ever such an enclosure on the hill at Lincoln? (photo and copyright, Dave Start and Heritage Lincolnshire)._

similar, hilltop, location at Lincoln before the Roman army took possession? At present the answer to this question seems to be negative; we have simply failed to find evidence for any iron-age enclosure, or indeed for any un-enclosed ritual site on the hilltop. The only sign of prehistoric monuments on the northern hilltop is the antiquarian reference to a large mound on the crest of the hill west of the Lawn Hospital, which was known as 'Giant's Grave' in the early 19th century and was recorded by Edward Willson (p. 188 and 220 below). It highly likely that this mound formed the base of a medieval windmill, but that does not necessarily mean that it was not a burial mound previously. The site has not yet been accurately located and remains enigmatic.

What then do these slight indications amount to? May's discussion (1988) of the significance of the finds from Lincoln points out that the city has produced no stratified iron-age coins, although the fact that it has produced any at coins at all is remarkable enough – given the rarity of such sites in the county (it has produced either two or three unstratified coins – May 1984, 21; 1994; White 1984a, 96). Nor has it produced any other finds of a type such as one might expect on

an occupation site. Whether these few remains could constitute an _oppidum_ according to the definition of that term by May (1996, 628–31) is doubtful. If we stress the role of the _oppidum_ as a gathering place for a political unit, however, a place which was singled out from the surrounding countryside for ceremonial activities, perhaps in association with a tribal 'sacred place', then the word _oppidum_ for the hilltop north of the river at Lincoln might start to look more credible. What we can say is that the place seems to have had sufficient status as a place to have merited a name, presumably _lindon_, from the stem _lind-_, for 'pool' or 'lake'; hence, the 'place by the pool' (Rivet and Smith 1979, 393; Cameron 1985, 1–3), later latinised to lindum. The fact that it was the pool (perhaps a sacred pool) which gave its name to the location as a whole probably suggests that this was its most distinctive feature, and that any activity on the hilltop (ritual or otherwise) was subordinate to the pool.

Of possible relevance to discussion of whether the title _oppidum_ is in any way appropriate to Lincoln may be the traces of an extensive linear ditch system, which has been noted in several locations to the north and north-east of the city (Everson 1978b; 1979; Field

1980; Palmer-Brown 1993; Boutwood 1998; Trimble 2000; 2001; 2002; Field and Armour-Chelu 2001) (Fig. 5.10). These multiple ditches and their associated banks, which were not continuous, formed a boundary system, which extended northwards from the cliff-edge in the Greetwell area, and then northwestwards, to the west of Nettleham. Boutwood suggested that the ditches east of Lincoln were components of a much larger system of ditches which divided up the 'highlands' along the Lincoln Edge to the north (1998). In her analysis, the lengths of ditch between Greetwell and Nettleham would have formed parts of the long multi-ditched boundary that ran along the dip slope of the hills. At intervals along its course it was joined by other boundaries running across the ridge from the cliff-edge to the west and dividing it into large rectangles (such transverse ditches have been reported in Grayingham, Willoughton and Hemswell parishes, towards Kirton-in-Lindsey). It is likely that east–west components of this ditch-system existed closer to Lincoln than Hemswell, and we should expect the discovery of further east–west boundaries, at right angles to the north–south system, closer to the city. Indeed a possible east–west line has been noted on an aerial photograph of 1988 (in the possession of the City Council) which suggests a further triple ditch joining the known north–south alignment near Bunkers Hill, east-north-east of the city centre.

Wherever the known north–south ditch system was joined by such hypothetical east–west ditches, or indeed by other natural or man-made features across the ridge, the 'headland' on which the Roman city was to be established would be effectively 'enclosed'. In this topographical respect the ditch system northeast of Lincoln invites comparison with that which isolated the *oppidum* of *Camulodunum* (Colchester) before the Roman Conquest, which also enclosed the promontory on which the Roman city was to be founded. Some of the best-preserved examples of these ditches, north-west of Nettleham, were more than 1.5m deep in places and were associated with counterscarp banks (as in the site excavated at Bunkers Hill in 2000). The banks would have been a very visible feature in the landscape and their fabric contained pottery of the 2nd and 1st centuries BC. Accordingly it was argued that the ditch-system represents an 'expression of territorialism at a time of increasing population and pressure on land' (Palmer-Brown 1993), but we should also consider multi-functional roles – including the symbolic – for such features. As well as barriers for controlling people and stock movement, and access to water, they can be seen as structures restricting access to reserved spaces and framing ceremonial. The gaps in the ditches, at which other features including possible fences were found, could have been connected with all of these activities; functional and symbolic. The most recent investigations at Greetwell, indicate that not all the ditches were in use at the same time, and that one was filled before the 2nd century BC. A date no later than the early or middle Iron Age for the construction of the system is proposed here, with final back-filling not occurring until the Roman period.

Of course, late iron-age occupation of whatever type at Lincoln must be seen within the context of the political geography of the region, especially that of the local tribe, the *Coritani*, or now more correctly the *Corieltauvi* (Tomlin 1983). The core-periphery model of the economic and social development of the tribes of southern and eastern Britain is a useful way of analysing the comparative systems, but may be too simplistic (Cunliffe 1988, 154–7; 1991, 175–9; Burnham *et al.* 2001). In recent years, the results of landscape study (e.g. D Jones 1988; ed. Bewley 1998) and excavation have identified many more settlements, and an impression of the Corieltauvi as a complex and sophisticated rural society is gaining acceptance. Amongst recent studies, the final report on excavations at the extensive settlement at Dragonby stands out (May 1996). May has also discussed the major settlements of the eastern area of the tribal region in the 1st century BC (i.e. those occupying Lincolnshire and at least eastern Leicestershire) and characterised them as 'open' sites, showing evidence of wealth and expansion (1984) (Fig. 5.12). Such prosperity may, he suggests, have been stimulated by early contacts with both south-east Britain and Gaul and it points towards a stable economic and social system. In more recent analyses, based on a study of abundant coin finds and on pottery types, May has developed his ideas on the late Iron Age in this region further (1994; 1996, 638–44). He argues that the area between the Humber and the Witham appears to have been the main area of development, where an economy based primarily on stock-raising existed on the chalk and limestone hills. The availability of iron ore and salt no doubt provided further sources of wealth and both were available within easy reach of Lincoln itself (Fig. 5.13). The occurrence of stamped and decorated pottery was confined to this northern area of the county until *c.*100BC, when, perhaps in search of better sea-passages, the area south of the Witham was also included and cultural and technological refinements spread. Lincoln sits, then, on the border of May's proposed two late iron-age regions, and before the likely presence of the Stamp End causeway had been identified, May and others presumed that it was later in origin than the sites further east along the valley. Viewed against May's proposals, the identification of the likely causeway at Stamp End now places Lincoln at the centre of the Corieltauvian polity; linking, as it were, its heartland with its dependencies.

Important work on the Corieltauvi, on a similar scale to May's work at Dragonby, has also occurred at Old Sleaford, however, and revealed an even more exceptional site, which was not only very large but also a major centre of coin production (Elsdon 1997).

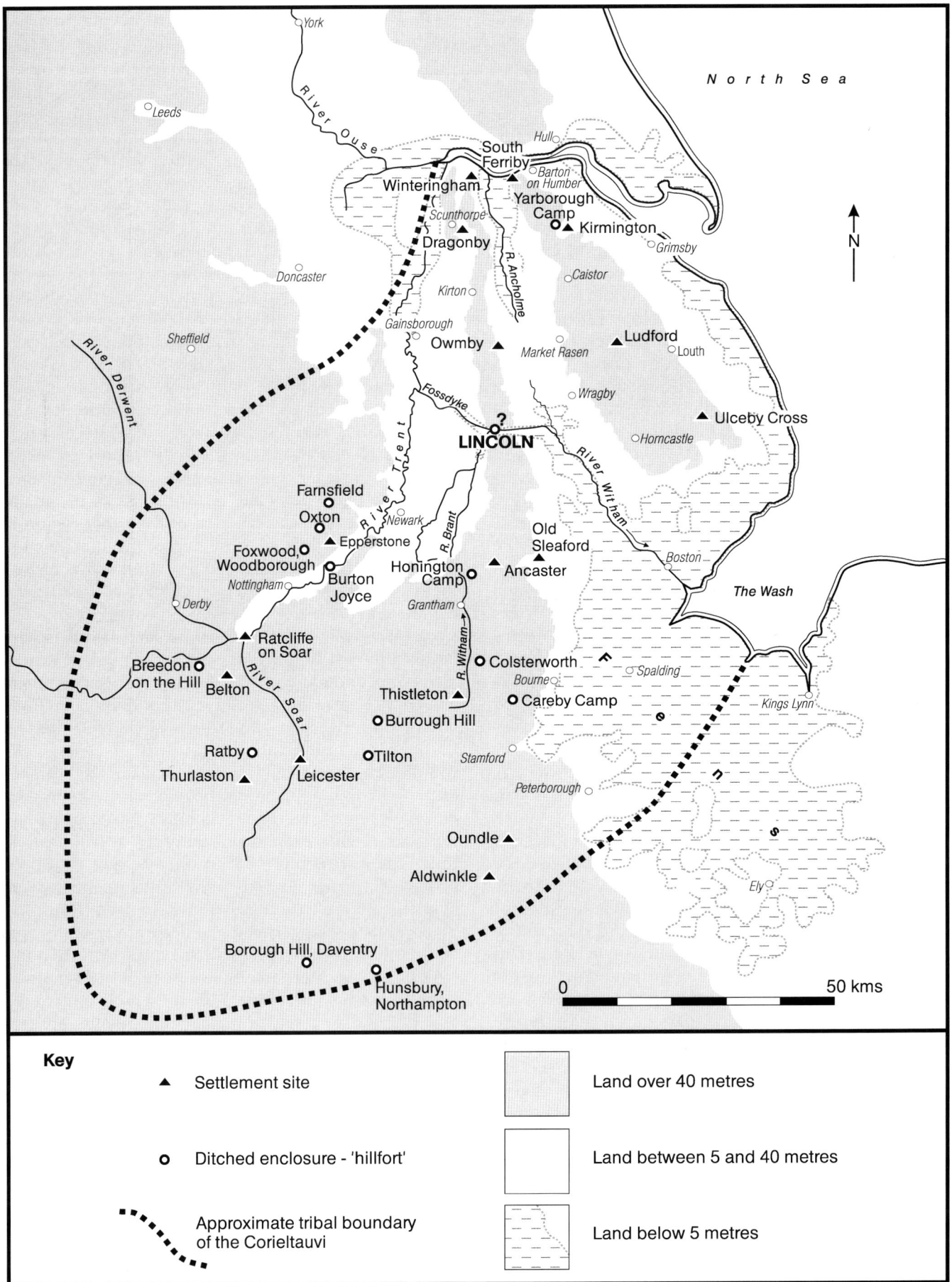

**Key**

| | | |
|---|---|---|
| ▲ | Settlement site | |
| O | Ditched enclosure – 'hillfort' | |
| ▬ ▬ ▬ | Approximate tribal boundary of the Corieltauvi | |

Land over 40 metres

Land between 5 and 40 metres

Land below 5 metres

_Fig. 5.12. The East Midlands in the Iron Age (sources, May 1976; 1984 and others – drawn by Dave Watt, copyright English Heritage)._

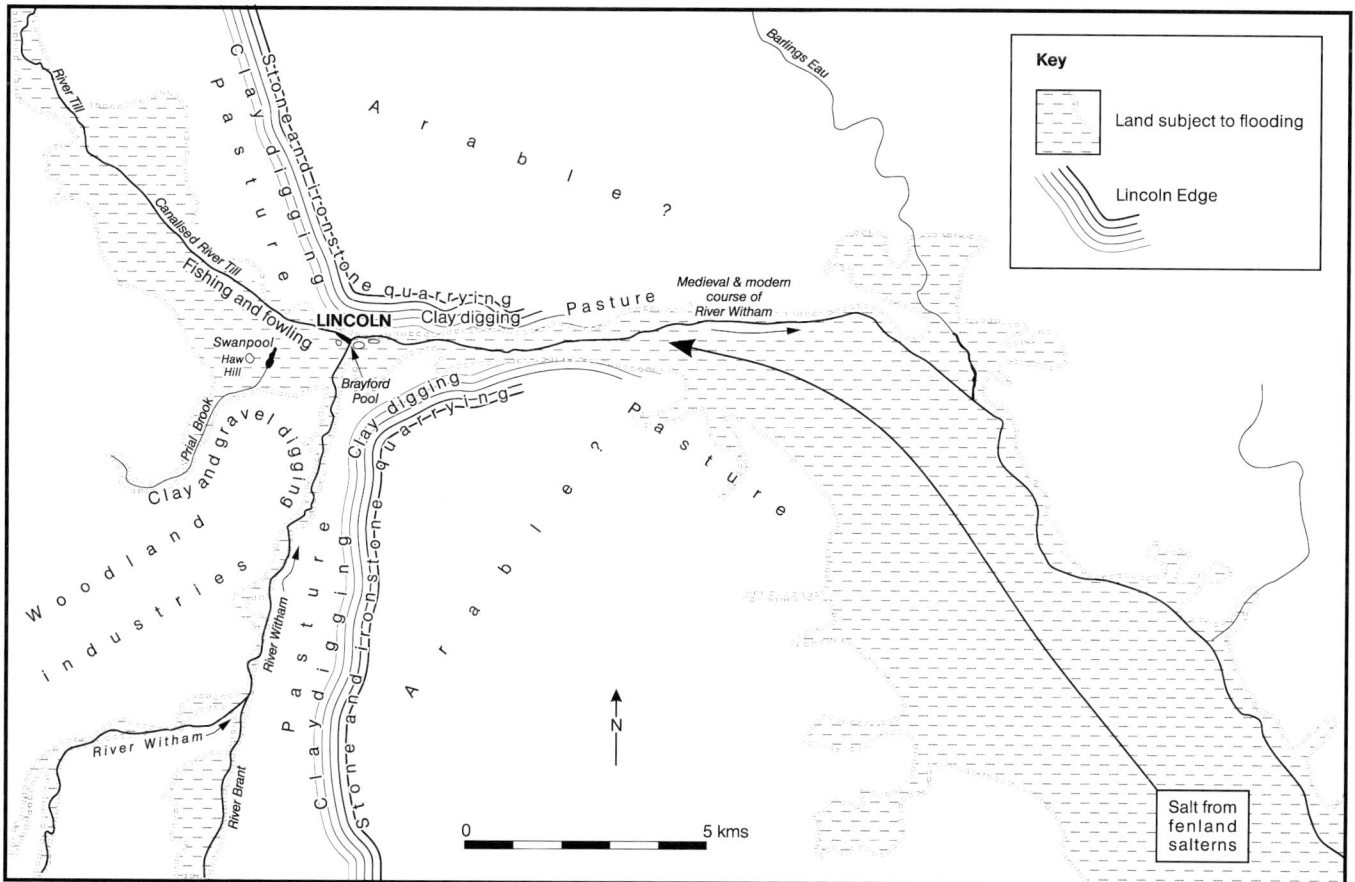

*Fig. 5.13. The likely availability of raw materials in the Lincoln area at the end of the Iron Age (drawn by Dave Watt, copyright English Heritage).*

If one takes an 'economic' definition of the term *oppidum*, there can be little doubt that Old Sleaford was the *oppidum* of the Corieltauvi (Millett 1990, 87). Yet Old Sleaford lies south of the Witham, outside May's proposed 'core' area of the tribe. For reasons we can only guess at, the Romans chose to relocate the 'central' place of the Corieltauvi to Leicester rather than Lincoln, even though Lincoln, perhaps a sacred, rather than an economic site of the Corieltauvi, was eventually recognised too by the foundation of the *colonia*. Lincoln was not, however, the only other potentially important location for the Corieltauvi outside Old Sleaford. The current project at Owmby (20km north of Lincoln) has yielded many late iron-age coins and an orderly series of enclosures (MacAvoy forthcoming). Owmby eventually became the next major Roman settlement site going north from Lincoln; that to the south was Navenby, which has also produced some evidence for settlement in the Iron Age. Furthermore both Owmby and Navenby may have seen early Roman military occupation.

In the Iron Age then, as in the Bronze Age, settlement in the area of the city should not be viewed as pre- or proto-urban, but rather as part of a local and regional tribal pattern, and one which contrasts with that found in other regions, for instance, in the Iceni tribal area of Norfolk (Davies and Williamson 1999). But, although Lincoln does not have evidence for a resident population in the late Iron Age, there are some hints that it was a place of significance for the Corieltauvi. The location derived its significance, and its place-name, from the sacred pools that were approached, we may propose, via the Stamp End causeway, which would itself have had a ritualistic as well as a functional character. With the exception of the enigmatic buildings on the island in the pool, there is no evidence for any other permanent occupation in the vicinity, but we might speculate that the hilltop was a place of some significance – if only on the evidence of topographical parallels such as Honington and Yarburgh Camps. No evidence has yet been produced for enclosures of this type at Lincoln, but the significance of this hilltop area might have been made visible to contemporaries as a sub-division within the known iron-age ditch system, by means of which the whole of the Lincoln Edge north of the gap was divided.

# B. The Prehistoric Era – The archaeological agenda. An introduction to the Research Agenda Zone entries (on CD-Rom)

## *David Stocker*

Although the evidence for settlement within the modern city boundary is both slight and late in date (RAZ 5.7), we should not take this to mean that the place was of no interest to prehistoric peoples. We can point to circumstantial and topographical evidence, as well as finds, to show that the river-crossing had been a focus of activity since at least the Bronze Age, as it had probably also been during the Neolithic. Naturally, we would expect the importance of the Lincoln river-crossing to be reflected in activity in the surrounding countryside. But we can hardly pretend that archaeology of the Prehistoric Era is thick on the ground and, therefore, establishing a research agenda is less complex than it is for later periods. Furthermore, any understanding of archaeological remains of this Era within the city boundary will be more dependent on the patterning of discoveries in the county nearby than is the case for better represented Eras. For these reasons, archaeologists working in the city should be greatly interested in prehistoric archaeology within a 10 or 20 mile radius; when viewed strategically, finds in this zone will have a very direct bearing on our understandings of Lincoln city sites and artefacts.

As our understanding of the city area in the prehistoric era is based so heavily on our understanding of the distinctive topography of Lincoln, palaeo-environmental studies will be particularly valuable here (RAZs 5.8; 5.9). Indeed, the much greater spans of time included within this Era, compared with later ones, will mean that landscape character within our study area will have changed enormously during its course and a basic dated sequence for prehistoric landscape development in the locality is still absent. The development of such a dated sequence is an urgent prerequisite for progress of archaeological research in this Era more generally.

In the light of our current knowledge, however, we can say that it was the distinctive character of the developing landscape around the area which was to become Lincoln that defined its role throughout the Prehistoric Era. In landscape terms this was a distinctive place in its region throughout prehistory and, consequently, we need to explore whether this distinctiveness was matched by equivalent regional cultural importance. We should also be aware that there may be fundamental cultural distinctions to be drawn within this long period. For example, it is possible that the distinction between the small groups of isolated finds of the Mesolithic–Early Bronze Age and the more elaborate finds and structures of the Late Bronze and Iron Ages represents a real difference in the cultural use of the area. The fact that there is little sign of occupation in the Lincoln gap much before the Roman period certainly does not mean that the site was of no importance, but it might mean that the site's importance was appreciated by peoples who actually lived elsewhere. Those peoples invested in the site only occasionally, but when they did so, the investment was, by contemporary standards, spectacular. The bronze- and iron-age metalwork finds from the river demonstrate the great scale of this investment in the valley at this point, even if they do not suggest occupation (RAZ 5.2). Similarly, in the Iron Age, the lack of occupation remains should not be interpreted as evidence that the place was forgotten. Indeed the evidence we have suggests that it was of considerable symbolic importance to the peoples in whose territory it lay - otherwise why demarcate it with such substantial boundary ditches (RAZ 5.6)? We need not get bogged down in the definition of *oppida* here, but we should bear in mind Martin Millett's advice on this subject, 'Whether or not it was permanently occupied, the focus of the tribe became identified with the central location' (1990, 26). The evidence we have so far suggests that Lincoln may have been just such a largely unoccupied central location in both the later Bronze Age and the Iron Age.

Within this Era, the District Council area has been divided into eleven distinct RAZs. The RAZ accounts, along with their mapped extent, can be accessed on the CD-Rom.

5.1   The Jurassic Way
5.2   Early crossing points and the Stamp End causeway
5.3   Hill top activity
5.4   Hill-side springs, streams and pools
5.5   Barrow fields north of Canwick
5.6   Ditched boundaries to west (and north?) of the city
5.7   Known settlement sites
    5.7.1   Settlement site on Burton Road

74

5.7.1

73

5.6

5.9.1

72

5.1

5.3

5.1

50 m

5.4

5.1

71

5.4

10 m

5.7.2

5.2

5.8 & 5.5

5.5

70

5.9.1

10 m

5.1

.8

50 m

69

10 m

N

68

67

0 1 2 km

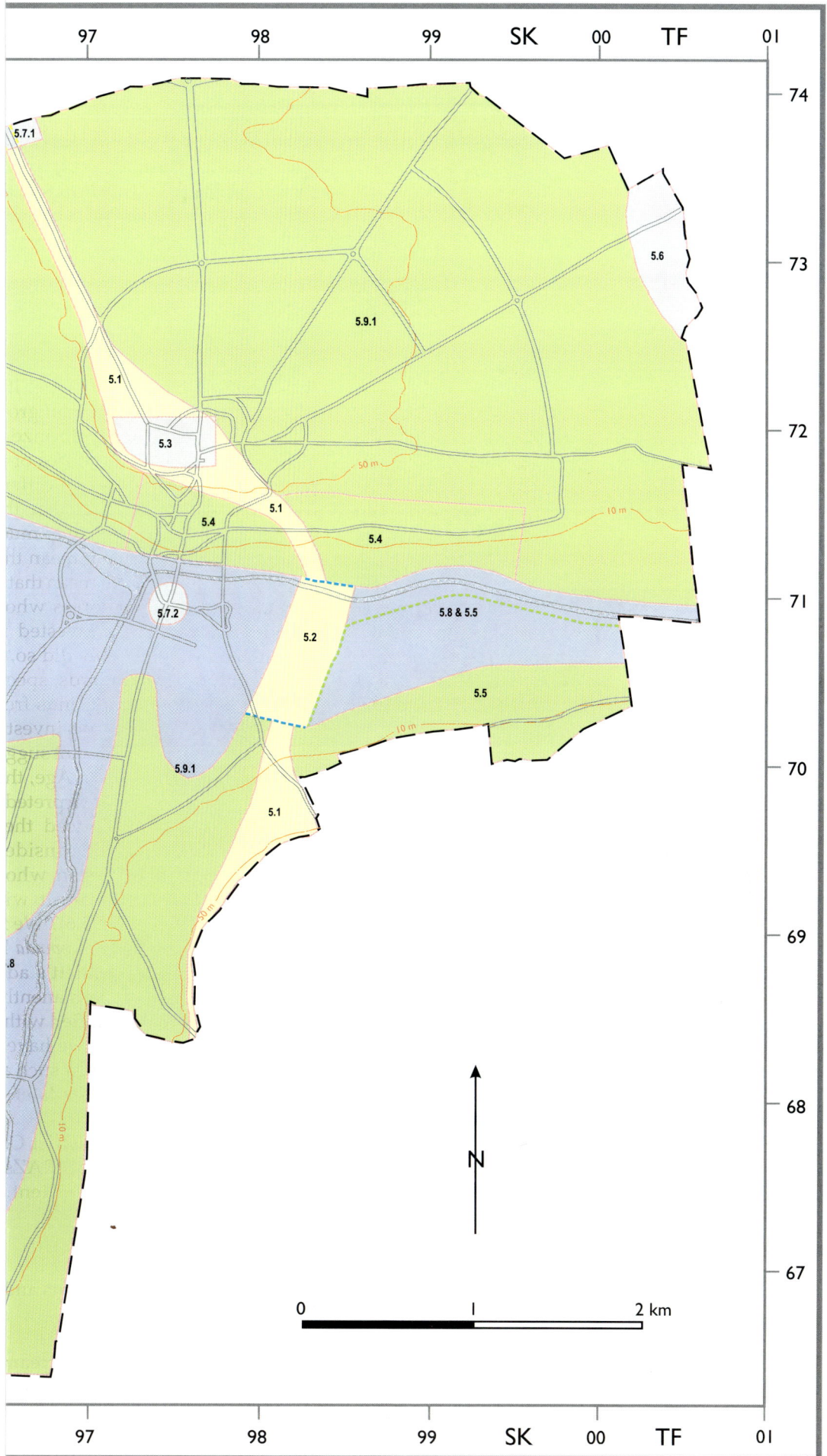

*Map 1. Research Agenda Zone locations for the Prehistoric Era – see CD-Rom for details (drawn by Dave Watt, copyright English Heritage and Lincoln City Council).*

The first two of these RAZs relate to known or suspected routeways, although, as we have seen in chapter 5A (above), the Stamp End route (RAZ 5.2) probably had an important ritual character as well as a functional one. This interrelationship between the ritual and the utilitarian will be a continuing theme through Lincoln's archaeology, and all future work, in every period, will have to bear it in mind. What is more, it is highly unlikely that we will be able to distinguish easily between the two motivations in most archaeological contexts. We are becoming accustomed to the idea that ritual activities in the past were not detached from daily life but were an integral part of it. Thus a river might be crossed for everyday purposes in a highly ritualised way. Similarly, we might argue, the construction of a well on the top of the hill (RAZ 5.3) or the collection of water from springs in the hillside (RAZ 5.4) might have both a ritual and a utilitarian aspect, and we need to be aware of this in our consideration of such features.

Conversely, if such utilitarian archaeological features can have a ritual dimension, we might think that overtly ritualised structures such as barrows (RAZ 5.5) should also be questioned about functional uses to which they might have been put. The same combination of ritualistic and utilitarian questions might also be asked of the ditched boundaries to the west and north of the city (RAZ 5.6), which could have served both to corral stock *and* to structure ceremonial.

Evidence for prehistoric settlement sites of a more conventional type (that is to say evidence for 'accommodation') has been extremely rare within the District boundaries (it has only been encountered at two places – RAZ 5.7.1 & 5.7.2), but that does not mean that we cannot identify favourable locations where settlement remains of this Era might be expected (RAZ 5.9.1), and further work here should aim to place such settlement within wider patterns in the region.

# 6. The Roman Military Era

# A. Archaeological account

## *Michael J Jones*

### Introduction: the conquest and occupation of the East Midlands

The Roman Conquest must have been a traumatic event in the life of the iron-age peoples of Britain. Prehistoric peoples of the southern and eastern seaboards had experienced many incursions, including one by the Romans in 55 BC, but few, if any, can have had the impact of the arrival of the Roman army in AD 43. Unlike previous invaders and infiltrators, whose armies were either composed of raiding parties who returned home after the raiding season, or land-takers, who eventually settled alongside their conquered neighbours, the Roman army was an army of occupation, a garrison, a projection of the political power of a remote people intent on assimilating Britain into their empire rather than assimilating themselves into Britain. Although many indigenous tribes had lived in nucleated settlements for nearly a millennium, and had been parts of European-wide trading networks for even longer, the disruption in cultural continuity was very great. Many fundamental forms of landscape, structure and artefact were redesigned and set on a new path of development. The impact of the Romans on the Witham basin at Lincoln, then, was radical, but not atypical. The apparently sacred character of the pools and meres (discussed in Chapter 5) underwent great physical changes in the early years of the Conquest, with the imposition of new forts and roads, and, although it would probably be a misrepresentation to say that the lifestyle of the peoples using the gap was completely destroyed, utilisation of the gap must have been changed beyond easy recognition in no more than a generation.

Today, the archaeological remains of the Roman military period are usually at the bottom of the sequence and, consequently, they are often quite fragmentary, but even so, remains surviving from this period include well preserved organic deposits in the waterlogged areas of the valley floor as well as the buried remains of streets and buildings (normally of timber at this date), and the interments of the population. The occupied areas were much smaller than they became later, but that does not mean that the impact of the Roman army was only felt on the hilltop and along the new causeway, which later formed the suburb of Wigford. Acting according to well-practised military protocols, the Roman army will have secured a much larger area of surrounding countryside for exercise, grazing and for the provision of supplies.

Roman military penetration into the tribal region of the Corieltauvi occurred in the first ten years or so after the Roman invasion's landing in AD 43. The date at which Lincoln was first selected and occupied as a military base remains unknown, and the question of whether that first base was the main hilltop fortress is, however, as yet unresolved.

There are several areas of uncertainty. We have, for example, no definite evidence regarding the attitude to the invading army of the local tribe (Todd 1991, 22–3; May 1976, 207). Its lands were situated between the ostensibly friendly client kingdoms of the Brigantes of northern England and the Iceni of East Anglia, both of whom gave trouble in due course. The presence of early garrisons, including those in the so-called 'vexillation-fortresses' of Longthorpe (Frere and St Joseph 1974), Osmanthorpe (Bishop and Freeman 1993), Newton-on-Trent (Welfare and Swan 1995, 67–9), and Rossington Bridge (Van de Noort and Ellis 1997, 275–8) probably indicates some fragmentation of the 9th Legion (Fig. 6.1). There are clear ceramic links between Lincoln and Longthorpe (Dan-

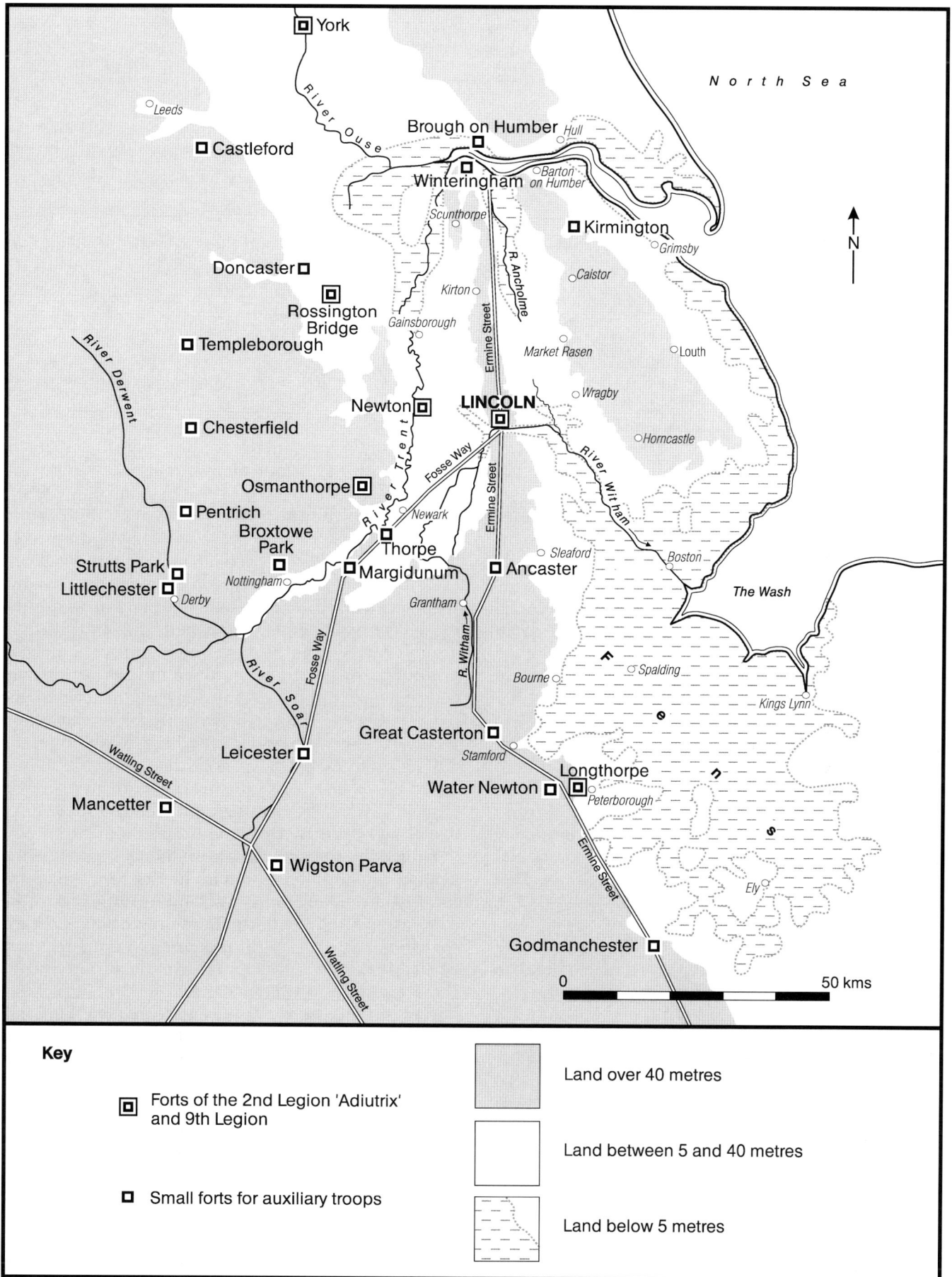

*Fig. 6.1. Roman forts in eastern England (sources, Jones and Mattingly 1990 and others – drawn by Dave Watt, copyright English Heritage).*

nell and Wild 1987) suggesting that potters making red-slipped wares moved from Longthorpe to Lincoln, and this makes it more likely that part of the legion had been at Longthorpe. Legionary vexillations may have been housed in winter quarters, perhaps together with auxiliaries in the campaigning seasons, but the function of these large sites is not known for certain (Bishop and Freeman 1993, 171–5). Hassall (2000, 64–5) has suggested that the so-called vexillation fortresses may actually have contained groups of auxiliary regiments, and that the 9th Legion could have been brigaded together with the 14th at Leicester from c.AD 43 – c.55. The implication of this hypothesis is that sites such as Longthorpe did not contain legionaries. Although the size of the barracks at Longthorpe cannot be used to argue against their housing auxiliary troops, nor is equipment diagnostic (Maxfield 1986, 72), the ceramic links noted above perhaps do make it likely that such sites did contain some legionaries. Other early forts are known, such as that at Kirmington, at a gap in the Wolds (Riley 1977), as well as several temporary camps.

These early sites were at important strategic points, but the developed military road system, which was subsequently created to control the tribe, largely ignores them. It has been proposed that the larger forts were intended to form a frontier line, soon abandoned (Jones and Mattingly 1990, 90–94). The roads – principally the Fosse Way and Ermine Street which joined south of the marshy land and the river crossing at Lincoln – were protected by a series of forts at regular intervals with extra bases at strategic points – a 'rearward communication route'. The details of their exact locations, garrisons and dating need not concern us here: few have been investigated in sufficient detail to reveal their detailed layout, while the military position was fluid and existing methods of dating are of only limited help in assigning them to particular campaigns. As a consequence, interpretations can differ (compare, for example, Webster 1980, 136–7, 162–4, with Todd 1991, 23–36).

Nevertheless, it does appear probable that some of these sites were occupied before the end of the Claudian period (Webster 1980, 1981). It may have been the case that the 9th Legion was subdivided and based in the various smaller fortresses for several years, and the various detachments (or at least most of them) only brought together when the hilltop fortress was constructed at Lincoln. The pottery dating from excavations both inside the uphill fortress and at the earliest sites of extra-mural occupation so far investigated would favour a date in the Neronian period (Darling and Jones 1988; Steane *et al.* 2001), and probably by c. AD 61, possibly following the suppression of the Boudiccan revolt. Webster (1988, 19–21) has suggested a later Neronian foundation with the reorganisation of the legions in c. AD 66 following the withdrawal from Britain of the 14th Legion. Hartley (1981) has proposed an even later date, in the early 70s. Most recently,

Manning's (1997) study of Ptolemy's sources would suggest a date before the mid 60s.

On historical and epigraphic grounds, an earlier, Claudian, base in the Lincoln area is a distinct possibility. The most contentious dating evidence takes the form of several legionary tombstones, most found last century in the Wigford area of Lincoln (Whitwell 1970, 17–18). Epigraphic experts have argued that the 9th Legion tombstones lacking *cognomina* – the third or sur-name – (RIB 1965, 254, 255, 257: below) should be no later than c.AD 50 and thereby indicate a legionary presence in the Claudian period (Birley 1979, 15, 83; Maxfield 1989, 20 and n). Webster would contend that the lack of *cognomina* cannot be taken to indicate such an early *terminus ante quem*, citing later examples (1981, 49). An earlier study of the use of the *tria nomina* by Chilver (1941, 59), covering a wider sample of the Roman citizen population, shows that use of the *cognomina*, though becoming increasingly common, was not universal till later in the 1st century than the Lincoln fortress. At our request Laurence Keppie has kindly re-examined the question in detail (2000, 87–9), consulting evidence from a number of 1st-century military bases, including those previously occupied by the 9th Legion. His study of 250 inscriptions (deliberately excluding those serving in Britain in the Claudio-Neronian period) shows that the practice of adding *cognomina* had begun by Augustus' time, and would argue for an early date for the legion's arrival at Lincoln, although this evidence cannot yet be considered conclusive. In Keppie's study, the material from Mainz in Germany was of some interest: all 13 tombstones of legionaries serving in the fortress at Mainz between AD 43 and 69 had *cognomina*. Christoph Rüger has also given his expert views on the evidence from Lower Germany, which supports an early date for the general use of *cognomina* (pers. com.).

Rüger also questions whether the dating of the first samian ware pottery should not be later than the fortress' foundations, as indicated from excavations at Remagen and Saalburg. Certainly there is a view that the arrival of the army took place a few years earlier than the samian pottery seems to indicate. Unfortunately, the coin evidence is of little help, although there are Republican issues and Claudian copies (Mann and Reece 1983). The *principia* site was the most productive of these early issues (below), which could therefore be explained as currency brought in by the army following the construction of the Neronian fortress, rather than providing an earlier date for its arrival.

Whatever conclusions are drawn, one question is begged by the location of most of the gravestones at a distance of c.2km south of the hilltop fortress, close to the point where the Fosse Way and Ermine Street joined (Fig. 6.2). Was this the cemetery of an earlier fortress, perhaps belonging to the Claudian period, as the author has proposed in several previous papers (Jones 1985; 1988)? There are certainly parallels for

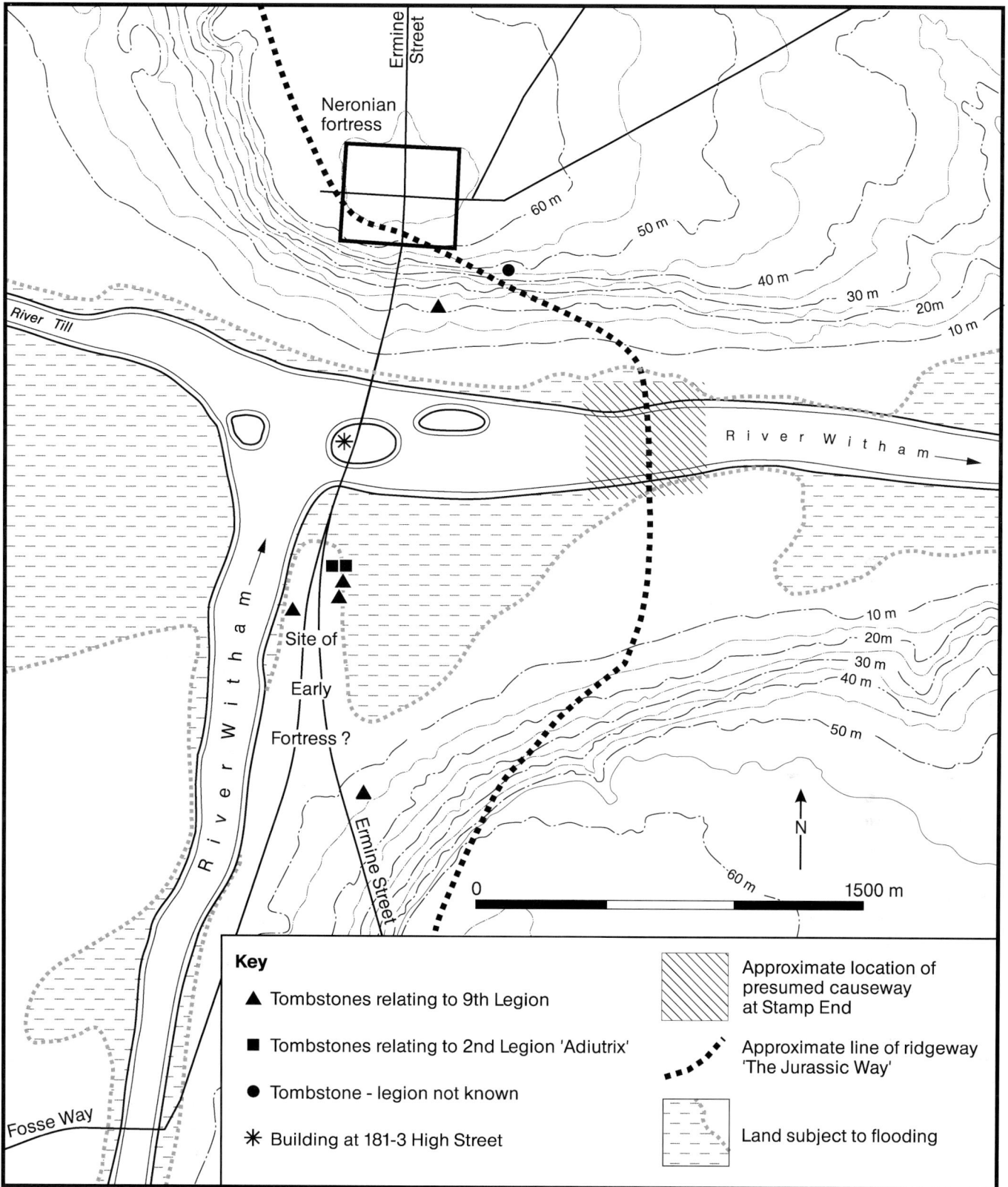

*Fig. 6.2. Lincoln Gap in the 1st century, showing location of legionary fortress and tombstones in relation to topographical features (drawn by Dave Watt, copyright English Heritage).*

similar changes of site, notably from the Claudian base at Kingsholm to the later fortress at Gloucester (Hurst 1988; 1999) – a case of especial interest since this relocation was previously considered to have been connected with the risk of flooding and the position of the river crossing, as may also have been the case at Lincoln. The discovery of a pre-Roman iron-age settlement now suggests rather that the original siting was intended to monitor the native population (Hurst 1999a). But the earliest pottery from the Wigford area of Lincoln appears to be no earlier than Neronian, and it would still be quite acceptable for a cemetery at this distance to have served the uphill base (as at Caerleon and Strasbourg). Certainly the cemetery in Wigford was still in use after the hilltop fortress was built. Moreover, unless the road lines changed later, there would have been little space for a fortress immediately north of the road junction – where it might be expected – and south of the marshy land in the St. Marks area. This still leaves open the possibility of a small base here, or of a larger base further south, especially if the lines of Ermine Street and the Fosse Way originally joined much further south. Its site might have been on the gravel terraces east of the river, and aligned on to Ermine Street rather than the Fosse Way. As yet, however, there is no real evidence apart from the tombstones and the arguments over discrepancies in dating to corroborate this hypothesis. Two ditches sealed by alluvium, and therefore thought to predate the late Roman period, were found running north–south for at least *c.*37m during construction works immediately east of Sincil Bank in 1994 (Trimble 1994b), indicating some form of activity here prior to the invasion, but no dating material was recovered. It is also conceivable that another base remains to be found elsewhere in the Lincoln area, where a construction camp like that at Wroxeter (ed. Chadderton 2002) was located – perhaps even on the hilltop.

In wider geographical terms, Richmond (1946, 26) noted the way in which the site of the Neronian fortress blocked access from the north to the Witham crossing, with the legion held in reserve behind the contemporary tribal and military frontier at the Humber and able to keep an eye on both the Brigantes and the Iceni. It was also possible to block the other route from the north, via the lowest crossing of the Trent at Littleborough/Marton, where a small fort was built; land to the north of that crossing included much wetland (Van de Noort and Ellis 1997). Lincoln was accessible by road from the south and south-west, and from the south-east by water. Perhaps the link with the Fosse Way and the presence of the Brayford Pool were decisive topographical factors in the establishment of the fortress on the hilltop. The natural defensibility of the hilltop site at Lincoln, with its steep scarp to the west as well as to the south, may have encouraged the Roman army to select a site here, rather than one a little further east, where the river crossing may have been easier and facilities already in existence. There were still difficulties with the hilltop fortress' site, which had to be accessed via a marshy valley and a steep climb to an area with poor water accessibility, but these were obviously considered secondary to other factors. Neither the low-lying land in the valley nor the steep, poorly draining hillside were options.

## The Legions at Lincoln

The discovery of several tombstones in the late 19th and earlier 20th centuries was the first decisive step forward in confirming the presence of legionaries at Lincoln (Whitwell 1970 ). They indicated successive garrisoning of a fortress by the 9th Legion and, probably from *c.* AD 71, the 2nd Legion *Adiutrix* (Figs. 6.3. and 6.4). The uncertain date of their arrival is discussed above. Their *origines* are of some interest: the legionaries of the 9th all came from regions close to the Mediterranean – Macedonia, Spain, and Italy (Birley 1979, 83). It is probable that the legion had previously been at Siscia (modern Sisak, in Croatia), in the province of Pannonia (Wilkes 2000, 102),

*Fig. 6.3. Memorial to Gaius Saufeius, soldier of the 9th Legion (Huskinson 1994, No.49). The inscription may be translated:*

To Gaius Saufeius, son of Gaius, of the Fabian tribe, from Heraclea *(i.e. Macedonia),* a soldier of the 9th Legion, aged 40 years and with 22 years' service. He is buried here.

*The stone was found in 1865 beside Ermine Street in Wigford and the drawing was made by Arthur Smith, the first curator of Lincoln Museum.*

*Fig. 6.4. Replica of memorial to Titus Valerius Pudens, soldier of the 2nd Legion (Huskinson 1994, No.53). The inscription may be translated:*

Titus Valerius Pudens, son of Titus, of the Claudian tribe, from Savaria *(south-eastern Austria)*, a soldier of the 2nd legion Adiutrix, the pious and faithful, and in the century of Dossennius Proculus. Aged 30 years, and with ... years' service. His heir erected this monument at his own expense. He is buried here.

*The stone was found in 1849 in Monson Street, off the High Street in Wigford. It is now in the British Museum (photo and copyright, Peter Washbourn).*

although confirmation of this is still awaited. After Lincoln, it went on to found the fortress at York in *c.* AD 71, and it may have been at Carlisle temporarily later in the century. The 2nd *Adiutrix*, as its name implies, was a specially-created force raised to supplement the existing army, and included ex-marines. One of its soldiers was from Lyon, the other with a documented *origo* came from *Savaria*, a colony in the province of Pannonia on the Danube (Birley 1979, 83–4). This legion moved from Lincoln in AD 77–8 to build a new base at Chester, which it probably left in AD 89, for *Aquincum* (Budapest), although it might

have left Chester a little earlier, and spent a short period at Inchtuthil (Hassall 2000, 62; Mason 2001, 41–6, 98–100).

Most of the tombstones were found in the area of Monson Street (see below), off Lower High Street, with one (or two) probably built into the east wall of the Lower City. The well known inscription of the standard bearer, Gaius Valerius (RIB 1965, 257), was found some distance south of Monson Street, towards the north end of South Common (Fig. 6.5). The find on South Common was made in 1909 to the east of the railway; the stone may have been previously disturbed by the digging of the cutting in 1865–7. There were other definite finds of early cremations in this area in 1911 and 1981, so that we can be confident

*Fig. 6.5. Memorial to Gaius Valerius, standard bearer of the 9th Legion (RIB 1965, No.257). The inscription may be translated:*

Gaius Valerius, son of Gaius, of the Maecian tribe, soldier of the 9th Legion, standard-bearer, in the century of the Hospes, aged 35. Service 14 years. He left instructions in his will for this monument. He lies here.

*The stone was not recorded until 1909, but it is thought to have been found close to the line of Ermine Street when the Lincoln-Grantham railway was cut through South Common in 1865 (Smith 1929, 9–11) (photo and copyright, Lincolnshire County Council, Lincolnshire Museums Service)*

that another part of the legionary-period cemetery lay here. It is these discoveries in particular, as well as the absence of *cognomina* on the tombstones, which pose the question of an early legionary base to the south of the Monson Street finds.

## The hilltop fortress

The principal clue to the location of the uphill fortress underlying the later *colonia* (Chapter 7 below) was the discovery of early pottery and artefacts, some of military association, in the area of Westgate and in particular at the Water Tower built in 1910 (ON 237, Webster 1949). Webster was able to identify the line of the fortress' northern and western defences during excavations in the 1940s (Fig. 6.6), and Thompson (1956) and Petch (1960) subsequently confirmed that eastern and southern lines also lay beneath those of the *colonia*. Little progress could be reported, however, in eluci-dating the internal arrangements – except close to the northern part of the western rampart, where Webster was fortunate to find legionary-period deposits close to the modern ground surface. Generally the fortress' slight remains are deeply buried, difficult of access and in places already destroyed. Whitwell's exca-vations close to the Bailgate Methodist Church in 1967–8 revealed a limited number of wall trenches for timber structures, but not sufficiently extensive or well-preserved to identify their functions (ON 261 – unpublished but noted in Whitwell 1970, 21). Similarly slight hints of early buildings were also noted by Petch during work on the nearby *colonia* baths (CP 56), a site

Fig. 6.6. Section through the Roman legionary ditch and, to its left (east), the front palisade trench for the rampart. A view (from the north-west) of the excavations undertaken in Westgate in 1945–6 by Graham Webster – the photograph was taken by I.A. Richmond (photo and copyright Lincolnshire County Council, Lincolnshire Museum Service).

which yielded much early pottery – presumably from rubbish pits and demolition deposits of the fortress structures. Remains of timber buildings on the site suggest that the fortress baths could not have covered quite the same area, and baths did occupy different locations in some fortresses – as, for instance, at Exeter. The relationship between baths and other fortress structures and their replacements or equivalents in the *colonia* period needs further exploration. The position of the *colonia* baths at Lincoln is, however, similar to those at the 9th Legion's fortress at York (Ottaway 1993, 31–3, fig.9), and to those at Caerleon (Zienkiewicz 1986). At Exeter and Usk, the baths were situated in the range to the rear of the *principia* (Henderson 1991; Manning and Scott 1989, 169). It was extremely rare at this period for legionary fortresses to have extra-mural baths, in contrast to auxiliary forts, where such a location was normal (Johnson 1983). The unfinished Flavian fortress at Inchtuthil is one exception; here a baths-suite was provided in the officers' temporary compound (Pitts and St Joseph 1985, 215–8). The scale of the building at Inchtuthil suggests a 'restricted clientele', and it may have been intended to construct a full-scale *balneum* in due course. Alternatively, the extra-mural location at Inchtuthil could have been connected with the problem of water-supply, and the same may have been the case at Lincoln.

The space available inside the defences identified by Webster, Thompson and Petch measured *c*.440m east–west by *c*.360m north–south. The postulated plan would allow for barrack blocks, plus the width of an adjacent street, to measure up to 300 Roman feet, although many contemporary examples were shorter (Maxfield 1986, 63). Two cohorts could be accom-modated to the north and south of the *via praetoria* in the blocks closest to both west and east gates, giving a total of eight cohorts. The first cohort – not yet double at this date (Frere 1980, 58) – might occupy some of the area to the south of the *principia*, and possibly some of the space to the north of it, fronting on to the *via principalis*. Part of what may have been the east–west street north of the *principia* was noted south of the famous length of standing Roman masonry known as the Mint Wall in 1979 (WB 80). There would then still be room for the final, tenth cohort. But the arrangement could be more complex, as at Exeter, where the barracks were shorter in length (*c*.200 feet), inside a fortress that was more elongated in shape than Lincoln, and for which a surveyor's blue-print has been proposed (Bidwell 1997, 32, fig. 16). Two cavalry *alae* also seem to have been fitted in at Exeter, and it is quite possible that in these early years of the Conquest the garrisoning of all bases had to be flexible. At Usk for example, there were *fabricae* (workshops), rather than first cohort barracks, adjacent to the *principia* (Manning and Scott 1989, 166–70).

Another metrological approach to the planning of the Lincoln fortress has been suggested, involving the use of proportions (Jones 1975, 54–60) and square roots, based on principles of geometry exemplified in the mitre square found at Canterbury (Ball and Ball 1988). By this analysis, the *praetentura* (the area east of the *via principalis*) at Lincoln would be of the proportion 1:2 (or the square root of 4), whilst the *retentura* would be 1:1.6216 (probably correctly 1.618, or the 'golden section'). Evans (1994) has also discussed military building techniques, with special reference to the application of modules, but Lincoln is too poorly understood as yet to test this hypothesis. Most recently there has been an impressive attempt to estimate the quantities of materials and manpower required in order to build a fortress (Shirley 2001). While it is accepted that precision is impossible, this careful analysis confirms that the Lincoln fortress' construction would have involved a good proportion of the Legion for a few years. In addition, a large team would be needed to supply them with building materials and with food.

The discovery and identification of the *principia* (below) indicates that the *via principalis* ran north–south (roughly along the line of modern Bailgate/Steep Hill), so that the legionary gates would have underlain those of the *colonia*. The remains of the east gate (RENO 76, Thompson and Whitwell 1973) would then represent those of the *porta praetoria*. Certainly this gate was a double one, while the west gate to the rear of the *principia*, the *porta decumana*, was only a single carriageway, at least in the *colonia* period (*Ibid.*,194–200). This seems to make perfect sense as far as it goes, but the absence of evidence for other identifiable structures or definite streets except those adjacent to the defences means that we can establish little else of the internal layout. The area covered by the fortress, at *c*.17 hectares (*c*.43 acres) is only some 80% of the normal size of later examples, but it is not clear whether it housed a full legion, or only part, since none of the barrack blocks has been investigated to any large extent – it may be that there were fewer ancillary buildings (Manning and Scott 1989, 161). A reconstruction (Fig. 6.7) can be attempted, however, using standard measurements as proposed by Crummy (1985; 1988), even though the pitfalls of this approach have been spelt out by others (Millett 1982). It seems probable that the fortifications and the streets were provided early in the construction process, while the soldiers were in temporary accommodation, either within the area of the fortress, or outside it. To the west, evidence of early structures in the grounds of the Lawn (L 86) might represent an earlier base rather than extra-mural occupation contemporary with the fortress.

More details of both the defences and the internal arrangements have been discovered since 1970. Information on the legionary fortifications up to 1979 – notably at Westgate School in 1973 – has already been collated (W 73, Jones 1980). The rampart was timber-fronted, although a turf or clay revetment may have been intended originally, and only a single ditch was provided. The use of timber fronts was comparatively rare in Britain and its use might have been occasioned by the friable nature of the soil, but it is equally possible that those who chose to use it had previously used timber in the Rhineland (Jones 1975, 82–8). Towers projecting beyond the original line were added subsequently (Jones 1980, 48–9). Subsequent work on the legionary defences took place at East Bight in 1980–81 (EB 80) and Chapel Lane in 1985 (CL 85), and the results from these sites are described elsewhere (Steane *et al.* 2003). In every case, although several sites produced quantities of pottery from the Neronian period, the amount of new information on building layout was modest. We can at least now confirm the presence of so-called 'rampart-buildings', between the rampart and the *via sagularis* on the line of the northern defences at North Row – evidenced here by waste dumps (Jones 1980, 30–1) – and at East Bight in 1964–6 (Whitwell 1980, 6–9) and in 1980–1 (EB 80). In some cases, these may have been 'cookhouses', possibly including bread-ovens (Marvell 1996, 71–3). At East Bight (EB 80), the 1980–1 excavations produced metalworking refuse from associated deposits, whilst at the earlier site (EB 66) copper alloy fragments were discovered, although these have yet to be analysed. It is possible that this rubbish was derived from a workshop undertaking repairs to metal equipment.

At both the Westgate 1973 and East Bight 1980–1 sites, the excavations extended inside the *via sagularis* into the fringes of the adjacent buildings, presumably barracks. The evidence from the Westgate site (W 73) appears to indicate up to three rooms of a block running east–west, and presumably therefore the centurion's quarters – although the function of none of the individual rooms is clear (Jones 1980, 29–30, fig. 37). Some good quality glass of 1st-century date came from this site, partly from residual contexts, it must be admitted, but perhaps representing something of the centurion's lifestyle (Hoffman 1995; Price *et al.* forthcoming). At East Bight, building construction techniques were similar, but it was impossible to determine if the structures ran east–west along the intervallum road or north–south. There were probably two phases of timber building here, both presumed to belong to the military occupation since they were sealed by what appears to be the military demolition dump. The dump contained a quantity of early pottery as well as many fragments of military equipment, including objects associated with cavalry: its function may have been for recycling copper alloy waste. The most notable object was a dagger-scabbard, with decorated panels of silver inlay (Scott 1985; Webster 1985b) (Fig. 6.8). The group includes the largest collection of armour from any site in the city.

Hints of other fortress structures came from a number of the other sites investigated since 1970. At Chapel Lane, there were two successive phases of timber buildings, with differences in internal arrangements, although both might still have been barracks

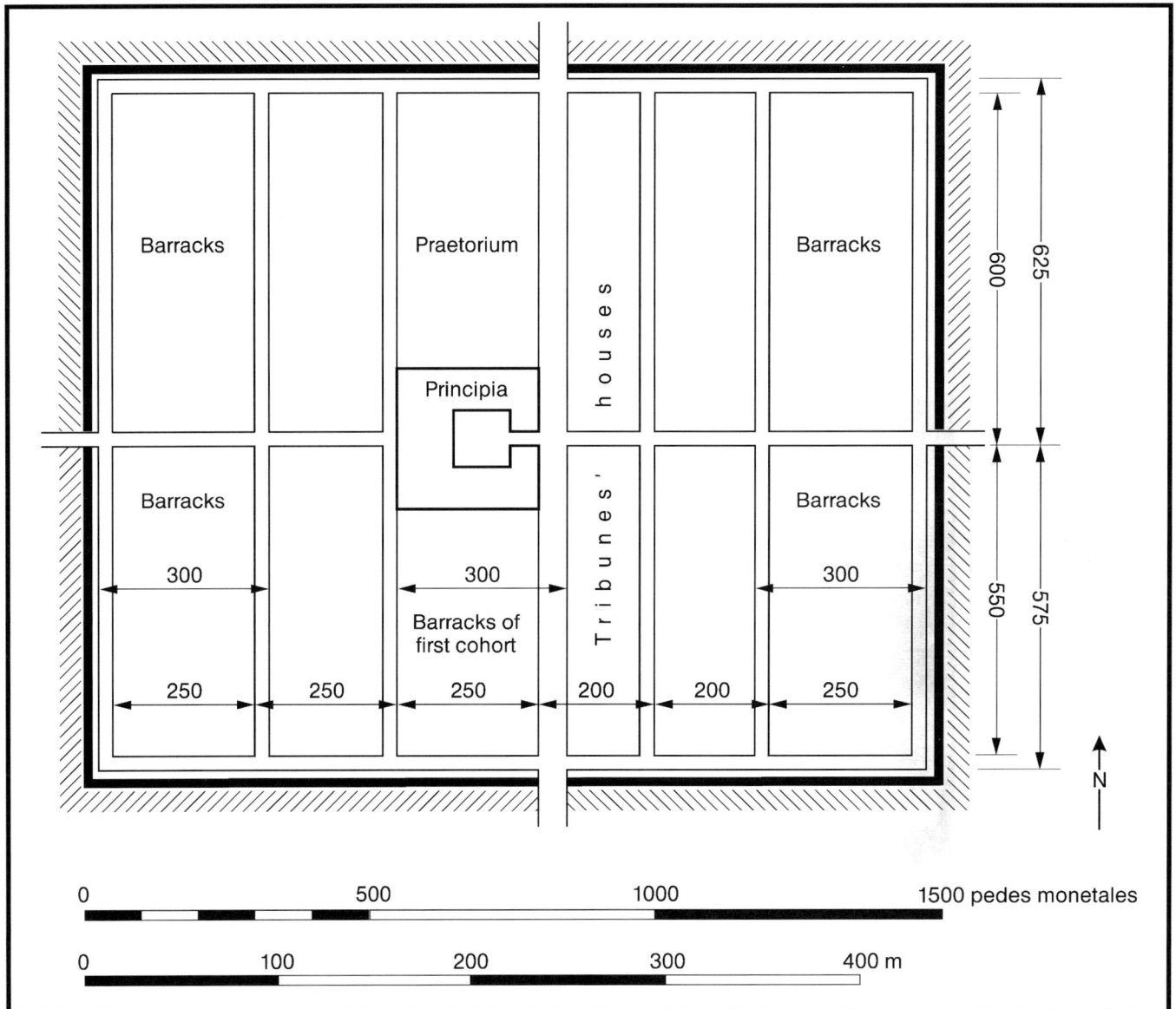

Fig. 6.7. Reconstruction of layout of Neronian fortress (sources, Jones 1988 and others – drawn by Dave Watt, copyright English Heritage).

(CL 85). The use of posts not set in wall trenches in its first phase may indicate a verandah. The earlier structure here was dismantled, the later burnt, perhaps at the end of the legionary occupation. Close to Chapel Lane, at West Bight in 1976 (WB 76), the demolition debris beneath the make-up for a *colonia*-period building included some wattle and daub, rendered prior to being given a plaster surface. It was associated with much 1st-century pottery. Remains of early stone buildings in similar locations to the legionary baths at Exeter and Usk were too slight to suggest a structure of the scale of a bath-house, and may actually represent the first *colonia* phase there. Similar demolition material came from nearby (WB 80) and the other side of the Mint Wall (MW 79) to its south, all three sites lying immediately north and

north-west of the *principia* and likely to represent, therefore, structures other than barracks.

With the exception of the *principia*, the constructional details of the legionary fortress buildings at Lincoln appear to indicate two different types of construction; continuous wall-trenches, or intermittent postholes (possibly indicating different functions), and white-painted wattle and daub walls. We cannot yet tell if the ground had to be cleared of trees, turf or other vegetation before building could begin. Several sites show traces of rebuilding, while repairs to the rampart front were noted at East Bight, and at Cuthberts Yard, to the north of the Westgate School site. The evidence for demolition, in some places involving fires, at the end of the fortress' life seems more definite (Steane *et al.* 2003).

There were tantalising fragments of evidence for water supply. A timber-lined channel, or long tank was discovered, towards the front of the basilica, reminiscent of that at Inchtuthil (Pitts and St. Joseph 1985, 78–9), and stone bases for water storage tanks in the courtyard, served perhaps by the well later capped in the *colonia* period (see below). The presence of the well at one end of the *principia* courtyard is found at a number of other major forts (Johnson 1983, 106). Its initial excavation might have been seen as a ritual foundation act, occupying a position more or less at the centre of the fortress.

Another minor but possibly significant feature may belong to the foundation phase of the *principia*. A small pit in the courtyard, previously assigned to the earliest church phases (see below chapter 8), may actually represent a ritual or sacrificial rite containing minute fragments of burnt bone, like that found roughly in the centre of the *principia* courtyard at Inchtuthil (Pitts and St. Joseph 1985, 59, 81, with Pl. XIIIB). A purely functional explanation is just as plausible, since the pit was not placed centrally in the courtyard at Lincoln, but what makes an early Roman date possible is the radiocarbon dating of the bones, with a medial date of Cal 43BC (Cal 370BC – AD 220). It is the case, however, that the radiocarbon date places this deposit more firmly in the late Iron Age, and it provides the clearest indication we yet have for the ritualistic occupation of the hilltop before the Roman invasion (p. 28 above).

Although fragmentary, the plan of the structures revealed can only be interpreted as that of the *principia* or headquarters. These were normally built to a plan similar to a civic *forum*, and were known to some Roman writers as such. The Lincoln example measured up to *c.*75m north–south (its northern boundary being marked by the potential street surface at MW 79, beneath the civic basilica) and up to *c.*70m east–west, with its courtyard *c.*30m (*c.*100 Roman feet) east–west. The layout can be compared with other legionary headquarters (von Petrikovits 1975, 68–75; Blagg 2000), but the closest parallels to the structural remains are the Augustan *principia* at Marktbreit near Mainz (Pietsch 1993) and that at Haltern (Hauptlager), on the river Lippe in Germany, excavated in 1905–7 (Fellman 1958, 98–102; 1984; von Schnurbein 1974, 56–9; 2000; Wells 1972, 183–5). Both Marktbreit and Haltern were occupied only for a short period, but with sufficient time at Haltern for major building alterations. The *principia* here measured *c.*54m by *c.*48m, excluding the rooms to the rear where the standards and the pay-chest were kept, a similar size to that at Lincoln, though possibly a little smaller. That at Marktbreit was a little larger than Haltern. There are also remarkable similarities between the constructional features of both the basilican aisled hall and the north range (Wells 1972, 184). But there are no records at Haltern of any water-channels, or of verandah posts; either they were not provided, or possibly the evidence was too slight to be

*Fig. 6.8. Legionary dagger-scabbard (possibly belonging to a centurion) with inlaid pattern in silver. It was excavated from within the north-east corner of the fortress (EB 80) (photo and copyright, City of Lincoln Archaeology Unit).*

## The *principia*

Descriptions and discussions of the excavations of the north-west part of the *principia* have already been published (Jones and Gilmour 1980; Jones 1988, 150, figs 7.3–5; Steane *et al.* 2003). What follows is largely a recapitulation of ideas put forward in these preliminary accounts, although some points now also require revision. The remains of the *principia* took the form of post-pits – intended to take squared posts generally 12 × 8 Roman inches – as well as postholes and wall-trenches, with pebbly external surfaces (Fig. 6.9). No internal floors survived. As at East Bight, two phases of construction were found, suggesting a remodelling of the timber cross-hall (*basilica principiorum*) but probably not a complete rebuilding of the whole complex. The area investigated measured almost 50m east–west, from the nave of the basilica to the inner wall of the east range fronting on to the *via principalis*.

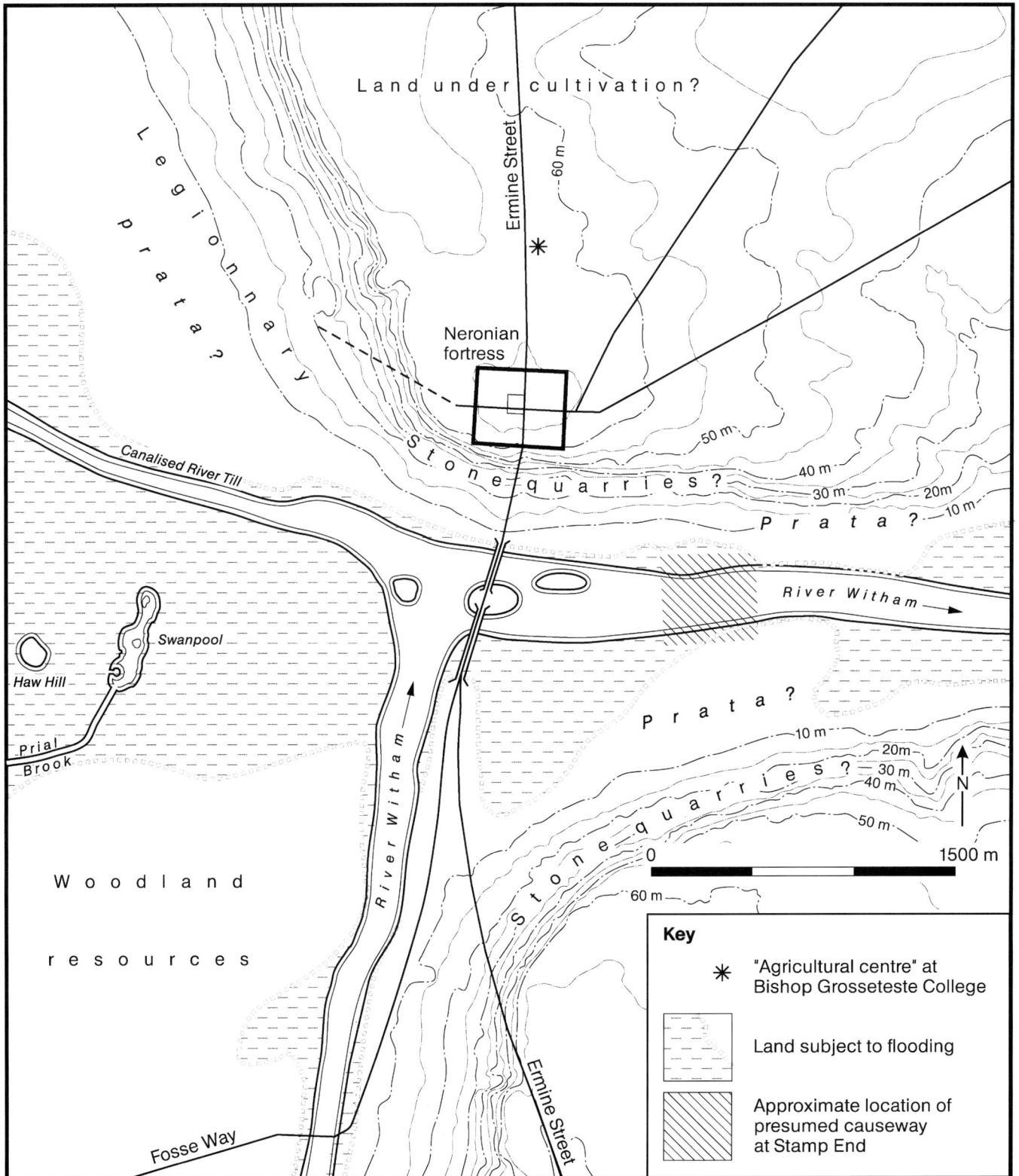

*Fig. 6.10. Resources in the hinterland of the Neronian fortress. Swanpool is shown in its modern location (drawn by Dave Watt, copyright English Heritage).*

a store building, between Silver Street and Broadgate (LIN 73c) is uncertain, but if the earlier dating is preferred, it could have been of legionary date. Certainly there was much early pottery from here, and it is probably significant that material of a similar date also came from the nearby Broadgate East site (BE 73). The fill of a north–south ditch here was no later than the mid 2nd century. In view of the presence of a possible Roman 'dock' to the south-east of the site (p. 98–9 below), it may be that the 'ditch' represents an early inlet of the river, or that there was a riverside focus to the south or south-east of these sites.

Several other sites on the hillside have yielded 1st-century pottery and other finds, from residual contexts, producing a peak in the amount of samian ware in the last decade of legionary occupation. This might be interpreted as indicating nearby structures as the *canabae* grew, or perhaps it merely reflects the reuse of legionary rubbish for levelling or terracing purposes. The deposit at Spring Hill (SPM 83) including a Rhodian amphora may represent such dumping.

It is from further south, beyond the river, that most stratified early material has been recovered. Here it is necessary to consider in turn the evidence for structures, cemeteries and roads. At the site of 181–3 High Street (HG 72), which overlay native structures built on a sand island, the artefactual evidence – including a spearhead – and the small collection of animal bones (for what they are worth) seem to indicate a clear discontinuity in material culture between the late Iron Age and the Roman periods. At least one rectilinear structure, with associated painted wall-plaster, belongs to the legionary period, and on this street-front site is best interpreted as a trader's house, although a directly military use cannot be ruled out.

To the south was a further area of marshy ground, not drained before the mid 2nd century, and the road appears to have crossed it via a causeway, before the two routes to London (Ermine Street) and to Leicester, Cirencester and Exeter (Fosse Way) diverged, in the vicinity of modern King Street. At St Mary's Guildhall (SMG 82), *c*.100m further south, pottery from an early road ditch for the Fosse Way seems to confirm its 1st-century origin. Unfortunately, it was not possible to excavate the earliest road surfaces here or those of the road to the east, provisionally interpreted as Ermine Street. Some of the cut features between the two roads dated to the late 1st century, but were not excavated over a sufficiently wide area to enable detailed interpretation or to give a more precise dating. At present we should probably accept that they did not pre-date the early *colonia*.

Even so, we should remember that this is one of the areas, on the gravel terrace south of Monson Street, where traces of any earlier military base are most likely to be found. The discovery of a 1st-century cemetery at Monson Street (on the east side of Ermine Street) in 1982 (M 82) confirmed the chance earlier finds of legionary tombstones and early cremation burials. The cremation graves consisted of shallow cuts into the natural sand, with human remains sometimes contained in pottery vessels, and other finds associated (Fig. 6.11). Small slots also cut into the sand may have held timber grave markers. Interestingly, although the analysis of those individuals found (at least four in number) indicated that only one was possibly a soldier, the burial rite had distinctively Roman elements rather than native (Philpott 1991, 8). The legionary stones show that soldiers were being buried here, but also

women, perhaps the legionaries' partners and children or those of traders. The significance of the presence, also, of some animal bones is less certain, but such finds are common in Roman Britain and probably represent sacrificial meals (Philpott 1991, 195–200). Hob-nails were common, as were glass containers (*unguentaria*) for anointing the corpse with oil or perfume (Fig. 6.12) (*Ibid.*, 117–8). The Monson Street glass vessels were normally placed on the funeral pyre, since most – but not all – had melted. A mirror, not an unusual item of grave furniture from the late Iron Age

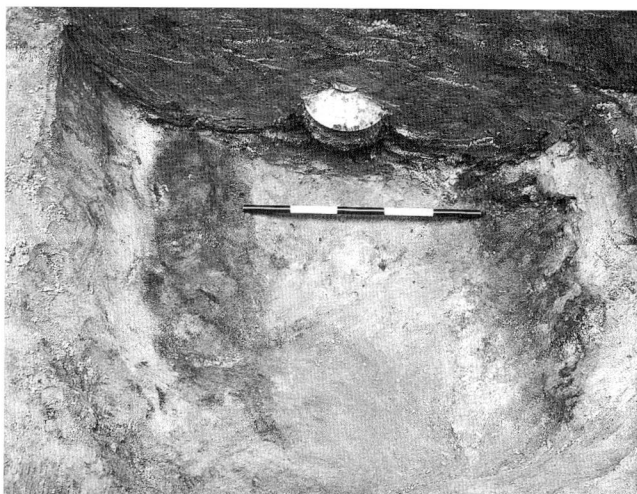

*Fig. 6.11. Early Roman burial pit containing a cremation in a rusticated pot, with lid, found in excavations at Monson Street (M 82), close to the line of Ermine Street, south of the pool (photo and copyright, City of Lincoln Archaeology Unit).*

*Fig. 6.12. Hob-nails and* unguentaria *(bottles and phials to contain liquid offerings) from the early Roman cremation burials at Monson Street (M 82) (photo and copyright, City of Lincoln Archaeology Unit).*

(Philpott 1991, 123), is a further indicator that those buried were of some status and wealth. A nearby stone building – unusual for this period – has been provisionally interpreted as a mausoleum for someone of even greater distinction, although no burials were found in the part that was excavated. Trollope and Trollope (1860) also noted an area of charcoal and soot nearby, perhaps the *ustrina* or pyre-site of the legionary-period cemetery (McKinley 2000; Polfer 2000), or possibly associated with the iron-working debris from later occupation of the site, which appears to date to the early *colonia* period.

A number of other burials is known from further south, by Gowts Bridge, *c.*200m south of Monson Street (and west of the Fosse Way), including the notable tombstone of Gaius Saufeius (Fig. 6.3), while that of Gaius Valerius (Fig. 6.5) came from South Common several hundred metres further south. Both Saufeius and Valerius had been soldiers of the 9th Legion. The South Common area has also produced two early cremations, both closer to the projected line of Ermine Street than that of the Fosse Way (Fig. 6.2). It appears, then, that much of the drier land south of the river crossing was designated for burial purposes during the legionary occupation. Whether the large gaps between the known burial sites contained further burials, other classes of structures, or even another military base, is unknown, although the possibility that this was where an early fort is to be found has already been canvassed (p. 39–40 above). These southern cemeteries appear to continue in use into the early *colonia* period, but probably not beyond.

These were not, however, the only legionary cemeteries. A legionary tombstone discovered incorporated into the rebuilt city wall north of the lower east gate suggests an area used for burial on the hillside south-east of the fortress – certainly both early cremations and later burials are known here. Cremations are also recorded for some distance to the east and north-east of the fortress's east gate, and south-west of its west gate, but they were early discoveries and cannot definitely be assigned to the legionary period. The finding of a cremation in a rusticated jar on Newland Street West, several hundred metres west of the lower west gate (NSS 97), gives some idea of the extent to which the cemeteries had spread by the early 2nd century. However, like many of these earlier finds, this cremation probably belongs to the early *colonia* rather than to the military occupation.

The engineers building the new military road system outside the fortress must have been much preoccupied with the junction of Ermine Street and Fosse Way and with the problem of constructing the new 'Wigford' causeway over the damp, low-lying ground, connecting the islands in the pre-existing pool. Observations in the 19th century indicated the presence and structure of this causeway in a number of locations, and mention, among other elements, a layer of 'concrete'. These were all assumed at the time to represent Ermine Street. The data from these observations and from those made by the engineer Michael Drury in 1877–8 (Drury 1890) can be used to suggest that the ground dropped steadily going northwards from St. Botolph's, but notably the concrete is not so substantial where there was a higher area of sand terrace in the region of Nos. 181–3 High Street (HG 72) (Figs. 6.13 and 6.14). Further north the causeway led to a wooden ramp and bridge based on timber piles.

The installation of such substantial engineering features is more likely to belong to the major re-development of this southern suburb in the late 2nd and early 3rd centuries than to an early military context, and the second phase roadside ditch at the St Mary's Guildhall site (SMG 82) had a fill dating from the early or mid 2nd century. We presume, however, that the road followed the same route in the 1st century and that it would have required some sort of embankment and surfacing over the lower ground. The recent investigation of a road crossing marshy ground at Scraftworth, near Bawtry, gives some idea of an alternative, presumably military, solution. Here, also, the road lies close to a fortlet (Van de Noort and Ellis 1997, 284) and large tree trunks were laid down as a base for a causeway of smaller timbers and brushwood, and then covered by turves. In due course a gravel road, supported either side by oak posts, replaced it. Perhaps similar technology was employed for the ramp leading to the river crossing at Lincoln.

The external boundaries of the *prata legionis* (literally the 'legion's meadows'), where military stock grazing and related activities took place, cannot easily be established. They must have lain somewhere within the territory taken over by the army (Mason 1988a; 1988b; 2001, 118–20), close to the fortress and including much land within the modern District. The area covered could well have been extensive, however – boundary-marker stones from Dalmatia and Spain indicate areas in excess of 500 km$^2$ (Mason 2001, 118). Evidence was found for use of the rural settlement at Claydon Pike (in the Thames Valley east of Gloucester) for storing foodstuffs, and the grazing of horses under military control, was apparently reorganised for the *colonia* there, but it seems that use of these lands to supply the city might have commenced in the legionary period (Miles and Palmer 1990). Hurst (1988, 68–9) originally suggested that the *prata legionis* at Gloucester was subsequently taken up as the colonial *territorium*. Consequently, it would have reflected the area required to feed the troops and their associated communities. He estimated its extent at *c.*50–90 km$^2$, but he has since accepted that it will be almost impossible to find definite evidence to confirm the location or size of the territory (1999a, 127). Other features of the *prata* might include groups of practice-camps and siege-works, and major sources of water serving the army, whilst it is also likely that potential military obstacles, such as the iron-age triple ditch-system at Lincoln, would be demolished. The Lincoln

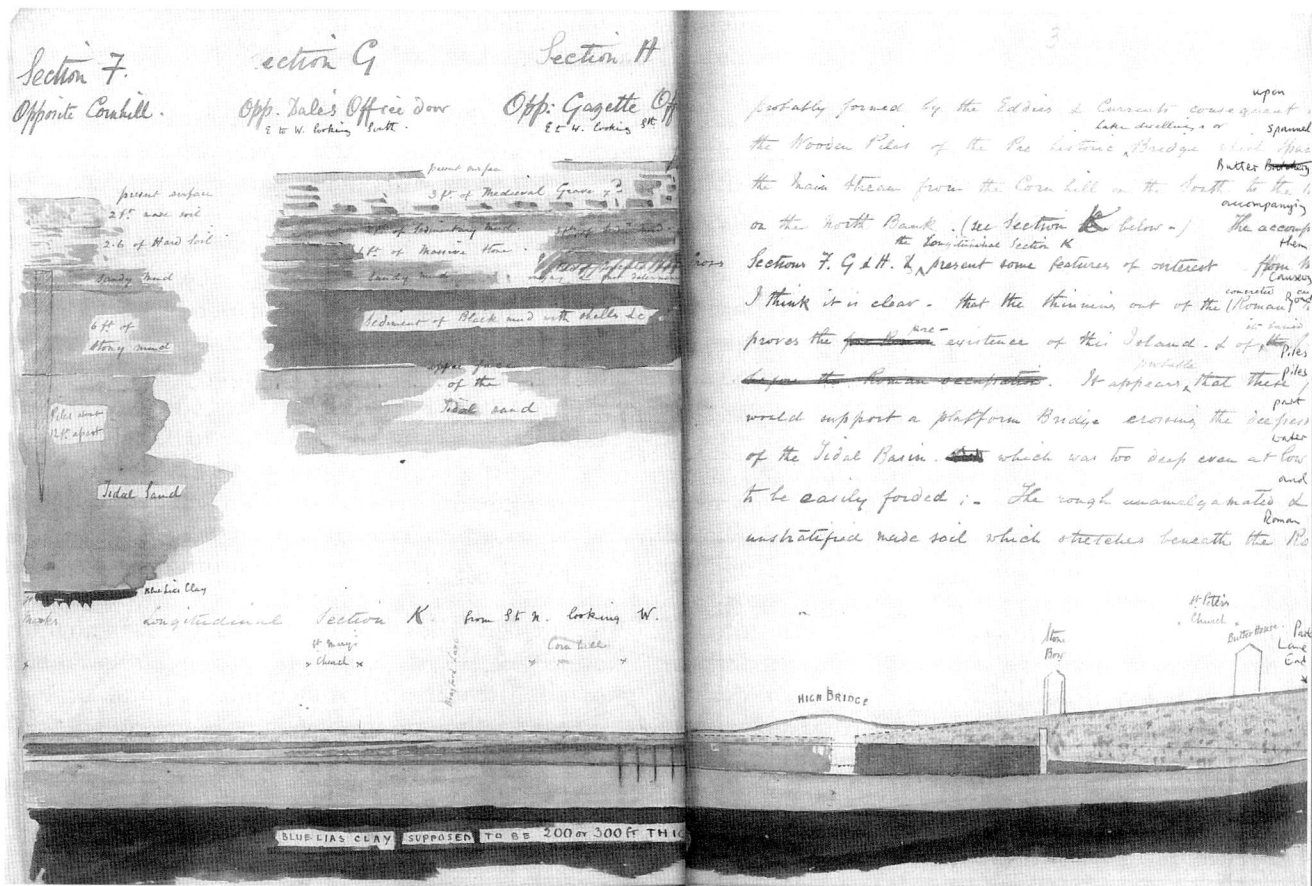

*Fig. 6.13. Pages from the notebook of Michael Drury made in 1887–8 recording the stratigraphical relationships between alluvial deposits in the Wigford area (Drury 1888) (Plate 1.1). The information contained is summarised in Fig. 6.14 (photo and copyright, Lincolnshire County Council, County Library Service, Local History Collection).*

ditch system does appear to have been slighted at about this time and this may reflect its inclusion within the *prata legionis*. Conversely, the survival of other types of features, such as iron-age rural settlements, into the Roman military period probably indicate that the *prata* did not extend this far. Recent aerial photography has identified what appears to be an iron-age forerunner of the Scampton villa, for example, and this probably suggests that here, 8km north-west of the fortress, we are outside the zone of close military control. Similarly, two settlements which continued in occupation from the late Iron Age into the Roman period were discovered in pipeline operations *c.*20km east of Lincoln in 2001, suggesting that the legion's area of control did not extend to the Wolds.

It is assumed that, for reasons of political expediency, the foundation of the *colonia* would have involved minimal further appropriation of land beyond the land already appropriated for the fortress (Richmond 1946, 65), so that there could have been a close relationship between the *prata legionis* and the *territorium coloniae*. Furthermore, it might be easier to establish the extent of the *territorium coloniae*, especially if it was distinguished by a formal land allotment system such as

'centuriation'. Some have assumed that the colony's territory would include both the Ancaster quarries – source of the Bailgate milestone (RIB 1965, 2241) – and supplies of iron and timber (Whitwell 1970, 39; Todd 1991, 37; Mason 2001, 170). If so, the extent of both *territorium* and *prata* would have been considerable. However, there is no obvious reason for thinking that all raw materials brought into the fortress would have been produced within either the *prata* or the *territorium*, and there were, anyway, supplies of good quality building stone in the immediate vicinity of the fortress, along exposures around the hilltop, and of timber, probably, in the valley floor in the Birchwood area south-west of the Roman settlement. We might see the early pottery found near Bishop Grosseteste College, *c.*600m north of the fortress, on the site of a later farm or villa as indicating one centre of agricultural activity within the *prata* but, like that from Britain in general, the evidence for Lincoln is insubstantial and inconclusive. Of course, the marshland in the valley floor would have been unsuitable for grazing, although the hill slopes and tops north and south of the city would have offered extensive pasture for the cavalry's horses as well as for cattle and sheep.

# B. The Roman Military Era – The archaeological agenda. An introduction to the Research Agenda Zone entries (on CD-Rom)

## *David Stocker*

At the time of the Conquest, it is clear that Lincoln was selected as one of a handful of locations for major Roman investment within the territory of the Corieltauvi (along with Leicester and, perhaps, Longthorpe). We need to ask why. Until recently, arguments based on the superiority of the Roman military engineers' appreciation of the defensive capacity of the place was offered as the principal, if not the only, explanation. Such arguments, rooted in military engineering and strategy, remain valid, but this *Assessment* has shown that, in AD 43, the site was already valued for other reasons. We have seen in Chapter 5 that, although there may have been no settlement at Lincoln in the late Iron Age, this did not mean that the place was unimportant to the peoples of the countryside round about. Indeed the little evidence we have suggests that it was a site of considerable symbolic importance to the Corieltauvi, and, we could argue, that importance may have been confirmed by the site's selection for major Roman installations.

But iron-age Lincoln was not the Corieltauvi's main political centre; that was probably at Old Sleaford and this centre was moved by the Romans, not to Lincoln, but to Ratae Corieltauvorum – Leicester. So, if we are correct to measure Lincoln's importance in the 1st century AD by characterising the Roman establishment here, we should be contrasting the legionary headquarters with the tribal capital and political centre. This reasoning should lead us to draw a clear distinction between the foundation of Lindum and Ratae Corieltauvorum. Lindum is clearly *not* the main political centre. Indeed, like Glevum, it seems to be a foundation of a distinctive military type, a long way (over 50 miles) from the centre of the political territory in which it sits.

In making the same observation, Martin Millett (1999, 193) thought that this indicated that distinctive 'tactical' factors resulted in the foundation of both Lindum and Glevum. Millett proposed that such military bases were located in 'quiet' areas deliberately, to keep the army away from the centres of tribal power. However, our preliminary understanding of the layout of the Witham gap in the late Iron Age, described in Chapter 5, suggests that the area of pools and meres west of the Stamp End causeway, or river

crossing, had a great ritual significance to the peoples who lived in the area. Indeed the significance of the pools for earlier peoples, rather than any other aspect of the topography, is preserved in the Roman place name *Lindon*, which derives from the Celtic *llyn* – 'a pool' (Cameron 1985, 1-3). To the Romans the pools were the most notable feature of the location, although the equation of *-don* with the word *-dun* (meaning a hill) is no longer thought valid (*Ibid.*). Given our new understanding of the symbolic importance of the Lincoln gap to the Corieltauvi, we should probably now suppose that motives other than tact were dominant in the Roman decision to establish a military base here. The pre-existing ritual significance of the site must affect our view of the impact of new military installations at Lincoln for their contemporaries. As the military details of the invasion and the Roman army are already studied so extensively at sites across the Roman Empire, it may be this interaction, between conquerors and conquered, to which the Lincoln case can contribute most effectively.

Within this Era, the District Council area has been divided into 27 distinct RAZs which attempt to address both the military agenda and the relationship between the Romans and their new imperial subjects. The RAZ accounts, along with their mapped extent, can be accessed on the CD-Rom.

Our research agenda for the Roman Military Era contains, first, a group of eight RAZs defined in order to address questions relating to the initial choice of site for the Roman fortress or fortresses. All of these RAZs ask what the choice of location for the new fortress might be able to tell us about the relationship between conqueror and conquered. Should the installation of a new fortress alongside the ritual pools, and the construction of a causeway across them, be seen as a sensitive gesture by a political ally; or alternatively, is it more likely to represent a deliberately aggressive act of desecration or humiliation?

6.1   The early fort
6.2   The Wigford causeway
6.3   Buildings on the sand islands in the Brayford

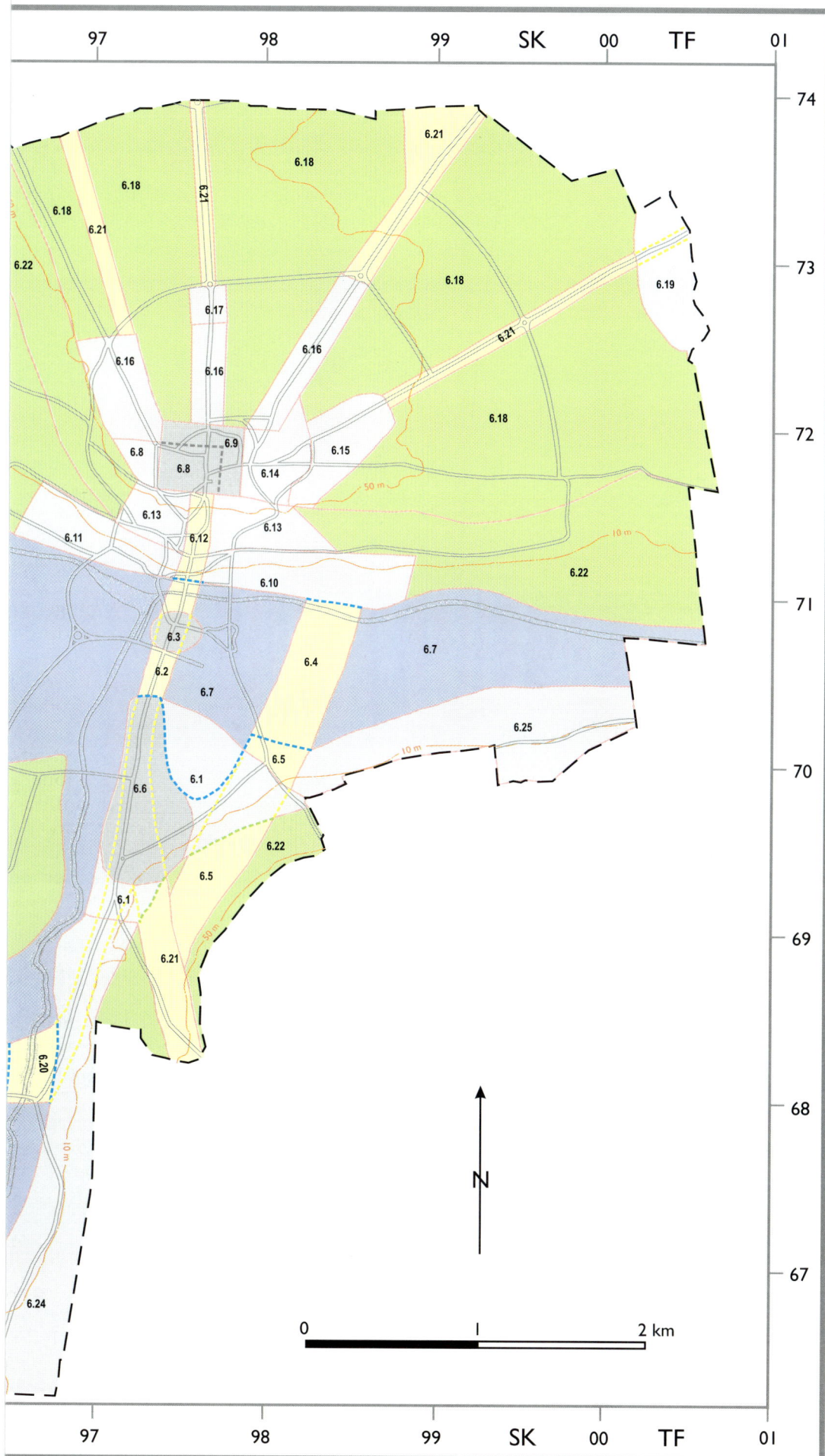

*Map 2. Research Agenda Zone locations for the Roman Military Era – See CD-Rom for details (drawn by Dave Watt, copyright English Heritage and Lincoln City Council).*

6.4  Stamp End causeway
6.5  Route way to the Stamp End causeway
6.6  Early cemetery in the Wigford area
6.7  Valley floor deposits
6.8  An early hilltop enclosure?

A second group of research questions within this Era are focused on issues related to organisation and planning within the Roman military base, or bases. First-century military organisation is a well-populated research area and future work in Lincoln can make a substantial contribution to the debate. Three RAZs have been identified which should help explore such matters:

6.9  The Neronian Fortress
    6.9.1  Fortifications
    6.9.2  *Principia*
    6.9.3  Barracks

A third group of RAZs have been identified which approach the difficult topic of how archaeological discoveries might tell us about the impact of the new Roman fortress on its immediate surroundings and on native populations. Because existing information is so scarce, these questions are poorly formulated at the moment. Nevertheless we can make preliminary proposals, based on our limited understanding of the topography of the Lincoln gap. The RAZs so far identified that cast light on these issues are as follows:

6.10  Waterside installations
6.11  Potential western quaysides
6.12  Road up the northern hillside
6.13  Northern hill slope area with springs and possible secular occupation
6.14  Training and recreational complex outside fortress east gate
6.15  Cemetery east of fortress
6.16  *Canabae* outside east, north and west gates
6.17  'Farm' at Bishop Grosseteste College
6.18  Legionary *prata* and *territorium*
6.19  Iron-age ditch system
6.20  Fosse Way crossing of Witham
6.21  Roads beyond the *Canabae*
6.22  Northern and southern hill slopes
6.23  Birchwood area and Boultham Moor
6.24  Upper Witham valley
6.25  Lower Witham Valley

# 7. The *Colonia* Era

# A. Archaeological account

*Michael J Jones*

## Introduction –
## The establishment of the *colonia*

Once the legions had left, in due course a decision was taken at the highest level, and requiring the Emperor's agreement, that the Lincoln fortress was to be converted into a veteran settlement. Like Gloucester (with which it has so many similarities in the Roman period) Lincoln was selected for the site of a military colony, or *colonia*. Although the chronology at Gloucester is disputed (Hassall and Hurst 1999), in Lincoln's case the foundation occurred within a decade or so of the departure of the army. Lincoln's prompt designation may have been connected with its relative distance from any existing major centre; it was Leicester (over 50 miles to the south-west) which had became the *civitas* (i.e. the local government) capital of the Corieltauvi.

The approximate date of the foundation of what was probably formally called *Colonia [Domitiana] Lindensium* is provided by the tombstone of Marcus Minicius Marcellinus at Mainz. It records a citizen of Lincoln origin, who notes his voting tribe – one belonging to the Flavian period (AD 69–96) (Fig. 7.1) (*C.I.L*, 13, 6679; Wacher 1995, 132). A Domitianic date is favoured because the army was busily engaged in the conquest of Wales and northern Britain until *c.* AD 78–85, but under Domitian (AD 81–96) the army in Britannia returned to barracks. Salway (1981, 152) argues that, if a colony had been founded by the governor Agricola (i.e. before AD 84), his son-in-law Tacitus would have mentioned it in his biography. There has been a tendency to push the foundation date of Lincoln towards the end of Domitian's reign, and to link it with that of Gloucester (which was probably founded – or re-founded – under Nerva, AD 96–8), so that the two similar settlements can be seen as elements of the same strategy. Although we

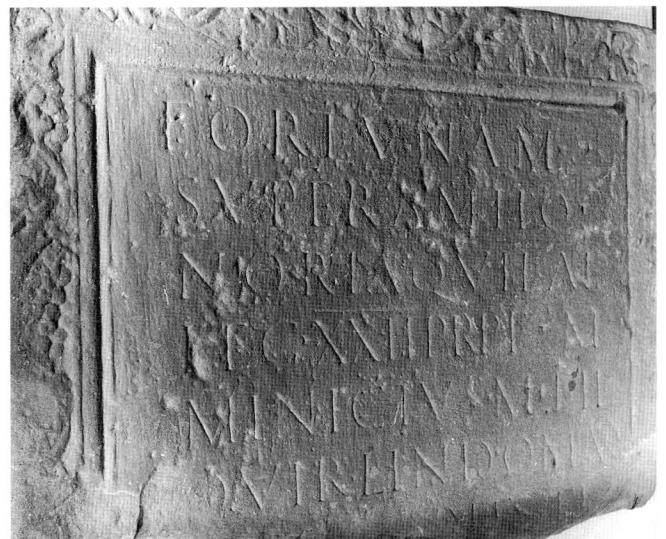

*Fig. 7.1. Dedication of a structure (perhaps a building) in Mainz to the goddess* Fortuna *by Marcus Minicius Marcellinus of Lincoln (CIL XIII, 6679). The inscription can be translated:*

*[This structure]* is dedicated to the honour of the goddess *Fortuna* by Marcus Minicius Marcellinus of Lincoln *[Lindo]*, leading centurion of the 22nd Legion, *Primigenia*, of the voting tribe of the Quirina.

*The dedication, which dates from 81–95 AD, is the earliest evidence we have for the name of the city (photo and copyright, Mittelrheinisches Landesmuseum, Mainz).*

have no information on the number of veterans settled at Lincoln, it is likely to have been several hundred, if not more, and there may not have been enough soldiers due for retirement in such a short period.

Indeed, there are instances where veterans from several legions had to be grouped together (Keppie 1984, 105). Others could have joined over the ensuing years. In such a case, the two *coloniae* at Lincoln and Gloucester may have been founded a decade apart.

One of the principal functions of the Italian colonies founded under Augustus was to provide land for families who were cramped in Rome itself, and indirectly to encourage a revival of the birth-rate (Levick 1967, 184–92; Salmon 1969, 145–57; Keppie 1984, 107). Colonies of the Lincoln and Gloucester generation were principally expedients to discharge legionaries on land which was already imperial property and involved minimal unpopular disturbance of the native community (Wacher 1995, 132). It is now considered less likely that they were also intended to form a defensible base in emergency, but they would have a value in administrative terms, for example in the collection of taxes, and in due course as a source of legionary recruits (Birley 1979, 104–5; Isaac 1992, 311–32).

We can assume that former soldiers of the 9th Legion (based in York from about AD 71 and only a few days' journey away) formed a major element of the new colonial population, perhaps together with others who had fought in campaigns in northern Britain. It is now clearly established that soldiers preferred to stay on retirement in the provinces in which they had served and where they had developed long-term relationships. Those being discharged in the mid 90s AD – if that *was* the date – were recruited about AD 70, immediately following the wars of AD 68–70 when many provincials (i.e. non-Italians) entered the legions. It is estimated that the proportion of Italians at Gloucester, for example, may have been only about 20%, as opposed to nearer 50% at Colchester (Hurst 2000). Since they had seen less of Italian towns, the later *coloniae* may have reflected less of the cultural influence of the Mediterranean. The veterans still had certain privileges, and held similar standing as members of the *colonia's* ruling *ordo* (Garnsey 1970, 245–51). Some might have savings, and they were rewarded with land (normal until the end of the century), or a cash grant, or even both.

There was presumably also a native element in the population, some of whom may have been derived from the extra-mural settlers of the legionary period. On the other hand, although the army would have created a substantial market, we have no indication as yet of more than a modest number of indigenous people in the urban area. The evidence in general for Romano-British towns indicates that the mature *coloniae* differed little from the *civitas* capitals in terms of economy and diet (Dobney *et al.* 1999). Such similarities might be expected by the 3rd century, but further research on the earliest colonial phases is likely to show greater distinctiveness in such areas.

There is no evidence from Britannia regarding the contents of the legal charter which regulated the

communities in such newly established *coloniae*, but details of those surviving from Urso (Hardy 1912) or those given in the *Lex Irnitana* (Gonzalez 1986), give us some indication of the arrangements for local government in Spain. There would normally have been a large council (*ordo*), possibly of 100 decurions, and these men were the local equivalents of the Roman senate. Selection for the *ordo* involved meeting social and financial criteria – although the decurions possessed a certain status and several privileges, they were expected to contribute financially to the development of their city (Garnsey 1970, 242–5). Moreover, to discourage absenteeism, they were normally required to maintain a house in or near to the *colonia*, perhaps a farm, or a *villa*, in the *territorium*. Recent excavations at some late Republican cities in Italy, notably Cosa and Fregellae, have identified the decurions' houses close to the *forum*, with less sumptuous residences for other groups further away. How far such essentially Italian, Republican, arrangements were reflected in the government of provincial colonies of the Imperial period is not yet clear. The duties of the various magistrates, who provided executive government, are known to some extent, but need not be discussed further here (Wacher 1995, 36–8).

Although it is not certain how far these earlier Italian models were followed in Britannia, two slight 'imperial' references are known from Lincoln. The city has produced only one definite inscription mentioning a decurion; that set up by Aurelius Senecio (Fig. 7.2), to his wife Volusia Faustina, who may have been descended from a veteran settler (RIB 1965, 250; Birley 1979, 117). This stone probably belongs to the 3rd century. The officer whose dedication stone provides the date for the foundation of Lincoln, Marcus Minicius Marcellinus (*C.I.L.* 13, 6679 – Fig. 7.1), was a chief centurion in the 22nd Legion *Primigenia* before he retired and he would have also been a prominent member of Lindum's civic elite – had he ever returned.

Soon after the departure of a majority of the legionaries of the 2nd Legion *Adiutrix* in about AD 78, the fortress would have been reduced to a mere shell. Perhaps a caretaker garrison was left in control, with the additional responsibility for dismantling the legionary buildings – a process that may have taken some time. The fortifications were left in position; the streets were useful for demolition work and as a basis for any future development. Some of the posts of the cross-hall in the *principia* were sawn off and the rotting of the stumps created rectangular voids, but most were actually withdrawn at the time of demolition and the whole area was subsequently levelled.

The site may have been mothballed. The Roman right to its ownership (as part of the public property of the state – the *fiscus*) and that of other nearby land used for military purposes was assured, but it probably required reassertion (Salway 1981, 153). At some other former fortress sites in Britain, like Colchester and Gloucester, the transition to a civil settlement occurred

*Fig. 7.2. Memorial to Volusia Faustina and Claudia Catiotus..., found re-used in the walls of the Lower City in 1859 (Huskinson 1994 No.57). The inscription may be translated:*

To the divine shades. Erected by the decurion Aurelius Senecio to his deserving wife Volusia Faustina, a citizen of Lincoln [*Lindum*], who lived 26 years 1 month and 26 days. Also to Claudia Catiotui ... who lived 60 years.

*The relationship between Volusia and Claudia is not clear. The monument dates from the 3rd century (photo and copyright, British Museum).*

## The Upper City in the *Colonia* Era

Within the confines of the legionary fortress defences and largely reusing its street layout, the new *colonia* emerged as a recognisable Roman city during its first half-century (Fig. 7.3). Impressive public buildings and works were developed, some presumably financed by the colonists, while town-houses were initially modest in scale. Like that of the fortress, the sequence of defences of the Upper City in the *colonia* period has been well-explored but there has been only limited investigation of the interior. This was even more apparent when Ian Richmond wrote in his classic essay in 1946, 'the tale of structures within the *colonia* is thus a sorry one. All too many opportunities have been missed' (Richmond 1946, 39). At the same time he could conclude (1946, 68): 'Roman Lincoln itself offers a glimpse of flourishing Roman urban culture in imported purity such as has not yet emerged on British soil'. That observation was based partly on the evidence of architectural and sculptural remains, on the cosmopolitan nature of the population as known from inscriptions, and on other artefactual evidence. It would not be made today, perhaps; not that Lincoln has ceased to offer further glimpses of *Romanitas*, but other towns can now boast similar details (Jones 1999a; Hurst 2000). Two substantial excavations have been undertaken since Richmond wrote, on the sites of the *forum-basilica* and the public baths, and both provided only limited information on plans and dating. Nevertheless, the limited indications of Roman structures and finds of associated artefacts reinforce the impression made on Richmond of architectural magnificence and sophisticated engineering works.

In the upper part of the *colonia* many of the more obvious opportunities for archaeological excavation have already passed. The whole area is now a well-maintained Conservation Area and has a very high density of listed buildings and, consequently, there is unlikely to be large-scale development here in the near future. In spite of the intensity of post-Roman occupation, Roman stratification here is in places close to the surface; in the north-western quadrant it is even found within the first metre of deposits. Consequently it is important that even minor and apparently trivial works are monitored archaeologically in order that our understanding of the Roman city can continue to develop.

### The Street System

The first attempt at understanding the detailed internal layout of the *colonia* was attempted by Baker (1938), partly using Haverfield's (1914) account and finds of sewers in the previous century as a basis. These ideas were further developed by Richmond (1946, 35–6) and updated by Whitwell (1970) and Wacher (1975). Excavations in the 1970s made it clear, however, that the layout of the town was no longer discernible in the

promptly after the departure of the garrison. This may have been the case at Lincoln also, but it is also possible that there was a hiatus of up to 15 years or so, which would have implications for the subsequent layout of *colonia* buildings. The impact of the military withdrawal on adjacent extra-mural settlements during any hiatus is uncertain, but those largely dependent on the legionary market must have been affected, if they did not depart with the legion itself.

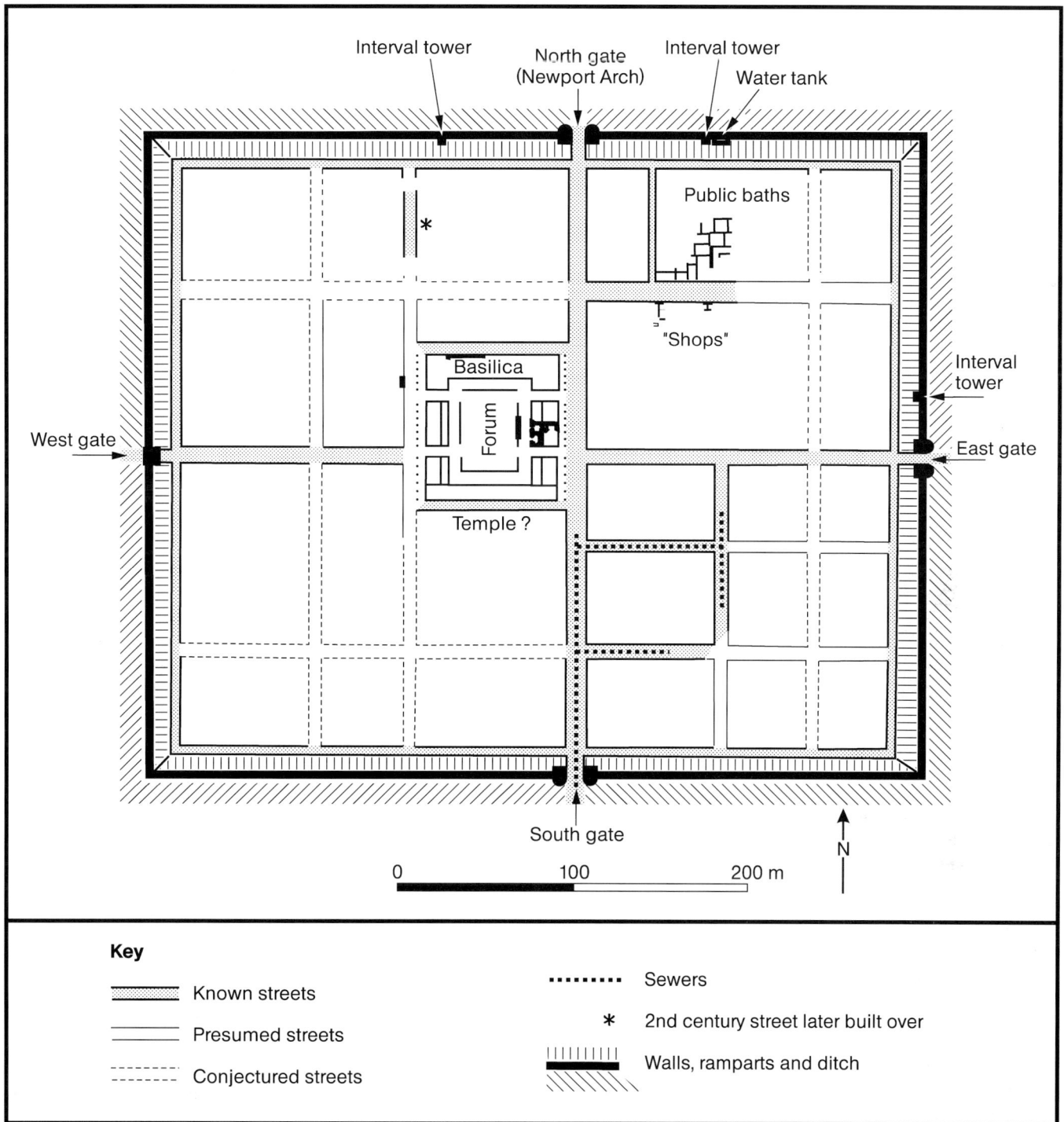

*Fig. 7.3. Reconstruction of plan of the Upper City in the* Colonia *Era (drawn by Dave Watt, copyright English Heritage).*

present layout – the Roman street-system had been largely lost in the post-Roman period (Fig. 7.3). Nor had it been imposed *de novo*, as happened on 'green-field' sites such as the early 2nd-century *coloniae* at Xanten (Precht 1986) and Timgad (Fentress 1979). Rather, the fortress was essentially converted into the city – not a unique phenomenon in Britain by any means (ed. Webster 1988). In some cases, the military streets may have been resurfaced, in other cases they

were abandoned (e.g. north of the *principia*), while there was certainly some reconstruction along existing lines to enable a drainage system to be put into place. Richmond (1946, 36) pointed out the potential of the Roman sewers for understanding the street pattern, but probably underestimated the practical difficulties of following their course. Little progress has been possible in recent decades in exploring this evidence.

Our knowledge of the locations, widths and character of various Roman streets has been obtained from a variety of sources over a long period, including the sewers to the west and north-west of the Cathedral. Drury (1888) observed the principal north–south street (the *cardo maximus)* in the Bailgate area, and estimated that it was about 27 feet (*c.*8.3m) wide. At roughly the same time, the discovery of the Bailgate colonnade (below) established that the width of the entrance into the *forum* was between 15 and 16 feet wide (*c.*4.5– 4.8m), – the column-centres being in the region of 20 feet (*c.*6.1m) apart. The entrance was between two double columns in the colonnade along the *cardo*, on the line of the street linking the east and west gates. To the east and west of the *forum* it may have been considerably wider. There were, however, wide porticoes in places, which may have encroached on to the road itself, reducing its width. The north and south gateways to the upper *colonia* were, in all, at least 40 Roman feet wide, which may reflect more closely the true width of the main streets, including the porticoes. A gap to the south of the colonnade, presumably marking a further street, was about 17 feet (*c.* 5m) wide. To the north of the colonnade and the Mint Wall, both now considered to belong to the early 3rd century, the new east–west street of similar date was found in 1980 to be at least 5m wide, but certainly less than 12m (WB 80).

Presuming that it really was a street and not merely a yard surface, the possible north–south street at Chapel Lane (CL 85) was at least 4 to 5m wide (*c.*14–16 feet). But, if it was a street, it only lasted a short while, and may have been subsequently shifted or narrowed to the east. A street to the west of the *forum* complex is likely, following a line a little to the west of the modern West Bight. The excavations at Cottesford Place (CP 56) revealed a further major east–west street (Fig. 7.4), up to 10m (over 30 feet) wide in places but narrower

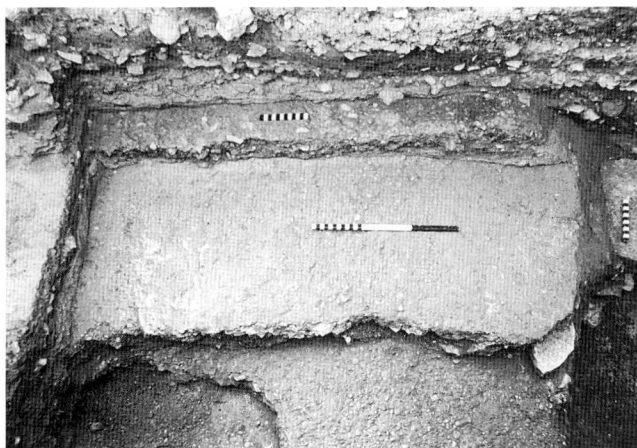

*Fig. 7.4. Road surfaces of the* Colonia *Era on the line of an east–west street in the north-eastern quarter of the Upper City, excavated at Cottesford Place in 1956–7 (CP 56). The larger scale is 3 feet long (photo and copyright, estate of D Petch).*

elsewhere. It led eastwards from the *cardo* to the south of the baths. A narrow north–south lane, perhaps of military origin, about 4m (13ft) wide, joined it to the street inside the fortifications, but this was later built over as the baths were extended. The intervallum road itself has been excavated on the north and south sides, at North Row (ON 257, Webster 1949), East Bight (EB 80) and at the Sub-Deanery in 1955–8 (ON 240, Petch 1960). These roads were all later resurfaced, and had widths not exceeding about 6m (20 feet), with indications of a narrow footway adjacent to the structures inside the street. Similar intervallum roads can be also presumed on the east and west sides of the upper *colonia.*

Most of the road surfaces appear to have been formed of small pebbles, but the principal north–south street was paved, and was noted most recently in a small trench in Bailgate in 1997 (RLB 97). This evidence corroborates that from records of the road adjacent to the Bailgate colonnade, and that from Michaelgate (MCH 84) on the hillside (presuming that this was a street rather than part of a building – p. 85 below). The principal east–west street may have been given the same treatment, which may not have extended beyond the gates, except for the line of Ermine Street through the lower *colonia.* Surfaces revealed in 1996 adjacent to and outside the north gate were of pebbles (NEB 96). Here the main carriageway through the arch was the standard 16 feet (*c.*5m) wide.

Our evidence for the street layout indicates that the known *insulae* of the upper *colonia* were of varying size, unlike the regular planning of the square domestic units at Timgad, for example. This irregularity is probably the product of the partial retention of some of the streets and structures of the fortress alongside the partial replacement of others. The plan (Fig. 7.3) identifies what is known and comparison with Fig. 6.7 shows how much may have been derived from the legionary layout.

## Drainage and Water Supply

The discovery of a sizeable sewer beneath the main north–south street, and of other smaller feeders linking into the system, belongs to the 19th century. The sewer was first traced in 1838 (RENO 3216), for some 15m and then, apparently in 1883, it was followed for several times this length (Richmond 1946, 36). The records of these explorations are confusing in places. In particular it is uncertain whether the main sewer was actually larger south of the intersections of the main streets, whilst one account appears to indicate a diagonal course southwards (perhaps to ensure a steady flow?) rather than one following the line of the main street. That further investigation of the sewers has not been possible is a matter of frustration and regret, not only for what we might learn about the system and its date (and, in turn, about the street pattern) but also for what the fills might contain in the way of artefactual and environmental evidence, as demonstrated at York (Buckland 1976). A further hint of the presence of the sewer continuing down Steep Hill was revealed in 1986 near to its junction with Wordsworth Street, and we might expect that the outflow went directly into the river (ON 27) (Jones 2003).

Excavations on East Bight (EB 80) and at Cottesford Place (CP 56) also revealed what are likely to have been surface- and storm-water drains beneath the two parallel east–west streets. That at Cottesford Place may also have carried the outflow from the public baths. The insertion of a drain at East Bight involved the complete reconstruction of the road (Fig. 7.5); the drain had stone sides and a slab cover, but its base was a elliptical channel cut into the clay – this shape apparently facilitating a constant velocity of flow to minimise silting.

Nearby on East Bight, excavations between 1968 and 1979 revealed a structure about 16m (c.55 feet) long added to the rear of the city wall (built in the early 2nd century) but predating the rebuilding of the wall in the late Roman period (EBS 70). It consisted of a solid rubble foundation c.5m deep, with a lining of *opus signinum.* An overhang on the adjacent surviving stretch of the city wall (Fig. 7.6) at a height of c.1.5m

indicates either an offset or the full height of its north wall (Jones 1980, 13–17, fig. 14). It may have been a vaulted structure. It seems most likely that it represents a water-tank, a *castellum aquae,* or *castellum divisiorum,* used to store water – presumably from the aqueduct (p. 116–8 below). Such tanks served various functions – to serve the public baths and perhaps the public fountain in the Lower City (p. 90 below), to flush out the sewers and, when sufficient water was available, also to service private establishments. A second aqueduct and tank may have been required to service facilities in the lower *colonia,* however, so the East Bight *castellum* may have been one of a series of such structures in the city. It may be compared with others in the Roman Empire, including that at the edge of the *forum* at Lucus Feroniae, c.20km north-east of Rome (Jones 1962, 197–201; Potter 1979, 113–14) (Fig. 7.7) and at Pompeii (Hodge 1992, 282–4). The size of the sewers would imply that a large volume of water was available (some, no doubt, rainfall), but some of the city's water supply would have come from wells, including that in the east range of the *forum* (p. 71 below), whose capacity

Fig. 7.5. Drain of the Colonia Era beneath the street inside the fortifications in the north-eastern quarter of the Upper City excavated at East Bight in 1980 (EB 80). The scale is 2m long (photo and copyright, City of Lincoln Archaeology Unit).

Fig. 7.6. Excavated remains of the 'castellum aquae' at East Bight as excavated between 1970–9 by K Wood. The slabs in the foreground are parts of the collapsed concrete lining of the great tank, whose foundations and superstructure are also visible (photo, H N Hawley).

*Fig. 7.7. Base for a 'castellum aquae' similar to that at East Bight (Fig. 7.6) at the Roman city of Lucus Feroniae (north of Rome) (photo and copyright, M J Jones).*

is estimated at 3,000 gallons (13,500 litres). The known pipeline built to bring water in the city from the north-east could not have supplied the whole city. The Lincoln aqueduct is frequently discussed, yet how the system of which traces have been found actually functioned remains problematical – it is described and discussed below.

### Fortifications

An account of discoveries on the upper *colonia* fortifications up to 1979 has already appeared (Jones 1980) and a companion volume on pottery has also been produced (Darling 1984). There have been some further discoveries since 1979, but these have only modified earlier conclusions in detail. Wacher (1998) now considers it unwise to think in terms of major periods of defensive building rather than a continuous programme of construction and repair; nevertheless, at Lincoln there are clear indications of some major building programmes.

The work at East Bight to the east of the *castellum aquae* (EB 80) showed that the late rampart dump had extended over the intervallum road, which was thus proven to have gone out of use during the 4th century (Jones 1980, 17–19; Steane *et al.* 2003). The evidence from other sites on the defences is too poor to confirm whether this was a local or general development. It may be that some of the dumps of material found on the rampart represented rubbish from the interior, including that from public buildings. Discovery of the east wall adjacent to the south side of the Cathedral (LC 84), and of the west wall across the line of the Castle west gate (CWG 86) served principally to confirm the exact line of the wall.

As at Gloucester, the circuit at Lincoln followed the line of the fortress defences. Colchester's new

enclosure was much bigger than the legionary base, however, as were those at Exeter and Wroxeter. Even so, there are parallels between Colchester and Lincoln since the hillside outside the fortress at both places seems to have formed part of the new town and was later walled. No traces of any capstones or cornices from the wall have come to light at Lincoln. The string-course from Cirencester (Holbrook 1998), and the evidence from Chester for these features (Strickland 1996) may be exceptional. The *opus quadratum* build at Chester, found also at Gloucester and Inchtuthil, may have been confined to bases of the 20th Legion. At Lincoln the sources of building materials and methods of construction were considered, and it was suggested that the non-oolitic limestones of the early wall were not of the same quality as the truer oolitic stone used later (Fenton 1980).

The sequence remains as set out in 1980 (Fig. 7.8). A stone front was built in the early 2nd century (probably during the Trajanic or Hadrianic periods) in front of the legionary rampart, before the timber revetment was removed and the gap filled. The legionary rampart was deliberately left in place for security, but the wall may also have been advanced forward in view of both the narrowness of the legionary bank and the wish to maintain the line of the intervallum road. A new ditch was also required, since the stone front rested on the rammed fill of the legionary ditch. Towers were added at intervals of about 40m to the inner face of the wall, but how much later is difficult to establish. They may date from the period when the rampart and wall were heightened in the late 2nd or early 3rd century, at the time when work may also have been taking place on the Lower City. A major refurbishment subsequently took place at some date after the late 3rd century, which involved thickening and raising the height of the wall and of the rampart bank, as well as the construction of a wide ditch. As study of Cirencester's fortifications has also shown (Holbrook 1994; 1998; Wacher 1998), we cannot expect to be too precise about the dating of urban defences, nor should we expect there to have been complete uniformity around the circuit. This latter *caveat* is more applicable to the developed circuits in the later period, when repairs of particular stretches might become necessary periodically. Only the *coloniae* obtained permission for early stone fortifications in Britain (Hurst 1986, 118–21), and with the early wall at Lincoln we might expect the initial build to have been fairly regular, even though it probably took several years to achieve.

The four gates of the fortress were replaced by four stone gates into the upper *colonia*, later developed into substantial structures, on the same sites. The east and north gates are both known from excavation (RENO 76, ON 208, Thompson and Whitwell 1973) and both eventually developed into large structures with several archways set in rectangular structures with flanking chambers (Plate 2.4). Over each gate in their developed phases were substantial chambers whose function

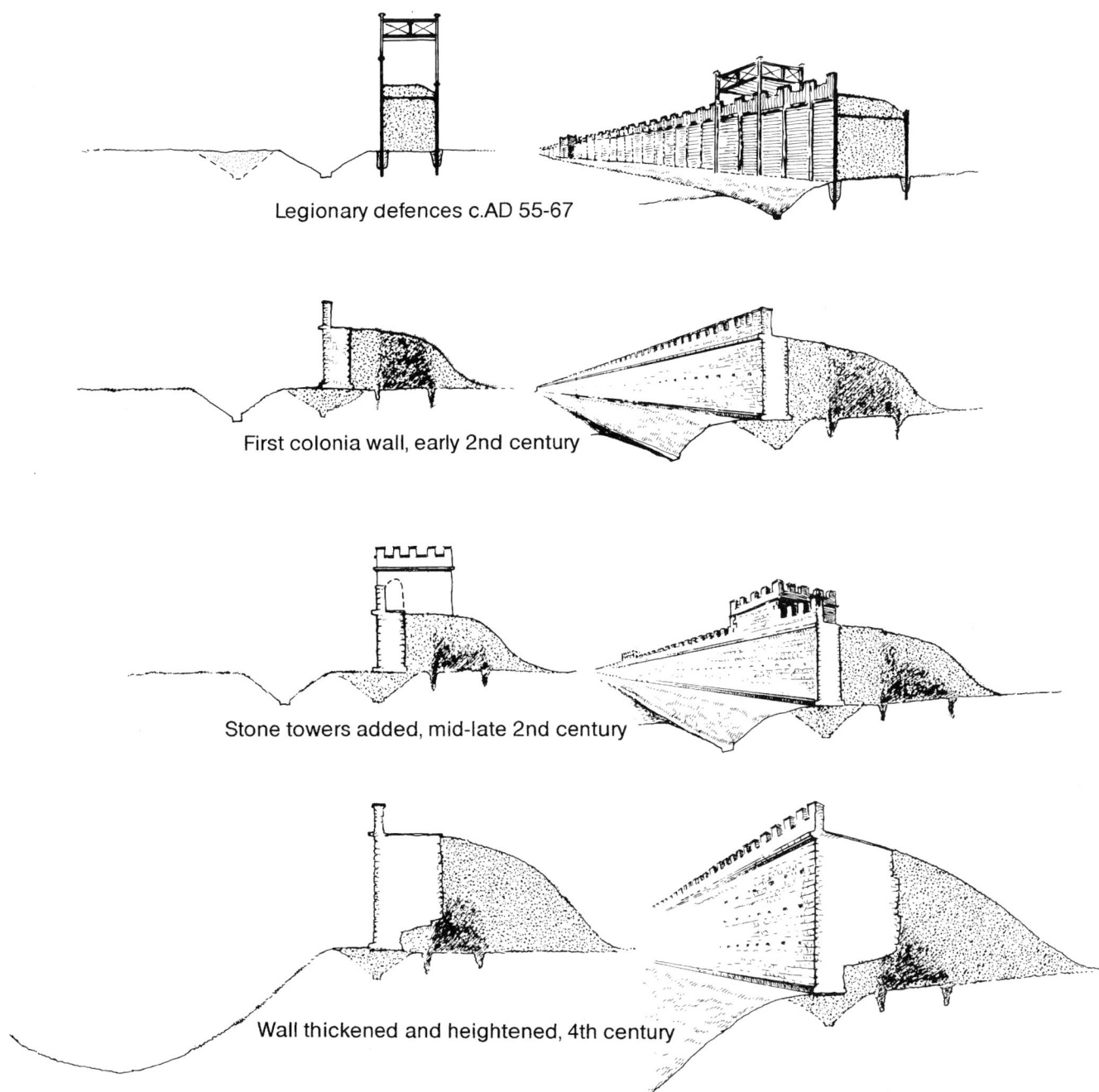

Legionary defences c.AD 55-67

First colonia wall, early 2nd century

Stone towers added, mid-late 2nd century

Wall thickened and heightened, 4th century

*Fig. 7.8. Diagram showing sequence of development of defences of the Upper City (source, Jones 1980 – drawn by Dave Watt, copyright English Heritage).*

remains uncertain, although they may have been re-used in the 11th century as great halls (Stocker forthcoming a). The west gate was seen to be different, however, at least in its final phase, when it was partially excavated in 1836 (RENO 3144, Thompson and Whitwell 1973, 194–200). As the 'back' gate, it was a smaller structure than the east and south gates, turriform in nature with a single archway beneath. The west gate also had a chamber over the passageway, but it was necessarily on a smaller scale.

The south gate is the least well understood of the four, and this may be because rebuilding early in the 3rd century, on a more monumental scale, transformed this structure in ways which did not affect the other three (Wacher 1995, 135). Wacher's suggestion has much to recommend it. However, the rebuilding operation would have taken several years, at a time when considerable construction work was being undertaken in the city as a whole – including that on extending the defences and the *forum*, as well as a major suburban development to the south of the river. No new excavations have been possible since 1979, but the discovery of two 18th-century representations of the east and south gates, by Nathan Drake (purchased

likely their presence indicates the former existence of an adjacent *exedra*, semi-circular or rectangular in plan (p. 73 below).

The Mint Wall has been standing above ground as a visible monument since its construction during the Roman period. It was drawn by Hieronymous Grimm (Fig. 7.13) from the south in 1784 and subsequently by E. J. Willson (London, Society of Antiquaries Ms 786/6, 29) – a view no longer so easily possible since the building of the North District School in 1852, which revealed remains of a 'beautiful pavement'. These two early depictions show the stub of a wall running southwards from its west end, but its appearance is more of tile work, and the recent discovery that the Mint Wall continued further to the west (ON 11) confirms that this was not the principal return. There was evidence of a further return of a wall '3½ feet thick' approximately 29.5m (97 feet) to the west of the colonnade (Mayhew 1879; Parker 1878, 396–8), and a more vague and possibly erroneous note of another 'about 54ft' west of the colonnade (Venables 1883, 317–19). An analysis of mortar from the wall (by Dr G C Morgan of Leicester University – unpublished) found it to be higher in lime than normal, suggesting that the wall may have been plastered. Apart from the additional tile courses at the west end, the Mint Wall retains few other indications of architectural features. There are, for example, apparently no traces of windows discernible.

Remains of the most northerly columns in the Bailgate colonnade, the second component of the *forum* fabric which can still be seen today, emerged in 1878 during the construction of a sewer beneath Bailgate (RENO 3204). Further elements in this impressive structure were still coming to light as late as 1897 (Fig. 7.14). These discoveries were described in a series of contemporary accounts (Parker 1878; Penrose 1878; Mayhew 1879; Venables 1883; Fox 1892). Mayhew recorded work by a Mr. Allis of 29 Bailgate in his own cellar which exposed the four columns, including the inosculating pair, at the northern end, as well as the north–south wall, of stone with tile bonding courses, and an adjacent cement floor, some 97 feet to the west. The rest of the colonnade of large columns, in all some 84m (275 feet) long, was found in 1891 and 1897 (Venables 1892; Fox 1892).

In total the colonnade contained 19 columns (some double and one triple), and their disposition indicates two entrances, one of which lay on the line of the *decumanus maximus* linking east and west gates, and another further north. The columns' dimensions, between 750mm and 850mm in diameter, suggest they rose to a height of between 6 and 8m, and their centres are generally *c*.4.8m apart, with wider spacing of nearer 6m where there were double or triple inosculating columns supporting (arched) entrances (Blagg 1996, 9). Blagg (1982a, 136–7) pointed out that the spacing of the columns (at 6.5 times the column diameter) is similar to those of the Leicester *forum* but that the intercolumnation at both Leicester and Lincoln are unusually narrow compared with the British norm (where the spacing of the columns is nearer 8 times the diameter). In terms of its architectural ornament generally, however, the Lincoln *forum* displays links with both southern Britain and the military zone (Blagg 1980). In particular, the column capitals are of the type

*Fig. 7.13. The Mint Wall from the south by S H Grimm, c.1784 (photo, H N Hawley, copyright British Library).*

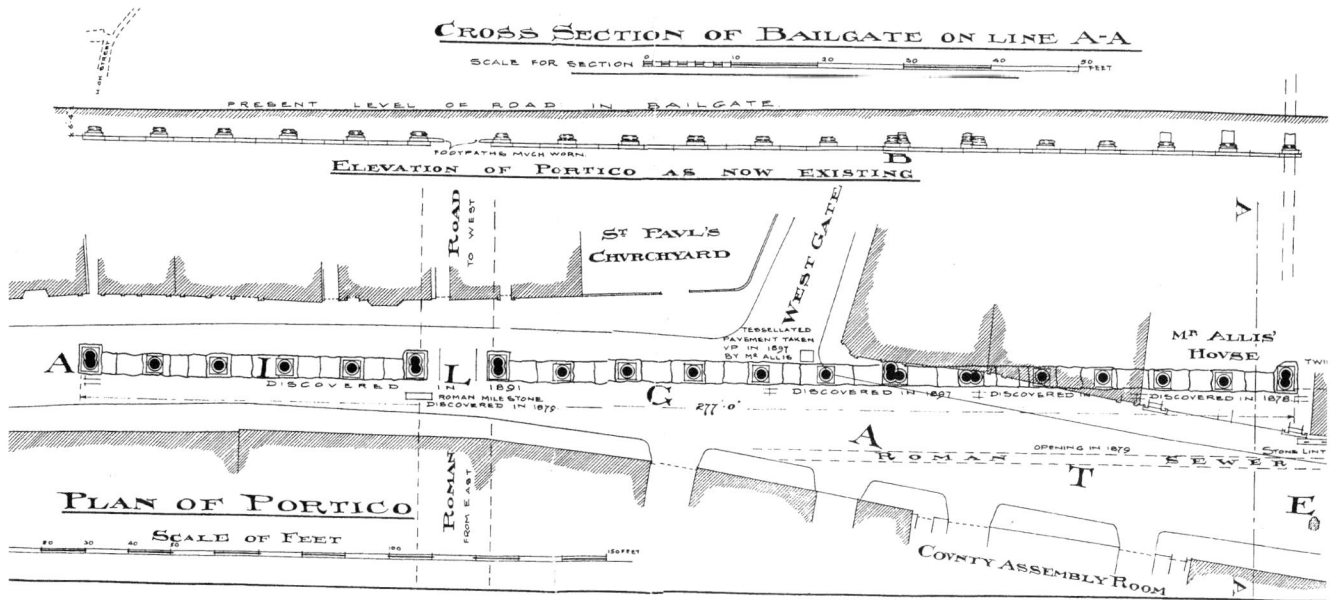

Fig. 7.14. *The remains of the colonnade along the east side of the* forum. *An engraving produced by Cuthbert Harding in 1903 to illustrate the discoveries of 1878. North is to the right (copyright, Lincolnshire County Council, Lincolnshire Museums Service).*

thought to derive from the north-east Gaulish 'form C' (Blagg 2002). The columns were not of limestone, but coarse sandstone. Fox (1892, 237) also noted a fragment of architrave beneath Bailgate indicating that the colonnade 'supported a horizontal entablature' rather than arches. To the south of the colonnade was a paved road, then a chamfered corner block. The bronze foreleg of a horse, thought to be part of an equestrian statue of an emperor, may also have come from this area (Richmond 1944).

Finds of tessellated pavements were made to the south of the Mint Wall (as noted above), during the rebuilding of St. Paul's church in the 1870s, and adjacent to the colonnade in 1897 (RENO 1439). A roundel with a head thought to be that of Mercury or *Fortuna*, or Summer, was removed to the Museum. In 1962, J B Whitwell excavated a small trench further south on Bailgate (to the rear of No. 19, now the Midland Bank – RENO 278), which revealed the junction of a north–south wall, with a gap for a doorway, with an east–west wall (Fig. 7.15). There were some disturbed flagstone fragments at a lower level, a later concrete floor and a black and white mosaic pavement (Whitwell 1963). These discoveries were of such limited scale that, although they indicated two phases of substantial building, the function of the structures was uncertain, but they can be incorporated into a hypothetical reconstruction of the south range of the *forum* (see Fig. 7.19 below). Richmond (1946, 38) noted Thomas Sympson's 1740 record of the SW corner of a building with tile bonding courses in what must have been the south-western part of the structure, but its exact position remains uncertain.

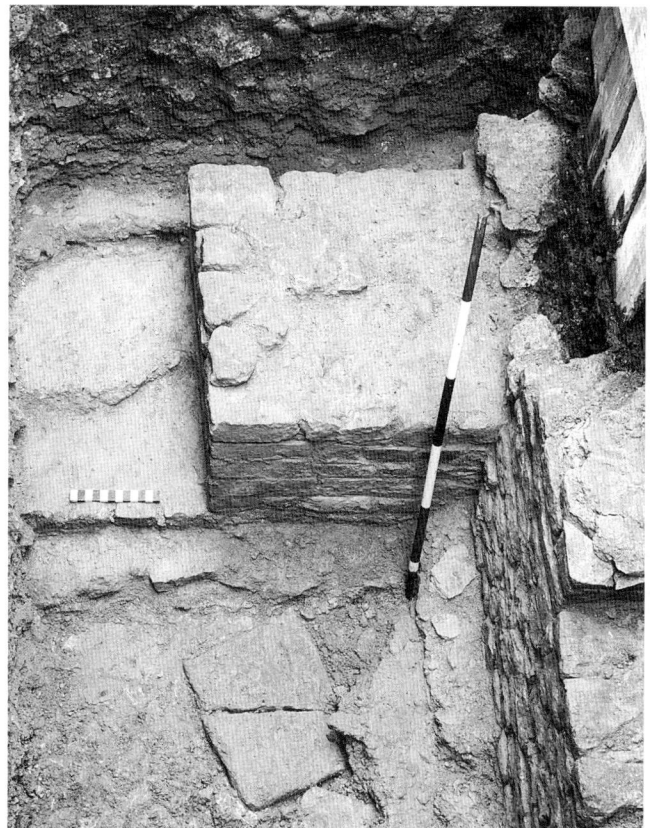

Fig. 7.15. *Remains of a major 2nd- or 3rd-century building to the south of the* forum *courtyard, excavated by B Whitwell in 1962–3. It may represent the junction between elements of the south and east ranges (see Fig. 7.19). The vertical scale is 6ft long (photo and copyright, Lincolnshire County Council, Lincolnshire Museums Service).*

The next investigation of the area after 1963 was a chance discovery made to the rear of No. 2 West Bight to the west of the Mint Wall when foundation trenches for a new house were dug in 1976 (WB 76). They revealed the western face of a substantial north–south stone wall (Fig. 7.16), including tile bonding courses, but to its west was an apparent floor of mortar, which may have been bounded by a structure such as a small portico parallel to the wall. Subsequently, a new, higher floor was laid over pitched limestone footings sealed by a pebbly aggregate, and later by slate flags, while quarter-round moulding in *opus signinum* occurred adjacent to the wall.

It was not surprising, therefore, that the layout of the major building complex defined on the north side by the Mint Wall and to the east by the Bailgate colonnade remained difficult of interpretation. The investigations carried out from 1976 until 1980 (WB 76, SP 72, WB 80, MW 79), supplemented by subsequent minor discoveries (MWS 83), and observations made during pipeline installations in 1982 and 1992–3 (ON 11), have added a great deal, however, and it is now possible to elucidate a clearer sequence.

The investigations of the Roman deposits beneath St Paul-in-the-Bail in 1978–9 (SP 72) were on a larger scale than previous work, covering an area almost 50m long and between 6m and 15m wide, and their impact on our understanding of the legionary occupation has already been described (chapter 6). The principal discovery of the *colonia* period in 1978 was of an extensive but badly-preserved surface, bounded to the east by a stone wall. It was originally pebbled but was later paved, at least in part. Excavations to the east of the stone wall in 1979 revealed more of the surface, but here it had gone out of use and had been replaced by a double range of rooms, each leading out on to a portico – on to the paved courtyard to the west, and towards the Bailgate colonnade and the principal street to the east.

The sequence, as recently re-analysed, involves some changes to the preliminary interpretation. In the first instance, the small rectilinear structure at the western edge of the excavations, initially considered to be a building of the early *colonia* (Jones and Gilmour 1980, 66), is now considered to represent the earliest church on the site, belonging to the late or sub-Roman period (Jones 1994). Second, remains of the early *colonia* phases are fragmentary and thus difficult to interpret with confidence. They include several phases of surfacing, and a possible north–south timber colonnade, similar to that at Exeter (Bidwell 1979, 73). Timber *basilica*s have been found at both Exeter (here as a temporary measure while the stone version was under construction – Henderson 1988, 110–11), and at Silchester (Fulford 1993; Fulford and Timby 2000). The south-eastern part of an early timber structure (formerly interpreted as part of the second-phase *principia*) may represent, alternatively, an ephemeral constructional phase, or a timber civic building. Subsequently, well-preserved

*Fig. 7.16. Remains of a major 2nd- or 3rd-century structure west of the* forum *complex, in modern West Bight (WB 76). These remains are west of the standing Mint Wall and it is presumed that they represent the building beyond the street on the west side of the* forum *(see Fig. 7.19). The longer scale is 2m long (photo H N Hawley).*

paving along with the statue bases and other incorporated features may have extended only as far west as the stone wall defining the later courtyard. This north–south wall (Fig. 7.17) was previously interpreted as contemporary with the later *forum*, but it is now considered possible that it was already in position. It may then have represented the western wall of a major public structure containing a paved floor, or precinct, with statues, which fronted on to the main street to the east. The make-up for its successor contained debris which may have been derived from this early building, for example fluted mouldings from columns (Blagg 1979; 1982a), and fine-quality painted wall plaster. Was the surface so well-preserved because it was covered with a roof rather than, as previously assumed, being in existence for only a short period? Or was it merely a surface that did not receive much wear?

Presumably the well, if of legionary origin, continued in use in the *forum*. There are no traces of any contemporary walls, but the paving had also been found about 30m to the south in 1962–3, and the Bailgate colonnade, or an earlier version of it, may have belonged to the same phase. The stone pier found beneath the Mint Wall to the north-west (WB 80) might have formed part of the same complex. Most probably the remains represent some form of civic centre; a *forum* with a temple and possibly also a *basilica*.

The major redesign of the complex, which probably involved the construction of the Mint Wall and possibly that of the Bailgate colonnade, now appears to have taken place at the end of the 2nd century or in the first decades of the 3rd (*contra* Jones and Gilmour

1980, 66). It involved a resurfacing, including at least some paving of the area to the west of the north–south wall, which was, or now became, a stylobate for a colonnade. To the east of the wall, the new layout consisted of a double range of rooms entered via internal and external porticoes. These rooms were constructed from the level of the early paving, although their floors were *c.*1m higher (Fig. 7.18). Three rooms leading on to the western, internal portico were identified, and others to N and S can be presumed (Fig. 7.19), while two rooms were found to the east.

The larger of these rooms appeared to contain the well-head perhaps constructed as part of the same scheme, although it appears to have been accessed from the west, where the foundations of two successive water-butts were found first by the room entrance, then adjacent to the well. The large eastern room, whose south wall only came to light during conservation work at the site in 1983, was at times subdivided (Fig. 7.20). The floors in this area leading on to the main street were not of *opus signinum*, but usually of clay, going through a whole series of phases indicating industrial or commercial use. Traces of copper- and silver-working at one time, and pottery, coins and vessel glass are all suggestive of a shop or refreshment area. Unpainted wall-plaster was found in the partially-excavated space to the north, which may also have been a shop. In subsequent deposits in this general area, finds of architectural fragments (including a moulded cornice), and a little imported marble hint at the quality of the building, but the *opus signinum* floors facing on to the internal courtyard were kept clean and produced little in the way of contemporary artefacts. The various rooms continued to be used at least into the late 4th century, and in some cases later.

Fortunately, it proved possible to excavate in the area to the south of the Mint Wall later in 1979 (MW 79) (Fig. 7.21), and to the north in the following year (WB 80). A further small investigation on the south side was undertaken in 1983 several metres to the east of the 1979 site (MWS83) and subsequently in 1987–8 a detailed survey of the standing wall itself was carried out. The work on the south side revealed an *opus signinum* floor similar to that found in the second phase *forum* at St. Paul-in-the-Bail (above), but at a higher level. To the south of an east–west wall 13m south of the Mint Wall, the floor level was about 800mm lower, that is to say it was at the same height as that of the portico around the inside of the courtyard (SP 72). The floor here had been heavily worn and repaired with cobbles (visible in Fig. 7.21) – it is fairly near to the projected centre of the structure, and perhaps it was close to an entrance and/or staircase. A further east–west wall was found some 7m to the south of the first;

*Fig. 7.17. Paving and statue base beneath the later walkway along the east side of the* forum *courtyard excavated in 1979 (SP 72)(looking north – see also Fig. 7.19). The scale is 2m long (photo and copyright, City of Lincoln Archaeology Unit).*

*Fig. 7.18. Remains of chambers within the east range of the later* forum *excavated in 1979 (SP 72)(looking west – see also Fig. 7.19). The scale is 2m long (photo and copyright, City of Lincoln Archaeology Unit).*

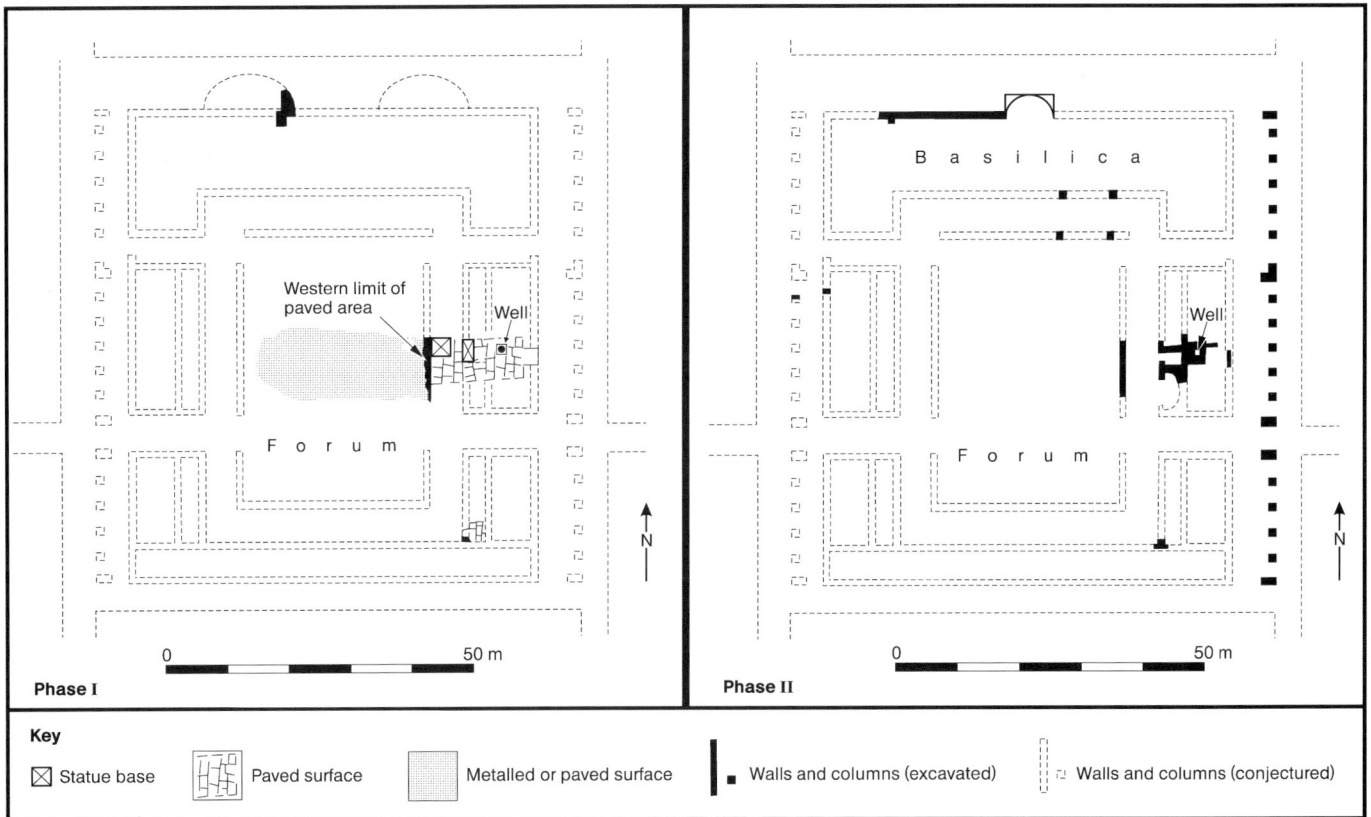

Phase I

Phase II

Key

⊠ Statue base | Paved surface | Metalled or paved surface | Walls and columns (excavated) | Walls and columns (conjectured)

*Fig. 7.19. Reconstruction plans of two proposed phases in the development of the* forum *complex. Phase I attempts to collect together known features of the early 2nd century. Phase II represents the better-known remains following the reconstruction of late 2nd- or early 3rd-century date (drawn by Dave Watt, copyright English Heritage).*

*Fig. 7.20. Remains of chambers within the east range of the* forum *complex, excavated in 1983 (looking south). Compare Figs. 7.18 and 7.19 (photo and copyright, City of Lincoln Archaeology Unit).*

it was the same width as the internal portico around the courtyard (SP 72). The floor and another more northerly wall were encountered further east in 1983 (MWS 83).

In 1979 the trench adjacent to the Mint Wall had revealed a wall surviving higher than the floor (MW 79) – could this be the remains of an earlier wall incorporated into the revised scheme? The answer was soon available. On the north side, a trench excavated in 1980 adjacent to the Mint Wall (WB 80) found that the Wall's base lay some 2m below the present ground surface, giving a wall total height to its surviving top of over 9m. The wall here was based on an early masonry foundation structure (Fig. 7.22), of which a quarter-circle was visible, but which probably representing a semi-circular projection facing northwards. It was presumably part of the same structure found in 1979 adjacent to the Mint Wall's southern face. Dating material suggested that the projection had probably been constructed in the early part of the 2nd century. Fragments of two ceramic antefixes with female heads, probably used as the gable end rather than along the eaves (Blagg 1979, 277–9), give some idea of its superstructure. The extent and purpose of the building to which it belonged cannot easily be determined. It was replaced by the building of which the Mint Wall was the northern limit. Remains of a street adjacent to the wall were found dating the wall itself to the late 2nd or early 3rd century – a date which ties in well with the evidence for the date of the reconstruction of the *forum* from excavations in the east range (SP 72).

Fig. 7.22. Semi-circular structure beneath Mint Wall, seen in excavations at West Bight in 1980 (WB 80) (looking east). The scale is 2m long. This structure is interpreted as part of an apsidal projection from the north wall of first phase of the early forum complex (Compare Fig. 7.19) (photo and copyright, City of Lincoln Archaeology Unit).

Fig. 7.21. Excavations to the south of the Mint Wall in 1979 (MW 79) looking north-west. The Mint Wall itself is visible behind the brick wall beyond the trench. The base of the trench is formed by the (greatly repaired) floor of opus signinum, which is very similar in character to the floor of the late 2nd- or early 3rd-century forum found in excavations in the east range further south. The scale is 2m long (photo and copyright, City of Lincoln Archaeology Unit).

the most reasonable interpretation, and enables us to suggest a *forum-basilica* complex running north–south for the length of the colonnade with the *basilica* itself across its northern end.

Two further aspects of the *forum* deserve consideration here. First, we have already noted that the stone-by-stone recording of the Mint Wall (MWS 83) drew attention to the more frequent tile courses at the eastern end of the standing fragment. These suggest that the wall is approaching an adjacent corner or opening, and such details might be expected if this was close to an *exedra*. Such features are usually either semi-circular or rectangular rooms or recesses in which the most significant deities of the city would be honoured (Fig. 7.23). *Exedrae* were usually centrally placed, however, and for this to be the case here, the Mint Wall should have extended further west than the present fragment. Some confirmation that this was indeed the case has come from observations of a number of service trenches. One already mentioned, in 1982, showed that the wall extended westwards for at least 1.5m beneath West Bight (ON 11). Our proposed layout for the developed *forum-basilica* (Fig. 7.19 phase II) also presumed that the east and west sides of the complex were symmetrical, and accordingly the wall found at West Bight (WB 76) was seen as the east wall of the building to the west of a north–south street west of the *forum*. Service trenches along Westgate in 1982 and 1992 (WEB 92, Wragg 1992) revealed remains of foundations which appeared to confirm a symmetrical arrangement, plus a major building to the west.

A second discussion followed on from Goodchild's suggestion (1946, 77) that Lincoln may have been one of the rare examples in Britain of a double precinct (or 'Gallo-Roman' *forum*). In 1980 the similarity between

The results of the work adjacent to the Mint Wall suggested that it formed the north wall of the large hall lying east–west, at least 13m wide, with an aisle, or at least a portico, to the south, which appears to be part of the same building as the colonnade and the remains of the east range to its west (SP 72). The identification of this east–west hall as the *basilica* – first put forward more than a century ago – still seems

*Fig. 7.23. Reconstruction of the late 2nd- or early 3rd-century* forum *from the north by David Vale, showing the* basilica *in the foreground with its projecting apse (or* exedra*) (drawing and copyright, estate of David Vale).*

the Bailgate colonnade and the example at Augst was noted (Jones and Gilmour 1980; Laur-Belart 1991). Furthermore, the fragmentary inscription found at SP 72 referring to the rebuilding of a temple by the priest of the imperial cult (Hassall and Tomlin 1979, 345) made it likely that a temple precinct did exist hereabouts. It has been suggested (but not proven) that a small temple occupied a position in the southern part of the *forum* at Velleia (Wacher 1995, 138; Ward-Perkins 1970, 7, fig.4) and Frere (1983, 68–9) considered the Flavian *forum* at Verulamium, with its double-aisled *basilica* and temples in the opposite range, to be a prototype for Roman Britain. Given the limitations on space indicated by the southern limit of the colonnade at Lincoln and the return wall found by Whitwell in 1962–3, however, it appeared that there was insufficient room to the south of the *forum* piazza here for a temple.

### The civic centre: interpretation and discussion

Many eminent specialists visited the various excavations at St Paul-in-the-Bail. Some had been initially sceptical about the identification of the site (in its developed form) as a *forum*, for similar reasons to those given by Richmond (1946, 37) – such as the great width of the east range. The double range of rooms and wide porticoes, giving a total width of about 27m, were, however, of comparable dimensions to that at Paris (Duval 1961; Velay 1992), and most scholars have now accepted the *forum* interpretation. Dr J B Ward-Perkins, for example, found the layout as proposed in the 1980 article 'very convincing', and suggested that room for a temple might be found within the west range, or for a small one in the south range; the double-precinct plan was, he thought, 'elastic' (pers. com. 6/11/1979).

We have some indications of internal partitions within the Lincoln *basilica*, and of a likely continuation of the internal portico, on the south side, which might have allowed for a clerestory arrangement here. The space between the portico and the *basilica* wall has been referred to in previous reports as an 'aisle', but there may also have been an aisle internally. It appears to be of fairly simple plan, and is similar to, for example, Djemila/Cuicul in North Africa (Ward-Perkins 1981, 40), but the hint of an *exedra*, whether rectangular or semi-circular, in the centre of the north wall is more distinctive. This feature could represent one of several possible rooms: a small temple, offices, the *curia* or council room (as at the second phase at Augst – Trunck 1991; Laur Belaart 1991), or merely an architectural recess housing a statue (as at St. Bertrand de Comminges: Badie *et al.* 1994). Such features had a long tradition, and are described in Vitruvius' account of the *basilica* at Fano. If not within the *exedra*, the *curia* might have been located at one end of the *basilica*, in the south range, facing it (as suggested at Verulamium), or even along another side. The floor with quarter-round moulding found adjacent to the north–south wall in the *basilica* may represent the higher level of the floor of a heated room. Such a raised floor would fit better the proposed level of the *basilica* floor derived from that of the portico.

There is still much to establish regarding both the general layout of the complex and the detailed arrangement of the *basilica*. For example, the relationship of the triple columns in the colonnade to an entrance into the courtyard and to the structure of the *basilica* still needs to be confirmed, and access arrangements from the courtyard to the portico and from the portico to the *basilica* need to be investigated. The *basilica* at Velleia had staircases towards both ends, for example, while at Caerwent and Glanum, and possibly at Exeter, steps continued along the whole length. At Lincoln, evidence for wear of the steps might indicate a central staircase (MW 79). Don Mackreth also pointed out the likelihood of a stone gutter at the perimeter of the courtyard adjacent to the internal colonnade, as at Wroxeter (Atkinson 1942, 88–9). At Lincoln, a 13th-century trench in this location probably represents its robbing. The building method used at the Mint Wall and in other elements, based on small squared blocks (*petit appareil*) and incorporating tiles, is found in many Gallo-Roman monuments from the end of the 1st century (Adam 1994, 143). These observations, however, all relate to the developed, second-phase, *forum*, while the evidence appears to suggest two or more major building periods. Although there are hints of structures in timber, which may represent elements of a temporary civic centre for the first generation of colonists, it is clear that a new precinct was built in stone in the early 2nd century. This structure underwent at least one major redesign by the early 3rd century. Furthermore, there are likely to have been modifications during the interval and some elements of the 'definitive' form may already have been built.

The earlier of the two *fora* included an extensive paved area with statues, perhaps a pebbled courtyard to the west and a structure incorporating a projection to its north-west which may have been attached to its perimeter wall – or may have formed part of a separate structure. *Fora* and temples occasionally display such projections, for example at Bavay in north-east Gaul (Bedon *et al.* 1988), St Bertrand-de-Comminges in south-west Gaul (Badie *et al.* 1994) and at the *Forum Caesaris* in Rome, remodelled early in the 2nd century (Claridge 1998, 148–52) (Fig. 7.24). The *Traianeum* (temple to Trajan) at Italica in Southern Spain is another structure worth close examination, since its outer precinct wall had a series of similar semi-circular and rectangular *exedrae* (Gros 1996; Leon 1988) (Fig. 7.25).

If the first phase at Lincoln was a temple precinct, the temple itself may have stood at the highest point, beneath the later *basilica*, or have faced east on to the main street. Although the remains of buildings of this phase have yet to be located, the discovery of plaster-casings for brick columns may be a clue to its appearance. Similar convex casings were found at the temple precinct at Colchester (Blagg 1990, 426). Blagg (1984) considered that the new community's religious requirements would be paramount, and Esmonde Cleary (1998) emphasised the high investment in religious structures in the early stages of Romano-British urban development. Dr J B Ward-Perkins (pers. com. 1979) noted that the so-called 'temple-forum' appeared to be more common when the imposition of Roman rule was 'quite recent', and that the temple, presumably dedicated to Rome and Augustus, would be prominently sited. Yet at Conimbriga (Alarçao and Etienne 1977), it was the later, Flavian *forum* which gave more emphasis to the temple. Certainly the huge precinct at Colchester – probably only dedicated to the emperor Claudius after his death in AD54 – may have been an expression of the godlike qualities of the Emperor who conquered Britain, as much as a reflection of the site's status as the early provincial capital and centre of the imperial cult (Drury 1984; Wacher 1995, 116–9; Crummy 1997, 59–61). The Roman victory was also commemorated through a monumental arch. The temple precinct at Colchester was further developed from the end of the 1st century, as the two new *coloniae* were being established (*Ibid.*, 99–100). Hurst (1999b) has suggested that the Westgate colonnade at Gloucester also belonged to a huge temple precinct up to 135m by 65m in plan, larger even than the *forum-basilica* there. It may be then, that there was a similar large precinct at Lincoln, possibly representing a 'temple-forum', or perhaps also incorporating a *basilica*. The British *civitas* capitals are normally excluded from discussions regarding temples of the imperial cult, apart perhaps from the *municipium* at Verulamium (Frere 1983), but it may be unwise to restrict our perspective unnecessarily. For instance, the open space south of the *forum* at Exeter (Bidwell 1979, 78–82) is worth re-consideration as a temple precinct, rather than a livestock market, and this may be equally true for other open areas close to *fora*. At Canterbury, for example, there was a temple precinct adjacent to the *forum-basilica*, but it was clearly separate (Wacher 1995, 193–4).

It was not unusual for public monuments to be modified or thoroughly redesigned, and sometimes enlarged, as at London (Milne 1992) and at Conimbriga

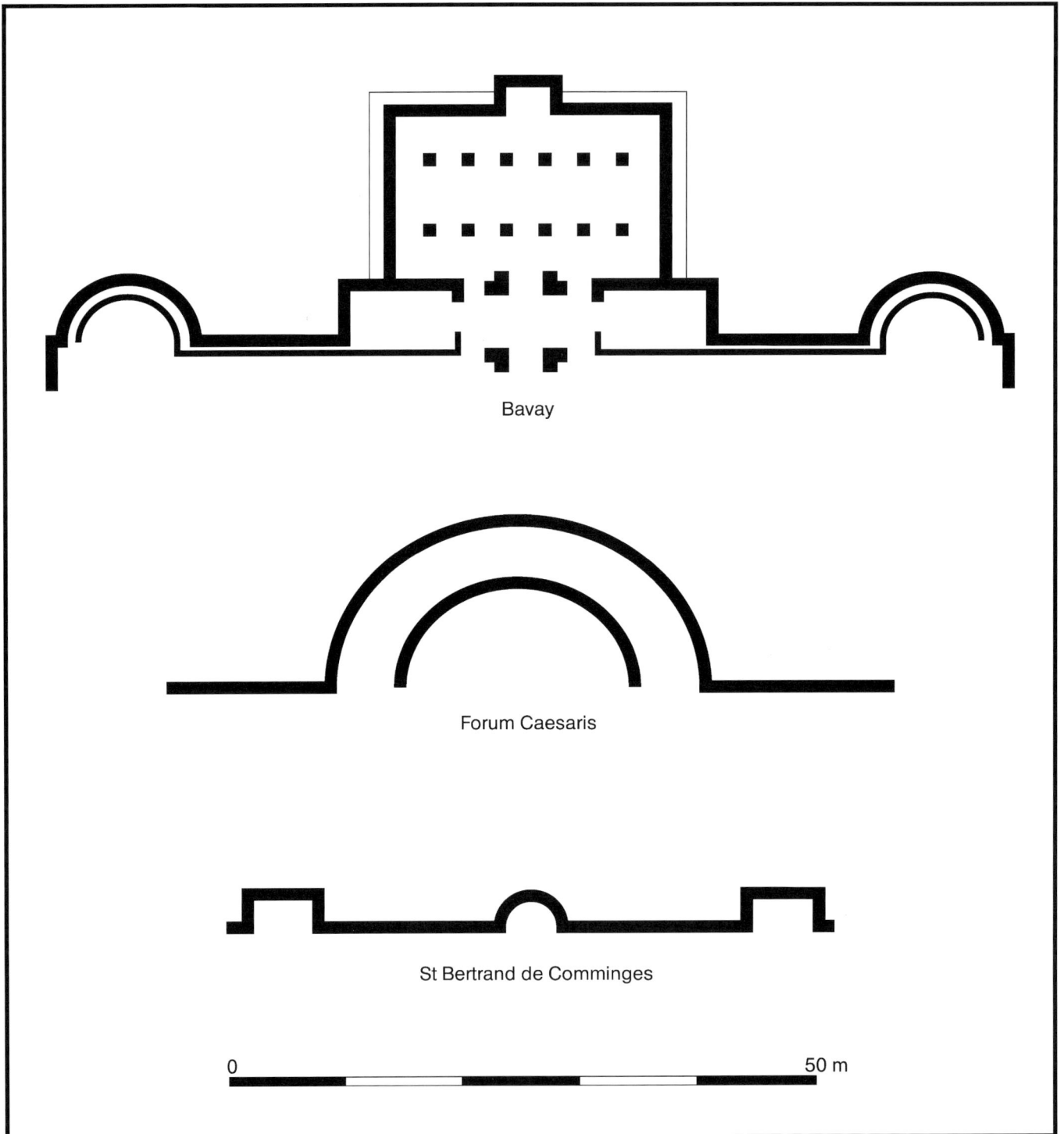

Bavay

Forum Caesaris

St Bertrand de Comminges

0                                                    50 m

*Fig. 7.24. Details of plans of walls around* fora *at Bavay (northern France), St Bertrand de Comminges (south-western France) and the* Forum Caesaris *in Rome (sources Wightman 1985, Badie et al. 1994 and Claridge 1998 – drawn by Dave Watt, copyright English Heritage).*

in Portugal (Alarçao and Etienne 1977). In the second period at Lincoln, a double range of rooms with wide porticoes may have surrounded the courtyard on two or three sides, with the probable *basilica* to the north. Such a structure would also have had a colonnaded frontage on to the *cardo*, now represented by the Bailgate colonnade, and probably also something similar to the west. Such wide ranges with double rooms and porticoes are also found at London, as well as at the Gallic *fora* of Augst, Paris and Nyon. The detailed arrangement of the south range at Lincoln, of which we have only the general outline, is uncertain

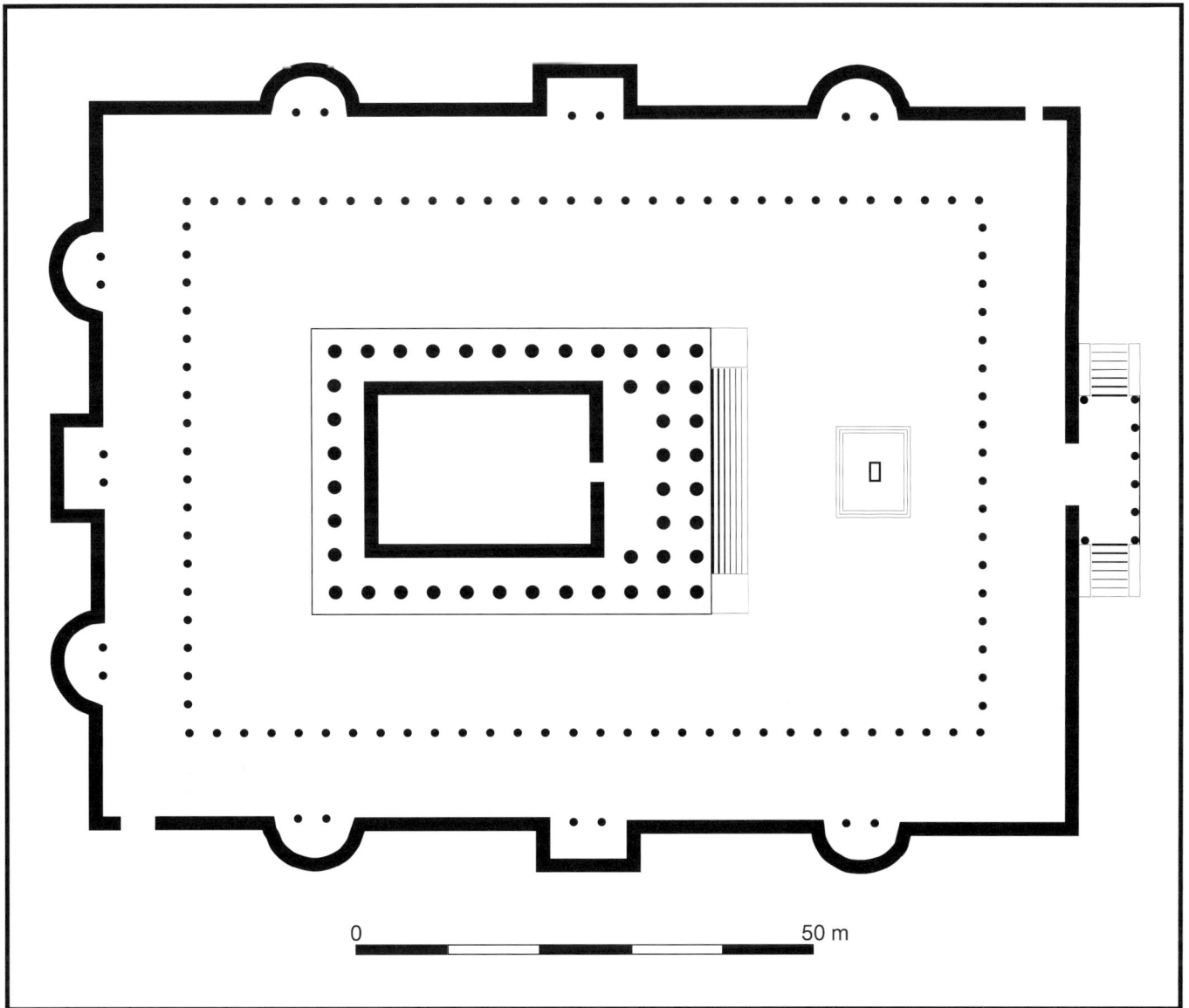

*Fig. 7.25. Plan of the precinct wall of the* Traianeum *at Italica (southern Spain) (drawn by Dave Watt, copyright English Heritage).*

and several reconstructions are possible – including an embedded small temple, or a separate temple precinct. The wall found by Whitwell in 1962–3 does not rule out any of these interpretations; there was, for instance, a wall separating the main courtyard from the temple precinct at Nyon (Rossi 1995) and a clear division also occurs at Virunum on the Danube (Mocsy 1974, 87–90). It is therefore possible that a temple precinct at Lincoln may have extended further to the south in this second phase. In view of the fact that it was a rebuilding, the temple to which the Purbeck marble inscription refers (above) is more likely to belong to a temple in this second phase of development of the *forum*. Indeed it might imply that it had been rebuilt in a different location from its original site. Having presumably started out with a prominent temple, it is unlikely that the *colonia* would dispense with such a feature when

the *forum* was remodelled. If not within the *forum* complex, it is likely that the cult site was adjacent.

The solid corner block to the south of the colonnade may, according to Mackreth, only represent a *spina* before the colonnade continued, but evidence casting light on this matter is lacking. What can be said is that, at less than 85m long, the Bailgate colonnade falls well short of the length of the normal length of the double precinct *forum*; that at Paris, for instance, measured 118m. The chamfered corner block to the south (above p. 69) is, however, best interpreted as that of a podium for a temple facing east (a type for which there are various parallels – Gros 1996, 124–98).

To conclude, the most important understanding to emerge from these detailed reconstructions of the Lincoln *forum-basilica*, made possible by recent work, is that we can now demonstrate that it stands apart from the so-called *"principia*-type" *forum* found at most *civitas* capitals in Britain (Fig. 7.26). Rather, the long colonnaded frontage, with double side entrances into the *forum*, and wide double ranges, suggests that it belongs to a different category of building, perhaps derived from continental models. Like many of these examples, the later *forum* at Lincoln may have contained a major temple.

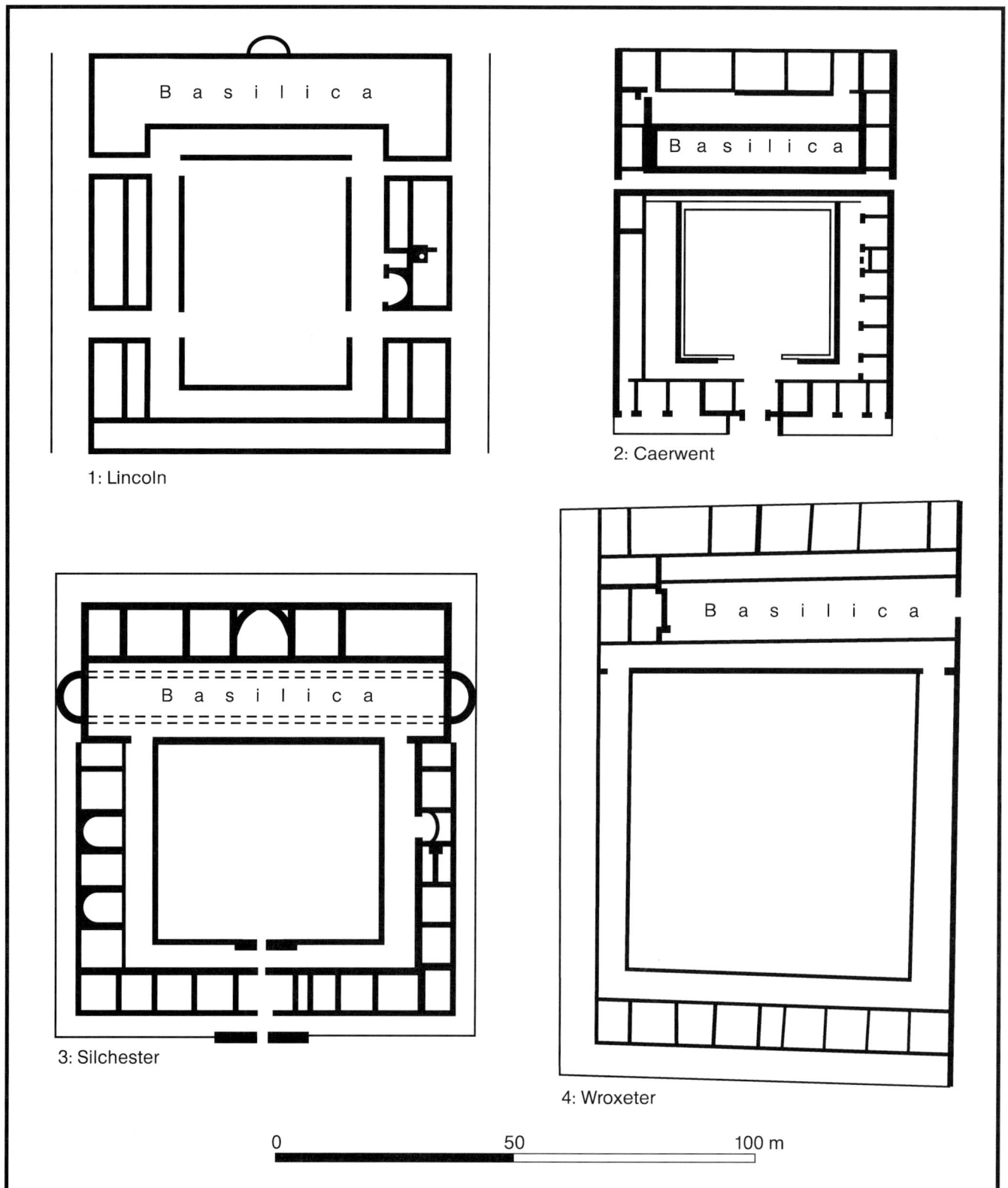

*Fig. 7.26. Simplified reconstructed plans of* forum *complexes in Britannia, compared with the late 2nd- or early 3rd-century example at Lincoln (source, Wacher 1995 – drawn by Dave Watt, copyright English Heritage).*

## Baths, temples and other structures

Indications of monumental structures along the two principal streets come from both antiquarian discoveries and more recent observations, while what appears to be the public baths was excavated to the north east of the *forum-basilica* in 1957–8 (CP 56). Apart from the substantial structure (perhaps a temple) immediately to the south of the known later *forum*, there was another across the main north–south street; a wall containing tile courses in its fabric appeared north of Eastgate in 1848. Further to the south, fragments of a fluted column were found in 1883–4 (Venables 1884). In 1985, during the cutting of a service trench into Bailgate a little to the north, the same wall was exposed, and the base of an engaged column was found (ON 323), and a further fragment of the wall was noted in 1992 during pipeline work (WEB 92, Wragg 1992). Tom Blagg suggested that these fragments are most likely to have formed part of a monumental entrance, or archway (pers. com.). Such a huge block as the engaged column base is likely to have been still *in situ*, but if it had been moved, it might have come from an entrance to the *forum* – a similar stone at Silchester had been displaced in this way (Boon 1974, 108). An alternative possibility is that it represents the *cella* of a temple – but it would be unusual for the *cella* to face on to the main street. Remains of a colonnade found further east, at Atton Place to the north of the west front of the Cathedral, may indicate another monumental frontage in this vicinity (RENO 3097).

In 1879, when the Roman sewer was discovered to the east of the Bailgate colonnade, the well-known milestone of Victorinus was found (ON 325), giving the distance to Segelocum, (Littleborough) as 14 miles (RIB 1965, 2241) (Fig. 7.27). In 1891, two double columns were found close to the site of the milestone, near the main east–west street (Fig. 7.14). Rodwell (1975, 86–7) suggested that the milestone was not in its original location, but this central location is very close to the stated distance from Littleborough and the suggestion lacks something in conviction.

A row of seven or eight brick piers, with semi-circular fronts, came to light further north, at the same time as the Bailgate colonnade, in 1878, but across the *cardo* and extending northwards from the northern limit of the colonnade. Its northern edge was presumably along the east–west street south of the baths. These structures could front a row of shops; Brodribb (1987, 54–6) and Adam (1994, 145–8) have shown how bricks were used to represent engaged columns in buildings of this type. In 1993 the foundations of a stone structure, presumably fronting on to the east side of the *cardo*, were found during pipeline works further north in Bailgate. This discovery helped to confirm the building-line, but little else.

The public baths were situated to the east of the main north–south street (CP 56). Their location may

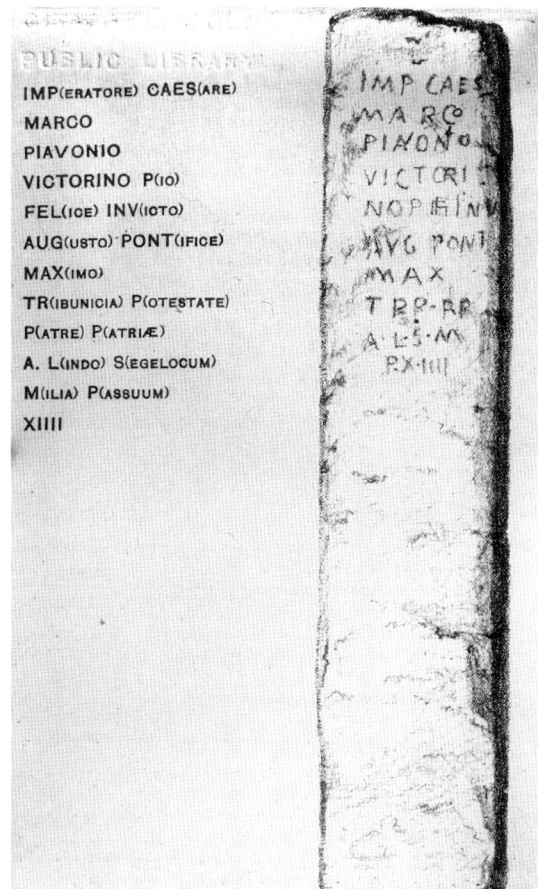

Fig. 7.27. *Drawing by Professor Haverfield of the inscribed milestone found in 1879 in Bailgate (RIB 1965, No.2241), close to the eastern colonnade of the* forum. *The inscription can be translated:*

To the Emperor Caesar Marcus Piavonius Victorinus, the pious, fortunate, unconquerable, Augustus, Chief Pontiff, invested with tribunician power, father of his country. From Lindum to Segelocum [*Littleborough?*], XIV miles.

*(Photo and copyright, Lincolnshire County Council, Lincolnshire Museums Service).*

have been influenced by the nearby *castellum aquae* on the northern defences (or vice-versa). It would be normal for a building as important as the baths to face on to the main street, but the limited evidence we have from Petch's excavations of 1957 failed to demonstrate this. These excavations have not yet been published, but Mr Petch has left us a draft report, which explains that, rather than the baths having a façade to the west, there was a colonnade on the N side of the street south of the baths leading eastwards from the *cardo*. Several rooms were uncovered, including some which were certainly heated, with deep hypocausts and tessellated pavements, as well as a douche (Figs. 7.28 and 29). Unfortunately the remains discovered tell us little about the plan-type (Gros 1996,

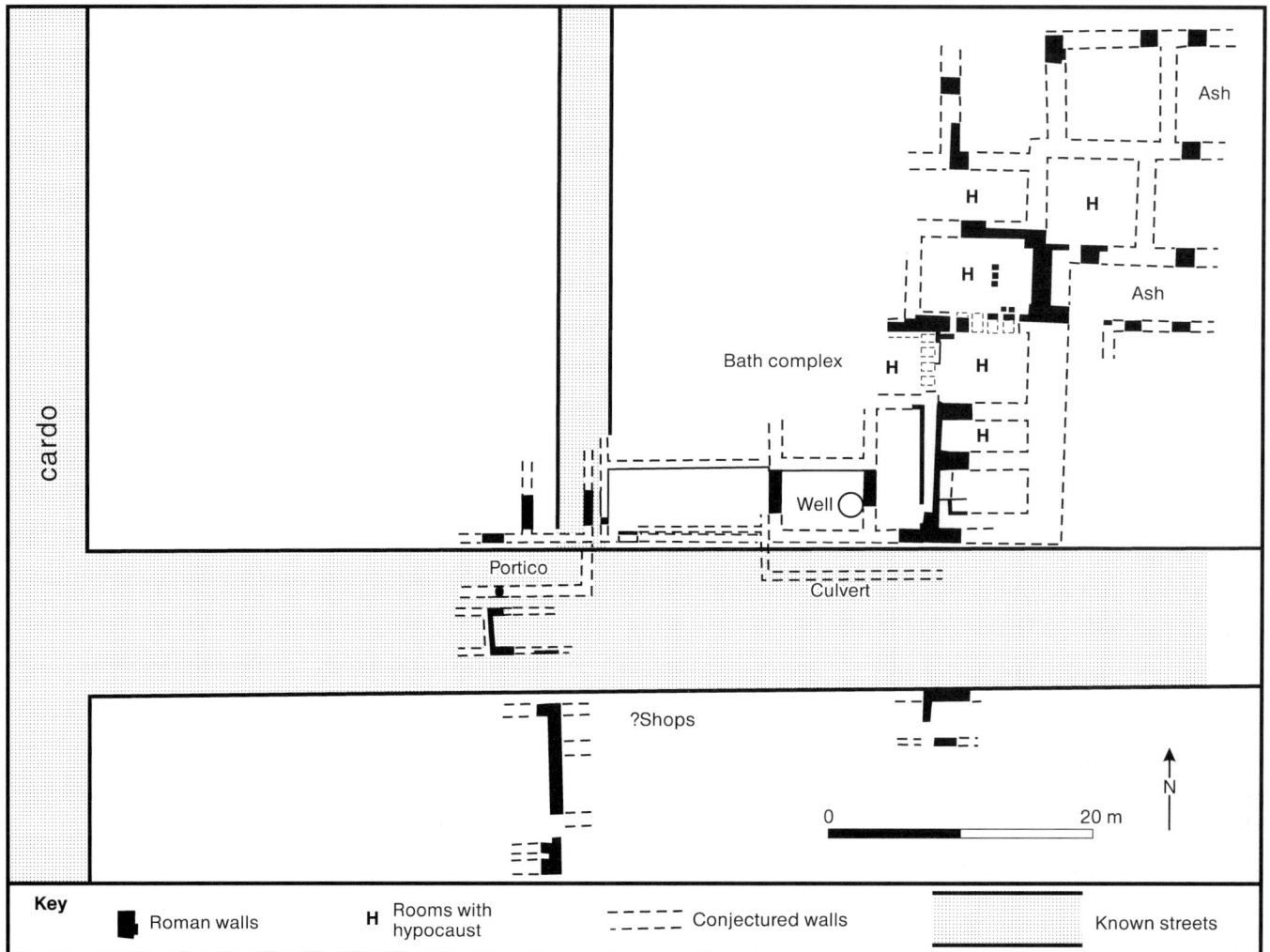

*Fig. 7.28. Plan of the Upper City bathhouse complex and nearby buildings, as excavated by Denis Petch at Cottesford Place in 1956–7 (CP 56) (redrawn from Mr Petch's 1987 plan by Dave Watt, copyright English Heritage).*

388–417; Bidwell 1979, 43–50). They covered an area of at least 60m by 45m, but there was clear evidence that they had been twice extended, sealing an early street in the process. This extension dated from the Hadrianic period or later, and it is clear that a major modification or rebuilding took place in the late Antonine period or soon after. Like the walls of the later *forum*, some of the walls incorporated brick courses. Whether any element of the earlier phase dated back to the legionary period remains uncertain, although this would not be an unusual location within the fortress for legionary baths. Parts of the site had previously contained legionary timber structures. The occurrence amongst the building materials of a number of stamped tiles, originally interpreted as products of the 5th Legion (Todd 1965), can no longer be accepted as evidence for a legionary baths. These were subsequently recognised as being of civil manufacture (Bogaers 1977) and are now considered to belong to the Hadrianic phase (Black 1996). The site also pro-

duced important collections of samian ware and vessel glass of late 1st- or early 2nd-century date, and this seems to confirm that the site was developed as a bath-house only in the *colonia* period.

Another public structure may be represented by several substantial walls to the west of the *forum*, all running parallel, north to south, some as much as 2m thick below the offset courses, and incorporating tile courses (WEB 92, Wragg 1992). These are best interpreted as the remains of a building facing southwards on to the main east–west street. The most easterly two walls of this group may represent the western colonnade of the later *forum* and the outer wall of the next building to the west. The second lines up with the substantial wall found at West Bight (WB 76). A mortar floor was noted between two of the walls, but since they could not be investigated beyond the area of the water-pipe trench in which they were found, we know too little of their plan to identify the building's function. Further west along Westgate, two

*Fig. 7.29. View of what the excavator interpreted as a 'douche' within the bath house complex east of Bailgate, excavated by Dennis Petch in 1957. Note the drainage gully around the edge of the chamber. The scale is 3ft long (photo courtesy of estate of D Petch).*

parallel north–south walls, about 5m apart, were noted in advance of and during construction work in 1989 (TG 89). Painted wall plaster was associated with this structure and these slight indications might imply a house. Well to the south of the *forum-basilica,* remains of a stone building with a mosaic floor were noted at the south side of the square known as Castle Hill in 1979 (ON 57). They indicate a structure on the west side of the *cardo,* but its function remains uncertain, and it is likely that it was also house, and so we move to consideration of the evidence for residential structures.

## Housing

Recent excavations at some Italian colonies have shown that the prestigious houses of the decurions were clustered close to the town centre, while those of the vast majority of the population were both smaller and situated further away from the *forum.* So

much is clear from Cosa and Fregellae, and in the colonial part of Pompeii. The towns of Roman Britain, whether *coloniae* or not, may not exhibit this characteristic; they were, after all, founded later, and few large town houses are known before the mid 2nd century (Walthew 1975; 1983). On the other hand, the picture gained from current work at Ostia of slow, evolutionary change rather than episodes of general rebuilding (Delaine 1996), may be more representative of what happened in Britain.

The earliest houses at Lincoln have not been investigated to the same extent as those at the other British *coloniae* at Colchester and Gloucester, where some seem to have been formed from modified barrack blocks. This phenomenon might be expected at Colchester, which had been a fortress for only six years before it became a *colonia*. At Gloucester, however, there may have been a shorter hiatus between the departure of the army and the foundation of the *colonia* than at Lincoln, and this might account for the reuse of barracks buildings there (Hurst 1988; Hassall and Hurst 1999). During the transitional period at Lincoln, the military buildings were dismantled, at least in part. Furthermore, in the earliest years of the *colonia*, new accommodation for the new administrative and religious centres would have been priorities. Such evidence as we have from recent excavations at Lincoln suggests both that the first houses were provided with walls of timber, in some cases on stone sills, and that they may well have been modest in scale (CL 85 and EB 80). Those of the 3rd and 4th centuries tended to be larger, with substantial stone walls and decorative painted plaster. They might include an area for business and their frontages could be used, even let out, for commercial purposes. Traders' houses, buildings devoted principally to commerce with accommodation attached, have been identified outside the north, west and east gates (L 86; WC 87). They took the form usually found in Britannia, of long narrow structures, gable end on to the street (Wacher 1995, 66).

Our knowledge of housing in the upper *colonia* is very limited, but it can be assumed that some of the mosaic pavements found in previous centuries belonged to the houses of the well to do (Richmond 1946, 38–40; Neal and Cosh 2002). They are recorded within the area of the Castle (Fig. 7.30), the Cathedral and its precincts, and at the east end of the plot occupied by the Methodist Church at the north end of Bailgate. The last mentioned, however, may have come from within the area of the public baths (CP 56). Black and white pavements were also found at the public baths by Petch, at the top of Steep Hill and at the south-east corner. Others are known near to, and beneath, the water tower to the north-west of the *forum*. Richmond did not consider these mosaics to be in the first rank. He thought they represented 'comfort rather than elegance' and they have not been shown to be the work of a local school of mosaicists. David

Neal confirms the fragmentary nature of the evidence, and notes that the Lincoln designs are limited to geometric patterns (*Ibid.*). Some of the buildings containing mosaics also had walls with decorated and painted plaster.

As Hurst (2000) has pointed out, the three early British *coloniae* may have all made use of the surviving military infrastructure created by the fortresses, but each went its own way in establishing a physical identity, based upon both military-inspired and civic designs within the context of their changing times. It does appear that the Lincoln *colonia* concentrated its initial investment on major public works, including a *forum*-temple, baths and fortifications, rather than on private housing. The new developments showed some continental influence and reflected Lincoln's colonial status. It is likely that major expenditure on monuments and services continued throughout the 2nd century, and the *forum*, the baths, and gates were all apparently being modified in the early 3rd century. At some stage, domestic housing was given greater investment, and

by the late Roman period there were few public building programmes, with greater resources devoted to finer houses (p. 90–3 and 130–2 below).

A quantitative analysis of the pottery from the Upper City undertaken by Margaret Darling is consistent with the other types of evidence. Most of the finer wares of the 1st and 2nd centuries, including the largest samian assemblage from the city, came from the public baths. Some trading took place from shops inside the walls. Later, the better-quality vessels are associated with the town houses – most of the excavated examples of which lie on the hillside, in the lower walled city. Based on the evidence available, the Upper City did not become more commercial as time went on, but like the Lower City, it probably also witnessed the growth of larger houses. Other material, such as marble inlay, corroborates the impression of first public, and later private, affluence.

## The lower walled city in the *Colonia* Era

By the mid 2nd century the hillside below the Upper City, and between it and the river shows evidence of formal planning and settlement over an extensive area. For instance, at The Park (P 70), on the line of the later western defences, there were timber buildings at right angles to Ermine Street in the early 2nd century, presumed to relate to a street-grid. With the exception of burials, it is thought likely that any military-period structures on the hillside had lined the road leading from the south gate of the fortress to the river crossing but, in the *colonia* period, development spread laterally across the hillside. It eventually spread so far east and west of Ermine Street that buildings, including those at The Park, had to be demolished to make way for the construction of fortifications. These fortifications involved extension of the uphill circuit almost to the line of the then riverfront and provided a rigid boundary for the whole *colonia* in the 3rd and 4th centuries (p. 86–8 below).

A substantial amount of evidence from antiquarian discoveries has now been gathered and placed alongside discoveries from more recent excavations (Fig. 7.31), and we can now say that the Ermine Street frontage, at least on the lower, gentler slope, was probably occupied by a range of public monuments, while the land to east and west was largely devoted to residential developments. By the 3rd century, public monuments were in place in the Lower City and the private houses were growing in scale. By the 4th century there were several large and well-appointed examples of such houses. Strengthening of the fortifications during the same period provided a considerable barrier, but must have required substantial resources. Hints from a number of Lincoln sites indicate the survival of urban life here into the early 5th century, but by this date there was probably a much reduced

*Fig. 7.30. The mosaic found within Lincoln Castle in 1845 in a coloured chromolithograph (from a drawing by G J Wigley) (Plate 2.3) (photo and copyright, Lincolnshire County Council, Lincolnshire Archives).*

Upper south gate

T e r r a c i n g        T e r r a c i n g

60m
55m
50m
45m
40m
35m
30m
25m
20m
15m
10m

Steps

House

Diversion for wheeled vehicles

House

House

Gatehouse

House

Gatehouse

Houses

Gatehouse

Lower west gate at The Park

Baths

Temple

House

Public fountain

Gatehouse

Postern gate

*R i v e r   W i t h a m*

N

*Sand island?*

*B r a y f o r d*

*P o o l*

0                    250 m

*Island*

**Key**

Land subject to flooding
(if not permanently underwater)

Road known

Road conjectured

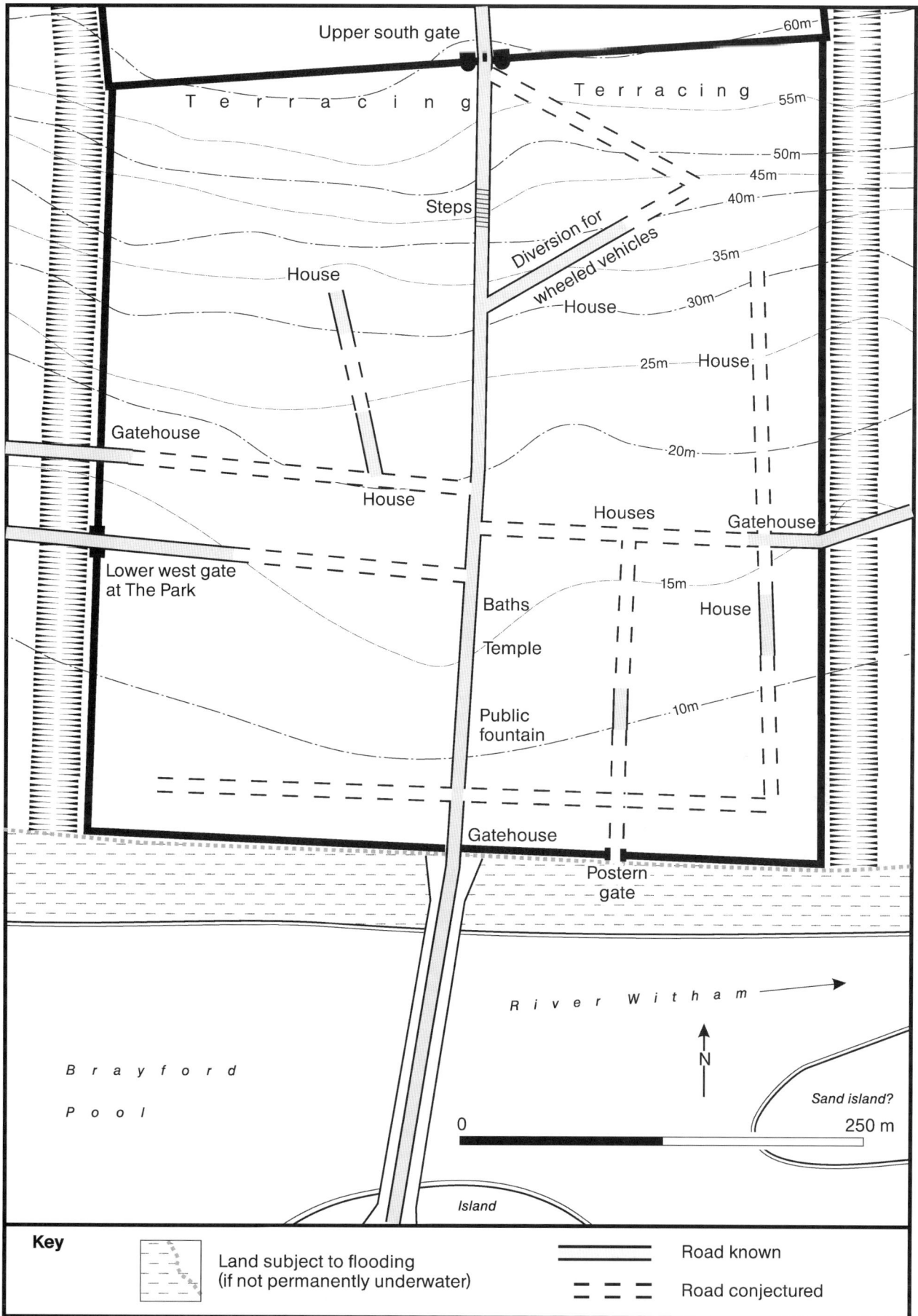

*Fig. 7.31. Reconstruction of layout of the Lower City in the Colonia Era, showing the principal features for which evidence has been recovered (drawn by Dave Watt, copyright English Heritage).*

population and little economic activity. By the second quarter of the 5th century, occupation had apparently ceased.

The combination of the very steep slope in the upper part of the hillside (in places about 1 in 6), plus the line of springs and the consequent risks of subsidence, meant that development here was fraught with practical difficulties. Evidence from excavations indicates the presence of culverts and drains; some of these ran parallel to the north–south streets, as on Silver Street (LIN 73b), where there was also a wooden water-pipe on the opposite side of the street. In spite of these measures, the amount of silt on the various road-surfaces suggests that the streets would have been awash during periods of heavy rain. The substantial stone drain at the house recovered from excavations in Hungate (H 83), also provided with wooden water pipes, had become blocked. Elsewhere, there may have been pools and flowing streams; the low-lying deposits at Saltergate (LIN 73f) might be best interpreted as a spring and a pool east of Ermine Street, between Silver Street and Free School Lane, feeding into the channel found in excavations in 1988 at Waterside North (WNW 88). Other streams or inlets may have existed outside the line of the defences.

The sandy terrace lower down the hillside was, of course, much less of a problem to Roman builders, being flatter, drier and better drained. Here we find often deeply buried deposits, with the Roman material regularly occurring at depths below the modern surface of between 3m and 5m. The bottom of the lowest feature at the Hungate site (H 83) was over 7m down, and preliminary investigations at the former St. Cuthbert's School to the north-east suggest even greater depths. By contrast, terracing operations on the steeper slope – some of them medieval and later in date – have resulted in Roman deposits occurring at the modern ground level in some places and several metres deep in others a few yards away. Towards the bottom of the slope, closer to the river, the Roman deposits again lie 3m to 4m down. Although nowhere near as well-preserved as the Upper City, the Lower City contains several listed buildings and Conservation Areas, which have restricted the size and depth of redevelopment. Consequently, our picture of the northern third of the Lower City is very partial, although further south, along Ermine Street, our understanding is much fuller. But even here no major discoveries on Ermine Street itself have been made under modern conditions. Our information is derived either from antiquarian investigations or from small-scale observations in more recent times. Even though some of the excavations in the Lower City in the 1970s and 1980s were on a large scale, they still covered only small parts of the total occupied area, and consequently we lack complete plans of the urban buildings, and thus the ability to analyse structures in the way that can be achieved elsewhere (e.g. Wallace-Hadrill 1994; Laurence 1996).

## Origins and Early Growth

As reported in chapter 6, several sites in the Lower City have produced 1st-century artefacts belonging to the military episode, although not all of the clusters are close to Ermine Street. In some cases, it is possible that legionary finds may have been contained within rubbish imported as make-up for 2nd-century development, for example at excavations at Spring Hill/ Michaelgate (SPM 83), where a 1st-century Rhodian amphora was discovered. It is presumed that in the military period the hillside was under the army's control and zoned for extra-mural settlement, and it is also likely that this area was subsequently included within the original boundary (*pomerium*) of the *colonia*. This may mean that the area of the Lower City was defined physically in some way prior to the erection of the walls in the 3rd century. While Richmond regarded it as a suburb subsequently rationalised by the construction of defences (1946, 40), Esmonde Cleary (1987, 109–10) considers that the imposition of a street grid implies that the Lower City was treated as part of the city proper, comparing it in this way with Colchester's expansion beyond the walls of the fortress. Wacher (1995, 143) has suggested that the immigrants and local traders formerly in the legionary *canabae* may have constituted the majority of the settlers on the hillside, with the status of a *vicus*, whose enfranchisement may have been effected only later – perhaps as late as Caracalla's general act in the early 3rd century, by which time fortifications were at least under construction.

It is generally accepted that the area of the Lower City was part of the new *colonia* from the start, in spite of ambiguous references to 19th-century finds of cremation vessels east of the Strait (Richmond 1946, 45) and on Free School Lane (ON 105). Since there are reasons to doubt the details of both, more definite evidence is required before we can accept that any of this area was ever used for adult burial. It seems more likely that the area was zoned for future expansion. It is also difficult to know what to make of Drury's record of 'cavern-like apertures' on St. Martin's Lane (1888). It remains possible that they were *loculi* for cremated remains, as was also suggested by Richmond for structures found off Newport (1946, 52), but in the context of more recent finds this seems increasingly unlikely.

Surprisingly, some of the earliest civilian occupation has emerged at, and beyond, the subsequent east and west limits of the walled city at Silver Street (LIN 73c) and The Park (P 70) respectively. This may have been merely because early deposits here had both survived and have been excavated, but these early clusters may point towards inlets of the river to the west and east of the later walls. Such an inlet might also help to explain the early ditch fill at Broadgate (BE 73). Other early structures are known at Spring Hill (SPM 83), Steep Hill (SH 74), and Swan Street (SW 82). What is notable, in most of these cases, is that the earliest structures appear to be aligned on a street grid, which lay at right angles to Ermine Street and which may have extended beyond the lines of the subsequent defences. In all, we now have evidence from eight different excavations suggesting a planned and partially occupied layout in the Lower City by the middle of the 2nd century, and in some cases the evidence points to the layout's establishment several decades earlier. This date fits well with the proposal that there was an early plan for the hillside, with street frontages being built up first and remoter areas being filled in only later. Most of the earliest structures were houses of timber, on a modest scale, but others might have been for commercial use. Some were well-appointed.

### Topographical development and street plan

Richmond (1946, 42–3) considered the parallel walls near to the top of Steep Hill noted by Drury (1888), the lower of which was *c.*4.5m thick, to represent a major terrace which ran across much of the hillside at that point, citing that at Tarragona as a good parallel. He subsequently suggested that it had created an artificial platform *c.*45m wide. Wacher (1995, 144) proposed as an alternative possibility that the terrace could have represented part of the theatre structure, with the *cavea* facing southwards – a good use of the slope. After all, one might expect a theatre to be found within the walls of the *colonia*, and if this structure were part of such a building, it would be good evidence that the hillside was part of the *colonia* proper from its beginning. Excavations elsewhere, however, have since established that there was frequent small-scale terracing within and possibly between properties – notably at Michaelgate (SPM 83), Flaxengate (F 72), Hungate (H 83), Danes Terrace (DT 74), and Spring Hill (SH 74). The fact that no major terrace structure, like that proposed at the top of Steep Hill, has yet appeared may be the result of the lack of excavations on the steepest part of the slope. Observations by the author in Steep Hill in 1985, near to where Drury noted the terrace walls, found the natural rock at a depth of only about 1m. Perhaps at this point the hill was so steep the bed-rock itself had to be excavated to create platforms for construction. By contrast, Roman deposits on the line of the main street lower down Steep Hill were at least 3m deep (MCH 84), whilst, to the east, adjacent to the line of the medieval and modern Steep Hill, they were again almost at the same level as the modern surface (SH 74). Drury also saw Lias clay 'at a depth of only 5 feet' opposite the Jews House, and suggested that remains of earlier periods had ended up 'at the hill base' further down.

We now have to abandon some earlier ideas about the street pattern (Wacher 1975, fig. 29; Coppack 1973, 97, fig.1), based on the idea that the Roman grid was largely re-used in the medieval period. It became clear in the 1970s that the Roman secondary street system

had largely disappeared, and that part of the town was re-planned in the 10th century (Jones 1985; Fig 9.34). Yet there has been substantial progress in locating streets of the Roman Lower City. First, Ermine Street, the major thoroughfare, deserves reconsideration. The line of Ermine Street itself appears to continue in a straight line up the hill from the bridge-head. Its approximate position, roughly on the present course of High Street (but a little to its west), is known from finds of public structures adjacent, and from an account made during drainage operations outside what is now Binns Store, 50m north of the lower south gate, in 1839 (Richmond 1946, 42). The question of whether it took a direct route up the steeper part was largely settled in 1984 when its course was discovered in between the lines of the modern streets Michaelgate and Steep Hill (MCH 84) (Fig. 7.32). Here Ermine Street was formed of monumental steps, interspersed with ramps, an impressive feat of engineering and a most unusual phenomenon for Roman Britain, although not without parallel in the more hilly towns of the Mediterranean (for example at Pergamon in Turkey – Bean 1979, 45–51). Such a grand topographical feature as these steps imply would have been entirely appropriate to Lindum's *colonia* status and will have formed a grand ceremonial approach to the Upper City. Unfortunately the dating of the staircase is problematical – we presume it was constructed in the 2nd century, but we have no proof of this.

*Fig. 7.32. Flight of stone steps in the course of Ermine Street as it climbed the steepest part of the hill in the Lower City – found in excavations at Chestnut House, Michaelgate in 1984 (MCH 84). The scale is 1m long (photo and copyright, City of Lincoln Archaeology Unit).*

A second north–south street was located running at least some of the way up the steep slope at Spring Hill (SPM 83), and it probably continues the line northwards of that indicated at the western edge of the Hungate site (H 83) – suggesting that Hungate also may follow a Roman street. However, this putative second north–south street would be at an obtuse angle to the line of Ermine Street, unless it lay a little to the west of Hungate. A third north–south street is known to the south of Silver Street, where a pavement (or a portico) lined its eastern side (LIN 73 a/b). This street was in existence from the early 2nd to the 4th century. A fourth north–south street is known to run northwards from the small gate found on Saltergate (LIN 73d), immediately west of Bank Street. Its northerly continuation was noted near Silver Street in 1976 (ON 1a). Yet another north–south street, roughly midway between the two known east of Ermine Street and within the walls, may be indicated by a gap between structures found by Mr D F Petch during foundation works in 1956 beneath the Co-op in Silver Street (sketch in the City and County Museum archives). If extended north it would run to the east of Flaxengate.

Some uncertainty remains about the principal east–west route across the hillside. Indeed, we may have to accept that any grids either side of Ermine Street were laid out without reference to each other separately, or at least offset, as they were, for example, at Cirencester (Holbrook 1994, 58–60, fig.18). It has proved difficult to project a line for the expected route across the hillside between the east and west gates, and consequently we may have to question the postulated positions of the gates themselves. There was certainly a gate where Clasketgate passes through the east wall by the 10th century (p. 183–4 below), but if the kink at the western end of Monks Road is post-Roman in date, the Roman gate may have lain even further north. If the putative east–west main street ran at right angles to the defences and to Ermine Street, it must have been several metres to the south of the line of Grantham Street (Fig. 9.34), as it was not found in excavations here (F 72, SW 82). Alternatively, the alignment of a stone foundation at Flaxengate (F 72) may actually have respected a street running on the same alignment, obliquely to the grid, and perhaps linking the east gate with Ermine Street further north. The existence of diagonal routes was established in 1987 when a street with several surfaces, some of them showing evidence of wheel-ruts, was noted immediately to the north of the Steep Hill site (SH 74), near to the point where the gradient becomes very steep. It was presumed that this represented a diversion for wheeled vehicles, and the possible extension of the Roman route to the east of Steep Hill is followed by the modern street called Well Lane. Discovery of the road helped to clarify why the house at this site lay at such an angle – it followed the alignment of the diagonal street. It is still uncertain whether the route of Ermine Street itself (as indicated by the steps at Michaelgate – MCH 84) and the diagonal

route east of Steep Hill were contemporary but, since they served different functions, they could have been in use contemporaneously. The discovery at Steep Hill suggested that wheeled traffic could avoid the stepped, direct route up to the Upper City by taking a zig-zag course, presumably bending back north-westwards towards the upper south gate. A good parallel for this type of switch-back road for wheeled traffic can be found at Cassino in Italy. There may have been several other streets taking easier gradients, but if so we have yet to explain how the major terrace observed by Drury at the top of Steep Hill was negotiated.

A further east–west street is possible on the line of a surface found outside the (later) eastern walls at Broadgate East (BE 73), close to where a postern gate in the defences was noted in Broadgate in 1994 (GLB 94). This may, however, have been a street confined to the outside of the city ditch. More certainly located than that at Broadgate was an east–west street on the line of the inserted gateway at The Park, in the western walls (P 70). The gate here lies some 100m to the south of the modern street called West Parade, which probably crosses the line of the wall on the site of a Roman gateway predating that at The Park. Burials are known from the extra-mural area nearby (Thompson and Whitwell 1973, 130). Roman buildings found hereabouts related to a nearby frontage of a north–south street which cannot be far from the line of the modern Beaumont Fee at this point. A final east–west street existed, outside the walls next to the riverside, on the north side of what later became Saltergate (LIN 73d), but, if Roman at all, this street must be dated no earlier than the 3rd century, following the construction of the southern defences.

It is worth noting that none of the roads in the Lower City system are in exact alignment with those in the former fortress above hill. They are mostly offset slightly north-west to south-east and this presumably came about because the line from the fortress south gate to the bridge-head does not continue, precisely, the north–south line of the *cardo*. This divergence indicates the priority of the Upper City, in terms of layout (which is easily demonstrated from other evidence) but it might also imply that the south wall line of the former fortress continued in use as a boundary throughout the Roman period. Where examined, all of the streets continued in use to the late Roman period, and some to the end of Roman occupation.

## Fortifications

As with the Upper City's defences, those of the lower city have been the subject of a recent study (ed. Jones 1999), while further details of the 1973–4 excavations at Silver Street and Saltergate (LIN 73 a–f) are found in the summary account of excavations in the Lower City (ed. Colyer and Jones 1979). It seems clear that construction of the defences began later than the layout of the street-system. Certainly it involved the demolition of existing buildings at The Park (P 70) on the west side and at Silver Street on the east (LIN 73c). Nor do the defences relate directly to the street layout, except in terms of their general alignment, which represents an extension of the line of the Upper City walls, but parallel to the (slightly modified) alignment of Ermine Street. They extended southwards to the contemporary riverfront – or even beyond it. Drury's section drawing through the exposed deposits (1888) suggests that *c.*20–30m of the river frontage was already reclaimed by the time that the walls were built (unless it indicates colluvial deposits).

There is, however, still uncertainty about the nature of the earliest fortifications. Whilst it is clear that a rampart about 7.5m wide and a contemporary wall 1.2m thick were provided on the west side, at Silver Street (LIN 73c) on the east there was some indication of a line of substantial posts on the rampart top, presumably for a fence or boxed structure. This is an unusual feature and may represent a rapidly-built temporary defence, filling-in whilst stone-wall construction progressed more slowly around the circuit. Moreover, indications from the Silver Street site suggest a date well into the 3rd century for construction of a stone wall along the eastern side, but evidence from a nearby site on the west side of Broadgate (GLB 94) favours a *terminus post quem* of the middle or later 2nd century, as on the west. Contamination of earlier deposits at the Silver Street site with later material does not seem likely, and the conflict in dates for the east wall remains unresolved.

It has been suggested that the Lower City wall was constructed in the early 3rd century, and that it was linked with the enfranchisement of the Lower City community by Caracalla (Hurst 1986, 121; Février 1969). Alternatively, it could be seen as part of a provincial policy of enclosure being applied to all major Romano-British towns. Of course, the fact that it happened at all acknowledges the growing importance of this part of the city. It could also have been connected with the development of the suburb to the south of the river (below), which may have allowed many of the traders to relocate, and thereby created more space for the Lower City's residents as well as for public monuments. The demand for aristocratic residential space, therefore, might have been a factor in the decision to fortify.

In addition to the rampart and wall, on both sides of the Lower City there was at least one ditch, later re-cut, and internal towers were added at intervals of 40m or 50m during the 3rd century (ed. Jones 1999, 259–62). There was a major late refurbishment of the Lower City wall at Lincoln in the 4th century. At The Park the wall was thickened and heightened, and a wide 'saucer-shaped' ditch some 25m wide is probably contemporary; its cutting may have encroached on to the cemetery where some of the tombstones once stood. A substantial number of inscribed and moulded stones was incorporated into the rebuilt wall, in-

cluding the tombstone of Volusia Faustina (RIB 1965, 250, Fig. 7.2). On the west side the rampart was further extended to a width of at least 16m, and more large groups of pottery, glass and other artefacts were found in the dumps, as well as butchers' waste (P 70). The rampart was probably also extended at other sites, and dumps containing large amounts of rubbish have also been found (LIN 73 c and d).

Gates are presumed in the southern wall on the line of Ermine Street, and in the east and west sides on the lines of West Parade and Monks Road respectively (ed. Jones 1999), but no structural evidence has been recovered from these locations, except for indications of strengthening of the wall adjacent to West Parade (WP 71). The sketch of the medieval Clasketgate Gate made by the Buck brothers in 1723 (Oxford, Bodleian Library Ms. Gough Lincs. 15, f.18v/19r – Fig. 9.24) shows a large rectangular building along the line of the wall with a single carriageway arch and a fine chamber over. The gate depicted here is unlike the city's other known medieval gates and it resembles the medieval form taken by the rehabilitated Roman gates to the north and east of the Upper City (Stocker forthcoming a). Clasketgate Gate, then, might have been a Roman survivor into the medieval period. The lowest courses of the gate structure south of the carriageway appear from the sketch to incorporate some reused (Roman?) blocks and such reuse is also seen in the towers of the lower west gate and parts of the 4th-century rebuilding of the wall (below). The possible remains of a tower on the north side of West Parade were also formed of re-used blocks and this might imply that a gate here took a similar form to the Clasketgate Gate structure (ed. Jones 1999, 193–4). Buck's sketch might also suggest that the Roman fabric could have included the carriage-way arch. The Roman city wall is known to have survived up to a height of 18 feet in this area at the time of the sketch (*Ibid.*, 255), and the fragment visible adjacent to the gate could therefore be of Roman date.

Although the fabric of the surviving Stonebow, which is on the site of the Roman south gate at the bridge-head, is now mostly that completed in 1520, it too takes a similar form to the medieval Clasketgate gate and to the east and north gates of the Upper City (Stocker 1997b). We know that there was a stone gate at Stonebow from 1147 (Cameron 1985, 41) and it may be that the late medieval rebuilding perpetuated the form of a pre-existing Roman gate.

The south gate of the Lower City may have been a different type of structure, in fact, since from the time of its construction it would have represented the main entrance to the walled city for most new arrivals. It is conceivable that a triumphal arch stood here before the walls were built – such a building is known to have stood in analogous locations at both Colchester and Verulamium (Crummy 1997; Niblett 2001). Such an arch would have been easy to incorporate into its medieval successor, and the plan of the Stonebow completed in the 1520s may have reflected that of an earlier structure over a millennium old. Posterns are also known in the Lower City circuit; the example at Saltergate, 100m east of the main south gate, is late Roman in origin (LIN 73d), but those in the east side at Broadgate (GLB 94) and in the west side at West Parade (WP 71) may be medieval.

For reasons as yet unclear, a new gate was also inserted about 100m south of the main west gate in the middle or later 4th century and was the subject of total excavation in 1970–2 (P 70) (ed. Jones 1999) (Fig. 7.33). Like the reconstruction of the wall itself, it incorporated re-used blocks of monumental scale, perhaps from a grand funerary monument rather than a temple, although some of the material incorporated into other parts of the city wall came from occupied buildings (Blagg 1999). Such re-use is fairly unusual in Britain (Blagg 1983). This small new gate consisted of a pair of square towers, including guard chambers, set either side of a single carriageway.

The contrast in design between the gates of the upper and The Park gate deserves comment. The two best known of the Upper City gates, the east and north gates, both appear to have been rebuilt between the early and mid 3rd century to a similar, but not identical, plan, with semi-circular fronted towers projecting in front of the wall and flanking the entrances. They belong to a well attested tradition of Roman gate-architecture, found in some of the most prominent gateways at Cirencester, Colchester, and Verulamium (Wacher 1995, figs. 28–30) and with an ancestry going back to the Mediterranean. As such, their designers and sponsors were making a significant statement on Lincoln's aspirations as an imperial city. While the plan of the upper south gate is uncertain, it could well have been similar, and being located in such a prominent position, above the ceremonial staircase, visitors were sure to be impressed. The west gate, however, always the rear and least important gate, was according to Thompson's reconstruction, essentially a tower projecting in front of the wall, incorporating a carriageway (Thompson and Whitwell 1973, 194–200). This more limited plan form might have been the model followed by the gates of the Lower City. It can be argued on the limited existing evidence that the east and west gates of the Lower City were of this type, but possibly not until their 4th-century refurbishment which involved re-used architectural fragments. The lower west gate (P 70) is the only unambiguous example, and we should note that this incorporated an earlier phase similar to that of the west gate of the Upper City (ed. Jones 1999, 16–18, 180). This is also a gate type found elsewhere, including at Gloucester's North Gate.

## Public monuments

Although the Lower City was far from the original heart of the colonia that saw the greatest flowering of architectural magnificence, it has become clear that the Ermine Street frontage, on the lower part of the hillside at least, was graced in due course by several major

Fig. 7.33. The late Roman gate on the western wall of the Lower City, excavated at The Park in 1970–2 (P 70). The photograph is taken from the outside of the city wall looking east. The footings of the two small towers flanking the gate passage are clearly visible projecting from the wall itself (photo and copyright, C V Middleton and Sons).

public structures. That similar buildings are not yet known from the steeper hillside may be due as much to the lack of modern excavation as to the problems of the slope, but it is now clear that, for 250m or so to the north of the lower south gate, Ermine Street was lined with temples, baths and a fountain. Most of the discoveries have been on a small scale and, apart from the fountain, only fragments have been fully investigated. Immediately east of Michaelgate and west of Ermine Street, remains of a mosaic pavement have been noted, but these probably represent a domestic residence. The most northerly structure likely to be public in nature was noted by Drury in the 1880s on the north side of Grantham Street, where it was represented by moulded stones (1888). At the western fringe of the Flaxengate site (F 72), the eastern end of what at first appeared to be a late Roman basilican building was revealed (Fig. 7.34). Whether its western wall was that noted by Drury cannot be proven – it seems more probable that Drury saw a classical frontage predating, and to the west of, the excavated

structure. If the structure noted by Drury was an extension of that found at Flaxengate it would be 60m long. Unfortunately, work to the west of the Flaxengate excavation site in 1981 (GP 81) and to its south in 1982–3 (SW 82) found no further evidence of this building; the deposits had apparently been destroyed. A Tuscan capital, *tesserae*, imported marble inlays, and window glass do, however, give some idea of its quality, while an example of corrugated glass and several late Roman conical beakers echo this impression. Its construction could be associated with the city's elevation to capital status, but its function remains uncertain, and its full plan similarly so. Nevertheless, its apparent scale and layout suggested to Thomas (1985, 168–9) that it might be a church; an alternative perspective would see it as an assembly or audience hall for official purposes, but less grand uses are also conceivable (p. 129 below).

Not far to its the south, during construction works at 274–7 High Street in 1997, damaged remains of what appeared to be a fluted column were pulled from a service trench on the edge of High Street (HSG 97). A

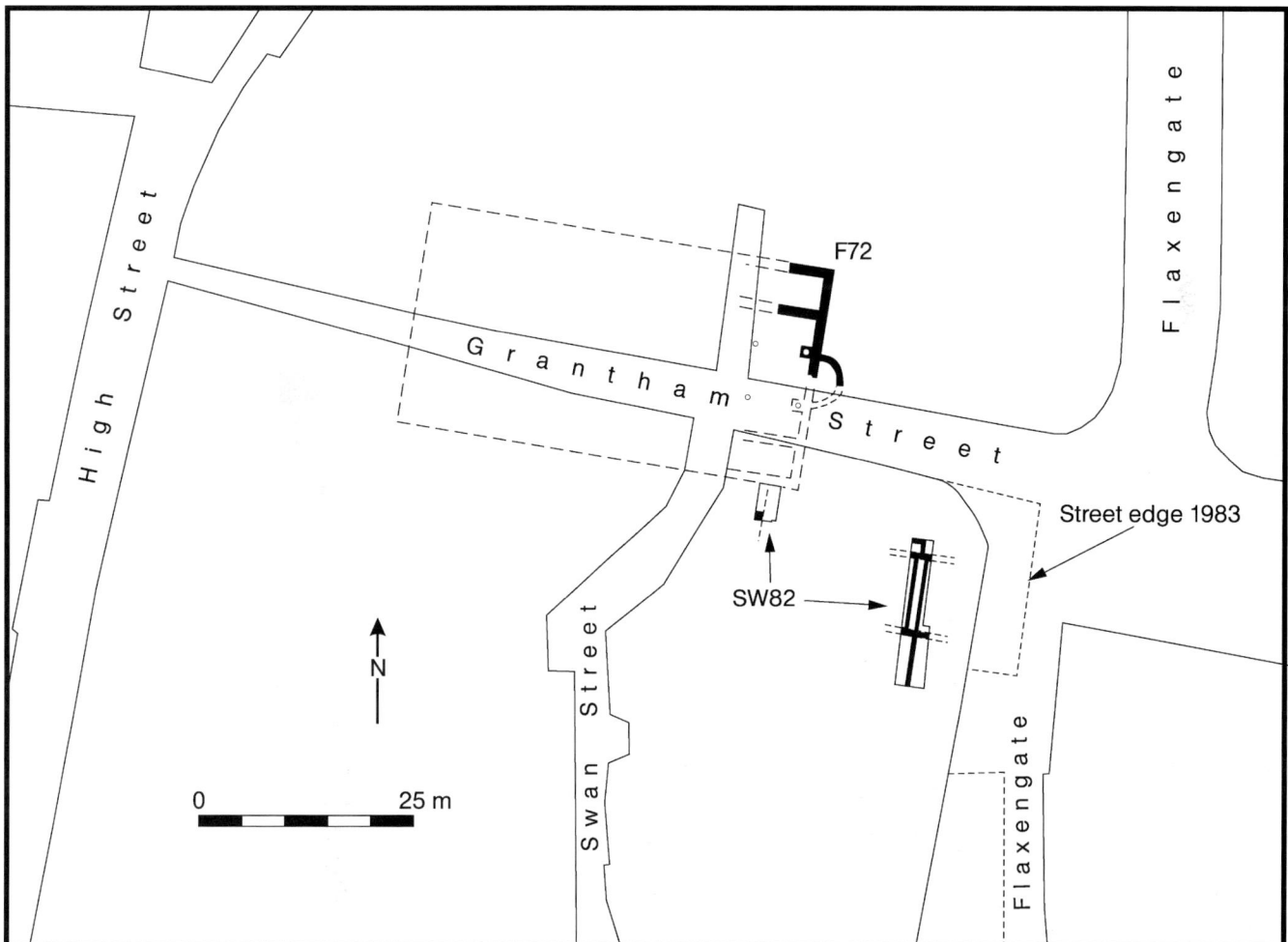

*Fig. 7.34. Plan of major Roman buildings near to Flaxengate in the centre of the Lower City, east of Ermine Street (F72 and SW 82). The outline of the reconstruction of the northern building, as a large basilican church in Thomas 1985 (Fig. 37), is shown as a broken line (drawn by Dave Watt, copyright English Heritage).*

little further south, discoveries in 1782 (ON 392) and 1924–5 (ON 258) are thought to represent a substantial baths building (or even two separate baths buildings). The earlier find, in the King's Arms Yard adjacent to the Theatre Royal, consisted of a heated room about 6m square. Under the corner of Clasketgate and High Street, near to where St. Lawrence's Church was subsequently built, the construction of a cellar for the original Boots store in 1925 uncovered a wall *c.*4.5m long, aligned north to south and incorporating two well-constructed flue arches with heads of radial tiles (Fig. 7.35 a and b).

A little further to the south, beneath No. 287 High Street (Ruddock's Bookshop – RENO 3087), column bases, plinth or architrave stones and other architectural fragments were recovered, plus a significant late 2nd- or 3rd-century inscription referring to the ward (*vicus*) of the guild of Mercury (RIB 1965, 270). The city would have been divided into such quarters or *vici*, and here, presumably, was the tutelary shrine of the god.

Only a short distance away, on the same side of the street, was a public fountain first found in 1830 but only investigated in 1953 (Thompson 1956, 32–6) (Fig. 7.36 a and b). It was an octagonal structure of massive limestone blocks, with a floor of *opus signinum*, and a later tile surround rendered in red painted plaster (ON 232). Thompson thought this secondary element necessary to seal the leaks from the main structure. It measured 6m in diameter, but probably did not stand much over 1m in height. It was clearly a public fountain – part of the channel for the outlet pipe was found, and it was presumably fed from uphill by an aqueduct. The pipeline found at Greestone Stairs in 1857 (RENO 3083, Richmond 1946, 37) might have been intended to supply it. Thompson recognised its function, and compared it with Richmond's study of the workings of the example at Corbridge (Northumberland – Richmond and Gillam 1950, 158–68). It belongs to a type also found in Gaul and Africa, sometimes associated with *nymphaea* – i.e. within temple complexes. It probably stood in its own open court, on the edge of the street, and good parallels are those at Metz and Timgad (Gros 1996, 435–8).

The fountain was in use until at least the end of the 3rd century. Unfortunately its construction date is not known, but its appearance in the townscape, together with that of the nearby temple(s) and baths mark the architectural maturity of the Lower City. Further discoveries of column-bases on both sides of the street just inside the south gate reinforce this impression of architectural splendour (Richmond 1946, 44), and such finds show that a monumental arch on the Stonebow site would not have been out of place.

## Housing

Although little of the public monuments has been revealed by the excavations of recent decades, large

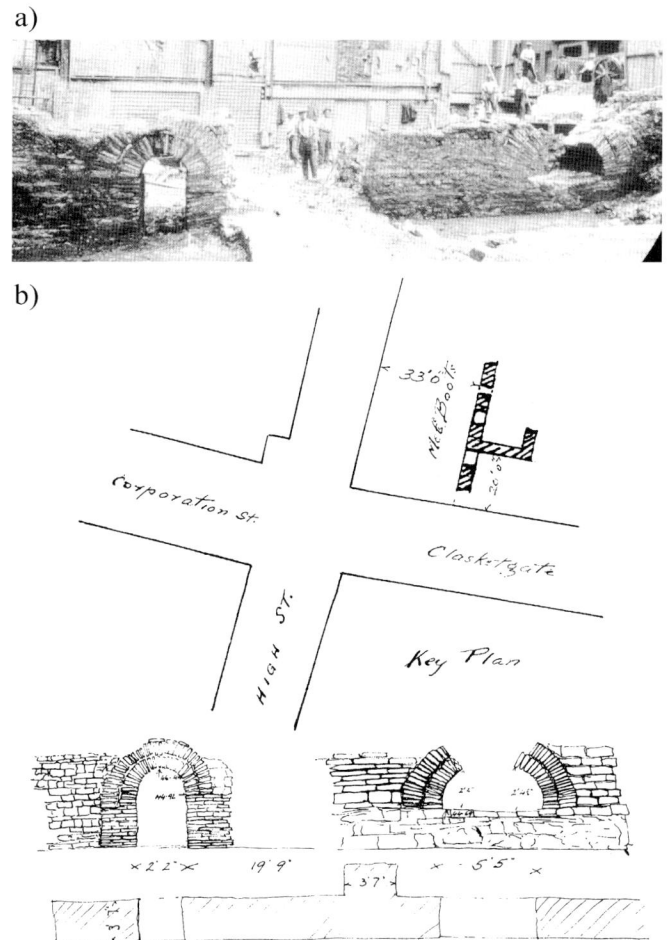

*Fig. 7.35. a) Excavations undertaken in 1925 for the basement of the new* Boot's *store at the corner of Clasketgate and High Street from the west. b) Record drawings made by Arthur Smith of the ruins of the Roman public building found in these excavations (photo and copyright (a. and b.), Lincolnshire County Council, Lincolnshire Museums Service).*

amounts of new information for residential development on the hillside has been forthcoming, to supplement that known already from chance finds and earlier investigations. The concentration of new discoveries reflects, of course, the location of rescue excavations, rather than the actual spread of houses and these investigations have been undertaken principally in the centre and the south-eastern quarter of the Lower City. There has also been some work near the limits of the walled area, and beyond, and it is now clear, for example, that occupation extended west of Orchard Street (ON 77 – Colyer 1975, 244–5, fig. 2) and east of Broadgate (BE 73). Even though almost no complete plans have been recovered, the largely residential character of this hillside area has been demonstrated (Fig. 7.31).

Even though the earlier deposits have not been examined at several sites, the evidence for chronological development of houses in the Lower City, from the earliest timber structures to increasingly large stone-built types, is not inconsistent with the picture derived from many Romano-British towns (Walthew 1975; 1983). The outstanding impression is of the size and quality of the later Roman houses, and it is tempting to associate those with the city's rise to capital status in the 4th century and the concomitant arrival of government officials. Certainly there is an impression of increased investment in residences after AD 200. The possibility that part of the city, even the Lower City, was comprehensively redeveloped to accommodate the requirements of the new government must be borne in mind, although some would argue that the Empire was by then too impoverished to afford such schemes – except at the principal imperial residences.

a)

b)

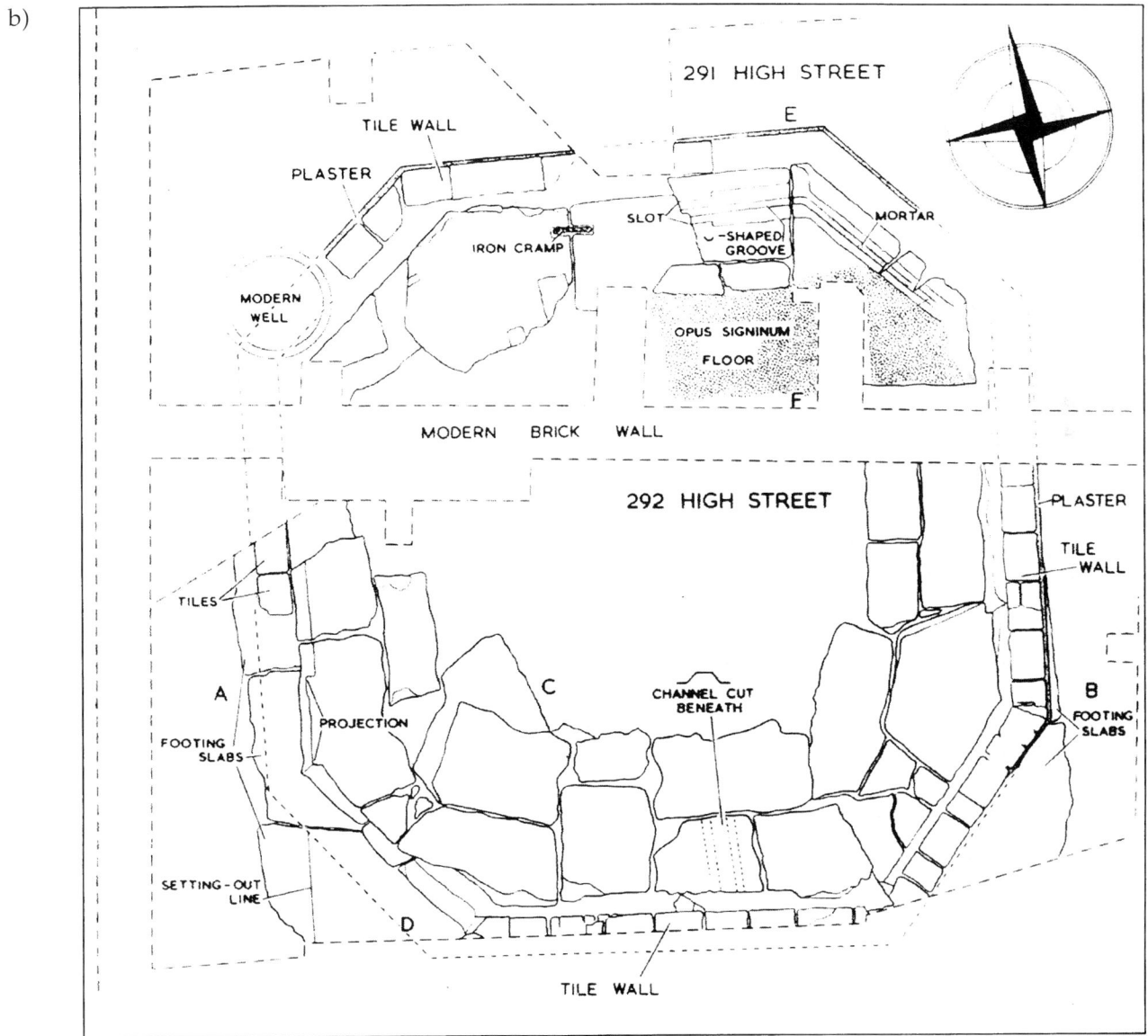

*Fig. 7.36. a) The base of the public fountain east of Ermine Street, found in 1830 and excavated in 1953 by F H Thompson, viewed from the north-west. b) Plan of the base made in 1956 (photo and copyright (a. and b.), Lincolnshire County Council, Lincolnshire Museums Service).*

Some houses were already known before 1950. A heated room with red-painted walls east of Bank Street was discovered in 1936 (ON 101); a room with a hypocaust on Grantham Street a little to the west of Danesgate was found precisely a century earlier (RENO 3208); and a house to the east of Flaxengate with marble inlayed surfaces was investigated in 1945–6 (RENO 3078, Coppack 1973). Petch noted remains of several stone walls beneath the Co-op store developed at Silver Street, to the north-east of the Bank Street finds, in 1956 (RENO 4715), but only a sketch of these discoveries survives (in the City and County Museum archives). They probably belonged to domestic structures but not even one complete room was recorded in the difficult working conditions.

Further eastwards along Silver Street, the work in 1973 to the east of Free School Lane uncovered a long sequence of structures, either side of the north–south street (LIN 73, a–c). Some of the earlier buildings were subsequently obliterated by the east rampart, which contained fragments of painted wall plaster indicating to Wacher (1979, 83) a house 'of some substance and elegance'. Among the better preserved or more extensively examined later houses, those at Spring Hill (SPM 83), Hungate (H 83), Swan Street (SW 82), and Saltergate (LIN 73) are most worthy of comment. The Spring Hill residence was discovered when a mosaic pavement, which extends beneath the modern street, was revealed. It had been first recorded – and saved – by Drury (1888), but although subsequent excavations uncovered a house of at least twelve rooms, including one with a hypocaust, its general layout and extent remain uncertain (Fig. 7.72). The house found at Saltergate in 1973–4 (LIN 73e) was not built before the end of the 3rd century, but may have replaced an earlier residence (Fig. 8.17). The new building was provided with a channelled hypocaust. Window glass of the late Roman blown type came from its demolition deposits. On the evidence of adjacent discoveries, it may have extended southwards as far as the fortifications, and eastwards to the street aiming for the late postern, and this would imply that it was at least 30m square. Some of this space probably included a garden. To the west of the area dug (LIN 73f) there were hints of a pond (with heron bones in the latest fill) – did this pond form part of a garden sharing a terrace with the adjacent house? Richmond (1946, 44) notes a wall hereabouts running 'east to west', found in 1924 and extending for at least 15m. A surviving illustration (in the City and County Museum archives) actually shows a north–south wall, longer than this, so Richmond may have been mistaken in recording its alignment, or two different walls have been found. The north–south wall seems to indicate that the house extended almost as far southwards as the back of the rampart. Other gardens, or at least open areas, are suggested at Flaxengate (F 72), at Steep Hill, and at Spring Hill. All of these appear to be late Roman in date. At the Hungate site (H 83), an open area a little to the west of Ermine Street had a

stone drain which had become blocked, and iron junctions for wooden pipes survived as evidence for its water supply. This site also produced a 2nd- or 3rd-century relief sculpture (below – Fig. 7.37), box-tile, painted wall-plaster and the largest collection of window glass from any site in the Lower City (only the public baths produced more). It continued in use into the late 4th century, as did at least one structure south of Grantham Street (SW 82), with late additions. There was also evidence from the West Parade site (WP 71), at a property close to the western defences and well to the rear of a street frontage to the east, of late expansion of a trader's residence, and occupation to the end of the Roman period.

The houses of the Lower City accordingly fill out our picture of the town, complementing the evidence for public monuments within the upper and lower cities. In general they suggest that the city expanded and developed most in the century or so following AD200. They are assumed to be associated with citizens of power and influence – the *curial* class – while some may perhaps have belonged to the government officials and others even to the wealthiest and most successful traders. Up to ten separate properties of this nature can be identified already in the Lower City, and twice this many may remain undiscovered, while there were clearly several more in the Upper City. This number would far exceed that at Caerwent and Silchester, where 12–15 such houses can be discerned, and is more in line with the figure of 20–30 suggested for Veru-

Fig. 7.37. Late Roman sculpture of Cupid and Psyche from excavations at Hungate, to the west of Ermine Street in the Lower City (H 83) (photo and copyright, City of Lincoln Archaeology Unit).

lamium (Todd 1993). Todd inferred that there would have been a stable but limited number of powerful families running the civic administration. Perhaps at Lincoln this elite should be extended to include the government representatives. The evidence for related social and economic activity is discussed in the next section, but without further information it is difficult to relate the quality and decoration precisely to social standing. It is worth pointing out, however, that most finds of marble inlay, as well as many other fine architectural details, come from the central part of the Lower City (Fig. 7.71), and this area seems to be dominated by public, not private buildings.

### Social and economic life

The range of artefacts and building materials associated with both public and private structures in the Lower City reflects the 'Roman' style of urban life there between the 2nd and 4th centuries AD. They included relief sculpture from the house at Hungate (Fig. 7.37) (H 83), found in late demolition deposits, though considered to belong to an earlier phase than the late Roman residence. It is now suggested that the scene depicted represents the mythical story of Cupid and Psyche, a local version of that described in Apuleius' *Golden Ass* (Martin Henig, pers. com.) rather than the Venus and Adonis myth, as earlier proposed (Blagg and Henig 1986). In addition to the inscription referring to the worshippers of Mercury found on High Street, a similar stone of the guild of Apollo (RIB 1965, 271) came from the rebuilt city wall (Lewis 1966, 71). Finds such as the late buckle (Leahy 1984, No.13) and a brooch of Free German origin (Mann J E 1999, No. 4) may indicate nothing more than the fashion of the day rather than Germanic soldiers, but should be noted as part of the global picture.

The Lower City wall also incorporated a large number of other inscribed and sculpted stones, some of them no doubt obtained from adjacent cemeteries. They included the tombstone of nonagenarian Claudia Crysis (RIB 1965, 263) and that of Volusia Faustina (Fig. 7.2 – already discussed) plus altars to Mars (RIB 1965, 248) and that to the 'Goddesses, Fates, and Deities of the Emperor' still visible in St Swithin's Church. The same church site produced the tombstone of the youth holding a hare (Huskinson 1994, 28, No.58), while deities associated with *cornucopiae* were found at Newland (Huskinson 1994, 2, No.4) and on Monks Road (Huskinson 1994, 1–2, No.3). The latter is interpreted as the personification of the city, and generally regarded as one of the finest pieces from Lincoln. While their place in the cemeteries is discussed below, the culture they express, and the quality of some of the finest pieces, reflect the presence of a literate Latin-speaking elite in Britain (Henig 1995). The city contained a variety of cultures – even in the later 4th century, with a Christian bishop long established in the city, the ritual inherent in the oven containing chicken bones at the lower west gate (ed. Jones 1999) is clear evidence of the contemporary vitality of pagan beliefs.

This evidence of 'high' cultural aspirations can be set against that of the pottery (Darling and Precious forthcoming), and other artefacts. The functional profile of pottery vessels shows the Lower City to have the highest proportion of table-to-kitchen wares for the city. There are fewer drinking vessels than the southern suburb, but the general profile is closer to the suburbs than to the Upper City. Superficially, the reasons for this may of course be due to the nature of the sites investigated – for instance, there has been little modern excavation of houses in the Upper City, and most of the deposits excavated in the Lower City have been of comparatively late date. But it is interesting to compare the ceramic assemblage with the glass. The later Roman vessel glass from the Lower City forms a large collection; it was especially plentiful at Flaxengate, Hungate and Silver Street (F72, H83, and LIN73 d–f). Many vessels were used for liquid consumption and for the display and serving of food, as might be expected.

Before the late Roman period, we have little evidence from the Lower City for industrial activity. This is likely to reflect the fact that, until well into the 4th century, industry seems for the most part to have been confined to extra-mural areas. A site to the east of the east walls, in Broadgate (BE 73), contained a furnace for iron smelting, in the grounds of a residence which later had a baths suite added. In the later period organised butchery was being practised on a large scale; dumps of waste were found at Flaxengate (F 72), on the rampart at The Park (P 70), and particularly at Waterside North (WNW 88). Much of the dumping occurred in the 4th century, when there was also iron-working at Hungate (H 83), possible gold- and silver-working at Flaxengate (F 72) and Saltergate (LIN 73d)(unless this was really late Saxon), and a trader's oven was found north of West Parade (WP 71). Some of this commercial activity could well have been confined to the last decades of the Roman period, when the nature of the town was changing rapidly and there may have been a shift to a different and more self-sufficient, economic basis. Were these the last throes of the Roman system, or was it merely suburban traders seeking security by moving inside the walls as others left?

## Extra-mural occupation in the *Colonia* Era

As we have seen in chapter 6 (on the Roman military period), settlement outside the walled town began as early as in any part of the city. The legal status of the Lincoln suburbs remains uncertain. Rodwell (1975) proposed the concept of the 'town-zone' in attempting to clarify how distances were measured from towns.

Mann (1987) found this difficult to accept, arguing that the only meaningful division was the *pomerium*, between those who lived inside the city boundary (later the walls) and those outside, although each may have had the same rights. Although the water was used for fishing and communication, and the adjacent land for settlement and storage, much of the land outside the city walls was devoted to cemeteries. The principal area used for burial in the legionary period lay to the south of the river, but also probably included the hillside to the south-east of the fortress. There is also equivocal evidence for burials on the hillside immediately below the fortress, along with structural remains which are best interpreted as the *canabae* (SH 74).

These areas, and others outside the other gates of the fortress, were also occupied in the 2nd century and later, following the establishment of the *colonia*, but it is difficult to prove that occupation was continuous. There is plenty of evidence for in-fill and expansion as the town flourished, and much of this evidence has emerged in the last quarter century – contrast Whitwell's (1970) discussion with that of Esmonde Cleary (1987). Richmond's account of extra-mural occupation (1946, 45–54) was principally concerned with the cemeteries, whilst he considered that finds such as those of mosaic pavements on Monson Street represented an outlier of the main settlement – hence the proposal that it indicated a villa. It is now clear that the Monson Street area, initially a late 1st-century cemetery, was subsequently swallowed up by the suburban spread. In this southern direction, the ribbon development characteristic of suburban topography extended for at least 1km beyond the walled area by the mid 3rd century. An area to the east of the Upper City was largely used for burial for up to 800m, mainly along the roads. The other suburbs are not so well studied, but some of them were similarly extensive (Fig. 7.38).

Lincoln now has much to offer the student of Roman 'suburbs' in Britain. The extent of the settlement at any one time and organisation of space are of considerable economic and topographical interest, and the extra-mural areas also contain much of the evidence for commercial activity and for the remains of the population. At Lincoln, the sites on the waterside and the low-lying land of the southern suburb have produced almost all the city's organic material, and evidence for the contemporary environment. Even so, attention also needs to be given to the suburban areas to the north, west and east of the walled city, where very much less excavation has taken place, and these areas are dealt with first. An examination is also made of the urban fringe, where industrial activity took place, the sources of water, the watercourses themselves and approach roads. There is finally some discussion, necessarily brief, of the related countryside. The cemeteries are also discussed in a section of their own (p. 108–14).

## The suburbs of the Upper City

There was extensive development on all sides of the Upper City from the 2nd century, with commercial structures along the streets immediately outside the walls, whilst areas beyond and to the rear were largely designated for burial grounds.

The evidence for legionary-period occupation to the west of the fortress has already been mentioned (p. 47 above). Since no structural evidence has survived, it is conceivable that deposits here indicate not settlement, but rather represent the later filling of pits of early *colonia* date with material derived from legionary rubbish dumps (L 86). Whether or not it came from here (and these pits have the character of irregular 'borrow-pits' rather than large-scale quarrying), stone would have been required both for the new front of the rampart and the range of public buildings being erected in the first half of the 2nd century. Similar quarry pits were found to the rear of the western rampart (W 73). Later in the 2nd century there developed a row of traders' houses along the south side of the street issuing from the west gate. There was further pitting, possibly also for stone quarrying, further west, and as with other parts of the city, the quarries may have preceded suburban development. Further south, but still in the grounds of the former Lawn Hospital, two cremations were discovered during construction work in the 19th century, showing that part of the suburban area west of the *colonia* wall was also being used as a cemetery. It can be presumed that there were also houses on the north side of the street close to the *colonia* wall, but unlike most of the roads issuing from the walled city, there is no solid evidence that this road was a long-distance route. It might have joined with the putative prehistoric trackway and taken a north-westerly course along the edge of the ridge, or a route which took it over the scarp and out into the carr lands – or possibly both.

To the east of the Upper City there was also a mixture of settlement and burial uses. A sequence of structures from the late 2nd century, probably of a commercial nature, was found near Winnowsty Lane (WC 87), *c*.200m to the east of the upper east gate. Stone buildings replaced timber here in the 3rd century. The standard of construction was clearly lower than that found elsewhere in the city or suburbs with no remains of internal decoration or window glass. Remains of other stone suburban buildings have been noted closer to the east gate, and the road issuing from the east gate was probably built up at least as far as the Winnowsty Lane site, but this site might be close to the edge of contemporary suburban development. Part of a stone structure about 100m to the south of Winnowsty Lane was noted in 1997 (PGB 97). In addition to this clear evidence for occupation in the western parts of the suburb, there is also evidence of cremations and inhumations further east and east-north-east along the two principal roads now repre-

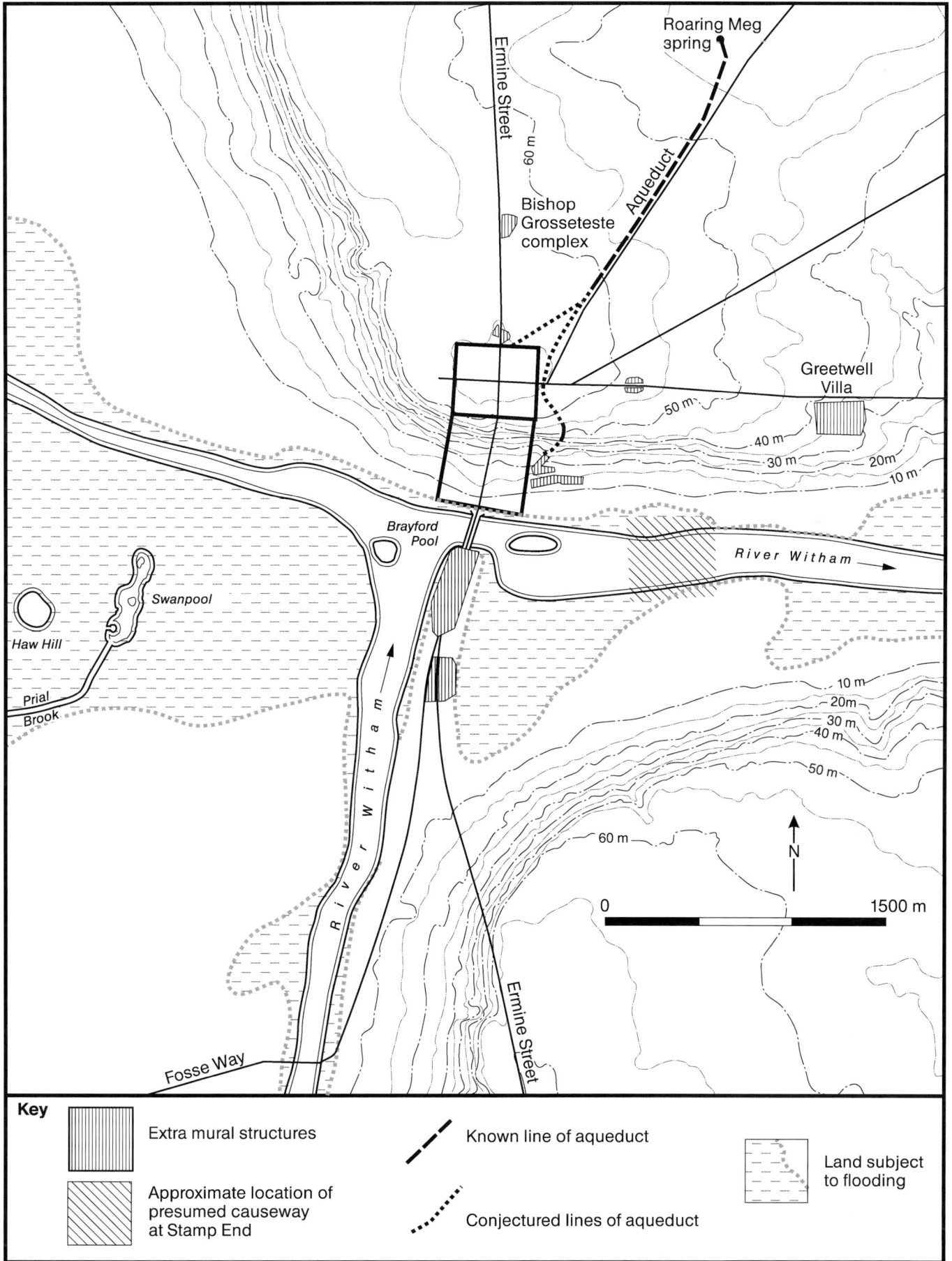

*Fig. 7.38. Known extra-mural settlement sites of the* Colonia *Era. Swanpool is shown in its modern location (drawn by Dave Watt, copyright English Heritage).*

sented by Greetwell Road and Wragby Road. These cemeteries extended along both for at least 800m (Richmond 1946, 50–1; p. 111 below).

The picture to the north of the *colonia* wall is similar, where remains of both a 3rd-century commercial property and disturbed inhumations were found in 1995 on the east side of Ermine Street about 50m to the north of the North Gate. The commercial property probably succeeded an earlier building on the same site (McDaid and Field 1996). There have been many finds of graves both east and west of Ermine Street for several hundred metres to the north of the walled area. Furthermore, the burials did not simply line Ermine Street, but some have been found well to the east, towards the line of Nettleham Road. Unfortunately, most of these cemetery remains were uncovered and destroyed during residential development in the 19th century, with only limited recording (Richmond 1946, 52–3). Structures partially excavated in the 1970s, and again in 1994–5, in the grounds of Bishop Grosseteste College (BGB 95), nearly 600m north of the walled area, appear to be isolated from the suburbs further south by these cemeteries (Fig. 7.39 and 7.66). These structures might, therefore, be best interpreted as remains of a farm rather than as commercial properties (p. 121 below).

### The suburbs of the Lower City

As with the Upper City, the suburbs to east and west of the lower walled area contained a mixture of commercial and industrial properties as well as cemeteries, with detached rural establishments beyond the limits of settlement. The extent of the burial grounds remains poorly defined, but they included at least one area of monumental tombs, which obviously influenced Richmond's views about the 'purity' of the city's *Romanitas*. We know of no boundary between the occupation on the hillside outside the walls of the Lower City and that to its north outside the Upper City, of course, but as they have a somewhat different settlement sequence, it is convenient to discuss the two groups of suburbs separately.

As with the Upper City suburbs, most of our evidence for settlement outside the Lower City relates to the roads which issued from the east and west gates. Remains of graves are known along both West Parade and Monks Road, but here some were found quite close to the gates, whilst others were at some considerable distance. There were cremations outside the presumed main west gate (on the line of West Parade), whilst a sequence of structures is known to their south in the Orchard Street area (ON 77; ON 128; ON 318). More recently an unsuspected cremation cemetery has been recorded on Newland Street West (NSS 97) several hundred metres to the south-west. It is possible that this last find might have been associated with a separate settlement focus to the west, rather than with the town itself.

To the east, to the north of Monks Road (which lies

*Fig. 7.39. Building excavated at Bishop Grosseteste College in 1995, part of a possible farm complex of the* Colonia *Era east of the Ermine Street and about 700m north of the walled city (cf. also Fig. 7.66) (photo and copyright, City of Lincoln Archaeology Unit).*

on the approximate line of its Roman predecessor), the hillside was clearly used for burial from an early date, and these burials extended as far south as the line of the road itself. Inhumations have been recorded here as well as cremations, including one in a lead coffin (found in 1978–9 and dispatched to the City and County Museum). This area produced the remains of some fine monuments, and others built into the refurbished city wall in the 4th century may have been derived from these high status cemeteries outside the east gate. The sites of the Sessions House and the adjacent Technical College have also yielded remains of a 2nd-century pottery kiln (Baker 1936); it was probably just one of a group of such facilities. These early investigations also produced moulds indicating large-scale production of counterfeit coins in the early 3rd century; a time when the dearth of small change meant that the manufacture of local issues became fairly common (Richmond 1946, 47–8). According to E J Willson, other coin moulds, of similar date, were apparently found at the top of Motherby Hill, close to the junction of the west walls of the upper and lower cities, in 1812 (London, Society of Antiquaries Ms 786, 6/9).

To the south of the road heading east from the Lower City, at Broadgate East (BE 73), occupation was documented from early in the *colonia* period – predating the construction of the defences. A timber structure was succeeded by a stone building, with an associated furnace for iron smelting. The addition of a baths suite to this building shows that a good level of prosperity was reached by the 3rd century (Fig. 7.40). If this property had fronted on to a street later cut off by the fortifications, the occupants' livelihood might have been affected, and the dating evidence for the demolition of the baths would not be inconsistent with such a sequence of events. Yet we have little

c
v
p
(
F
'
t
tl
a
h
n
n
tl
p
fi
h
r
tl
N
L
a
w
F

h
o
s
a
i
l
q
c
o
w
t
b
sl
c
1
8
r
w
f
8
p
w
P
q

H
R
t
li
a
e
d
2
la
p

*Fig. 7.40. Remains of a late Roman plunge-bath excavated within a domestic complex at Broadgate East, east of the Lower City wall in 1973 (BE 73). The view is from the north and the scale is 2m long (photo H N Hawley).*

information about the topography of those areas away from the main east–west road. Remains of a surface in the south-west part of the Broadgate site could represent either an east–west street (linked to the town grid), or a north–south road outside the ditch. The fill of the north–south ditch found here, however, contained pottery no later in date than the mid 2nd century, i.e. it was earlier than the known defences. The comparatively early finds known from the Silver Street site (LIN 73a–c), which is within the later walls and not far to the west of Broadgate East, might mean that there was an early focus here. Although the origins of this early focus are more probably related to the military occupation (p. 47–8 above), this may be a misjudgement and it is not impossible that occupation in this general area may have begun in the early *colonia* period, even though it was to become separated by the city wall.

Our only other evidence for buildings in the suburb east of the Lower City is a stone wall at least 9m long, aligned east–west, and located about 250m to the east of the gate, noted in 1968 (Whitwell and Wilson 1969, 103–4). Presumably this belonged to a building on the south side of the road marked today by Monks Road. This is the farthest out that evidence for buildings has been reported, but the original extent of suburban development might have been considerably greater.

Almost a mile out, on the hillside and along its crest, the extensive remains of the so-called 'Greetwell Villa' were uncovered during ironstone mining in the 1880s and 1890s (Figs. 7.41 and 42. See also p. 355–6 below).

The tantalisingly brief early accounts noted the opulence and quality of decoration, with a baths-suite, and painted wall-plaster including the figure of a swallow (RENO 3084). More was found during subsequent mining operations. Detailed study of its mosaic pavements by David Neal (Neal and Cosh 2002, 69, 70, 119, 162–83; Rainey 1973, 109–10) has pointed out that they are of palatial quality, and at 87m, the mosaic in the east–west veranda was among the largest known in Roman Britain. Furthermore, it deployed techniques, including 'reticulation', which were probably peculiar to continental mosaicists, which also make it remarkable for Britain. It is a pity that their discovery, though recorded, occurred during quarrying work and in a period when only a limited archaeological response was possible (Venables 1884; 1891). Consequently we have no stratigraphic information and little dating evidence. The wealth display apparent from the scale and quality of the mosaics does however indicate either a very wealthy citizen, or perhaps a government official, possibly even the 4th-century provincial governor.

### The southern suburb: the waterside

Our analysis of occupation of the suburban area south of the city can be more extensive than that of the other extra-mural suburbs, and it includes discussion of evidence for both the use of the waterside and the extensive ribbon development further to the south. Furthermore, it is possible that these suburbs were distinguished in Roman times from those around the other gates of the city. The waterside itself and the Wigford causeway were of such strategic significance to the city itself that we might suspect that it was given a distinctive legal status. Although inextricably tied to London, the extensive ribbon development at the south end of London Bridge at Southwark, which was also based around a causeway of similar type to that at Wigford, is known to have held a distinct sub-civic status, which permitted it some level of liberty and perhaps self-government (ed. Watson 1998; Sheldon 2000). Esmonde Cleary has suggested a parallel between this aspect of Lincoln and Lyon, where the *colonia* was largely on the hilltop, and the trading settlement by the river (pers. com.). In Lincoln, the amount of new information on this southern suburb since Richmond's (1946) article, and even since Whitwell's (1970) and Wacher's (1975) syntheses, is considerable. Yet the archaeology of suburbs and of waterfronts is itself a topic which has only been studied intensively since the 1970s, and although not fully analysed, the evidence from Lincoln has its part to play in the continuing debate. In particular, the extensive investigations in 1987–91 at Waterside North, between the city wall and the river east of Ermine Street (WN 87, WNW 88, WF 89, WO 89), have provided much new information and the following discussion incorporates the preliminary results.

a)

b)

c)

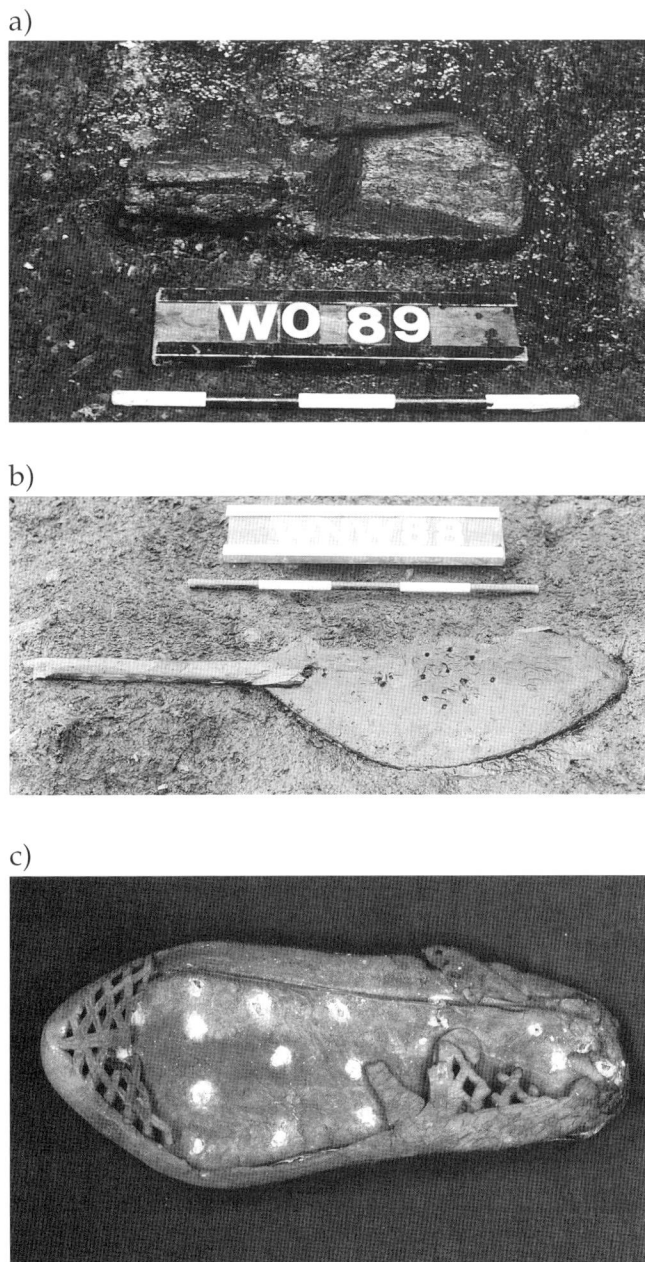

*Fig. 7.45. Three organic objects preserved within the extensive late Roman rubbish-dumps along the northern shoreline, south of the walled city: a) wooden scoop, b) bakers' shovel (?) for placing loaves in the oven, c) shoe with pierced leather-work (photos and copyrights, City of Lincoln Archaeology Unit).*

*Fig. 7.46. Fragment of cedar-wood writing tablet from late Roman rubbish dumps along north bank of the River, south of the walled city (photo and copyright, City of Lincoln Archaeology Unit).*

domestic animals involved, and to butchery practices and diet. The most notable collection was of the remains of 4th-century cattle, which constitutes the largest vertebrate collection to date from any Roman site in Britain, and appears to indicate butchery on such a large scale that it probably involved the civic authorities. The rubbish dumps appeared to contain many mandibles and shoulders of beef, dumped while they were still fairly fresh, and used essentially as

hardcore (Fig. 7.48). Two types of butchery operation can be discerned; on the one hand there was marrow extraction for such purposes as lamp-oil and cosmetics, and, on the other, there was de-fleshing and dismemberment of joints for cheaper cuts of meat, as well as clear evidence that shoulders were being provided for smoking. The cattle slaughtered were of moderate age and had probably been used for various purposes, including as draught animals, before being brought into market from outside the town.

In addition to the cattle bones, there were some sheep, mainly but not exclusively kept for wool, a few pigs, and chickens and even dogs appeared to form part of the diet. Other mammals found included hare, red and roe deer, and the Roman import, the black rat. Among the bird bones from the city were cranes as well as geese and ducks. The fish species at Waterside North included the earliest British examples of carp and bitterling, and one concentrated group of

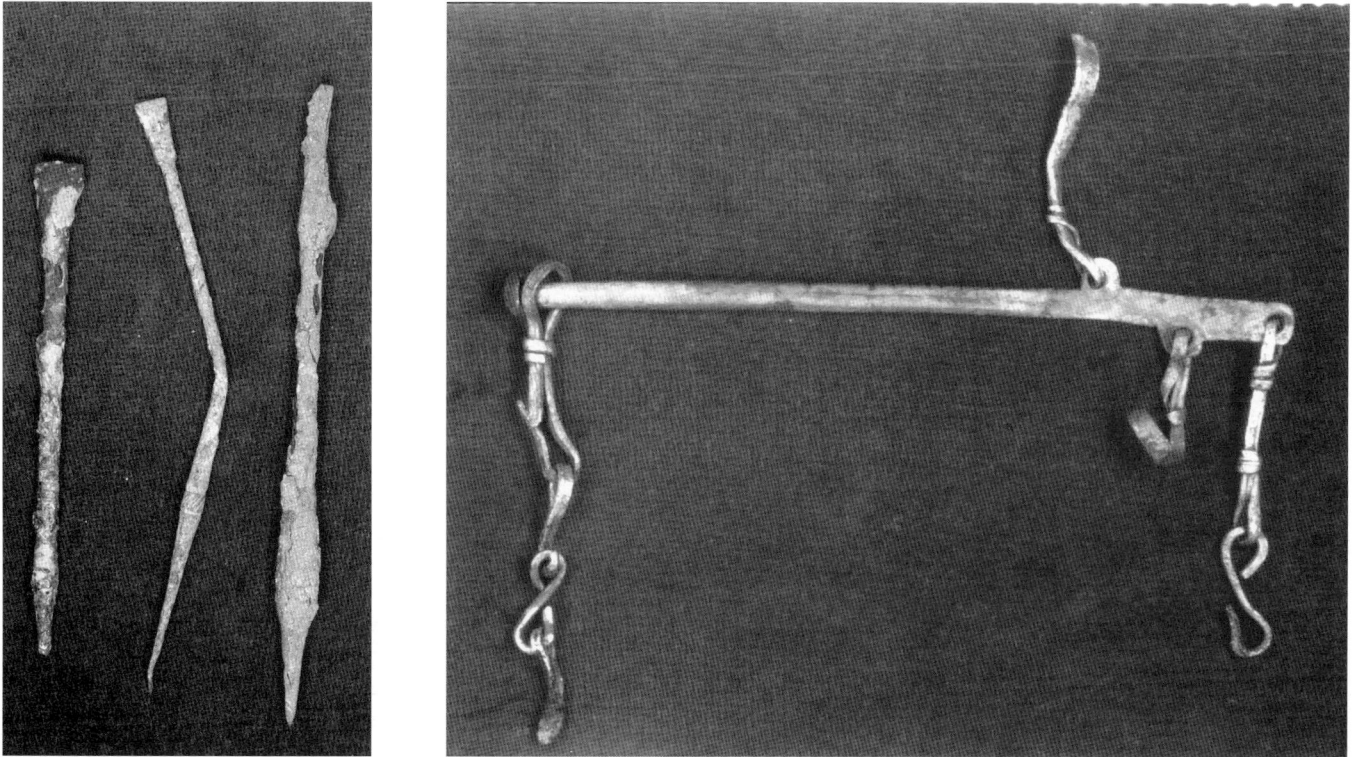

Fig. 7.47. Group of stili and a steelyard from late Roman dumps north of the river, south of the walled city (WNW 88) (photo and copyright Lincolnshire County Council, Museums Service).

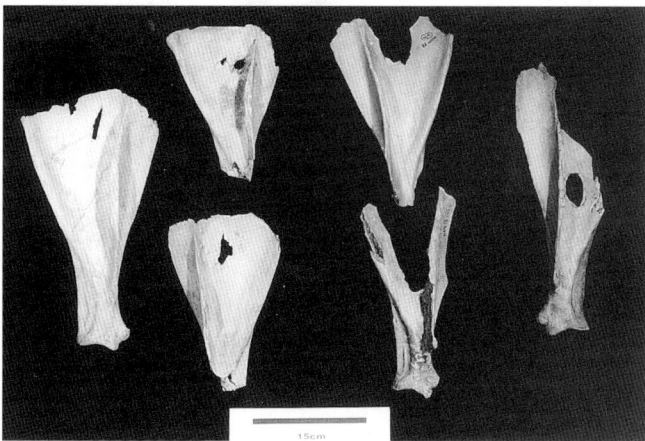

Fig. 7.48. Scapulae of cattle from late Roman rubbish-dumps along the northern shoreline, south of the walled city, showing holes made by butcher's hooks (photo and copyright, City of Lincoln Archaeology Unit).

the insect remains (Kenward 1995; Dobney *et al.* 1998). The presence, for instance, of a cockroach (again the earliest find from Britain) implies heated buildings, such as granaries, and this is a location where warehouses might be expected. Like the evidence for mass-market butchery, these finds suggest working granaries and continuing organisation of the food supply until the late 4th century. Some insect remains may have been associated with manure from stables and this suggests that horses were still being quartered here in later Roman times. The insects also confirm that water conditions were largely still or sluggish, or at least they represent areas of stagnant pools in a river of low to moderate energy flow – something also suggested by analysis of the sediments and the molluscs. This picture of the river conditions is completed by the evidence from plant remains (Greig 1989), which suggest a rich and varied local flora with many species associated with wetland or marshland, and a number of crops as well as grasslands and damp meadows upstream. The rural landscape nearby was essentially an open one. Finally, various species were indicative of a largely freshwater environment, with occasional hints of tidal influence reaching the city.

It was noted above that there were indications from several sites that the river level had risen by between 1.5 and 2 metres during the late Roman period. We have argued above that this is most likely to have

sand-eel bones is thought to represent either residue from manufacture of a local variant of *garum* (a fish sauce), or the processing of larger species for whom sand-eel were prey or bait.

Similarly interesting, both from the point of view of the site, and the river environment generally, were

arisen through the installation of a water control system at Stamp End, but the effect of this engineering would have been enhanced by canalisation of the watercourses above Lincoln, for which we have no real evidence as yet. One such canalisation would have that of the River Till east of Lincoln to form the easternmost 5km of the Fossdyke. It is still not known when the Fossdyke canal, connecting the Witham with the Trent at Torksey, was constructed. It has frequently been presumed to be Roman, but there is no satisfactory evidence for this theory at present and the discussion based on pottery evidence from the High Medieval Era (p. 116 and 241 below) suggests that the Fossdyke route was not significant for the city's trading links in the Roman period.

### The southern suburb: development south of the river

At 181–3 High Street (HG 72), on what was an island in the river before the Wigford causeway was built, the early Roman timber structures fronting Ermine Street may have served the military, or they may have been connected with cult uses of the pool, and the artefactual material from this site suggests a link with the legions rather than a native source (Darling and Jones 1988; Steane *et al.* 2001a, 106–7). The earliest deposits on sites between here and the river to the north have not been investigated, whilst over an area extending several hundred metres to the south it was too damp and low-lying for settlement. The next definite site to the south to yield occupation was beyond the postulated fork in the road system, at Monson Street (M 82), again on higher land, which was used as a cemetery in the 1st century. There may have been a chronological gap in the sequence at the site before it was levelled and used for industrial activity, including smithing, in the early 2nd century. At the nearby St Mary's Guildhall (SMG 82), about 50m further south, there was some sort of occupation by the early 2nd century, probably, like that at Monson Street, industrial in nature. The earliest pottery is too late to support the idea that an early legionary base occupied the site, but it seems likely that the combination of drier ground and the proximity of the two main roads to the south made this a favourable location for trading.

Further north by contrast, opposite St Mary-le-Wigford (HG 72), there may have been almost continuous occupation from the legionary period, the first *colonia* structure being in place by about AD 100. The coin list from the site indicates commercial activity in the previous decade. At some stage in the 2nd century, the quantity of pottery vessels used for pouring and drinking suggests a tavern, or a temple where libations were poured. The existence of a cellar for storage corroborates this interpretation. Later in the 2nd and into the 3rd century, there is an emphasis on dining as well as drinking on this site, now associated with an unusual circular structure, although there were also some signs of commercial or industrial activity (Fig. 7.49).

How far southwards commercial properties extended before the late 3rd century we cannot say, although the cemeteries give some clue (see below). The whole area either side of the causeway was subsequently transformed by major landfill operations which facilitated the development of extensive ribbon development for at least 1km to the south of the river. This might have been either a municipal or a private enterprise. This landfill operation and the sequence of occupation which followed are best exemplified by the evidence from the site of St Mark's Church (SM 76). Here the lower terrace, at about 3.5m OD, was drained using a system of channels; their fills and other earlier deposits at the site produced waste from shoemaking, horse-bones, and freshwater molluscs. Similarly marshy conditions were found across Ermine Street to the south-east (ZE 87). The ground level was then raised by a metre or so bringing it to a similar level as the drier ground to north and south. It is possible that the first commercial structures against the main road were modest stalls – they were certainly of timber. But at some stage between the late 2nd and the early 3rd century a row of at least four adjacent traders' houses was constructed, measuring *c.*8–9m wide and *c.*25–30m long (Fig. 7.50). They were subsequently rebuilt at least twice, first with narrow stone sill walls, intended to support timber framing, and later completely in stone. Until there were load-bearing stone walls, the roofs were supported principally by aisle-posts. Tiles were commonly used for roofs, apart from one late building, which produced many stone slates in its demolition levels.

Normally the working areas were in the central part of the building, behind the shop and in front of the living accommodation. Corridors provided ways through from the shop to the domestic quarters, and from the workshop to the rear yard. Over a century or more the buildings may have served several different functions. Remains of ovens, hearths and possible vats may indicate the heating and/or cooking of food, or metallurgical activity (Fig. 7.51), but little survived in the way of waste products – it was probably removed to the rubbish dumps behind the buildings, unfortunately outside the excavated areas. Some indications of commercial activity survived. A large stone with two differently-sized, bowl-shaped hollows had been set into the floor in one phase – it was possibly used to provide standard measures (Fig. 7.52). Examples of table-tops with similar depressions are known from Pompeii (Richardson 1988, 89) and Tivoli (Giuliani 1970, 61–6) in Italy and from Nyon in Switzerland (Rossi 1995, 50, 161). They were known as weighing tables (*mensae ponderariae*) and were often set up in prominent positions such as adjacent to the *forum*. The stone from Lincoln was presumably in a secondary position and it may have come from a secondary market in the city rather than the *forum*.

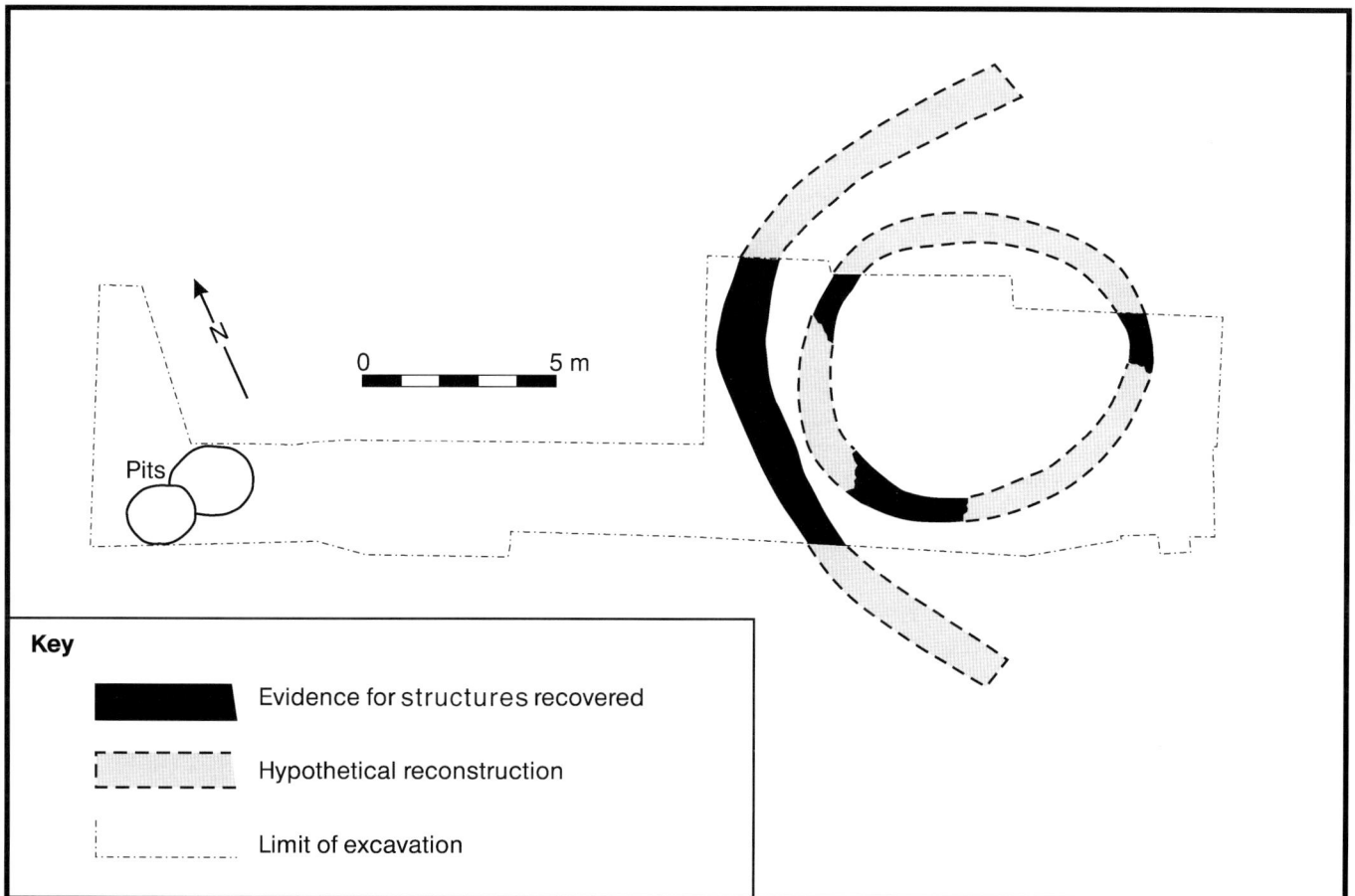

*Fig. 7.49. Plan of unusual sub-circular structures of later Roman date excavated to the west of Ermine Street, on the site of the late iron-age buildings, on the former sand-island in the Witham (HG 72) (drawn by Dave Watt, copyright English Heritage).*

Pottery vessels with representations of the smith-god, a phallic-shaped pot and a face pot were found in one building, in 3rd-century contexts, and probably indicate a household shrine for a blacksmith (Darling 1990; Darling and Precious forthcoming) (Fig. 7.53). Further evidence for smithing, in the form of hammer-scale, was also found in the late 2nd – or 3rd-century deposits at St Mark's, as well as at other buildings in the suburb. In the 4th century, individual pots were probably used as safety deposit boxes buried in the successive floors against a wall. Two still had lids in position – a stone and a dish. In yet another 4th-century phase the layout of the building was reversed; a series of rooms towards the street front was decorated and one contained a phallic object – probably from the shrine. The provision of a decorated suite towards the street end, rather than at the rear, is evidence for a change of trade to one involving guests. At the same period, a tile possibly indicates another industrial process using an oven or furnace elsewhere in the building. Later in the sequence, imported marble veneers were found, and could have been incorporated into the structure, if not derived from another context.

The sequence of re-buildings, to a similar pattern

but at different times, may suggest that the traders sooner or later owned their own houses. Some re-buildings were probably occasioned by fires. The pottery from the site would suggest that these houses flourished between the late 3rd and the early 4th centuries; one structure reached its maximum size about AD 320. Some houses were abandoned by *c.*370, but others continued in occupation, or were reoccupied, almost to the end of the Roman period. Yet a decline in building standards in the latest phases is discernible when evidence of habitation was confined to the eastern part of the house. By this date, the ground level had been raised again, against the rising river.

The boundaries between houses remained stable at St Mark's Church, but this was not so at St Mark's Station to the south (Z 86), where a mid or late 2nd-century timber house, probably on higher, drier ground, had stood to the north of an east–west watercourse that contained an oak ladder (Fig. 7.54). This 'drain', possibly a development from a natural predecessor, may have continued across Erminc Street.

In addition to the four 'traders' houses' found at St Mark's Church to the north, four or perhaps five

Phase I

N

Building I

Living area          **Building II**          Workshop

Shop

Partitions with
painted plaster

Oven

Aisle posts

Partitions with
painted plaster

**Building III**

Building IV

0                              10 m

Phase II

N

Building I

Corridor?

Living area          Workshop

**Building II**          Partitions

Oven

Shop

Corridor

Partitions

**Building III**

Oven

Building IV

0                              10 m

Ermine Street

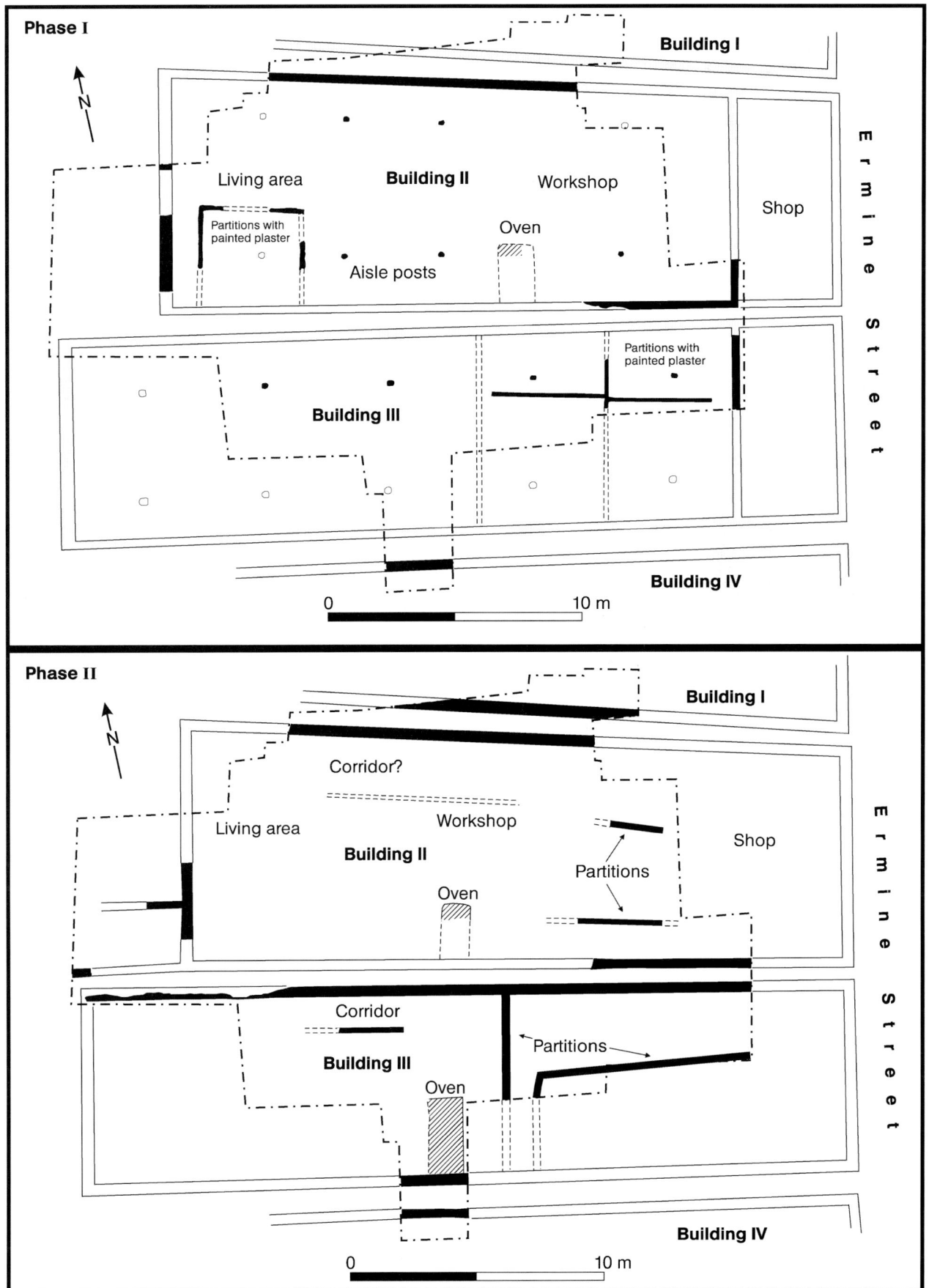

*Fig. 7.50. Reconstruction plans of strip buildings to the west of Ermine Street, built on reclaimed land in the later Roman period. Phase I dates to the early 3rd century, phase II to the late 3rd century. The site (SM 76) lay about 500m south of the walled city (drawn by Dave Watt, copyright English Heritage).*

adjacent traders' houses are known from the St Mark's Station site, when the more recent investigations of 1994–6 are added to those of 1986. However, these represent only about half the total number now discovered extending about 700m southwards from the most northerly site opposite St Mary-le-Wigford (HG 72).

The most southerly structures found to date are those to the north and south of Monson Street (M 82, SMG 82), fronting on to Ermine Street as well as to the

Fig. 7.51. Late Roman oven in 'building III' on the St Mark's site (see Fig. 7.50), looking south. The scales are 2m long (photo and copyright, City of Lincoln Archaeology Unit).

Fig. 7.52. Stone 'measure' excavated within the late Roman strip buildings on the St Mark's site (see Fig. 7.50). The scale is 0.5m long (photo and copyright, City of Lincoln Archaeology Unit).

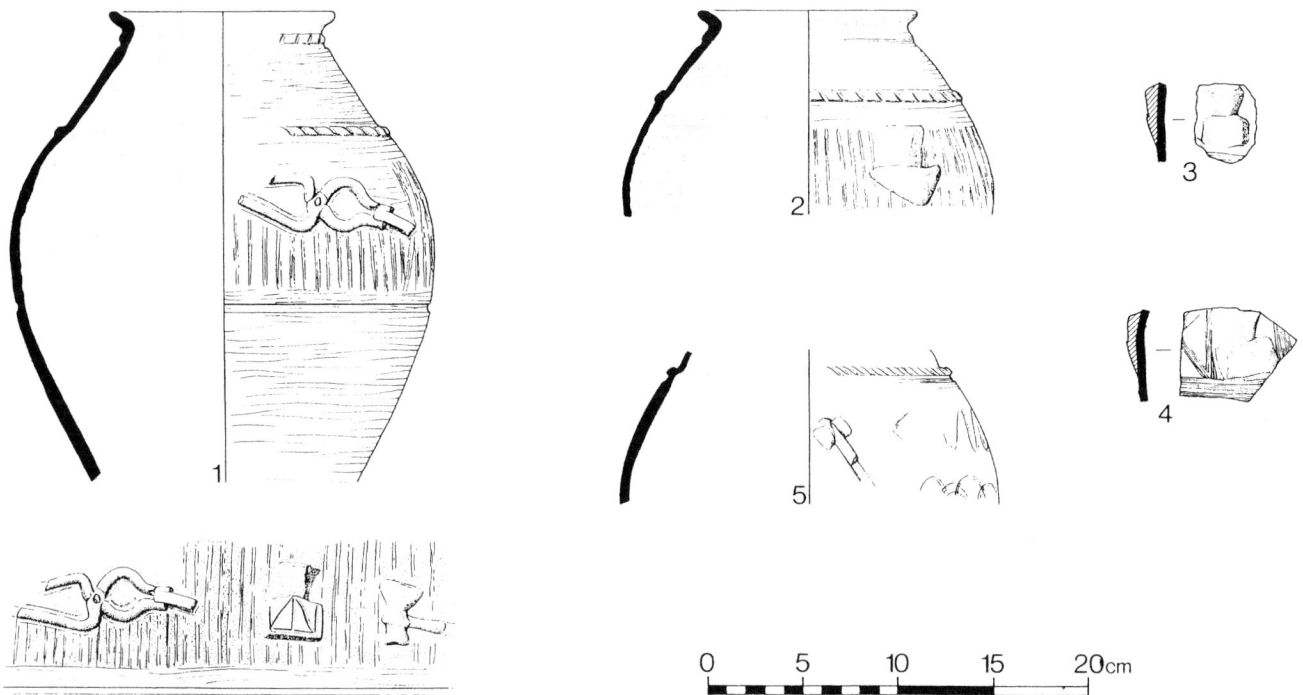

Fig. 7.53. Late Roman pots from excavations at the late Roman workshop buildings west of Ermine Street shown in Fig. 7.50 (SM 76). Margaret Darling has suggested that these pots may have been used in ceremonies dedicated to the gods of metalworkers (drawing, Margaret Darling, copyright City of Lincoln Archaeology Unit).

Fig. 7.54. Roman ladder, excavated from the edge of a drain behind buildings fronting onto Ermine Street at the former St Mark's Station (Z 86). Looking north; the scale is 0.5m long (photo and copyright, City of Lincoln Archaeology Unit).

Fosse Way (Fig. 7.55). At Monson Street a lane ran between two examples, apparently dating from the early or mid 3rd century – several decades earlier than those at St Mary's Guildhall further south, but with evidence for a significant re-planning during their life. The Monson Street houses were adjacent to the site of mosaic pavements, discovered in the 19th century and taken to be associated with tombs (Trollope and Trollope 1860, 16–17) or with a villa (Richmond 1946, 46), until it became clear in the 1980s that the town had extended this far. Since the documented find-spot of the first mosaic was more or less precisely that of a possible mausoleum found in 1982 (p. 49–50 above and 111 below), and Trollope also noted some inhumations here, it is quite possible that the mosaic(s) belonged to this structure rather than to the later commercial buildings. The fact that the mosaic is likely to date to the 2nd century (Neal and Cosh 2002, 175–83) also favours the cemetery context above the domestic. The Monson Street excavations also found rooms of the traders' houses with painted walls and stone roof slates. Which trade generated this wealth is unknown. Fragments of a ceramic figure of a god (perhaps a household god) turned up in mid or later 3rd-century material. At St Mary's Guildhall, the 3rd-century pottery from one house, associated with copper-working, includes high-status dining vessels, while the adjacent building produced more of a concentration of kitchen wares. This pattern may be due simply to the location of those rooms investigated.

No site further south than St Mary's Guildhall has been the subject of modern excavations, so the southerly limit of suburban growth is as yet undefined. A recent interpretation of a stone sculpture incorporated into the 11th-century tower of the church of St Peter at Gowts, has speculated that it represents the Mithraic god Arimanius, and as such, is evidence for a temple of Mithras in the city (Stocker 1997a). Such temples would most likely be found in the 2nd century associated with the former legionaries, but located at the settlement fringe and close to water; the location is accordingly appropriate and the stone need not have been moved far. Of course, we still lack any structural evidence for such a temple.

Some evidence for the use of land to the rear of the street frontages was obtained at Chaplin Street (CS 73), where 2nd- or 3rd-century features parallel to the main street may indicate either drainage or agricultural activity. We understand too little of the suburb this far south, however, to explain how any drainage system was managed. Some early discoveries may suggest that the burial grounds continued beyond, and it is to these that we now turn.

### The cemeteries of Roman Lincoln

The existence of cemeteries outside the fortress and the subsequent walled city was noted by 18th-century antiquarians, just as the reviving town was beginning to expand again and adjacent stone quarries were coming back into operation. Over the next century or so, many finds of both cremations and inhumations came to light, together with a remarkable range of grave goods and several tombstones and other monuments. Records of these discoveries are valuable in establishing the location, date and burial rite, and in some cases the individuals involved, but unfortunately little analysis was undertaken of the human remains found. The fact that the sites were on the fringe of the town, beneath a relatively slight accumulation of later deposits, meant that much was damaged without record, and those to the north and east of the Upper City, discovered during stone-quarrying, will have been totally destroyed. The documentation of the early discoveries and their study can be summarised chronologically. William Stukeley noted the position of some of the cemeteries to the south, east and north-east of the Roman town when preparing his map of Lincoln in 1722 (Fig. 7.56). 'Urns' and 'burial places' close to Nettleham and Wragby Roads are specifically noted on the map but three mounds recorded in the so-called 'Greetwell Fields' are now considered to represent the sites of late medieval and later windmills (p. 272–3 below).

Others including Pownall (1792) and O'Neill (1892) recorded burials, while Edward and Arthur Trollope also made useful contributions (1860). With the aid of F T Baker, Richmond was able to summarise knowledge in 1946 (48–54), and could point also to the primary locations of the legionary-period cemetery in the

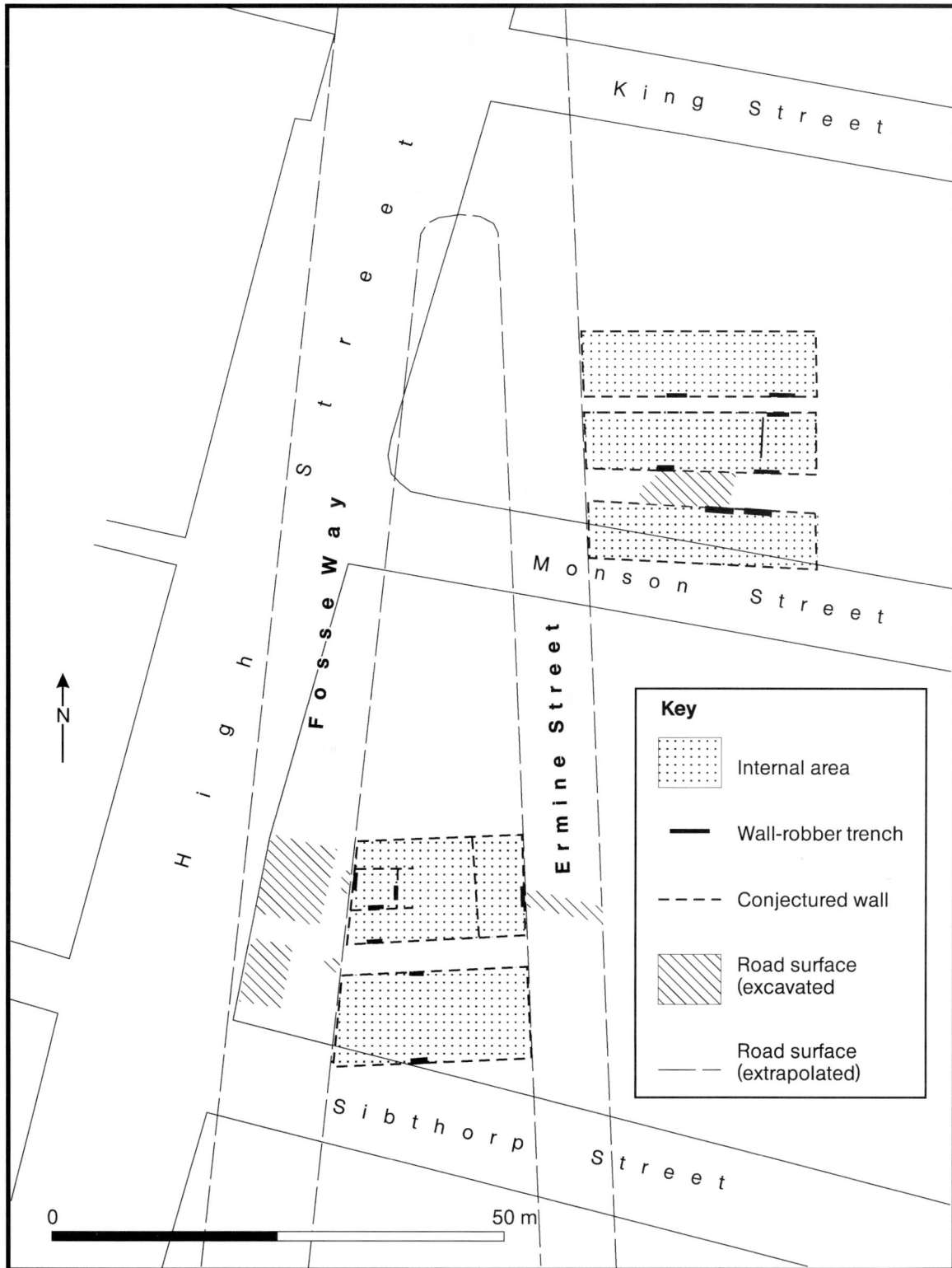

*Fig. 7.55. Reconstruction of local topography south of the junction between Ermine Street and the Fosse Way, based on excavations in 1982 at St Mary's Guildhall and Monson Street, 800m south of the walled city (source, Magilton and Stocker 1982, drawn by Dave Watt, copyright English Heritage).*

Monson Street and South Common areas, as well as other finds of both cremations and inhumations on all sides of the city walls. Apart from Thompson's work on the late 1st-century barrow at Riseholme (1954b),

*c.*3 km north of the city, Whitwell, in his volume on *Roman Lincolnshire* (1970), could add little to Richmond's account. Immediately after it appeared, however, Glyn Coppack went into the subject in greater

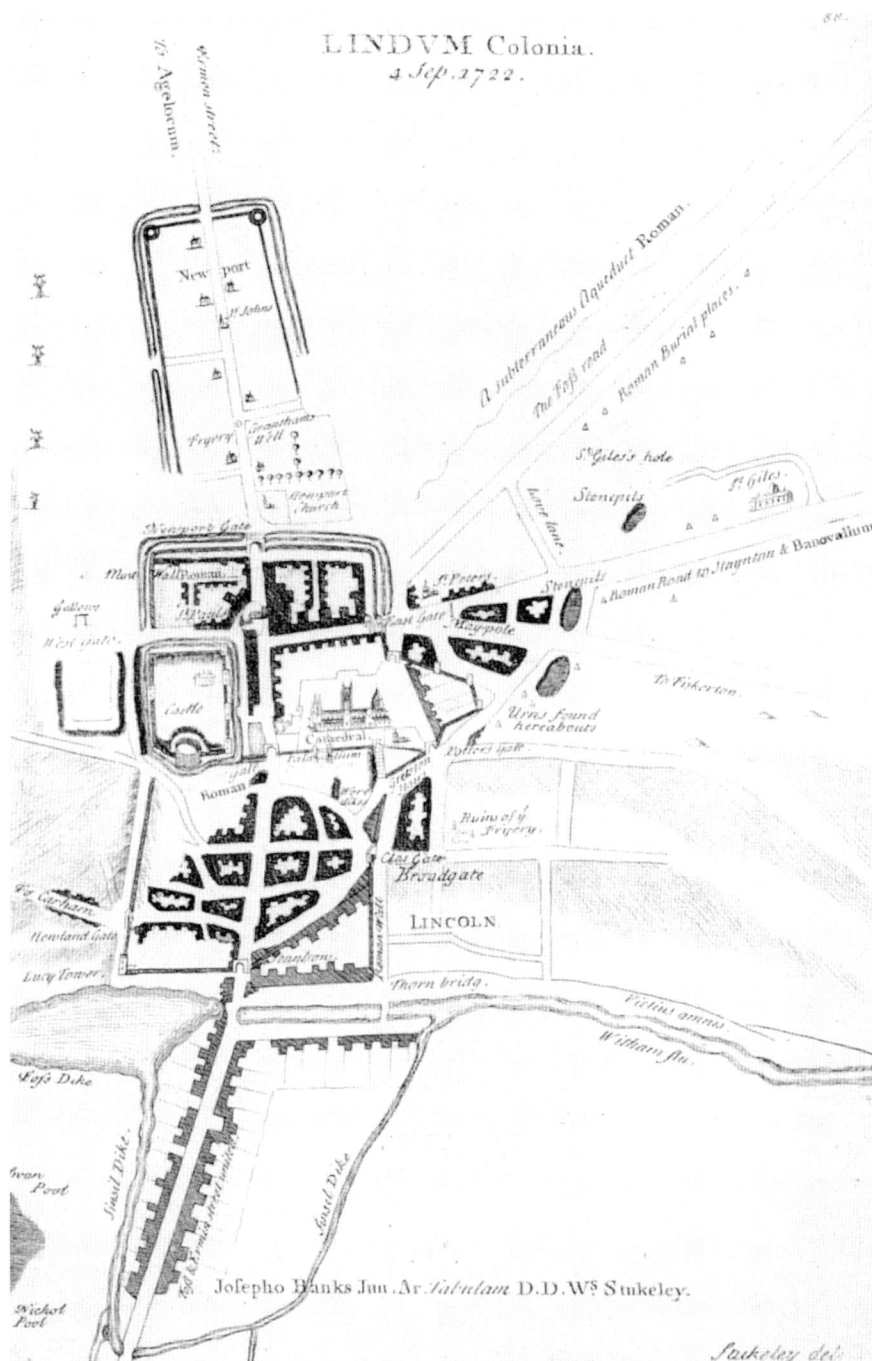

Fig. 7.56. *Map of Lincoln drawn in 1722 by William Stukeley (published in 1724), showing many Roman remains including burials (Stukeley 1724 plate 88).*

depth, searched out some of the cremation vessels recorded (including some in the British Museum), and produced a draft article on the subject (copy in City and County Museum archives). They convey the expected impression that burial location and practice at Lincoln was fairly orderly, typical of the major towns of Roman Britain (Esmonde Cleary 2000a).

Coppack's notes, which have also been studied by Margaret Darling, form part of the basis for the outline account presented here, but the subject requires further research before a detailed study can be published. In the meantime, since Coppack's work, there have been further finds. Among these are burials in the modern Newport Cemetery (White 1976, 55; 1977, 80–1), and fragments of a re-used tombstone from the foundations of the medieval church of St Mark's in Wigford (Hassall and Tomlin 1977, 428), possibly referring to a *decurio* (Fig. 7.57). Another was discovered behind the northern defences at East Bight (EB 80) (Hassall and Tomlin 1982, 410). Finds of cremations and inhumations have been made on Wragby Road, close to Lee Road (ON 365), and to the west of the Lower City at Orchard

Street, where a relief of Mother Goddesses was recovered (Blagg 1982b) (Fig. 7.58). Further burials have been found west of the city at Newland Street West in 1997 (NSS 97), and, of course, at the excavations already referred to at Monson Street in 1982 (M 82), on the site of the 1st-century cemetery. This information has been summarised by the author and a map, based largely on Coppack's work, showing all approximate cemetery locations is presented here (Esmonde Cleary 1987, 106–113) (Fig. 7.59).

The map provides some clue to the definite locations of burials, which probably represent only part of the actual extent of the cemeteries. Most, but not all, lay close to the major roads issuing from the city. There appears to have been overflow into open land in the north-east quadrant, between Newport, Nettleham Road, Wragby Road and Greetwell Road, as well as in parts of the hillside. The cemeteries appear to have

taken up large tracts of extra-mural land not used for official or commercial buildings – although finds of late Roman vessels cannot be taken to imply burial since there appears to have been a change to inhumation at Lincoln during the 3rd century. Information about the belief-systems involved, and details of burial rites and the reasons for this empire-wide change in practice, can be found elsewhere (Toynbee 1971, 43–54; Jones R F J 1987; Philpott 1991; Pearce *et al.* 2000). At Lincoln, the early cemeteries south of the river appear to have been in use, to some extent, in the 2nd and 3rd centuries, although parts of them were swallowed up by the burgeoning commercial suburbs. The analysis of the cremations from Monson Street has been mentioned above in chapter 6. The Monson Street excavations also revealed the north side of a stone building of comparatively early date, which has been interpreted as a mausoleum (Steane *et al.* 20001a, 19), and which was possibly the context for the mosaic pavement found *c.*1845 (p. 108 below). Trollope and Trollope (1860, 16) also noted several inhumations aligned north–south nearby. More recently, other north–south burials have turned up; two were found to the rear of the traders' houses east of St Mark's Station (ZE 87), and another in the grounds of Bishop Grosseteste College (BGB 96). Stukeley considered that an area further south along High Street (here the Fosse Way) contained many 'funeral monuments', and Richmond interpreted a find noted by Drury as one of them (1946, 49–50).

Most of the burials encountered to date have been cremations, but most cemeteries also seem to have contained later inhumations, although caution must be exercised in identifying finds of inhumations as Roman, since the medieval suburb of Wigford here contained many parish churches and their graveyards, and the same is true for other areas of the city. Some special characteristics deserve comment. In addition to

*Fig. 7.57. Monumental Roman inscription re-used in the walls of the 11th-century church of St Mark (SM 76). The inscription dates from the 2nd or early 3rd century and can be translated:*

To the divine shades, *[names of commemorated],* from Sav*[aria],* …, *[de]*curion *[?]…*

*(Photo H N Hawley).*

*Fig. 7.58. Relief sculpture of the mother goddesses (Deae Matres) found in Orchard Street in 1980 (Huskinson 1994, No.17) (photo H N Hawley).*

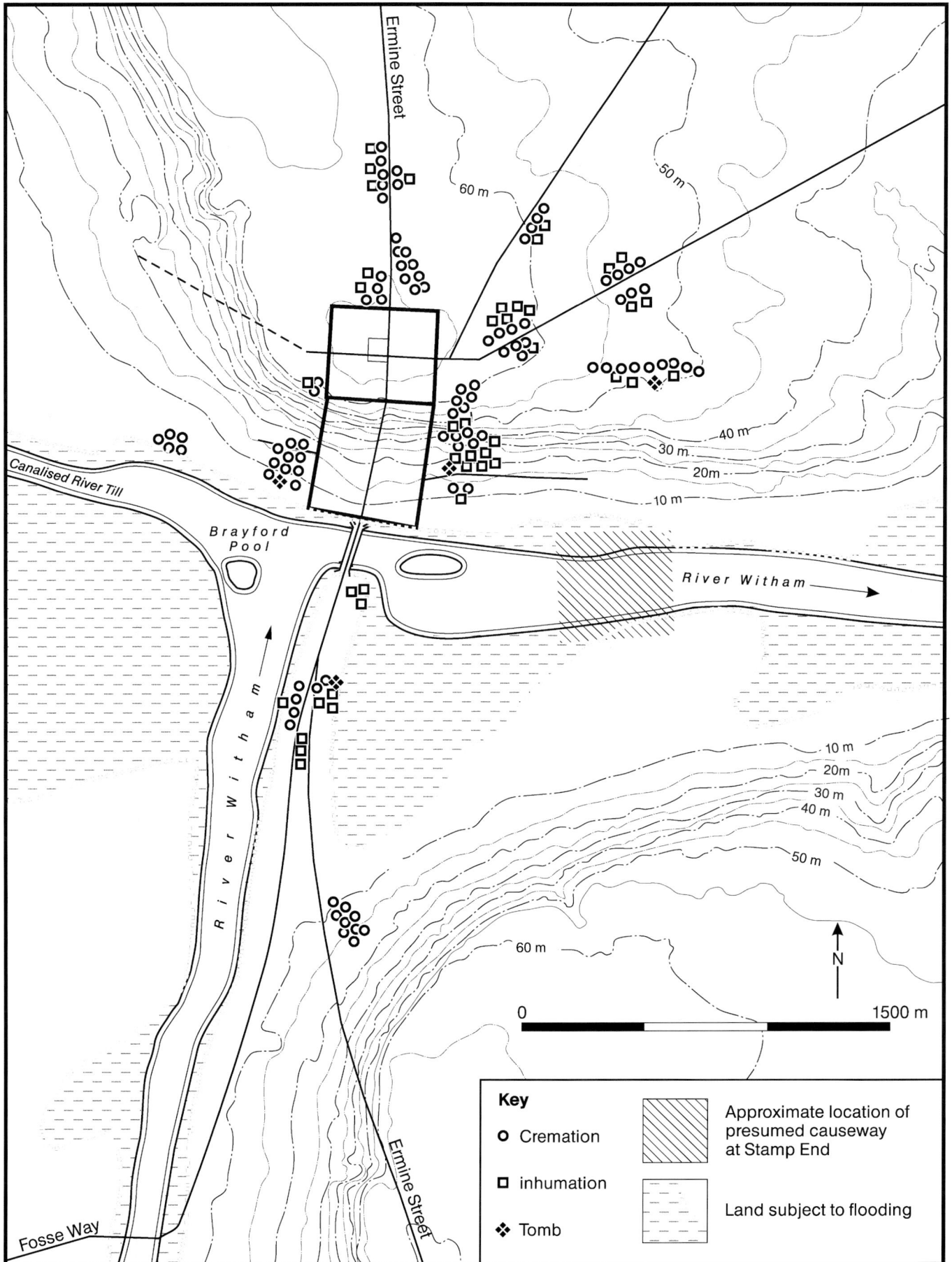

*Fig. 7.59. Known cemeteries of the* Colonia *Era (source G. Coppack, and others. Drawn by Dave Watt, copyright English Heritage).*

the Roman barrow at Riseholme, there was possibly another outside the original west gate of the Lower City, close to West Parade (Richmond 1946, 53). There were also burials in lead coffins, in stone sarcophagi, in tile-lined coffins, and another subterranean mausoleum (more exotic than that suggested for the Monson Street site). Richmond (1946, 52) identified *loculi* (literally 'small receptacles') on Newport not far outside the north gate, which accommodated rows of burials belonging to a burial club (ON 354). The discovery of the tombstone of C. Antistius Frontinus (RIB 1965, 247), a treasurer of a guild – probably for such a burial club – is adduced as evidence for such arrangements within the city. The impression conveyed by these sepulchres could be indicative, at first sight, of the metropolitan and Mediterranean cultural influences, as commented on long ago by Richmond and more recently by Esmonde Cleary (1987, 113). Increasingly, however, parallels are recognised between this type of material and the north-western provinces of the Empire. Even so, issues of cultural identity are now recognised to be more complex (Pearce 2000), and Struck (2000) has shown that, in tribal areas remote from South-east Britain, such monuments were almost invariably associated with incomers – either with immigrant Romans or with those who aspired to Roman identity. The cosmopolitan nature of the archaeologically visible component of the population is reinforced by the inscriptions on many tombstones, including that belonging to Flavius Helius, a Greek (RIB 1965, 251). Like the legionaries, the *origines* of some *colonia* citizens were widely scattered. Of these the monument of M Aurelius Lunaris tells particularly of the fame and influence of *Lindum* across the western empire (Fig. 7.60). His link with Bordeaux is considered to indicate that he operated as a wine-merchant, and was sufficiently proud of his rank as *sevir Augustalis* (a priest of the imperial cult) of Lincoln and York to recount the fact in the altar he set up in his home city in AD 237.

We cannot pass over the subject of burial without a reference to several finds of infant remains. These are known from several extra-mural houses at the Lawn (L 86) west of the Upper City, at Bishop Grosseteste College (BGB 95) at the edge of the northern suburb and especially to the south, at St Mary's Guildhall (SMG 82), 181–3 High St (HG 72), and in the St Marks area (SM 76, Z 86, ZE 87). Of the 14 examples found in the southern suburb, the extent to which the remains survived varied, but all the femora bones were present, and have been used for comparative analysis (Boylston and Roberts 1995). All had apparently died in the late foetal or perinatal periods. As a result, we cannot have any certainty as to whether death occurred at birth or subsequently, or in what circumstances. Thus the small Lincoln sample cannot resolve the problem of whether infanticide, perhaps merely by exposure, was common in Roman Lincoln (Harris 1994; Mays 1997). There is evidence to indicate that infants were not viewed as fully human until their soul existed, which according

to Pliny was at the age of teething. The Lincoln examples were normally placed under eaves or floors, which may itself reflect a kind of ritual (Watts 1989). Two cremations placed in pottery vessels on the rampart of the Park (P 70) may also have been infants, but no analysis has been possible.

As Watts has also noted, there was a marked change in attitude towards the burial of infants in the late Roman period, which, she argues, reflects the arrival of Christian values affording more respect to the human corpse. Unfortunately insufficient material from Lincoln has been discovered to test this idea. Some of the infant burials may have been 4th-century in date, but

*Fig. 7.60. Inscription recording the dedication of a temple by Marcus Aurelius Lunaris at Bordeaux in AD 237. Lunaris was a priest of the imperial cult in both Lincoln and York. The inscription may be translated:*

In honour of the goddess Tutela Boudiga, M. Aurelius Lunaris, priest of Augustus *[sevir Augustalis]*, of the *coloniae* of York and Lincoln *[Lind]*, in the province of Lower Britain, set up the altar in fulfilment of the vow he made on starting from York. Willingly and rightly did he fulfil his vow, in the consulship of Perpetuus and Cornelianus.

*(photo and copyright Musée d'Aquitaine, Bordeaux)*

since there is no inherent indicator of Christian belief, it is not possible to say whether their burials derive from Christian rites. Adult burial tends to be more visible in this late period, since ordered inhumation cemeteries were common, and the standard burial practice was that adopted by Christian communities (Philpott 1991, 239–40). The late Roman cemeteries may therefore have contained some Christians, although the evidence that pagan tombs and temples were being demolished between the mid and late 4th century for re-use in the city wall does not in itself imply that pagan beliefs were in serious decline. They may have merely become mixed with some Christian ideas and practices (Watts 1991). The presence of two late Roman burials east of St Mark's Station (ZE 87) may suggest that, as the commercial properties were being abandoned, their sites were being used for burial. Subsequently, burials move inside the city walls; this significant phenomenon, dating not earlier than the turn of the 5th century, is discussed in the penultimate section of this chapter.

In summary, Lindum Colonia's cemeteries have yielded much in the way of artefactual evidence, but some of it has yet to be analysed fully. The potential for studying the population and linking the skeletal evidence to the cultural is apparent (Pearce *et al.* 2000), but large-scale excavations under controlled conditions are necessary to realise it. The epigraphic and artefactual evidence already at our disposal tends to cover only part of the population and provide an unbalanced picture (Jones R F J 1993). Moreover, future studies could also make use of social theory as, for instance, elucidated by Morris (1992). It has been estimated that, for an average population of about 10,000, some 350 burials would take place each year. In Lincoln's case, assuming a smaller population (which may be an underestimate), there would have been at least 50,000 individuals buried during the Roman period.

*Communications: roads, rivers, canals*

The presence of a legion in the city had ensured good communications; the construction of both Ermine Street – possibly replacing a prehistoric routeway along the edge of the ridge – and the Fosse Way belong to this period. Tillbridge Lane, the route deviating north-westwards from Ermine Street some 5km north of Lincoln, could also be of military origin. This military road system was consolidated with the foundation of the *colonia*; the likely destinations of roads issuing from other city gates is shown on Fig. 7.61. Some of the roads leading from the city can only be plotted with certainty for a short distance but may have extended much further. For example the road east towards Greetwell has cemeteries extending for more than 800m away from the city wall, but has yet to be identified in excavation. To the west of the Upper City it is not clear whether the road ran along the

Edge to the north-west or down the scarp towards Long Leys Road. There is still also a possibility that a Roman road ran along the Lindum Road – Pottergate route from the east gate of the Lower City to the east gate of the Upper City, although no trace of such a road has ever been found. Roads north and east towards the coast, and southwards to the east of Sleaford (Mareham Lane) may belong to this secondary development, since they do not appear to link military bases or their early civilian successors.

Within and adjacent to the city, roads were constructed and repaired according to need. Drury (1890) described the road surface running through the southern suburb on the causeway. The Fosse Way and Ermine Street appear to have converged at the point where the higher terrace gave way to lower ground (Fig. 7.55). Drury described the Roman causeway construction as 'concreted', i.e. with mortar between the stones, but whether the concrete was a surface or make-up was not clear. It is presumed that the army had constructed some sort of causeway over the damper ground shortly after their arrival (p. 50 above), but the concreted construction appears to belong to the *colonia* period (Davies 2002). Its appearance may be connected with the development of the southern suburb for commercial activity, or simply with the increase in wheeled traffic from the south. Excavations at St Mary's Guildhall (SMG 82) suggested that the surface of pebbles was mortared in the mid Roman period, and there are other examples within the city of this type of construction – the earliest (4th-century) road through the gate at The Park (P 70) was of this type. The later road surfaces at St Mary's Guildhall were of larger pebbles (Fig. 7.62), as they were at The Park, but we have seen that the main street of the city within the walls was paved. Within the city, the successive surfaces of the main roads could accumulate until the stratigraphy became nearly 1.5m thick, whereas on the fringes it might be only as thick as a single surface. Roads at East Bight (EB 80) and Silver Street (LIN 73b) appear to have sidewalks for pedestrians, whilst porticoes served a similar function, on a monumental scale, along the principal streets in the upper and lower towns. The Fosse Way at St Mary's Guildhall (SMG 82) was c.7–8m wide with a central drain, Ermine Street here perhaps a little narrower but also with a drain. Wheel ruts were visible on the stretch of the Fosse Way excavated in 1982 and are now exposed within the building, but they were not so clear on the latest surviving surface. No trace has yet been found of the 'top-dressing' of gravel which Davies (2002) speculates was used to ease the strain on vehicles.

Examples of roads which apparently suffered little wear from traffic include those at the Lawn (ON 159), and at Kennington House on Wragby Road (Trimble 1994). Since even major roads can be so much less substantial outside the settlements, it is no wonder that we cannot define the precise line of Ermine Street in the South Common area. Milestones were provided

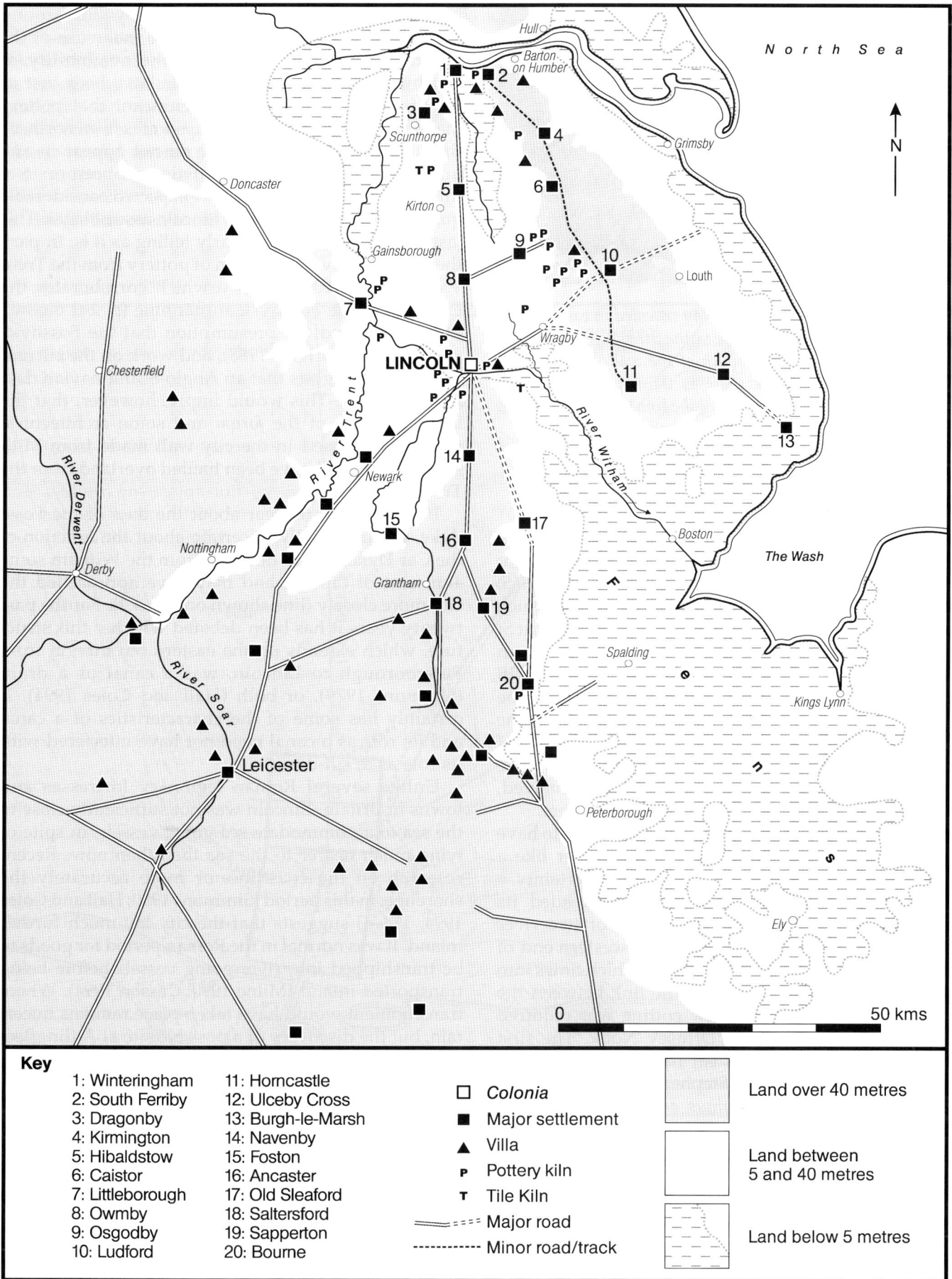

*Fig. 7.61. The East Midlands in the later Roman period (drawn by Dave Watt, copyright English Heritage).*

a)

b)

*Fig. 7.64. a)* In situ *section of the aqueduct along Nettleham Road, as seen in excavations near the Roaring Meg spring in 1973. The scale is 2 feet long. b) Cross-section through aqueduct pipe and* opus signinum *jacket (a) photo H N Hawley. b) photo and copyright, M J Jones).*

is that the source was at greater distance, on higher ground. Wacher (1995, 140–1) has suggested that this might be as far away as the Wolds, at least 25 km to the north-east. Although there is, as yet, no evidence that the pipeline extended beyond the Roaring Meg, other authorities have suggested that an inverted siphon would represent the most appropriate technology, as exemplified by those at Lyon and Aosta in Gaul and at Aspendos and Pergamon in Turkey (Wacher 1975, 131; Stephens 1985, 202 and n.74; Hodge 1992, 147–60). N A F Smith would prefer a bucket-chain system to an inverted siphon, as suggested for Cosa in Italy (1976, 45–71; 1991; Oleson 1984). The argument put by Thompson that the foundations exposed were too insubstantial to carry a tower 20m high, even a timber one, is not accepted by Smith, and his point of view has some merit. There is clearly great benefit in involving hydraulic engineers in solving the problem – but not all agree (Isaac 1980). There are certainly good precedents for bringing water to the town from a considerable distance (for example at Cologne – Haberey 1971), and some pump-based systems have been recently discussed (Oleson 1996). The author of the standard work on Roman aqueducts even speculated that the water might have flowed away from the city (Hodge 1992). Certainly, the sections of pipe excavated show no trace of the lime-scale which would be expected and several authorities accordingly question whether the system ever worked! It is clear that this is one problem, of considerable significance, which demands targeted research (Jones 2003).

The capacity of the single pipe-line found to date could have coped with the demands of the public baths, but probably not much beyond. There may have been other pipes – one was noted on Greestone Stairs, possibly intended for the public fountain in the Lower City – but wells such as that in the *principia* and subsequent *forum* may have been more widely provided. Spring water was favoured if it could be obtained, so that the Roaring Meg, as well as sources on the steep hillside, may both have been exploited.

### The urban fringe and surrounding industry and agriculture

Like all major urban settlements, *Lindum colonia* was dependent on a rural hinterland for providing many of its requirements, from raw materials to food and manufactured goods. Many of these were obtained locally, and some from very close to the city. Moreover, there were close relationships, socially as well as economically, between the town and the surrounding countryside: for instance, some of the leading citizens would have lived for much of the time on rural estates whilst, by contrast, some of the farmland close to the city may have been run from urban residences. The purpose of this final section is to discuss the evidence both for land use at the urban fringe, in particular the exploitation of natural resources and the industries which they served, and to consider what we know about the organisation and occupation of the city's agricultural hinterland. Some useful research has been undertaken recently on the first of these questions, but the second aspect is still problematical and much remains to be done.

Lincoln's situation on the Jurassic ridge has meant that the site of the city and adjacent land has served as a source of building stone intermittently since the Roman period. With notable exceptions, including the Millstone Grit (obtained from the Pennines) employed for the Bailgate colonnade and some other architectural features re-used in the rebuilding of the city wall, the Roman city was largely constructed out of local Jurassic limestone, probably obtained from quarries very close to the city. Millstone Grit was also employed extensively in York from the early 2nd century, probably both for decorative and load-bearing purposes (Buckland 1988). Although there has been only limited study of Lincoln's building stone, to compare with studies such as that of late Roman York (Buckland 1984), Lincoln is far from unusual in this respect amongst the Roman towns of Britain. At Lincoln, analysis of the sources of imported luxury marble veneers has been possible (Peacock and Williams 1992), but detailed examination of the more common materials has been confined to the defensive walls of the Upper City (Fenton 1980). This study was able to distinguish between the various local limestones and revealed that true oolitic stone (i.e. those which have at least 80% oolith inclusions), including the famous 'Ancaster' freestone, was not employed. The results of the analysis did suggest, however, that the better beds of the Lower Lincolnshire limestone (i.e. those which have 'peloidal' inclusions rather than ooliths) quarried in the immediate vicinity of the city, were only employed for the city wall from the mid Roman period onwards. Earlier masonry structures, therefore, may have been restricted to the use of poorer quality stones, from the upper levels of local strata.

Identifying the precise locations of the Roman quarries is notoriously difficult – both because they were re-opened, enlarged and used extensively in the high medieval and later periods, and because many have since been built over, some on more than one occasion. Furthermore, different quarries contain various types of stone in beds of varying thickness (Ussher *et al.* 1888). It may be that outcrops of stone on the western and southern scarps of the northern ridge terminal, and the equivalent northern and western scarps of the southern terminal were exploited first, since they were so accessible. Excavations at Westgate, immediately inside the western defences (W 73), and outside them at the Lawn (L 86), revealed deep pits cutting well into the tabular bedrock which appear to be quarries, some filled with 1st-century rubbish but continuing into the early 2nd century. These might have provided some stone for the first stone fortifications and/or public buildings, but they

are no more than small 'borrow pits' and are unlikely to have produced it in very large quantities. Much of this part of the hilltop may have been quarried in the same way. The likely presence of quarries was noted on Langworthgate (LG 90) east of the Upper City, but the few archaeological excavations in this area have hardly penetrated to the necessary depth. In the medieval and post-medieval periods, land to the north and east of the city was quarried, but there is little prospect of showing how much if any of this activity originated in the Roman period.

Fenton's study of the upper defences also included a consideration of the mortars (1980, 45–6), but only limited work has been possible on those of the Lower Defences (Morgan and Jones 1999). Again, there was a distinction between the gravel used in the earlier and later walls, suggesting different sources. Whilst the earlier source was located along the rivers to the south and west of the walled city (including along the course of the Fossdyke), the later sources, of older river sand and gravel, lay further to the south-west (Fenton 1980, fig 48). This also happens to be the area of the city – Boultham and Swanpool – where the major pottery industry of the 3rd and 4th centuries was also situated (Darling 1977, 32–7; Darling and Precious forthcoming).

An outline account of the origins and development of the pottery industry at Lincoln is in order here as part of a summary of the land-use on the urban fringe (Fig. 7.65) (Swan 1984; Darling and Precious forthcoming). Several kilns were to be found at some distance from the city, for example the Flavian-Trajanic kiln at North Hykeham is some 7km to the south-west, and the Antonine industry at South Carlton, which served a military market on the Northern Frontier, is a similar distance to the north-west. The Hykeham and Carlton industries may have owed their location primarily to easily-accessible clay sources. Others, such as the Racecourse kiln(s), north of the Fossdyke less that 2km west of the city, and that close to the town's east wall at the Technical College, could be related rather to ease of transport to market. The 3rd-century kiln at Bracebridge Heath, on the ridge to the south of the Witham gap, may have related to a settlement in that area, evidenced otherwise by artefact scatters (Donel 1992b). The Swanpool industry appears to derive from an existing East Midlands (possibly Corieltauvian) tradition, developed to serve the needs of the city and surrounding hinterland, competing with that based in the Nene Valley. It survived almost to the end of the Roman period, as long as the city provided a market. The kiln-types found were already in use in the Lincoln area, suggesting that the potters had not migrated from another region. Whether the industry moved to this site because suitable clay was discovered in the course of gravel quarrying, or vice-versa, we cannot say at this stage, and the presence of iron slag in the Swanpool mortaria (Darling and Precious forthcoming) might even suggest that iron-working was taking place

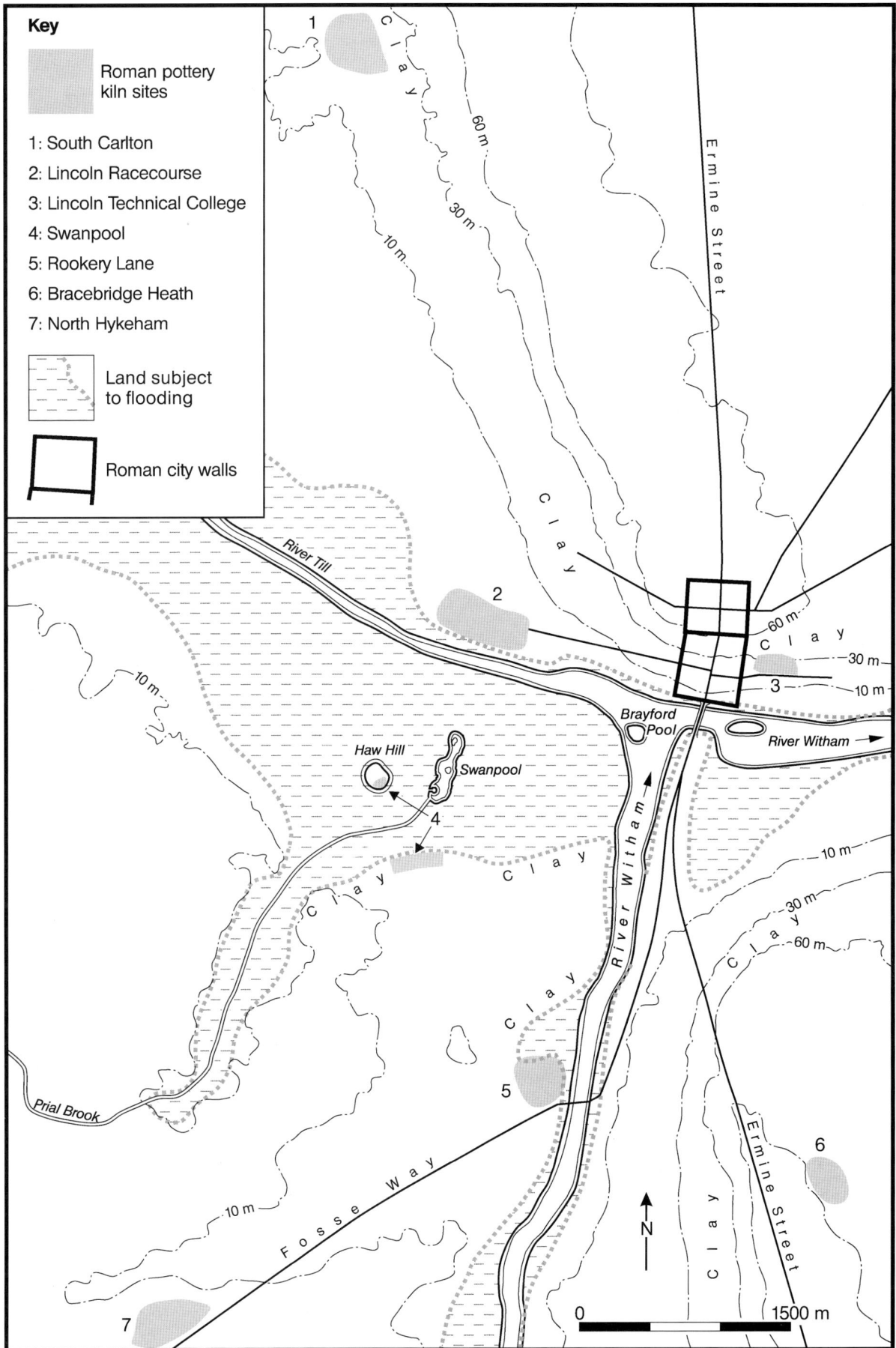

*Fig. 7.65. Later Roman pottery kilns in the Lincoln vicinity. Swanpool is shown in its modern location (sources, Darling and Precious forthcoming and others – drawn by Dave Watt, copyright English Heritage).*

nearby. This *Assessment* has highlighted the close correlation between kiln-sites and exposed clay next to the waterways. Only one local tile-kiln of Romano-British date has been identified, in Heighington parish, close to the Car Dyke (Darling and Wood 1981). It is unlikely that this was the only such kiln exploiting the market offered by the city and further examples, perhaps closer to the city, might be expected.

It was noted above that there may have been an iron-smelting industry in the Swanpool area, presumably based on the ferrous content of the local limestones, and iron-working may have been undertaken at the same time as potting (Darling and Precious forthcoming). It is certainly true that such industries might achieve economies of scale by working side by side in this fashion, and this might locate any Roman smelting industry in this area between the lower Witham and the River Till. Land and taxation costs were presumably lower for rural sites, coppicing for fuel would have been possible close by, and out of the city the nuisance to citizens would be reduced (Millett 1990, 165–74.)

Beyond the quarries and potteries, we now have some information about the limit of urban land-use and the start of rural occupation (and here we disregard Rodwell's idea of an official 'town-zone', put forward in 1975). The remains of stone buildings in the grounds of Bishop Grosseteste College (BGB 95; Wragg 1997) adjacent to Ermine Street *c.*600m to the north of the city, provide new data, but also present problems of interpretation. This site (Fig. 7.39 and 7.66) lies immediately beyond an area used for burial, and as such might be considered to be outside the urban limits. Although it has produced some 1st-century pottery in residual contexts, occupation appears to have intensified in the mid 2nd century, with an apparent *floruit* in the mid or later 3rd century, but not lasting beyond the mid 4th century. Parts of two structures are known, separated by a yard. The quality of the pottery, with a good number of fine wares and imports, suggests a degree of prosperity and status, while the environmental evidence provides further clues as to function. The range of molluscs indicates that it was located in a mixed environment, i.e. in open land with some shade, and there are traces of cereal grains and of spelt wheat. The occurrence of neonates among the sheep and cattle suggests that some were kept and bred. This may be a part of a villa estate, or more accurately a farm, no doubt serving the town.

Although it is possible that land to the rear of traders' houses in the southern suburb was used for small-scale agriculture, the nearest identified villa to the city is the so called 'Greetwell Villa' on the north side of the Witham Valley 2km east of the walls (RENO 3084). However, there are reasons for thinking that this might not be a typical example of such establishments (p. 97 above and p. 130 below) and we have no evidence to suggest that it was the centre of an agricultural estate serving the city. Other, more traditional villas are

known within a few miles of the city, especially on the Lincoln Edge overlooking the valley to the west, close to Burton, Glentworth, and Scampton. Some of these sites have been known for centuries; that at Scampton was first published in 1810 (Illingworth 1810; Todd 1991, 86–9; Winton 1998, 53). They all lie to the north of the city but a similar pattern might be expected to the south, and one is also known in Canwick parish. Like the villa at Norton Disney to the east of the Fosse Way, south-west of Lincoln, they would have had good road links. It is considered likely that some of those close to Lincoln were occupied by the colonists who served as the city's magistrates and provided their principal source of income. We cannot really say how far removed from the original settlers were the families who represented the civic and rural elite at the time of their greatest development in the 4th century.

A site recently investigated some 2km to the east of the Upper City, close to the modern Greetwell Quarry (Field and Armour-Chelu, 2001), was occupied by the mid 3rd century AD. It contained a rectilinear pattern of field boundaries, within which were some structures, thought to be grain-stores on the basis of environmental samples, corn-driers, and stone-lined drains. This is clearly a small agricultural establishment which must have played some role in provisioning the city. There was also a small inhumation cemetery aligned principally on a nearby north–south ditch, perhaps representing the edge of the settlement, which may have lain mainly to the south of the excavated area where geophysical survey had suggested the presence of similar features (Johnson 1997). North-west of the walled city, remains of stone buildings perhaps belonging to a villa estate were found on Long Leys Road in 1984 (Field 1985). Like that near Greetwell Quarry, this site also contained inhumations, which dated to the 3rd century.

### Town and country relationships and the territorium

It goes without saying that, in the pre-industrial but urbanised society of the Roman Empire, much of the surrounding countryside would have been organised to serve the needs of the city. The problem of the extent to which towns were more consumers than producers, and what the town could offer in return for agricultural produce has been a subject of long debate, (e.g. Finley 1981; Fulford 1982; Engels 1990; Wacher 1995, 70; Roskams 1999). One of the keys to this problem can be found in environmental evidence such as that from animal bones (King 1978; Maltby 1979; Dobney *et al.* 1996). Central to our understanding is the economic interrelationship of the various settlements, which can be addressed partly by examining the source of material (e.g. pottery) found in the city (Millett 1982). Some evidence from nearby 'small towns' or 'market centres' (Fig. 7.61) is already available; at Ancaster (Todd 1981), on nearby sites along the Fosse Way (Walker *et al.* 1991), on the sites to the north of Lincoln (Whitwell

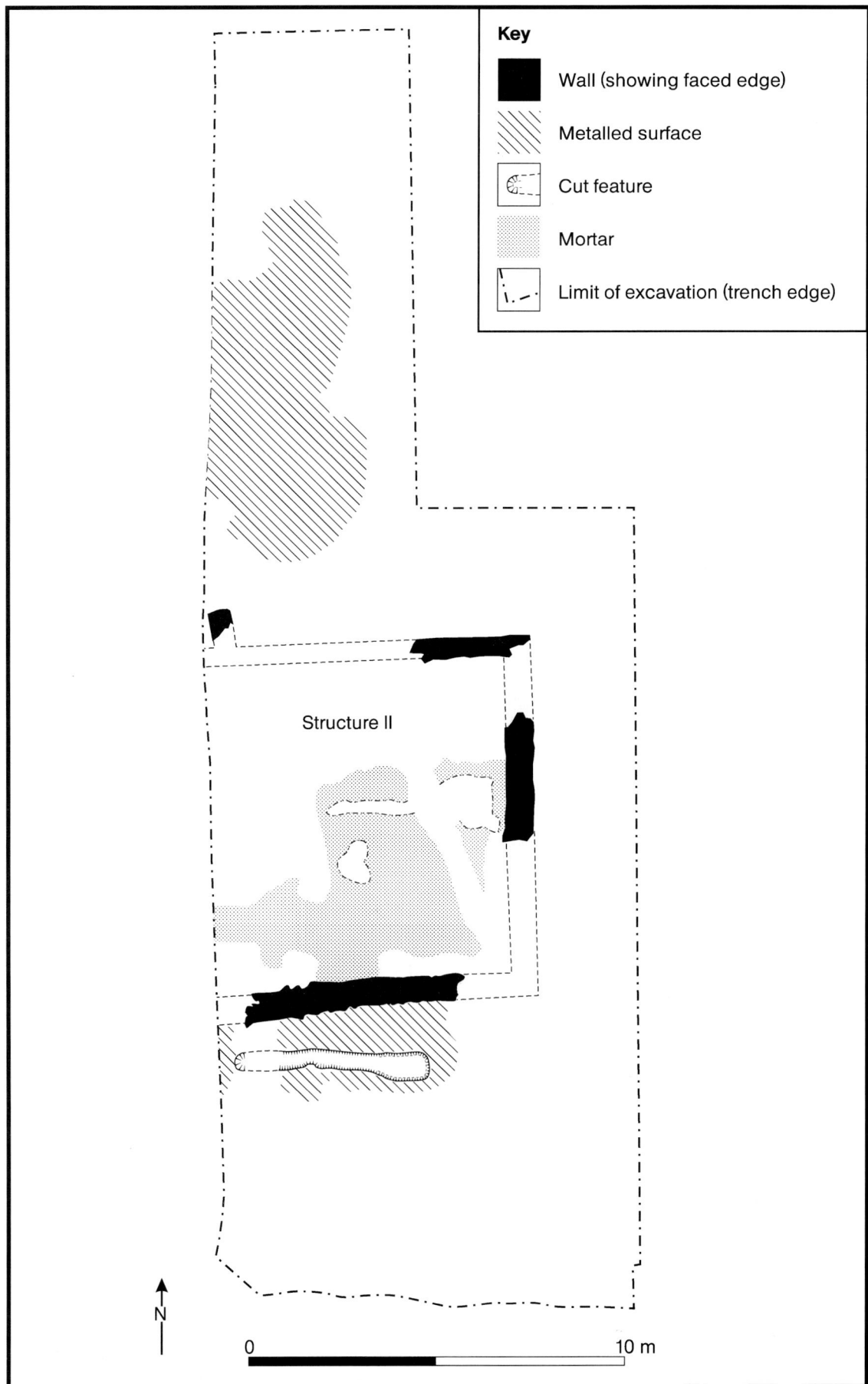

Key

Wall (showing faced edge)

Metalled surface

Cut feature

Mortar

Limit of excavation (trench edge)

Structure II

N

0                                                        10 m

*Fig. 7.66. Plan of later-Roman building excavated at Bishop Grosseteste College in 1995 (see Fig. 7.39) (source, Wragg 1997 – drawn by Dave Watt, copyright English Heritage).*

1995), and on small towns in eastern Britain more generally (Burnham and Wacher 1990). The centre-periphery model could be tested by comparing Lincoln finds with those from these outlying sites. In this case we should be looking to see whether commercial activity shows any sign of decentralisation from the major urban centres to the smaller markets (Millett 1990, 147–9). Our present understanding, unfortunately, sheds almost no light on such issues. Lincoln provides little evidence that it lost its function as a commercial centre to these smaller satellites until the Romanised economy in Britain was in decline generally. Its special status as a *colonia* and later as a centre of imperial government may have strengthened its position and ensured that it was always the dominant centre of importance, regardless of the fluctuations in the relative economy of the region.

In developing strategies for studying Lincoln's hinterland, we can learn from the current research project being undertaken on the Wroxeter Hinterland (White and Leusen 1997), and from the 'Urban Hinterlands' project (Perring 2002). This second project has identified suitable case studies for analysis (the Lincoln area was not one of those selected for the Roman period). It is suggested that there is much scope for the study of networks for exchange (e.g., from patterns of coin loss), power and authority, and the influence of extended families. Roskams (1999) seeks to move to a new interpretative framework based on a study of how surpluses were extracted. Before we can apply any of these analytical approaches in the Lincoln area, more study of pottery assemblages, building materials, and other groups of dated artefacts is needed from a wider area around the city, in order to understand the extent to which various Lincoln products travelled. With regard to the city as a consumer, much useful information on the exploitation of natural resources resides in excavation data still to be analysed. We should also recognise that in looking at the interdependence of urban and rural sites, as in other aspects of settlement studies, account will have to be taken of regional variations, and the pattern around Lincoln may not be found commonly elsewhere.

The question of urban influence on the countryside in Lincoln's case is connected to some extent with its *territorium*, land which lay directly under the control of the *colonia* – but this is to be distinguished clearly from what is meant by the hinterland as a whole. The *territorium* may have corresponded closely to that of the 1st-century military occupation, the *prata legionis* (p. 50–1 above). How or whether the *territorium* can be defined is an interesting problem in itself and it may not be visible in the archaeological record at all. We must leave open the question of whether its lands were centuriated, i.e. divided into areas of standard size (normally squares 2400 Roman feet long), as was common in Italy and some Mediterranean provinces (Dilke 1971). Keppie (1984) would argue that cen-

turiation would be expected at Lincoln, and the other early military colonies in Britain. Others are not so sure (e.g. Hurst 1988, 68), and it does appear that the process was ceasing to be normal after the Hadrianic period (Potter and Johns 1992, 250–51). In these circumstances, we cannot be sure that the process would have been applied in Lincoln's case.

Certainly the existing aerial photographic coverage of the heath to the north and south of the city reveals no evidence for features underlying visible field-patterns which could be interpreted as representing formal Roman land-allotment, although Winton refers to sites at some distance from Lincoln, which may require further attention (1998, 62–3). Several researchers have spent many years searching for evidence of centuriation in Britain, but none has come forward with ideas meriting scrutiny, until recently. Mr A Syme, a retired engineer from Leicester, and Dr J W Peterson (1993) of the University of East Anglia at roughly the same time both proposed that the alignment of fields to the north and south of the city derives from their Roman layout. They are at an oblique angle to the *colonia* street grid, but rather follow the line of the coast road issuing from the east gate. We now have to test these hypotheses, but dating may be difficult. There is no evidence as yet from the Lincoln area for a site like that at Claydon Pike, Gloucestershire, where a settlement under official control seemed to be aimed primarily at collecting food. Recent work at West Deeping indicated a major reorganisation of settlement in the 2nd century and, although it is at least 50km to the south of Lincoln, it would fall within Peterson's area of centuriation, At the same time, it is quite conceivable that if there were existing field-systems, these continued to be used (Taylor 1975, 57–8).

Richmond (1946, 65–6) considered, on the basis of Italian parallels, that the Lincoln *territorium* would have covered an area of not less than 100 square miles, and that it must have included both land along the ridge and a great deal more in 'the marshes'. Newly drained land is a possible location and the area of the Fens adjacent to the Car Dyke worthy of consideration as a contender (Potter 1981). Here the work of the Car Dyke Research Committee and the Fenland Survey Project (Hall and Coles 1994, 105–21) has confirmed that there were major engineering works from the late 1st century, including canals and roads, as well as intensified settlement from the Roman period. This implies an intensification of land use, and it is also the implication of the re-interpretation of the Car Dyke as a land drain as well as a canal (Simmons 1979).

Others since Richmond have considered a smaller area, extending at least 20 miles in different directions, more appropriate (Whitwell 1970, 24; 1982, 57–8). In various studies of Gloucester, Hurst (1988; 1999a) has moved away from trying to define the legionary and *colonia territoria*, for which he had previously suggested an area of 10 by 5 km, towards examining the relationship of the *colonia* to its hinterland (Reece 1999;

Roskams 1999). Some current thinking argues rather that we should be trying to establish whether there were any ways in which the British *coloniae* were different from the other major towns in all but legal status (Reece 1999; Millett 1999), and the pursuit of what may be an anachronistic goal – a clearly centuriated and defined landscape – may well turn out to be a fruitless exercise.

Another indication of the official territory of the *colonia* may be the distribution of settlements, milestones, temples, etc., which seem to imply some dependence on Lincoln. Sites such as the shrine at Nettleham jointly dedicated to *Mars Rigonemetos* and the *Numina Augustorum* (Fig. 7.67) must indicate a link with the *colonia* (Esmonde-Cleary 1987, 113; Wacher 1995, 145). Some would like to see settlements such as that on the Trent at Littleborough (Riley *et al.* 1995) and that at Ancaster (Todd 1981; Wacher 1995, 146) as part of the *territorium*, since distances are measured to them on milestones *from* Lincoln. A petrological analysis of milestones (Sedgeley 1975) seemed to suggest that, if the *colonia* was responsible for their provision, Lincoln's *territorium* was even more extensive than many expected, and we have already seen that Peterson's scheme for centuriation covers a huge area. Changes in the macro-patterning of land-use of the countryside around might also help to define Lincoln's *territorium*, much as those identified several miles to the east of Gloucester have suggested to some the imposition of a Roman land use system for grazing horses (Miles and Palmer 1990). There are also clear changes in landscape division around York, but some changes could be datable to the pre-Roman period, and others occur in the 2nd century (R F J Jones 1988; Roskams 1999).

## Lincoln in the 4th century

The administrative reforms introduced by Diocletian at the end of the 3rd century, and continued by his successor Constantine I, had implications for Lincoln, since the city now probably became a provincial capital. It was one of four capitals in the new Diocese of *Britannia*, and we presume that it was this capital status that influenced the establishment of a bishopric here (Barnes 1982; Potter and Johns 1992, 190–91). For a century, Lincoln had had to play second fiddle to York in *Britannia Inferior*, but now the two cities now took control of their own provinces; York of *Flavia Caesariensis*, whilst Lincoln was promoted to be the capital of *Britannia Secunda* (Mann J C 1998). The boundaries of the new province are unknown. It cannot have extended further north than the Humber, but must have included the modern East Midlands and perhaps more land to the west, and possibly also some of East Anglia (Fig. 7.68).

The reasons for Lincoln's elevation to provincial capital, at the expense of Leicester or Caistor-by-Norwich, are not known, but its status as a *colonia*

*Fig. 7.67. Inscription dedicating an arch to the local god* Mars Rigonemetos, *found at 13 Willowfield Close, Nettleham, in 1961. The inscription can be translated:*

To the god Mars Rigonemetos and the divine Emperor, Quintus Neratus Proxsimus has given this arch at his own cost.

*(Photo and copyright, Lincolnshire County Council, Lincolnshire Museums Service).*

may not have been the key factor. It has been traditionally accepted that the *colonia* at Gloucester, similar in so many ways to Lincoln, was not promoted in this way, although an argument has been advanced for its promotion rather than that of Cirencester (Reece 1999, 77–8). The choice of Lincoln may rather have been related to its economic dominance of a wide region, whilst Gloucester had a large prosperous rival relatively nearby in Cirencester, which may explain why it had not become pre-eminent in its region by the 4th century. Although secondary to York, Lincoln may also have benefited from this close relationship with the capital of Northern Britain from the early 3rd century. The fact that they shared *seviri augustales* might reflect Lincoln's aspirations or its recognised standing as a 'joint-capital' (Richmond 1946, 67–8; 1969, 62–79, Fig. 7.60).

The re-organisation of the church following Constantine's Edict of Milan in AD 313 seems to have followed that of the provincial administration, and was centred on the major urban centres (Mann J C 1961; Rivet and Smith 1979, 49–50; Thomas 1985, 197). Lincoln's first known bishop, Adelphius, attended the inaugural gathering of the Western bishops in Arles in 314. Whether the city also served as a base for the reorganised field army or for any *foederati* is uncertain; the documentary sources are not specific on this point and the archaeological evidence is negligible and ambiguous (James 1984; Tomlin 1987; Leahy 1984, 1993). In a recent paper, as yet unpublished, Mark Corney and Nick Griffiths note the concentration of 'Germanic' belt and related fittings in the area of *Britannia Prima*, including in areas close to towns with late fortifications, and suggests that these were fittings issued to the field

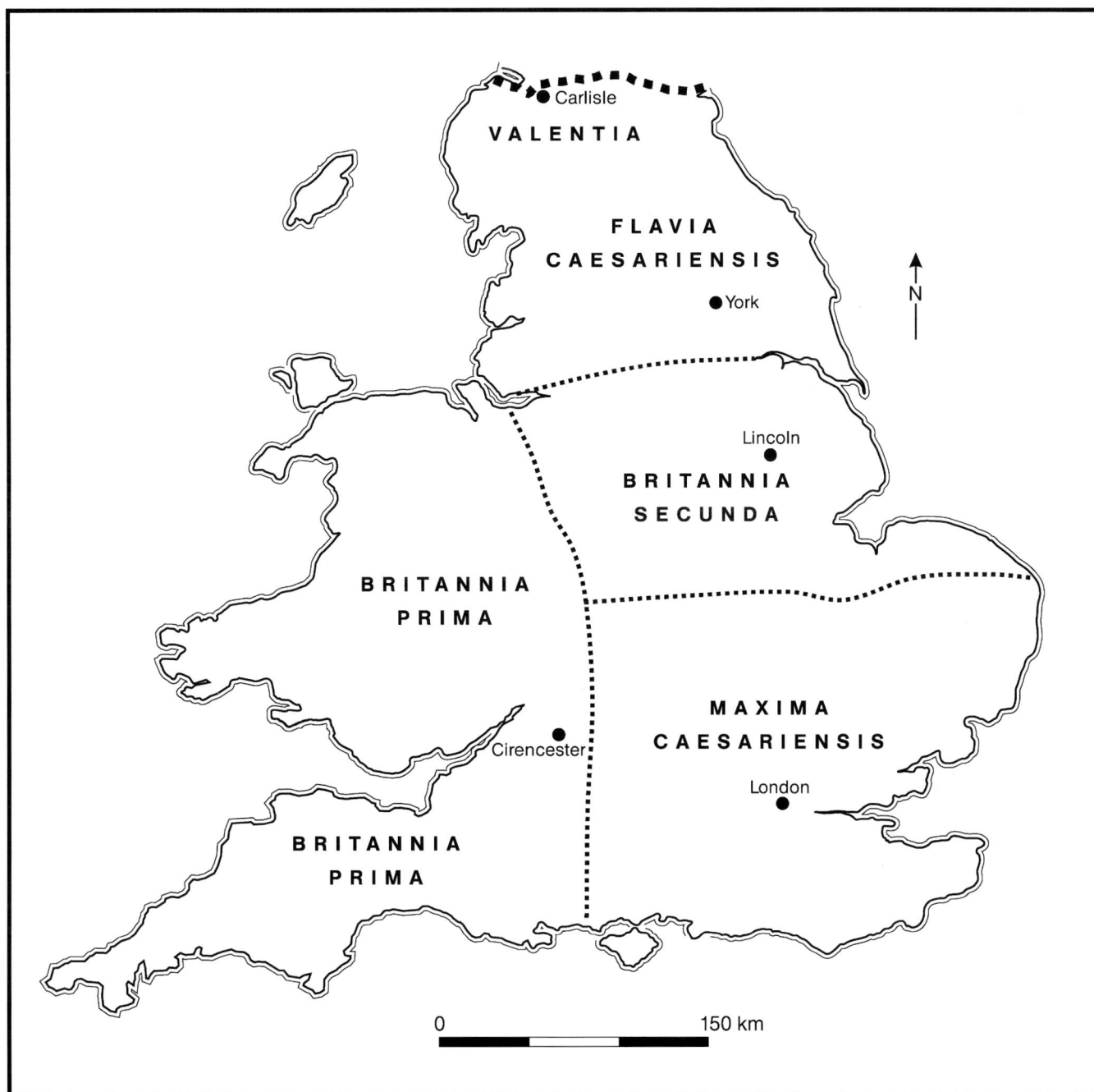

*Fig. 7.68. Our most recent understanding of the division of Britannia into four provinces in the 4th century (source, Mann 1998 – drawn by Dave Watt, copyright English Heritage).*

army, or to civil officials (forthcoming). At the same time, Lincoln's administrative importance, strategic location and strong fortifications would mean that it could have provided an optional stop-over or temporary base for military units (Mann J C 1977).

The nature of late Roman towns, and in particular those in Britain, has been the subject of much debate, especially since Reece's provocative suggestion of comparatively early physical decline, indicating a significant change in the function of urban centres (1980). These ideas have since been refined by Reece

himself (1992), and he has reaffirmed his view that urban-based life was only ever superficial. Because it was not deep-rooted, he argues, Romano-British towns gradually became little more than 'administrative villages' as the late Roman period wore on. Building on Reece's radical approach, a different emphasis has been offered by Faulkner in a systematic, quantitative analysis of the population densities of Colchester (1994) and Verulamium (1996), as well as a more general study of sixteen separate towns, including Lincoln (though here based on data which is to some extent out of date) (2000). Faulkner employs the term 'post-classical urbanism' to indicate 'urban' occupation continuing, and still involving an aristocratic centre for administrative, religious and military purposes. Yet he considers that it is also characterised, from as early as about AD 325 in Colchester, by a reversion to poorer quality housing, often of timber, reduced maintenance of civic functions and facilities, and a considerably smaller population. Such transformations occur at different dates in different towns, however, and Faulkner (1998) sees it occurring several decades later in Cirencester. Crummy (1999, 94–5) corroborates the impression of continuing urban occupation at Colchester into the early 5th century. One of the great values of Faulkner's studies is his estimation of relative building costs, which indicates how much was being spent in different periods on public and private construction – initially on public works, then mainly on private houses. The value of these estimates is apparent even though they are complicated by the need

in the 3rd century to build stone fortifications (Fig. 7.69). Without resorting to the same detail, we can see a similar picture for Lincoln. Obviously the building of the city walls, later including the Lower City, and their subsequent repairs and refurbishment, was a continual drain on resources. Public amenities would have occupied a similarly large proportion of available funds, where not paid for privately, until the early 3rd century and by this time a greater share of wealth was being devoted to housing. The trend for houses to be enlarged at the expense of the reconstruction of public buildings continued through the late 3rd and 4th centuries. A further factor at Lincoln was the effort required to develop the southern suburb over marshy ground.

Reece and Faulkner's views are certainly valuable, but do they exaggerate the speed and extent of 'decline'? The evidence from 4th-century Britain does give the impression of reduced spending on public works, apart from fortifications and, later in the

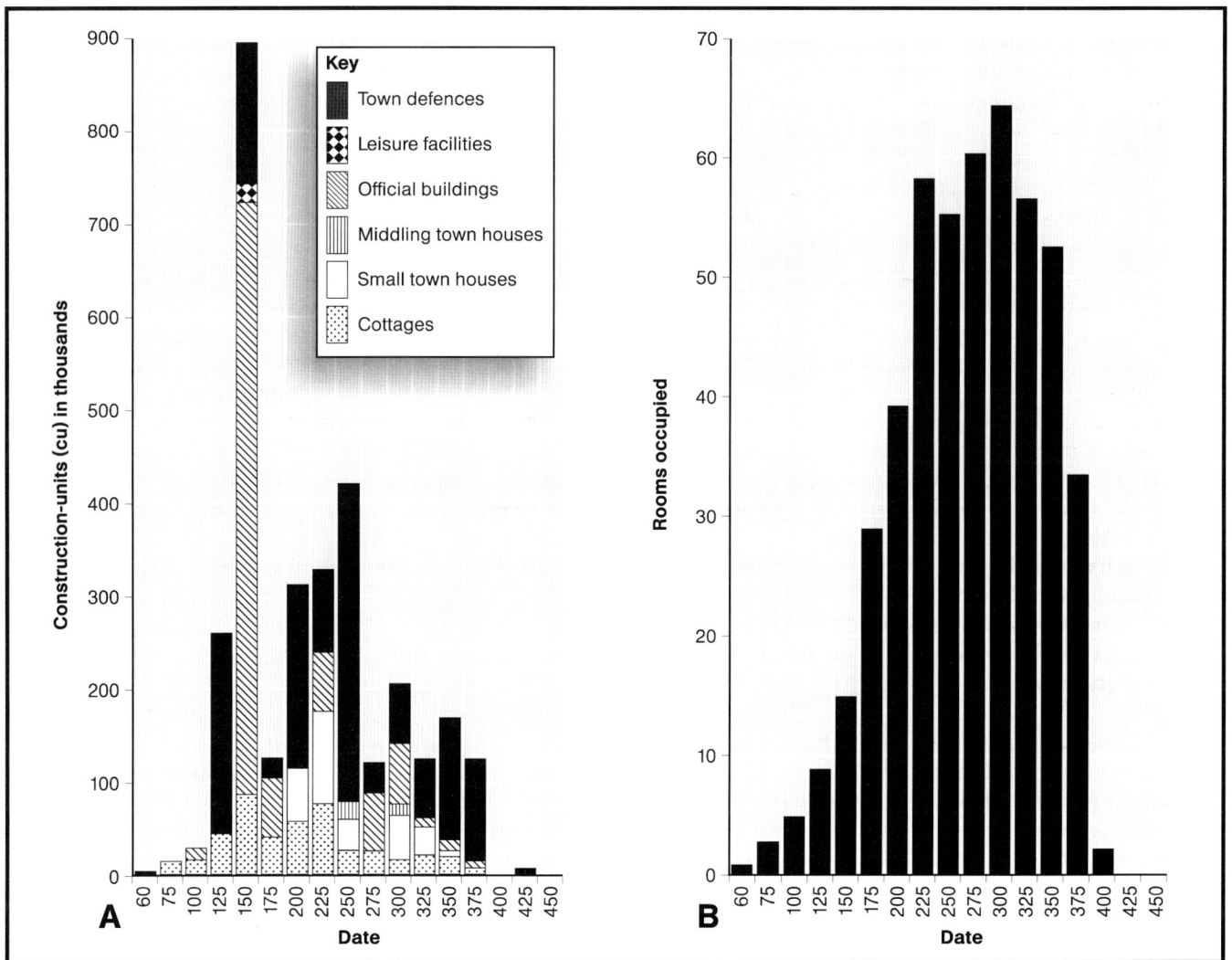

*Fig. 7.69a and b. Bar-charts to illustrate a) the estimated approximate proportions of different types of urban construction project through the Roman period; and b) the total numbers of rooms across the city which excavations have shown were occupied through the Roman period (source, Faulkner 2000, drawn by Dave Watt, copyright English Heritage).*

century, a few churches, but there is also plenty of evidence for private wealth, commercial activity, and conspicuous consumption until the latter part of the 4th century. A similar pattern appears in Italy at an earlier date as the local nobility became less available and towns less dynamic, but this did not necessarily mean an economic crisis (Whittaker 1995).

The economic context is one of increasing demands from Rome. The imperial coffers were under pressure from the costs of the army and the maintenance of the administrative and economic system, and this exerted pressure on the provinces to pay high taxes. Taxes were collected through the major towns, which for this reason alone had to be protected, although the 4th century is also the period when the smaller market towns in Britain also showed most economic vibrancy (Millett 1990, 143–51). The government dependence on an urban network (and vice-versa) is acknowledged in Esmonde Cleary's model of late Roman towns in Britain, a study well-informed on the economic realities of the imperial system (1993). The days of investment in most public works were largely over by the 4th century, and those public structures which had previously symbolised Roman urban culture – *fora*, baths, temples – were generally in terminal decline in the later part of the century, or in certain cases put to different use. The dominant physical structures were rather the city walls and the large town-houses. Outside Britain, churches were an additional feature from the late 4th century, but never had time to become so important here before the Roman withdrawal. Trading and manufacturing functions continued, and were in some cases facilitated by communications systems set up principally for administrative purposes.

What did this mean for Lincoln and what has the archaeological evidence to tell us? The present account supersedes an earlier discussion of the evidence (Jones 1993), taking into account more recent results from site work and analysis, as well as new interpretations. First of all, Lincoln's newly acquired capital status, the arrival of government officials with resources and requirements, and the corruption that went with this power, would have benefited the city more than those without this status. Moreover, their presence demanded a secure base – requiring strong fortifications, new residences, a certain standard of living, and maintenance of communications. The city's functions as a tax-collection centre and as a bishopric would have brought further benefits. As long as the system was maintained, Lincoln's survival and a measure of prosperity were guaranteed, and this prosperity in turn acted as an attraction for further settlers and traders.

## Public buildings

Whilst a considerable amount of evidence is available for late Roman occupation in the city, for the study of

some aspects it hardly represents a valid sample. Moreover, precise dating is also difficult, and there is the usual problem of residuality. It is true that new pottery types and coinage appear in the later 3rd century, but towards the end of the 4th century, there are serious dating problems, which are dealt with in the following section.

Probably the most costly undertaking was the refurbishment of the fortifications, involving the heightening, either by thickening or complete re-building, of the city wall, the creation of a single wide ditch and work at some of the gates, which included at least one new entrance (Figs. 7.8 and 7.33). These operations may have commenced as early as the late 3rd century in the Upper City (Jones 1980). The work was still in progress on the lower circuit after the mid 4th century, a length of over 2km in all (ed. Jones 1999). In places, particularly in the Lower City's southern walls, tombstones and architectural fragments were incorporated; an unusual phenomenon for Britain although it is also seen in the riverside wall at London now re-dated to the late 3rd century (Hill *et al.* 1980; Sheldon and Tyers 1983; Blagg 1983). Lincoln also differs from most other major cities in Britain in the absence of external semi-circular towers, except at the 3rd-century gate structures. The style of the later walls is generally conservative, and does not even resemble some of the other circuits in the region. This may argue against their construction by the army, but the closest parallel to the Lincoln style are forts on Hadrian's Wall and this might suggest that the army based in York was responsible for both. It is possible to link this huge investment with the city's elevation to capital status, and to see it partly as a symbol of Roman authority. Although many other towns were also building new walls, which could also provide refuge in case of crisis, the Lincoln enclosure was large compared with those at Ancaster, Horncastle, or Caistor, for example, and would have taken much greater manpower to defend. Perhaps the primary intention was to impress and to deter attack.

At East Bight on the northern defences, the late rampart extended over the street immediately inside (EB 80), but on the whole it does appear that the street system was maintained. At the two new gates in the lower circuit at the Park (P 70) and Saltergate (LIN 73d) resurfacing of the roads continued throughout the century. At the *forum* site (SP 72), a unit facing on to the street seems to have been used in the 4th century for metalworking then subsequently as a shop where cash was paid over. The public-baths east of Bailgate (CP 56) appear to have continued in use in the 4th century but not beyond about AD 350 (although the quality of the evidence for the late Roman period at this site is poor).

There is much uncertainty about other public buildings too. Amongst new edifices, we might expect to be able to identify a new church structure to house the newly-recognised Christian community, and the discovery of two churches of potentially episcopal character and of potentially late Roman date at the *forum* (SP 72) represents an archaeological find of the utmost importance (Fig. 7.70). As first interpreted, the second church was identified as that built by Paulinus in AD 628 and documented by Bede. The subsequent radiocarbon dating of the earliest graves, including some cutting into its wall-line, made this idea less supportable and introduced the possibility of a late Roman or Sub-Roman construction date, with various possible historical implications (Fig. 8.8). First of all, St. Paul was a popular dedication in the last few decades of the 4th century (Sullivan 1994). Nor is it impossible that burials should appear in this location at the end of the Roman period; burials began to appear within the walls of Roman towns from as early as the end of the 4th century, linked to the cult of saints, and their relics (Brown 1981, 4–5; Harries 1992; Galinié and Zadora-Rio 1996). Indeed it has been said that the acquisition of the relics could

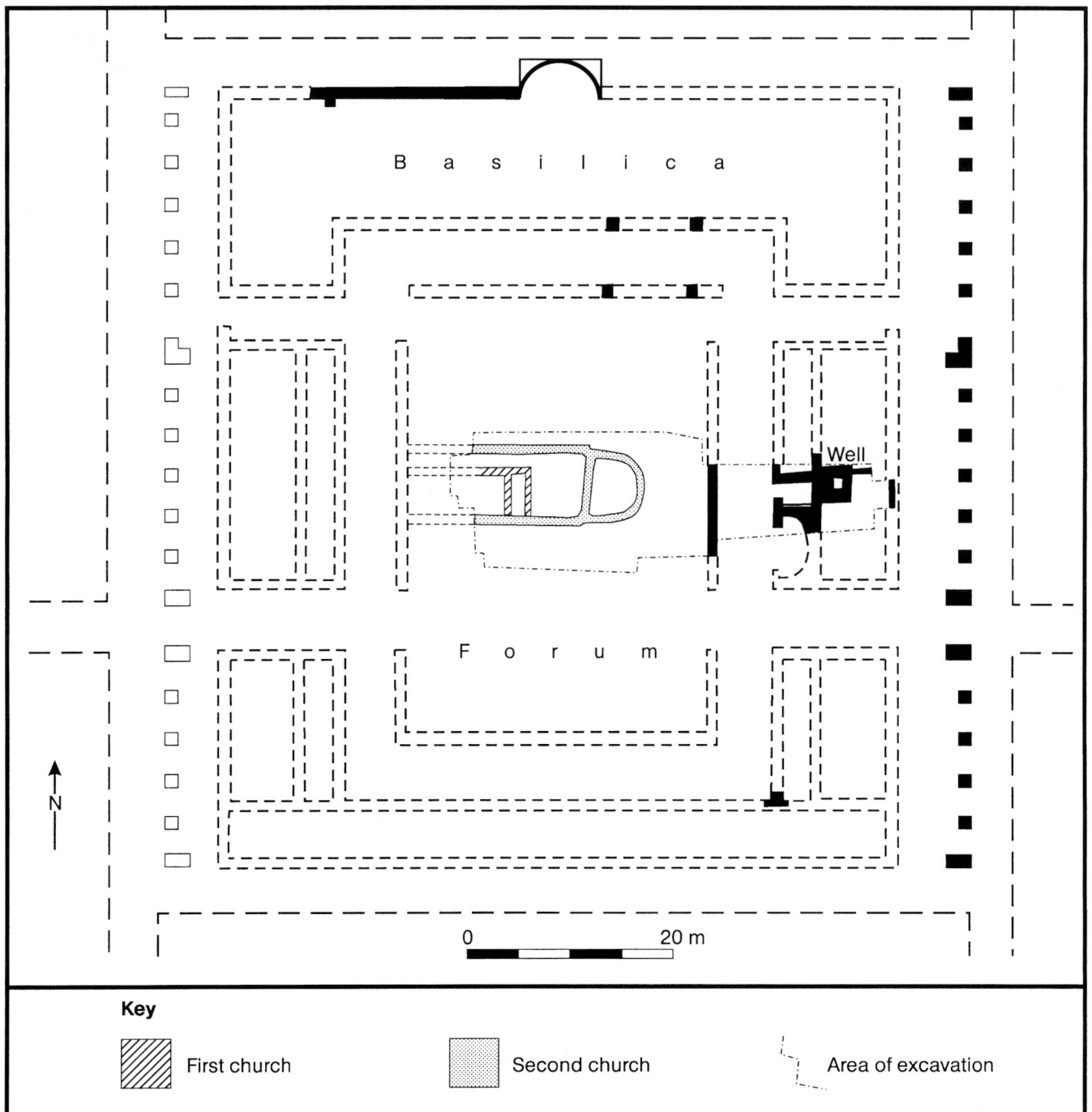

Key

First church          Second church          Area of excavation

*Fig. 7.70. Plan of the reconstructed* forum *of the late 2nd or early 3rd century, with locations of the two early church structures (perhaps of 4th-century date) superimposed (drawn by Dave Watt, copyright English Heritage).*

compensate to some extent for urban decline (Loseby 1992).

Although the phasing of the site is now fairly clear, we have yet to reach agreement on the dating of the respective phases and, whilst Dr Vince makes a case that the churches themselves are most likely to be of 7th-century date (p. 147–51 below), it is the view of this author that a late Roman or sub-Roman context must also be seriously considered for the first two phases of church building here. Such separate church structures did not become normal in Britain before the end of the 4th century, but despite the fact that they cannot be dated precisely, nevertheless the two successive timber structures built in the *forum* courtyard could belong to the very last decades of the Roman occupation and/or to the following century or so (Jones 1994b). A Roman date, especially one of about AD 400, cannot be dismissed lightly on the grounds of probability; we know that there was a bishop housed within the city at the time, who attended the Council of Arles in AD 314. Nor can it be said that the plan of the second church at the *forum* site is uncharacteristic of the Roman period; the broad nave with stilted apse and 'choir screen' here is very comparable with European examples of late Roman date – like that at St. Blaise at the Roman town of Ugium in Provence (Rolland 1951), dated to about AD 500. The plans of the churches do not help us to be more precise about the dating, however, as close parallels are found across Europe between the 4th and the 7th centuries (Jones 1994b). There are, admittedly, few close parallels for churches in the courtyards of *fora* – and most examples are in Turkey and North Africa (Jones 1994b; Potter 1995; Duval 1977).

Both of the Lincoln buildings could be seen, then, as churches, entered from the *forum* western portico. Their western ends lay beyond the limit of excavation, but presumably related to the intercolumniation of the surviving west portico of the *forum*. The earlier, rectangular building is much smaller than the more distinctive apsidal ended structure, which could have held at least a hundred worshippers. Both structures had chancel screens indicated by a post-in-trench construction, the earlier chancel being very short and square-ended, the second roughly semi-circular. What may have been a foundation deposit (of relics?) from a feature immediately west of the second church's screen, i.e. beneath the altar, gave a medial date of CAL AD 441 (Har 4177) (Fig. 8.8 No. 34). The only other item of dating evidence, a coin of Arcadius, cannot be directly associated with the church structure rather than use of the *forum* surface. The dating of the whole sequence is therefore to some extent floating, and has to be interpreted on grounds of probability.

So, nothing about the structures in the *forum* courtyard should rule out a late Roman date, and the key radio-carbon dates do provide a scatter of appropriate dates, both for the postulated 'foundation deposit' and for the burials cut into its robbed footings, which would be consistent with the building's con-struction in the late 4th century and its removal by the 6th century. However the evidence of these radio-carbon samples, although most persuasive, is not conclusive, and the alternative case, that the second church structure (at least) was erected in the 7th century has some points in its favour.

The discovery over recent years of a number of late Roman artefacts, including lead tanks, implying Christian ritual at nearby settlements, makes it more likely that a group of worshippers existed in Lincoln (Jones 1993, 138; Watts 1995). The bishop based at Lincoln may have visited these sites to carry out baptisms by the affusion method (pouring water over the head) as illustrated on the Walesby lead tank (Thomas 1985, 220–27; Painter 1999). Burial patterns of the 4th century are not easy to distinguish from those of the late 3rd century, although the 4th century tends to see more orderly cemeteries generally (Philpott 1991). Certainly there is little direct evidence of the impact of Christianity on burial rite, but the increasing number of inhumations as compared with cremations might indicate the influence of Near-Eastern religions on concepts of the afterlife and engender greater respect for the human corpse.

The earlier discovery of a building at Flaxengate (F 72), which was provisionally interpreted as a church (Thomas 1981, 168–9), remains problematical (Fig. 7.34). The masonry discovered in 1976 appeared to represent the NE corner of a possible aisled *basilica* with an apse, and floors either mortared or tessellated, and there are some high status finds from the site. Unfortunately, excavations on adjacent sites to south and west have failed to find what was expected on the basis of Thomas' reconstructed plan (1985, 199, fig 37). The scale of the remains found in 1976 do suggest a building of some scale, and a domestic structure seems unlikely. If the building is not interpreted as a church, another possible interpretation – that it served as a barn – should probably also be discounted on the grounds that the architectural detail is too grand. Some large late Romano-British barns are known, at Colchester for example (Crummy 1992, 33–4), and a massive building in London has been interpreted as either a possible Cathedral church or a granary (Sankey 1998).

An alternative interpretation might be as the governor's assembly or audience-hall, and this raises the whole question of the accommodation required by the new provincial administration. The question has been little addressed until recently, especially for Britain. A general survey of governors' palaces by Richmond (1969, 260–279) explored the available evidence for the whole imperial period, including the palaces of 1st-century legionary legates. The remains of that at Carnuntum on the Danube, where the imperial court was based AD 171–3, are of great interest, and included a large basilican audience hall. At Aquincum, where it resembled a great country house, the imperial complex allowed scenic views over the river, and a similar situation was found at Cologne. Those at Dura Europos (built in the early 3rd century) and Split (built for Diocletian's retirement in the early 4th century) were also adjacent to great expanses of water, but more tightly planned (Wilkes 1993). A huge complex was created at Trier for the late Roman base of the western empire, including a basilican audience chamber, which represented a rebuilding on a much larger scale of the 2nd-century procurator's residence. This structure formed merely one element of a whole area carved out of the city, including a new baths complex linked with imperial villas along the valley (Wightman 1985, 234–9). Elements of palatial structures still surviving in standing fabric have also been identified at Arles.

In a recent survey, Ward-Perkins (1998) draws attention to the fact that the Roman government was spending resources in favoured capitals, at the expense of other urban centres. There is now some evidence for this phenomenon, especially in the Eastern Empire, for example at Aphrodisias (Roueché 1989). Within this context Lavan (1999) has studied the physical impact of provincial status on urban centres in great detail, and notes examples of public expenditure by provincial governors. In some capital cities, such governors may have appropriated the civic treasury and even taken over the curial administration (Liebeschuetz 1992). Lavan has pointed out that governors also seem to have spent public resources on some non-capital cities, and would argue that it was only the presence of the imperial court that stimulated the release of huge investment.

There is little evidence for palace architecture to date from Britain, and of course it is questionable whether major new structures could be afforded. After all, three British bishops who attended the Council of Ariminium in 359 are recorded as having requested their travelling expenses (Thomas 1985, 197–8), although this evidence should be treated carefully (Esmonde Cleary 1989, 121). The building at one time considered to be the governor's palace in London is now interpreted differently (Milne 1995, 91–3; Wacher 1995, 92–4). On the other hand, Williams (1993) has provisionally identified a palace in London built by Allectus. A Severan Palace is thought to exist at York on documentary evidence, but this might be a reference to the residence of the legionary legate (Ottaway 1993, 62–3). Wacher (1995, 314–5) has suggested that the late wall dividing the forum into two at Cirencester may have been constructed to provide space for provincial administration. Lavan (1999), while accepting that the new governors from the time of Diocletian may have had to find accommodation within the existing administrative buildings, is not convinced that the reordering of the Cirencester *forum* was linked to the governor's presence. The alternative interpretation, as the boundary for a temple precinct along the lines of the *forum* at Nyon, seems unlikely (Rossi 1995) and Wacher's idea proposes an expedient measure which may have been necessary to accommodate the new officials.

At Lincoln, the only possible evidence to date for use of the civic centre by the provincial administration consists of the potential church(es) in the *forum* courtyard, but of course much more of the complex remains to be explored. It is, however, worth considering the possibility that the civic administration ceased to work, and that the site was subsequently handed over to the provincial governor who in turn passed it on to the bishop, as happened to the church on the site of the palace at Cologne (Brühl 1988). The proposed basilican hall at Flaxengate and the nearby late residence (excavated in 1945–6) terraced over earlier houses are other possible candidates. Unless they were subsequently collected for re-working, the finds of marble wall veneers and exotic glass vessels from the Flaxengate site do, however, hint at a high level of expenditure.

Nor should we forget that the Greetwell villa, even though not investigated under modern conditions, was exceptional for several reasons. The quality of its mosaics was such that they required imported craftsmen; the huge, almost unrivalled, scale of its main corridor – providing an impressive pavilion overlooking the Witham Valley – and the fact that the coins found at the site form one of the latest groups from the city. In this context, the recent suggestion that the villa at Woodchester near to Cirencester was also a palace (Smith 1997, 172–95) may suggest a parallel. There is no distinctive evidence that would identify such large, sumptuous villas as palaces, but given the nature of the late Roman bureaucracy, the Greetwell Villa is a good candidate for the governor's residence.

### Private residences and commerce

The presence of a number of well-appointed townhouses of some size – that at Spring Hill had at least twelve rooms, for instance – within both the upper and lower cities has been noted in the appropriate sections above (Fig. 7.71). Both the style of the mosaics (Rainey 1973, 108–10; Neal and Cosh 2002), and dating evidence for excavated structures, suggest that these residences of the urban elite reached their maximum development in the 4th century (Fig. 7.72). Some no doubt belonged to the local aristocracy involved in civic administration who were now competing with each other politically and economically, and investment in impressive reception areas was a more successful strategy than the earlier emphasis on funding public works (Perring 1991a). At least six large houses of late Roman date are known from the Lower City – in fact, apart from the principal street frontage, the hillside seems to have been covered largely by houses and their gardens. The point should be made, however, that the larger residences could always include a commercial element, if only by letting out their street frontages as shops.

There is also some evidence of contemporary

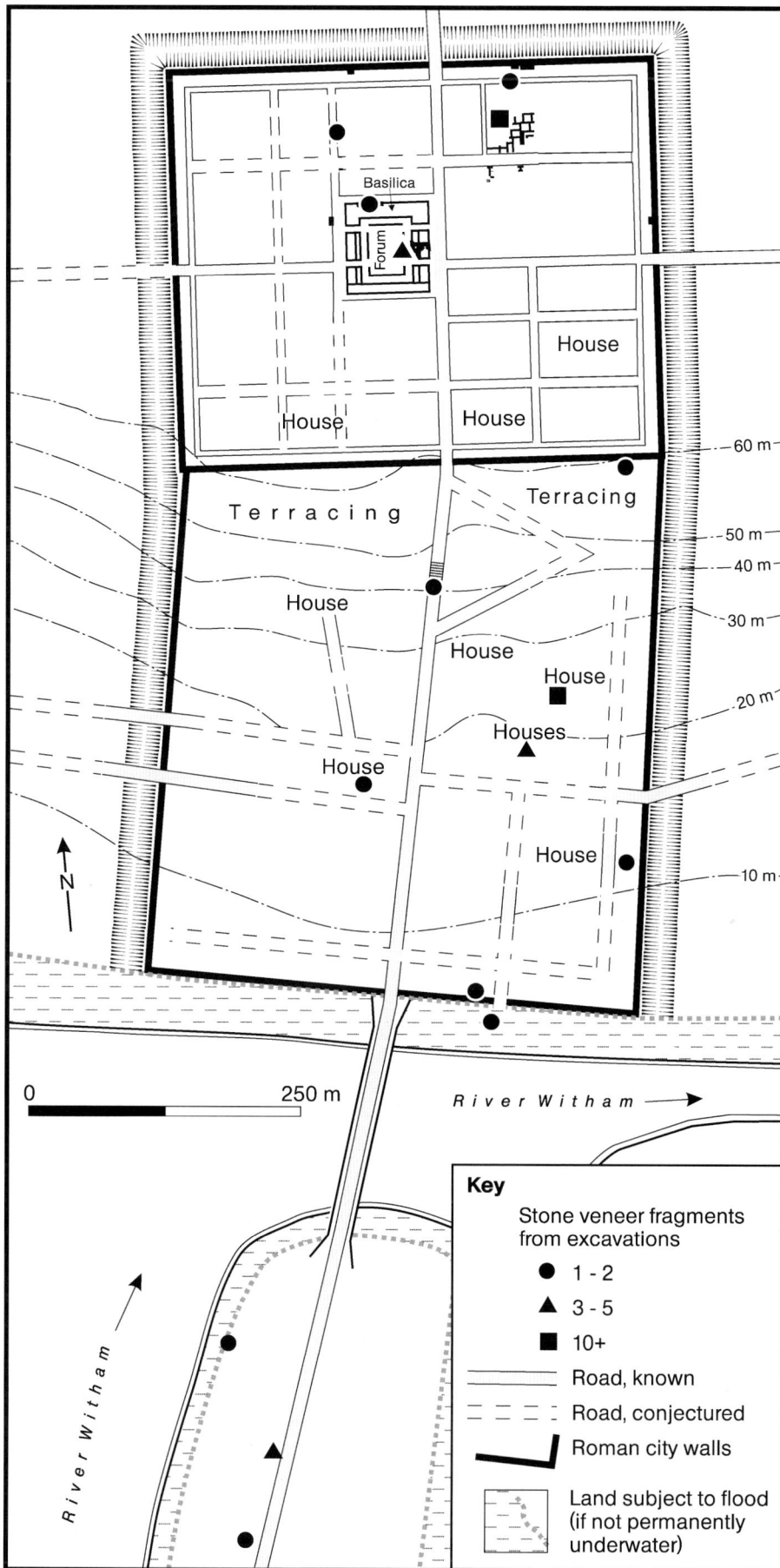

*Fig. 7.71. Distribution of later Roman town-houses and finds of wall veneers within the walled city (drawn by Dave Watt, copyright English Heritage).*

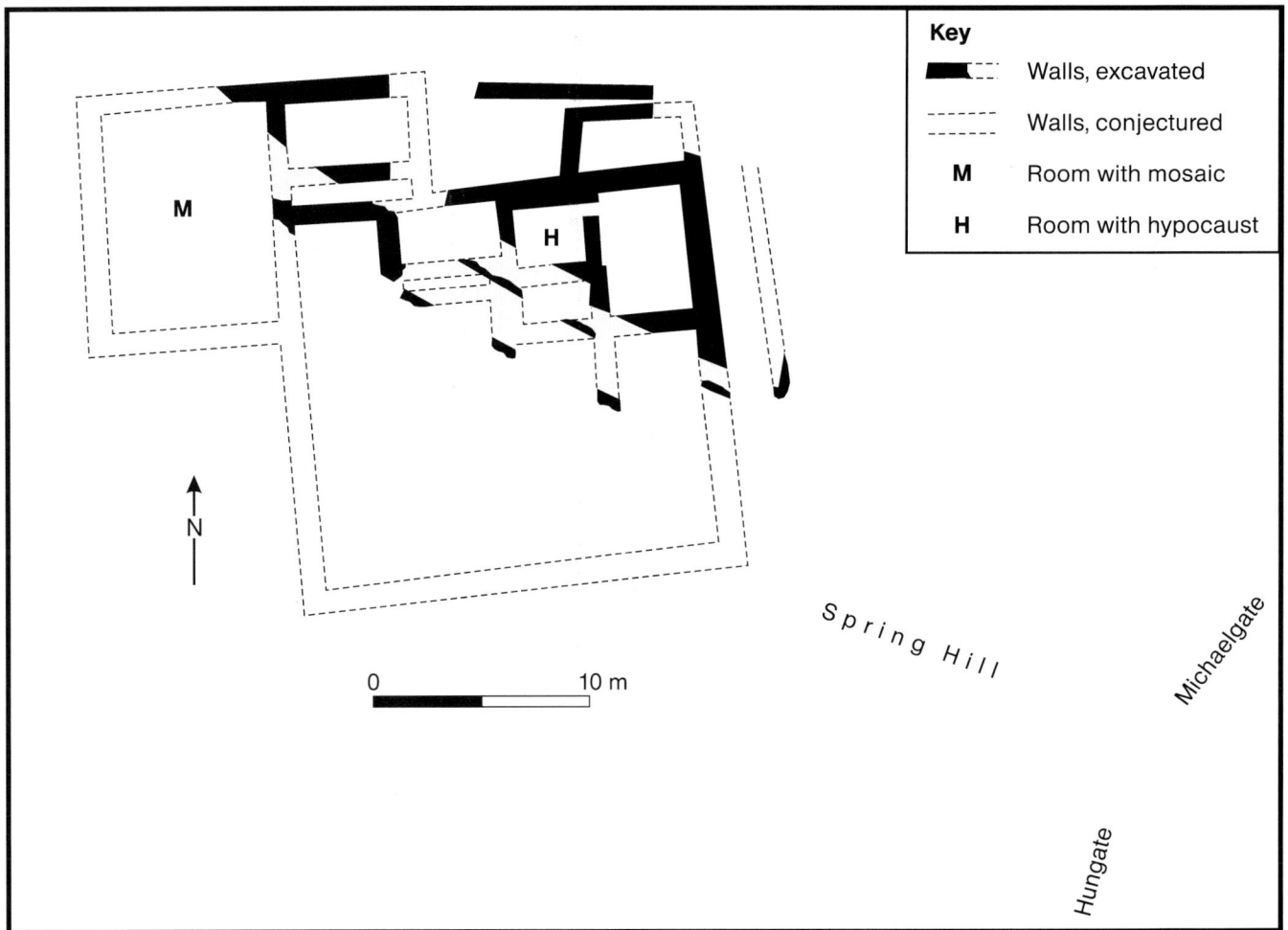

Fig. 7.72. Plan of late Roman town-house partly excavated on modern Spring Hill in 1983–4 (source, Snell 1984, fig.3 – drawn by Dave Watt, copyright English Heritage).

industrial activity, and several properties, which may have been primarily commercial rather than residential in nature, were still seeing expansion taking place in the 4th century; for example the buildings at West Parade (WP 71) acquired a rear extension at this time (ed. Jones 1999, 195–8). As we have seen already (p. 104–8 below), most properties occupied by artisans and devoted largely to their trades were actually situated along the roads outside the walls. The creation of the new commercial suburb to the south of the river may have involved relocating some traders, so facilitating further expansion of the intra-mural residences. There is some indication of abandonment at the fringes by the middle of the 4th century, for example at Greetwellgate east of the Upper City (WC 87) and at Chaplin Street in Wigford (CS 73), but most seemed to have survived well into the 360s or 370s, if not beyond.

A feature of some of the late Roman sites was further landfill, especially in the lower-lying parts of Wigford (SM 76; Z 86), and dumping was also found along the waterside with the construction of a new timber revetment (BWE 82; SB 85; WNW 88). We have already noted that these riparian operations may have been a response to a rise in the river-level, which, as we have seen, may have been the intended effect of major changes in the layout of the port (p. 100 above). But whether the landfill was a response to natural inundation, or part of an extensive hydrological engineering project, it implies a determination by the community to invest in future prosperity. The butchers' waste, stable manure, and grain pests which derived from these dumps indicate, as has already been said, organisation on a municipal scale, including controlled storage facilities (p. 101–3 above; Dobney et al. 1998), and this provides some of the best evidence we have for the city's continuing role as a major centre of processing the produce of the surrounding area until almost the end of the 4th century. Similarly, pottery production in the 4th century is not greatly different from that in the 3rd century, until the last decade or so, when it may have ceased with the ending of the money supply. Margaret Darling's and Barbara Precious's analysis does, however, show an increasing dependence on local Swanpool products throughout the period (forthcoming).

# The end of Roman Lincoln

## The city in transition

How the Roman urban settlement came to an end, or rather how it developed into a different type of settlement, by the mid 5th century, is the subject of this final section on the Roman period. The factors which led to this transformation have been the subject of several recent studies, and predictably for such an intractable period there are divergent views (Brooks 1986; Esmonde Cleary 1989; Higham 1992; Wacher 1995, 408–21; Jones M E 1996). Whether, as suggested by Wacher and Jones, factors such as disease and a native revolt were significant is difficult to prove. It is at least clear that the termination of coin supply at the beginning of the 5th century, severing Britannia from the imperial economic and taxation system, was the final nail in the coffin of its urban material culture.

To a different degree and at different dates, this phenomenon is of course found in other western provinces, although there has been some anxiety recently about referring to it categorically as 'decline', rather than as a 'transformation' (Liebeschuetz 1992; Cameron 1993, 129; eds. Christie and Loseby 1996; Bowersock 1996). The reasons for this may have much to do with political correctness, post-imperial perspectives and attitudes to 'progress', and to our changing concepts of civilisation. As our former concepts of 'civilisation' as something connected to classical, urban, models in Greece and Rome have been discarded, so we are now ready to accept that rural, barbarian, models of society are just as 'civilised' when viewed in their own terms, rather than against terms laid down by classical and neo-classical authors (Hingley 2000). Whatever value-judgements are placed on the period, we are principally concerned here with understanding the meaning of the archaeological evidence, which is difficult to date precisely after about AD 380, and its relationship to the scarce historical references. At least, there is now an acknowledged value in studying transitional periods, often dignified as 'social transformations', and a healthier respectability about this period, known as 'Late Antiquity' in some countries but not generally so in Britain (Esmonde Cleary 2000b; Jones 2001). It is clear that, in the Western Empire in general, terminal fault-lines are discernible in the late 4th century, caused and/or aggravated by serious problems on the frontiers, and that the empire had to accommodate some former enemies – 'barbarians' – in an attempt to survive. Some argue that internal political and social problems and climatic change within Britain were also major factors (Wood 1991; Jones M E 1996).

When and why all these changes occurred is a matter of continuing debate. Reece argues for a clear distinction between the east and west of Britain (1995), and this may imply that we should be comparing Lincoln with Colchester and York, but not, perhaps, with Gloucester. Our concern here is to elucidate the sequence at Lincoln and consider what it contributes to that debate. Gauging the extent and timing of the abandonment of buildings is, however, an exercise fraught with problems, owing to problems of dating the final occupation deposits – if indeed they survived subsequent disturbance (Steane and Vince 1993, 71; Faulkner 1994; 1996; 1998; Darling and Precious forthcoming ). Attempts to date the length of time for which occupation continued over several structural phases after that of the latest datable artefact using 'dead reckoning' have been made at Bath (Cunliffe and Davenport 1985) and Wroxeter (Barker *et al.* 1997), partly based on wear pattern. But a distinction must be made between surfaces which could easily be kept clean of artefacts – such as the public buildings at Bath and Wroxeter – and other contexts. Faulkner argues for an earlier termination date for certain buildings at Verulamium (1996, 88–91). In the process, he has highlighted the problem of dating site abandonment (1994, 102–3).

The dating evidence for the abandonment of sites investigated in Lincoln has been recently rehearsed (Jones 1993) but an update is in order. The coins and pottery are generally in agreement that some sites in the Upper and Lower Cities as well as the suburbs were being deserted between the mid and the late 4th century, and several buildings were demolished while others continued – and in certain cases structures were rebuilt. Quantitative analyses of coin loss (Mann and Reece 1983; Davies 1995) highlighted a 'high point' in the 360 or 370s, relatively later than other towns, followed by a sharp drop (Fig. 7.73). This might reflect the start of a serious contraction of the money economy from *c.*375 (Fig. 7.74). With the single and notable exception of the Greetwell Villa, most of the coins of the very late 4th century or the beginning of the 5th (House of Theodosius) were produced by two sites on the hillside at Flaxengate (F 72) and Hungate (H 83), and from the nearby riverside, and in general these finds are a clear indication that organised urban life, although more impoverished and reduced in scale, went on into the early 5th century. Activity was not merely reduced to this core area of the town, however. At one of the traders' houses in the southern suburb at least 500m south of the south gate (SM 76), the building was reduced in scale by the construction of a new back wall much closer to the street. The road surface adjacent to the river immediately east of the Ermine Street bridge (WO 89) received a new surface after the 380s, while at the lower west gate (P 70) the road through the gate was resurfaced around AD 400, with a coin of Arcadius (395–408) being found in the penultimate surface. By this date, however, dumping of rubbish – including material of about AD 390 – was allowed adjacent to the city wall, whereas previously the rampart alone had been used for dumping (Darling 1977; ed. Jones 1999, 10). More evocative is the gradual decay of the interval tower at West Parade (WP 71), which was used for the dumping of dead dogs. But unfortunately this process

et al, 1992), or as evidence for gardening compost being generated within pits at Rouen (Jaques Le Maho, pers. com.).

At Lincoln, several sites on the less steep, more southerly part of the hill where the deeper stratigraphy tends to be intact, and also in the southern suburb, have contained deposits which might be considered as dark earth (Vince 1990). They are not all derived from the same processes, but it is clear that some of them were dumped (Fig. 7.75). In certain cases, such dumping may have been related to the consolidation of the quaysides, in others it seems to act as a level platform between the ruins of stone walls so that timber buildings might be erected. The 'dark earth' deposits seem, if anything, to date to the last generation or so of the Roman period, i.e. between *c.*AD 375 and 410. They suggest continuing occupation of an urban nature, which is consistent with the large amounts of butcher's waste found at Flaxengate (F 72) within this material, implying the provisioning of a large, local, population. The fresh condition of the pottery, and its general level of residuality, as well as the absence of any impact by roots on animal bones, all militate against cultivation within the 'dark earth' deposits. Some of it appears to have been derived from nearby middens, and this implies both a substantial population (to create the middens) and also, perhaps, it may imply changes in the method of refuse disposal. Certainly it tends to suggest that the population had shifted within the settlement such that former dwelling sites were now used for rubbish disposal and vice-versa. The character of the Lincoln 'dark earth' deposits indicates subsequent weathering and biological reworking, as well as the impact of fires and, possibly, flooding of the valley and the growth of scrub.

Overall, the 'dark earth' deposits seem to mark the end of the large-scale town residences, and their replacement by a new community of lower architectural aspiration – Faulkner's 'shanty town' – and a more mixed economy. Unlike Northern Gaul (Halsall 1996), Britain had not been seriously affected by the invasions of the 3rd century, but it was not so well equipped to withstand the crises of the next century. The abandonment of the larger residences in Lincoln as the 4th century went on, was, perhaps, partly compensated for in Britain by renewed investment in rural villas, but this was only a temporary reprieve. At several Romano-British villas, the final phase of occupation appears to be at 'squatter' level, the original occupants presumably having departed westwards or across the Channel. The plethora of coin and other precious hoards dating to the last few years of official Roman control is witness to the flight of several very wealthy groups (Bland 1997). By contrast, the significant 'villa' site at Greetwell stands out from the norm of British examples, and its late coin series demands a special explanation, such as that it belonged to the machinery of state.

What evidence we have for the changes in economic

*Fig. 7.75. A deep deposit of 'dark earth', typical of the latest Roman deposits in Lincoln (from excavations at Hungate, west of Ermine Street – H 85). The scale is 0.5m long (photo and copyright, City of Lincoln Archaeology Unit).*

activity could be interpreted as a reflection of serious disruption in the Roman supply system from about AD 370, which some historians would attribute to the *barbarica conspiratio* (Wood 1991), but the causes were more complex. The effects included a greater reliance on using available materials, hence perhaps the spate of demolition and intensification of metalworking at Lincoln. Similar metalworking and demolition has also been observed in other towns, including York (Carver 1995, 187–95). In the meantime, the imperial officials and civic administration endeavoured to keep the system working. Surviving foci discernible at the forum and at the Greetwell 'villa' may have been connected with just such officials. There may have been other such establishments in the Upper or Lower City, and the Bishop's church, wherever it was, might have attracted a community around it (Potter 1995, 99–102). After about AD 410, however, the town could not survive for long, even in its reduced state, but there are indications that some sort of community did continue.

### Continuity of institution? Christianity and power

The existence of a bishopric at Lincoln and its physical manifestation in the 4th century have already been discussed briefly (p. 127–9 above). By analogy with practice elsewhere, Christian worship in Lincoln may have taken place in private houses until the resources and a site became available for a separate *ecclesia* (Wightman 1985, 286–296; Esmonde Cleary 1989, 34–40; Testini *et al.* 1989; Duval *et al.* 1991; Loseby 1992). Gallic bishops, at least, did not become wealthy and influential before the late 4th century, but subsequently there was a spate of construction work lasting for the next century or so. By contrast the evidence for 4th- and 5th-century churches in Britain is both slight and highly contentious. Most buildings proposed as churches have been subject to alternative interpretations, as can be seen when we compare Thomas's discussion of them (1985), with Potter's and Johns' (1992, 205–9). Nevertheless we have no reason to think that Bishops did not become powerful figures in the secular world, as Gregory of Tours shows they clearly did in Gaul. The centralisation of the Christian church and its insistence on dogmatic discipline might have appealed to the centralising tendencies of sub-Roman rulers, who were both more itinerant than their Roman predecessors and who attempted to focus local power in the hands of their personal kinship group. The presence of a bishop within the ruler's entourage would have ensured a level of control over sacral powers within his jurisdiction. This would have been difficult to maintain if such powers had been diffused through a great variety of disparate cults, with little or no relationship to each other and no hierarchy of dogma and control.

The extent to which Christianity was practised and flourished in Britain is also a problem fraught with difficulties, in view of the nature of the evidence (e.g. Painter 1999). Some artefacts which have previously been presumed to indicate Christianity do not necessarily do so; most that are convincing appear to come from East Anglia (Mawer 1995; Millett 1994a). Outside the 'intellectual classes' at least, early Christian practice in Britain incorporated some pagan beliefs and rituals (Potter and Johns 1992; Watts 1991). Moreover, the actual display of Christian artefacts could be inspired not so much by belief as social aspiration. Frend (1992) has suggested that the church in Britain atrophied in the later 4th century, but this is an argument *ex silentio*, and there is in fact an increasing amount of evidence for Christian practice, for instance, the growing number of lead tanks (Jones 1998). Further, it is quite justifiable to claim that the church continued to develop, especially in the west, and that this trend continued between the 5th and 7th centuries (Bassett 1992; Dark 1994). Certainly, in parts of Wales and of north-west Britain there was considerable expansion of Christian establishments at some locations. The site at Whithorn has been interpreted as a 5th-century monastery (Hill 1997) or as a bishopric surviving from the Roman period (Thomas 1985). Thomas also argues that St Patrick's career was an outcome of a Latin-reading, Christian elite originating in this part of Britain. This notion may be corroborated by recent, controversial suggestions that there exists cryptic epigraphic evidence for a literate Christian elite, which survived the end of the Roman occupation (Howlett 1994; 1997; Thomas 1994; 1998). From another perspective, new pagan temples were rare by the 4th century. Their popularity had probably peaked around 300, but although the reuse of their sites or their fabric may both reflect the official attitude and the 'Christianisation' of belief or display, it may also be a sign of the increasing influence of the Germanic peoples within the town, as much northern European paganism was not focused on buildings, but on natural phenomena.

In spite of the apparently impoverished nature of Romano-British Christianity, both materially and spiritually, it is reasonable to assume that there was a network of urban-based bishoprics before the Roman withdrawal. Each needed accommodation as well as a place of worship – perhaps provided by the civic or provincial administration, or by well-to-do adherents. The sequence of two successive timber churches, respectively about 15m and 25m long, and subsequent burials in the *forum* courtyard at Lincoln has already been noted (p. 127–9 above) (Gilmour 1979; Steane 1991; Jones 1993, 25–6; Jones 1994b). On the basis of the radiocarbon dating, we have argued that both structures could represent churches erected before the end of the Roman period, or alternatively in the sub-Roman period. In the case of the smaller, earlier church, at least, it may have been associated with the bishop, perhaps forming one element in an 'Episcopal group' of churches (Jones 1994b, 337–9). Such groups sometimes consisted of two churches, one of which might be used for relics or other purposes, a baptistery – presumably here using the nearby well in the east range – and accommodation nearby. It is possible that the civic *basilica* was converted to one of these churches. If the church in the *forum* was in fact Roman, its prominent site would suggest that it was part of Bishop's establishment. Lincoln's capital status may have enabled the Bishop to locate his Cathedral in such a prestigious position, especially in the political conditions of about AD 400. The Bishop might also order the construction of a church as a symbol of authority, and such an act might be just as plausible soon after the official withdrawal from Britain as before it. An alternative construction date in the 5th or 6th centuries is, however, just as likely for these two churches and is more consistent with the radiocarbon dates. Even an early 7th-century one is not yet out of the question, and is still favoured by some specialists (Sawyer 1998, 226–30, p. 147–51 below). Finally, then, we should recognise that, even if the church in the *forum* at Lincoln had its origins in the Roman period, we have no grounds for presuming that the sequence was interrupted with the ending of Imperial support for Britain. It is quite conceivable that one or more of the churches was constructed by a bishop himself acting as leader, or chief support to, a 'princeling' of a small community during the 5th century. There were after all continuing contacts between British and Gallic bishops, with hints of persisting Roman attitudes (Wood 1987).

Of course, the early 'Cathedral' may have lain elsewhere in the city, wherever there was more space or where space was made available – perhaps as a gift by a local aristocrat (Loseby 1992). One possibility is in the Lower City. While the basilican structure at Flaxengate is probably to be discounted, what may be a pre-Viking church complex, including the twin churches of St. Peter's with the nearby fountain available as a baptistery, might form another 'Episcopal group'. Here, however, there is no evidence for any form of church before the 8th century, and that evidence is itself highly debatable (p. 154–6 below).

### The Roman legacy

A surviving community attempting to maintain a Roman identity appears to be reflected by the almost complete absence of evidence for early Anglo-Saxon penetration into the city (Myres 1986, 177–82; Eagles 1979; 1989; Leahy 1993, 36). Exceptional finds which might cast light on the question of continuity include a handmade vessel from the Greetwell 'villa' (Myres 1946, 87–8) and another from the flue of one of the Swanpool kilns. The latter was recently considered to show that the industry continued to operate until the 6th century (Dark 1996, 58–9), but it is unrealistic to propose such a radical idea on such slight evidence. Although the amount of 6th-century pottery from the city is no longer negligible, it cannot be taken to imply continuity, when the urban population, and with it the mass market which the kilns had served, had clearly been so low for a century or more. How quickly the city was incorporated into the emerging Anglo-Saxon kingdom of Lindsey is one subject of the next chapter.

The Roman occupation of Lincoln passed on a fortified site dominating the effective communication routes, with some surviving buildings as well as decaying ruins, which was useful both as a symbolic base and as a refuge. Much of the former city would have reverted to waste ground. Whilst we know too little of the political structure of the 5th century, most authorities agree that there was a return to a tribal or kin-based society, whose leaders may have found the former capital city expedient for legitimising their power (Wilmott 1997; Phythian-Adams 1996). This widespread transformation saw forms of display other than towns and trade at market sites used to maintain social and military stability and to cement political alliances (Carver 1993, 1997). In this new world it is entirely possible that the physical survival of the *forum-basilica* at Lincoln provided not only an ecclesiastical focus but a political centre too, and that the persistence of the Roman name marks it out as always having had a 'central place' function. Leahy (1993, 38) speculates that a *tyrannus* descended from Germanic mercenaries kept the incoming Anglo-Saxons out of Lincoln and its immediate surroundings for several decades, but this proposal is entirely without archaeological support as yet. Evidence for continuing occupation at former Roman sites in Britain is increasing, but remains problematical. For the mass of people we may be sure that a subsistence life style continued, whether within the town walls or in rural settlements. The mass-market economy allowing easy access to a range of material goods was at an end.

# B.  The *Colonia* Era – The archaeological agenda.
## An introduction to the Research Agenda Zone entries (on CD-Rom)

### David Stocker

The traditional view, which held that urbanism in Roman Britain was a mechanism frequently initiated by the foundation of a military base, and that a town inevitably developed from the *canabae* of the fort, has been challenged by several writers in the last twenty years (e.g. Millett 1990, 65). In our research agendas for the Prehistoric and Roman Military Eras, above, we have started to move towards a different explanation of for the establishment of urbanism at Lincoln. We have indicated that we are only now starting to understand that Lincoln's importance as a tribal ritual centre was an important (perhaps the dominant) factor in the foundation of the Roman fortress. In the *Colonia* Era then, logically, we should go on to ask whether it was this ritual importance, alongside the military base

and its associated secular settlement, which enabled a form of urbanism to become established here.

Martin Millett has warned against our seeing all *Coloniae* as directly comparable site types (1999, 192–4) and, in the *Colonia* Era, we can follow the development of Lindum's distinctive ritual importance, alongside many more conventional domestic and economic characteristics of urbanism. Consequently, in compiling the research agenda for the *Colonia* Era it seemed appropriate to lay stress on the need to investigate the ritualistic backgrounds to many aspects of the *Colonia*'s archaeology in future work. In doing so, of course, we can reveal connections and understandings which have not been made before, but also, in approaching domestic and economic questions from this unaccustomed angle, we are forced to view old certainties in a new light.

The archaeology of the Roman city in the *Colonia* Era demonstrates, of course, life-styles in which ritual, commercial and other motivations were inextricably intertwined. Even so, archaeologists coming from the modern secular world have been inclined to separate these inextricably linked motivations and to pigeon-hole sites and activity in the city into two distinct categories; those which retain evidence for, and the setting of, 'ritual' activity (usually labelled temples) or those which demonstrate a purely 'utilitarian' motivation. Our distinctively modern segregation of motivations into either 'ritual' or 'secular' seems easy to apply to the Roman period, and it may be that this apparent ease of segregation has appealed particularly to post-Enlightenment scholarship. However, the impression that the Romans compartmentalised their lives so strictly into adjacent but unconnected 'ritual' and 'secular' spheres is an interposition of modern scholarship. The Romans did not segregate motivations in such ways. To the Roman citizen of the *Colonia*, arguably, the distinction between 'public' and 'private' motivation and activity would probably have been more meaningful, than that between 'ritual' and 'secular'. Much of Roman 'public' life was highly ritualised, although it would be misleading to think of 'private' life as being 'more secular'.

As it happens, Lindum provides a very useful example for the study of these interrelationships between 'ritual' and 'public', 'private' and 'secular' spheres of Roman life. Within the city there were clearly buildings and areas more-or-less exclusively devoted to one aspect of life rather than the other, but there are also many zones of the city where the two motivations jostle each other for prominence. Through time, the structures of Roman Lindum may demonstrate a shift in motivation from the 'public' (expressed most obviously in the *forum* itself and many other public buildings) to the 'private' (expressed in the increasing sophistication of private houses, for example). Such a shift in motivation, some might argue, is also demonstrated in the change from expressions of 'public' ritual in the official temples towards the more 'private' rituals associated with Christianity.

This exchange between Lindum the economic centre and Lindum the sacred centre, already noted as an important aspect of the Military Era, has also informed much of the discussion leading to the identification of the 30 RAZs for the *Colonia* Era (which can be accessed on the CD-Rom). First, a group of 12 RAZs has been identified in which the 'public' or 'ritual' motivation is clearly dominant over all others:

7.15 The *forum*
7.16 The baths
7.17 The aqueduct
7.18 The sewer system
7.19 Springs and pools on the hillside
7.20 Temple complexes in the Lower City
7.21 Possible temple complexes on islands in the lake
    7.21.1 The possible Wigford island temple
    7.21.2 Potential religious site on Hartsholme
7.22 Upper Ermine Street
7.23 The Greetwell villa
7.24 Cemeteries
7.25 The late pre-Roman iron-age ditch system

Not surprisingly, this group of sites and areas contains many of the most famous, and most characteristic, archaeological features of the later Roman city – demonstrating, presumably, that Roman urbanism has been characterised in the past by its ritualistic and public buildings, rather than by its more 'private' or 'secular' ones. But the debate between 'public' and 'private' function in the later Roman city cannot be restricted to motivations for the construction of individual buildings. It has, also, to confront our whole concept of urbanism in the Roman period. The accepted model of the early city as a large, commercially oriented, conglomeration of more or less autonomous individuals, representing all classes and activities in society, owes a great deal to the experience of later Western European urbanism in the Renaissance and in the 19th century. But although this 'Liberal' model may be applicable to many southern European cities of the Roman period, it is not so clear that there were many such cities in Britannia. Londinium may well have been such a place but increasingly excavation, even at major cities such as Colchester, is showing us that urban centres, laid out in imitation of Rome itself in the 1st century had become, by the 4th century, little more than defended enclaves of a governing elite. The remarkable thing about 3rd- and 4th-century Colchester is not so much that it possessed a group of fine, classically-inspired, 'public' and 'ritual' buildings, but that these seem to have been the only buildings of any sort within the walls, apart from the houses of the officials who maintained the cult. The city may not have been a free-standing, self-reliant, community at all – it might be more accurately characterised as an 'administrative village' (Reece 1980) – a sort of shrine at which 'government' itself was celebrated.

Government itself, of course, was the whole *raison d'être* of the later Roman city. Although the city might have an economic function as the meeting place at which it was ordained that markets should be held, such markets could have been held there precisely because of the symbolic importance of the place, and not necessarily because there was a large population requiring this service. In this respect it might have functioned more like some early medieval *wics*; as a licensed market where traders were gathered together, temporarily, at places where political power was symbolised. Roman traders were certainly called to the city to ensure that their appropriate economic dues were paid to the Imperial power, but did they necessarily live there? Such tax-collection was the main business of the Empire, and this function was represented in physical form by the buildings of the City itself. Certainly the implication of both the good supply of late Roman coinage commented on by Mr Jones (above) and of its abrupt termination in the early 5th century, would be that Lindum was a focus for fiscal affairs, but not necessarily economic ones. City buildings of the late Roman Empire, then, had a symbolic and 'public' role to fulfil. This may have been true even of the so-called 'private' houses of the city's officers who serviced the Imperial governmental structures represented by the 'public' buildings, and so, strictly, we should ask whether late Roman towns like Lincoln were not more like large ritual sites than large settlement sites. We must ask whether late Roman Lincoln, then, might not be viewed more like a large walled monastery; a community dedicated more to the maintenance of the concept of the Roman *Imperium*, than to any other end. Certainly viewing these sites in this way would help our understanding the transition from the 'towns' in the 4th century to the 'monasteries' that many of them became in the 7th century.

It would be convenient to assert that research into gender issues in Lindum is simply an aspect, or a reflection, of the debate about 'public' and 'private' space. But the fact is that none of the research which has been undertaken here so far has investigated any gender issues at all. The military background to the foundation of the *Coloniae* must have resulted in an essentially male 'public' arena (Millett 1999, 196), but even if the women and children were invisible in the 'public' realm, their presence should be detectable in the 'private' sphere. We need to look at some of our information about 'private' space in a more sophisticated way to see if it is, in fact, gendered. In practice, however, the greatest progress in gender studies might be made most easily in study of the cemeteries (RAZ 7.24).

Our thinking about the dominance of 'public' buildings and structures in later Roman Lincoln has helped us to identify a second group of ten RAZs, in which 'public' and 'private' aspects of life in the later Roman city seem to be more interrelated. In these RAZs the interactions between ritualised 'public' behaviours and less ritualised 'private' ones can be studied, and we can ask to what extent the city really was a functioning town, as opposed to a symbol of Empire with its necessary support systems.

7.8  Quayside east of High Bridge
7.9  Riparian deposits
7.11 Housing areas
     7.11.1 Houses within the Upper City

7.11.2 Suburban development north and
       west of the Upper City
7.11.3 Suburban development east of the
       walled city
7.11.4 Houses within the walled Lower
       City
7.11.5 Houses within the southern
       suburb
7.12 The defences
7.13 Stamp End causeway
7.14 Area of *centuriation* around the city

To investigate the relationship of 'public' to 'private' space further we should compare our later Roman town-houses with surrounding villas. If our distinctions between 'public' and 'private' space in the town have any validity, then the villas should represent a much greater level of seclusion and a privatisation of space. We might expect even the most 'private' of houses to have filled a 'public role' in the town, even if it was merely through the external display of status relative to buildings round about. Whereas, in the countryside there was, presumably, no obvious need for such competitive displays and accommodation could be more truly 'private'. Unfortunately, the only example of a villa within the city boundary, at Greetwell, is evidently far from typical and may not be a 'villa' at all in any helpful sense (RAZ 7.23). Work in the county beyond the District boundary can help us here and future explorations of nearby villa sites could make an important contribution by comparing their results with the 'private' city houses.

The final group of eight RAZs we have defined for this Era can cast light, primarily, on the economic background to, and on economic motivations within, later Roman Lincoln, and by definition, most of them are critical to our understanding of the relationships between the city and its surrounding countryside. They too have an important role to play in our understanding of urbanism in the city, as, handled carefully, results from future work here should inform the debate about whether the late Roman town was really an economic dynamo for the surrounding territory, or more of a 'shrine' to the concept of imperial government.

7.1  Roads entering the City
7.2  Newark Road bridgehead
7.3  Industrial belt south-west of the city
7.4  Kilns
     7.4.1  Racecourse kiln and associated
            industrial zone
     7.4.2  Technical College kiln
7.5  Potential industrial area around South
     Common
7.6  Upper Witham valley
7.7  Newport 'farm'

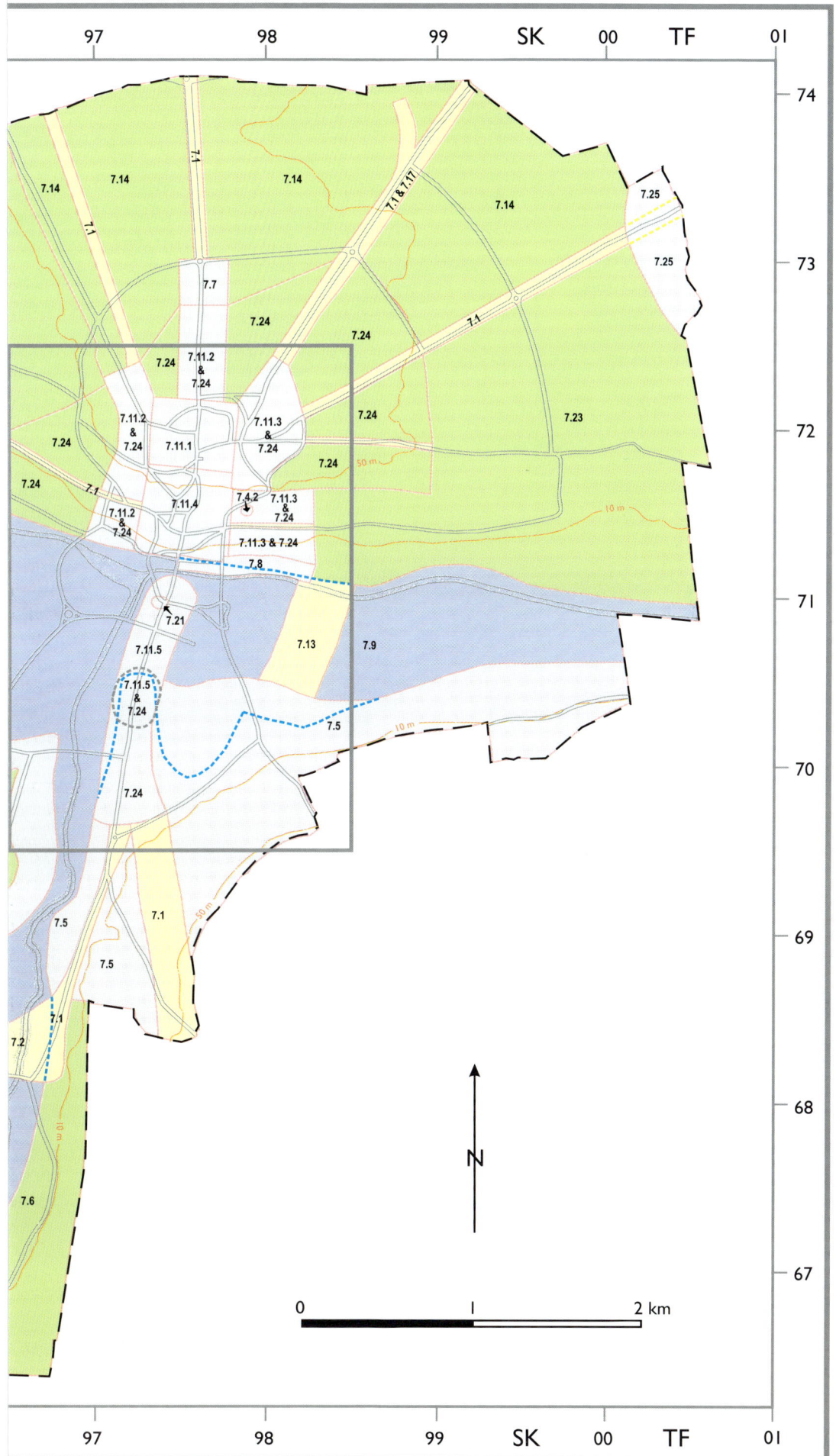

*Map 3. Research Agenda Zone locations for the Roman* Colonia *Era – See CD-Rom for details (drawn by Dave Watt, copyright English Heritage and Lincoln City Council).*

98

7.1
&
7.17

7.24

7.11.2
&
7.24

7.11.3
&
7.24

7.1

7.12

72

7.16

7.1

7.11

7.1

7.15

7.11

7.12

50m

7.12

7.22

7.11.4 & 7.19

7.4.2

7.11.3
&
7.24

7.11.4

.20

7.1

10m

7.11.3 & 7.2

7.20

7.8

7.9

71

7.13

7.5

70

N

7.5

10m

1 km

50m

98

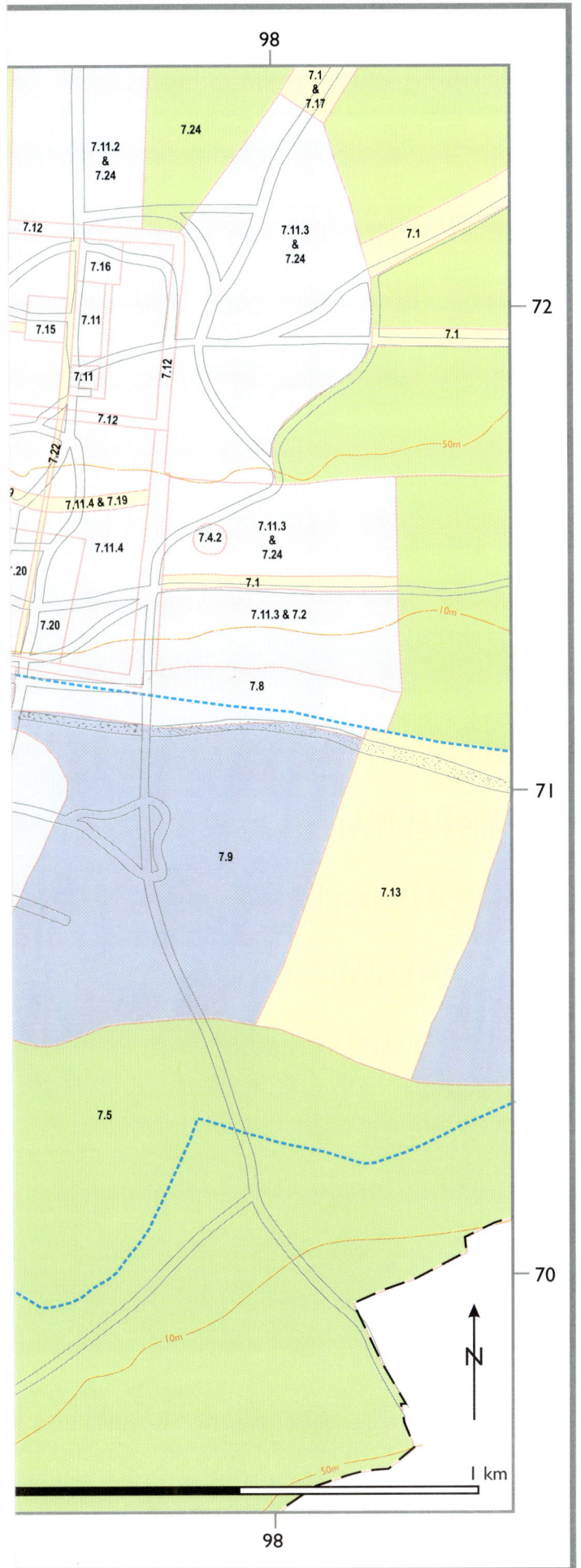

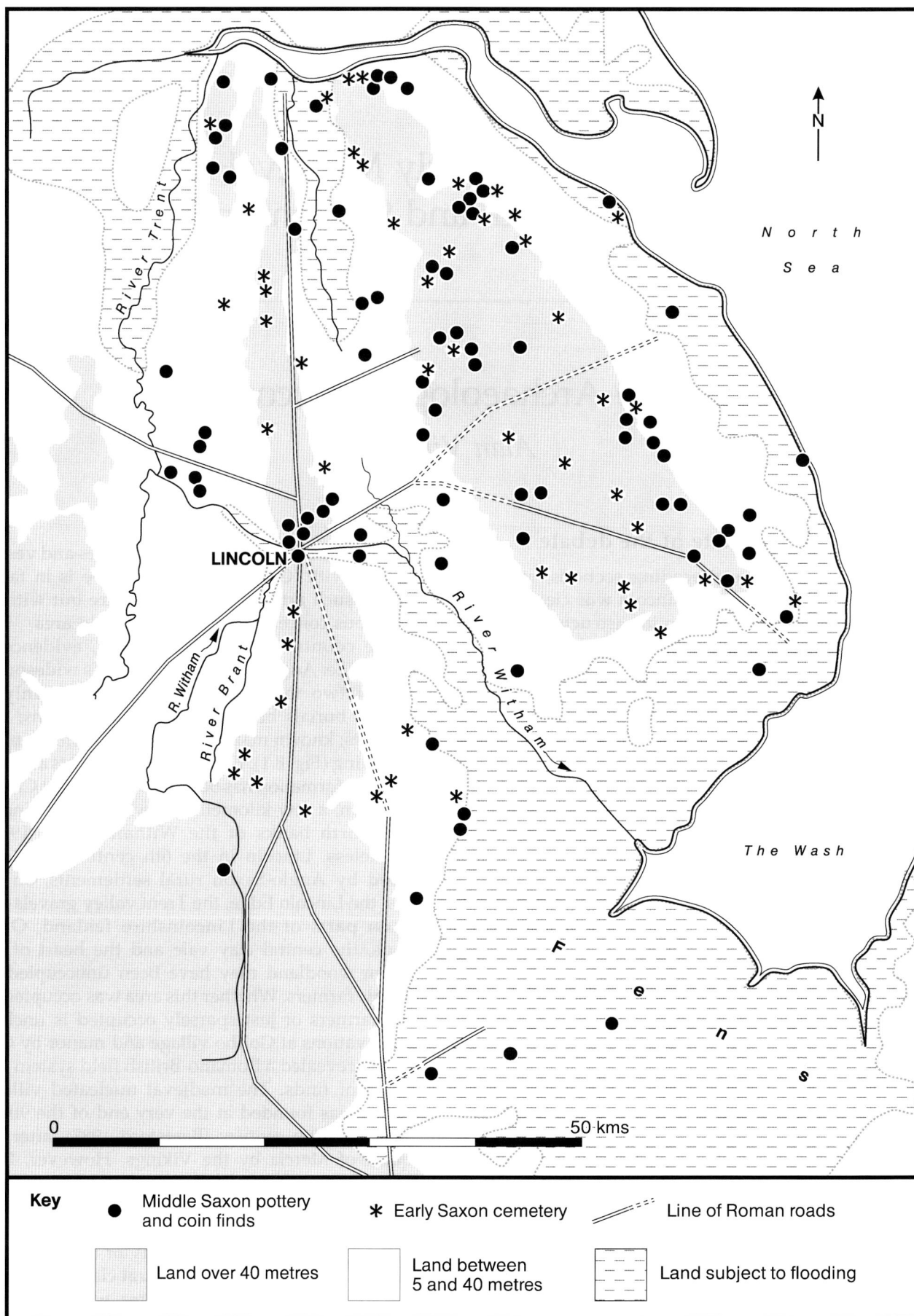

*Fig. 8.1. Features dated to the period between the 5th and 8th centuries in Lincolnshire (drawn by Dave Watt, copyright English Heritage).*

vale, therefore, and other areas of clay vale such as the Trent valley, may have been essentially woodland landscapes whose resources were mainly exploited by agricultural settlements on the surrounding lighter soils, or they may have been waste, or occupied by descendants of the Romano-British farmers. It is worth noting that the hagiography of St Guthlac states that when the saint first came to the island upon which Crowland Abbey was later built, it was haunted by demons who spoke in Ancient British (Stocker 1993). There was therefore an association in the minds of the hagiographer's readers between British and marginal areas. Even if there were British enclaves in the surrounding countryside, it is still not certain that they would have owed allegiance to a British authority based in Lincoln rather than being subject to Anglo-Saxon lords. Nevertheless, should a British Christian community have survived in the ruins of the Roman city then it must have been supported in some way by a larger community beyond the city walls.

By the end of the 7th century, or at the latest early in the following century, Lincolnshire had become Christian – to the extent that burial using pagan rites had ceased and there is evidence for the existence of Christian communities both living the monastic life and ministering to the people (*Ibid.*). Whilst it is conceivable that some of the latest Anglo-Saxon cemeteries may have continued in use into the early 8th century, no artefactual evidence has yet been produced to document this. Consequently, archaeological evidence for this period is almost entirely from settlements, although excavation in Lincoln itself has revealed two cemeteries which were probably in use at this time, one in the centre of the Upper City and the other in the south-eastern quarter of the Lower City (SP 72, LIN 73e–f). With the exception of a very few excavated sites, such as those at Flixborough (ed. Loveluck forthcoming) and Normanby-le-Wold (Addyman and Whitwell 1970) this evidence is almost entirely in the form of potsherds, metalwork and coins. Unfortunately very little of this material is as yet fully published, since much has been discovered through the activities of metal detector users, rather than through archaeological fieldwork.

Consequently, one might expect that we could recognise settlement in Lincoln both in the earlier part of this era, colloquially known as 'the pagan Saxon period', and in the later part (the middle Saxon period) through the presence of artefacts whose general character and range is known from a number of sites in the surrounding countryside. Such finds have, indeed, been recovered from in and around the city of Lincoln, but in such small quantities that they really only emphasise that whatever was happening in the city was extremely localised and small-scale. Similar patterns of almost complete abandonment have been found in other Roman cities, such as York and London. In both these cases, however, it is now known that there was a thriving community in the vicinity, but

that this community was living *outside* the Roman walled city. In the case of York, this community is known from excavations at Fishergate, downstream of the city (Kemp 1993) whereas in London it was situated upstream, stretching back from the Thames between Charing Cross to Fleet Street (Vince 1990b). Both the York and London settlements had contemporary place-names incorporating the element -*wic* – *Eorforwic* and *Lundenwic* – and much has been made of the existence at Lincoln of the suburb of Wigford, whose first element is clearly shown by medieval written sources to have been *Wic*- (Cameron 1985, 45). Further comparison between London and York indicates that the latter's trading settlement must have been on a much smaller scale, and of shorter duration, than that along the Strand, and it is also likely that any equivalent settlement in the Lincoln area would have been smaller and later in origin than that at *Lundenwic*.

Nevertheless, there is evidence that such a river port did exist in the Lincoln area – in the Trent valley at Torksey. Finds of middle Saxon metalwork and coins have been found by metal detector users to the north of the medieval town (Sawyer 1998, 197, 260), which was itself already a centre for pottery production in the late 9th or early 10th century (Barley 1964; 1981). Whilst many of these are 'contact period' finds, which could have formed an element of Viking spoils, there are five 'Series E' *sceattas* from 'Torksey' recorded in the Early Medieval Coin Database (*EMC* 2001). It may be that the existence of a pre-Viking trading settlement on the Trent explains why it was at *Tiowulfingcastre* (i.e. perhaps the former Roman settlement at nearby Littleborough) that the people of Lindsey were given their mass baptism by St Paulinus in the 620s, and why it was that the Viking army over-wintered at Torksey in 873/4 rather than at Lincoln. The close connection between this area of the Trent valley and Lincoln is reflected in the evident status of Torksey in the later 11th century in *Domesday Book* (eds. Morgan and Thorn 1986, T1). There, it is stated that Torksey burgesses paid their geld at Lincoln, amounting to a fifth of the total. This proportion is in accord with the number of burgesses recorded, 213 out of a combined total of 1183, or 18%. Clearly for some purposes the two settlements were treated as one and, since Torksey at that time was in the hands of the Queen rather than the King, this is unlikely to have been a recent, late 11th-century, arrangement.

Much of the interest in Lincoln between the 5th and 9th centuries, therefore, lies in assessing the likelihood of an, as yet undiscovered, extra-mural trading settlement on the Witham and in trying to second-guess where such a settlement might be (Fig. 8.2). Meanwhile, a second strand of interest is the role of Lincoln as an ecclesiastical centre. In the 4th century, Lincoln was one of four bishoprics in the British provinces, which were presumably allocated one per province. Elsewhere in the Empire, it was often the Cathedral and bishop's palace rather than

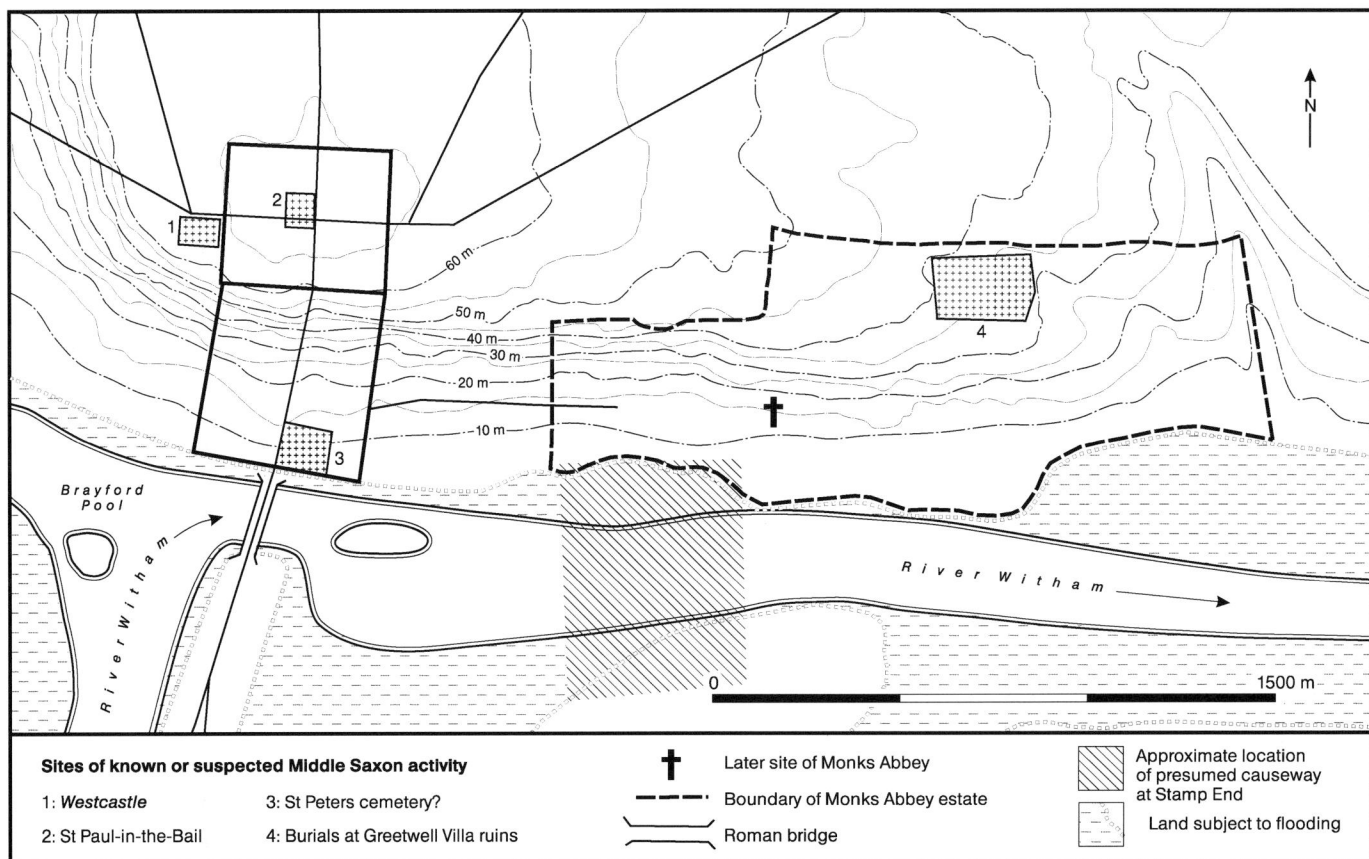

*Fig. 8.2. Identified and suspected sites of the period between the 5th and 8th centuries (drawn by Dave Watt, copyright English Heritage).*

the walled Roman city which formed the focus for later settlement and around which medieval towns grew (as at Tours and Xanten – Galinié 1988; Janssen 1988). No such pattern has been detected in England, although it has been considered at Verulamium/St Albans. However, it is at present thought that the medieval town of St Albans is a 12th-century foundation and that until this date the focus of settlement remained the old Roman town (Niblett and Thompson forthcoming).

Since the seat of the bishopric was transferred from Dorchester-on-Thames to the minster church of St Mary of Lincoln in the early Norman period, the antiquity of the site of the new Cathedral cannot be presumed. The move itself, however, was merely a reversion to an earlier pattern, since the bishopric had only been administered from Dorchester as a result of the acquisition of Lincoln by pagan Vikings in the mid 9th century. It is quite possible that St Mary was chosen for the site of the Norman Cathedral because of historic associations with the pre-Viking bishopric, but it cannot be assumed that this was the case, and other potential sites for the pre-Viking Cathedral have been put forward. It has also been suggested that Lincoln's bishop actually had two or more churches

(based on the evidence of a single charter) or even that the nature of 7th- and 8th-century dioceses was so different from those of later times (or contemporary times in continental Europe) that we should not be looking for a Cathedral site, as such, in any case (Gem 1993; Stocker 1993). Another clue to the ecclesiastical provision of Lindsey is given by a lost inscription, recorded by Bede in his *Liber Epigrammatum*. This inscription is said to have been set up by bishop Cynebehrt (*c*.720–734) in a church (*basilica*) dedicated to an apostle within the town (*urbs*) that is the mother seat of the bishop and his successors (*Ibid.*; Everson and Stocker 1999, 306–7). Most scholars agree that Lincoln is the likely site for this inscription but the inscription does not specifically state that the dedicated church is itself the bishop's seat, indeed, its wording lends support to the model of the bishopric being served by several churches.

Four main contenders for the site of the bishop's churches have been put forward: first is that of St Mary's church, whose remains presumably lie under the nave of the medieval Cathedral. The most convincing strand of argument here is that certain medieval churches in the county of Lincolnshire were obliged to pay a tithe, 'Mary Corn', to the minster. Such obligations often resulted from the recipient church having been, at one time, the mother church of the donor. Such relationships could either be between minster churches and their Cathedrals or between more junior churches ('proto-parish churches') and their local minster church. In either case, St Mary's minster in Lincoln would appear to have been of higher status than those around it. But, as 'Mary Corn' was collected across Lincolnshire and not just within Lindsey, it seems likely that it dates from after the foundation of the county around the year 1000 (Owen 1971, 37–8; 1984; 1994, 12). The giving of 'Mary Corn' was not of comparable antiquity to other English cases and could have even originated in the later 11th century.

The second contender for the site of the early bishop's church is St Paul-in-the-Bail. Early antiquarian speculation had it that this church was originally dedicated to St Paulinus, who converted the people of Lindsey in the early 7th century and whose church, according to Bede, writing just over a century later, could still be seen in Lincoln, although ruinous. Excavation has indeed shown (SP 72) that there was a church nearby during the middle Saxon period, and arguably even earlier (see below). Nevertheless, it is not possible to make Bede's account fit the archaeological evidence without some damage to one or the other and there is plenty of room for speculation and doubt. The third contender is St Peter's church, or to be precise St Peter's churches, since it has been shown that the two churches dedicated to St Peter (-at-Arches and -at-Pleas) situated just inside of Stonebow must have originally shared a single churchyard and may have begun life as a single religious precinct (Gem 1993). There is a little evidence for this church in the archaeological record, in the form of C14-dated burials from a site fronting onto the south side of Silver Street (see below). The fourth and final suggested site for the early Episcopal church is St Mary-le-Wigford – most recently proposed by Steven Bassett as part of an elaborate theory, central to which is the suggestion that Wigford is, indeed, the middle Saxon *wic* of Lincoln (Bassett 1989). Given that we now know, as a result of the post-excavation analysis of a dozen excavations in Wigford, that there is no middle Saxon occupation in the central or northern part of that suburb it seems safe to say that this is the one contender which can definitely be removed from consideration.

Finally, before considering the known sites in more detail, we must mention the role of Lincoln as a royal and administrative centre in the pre-Viking period. Lindsey certainly existed as a distinct entity in the 7th century, when its people are listed in the *Tribal Hidage*. There are, however, no documentary sources in which Kings of Lindsey are recorded. Its status is always that of a province or sub-kingdom. The most recent consideration of the early Kingdom concludes that it probably existed but was always heavily restrained by powerful neighbours to the north and south (Foot 1993). Any Kingdom of Lindsey ceased to exist before

the end of the 8th century and from that period onwards Lindsey was a region or province of Mercia, and was presumably ruled on behalf of the Mercian King by a sub-king, duke or ealdorman. The exact status of these local rulers seems to have varied from province to province and probably also from individual to individual. They would have derived their power from a range of sources: membership of a local elite lineage, direct authority granted by the Mercian King, or by personal prowess. In any case, the nature of the places where such men lived is in doubt. A survey of 'palace' sites identified by archaeologists has led John Blair (1992) to conclude that they are merely the upper end of a continuum of rural settlements and that they were dominated by one or more timber halls. It was rare for these settlements to form the nuclei for later towns and a large number seem, like their lesser counterparts, to have been abandoned during, or at the end of, the middle Saxon period. Many of the functions which early interpretations of the documentary sources took to have been fulfilled by these royal estate centres are now seen by Blair as having been supplied by minster churches, which consistently did end up as the nucleus of a town or village. According to such a view, *Blaecca*, the local ruler of Lindsey at the time of Paulinus, is more likely to have circulated between a number of settlements scattered around Lindsey, of which Lincoln would be merely one. Nevertheless, at least one such settlement might have existed close to Lincoln, for the use of the reeve when attending the church in Lincoln.

Even if we accept that Lincoln was more likely to have been an ecclesiastical than a royal power centre at this period, it seems that even ecclesiastical power was less centralised at this period than later. The Bishops of Lindsey, for example, often styled themselves as bishop of the people of Lindsey (as did those of the East Saxons or Deirans) rather than bishop of a place (such as London or York). This should be no surprise since both systems of authority were influenced by each other and were themselves affected by social expectations of the limits of power and its expression.

## The Upper City and its suburbs

Early Anglo-Saxon pottery has been found on several sites in and around the Upper City, although never in large quantities (Fig. 8.3). Only a single sherd was found on the St Paul-in-the-Bail excavations (SP 72), four sherds were found on the West Bight excavations north of the Mint Wall (WB 80) and five sherds were found in three separate excavations along the defences at East Bight (EB 80). Although by no means a large scatter these sherds do suggest activity, if not settlement, inside the walls between the 5th and the 7th centuries. Little is known of the chronology of early Anglo-Saxon pottery, except where large fragments of

**Key**

**Site code**
1: BE73i
2: BE73v
3: BN89
4: CL85
5: CWG86
6: CY89
7: DT74ii
8: EBii80
9: F72
10: FLAX69
11: H83
12: L86
13: LA85
14: LH84
15: LIN73a
16: LIN73c
17: LIN73di
18: LIN73f
19: M82
20: MW79
21: MWS83
22: ON116
23: ON36
24: P70
25: SMG82
26: SP72
27: TC93
28: W73
29: WB80
30: WF89

Land subject to flooding

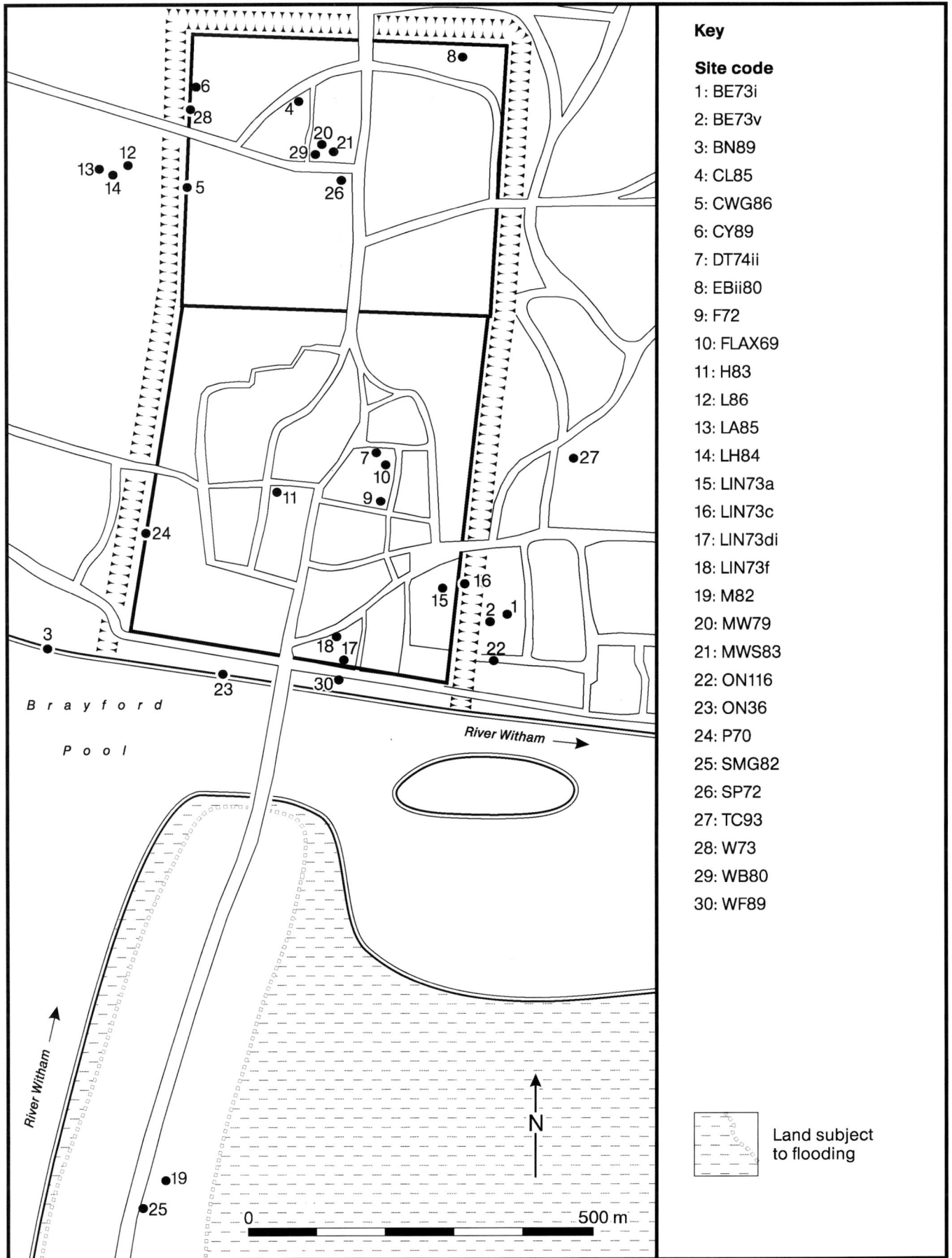

*Fig. 8.5. Finds of 7th- and 8th-century (i.e. middle Saxon) pottery in Lincoln. The street plan is later medieval (source, Vince and Young forthcoming, drawn by Dave Watt, copyright English Heritage).*

| Sitecode | Ware name | Sherds | Broad source |
|----------|-----------|--------|--------------|
| *a)* | | | |
| CL 85 | ELFS | 2 | Local |
| CWG 86 | ELFS | 1 | Local |
| CWG 86 | MAX | 3 | Local - not yet identified to group |
| CWG 86 | MSAX | 1 | Not yet identified |
| EBU 80 | MAX B | 1 | Local |
| MW 79 | MAX B | 1 | Local |
| MW 79 | MAX B | 1 | Local |
| MWS 83 | MAX B | 1 | Local |
| SP 72 | MAY | 1 | Imported |
| WB 80 | ELFS | 1 | Local |
| WB 80 | MAX C | 1 | Local |
| *b)* | | | |
| CY 89 | ELFS | 1 | Local |
| CY 89 | MAX B | 3 | Local |
| L 86 | MAX A | 2 | Local |
| L 86 | MAX B | 5 | Local |
| LA 85 | MAX A | 5 | Local |
| LA 85 | MAX B | 8 | Local |
| LH 84 | MAX A | 15 | Local |
| LH 84 | MAX B | 33 | Local |
| W 73 | MAX B | 1 | Local |

*Fig. 8.6. Totals of sherds of 7th- and 9th -century pottery from sites inside (a) and immediately outside (b) the Upper City walls (source, Vince and Young forthcoming).*

foundations were cut. It is quite possible that the late metalling was a floor within the second structure, but it is perhaps more likely that it was simply the last, or at least the latest surviving, surface of the *forum* courtyard. If this was the case, the second building would date to the later 4th century or later.

The identification of the second building as a church depends partly on the later history of the site but partly on the ground plan, the orientation, and the identification of the north – south deposit as a dedicatory foundation burial; saintly bones buried under the site of the altar. If this identification is accepted, then the first building can be seen as the second building's predecessor. The evidence for the character of this first building, however, is much less strong, whilst the historical context of both buildings remains uncertain. Following the adoption of Christianity as the official religion of the Roman Empire in the early 4th century it would not be impossible for these buildings to have been the successive Cathedrals of the provincial bishop (as suggested by Mr Jones above). But it must be pointed out that an early 7th-century context would also be possible for the second church, and would perhaps fit the construction method better. Earth-fast plank walls are found in some 7th-century secular halls whilst the early Carbon-14 date from the 'foundation burial' might be explained as being due to the reburial of a Roman saint's remains. Even so, such a re-dating would still leave the first church pre-dating the Pauline mission; it would have to be either Roman or Romano-British.

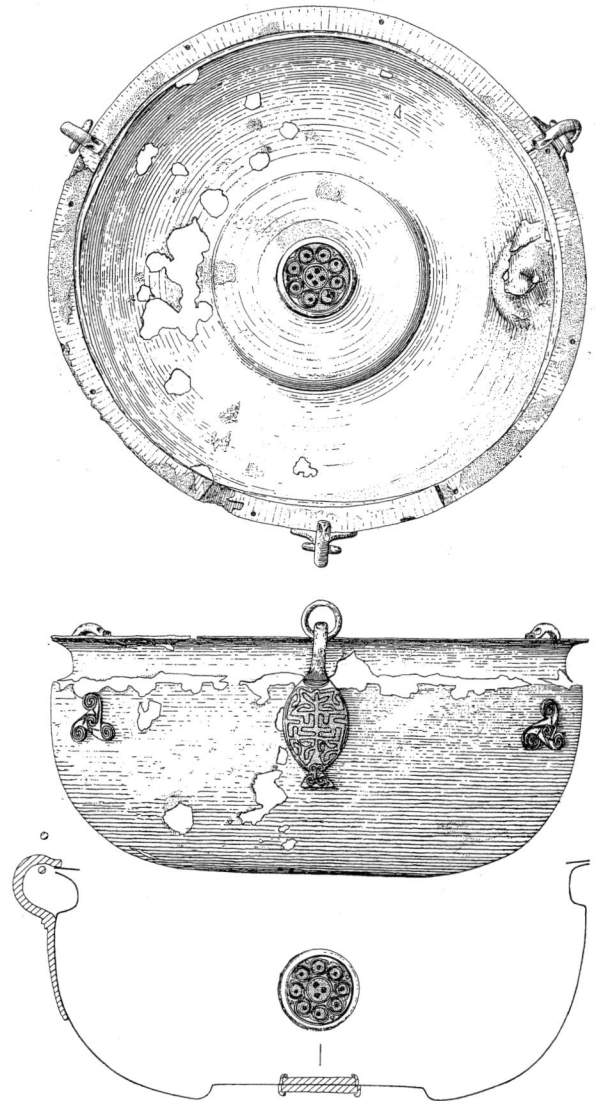

*Fig. 8.7. Hanging-bowl of 7th -century date from St Paul-in-the-Bail (SP 72), Lincoln (drawing and copyright, City of Lincoln Archaeology Unit).*

The possibility of the survival of a Christian British community in Lincoln, in the midst of an Anglo-Saxon, pagan countryside, is not as far-fetched as it might seem. There is historical evidence to suggest that this is precisely what happened at St Albans, although in that instance it is likely that there was also a British enclave in the surrounding countryside occupying the whole of the Chiltern Hills. Various writers have suggested that the Lincoln area, similarly, was avoided by 5th-century pagan Anglo-Saxon settlers because of a strong Romano-British presence here, and this lacuna can be seen in Leahy's 1993 map of 5th-century cemeteries in Lincolnshire (Leahy 1993, fig. 4.2).

The subsequent history of the burial ground at St Paul's provides further hints of its earlier importance. Immediately to the west of the 'foundation burial' on the chord of the apse was a large, stone-lined, grave.

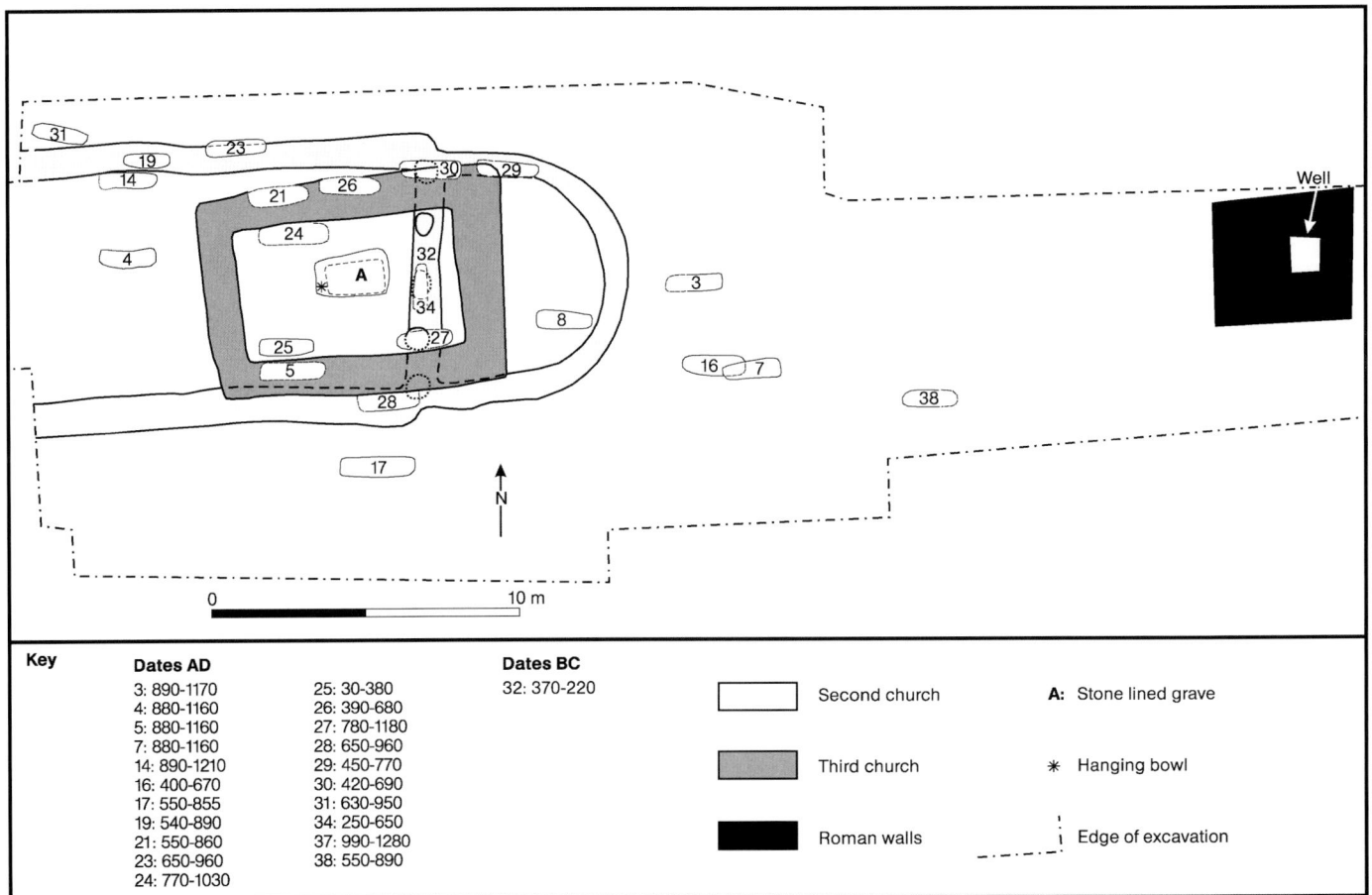

*Fig. 8.8. Plan of second and third churches at St Paul-in-the-Bail (SP 72), showing locations of graves selected for radiocarbon dating and the results to two standard deviations (drawn by Dave Watt, copyright English Heritage).*

The grave itself was empty, almost all the human bones had been removed, perhaps translated, but missed within the stone packing was a copper alloy hanging bowl (Fig. 8.7). This bowl appeared to have been in a poor state when buried, since one of the enamelled escutcheons was found detached from the bowl's base, which subsequent study shows had previously had its rim repaired. The bowl was studied by Rupert Bruce-Mitford and placed in the 7th century (1993, 52–3). One could argue that both the church's altar and this burial were independently sited at the centre of the *forum* courtyard, but the grave cut shows the same slight deviation from the orientation of the *forum* as the earlier church. In the author's view, this gives powerful support to those who would identify the second church as that of Paulinus. It is, of course, not possible to say whether the bowl was buried in the 7th century or later but the later the date of burial, the more likely it is that the church is of 7th-century construction.

A counter-argument comes, however, from a study of the cemetery that overlay these remains and was, in the main, dated to the late 10th century or later and associated with the parish church of St Paul. A group of burials, thought on stratigraphic grounds to be the earliest in the cemetery, were submitted for Carbon-14 dating. Whereas some of these gave determinations centred in the 11th or 12th centuries, as expected, there was also a series of burials with much earlier Carbon-14 dates and some of these early burials lay across the line of the second church's walls (Fig. 8.8 Nos. 19, 23, 28, 29, 30, 34). Even allowing that the actual date of some of these burials could be at the very latest end of their two standard deviation range, it is still difficult to reconcile these dates with a 7th-century date for the second church. Unfortunately, the burials were subsequently re-buried and it is not possible to undertake further Carbon-14 determinations.

A further and final contradiction is contained in the exact text of Bede's description of Paulinus' church. Writing in the 730s, Bede reports that this building was stone-built, and in ruins. As the remains at St Paul's indicate a timber building at the relevant period, either Bede must be in error, or this is not the church referred to. Professor Sawyer has suggested that the excavated church was that of Paulinus but that Bede was mistaken about its construction (1998, Appendix 4). However, there is evidence to suggest that the construction of a church *in stone* was itself of symbolic importance in the 7th century, in Bede's time (Hawkes forthcoming; Stocker forthcoming b). Given the availability of Roman masonry throughout the Upper City in the 7th century there is no reason for Paulinus not to have built in stone, and every reason for him to do so. If we follow this line of reasoning, then Paulinus' church must lie elsewhere. There is no doubt, however, that the St Paul's site was of great significance to the early church and that in the 7th century or later, a rich burial had been made there.

Artefactual evidence for post-Roman, pre-Viking activity at St Paul-in-the-Bail is equally ambivalent. There is no doubt about the approximate date or context of the hanging bowl, although its burial date is less certain. The bowl was certainly old when buried, and had been repaired. But there is a group of other finds which, taken together, suggests significant mid 9th-century activity. However, all of these were recovered from deposits also containing medieval and later finds and their original stratigraphic context, or contexts, is unknown. First, there is a group of four silver pennies dating to the early 870s (Blackburn, Colyer and Dolley 1983, 10–11, figs. 14–17). Secondly, there are three high quality dress fittings of probable 9th-century date. A cast silver buckle and strap slider (Fig. 8.9) appears to be of Carolingian manufacture. Its buckle loop was replaced with a substitute of much lesser quality, although also made of silver. A second silver buckle is decorated with Trewhiddle-style ornament set against a niello background (Fig. 8.10) and a silver strap end also had a Trewhiddle-style niello panel, although its subject, two animals with interlaced tails, is of finer quality than those on the buckle. The rounded ears on the animal head terminal place this buckle into an East Midlands group defined by Leslie Webster on distribution evidence (pers. com.). Lastly, there is a fragment of carved stone, identified by Everson and Stocker as being mostly likely from a stone coffin with decorated sides (Everson and Stocker 1999, 219–21). The stone was found redeposited in a late Saxon or medieval burial. The dating of the piece is uncertain and could be as early as the end of the 7th century or as late as the 11th century. These finds might have originated in a disturbed burial or burials; they might have been loot or simply casual losses from nearby occupation. In any event, the coins and metalwork are probably to be placed in the main period of Viking activity in the Lincoln area and may therefore not be relevant to any discussion of the use of the church site in the middle Saxon period proper. The coffin, however, may be a different matter and it is tempting to see this find as being evidence for a high status mausoleum in the middle Saxon period, even though the suggestion cannot be taken further without a more precise date for the monument represented by the fragment.

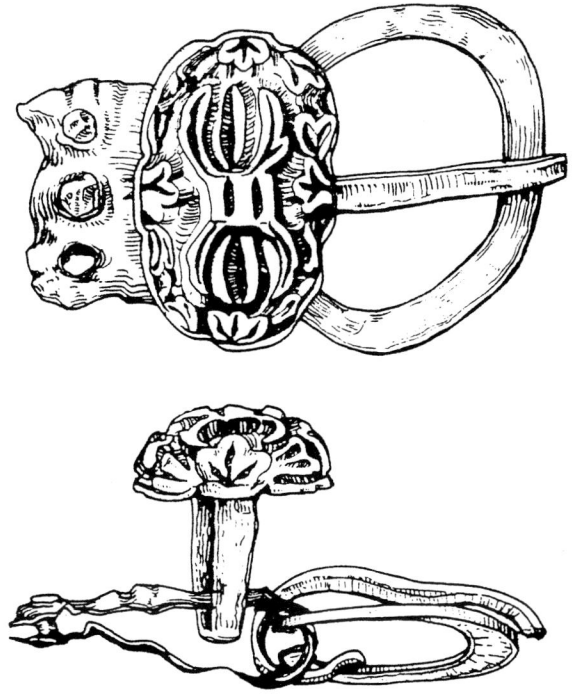

*Fig. 8.9. Cast silver belt-slider and buckle of 9th-century date from the St Paul-in-the-Bail site (SP 72) (drawing and copyright, City of Lincoln Archaeology Unit).*

*Fig. 8.10. Buckle (above – c.30mm across) and strap-end (below – c.60mm long) of 9th-century date from the St Paul-in-the-Bail site (SP 72) (drawing and copyright, City of Lincoln Archaeology Unit).*

## A possible settlement outside the former Roman west gate

The area outside of the west gate of the Upper City has produced a few sherds of early Anglo-Saxon pottery, found in the 1984 excavations at The Lawn (L 84–6) (Figs. 8.3–6). This pottery was found in later deposits and any stratigraphic context that they might have once had was clearly destroyed by the extensive medieval cemetery that occupied most of the excavated area. This must also be true for the middle Saxon pottery scatter from this same site, which is, however, of much higher density (Fig. 8.6). In fact, the total of 69 sherds is comparable with most other middle Saxon settlement sites in Lincolnshire (although this observation is put into perspective by the number – over five thousand – of middle Saxon potsherds from recent excavations at Flixborough). The presence of middle Saxon sherds at Cuthbert's Yard (CY 89), on the other side of the modern Burton Road (which did not exist in the middle Saxon period – see Fig. 9.59) offers the possibility that parts of this settlement (if such it was) have survived the destruction wrought by the medieval cemetery. Trial excavations in advance of the layout of the Lawn kitchen-garden (LKG 91; LKGa 92), however, failed to produce any Anglo-Saxon finds. Nor were any found during the watching brief which accompanied the conversion of The Lawn Hospital into a conference centre. Furthermore, it is quite possible that the sherds found in the Cuthbert's Yard excavations represent rubbish derived from occupation within the walls rather than settlement activity at The Lawn. In view of the later date range (within the middle Saxon period) of the four sherds, perhaps, this is the more likely explanation.

## Early and middle Saxon activity in the Lower City and its suburbs

Early Anglo-Saxon activity in and around the Lower City is represented almost entirely by finds of potsherds, none of them apparently stratified (Figs. 8.3 and 8.11). The scatter of finds has no apparent focus, and includes parts of the Lower City that might have been thought of a peripheral – such as the western defences (at The Park, for example – P 70). There are, however, too few finds to say that there was a concentration on the defences. The large number of finds from Flaxengate (F 72) is only partly explained by the size of the 1972–76 excavations and the large quantity of 'dark earth' excavated there, since early Anglo-Saxon potsherds were also found in the 1945–47 and 1969 excavations. There is no apparent correlation between these finds and the duration of Roman occupation, since sites such as Hungate, with some of the latest and largest late 4th-century finds assemblages, have not produced early Anglo-Saxon potsherds. Five sherds have been found on waterfront sites (WNW 88, WO 89 and LT 72), which were

| Sitecode | Ware name | Sherds | Broad source |
|---|---|---|---|
| WNW 88 | ESAX | 1 | Local |
| WNW 88 | ESAXLOC | 1 | Local |
| WO 89 | ESAXLOC | 1 | Local |
| WO 89 | SST | 1 | Regional |
| LT 72 | ESGS | 1 | Regional |
| LIN 73f | SPARC | 1 | Regional |
| LIN 73ei | ESAXX | 1 | Regional |
| LIN 73ei | SPARC | 1 | Regional |
| ON 211 | CHARN | 3 | Regional |
| P 70 | SAXON SANDY | 1 | |
| Flax 69 | ESAXLOC | 1 | Local |
| Flax 69 | ESGS | 1 | Regional |
| Flax 69 | SST | 2 | Regional |
| F 72 | CHARN | 6 | Regional |
| F 72 | ESAXLOC | 4 | Local |
| F 72 | ESAXX | 5 | Regional |
| F 72 | ESGS | 3 | Regional |
| F 72 | SPARC | 6 | Regional |
| F 72 | SST | 3 | Regional |
| Flax 45-7 | SST | 2 | Regional |
| SH 74 | ESAXX | 7 | Regional |
| MCH 84 | ESAX | 1 | Local |

Fig. 8.11. Totals of sherds of 5th-and 6th-century pottery from sites in and around Lower City (source, Vince and Young forthcoming).

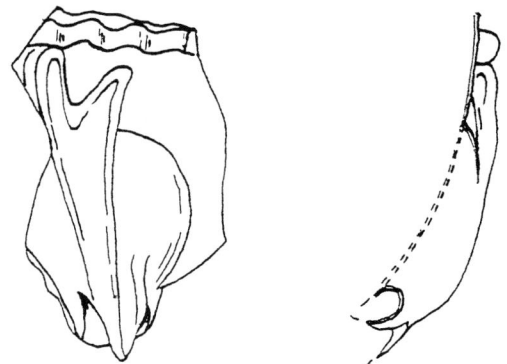

Fig. 8.12. Fragment of glass bowl (c.60mm tall) of late Roman or early Anglo-Saxon date from Spring Hill (SPM 83) (drawing and copyright, City of Lincoln Archaeology Unit).

probably either under water or seasonally flooded during the early Anglo-Saxon period. In addition to these meagre pottery finds, however, Professor Evison identified two pieces of vessel glass as of either very late Roman or early Anglo-Saxon date (1996). A bowl fragment from Spring Hill (SPM 83) was decorated with trailing and a claw (Fig. 8.12) and a body fragment from Hungate (H 83) was decorated with trailing. In both cases a late Roman date is more likely than an Anglo-Saxon one.

Middle Saxon activity in and around the Lower City is also represented almost entirely by potsherds found in later deposits (Figs. 8.5 and 8.13). In two cases it is

*Plate 1*

*Plate 1.1  Pages from the notebook of Michael Drury made in 1887-8 recording the stratigraphical relationships between alluvial deposits in the Wigford area (Drury 1888).*
*(Photo and copyright, Lincolnshire County Council, County Library Service, Local History Collection).*

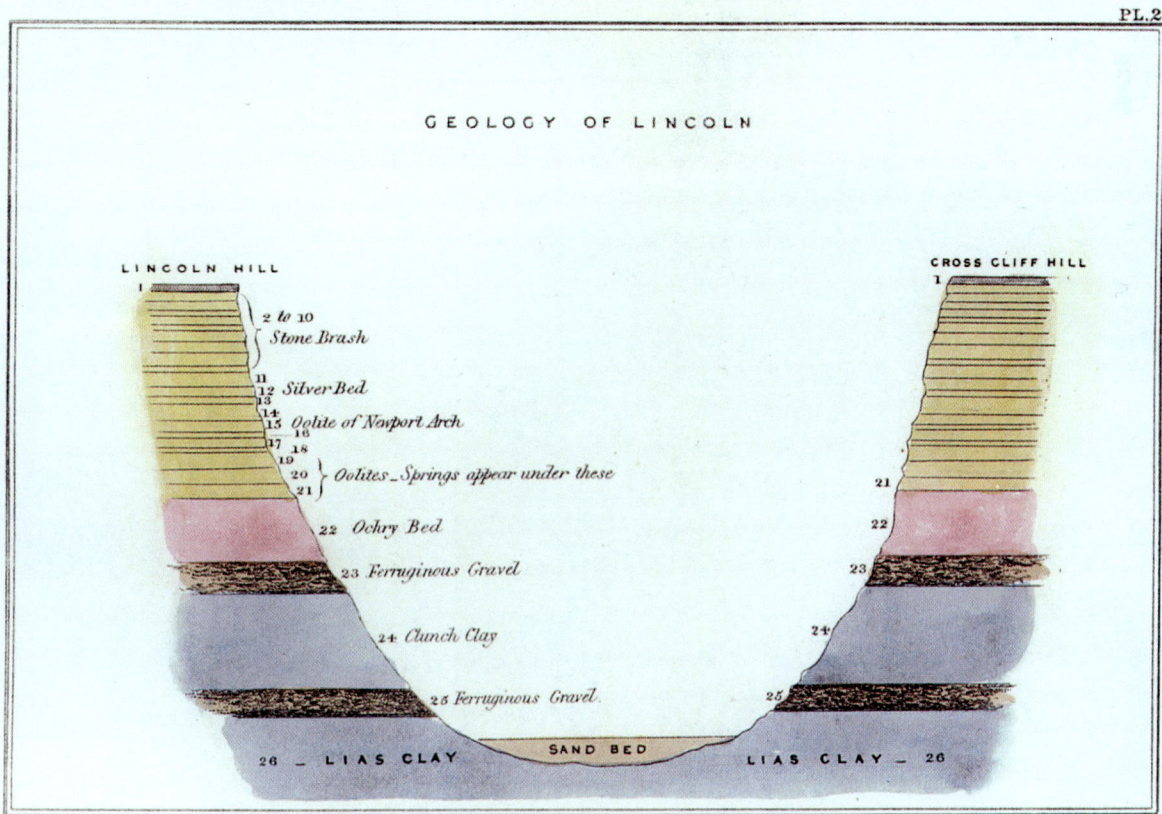

*Plate 1.2  Simplified section north-south through the Witham Valley at the Lincoln gap. Not to scale*
*(Bedford 1843 plate 2).*

*Plate 2*

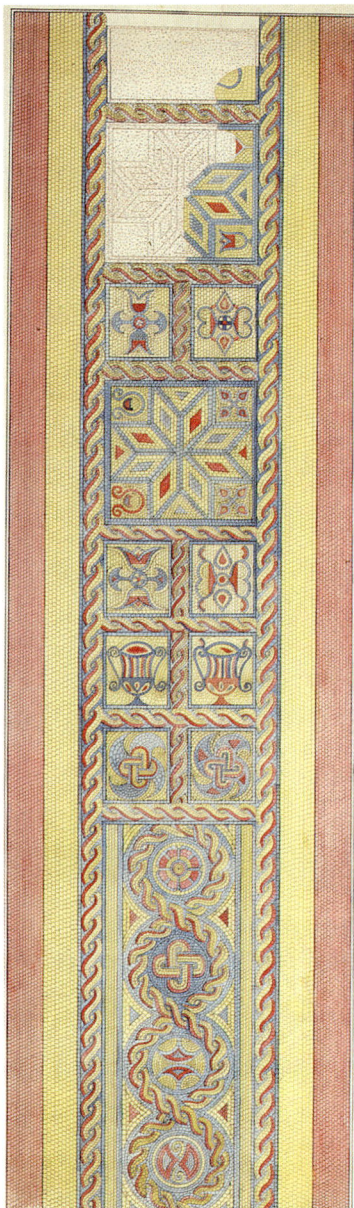

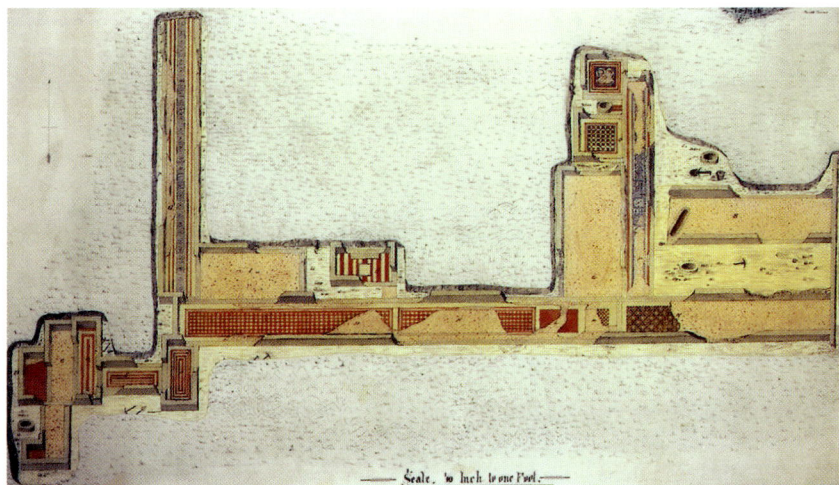

*Plate 2.1   Plan made by B Ramsden in the 1880s of the spectacular remains of the late Roman 'villa' on the brow of the cliff south of the modern Greetwell Road, about 1.5km east of the walled city. North is at the top. (photo and copyright, Lincolnshire County Council, Lincolnshire Museums Service)*

*Plate 2.2   Mosaic in the east corridor at the Roman 'villa' south of Greetwell Road. A drawing made by B Ramsden in the 1880s as a detail of plate 2.1. (photo and copyright, Lincolnshire County Council, Museums Service)*

*Plate 2.3   Mosaic found within Lincoln Castle in 1845. Chromolithograph from a drawing by G J Wigley. (photo and copyright, Lincolnshire County Council, Lincolnshire Archives)*

*Plate 2.4   The Newport Arch from the south. Built in the 3rd century, it served as the fortified north gate of Roman, medieval and early-modern Lincoln. (photo and copyright D Stocker)*

*Plate 2.5 – 'Basal escutcheon' of the 7th-century hanging bowl excavated at St Paul-in-the-Bail (SP 72). It is decorated in enamels and 'millefiore'. (photo and copyright City of Lincoln Archaeology Unit)*

Plate 3

Plate 3.1 Lincoln Castle from the Cathedral showing the eastern curtain, from the Observatory tower (left) to Cobb Hall (right), with the East Gate placed between the two. The chimneys of prison buildings of 1787 and 1847-8 are visible behind the East Gate and towards the rear of the courtyard is the façade of the Assize Courts of 1823-6. (photo and copyright D Stocker)

Plate 3.2 West Gate of Lincoln Castle from the west in 1983 before restoration. (photo and copyright D Stocker)

Plate 3.3 East gate of Lincoln Castle. The original 12th-century gate is almost invisible behind the arch and bartizans added, probably, in the1230s.

Plate 3.4 West tower of St Peter-at-Gowts from the south-west. The tower is very similar in type and date to St Mary-le-Wigford, but has details of finer quality. (photos and copyright D Stocker)

Plate 3.5 West tower of St Mary-le-Wigford from the west. The tower dates from the final quarter of the 11th century. The elaborate building in the foreground is St Mary's Conduit, built out of masonry reused from the Whitefriary in about 1540.

Plate 4

Plate 4.1   West gate-arch of St Mary's Guildhall in Upper Wigford. The arch is the most impressive of the truncated remains of a mid 12th-century town-house of great size and quality, which had connections with the Crown and was the subject of a major archaeological study 1982-6. (photo and copyright D Stocker)

Plate 4.2   Details of the sculpted string-course decorating the west façade of St Mary's Guildhall.  This work is of the highest quality and as accomplished as contemporary work at the Cathedral. (photos and copyright D Stocker)

Plate 4.3   Late 12th-century doorway into Nos. 46–7 Steep Hill.

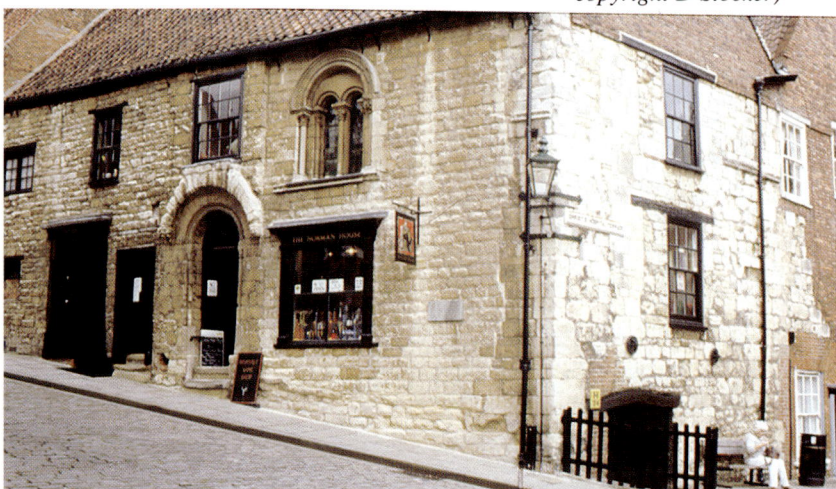

Plate 4.4   Late 12th-century house at Nos. 46–7 Steep Hill, from the south-west. (photos and copyright D Stocker)

Plate 4.5   12th-century house known as St Andrew's Hall in Upper Wigford from the north-east. A water-colour by Moses Griffiths made before demolition in 1783. (photo and copyright Lincolnshire County Council, Usher Art Gallery)

Plate 4.6   'The Jew's House' at the foot of Steep Hill. One of the few 12th-century English domestic stone buildings with which a contemporary Jewish connection can be demonstrated. (photo and copyright D Stocker).

Plate 5.1 Lincoln Cathedral from the Castle, by Frederick Mackenzie (1787–1854). (photo and copyright Lincolnshire County Council, Usher Art Gallery)

Plate 5.2 The top of Steep Hill looking north. The surviving masonry of the south gate of the Bail is just visible below the street-lamp half-way up on the left (west) side. (photo and copyright D Stocker)

Plate 5.3 Tower on the northern sector of the Close Wall. The tower was the subject of an archaeological recording project and conservation programme in 1992, which demonstrated that it was built in the late 13th century. (photo and copyright City of Lincoln Archaeology Unit)

Plate 5.4 The Sincil Dyke in flood, looking north-eastwards towards Bargate Bridge. The dyke itself was probably cut in the 11th-century, but the terraced housing on the left (north) side is typical of much built in Lower Wigford in the second half of the 19th-century. (photo and copyright D Stocker)

Plate 6

Plate 6.1    The Chancery. The brick-built street range of c.1500 forms only one part of one of the finest Close houses. (photo and copyright D Stocker)

Plate 6.2    The late-medieval inn at the top of High Street known as The Cardinal's Hat. The building was restored in 1953 by the St John's Ambulance Brigade. (photo and copyright D Stocker)

Plate 6.3    High Street approaching High Bridge from the south c.1825 by A C Pugin. The view shows a number of surviving medieval timber-framed buildings provided with brick fronts at later dates (photo and copyright Lincolnshire County Council, Usher Art Gallery).

Plate 6.4    A late 17th-century 'row' near St Mary's Guildhall in Wigford. These rare survivals of early vernacular buildings were in a semi-rural setting when constructed. (phot and copyright D Stocker)

Plate 6.5    High Street approaching High Bridge today from a similar vantage point to 6.3 (photo and copyright D Stocker).

*Plate 7*

*Plate 7.1  The new County Court and Gaol building designed by John Carr of York and William Lumby and built in 1787. Behind is the forbidding prison building of 1847-8. (photos and copyright D Stocker)*

*Plate 7.2  Ellis' Mill, Mill Road. The last of the line of windmills which had stood along the cliff edge since the medieval period. Rebuilt in brick in 1784 and restored by Lincoln Civic Trust in 1977.*

*Plate 7.3  The spire of St Swithin's church, the grandest of all the Anglican structures in the city of Victorian date. It was designed by architect James Fowler of Louth and erected in 1884–7 as a memorial to Lincoln ironmaster Joseph Shuttleworth by his son Alfred.*

*Plate 7.4  Former Baptist chapel, Mint Lane designed by architects Drury and Mortimer and built in 1870. (photos and copyright D Stocker)*

*Plate 7.5  Doughty's Mill from the north, across the Witham. The finest of the remaining buildings of Lincoln's once extensive milling industry, the western mill (right) was built in 1863, whilst the eastern 'tower' mill dates from 1891. The building was carefully sited and designed to make maximum use of water transport. (photo and copyright D Stocker)*

*Plate 8*

*Plate 8.1   Uphill and Downhill. This view of the city from the south-east shows the cathedral surrounded by medieval buildings floating above the industrial city in the valley, represented by the impressive southern façade of Robey's Globe Engineering Works (currently a building supplies warehouse).  Robey's workforce and their families now lie in the adjacent civic cemetery (laid out in 1856) alongside their contemporaries (photo and copyright P Everson).*

*Plate 8.2    Today's city from the south-west in 1996. The Brayford Pool is now a backdrop for buildings of the leisure industry, whilst the railway marshalling yards have been replaced by the new university (photo and copyright M J Jones).*

| Sitecode | Ware name | Sherds | Broad source |
|---|---|---|---|
| BE 73I | MAX B | 1 | Local |
| BE 73I | MAX C | 1 | Local |
| BE 73v | MAX B | 1 | Local |
| BN 89 | ELFS | 1 | Local |
| DT 74ii | MSAX | 1 | Not identified (missing) |
| F 72 | BLSURF | 2 | Imported |
| F 72 | BRBURN | 1 | Imported |
| F 72 | ELFS | 39 | Local |
| F 72 | IPS | 1 | Regional |
| F 72 | MAY | 1 | Imported |
| F 72 | MSAX OC | 14 | Local |
| F 72 | MSAX X | 2 | Regional |
| F 72 | ORP | 1 | Imported |
| Flax 69 | ELFS | 1 | Local |
| Flax 69 | MAX A | 1 | Local |
| H 83 | ELFS | 85 | Local |
| LIN 73a | BLBURN | 1 | Imported |
| LIN 73c | MAX | 3 | Local |
| LIN 73di | MAX A | 4 | Local |
| LIN 73di | MAX B | 1 | Local |
| LIN 73di | MAX C | 4 | Local |
| LIN 73di | MSAX X | 1 | Regional |
| LIN 73f | MAX | 1 | Local |
| LIN 73f | MAX C | 2 | Local |
| ON 116 | MAX | 1 | Local |
| ON 36 | MAX B | 1 | Local |
| P 70 | MAX | 1 | Local |
| TC 93 | MAX | 1 | Local |
| WF 89 | ELFS | 1 | Local |
| WF 89 | MAX B | 1 | Local |

*Fig. 8.13. Totals of sherds of 7th-, 8th- and 9th -century pottery from sites in and around the Lower City (source, Vince and Young forthcoming).*

taken as evidence for middle Saxon activity. Only two sites produced definite early middle Saxon pottery (MAX A ware), the 1969 excavation at Flaxengate (F 69) and a trench at Saltergate (LIN 73d), situated just north of the southern wall of the Roman city and immediately north of the contemporary waterfront. Given the small size of most excavations, and the low frequency of these middle Saxon sherds, it is difficult to make much of their absence unless a wider pattern is visible. It does, however, seem to be significant that middle Saxon pottery is absent from sites in the western part of the Lower City. None was found on The Park (P 70) and West Parade (WP 73) sites and on sites on the hillside, such as Spring Hill (SPM 83) and Steep Hill (SH 74).

The presence of middle Saxon pottery outside the walled area to the east of the city may be significant, although only one or two sherds have been present per excavation to date. Finds from sites to the south of the Roman wall are likely to have been deposited in an area which was either permanently or seasonally under water in the middle Saxon period and must reflect either the use of the river or activity on the waterfront.

Other middle Saxon finds from the Lower City have been very rare and their assignment to this period is in most cases doubtful. With the exception of a buckle with triangular buckle plate from Michaelgate (MCH 84), found in a medieval context (Fig. 8.14), they are all from Flaxengate (F 72). An antler die is of a type known

possible that the figures are biased because of the inclusion of vessels of ELFS ware. At Hungate, 85 sherds from a single bowl were found in 10th-century contexts (which were the earliest post-Roman deposits on the excavation). Clearly, there is a difference in the significance of a complete smashed vessel as opposed to single sherds and it is very likely that this vessel was broken on site. As to when it was broken, the excavation at Flaxengate may be significant, in that it too has a high concentration of ELFS ware sherds, although in this case there is no suggestion that they are from a single vessel. However, they too occurred in later deposits, dating in this case to the late 9th century. It is thought likely that ELFS ware continued in use in Lincoln after the Viking take-over of the town, but its rarity in other early 10th-century deposits, together with the presence of sherds of definite late 9th-century date at Hungate, suggest that the Hungate bowl was used in the late 9th century, rather than in the 10th century. The various imported vessels found at Flaxengate (F 72), and at Silver Street (LIN 73a) are also potentially examples of ceramics used at the very beginning of the Anglo-Scandinavian period, although they are also types which are definitely known in pre-Viking contexts, and in other circumstances would be

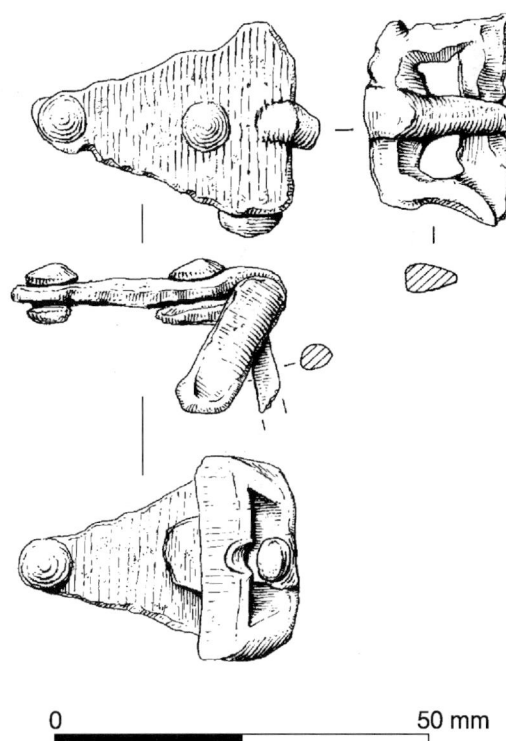

*Fig. 8.14. Buckle of middle-Saxon date from medieval deposits at Michaelgate (MCH 84) (drawing and copyright, City of Lincoln Archaeology Unit).*

from both middle and later Saxon contexts, as is an antler counter. A copper alloy pin with polygonal head decorated with ring and dot is equally likely to be of late Saxon as middle Saxon date. There are two possible ansate brooches, of a type best known from contexts on continental sites dated between the 7th and 9th centuries, but whose date range may extend to the end of the 9th century. Although one of these brooches was unstratified, has no evidence for mounting and must be regarded as a suspect identification, the other, found in Wigford (SM 76), is an undoubted example and was probably produced before the Viking settlement (Mann 1986, 41, fig. 30) (Fig. 8.15). When it was first deposited in Lincoln is uncertain, however, as it was recovered from a medieval deposit and might have arrived on the site long after its period of use. Finally, the rim of a glass cup or beaker with a trail below the rim, from Flaxengate (F 72), has been dated by Professor Evison to between the 8th and the 10th centuries (Fig. 8.16).

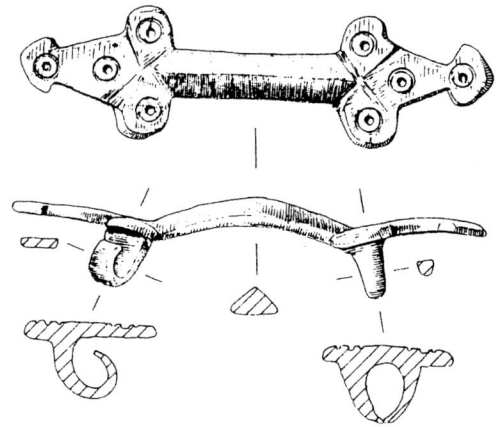

Fig. 8.15. 'Ansate' broach (c. 80mm long) of middle Saxon date from the excavations at St Mark's church (SM 76) (drawing and copyright, City of Lincoln Archaeology Unit).

## The Silver Street burials –
## An early church centre in the Lower City?

At least five inhumation burials were found in excavations in the early 1970s between Silver Street and Saltergate (LIN 73e) (Fig. 8.17). The burials were situated in the north-eastern part of the excavated area and did not extend further east, south-east or south-west. One of the burials was identified in the northern section of the trench underneath what is now the southern pavement of Silver Street and it is possible that further burials lay to the west and north, underneath the road. This may be important evidence for the dating of the burials, as the road was certainly in existence in the early 10th century and most likely also in the late 9th century. One of the burials was on its back but with the legs flexed (Fig. 8.18). This 'supine-flexed' position was common during the 7th-century phase of burial at Castledykes, Barton-Upon-Humber (Drinkall and Foreman 1998, 333) but it was not present in the cemetery of St Guthlac's Monastery in Hereford (dating from the middle Saxon period to the 12th century – Shoesmith 1980), the late Saxon monastery of St Oswald in Gloucester (Heighway and Bryant 1999) nor the Anglo-Scandinavian parish church graveyards of St Mark's (SM 76) or St Paul-in-the-Bail (SP 72) in Lincoln. Three of the Silver Street burials could be aged and sexed, the fourth being too fragmentary for study. Three were females ranging in age from young, through young/middle aged to mature adult (Boylston and Roberts 1995). Loose adult human bones found in the excavation suggest that a further burial, or burials, may have been destroyed by later activity. The presence of neo-natal human bones either shows that an infant (or infants) was also buried in this cemetery or that there might conceivably have been a Roman infant burial within the Roman town house into whose remains the later burials were cut. A Carbon-14 determination of AD 780±90 was obtained from one of

Fig. 8.16. Fragment (c.25mm wide) of glass cup or beaker of middle-Saxon date from excavations at Flaxengate (F 72) (photo and copyright, City of Lincoln Archaeology Unit).

the burials (Har. 863, uncalibrated). Stratigraphically, the burials must be very late Roman or later and they are sealed by late 9th- or early 10th-century deposits. The Carbon-14 date, and the supine-flexed burial, suggests that they belong to the middle part of this period and are probably early or middle Saxon in date. No grave goods were present, unless the remains of an iron knife in one of the graves and lead sheet (possibly part of a vessel) from another were deliberate inclusions, and there is scant evidence for coffins (iron nails were present in two of the graves but were not noted as being coffin nails during excavation).

Whilst it is possible that the burials were isolated, perhaps even being hurried burials following a disaster (such as a Viking raid), it is more realistic to link them to the churchyard of St Peter-at-Arches church (which lay some 50m to the west). Consequently, it is not impossible to imagine that, at an earlier stage in the development of the town, the graveyard might have extended this far east, and may have included the Silver Street burials. The church of St Peter-at-Arches, and its fellow church in the same graveyard, St Peter-at-Pleas, have long been thought potential early church sites (Hill 1948, 60, 130–1) perhaps representing a middle Saxon monastic community ruled over by the bishop of Lindsey. Docu-

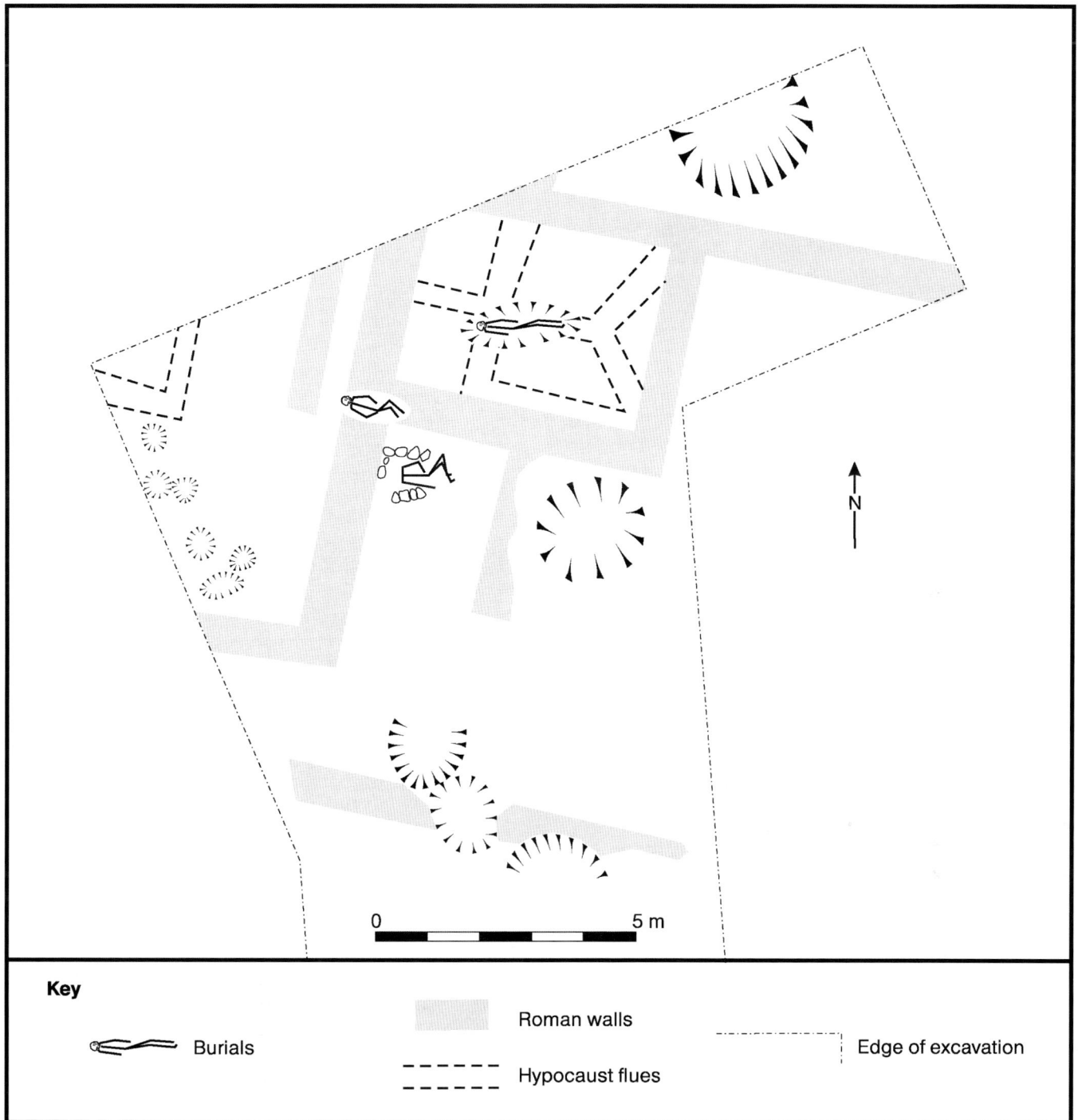

*Fig. 8.17. Plan of early or middle Saxon burials cut into Roman buildings in the south-eastern part of the Lower City (LIN 73 e and f) (source, J. Wacher – drawn by Dave Watt, copyright English Heritage).*

mentary sources show that the bishop presided over two communities and Richard Gem has argued that at York, Canterbury and London the 8th-century bishops also presided over two communities, one of regular canons and the other monastic. He further points out that at least one of the bishop's churches was dedicated to one of the apostles and that, in the late 7th and early 8th centuries, dedications to Paul, Peter or Andrew would be most likely, whilst sub-

ordinate churches were often dedicated to the Virgin Mary (Gem 1993, 126). On these, admittedly flimsy, grounds we can suggest that St Peter-at-Arches, together with St Peter-at-Pleas, could have formed the core of a monastic community ruled by the bishop of Lindsey. An alternative hypothesis, advanced by David Stocker, suggests that Bardney may have been the site of this second community and the presence at Bardney of the head of St Oswald does indeed suggest

*Fig. 8.18. Burial in a 'flexed' posture of early or middle-Saxon date cut into Roman buildings in the south-eastern quadrant of the Lower City (LIN 73e) looking south-west. See Fig. 8.17 (photo and copyright, English Heritage).*

that this monastery was of considerable importance during the middle Saxon period.

Further evidence in favour of an early church at the site of the two St Peters has been put forward during the progress of this *Assessment* work by Mr Jones. He suggests that the complex of public buildings in this general vicinity in the *Colonia* Era, which included at least one temple, might have been reused in middle Saxon times. It is possible, he suggests, that some of the stone structures within this complex were adapted for a later purpose – for instance, the public fountain (ON 217) may have become a baptistery associated with either, or both, the churches dedicated to St Peter (p. 137 above). Mr Jones also notes that the proximity of two buildings both dedicated to the same important early saint may point to the existence of a double church separated by a baptistery, in the form now known in considerable number on mainland Europe (Duval *et al.* 1991). Although if this is the case, they might be no earlier than 7th-century in origin. In other former Roman provinces baths buildings were frequently converted into churches; examples at Jublains and Cimiez are only two amongst several in Gaul (*Ibid.*). The fact that standing remains of the baths were encountered in 1924, near to the site of the later St Lawrence's church further to the north may suggest that the Lincoln bath ruins were also reoccupied in the post Roman centuries, as they were at Leicester, where they formed an annex to St Nicholas' Church.

## The traditional site of Icanho

Another hint that Lincoln was occupied by a church in the middle Saxon period is given in John Leland's *Itinerary*, written in the 1540s. He recounts that there

was a local tradition that the cell of St Mary of York to the east of the Lower City was the site of the monastery of *Iccenhoe* (*Icanho*), famous as the house of St Botolph in the 7th century (Toulmin Smith 1910, I, 30). In many cases, these late traditions have a grain of truth within them. For example, the location of *Hamwic*, the middle Saxon predecessor of Southampton, was recorded, in jumbled form as a local tradition, in Leland's account of St Mary's church there. However, in that case there was plentiful corroboration of the previous importance of the suburb of St Mary, not least the fact that the church had retained its status as mother church of Southampton. In the case of Lincoln there is no other evidence, archaeological or historical, to suggest that there had ever been a middle Saxon monastery east of the city. However, the monks of the York abbey often acquired sites with an earlier Christian association and were given a large estate in Lincoln in the early 12th century. Their initial holding seems to have been bounded by the *Butwerk* suburb to the west, the limestone scarp to the north and east and the Witham to the south.

Another reason not to dismiss Leland's report of the tradition entirely is the fact that this area shares a topographic similarity to Fishergate in York, the Strand in London and St Mary's suburb in Southampton, all of which have been shown by archaeological excavation to have been occupied by middle Saxon trading settlements. The presence of single sherds of middle Saxon pottery from three sites in the *Butwerk* suburb does suggest that the area might have seen activity at this time, but the area itself has yet to be investigated archaeologically and is now covered by a 19th-century suburb.

## Evidence for early and middle Saxon activity in Wigford

There is no stratigraphic evidence for post-Roman, pre-Viking activity in the Wigford suburb and in most cases the stratigraphic hiatus continues to some point in the early or mid 10th century. The Wigford suburb is also almost devoid of finds of early or middle Saxon date. The only exceptions are from Monson Street (where an imported Grey Burnished Ware vessel was discovered, represented by nine sherds from two contexts – M 82); a sherd of MAX B ware from excavations at St Mary's Guildhall (SMG 82) and the ansate brooch from St Mark's Church mentioned above (SM 76) (Fig. 8.15). All three finds could belong to a transitional phase in the mid 9th century, but they do suggest there was some activity south of the Witham in either the middle Saxon or very early in the Anglo-Scandinavian periods. It may be significant that these sites are the most southerly of the Wigford excavations, two of them being situated at a point where the sand terrace rises up above the Witham flood plain.

# B. The Early Medieval Era – The archeological agenda. An introduction to the Research Agenda Zone entries (on CD-Rom)

## *David Stocker*

Whatever its character, in the area formerly occupied by the Roman city, the early medieval presence was minimal. As Dr Vince shows (above), the evidence is confined, almost literally, to a handful of pottery and a small number of burials, some of which were rather inadequately recorded. Whatever else, then, there was no continuity of anything we could describe as civic life between the later Roman period and the arrival of the Vikings. The scale of activity for which we have evidence at present is simply too small to sustain any other view and, whilst it could be objected that not enough work has been done in key locations of the city, as time goes on and sites are monitored by an increasingly vigilant planning system, the chances of any such evidence being found are reducing each year. The practical result of this lack of evidence is that we have been able to identify only a small number of RAZs (ten) compared with both earlier and later periods and, perhaps, a much less well-targeted research agenda. These RAZs can be accessed through the CD-Rom.

## The city of the dead

Clearly our primary concern in future work will be to build on the slight evidence we have already for the early church within the city, and to investigate whether or not there was a continuous Christian community in the city between the presumed Christian community of the 4th century and the documented arrival of St Paulinus in 628. This debate necessarily focuses, at present, on the known early church site at St Paul-in-the-Bail, but we should not lose sight of the possible presence of a second early church site in the Lower City and a third potentially important location to the east.

Accordingly, three RAZs have been identified in which these issues can be explored:

8.1 Burial sites
  8.1.1 St Paul-in-the-Bail
  8.1.2 The churches of St Peter and the Silver Street burial ground
  8.1.3 Greetwell villa estate and potential *wic*

The results from the excavations at St Paul-in-the-Bail (SP 72) have proved intractable, and no consensus has yet emerged, or is likely to. Our best route forward may not lie in continual re-examination of the same few items of excavated data but, rather, in establishing a research agenda that addresses the context in which the site at St Paul's developed (RAZ 8.1.1). Our first step down this road must be to recognise that we have evidence for two other early Anglo-Saxon burial grounds in Lincoln; at Silver Street (RAZ 8.1.2) and at the Greetwell 'villa' (RAZ 8.1.3). Taken as a group, some additional reflected light is cast on the individual sites. All seem to represent examples of the same ritual behaviour that has been observed on dozens of other former Roman sites. That is to say, a space was cleared within the ruins of the buildings and a small number of burials were carefully dug into the rubble. This type of early Anglo-Saxon burial is ubiquitous on former villa sites, and it comes as no surprise that it occurs also at the Greetwell 'villa'. So, before we make special claims for the burials at the St Paul's site, we have to ask why we should consider them any differently from those at Greetwell 'villa' or at Silver Street.

This category of Anglo-Saxon burial has been the subject of considerable study in recent years. It is clear, for example, that the burials within villas should be compared with burials carefully placed in Neolithic and Bronze Age barrows and in other features of what was, to the Anglo-Saxons, their own historic landscape (Williams 1997; Bell 1998). Williams, in particular, shows that, whilst this burial behaviour is very deliberate, the wide range of Roman sites selected for re-use as burial grounds makes it unnecessary to imagine that the Roman function of the structure re-used influenced its selection as an Anglo-Saxon burial ground. It is the generalised association with previous generations, he argues, that was sought out by the Anglo-Saxons, rather than a specific connections with remembered Roman cult practises. Furthermore, such re-use of Roman monuments can occur at any date between the 5th and 8th centuries, so this behaviour cannot be used as a dating mechanism at St Paul's. Even so, it does indicate that the ruins of Roman Lincoln were not merely abandoned in the Anglo-Saxon period. They may have become a liminal location, between the living and the dead, but they were evidently not without meaning or function.

Unfortunately, although this burial behaviour clearly indicates a desire to appropriate the ancestors and to 'impose a ... sense of the past' (Williams 1997, 26) on contemporary Anglo-Saxon society, it cannot be said that such burials represent any specific cultic meaning, either pagan in character or Christian. At least one of the Silver Street burials was in a crouched position (Steane and Vince 1993, 75), however, and is thus unlikely to be Christian, in any conventional sense. It is very tempting to think that, because the Anglo-Saxon burials at St Paul's were made on a site which (according one view of the sequence) had previously contained a late Roman church, then the burials of the 5th and 6th centuries here were Christian – 'keeping the flame alive' as it were. However, analyses such as that by Howard Williams would strongly suggest that the forum space at Lincoln was selected for burials because it was at the centre of the walled Roman enclosure, and because the former forum was presumably clearer of rubble and offered less intractable soil conditions, rather than because it was known that it was once a church site. And this, in its turn, also suggests that the burials may have been pagan rather than Christian – although we must bear in mind that these two terms may not be antithetical.

Even though the burials at St Paul's are aligned east – west, this may be because they are aligned with their feet towards the ever-present well-head, known to be open in both previous and succeeding Eras and so almost certainly still in operation at the time the burials were made. Furthermore, east – west burial, with the head towards the west, is also a characteristic of the 'final phase' of early Anglo-Saxon burials in England (Leeds 1936, 96–114) and is a clear 'trend' in the 'final phase' burials from the cemetery at Castledyke in Barton-on-Humber (Drinkall and Foreman 1998, 335–7). Unfortunately, the posture of the burials excavated at St Paul's was not recorded in sufficient detail to detect unusual aspects of the inhumations which may have indicated any non-Christian characteristics. Even though the burials are without grave-goods, such unfurnished burials are more common than furnished ones in Anglo-Saxon inhumation cemeteries, and they are certainly the norm amongst burials made in the ruins of Roman buildings. One of the burials was furnished, however, with the St Paul's hanging bowl (Fig. 8.7), and in Lincolnshire more widely (where such finds have any sort of context at all) they are associated with known pagan Anglo-Saxon burial grounds (Bruce-Mitford 1993). In addition to following lines of research aimed at elucidating either an early Christian interpretation for the St Paul's burials, therefore, we should also pay more attention to the possibility that these burials might simply be pagan burials of this widely distributed and comparatively well-understood class.

## A city for the living?

In the darkness brought about by our lack of information about the city area at this date, we can have only suspicions about settlement sites in the vicinity. What little is known from the wider county suggests that major settlements of the early Anglo-Saxon communities in Lincolnshire are not dissimilar to communities of similar date elsewhere in the country – for example at Mucking (Essex – Hamerow 1993). It has not proved difficult to identify such sites at places like Quarrington near Sleaford (Coupland and Taylor 1995), but nothing remotely comparable to the Quarrington type of site is even hinted at within the Lincoln City boundary. The nearest potential settlement sites of this date are those at Cherry Willingham (5km east) (Field 1981) and Middle Carlton (Everson *et al.* 1991, 8–9), but their character remains to be elucidated. A single RAZ (8.2 – Possible occupation site near Roman upper west gate) has been identified within the City boundary, but as Dr Vince shows, it is not at all clear that it represents settlement of the character seen at Cherry Willingham or Middle Carlton.

Perhaps then, after a period in the Roman Era when the city's development was strongly influenced by southern European concepts of urbanism, Lincoln in the sub-Roman period quickly reverted to the natural role it had played since the Bronze Age; that of a cult-centre. An important symbolic place for local peoples, but not one which was used for settlement. A site at which, perhaps, settlement may even have been taboo. This line of thinking suggests we should be exploring Lincoln as a symbol of power, in its distinctive and highly visible location, dominating the rural communities who lived round about. This theme runs through all of RAZs identified for the Early Medieval Era, but it can be investigated most readily, perhaps, in the three RAZs that have been drawn around known burial sites (RAZs 8.1.1, 8.1.2, and 8.1.3) and in a group of RAZs which aim to look at the way in which the former Roman infrastructure was managed in the Early Medieval Era:

8.3 Re-use, abandonment and other treatments of Roman roads and other Roman monuments:
 8.3.1 Central elements of former Roman city and Roman network
 8.3.2 Stamp End causeway
 8.3.3 Triple boundary ditch
 8.3.4 'Reserved' enclosure(s) defined by the Roman city walls

The view of the city taken by the surrounding local peoples in the Early Medieval Era can also be assessed, at a simple level, by looking at the pattern of settlement and agriculture beyond the area dominated by the Roman ruins. Was the land beyond the ruins cultivated or settled at all? Or was there some kind of cordon, marked by natural or man-made features, perhaps, that indicated a change in land use around the city? Two RAZs have been identified which aim to approach these questions.

8.4 Land around city potentially usable for settlement and agriculture
8.5 Riparian deposits.

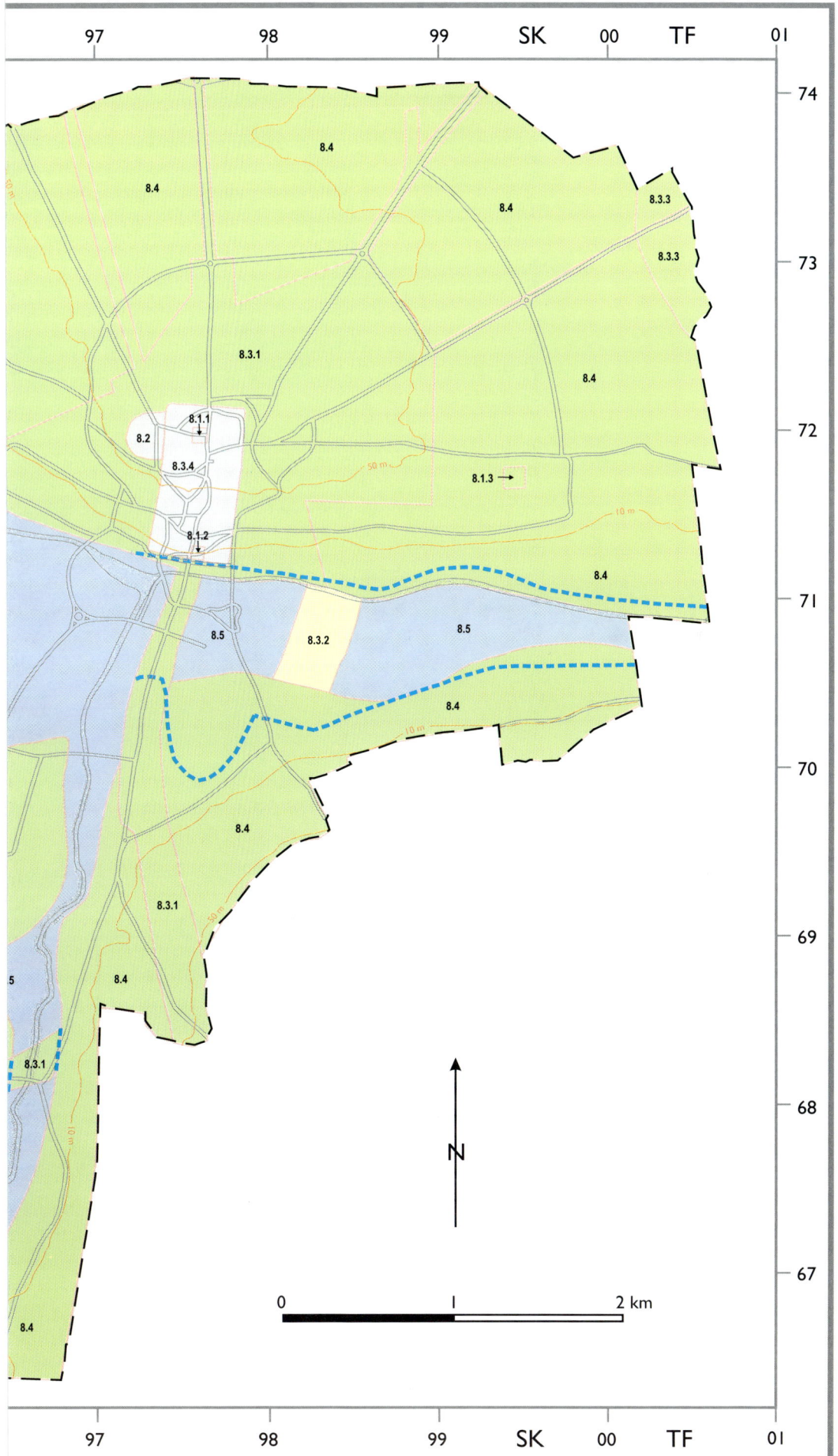

97    98    99    SK    00    TF    01

74

8.4

8.4

8.3.3

8.4

8.3.3

8.3.1

8.4

8.1.1

8.2

8.3.4

8.1.3 →

8.1.2

8.4

8.5

8.3.2

8.5

8.4

8.4

8.4

8.3.1

8.4

5

8.3.1

N

0          1          2 km

97    98    99    SK    00    TF    01

*Map 4. Research Agenda Zone locations for the Early Medieval Era – See CD-Rom for details (drawn by Dave Watt, copyright English Heritage and Lincoln City Council).*

# 9. The New Town: Lincoln in the High Medieval Era (*c*.900 to *c*.1350)

## A. Archaeological account

### *Alan Vince*

## Narrative outline

The history of medieval Lincoln was extremely well covered by Sir Francis Hill whose *Medieval Lincoln*, published in 1948, has stood the test of time, and it has now been joined on the shelf by the four volumes of the Civic Trust's *Survey of Ancient Houses in Lincoln* (chapter 1 above). Archaeology too has added to our knowledge of medieval Lincoln in the past thirty years, and the account that follows represents a considerable revision of the narrative presented by Hill. This success has been made possible through conscious targeting of areas where there are no sources other than archaeological ones. Apart from occasional references in the *Anglo-Saxon Chronicle* and in one or two other sources, for the first 150 years of Anglo-Scandinavian Lincoln, results from excavations are the only reliable sources of evidence. From the middle of the 11th century onwards, however, it is possible to make closer associations between surviving monuments and landscape features in documentary sources, and to make reasonable conjectures about the topography of the city based on the post-medieval street pattern and early modern plot boundaries (Fig. 9.1). However, to provide a more detailed chronological explanation for how this map developed we require archaeological evidence, and in particular pottery. Jane Young has divided the pottery of the mid 9th to mid 12th centuries into eleven Ceramic Horizons, including transitional horizons and the beginning and end of the period (Fig. 9.2).

The archaeology of the long period between the re-emergence of the town at the end of the 9th century and the disintegration of the urban economy in the early 14th century is discussed here as a continuum although, naturally, different phases are easily detectable during its course. Strangely enough, although the greatest political change within the Era – the Norman Conquest of 1066 – made an impact on the townscape of the Upper City through the foundation of the Castle and Cathedral, it is not immediately visible within the material culture of the city derived from excavations. Consequently we have not chosen that decisive political date for a division in our account. Instead we have identified a much more decisive break in the city's material culture in the decades around 1300, connected with seismic shifts in the city's economy. Within the period between *c*.900 and *c*.1350, however, there are other marked changes in material culture – in particular a change in the appearance and lifestyle of the city in the central part of the 12th century. Consequently, in the sections that follow, it often seems appropriate to subdivide the High Medieval Era into two basic blocks, the periods before and after *c*.1150.

### *Lincoln between the late 9th and the mid 12th centuries*

The period from the late 9th to the mid 12th centuries saw the re-establishment of Lincoln as a town. Almost every excavation carried out in the town or its suburbs has produced evidence for occupation during this period and the archaeological evidence for a large population is confirmed by estimates of the population based on documentary sources (p. 163–7 below, Fig. 9.6). It is not controversial to say, then, that the city was re-founded towards the end of the 9th century as an urban location and that, within a period of no more than 200 years, it prospered greatly and spread beyond the Roman walled area and into new suburbs to the north, north-east, west, east and south.

At the beginning of this period Lincoln was, perhaps, the central place of the province of Lindsey, although there is considerable uncertainty as to how centralised Middle Saxon settlement hierarchies were and it may

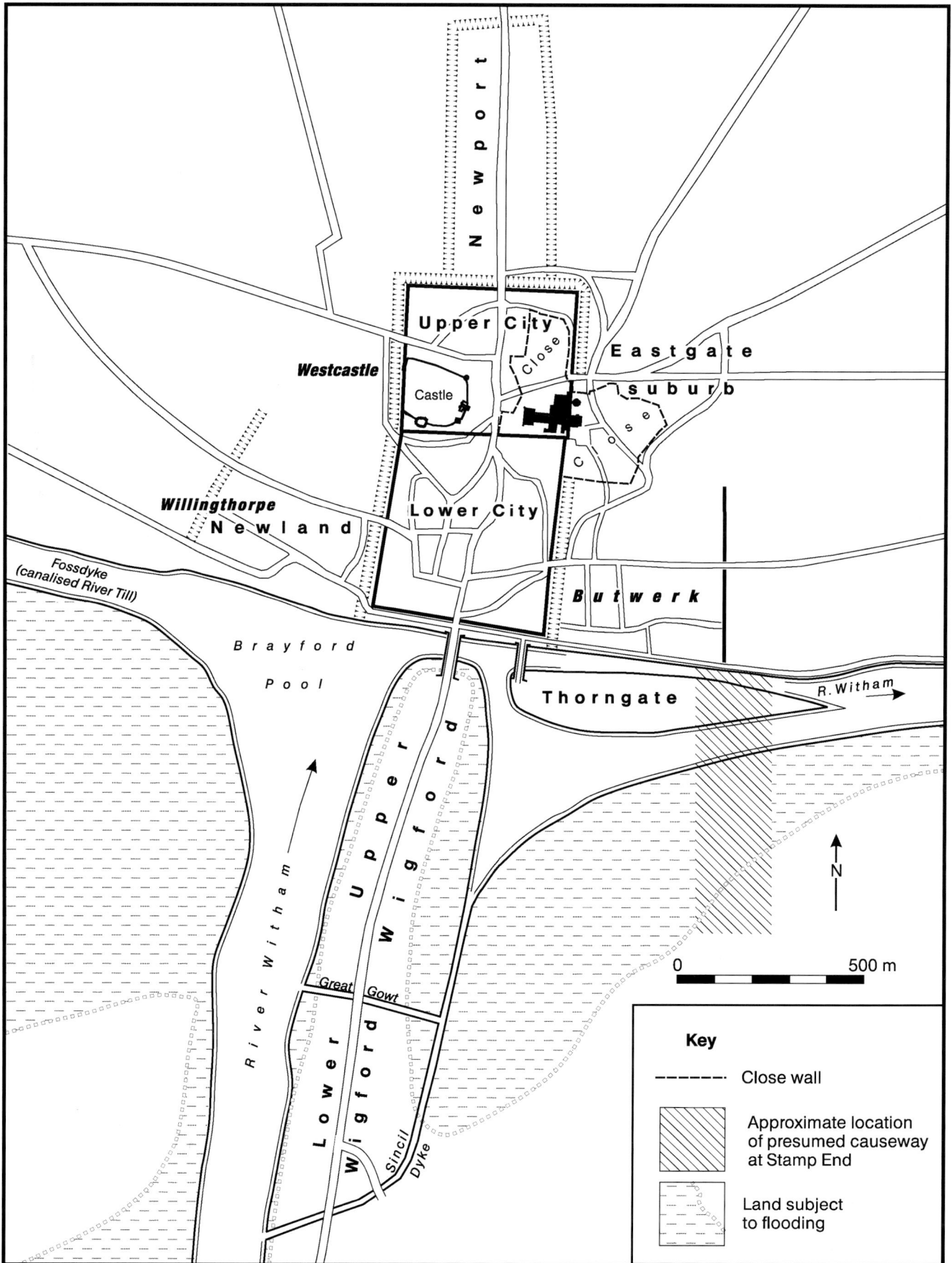

*Fig. 9.1. Lincoln in the High Medieval Era, showing its principal elements. The topography and street pattern incorporates the most recent opinions, discussed in this volume, but some elements remain entirely conjectural (drawn by Dave Watt, copyright English Heritage).*

| Ceramic Horizon | Suggested absolute dates | Comments |
|---|---|---|
| ASH 6 | Mid to late 9th century | Transitional phase. No clean assemblages in the city. |
| ASH 7 | Mid/late to late 9th century | Type fossil: LG |
| ASH 8 | Late 9th to early 10th century | Type fossil: LSLS |
| ASH 9 | Early/mid to mid 10th century | LKT dominant |
| ASH 10 | Mid to late 10th century | LKT dominant |
| ASH 11 | Late 10th century | First appearance of TORK and SNLS |
| ASH 12 | Early to early/mid 11th century | LKT out of use |
| ASH 13 | Early/mid to mid/late 11th century | Mainly distinguished from ASH12 by the fabric of the Stamford wares |
| ASH 14 | Mid/late 11th to early 12th century | TORK and SNLS out of use |
| MH1 | Early/mid to mid 12th century | Glazed wares become common (NSP) |
| MH2 | Mid 12th to mid/late 12th century | Locally produced glazed wares appear (LSW1) |

*Fig. 9.2. Pottery groupings between c.850–c.1150 (source, Vince and Young forthcoming).*

well be that there was little to choose between Lincoln and other ecclesiastical and aristocratic centres in Lindsey, or elsewhere in the East Midlands. By the end of the 12th century, however, Lincoln was undoubtedly the largest urban centre in the East Midlands, far exceeding Nottingham, Derby and Leicester in size. It grew to become comparable to places such as York, Norwich, Chester and London, all towns which acted as the central place for a large region and which, by dint of their size, also acted as markets for rural produce and the products of rural and urban artisans. One of the tasks for urban archaeology is to chart the city's phenomenal growth and to find explanations for it.

Politically, the primary event as far as the city was concerned was the arrival of the Viking Army in 873/4 and the subsequent division of the Anglo-Saxon Kingdom of Mercia into English Mercia, which within a generation had been adsorbed into a Greater Wessex, and Danish Mercia. The internal organisation of the flourishing independent Viking states, of which Danish Mercia was composed in the late 9th and early 10th centuries, is poorly known. The Viking Northumbrian state was certainly heavily centralised and based on the city of York, whilst the East Anglian Kingdom under the Vikings was probably centred on Ipswich. There was occupation at Norwich during the Viking period but it appears to have been small scale – the medieval town's origins are much later, in the late 10th or early 11th centuries. Danish Mercia, however, seems to have been more federal in its organisation. The frequent references to the Mercian Danes in the *Anglo-Saxon Chronicle* mention the armies of several towns (such as Bedford, Leicester and Northampton) but no king or other pre-eminent leader. It is likely, therefore, that royal power did not survive the dismemberment of Mercia and that either new structures were set up or power reverted to the second level, that of the province or region. As far as Lincoln is concerned, this would have meant that the Trent was a major boundary as, presumably, was the river Witham. Thus, Lincoln would have been on the southern fringe of the territory it controlled, standing in a similar relationship to Lindsey as Stamford did

to the territory it controlled – later known as Kesteven. Exactly where the southern boundary of the army of Lincoln's territory ran may have vital significance for the development of the early town, since a strict interpretation would place the suburb of Wigford within Kesteven, the territory of the army of Stamford. In fact a similar situation existed at Stamford, where the Welland probably formed the boundary between territory looking to Stamford and that looking to Northampton, isolating Stamford's southern suburb in a separate polity (Mahany *et al.* 1982, 2–10, 178).

In the second decade of the 10th century, between 911 and 923, the English won back much of Mercia, including Nottingham and Stamford in 921 but there is no record of the capture of Lincoln. Furthermore, stray coin finds indicate that Lindsey was strongly linked economically with the Viking Kingdom of York (Blackburn *et al.* 1983, 13) whilst Everson and Stocker's analysis of stone sculpture emphasises this same alignment (Everson and Stocker 1999, 80–84). In 923 Edward was accepted as overlord by the Vikings of Northumbria and there seems to have been peace between the Danes and the English for a couple of decades, until 943, when Anlaf Sihtricson came south to fight the English at Leicester. Hostilities lasted until 954, when Eric Bloodaxe was deposed as King of Northumbria, marking the end of the Kingdom, which henceforth was ruled by English kings.

The period following the incorporation of Northumbria and the East Midlands into England is seen by some historians, notably David Roffe (2000), as being the time when many of the administrative institutions seen in the mid 11th century in *Domesday Book* came into existence. Counties, for example, replaced the old regions during this period and in parts of old Mercia these new divisions seem to have cut across old boundaries. Lincolnshire, however, may initially have equated to the boundaries of Lindsey, with the southern part of the county, Kesteven, forming a 'Stamford-shire'. There is, however, no documentation for this intermediate stage of development, and before 1066 Lincolnshire had assimilated Kesteven and assumed the form which was to last until 1974. This had the effect of shifting Lincoln itself from a peripheral position in relation to its administrative territory to a more central one. To judge by later disputes over the southern administrative boundary of the city, the presence of an ancient boundary along the Witham continued to affect the development of the city until modern times, causing the Wigford suburb to be given special treatment. For example, the open fields of

Lincoln are all to the north of the river, which might imply that they were allotted in the late 9th or early 10th century, before the occupation of the Wigford suburb (Fig. 9.3).

Superimposed upon the county level of organisation was the earldom, introduced by Cnut in the early 11th century and replacing the ealdormanries of the 10th century. The position of the earl was equivalent to the

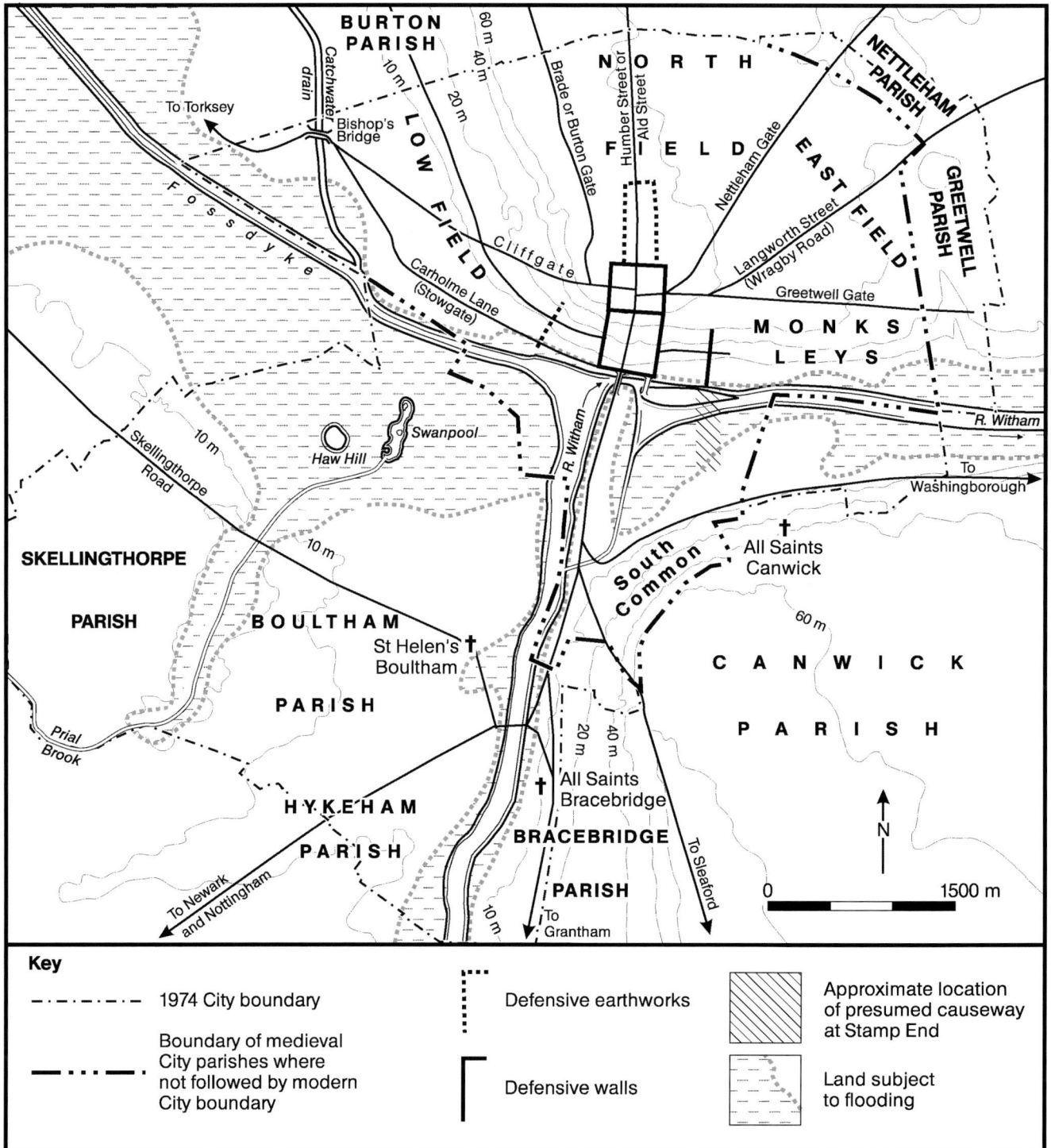

**Key**

– - – - – - –  1974 City boundary

– - – - – - –  Boundary of medieval City parishes where not followed by modern City boundary

⋮⋮⋮  Defensive earthworks

Г  Defensive walls

▨  Approximate location of presumed causeway at Stamp End

▨  Land subject to flooding

*Fig. 9.3. The layout of Lincoln's medieval open fields, meadows and the extent of its medieval parishes, in relation to modern administrative boundaries (sources, Hill 1948 and others – drawn by Dave Watt).*

ealdorman of earlier times but there was a shift in power towards the King so that the earl was a more powerful figure, owing less to local factions than his predecessors and in general commanding a larger area. To what extent this increase in power was reflected in the topography of the city is a further area of interest. In particular we might expect the layout of the Upper City to be affected by the introduction of a new centre of county administration.

Many aspects of the Old English state survived the Norman Conquest and *Domesday Book* provides detailed evidence for the state of Lincoln in 1066 and 1086. Local power, in the main, seems to have remained in the hands of the Anglo-Danish elite but the impact of the conquerors should not be down-played. Normans and their allies formed an important new element in the land-holding elite and it is to be expected that these newcomers were not alone. Their retinues could have provided a channel for new ideas and fashions. Some indication of the continuity before and after the Conquest is provided by the list of Lawmen given in *Domesday Book* (Fig. 9.4). Four of the twelve lawmen served both under Edward and William and a further

four inherited their positions from their fathers. In two cases, Wulfnoth the priest and Leodwine son of Rafn, there is no obvious connection between the holders of the position under William and their predecessors but the later holders were Anglo-Scandinavian and in only two cases were the later holders obvious newcomers: Norman Crassus and Peter of Valognes. Both were members of the Norman court (Hill 1948, 52), but whereas Norman Crassus may well have been resident in Lincoln, Peter of Valognes clearly acquired the office of lawman along with the lands of Godric son of Eadgifu. It may well be, therefore, that even the two lawmen seemingly unrelated to their predecessors in *Domesday Book* held their positions through holding the lands of Siward and Halfdan. In this regard we should also note that Siward's heirs (his wife and son Norman) were in dispute with Wulfnoth over Siward's share of a carucate in the fields of Lincoln (ed. Morgan and Thorn 1986, 336b).

In addition to the 12 lawmen of Lincoln, *Domesday Book* lists some of the major landholders, before and after the Conquest. (Fig. 9.5). As Hill notes (1948, 42), they were probably only listed because they were

| | Lawman in 1066 | Lawman in 1086 | Comments |
|---|---|---|---|
| 1 | Harethaknutr | Svertingr son of Harthaknutr | Inherited |
| 2 | Svertingr son of Grimbald | Svertingr | Survived |
| 3 | Svartbrandr son of Ulf | Svartbrandr son of Ulfr | Survived |
| 4 | Valhrafn | Agmundr son of Valhrafn | Inherited |
| 5 | Alwold | Alwold | Survived |
| 6 | Beorhtric | Godwine son of Beorhtric | Inherited |
| 7 | Guthrothr | Crassus | Evidently an Anglo-Scandinavian replaced by a Norman incomer |
| 8 | Wulfbert | Wulfbert | Survived |
| 9 | Godric son of Eadgifu | Peter of Valonges | The Norman Peter also acquired Anglo-Scandinavian Godric's carucate in the fields |
| 10 | Siward the priest | Wulfnoth the priest | ? Inherited |
| 11 | Leofwine the priest | Burgwald son of Leofwine | Inherited |
| 12 | Halfdan the priest | Leodwine son of Rafn | Descent not known |

*Fig. 9.4. The fate of Lincoln's 12 'Lawmen'* (Laguna, ides habentes sacam et socam) *between 1066 and 1086 (source, Foster and Longley 1924).*

| Estate owner 1066 | Estate owner 1086 | Outline of holding |
|---|---|---|
| Tochi son of Outi | Geoffrey Alselin and his *nepos* Ralf | Hall, 30 messuages, 2.5 churches. The 30 messuages held on privileged terms |
| Merlesuen | Ralf Pagenel | 1 messuage (quit of all custom) |
| Earl Morcar | Earnwine the Priest | 1 messuage (with sake & soke) |
| Ulf | Gilbert of Gant | 1 messuage (with sake and soke) |
| Earl Harold | Earl Hugh | 1 messuage (with sake and soke) |
| Suen son of Suaue | Roger de Busli | 2 messuages (with landgable) |
| Stori | Countess Judith | 1 messuage (with sake and soke) |
| Probably not a single holding before 1072 | Bishop Remigius | 1 messuage (without sake and soke)<br>1 little manor with 1 carucate (with sake, soke, toll and team);<br>1 messuage (with sake and soke and not subject to King's geld);<br>2 messuages (with sake and soke and subject to King's geld);<br>2 churches (with sake and soke). Soke of 78 messuages but suject to King's geld). |

*Fig. 9.5. The fates of major Anglo-Scandinavian landholdings in Lincoln after 1066 (source, Foster and Longley 1924).*

the summer until, in September, King John and his army arrived, at which point Gilbert fled and John entered the city. However, in October John fell ill and died in Newark whereupon Gilbert de Gant resumed his siege of the Castle on behalf of Louis, being joined by the baronial army, which was quartered in and around the city. William the Marshal, acting for the new infant King, Henry III, mustered troops at Newark and mounted an assault on the city, approaching by way of Torksey and Stow, so as to join up with the defenders of the Castle whilst avoiding the town and its suburbs. This stratagem worked and the royal forces mounted a two-pronged attack on the French forces in the city; the smaller party entered the Castle, via the west gate, and were then able to fire arrows onto the besiegers. Meanwhile, the rest of the royal forces stormed the north gate (i.e. Newport Arch – which implies that the defences of the Newport suburb offered no resistance) and entered the city, driving the besiegers southwards until they were clear of the city. The defences of the Castle, and the city, clearly took some battering during the siege and battle, known thereafter as *The Fair of Lincoln*, and subsequent developments were concerned both with repairing the walls and strengthening weak points in the Castle defences. By this time, the market place outside the Castle east gate had been almost filled with housing whilst the southern stretch of the Castle wall was overlooked by two towers, and defended by the natural hill slope. Consequently, repairs and modifications were confined to the east and west gates and the north-east corner of the curtain wall – where a large tower was erected (p. 177 below). A further feature which was certainly constructed later than the battle, but which may be only an indirect result of it, was the construction of a second gate across Steep Hill, to the south of the Roman gate (Johnson and Vince 1992).

### Lincoln's new urban economy c.900–c.1350

No direct measure of the relative wealth or size of Lincoln in the Anglo-Scandinavian or early Norman period exists and it is therefore difficult to make comparisons with the situation between the mid 12th and mid 14th centuries. We have already noted that Lincoln was much the largest in terms of population amongst the Five Towns of the East Midlands in the 10th century, and nothing expresses its pre-eminence so clearly as the output of the mints, which all these towns had. With 95 moneyers, Lincoln from 979–1066 had a much greater output of coin than Nottingham (13), Stamford (52), Derby (13) and Leicester (21). Indeed, in this ranking, Lincoln is second only to London nationally (with 141 moneyers) and it stands just above York (with 91) (Hill 1948, 30–1). The later 10th and early 11th centuries were times of exceptional growth and importance for the city. However, it is clear that this rise to wealth and influence did not cease at the Conquest. As we have seen, the city was still expanding between 1066 and 1086, and in terms of size and wealth, Lincoln was one of the five most important cities in William's new realm. The establishment of a Cathedral and Castle ensured that the 12th and early 13th centuries were periods of continuing prosperity for the city, both in absolute terms and in relation to other cities in England. By the 13th century, Lincoln's only rival within the East Midlands was the newly-founded market town of Boston, but there can be little doubt that it was the dominant urban place in the region. This is dramatically demonstrated by a recent study of place-names used in personal names in the Lay Subsidy Rolls in the early 14th century, carried out by Paul Bischoff (pers. com.). Bischoff shows that Lincoln attracted immigrants from much further afield than other East Midlands county towns (Nottingham, Leicester) whereas the smaller, newer towns, such as Retford, were populated mainly by people from surrounding villages. This large 'population catchment zone', which shows Lincoln pulling in people from all over the East Midlands demonstrates that, in effect, between the 12th and 14th centuries, Lincoln was the regional capital, unrivalled south of the Humber until (on the southern edge of the Fens) its hinterland ran into that of London. From the middle of the 13th century onwards, however, Lincoln started to slip rapidly down the ranking, and was, for example, unable to pay its fine for pardon after the Baron's War, and that led to the holding of a royal enquiry into the city's poverty in 1267. During the production of this *Assessment*, the very visible evidence for this decline, or more likely, collapse, of Lincoln's economy in the late 13th and early 14th centuries was thought sufficiently marked to represent a change of 'Era' and, consequently, it is discussed at much greater length in chapters 10a, 10b and 10c below.

Although precise figures are unobtainable, Lincoln's population trends reflect the city's dramatic boom between the 10th and 12th centuries, followed by its equally startling decline from the late 13th century onwards (Fig. 9.6). These trends are seen in many other towns in England, but Lincoln's rise is more dramatic than most and its collapse similarly so. The population of the Lincoln area at the end of the 9th century is unknown but, if we exclude the possibility of an undiscovered extra-mural trading settlement, it is likely to have been in the low hundreds at most. But, at the time of the *Domesday Book* inquest in 1086, it is estimated that there were between six and ten thousand inhabitants, depending on what multiplier is used for the size of a household and whether or not certain categories of inhabitant are excluded. The late 12th century saw, in England as a whole, an increase in population which was both caused by, and itself the cause of, the growth of new towns and markets. The estimated population of the country grew steeply during the 13th century until, by the early 14th century, it seems that the carrying capacity of the land, under the existing agricultural

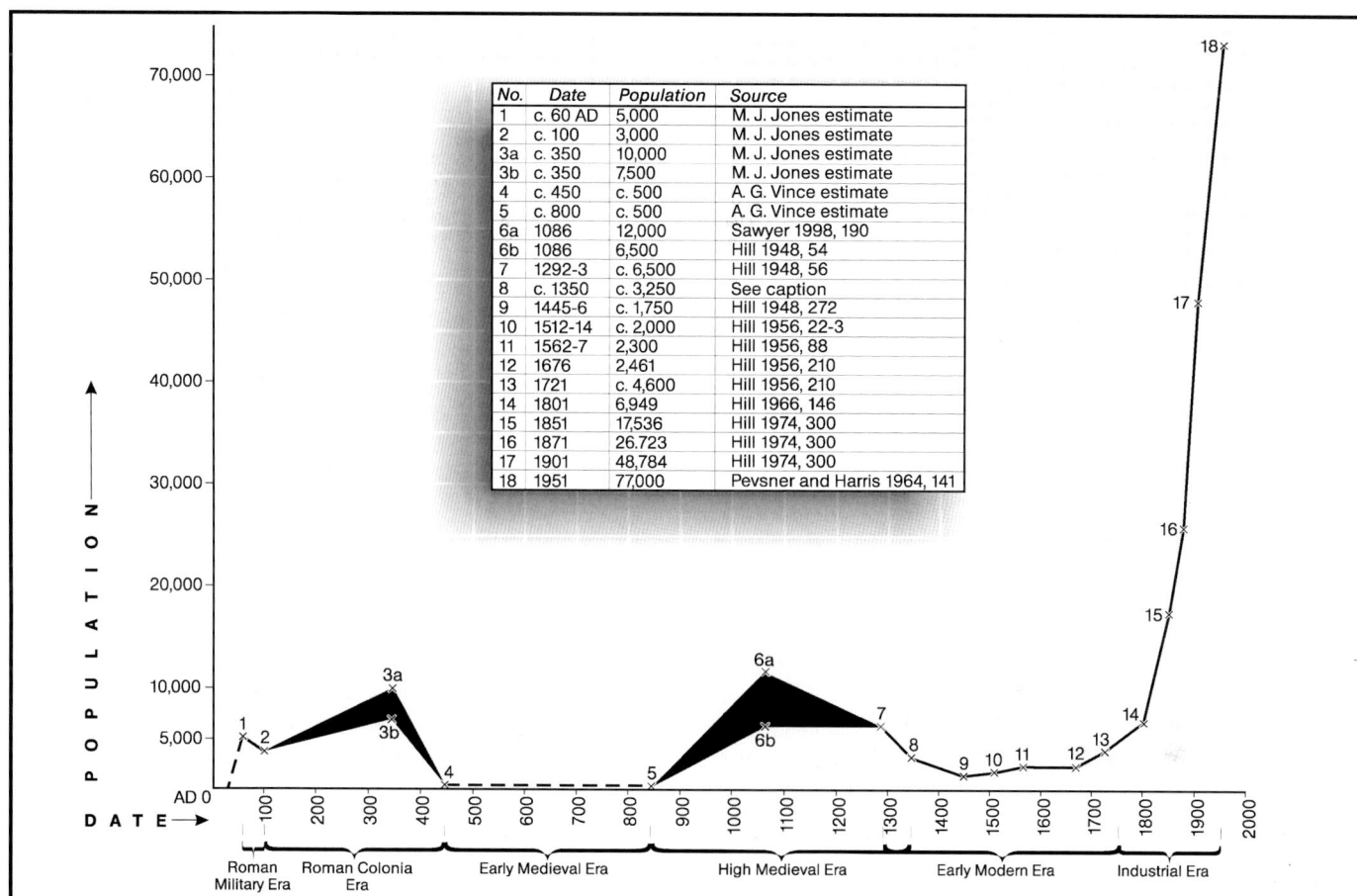

| No. | Date | Population | Source |
|-----|------|-----------|--------|
| 1 | c. 60 AD | 5,000 | M. J. Jones estimate |
| 2 | c. 100 | 3,000 | M. J. Jones estimate |
| 3a | c. 350 | 10,000 | M. J. Jones estimate |
| 3b | c. 350 | 7,500 | M. J. Jones estimate |
| 4 | c. 450 | c. 500 | A. G. Vince estimate |
| 5 | c. 800 | c. 500 | A. G. Vince estimate |
| 6a | 1086 | 12,000 | Sawyer 1998, 190 |
| 6b | 1086 | 6,500 | Hill 1948, 54 |
| 7 | 1292-3 | c. 6,500 | Hill 1948, 56 |
| 8 | c. 1350 | c. 3,250 | See caption |
| 9 | 1445-6 | c. 1,750 | Hill 1948, 272 |
| 10 | 1512-14 | c. 2,000 | Hill 1956, 22-3 |
| 11 | 1562-7 | 2,300 | Hill 1956, 88 |
| 12 | 1676 | 2,461 | Hill 1956, 210 |
| 13 | 1721 | c. 4,600 | Hill 1956, 210 |
| 14 | 1801 | 6,949 | Hill 1966, 146 |
| 15 | 1851 | 17,536 | Hill 1974, 300 |
| 16 | 1871 | 26.723 | Hill 1974, 300 |
| 17 | 1901 | 48,784 | Hill 1974, 300 |
| 18 | 1951 | 77,000 | Pevsner and Harris 1964, 141 |

*Fig. 9.6. Graph showing estimated development of population of Lincoln from c.AD50–1945. The figure for c.1350 (point 8) is 50% of the 1292–3 figure and is based on Thompson's 1911 study – moderated by Hill 1948, 251–2. These assessments suggest that 60% of the clergy in the city died in 1349 and that civilian mortality was likely to have been between 40% and 50%. Although the figure might be an overestimate, and there will have been some recovery in population numbers, nevertheless, this figure conforms to the clear trend in the city's population during the 14th century and is supported by Bishoff's economic analysis (1975) and Platts' economic study of the county as a whole (1985, 162–9) (drawn by Dave Watt, copyright English Heritage).*

regime, had been reached. A series of famines during the early 14th century show that there was no surplus that could be used as a safety net in times of crisis. Population growth, then, faltered and then in 1348 fell dramatically in the wake of the great plague. Of course, the growth in rural population in the 12th and 13th centuries provided a larger market for goods, such as those made and traded through Lincoln, but the decline in rural numbers in the county in the 14th century hit the city hard, just at a time when its place in the international economy had also been compromised.

The archaeological evidence as to how the city fared in the 13th century is not clear-cut. On the one hand, there is evidence for the *increased* use of the backs and interiors of plots for housing, although much of this was also taking place in the 11th century, and on sites in the Wigford suburb this may be the period when lanes were constructed linking the High Street to the

Brayford Pool, as at St Mark's Station (Z 86). On the other hand, there is no evidence for any new area coming into occupation later than the late 12th century, although the extremities of the settlement have yet to be satisfactorily investigated archaeologically. Documentary sources show that both the fringes of the Eastgate and Wigford suburbs were occupied in the later 12th century (St Leonard's and St Botolph's parishes), but we cannot yet say whether this was an expansion of the 12th century or one which occurred somewhat earlier, in the later 11th century, as at *Butwerk* and Newport. A survey of suburban development by Derek Keene has shown that Lincoln follows the pattern of many county towns, founded in the pre-Conquest period and growing continuously during the 11th and 12th centuries (Keene 1975). By the later 12th century these places had ceased to expand outwards, although they may have been more intensively occupied within their existing limits. Keene suggests that this arrest in growth may be because the distance to the centre of town from the outer limits had become intolerable (from the northern end of Newport to the southern end of Wigford was a distance of 3.25 km, for example), or that land rents at the centre were driven up to such a point that certain trades could not operate. In his important thesis on the decline of Lincoln in the 13th and 14th centuries, however, Paul Bischoff (1975) has suggested that the collapse of the cloth trade was responsible for calling expansion to an abrupt halt. He shows that the fine cloths made in Lincoln and shipped all over Europe were suddenly out of fashion and simply unsaleable. Furthermore, this was not just a shift in fashion to which Lincoln might have adapted, it was a structural shift brought about by the growth of the Flemish cloth industry at the expense of the English one. Lincolnshire still remained an important wool producing county, but the profits of that trade went to a few wool merchants, rather than being distributed amongst a much larger group of weavers (not to mention the service trades which catered for the weavers). Paul Bishoff shows that these profound changes in the structure of the cloth industry lead directly to a rapid and dramatic decline in the city's population. Furthermore, the growth of new towns (like Boston) in the 12th and 13th centuries took away potential new citizens from Lincoln and also provided competition for its services and industries. An example of this is the pottery industry, where new regional production centres sprang up during this period, at Toynton All Saints, at Bourne and, across the Trent, in Doncaster, for example, nibbling away at the market for Lincoln wares.

Even if we are uncertain of its size in the 11th and early 12th centuries, Lincoln's port certainly declined in the middle of the 13th century. Again, this is most graphically shown through the study of pottery. In the later 12th and 13th centuries, a range of imports is found in the city, albeit in small quantities, but from the middle of the 13th century onwards their number declines dramatically. Presumably this is due to ships which used to come directly to Lincoln unloading instead at Boston and Kingston-upon-Hull. Since Boston had been in existence in the later 11th century it is likely that the main reason for the absence of

imports is the foundation of Hull in the 1260s. A comparison of gross figures for pottery sherds found in the three main zones of the city shows that there is hardly any difference between the quantities of late 11th- to mid 12th-century and late 12th- to mid 13th-century pottery in any area. The overall figures are heavily skewed because of the inclusion of the predominantly late 9th- to 12th-century Flaxengate site (F 72) and the Silver Street pottery production site in the Lower City (LIN 73b) and of waste from the late medieval pottery production site east of St Mark's Station (ZE 87) in the Wigford totals. If we correct the table for these imbalances (Fig. 9.7), we see that pottery use reflects the economic decline only in Wigford. We should note that it is not apparent in the Lower City, however, where the weaving trade was apparently centred and where one might expect to see any signs of decline most dramatically. Furthermore, the figures for both the Upper City and Wigford figures are higher in the late 13th and 14th century than in the preceding century. Such figures are, of course, potentially misleading not just because of biases within the samples from excavations, but also because they take no account of the increased use of glazed jugs during the medieval period – whether or not there were fewer people, those that were present in the later periods certainly had a richer material culture.

## The fight for power – civic government and society c.950–c.1350

A theme running though the history of medieval Lincoln is the struggle for control of the city between three separate groups: the custodian of the Castle, the Cathedral and the citizens of the town. But this is essentially a post-Conquest division of power, and there was probably already an elaborate social stratification within the Anglo-Scandinavian town. The paucity of evidence for occupation within the Upper City before the Conquest actually argues for the high status of that area, as a reserved aristocratic and religious enclave. There is less evidence for any difference in character between the extra-mural suburbs of Upper Wigford and *Butwerk* and the intramural settlement in the Lower City, although it is likely

| Period | Lower City | Lower City (corrected) | Upper City | Upper City (corrected) | Wigford | Wigford (corrected) |
|---|---|---|---|---|---|---|
| L 9th /11th | 94.94% | 75.15% | 0.58% | 2.97% | 4.48% | 21.89% |
| L 11th /M 12th | 90.63% | 78.77% | 3.45% | 8.15% | 5.92% | 13.08% |
| L 12th /M 13th | 89.61% | 84.92% | 5.01% | 7.40% | 5.36% | 7.66% |
| L 13th /M 14th | 73.60% | 69.22% | 12.18% | 15.29% | 14.19% | 15.46% |
| L 14th /15th | 48.46% | 75.14% | 4.66% | 9.13% | 46.85% | 15.67% |
| Grand Total | 87.23% | 76.87% | 2.95% | 7.95% | 9.82% | 15.15% |

*Fig. 9.7. Pottery finds, by source, for various areas of the city from the 11th to the 15th centuries. The 'corrected' columns exclude atypical collections (source, Vince and Young forthcoming).*

that certain industries were located mainly in these suburban properties. This can be demonstrated for the pottery industry but not, so far, for any others. Furthermore, there is evidence for the practice of small-scale crafts on many properties within the Lower City.

However, despite the lack of recognised archaeological differences, David Stocker (2000) has recognised a difference in the number and character of the grave monuments from churches in northern Wigford – specifically St Mark and St Mary-le-Wigford. He sees the high number of recorded monuments at these two churches and the low numbers recorded from churches elsewhere in the city as a reflection of the original situation rather than an accident of survival and posits a different social structure in the two Wigford parishes, which he suggests might reflect a mercantile quarter in this part of the town.

By the mid 12th century the constableship of the Castle had become hereditary within the De la Haye family (who may have been descended from Colsuein, a great figure in late Anglo-Scandinavian Lincoln) and they continued to hold this office until the early 14th century when the family was joined by marriage to the earls of Lincoln. Hill (1948) has charted the convoluted relationships of the Earldom and the constableship of the Castle and has shown that two families; that of Countess Lucy and the De la Hayes, held the constableship throughout the 12th and 13th centuries and that the families were finally united in the late 13th or early 14th century by marriage. The Earldom did not in itself give any rights over the Castle, although both Lucy and her son Ranulph had fortified and held towers here and Ranulph had also held the constableship. The office of Constable brought with it both rights and duties. In 1311 the constable had to provide 'castle-guard' and held the keepership of the prison in the Castle, the wardships, all other profits issuing from the Castle, rents from tenants in the Bail and rent from foreign tenants in Lindsey and Kesteven. The 'other profits' must have included the toll from the market held at Castle Hill and the right to administer justice within the Bail court. The King, on whose behalf the Constable held these rights, also had the right to administer justice to any lawbreaker on the King's highway or the town walls.

The right of the Dean and Chapter to conduct their own affairs was hard won and a series of charters for land in the Bail and the Pottergate suburb show that, in the mid 12th century, office holders and others in the Cathedral had to provide their own accommodation and held land in the same way as other citizens of the town. Inexorably, however, the Cathedral gained more and more control over its office holders' private dwellings. In some cases, as with the property which later became the Angel Inn, on the northern corner of Eastgate and Bailgate, a property became associated with an office, in that case, the office of Archdeacon of Lincoln, but was transferred to the next incumbent of the office by being sold by the late

official's executors. In other cases, however, the property was granted to the Dean and Chapter who then provided a tenancy for its previous owner until his death. Once the Cathedral was in possession of land, stipulations were laid down as to who might live in the property, to bar sub-letting to any not working for the Cathedral. Certain properties were then provided for particular officials – the Dean, the Subdean, the Precentor, the Sacrist, the Vicars-Choral, the Chancellor and various chantry priests amongst others. Rents obtained on other property in the town were used for the construction and upkeep of these houses, some of which were accounted for separately and others out of the common fund. Ultimately, the Cathedral gained the right to construct a wall around their property and passed on the duty to build and maintain this Close Wall to those holding land within it. The first grants date to the later 13th century and by the middle of the 14th century a continuous circuit had been achieved, enclosing not only Pottergate, the southern part of the Eastgate suburb, but also the majority of the south-eastern and north-eastern quarters of the Bail. The archdeacon's houses on the Bailgate/Eastgate corner were actually outside of the Close Wall but the great majority of Cathedral properties were included within it (Fig. 9.18). The Dean and Chapter retained their separateness throughout the medieval period and, indeed, when in 1815 the medieval northern gate in Pottergate was demolished, an open archway replaced it on the site, to ensure that the symbolic enclosure of the Close retained its integrity.

The citizens too gradually gained power during the later 12th century. Their affairs had been run by twelve lawmen and the Burwarmote Court from the late 11th century onwards, but a major advance took place in the late 12th century, following the granting of liberties and customs to the city by Richard I in a charter of 1194. In 1206 we hear of Adam, Mayor of Lincoln, and soon after that of a Council, composed of 24 citizens. In the 11th century, the Burwarmote had met in the churchyard of St Peter-at-Pleas, or perhaps in a hall nearby, but by the early 13th century, the Council had a guildhall in the south-east corner of the Lower City, which in 1237, at the King's request, they gave to the Franciscan friars for the site of their new friary and were, in return, given the chamber above the Stonebow, overlooking the site of the old court. Hill makes the point that the medieval Council was elected from within a small circle, since a very few families seem to have retained the office of mayor (*Ibid.*, 295–8). The Council's jurisdiction stretched to the city limits, excluding the Bail and the Close, so that neither the boundary between the Lower City and its suburbs, nor that between the area in occupation and the open fields and countryside surrounding it had any legal significance. Thus, over time as the city grew and contracted the boundaries of settlement shifted and the old formal limits were gradually obscured.

## Topographical description of the city

### *Civic defences c.900–c.1150*

In the mid 9th century the defences of Lincoln consisted of the Roman walls and ditches of the upper and lower cities. On most sides of the city these walls (and their associated ramparts and ditches) survived as defensive works, although it is possible that they had been breached in places and the ditches silted. We have no excavated evidence for the condition of the late Roman ditches in the 9th century (the evidence from Motherby Hill west of the Lower City – MH 77 – is ambivalent) but it is likely that they still formed a real barrier. Similarly, we have no evidence from any of the many sections cut across the defences for any 9th-century construction activity on the walls. But it is also the case that there is no archaeological evidence that any medieval work at all took place on these defences after the Roman period, except for the insertion or renovation of gateways. It is doubtful, therefore whether such negative evidence is reliable.

Only in two places is the survival of the Roman walls into the 9th century thought doubtful. The wall between the Upper and Lower Cities, the south wall of the original Roman fortress, had ceased to have a defensive function in the 2nd century with the construction of the Lower City defences. Nevertheless, it may have served a symbolic function, separating ceremonial and religious from domestic functions perhaps. Documentary sources show that the eastern part of this wall and ditch was considered to be part of the Castle defences in the early 12th century, when Stephen granted the Bishop the right to build his palace on ground immediately south of the ditch (ed. Foster 1931, 54–5, RA87). This ditch may, however, have been a Norman re-cutting, undertaken at the foundation of the Castle in 1068 and we have no earlier evidence for its survival. Two excavations have taken place along this stretch of wall, both directed by Denis Petch in the 1950s (Petch 1960). From this work it seems clear that the Roman rampart survived to some height in the Middle Ages, but that the build-up of deposits inside the fortress masked its height. The upper parts of Petch's sections were not recorded in detail (at least, not in the published versions). There is still today a considerable drop to the south of the rampart, and Petch's work shows that the Roman wall lay halfway down the existing slope outside the medieval Upper City, and inside the Bishop's Palace. The eastern part of the south wall of the Upper City, then, was rebuilt further north in the Norman period, either when William I constructed his castle or when the wall, effectively, was given to the Bishop together with the grant of the ditch, which initially separated the Cathedral from the Bishop's Palace. This rebuilt wall formed the southern boundary of the Close.

To the west, much of the line of the fortress south wall was removed in the Norman period for the construction of the Castle but small stretches ought to survive in the southern side of the Lucy Tower motte and between the observatory tower motte and the south gate. A fragment of wall, traditionally identified as the Roman city wall, is exposed in the grounds of Hilton House but an examination of early maps of this area suggest that wall was curved, and concentric with the Lucy Tower. Most probably, it was part of a rebuild of the city wall following the outer edge of the motte ditch, before heading southwards to join the western wall of the Lower City. From the location of the Lucy Tower motte itself and the likely position of the earliest inner bailey curtain wall (now incorporated into the Observatory Tower motte) it is likely that the Norman Castle defences lie slightly to the east and north of the original Roman line. On both sides of the south gate, then, it seems that the defensive line marked by the south wall of the Roman Upper City was important in the Norman period, but that the wall itself had become disused, possibly because it had suffered considerable erosion in the intervening centuries.

As with the former south wall of the Roman fortress, the extent of survival of the Roman wall along the Witham waterfront is also uncertain. The Saltergate excavations (LIN 73d) showed that the Roman wall here was used as foundations for a medieval masonry building, although this building is undated. No records, and few finds, survive from the excavation of the Saltergate postern gate, but it is likely that a 10th-century 'jetty' with stone foundations retained by timber revetments, found in excavations in 1988–9, was approached through this gate (Donel and Jarvis 1990; Donel 1991b; Chitwood 1991). This jetty was cut away in places by rubbish pits containing 11th-century pottery and it may be that they indicate the closure of the gate at the end of the 11th century (and perhaps the construction of the predecessor of Bank Street slightly to its east). On this rather flimsy evidence, however, we presume that the Roman riverside wall was still standing and defendable in the mid 9th century but was already breached in the 11th century, although we cannot be sure whether this was before or after the Norman Conquest.

The Roman defences were inherited by the Anglo-Scandinavian and Norman inhabitants of Lincoln, then, but any works carried out between the 9th and 12th centuries must have been very limited in scale and extent. Having said that, large areas of the defences, and especially the city ditch, have not been examined archaeologically, whilst many of those excavations which have taken place have been in areas where we might not expect post-Roman activity to survive.

### *The first Castle, 1068–c.1130*

Lincoln Castle was a royal foundation erected as a response to a rising in the North in 1068. The *Anglo-*

*Saxon Chronicle* suggests that it was raised in the same campaign as Nottingham, York and 'many other places in that part of the country'. The first Castle therefore seems to have been erected as part of a hasty campaign designed to house a garrison and provide a secure base for the King and his retinue when in Lincoln. At its foundation, the need for a fortified enclosure within which military and civil government could be based would have been paramount and the intact Roman fortress would have provided just such an enclosure ready-made. It has always been presumed, since the earliest antiquarian accounts, that the present ditched, banked and walled enclosure represents the Castle of 1068. However, the post-excavation work on several projects, especially those at the west gate (CWG 86), has raised the likelihood that the present castle enclosure is a somewhat later feature in the topography. The west gate excavations revealed the Roman wall, the Norman gate foundations and a succession of medieval street surfaces, which show that the ground level inside the Castle had been raised considerably during the medieval period, leading to the survival of Norman structures to some height below ground.

Detailed analysis of the excavation records has not yet taken place but an initial survey of the pottery from the excavation shows that there is virtually no 11th-century material present; the post-Roman sequence starts with the 12th century. This cannot be simply due to the fact that levels of 11th-century date were not reached and, indeed, four sherds of middle Saxon pottery were present. It implies that the curtain wall, the bank upon which it is built and the west gate itself date to the 12th century.

This means that we have to reconsider exactly what the Castle founded in 1068 looked like (Fig. 9.8). Parallels at other urban castles of early Norman date (such as the Tower of London or Gloucester Castle), might suggest that the initial defences consisted of a small bank and ditch cutting off a corner of the Roman defences. At Gloucester this small space was almost entirely filled by a motte. At Lincoln, however, we have the record of *Domesday Book*, which informs us that in 1086 the Castle covered ground equivalent to 166 households. And it is the reinterpretation of this account that shows us that the first castle at Lincoln occupied the whole of the upper Roman enclosure

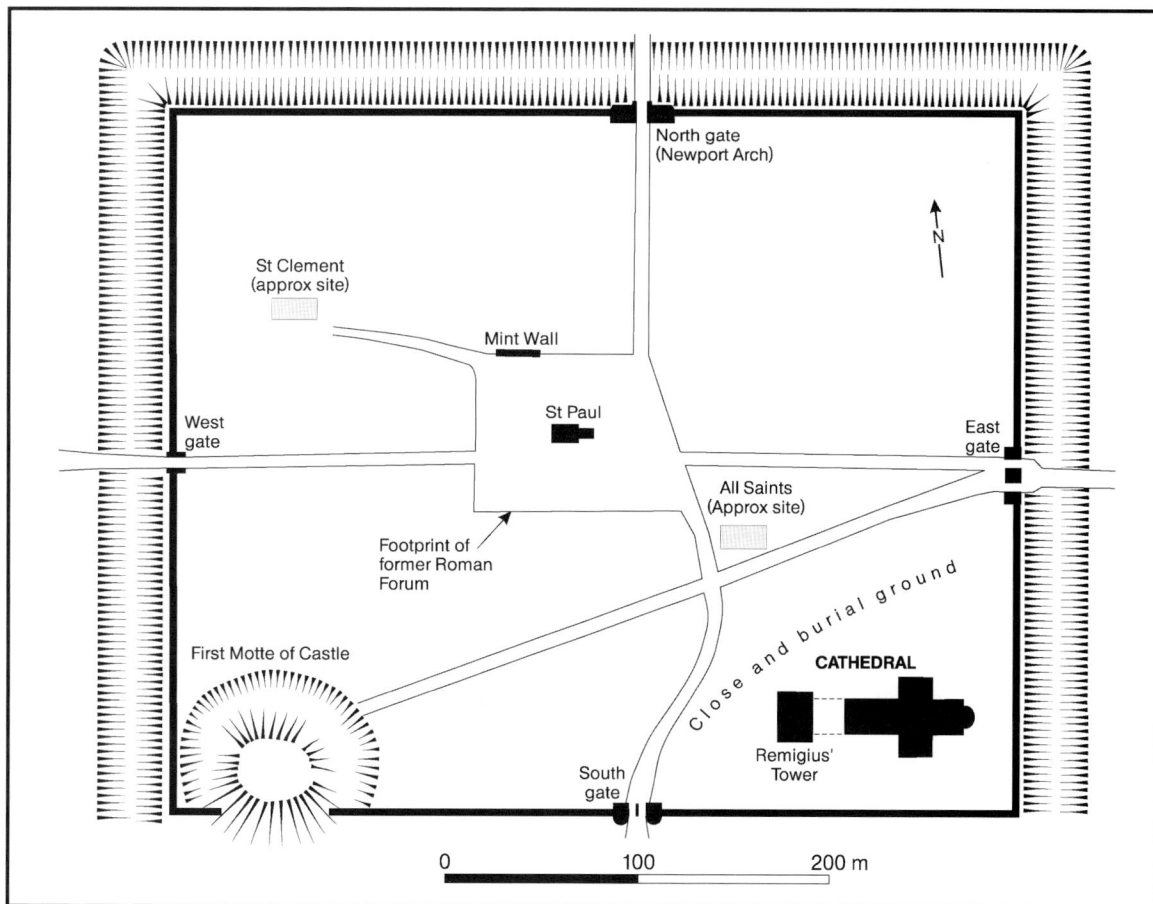

*Fig. 9.8. Reconstruction study of the Upper City plan c.1090. It is argued here that the whole of the former Roman enclosure served as the Royal castle founded in 1068 (sources, Stocker and Vince 1997; Stocker forthcoming a – drawn by Dave Watt, copyright English Heritage).*

(Stocker and Vince 1997; Stocker forthcoming a). *Domesday Book* states that Lincoln was assessed as having 970 occupied residences in total in 1066 and only 760 in 1086, and that of the 240 unoccupied residences 166 were 'waste' on account of the Castle. These figures clearly imply that 17% of the city's taxable property in 1086 was located in the area of the Castle and, as it happens, the area of the Upper City accounts for between 14% and 21% of the occupied property in the city at this date (including the Eastgate, *Butwerk* and Wigford suburbs, but excluding Newport, Newland and the *Westcastle* suburb – depending on whether one takes the city to include or exclude the city ditches). It seems highly likely then, that the Castle in 1086 was not the 12th-century enclosure which we have grown to think of as Lincoln Castle (which is less than 5% of the occupied area of the city) but rather that it was the whole of the former Roman Upper City. The area, in fact, known throughout the medieval period as the Bail. The only other explanation of the *Domesday Book* entry would be that land in the south-west quarter of the Bail was taxed at about four times the standard rate – but the actual land-toll values recorded in medieval documents are consistently at the standard rate of one penny (Hill 1948, 58–9).

We suggest then, that, in 1068, the King expropriated and removed from taxation the entire Upper City, which was previously assessed as being equivalent to 166 residences, or units of taxation, and devoted it to the newly-founded Castle. Lincoln Castle has, therefore, a two-stage development. The first stage in this development, in 1068, was the expropriation of the whole Upper City, the former Roman fortress. A motte was thrown up in the south-west corner and, defending this motte, some refurbishment of the Roman defences, especially on the exposed southern stretch may have been necessary. A recent study has looked at the north and east gates and concluded that the Roman gates were re-edified during this initial phase of castle building (Stocker forthcoming a).

In 1072×5 the new Cathedral was, therefore, founded *within* the new Royal Castle, and the early bishops of Lincoln had their palace inside the King's fortification. Indeed, in addition to being the sacerdotal head of the diocese, they were also, legally, the principal secular barons in the new Castle, owing a service of 20 knights to the King (*Ibid.*; Hill 1930; 1948, 86–8). Consequently it was in the Roman Upper City wall (and not in the later Castle enclosure wall), between 1101 and 1115, that the Bishop was allowed to make a door by the King to give him access to his house (ed. Foster 1931, 20, RA21).

Then, in the early 12th century, the decision was taken drastically to reduce the area of the Castle and to exclude the Cathedral. Work began on the construction of the massive earthwork ramparts and curtain wall we see today. Construction of the new ramparts involved the blocking of the original Roman west gate to the Upper City (it still survives buried in the rampart), and the construction of a postern gate into the city from the west (Fig. 9.9). A new street following the line of the new ramparts and ditch was laid out on the line of modern Westgate.

### The Castle between the early 12th and the early 14th centuries

The new enclosure, begun in the early 12th century, is the complex we recognise as the Castle today (Fig. 9.9) (Plate 3.1). The defences consist of two keeps (the Lucy Tower and Observatory Tower), both sitting on mottes, a curtain wall on top of an earthen bank, a corner tower (the Cobb Hall) at the north-east angle of the circuit, the east gate, the west gate and the ditch. Although from the middle of the 12th century the area within the Roman walled circuit but outside the new Castle was demilitarised, it continued to be known as 'the Bail', and it had the status of the outer bailey of the Castle.

Exactly when the change in the Castle's size occurred remains uncertain, and it may, anyway, have been a developmental process (Stocker and Vince 1997; Stocker forthcoming a). It is clear however that, whereas in the last quarter of the 11th century, the entire Roman enclosure was looked upon as the Castle of Lincoln, with its defence being shared by the Bishop, the Earl and the Sheriff, by the mid 12th century the Castle was considered to be the inner bailey alone and the responsibility of lay lords holding the office of 'custodian' of the Castle. A significant point had been reached in the early 1130s when the bishop was given leave for his knights to undertake their 'castle-guard' at the bishop's castle at Newark (ed. Foster 1931, 35, RA51) and the King gave the east gate of the Bail to the bishop for use as his palace (ed. Foster 1931, 43, RA49). The relative sequence of construction of the inner bailey defences is fairly clear but the precise chronology is not. Both the west gate and the earliest phases of the east gate can be dated by their architectural form to the early years of the 12th century, a conclusion which is supported, in the case of the west gate, by excavated pottery.

The west gate was built to accommodate the massive western earthwork rampart and so is probably contemporary with it, whilst the equally massive northern earthwork rampart looks similar in type and scale and is unlikely to be significantly later in date. Both are very high and broad, rising at least 6 metres above the bailey and even higher above the surrounding Bail (Figs. 9.9 and 9.10). Along the eastern side of the enclosure the earthwork is quite different in scale and character, being less massive. To the north of the east gate it reaches only about 3 metres high and to the south of the east gate there is no rampart at all, merely the motte on which the Observatory Tower stands. The eastern defences may be somewhat later in date than their northern and western counterparts – perhaps belonging to the second quarter of the 12th century. The two lengths of wall on the eastern side are unlikely

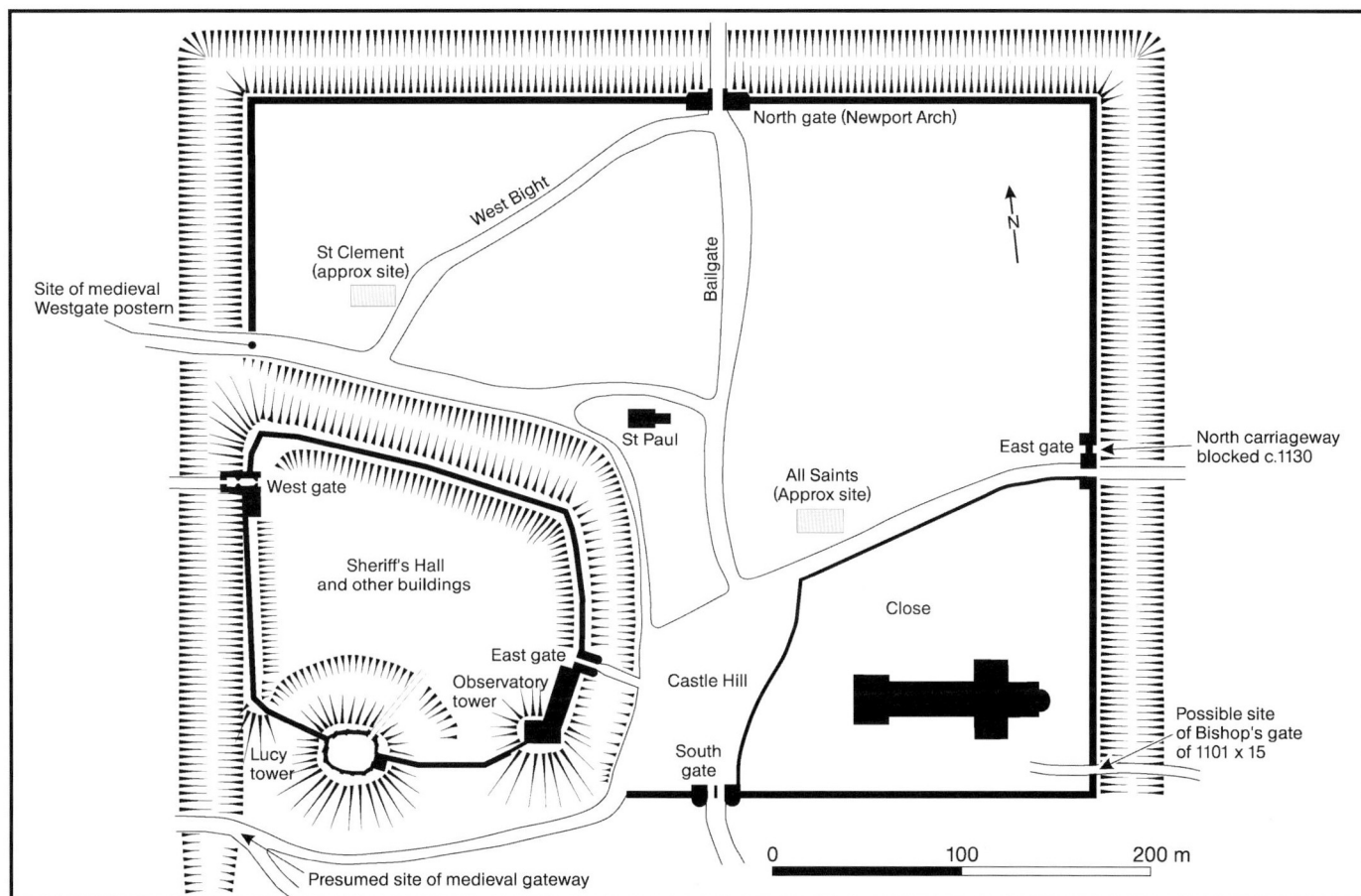

*Fig. 9.9. Reconstruction study of the Upper City plan c.1150, following the withdrawal of the Castle to the newly constructed enclosure in the south-western corner of the Roman enclosure (sources, Stocker and Vince 1997; Stocker forthcoming a – drawn by Dave Watt, copyright English Heritage).*

to be contemporary with each other, however, as they are on markedly different alignments. It is worth observing that the eastern wall, from the east gate northwards until just before Cobb Hall, runs on the alignment of the Roman street grid and follows the projected line of the north–south street bounding the Roman *forum/basilica* complex on the west side. Its precise position may therefore have been determined by the survival of an element of the Roman topography. This length of curtain wall is also free of herringbone work and so could also be a generation later in date than the northern and western walls. This stretch may, however, be somewhat earlier than that from the east gate to the Observatory Tower, as the latter stretch seems to have been built of a piece with the tower. This stretch incorporates mid 12th-century windows, which belonged to a range built against its west face. This wall, like the range built against it, is likely to belong to the same mid 12th-century campaign of building as the Observatory Tower itself. There is little doubt that the Observatory Tower, in the south-west corner of the inner bailey, is that built by Ranulph and referred to in the charter from Stephen given in 1149. Ranulph was,

however, in intermittent control of the Castle throughout the civil war and it may be that the 1149 grant was to a certain extent retrospective permission for works already underway. Even so it seems clear that the defensive circuit was largely complete by the middle of the 12th century.

The new inner bailey earthworks were surrounded by a wide, rock-cut ditch, which runs parallel with the earthworks, including those parts that are thought to be mid 12th-century features. Descriptions of this ditch in the 17th century and later show that it remained a recognisable feature throughout the medieval period (Hill 1948, 99). The spoil from the ditch is likely to have provided the material for the earthwork ramparts themselves and, consequently, they will contain much inverted Roman and early medieval evidence. It may therefore be of some significance that the 1974 excavations on the Observatory Tower site produced a significant quantity of early and middle Saxon potsherds.

The massive earthworks of the new inner bailey of Lincoln Castle were topped by masonry walls (Fig. 9.10). Almost all the curtain wall was refaced on both

*Fig. 9.10. The north side of the Castle earthworks from the north-west shown in a watercolour in the Willson Collection (Lincoln Cathedral Library, portfolio D. No 20). The watercolour was made later than 1801, when the Chapter House roof was altered, but before 1815, when the tiled roof of Cobb Hall was removed. It shows the truly enormous scale of the early 12th-century earthworks. The view shows the unrestored state of both Cobb Hall and the northern curtain wall, whilst the small stone barn behind the flock of sheep might have been built on the site of the church of St Clement-in-the-Bail (photo Lincolnshire County Council Archives Office, copyright Lincoln Cathedral Library).*

return on the south side and much of the north wall can also be assigned a date in the early 12th century, although given the extent of replacement of the wall face in the last two centuries, it is possible that herringbone work was once more prevalent. The curtain wall along the south side of the enclosure is undoubtedly later; it must have been constructed as part of the work on the towers crowning the two mottes, in the middle years of the 12th century.

Two minor postern gates are visible in the circuit today, near the centre of the north wall and in the base of the ditch surrounding the Lucy Tower, on the eastern side (between the Lucy and Observatory Towers). Both have been reconstructed with two-centred heads, but in their surviving form the masonry is wholly 19th century or later. Even so, it is likely that these two doorways indicate the locations of medieval posterns, but further work is needed to establish whether they were original features of the wall itself, or whether they were punched through in the 13th century or later, as the forms of their replacement arch-heads would suggest.

A rectangular early Norman gate tower with a rounded gate arch survives within the later work at the east gate (Fig. 9.11). Its plan and construction

sides in the late 18th and early 19th centuries, as part of refurbishment associated with the prison, and has been refaced again in the last thirty years. In several places the masonry curtain wall running along the crest of these earthworks has been observed to sit on a timber framework resting directly on the Castle bank (Elliott and Stocker 1986, 28–30). It has been suggested that this feature indicates that the wall is later in date than the bank, but there is no reason to think this is so. Furthermore, the complete absence of 11th-century pottery from both the Castle west gate (CWG 86) and The Lawn excavations (which investigated the small extra-mural suburb which grew up outside the west gate – LH 84/LA 85/L 86) suggests that the earthworks are of 12th century date. By contrast, both sites produced quantities of pottery of the early 12th century. The presence of herringbone work in the curtain wall skins towards the north-west corner has been noted by antiquarian authors and its significance for the dating of the Castle has long been debated. Sometimes its presence has been taken as a sign that the walls are 11th-century in date, but herringbone work is present in several Lincolnshire churches constructed *c.*1100, although would be anachronistic if much later (Stocker and Everson forthcoming). It therefore seems that the entire west wall, the eastward

*Fig. 9.11. The Castle east gate from the east (photo and copyright, D Stocker).*

suggest that it is contemporary with the larger Castle west gate rather than being the original late 11th-century gate as argued by Foster and subsequent writers (1931, xxii–xxiii). The gate was extensively repaired between 1224 and 1229, but it is far from certain that the extensive barbican is this early in date. It was the subject of a brief survey in 1986 (CEG 86). The barbican consisted of a pair of drum towers seated in the bottom of the ditch that fronted a long rectangular, enclosed 'killing space' in front of the main gate. The vaulted lower chambers in both towers survived their demolition in 1791, although access is difficult, but they are marked out at ground level in the pavement cobbles.

The Castle west gate has been intensively investigated in recent years (Plate 3.2) (CWG 83/86) and a report is in preparation (Donel and Jones forthcoming). The detailed results of the excavation, with the exception of the pottery, are not available at the time of writing but it seems that the first Norman roadway was constructed over the stump of the Roman wall and rampart so that the road rose up to enter the Castle and then dropped steeply down once over the rampart (Fig. 9.12). Within the following two centuries a considerable build-up took place, so that by the middle of the 14th century the ground surface within the Castle was level with the base of the Norman arch. This has led to the burial of at least one substantial masonry building that survives to window height on the south side of the roadway. A revetment wall and a set of steps leading up to the wall walk formed the northern boundary of the roadway. These seem to have been constructed late in the sequence and are probably later 13th or 14th century. On the exterior (west) of the gate an early type of barbican, consisting of a simple fore-space surrounded by walls, had formed part of the original layout. Survey and excavation of this structure (CWG 82) showed that the original rectangular barbican had been enlarged with a low rectangular tower on the north side (Stocker 1983). This tower might have been contemporary with the construction of a second gate arch within the passageway, designed to accommodate a portcullis. This extensive reconstruction probably dates from 1233–4, when £54.6s.4d. was spent on fortifications here.

The Lucy Tower is a polygonal masonry 'shell-keep'

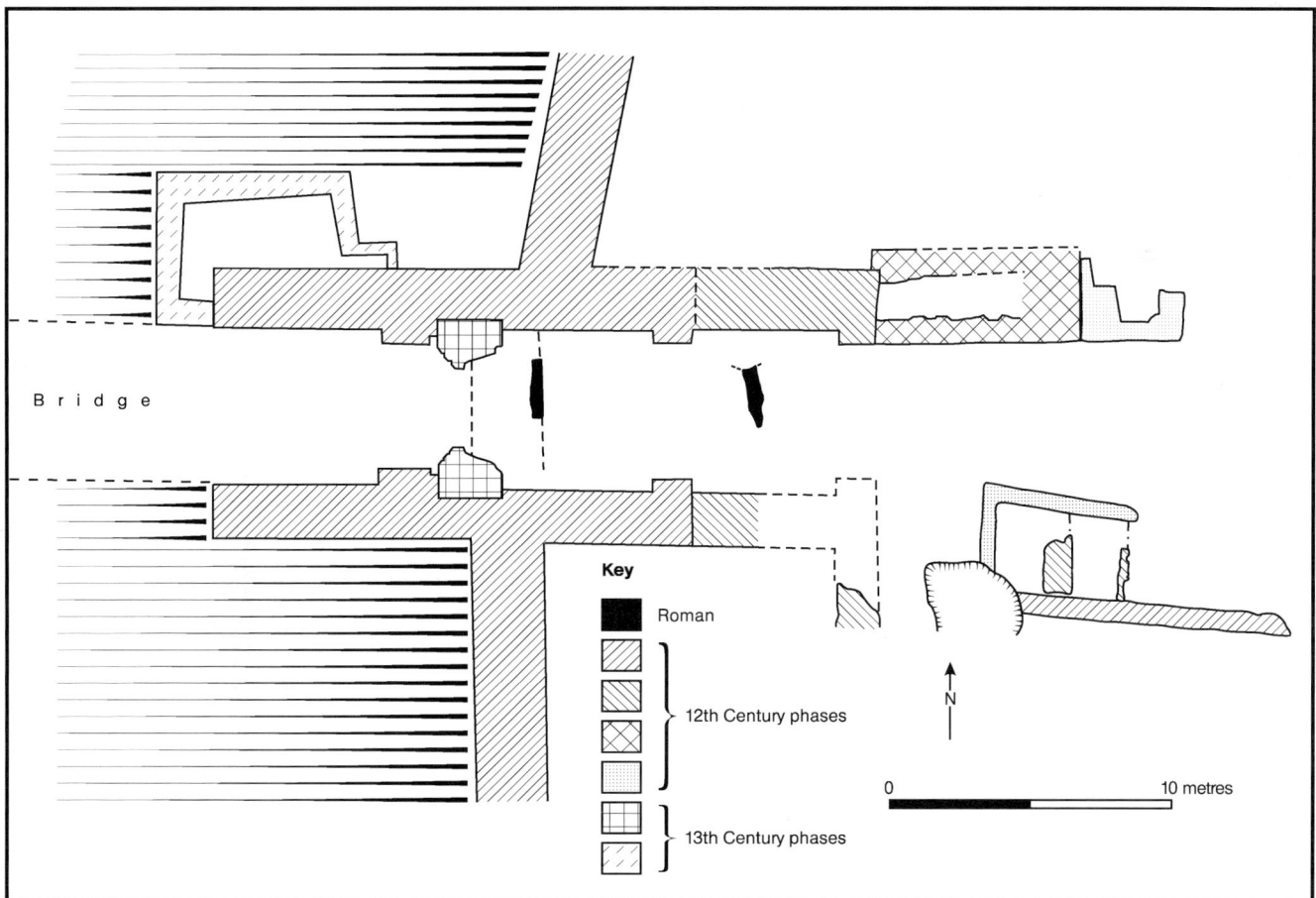

*Fig. 9.12. Plan showing the development of the Castle west gate, as revealed in excavations between 1983 and 1989 (CWG 83–9). For location within the Castle enclosure see Fig. 9.9 (sources, Stocker 1983; Otter 1989 – drawn by Dave Watt, copyright English Heritage).*

*Fig. 9.13. The shell-keep of Lincoln Castle (known as the Lucy Tower) from the south-west. Engraving by S and N Buck, published in 1724.*

which sits on a large conical motte (Fig. 9.13). Buck's view of the motte suggests that it may have been constructed with bands of stone alternating with soil, whilst observations in the 1990s carried out by Lisa Donel have shown that, at its summit, the mound consists of loosely-packed limestone rubble (ON 400). The motte was originally surrounded by a deep, rock-cut ditch, the north-eastern part of which can still be seen within the cellars under the Prison building of 1787, parts of which were built over the ditch. Although no absolute dating has yet been recovered, (and although trial excavations have proved inconclusive – Donel 1991a), it is thought likely that the Lucy Tower motte has survived from the first castle of 1068 (above). This is partly because of its dominant position within the city, but also because it seems likely that the first line of Eastgate was intended to link the motte to the principal gate in the Upper City, before the present curtain wall and is earthworks had been constructed (Stocker and Vince 1997; Stocker forthcoming a; see p. 170–2 above and also below p. 201–3).

The masonry of the shell keep itself has been reduced in height by a storey. It retains two original doorways into the ground storey. The main gate is on the north-east side and a smaller gate, leading onto the berm of the motte on the south side, is of a similar date but without decoration. Ranges of buildings, including at least one garderobe, evidently existed to the east and west of the keep, built into the curtain wall, which runs up to the keep on both sides. It seems, however, that there was no means of access between the wall walk of the curtain wall to east and west and the first floor of the keep itself.

If, as seems certain, this is the location of the tower fortified by Countess Lucy, then it is most likely to have been built after the death of her third husband, in 1129, and was perhaps unfinished by her own death in 1136. It is not yet known, however, whether the work carried out by Countess Lucy between 1129 and 1136

was the construction (or re-construction) of the motte on top of which the present Lucy Tower sits, the construction of a timber tower or the construction of the masonry tower we see today. However, the main gate of the surviving keep is decorated with a moulding that links it, amongst others, with work at the Cathedral and St Mary's Guildhall (Stocker 1991, 37 and 87). In Stocker's discussion of the mid to late 12th-century architectural mouldings at St Mary's Guildhall he follows Professor Zarnecki in accepting that their earliest appearance locally should be dated between 1145 and 1155, i.e. later than the Countess's death. Since neither Henry II nor Richard I are recorded as spending large sums on Lincoln Castle it is unlikely that either king was the builder of the Lucy Tower keep (Colvin, Allen-Brown and Taylor 1963). The architectural detail may therefore suggest that the polygonal keep was built, or completed, by Ranulph Gernons, Lucy's son. The possibility of an earlier timber keep must, however, be borne in mind. It is likely that any timber tower would have involved the use of massive posts whose postholes may have survived the use of the interior of the keep as a burial ground during the use of the Castle as a prison in the 18th and 19th centuries.

The Observatory Tower and its motte was investigated in 1974 by Nicholas Reynolds (Reynolds 1975), who was able to demonstrate that the motte contains within it, a square, rubble-filled tower, which could only have been built before the motte was piled up against it. Parallels for this construction technique can be found at Totnes, Farnham and Ascot Doilly. Reynolds recovered sherds of glazed pottery from the original mortared rubble backfill of the tower which at that time were best paralleled with material from the Bishop's Palace, dated to the 1170s (Reynolds 1975, fig 79). These vessels are now classified as LSW1 and attributed to the ceramic horizon MH2 (Fig. 9.2). The sherds are clearly not attributable to the early 12th century but they might just be dated to the 1130s (making this Lucy's tower). They are much more likely, however, to date from the 1150s, confirming that the Observatory Tower is that built by Ranulph and referred to in 1149.

The free-standing tower above the motte was built on the stone foundations of the rubble-filled tower, and may have had either a timber or stone super-structure (Fig. 9.14). A doorway into this tower from the west is datable to the 14th century, whereas two round-headed arches are present in a cross wall sitting on the rubble fill, suggesting that by the later 12th or early 13th century there was a stone tower sitting on this base (Reynolds 1975, fig 78 and Plate XVb). This tower was connected with a range of buildings to the north, to which the 12th-century windows incorporated into the curtain wall belonged. To the west of the tower it was originally possible to access the wall walk, or another range of buildings, via a circular staircase rising through the tower which communicated with a passageway within the tower walls, below the level of the motte platform (Hill 1948, 85).

The semicircular, three-storied tower at the north-east corner of the curtain wall, known as 'Cobb Hall', is a later addition to the defences, and has been the subject of a recent study by Derek Renn (Renn forthcoming) (Figs. 9.10 and 9.15). Renn believes it most likely that the tower was added to the circuit during the same phase of repairs between 1217 and 1229 that also included the reconstruction of the east gate (above). Certainly the new tower would have commanded a view across the churchyard of St Paul's church, so as to cover any approach south from Newport Arch, as well as commanding a view along Westgate to the west postern gate, and it was from these directions that the besieging force came during the so called *Fair of Lincoln* in 1217.

### The outer bailey or Bail defences, c.1130–1350

There is no evidence for work on any of the gates of the outer bailey between the later 12th and the mid 14th centuries. There are reasons to think that the south gate of the Bail retained Roman fabric throughout the medieval period (p. 63–5 above) whereas the Newport Arch (Fig. 9.16) and the east gate of the Bail, with its two arches (Figs. 7.9 and 9.43), seem to be structures of the late 11th or early 12th century (Stocker forthcoming a). The form of the western postern, north of the north-west corner of the Castle enclosure, is unknown but is likely to have been a single arch of early 12th century date, probably contemporary with the construction of the inner bailey itself.

The *Hundred Rolls* record that Aaron the Jew (active in Lincoln c.1166–85) encroached upon the stretch of the south wall of the Bail, running westwards from the south gate to the inner bailey ditch (ed. Illingworth 1812–18, I, 322a; Johnson and Vince 1992, 12). As we have seen, Petch's 1955 excavations in the Old Dean-

Fig. 9.14. The south-east angle tower of Lincoln Castle (known as the Observatory Tower) from the north-east on its distinctive motte. Both the tower and the wall adjoining it have been greatly restored and little of the original 12th-century fabric is now visible (photo and copyright, D Stocker).

Fig. 9.15. The north-east angle tower of Lincoln Castle (known as 'Cobb Hall') from the east (photo and copyright, D Stocker).

ery Garden, to the east of the south gate of the Bail, demonstrated that the entire line of the Bail wall between the gate and the south-east angle, was rebuilt north of its Roman line, but whether this rebuilding

predates the royal licence to pierce the Bail wall, given to Bishop Chesney in 1155–8 (ed. Foster 1931, 86–7, RA137), or was part of the same operation is unknown. The eastern wall of the Bail has been investigated at several points but only at the southernmost site was medieval work surviving (LC 84). This excavation revealed what may be the southern jamb of a postern gate, together with a stub of a projecting wall. The wall above these features had been rebuilt (Fig. 9.17). One interpretation of these features is that they represent two separate structures: a simple gate followed by a tower (Stocker 1985a, 42, fig. 34 b and c). Another possibility is that the jamb is part of a medieval postern gate, perhaps that which Bishop Bloet was given leave to cut in the Castle wall by Henry I sometime between 1101 and 1115 (ed. Foster 1931, 20–1, RA21). That gate, significantly, was intended to give access to the Bishop's house, which would either imply that his house lay east of the Bail before its relocation to the upper chamber of the east gate of the Bail in 1130–3 or, as David Stocker has suggested, that the Bishop's house at that time was within the Bail, perhaps at the west end of the Cathedral church (ed. Foster 1931, 34–5 RA49; Hill

*Fig. 9.16. Newport Arch from north. An engraving made from a drawing by R D Poilicy prior to 1784 (photo and copyright D Stocker) (See also Plate 2.4).*

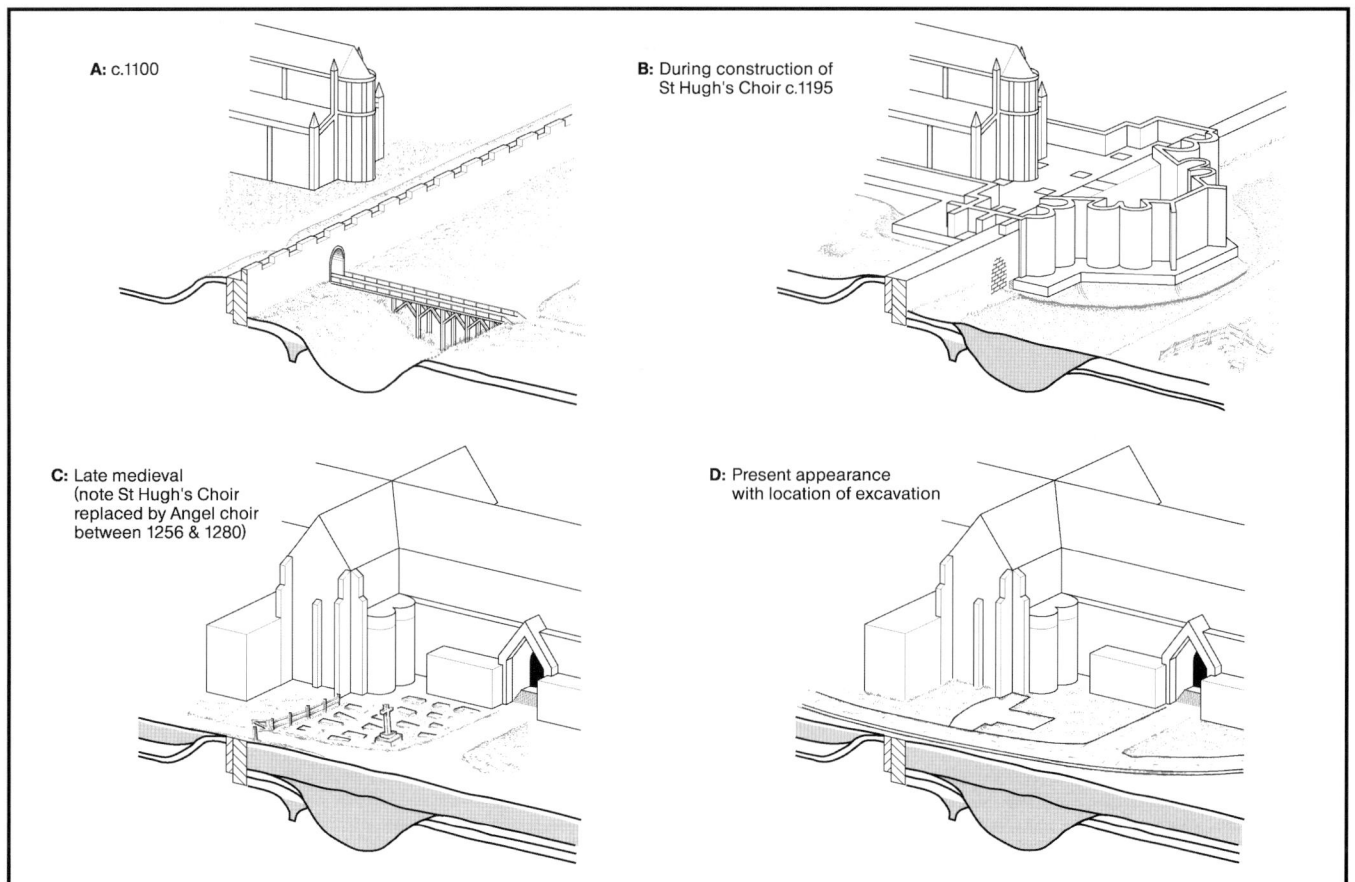

*Fig. 9.17. Proposed sequence of development of east wall of Upper City, showing the encroachment of the east end of the Cathedral, based on excavations in 1984 (CWG 84) (source, Stocker 1985. Re-drawn by Dave Watt from an original by Alan Smith. Copyright English Heritage).*

1948, 127; Stocker forthcoming a).

The Bail ditch survives today as an earthwork on the northern and north-eastern sides of the Bail. On the western side it survives west of the Castle but not further north, where its position was roughly determined during investigations at Cuthbert's Yard (CY 89). To the east of the Cathedral the western lip of the ditch was seen in 1984 (LC 84 – Fig. 9.17) whilst to the south of the Bail the northern lip was noted by Petch (1960). The existence of a ditch along this southern stretch of wall is also confirmed by a mention in King Stephen's grant of land to Bishop Alexander for the construction of his palace in 1135–8 (ed. Foster 1931, 54–5, RA87). The width of this ditch can be roughly gauged from the boundaries of the roads and other features which respected its outer lip, but its depth and profile are not known. It is not clear, either, whether the ditch was merely a clearing-out of the late Roman ditch or an entirely new Norman construction. At the western end of the south side, however, it respects the Lucy Tower and must have been re-dug as part of the construction of the motte.

The circuit of ditch from the Westgate postern around to the east gate of the Bail remained under the control of the King but the stretch from the east gate southwards, round to the south gate, must have been abandoned during the 12th century. The construction of the new east end of the Cathedral (begun in 1192) occupied a large part of the ditch on the east side (Fig. 9.17b; Stocker 1985a), whilst the grant of land for the Bishop's Palace, issued by Stephen (probably in 1137) and confirmed with the same boundaries by Henry II in 1155–8, specifically includes the ditch. And in the latter grant the Bishop is allowed to build over its line (ed. Foster 1931, 54, 86, RA87 and 137). The stretch of ditch between the west wall of the Bishop's Palace and the south gate of the Bail must have been backfilled soon after this. The Norman House on the corner of Christ's Hospital Terrace and Steep Hill has architectural features dating to the 1170s, and it lies over the probable terminal of the ditch (unless the ditch crossed the line of Steep Hill and was crossed by a drawbridge). Furthermore, properties to the east of the Norman House are said in 13th-century documents to lie in the cemetery of St Michael-on-the-Mount rather than in the King's ditch (Johnson and Vince 1992). It is possible that these properties encroached upon the ditch, but they do not appear to be included in the list of encroachments on the east side of Steep Hill noted in the *Hundred Rolls*, whereas the encroachment of Aaron the Jew upon the King's wall to the west of the road is noted, and must have been contemporary (ed. Illingworth 1812–18, I, 322a). There is no mention of the King's ditch or encroachment upon it to the west of Steep Hill and yet here too we appear to have documentary evidence for the existence of properties on its line in the 12th century (Johnson and Vince 1992, 15). It seems likely, therefore, that the ditch on both sides of the south gate of the Bail was back-filled with per-mission of the King, or at least that encroachment upon it was not regarded in the late 13th century with the same seriousness as encroachment upon the walls themselves.

### The Close Wall c.1280–c.1350

Many studies of later medieval defences confirm that they were only nominally defensive in purpose; the desire to erect defences being stimulated by concern for status rather than security (Coulson 1982, 74–7). This motivation seems particularly clear in the case of Lincoln Cathedral precinct, where both the height and nature of the defences were governed by royal licences. The first of these was in 1285, then a second in 1316 appears to be merely a confirmation of the earlier licence, whilst a third, in 1318, grants permission for the wall to be higher than 12' and for turrets to be built. In 1329 the bishop was given licence to extend and raise the walls of the palace enclosure (*CPR*). Thus, by middle of the 14th century both the precinct and the Bishop's Palace were enclosed by defensive walls.

Once complete, the Close Wall snaked through the existing properties around the Cathedral, defining large areas north and east of the Cathedral (Fig. 9.18). It had at least ten gates, most with impressive gatehouses – including three with pairs of gatehouses. Starting at the south-west corner, the Close Wall formed the eastern boundary of the properties fronting onto the northern end of Steep Hill as far as the two Exchequergates (Fig. 9.19a and b). St Mary Magdalene's church and the White Hart to the north lay outside the Close, but at the western end of Eastgate was a second double gatehouse (Fig. 9.20). The wall then headed north to include properties on James Street before following the south and west sides of East Bight in returning to Eastgate. It seems likely that there was a door through the wall allowing access between James Street and East Bight. Where the wall crossed Eastgate, just to the west of the former Roman east gate, there was another gatehouse and, to the south-east of the gatehouses, the wall again followed the property boundary along the rear of properties facing onto Eastgate, outside the Bail. Another gatehouse stood across the northern end of Pottergate (Fig. 9.21). The wall emerged from behind properties at Winnowsty Lane, which ran along its north-eastern limit. The wall then turned south-west and ran along the western side of Wragby Road, back towards the southern end of Pottergate, where stood another gatehouse (Fig. 9.22). From here, after a short length extending due south, the wall turned due west, joining the Roman wall of the Lower City at the south-western corner of the College of the Vicars-Choral. Another small postern gate existed where the lane now called Greestone Place (but formerly known as *Boune Lane*) crossed the wall line at the south-east corner of the Vicars-Choral property. The Close boundary then followed the existing wall of the Lower City northwards and the

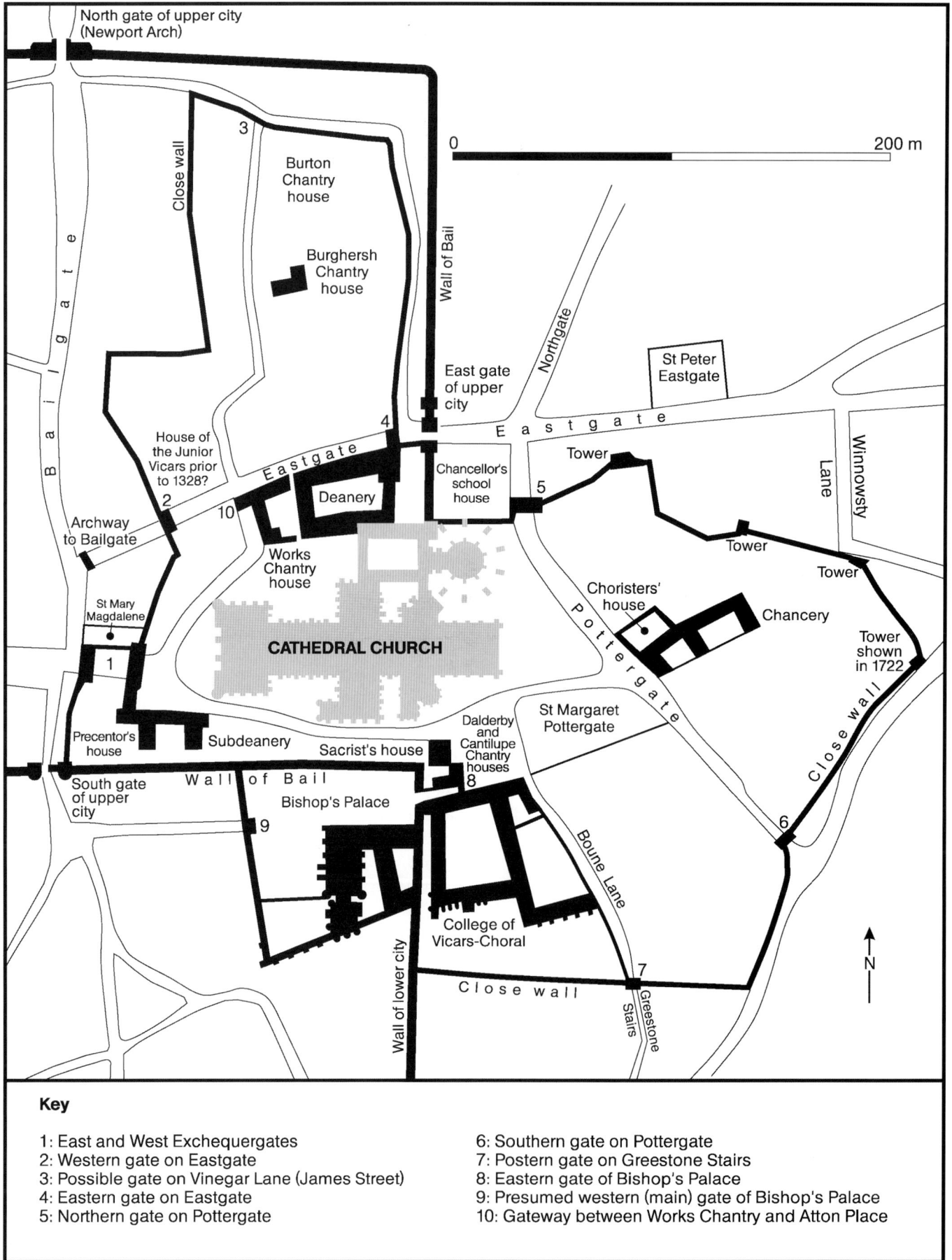

Fig. 9.18. Lincoln Cathedral Close, showing the wall, gates and main residences (source, Jones S R. et al. 1984–96 – drawn by Dave Watt, copyright English Heritage).

**Key**

1: East and West Exchequergates
2: Western gate on Eastgate
3: Possible gate on Vinegar Lane (James Street)
4: Eastern gate on Eastgate
5: Northern gate on Pottergate

6: Southern gate on Pottergate
7: Postern gate on Greestone Stairs
8: Eastern gate of Bishop's Palace
9: Presumed western (main) gate of Bishop's Palace
10: Gateway between Works Chantry and Atton Place

a)

b)

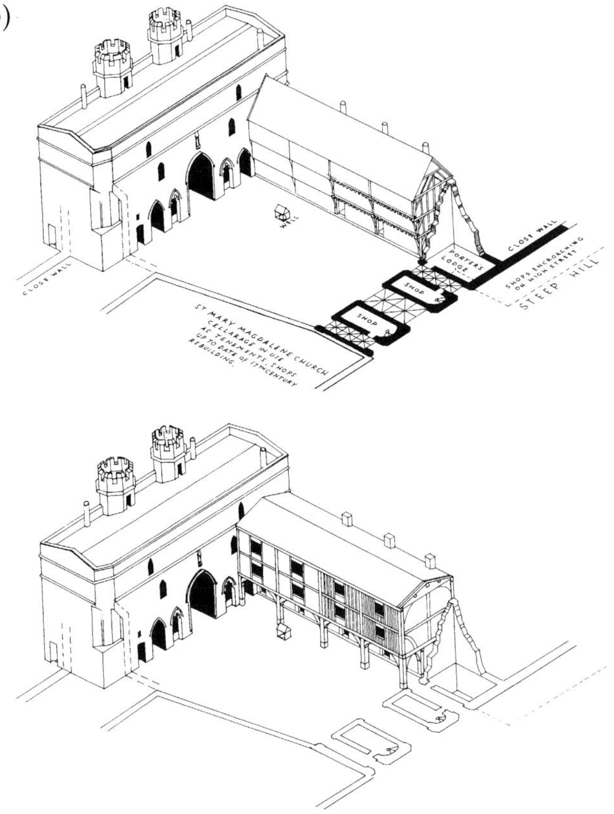

*Fig. 9.19. a) The western gatehouse of Exchequergate complex from the north-west in a drawing made before 1796 from the Willson Collection (Lincoln, Cathedral Library, portfolio D. No 13). b) Reconstruction of medieval Exchequergate complex by Stanley Jones (1987, fig. 101). The demolished western gatehouse is shown here only in plan. Above c.1400, below c.1500 (copyright a) Lincoln Cathedral Library. b) S R Jones and Lincoln Civic Trust).*

*Fig. 9.20. The view looking eastwards along Eastgate through the arch across the street at its western end, looking towards the western face of the western Close gatehouse. A drawing with sepia wash by Peter de Wint, made prior to 1812 (photo and copyright, Lincolnshire County Council, Usher Art Gallery).*

*Fig. 9.21. Close gatehouse at north end of Pottergate from the south, a drawing made by Edward Willson made prior to 1815 (London, Society of Antiquaries Ms, 786, portfolio A) (copyright, Society of Antiquaries of London).*

existing (rebuilt) south wall of the Bail eastwards to rejoin the wall behind the properties fronting onto Bailgate. The wall was of stone, but the surviving lengths indicate many different builds and repairs. As one might expect, the more impressive stretches seem to have been those which looked onto large gardens, or open country along Eastgate outside the Bail, Win-

*Fig. 9.22. Surviving Close gatehouse at the south end of Pottergate, from the north (photo and copyright, D Stocker).*

*Fig. 9.23. Mural tower on the northern sector of the Close Wall between the Cathedral School playing field and Disney Place Garden, looking north-west (Plate 5.3) (photo and copyright, City of the Lincoln Archaeology Unit).*

nowsty Lane and Wragby Road. Here the wall had a crenellated parapet and a wall-walk as well as square projecting mural towers (Fig. 9.23).

As we have seen, the Dean and Chapter had acquired responsibility for the upkeep of the defences in the south-east corner of the Bail at an early date, and rebuilt the wall between the Bishop's Palace and the Cathedral in the early or mid 12th century, but there is apparently neither documentary nor archaeological evidence for the defensive arrangements which accompanied the breaching of the wall at the east end of the Cathedral in the 1190s. It has been suggested that the east end of St Hugh's Cathedral might have, itself, formed the Bail defence as at Avila Cathedral in Spain (Stocker 1985a, fig 34d). The 1984 excavations at the point where the Bail wall became incorporated into Cathedral foundations neither confirm nor refute this interpretation. It is equally possible that the Bail wall was simply removed down to the new ground level outside the wall, which was raised to the same height as that within the Bail. However, it does seem from the royal grant of 1255 to the Bishop that the Bail defences were considered to be intact at that date.

Documentary sources (ed. Major 1973, 194–200, RA2863–9) make it clear that land to the east of the Cathedral was being sought *c.*1260, for the extension of the Cathedral cemetery and this would be consistent with the date and character of the earliest burials excavated in 1984 to the east of the Roman wall (LC 84), although the archaeological evidence would also suit an earlier 13th-century date. This extension seems to have been linked with the construction of the Angel Choir, built between 1256 and 1280. The grant of land for the College of the Vicars-Choral, dated between 1266 and 1272, gives as their southern boundary the new wall of the city (ed. Major 1973, 200, RA2870).

This new wall is that running east–west across the line of the *Werkdyke* to the south of the College, which later on certainly formed a part of the Close Wall. The implication of this is that the Close Wall was certainly started at or before the time of construction of the Angel Choir. It could for example, have been begun when the first breach in the Bail wall took place, in 1192. Whichever date is taken, however, there is no doubt that the 'new wall of the city' on the south side of the college of Vicars-Choral predates the royal licence to crenellate the Close.

Indeed, the extent to which the Close Wall was built following the royal licences, rather than those licences being a recognition and legitimisation of existing structures, is a question raised by the dendrochronological analysis of timbers from the floor of one of the Close Wall towers in Winnowsty Lane (Hall 1992). These indicate a felling date between 1249 and 1284 for timbers used in a tower for which permission to build was not granted until 1318 (*CPR*, 257). The timbers could, of course, have been reused, and indeed some of the timbers from the sampled roof (if not the sampled timbers themselves) have evidence for reuse (Brann and Donel 1997, fig 3). Despite this, a detailed survey of parts of the Close Wall, carried out over a number of years has failed to find convincing evidence for either the heightening or crenellation of the defences. Hall suggests, however, that there is evidence for differences in date for some parts of the Close Wall on the basis of their differential use of large faced ashlar, as opposed to coursed rubble. If this is so then the stretch in Winnowsty Lane would be earlier that the stretch immediately to its west, to either side of No.2 Minster Yard (Hall 1993, 3).

### The defences of the Lower City, c.1150–c.1350

The *Hundred Rolls*, drawn up in 1274–5, recorded encroachment on the King's wall on both the west and south sides of the Lower City (Gilmour and Roffe 1999, 265–6). In the north-eastern corner the Bishop had been allowed to incorporate part of the city wall into his palace in the mid 12th century (ed. Foster 1931, 269–76) whilst in the later 13th and 14th century the Vicars-Choral were given a stretch of the city ditch in the 13th century (ed. Major 1973, 200, RA2870; Jones, Major and Varley, 1987, 40–64). The sequence by which the eastern defences fell out of use to the south of this, to either side of Clasketgate, is unclear but apart from a stretch which today lies in the grounds of the Usher Art Gallery, there is no trace above ground and every reason to believe that, with the early growth of the *Butwerk* suburb, the eastern defences soon became redundant. Be that as it may, work was carried out on the Lower City defences during the medieval period, at Stonebow, Newland Gate and Clasketgate Gate and at the south-east and south-west corners, where extensions to the wall and ditch followed the expansion of the city southwards along the waterfront. All these works, however, are likely to have been as much a matter of civic pride as of defence.

There is no evidence for medieval refurbishment of the Roman wall to the east or west of the city. At West Parade (WP 71), The Park (P 70), Silver Street (LIN 73c) and, more recently, on the site of the Central Library (GL 91; GLB 94), wherever evidence for the wall or rampart in the medieval period has been recovered, it demonstrates the survival of the Roman work. Whatever works took place to repair or rebuild were clearly no more than cosmetic and it seems that the medieval Lower City was defended by a wall and rampart mainly of Roman fabric. On the south side of the Lower City, medieval work was found overlying the Roman city wall (LIN 73d) but it is quite clear from an examination of this walling that it is domestic, forming the back of a building fronting onto Saltergate. We have already seen the circumstantial evidence that the Roman postern gate here remained open in the 10th century but had gone by the 11th century (p. 170 above). The closure of the gate does not prove that the wall had

been removed by that date, but it is clear that the Roman wall line cannot have been a working defence for long after occupation spread onto the old foreshore on its south side. On this southern side of the city, encroachment along the entire wall line from Newland to Greyfriars was recorded in Edward II's charter of 1315, although it is also stated that the houses built on the wall were for the improvement of the city and were allowed to remain (Hill 1948, 157). The *Hundred Rolls* also record encroachment on the southern part of the western stretch of defence (Gilmour and Roffe 1999, fig. 125). This took the form of extensions to the rear of properties fronting onto Beaumont Fee assimilating the rampart and perhaps also the wall. Two gates are known for certain to have existed in the Roman Lower City defences during the medieval period; the Clasketgate Gate on the eastern side and Stonebow on the south, and there is a strong likelihood that at least one further gate once existed in the western defences.

The bishop's manor of *Willingthorpe*, which lay to the west of the Lower City (p. 228 below), was organised around three east–west streets. In the later 11th century, the southernmost street would have run along the south side of the Roman wall, but the other two, presumably, would have been entry points into the city, with gates at their eastern ends. What may be the northern end of a medieval gate at West Parade was found in 1971 during excavations (WP 71). The proposal that there was a gate serving the central of the three *Willingthorpe* streets, giving access to *Midhergate*, is more problematic since there is neither documentary nor archaeological evidence for its existence. However, Park Street, within the walls, and Newland Street West (the presumed *Midhergate*) outside them, are roughly aligned (Fig. 9.65). It is easy to envisage a gate having existed during the 12th and 13th century at the west end of Park Street, with the church of St Stephen (sometimes called – in *Midhergate* – Cameron 1985, 135) lying immediately outside it. Any such gate could have easily been lost during the later medieval period, following the decline in population of the western side of the Lower City and in the Newland suburb. A watching brief in Orchard Street by CLAU failed to observe this hypothetical street but burials have been found both to the south and north of its proposed line (ON 10; ON 77). When this site was investigated by Bob Jones in 1980, he noted that these burials were much denser to the south and it is possible that the cemetery expanded northwards over the line of *Midhergate* once the road had been abandoned (Jones R H, 1981).

More is known of the large gatehouse in the centre of the eastern defences of the Lower City, Clasketgate Gate. The first element of the street-name *Clasketgate* is apparently based on the Old English *Klakks hlith* (Klak's Gate) and, although not recorded until the mid 13th century, it is strong evidence for the existence of a gate in the centre of the eastern defences in the 11th or 12th century if not earlier (Cameron 1985, 58–9). We know, in any case, that it was possible to pass through the Roman wall at this point by the late 9th century, because such an access was clearly utilised by Silver Street (one of the earliest Anglo-Scandinavian streets) as it left the Lower City. A sketch of the medieval gate by Buck (Fig. 9.24) shows a round-headed arch with large chambers to either side and a hall above, lit by arrow slits on its east side and a doorway at the south end. The doorway looks as though it may have been of 13th-century or later date, but the remainder of the structure is clearly of earlier date. It may be that, like the upper east and north gates, medieval Clasketgate Gate was formed around a surviving Roman structure (p. 87 above). No trace of the gate remains, although its foundations are reported have been seen in road-works at the junction of Silver Street and Clasketgate.

Like the name Clasketgate, the name 'Stonebow' (OS *Stein-bogi* – stone arch), the central gatehouse in the southern walls of the Lower City, suggests an early gatehouse. It is first recorded in 1147 (*Ibid.*, 41). At that date, a stone arch could as easily be of Norman as of Roman date and it is not clear whether the medieval Stonebow was a Roman or later structure, since it was partly taken down in the late 14th century and rebuilt or refaced in 1520 (Fig. 9.25) (Stocker 1997b). The Roman gate is known, from observations of the line of the wall, to have lain slightly north of the early 16th-century gateway (Richmond 1946, 41) and the 16th-century structure lies immediately south of the projected line of the Roman wall. The gate was in royal hands in the early 13th century and permission to use its upper floor as a council chamber was given by the King in return for the city giving its own guild hall to the Greyfriars (Hill 1948, 207and n.). Given that the *Burwarmote* Court traditionally met immediately north of Stonebow, near St Peter-at-Pleas (called *ad Motstou* – *i.e. at Mootstone* – in *c*.1200 – Cameron 1985, 132) it is perhaps surprising that the Council was not earlier granted the use of the Stonebow. It may be that the establishment of the Council's hall at the south-east corner of the city was a recent event, brought about by the uncertain relationship between the King and the Council at a time when city government was in the process of change.

As the southern limit of the Lower City moved southwards beyond the line of the southern Roman wall, so the city ditches to east and west had to be extended too (eg. Figs. 9.65, 9.66 and 9.67). This may originally have had no defensive implications; it may simply have been a practical consideration, demarcating boundaries. The Lucy Tower Street excavations (LT 72) revealed that the 13th-century stone wall extending the line of the Roman west wall towards the river was built in a silted-up ditch, which must be the continuation of the city ditch running down the western side of the Lower City defences (Fig. 9.26). The ditch had been cut through dumped deposits of 12th-century date, which overlay what was taken to be naturally-deposited peat containing 11th- or 12th-

*Fig. 9.24. Clasketgate gate from the south-east in 1724 by S and N Buck (Oxford, Bodleian Library Ms, Gough Lincs. 15, f.18v–19r)(photo and copyright Bodleian Library, Oxford).*

*Fig. 9.25. Stonebow from the south in c.1784 by S H Grimm (photo and copyright, British Library)*

*Fig. 9.26. Excavations at the Lucy Tower on the Brayford in 1972 (LT 72) from the east (photo and copyright, City of Lincoln Archaeology Unit).*

century pottery. The lower fills of this ditch contained 12th-century pottery, whilst its profile – a wide U-shape – suggests that it was a boundary and water-course rather than defence. There is no evidence for the existence of a bank on the eastern side of the ditch, but one could have existed outside the excavated area. Whilst it is likely that this ditch acted as an outlet for the city ditch running from Motherby Hill down to Newland, it is positioned slightly to the east of a straight projection of that ditch (a discrepancy of 33m). Probably the city ditch curved eastwards, around the corner of the Roman walled circuit, and then followed a course in line with the Roman wall. The present Lucy Tower Street occupies the projected line of the ditch, which may have been preceded by the earlier outflow during the 10th and 11th centuries, whilst this area was being reclaimed from the Brayford Pool. The ditch has been associated with the siege of Lincoln during the Anarchy, or with an attempt by the Council to make good a perceived weakness in its defences in the early years of Henry II's reign. It is thought likely that a similar ditch will have existed in the equivalent position on the eastern side of the city.

In the late 13th century, however, these ditches were replaced by stone walls extending the city circuit into the river, and with new towers and gates. The new western defences are much better understood than the eastern. Antiquarian sketches survive of both the 'Lucy Tower on the Brayford' (not to be confused with the shell keep in the Castle) (Fig. 9.27) at its southern end, and the Newland Gate to the north (Fig. 9.28). The Lucy Tower itself, along with a section of the wall and successive ditches provided the centrepiece of the 1972 excavations (LT 72 – Fig. 9.26). The wall, where investigated at its southern end, rested on carefully laid foundations which filled the earlier ditch. Pottery from these dumps shows that the backfill of the ditch and preparation of the surface for building took place in the late 13th or early 14th century, probably later than the first documentary mention of Newland Gate in the *Hundred Rolls* (ed. Illingworth 1812–18, I, 318b, 29). The Lucy Tower was a circular drum with a chamfered plinth, contemporary with the defensive wall. A wall running east from the tower is stratigraphically later, but apparently nearly contemporary. It is likely that the tower and this east–west wall formed the water-front. A small ditch was dug along the west side of the new tower and wall and there is evidence for its maintenance, in the form of re-cuttings. It was finally allowed to silt up in the 16th century.

The Newland Gate was used as a boundary in the *Hundred Rolls* when describing encroachments upon the southern wall of the Lower City (*Ibid.*). A gate of some sort therefore existed here in the later 13th century, towards the northern end of the new defensive wall, which terminated in the Lucy Tower on Brayford. Buck's sketch of the gate (Oxford, Bodleian Library Gough Ms. Lincs. 15) (Fig. 9.28) indicates that it had a single chamber above, roofed at right-angles

*Fig. 9.27. The Lucy Tower on the Brayford from the south in 1724. Coloured drawing by S and N Buck (Oxford, Bodleian Library Ms, Gough Lincs. 15, f.51r) (photo and copyright Bodleian Library, Oxford).*

*Fig. 9.28. The Newland Gate in 1724, from the west, by S and N Buck (Oxford, Bodleian Library Ms, Gough Lincs. 15, f.9r) (photo and copyright Bodleian Library Oxford).*

to the curtain. From what can be seen of the architectural details, the gate arch could be later 13th-century in date with some later modifications, such as the late or post-medieval mullioned window over the arch.

The eastern companion to the Lucy Tower on the Brayford, the gate leading eastwards and the wall that joined it to the Roman defences, is comparatively poorly known (Fig. 9.67). It is thought, however, that the locations of the gate and the tower were reversed. The gate seems to have been at the southern end of the wall, gaving access to *Butwerk*, and is first mentioned in a lease of 1383 (Hill 1948, 158, citing *CPR* 1381–5, 302). Presumably, this gate stood immediately south of the south-east corner of the late medieval timber-framed building called the Green Dragon, which occupies the site today and seems to have encroached on the wall line. The tower corresponding to the Lucy Tower, however, was still standing in the 18th century and lay somewhat to the north, in the yard north of the Green Dragon. The tower, then, was apparently set back from the waterfront, with the gate between it and the river. It is possible, however, that the tower marked an earlier, (possibly 13th century) river bank and that the river itself has been pushed southwards making room for the gate to *Butwerk* (and subsequently the Green Dragon) to be built on reclaimed land. A strip of land to the east of the Green Dragon was known in the 18th century as Tower Garth and is probably the same 8.5-by-72 ell plot leased by the corporation (the Mayor and citizens) to John Norman in the late 14th century (Hill 1948, 157). The southern part of this plot is recognisable on Padley's 1819 map of Lincoln, where it measures *c*.11m wide (as opposed to the 9.7m it should be at 45 feet to an ell). By this time the northern part of the plot had been taken to widen Broadgate. Hill surmised that this land probably comprised part of the city ditch, and viewed on the map it is likely that the entire width of the city ditch at this point was leased, making the ditch *c*.11m wide.

### The Castello de Tornegat

A single charter records that Thorngate Castle (*Castello suo de Tornegat*) was given to Bishop Alexander in 1141 (ed. Foster 1931, 61, RA99). Hill thought that this castle should be equated with the later references to 'Kyme Hall', which can be placed somewhere in the area between Thorngate, Waterside North and Saltergate, i.e. north of the river (1948, 157). Chris Johnson, on the other hand, has determined that it probably lay at the western end of the Thorngate suburb, to the south of the river (Lincolnshire Archives Office, TLE 36/1/9 and LD 57/1/4). He suggests that it may be equated with a tower that seems to have been the companion of that north of the Green Dragon which, as we have seen, is likely to be of 13th-century date. Unless further archaeological or documentary evidence is forthcoming, it is impossible to choose between these two options. In any event, this castle clearly had little lasting influence upon the topography of the city.

### Suburban defences and boundaries

The existence of an earthwork around the Newport suburb has been known since the 18th century, when it was planned by Stukeley (Fig. 9.29). At its northern

end the earthwork survived into recent times, by which time it was much disfigured; its north-west corner had been quarried on both the north and west sides, and there were also quarries within the line of the earthwork. On the north-east side, however, the earthwork could be traced in the grounds of Bishop Grosseteste College well into the 20th century and the one archaeological investigation of the earthwork was carried out here by Tom Baker in 1937 (ON 256). This apparently confirmed the medieval date of the earthwork and disproved the implication of Stukeley's plan, that the earthwork had circular corner towers and stood outside a stone wall.

There is no documentary evidence for the construction of the earthwork, nor it is clear from the contemporary descriptions of the 12th- and 13th-century sieges of Lincoln whether it was in existence at that time. Similarly, there is no evidence for the nature of the barrier at the north end of the suburb. Presumably there must have been a gate, or at least a bar, across Ermine Street. Nor is there any evidence for the arrangements where Church Lane crosses the line of the earthwork. There should also be access points in the earthwork on the western side where at least one route from the west joins Ermine Street. It is

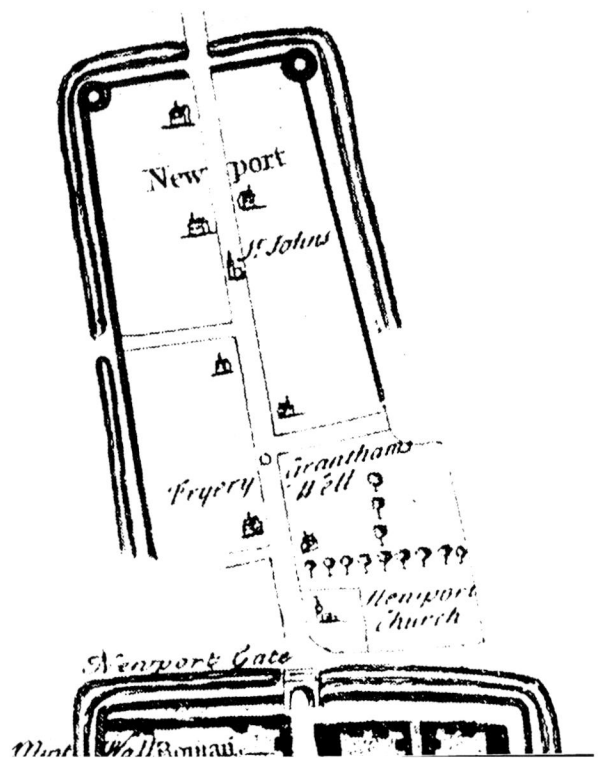

Fig. 9.29. Detail of Newport area from the map of Lincoln by William Stukeley, dated 1722 and published in 1724. Note the large ditch surrounding the suburb to east, west and north. The map also depicts walls and corner towers, which have been searched for in excavations but never found (source, Stukeley 1724, plate 88).

presumed that the ditch of the earthwork was joined to that surrounding the Upper City but this point too, and the nature of the termination of the accompanying bank, are unknown.

It is suggested below that the Wigford suburb south of the walled city was laid out in two stages (p. 242 below – Fig. 9.69). The northern of these components (which we have called 'Upper Wigford'), dating to the early or mid 10th century, extended southwards to a point just beyond St Peter's church. The western side of the suburb would have been formed by the Brayford Pool, which in the early 10th century would have extended quite close to Ermine Street, and the eastern side would have been marked by marshy ground, like that revealed by excavations south-east of St Marks' Station in 1987 and 1990 (ZE 87). The southern boundary of Upper Wigford would have been close to the line of the drainage ditch known as Great Gowt. In its present form, the Gowt is clearly an artificial cut but it is possible that it was originally a recutting of a natural river channel. Be that as it may, it seems likely that the ditch originally formed the boundary of the early, northern, part of the suburb and therefore, that it is another suburban demarcation line. In this case the Great Gowt itself might have consisted of a narrow cut and bank perpendicular to the line of Ermine Street and would have formed quite a considerable obstacle.

The southern extension to the Wigford suburb, Lower Wigford, consisted of a funnel-shaped green or market which may have been laid out at the same time as Upper Wigford, or it may have been later (Fig. 9.83a). Whether it was laid out in the 10th century or later, Lower Wigford was soon given a new southern boundary, marked by a new ditch, known as Sincil Dyke (Plate 5.4), a wall, probably with a rampart behind it, and two gates: Great and Little Bargate. The first references to any of these features is in the late 12th century (Cameron 1985, 13); however, the existence of hospitals on either side of the green, immediately south of Sincil Dyke from the very end of the 11th century suggests that this line was the suburb's boundary from that date. How defensive this ditch was intended to be at this early date, however, is less certain. Documentary sources (e.g. *HMC*, 60) show that for at least part of its circuit the ditch was accompanied by an internal bank, and furthermore, Speed's map shows what appears to be a defensive wall linking Great and Little Bargate. It probably extended the whole length of Sincil Dyke in Lower Wigford south of Great Gowt although excavations at Knight Place (KP 92) (Donel 1993) failed to find any trace of it. These excavations did show, however, that the present line of the ditch is further east than its late medieval or early post-medieval line. The recutting of the ditch clearly took place later than the establishment of the tenement boundaries to the east of the High Street resulting in the creation of strips of land on the line of the original ditch which were leased

out by the city. Illustrations of the two Bargates indicate that they were probably of 13th-century or later date (Figs. 9.30 and 9.31) and show that the Little Bargate was a surprisingly elaborate structure. This probably indicates that the route leading towards this gate, from Canwick, was originally of similar importance to that from Bracebridge. However, within the defences, this route was termed a 'lane' rather than a street or King's highway from the 13th century, and there is no doubt that the west or Great Bargate was always the main entrance to the city.

In the eastern suburb of *Butwerk*, there is docu-

*Fig. 9.30. Great Bargate from the south-east in 1724 by S and N Buck (Oxford, Bodleian Library Ms, Gough Lincs. 15, f.20r) (photo and copyright Bodleian Library Oxford).*

*Fig. 9.31. Little Bargate from the south in 1724 by S and N Buck (Oxford, Bodleian Library Ms, Gough Lincs. 15, f.41r) (photo and copyright Bodleian Library, Oxford).*

mentary evidence for a stone wall, running from The Stamp northwards during the medieval period (Fig. 9.32). In 1371 a *Baggerholme* gate (*porta*) is mentioned, which presumably marked the formal limit of the *Butwerk* suburb (Cameron 1985, 49). This gate may have been a bar at which toll was collected, but a charter of 1240x50 makes it clear that there was (by that time) a wall associated with the gate (ed. Major 1973, 297–8, RA2959). Even so, the wall may not have been continuous, and we may doubt whether it was intended as a serious defence. Furthermore, it is likely that the wall had ceased to have any serious function by the 15th century. It seems more likely that these features represented a formal administrative boundary to the suburb, provided either at its foundation in the mid 11th century, or later. Neither ditch nor gate are accurately located, but the 1240x50 charter seems to indicate a plot on the hillside, since its northern boundary was the *Wyngard*, probable the same *vinyard* given as a boundary for a property in Holy Trinity Greestone Stairs parish given to the Blackfriars (ed. Major 1968, 291–3, RA2954–5; 297–8, RA2959). The street called *Bagerholme* in this charter is Monks Road, rather than Cameron's suggestion of modern Baggeholme Road, since the 1240x50 charter is quite clear in stating that the highway is running east–west. Other charters confirm this identification. It is probable that the 1455 agreement between the Council and the Black Monks describes this same suburb boundary at its northern and southern ends (Lincolnshire Archives Office, Lincoln City Charters 6/54). There, the southern part is described as a stone wall (Cameron 1985, 102) and the northern part is the 'stone wall called *Chiviotwall*' (*Ibid.*, 58). The southern wall was said, in the 1455 agreement to have been built by the Friars of the Sack. It probably formed the eastern boundary of their property, which seems to have run along the west side of modern Baggeholme Road. By 1455 the suburb would have suffered substantial depopulation, of course (see chapter 10 below), and it is possible that the boundary might have been rendered meaningless by that date, with agriculture on both sides. The very fact that an agreement between the Council and St Mary's Abbey was necessary in 1455, however, indicates that the boundary between the two estates was disputable and that it was still regarded as important.

There is also evidence for a similar boundary to the Newland suburb, to the west of the walled city (Fig. 9.33). The western limit of the Newland suburb in the medieval period is given by a 13th-century documentary reference in the cartulary of Welbeck Abbey to a gate located by C Johnson just to the west of the junction of Newland Street West with the modern Nelson Street (London, British Library Ms., Harl. 3640, f106). A second charter, of *c*.1200, refers to selions in the open fields lying next the King's ditch at Newland (ed. Major 1968, 235, RA2646). There seems little doubt, therefore, that the Newland suburb was also defined

by a bank and ditch, with a gate set centrally within the defensive line, although at what stage in the suburb's history it gained its boundary or defence is unknown. The roads which later became Carholme road and West Parade also extended beyond the boundary, and must have breached it at crossing points about which nothing more is known. It is not clear, either, whether the ditch would have simply run up the slope to the foot of the cliff and terminated. However, a reference in Willson's notes (London, Society of Antiquaries, Ms. 786/5, 25) to a lane, running along the boundary of St Mary-le-Wigford and St Martin's parishes north out of Newland towards the *Giant's Grave*, may suggest that it survived into the 19th century. *Giant's Grave* might have been an old post mill mound west of St Bartholomew's church (see also Fig. 9.59 below). Furthermore, an area of organic silts observed during pipe laying in Newland Street West is in the appropriate position to have been a ditch in front of the gate, although it was by no means certain that it was a linear feature, rather than, say, a pond or back-filled clay pit (NSS 97; Wragg 1998). As in *Butwerk*, there is no evidence in the 19th-century tenement and field boundaries to indicate a major differences in land-holdings either side of this boundary line, nor is the line clearly marked on the Enclosure Award map of 1803. In Newland too, therefore, the existence of a suburb boundary or defence on this line seems likely, although it was clearly of little significance to late medieval and later topography.

There is no evidence that the eastern and western suburbs of the Bail (Eastgate and *Westcastle*) were ever defended nor that they ever had formal or symbolic boundaries. Whether this denotes a difference in their status, being suburbs of the King's Bail rather than of the city, is uncertain. However, the fact that 'uphill' Newport (which was administratively a city suburb rather than a Bail suburb) was defended suggests that (as Eastgate and *Westcastle* were linked to the Bail) their lack of defences may have been due to the different priorities of their respective lords. Whether the 'new wall of the city' reported to have formed the southern boundary of the college of Vicars-Choral (p. 182 above, ed. Major 1973, 200, RA2870) can be seen as evidence for an eastwards extension of the walled city, pre-dating the Close Wall and perhaps including a planned Eastgate suburb, remains unknown.

## Development within the walls in the Anglo-Scandinavian period

At least one of the Roman streets of Lincoln survived into the mid 9th century, Ermine Street, but much of the Anglo-Scandinavian street system seems to have been laid out with little regard to the known Roman streets of the Lower City (Fig. 9.34). There was no evidence for post-Roman, pre-10th century, metalling of the street at Michaelgate (MCH 84) and there are

Black Friars
precinct

'Chiviotwall'

St Mary's Abbey estate

Bagerholmegate

Gate

Baggerholme
Close

St Hugh's
Croft

Baggerholme Leys Wong

W a l l

N

Bedern Lane

Sack Friars
precinct

The Stamp End

0                    200 m

Area of Blackdyke dock

*River Witham* ⟶

**Key**

— · — · —  Boundary of
St Mary's Abbey Estate

· · · · · · · · · ·  Precinct boundarys

▨  Approximate location of
presumed causeway
at Stamp End

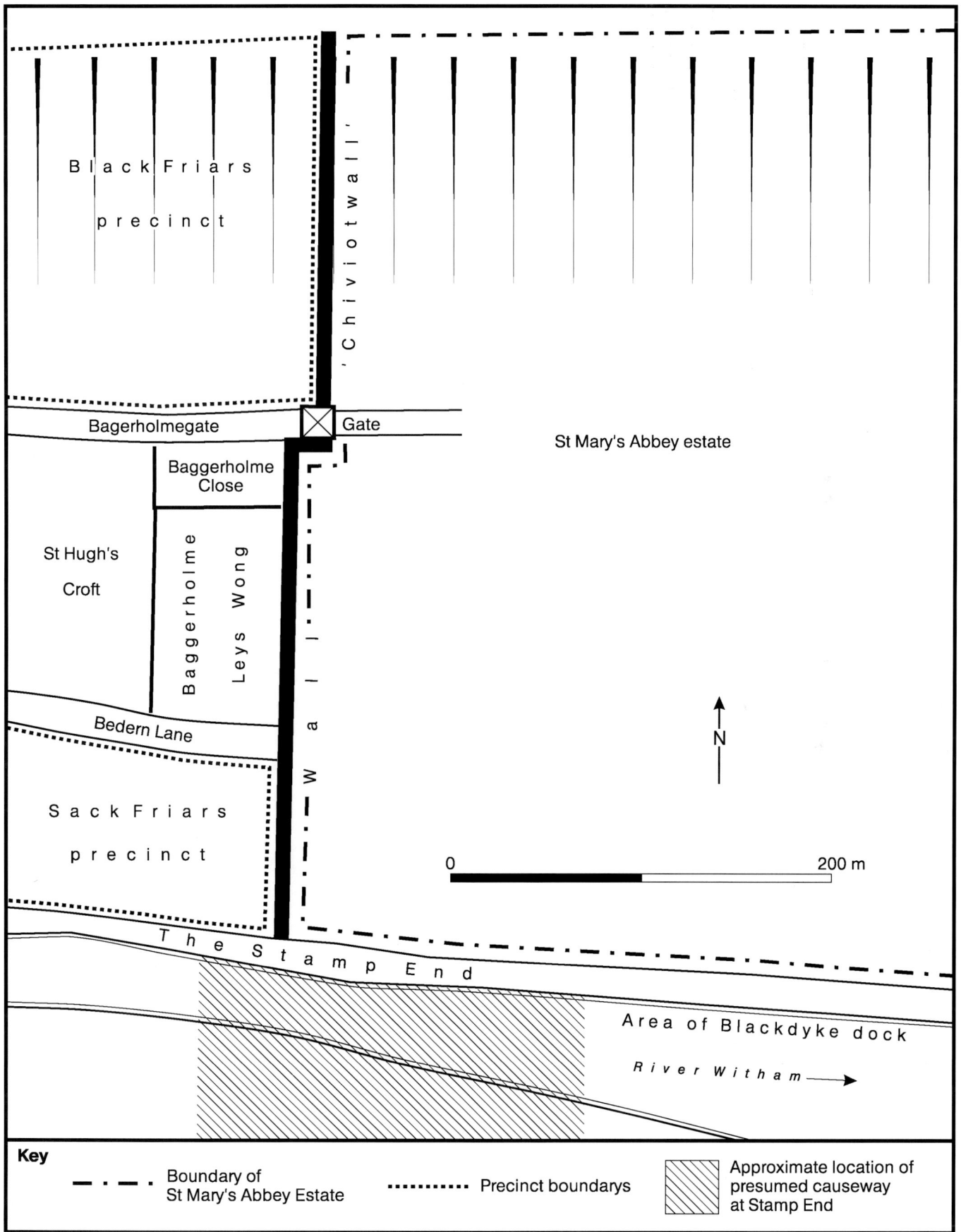

*Fig. 9.32. Reconstruction study of defensive or boundary features along the eastern side of the suburb of* Butwerk *(drawn by Dave Watt, copyright English Heritage).*

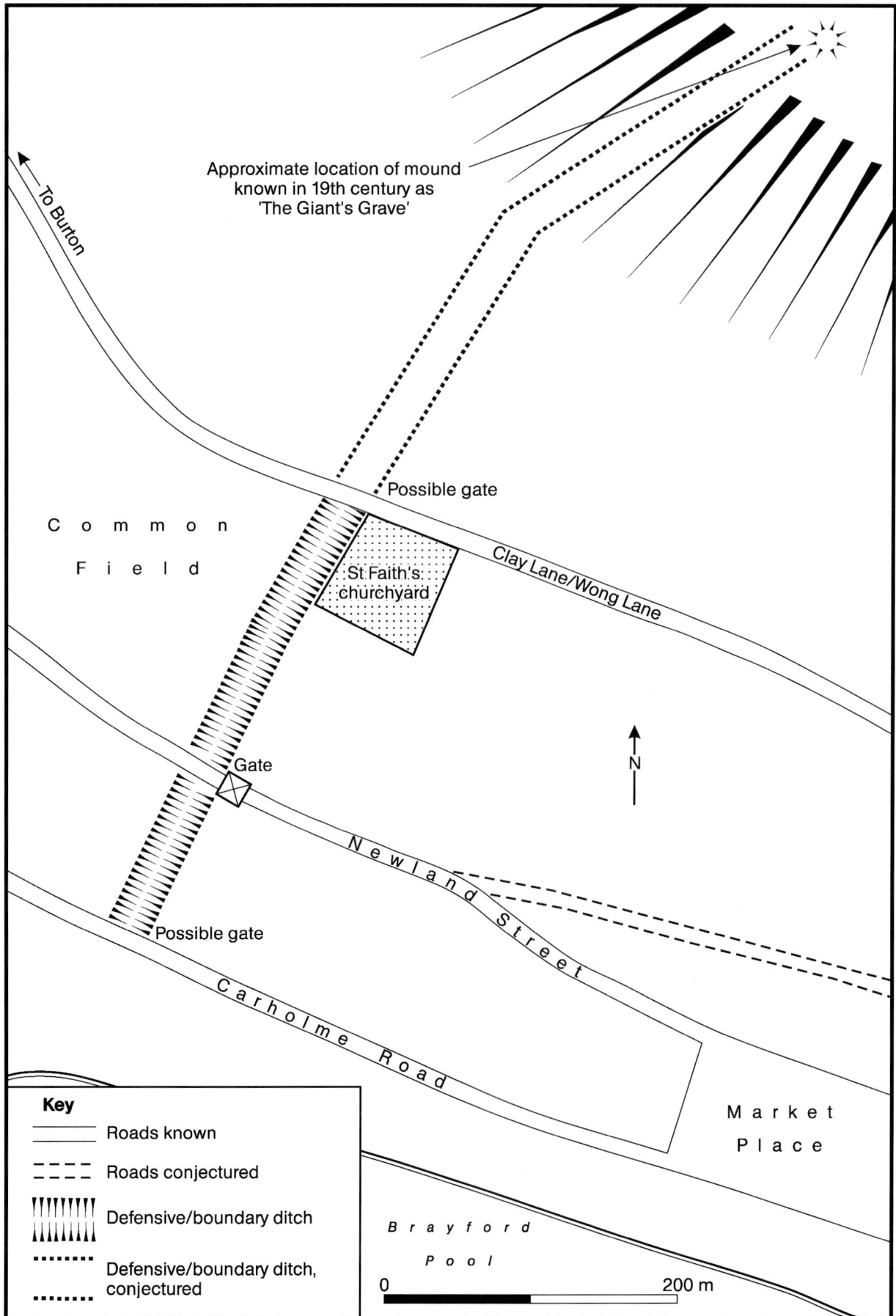

*Fig. 9.33. Reconstruction study of defensive or boundary features along the western side of the suburb of Newland (drawn by Dave Watt, copyright English Heritage).*

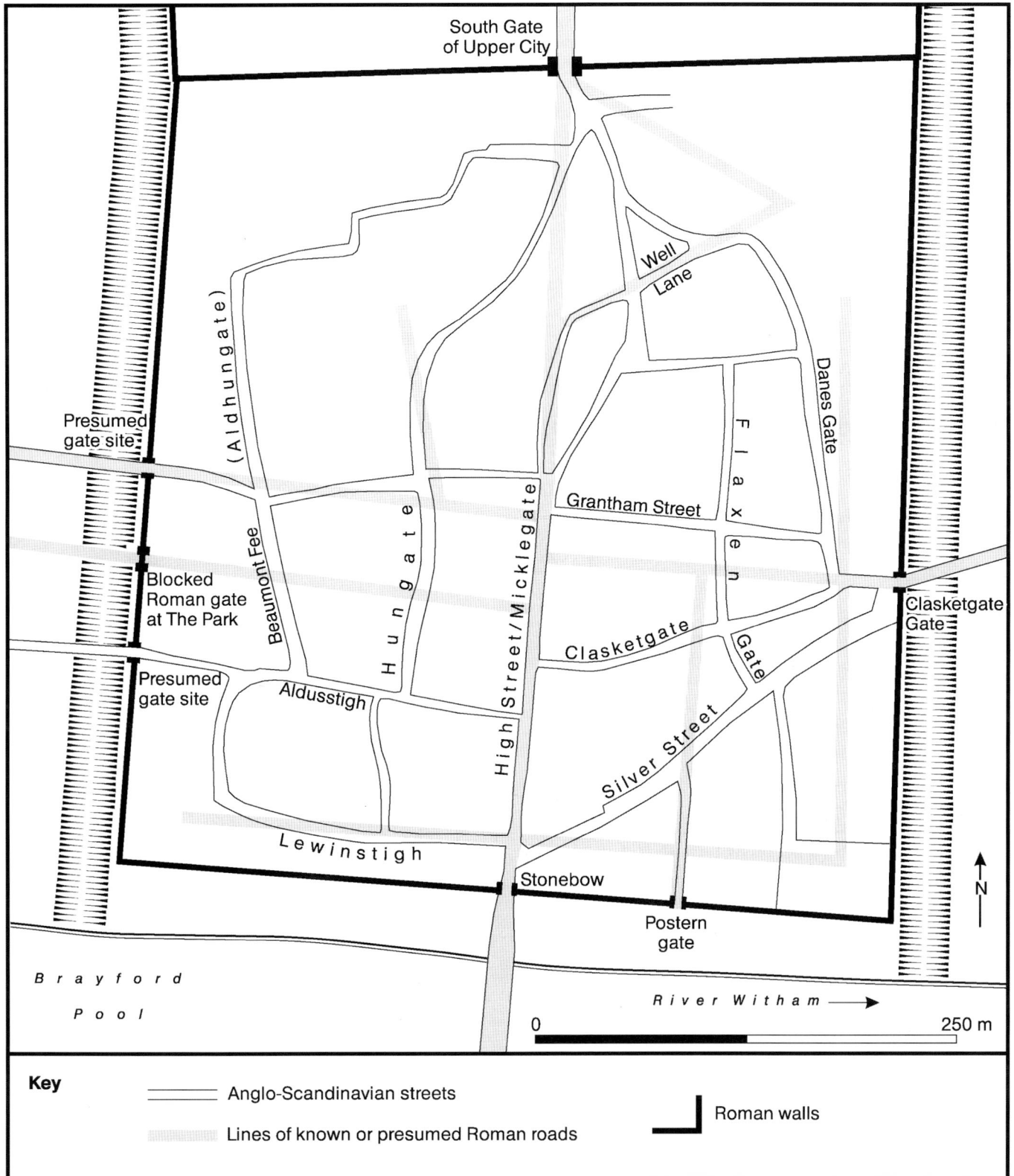

*Fig. 9.34. Probable Anglo-Scandinavian street pattern within the walls of the Lower City relative to its Roman predecessor. The lines of the presumed Anglo-Scandinavian streets are based on Padley's 1842 map (drawn by Dave Watt, copyright English Heritage).*

two cases where Theodosian coins have been found below the latest Roman street surface, at The Park and Waterside North (P 70 and WO 89). In the latter case, however, the surface represented a 'hard' running down from Ermine Street to the waterfront, rather than the main thoroughfare itself. These late Roman coin finds suggest that the street could not have had much traffic during the five centuries between the 4th and the 9th; it would otherwise have been repaired, resurfaced or worn away to form a hollow way, especially where it climbed the hill towards the old fortress. It has been surmised that certain Roman side streets may have been brought back into use in the 9th or 10th centuries, whilst that underneath Well Lane, appears to have been a late Roman diversion of, or alternative to, Ermine Street (Fig. 9.34). Grantham Street, Hungate, *Lewinstigh* (Mint Street) and Flaxengate run parallel to the presumed lines of Roman roads. Grantham Street itself might have been laid out along the line of a Roman east–west street, for which there is no other evidence. A comparison of ground levels on sites immediately north and south of the street indicate that a major terrace must have existed somewhere under it, although there are problems reconciling this proposal with the observations by Edward Willson locating Clasketgate Gate. More certainly, the northern part of Hungate follows a Roman alignment, as road metalling of 2nd-century date was found just to the east of the street (H 83). What might have been a northerly continuation of this street, was excavated higher up the hill (SPM 83). Excavations to the south of the Saltergate postern demonstrate that it continued in use into the 10th century and it seems likely that Flaxengate was originally aligned on this gate. However, no sign of a Roman predecessor to Flaxengate was found during the 1972–6 excavations (F 72) and it may be that the Roman street only went as far as Grantham Street (SW 82) and that the stretch of road linking Grantham Street and Danes Terrace was a 10th-century extension. The eastern part of the modern Mint Street (known in the medieval period as *Lewinstigh*) also follows a hypothetical Roman intramural road, but the relationship between the two streets has not been investigated archaeologically.

The Anglo-Scandinavian street pattern was influenced not only by surviving Roman street lines but also by Roman ruins. Roman terracing probably survived to influence the topography of the northern part of the Lower City, for example at Danes Terrace, and the survival of the ruins of the *forum basilica*, a focal point in the Upper City, and their possible influence on middle Saxon topography has been described and discussed in detail in chapter 8.

Only two sites have produced stratigraphic evidence for occupation in the first phase of Anglo-Scandinavian settlement in the form of distinctive ceramics (ASH 7). These were the 1945–8 excavations on the east side of Flaxengate, which produced a rubbish pit containing pottery of this date, and those on the south side of

Silver Street (LIN 73f). In both cases the evidence is too slight to demonstrate which street, if either, the properties bounded, nor can anything be said about property size or layout in this earliest phase. Even so, neither site is served by a known Roman street and within a generation at most, the buildings in this area were fronting onto Flaxengate, Danesgate and Silver Street, none of which had Roman origins. The distribution of pottery dating to ceramic horizon ASH 7 is wider than these two sites (seen for example the distribution of Lincoln Gritty ware, (LG) – Figs. 9.35 and 9.36), but there is always the possibility that early sherds found at other sites were residual, brought onto site at a later date. The earliest post-Roman activity at Hungate (H 83), for example, consisted of unintelligible scoops and slots cut into late Roman deposits. These features were filled with a deposit laid down in preparation for the first known building, fronting onto Hungate. There is no doubt that this construction occurred in the early to mid 10th century (i.e. ASH 9), but amongst the pottery from its construction were sherds from earlier Anglo-Scandinavian phases, including many sherds from an ELFS bowl. The bowl is of a type in use in the pre-Viking period and we would not expect to find it on any but the earliest occupied Lincoln sites. Similar finds occurred at Flaxengate (F 72) and it is at present impossible to provide a secure context for them. Their existence demonstrates activity nearby, however, and this might even have been on the site itself, but strictly speaking, at both Flaxengate and Hungate Anglo-Scandinavian occupation sequences start about AD 890, rather than in the very earliest ceramic phase. It is likely that in this earliest phase of occupation both of these sites were parts of large plots fronting on to the High Street, where occupation of this early period might logically be sought. Nevertheless, this evidence for the very earliest phase of Anglo-Scandinavian activity occurring in the Flaxengate/Silver Street area is compelling, whilst the total lack of similar finds from the Upper City, Wigford or any of the extra-mural suburbs, also suggests that in the late 9th century the occupied area of Lincoln was confined to the southern part of the lower walled city (see Fig. 9.45). It is unlikely that the Upper City would have been totally ignored in this period, not least because of its clear symbolic and strategic importance, but the large number of excavations within this enclosure have failed to produce comparable finds of this period, and it would be surprising if it had been extensively occupied.

By the early or mid 10th century (ceramic horizon ASH 9) we can certainly add Hungate and Flaxengate to this list of occupied streets, together with most of the excavated sites in the Wigford High Street (i.e. from Holmes Grain Warehouse – HG 72 – in the north to St Mary's Guildhall – SMG 82 – in the south), demonstrating that at least the central and northern parts of this suburb were occupied, southwards as far as Great Gowt. The best indication of the extent of

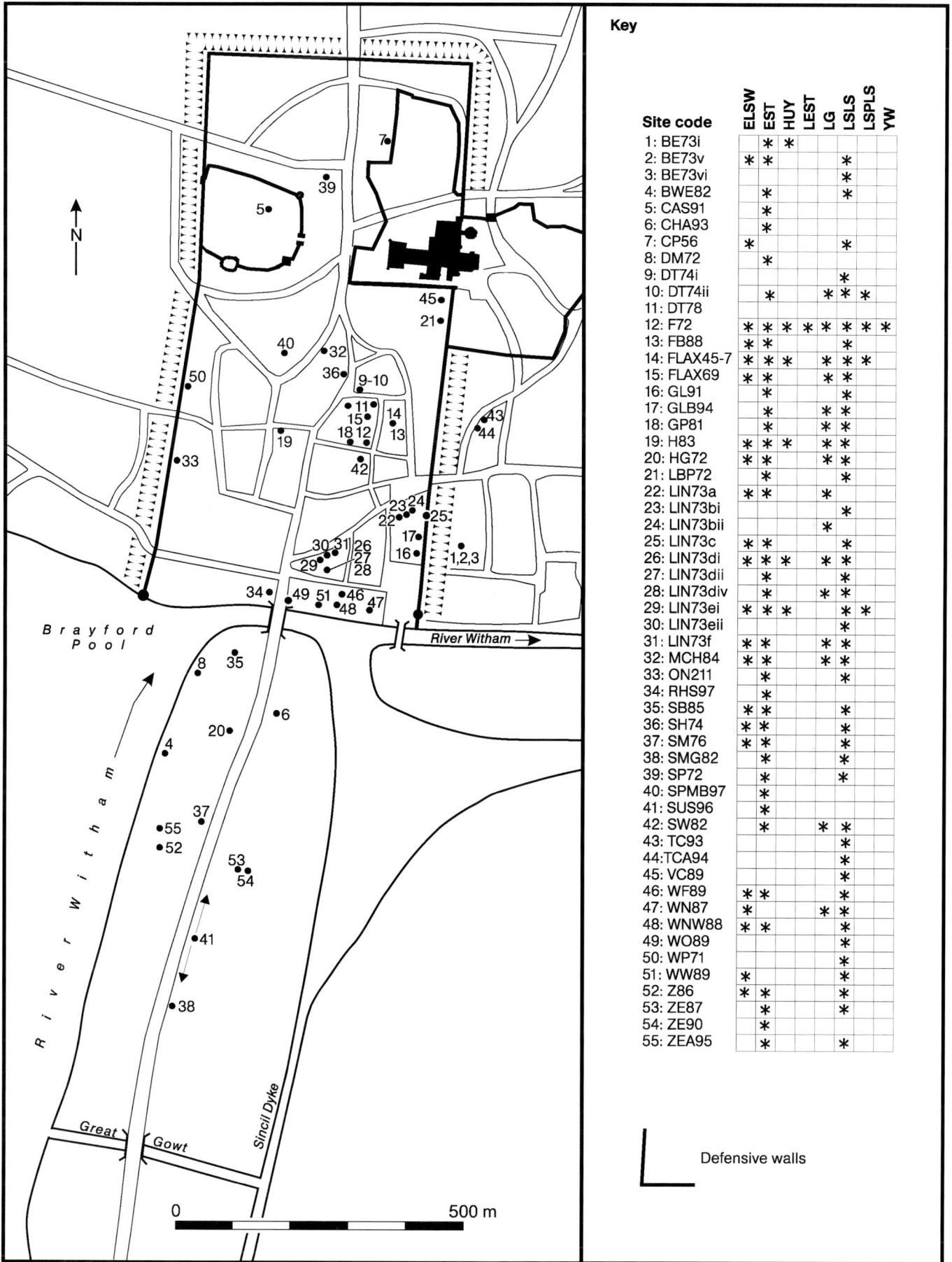

| Site code | ELSW | EST | HUY | LEST | LG | LSLS | LSPLS | YW |
|---|---|---|---|---|---|---|---|---|
| 1: BE73i | | * | * | | | | | |
| 2: BE73v | * | * | | | | * | | |
| 3: BE73vi | | | | | | * | | |
| 4: BWE82 | | * | | | | * | | |
| 5: CAS91 | | * | | | | | | |
| 6: CHA93 | | | | | | | | |
| 7: CP56 | * | | | | | * | | |
| 8: DM72 | | * | | | | | | |
| 9: DT74i | | | | | | * | | |
| 10: DT74ii | | * | | | * | * | * | |
| 11: DT78 | | | | | | | | |
| 12: F72 | * | * | * | * | * | * | * | * |
| 13: FB88 | * | * | | | | * | | |
| 14: FLAX45-7 | * | * | * | | * | * | * | |
| 15: FLAX69 | * | * | | | * | * | | |
| 16: GL91 | | * | | | | * | | |
| 17: GLB94 | | * | | | * | * | | |
| 18: GP81 | | * | | | * | * | | |
| 19: H83 | * | * | * | | * | * | | |
| 20: HG72 | * | * | | | * | * | | |
| 21: LBP72 | | * | | | | * | | |
| 22: LIN73a | * | * | | | * | | | |
| 23: LIN73bi | | | | | | * | | |
| 24: LIN73bii | | | | | * | | | |
| 25: LIN73c | * | * | | | | * | | |
| 26: LIN73di | * | * | * | | * | * | | |
| 27: LIN73dii | | * | | | | | | |
| 28: LIN73div | | * | | | * | * | | |
| 29: LIN73ei | * | * | * | | | * | * | |
| 30: LIN73eii | | | | | | * | | |
| 31: LIN73f | * | * | | | * | * | | |
| 32: MCH84 | * | * | | | * | * | | |
| 33: ON211 | | * | | | | * | | |
| 34: RHS97 | | * | | | | | | |
| 35: SB85 | * | * | | | | * | | |
| 36: SH74 | * | * | | | | * | | |
| 37: SM76 | * | * | | | | * | | |
| 38: SMG82 | | * | | | | * | | |
| 39: SP72 | | * | | | | * | | |
| 40: SPMB97 | | * | | | | | | |
| 41: SUS96 | | * | | | | | | |
| 42: SW82 | | * | | | * | * | | |
| 43: TC93 | | | | | | * | | |
| 44: TCA94 | | | | | | * | | |
| 45: VC89 | | | | | | * | | |
| 46: WF89 | * | * | | | | * | | |
| 47: WN87 | * | | | | * | * | | |
| 48: WNW88 | * | * | | | | * | | |
| 49: WO89 | | | | | | * | | |
| 50: WP71 | | | | | | * | | |
| 51: WW89 | * | | | | | * | | |
| 52: Z86 | * | * | | | | * | | |
| 53: ZE87 | | * | | | | * | | |
| 54: ZE90 | | * | | | | | | |
| 55: ZEA95 | | * | | | | * | | |

Key

⌐ Defensive walls

*Fig. 9.35. Distribution of late 9th- and early 10th-century pottery types. The topography and street plan is later medieval (source, Vince and Young forthcoming, drawn by Dave Watt, copyright English Heritage).*

| Ware types | ASH7 | ASH8 | ASH9 | ASH10 | ASH11 | ASH12 | ASH13 | ASH14 |
|---|---|---|---|---|---|---|---|---|
| Lincoln Late Saxon Shelly ware (LSH) | Other | Main | Main | Main | Main | Main | | |
| Lincoln Kiln-type Shelly ware (LKT) | Main | Main | Main | Main | Main | Other? | | |
| Lincoln Gritty ware (LG) | Main | Main | | | | | | |
| Late Saxon Crucible fabrics (LSCRUC) | Main | | | | | | | |
| Torksey ware (TORK) | | Other | Other | Other | Main | Main | Main | |
| Stamford ware (ST) | | | | Other | Other | Other | Main | Main |
| Lincoln Fine-Shelled ware (LFS) | | | | | Other | Main | Main | Main |
| Lincoln Saxo-Norman Sandy ware (SNLS) | | | | | Main | Main | Main | |

*Fig. 9.36. Named wares related to Lincoln's ceramic horizons between c.850–c.1100. 'Main' indicates that the ware is a primary indicator of the ceramic period; 'Other' indicates that the ware is found, but is not a primary indicator of the ceramic horizon (source, Vince and Young forthcoming).*

occupation in ASH 8 or ASH 9 (i.e. by the central part of the 10th century) is given by comparing the distributions of the pottery type known as LG with its successor, LSLS (Fig. 9.35). These are clear signs of expansion, and most of the sites that had previously produced only a sherd or two of LG pottery now produced much more substantial quantities of LSLS. The predominance of Silver Street and Flaxengate is still evident, but now activity clearly moved down towards the Witham waterfront. LSLS was found in the Waterside excavations, deposited in the main on the foreshore. Occupation had reached Michaelgate, towards the top of Ermine Street in the Lower City (MCH 83) and a few finds from Cottesford Place and St Paul's in the Upper City (CP56 and SP72) are perhaps refuse from occupation sites. Both sites are later within plots fronting onto Bailgate.

Whether Grantham Street was occupied at this stage is also doubtful. Finds of early Anglo-Scandinavian pottery from the GP81 site might well derive from refuse disposal by households with buildings fronting onto Flaxengate or Ermine Street. Other sherds elsewhere in the city are so sparse, and all in residual contexts, that they cannot reliably be used to indicate the extent of settlement. Results from the site at Broadgate East (BE 73) hint, however, that occupation immediately outside the lower eastern defences may have begun in the early Anglo-Scandinavian period. Such occupation might have fronted onto Friars Lane, which can be seen as a southerly continuation of 'Pottergate', the route that, until the 18th century, wound its way up the hill from Clasketgate to Eastgate.

Three mechanisms may have led to the spread of occupation debris away from the occupied area. First, rubbish middens may have ringed the settlement. It is thought that at Flaxengate such middens were the source of much of the material used as levelling at the beginning of each new building phase. Later on, the existence of such middens, or *laystalls*, is known from documentary sources. Secondly, manure derived from these middens may have been used on the town fields. This is a possible explanation for some of the early finds from Broadgate East and other sites in what later became the *Butwerk* suburb. Thirdly, much of

the ground fronting the Witham, on both north and south banks, required reclamation before it could be settled and many of the early sherds may have been imported in material used as make-up during such reclamation episodes.

The spread of settlement from the mid to the late 10th century (Fig. 9.46) is difficult to study because the ceramics of this period were, in the main, a mixture of earlier types and new types that continued in use into the 11th century. Stratified assemblages can be assigned to ceramic horizons ASH 9, ASH 10 or ASH 11 through a study of the typology and manufacturing methods used for the principal wares, but unstratified finds, which are in the majority in this period, cannot be precisely dated (Fig. 9.36). A rough indication of the extent of settlement by the end of the 10th century can be gained by comparing the Figs. 9.35 with 9.37, and the results of this comparison have informed Fig. 9.46. Figure 9.39 indicates the frequency of ceramic fabrics LKT and LSH as a percentage of all Anglo-Scandinavian pottery and shows that there is, for the first time, a significant quantity of pottery on a site in the Upper City, St Paul-in-the-Bail church (SP 72). There are also finds from two sites at the western edge of the *Butwerk* suburb (TCA 94 and BE 73). The frequency of LSH sherds is highest on sites along the waterfront on both sides of the river (at St Benedict's Square – SB 85 – and the Waterside sites WO 89, WN 87 and WNW 88) and this clearly indicates that they were reclaimed at a time when this ware was at its height of popularity, in the mid 10th century. Two other sites with high frequencies of LSH sherds are those at Spring Hill (SH 74) and the 1994 excavations at Cathedral Street (TCA 94), which revealed evidence for production of this ware. The presence of LSH and the earlier LSLS wares at Steep Hill, at its junction with Well Lane, is significant. There is no evidence for occupation on the site before the 11th century, when it is thought the line of Steep Hill itself was established, but equally there is no evidence from this site for the raising of the ground level by terracing, which might have led to the importation of 10th-century pottery at a later date. This pottery may be evidence, therefore, for activity fronting onto Ermine Street at an earlier date than the first built structures.

**Key**

**Site code**

| | |
|---|---|
| 1: BDW96 | 39: LIN73f |
| 2: BE73i | 40: LT72 |
| 3: BE73v | 41: MCH84 |
| 4: BE73vi | 42: ON211 |
| 5: BE73x | 43: ON217b |
| 6: BGB95 | 44: ON244 |
| 7: BWE82 | 45: ON247 |
| 8:CAT86 | 46: ON343 |
| 9: CL85 | 47: ON486 |
| 10: CP56 | 48: ON487 |
| 11: CS73 | 49: P70 |
| 12: DM72 | 50: SB85 |
| 13: DT74i | 51: SES97 |
| 14: DT74ii | 52: SH74 |
| 15: DT78 | 53: SM76 |
| 16: EB70 | 54: SMG82 |
| 17: EB74 | 55: SP72 |
| 18: EB80 | 56: SPM83 |
| 19: EB82 | 57: SPMB97 |
| 20: EME92 | 58: SUS96 |
| 21: F72 | 59: SW82 |
| 22: FLAX45-7 | 60: TC93 |
| 23: FLAX69 | 61: TCA94 |
| 24: GL91 | 62: VC89 |
| 25: GLB94 | 63: W73 |
| 26: GP81 | 64: WB80 |
| 27: H83 | 65: WF89 |
| 28: HG72 | 66: WN87 |
| 29: LBP72 | 67: WNW88 |
| 30: LIN73a | 68: WO89 |
| 31: LIN73bi | 69: WS82 |
| 32: LIN73bii | 70: WW89 |
| 33: LIN73c | 71: Z86 |
| 34: LIN73di | 72: ZE87 |
| 35: LIN73dii | 73: ZE90 |
| 36: LIN73div | 74: ZEA95 |
| 37: LIN73ei | 75: ZEB95 |
| 38: LIN73eii | |

Defensive walls

Brayford Pool

River Witham

Sincil Dyke

Great Gowt

River Witham

0     500 m

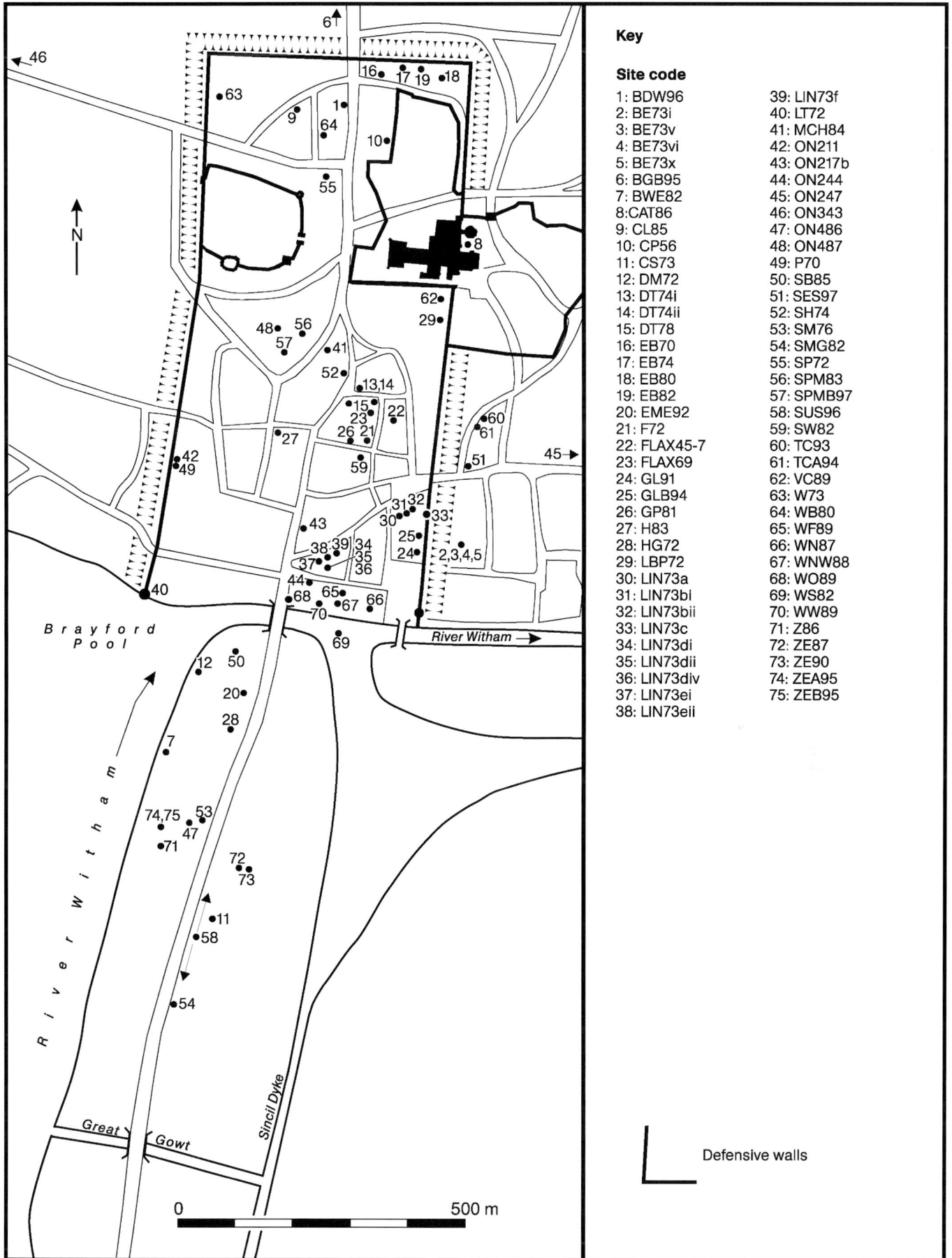

*Fig. 9.37. Distribution of* all *pottery types to the end of 10th century. The topography and street plan is later medieval (source, Vince and Young forthcoming, drawn by Dave Watt, copyright English Heritage).*

At the end of the 10th century, shell-tempered wares ceased to be manufactured in Lincoln and the city turned to sand-tempered wares which were either locally-made (like ceramic fabric SNLS) or imported from Torksey (TORK), together with shell-tempered wares probably brought into the city from the surrounding countryside (LFS). These sandy wares have a limited period of use in the early to mid 11th century and their distribution therefore gives a good indication of the extent of occupation in Lincoln immediately before, and at the time of, the Norman Conquest (Fig. 9.38). Increasingly, however, local wares were supplanted by Stamford ware cooking pots and we find that, usually, sites with high percentages of the latter ware are likely to have been first occupied later than those where local wares predominate.

When the incidence of finds of these 11th-century sandy wares is compared with that of 10th-century shelly wares (Fig. 9.39) we see that, in most cases, excavated sites produced more shelly than sandy wares (which, given that the shelly wares were in use for over twice as long, is not surprising). Sites with more sandy than shelly ware are restricted to the fringes of the 10th-century settlement. The highest percentages of sandy ware came from sites at the fringes of the Lower City such as The Park, West Parade and the Bishop's Palace (P 79, WP 71 and LBP 72), and the Upper City at Chapel Lane and Cottesford Place (CL 85 and CP 56). The Upper City finds include some from sites that, later in the medieval period, fronted onto West Bight, the north–south lane parallel with Bailgate.

A similar comparison between Stamford ware (ST) and 11th-century sandy wares (TORK and SNLS – Fig. 9.40) shows that two areas of the city stand out as having low ratios of early to mid 11th-century pottery compared with pottery of the late 11th or 12th century. These sites lie around the Brayford Pool waterfront and in the Newport suburb (BgB 95 and BN 89) and on the periphery of the Upper City and *Westcastle* suburb (EB 53, L 86, W 73). Unfortunately, the pottery from the later 11th and early 12th centuries, which has been divided into ceramic horizons ASH 13, ASH 14 and MH 1 by Jane Young (Fig. 9.36), includes few common diagnostic types so it is not possible to use pottery to locate shifts in activity in the same way following the Norman Conquest as it is for earlier periods. As in the late 10th century, this period is marked by the phasing-out of earlier wares and the appearance of new ones. From this period, however, it becomes increasingly possible to use documentary sources for topographic reconstruction, and from such sources it is clear that, from just before the Conquest until the first few decades of the 12th century, the city continued its suburban expansion. Most of the *Butwerk* suburb probably dates from this period, although new development here incorporated and overlay the earlier activity along the outer berm of the city ditch. Newport seems to have come into existence during this period, as did the

Newland suburb (although its name is 12th-century). This is also the period when we can first show that the Wigford suburb extended as far south as St Botolph's church and it is also clear from *Domesday Book* that the Eastgate suburb was in existence by this date. The main excavation in this area (WC 87) seems to confirm that the suburb is a later 11th-century foundation. Finally, it is suggested here that the small suburb of Thorngate may have started life as a natural eyot, which may, or may not, have been occupied in the later 11th or early 12th century. The precise nature of these suburbs and their topographic development is considered in detail below, but here it is important to note that, between them, they probably doubled the area of settlement in the city.

### Settlement within the Bail c.900–1150

From the mid 9th century (when a scatter of high status artefacts was deposited at St Paul-in-the-Bail) until the end of the 10th century there is little evidence for the character of activity in the Upper City. None of the excavations in this part of the city have produced strata or finds dating from the late 9th or mid 10th centuries. Given the size of the excavated area at the St Paul's church site (SP 72), this is clear evidence that, whatever use the area might have been put to, it cannot have been part of the commercial settlement centred on the Lower City. Much of the area must have been filled with standing Roman ruins and large earthworks. In addition to the walls of the fortress, parts of the *basilica* walls survived, including the 'Mint Wall' (Fig. 9.41). It is possible that the outline of the *forum* complex was also still discernible, with a chapel or mausoleum, surrounding the hanging bowl burial at St Paul-in-the-Bail, centrally placed within this area. The four Roman gates were still standing and probably in use at this period. However, Nathan Drake's sketch of the east gate in the early 18th century (Fig. 7.9) shows that the Roman arch was considerably lower than the Norman one. Clearly, there had been a substantial rise in ground level in this part of the Upper City, although there is no evidence for when this took place, despite the excavation of the north and south chambers of the gate and some of the street levels between.

Four churches are likely to have existed in the Upper City before the Conquest. That at St Paul-in-the-Bail may have been only a chapel during this period, since it lacked a chancel (Fig. 9.42). Although still open to some doubt, the archaeological evidence suggests that this single-celled stone structure was built in the 10th century, corresponding to the sudden increase in 10th-century pottery on the site. St Clement-in-the-Bail may have started life as a private chapel too, although finds from Chapel Lane (CL 85) and West Bight (WB 80) could be used to suggest that this was a parochial foundation of the 11th century. St Clement was also the dedicatee of one of the two churches founded by

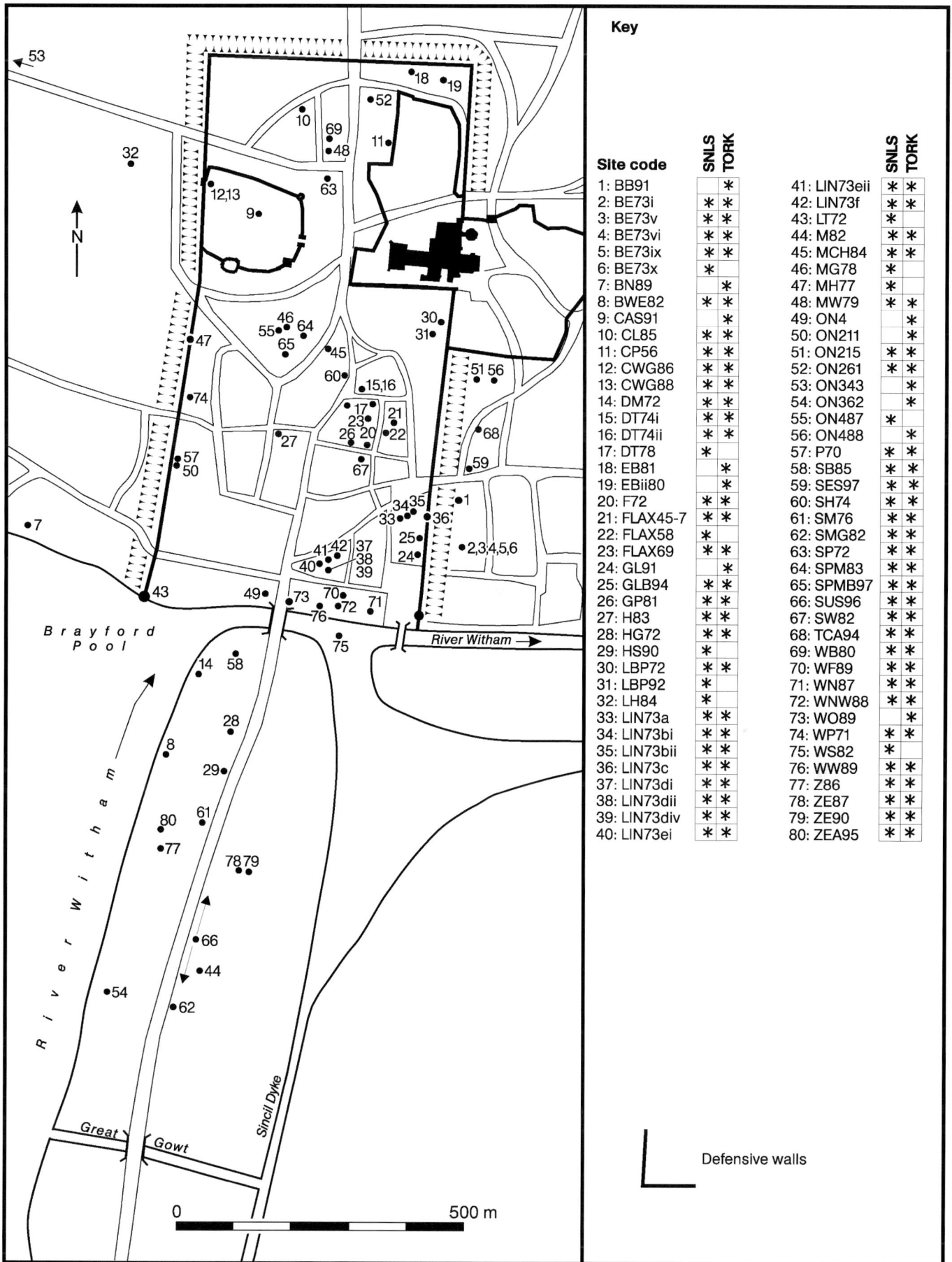

| Site code | SNLS | TORK |
|---|---|---|
| 1: BB91 | | * |
| 2: BE73i | * | * |
| 3: BE73v | * | * |
| 4: BE73vi | * | * |
| 5: BE73ix | * | * |
| 6: BE73x | * | |
| 7: BN89 | | * |
| 8: BWE82 | * | * |
| 9: CAS91 | | * |
| 10: CL85 | * | * |
| 11: CP56 | * | * |
| 12: CWG86 | * | * |
| 13: CWG88 | * | * |
| 14: DM72 | * | * |
| 15: DT74i | * | * |
| 16: DT74ii | * | * |
| 17: DT78 | * | |
| 18: EB81 | | * |
| 19: EBii80 | | * |
| 20: F72 | * | * |
| 21: FLAX45-7 | * | * |
| 22: FLAX58 | * | |
| 23: FLAX69 | * | * |
| 24: GL91 | | * |
| 25: GLB94 | * | * |
| 26: GP81 | * | * |
| 27: H83 | * | * |
| 28: HG72 | * | * |
| 29: HS90 | * | |
| 30: LBP72 | * | * |
| 31: LBP92 | * | |
| 32: LH84 | * | |
| 33: LIN73a | * | * |
| 34: LIN73bi | * | * |
| 35: LIN73bii | * | * |
| 36: LIN73c | * | * |
| 37: LIN73di | * | * |
| 38: LIN73dii | * | * |
| 39: LIN73div | * | * |
| 40: LIN73ei | * | * |

| Site code | SNLS | TORK |
|---|---|---|
| 41: LIN73eii | * | * |
| 42: LIN73f | * | * |
| 43: LT72 | * | |
| 44: M82 | * | * |
| 45: MCH84 | * | * |
| 46: MG78 | * | |
| 47: MH77 | * | |
| 48: MW79 | * | * |
| 49: ON4 | | * |
| 50: ON211 | | * |
| 51: ON215 | * | * |
| 52: ON261 | * | * |
| 53: ON343 | | * |
| 54: ON362 | | * |
| 55: ON487 | * | |
| 56: ON488 | | * |
| 57: P70 | * | * |
| 58: SB85 | * | * |
| 59: SES97 | * | * |
| 60: SH74 | * | * |
| 61: SM76 | * | * |
| 62: SMG82 | * | * |
| 63: SP72 | * | * |
| 64: SPM83 | * | * |
| 65: SPMB97 | * | * |
| 66: SUS96 | * | * |
| 67: SW82 | * | * |
| 68: TCA94 | * | * |
| 69: WB80 | * | * |
| 70: WF89 | * | * |
| 71: WN87 | * | * |
| 72: WNW88 | * | * |
| 73: WO89 | | * |
| 74: WP71 | * | * |
| 75: WS82 | * | |
| 76: WW89 | * | * |
| 77: Z86 | * | * |
| 78: ZE87 | * | * |
| 79: ZE90 | * | * |
| 80: ZEA95 | * | * |

*Fig. 9.38. Distribution of* Torksey *(TORK)* and *Saxo-Norman Lincoln Shelly (SNLS) wares (of late 10th- and early 11th-century date). The topography and street plan is later medieval (source, Vince and Young forthcoming, drawn by Dave Watt, copyright English Heritage).*

| Site code | LKT | LSH | TORK | SNLS | % of sandy ware |
|---|---|---|---|---|---|
| EB 53 | 14 | 0 | 0 | 0 | 0% |
| W 73 | 1 | 2 | 0 | 0 | 0% |
| BG 95 | 9 | 2 | 0 | 0 | 0% |
| GL 91 | 291 | 11 | 3 | 0 | 1% |
| WO 89 | 130 | 141 | 7 | 0 | 3% |
| GP 81 | 570 | 12 | 9 | 15 | 4% |
| WF 89 | 868 | 64 | 16 | 24 | 4% |
| Flax 69 | 456 | 125 | 10 | 20 | 5% |
| SB 85 | 637 | 586 | 46 | 33 | 6% |
| GLB 94 | 391 | 4 | 16 | 14 | 7% |
| WN 87 | 49 | 93 | 2 | 9 | 7% |
| TCA 94 | 4 | 227 | 1 | 22 | 9% |
| WW89 | 52 | 45 | 4 | 8 | 11% |
| Flax 45-7 | 33 | 23 | 2 | 5 | 11% |
| F 72 | 45899 | 4159 | 3151 | 4088 | 13% |
| MCH 84 | 2598 | 66 | 144 | 300 | 14% |
| WNW 88 | 664 | 408 | 56 | 142 | 16% |
| BWE 82 | 159 | 46 | 19 | 32 | 20% |
| H 83 | 656 | 91 | 102 | 104 | 22% |
| SH 74 | 226 | 105 | 60 | 41 | 23% |
| Z 86 | 501 | 73 | 90 | 98 | 25% |
| HG 72 | 1130 | 106 | 232 | 227 | 27% |
| DM 72 | 107 | 27 | 24 | 29 | 28% |
| SP 72 | 1383 | 69 | 147 | 465 | 30% |
| SMG 82 | 271 | 77 | 56 | 99 | 31% |
| SW 82 | 169 | 14 | 25 | 65 | 33% |
| ZE 87 | 187 | 21 | 41 | 63 | 33% |
| SM 76 | 103 | 48 | 24 | 60 | 36% |
| SPM 83 | 80 | 4 | 47 | 9 | 40% |
| BN 89 | 4 | 0 | 3 | 0 | 43% |
| P 70 | 57 | 7 | 59 | 5 | 50% |
| IBP 72 | 32 | 4 | 24 | 13 | 51% |
| CL 85 | 51 | 21 | 33 | 99 | 65% |
| CP 56 | 16 | 1 | 8 | 25 | 66% |
| CWG 86 | 2 | 0 | 1 | 3 | 67% |
| WP 71 | 36 | 0 | 147 | 36 | 84% |

*Fig. 9.39. Comparison of total numbers of sherds of selected 'sandy wares' (SNLS and TORK) with selected 'shelly wares' (LKT and LSH), arranged in order of the percentage of the site's 'sandy ware' (source, Vince and Young forthcoming).*

| Site code | TORK | SNLS | ST | % Stamford |
|---|---|---|---|---|
| L 86 | | | 13 | 100% |
| W 73 | | | 18 | 100% |
| EB 53 | | | 13 | 100% |
| LA 85 | | | 20 | 100% |
| BGB 95 | | | 49 | 100% |
| BN 89 | 3 | | 70 | 96% |
| WP 71 | 147 | 36 | 1352 | 88% |
| GP 81 | 9 | 15 | 87 | 78% |
| Flax 45-7 | 2 | 5 | 25 | 78% |
| CWG 86 | 1 | 3 | 13 | 76% |
| IBP 72 | 24 | 13 | 95 | 72% |
| SW 82 | 25 | 65 | 196 | 69% |
| GLB 94 | 16 | 14 | 60 | 67% |
| Flax69 | 10 | 20 | 55 | 65% |
| H 83 | 102 | 104 | 358 | 63% |
| GL 91 | 3 | | 5 | 63% |
| SPM 83 | 47 | 9 | 80 | 59% |
| WF 89 | 16 | 24 | 53 | 57% |
| P 70 | 59 | 5 | 72 | 53% |
| WN 87 | 2 | 9 | 11 | 50% |
| CP 56 | 8 | 25 | 25 | 43% |
| Z 86 | 90 | 98 | 128 | 41% |
| BWE 82 | 19 | 32 | 33 | 39% |
| F 72 | 3151 | 4088 | 4437 | 38% |
| WNW 88 | 56 | 142 | 110 | 36% |
| SH 74 | 60 | 41 | 53 | 34% |
| MCH 84 | 144 | 300 | 218 | 33% |
| DM 72 | 24 | 29 | 22 | 29% |
| SM 76 | 24 | 60 | 31 | 27% |
| WW 89 | 4 | 8 | 4 | 25% |
| SB 85 | 46 | 33 | 20 | 20% |
| SMG 82 | 56 | 99 | 39 | 20% |
| ZE 87 | 41 | 63 | 25 | 19% |
| SP 72 | 147 | 465 | 132 | 18% |
| CL 85 | 33 | 99 | 24 | 15% |
| WO 89 | 7 | | 1 | 13% |
| TCA 94 | 1 | 22 | 1 | 4% |
| HG 72 | 232 | 227 | 14 | 3% |

*Fig. 9.40. Comparison of totals of sherds of selected 'sandy wares' (SNLS and TORK) with 'Stamford ware' (ST), arranged in order of percentage of 'Stamford ware' (source, Vince and Young forthcoming).*

Colsuein in the mid 11th century in *Butwerk* and recent research suggests that the dedication was particularly popular amongst the Danish elite who became established in England following the accession of Cnut in 1014 (Crawford 1999). All Saints-in-the-Bail was clearly an important church in 1066, endowed with lands outside the city, and a documentary study has demonstrated that its churchyard originally extended at least as far as Bailgate and Eastgate, a conclusion recently confirmed through excavation (Jones *et al.* 1990, 50–51; 1996, 144–5; Wragg 1997b).

The status of the fourth church in the Upper City, the minster church of St Mary of Lincoln, located on the site now occupied by the Cathedral, remains controversial (Owen, D 1984, 1994). Parts of its cemetery have been found outside the west end of the Cathedral (Everson and Stocker 1999, 194–5) and, although Bassett

proposed that it might have been situated to the west of the Norman west front (1988) it is now postulated that the church itself was located under the nave of the Cathedral church (Stocker and Vince 1997). There are several English cases of an Anglo-Saxon minster church remaining in use whilst its Norman successor was being built, but in most of these cases the two structures were of equivalent status – Cathedral replacing Cathedral or abbey replacing abbey. It would probably not have been thought appropriate for the Bishop and the new chapter to use a single- or double-cell church of the size of the 11th-century structures known at St Paul, St Peter Stanthaket or St Mark. But the new Norman clergy could have continued to use the Anglo-Saxon minster had St Mary of Lincoln been of comparable size to the Bishop's minster at Stow. If, as is now suggested, the pre-Conquest church of St Mary was used for some

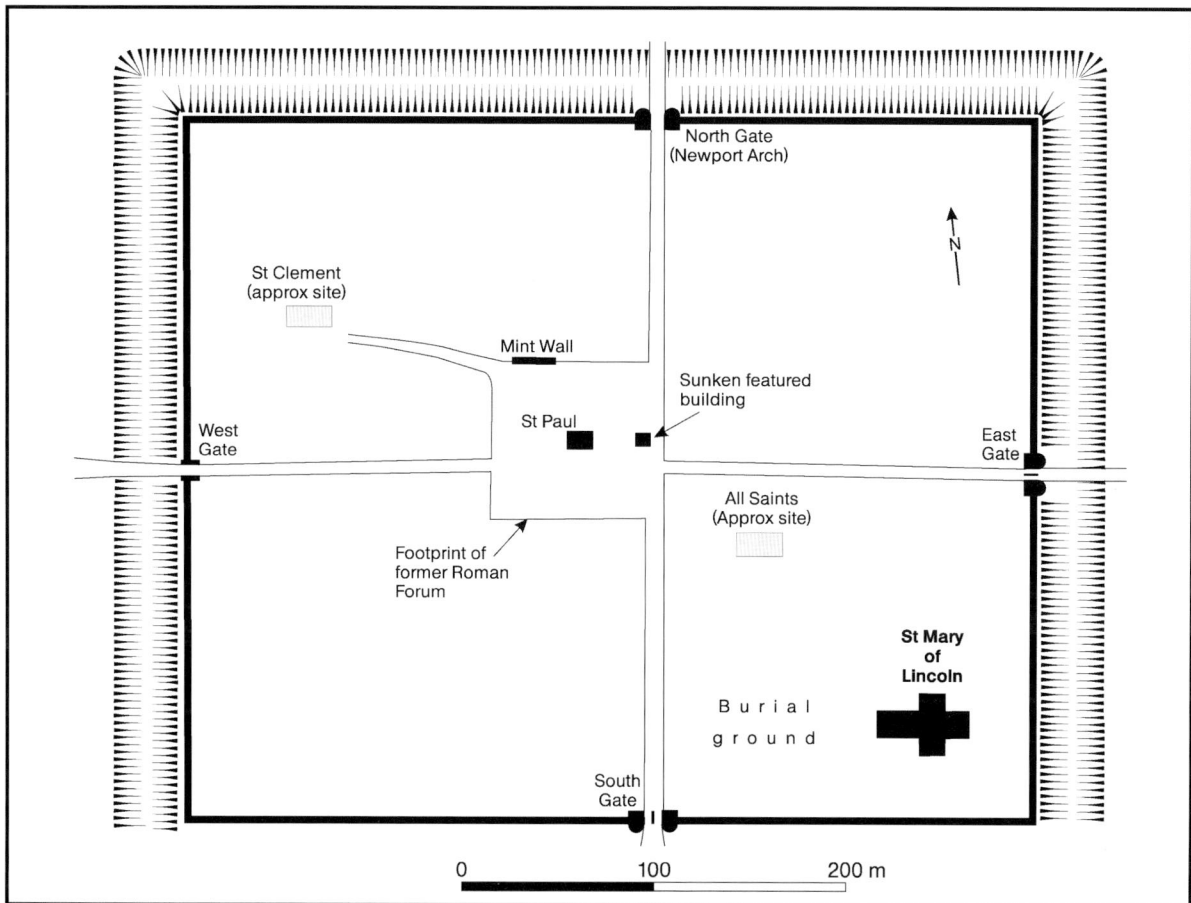

*Fig. 9.41. Reconstruction study of the layout of the Upper City in the late Anglo-Scandinavian period. There is no excavated evidence that the lines of any of the Roman roads were in use at this period, but those shown were probably extant, at least as informal routes between gates (drawn by Dave Watt, copyright English Heritage).*

time by the Norman clergy then it must have been of some size. Owen has suggested that it would have housed seven or eight canons (1994, 13), which suggests not just a building of some size, but a large domestic complex also.

Plans to build a new Cathedral must have been made as soon as the decision was taken, in 1072, to move the see from Dorchester-on-Thames to Lincoln. As Bates notes (1992), Remigius, the first Norman Bishop of Lincoln, was still styled *Bishop of Dorchester* in 1072, in 1074/5 he was *Bishop of Dorchester or Lincoln* and from 1081 onwards was always termed *Bishop of Lincoln*. There is thus only a gap of four years from the start of construction of Lincoln Castle in 1068 and the decision to move the see. The boundaries of the *atrium* of the Norman Cathedral are clear. The south and east boundaries were formed by the Roman wall, which was still considered the King's wall in the mid 12th century, whilst the western boundary was probably formed by the boundary noted above, running behind the White Hart to the south gate of the Bail (Fig. 9.8 and 9.9). West of this was the King's highway. The north boundary was the south side of Eastgate

(Jones *et al.* 1996, 156 – Fig. 9.9). The layout of individual buildings within the early Cathedral precinct is not known, although several finds between Exchequergate and the west front show that this area remained the site of the Cathedral graveyard, as it had been in the pre-Conquest period.

We remain unsure what road system was in use in the Upper City before the Conquest. Both Chapel Lane and East Bight have been claimed as pre-Conquest route-ways, analogous with streets like Silver Street, which may have linked the Roman gates in the Lower City, and with similar changes of alignment found in other reused Roman towns. The southern stretch of the modern Chapel Lane still runs close to a right angle to the line of the Roman east–west street, and it joins the modern Westgate at an angle. This might suggest that it preserves, in part, a Roman alignment – perhaps indicating a measure of continuity. If this proposal has any value, then the southern part of the original West Bight will have been cut by the construction of the Castle ditch (Fig. 9.59 below). However, the scanty archaeological evidence seems to suggest that the southern stretch of Chapel Lane is

**St Paul-in-the-Bail** - Development of the church before 1301

Nave
(based on single
celled chapel)

Chancel

N

South    aisle

South door

0                    5 m

| | Anglo-Saxon 8th-10th C. | | 12th C. I | | 12th C. II | | 12th C. III | | 12th C. IV |
|---|---|---|---|---|---|---|---|---|---|
| | 12th-13th C. I | | 12th-13th C. II | | 13th C. I. | | 13th C. II | | 13th C. III |

**St Paul-in-the-Bail** - Development of the medieval church after 1301

Porch ?

Tower

Nave

Chancel

N

South    aisle

Chapel

South door

0                    5 m

| | Pre-1301 | | 1301 (demolished 1786) | | 1301 (demolished 1700) |
|---|---|---|---|---|---|
| | Date uncertain | | Late 14th C. | | 1700 |
| | | | | | Georgian church (built 1786) |

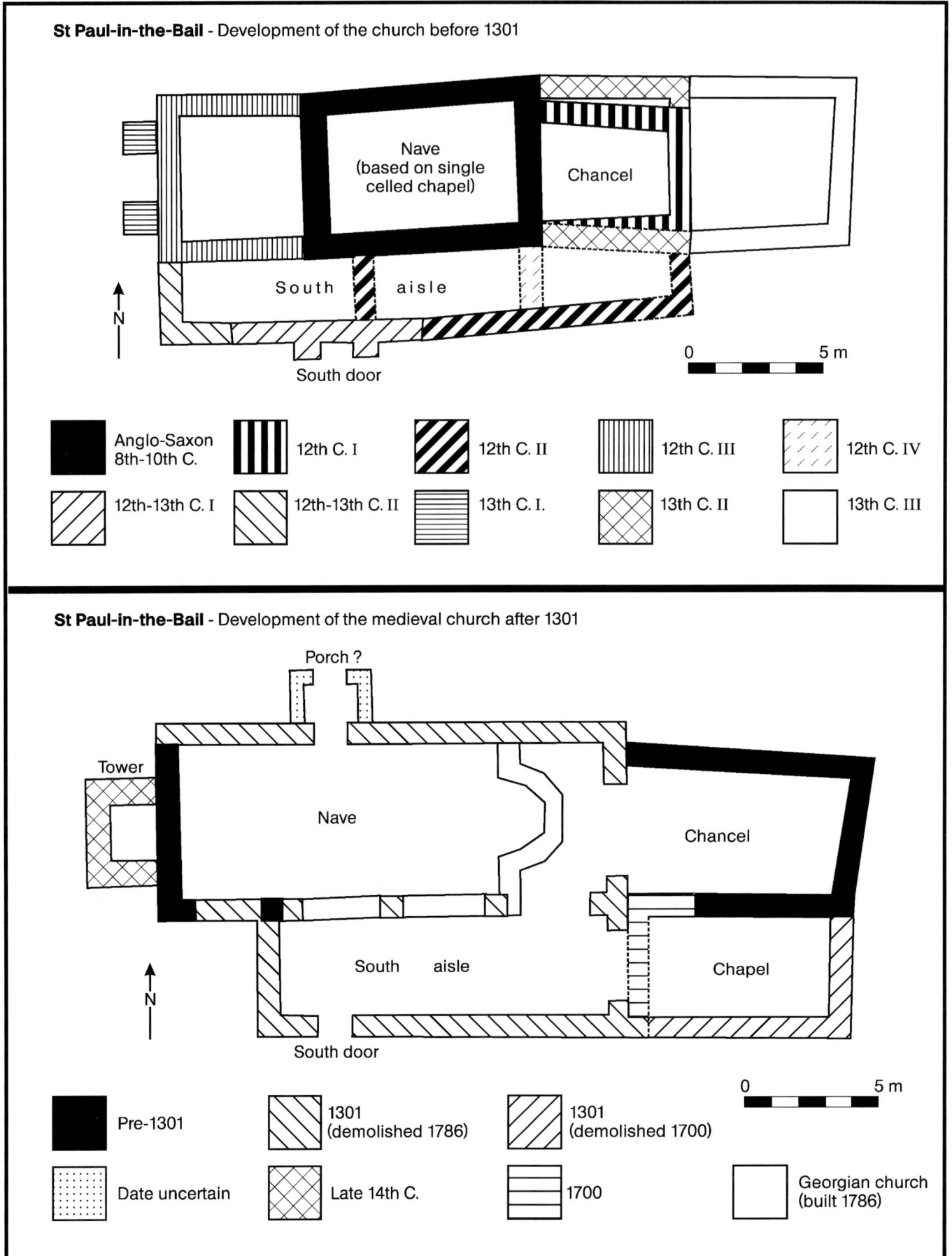

*Fig. 9.42. Development plans of the church of St Paul-in-the-Bail (drawn by Dave Watt, copyright English Heritage).*

more likely to be of post-Conquest date and it prob-ably formed the western boundary of the churchyard of St Clement's church. In this interpretation, the northern part of Chapel Lane can be seen as an access route running from the north-east corner of the churchyard towards Newport Arch.

The antiquity of Chapel Lane was not confirmed by excavation (CL 85) and work in the modern lane called West Bight (WB 80) suggests that this street, now a mere footpath was the more important street in the medieval period. At Chapel Lane, 11th – or 12th-century pits and associated robber trenches suggest that this site lay within an occupied tenement. It may be significant for the dating of Chapel Lane that none of these pits reflect its diagonal alignment but instead follow the Roman orientation, a line also followed by the modern lane called West Bight. The medieval activity found in the northern trench in excavations at West Bight (WB 80) was, however, less certainly domestic and was perhaps associated with quarrying limestone and the production of lime. Although it follows the alignment of the Roman grid there was no evidence for the lane having a Roman origin and, indeed, at its southern end it would have run across the west end of the *basilica* and the western range of the *forum*. The date at which these two streets were laid out, then, remains poorly defined. It is clear that they were not survivals of Roman streets, but they may have been laid out just before the Conquest, although a date in the 12th century is equally likely. The debate over the antiquity of these streets has not been assisted by the fact that the terms *East Bight* and *West Bight* were used in medieval documents to refer to areas, the north-west and north-east corners of the Bail respectively, and not to streets at all (numerous references in Jones *et al.* 1990 and 1996).

In the north-east quarter of the Upper City the pre-Conquest topography is equally unclear. Jones *et al.* suggest that the northern part of James Street originally terminated at the Roman east–west street and was subsequently extended southwards to Eastgate (1996, fig 2) and it is tempting to see this part of James Street as a mirror image of West Bight. Here too, medieval tenements fronting onto Bailgate do not ever seem to have extended back to the parallel street, which, instead, served a series of large plots some of which, in the 13th century, were used as orchards and gardens. But even if we argue that James Street is the same date as modern West Bight, it is still far from certain that we are suggesting a pre-Conquest date.

The nature of pre-Conquest occupation in the Upper City is difficult to distil from these scanty remains. In the late 9th and 10th centuries, it is highly likely that the area was an ecclesiastical and aristocratic enclave, as it may well have been before the arrival of the Danes in the late 9th century (Stocker forthcoming a). But the density and nature of settlement within the enclosure in the 11th century remains unclear. The cellared building at the eastern end of the St Paul's church site

(SP72 – Fig. 9.41 and 9.81a), the only near-complete excavated building of this date in the Bail, represents some sort of domestic occupation in the central part of the enclosure in the early to mid 11th century. It may have been constructed behind a frontage on the line of Bailgate or its Roman predecessor. If we view the St Paul's building as evidence for conventional settlement here in the 11th century, then it may be possible to link such settlement with the rubbish pits excavated at Chapel Lane (whose date is less certainly fixed) and propose a conventional urban settlement uphill to match that well-established downhill.

There was, however, clearly a major transformation of the Upper City in the years following the Norman Conquest, and the foundation of the Castle and the Cathedral (Fig. 9.8). Without a program of targeted excavations it is not yet possible to date the major topographic features of the Upper City, but never-theless, the following hypothetical scheme would explain the development of the surviving medieval topography (Vince and Stocker 1997; Stocker forth-coming a). At least two of the four gates to the Upper City were rebuilt in the Norman period. The east gate was clearly the more important of the two, with two archways, implying the existence of a double carriage-way, as in the Roman gateway (Fig. 9.43). The new north gate consisted of an addition to the Roman Newport Arch and had a single archway (*Ibid.*). There was apparently no comparable work at the west gate, which retained its Roman form at the time when it was taken out of use and buried under the inner bailey bank. No evidence concerning any rebuilding of the south gate in the early Norman period has come to light.

The northern archway of the new Norman east gate overlay the northern arch of the Roman gate but the southern archway was constructed to the south of the Roman southern arch, implying that the medieval street was wider than its Roman predecessor. Although it is possible that the street leading into the Upper City through the east gate in the early Norman period origi-nally followed the Roman line we shall see that there is evidence that, by the mid 12th century, the medieval street called Eastgate was in existence. This diagonal route does not make sense as a convenience route join-ing the south and east Roman gates, for which it would have to head more towards the south, but instead it heads towards the new motte in the south-west corner of the Upper City (Fig. 9.8). This seems further good evidence for the proposal that a new main route across the Bail was laid out in 1068 through the new east gate aiming for the new Norman motte. This is, of course, further evidence for the Upper City having been adopted entire to serve as Lincoln's first castle (p. 170–2 above; Stocker and Vince 1997; Stocker forthcoming a).

Although an origin for Eastgate following the establishment of the Castle in 1068 seems likely, this means that it will have been truncated in the early 12th century when the new inner bailey was constructed.

Westgate may be later than we have suggested. The orientation of the south boundary of Nos. 1–4 Chapel Lane might offer some support for the idea that this lane was heading towards the new postern gate on Westgate and it might also locate the church itself in the north-west angle between this lane and Chapel Lane (see Fig. 9.10).

By the middle of the 12th century we have the first evidence for the existence of the stretch of Bailgate south of St Paul-in-the-Bail churchyard (which will be discussed later – p. 209–14 below), but not for any of the properties around Castle Hill and Steep Hill. In Fig. 9.9 this area is reconstructed as being an open area or a market place with its northern boundary being the parish boundary between St Paul and St Mary Magdalene. Castle Hill, the centre of this space, was the site of a market of unknown antiquity in the 19th century (Jones *et al.* 1996, 55). The south-east boundary of this hypothetical space is marked by the precinct wall of the Cathedral. This survives as the back wall of cellars of buildings on the east side of Steep Hill and from the *Hundred Rolls* we can surmise that this wall was in existence in the early 13th century, when this row of houses was said to have been built as an encroachment on the King's highway. The northern continuation of this line forms the Bailgate frontage of the White Hart Inn, suggesting that this frontage has remained stable since the early 13th century.

Although individually some of these probable Norman features could have been influenced by pre-existing features, either of Roman or Anglo-Scandinavian date, taken as a whole they provide evidence for two phases of large-scale re-planning of the area within the Roman walls. The first, we suggest, dates from the establishment of the first Castle in 1068 and the construction of the Lucy Tower motte and includes the reconstruction of the Bail gatehouses and the laying out of Eastgate. The second dates from the superimposition of the smaller Castle enclosure on the Bail, in the first half of the 12th century, and includes not just the truncation of Eastgate but the provision of a network of new roads around the new fortification.

### Settlement in the Lower City within the walls c.900 – 1150

Little evidence has been recovered in the Lower City for its internal development or topography between the late 9th and mid 12th centuries, and what has been discerned on the basis of the distribution of short-lived and locally made pottery types has been described above (Fig. 9.45) (p. 192–6 above). The 10th-century settlement based around Silver Street, the High Street as far north as St Martin's church, Flaxengate, Hungate and Grantham Street, was organised around only two newly constructed streets, Flaxengate and Silver Street (and even Flaxengate may simply be a continuation northwards of a Roman alignment). The character of

this settlement has been analysed in Perring's monograph (Perring 1981) and its appearance is reconstructed in Fig. 9.47.

It is likely that this 10th-century settlement was served by several churches. Central to the settlement were the two churches dedicated to St Peter (St Peter-at-Arches and St Peter-at-Pleas), which lay side-by-side on the main street immediately inside Stonebow. The churches of St Lawrence and St Martin on the High Street are also likely to be primary. An alternative name for St Peter-at-Pleas indicates that the moot place was nearby, presumably being held in the open space at the southern end of High Street. Some areas of this settlement remain unexplored. In particular, the south-western quarter of the settlement is entirely hypothetical. The church of All Saints, Hungate, may have been in existence and on Fig. 9.45 Mint Lane (*Lewinstigh*) and Mint Street are shown. The church of Holy Trinity Clasketgate is also within this early zone of settlement, occupying an area bounded by Silver Street, Flaxengate and Clasketgate, but it could be a later foundation.

The reconstruction of the settlement layout in Fig. 9.45 emphasises that the settlement was bounded on the southern side by a large expanse of water – though its depth and navigability are unknown. It is also not clear how the Witham was crossed by foot and wheeled transport at this date. It is likely that the original *broad ford*, which gave its name to the Brayford Pool, was located in this area. If a ford indeed existed across the river on the line of Ermine Street, however, clearly large boats could not be floated downstream from the pool into the Witham. To the south of the line of the south wall of the Roman Lower City a waterfront developed at a very early stage in the settlement's Anglo-Scandinavian history. Its development is considered along with the port more generally below (p. 235–42 below).

A major change in the layout of the settlement in the Lower City took place in the 11th century, apparently in the generation before the Norman Conquest (Fig. 9.46). These changes included the diversion of Ermine Street as it climbed the hill and the laying out of The Strait and Steep Hill (as shown by excavations at MCH 84, DT 74 and SH 74). There was also expansion of settlement south of the Roman city wall (and perhaps in some cases over the line of this wall). This development was probably contemporary with the laying out of Bank Street, Free School Lane and Saltergate (although this may well be slightly later). And finally the roads around the edges of the settlement core (such as Beaumont Fee and Danesgate) were probably constructed at this date. Eight churches are likely to date from this period: St Mary *Crackpole*, St Edmund, St Swithin, St George, St Cuthbert, St Andrew, St Michael, St John-the-Poor and St Peter Stanthaket.

Another feature of the Lower City which may have come into existence at this time were a number of subsidiary markets (Fig. 9.83d, f and h). In most cases these were located in streets, rather than in dedicated rectilinear areas, such as may have existed in the

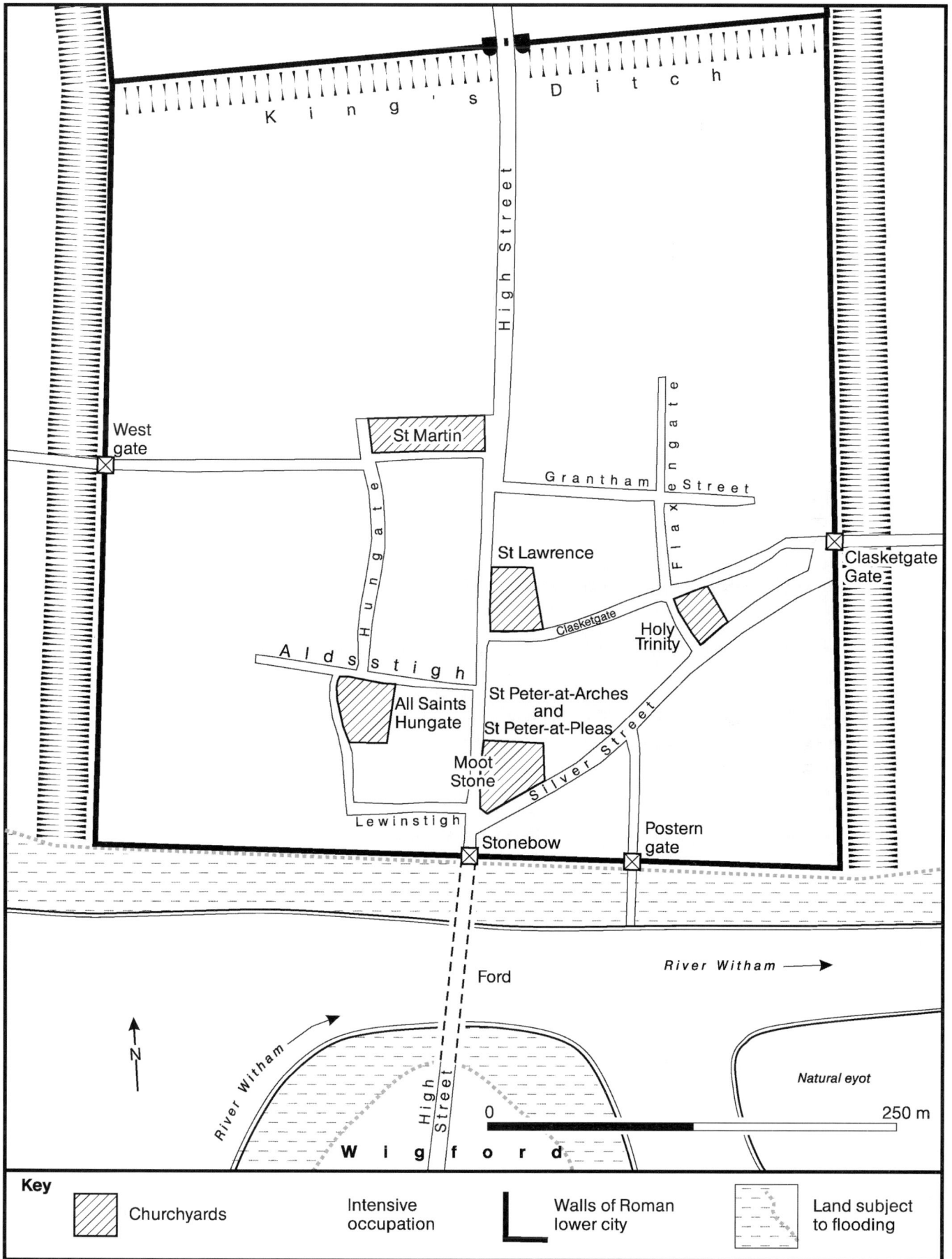

*Fig. 9.45. Reconstruction study of the Lower City in the 10th century (drawn by Dave Watt, copyright English Heritage).*

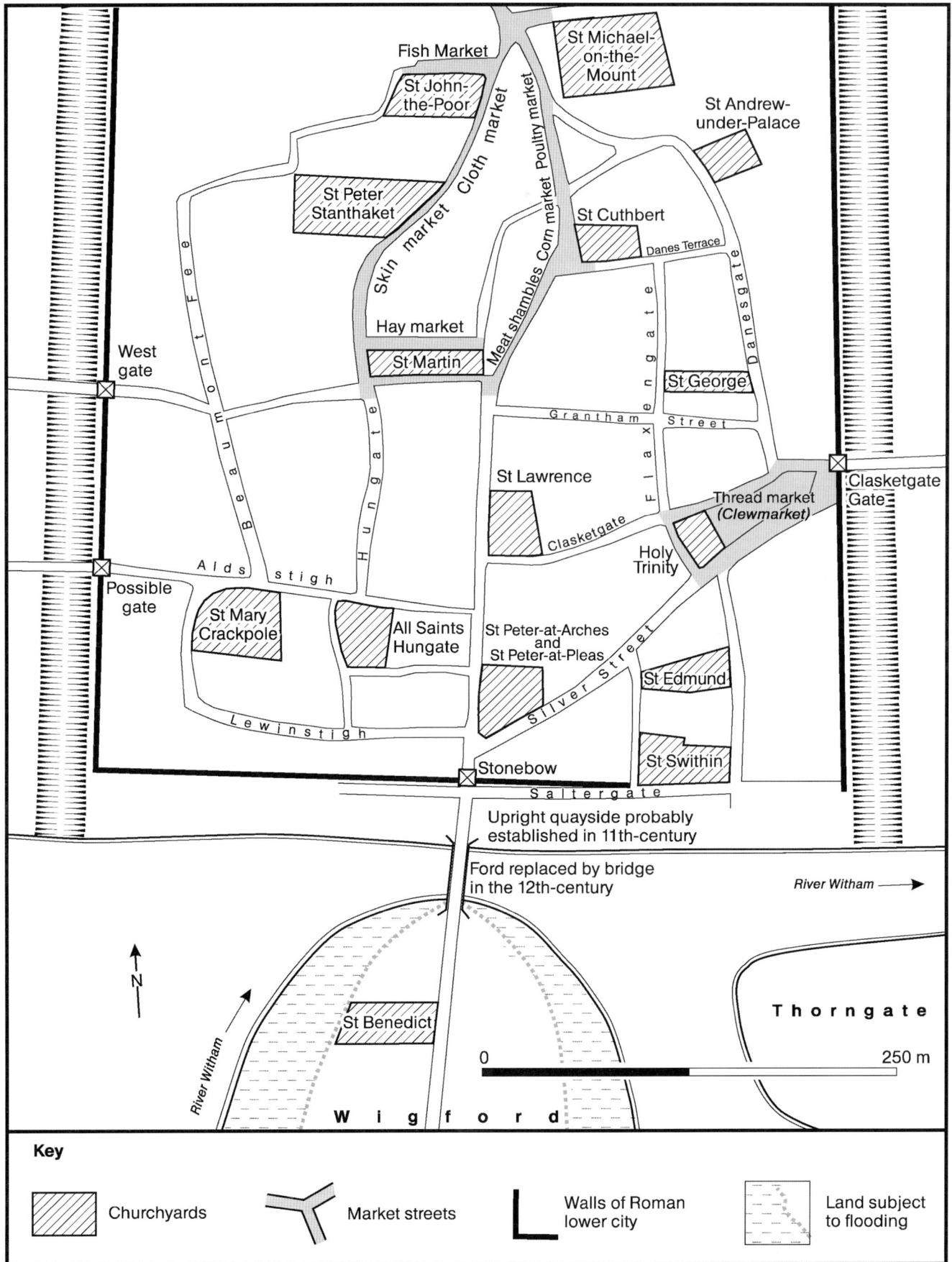

*Fig. 9.46. Reconstruction study of the Lower City in the first half of the 11th century, following expansion and re-planning. The evidence for the locations of market places is documentary and mostly late medieval in date (drawn by Dave Watt, copyright English Heritage).*

*Fig. 9.47. Reconstruction of 10th-century houses from excavations at Flaxengate (F 72), looking north (drawn by Tig Sutton, copyright City of Lincoln Archaeology Unit).*

Upper City at Castle Hill in the early Norman period. In the late medieval period some of these had developed into specialised markets: the skinmarket at the northern end of Hungate; the *clewmarket* (thread market) between Clasketgate and Silver Street; the corn market at the junction of Danes Terrace and The Strait; the hay market around St Martin's church and the malt market south-east of St Swithin's church. It may be significant that these markets were located at the edges of the 10th-century settlement. These markets, seemingly, remained in these locations until the 16th century, and, as far as can be seen, this was made possible by a lack of major changes in the topography of the Lower City settlement from the middle of the 11th century onwards. This apparent stasis through the 12th and 13th centuries, suggests that Lincoln might have reached its apogee, at least in terms of the extent of settlement, around the time of *Domesday Book*.

## The development of the walled city c.1150–c.1350

A large number of archaeological excavations have taken place on sites within the walled city which cast light on the settlement following the imposition of the second Castle enclosure. In the Upper City the most important of these was at St Paul-in-the-Bail church where several phases of alteration and rebuilding of the pre-Conquest single-celled church were recorded (SP 72 – Fig. 9.42). Small-scale but informative work has also taken place at several sites in and around the Cathedral and the Castle (Reynolds 1974; CWG 82/6).

Elsewhere in the Upper City, the most informative site for this period lay immediately to the north of the Mint Wall (WB 80), where the history and layout of a large part of a single medieval tenement was uncovered. Evidence for stone digging was found on a site to the west of St Clement's church (W 73). Other Upper City excavations, however, were located in peripheral parts of the enclosure, such as the north rampart (EB 80) or the land west of West Bight and south of Chapel Lane (CL 85). Excavations on properties fronting onto the main streets of the Bail (Bailgate and Eastgate) have been confined to small-scale observations. Unfortunately, only the 1956 excavation by Dennis Petch at Cottesford Place (the site of one of the large residences in the Close occupied mainly by canons – Jones *et al.* 1990, 86–90) can be used to compare archaeological with documentary sources for this period.

The main sources of information on the Lower City's archaeology in the 12th and 13th centuries are the area excavations at Flaxengate (F 72 – Perring 1981; Jones 1980), West Parade (WP 71 – ed. Jones 1999), Danes Terrace (DT 74, DT 78), and Hungate (H 83). These results are augmented by excavations on the site of St Peter Stanthaket church (SPM 83); on land at the back of properties fronting onto Steep Hill and Michaelgate (MCH 84); at a property at the junction of Steep Hill and Well Lane (SH 74) and in excavations on the site of the Greyfriars, fronting onto Silver Street and Free School Lane (LIN 73a–c, GL 91, GLA 94 and GLB 94).

As in the earlier part of this Era, pottery provides the most plentiful source of information on the extent and character of settlement within the walled city (Fig. 9.48). Much of the city's pottery between the mid 12th and mid 13th centuries was supplied by Stamford (ST) and by local industries producing handmade shell-tempered wares (LFS). Early in the 12th century, the first evidence for the re-emergence of an indigenous Lincoln pottery industry is found. These early vessels were glazed jugs and pitchers (LSW1), but were initially outnumbered by vessels from Nottingham (NSP). Changes in rim form, decoration and glaze occurred during the 12th and 13th centuries and these are usually sufficient to distinguish 13th – to 14th-century Lincoln glazed ware (LSW2). Shell-tempered wares from Potterhanworth (POTT) first occur in early 13th-century deposits but only become common in the second half of the century. On the basis of these various changes, ceramic horizons MH1 to MH4 have been defined. As currently dated, these correspond to the early 12th century (MH1), the middle or later 12th century (MH2), the early 13th century (MH3) and the later 13th and earlier 14th centuries (MH4).

Thirty-five numismatic finds from excavations in Lincoln between 1972 and 1987 were minted in the period c.1150–1350. No coins minted in Lincoln before the reign of Henry II have been found in excavations, but this is consistent with the national pattern and not necessarily any reflection on the scale of monetary

| Ware name and type code | MH1 | MH2 | MH3 | MH4 | MH5 |
|---|---|---|---|---|---|
| Early Medieval Handmade fabrics (EMHM) | Other | Other | Other | Other | |
| Lincoln Glazed ware – Fabric A (LSWA) | Other | Other | Other | Main | Main |
| Pingsdorf-type ware (PING) | Other | Other | Other | | |
| Sparsely Glazed ware (LOCC) | Other | Other | Other | | |
| Developed Stamford ware (DST) | Other | Other | Main | Main | |
| Andenne-type ware (ANDE) | Other | Other | | | |
| 12th/13th-century Lincoln Glazed ware (LSW1) | Other | Main | Main | Main | |
| Local Early Medieval Shelly ware (LEMS) | Other | Main | Main | Main | |
| Thetford-type fabrics (THETT) | Other | | Other | | |
| York-type Splashed wares (YORKSPL) | Other | | Other | | |
| Stamford ware-type crucibles (STCRUC) | Other | | | | |
| Stamford ware (ST) | Main | Main | Main | Other | |
| Lincoln Fine-Shelled ware (LFS) | Main | Main | Main | | |
| Nottingham Splashed ware (NSP fine fabric) | Main | | | | |
| Beverley ware (BEVO) | | Other | Other | Other | |
| Brunnsum-type flasks (BRUNS) | | Other | Other | | |
| Doncaster Hallgate-type ware (DONC) | | Other | Other | | |
| Nottingham Splashed ware (NSP fine and fine/sandy fabrics) | | | Main | | |
| North French wares (NFREM) | | | Other | Other | Other |
| Paffrath-type ware (BLGR) | | | Other | Other | |
| Gritty ware (YG) | | | Other | | |
| York Glazed ware (YORK) | | | Other | | |
| Nottingham Splashed ware (NSP sandy fabric) | | | Main | | |
| Nottingham Glazed ware (NOTG) | | | | Other | Other |
| Rouen-type ware (ROUEN) | | | | Other | Other |
| Scarborough ware (SCAR) | | | | Other | Other |
| Potterhanworth-type ware (POTT) | | | | Other | Main |
| 12th/13th-century Lincoln Glazed ware (LSW1/2) | | | | Other | |
| Bourne-type ware (BOUA) | | | | Other | |
| Medieval Local fabrics (MEDLOC) Fabric A | | | | Other | |
| Nottingham Splashed ware (NSP) | | | | Other | |
| Tile fabric (TILE) | | | | Other | |
| 13th/14th-century Lincoln Glazed ware (LSW2) | | | | Main | Main |
| Saintonge ware with a mottled glaze (SAIM) | | | | | Other |

*Fig. 9.48. Named wares related to Lincoln's ceramic horizons between c.1150–c.1300. 'Main' indicates that the ware is a primary indicator of the ceramic period; 'Other' indicates that the ware is found, but is not a primary indicator of the ceramic horizon (source, Vince and Young forthcoming).*

exchange in Lincoln. Twenty *short-cross* pennies were found, all demonetised by the 1270s, and 19 *long-cross* and *Sterling* pennies. Of these, however, a number were probably in use in the second half of the 14th century and are therefore not strictly relevant to the study of settlement in this Era. The coins rarely, if ever, occurred in deposits which are likely to be closely dated and merely provide confirmation that activity between both the late 12th and mid 13th century and the later 13th and earlier 14th century was present on the sites in which they were found. The distribution of the *short-cross* coins is mostly in the Lower City (eleven coins), with three coins in Wigford and only one or two coins each from the Upper City, *Westcastle* and *Butwerk*. The distribution of the later coins is also largely in the Lower City (eleven coins), although there are four in the Upper City and two coins each from *Butwerk* and Wigford. Given the disparity in the intensity of investigation between the different parts of the city it is not possible to say much more about these distributions.

A range of other artefacts dating from between the later 12th to the mid 14th century was found in excavations between 1972–87. There are very few identifiable bone, antler or stone artefacts and also virtually none made from perishable organic materials, such as textile, leather or wood. This is due to the lack of suitable excavated deposits. A total of 91 domestic artefacts can be dated stylistically to this period (there is too much residuality to use non-diagnostic artefacts). Of these, 28 could be dated between the mid 12th and early 13th centuries and 57 between the mid 13th and mid 14th centuries. As with the coins, the majority of the finds (a total of 24) came from Lower City sites, with Wigford sites producing three and *Butwerk* one. The majority of these items are dress fittings (which always exhibit the greatest typological variation, and are therefore easiest to date) but the collection includes casket mounts of bone and copper alloy and a glass vessel from the back of a property fronting onto Steep Hill or Michaelgate. The finds also include one gold item, a pin from Flaxengate (F 72). The predominance of the Lower City sites is less marked amongst the later finds, with Wigford sites producing ten, Upper City sites, four, and *Butwerk* two. The later finds are also mainly dress items but include harness fittings, jetons, a lead alloy token, glass vessels (from three sites, all from the upper part of the Lower City) and a lead alloy weight.

The Upper City is renowned for the survival of its medieval housing and the *Survey of Ancient Houses in Lincoln* devoted three volumes to the Close (Jones *et al.* 1984; 1987; 1990) and one to Bailgate and the north-west quarter of the Upper City (Jones *et al.* 1996). In the Lower City buildings of the High Medieval Era have survived much more rarely, but even so, the Bishop's Palace (Brann forthcoming), St Mary's Guildhall (Stocker 1991), Garmston House (Jones SR 1992a) and the Norman House at Nos. 46–7 Steep Hill (Jones SR 1992b – Fig. 9.49) have all been the subject of recent archaeological recording. Compared with the buildings of the Close, however, surviving buildings in the Lower City tend to have less comprehensive documentary records, since a significant proportion of the properties remained in lay hands throughout the medieval period. Nevertheless, the *Registrum Antiquissimum* contains information on a large number of 12th- and 13th-century properties fronting the High Street, The Strait and Steep Hill. Wills and other documents recorded in the City Council register known as *Burwarmote Book* (Lincolnshire Archive Office, D&C Ms. 169) provide similar evidence, although mainly for the 14th century. However, unlike the *Registrum Antiquissimum*, *Burwarmote Book* has yet to be transcribed, edited and printed. Unedited transcriptions are available for many of these properties, however, and they have been used here, for example, to reconstruct the tenement histories of several High Street properties in the parishes of St Peter-at-Arches and St Peter-at-Pleas.

Studying the distribution of the population of Lincoln between the 12th and 14th centuries is impossible with any degree of accuracy. Global estimates of the population have been made based on a variety of measures, all one step removed from the population itself and usually a measure of wealth rather than population. Nevertheless, these figures lead us to expect a rapid rise during the 12th century and perhaps a slowing down during the 13th century, followed by a sharp decline in the 14th century (Fig. 9.6). Archaeological sources are a very blunt weapon with which to attack the study of population and in this section we will be concerned almost entirely with relative densities. The infrastructural skeleton of the city had been completed by the middle of the 12th century and there was little further expansion beyond its boundaries, but a number of further developments took place within the settled area between *c*.1150 and the early 14th century. We can distinguish, in particular, a sequence of major internal changes in the topography of the Bail and its associated suburbs, and these developments contrast with activity in the Lower City, where to a large extent the layout of the city

*Fig. 9.49. Late Norman house at Nos. 46–7 Steep Hill, from the south-west (photo and copyright, D Stocker).*

established by the end of the 11th century remained unaltered.

### Settlement in the Bail, c.1150–c.1350

As we have seen, the Bail was transformed twice after the Norman Conquest, first by its requisition as the Norman Castle in 1068, and secondly by its division into the Close in the south-east quadrant and new Castle enclosure in the south-west (p. 170–7 above). In the later 12th and 13th centuries we can see the construction of houses along Eastgate in the wake of these changes, followed by the expansion of the Close north of the street. We can also see the laying-out of tenements fronting onto the north part of Bailgate and the infilling of the proposed marketplace in the central and southern parts of Bailgate and Steep Hill. The documentary sources and surviving architecture make it clear that the Bail in the 12th and 13th centuries was a mosaic of different land uses and social groups. With the exception of a small quantity of material recovered from excavations in and around St Mary of Lincoln, the archaeological evidence from the Bail comes mainly from areas that we might expect to be peripheral, around the defences and in the West Bight. Only one excavation whose results are available is close to the social centre of the Bail (SP 72), and this site is clearly atypical, at least in its early history.

Over 1300 sherds of later 12th- and early 13th-century pottery have been recovered from excavations in the Bail, compared with just over 900 from the preceding period. However, whereas in the earlier period over half of the pottery from the Bail came from St Paul's, in this period the finds are more evenly spread, with sites at Castle west gate (CWG 86) and West Bight (WB 80) both producing more than 10% of the finds. The various excavations at the east end of the Cathedral also, naturally enough, produced more pottery of this period than the preceding one. In fact,

by St Botolph's church) and Broadgate (where the street was widened over the site of the city ditch in the 16h century). The evidence from properties south of the highway for its original width, however, is equivocal, although we do have evidence for the line of the medieval frontage running from Atton Place to the Old Deanery. None of the properties fronting onto Eastgate retains any documentary or architectural evidence for an earlier date than the late 12th century. Furthermore, these properties are sometimes said to be in the *atrium* of the Cathedral, assumed to have been a wide forecourt surrounding the church, and occupied in part by a cemetery. In the case of the Old Deanery, however, there is some evidence for encroachment onto what was originally a wider street on the line of Eastgate. In 1226 a *purpresture* was recorded but unspecified, and in 1274 the *Hundred Rolls* are specific in saying that the Dean had encroached five or six feet upon the King's highway (Jones *et al.* 1990, 20). It seems likely, then, not only that, in the later 11th and 12th century, Eastgate ran south-west – north-east on its present line, but also that it was originally even wider than at present on its south side. It may even have been funnel-shaped, widening out as it ran eastwards. As it serviced much the grandest gate and was much the widest street in the Upper City, there seems little doubt that Eastgate was the primary route-way in the Bail in the late 11th and early 12th centuries.

On the northern side of the street, at the extreme western end, a house built in the 1160s–70s on a part of All Saints cemetery also seems to have encroached southwards onto the highway. In 1881 the last remnants of this house were destroyed and the frontage pushed back to something approximating its original line (Jones *et al.* 1996, 151, figs. 140 and 143). Further east, properties with important stone houses, such as the Angel (Fig. 9.52) and Atherstone Place (Fig. 9.53), lined the northern side of this highway from the mid 12th century onwards (Fig. 9.54, documented in Jones *et al.* 1990). The construction of these houses, and any encroachment onto the highway, may be contemporary with the blocking of the northern gate passage, which is most likely to have occurred when the gate was acquired by the Bishop in the early 1130s for his lodging (*hospitandum*) (ed. Foster 1931, 34, RA 49; Stocker and Vince 1997; Stocker forthcoming a). The blocked gate passage was probably adapted to form ancillary rooms, for food preparation or storage, for example.

The development of the other main street in the Bail following the creation of the Castle enclosure and the Cathedral Close, Bailgate, has to be considered in three separate blocks, and a 'plan-form analysis' (Conzen 1960; 1968) of its components is given in Fig. 9.54. The southern third, from the Eastgate junction southwards (Fig. 9.54 Zone III), may not be any older than the late 12th or 13th century. It is likely that this entire area was initially an open space, later divided into Steep Hill, Castle Hill and Bailgate. There is also documentary evidence for a subsequent encroachment

*Fig. 9.53. South façade of the large, partly 12th-century, residence on the north side of Eastgate, now known as Atherstone Place (photo and copyright, D Stocker).*

(Fig. 9.54 Zone IV) on the east side of Steep Hill. A 'row', of 17 shops probably represent a single encroachment on the highway, using the Close Wall to the rear (Fig. 9.54). *The Hundred Rolls* indicate that the shops were between 10' and 16' wide and give the names of the holders, from which fixed point their subsequent histories can be reconstructed (Jones *et al.* 1996, 8–9; ed. Illingworth 1812–18, I, 218, 312, 318, 324b). The 17 shops were held by 12 people, some of whom are known to hold other land in the city. These landholders include a cutler (or scyther), a mercer, a porter and an apothecary.

On the west side of Steep Hill, the original encroachment (Fig. 9.54 Zone III) can, in part, be dated to the time of Aaron the Jew (active in Lincoln from *c.*1166 to 1185) (ed. Illingworth 1812–18, I, 322b; Jones *et al.* 1996, 8–9). North of Castle Hill, the first few properties (ed. Illingworth 1812–18, I, 322a; Jones *et al.* 1996, 8–9, 56–62) have little early documentation and contain no fabric earlier than the 15th century. However, the next property, No 3 Bailgate, has a vaulted basement of the 13th century and a ground plan suggesting that it formed part of a row of buildings, not a corner. Since Nos. 1 and 2 Bailgate are thought to have originally formed a single property, it seems that the corner between Bailgate and Castle Hill has been in approximately the same position since the 13th century. This sequence of buildings north and south of Castle Hill allows us to suggest, then, that the large open space, originally created in the early 12th century and defined by the hypothetical westward extension of Eastgate on the north, the boundary of the Cathedral precinct on the east and the south wall of the Bail on the south (Fig. 9.9), must have been rapidly filled in with housing in the later 12th century.

To the north, the section of Bailgate between Eastgate and St Paul-in-the-Bail initially runs at right angles to

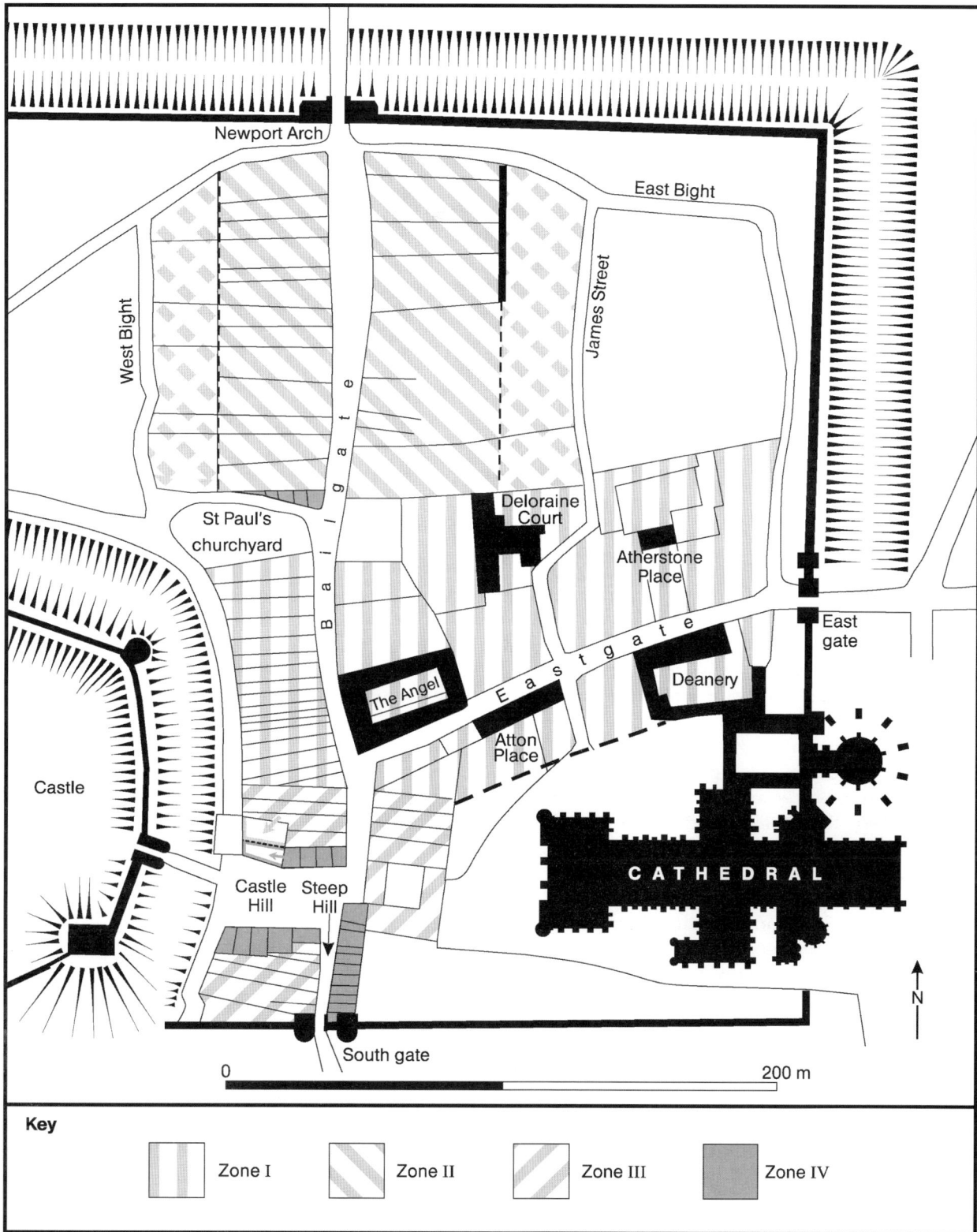

*Fig. 9.54. Plan-form components diagram of the Bailgate/Eastgate area. Zone I is a block laid out orthogonally on the line of Eastgate, a street which we argue was established in 1068. The earliest evidence for building within this block, however, is mid 12th century and we suggest that this development post-dates the contraction of the Castle and the construction of the inner bailey. Zone II is a planned unit either side of northern Bailgate. This block had been established by the late 12th century, but, we suggest, it was subsequent to Zone I. Zone III is thought to be 'infill' of the open space established between the Castle wall and the western boundary of the Close. This space was open in the mid 12th century but the southern part may have been infilled by Aaron the Rich (amongst others?) towards the end of the 12th century. Zone IV represents booths and shops encroaching on streets and markets at later dates. Those along Steep Hill were present by the late 13th century (based on Padley's 1842 map, drawn by Dave Watt, copyright English Heritage).*

Eastgate, suggesting that it was laid out either contemp-oraneously or subsequently, and then bends westwards to provide the east boundary of St Paul's churchyard (Fig. 9.54, Zone I). A route along this line may have serviced the property indicated by the cellared building in the eastern part of the St Paul's (SP 72) site during the pre-Conquest period, but any such property could equally have been accessed from the reconstructed lane adjacent to All Saints church yard. Furthermore, the early or mid 11th-century cellar next to St Paul's was infilled, and a metalled area was laid out, associated with 11th-century metalworking. This indicates, quite clearly, that if there ever was a through route on this line in the pre-Conquest period it was soon discontinued. When it was eventually re-established, the new street was orthogonal with the new line of Eastgate its fine new buildings here suggest a mid or later 12th-century date (ed. Jones *et al.* 1996).

The final length of Bailgate runs from the junction with Westgate northwards (Fig. 9.54, Zone II). All of the properties, on either side of the road, appear to have plots with similar widths. Of those on the west side, No. 34 ran, in the mid 17th century, from Bailgate to West Bight, but all the rest were bounded on their west sides by other property (Jones *et al.* 1996, S131). Even No. 34 was bounded in the late 14th century on its west by other property, not a lane. Excavation at West Bight (WB 80) revealed a medieval plot with a stone founded building at its west end, fronting onto the north–south lane called West Bight, and pits and industrial features at its east end, bounded by a stone wall of 13th- or 14th-century date. The line of this eastern boundary can be seen further north, and it is clear that, by the end of the 13th century all of the properties extending back from Bailgate were bounded by a single wall to the west. They were all plots between 50m and 53m long. Furthermore, it is also possible that the properties running back from the east side of Bailgate were originally laid out to respect a similar boundary, running parallel to James Street. This boundary is fossilised in its northern part by the early 14th-century Close Wall and is probably referred to in charters relating to properties which made up the Cottesford Place estate from the 1270s (e.g. ed. Major 1968, 131–3, RA2530). South of this point, however, the orientation of land divisions reflects the influence of the Eastgate alignment. In this southern area the properties are known from documentary sources to have been residences of the canons of the Cathedral, from the middle of the 12th century onwards.

The layout of the plots on either side of Bailgate, north of Westgate, then, is remarkably uniform and could represent a single episode of urban planning. If this is correct, the surviving documentation for these properties (brought together in Jones *et al.* 1996), suggest that the area had been laid out in the mid 12th century. No deeds are known before the late 12th century, but the surviving deeds hint that the properties were already a generation old. The street line itself has a

gentle sweep to it, curving slightly to the west and narrowing as it approaches St Paul's church. This may in part reflect the desire on the part of the 12th century urban planners to provide plots on the corners with the early east–west lane with an approximate right-angled corner.

The final street in the Upper City to be considered is East Bight. Starting at the north-west, this street runs at right angles to Bailgate until it meets the property boundary forming the rear of plots fronting onto Bailgate. From that point as far as the east gate of the Bail, the street consists of five straight segments, each segment being marked by the junction of property boundaries, and the north-east corner of the Bail. At its junction with the Close Wall, the street takes a sharp angle southwards until it meets its former junction with James Street (blocked in the early 14th century). It then takes on an alignment at right angles to James Street until it turns southwards heading for Eastgate. The last stretch of East Bight is characterised by two straight sections running towards a point on the back of the rampart, midway along this stretch. It looks very much as though East Bight, in its present form at least, took its line from pre-existing topography rather than itself setting the lie of the land. In other words, it does not have the appearance either of a convenient route between Newport and the east gate of the Bail (which might have come into existence at a time when this quarter of the Bail was little used). Nor does it have the appearance of an intramural street (such as might have been constructed in the Anglo-Scandinavian or early Norman periods, and has been claimed at several West Saxon *Burhs*). Elsewhere in Lincoln similar intramural streets, like Beaumont Fee and, possibly, Danesgate, are thought to be secondary Anglo-Scandinavian, perhaps dating to the mid 11th century and, like East Bight, they are clearly not related to the defences. Excavations to the north of East Bight provide no evidence for medieval occupation fronting onto it, and unlike the two Lower City roads, East Bight may have only ever been a route-way, rather than an occupied street. The earliest documentary reference to the street now known as East Bight is datable to the middle of the 13th century and concerns a garden, later known as *Scotgarth*, which was located somewhere to the east of what became the Burghersh Chantry House (ed. Major 1968, 118–120, RA2517).

### Settlement in the Lower City, c.1150–c.1350

The best evidence for occupation in Lincoln between the 12th and the 14th centuries comes from the Lower City, both from the centre of the settlement (SH 74, DT 74, DT 78, SW 82, H 83, LIN 73d–f) and from the eastern and western peripheries (LIN 73a–c, WP 71, P 70, MCH 84). Excavations in the central area of the Lower City show that there were buildings fronting the main streets and principal side streets and, by the beginning of the 13th century, all excavated buildings had stone foun-

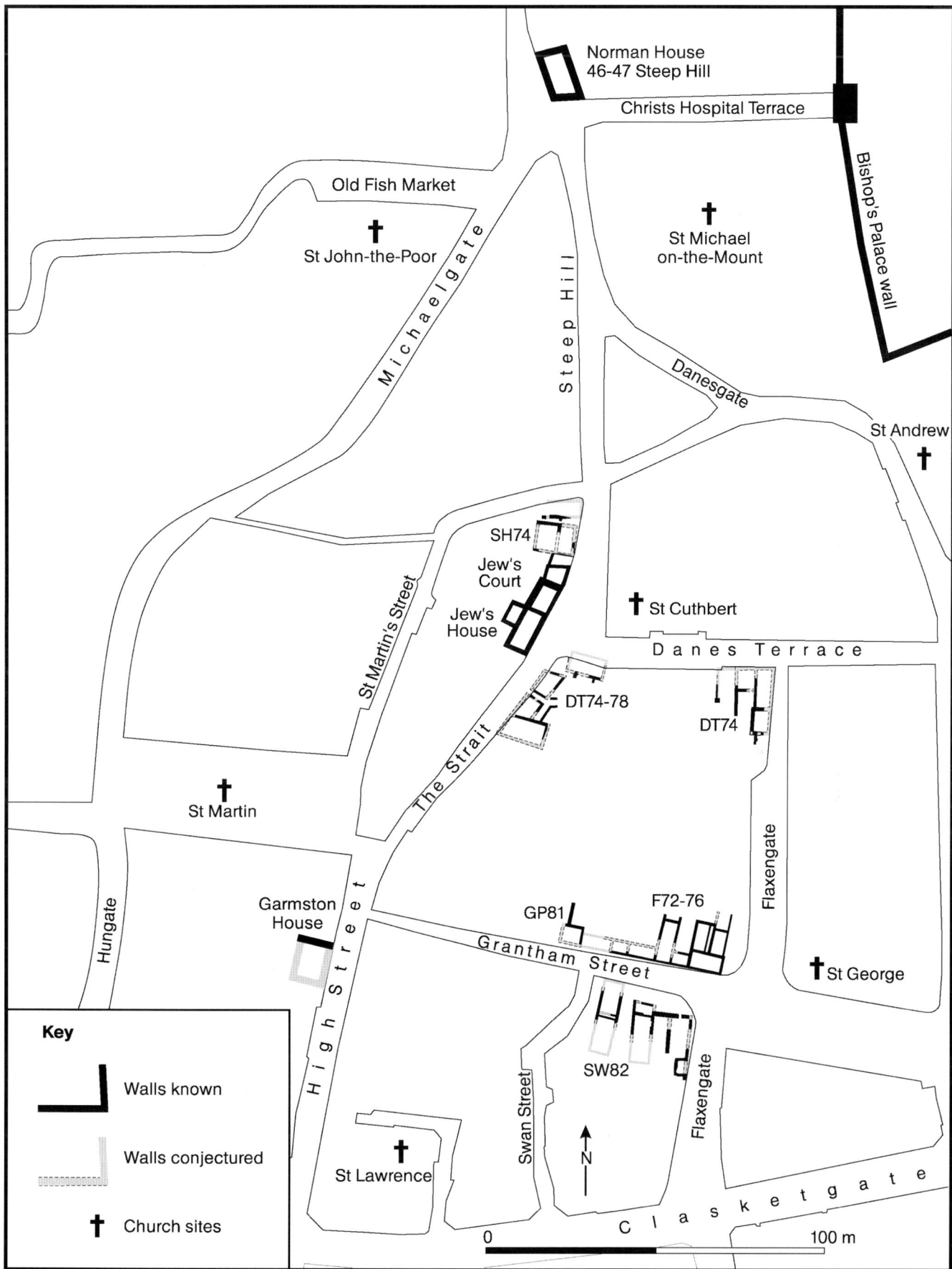

*Fig. 9.55. Plans of stone houses, both excavated and standing (generally of mid 12th- to mid 13th-century date), in the central part of the Lower City. The street plan is modern (source, Magilton 1983 with additions – drawn by Dave Watt, copyright English Heritage).*

dations, and probably masonry superstructures too (Fig. 9.55). Excavations in Hungate (H 83) suggested that, here, the change to stone construction took place around the middle of the 12th century, whereas the date of the first stone buildings at Flaxengate has been placed either in the later 12th or early 13th centuries. Unfortunately the disruption to the stratigraphy caused by the digging of the foundations and cellars of these Flaxengate buildings has meant that this critical date cannot be more closely determined, although, at present, the later date is preferred. Even so, few buildings on Flaxengate, or elsewhere, are likely to have been as impressive architecturally as the surviving so called 'Jew's House' at the foot of Steep Hill (Fig. 9.56), even though the ground plans of contemporary buildings demonstrate that many were of the similar scale. More peripheral sites around the Lower City also reveal evidence for occupation between the 12th and 14th centuries, but, although often also of stone, there are several indications that buildings in such locations were less well-built than those in the centre.

Just inside the western city wall, excavations at West Parade (WP 71), produced finds of later medieval date, but from a thick soil overlying the earlier buildings and pits, which was interpreted as a horticultural horizon, perhaps deriving from the dumping of night-soil and the use of the land as a garden or orchard. On the eastern side of the city (LIN 73, GL 91, GLA 94, GLB 94) occupation of 12th- and 13th-century date was superseded by walls and burials associated with the Franciscan friary, which had a substantial impact on the topography of this part of the town. The Franciscans first arrived on the site before 1231 and were given grants of land in at least three stages. Before 1231 they had a grant from William de Beningworth, and, in that year, the citizens allotted them land near their guildhall. As we have seen, in 1237 the guildhall itself was granted to the friars, in return for the Crown's gift to the citizens of use the chamber over Stonebow for civic affairs (p. 184 above; Hill 1948, 149). The location of the early guildhall building is not known, but it must lie somewhere within the Friars' precinct in the south-eastern corner of the Lower City. The Friary grew rapidly after 1237 and, by the end of the 13th century, occupied the entire block between Silver Street, Free School Lane and the north side of what is now St Swithin's church. This last was a market in the medieval which later specialised in sheep. *The Hundred Rolls* report that, in the later 13th century, Lord Phillip de Kyme appropriated and obstructed a lane in the parish of St Swithin, where there used to be a common passage between the market and the Witham (ed. Illingworth 1812–18, I, 310). A single Friary building survives (Fig. 9.57), which was the subject of a study in 1982 (Stocker 1984b). The study demonstrated that, in its later phases, the building was the fraternal infirmary, and that it had probably played that role since its construction in the years around 1240. Such a role was confirmed by excavations that have taken place over much of the site

*Fig. 9.56. The so-called 'Jew's House' (No.1 The Strait and No.15 Steep Hill) viewed from the east (see also Plate 4.6) (photo and copyright, D Stocker).*

*Fig. 9.57. The surviving building at the southern end of the Greyfriars' precinct from the south-east by S H Grimm (c.1784). Excavations in the 1990s (GL 91 GLA 94 GLB 94) confirmed that this range relates to the infirmary cloister (to the north) and was probably the infirmary hall. Note the ruined east gable of the parish church of St Swithin (photo and copyright, British Library).*

of this friary (LIN 73a–c; GL 91; GLA 94; GLB 94). The 1973 excavations recovered evidence that the church was at the northern end of the site, and preliminary study of the 1994 excavations suggest that the friary was substantially re-planned at least once.

Even taking such 13th-century developments into account, however, the street pattern of the Lower City seems to have reached its final, medieval form before the Norman Conquest and there is little evidence for its later modification or extension. This may not be quite such a valid generalisation in the south-eastern corner of the city, however, where it is possible that streets linking Silver Street to Waterside North were laid out or extended in the 12th century. Even here, however, it is possible that the pattern is of pre-Conquest date – the excavation at Free School Lane (LIN 73a) discovered occupation fronting onto the north–south street in the pre-Conquest period. On the other hand, a watching brief in Saltergate (SLG 89) might suggest that the understanding we have developed of the development of the quaysides in this part of town might be faulty (p. 235–9 below – Fig. 9.68). This watching brief revealed wattle fencing and organic dumped deposits identical to those found further south, in the Waterside excavations (WO 89), but associated with 12th-century and later pottery. It is not clear what we would should make of this finding, but it seems to raise the possibility that Bank Street and Free School Lane were originally bounded to the south by the Roman wall, and that they were not extended through the line of the wall to join the new street on the line of Saltergate until the 12th century.

The possibility that the south-west corner of the Lower City also saw medieval expansion connected with the development of the port, between *c*.1150 and *c*.1350 is considered further below (p. 239–40 below). But, with the exception of the undated sequence at Brayford Wharf North (BWN 75) and the evidence for 12th-century activity at the southern end of Lucy Tower Street (LT 72), there is no good archaeological evidence for the medieval topography of this area. A tenement in this quarter of the city was, in any case, described in the early 14th century as a 'waste in a waste part of the city' (ed. Major 1958, 170–1, RA2362), and goes some way towards explaining why so little of the medieval topography is reflected in the modern street layout. Even so, a series of charters record the assembly of an extensive holding in the Lower City during the late 13th century, which was finally acquired by the Dean and Chapter following the death of Thomas de Sancto Laudo in 1316 (ed. Major 1958, 172–88, RA2364–79) (Fig. 9.58). They indicate that a row of properties existed on the south side of a lane/highway called *Lewynstigh* which had, as their southern boundary, either the King's wall or the highway of *Walkergate*. At least three of these properties were amalgamated during the 13th century to form an urban estate containing a hall, chapel, cellar and garden. Two charters, dated 1291 and 1293 record the grant by the City Council of a plot of land, ten royal ells long and between three-and-three-quarter and five ells wide, 'under the King's wall' in *Walkergate* to Hamo de la Dale and its subsequent granting to Thomas de Sancto Laudo. These grants seem to record encroachment on yet another stretch of the city wall and it is probably significant that charters of 1271–2 give the King's wall as their southern boundaries whereas those of 1276–9 give *Walkergate* instead. The precise boundary of these properties has not yet been determined but it is clear that *Lewynstigh* must have run east–west just north of the city wall whereas *Walkergate* either ran on the line of the city wall or immediately to its south. The plot of land lying between Mint Lane and Guildhall Street is almost

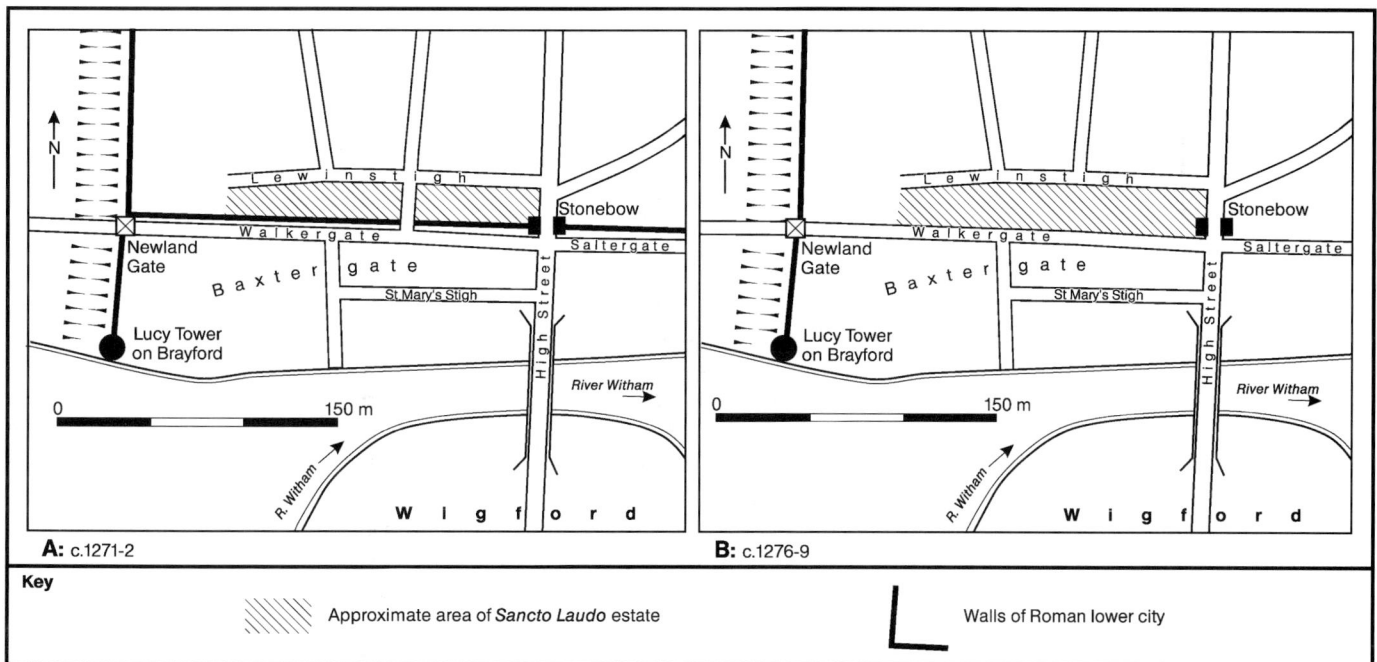

*Fig. 9.58. Location of the* Sancto Laudo *estate in the south-west corner of the Lower City, relative to the southern city wall – a) layout in about 1271–2; b) layout in about 1276–9 (drawn by Dave Watt, copyright English Heritage).*

certainly included within this estate. Further east, charters relating to properties in the parish of St Mary *Crackpole* often include the King's wall as their western boundary and either the King's highway (probably *Aldhungate*, now Beaumont Fee) or other properties as their eastern boundary (ed. Major 1958, 156–172, RA2347–2363).

## Settlement in the suburbs of the Upper City *c.*900–*c.*1350

The term 'suburb' (*suburbium*) is found in documents relating to property in Lincoln from the 12th century onwards and the distinction was clearly already present in the mid 11th century, since Colsuein's estate in *Butwerk*, in the Lower City, is described as being outside the city (*extra civitate*). Toki's estate in *Domesday Book* also included one property noted as being outside the wall. Some of the medieval suburbs developed clear identities, such as Wigford, *Butwerk*, Newport and Newland (Fig. 9.1) but, in others, it is less clear whether documentary sources refer to land fronting onto a street or whether some street names also connoted an area (e.g. Eastgate and Pottergate). Suburbs lay outside all three external gates of the Upper City. The Eastgate suburb may well be of pre-Conquest origin but it seems to have been re-planned and enlarged in the Norman period. The Newport suburb appears, by contrast, to have been a *de novo* development of the late 11th or early 12th century, whilst the history of the suburb outside the Upper City west gate appears to have been confused by its misidentification with the suburb of *Westgate* – a name used in some documentary sources when discussing Newland. Here we have distinguished this suburb from its downhill neighbour by using its medieval name – *Westcastle.*

### The suburb of **Westcastle**

Archaeological evidence, combined with a reconsideration of the documentary sources, suggests that *Westcastle* is of post-Conquest, perhaps even 12th-century, origin. We have seen that there is evidence for early and middle Saxon activity to the west of the Upper City (chapter 8 above), but, the residual pottery assemblage, which is the only evidence for this activity, contains no sherds of mid 9th-, 10th- or 11th-century date and the remaining pottery from the Lawn excavations (L 86) is definitely post-Conquest. It may even belong to a period quite late in the 12th century. The western approach to the Upper City must, therefore, have suffered considerable dislocation in the Anglo-Scandinavian and early Norman periods. If this dislocation had occurred after about 1100, the apparent gaps in settlement in the suburb might have been thought due to temporary blocking of the original Roman west gate, and the consequent diversion of the approach road to enter the city through the west postern

of the Bail. But, as the distribution of pottery types suggest that it was in decline before the Castle was founded, it may be that the Roman west gate was already blocked or superseded before the foundation of the Castle. As far as we can tell from present evidence, the sequence of occupation in the suburb is as set out in Fig. 9.59.

St Bartholomew's church served the suburb and is first recorded *c.*1189 (Hill 1948, 96n, 145). The site of the church has been excavated but very few traces remained, mainly as a result of landscaping of the site after its incorporation into the grounds of the Lawn Hospital (LH 84). A leper hospital, also dedicated to St Bartholomew, and certainly attached to the church, is a later medieval foundation (first recorded in 1312). The precise location of the hospital buildings is not known, they were not discovered during the excavations and there is a suggestion that the Union Workhouse may have occupied part of its site (Fig. 9.59c). A leper hospital dedicated to St Leonard also appears to have existed *extra castrum civitatis Linc.* in 1301 and 1312 (Cameron 1985, 125 – citing the Bishop's Register for 1312). These references have caused much difficulty in the past. It seems that, either we have two leper hospitals next to each other on the road leading out of Westgate postern, or, alternatively, the hospital of St Bartholomew was also known as St Leonard's and the references are to the same institution. A more detailed description in a will of 1299, of the location of one leper hospital *bywestcastle* and next to *westpittes*, which was probably a part of the open field lying west of Newport, suggests that it may have lain north of *Cliffgate*, (ed. Major 1968, 238–40, RA 2906). Unfortunately this will does not give the dedication of the hospital concerned, and it could refer to St Bartholomew. However, even if it does not represent a second hospital, it may provide evidence for 13th-century activity north of *Cliffgate*.

*Cliffgate* is one of two medieval routeways approaching the Upper City on its western side. St Bartholomew's stood to the south of this road, which survived into the 18th century but was finally closed as a result of the enclosure of the open fields in 1803 and the construction of the modern Burton Road. The metalling of *Cliffgate* was exposed in excavations in the Lawn Hospital kitchen garden, and the line of the road can be followed as property boundaries westwards to its junction with Long Leys Road and the north-eastern corner of West Common. In the later medieval period, entry to the Bail from the eastern part of *Cliffgate* was through a postern at the west end of modern Westgate, but it seems that, originally, *Cliffgate* was aligned on the Roman gate, which was buried *c.*1100 (p. 172 above). This suggests that the road itself, though not the suburb, is of pre-Conquest origin. Rubbish pits containing late 12th-century material, found in the Lawn excavations (L 86) are probably too far south to be associated with properties fronting onto *Cliffgate*, as diverted towards the west

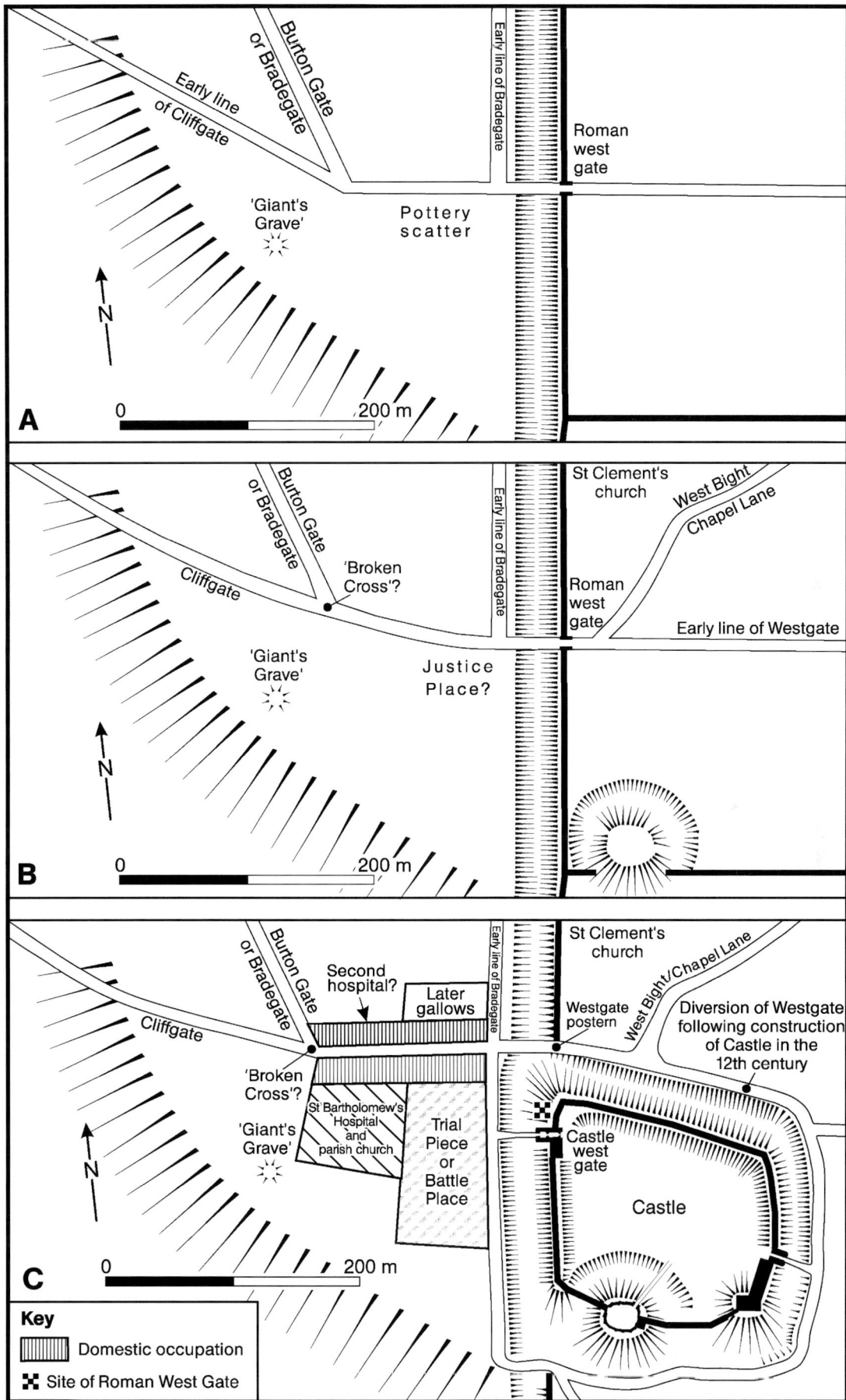

*Fig. 9.59. Reconstruction studies to explain proposed development of suburb of* Westcastle. *A) middle Saxon. B) c.1068. C) late 12th century, at the time of maximum expansion of the suburb (drawn by Dave Watt, copyright English Heritage).*

postern gate (about 55 metres to the north), but they could have been within properties fronting onto a road along the outer edge of the Castle ditch, or even one issuing from the Castle west gate (for which we have no documentary evidence). These pits suggest that, despite the poorly developed street network, there was some domestic occupation outside the Castle west gate, before this area became dedicated exclusively to assemblies associated with justice.

A late 18th-century map of Lincoln shows Mill Lane, rather than the modern Burton Road, as the main approach route to Lincoln from the north-west (Armstrong 1779; Hill 1948 fig 22). It seems likely, then, that the long-distance route from the north-west entered the built-up area along this line, joining *Cliffgate* just to the west of The Lawn kitchen garden. A plan of Lincoln Castle in the Duchy of Lancaster archives, made in 1783 (*Ibid.*, Plate 2), and other views (such as Fig. 9.89), indicate that the open fields ran right up to *Cliffgate*. Furthermore, excavations alongside Burton Road (CY 89) and observations during road-works suggest that this north-western route is post-medieval in origin. Hill's reconstruction of the fields and roads of Lincoln, based on cartographic, documentary and place-name evidence shows that the original road from Burton was known both as *Burtongate* and *Bradegate* (*Ibid.*, fig 22). From its junction with *Cliffgate* it ran along the cliff edge in a north-west direction before it turned north-eastwards, crossed the line of the modern Burton Road, to run on a divergent course in a very straight line to the north-east of it. The antiquity of this earlier route of the road towards Burton is unknown. The straightness of the section of the newly identified road north-east of the modern Burton Road suggests it may in fact be of Roman origin. There are a number of Romano-British sites to either side of the road line and a fieldwalking survey of land at Ellis's Farm, Burton, shows that Roman potsherds concentrate on the road line. However, it clearly survived into the medieval period and *Bradegate* is first noted in documents of the late 13th century (Cameron 1985, 53). The length of road along the cliff-edge (modern Mill Road) is clearly a diversion from an original more or less straight line taken by *Bradegate* into the city (a line which was still marked by field boundaries at enclosure heading for the north-west corner of the Bail ditch), but the date of the diversion is not known. The diversion was presumably connected with the establishment of windmills on the cliff, likely to have been in the late 12th century or later.

Hill's reconstruction of *Bradegate*, showing it joining *Cliffgate* before entering the city through the west postern gate, probably represents the original layout. However, an isolated reference in a 13th-century charter concerning land in St Nicholas's parish in Newport shows that there was a right of way running through a property on the west side of the street which had been used as a route from Newport to the Castle west gate since the mid 12th century (ed. Major 1968,

244–6, RA2658). It may be, therefore, that *Bradegate* originally bifurcated at the north-western corner of the Bail, with branches running parallel with both the western and northern ditches of the Bail, to enter either through Newport arch or through the west postern gate. *Bradegate* would be, therefore, be a mirror image of Nettleham Road, Church Lane and Northgate on the eastern side of the Bail.

By the late Middle Ages the area immediately outside of the Westgate postern, was used as the gallows, commemorated by the name *Hangman's Dyke* given to part of the Castle ditch (Hill 1948, 99) and by the name *Gallowtree shorts* given to part of the open field. No doubt this association with judicial process was related to the presence immediately south of the road, in front of the Castle west gate, of *Battle Place* (first recorded in 1275), interpreted by Hill as the site of trials by battle (Hill 1948, 359). Both the gallows and the *Battle Place* suggest an association with the shire court, held within the Castle, and injuries found on some of the burials excavated at the Lawn (L 86) suggest that executed prisoners were buried there (Boylston and Roberts 1994). The precise position of the gallows is first recorded in the late 18th century, at which time it lay west of the Bail ditch, and it is visible in Fig. 9.89. This gallows was originally for the execution of those condemned by the sheriff of the county whereas a gallows on Canwick Hill, was used by the City Council (Hill 1948, 231n). The *Hundred Rolls* record that *Battle Place* had recently been appropriated by the Castle and used to be a site of recreation and entertainment. Moorfields in 12th-century London, immediately outside the walled city on the north side (trans. Butler 1934), provided a similar facility there and both are similar in function to the butts provided for archery practice on the edge of most medieval and post-medieval towns. The site of *Battle Place* itself seems to have been retained as open ground and grazed by the Lord of the Bail, but it was also used for preaching (ed. Page 1906, 220), and for stalls in times of markets and fairs (Hill 1948. 262).

To the west of St Bartholomew's church and *Battle Place*, was a windmill, first recorded in 1505 (*Ibid.*, 336–7). It is unlikely that even the most southerly mill in Mill Road would have been described as being west of St Bartholomew's, although given the lack of landmarks in this area of open fields it is not impossible. The mound associated with this windmill might have been the *Giant's Grave*, which we have already noted in our consideration of the western boundary of Newland suburb (p. 188 above). Alternatively, *Giant's Grave* could have been a much earlier prehistoric burial mound (p. 30 above), or it could have served both purposes. From Willson's account, it was evidently visible from the Newland suburb, and must therefore have lain south of *Cliffgate* on the crest of the hill.

This small suburb of *Westcastle* has frequently been identified with the manor of *Willingthorpe*, belonging to the Bishop and mentioned in *Domesday Book* and elsewhere (*Ibid.*, 61–2). Foster used this identification to link the Castle west gate with that built by the Bishop with the King's permission at the start of the 12th century, to give the Bishop access to his estate (ed. Foster 1931, 20–1, RA21). Given the total lack of 11th-century finds from the extensive excavations in the area, this proposal must now be seen as inherently unlikely and it is argued here that the suburb of *Westgate* was located to the west of the lower walled city and was also known as *Willingthorpe*. It was later subsumed into the Newland suburb, as David Roffe has already argued in his discussion of downhill sites (Gilmour and Roffe 1999).

The implication of this relocation of the *Willingthorpe* suburb further south, and of the dates of pottery recovered from excavations, is that the *Westcastle* suburb, known to have been outside the Castle west gate by the end of the 12th century, was probably a re-foundation. It seems to have been short-lived, however, and as early as 1295 both the Dean and Chapter and the Constable were given leave by the rector to bury their dead in the cemetery of St Bartholomew's church (Hill 1948, 145–6). Within the year, negotiations were begun to transfer the church and its property to the Dean and Chapter and two years later, in 1297, the bishop gave the church to the Dean and Chapter as a burial ground, stating that for a long time the parish had had no parishioners (ed. Foster 1933, 165–71, RA465–472). The early demise of the suburb and its use as overflow cemetery and area of justice probably led to changes in the road pattern, which themselves would have increased the isolation of the area. St Bartholomew's itself was given to the master of the Cathedral choristers and, in 1391 the Pope granted an indulgence to those visiting the church on St Bartholomew's day or vigil since by that time oblations did not exceed one mark (ed. Foster 1933, 177–8, RA 479–80).

## The suburb of Eastgate

The Eastgate suburb, on the other side of the Upper City, is both larger and earlier than *Westcastle* on the west (Figs. 9.60 and 9.61). It was served by four churches: St Peter Eastgate, St Leonard, St Giles and St Margaret Pottergate. Of these, St Margaret is the earliest known (Fig. 9.62). An inscription (*corpus sifordi presbiter sce elene et sce margarete titulatus hic iacet*) found in a stone coffin on the site of this church has been dated to the 11th century and suggests that the church was originally dedicated to both St Margaret and St Helen (Hill 1948, 143). The remaining three churches all appear in documentary sources in the mid 12th century. Dedications to St Giles and St Leonard are particularly common in the 11th and 12th centuries, although of course, such churches could be rededicated.

The suburb was laid out along a series of roads leading to the east gate of the Bail. Taken from north to south the first of these was Northgate. The name Northgate was applied in the 19th century to the road crossing Eastgate at right angles, from the Priory arch on the south and which branches into Church Lane and Nettleham Road, but originally it ran north-north-eastwards along the line of Nettleham Road. Next Langworthgate ran north-eastwards becoming what is now called Wragby Road. Greetwellgate ran, as it still does, due east, whilst Winnowsty Lane originally ran directly south-eastwards (at which stage it was known as *Wainwellgate* – Fig. 9.60). Pottergate and *Boune Lane* (now Greestone Place and Stairs) arrived at the east gate of the Bail from the south-east and south-south-east respectively. The relative chronology of these roads is unknown. All were probably in existence by the 11th century and, in the case of Pottergate, properties on its north-eastern side have documented tenement histories extending back to the 12th century. The street name Pottergate must surely refer to the potters who worked outside of Clasketgate below hill (p. 230–1 below) and whose properties fronted onto the south end of this street (which was replaced by New Road/Lindum Hill in 1786). This pottery industry began in the 10th century and had disappeared by the end of the 11th century indicating the latest possible date for the formation of the street name.

A feature of the development of the Eastgate suburb was the progressive filling in of the city ditch and the extension eastwards of the Cathedral. Documentary sources make it clear that there was a distinction between the King's ditch, surrounding the bailey of Lincoln Castle, and the city ditch (even though *The Hundred Rolls* make it clear that the city ditch was also seen as the King's property, to whom citizens encroaching upon it were liable to pay a fine). The Castle ditch is distinguished, for example, from the ditch along the west side of the Lower City (ed. Illingworth 1812–18, I, 311b–312a, 318b, 325a–b; Gilmour and Roffe 1999). Along the eastern side of the city the ditch was known as the *Werkdyke* and a part of it was granted by the Dean and Chapter for the construction of the college of Vicars-Choral in the late 13th century, showing that by this time it was in the hands of the Cathedral (Stocker forthcoming c). The northern boundary of the vicars' land was the 'road from St Margaret's church towards the Bishop's Court', showing that the road had already bridged the *Werkdyke* by 1266–72 (ed. Major, 1973, 200–1, RA2870). Excavations at the southern end of the Vicars Court plot by Lindsey Archaeological Services suggested that, in the central part of the vicars' plot the ditch was still open at the time of construction (VC 93). Further north, the east end of St Hugh's church was built over the ditch in the 1190s.

We have seen that excavations at the southern junction of the city wall and St Hugh's church in 1984 suggest that this construction entailed the destruction of a postern gate (p. 178 above, Fig. 9.17). This gate is now thought to be that for which the Bishop was given permission to construction through

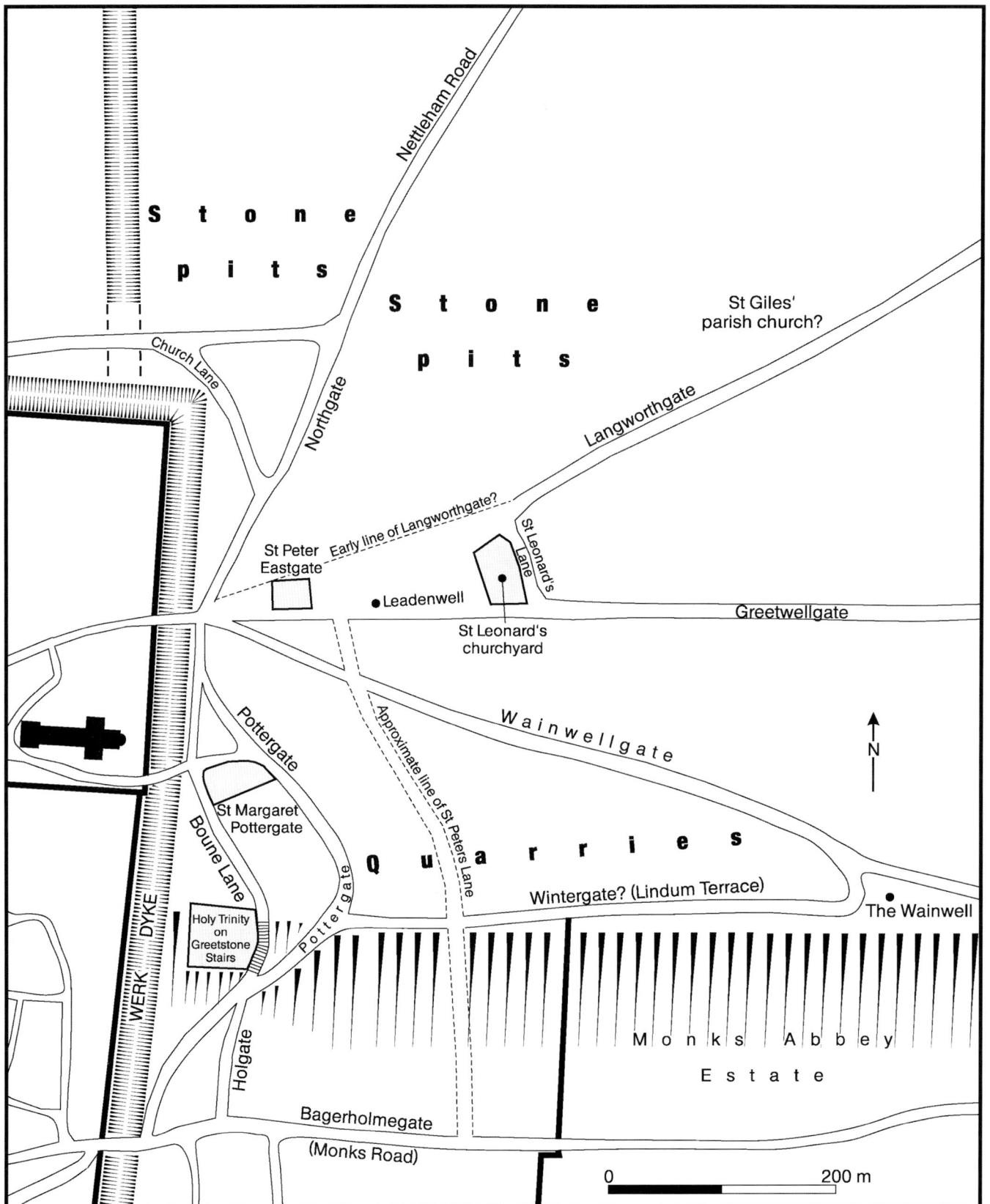

*Fig. 9.60. Reconstruction study of the layout of the Eastgate suburb in about 1150, i.e. before the extension of the Cathedral and the construction of the Close Wall (drawn by Dave Watt, copyright English Heritage).*

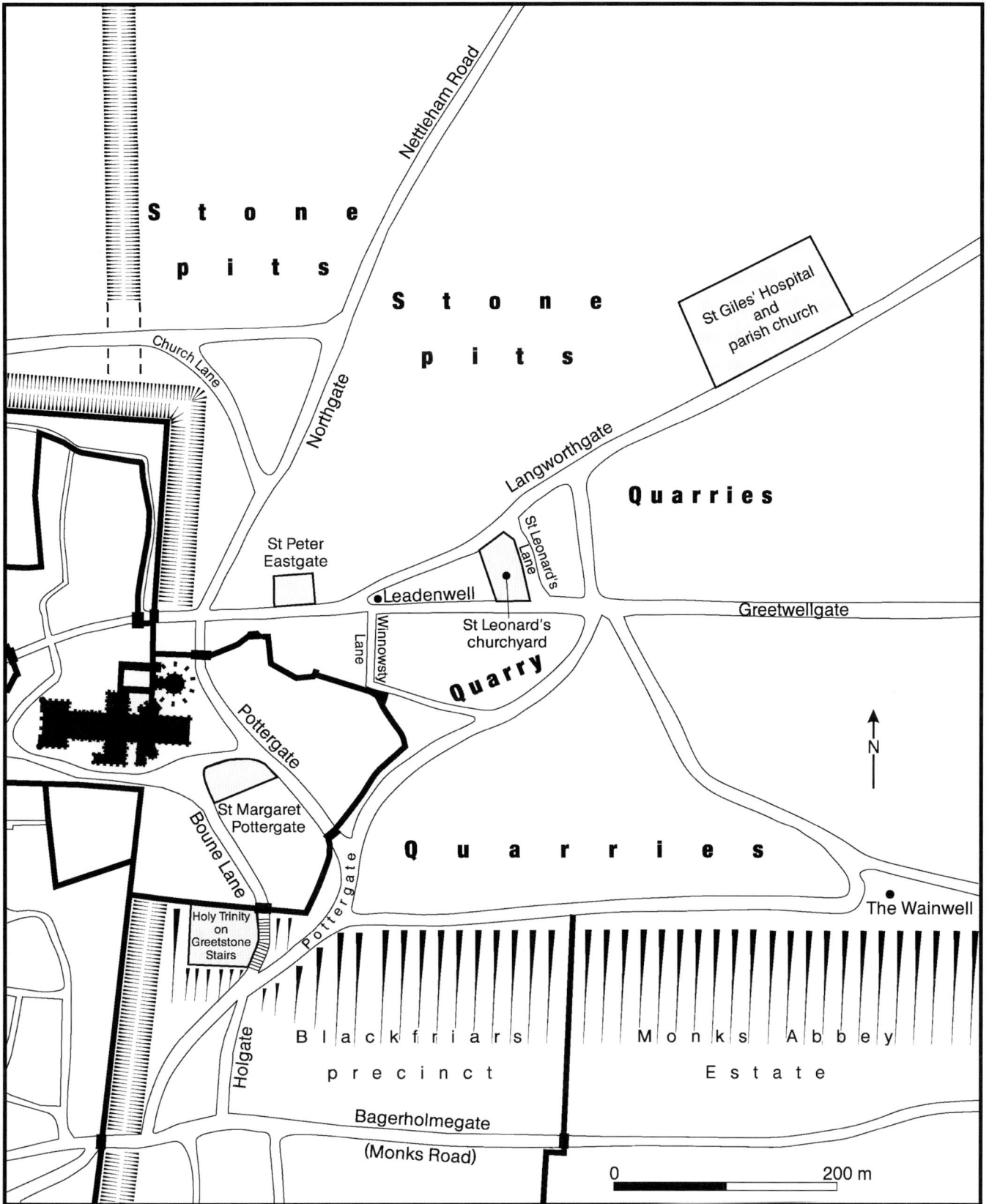

*Fig. 9.61. Plan of Eastgate suburb at its maximum extent (around 1300) (drawn by Dave Watt, copyright English Heritage).*

*Fig. 9.62. St Margaret's church Pottergate from the north-east; an undated drawing in the Willson Collection. This is probably a copy by Willson of a drawing of about 1780 (Lincoln Cathedral Library portfolio B No. 7a)(photo and copyright, Lincoln Cathedral Library).*

the King's wall in the early 12th century (Stocker and Vince 1997). Several 13th-century grants of land in this general area mention a postern gate (ed. Major 1973, 117, RA2783, 165, RA 2834, 263–4, RA2928), but by the 13th century, Bishop Hugh's new east end had already breached the Roman wall and any postern south of it would have been rebuilt. To extend his property in 1227, Geoffrey, the owner of a plot in this area made fine with the King, for land next to his plot, showing the site of the ditch was still regarded as the King's ditch subsequent to Hugh's work (Jones *et al.* 1987, 65; *CRR* xiii, No. 467). In 1255, following a commission, the King gave licence for the removal of the east wall of the city (*CPR* 1247–58, 506; Hill 1948, 120). This presumably referred to the stretch of wall from the point where Hugh's church originally breached the wall to the north-east corner of the Bishop's Palace. The inner lip of the ditch was seen during the 1984 excavations at the south-west corner of the Cathedral (LC 84 – Stocker 1985a) and parts of the fill of the ditch were exposed on the east side of the 1986 excavation of the rectangular chapel on the north-east side of the Cathedral (CAT 86). In both cases the only fills seen appear to have been deliberate backfill of 12th- and 13th-century dates.

Further north still, in the early 13th century, the Chapter House was built over the line of the Bail ditch. The northern end of *Boune Lane* was, evidently, truncated by the new Chapter House (if it had not already been terminated a generation earlier by St Hugh's Choir). Furthermore, in the 1220s, a chapel was built east of the north-east transept, again across the infilled ditch, and crossing *Boune Lane*'s original line. This chapel was excavated in 1986 (CAT 86) and

it is thought to have been built to house the shrine of St Hugh before the Angel Choir was constructed (Stocker 1987). The part of the Bail ditch immediately south of the Bail east gate and north of the Chapter House was, however, already in private hands by the end of the 12th century. It lay next to the land of Ralf the Ointment seller (Jones *et al.* 1990, 19). From these various references, then, it seems likely that the eastern Bail ditch south of the east gate was open and functional between the 9th and 12th centuries, with *Boune Lane* running parallel with it, but that between the east gate and the Close Wall south of Vicars Court, it was filled-in in stages between the later 12th and mid 13th centuries. To the north of the east gate the ditch still survives as an earthwork, maintaining the distinction between the Bail and the Eastgate suburb outside.

The documentary and architectural evidence for that part of the Eastgate suburb which lay within the Close has been published in *The Survey of Ancient Houses in Lincoln* (Jones *et al.* 1984; 1987). The original layout of the streets here was partly fossilised and partly modified by the incorporation of much of the suburb into the Close (Fig. 9.61). From both documentary and topographical evidence we can see that the construction of the Close Wall in the late 13th and early 14th centuries necessitated the closure of *St Peter's Lane*, whose line can probably be reconstructed, running southwards from the south-east corner of St Peter's church and then running parallel to Pottergate until its line is lost at the cliff edge (*Ibid.* 1984, 4 – Fig. 9.60). This lane may have served primarily as a back lane to properties fronting onto Pottergate, and the properties on either side were described as 'closes' before their acquisition by the Cathedral. One was held by a carter and another contained a barn, suggesting that they may have been used as paddocks (*Ibid.*, 51). In some cases the church acquired properties in Pottergate, and in *Boune Lane*, by purchase from lay owners, but in others land was already in ecclesiastical hands. In most cases, however, the development of plots can only be documented from the 13th or 14th centuries, and usually only in outline.

The expansion of the Cathedral eastwards had a great impact on the suburb. As we have seen, until the 1190s the Cathedral precinct was bounded by the Upper City wall but Bishop Hugh's rebuilding of the east end of the church, starting in 1192, involved breaking through of the wall. No firm evidence has yet been produced, however, to suggest that there was any commensurate extension of the Close eastwards. Even so, when the east end of the Cathedral was rebuilt again, on an even grander scale between 1255 and 1280, the expansion was accompanied by a cemetery east of the Upper City wall, on the south side of the church, revealed in 1984 (LC 84 – Stocker 1985a). Land for this purpose, to the south-east of the Cathedral, was described in charters of 1258–1264 as being either on the west side of Pottergate or in the cemetery of St Margaret (ed. Major 1968, 194–202, RA 2863–73). One of these properties appears not to have had a Pottergate frontage but was presumably accessed via *Boune Lane* and a lane running east–west from the postern in the city wall south of the Cathedral to Pottergate along the north side of St Margaret's churchyard.

Between the 12th and 14th centuries, the Eastgate suburb outside the Close is known mainly from documentary sources, together with slight evidence from three excavations (WC 87, LG 89 and LG 90), and has undergone several changes to its topography. The main east–west street, Eastgate/Greetwellgate, is on a Roman alignment. A number of medieval properties ran south from this street to *Wainwellgate* and traces of one of these were found in excavations in 1987 (WC 87). Today the western boundary of these plots is formed by Winnowsty Lane, after it turns north to join Eastgate. It is clear, however, that originally (i.e. before the construction of the Close Wall) this lane ran further east, to cross *St Peter's Lane* and probably continue on to the city gate (Fig. 9.60). Both the western end of *Wainwellgate* and the whole length of *St Peter's Lane* were closed following the construction of the Close Wall and the latter was incorporated into the Chancellor's garden (Fig. 9.61).

No documentary sources are known for properties north of the western part of Greetwellgate and in the 13th and 14th centuries, and subsequently, this area seems to have been an open triangular green, with a public well called the *Leadenwell* (and site of a Maypole) at the west end, and the church and cemetery of St Leonard situated centrally at the east end. A row of properties, fronting onto a road running north–south, was located to the east of St Leonard's church. This open space may have been bounded on the northern side, originally, by an early line of Langworthgate, running considerably further to the north than it does today. This hypothetical route would have run along the north side of St Peter's church (which was not on its modern alignment) leaving the church and churchyard to its south (Fig. 9.60). Evidence in support of the more northerly original line of Langworthgate came from the 1989 excavations on the north side of the street (LG 89). These showed that a Roman building aligned on Eastgate underlay the present street, which cannot therefore be on the line of the Langworthgate-Eastgate street. Medieval pottery finds from this site were mainly late medieval, consistent with this area having been part of the green until quite a late date. Deeds survive for several properties on the north side of Eastgate/Langworthgate, but all appear to be later and post-medieval, and of course they don't locate the precise line of Eastgate/Langworthgate in their boundaries relative to the remainder of the topography. Several of these properties appear to have been modest in size (described as cottages) or to have agricultural characteristics and may be characterised as 'squatter' settlement on the edges of the former green. To the north and east of the Roman (and high medieval?) road line, a series of crofts and green lanes are marked on early mapping, and these seem to fossilise the proposed northerly alignment of this road in their boundaries. We can suggest that they were laid out along the earlier, more northerly, line of Langworthgate, before encroaching onto the green to the south at some date in the late medieval period.

Only at the western end of this northern part of the suburb is there any sign of the elite town houses of the 12th and 13th centuries that characterise the Bail, Pottergate and the southern side of Eastgate at this period. In addition to those within the Close documented by Jones *et al.* (1984–1996) such houses also existed along the western side of Northgate, and within the triangle formed by Northgate, and the modern streets Church Lane and Nettleham Road. The original name for Church Lane remains uncertain, but one possibility is that it originally crossed the junction with Northgate to continue south-eastwards towards the north-western corner of St Peter's churchyard. From there, presumably, it ran on to Eastgate.

In its earliest manifestation, then, the Eastgate suburb seems to have been laid out along a funnel-shaped road or green on the line of modern Eastgate, which can only really be explained as a purpose-built market place (Fig. 9.83c). The green had churches placed within the open space at either end. A smaller triangular green or market place remained at the junction of Greetwellgate and Langworthgate long after the filling in of most of the green west and north-west of St Leonard's church. The location of the *Leadenwell*, in the centre of this large triangular space, may suggest that it was dug before the contraction of the large green. We know little of the character of this part of the suburb in the 12th to 14th centuries from documentary sources, although it is likely that the western part of the suburb, within the parish of St Peter, was sought out by officials of the Cathedral and other high status individuals. Plots in St Leonard's parish, however, seem to have been of more modest size. There is documentary evidence for occupation here from the late 12th century onwards.

The charters dealing with the east–west properties to the east of St Leonard's Lane (above) were bounded on their east sides variously by the fields of Lincoln, a common lane and the King's highway. It seems likely that, between the 12th and 14th centuries, this block was always bounded on its east by a route-way with the open fields to its east. The road in question probably branched off from Pottergate at the South Pottergate Gate and determined the location of the stretch of Close Wall that ran from the gatehouse to its junction with Winnowsty Lane – i.e. the line of the modern Wragby Road. There is no documentary evidence that this route was occupied. The un-located medieval street called *Wintergate* mentioned in *The Hundred Rolls* (Cameron 1985, 111) must have been somewhere here, but it is more likely to have run along the cliff edge, on the line later followed by Lindum Terrace.

On the 1803 enclosure award map, the crofts running back from Langworthgate exist as far east as St Giles church, beyond which were the open fields. The eastern limit of the suburb may have been the church itself, which is only once referred to as parochial. It was one of the latest churches to be acquired by the Cathedral (ed. Foster 1931, 207, RA 255), sometime between 1148 and 1163, and may, on those grounds, have been founded in the late 11th or early 12th century. Although it became a hospital in the 13th century, there was already a community of some sort there earlier, and it is possible that the parish failed to attract parishioners. Certainly there is neither documentary nor archaeological evidence for medieval occupation much to the east of the modern junction between Langworthgate and Wragby Road. It may be that parts of the area were already used for quarrying, as they continued to be into the 19th century. In 1275–80 St Giles was given to the Vicars-Choral, who were to sing masses for the benefactors of the house, but were given the right for weak and infirm vicars to live there (ed. Page 1906, 233).

The small quantity of pottery recovered from the three excavations in the suburb is mainly late medieval and later (Fig. 9.63). There is, however, a difference between the assemblages from the two sites in Langworthgate (LG 89 and LG 90) and that between Winnowsty Lane and Greetwellgate (WC 87), which includes small quantities of pre-Conquest and early medieval wares. To some extent the differences between the assemblages can be attributed to their methods of collection (the Langworthgate sites were on a smaller scale than the Winnowsty Lane excavation) but the small quantity of medieval finds in general from the Langworthgate sites does fit the interpretation of this part of the suburb as being both

relatively poor and sparsely occupied. The presence of pre-Conquest pottery at Winnowsty Lane leaves the dating of this suburban development uncertain. On the one hand, the site fronts onto a former Roman street, and it may be that simple ribbon development took place in this area before the Conquest, to be superseded by a more ambitious development afterwards. On the other hand, it is quite possible that the junction of the two former Roman streets, Langworthgate and Greetwellgate, was used as a market place before the Conquest and that the Norman contribution was merely to build St Lawrence's church and the block of properties to its east. In either case, the extent of the crofts north of the suburb and the location of St Giles church so far east, point to this being a shrunken suburb which may have been of much greater size and significance between the 11th and 13th centuries than is now evident.

### The Newport suburb

The Newport suburb (Figs. 9.29, 9.64 and 9.83b), outside the north gate of the Upper City, appears at first glance to have had a more straightforward history than Eastgate. It was part of the city and administered by the Council with little interference from either the Castle or the Cathedral (although the Dean and Chapter did hold land there, as elsewhere within the city). Unlike those to the east and west of the Upper City, this suburb had a formal boundary – a bank and ditch, which survived intact into the

| End date of ceramic period | Site Code LG 89 | Site Code LG 90 | Site Code WC 87 | % of total assemblage |
|---|---|---|---|---|
| AD 450 | 3.33% | 0.00% | 0.00 % | 0.36% |
| 850 | 0.00% | 0.00% | 0.85% | 0.71% |
| 1000 | 0.00% | 0.00% | 4.70% | 3.93% |
| 1150 | 0.00% | 0.00% | 7.69% | 6.43% |
| 1250 | 0.00% | 6.25% | 11.54% | 10.00% |
| 1350 | 13.33% | 18.75% | 27.78% | 25.71% |
| 1500 | 6.67% | 31.25% | 42.31% | 37.86% |
| 1700 | 76.67% | 37.50% | 2.56% | 12.50% |
| Uncertain | 0.00% | 6.25% | 2.56% | 2.50% |

*Fig. 9.63. Percentages of pottery, by date, recovered from three excavations in the Eastgate suburb (source, Vince and Young forthcoming).*

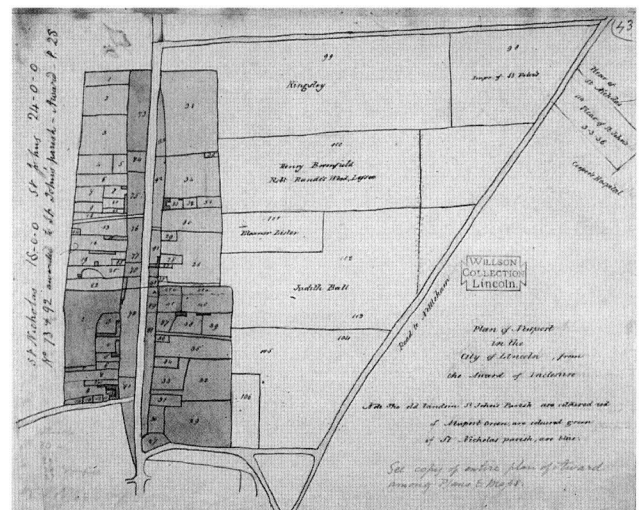

*Fig. 9.64. Map of Newport suburb by Edward Willson (based on J S Padley's surveys of c.1840 – London Society of Antiquaries Ms, 786/5, 45–6) showing the layout of properties and parish boundaries in Newport area (photo, Lincolnshire County Council, copyright Society of Antiquaries of London).*

18th century (Fig. 9.29). Excavated evidence for the Newport suburb is limited to excavations at Bishop Grosseteste College by Baker in the 1930s (on the medieval defences – Stanwell and Baker 1938) and by Rollin and Wragg (Wragg 1995, 1996, 1997; BGA 95, BGB 95 BGC 96).

Both of the churches serving the suburb, St John the Baptist and St Nicholas, came into the hands of the Cathedral between 1146 and 1163 and Hill thought this indicated that they may have been amongst the latest parish churches to have been founded in Lincoln, perhaps during the late 11th or early 12th centuries (1948, 169). St Nicholas' parish, as mapped on Padley's map of 1842 (Figs. 9.64 and 10.1), included the whole of the former North Field and parts of Low Field, whereas St John's parish was confined to only a part of the area within the earthen defences of the suburb. This unequal distribution of land probably indicates that St John was a later parish, carved out of that of St Nicholas. Padley's detailed maps of the 1840s also show that the site of St John's churchyard did not lie within St John's parish, an anomaly confirmed (if not explained) by Willson in the mid 19th century (London, Society of Antiquaries Ms. 786/5, 45–6 – Fig. 9.64).

Padley's maps also show a wide strip on the west side of the street and two narrower strips on the east side, within St Nicholas' parish. These strips preserve the original boundaries of the long, narrow, cigar-shaped market place, known as *Newport Green*, which formed the backbone of the suburb (Fig. 9.83b). The church and churchyard of St John were clearly placed within this elongated space, near its northern end. It has recently been investigated archaeologically and its location here has been confirmed (NP 93, NPB 94). Indeed, a charter of *c*.1223 actually refers to land 'in the street' of Newport 'on the east side of the church' and with another property on its south side, suggesting that the church may have been joined in the centre of the green by domestic buildings (ed. Major 1958, 20–1, RA2205). There was also a public well, which Stukeley identifies as *Grantham Well*, to the south of the church. This great green was the location of the Newport Fair held between the feasts of St Botolph and Sts Peter and Paul (17th to 29th June), which was given its charter in 1330, but which was certainly in existence well before that date (Bischoff 1975, 162–3). The fair was one of the known locations for the sale of Lincoln cloth, produced in the city, but by this late date these sales were of poor-quality local products produced for the domestic market. Similar elongated markets can be seen in post-Conquest planned towns elsewhere in England, often with a thoroughfare on one side of the market place kept clear whilst the remainder is periodically used for the market. Encroachment onto Newport Green, especially from the west and around St John's church during the medieval period, followed by the decline of the suburb in the late medieval and post-

medieval periods has led to the shape of the market place being completely lost.

Documentary evidence for the suburb is quite plentiful and starts in the 12th century, when witnesses to deeds with the surname *of Newport* are to be found. Charters show that land on both sides of the main market was usually divided into plots running from the highway to 'the ditch of Lincoln'. A series of charters dating from the early or mid 13th century show how Cathedral canons were able to assemble sizeable estates here (ed. Major 1958, 34–43, RA2220–2229). At his death, William de Winchcombe held what had been five separate plots on the west side of the street, in St John's parish, at least three of which were contiguous. Whether they were physically amalgamated in order to form a large building plot or kept separate and merely used as a source of income is not known. Excavations at Bishop Grosseteste College towards the northern end of the suburb (BGB 95) showed that the earliest medieval occupation here was of early 12th-century date, but is it possible, indeed quite likely, that the earliest occupation in the suburb would be further south, closer to the Upper City.

The only major institution in the suburb was the Augustinian Friary, which was founded in the later 13th century and received oaks in 1280 (Hill 1948, 151). Little detail is known of its extent, internal features or history, although it is said to have been situated in the northern angle between Newport and Rasen Lane. Rasen Lane is likely to be the successor to a minor medieval street in the suburb, known as *Sexstangate*, first recorded in the late 12th century (Cameron 1985, 98). Since its name contains an Old English personal name as its first element, it is likely that this street is of late 11th- or early 12th-century date and, as there is no reason to believe the suburb predates the Norman Conquest, it is likely that *Sexstangate* is a primary feature. Other lanes or paths extending back from the market street also existed within Newport and were used as boundaries in charters. The path next the dale of William Harefoot, for example, formed the southern boundary of a property granted *c*.1200 (ed. Major 1958, 1, RA2185) and lay on the east side of the market, in St John's parish. The modern Church Lane, which forms the southern boundary of St Nicholas' churchyard, is first mentioned as the northern boundary to a property in the Eastgate suburb in the 16th century. Its southern branch originally ran towards Northgate and St Peter Eastgate churchyard, but the existing branch north-eastwards, into the open fields, may also be of considerable age. Some, perhaps a majority, of the properties in Newport were involved in agriculture (and had barns, for example), and consequently, there were probably several tracks leading into the fields between the properties on both sides of the road. Such tracks, however, would have to cross the boundary bank and ditch, and this may suggest that they belong to a later phase of occupation.

## Settlement in the suburbs of the Lower City *c*.900–*c*.1350

Like the Upper City, the Lower City developed suburbs outside each of its gates between the 10th and 12th centuries (Fig. 9.1). The grandest, of course, was the populous area of the city south of the Witham, along Ermine Street, known as Wigford. But before we turn to look at this important area we should discuss the lesser suburbs of Newland, west of the Lower City, *Butwerk*, to its east, and Thorngate, to the south-east. At the junction of all four of these suburbs lay the narrow strip of land along the north bank of the Witham south of the city wall. This critical, but poorly-understood, area formed the heart of the port of Lincoln, at least at certain times, and it requires separate consideration.

### *The suburb of Newland*

To the west of the Lower City lay the suburb of Newland (Fig. 9.65). No controlled excavations have taken place in this suburb, except on reclaimed ground along the river at Brayford North (BN 89), which is unlikely to be typical. A model for its development can, however, be pieced together using documentary and cartographic sources. The place-name Newland in the medieval period undoubtedly referred to the entire suburb, from the Brayford Pool and Fossdyke northwards to what is now West Parade. However, two other place-names probably refer to either the whole suburb or to parts of it – *Willingthorpe* and *Westgate*. Traditionally, *Willingthorpe* is identified as the Bishop's soke of *Westgate* and both have been placed outside the west gate of the Upper City. But, now that archaeological excavation at The Lawn has made this attribution untenable (p. 220–1 above) another location must be found for this settlement. The description of the Bishop's estate in *Domesday Book* is not particularly informative: 'Bishop Remigius has one small manor with one carucate near to the city of Lincoln, with *sake* and *soke* and with *toll* and *team* over it' (trans. Hill 1948, 369). From the *Domesday Book* entry it is not possible to identify the owner of this manor in 1066, or even whether it existed then. *Willingthorpe* as a place-name disappeared during the 12th century (Cameron 1985, 46, cites a final instance in 1163–6) whereas 'Newland' is first recorded as a place-name at approximately the same moment – the earliest securely dated example is from *The Pipe Rolls* of 1181 (*Ibid.*, 85). Even so, deeds for properties in Newland included in the *Registrum Antiquissimum* distinguish between those in the Bishop's soke and those without (ed. Foster 1931, 188–90, 194, 196, 202, 267–8, RA 248, 250, 254). It is suggested here that the Bishop's soke in Newland was coterminous with the original settlement of *Willingthorpe*, a place-name which means 'the subsidiary settlement by the willow copse' (Cameron 1985, 46). The place-name is well suited to the likely medieval topography of this area, outside the city walls and on thin sandy soils developed on river terrace gravels. If correct, this implies that *Willingthorpe* was subsumed within a larger suburb of *Westgate* during the later 11th and 12th centuries, although the Bishop's Manor remained a separate legal entity (Hill 1948, 328–9). Finally, the name Newland was applied to the whole of this suburb; the Bishop's soke, the suburban development outside the west wall of the Lower City, and the presumably newly reclaimed ground in the southern part of the suburb, which probably gave the whole area its new name.

Two churches served the Newland suburb, St Faith and St Stephen. Neither survives, but their positions can be reconstructed through documentary sources and, in the case of St Stephen, through the discovery of burials on the west side of Orchard Street (ON 10). St Faith's church is said to be 'in the Bishop's soke' in 1163 (ed. Foster 1931, 205, RA255) and in 1230–4, but it is recorded as 'in Newland' from 1210–20 onwards (Cameron 1985, 121). St Stephen's church has no qualifying attribute in its earliest documentary references (from 1163 onwards) but is given the attribute 'in *Midhergate*' in *c*.1227. It is called 'in Newland' from this point on (*Ibid.*, 135).

Newland was served by three east–west streets. The northern one is now West Parade, was previously *Clay Lane* and before that *Wong Lane* (*Ibid.*, 59, 109). *Wong* is a Scandinavian dialect word for 'in-field', and a common medieval field name locally, and the field in question here was probably east of the modern West Common (*Ibid.*, 109). The southern street is Carholme Road, previously *Carholme Lane*. *Carholme* itself is a place-name first recorded in the 13th century but probably originally an Anglo-Scandinavian formation meaning 'Kari's water-meadow' (*Ibid.*, 20). On the 1803 enclosure map *Carholme* is a large field bounded by the Fossdyke on the south and its northern boundary is marked today by a stream-bed, often flooded during wet weather. The suburb's middle road is now called Newland Street West. On Padley's 1842 map, as it approaches the city wall, this street appears to have been widened and diverted south-eastwards to head for Newland Gate, at the south-west corner of the walled circuit (Fig. 9.83e). On the same map, Carholme Road also swings northwards to join this wide street, labelled *Far Newland*. This road layout looks very much like a market place inserted into the pre-existing street pattern at this corner of the suburb, and some confirmation of this is provided by the fact that the *Buttercross* once stood at its eastern end. This proposed marketplace cut across, and partially obliterated, an earlier street pattern and so must be of relatively late date – certainly post-Conquest. In 1842 the street was 230m long but only 24–7m, but in Fig. 9.65 we reconstruct an original width approaching 100m. The *Buttercross* is not recorded until the 16th century (ed. Foster 1914, 35) but the market's plan, and the long

Mound known as
'Giants Grave'

Common fields
subject to
early enclosure

Bishop's garden above Newland
under the hill, behind the Castle.
(18 acres)

West Parade/Clay Lane/Wong Lane

St Faith's
churchyard

Original area of
Willingthorpe?
Gate?

To Burton

To Torksey

Newland Street West

former Midhergate?

St Stephen's churchyard
(extended over line
of former road?)

West
gate

Motherby Lane

Orchard Street

Carholme Lane

Possible
gate?

Park Lane
(Aldusstigh)

Area of reclamation?

N

Buttercross ●

Market place inserted
into the street pattern
(perhaps in the 12th century)

Newland
Gate

Lucy Tower
on Brayford

*B r a y f o r d*

0          200 m

*P o o l*

**Key** ———— Roads, known

- - - - - Roads, conjectured

|||||||||| Defensive/boundary ditch-documented

••••••• Defensive/boundary ditch-conjectured

Lower City walls

Land subject to flooding

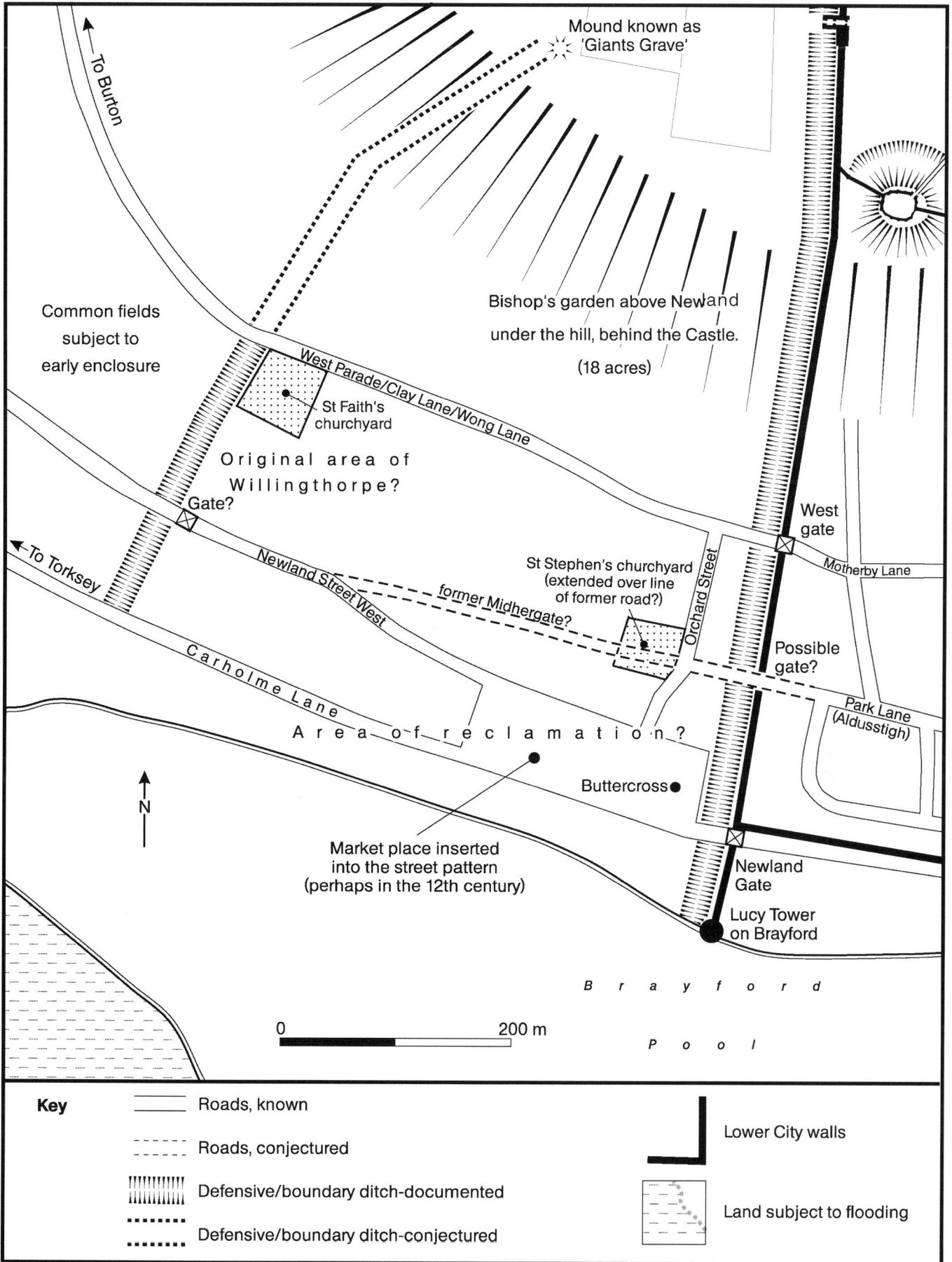

*Fig. 9.65. Reconstruction study of Newland suburb in the High Medieval Era (drawn by Dave Watt, copyright English Heritage).*

narrow plots which front onto it, suggest an earlier origin, and excavations on the southern part of such a plot (BN 89) indicate that there was reclamation and industrial activity here in the later 12th century.

If the Newland market place is a 12th-century alteration of an earlier street pattern, the early descriptions of St Stephen's church as 'in *Midhergate*', makes more sense. Cameron (1985, 87) suggests that the street-name *Midhergate* derives from 'middle army road' and, this could refer to the street's location 'in between' Carholme Road to its south and West Parade to its north. Originally, we can suggest, Carholme Road followed the northern bank of the Fossdyke to run along the outside of the Lower City south wall, whilst West Parade would have entered the city at the presumed gate at Motherby Lane. *Midhergate* also heads for the city wall, however, but its original entry point remains uncertain. It seems to be heading for the vicinity of the lower Roman west gate, but no evidence for the post-Roman use of the Roman lower west gate was recorded during the excavations here (P 70). Even so, Park Street inside the wall and Newland Street West outside it align well with the proposed line for *Midhergate* and, furthermore, the junction between its projected line and Orchard Street is marked by a distinct kink in Orchard Street itself. To the north Orchard Street runs at right angles to West Parade (and to the proposed *Midhergate*), whilst to the south it runs at right angles to Far Newland. The chance find of a medieval stone coffin, presumed to be an in situ burial in the graveyard of St Stephen's church, was made immediately south-west of the junction of Orchard Street (ON 10) and, consequently, St Stephen should be located immediately south of the proposed line of *Midhergate*. Park Street is the medieval street of *Aldusstygh* which runs directly from the west wall of the Lower City to the High Street, forming the boundary between the parishes of St Peter-at-Pleas and St Lawrence (Hill 1948, 359), and is clearly an ancient feature in the townscape. The name incorporates the Middle English feminine name, *Aldusa*, but the *-tigh* element denotes a lane or path, not a major route, and if this was originally connected with *Midhergate*, forming a major exit from the city to the west, its medieval name will have been assigned after it had lost that role.

We have already noted that the western limit of the Newland suburb in the medieval period was marked by a gate and probably a ditch situated just to the west of the junction of Newland Street West with the modern Nelson Street. It is presumed that the roads which later became Carholme Road and West Parade extended beyond the defences and, as they are depicted on Padley's 1842 map, a further development can be seen in the property boundaries in the western part of the suburb. Here a clear difference can be seen between recently enclosed land on the edge of West Common and earlier enclosures, whose fields have a curving edge running from south of Carholme Road north-

wards to Carline Road. North–south boundaries within this block of enclosures rarely if ever extend for more than one toft, but the east–west boundaries are formed either by Newland Street West, Carholme Road or West Parade, or by two intermediate lines, one running at the base of the cliff (part of which now forms a back lane behind properties on the south side of Alexandra Terrace) and the other running between Newland Street West and West Parade. The northern side of this boundary was divided into much smaller, roughly square plots, one of which has been identified as the site of St Faith's church (Lincolnshire Archives Office, parish file). In size, these plots are similar to those interpreted as tofts in Newport and *Butwerk*. There is no sign of a change in plot size, shape or orientation on either side of the putative boundary of the suburb, which suggests that they were laid out after this boundary had ceased to be important. Most likely, therefore, these were crofts rather than occupied plots and we know that such crofts were created in the Bishop's soke (Hill 1948, 330). On the other hand, the King's ditch at Newland seems to have been the boundary between the suburb and the open fields in *c*.1200, so these enclosures must be 13th-century or later in date. Most likely, the similarity of the enclosures to either side of the suburb boundary indicates that both the suburb itself and the open fields were being enclosed following the decline of the suburb in the later medieval period.

### The suburb of Butwerk

The earliest suburban activity in the Lower City was to be found outside the eastern rather than the western defences, in the suburb of *Butwerk* (Fig. 9.66). The suburb was approached via Clasketgate and was separated from the Lower City by the city ditch, the *Werkdyke*. Monks Road (known as *Bagerholmegate*), which leads eastwards out of Clasketgate is very likely of Roman origin (chapter 7 above). Certainly, an exit from the city on the site of the Roman Clasketgate Gate must have been in use in the mid 9th century, to account for the existence of Silver Street. Silver Street was probably important because it led to Pottergate, via a hollow way, *Holgate*, which ran up the hillside at a right-angle, 100m to the east of Clasketgate. *Holgate* led to the foot of the Greestone Stairs, whence the traveller could either ascend the stairs directly ahead, or turn north-eastwards along Pottergate before making a dog-leg turn north-westwards, towards the east gate of the Upper City. Most of the wheeled traffic from the Lower City to the Upper City must have travelled along this route, as must traffic heading to Wragby, via Northgate to Nettleham Road and round to Newport.

There seems to have been a difference in land-use north and south of *Bagerholmegate* in the 10th and 11th centuries, probably because the land to the north was much steeper and, therefore, more marginal. Exca-

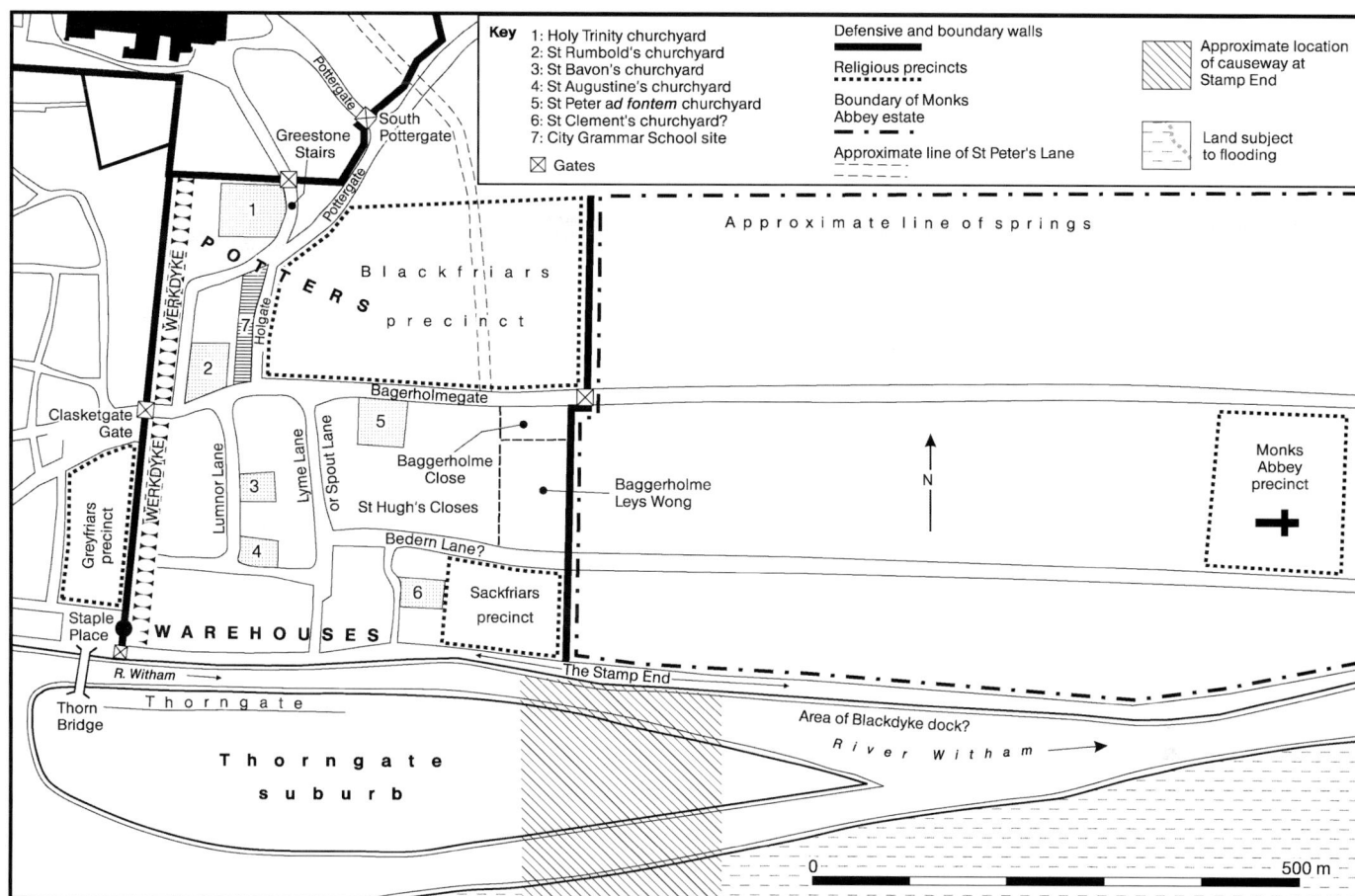

*Fig. 9.66. Reconstruction study of* Butwerk *suburb in the High Medieval Era (drawn by Dave Watt, copyright English Heritage).*

vations on the site of the Sessions House and Cathedral Street (SES 97, TC 93, TCA 94) have produced both waster dumps and evidence for pottery kilns dating from between the early or mid 10th century and the 11th century (and producing fabrics LSH and SNLS). This potting presumably gave its name to Pottergate, which lead to these sites from the north. There is no evidence for the continuation of pottery production here after the early 11th century and, although it is possible that production continued behind the church of St Rumbold, which fronted onto *Bagerholmegate*, it is perhaps more likely that the church and its churchyard were established here after pottery production had ceased. Meanwhile, the excavations at Broadgate East (BE 73) revealed evidence for timber buildings south of *Bagerholmegate* beginning in the 11th century and at least one earlier pit, together with a substantial scatter of 10th-century pottery. The presence of LSLS ware amongst this pottery suggests that activity began here in the late 9th or early 10th century. The character of this activity south of *Bager-holmegate* between the late 9th and 11th centuries is difficult to determine. The pottery of this date discovered here is unlikely simply to reflect manuring

and it would be somewhat surprising if inhabitants of the Lower City felt the need to dispose of rubbish outside the walls at this early date. It is more likely, therefore, that there was occupation in the area at this early period in the development of the settlement. Whether this occupation was also of an industrial nature, like the potteries north of *Bagerhomegate*, or related to waterside activities, or merely 'overspill' from the Lower City is not known.

By the middle of the 11th century the area to the south of *Bagerholmegate* was being developed or redeveloped. This is demonstrated most clearly by and entry in *Domesday Book*:

> Colsuein has … outside the city … 36 houses and 2 churches to which nothing is attached, which he settled on waste land which the King gave him and which had never been settled before. Now the King has all the customary dues from them.

The identity of one of these churches, St Peter *ad fontem*, is known from its subsequent history (Hill 1948, 133–4). The position of St Peter's church, on the eastern side of the suburb is also clear from documentary sources, whilst its precise location is provided by the discovery of burials on the south side of Monks Road, east of Rosemary Lane, and the recording of both burials and masonry in the area of Spa Close in the mid 19th century (Lincoln City Library, Ross Ms. *Annales Lincolniensis* III, 112). Hill suggests that Colsuein's other church might be St Augustine, on the assumption that this church too was located at the eastern end of the *Butwerk* suburb. But current opinion is that St Augustine's church was situated in St Rumbold Street (Johnson 1992). The identity of Colsuein's second church cannot be demonstrated for certain, but the site of every church in *Butwerk* is now established, except St Clement-in-*Butwerk*, and on topographical grounds therefore, it seems likely that this should be the missing church. A record in the Barlings cartulary records that land in St Clement's parish was disputed with the monks of St Mary of York and it is known that the monks' land was situated at the eastern end of the suburb, since the exact boundary was subject to an agreement between St Mary of York and the city (Hill 1948, 340). Land in the parish of St Clement-in-*Butwerk* also lay next to the suburb boundary, north of *Bagerholmegate* (ed. Major 1973, 295–8, RA2957–2959). It seems likely, however, that the church itself lay south of the road (below), suggesting that the parish was a long strip running from the cliff to the Witham and this may also have been the case for St Peter's parish.

In Colsuein's estate, then, we have unusually direct evidence for a planned extension to an existing pre-Conquest suburb in the middle of the 11th century. The *Domesday Book* entry makes it quite clear that the 2 churches were founded by Colsuein, together with accompanying houses, and that the land had previously been 'waste' (*vasta*). The term 'waste' in *Domesday Book* is usually thought to refer specifically to land that had once been occupied, yet here in Lincoln, it is said never to have had 'dwellings' (*hospitata*) before. In *Butwerk*, this apparently self-contradictory entry could be referring, however, to the former seasonal occupation of the site by a traditional market or fair, thought to have existed here because of the ancient place-name *Baggerholme*. This place-name, which is used as an attribute of St Augustine's and St Peter's churches from the 13th century, is derived from *Baggere* and *holmi* and means 'the water-meadow of the hawkers' (Cameron 1985, 13). Presumably St Mary's Abbey York would have had some control over this market. The abbey held their estate with the right of *toll* and *team*, from the late 11th century onwards, indicating that a market or fair could have been held on their extensive holdings on this margin of the town. We have no evidence for the fair's origin but it could have been held in the *Butwerk* area long before the foundation of the suburb, perhaps being pushed further and further east with the advance of settlement, in the manner glimpsed in *Domesday Book*. Certainly, the place-name suggests that this area was originally a fair or market ground, and such an interpretation might explain the use of the term 'vasta' for the land on which Colsuein's new estate in *Domesday Book* was built.

By the mid 15th century the name *Beggarsholme* was applied to closes situated to the east of the built-up area, beyond Rosemary Lane and Stamp End. *St Hugh's Croft*, is documented as the site of a fair since 1409, which later specialised in cattle, and it may be that this was the direct descendant of these early markets. *St Hugh's Croft* lay to the east of St Peter *ad fontem* churchyard and west of *Baggerholme Close* (Hill 1948, 270). *Baggerholme Leas* and *Baggerholme Wong* lay to the south between the *Baggerholme Close* and the river, indicating that when not used for trading this area was probably under the plough (Cameron 1985, 49). Since St Augustine's church (now thought to be located nearer the western end of *Butwerk* – Fig. 9.66) is also sometimes said to be *in Baggerholme*, the name clearly came to apply to a wider area, perhaps even the entire area of the *Butwerk* suburb south of *Bagerholmegate*.

By the 12th century there was also extensive occupation north of *Bagerholmegate* as well as south of it. Indeed, apart from a necessary break due to the steep nature of the cliff, it is clear that suburban settlement was continuous between the *Butwerk* suburb and the Eastgate suburb. The two suburbs were linked by *Holgate*/Greestone Stairs/*Boune Lane*, by Pottergate, and originally by *St Peter's Lane* also (p. 224 above). *St Peter's Lane* is probably the public highway which the Blackfriars were given permission to close in 1292 (ed. Page 1906, 220). With the expansion of the Close in Eastgate and the Blackfriars precinct in *Butwerk*, then, this last route was impassable by the end of the 13th century, but it may have been re-established further east, to run north–south just inside the suburb boundary. Certainly a north–south route in this location was confirmed in the 1455 agreement between the Council and the Black Monks (Lincolnshire Archives Office, Lincoln City Charters 6/54; Hill 1948, 341). Pottergate was undoubtedly the most important of these roads up the hill, however, as it took a gentler, diagonal route up the slope – suitable for wheeled vehicles – whereas the other lanes, may have been suitable for foot transport or packhorse only.

On its western side, the suburb *Butwerk* was clearly distinguished from the Lower City by the defences. It is possible, however, that the ditch was less of a barrier than might be imagined. Encroachment onto the ditch apparently took place on either side of *Bagerholmegate* outside Clasketgate Gate, and Hill suggests that documentary sources continued to use the name *Werkdyke* after it had been filled in and a roadway constructed over its site (1948, 33). Cameron noted a series of references to a street running outside or next to the King's ditch, however, starting with one of the late 12th century and extending into the 14th (1985, 54). The name of the street that now occupies the line of the city ditch, Broadgate, does not appear until the late 16th century (*Ibid.*). It is likely, then, that although there were earlier encroachments, the city ditch survived as an earthwork throughout its length from the College of Vicars-Choral, southwards to the Witham into the Early Modern Era. Certainly the impression gained from the Broadgate East site (BE 72) was that the *Lumnor Lane* frontage was the more important than that towards Broadgate throughout the medieval period, and leases for properties fronting onto Broadgate only start in the late 16th century.

The *Butwerk* suburb seems to have reached its maximum extent by the mid 12th century and, indeed, may even have failed to fill its original allotted space, since there was pasture land within the boundary of the suburb, to the west of Stamp End, in the 13th century. Even so, the Broadgate East excavations (BE 73) demonstrated intensive occupation throughout the 12th and 13th centuries. Like the Eastgate suburb, then, the western part of the suburb, closest to the city, saw more activity than parts further east. Documentary sources indicate the existence of several streets and lanes in *Butwerk* between the 12th and 14th centuries. South of *Bagerholmegate* these streets formed a rough grid. The road which today survives as Winn Street and Croft Street originally ran at least as far east as Monks Abbey, where it formed the southern boundary to the monastic precinct, and as far west as Rosemary Lane, where it formed the northern boundary to St Augustine's churchyard (Johnson 1992). Further south, it is unclear whether the modern St Rumbold Street is of medieval or later date but it is clear from *The Hundred Rolls* that there was a public highway running along the riverfront (Cameron 1985, 114). Much of the area between St Rumbold Street and the Witham is undoubtedly reclaimed land (the Roman 'Quay' found on the Telephone Exchange site lay immediately to the south of St Rumbold Street – p. 98–9 above). Unfortunately we have no archaeological information from *Butwerk* to document this reclamation. Only two north–south streets are documented in the medieval period. These survive today as Friars Lane (called *Lumnour Lane* at one stage in the medieval period) and Rosemary Lane (called *Lyme Lane* and, probably, *Spout Lane*). *Holgate* may originally have crossed Monks Road to run down to the Witham but in its latest phase there is a clear disjunction between *Holgate* on the north side of *Bagerholmegate* and *Lumnour Lane*. *Lyme Lane* seems never to have extended north of *Bagerholmegate* but did run south to the Witham. Further east, Sparrow Lane might have continued further north than its modern junction with Croft Street, to run along the eastern side of St Peter *ad fontem* churchyard, but there is no evidence that it ever ran further north than *Bagerholmegate*. In any event it could not have done so after the establishment of the Blackfriars precinct in the 13th century.

It is likely that, as well as being the southern limit of the suburban boundary ditch, The Stamp End would also have been the south-eastern limit of the suburb. The southern limit of the suburb seems to have been the Witham throughout, or at least this is the implication drawn above from the location of the tower in the yard of the Green Dragon Inn (p. 186 above). During the discussion of this tower we noted the presence of a road along the riverbank in the late medieval period, and this road is, presumably, the ancestor of Waterside North. If the riverbank was indeed moved south in the period between the 10th and the 14th centuries, then this road will have been built on newly reclaimed land. Its precise date might be provided by the construction of the new gate to the south of the Green Dragon Inn tower. We have no absolute date for this gate, but the tower, with which it may have been contemporary, was probably of early 14th-century date, like its companion the Lucy Tower on the Brayford. If the road on the line of Waterside North was a new construction of the 14th century, previously access to the *Butwerk* river front river and to the Stamp End causeway would have been by way of lanes leading south from St Rumbold's Lane. By c.1300, however, a line of warehouses faced the river on the north side of the road. These were the wool-houses in which the clip belonging to the Lincoln wool-merchants was sorted, packed and stored prior to sale at the Staple Place just inside the gate near the tower in Green Dragon Yard (Bischoff 1975, 200).

The present course of the Witham east of Stamp End is much further south than its medieval predecessor. An extensive watching brief carried out to the east of Stamp End, at Spa Road Old Power Station site (PS 94) revealed plentiful evidence for the course of the river but no signs of human activity nor any other means of dating the riverine deposits. To the north of Stamp End, the eastward expansion of the *Butwerk* suburb, was perhaps curtailed by the monks of St Mary of York, who acquired all the land to the east of it at the end of the 11th century. The Black Monks' estate had been given to them by Rumfar and was held by burgage tenure (Hill 1948, 59, 338–41). Their estate included the entire south-east corner of the city, north of the Witham and south of the cliff and was the third largest religious holding in Lincoln in the 1291 *taxatio* (Hill 1948, 152). The estate was run from a cell, dedicated to St Mary Magdalene, now known as Monks Abbey. Extensive trial excavations on the site (MA 83) produced no evidence for activity earlier than the earliest architectural fragments from the site (of the mid 12th century), whilst the standing church structure dates from the early 13th century, with substantial later medieval alterations (Stocker 1984a). The monks seem to have used this land mainly for agriculture (principally pasture) rather than urban development. A single reference, however, to a feature known as the *Blackdyke* (which Hill interprets, convincingly, as a dock, and which it is recorded in the late 14th century – 1948, 341–2, 360) shows us that the citizens used, of ancient custom, to come into this southern part of the Monks' estate to load and unload their boats, just below

The Stamp causeway. This facility, used by the citizens but perhaps partly on the monks' land was critical for the whole economic life of the city and was a source of constant friction between the Council and the monks and will be considered further below (p. 241–2 below).

Two further important ecclesiastical foundations were made in *Butwerk* in the 13th century. The Dominican Friars (Blackfriars) were established on the north side of *Bagerholmegate* in 1238. Its original, mid 13th-century, precinct was probably in the south-west corner of the later precinct, adjoining *Holgate*. Eventually the friary precinct extended from west to east along the whole frontage of *Bagerholmegate* from *Holgate* to the suburb boundary, the south-east corner being at a point close to the junction of modern Arboretum Avenue with Monks Road. The friary also expanded up the hillside. It gained permission to enclose a piece of land in 1284–5 and, as we have seen, a lane in the parish of Holy Trinity Greestone Stairs in 1291–2.

A second convent was founded in the south-east corner of *Butwerk* by the Friars of the Sack (Hill 1948, 151). The Sack Friars had established an oratory here before 1266, when the Council sold them a plot of pasture land west of Stamp Causeway and south of St Hugh's Croft, to extend their holding. The Friars had ceased to occupy the house by 1307, their order having been abolished, and the city had then to decide between competing requests for the site. The Abbot of Barlings, for example, wished to set up warehouses on the site for holding tanned hides, wool, corn and other products prior to selling them. Although the abbot was refused, a meeting of the abbots of the Premonstratensian Order took place in the church in 1310. After 1313 the site seems to have been in lay hands (the de Kyme family) until the foundation in 1358 of a chantry dedicated to St Peter (*Ibid.*). This oratory gave rise to the name *Bedern Lane* (in St Augustine's parish and therefore perhaps an early name for Croft Street) by the late 14th century (Cameron 1985, 51). In the early 19th century, Edward Willson was told that a church had stood until recently, to the east of Sparrow Lane with a gable end comparable to that of the Greyfriary (London, Society of Antiquaries Ms. 786/5, 101). This is likely to have been either the Sack Friars church or the parish church of St Clement-in-*Butwerk*.

Six parish churches served the *Butwerk* suburb (Fig. 9.66) (Johnson 1992, 1–4). Burials and the remains of a church recently found on the site of the Sessions House car park (SES 97; SESA 97) probably represent St Rumbold's church, whilst a location for St Bavon's church to the east of modern Unity Square would fit the description given in a document of 1180–90 – which places St Bavon's church to the south of St Rumbold (ed. Major 1973, RA2899, 232–3). Later documentation shows that St Bavon stood to the north of St Augustine. St Augustine's church, therefore, is probably to be located where burials were located in the early 1990s, on the north-east side of the junction of St Rumbold Street and *Lumnour Lane*.

The traditional location of Holy Trinity church is at the foot of Greestone Stairs, near the junction of *Holgate* and Pottergate. It probably lay north-east of St Rumbold, under the modern Art College or in the eastern part of Temple Gardens, but no direct archaeological evidence for the church or churchyard has been found, despite excavations on both sides of Greestone Stairs. Unlike other *Butwerk* parish churches, the boundary of its parish is known, since it was amalgamated with St Peter Eastgate rather than St Swithin and is therefore plotted on Padley's 1842 map of Lincoln. The entire parish was located on the steeply-sloping hillside and this may be good reason to suppose that the church, and associated settlement, would be later here than on the flatter ground to the north, around St Margaret Pottergate, or to the south. It may be that (as we have suggested may also have been the case with St Rumbold's) Holy Trinity Clasketgate church, was only created once the potting industry which had occupied much of the parish had ceased (i.e. sometime in, or after, the mid 11th century).

Hill thought that, because two of the *Butwerk* churches (Sts Rumbold and Bavon) were apparently dedicated to Flemish saints, and because of the evidence for a fair or market and the location of the suburb downstream of the High Bridge, this suburb may have supported a trading community in the 11th century. A further possible indication of Flemish settlers in 11th-century Lincoln comes from the personal name *Druelin*, recorded in *Drulinlide*, the name of a gate (perhaps the postern gate on Saltergate?) in the parish of St Edmund (Hill 1948, 361). However, David Stocker suggests here (RAZ 9.60.9) that the Rumbold dedication could be to the Mercian boy-saint, whose cult could have been current within a ruling class in Lincoln in the later 10th and 11th centuries. He points to the presence of several other city dedications, such as that to St Swithin, which might have been appropriate when the West Saxons were in ascendancy in Lincoln, i.e. between *c*.950 and *c*.1014.

In summary, then, it seems that the *Butwerk* suburb began in the early 10th century as an industrial area on the edge of *Werkdyke*, north and south of *Bagerholmegate* (modern Monks Road), and contained an important pottery industry. We have made the case here, also, that there was probably a fairground or market to the east of the industrial activity – which may have been of greater antiquity. During the later 10th and 11th centuries, the suburb developed into a commercial and residential area, with the fairground being pushed eastwards by settlement. The new suburb had planned components (such as that established by Colsuein between 1066 and 1086) and came to be centred around both *Bagerholmegate* and north–south streets, known by various names in the medieval period (*Holgate, Lumnour Lane, Lyme Lane*). At its maximum period of expansion, probably around *c*.1100 or a little later, it was served by as many as six parish churches. It was bounded on the east not just by a physical barrier but by the land-holdings of St Mary's Abbey York, who also eventually acquired much of the land within the eastern parts of the suburb also. These large-scale acquisitions imply that the eastern parts of the suburb (including Colsuein's new foundation) were not successful settlements over the long-term and they may have been occupied only for a short period in the late 11th and 12th century.

## The suburb of Thorngate

Despite its location south of the Witham, the small suburb of *Thorngate* was clearly more closely connected with the Lower City than with the Wigford suburb to its west (Fig. 9.67). Known as *Thorngate* by the 13th century, it seems likely that the suburb lay on an island originally called *Thorn*, suggesting an unoccupied eyot covered in scrub (the name *Thorney* is common in the Anglo-Saxon period, being, for example, the original name of the riparian island site of Westminster Abbey). Foster thought it likely to have been land reclaimed from the Witham (1931, 277–8). There may, for example, have been a gravel eyot in the Witham from which reclamation could have started. Furthermore, the description of the southern boundary in some instances as the *Oldeye*, 'the old river', strongly implies that the suburb lay on an island between two channels of a braided Witham.

Almost all that is known of this suburb is summarised by Canon Foster, who used John Ross' unreliable manuscript history, *Annales Lincolnienses*, for much of his information (1931, 277–82). Documentary sources for the suburb are almost entirely later 12th- or 13th-century in date, except for single a reference to a mid 12th-century castle of Thorngate (p. 186 above). In the mid 12th century, the suburb might have been adapted to form a private castle which, after the Anarchy, was acquired by the Cathedral and developed as a commercial suburb. Hill, however, considered that *Thorngate Castle* might have become *Kyme Hall*, which lay north of the Witham (Hill 1948, 159–60) and there was certainly a possibility of confusion between the suburb of *Thorngate*, to the south of the Witham, and the road *Thornbridgegate*, which ran along the north bank of the river from the Thorn Bridge eastwards towards Stamp End. (Hill 1948, 158).

The suburb was approached either by water or over *Thorn Bridge*, apparently the principal access route. The original location of *Thorn Bridge* has been the subject of much confusion. The modern Thorn Bridge, at the south end of Magpie Square, seems to have been constructed at the same time as Melville Street in 1847. Foster places the medieval *Thorn Bridge* at the south end of the present-day Thorngate and notes that it survived long enough to be included on Speed's map of Lincoln in 1610 (Fig. 9.91), whilst Sympson recorded that the bridge in this location had a datestone of 1602 (ed. Foster 1931, 280). A single street, *Thorngate*, is indicated in the 13th-century docu-

mentary sources, running along the line of the modern south bank of the Witham, eastwards from the bridge-head, with properties running north–south to the *Oldeye* or to the marsh – a line now marked approximately by the north bank of Sincil Dyke (Hill 1948, 158). According to Foster, the suburb was bounded on its west side by 'Wigford Causeway', which he says was a structure which ran north–south on the line followed by the modern Sincil Street. It is, however, hard to envisage a north–south causeway on this (still very low-lying) alignment and it seems much more likely that 'Wigford Causeway' refers instead to the causeway along which Wigford High Street itself ran. The occupied area of the suburb seems not to have extended as far east as Stamp End, and the character of the the eastern part of the presumed island is quite unknown.

No church is known to have existed in the suburb but a single burial was recorded in 1977 on the site of Doughty's Mill, to the east of Melville Street, and perhaps approaching the eastern edge of medieval settlement (ON 82). A single sherd of medieval pottery was associated with the burial, which was prone and isolated. Notwithstanding this discovery, references to a supposed church dedicated to St Denys appear to be a post-medieval historical confusion and in the 13th century the area lay in the parish of St Swithin, as is shown by charters in the Bardney Abbey cartulary (ed. Foster 1931, 281).

## Stamp End and the Port

By the time of the first relevant documents, in the 12th century, Lincoln was connected by water to the Trent, via the Fossdyke, and to the North Sea at the Wash via the Witham through Boston, whilst at the city's centre lay the Brayford Pool, where these water-courses met (Fig. 9.67). Understanding the dates and character of these various waterways is fundamental to our understanding of the start of the early Anglo-Scandinavian town and of the development of its later medieval successors. The results of excavations on the quaysides of Lincoln over the last thirty years has led to the realisation, whilst conducting this *Assessment*, that a central role was played throughout Lincoln's history by the previously disregarded structures in the river at Stamp End. It is now clear that there had been a barrier of some type across the river here since the Prehistoric Era (p. 22–4 and p. 100 above – also Stocker and Everson 2003) and that, from time to time in the Roman and medieval periods, river levels upstream may have been controlled at this point, by means of a dam, or dams, and weirs across the river. Sir Francis Hill suggested that the topographical feature called *The Stamp* in late medieval documents got its name from a boundary stone (1948, 41), but Ken Cameron showed us that it really derives from a word for a weir or dam (1985, 102 – although, unfortunately, the place-name is not recorded until the mid 15th century). Some references

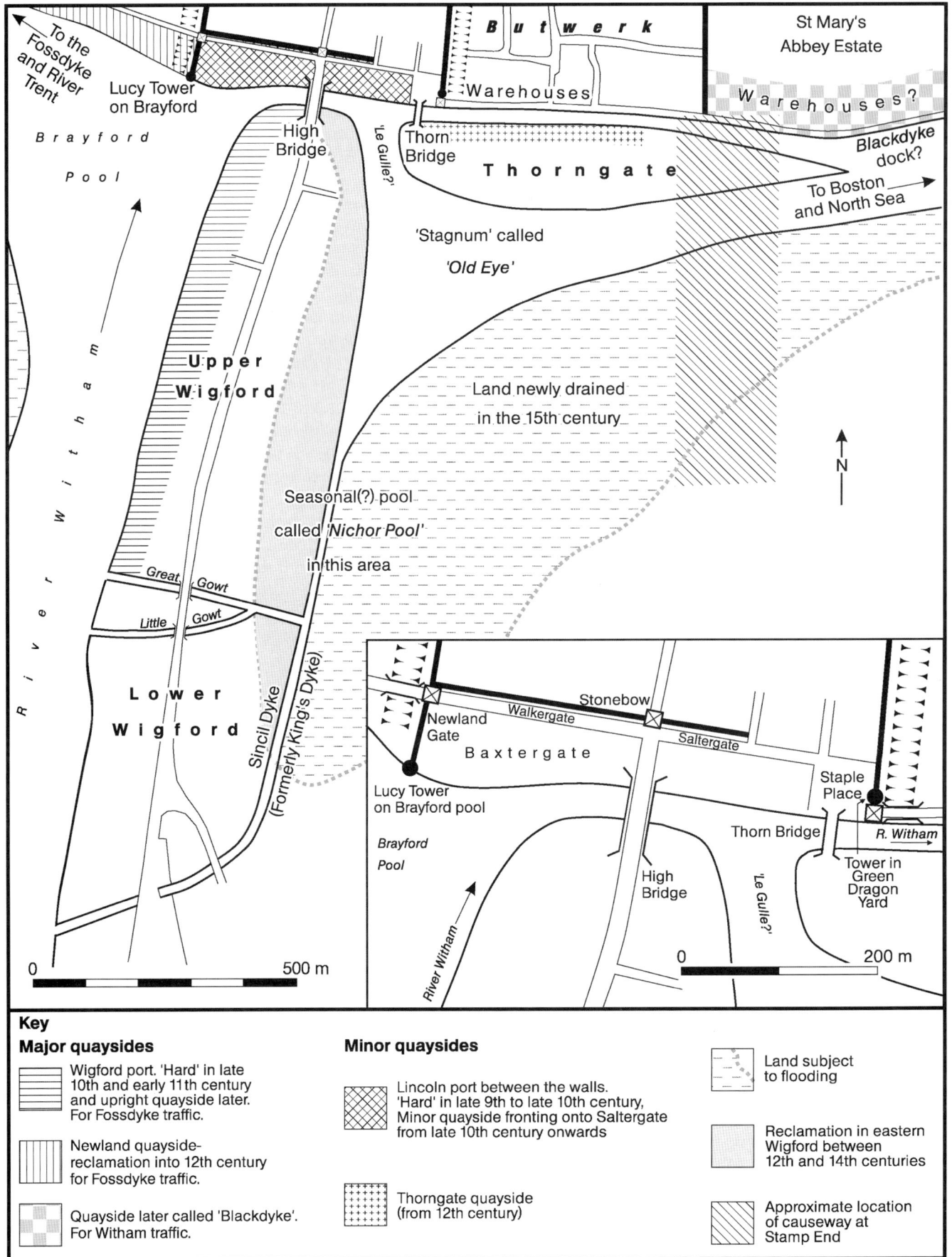

## Key

### Major quaysides

Wigford port. 'Hard' in late 10th and early 11th century and upright quayside later. For Fossdyke traffic.

Newland quayside-reclamation into 12th century for Fossdyke traffic.

Quayside later called 'Blackdyke'. For Witham traffic.

### Minor quaysides

Lincoln port between the walls. 'Hard' in late 9th to late 10th century, Minor quayside fronting onto Saltergate from late 10th century onwards

Thorngate quayside (from 12th century)

Land subject to flooding

Reclamation in eastern Wigford between 12th and 14th centuries

Approximate location of causeway at Stamp End

*Fig. 9.67. Reconstruction study of waterway and quayside layout forming the port area in the medieval period. The map is based on a combination of archaeological and documentary evidence and supposition (drawn by Dave Watt, copyright English Heritage).*

call this feature a causeway (*Ibid.*), suggesting that, in the late medieval period, it was sufficiently substantial to carry a route way across the valley from north to south. The dam is still visible as a great earthwork bank on 18th-century views of the city from the south-east, and may be marked by a dyke along one side on Padley's map of 1819. In the 15th century, the Friars of the Sack were credited with actually building the causeway (Lincolnshire Archives Office, Lincoln City Charters 6/54), but archaeological understanding of the development of the quaysides upstream allows us to propose that some form of dam and, perhaps, a causeway across the river at Stamp End was an ancient component of the Lincoln townscape and that it had been reconstructed many times before.

Part of the evidence confirming that there was a dam and/or weirs at Stamp End controlling the level of water upstream from the 10th century onwards comes from the results of excavations up-river, along the watersides of medieval Lincoln. Excavations have taken place in several parts of the port area: at Brayford

North to the west of the Lower City (BN 89); Lucy Tower Street and Brayford Wharf North on the western side of Stonebow (LT 72, BWN 75); the Waterside development to the east of Stonebow (WO 89, WNW 88, WN 87, WW 89) and a single observation to the south of St Rumbold Street (ON 116). Results from these sites make it clear that the late Roman waterfront consisted of a gently sloping foreshore extending at least 50 metres south of the south wall of the city (Fig. 9.68). Close to the wall, and to Ermine Street, this foreshore was metalled, and a Theodosian coin was recovered from below this metalling (WO 89). Lying above this metalling was a thin deposit composed of re-deposited river silt together with refuse, held in place by a series of shallow wicker hurdles. These hurdles are not thought to represent successive water-fronts, it is more likely that they were simply a lattice placed on the foreshore to stop dumped material from being eroded. In other words they seem to indicate that, after the Roman period, the foreshore consisted first of a gently sloping river bed, which is believed to

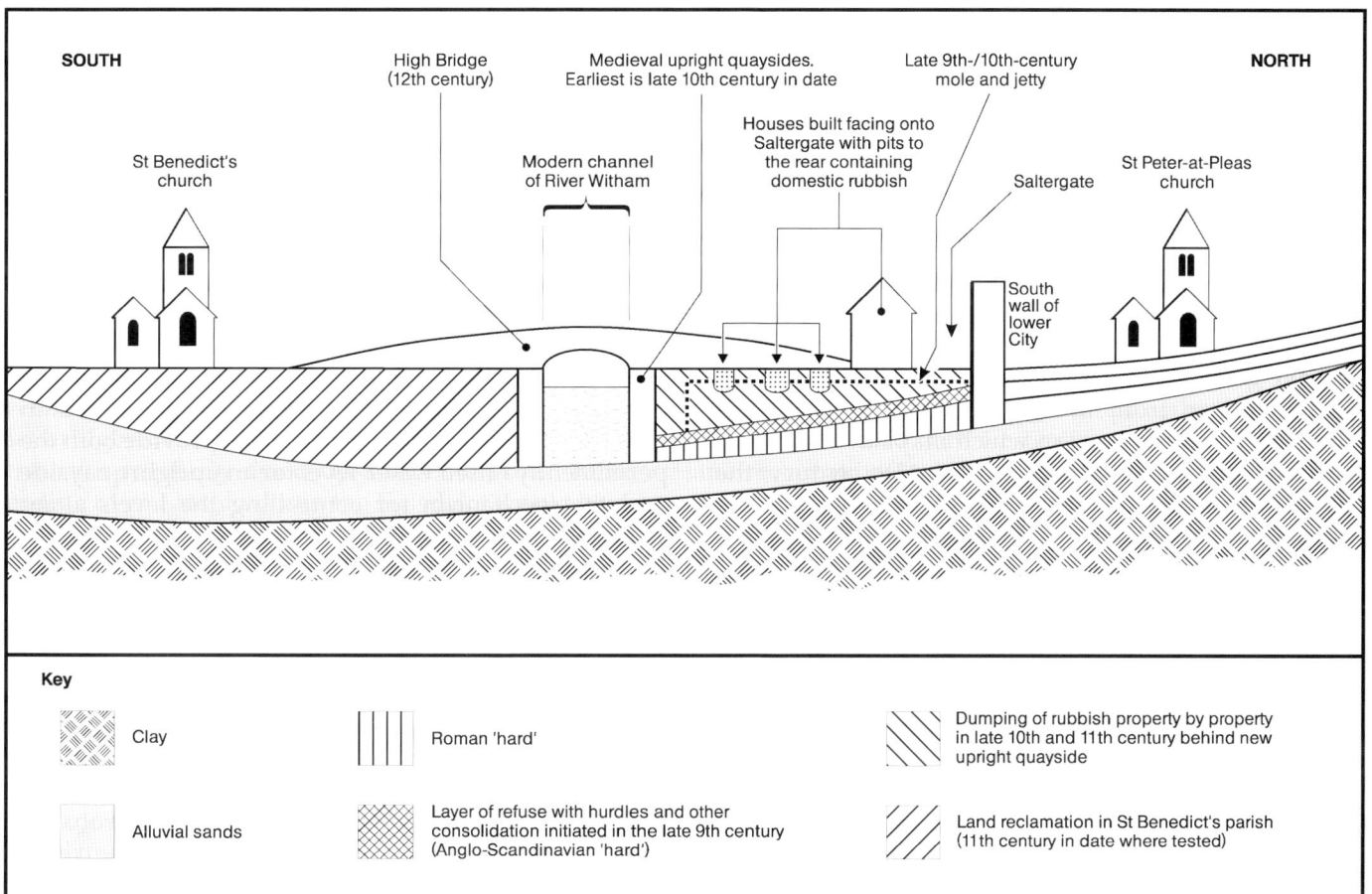

*Fig. 9.68. Greatly simplified sketch section (north to south) through the port area (from St Peter-at-Pleas' to St Benedict's parishes), demonstrating our current understanding of the development of the 'hards' and quaysides between the city's east and west walls. The horizontal scale is somewhat contracted, the vertical scale is greatly exaggerated (sources, Drury 1878 (Fig. 6.13) and unpublished excavations along Waterside North – drawn by Dave Watt, copyright English Heritage).*

provide space for it, as seems to be the implication of the Lucy Tower Street excavation. Elsewhere, industrial activity of some kind was taking place at the waterside end of properties running back to the Pool from Newland, to the west of the city wall (BN 89). Documentary sources suggest that dyers may have been concentrated in this area, at least until the collapse of the Lincoln cloth industry (p. 287–91 below).

To the east of Lucy Tower a stone riverside wall has been discovered (LT 72, BWN 75 – visible in Fig. 9.26), which could have acted as a wharf. The history of the *Baxtergate* area, which lies immediately behind these waterfront structures, and between them and the city wall, may be an example of a place-name which changes its meaning in the course of the medieval period. Several documents refer to land in *Baxtergate* in the parish of St Peter-at-Arches as being in the suburb of Lincoln. Where these properties can be located they are all to the south of the Roman wall, on land reclaimed from the Witham from the late 9th century. In some of these documents the land is said to be in *Baxtergate* – the street of the bakers. Once plotted, it seems that *Baxtergate* could refer to land immediately south of the Roman wall. Hill (and, subsequently, all other writers) took *Baxtergate* to be the medieval street-name of what is now Guildhall Street. But the documents show the name could also refer to land south of *St Mary's Stigh* (now Much Lane) and even land to the east of High Street (Fig. 9.58 and 9.67). Street-names in this period, of course, were mobile (and we do indeed have evidence for several changes of street name in medieval Lincoln). Elsewhere in the walled city there is some evidence for the use of such street names being applied to districts (e.g. *Hungate* is used both for a street and a district and zones of the Bail are sometimes called both *East Bight* and *West Bight*). One consequence of this is that there were in the medieval period two Hungate streets, later distinguished as *Aldhungate* and *Hungate*; whilst there are no clear-cut cases of documents from the Bail using the terms *East Bight* or *West Bight* unambiguously as street names. It is not unreasonable to suggest then, that, having started as the name for a street, *Baxtergate* became associated with an area corresponding to the suburb south of the wall, and north of the Witham, which was, or had become, the main location for bakers in the city. Indeed we might speculate that the transfer of the name from a street to an area may have occurred precisely because the waterfront was being reclaimed and new lanes, with new names, were being constructed.

The evidence for the sequence of waterfronts on the north side of the river can be instructively compared with the evidence from the south of the river. A structure at Dickinson's Mill (DM 72) is similar in many respects to the late 9th- and early 10th-century 'hard' seen on Waterside North (above). It consisted of a linear spread of limestone rubble laid on the sloping foreshore of the Pool. Although it is best interpreted as a stone-founded 'hard', however, we must acknowledge that

it could also have been the equivalent of the paved lane and jetty structure which extended into the water at Waterside North. Part of the reason for preferring to think that the Dickinson's Mill surface represents a 'hard' rather than a trackway is that it too was eventually reclaimed, although the process seems somewhat later in date than the very similar works further north, but still on the south side of the river (SB 85). There is no hint that the stone structure at Dickinson's Mill is Roman in origin, however. It appears to belong to the later 10th century and this might suggest that, whilst the principal hards in late 9th and early 10th century Lincoln were the re-used Roman ones along Waterside North, by the later 10th century they were starting to become established along the western Wigford shoreline. A similar conclusion and date has been reached using entirely different arguments based on the distribution pattern of 10th-century sculpture (Stocker 2000).

The apparent time-lag in establishing 'hards' on the south side of the river, compared with the north side, is interesting, and may suggest that there was more intensive use of the Wigford foreshore at precisely the same time that Waterside North was falling out of use as the city's major landing place. As on Waterside North (WO 89), wattle structures found at Brayford Wharf East (BWE 82) and at St Benedict's Square (SB 85) are probably associated with subsequent reclamation or stabilisation of the waterfront represented by the 'hard' at Dickinson's Mill. Furthermore, this reclamation might also be associated with the provision of substantial upright quaysides. A short stretch of vertical quayside was discovered, apparently replacing the 'hards' of the 10th and 11th centuries. Like the quayside at Waterside North it was also constructed from the side of a boat. It must be said, however, that these waterside structures on the Wigford shoreline have also been associated with fish farming, even though there is no direct evidence for the activity (Steane *et al.* 2001, 168). If this were a correct understanding, then interpretation of the Wigford side of the Brayford as a port will have to be re-considered; fish weirs are incompatible with active 'hards'. Unfortunately these excavations at the northern end of Wigford's western shoreline may be too far north to give a representative view of the development of the waterfront. Stocker's paper suggests that the focus of the port in the second half of the 10th century was further south, in the parishes of St Mark and St Mary-le-Wigford. Some slight evidence for a similar pattern of reclamation of land further south in Wigford, which saw 'hards' replaced by measures aimed at raising of an upright quayside, was found in trial excavations at Firth Road (ON 362).

The alterations in type of riverside facilities in Wigford seem to replicate the changes made at Waterside North – at both sites there is a transition from a 'hard' to a quayside between the mid 10th and the 11th centuries. Like the changes at Waterside North, this transition in Wigford can be seen as further evidence for a controlled rise in the water level in the Witham and the control of flood waters resulting from tidal variations in the Wash, down-river, achieved by the (re-)construction of the dam at Stamp End. Indeed the proposed (re-)construction of the dam, raising the levels of water in the upper Witham in the 10th century, may have been the key factor in the development of the Wigford shoreline. The reconstructed dam would, presumably, have allowed a sufficiently high level of water and sufficiently close control, to facilitate the construction and use of the Fossdyke, to the west of Brayford Pool. It is unlikely to be co-incidental that it is only once the water-levels had been raised that Lincoln starts to receive large quantities pottery produced at Torksey (TORK). Although the first imports of Torksey ware arrived in Lincoln at the start of the Anglo-Scandinavian period, it suddenly becomes the dominant pottery type in the late 10th or the start of the 11th century (p. 191–6 above and 276–81 below), i.e. at exactly the same time that the water levels in the Brayford Pool were being raised and that we think the 'hards' along the Western Wigford shoreline were being laid out. With a sufficient head of water, created by the water control features at Stamp End, the canal through to Torksey, on the Trent could be opened and the pottery could be brought along it. Vertical quaysides soon followed, at both Wigford and Waterside North.

The earliest documentary sources report that the Fossdyke was opened for traffic after some un-reported blockage in 1121 (Hill 1948, 173) and they confirm that the Fossdyke was in use throughout the 12th and 13th centuries, although it seems to have fallen into disuse, temporarily or permanently, in the early 14th century (*Ibid.*, 311–2). The lack of good evidence from the excavated sites around Brayford Pool (e.g. BWN 75, LT 72 and BN 89) for the loading or unloading goods in these later medieval centuries is mainly due to the lack of appropriate excavated strata and dating evidence rather than to the absence of activity. Only the Dickinson's Mill excavation has examined the water-front on Brayford Pool between the 12th and 14th centuries, but little helpful information was recovered.

Although it would have opened up transport to the Trent along the Fossdyke, the (re-)construction of a dam and weir across the Witham at Stamp End in the 10th century would have made movements by water upriver from the lower Witham into the Bray-ford Pool more difficult. There is, however, no reason to think that it would have blocked this eastern trade route completely; a flash-lock would have allowed boats to journey from the Brayford Pool down river, whilst man-handling the ship around the weir (a 'portage' – commonplace on many of the long-ships' trade-routes in 10th- and 11th-century Europe) would have allowed boats from the lower Witham into the Brayford Pool (Westerdahl 2002). Even so, as time went on and ships became larger it would make more sense for boats to unload immediately below the

Stamp End causeway and for goods to be taken along the river-side road into the town by cart. Perhaps it was the value of this land around the north end of the Stamp End causeway as a wharf and dock which motivated St Mary's Abbey York to hold onto the facility here, although they usually rented it out to local traders. In 1276, for example the York monks leased their wharf in *Calfcroft* to Kirkstead Abbey (Bischoff 1975, 95).

More significantly, perhaps, a dock called *Blackdyke*, evidently also on the St Mary's Abbey estate, is first mentioned in the agreement between the Council and the Black Monks in 1455 (Lincolnshire Archives Office, Lincoln City Charters 6/54; Hill 1948, 341; Cameron 1985, 15). In the earlier agreement between these two parties, struck in 1377, the same dock is called *The Ryvall*. The landing place represented by these place-names is very likely to have been in use between the 12th and 14th centuries, because by the 15th century, all citizens had a customary right to use it – a right which probably reflects a long-established practice (Hill 1948, 341–2). It seems clear that, in the 12th and 13th centuries, the bulk of the city's wool was loaded downstream of The Stamp, presumably at the *Black-dyke* or an adjacent dock, to be taken to the markets at Boston, where it would be transhipped to the continent (Bischoff 1975, 258), although we should note that the quantities of wool shipped from Lincoln via Boston represent only a small fraction of the total quantity shipped from that port. In fact, not all of Lincoln's wool went to Boston; some was always shipped from the Humber ports, to which it was carried by the Fossdyke between the 12th and 14th centuries (Hill 1948, 14). These cargoes would have been loaded upstream of The Stamp, perhaps on the Wigford waterfront, at least until the Fossdyke became impassable in the mid 14th century. By then however, much of the citizen's wool was apparently going to Hull and Boston by road (Hill 1948, 311). In 1411, the citizens complained to the King that they could no longer send their pack-horses to these ports because Sir Walter Tailboys was attacking the caravans (Hill 1948, 274). The picture provided by the export of wool suggests that we can overestimate how many ships were loaded and unloaded at Stamp End, and it may be that activity at the *Blackdyke* was simply not intensive enough to pull the city decisively towards the east, and explain why *Butwerk* did not develop into the city's major commercial centre. Another implication may be that, after the 13th century, the quantity of traffic to the east of Lincoln was minimal compared with traffic by road north and south and by river to the west.

At last, then, we are starting to understand the developing use of the Lincoln port through the High Medieval Era. Early on, in the late 9th and for much of the 10th century, it seems that the former Roman hard to the south of the walled city was the principal, if not the only, landing place in the settlement. Towards the end of the 10th century, however, 'hards' were laid out on the western shoreline of Wigford, apparently to take advantage of the (newly-constructed?) Fossdyke. Both developments (the construction of the 'hards' upriver and the Fossdyke) may have depended on the (re-)construction of the Stamp End causeway in the second half of the 10th century. Consequently, between the 11th and 14th centuries, it seems increasingly likely that the Witham, from Brayford Head eastwards to Stamp End, was used only for small boats (dealing mainly with locally caught fish, perhaps?). During this period, for conducting longer distance trade, the city had two quite separate dock areas – on the western shoreline of Wigford, facing Fossdyke and the west, and below Stamp End, facing Boston and the east. It would have made much better sense to load and unload ships trading with Boston here, at *Blackdyke*, rather than man-handling boats around the Stamp End causeway – even though that would certainly have been possible. In fact much unloading and transhipment onto carts of commodities coming upriver from Boston may have taken place even further east of the city. There is a remarkable collection of finds from the junction of the Barlings Eau and the Witham at Short Ferry, in Fiskerton parish, which suggests that the site was acting as an out-port for Lincoln (White 1976). Important finds of pottery, both from Lincoln and elsewhere, have been made here and they probably indicate a landing point, from which goods were carried overland to the city. It is known that the City Council also set up a toll-booth on the Witham at Dogdyke, immediately down-river of the junction between the Witham, the Kyme Eau (serving Sleaford) and the Bain (serving Horncastle) (Hill 1948, 215–6).

### Wigford, the 'Great Suburb'

The suburb of Wigford was little more than a long street, with properties along both sides, extending southwards from the bridge for more than 1.5km (Fig. 9.69). It was eventually defined, along its southern and eastern sides by the Sincil Dyke and on the western and northern by the Witham. The suburb had a clear identity throughout the medieval period and is given as the attribute of all 12 churches that served its parishes. Significantly, perhaps, the name Wigford was never associated with the parish church of Holy Innocents, or the priory and hospital of St Katherine south of Sincil Dyke, which are instead usually located 'next to Lincoln' or 'outside the walls' (e.g. Cameron 1985, 124).

Although the southern part of the suburb was clearly defined from the 12th century onwards by Sincil Dyke, it is not clear that this was the case in the late 9th or early 10th century, when the first evidence for occupation in the suburb is to be found. At this early date we suspect that the northern part of the suburb (which we have called Upper Wigford) extended only as far south as the Great Gowt (p. 187 above). South of the Gowt (in Lower Wigford), settle-ment may have been absent. The first element of the place-name Wigford comes from – *wic* (Cameron 1985, 45–6), an element with several distinct meanings when used in place-names (Ekwall 1930; Gelling 1987). It can be a direct translation of the Latin *vicus*, when used of un-walled Roman-British settlements, but it can also have the meaning of 'dairy farm' and is therefore a common name form for villages in river valleys. It is probably used in this sense in six examples amongst the Lincolnshire entries in *Domesday Book*: Anwick, Butterwick, Canwick, Casewick, Hardwick and Scopwick. However, – *wic* also had a specialised meaning, applying to trading and industrial settlements, as at Ipswich, *Harwich* (near Southampton) and Droitwich. This specialised usage was most common between the 7th and 9th centuries, although some of the salt extraction settlements in Cheshire and the West Midlands (like Nantwich) which incorporate this element may be of later date. The -*wic* element is indicative that in the original place-name, the term was used in the plural and Dornier (1987) has pointed out that the trading/industrial meaning is always, where it can be checked, a dative plural, i.e. it means something like 'at the *wics*'. The element -*wic* was also in use on the continent (e.g. Schleswig, Brunswick) and, in the case of Schleswig, may not predate the foundation of the town in the mid 11th century. In the English Danelaw, Old Norse influence on the language hardened the element to -*wik* or -*vik*, thus we get *Yorvik* (for Anglo-Scandinavian York) when the original Anglo-Saxon element was *Eorforwic*. In the case of Wigford, the first element is often spelt *wik-* or *wyk-*. Consequently the name Wigford shows strong Anglo-Scandinavian influence and it could well indicate a trading/industrial settlement, but it is not clear whether it is a novel coinage in the Anglo-Scandi-navian period, or a conversion of a pre-existing term.

Better evidence for the date of foundation of the suburb is provided by finds of pottery, which clearly indicate that the central and northern parts of Wigford (Upper Wigford) may have been occupied in the late 9th or early 10th century. Very few finds of earlier Anglo-Saxon pottery have been made (Fig. 8.5) and this may suggest little or no activity here in the pre-Viking period. Furthermore, the earliest pottery types found in quantity in Wigford (belonging to ceramic horizon ASH8) (Figs. 9.36 and 9.70) date from the very end of the 9th century, even though the earliest post-Roman stratification yet discovered on Wigford sites dates to the early to mid 10th century (ASH9). Early ware type LSLS, of the late 9th or early 10th century, was discovered on all but three sites in Wigford. These were Dickinson's Mill (DM 72) and Waterside South (WS 82), which in the late 9th and early 10th century were within the Brayford Pool and the river Witham, and the site at Monson Street (M 82), where only a small quantity of post-Roman pottery was collected in total.

Later Anglo-Scandinavian pottery from sites in

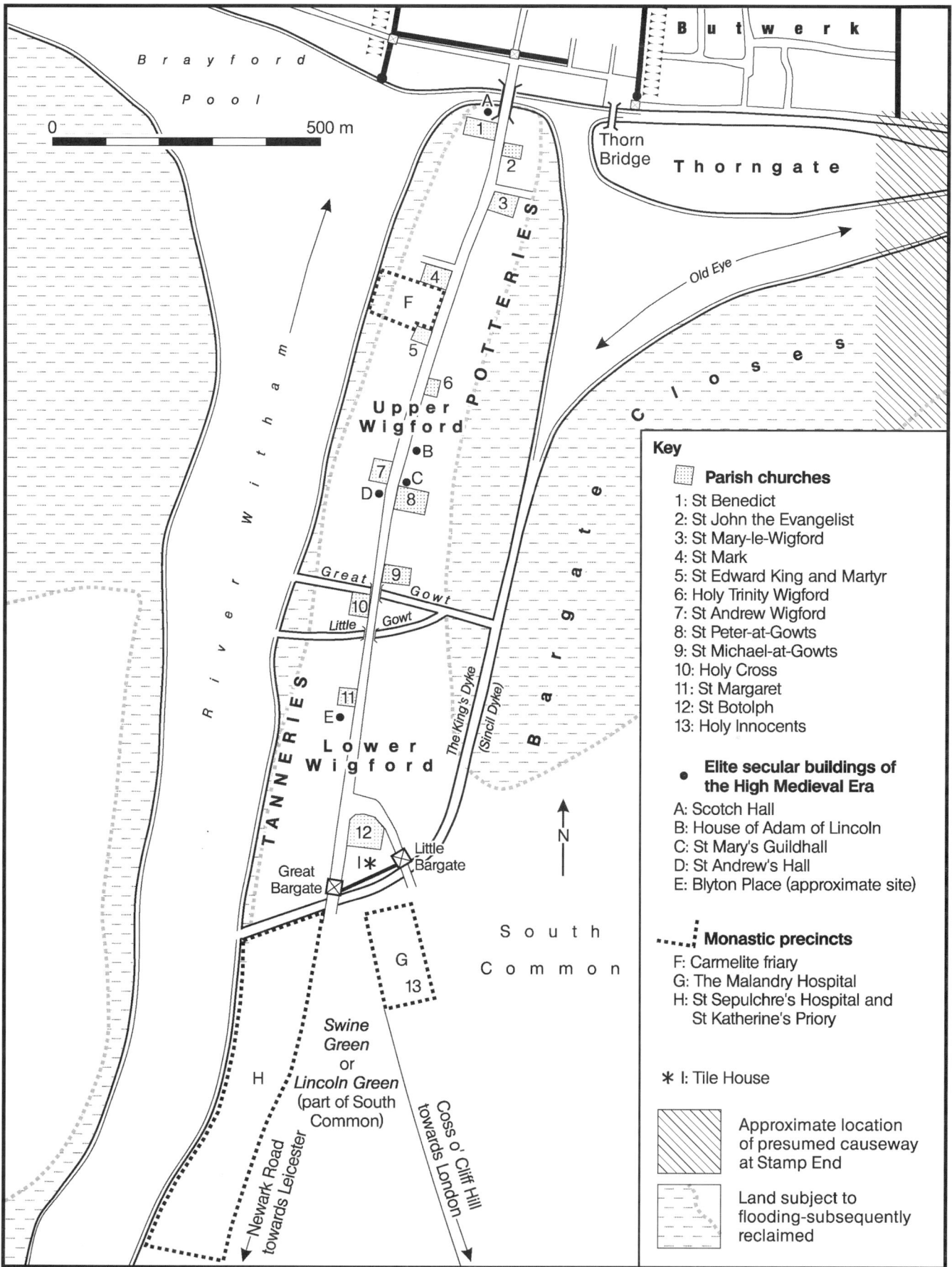

*Fig. 9.69. Reconstruction study of Wigford suburb in the High Medieval Era (drawn by Dave Watt, copyright English Heritage).*

| Site Code | ELSW | ESG | EST | LG | LKT | LSCRUC | LSH | LSLOC | LSLS | LSX | NOTS |
|-----------|------|-----|-----|----|----|--------|-----|-------|------|-----|------|
| BWE 82 | | | 1 | | 159 | | 46 | 5 | 1 | | |
| DM 72 | | | 5 | | 107 | | 27 | 2 | | | 9 |
| HG 72 | 2 | 1 | 10 | 1 | 1130 | | 106 | 15 | 12 | | 14 |
| M 82 | | | | | 7 | | | 1 | | | |
| SB 85 | 1 | | 1 | | 637 | 1 | 586 | | 1 | | |
| SM 76 | 3 | | 17 | | 103 | | 48 | 26 | 16 | | 1 |
| SMG 82 | | | 7 | | 271 | | 77 | 9 | 7 | 1 | |
| WS 82 | | | | | 12 | | 2 | | | | |
| Z 86 | 1 | | 4 | | 501 | | 73 | 4 | 6 | 1 | |
| ZE 87 | | | 3 | | 187 | | 21 | 1 | 7 | | |

*Fig. 9.70. Total numbers of sherds of various ceramic fabrics found at various sites in the Wigford suburb (source, Vince and Young forthcoming).*

Wigford is mainly found in similar quantities to earlier types, so we can conclude that occupation was more or less continuous following the suburb's foundation. However, the exceptions to this pattern are significant. At St Benedict's Square (SB 85), at the northern end of the suburb, seven times as many sherds of 11th- or 12th-century date were recovered, as sherds of the 9th or 10th centuries, whilst at Holmes Grain Warehouse (HG 72) a little further south, the equivalent ratio is two to one. It seems clear that, in the northern part of the Wigford suburb, from St Peter-at-Gowts northwards, settlement developed in the 11th and 12th centuries on either side of the High Street. We have seen that the western waterside of Wigford shows a similar sequence of development to the waterside south of the walled city (p. 240–1 above). The somewhat later date of reclamation of land from the Brayford to the south-west of St Benedict's Square (SB 85), compared with sites further south in Wigford, suggests that the suburb may have been extended northwards at a relatively late stage in its development, from an earlier core established a century earlier in the general vicinity of St Mary-le-Wigford.

The 11th-century waterfront at Dickinson's Mill (DM 72) was c.120m from the High Street frontage and further south at Brayford Wharf East (BWE 82), by the same date, the waterfront already extended yet further to the west – to at least 140m from the High Street frontage. Further south again, dumps of 13th-century pottery waste and other material were found in trial excavations in Firth Road (ON 362), though it was not clear whether these were dumps on low-lying, but dry, ground or part of a reclamation behind a quayside. No archaeological observations have taken place to the south of this site, but it is clear that the width of 'reclaimed' land behind the western side of High Street reaches its maximum to either side of the Great Gowt ditch, at 311m. However, it may be that, this far south, the natural gravel terrace, on which the central and southern part of the suburb lies, extended further to the west of High Street.

It seems clear, then, that to the north of Great Gowt (in Upper Wigford) the suburb developed, from the early 10th century, as a single street probably lined with properties on both sides. Furthermore we strongly suspect that the Great Gowt ditch formed the southern boundary of Upper Wigford (p. 187 above). Unfortunately, as there has been remarkably little excavation south of the Great Gowt, this conclusion is based on a plan-form analysis of the early mapping of the suburb. As mapped by Padley and others, to the south of the Great Gowt the High Street gradually widened out, to form a long, funnel-shaped, triangular space in front of St Botolph's church known in the 19th century as *Botolph's Green* (Cameron 1985, 35 – Fig. 9.83a). Padley's 1819 map shows St Botolph's church sitting on the green, the eastern boundary of which clearly continues southwards on the south side of the church. South of Great Bargate the eastern boundary of this green is also continued by the west boundary of the Malandry leper hospital, whilst the western boundary is reflected in the line of Newark Road. Between the two boundaries the large triangular open space was known as *Spital Green* or *Swine Green* (Cameron 1985, 41); it may be the *Lincoln Green* of medieval legend and mentioned in *Havelock the Dane* (ed. Skeat 1868, 80, line 2828).

Since the widening road and green north of St Botolph's and the large space outside Sincil Dyke are clearly coterminous, Sincil Dyke, which cuts across the middle of the space from west to east, must be a later feature than the funnel-shaped space itself. The Dyke must have existed when Little Bargate was built, probably in the 12th century, and it must also have been established (or at least intended) by c.1100 when the Malandry (Holy Innocents) Hospital and St Sepulchre's Hospital were founded 'outside' the city (Hill 1948, 343–6). From all this we can conclude that the properties lining the High Street, from the Great Gowt southwards, and the huge funnel-shaped green were part of a new development, which was presumably somewhat later in date than the 10th century reclamation and settlement layout in Upper Wigford, but earlier in date than the construction of a formal southern boundary to the city at Sincil Dyke, which must have occurred before *c.*1100.

The original huge, funnel-shaped, green was very probably a market place (Fig. 9.83 below), and it was, it seems therefore, an 11th-century development. It represents the same type of expansion at the south end of the city as is represented by the (smaller) market layout at Newport along Ermine Street to the north. As with Newport, it is hard to say whether this market existed before the Norman Conquest, and political circumstances might suggest that a date after the Conquest is more likely than one before. However, as probably at *Butwerk* also, it is possible that the extension of the suburb south of the Great Gowt was preceded by the use of the area for informal trading and common pasture. Whether St Botolph's church was constructed in the centre of the green, like St John Newport, or whether the green was laid out around a pre-existing church remains unclear. The medieval church had a cruciform plan (ed. Cole 1911, 54), the only parish church in Lincoln to do so, and such plans are frequently indicative of churches of higher status.

The Sincil Dyke, cutting across the enormous green and linking the river Witham above and below Lincoln, can be seen both as part of the water management system in the valley bottom and as a defensive structure in its own right. Several deeds for property on the east side of the northern part of High Street Wigford, and in the Thorngate suburb, show that, whilst the southern part was a clearly defined ditch, the northern part of Sincil Dyke's route was marshy. At its northern end, south and south-west of the island of Thorngate, and in the parishes of St John and St Mary-le-Wigford, it seems that the area was so wet at times that it was called a lake. In 1409 this marsh was clearly coterminous with *Le Gulle* extending southwards from the Witham along the east side of the Wigford suburb (Hill 1948, 349). In the 15th century this expanse of open water sometimes also extended far to the south of the Thorngate island and, though also known as *Old Eye*, was apparently also called *Le Gulle*, as both watercourses are given as the north boundary of a meadow called New Meadow (*Ibid.* and n). To the south of this point, from the parish of St Mark southwards, however, the Dyke cut through the meadowland, eventually called the *Bargate Closes*. This meadow seems to have been periodically flooded, too, and a watching brief carried out on the site of the football stadium (CFC 94; Trimble 1994a) revealed a podsolised sandy soil, cut by several features of Roman date, and sealed by a thin deposit of silty alluvium. Another pool, known as *Nickerpool*, ('the pool of the water-sprite' – Cameron 1985, 31) was situated near the junction of the Great Gowt and Sincil Dyke, slightly to the north of the Football Stadium site.

On the eastern side of Upper Wigford, northwards and north-eastwards to the island of Thorngate, then,

was a large area prone to flooding and, at its core, there was a more-or-less permanent lake of open water, extending southwards from the Witham to the west of Thorngate island and perhaps extending as far south as Great Gowts, when the weather was wet (Figs. 9.67 and 69). It was through this area that the northern part of Sincil Dyke was to be cut in the Early Modern Era (Fig. 10.15), as part of works aimed primarily at draining the lake and marsh here. Unfortunately we have no precise date for the completion of this northern part of the dyke; it had not been undertaken in the mid 15th century but it had been completed by Speed's map of *c.*1600.

The proposed two-phase development of the suburb, put forward above, is reflected in a two-phase development of the Sincil Dyke, except that it is the later phase of the suburb (Lower Wigford) which acquired the boundary dyke first. In its initial phase (apparently in the 10th and early 11th centuries), we can suggest that the suburb of Upper Wigford was bounded on its south side by a dyke which became Great Gowt. Outside the dyke a market was established and the suburb extended southwards around it. By the end of the 11th century this extension to the suburb had become sufficiently well established that a second boundary ditch was cut across the neck of the peninsular. This second dyke, probably of late 11th-century date, is represented by the curving southern section of modern Sincil Dyke, which cuts across the great green of the earlier extramural market and links with the eastern end of the Great Gowt, defining a new southern boundary for the settlement. The final phase of dyke construction, then, which did not occur until the end of the medieval period, simply extended these two dykes northwards through the low-lying marsh and lake, towards the Witham at Stamp End.

Within its dykes, even at its maximum extent, Wigford is essentially a one-street suburb. Now that we have a clearer understanding of the layout of the waterways east of Upper Wigford, it is no longer surprising that there is no evidence for the existence of Waterside South (nor of any other route-way running along the southern bank of the Witham) until a very late date. The first occurrence of the name noted by Cameron was not until Padley's 1842 map (Cameron 1985, 44). There is, however, plentiful archaeological and documentary evidence for side lanes, giving access to the Witham and Brayford on the west side and to the Dyke (for example, *Brayford Street*, first recorded in the late 13th century – *Ibid.*, 54) and other areas of water on the east. Two of these side streets appear to have been of greater significance; they ran immediately south of the Great Gowt, to east and west. That in St Michael's parish, on the east side of the High Street, called *Watergang*, might have been a lane running north–south on the inside of Sincil Dyke, but it is more likely to have run along the south bank of Great Gowt towards a bridge over Sincil Dyke. In the post-medieval period a footpath ran from a small bridge over the dyke at this position across the *Bargate Closes* towards Canwick. A bridge also existed at the end of St Mary's Lane (first recorded in the 16th century – *Ibid.*, 95). To judge by the depiction of St Mary's Lane bridge on Speed's map of 1610, these could have been simple affairs constructed in timber. Lanes running from the High Street to the water on either side were probably plentiful throughout the medieval period. Their legal status seems to have been sometimes as rights of way within a property in private ownership and sometimes as common lanes, which occur as boundaries between properties. Responsibility for these common lanes, presumably, lay with the commonality or parish, as did that of the highways, whereas the rights of way were the responsibility of the landholder. Archaeologically, however, there may be little difference between the two, except that the common lanes were more likely to survive for longer. Nevertheless, both rights of way on the south side of the Great Gowt survived the medieval period and were eventually upgraded to roads.

Once Sincil Dyke had cut the great green to the south of Great Gowts in half, there may have been a tendency to build on the area of former green north and south of St Botolph's church. This process of in-fill would also have been encouraged by the presence of the road that split off from High Street and headed for Little Bargate, north of the church. This road became the route to Canwick, and left the city defences via a stone bridge. It gradually lost status during the medieval period, ending up as a footpath, but there is no reason to doubt that it was an important carriage-way earlier on. It must be at least as early as the gate through which it passed, and although it is not recorded until the late 13th century (*Ibid.*, 14), its origins can probably be taken back to the 11th century. The High Street (on the line of the Roman Fosse Way), continued southwards and left the city through west or Great Bargate over another stone bridge.

Minor changes to the alignment and width of High Street have taken place over time. Structures of 10th- or 11th-century date, predating St Mary's Guildhall, appear to have encroached upon the Roman Fosse Way (Stocker 1991, 16). Further south, the projected line of Fosse Way runs underneath the western tower of St Peter-at-Gowts church, and probably therefore ran past the western doorway of the 11th-century church. There is a pronounced change in direction of the High Street at the southern corner of that church-yard and it is likely that this encroachment was started by the church, perhaps in order to build the tower. This encroachment may have been imitated subsequently by the Guildhall's predecessors. Once the construction of stone houses became commonplace in Wigford, by the late 12th century, it is likely that the street frontage was more or less fossilised for the remainder of the medieval period.

Perhaps the most significant change to take place

in Wigford in the 12th century was the gentrification of the suburb. It is quite possible that from the beginning of settlement, Wigford contained a mixture of the social and commercial elite and artisans (Stocker 2000) but there is spectacular evidence for the presence of high status residences from the middle of the 12th century. The earliest of these buildings may have been St Mary's Guildhall itself, which lay to the south of the residence of Adam, the first Mayor of the city, and across the road from *St Andrew's Hall*. The Guildhall itself is thought to have been, initially, a residence of a magnate of the highest order, constructed in the 1150s (Fig. 9.71 and Plates 4.1 and 4.2). The building might represent the remains of the Royal *hospicium* mentioned in *The Pipe Rolls* in 1157, built by Henry II to accommodate the royal crown wearing in the city (SMG 82; Stocker 1991). *St Andrew's Hall*, opposite, was a grand 12th-century town house of similar character (Plate 4.5); but even though of much greater scale than those surviving in Steep Hill, it was small compared with St Mary's Guildhall. There were elaborate medieval buildings throughout the central and northern part of the suburb, for example *Scotch Hall*, near the south-west corner of High Bridge (Stocker 1999, 7 and n.), although not all are thought to have had 12th-century origins. It seems, however, that this trend intensified during the period, and indeed continued into the Early Modern Era.

Another such high status building plot was partly excavated in 1986 (Z 86), in the central part of the suburb on the west side of the Wigford (just to the south of St Mark's church and partly on the site of the former St Mark's Station). In 1269 this plot became the focus of the Carmelite Friary, when it was founded by Bishop Odo of Kilkenny (ed. Page 1906, 224). The friary was extended in 1280 when Edward I authorised the friars to receive adjoining lands. At least one of these lands was acquired from Thurgarton Priory, whose cartulary preserves the agreements (ed. Foulds 1994, 600, No 1055). This new land lay in the parish of St Edward, and therefore to the south of the original precinct. The southern boundary of the friary, all within this extension, was investigated in 1986, whilst the northern part was briefly seen during a watching brief in 1985 (BR 85) and was more extensively investigated in the 1990s (ZWB 94, Wragg 1995a; ZEA 95/ZEB 95, Trimble and Jarvis 1998). Although the results from these latter sites are not yet available. The 1980s excavations demonstrated the development of a convent with a large church in the centre of the fully extended precinct and a cloister to the north.

South of the Sincil Dyke was a grouping of important religious communities around the (now extra-mural) green. The hospital of St Sepulchre was located immediately south of the bridge outside Great Bargate, on the west side of Fosse Way and it was a relatively ancient institution – being founded as early as the episcopate of Bishop Bloet (1094–1123) (ed. Page 1906, 189). On the east side of the green, alongside the parish

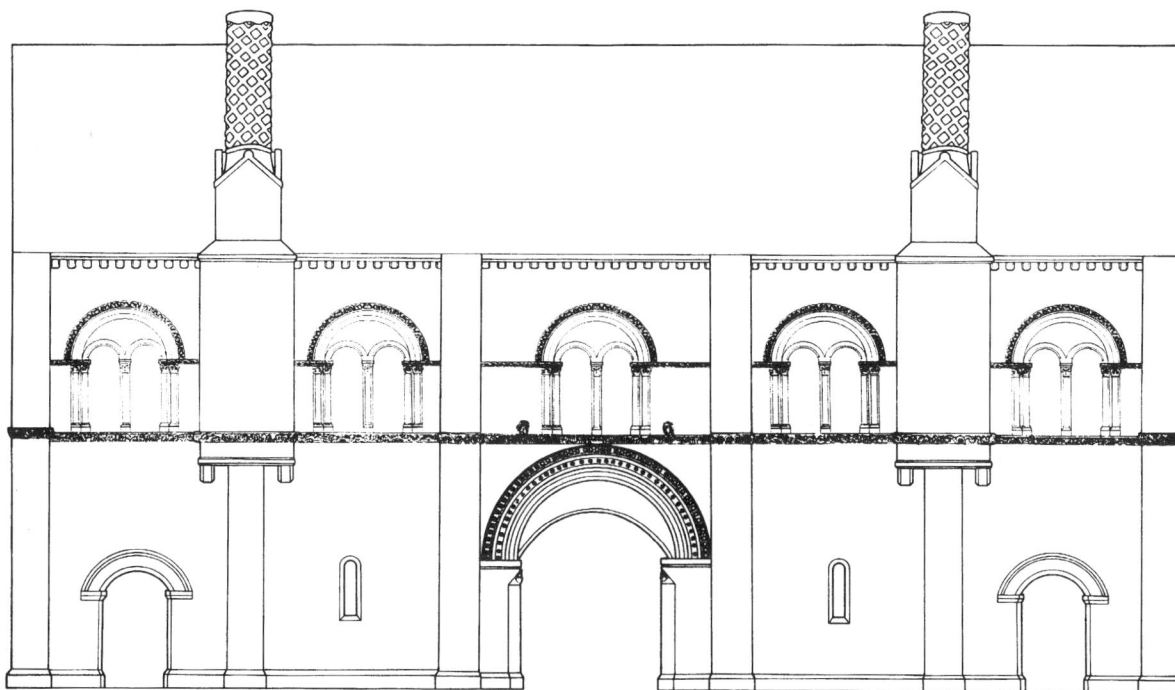

*Fig. 9.71. West façade of the residence known as 'St Mary's Guildhall', as reconstructed following excavation and survey (SMG 82) (see also Plates 4.1 and 4.2) (source, Stocker 1991, drawing by Alan Smith and Dave Watt).*

church of the Holy Innocents, was the well-endowed leper hospital of the Holy Innocents, usually known as The Malandry, which was probably not founded by Bishop Remigius (1067–1092), as was claimed by Dugdale, but by Bloet or Alexander (1123–48) (ed. Page 1906, 230). By *c.*1300, however, the most important institution around the green was also the most recently founded – the Gilbertine Priory of St Katherine, which was founded by Bishop Robert de Chesney shortly after 1148 (ed. Page 1906, 188). Its church and cloister were located south of St Sepulchre's, for which hospital the canons became responsible on the foundation of the Priory.

## Outlying settlements

Lincoln is, of course, surrounded by medieval settlements, many of which would have been inextricably linked to the city. A study of the names of hucksters, alewives, bakers and other minor tradesman (and women) in late 13th-century Lincoln has led Bischoff to suggest that many of these people were living in these villages and travelling in to the city on market days (forthcoming). However, there have been no recent excavations in any of these settlements and, therefore, our archaeological account of them can only be very limited. Although Bracebridge, Branston and Mere, Canwick and Washingborough parishes all lay within the 'County of the City' from 1409, amongst

these settlements, only Bracebridge lies within the modern administrative District of the City of Lincoln. Boultham parish, which was never within the County of City, is now within the City District however, along with fragments of the medieval Hykeham, Skellingthorpe, Greetwell and Nettleham parishes, but not including the settlements on which the parishes were centred. Because they are now administered by City government, the structure of this *Assessment* calls for a brief archaeological account of the settlements at Boultham and Bracebridge to prepare the ground for the research agenda put forward in chapter 9b (below). The account of Bracebridge below relies heavily on that produced for Stocker and Everson's study of 11th-century churches and settlement in Lincolnshire (Stocker and Everson forthcoming).

### Bracebridge

In *Domesday Book* Bracebridge was accounted together with the adjacent settlement of Canwick, and there were a total of three manors between the two settlements. Two of these manors were held by Geoffrey, Bishop of Coutance, and the third was held by Roger of Poitou. Even though Roger's holding was the least valuable (at only 40/−), he is reported as having held a church and a priest on his manor here. Presumably the Bishop of Coutance held a manor at both Bracebridge and Canwick (why otherwise would the two vills be accounted together?), but Roger's manor is not located specifically in one or other settlement. In the later Middle Ages, however, there was only a single manor in Canwick vill whereas there were two manors in Bracebridge, which very probably perpetuated a division that was earlier than 1086. One was called *North Hall* (occurs 1433) and the other *South Hall* (first occurring in 1400) (Cole 1904, 318; Cameron 1985, 192). Therefore, if our assumption that the Bishop of Coutance would have held manors in both Bracebridge and Canwick is correct, one of the two manors at Bracebridge must have belonged to Roger of Poitou. All Saints church Bracebridge was given to the Cathedral in the first half of the 12th century by one Albert Grellei (ed. Foster 1931, 89–90, No.141), and Bishop de Chesney gave the advowson to the Priory of St Katherine, Lincoln in c.1148 (ed. Page 1906, 188–190; ed. Foster 1931, 120–1, No.194). This Albert Grellei is likely to be the same Albert de Gresley, co-founder of Swineshead Abbey in c.1148 and son of Robert de Gresley, founder of Sixhills Priory (ed. Page 1906, 145–6, 194–5; Hallam 1965, 58). It has been suggested that Roger de Poitou's manor at Bracebridge, with its church, subsequently belonged to the de Gresley family (Stocker and Everson forthcoming). Although we can have no confirmation, then, that All Saints is the successor of Roger of Poitou's church, of 1086, nevertheless this appears very likely. All Saints Bracebridge is partly pre-Conquest in date (Brown 1925, 445 etc.) and it has a tower of the well-known 'Lincolnshire' type (Thompson 1907–8; Stocker and Everson forthcoming).

Little more seems to be known of the village's history in the medieval period. It was evidently a typical nucleated vill (vills with more than one manor were the norm in medieval Lincolnshire), and, like many settlements close to a large river, it drew additional support from the waterway. Render from a 12th-century mill was given to The Malandry by Ranulph Earl of Chester, and this may have been the same mill reported by the Hundred Roll jurors in the late 13th century (Hill 1948, 345, 347). A second mill, known as *East Mill* was an obstruction to the river in 1363 and its owners, the Knights Hospitalers, were required to remove it (*Ibid.*, 314). The river here contained many fisheries, including those belonging to St Katherine's Priory at the Dissolution (*Ibid.*, 348). The vill must have had rich water meadows by the river, and grazing on the limestone scarp, but its arable was mostly on top of the cliff, outside the modern city boundary.

There is little early mapping of the village, but the *Tithe Award* of 1842 (Lincolnshire Archives Office J272), shows what seems to be a small triangular market place at the north end of the settlement, in the angle between the original road to Brant Broughton and that to the bridge, facing northwards from the modern war memorial. Lining the road to the north, are rows of long narrow properties, which look very much like tofts. The south side of the market place,

closing the triangle from the south, is a large rectilinear plot which may represent part, or all, of the *curia* belonging to the original manor of *North Hall*, although this could have been located further south.

All Saints is strangely placed relative to the bridge crossing the Witham at Bracebridge, where the Roman Fosse Way from Lincoln turns sharply west to cross the river and heads for Newark. The church originally sat to the west of the old road to Brant Broughton, 300m south-east of this important river crossing. The river-crossing point seems securely located, and one would expect the settlement in Bracebridge to have focused upon it, rather than along the road to Brant Broughton to the south. The fact that the church is located near what must have been the south extremity of the medieval settlement, and not by the bridge, and the fact that we know that there were two manors in medieval Bracebridge, suggests that it might have been established near a second settlement focus. If the two later medieval manors reflect the early division of the settlement at Bracebridge into two foci, as seems likely, we can presume that the church represents settlement around the *South Hall* and that near the bridge, the *North Hall*. If All Saints is equated with the church mentioned in *Domesday Book*, then, it follows that Roger of Poitou's manor was represented in the later Middle Ages by the *South Hall* and the Bishop of Coutance's by the *North Hall*, which was probably sited in the vicinity of Bracebridge Hall. Unfortunately, apart from knowing that the vicarage was established to the east of the church by the 13th century (Cole 1903–4, 274 and n), we know little about the layout of the medieval settlement of Bracebridge (Hill 1948, 343–58), particularly about the area around All Saints church.

## Boultham

The settlement of Boultham is little known either archaeologically or historically. In contrast to Bracebridge it appears to have been a small and relatively insignificant settlement, though it was important enough to have been the focus of a medieval parish, based on the church of St Helen, which still survives in a greatly altered state. In *Domesday Book* the vill was formed from a single manor held by Robert of Stafford. It was small even then, with only a single tenant, Osmund, and a single nameless villein recorded, even though the manor was thought to be capable of supporting six oxen. It was worth less in 1086 than it had been in 1066, but in neither case was its value great (6/– as opposed to 13/4d). Robert's other holdings were mainly in the south of the county, but there is no reason to believe that Boultham ever served as a Lincoln base for the Stafford fee. Instead it should probably be seen alongside Skinnand, Metheringham and Thurlby as part of a small northern group of manors in his ownership.

Although Boultham was clearly well wooded, early

mapping of the settlement (for example the Armstrong map of 1779) shows two rows of houses extending along the Skellingthorpe Road, away from the church, in the area now covered by the grounds of Boultham Park. There was also a small group of houses to the east of the church. At the church this road was joined by another coming north from the main Lincoln – Newark Road. This latter road is not represented in the modern topography, although it must have crossed the small stream south of the church at approximately the same point at which the stream was later dammed to form the lake in the park. This dam may have been constructed using the small causeway that must have carried this minor road across the beck.

Strictly speaking, the precise location of St Mary Magdalene's Hospital 'outside Lincoln' remains unknown, even thought there are several references that probably refer to it between 1311 and 1402 (ed. Page 1906, 234; Cameron 1985, 147). It is probably the same institution as St Mary, Hartsholme, however, which was a cell of Bardney Abbey in the 12th century (Thompson 1913–14, 46–7). If this connection is correct, the hospital-cum-monastic cell should be located on the island of Hartsholme, which remains to be properly defined, but which was situated somewhere north of Boultham and west of Wigford. It has been suggested that Hartsholme might be identified with Haw Hill, an island in the carr land south west of the modern Swanpool in the Middle Ages and probably in the medieval Boultham parish (Hockley 1992).

## The city within: life and work in the medieval city

### Parish churches

A small number of Lincoln's 47 parish churches (Fig. 9.72) may have been in existence in the pre-Viking period. However, it is likely that the majority of them came into existence between the late 9th and the mid 12th centuries. Many have already been mentioned, as they provide important evidence for the topography and development of the city (especially the suburbs). Three were examined archaeologically between 1972 and 1987: St Paul-in-the-Bail, St Peter Stanthaket and St Mark (SP 72, SPM 83, SM 76, Gilmour and Stocker 1986). A fourth, St Bartholomew, may well have been excavated but the remains were so ephemeral that little can be said about them (LH 84, LA 85, L 86).

Although it might be identified as the site of the Lincoln church mentioned by Bede in the 7th century (p. 144–51 above), the earliest documentary reference to St Paul-in-the-Bail is about 1200 (Hill 1948, 103). St Mark and St Peter Stanthaket, like many of the churches in the city and its suburbs, are first mentioned by name in 1147–8 (ed. Foster 1931, 262–3, RA302), although this documentation suggests that they had already been in existence for some time by that date. In each case archaeological evidence confirms that the church was already a century old, or more, by the date of its first surviving documentary record. Documentary sources are therefore of little use when discussing the origins of Lincoln's churches. Topographical inferences may also be drawn to suggest that some churches are earlier than the first reference we have to them. It is tempting to assume that, as we have suggested was the case with Colsuein's *Butwerk* churches of St Peter *ad fontem* and St Clement (p. 231–2 above), church building went side-by-side with the spread of urban settlement. By and large this may be true, although some of the outlying churches, like St Faith-in-Newland or St Botolph in Wigford, may have had an existence as rural churches before they were engulfed in the suburbs of the city. In the end, however, excavation is the only reliable means of establishing church history before the early 13th century, when the wealth of documentary evidence for the city is so great that it is unlikely that a parish church could have existed without being mentioned in documentary sources.

All three excavated churches were built in stone, although at different times. The single cell church at St Paul-in-the-Bail is now thought to date from the later 10th century, although its coincidence with the hanging bowl burial suggests that it might be a direct replacement for an earlier timber structure, or at least that the site of the burial was still clearly marked in the 10th century (Fig. 9.42). The church of St Mark was originally constructed as a two-cell masonry building in the early to mid 11th century (Fig. 9.73). This date is determined both by the date of pottery in layers within and cut by the foundations and by the late 11th-century date of pottery in a dump of material deposited against the west end of the church, into which the tower foundations were cut. In both of these cases the masonry church was not the first religious use of the site. We have seen that the cemetery at St Paul was in use in the Middle Saxon period, perhaps even earlier (p. 149–51 above), whilst the cemetery underlying St Mark's church appears to have started in the mid 10th century with the raising of the ground level in a strip of land about 20 metres wide. Several generations of burials took place before the construction of the stone church and were marked by an important group of carved stone burial markers (Stocker 1986b; Everson and Stocker 1999). By contrast, the mid 11th-century masonry church at St Peter Stanthaket is the first evidence for the ecclesiastical use of the site, which may previously have had domestic occupation (Fig. 9.74). This sample of three churches therefore reveals three very different early histories. The only real similarity in their origins is that all three pre-dated the Norman Conquest.

This growth can be effectively illustrated in tabular form (Fig. 9.75). The suggested sequence of development given here can only be a model based on the

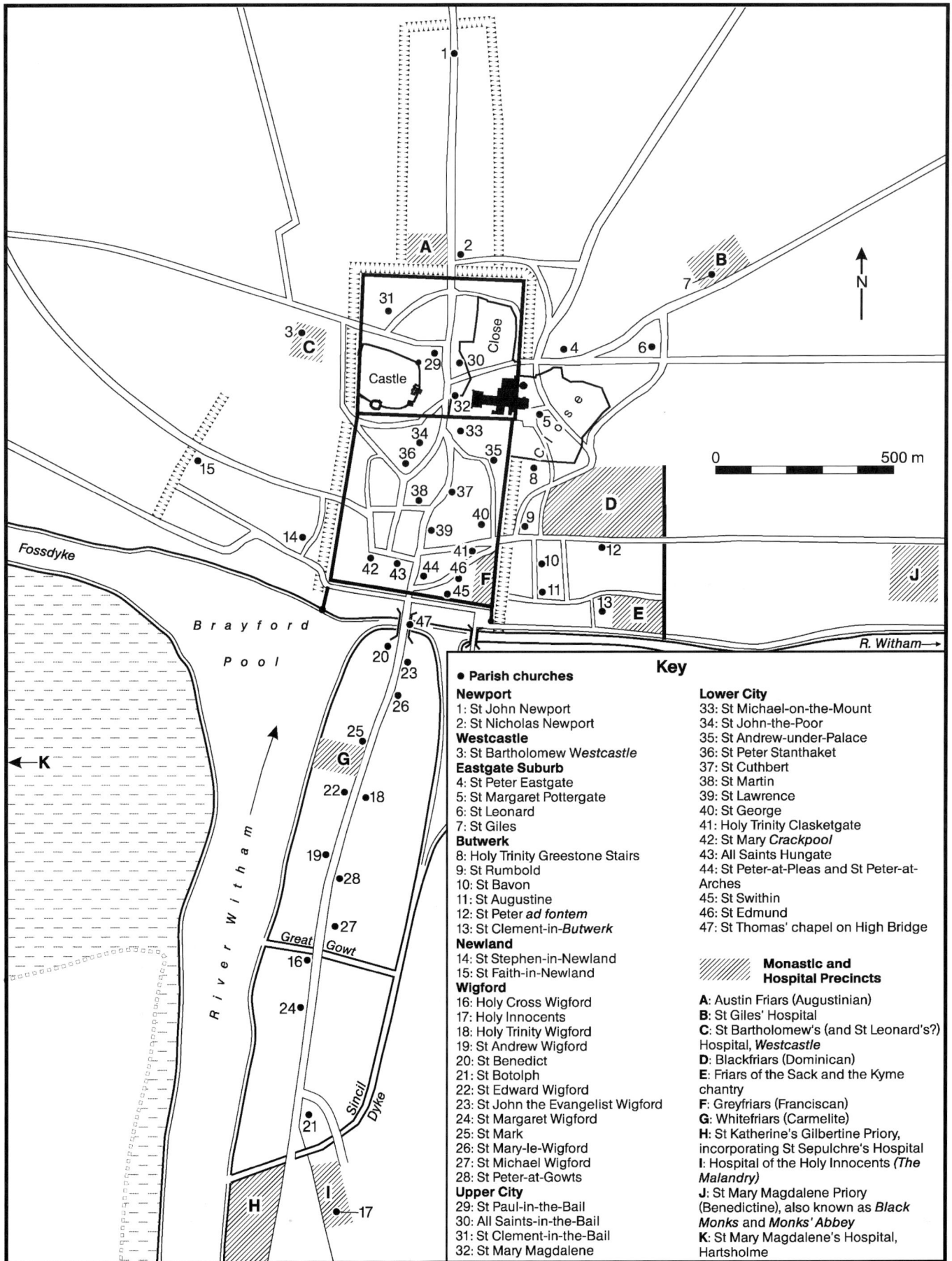

**Key**

**● Parish churches**

**Newport**
1: St John Newport
2: St Nicholas Newport
**Westcastle**
3: St Bartholomew Westcastle
**Eastgate Suburb**
4: St Peter Eastgate
5: St Margaret Pottergate
6: St Leonard
7: St Giles
**Butwerk**
8: Holy Trinity Greestone Stairs
9: St Rumbold
10: St Bavon
11: St Augustine
12: St Peter *ad fontem*
13: St Clement-in-*Butwerk*
**Newland**
14: St Stephen-in-Newland
15: St Faith-in-Newland
**Wigford**
16: Holy Cross Wigford
17: Holy Innocents
18: Holy Trinity Wigford
19: St Andrew Wigford
20: St Benedict
21: St Botolph
22: St Edward Wigford
23: St John the Evangelist Wigford
24: St Margaret Wigford
25: St Mark
26: St Mary-le-Wigford
27: St Michael Wigford
28: St Peter-at-Gowts
**Upper City**
29: St Paul-in-the-Bail
30: All Saints-in-the-Bail
31: St Clement-in-the-Bail
32: St Mary Magdalene

**Lower City**
33: St Michael-on-the-Mount
34: St John-the-Poor
35: St Andrew-under-Palace
36: St Peter Stanthaket
37: St Cuthbert
38: St Martin
39: St Lawrence
40: St George
41: Holy Trinity Clasketgate
42: St Mary *Crackpool*
43: All Saints Hungate
44: St Peter-at-Pleas and St Peter-at-Arches
45: St Swithin
46: St Edmund
47: St Thomas' chapel on High Bridge

▨ **Monastic and Hospital Precincts**

A: Austin Friars (Augustinian)
B: St Giles' Hospital
C: St Bartholomew's (and St Leonard's?) Hospital, *Westcastle*
D: Blackfriars (Dominican)
E: Friars of the Sack and the Kyme chantry
F: Greyfriars (Franciscan)
G: Whitefriars (Carmelite)
H: St Katherine's Gilbertine Priory, incorporating St Sepulchre's Hospital
I: Hospital of the Holy Innocents *(The Malandry)*
J: St Mary Magdalene Priory (Benedictine), also known as *Black Monks* and *Monks' Abbey*
K: St Mary Magdalene's Hospital, Hartsholme

*Fig. 9.72. All known parish churches, hospitals and monastic precincts in medieval Lincoln. The street plan is medieval (drawn by Dave Watt, copyright English Heritage).*

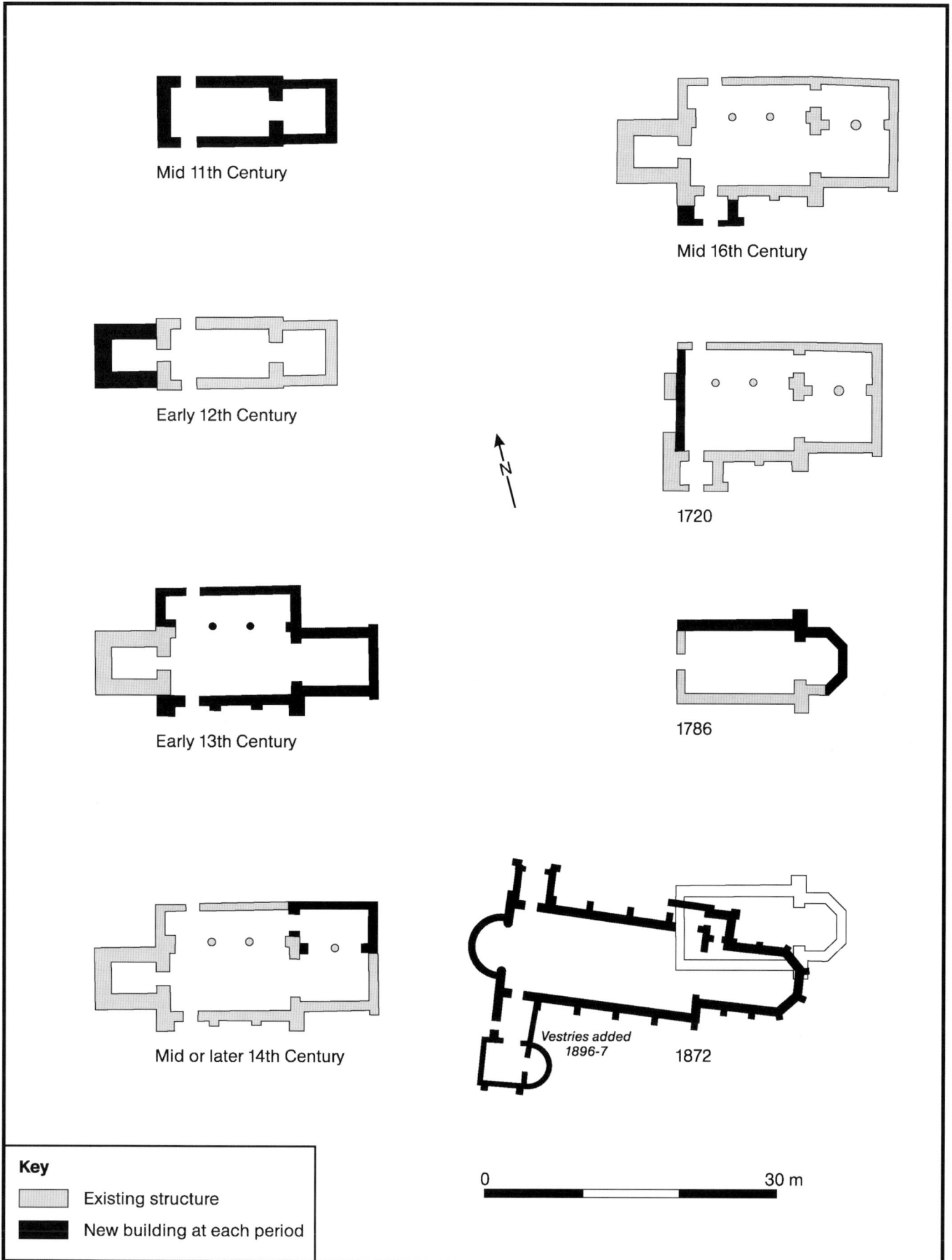

Fig. 9.73. *Development plans of St Mark's parish church, from excavations in 1976 (SM 76) (source, Gilmour and Stocker 1986 – drawn by Dave Watt, copyright English Heritage).*

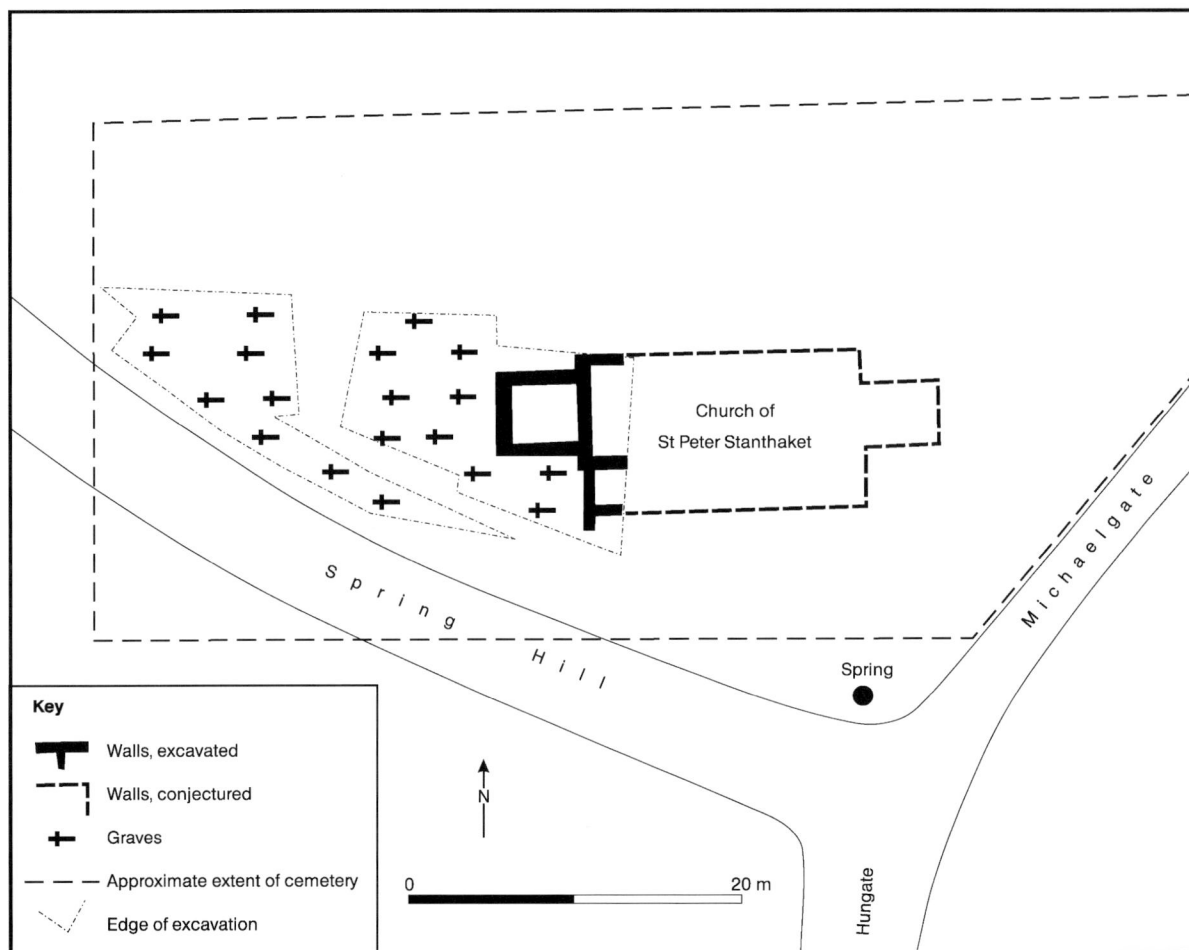

*Fig. 9.74. Partial plan of parish church of St Peter Stanthaket, recovered in excavations in 1983–4 (SPM 83) (source, Snell 1984 – drawn by Dave Watt, copyright English Heritage).*

| Date | National trend | Lincoln churches | Total |
|---|---|---|---|
| pre–late 9th century | Few but large churches, extensive cemeteries | St Paul, St Peter (at Arches and at Pleas), St Martin | 3 |
| Late 9th/early 10th century | Church under threat in the Danelaw. | Head of St Oswald taken by English from Bardney to Gloucester | 3? |
| mid 10th to mid 11th century | Explosion of church building, with burial rights | Upper city and lower city churches, Wigford and Butwerk and Eastgate suburb churches | 39 |
| Late 11th to mid 12th century | Trend towards fewer, better endowed churches | Westcastle, Newport and Newland churches | 46 |

*Fig. 9.75. Trends in parochial church development in the medieval city.*

assumption that the provision of churches and grave-yards changed significantly during the period of Lincoln's rapid growth. In general, in England, the process of formalisation of parish boundaries seems to have been taking place in the 11th and 12th centuries, although many of these parishes are likely to have been in existence as estates, or groups of estates, at a much earlier date. In Lincoln, the amalgamation of many of the smaller parishes during the 15th and 16th centuries means that we only understand the original boundaries of parishes where the amalgamation of

neighbouring parishes is adequately documented. The picture is complicated further by the fact that some parishes were divided and amalgamated with two or more neighbouring parishes. Some indication of the original layout of parishes might come from the detailed study of tenement histories and this work is underway as part of *The Survey of Lincoln*, but no results are yet available. What can be shown, with very little work, is which parishes extended into which *insulae*. For example, it seems that St George's parish extended south of *Brancegate* (Grantham Street) and St Andrew-under-Palace parish included land south and west of Danes Terrace. In fact, it seems to be the rule in the Lower City that parishes were not bounded by streets but cut across them. It is also clear that, with two exceptions (St Michael-at-Gowts and Holy Cross), the Wigford parishes originally ran across High Street as strips (pers. com. C Johnson).

The Lower City is likely to have seen the earliest post-Viking church foundation, given the archaeo-logical evidence for the date of settlement. However, neither Flaxengate nor Silver Street, the two streets which contain the earliest known settlement evidence, appear to have had early churches on their frontages. If there was a need for churches in the earliest phase of Anglo-Scandinavian settlement, then, this need was either satisfied by postulated pre-Viking churches such as St Martin and St Peter, or perhaps by the use of the St Paul-in-the-Bail site (despite the lack of structural evidence for the church within the exca-vated area before the late 10th century). Subsequent church foundations are likely to have accompanied the growth of settlement. Churches in the more northerly parts of the Lower City therefore ought not be earlier than the mid 11th century, since that appears to be the date of the first occupation in this area (p. 204–7 above). Such churches would include St John-the-Poor, St Peter Stanthaket, St Michael-on-the-Mount, St Cuthbert and St Andrew-under-Palace. One might further suggest that, since St John and St Andrew were such small and insignificant parishes, they might be the latest of this group to be founded. Even St Andrew, however, was in existence by 1155–8, since its churchyard is mentioned as a boundary in the second grant of land from the King to the Bishop for the construction of the Bishop's Palace (ed. Foster 1931, 86, RA137).

The relative chronology of the Bail churches may also follow the spread of settlement, although David Stocker pointed out that several middle Saxon mon-astic sites in Lindsey may have consisted of an extensive sacred area in which several foci were present. Although Stocker claimed Bardney (10km east) as an example of this layout, he did not go so far as to suggest that the Bail was an example of such an early *familia* of churches (1993, 107–110). If St Paul-in-the-Bail was part of a similar religious precinct, enclosed by the fortress walls, then any, or all, of the four churches might be of pre-Viking date. The plan of the 10th- and 11th-century church at St Paul (Fig. 9.42) might indeed suggest that it was a subordinate church, as it had no chancel before the 12th century. It may also be significant that the church is not named in any of the papal confirmations of city churches to the Cathedral. It seems likely that this was because it still belonged to a particular family (the ancestors of William son of Warner) whereas only those which were either in the King's hands, or which were not claimed by any other lord were granted to the Cathe-dral by the King. As late as the 12th century, then, St

Paul's may have been a chapel subordinate to another nearby church, of which the most proximate candidate would be All Saints. Assuming, however, that St Clement-in-the-Bail, St Mary of Lincoln and All Saints-in-the-Bail were more typical urban churches than St Paul, one would still guess at an earlier date for St Mary than for St Clement or All Saints, on grounds of dedication and its subsequent history. The finding of a grave-cover of about 1000 AD west of the Cathedral, apparently *in situ*, along with a second marker of about the same date, is an indication that the church there dates from at least the late 10th century (Everson and Stocker 1999, 194–6). All Saints-in-the-Bail is recorded in *Domesday Book* and was definitely in existence before 1066 (Hill 1948, 46). However, the church and lands attached to it were both in private hands in 1086, which might suggest that it was not of any great antiquity at that time and might have been founded in the late 10th or early 11th century. Finally, St Clement-in-the-Bail is taken by Jones *et al.* to be a post-Conquest foundation, on the grounds that this quarter of the Bail was occupied mainly by people owing service to the Castle (1996, 127). However, excavations at Chapel Lane and at Westgate School (CL 85, W 73) both produced pottery of early-to-mid 11th-century date and it is likely that this quarter was occupied before the Conquest and certainly well before the construction of the inner bailey rampart of the Castle in the early 12th century. There is therefore no reason why the foundation of St Clement's church should not also have occurred between the late 10th and mid 11th centuries.

The absolute and relative chronology of the six *Butwerk* churches has been discussed already (p. 230–5 above), and we have seen that St Peter *ad fontem* and, possibly, St Clement-in-*Butwerk* were probably associated with the foundation of Colsuein's extension to the suburb between 1066 and 1086. Holy Trinity Greestone Stairs may also have been founded at a similarly late date (i.e. around the Conquest). This implies that St Rumbold, St Bavon and St Augustine were slightly earlier foundations, but they still need be no earlier than the early to mid 11th century.

In the Eastgate suburb there is no indication of the foundation dates of the four churches (St Peter East-gate, St Margaret Pottergate, St Leonard and St Giles). We have already noted that the inscription found in a stone coffin at St Margaret Pottergate has been dated to the 11th century (Hill 1948, 143) (Fig. 9.62). On topographical grounds, however, we might presume that, since St Peter's church has the prime position on Eastgate (as well as a dedication of higher status than either Margaret or Leonard), it is the earliest of the three churches. No further parishes were created in Lincoln after the early 12th century and, indeed, it seems that the status of some of the existing parishes may have been in doubt from quite an early date. St Giles, for example, is only mentioned as a parish once (in 1453) and it is likely that any early parish church here became the chapel of the hospital of St Giles, founded before the late 13th century (Hill 1948, 147). Even the status of St Leonard's church seems to have been doubtful, with occasional references to the church as a chapel and with land within its parish recorded as being also within the parish of St Peter Eastgate.

Although no new parishes were created in Lincoln after the 12th century, new chapels were built. Some of these were for public use, as was the case with the bridge-chapel of St Thomas situated on a purpose-built extension to the east of the High Bridge. But some were for private use, as oratories within high status properties, such as that still surviving in the Chancery (Plate 6.1) (Jones *et al.* 1984, 63–4) or that constructed within the St Loe (*Sancto Laudo*) estate to the south of *Lewinstigh* (ed. Major 1958 182, RA2373) (Fig. 9.58).

We can say a great deal about the architectural development of the city's three surviving medieval churches at St Benedict (Fig. 9.76), St Mary-le-Wigford (Fig. 9.77) and St Peter-at-Gowts (Fig. 9.78) although even in these cases there has been substantial re-building in the Victorian period and before. At St Benedict's church, for example, the two-light belfry openings in the tower have been shown to be entirely constructed (or re-constructed) from re-used late medieval mouldings (Stocker 1982). The towers of both St Mary-le-Wigford and St Peter-at-Gowts appear to be original work but in both cases the remainder of the churches has been substantially altered in the Victorian period (Plates 3.4 and 3.5) (Hill 1948, 135–141). For the appearance and structural development of the other city churches we are dependent on two sources of information. Antiquarian reports and other documents, including early views, and the occasional finds of re-used stonework. We have early views of

the churches at St Peter Eastgate, St Margaret Pottergate, St Mary Magdalene, St Martin, St Swithin and St Botolph, all of which can help, to varying degrees in building up their architectural histories.

In addition to the large collections of architectural

Fig. 9.77. St Mary-le-Wigford church from the north-west by S H Grimm, drawn in c.1784. Note St Mary's Conduit-head in the south-western corner of the churchyard (photo and copyright, British Library).

Fig. 9.76. Drawing of about 1820 by Edward Willson of St Benedict's church from the south-west (Lincoln Cathedral Library Portfolio A, No. 15) (photo, Lincolnshire County Council, copyright Lincoln Cathedral Library).

Fig. 9.78. St Peter-at-Gowts church from the south-east. The separately roofed chapel housed the Jolyff chantry, founded 1347 (photo and copyright, D Stocker).

fragments from the excavations at St Paul-in-the-Bail and St Mark (Stocker 1986b) important fragments have also been identified from St John's Cornhill, St Botolph, St Peter-at-Arches and St Benedict's. A group of loose moulded stone fragments excavated at the site of St Mark's church were interpreted as having come from an ecclesiastical building on another site which was distinguished by having had a stone vault of 12th-century date as well as 13th century details (*Ibid.*, 48–9). Unfortunately it is unclear which building is represented, but the stones were reused in the rebuilding of the south porch of St Mark's, probably in the 16th century. Since grave markers were also present in these foundations it seems that the vault came from a church site, perhaps the nearby church of St Edward (Gilmour and Stocker, 1986, 89).

These records and observations provide plenty of evidence for the investment in the city's churches and for their growth. Complex forces are at work here, as can be seen at two of the excavated church sites, St Paul-in-the-Bail and St Mark (SP 72, SM 76). St Paul seems to have had a lowly status during the 11th and early 12th centuries. Its chancel was added east of the 10th-century stone cell in the 12th century, although the only reliable evidence for its date, is an undistinguished fragment from a stone coffin of probable 12th-century date. The acquisition of the chancel in the 12th century might be a sign that it was accepting more conventional parochial responsibilities, and the patronage was eventually acquired by Trentham Priory in Staffordshire (Jones *et al.* 1996, 101–2). In the early 13th century, however, the church was rebuilt, and provided with a south aisle with finely sculpted arcade details, which suggested to Pam Graves that the masons who worked on the job had been trained at the Cathedral. This work will have coincided with a period when the rector was one of the city's richest citizens, William, son of Warner (Jones *et al.* 1996, 101), and the aisle was added to the standing church without having to demolish the existing building, in a manner characteristic of surviving medieval churches.

In two of the three excavated Lincoln churches, however, in addition to piecemeal additions, substantial rebuilding has taken place. At St Paul-in-the-Bail documentary sources imply a date of 1301 for a complete rebuilding (Hill 1948, 104) and archaeological excavation confirms that the church was indeed substantially rebuilt around 1300 (Fig. 9.42). It seems clear, however, that the new aisle reused fabric from the earlier aisle as the westernmost arch of the later aisle is shown, filled in and acting as the south wall of the later building on an 18th-century drawing of the church (Fig. 9.79). Even though the foundation trenches for the aisle proved in excavation to date from shortly after 1301, the drawing clearly shows the early 13th century arcade arch details reused in the later fabric. At St Mark's church the evidence for the north aisle was also clearly recorded, although no precise date has survived, architectural fragments make a date in

the second or third quarters of the 13th century probable (Gilmour and Stocker 1986, 23–6). Here the original 11th-century south wall foundations of the nave were reused, and it may be that parts of the superstructure were also retained, as the western tower certainly was. The 11th-century chancel, however, was razed to the ground and its replacement built on a much larger scale, not using any of the original walls.

In total at least twelve Lincoln churches had acquired aisles by the 14th century. The need to supply an aisle, on the south side of the nave at St Paul-in-the-Bail and St Peter Stanthaket, but on the north side at St Mark, seems to have been mainly a reaction to changing liturgy and the need to create additional altar space, and need not imply that the parish numbers had outgrown the space available in the earlier nave. Furthermore it is also likely that the expansion of the chancel at St Mark's was made necessary by the elaboration of liturgy. The aisles at all three excavated churches were of late 12th or 13th-century date. In addition to fully developed aisles, chantry chapels were added to several of the Lincoln churches. Those at St Mary-le-Wigford, St Benedict and St Peter-at-Gowts still survive; the first two date from the 13th century and were built to be continuous with northern aisles, although having separate roof structures. The chantry at St Peter-at-Gowts was founded in 1347 by the Jolyff family (Fig. 9.78). The proliferation of chantries during the 13th and 14th centuries is reflected in surviving wills and other records. Large numbers of priests were employed, and in the 1377 clerical poll tax St Benedict's declared 11 priests, of whom maybe eight might have been chaplains (ed. McHardy 1992, 23). At St Andrew Wigford, which later disputes suggest had become virtually the private chapel of the Sutton family, there was a chapel dedicated to St Anne (Hill 1948, 166).

The regional tradition for building Romanesque

*Fig. 9.79. St Paul-in-the-Bail church from the south in the mid 18th century. A drawing (now apparently lost) formerly in the possession of the rector and churchwardens (source, Hill 1948, fig. 6).*

towers at the west end of a church is well-represented in Lincoln (Stocker and Everson forthcoming). There are surviving structures at St Mary-le-Wigford and St Peter-at-Gowts (Plates 3.4 and 3.5), although survey work undertaken during repair at St Benedict in 1981 showed that, although previously listed as such a tower, the structure here is entirely of the 17th century although incorporating late medieval fabric (Stocker 1982). Excavated examples are known from St Mark, St Paul-in-the-Bail, St Peter Stanthaket and further examples are known from early views of St Margaret Pottergate and St Peter Eastgate. The tradition extended from the late 11th century (St Mary-le-Wigford, St Peter Eastgate and St Peter-at-Gowts), through the 12th century (St Mark's, St Margaret Pottergate, St Peter Stanthaket) and into the 13th century at St Paul-in the Bail.

## Vernacular buildings

With very few exceptions, the secular buildings of Anglo-Scandinavian and Norman Lincoln were made of timber. The best-known examples are those from the Flaxengate excavation (F 72; Perring 1981). These range in date from the end of the 9th century to the mid 12th century and include both main dwellings, fronting onto the streets, and ancillary buildings in the yards behind. Only two other types of building might be expected in the city during this period; cellared buildings and halls. Even in the open area excavation at Flaxengate, however, it proved impossible to recover full plans of any of the buildings, both because of the size of the excavated area and because of later disturbance (Fig. 9.80).

It is difficult to determine the length of any of the buildings at Flaxengate, or elsewhere in the city, with any accuracy but it is clear from Fig. 9.80 that their lengths varied. Widths, however, were quite standardised – all were between four and five metres wide. The superstructure of the buildings is not always easy to understand, although the presence of stake holes and well as post holes on the lines of the external walls suggests that the earliest buildings probably had wattle and daub infilling, between the structural members. There is no evidence for coupling of posts across the building, which might indicate roofs supported by

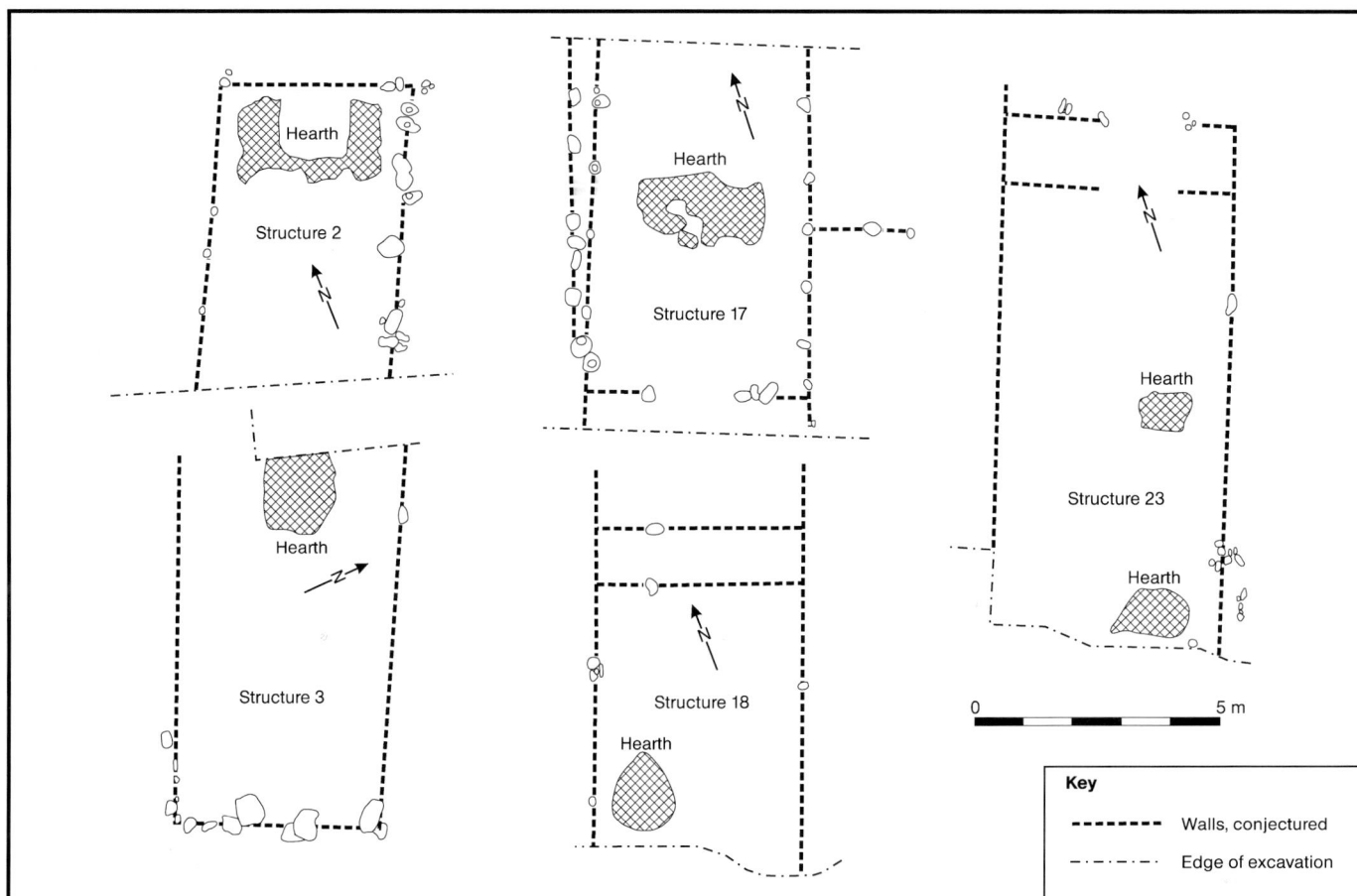

*Fig. 9.80. Plans of 10th- and 11th -century buildings excavated at Flaxengate (F 72). The walls (represented by the pecked lines) were built using several constructional techniques, with timber, wattle and daub (source, Perring 1981 – drawn by Dave Watt, copyright English Heritage).*

trusses, nor are the corner posts more prominent than the remaining wall posts. Later buildings at Flaxengate had one or more walls constructed with posts set in trenches and several buildings could only be recognised through the spread of ash and charcoal from their hearths. Their walls must therefore have been set into ground-laid beams. Since this method of construction usually leaves little evidence, it is possible that it was more common than the evidence would suggest. At Hungate (H 83), for example, the back wall of a 10th-century building fronting onto the street was represented only by small groups of stones, interpreted either as post pads or as material laid under a ground beam to level it. In a few cases there is definite evidence for the replacement of posts, indicating either repair or re-organisation of the structure. Several buildings at Flaxengate, especially in the 11th century and later, had a single wall line marked by a gully or slot. These might be interpreted as drainage gullies, but similar features also appear to mark internal divisions, whilst some gullies were clearly discontinuous and could not have effectively acted as drains. Internal divisions were noted in several buildings, marked by stake holes, post holes or slots. In a few cases these divisions consisted of vertically-set planks, as in Structure Seven at Flaxengate (Perring 1981, 8–9). Where present, these divisions seem to mark out a small area at one end of the building, perhaps used for storage or sleeping.

Access to these buildings was not always clear during excavation. In the Flaxengate (F 72) building known as Structure Three, two post holes set centrally in the gable end were interpreted as marking a doorway leading directly on to Flaxengate (Perring 1981, 7). Such evidence is extremely rare and access in most cases has to be surmised from a study of the layout of internal features, such as hearths and ovens. In the absence of scientific analysis of the ash and residues associated with these hearths and ovens, it is difficult to be certain of their function. The evidence from many occupation sites in the city suggests that crafts such as metal-working and glass-working were ubiquitous between the late 9th and 12th centuries, however, so the possibility that several features interpreted by excavators as hearths and ovens were used for industrial purposes should not be overlooked (but not overstated either, see Perring 1981, 42).

Nevertheless, it seems that every dwelling house at Flaxengate contained a hearth. In the earlier buildings these are thought to have been equidistant from each longitudinal wall and, in buildings set gable end onto the street, situated closer to the far gable end. In most cases the hearth was formed from a deliberately laid circular or oval patch of clay. In many cases this hearth was replaced by laying a new one on top, although in small keyhole excavations, as at Hungate (H 83), it is not possible to be sure that only the hearth was replaced, as opposed to the entire building. At both Flaxengate and Hungate it seems that major re-buildings were accompanied by the levelling-up of the entire building plot (or at least that part of it underlying the proposed new buildings) and similar make-up deposits have been recognised on many other sites.

From the mid 11th century onwards, to judge from Flaxengate, however, there was a tendency for hearths to be located eccentrically. Perring also notes a number of sunken hearths, which he distinguishes from ovens through their not having stoke-holes and he presumes they had no covering. Ovens worked by heating an enclosed dome, formed either of daub or stone and clay, by lighting a fire within. Once the structure was sufficiently hot, the ashes were raked out and the loaves or grain were inserted, to be baked or dried by the heat radiating from the walls and floors of the oven. The floor of an oven therefore needed to form a 'heat reservoir' and so it was thicker and more complete than a hearth. The feature termed a 'flue' or 'stoke-hole' by Perring is more accurately termed a rakings pit, a shallow pit in front of the oven into which the hot embers could be raked without danger of catching the floor on fire. Such ovens are rare on Lincoln excavations in the late 9th to mid 12th centuries.

On Flaxengate (F 72), floors within buildings were initially formed of beaten earth (often dark coloured when excavated as a result of contamination by charcoal and ashes from the hearth) and/or grassy material (Perring 1981, 39). This organic flooring normally only survived where the building had been destroyed by fire, and even in these circumstances it was not possible to distinguish scattered straw from woven matting. Clay floors were also present from the beginning of Anglo-Scandinavian settlement at Flaxengate but elsewhere clay floors appear to be a later introduction, mostly of post-Conquest date. As noted by Perring, barring exceptional circumstances it would not have been possible to recognise plank floors in these buildings. Nevertheless, where a building has a hearth, and ashes from that hearth lay directly on an earth surface, it is clear that no plank floor existed. Given the large number of hearths found in the city, it is likely that raised floors were rare.

Sites in Lincoln have simply not been excavated on a sufficiently large scale for us to consider the relationship of one building to its neighbour, and it is not even possible to understand access to the rears of most excavated properties. At Flaxengate (F 72), however, it seems that each timber building was free-standing and separated from its neighbour by a gap of a metre or less. These gaps could have formed passageways between the buildings and would have been wide enough for a person on foot. It is almost certain, however, that access was also possible through the buildings. Perring (1981, 39) suggests that some of the Flaxengate buildings may have had opposed doors midway along their longitudinal walls, although unusually, one of his examples (Structure Twenty-three), is aligned gable end-on to the street so that any doorways would have opened onto the putative side passage. There is no evidence at this period for the metalling of the passageways between buildings or their formalisation into lanes.

Although the excavations at Flaxengate (F 72) provided by far the best examples of such pre-Conquest buildings in Lincoln, there are other sites with comparable evidence. In the Lower City these include excavations at Hungate (H 83) and Silver Street (LIN 73e), both of which produced evidence for timber structures fronting the streets. At Hungate, it seems that the earliest structures were set parallel to the street but that, in the 11th century, a range was constructed at right angles to it. It is possible that this range faced onto a lane running along the south side of the churchyard of St Martin but it is equally likely that the range was accessed via Hungate. At Silver Street the frontage of the street had been pushed southwards in recent times so that only the back of the structure was excavated and its orientation is unclear. Similar evidence was also excavated in the Wigford suburb. At 181–3 High Street (HG 72) parts of two tenements were excavated. The frontage along the High Street did not survive but it is presumed to have been occupied in the 10th century by timber structures, since refuse pits occupied the area behind. In the late 10th- or early 11th-century timber structures were erected behind the frontage, although their disposition is unknown. There was a gap between the two structures (Nos. 7.1 and 8.1), occupied by a

party wall, if the structures were contiguous, or by a passageway if not. At St Benedict's Square (SB 85) the excavated areas were well behind the street frontage, close to the Brayford Pool river frontage. Traces of activity here may have either related to the Pool bank or to a lane running along the south side of St Benedict's churchyard. Interestingly, this activity began in the mid or later 11th century – the likely period of foundation of the church.

Unlike many English towns between the late 9th and mid 12th centuries, Lincoln does not have a large number of cellared buildings. Only three are known, two of them utilising Roman structures to form one wall and having superstructures supported on posts with stone infill between (Fig. 9.81). The two examples from Silver Street (LIN 73d) may date from quite early in the re-occupation of the city, and were certainly back-filled in the 10th century, whilst that at St Paul-in-the-Bail (SP 72) may have been constructed in the later 10th century but was certainly used into the 11th century. It was probably to the rear of a larger building to the east and was approached by steps from within this putative building. The Lower City examples appear to have been set at either end of a property fronting on to Silver Street, although it is just possible that the southern example, built against the back of the city wall, was approached from a north–south lane which ran through the Roman Saltergate postern gate to the waterfront.

The lack of other examples of sunken-floored

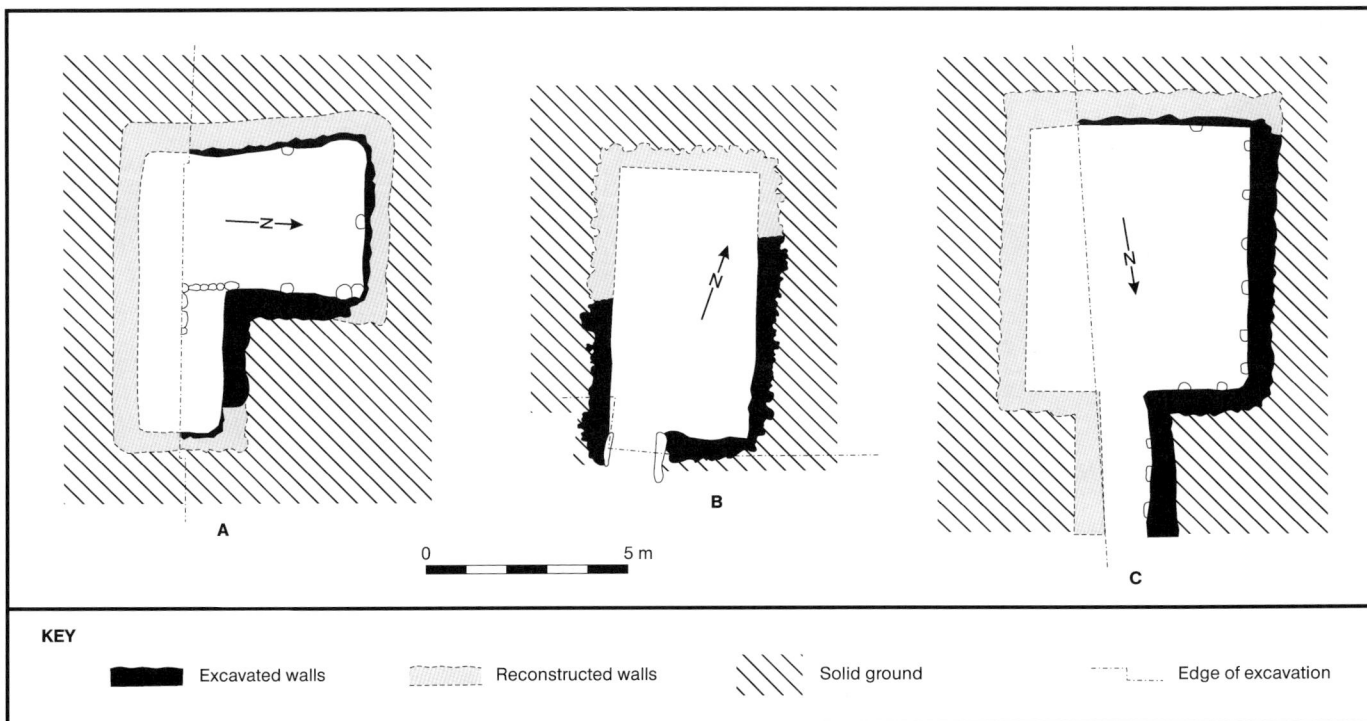

**KEY**

| ▬▬ Excavated walls | ░░░ Reconstructed walls | ╲╲╲ Solid ground | ‒‒‒ Edge of excavation |

*Fig. 9.81. Plans of sunken-floored buildings of 11th-century date from excavations at A) St Paul-in-the-Bail (SP 72) and B and C) Silver Street (LIN 73d) (drawn by Dave Watt, copyright English Heritage).*

buildings is probably related to their function. Previous discussion of such buildings has centred around their reconstruction and their function. Those in London, for example, range from semi-subterranean structures, in which the earth walls may simply have provided insulation to a dwelling house, to those where the below-ground structure was used for storage with the living area on an upper floor (Horsman *et al.* 1988). In London these structures are consistently late in date, being of the late 10th or 11th century in date. By the late 11th century, apparently, masonry cellars were being constructed. Elsewhere, at Coppergate, York, and in Chester and Gloucester for example, fully cellared timber buildings appear in the later 10th or 11th century (Mason 1985, 15–23). This may be related to the commercial character of the sites investigated at these places, but it may also reflect differences in the types of goods stored and the purpose in storing them. In Gloucester, for example, timber cellars were found on street frontage sites along the cardinal streets of the town in the late 10th and early 11th centuries (Heighway *et al.* 1979). Slightly later examples were excavated at Berkeley Street, however, which were set back from the street frontages and may have been used to store provisions for a large wealthy household whose residence lay above the cellar (Hurst 1975). The sunken-floored building at St Paul-in-the-Bail probably survived because the area in which it was built was taken back into the churchyard in the later Middle Ages, whereas equivalent locations along Bailgate are now occupied by medieval masonry undercrofts.

Cellars, therefore, were probably used either by traders for storing their stock or by wealthy households for storing goods for future consumption within the household. The three Lincoln examples probably fall into the commercial category and their absence from sites at Flaxengate and Hungate may be an indication that properties in these streets were not directly involved in trading, perhaps being occupied by artisans who sold their goods at markets and fairs

rather than from their workshops. However, there is also the possibility that at least the St Paul-in-the-Bail example, possibly the others too, were actually located within large urban estates and used for the storing of goods used within those estates.

Ancillary buildings, i.e. those which appear not to have been dwellings, have been rarely found (or at least, rarely recognised) in Lincoln excavations. Structure Nine at Flaxengate (F 72) is clearly such a building (Perring 1981, 11). It had cobbled floors and timber-framed walls supported on a sill beam set upon low dwarf walls. It is possible that the approximate alternation of buildings aligned with Grantham Street represents a pattern of L-shaped building layouts within plots of which only those at right angles to the street were found in the Flaxengate excavation. Interpreted in this way, Flaxengate would represent an early example of a common later medieval urban property layout, with two ranges forming an L-shaped layout within each plot, and with different functions undertaken in each arm of the 'L' (see, for example, the stone structures at Flaxengate, laid out in the late 12th or early 13th century – Jones, R J 1980, 51–54). Unfortunately, there is no evidence from the internal features of the Flaxengate examples to confirm that this layout existed here any earlier.

Lincoln is rightly renowned for the quality of its medieval domestic architecture, surviving from the second half of the 12th century onwards. These buildings fall into two main classes: commercial and high status domestic. Both are represented amongst those described and studied by the *Survey of Ancient Houses* (Jones *et al.* 1984; 1996). Excavation has added at least thirty new buildings, or parts of buildings, to this corpus, most of which can probably be classified as commercial, in that either trading or manufacture were carried out within them (Fig. 9.82). However, with only partial ground plans available it is often not possible to determine in detail the function of these buildings. The replacement of timber by stone from the 12th century had the unfortunate side effect

*Site Name and Site code*

| Lower City: | Upper City: | Butwerk: |
|---|---|---|
| Danes Terrace (DT 74, 78) | East Bight (EB 80) | Broadgate East (BE 73) |
| Flaxengate (F 72) | Mint Wall (MW 79) | |
| Garmston House (GC 90) | Westgate (W 73) | *Eastgate:* |
| Grantham Place (GP 81) | | Winnowsty Cottages (WC 87) |
| Hungate (H 83) | *Wigford:* | |
| Silver Street (LIN 73) | Dickinson's Mill (DM 72) | *Newland:* |
| Saltergate (LIN 73) | 181–3 High St. (HG 72) | Brayford Wharf North (BWN 75) |
| Michaelgate (MCH 84) | St Benedict's Square (SB 85) | Lucy Tower Street (LT 72) |
| Steep Hill (SH 74) | Waterside South (WS 82) | |
| Spring Hill (SPM 83) | St Mark's Station (Z 86) | *Westcastle:* |
| Swan Street (SW 82) | St Mark's Station East (ZE 87) | The Lawn (L 86) |

*Fig. 9.82. List of excavation sites in Lincoln that have produced discoveries of hitherto unknown stone-built houses of the 12th and 13th centuries (source, City of Lincoln Archaeology Unit).*

for archaeology of bringing a halt to much of the stratigraphic deposition which characterises sites of the
10th and 11th centuries, and there are numerous
examples of sites where the overall ground level has
hardly risen since the 12th century. At Hungate indeed
(H 83), 12th-century deposits survived at a higher
level than the surrounding pavement. A distinction
might be drawn, perhaps, between masonry buildings
constructed by professional masons and incorporating
stone architraves, and other details, and poorer
dwellings. However, even this simple division is
difficult in a city like Lincoln, where large amounts
of medieval masonry was available for reuse during
the later medieval and post-medieval periods and
when, as a consequence, a proportion of the moulded
stone found on a site might come from other sites
(Stocker with Everson 1990).

One of the distinctions between commercial and
high status domestic buildings in Lincoln is their
situation relative to the highway. The vast majority
of commercial buildings were set alongside the street,
as their timber predecessors had been. By the 12th
century, however, there were several streets where
buildings formed a continuous line, with no means of
access to the back of the property without going
through the house. In the case of the Jew's House in
Steep Hill, there were two distinct zones of activity
within the property (Wood 1974, 40–2; R. Harris pers.
com.) (Fig. 9.56). The first floor hall, and presumably
the ancillary ranges or free-standing buildings to the
rear, were accessed via a passageway running right
through the building from the street and giving access
to the upper storey by means of stairs at the back.
Meanwhile, the large spaces on the ground floor, to
either side of the passageway, were open to the street
and were probably rented out as shops. 'Jew's Court',
next door to the north, may be substantially post-
medieval in fabric but its ground plan too reflects
this same division. In some cases undercrofts, lying
below the shop, were probably also used for commercial storage and accessed by stairs within the
building – as at the stone built 'Norman House' at the
corner of Steep Hill and Christ's Hospital Terrace,
which was the subject of a survey done in 1992–3
(Jones S R 1992b; NH 92; NHA 93) (Fig. 9.49).

Reconstructing the original layout of such buildings, from surviving fabric, is a complex and time-
consuming process; shop fronts, which would originally have been open to the elements, have been
filled in, new access doorways have been inserted into
side passage walls and the back walls of shops have
been taken down. Fragments of 12th- and 13th-century
masonry continue to come to light during refurbishment, for example at Garmston House at the top of
the High Street in 1990 (GC 90 – Jones S R 1992a).
Even though so much is fragmentary, Lincoln (especially Bailgate and Steep Hill) still has few rivals in
England as a place to study the development of 12th-
and 13th-century commercial property.

## Streets and markets

The layout and development of the street pattern has
been described already, but the circumstances under
which the streets were formed and the means adopted
for their upkeep and use remain to be considered.
However, only one excavation, Flaxengate, has actually
produced physical evidence for a street (F 72; Perring
1981, 44). A length of Anglo-Scandinavian and later
medieval roadway was present in the excavated area,
as a result of the diversion of the street carriageway
eastwards in 1969–70. Despite some encroachment onto
the street in the 11th century, its western limit was still
respected in the 20th century. Perring's analysis of the
stratigraphy of the street surfaces and their relationship
to that of the buildings lining its frontage suggested to
him that the resurfacing of the street, and the rebuilding
and maintenance of the buildings fronting it, were
carried out by different bodies. Upkeep of buildings
along a street frontage was almost certainly a matter
for owner and tenants whereas the resurfacing of the
street may have been a collaborative effort, perhaps
carried out as a labour service. By the later medieval
period certainly, contributions were sought by the City
Council from the owners of tenements along the streets
under repair. In 1286 four citizens has been commissioned to 'arrange for the paving of the high road
running through the said town, taking care that the
better sort who have tenements on or abutting upon
the said road contribute thereto in proportion to their
tenements' (*CPR* 1281–1292, 260).

The first road surface at Flaxengate, dating from
the late 9th or early 10th century, was apparently
formed by laying an even thickness of limestone
rubble, about 140mm thick, directly onto the old
ground surface. The surface had no obvious kerb, no
camber nor any other provision for surface water run-
off. Within the first building phase on the site this
surface was replaced by a wider, cambered surface
that incorporated a stone-lined drain, about 120mm
wide and 200mm deep. A third resurfacing took place
in the early 10th century, immediately after the
destruction or demolition of the timber buildings of
Period II. Stratigraphic evidence suggested that this
street surface remained in use for about a century,
during which time occupation debris encroached upon
its edges and stones were dislodged from its surface.
A fourth resurfacing took place in the mid 11th
century (Period VI), corresponding in time to the
wholesale rebuilding of buildings on the street frontage. This surface appears to have been of poorer
quality than its predecessor and was allowed to wear
away completely in the middle of the street apparently
without attempts at resurfacing. At the end of Period
VI the road was covered by loam dumps, as was the
area once covered by buildings on the street frontage.
However, no attempt to lay down another street
surface was made and, instead, the former street limit
was marked by a fence, represented by a row of about

55 circular stake holes. No further evidence of activity on the street was found until Period XI, at the very end of the 12th century. At that stage, buildings no longer fronted onto Flaxengate, but onto Grantham Street and three pits were dug up against the street frontage.

Although we have been able to propose dates for the construction and development of much of the street pattern in the Anglo-Scandinavian and Norman periods in our consideration of the topography of the city above, only in the Flaxengate example do we have concrete archaeological evidence to set alongside the more general development of the street system. Furthermore it is possible to explain much of the early history of the Flaxengate street with reference to very local factors, like the reversal of importance from Flaxengate to Grantham Street, which may have had little to do with large scale town planning. One clear conclusion, however, is that in the late 9th and early 10th centuries considerable effort went into the maintenance of the street surfaces even though we may not be justified in contrasting this with the subsequent treatment of the street.

We know of only a few cases of new highways being established after the middle of the 12th century and many of these are in the Bail following the contraction of the Castle and the definition of the Cathedral Close (p. 209–14 above), although none have been excavated. Some of the buildings along the new 12th-century Bailgate, we can suggest, were designed for commercial use, but from our topographical description is it clear that much of the trading in the city was undertaken is specially formed market places. Such market places were established all around the city, mostly it seems in the period between the 10th and the 13th centuries (Fig. 9.83). Such markets are now thought to have been established outside the north, east and south gates of the Upper City, outside the gates of the Lower City at Newland, and outside the original southern boundary of Wigford at Great Gowts. Furthermore, the (apparently later) markets at Castle Hill and the malt market on Waterside North were also established in proximity to gates, although, like the *Clewmarket*, they were inside the walled enclosure. The evidence for a 'fair' outside the Lower City east wall in *Butwerk* is also important, but whilst it probably became a market of similar character to these others, it seems to have had a different origin and is not visible as a topographical feature in the townscape. The market places in Eastgate, Steep Hill, and in Lower Wigford were all funnel-like plans, set out between converging roads. Those in Newport and Newland were more like broad rectangular streets. There may a difference in date or the circumstances of foundation reflected in the two market layouts, as Newport and Newland are both thought be somewhat later developments than Lower Wigford, Steep Hill and Eastgate.

The only case of the creation of a possible new street

later than the mid 12th-century reconstruction of the street pattern in the Bail is at Waterside North and called *Thornbridgegate*, whose eastern end, from modern Thorngate to Stamp End, may lie on ground reclaimed late in this period (p. 233 above). Lanes, on the other hand, were probably established and lost with some regularity. Typically they gave access from one part of the city to another and allowed access to the sides and backs of properties fronting the highway. They will have changed with changes in ownership and use of the properties to either side. Documents abound with the names of lanes in Lincoln from the 13th century, and although a few may be new lanes, most of those recorded are likely to be considerably older. In some cases we can probably see the demotion of highways to lanes, and, in a few, the documents record the actual blocking of what was once a right of way. We have seen that *St Peter's Lane*, for example, which ran along the back of properties fronting onto the north-east side of Pottergate, was enclosed in the 13th century and extinguished in the early 14th (p. 224 above Jones *et al.* 1987, 51; ed. Major 1973, 76–83, RA2748–53). We have also already noted some of the numerous lanes running back from Wigford High Street to the water on either side (p. 245–6 above).

Some medieval documents referring to these lanes suggest that they may have had a dual status, as rights of way but included within the property as opposed to common lanes used as boundaries. There are three such cases in the Wigford suburb, all in the southern extension. Two 13th-century examples were in St Botolph's parish (Lincolnshire Archives Office, Eton College Muniments, ECR47/128 1280AD; ed. Foulds 1994, 614, No.1083) and a third (also of 13th-century date) was in St Margaret's parish in Wigford (ed. Major 1968, 69, RA2464). In a few cases, not unexpectedly, such lanes ran along the sides of churchyards and it may be that the modern St Benedict's Square has its origin in lanes which ran east to west across the churchyard towards the Brayford. There was clearly some right of way through St John's churchyard in Wigford to serve a property at the rear (Lincolnshire Archives Office, D and C Ms.169, fl256v), and Willson noted a lane running between Cornhill and Sincil Street, although this could post-date the use of the church (London, Society of Antiquaries Ms. 786/5, 26, 41). The north boundary of Holy Trinity Wigford churchyard was a lane, owned by St Peter's parish, although Mr Johnson reports that this is not documented until the 18th century (Lincolnshire Archives Office, LPC 1/13). Documentary evidence for lanes which later led to bridges across the Witham and Sincil Dyke are late in date, but it is possible that St Mary's Street (first mentioned in 1461–3 – Cameron 1985, 95) and St Mark's Street (first mentioned 1685 – *Ibid.*, 95) are much earlier in origin and led across their respective churchyards towards river crossings. As the city became more and more intensively occupied, of course, churchyards would have provided the only available open space

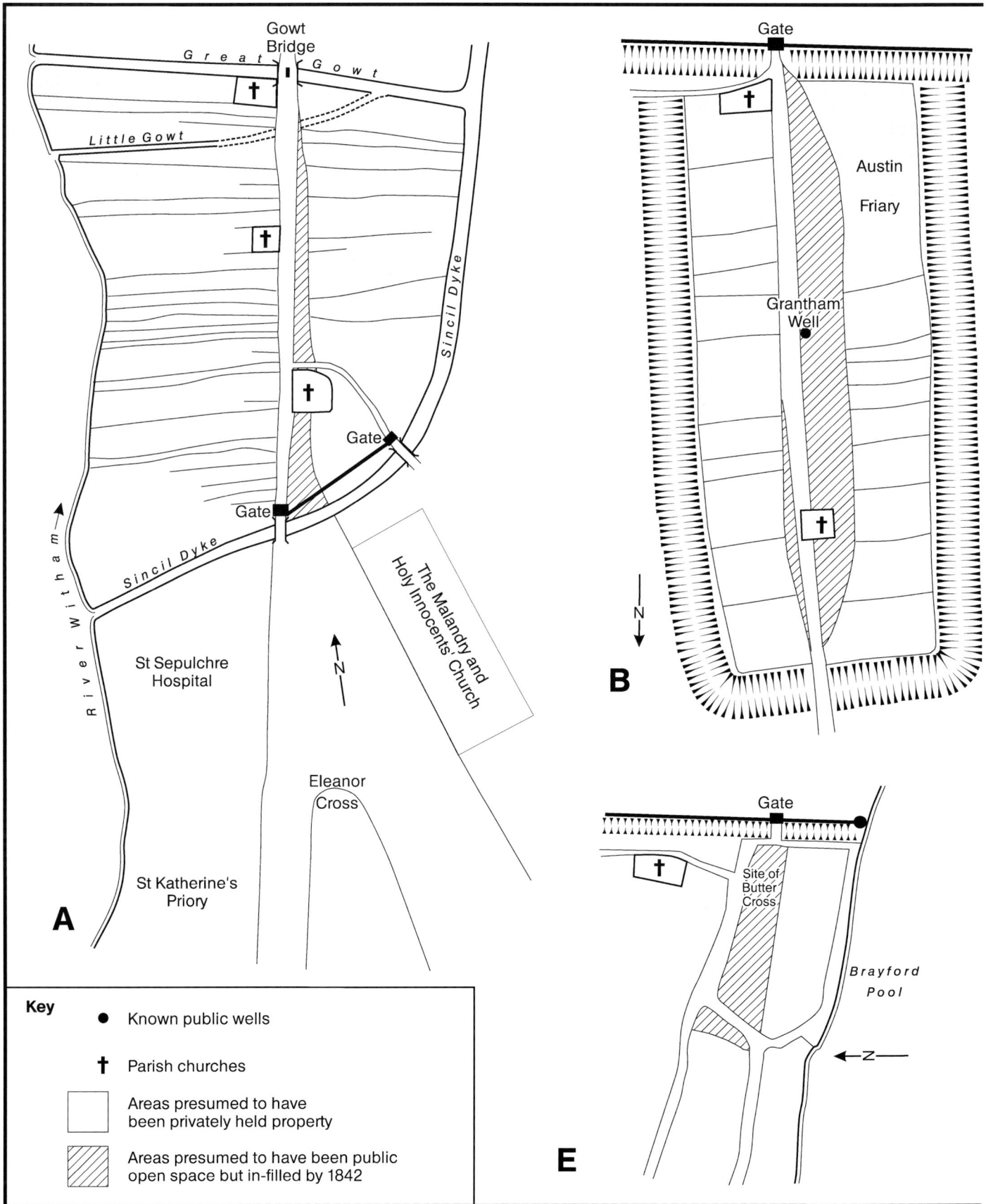

Fig. 9.83. Reconstructed plans of the medieval market places of Lincoln compared. The street plans are derived from Padley's 1842 map and the market places have been defined during the course of this study. A) Lower Wigford market (St Botolph's Green and Lincoln Green or Swine Green); B) Newport market; E) Newland market. A–D are markets of probable 10th- or 11th-century date; E–H are markets of unknown or later medieval date (drawn by Dave Watt, copyright English Heritage).

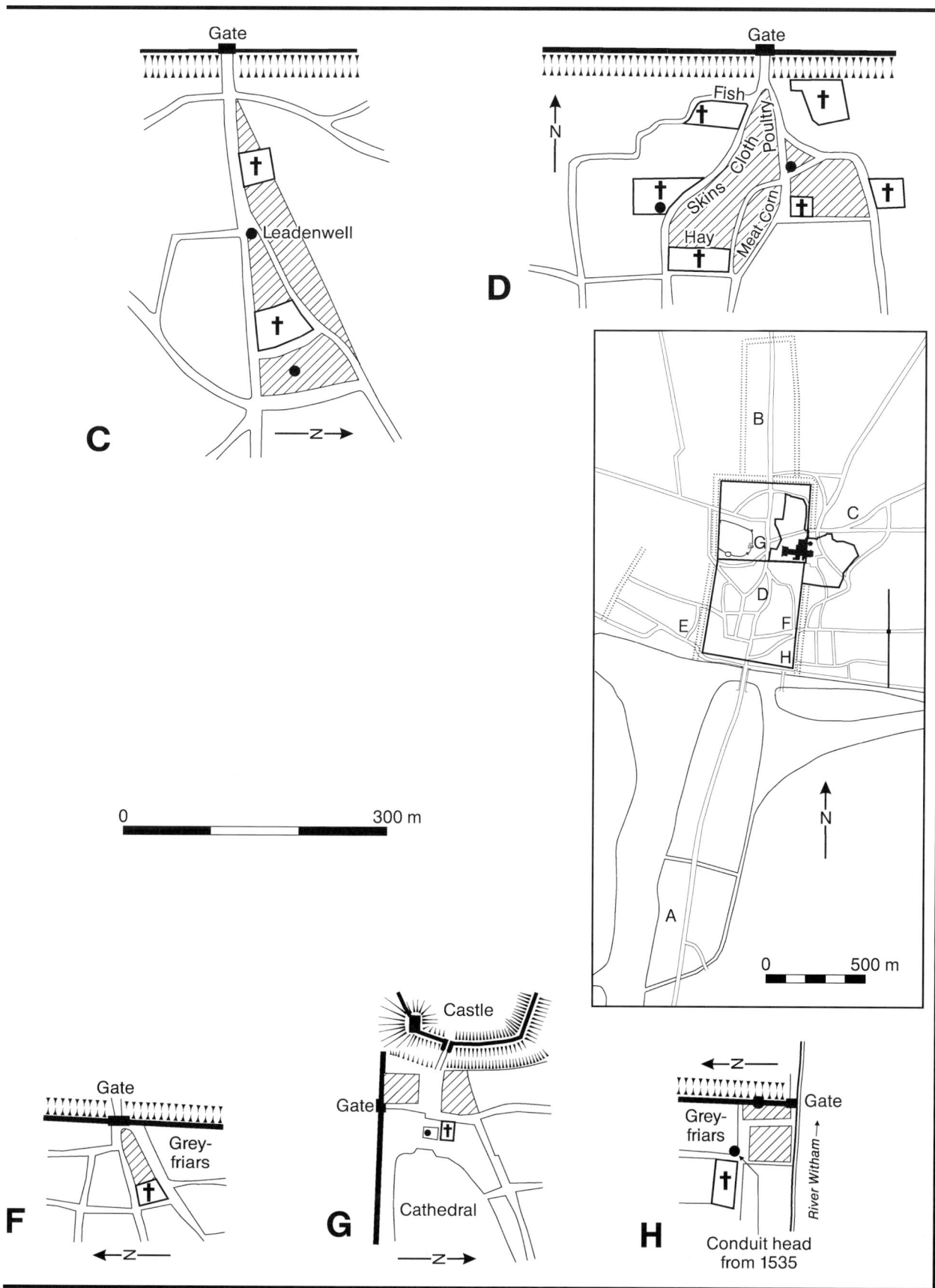

Fig. 9.83. *Reconstructed plans of the medieval market places of Lincoln compared. The street plans are derived from Padley's 1842 map and the market places have been defined during the course of this study. C) Eastgate market; D) Old High Market of the Lower City (showing the documented locations of individual traders in the late middle ages); ; F) Clewmarket (Thread-market); G) market place on Castle Hill (Duchy of Lancaster); H) Malt-market? followed by Staple Place (Wool-market); A–D are markets of probable 10th- or 11th-century origin; E–H are markets of unknown or later medieval date (drawn by Dave Watt, copyright English Heritage).*

from which to get access to the backs of properties, but it is also possible that such lanes across churchyards are as old as the churchyards themselves, and this may take their establishment back to the 10th century.

Place-name sources also contain information concerning the relative status of routeways. *Haraldsty* is the earlier name for Flaxengate, for example, and is therefore a case of a lane (*tigh*) being upgraded to a street (*gate*). It is not until the 16th century that we have any evidence for the involvement of the city in the naming of streets and lanes, although we cannot necessarily infer that, earlier, street names evolved only through common usage. Nevertheless, it is likely that recorded names do have a close relationship to the perceived status of routeways with a fundamental legal distinction between highways and the rest. The clearest case for the demotion of routeways comes from the Eastgate suburb where the modern Winnowsty Lane is the remains of a important routeway that has been demoted. Here a large quarry cut across its line just outside the suburb, and the Close Wall caused it to be diverted northwards within the suburb (Figs. 9.60, 9.61 and 9.92), both events making the road unusable for its original purpose, to go directly from the east gate of the Upper City to the *Wainwell* – from which it originally took its name *Wainwellgate*. In this case Cameron's researches show that the change of name is clear-cut and precisely dated -*strete* and -*gate* endings are found from 1212 to 1273 whereas -*tigh* endings occur first in 1272 and then run through the medieval period (1985, 110). The construction of the Close Wall at this point was dated by dendrochonology to between 1249 and 1284 and accords precisely with this change of name (Hall 1992), even though the documentary evidence for the date of the wall suggests a later date.

### Water supply and rubbish disposal

The provision of fresh water and the disposal of waste would have posed an increasing problem for the early town. It is arguable whether the sophisticated Roman water supply and disposal system, based on wells, aqueduct and sewers even survived to the end of the Roman occupation of the city, let alone until the late 9th century. In the absence of communal supply, water could be obtained by collecting rainwater, from the Witham, from springs, or by cleaning out Roman wells or digging new ones. There is, naturally enough, no archaeological evidence for the collection of rainwater in water-butts, but even in Lincoln's climate, the contribution made from this source must always have been limited. The Witham, on the other hand, would have supplied an unlimited amount of water, but whether it was safe to drink, even in the late 9th century, is doubtful. It is possible, however, that the inhabitants of Wigford obtained their water from the Upper Witham above the city. The natural springs in and around the city, however, must have been an

important, perhaps the most important, source of fresh water (Fig. 9.84). The spring line can be followed around the scarp of Lincoln Edge, following the junction of the Lincolnshire Limestone and the underlying clay. Below this line, ponds could form on the Liassic clay shelf above the river and be used for watering livestock, keeping ducks and the like. The Liassic clay shelf was capped with sands and gravels and water could be obtained higher up the hillside by digging a well through the sands into the clay, which could then act as a sump. On top of the hill, however, the water table is beneath at least 12m of limestone and here, the only possible source of water in usable amounts was to be found by digging wells. Digging a well through the limestone in the Upper City would have been a major engineering undertaking and identifying and rehabilitating Roman wells, like that at St Paul-in-the-Bail, would have made good practical sense. The well at St Paul-in-the-Bail (SP 84) was over 16m deep and, in the post-medieval period, only the bottom 4.5m were permanently wet.

It is possible that the ease of water supply was a governing factor in the location of the late 9th- and 10th-century settlement, located as it is in the optimum position for water supply – along the shelf of gravel capping to the Lias clay, between the springs in the hillside above and the river below. Only one well of late 9th construction has been excavated, in the Lower City (LIN 73c). It was backfilled in the late 12th century and its site preserved as a result of the acquisition of the area by the Greyfriars in the 13th century. Nevertheless, it is frequently difficult to date the first construction of wells and it is likely that many wells active in the later medieval and later periods started life during the initial development of the settlement. The construction of a stone-lined circular well at the Hungate site, however, was dated to the mid 16th century (H 83), and there is no indication that it had any earlier origin.

Public wells certainly existed, during the period between the 12th and the 14th centuries (they are occasionally used as boundaries in charters and elements in place-names) and there is no reason to think that they were not provided earlier. The term 'well' seems to have been used both for a shaft and a spring in which the water issues out of the aquifer under its own pressure. Public wells in use during the medieval period include the well in St Paul-in-the-Bail churchyard where there is circumstantial evidence for the construction of a new circular well-head in the 13th or 14th century (SP 72). A public well was also incorporated in the layout of the new Exchequergate complex when that was built in the early 14th century (Jones *et al.* 1987, 92–101) (Fig. 9.19b), and, although there seem to be no documentary references to it, the *Leadenwell* at the junction of Langworthgate and Greetwellgate, serving the putative market, is also likely to have been a public well in the medieval period (it is first recorded in

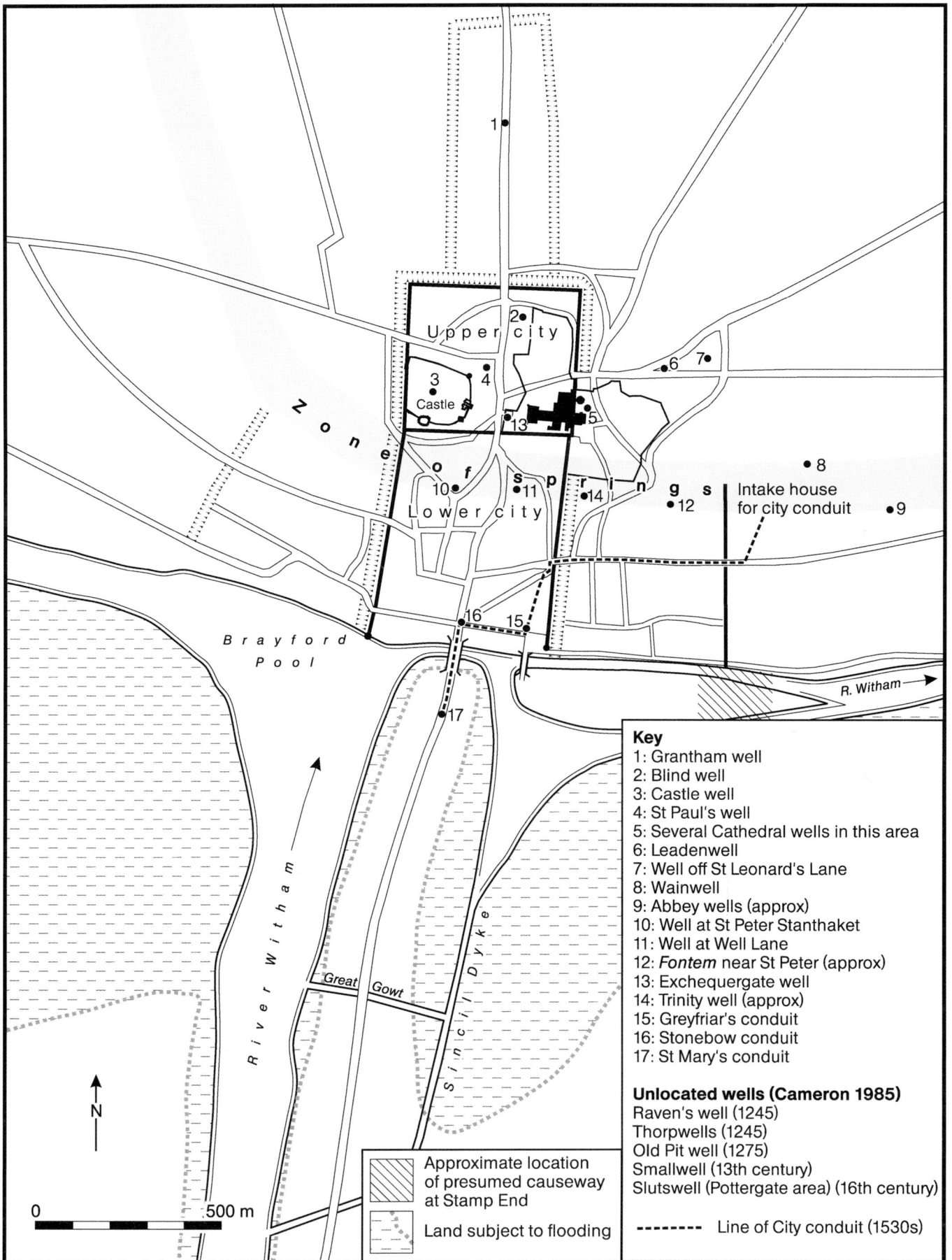

**Key**
1: Grantham well
2: Blind well
3: Castle well
4: St Paul's well
5: Several Cathedral wells in this area
6: Leadenwell
7: Well off St Leonard's Lane
8: Wainwell
9: Abbey wells (approx)
10: Well at St Peter Stanthaket
11: Well at Well Lane
12: *Fontem* near St Peter (approx)
13: Exchequergate well
14: Trinity well (approx)
15: Greyfriar's conduit
16: Stonebow conduit
17: St Mary's conduit

**Unlocated wells (Cameron 1985)**
Raven's well (1245)
Thorpwells (1245)
Old Pit well (1275)
Smallwell (13th century)
Slutswell (Pottergate area) (16th century)

-------- Line of City conduit (1530s)

Approximate location of presumed causeway at Stamp End

Land subject to flooding

*Fig. 9.84. Known public wells and springs in use during medieval period (drawn by Dave Watt, copyright English Heritage).*

1612 – Cameron 1985, 27). The same may have been true of the *Grantham Well* in Newport (which is, however, apparently not recorded until 1722). These public wells may also have helped to serve the Bail. A large well also served the inner bailey of the Castle.

There is plenty of evidence for provision of public wells in the Lower City and in *Butwerk*, although there is much less for the other suburbs. Well Lane, in the Lower City, was so-called by about 1240 (*Ibid.*, 108), perhaps from a predecessor of the well situated at the corner of Well Lane and Steep Hill. We have place-name evidence for interest in springs all along the cliff edge from the parish of Holy Trinity Greestone Stairs to the Monks Abbey estate. St Peter *ad fontem* is first so-called in a mid 14th-century transcription of a document of *c.*1189 and occurs in several sources of 13th-century date, alongside the name *at Wells* (*Ibid.*, 131). This well presumably lay in the close called *Spa Close* in the 1851 Tithe Award (*Ibid.*, 41). The Blackfriars brought water by conduit to their precinct from a spring source on the cliff edge further to the east in 1260 (ed. Page 1906, 220), although they themselves were on the spring line. Further east still there were at least two springs nearer the Black Monks' cell, rising to the north-east of the church and giving rise to the street name Spa Street. *Halliwellgate* seems to have been an alternative name for the original eastern end of *Wainwellgate* (now Sewells Road) along the cliff towards the *Wainwell* (the 'wagon well' *Ibid.*, 110 – Figs. 9.60 and 9.61), which was the medieval name for the strong spring later known as *Coldbath* just below the cliff and now within the Arboretum. Presumably then, the *Wainwell* was also considered to be a *Halliwell* or 'Holy Well'. There was a well or spring in the parish of Holy Trinity Greestone Stairs, giving its name to *Trinity Well Street* (Cameron 1985, 106) and on the boundary of this parish, apparently in Pottergate, was *Slutswell*, first recorded in the mid 16th century (Cameron 1985, 39). The *Slutswell* could have been a well on the top of the hill, but as Pottergate extended over the cliff edge and down the scarp, the name may have referred to one of the springs along the cliff-foot. Finally, on this side of the city, we should not presume that every medieval reference to *Greetwell* refers to the medieval settlement east of the city. It is possible that some of these references are to a 'Great Well' somewhere between the village and Eastgate. A very similar spring-line exists in the cliff-face to the south of the city, on South Common, and in 1306 the canons of St Katherine's Priory gained a licence to channel water from a spring here directly into their house through a conduit (Hill 1948, 248).

The disposal of refuse and cess would have presented different problems in different areas within the city, and such problems would also have changed with time. There is evidence to suggest that the properties excavated on the Flaxengate site (F 72) had middens – refuse heaps – in their yards in the 10th and 11th centuries. If horticulture took place at the rear of these plots then rotted refuse, including human cess, could form useful manure. Only once occupation had reached a certain intensity would the presence of large stinking rubbish heaps have been thought a problem – perhaps as much for the flies and vermin which would have lived in and on the middens as for the smell emanating from them. Even then, perhaps, cess and rotted refuse might have been buried in pits in the yards, rather than removed from the site, only to be dug out subsequently for use as manure either within the plot or elsewhere. A cycle of this type of 'composting' may be one reason why in many cases we find such extensive inter-cutting complexes of pits at the backs of properties from the 10th century onwards. There was certainly a desire to place these pits as close as possible to the boundaries of the properties, and on several excavations such lines of pits have been found, for example on a site fronting onto the High Street (WO 89).

Many of these pits were probably unlined; dug, filled and backfilled over a short period of time (Fig. 9.85). However, the lack of evidence for a lining does not mean that one was never present. On most Lincoln sites, where there was no organic preservation, a wicker or plank lining would leave no trace. We have a similar lack of information about the function served by these pits, before being used for rubbish disposal. It is now possible to distinguish the remains of human cess from those of other organic rubbish, through the presence of parasite eggs in soil samples, but the major excavations of this type of site in Lincoln (between 1972 and 1987) took place before the identification of parasite eggs became standard practice. Such information is only available for the pits on the waterside excavations (WNW 88, WO 89) (Carrott *et al.* 1994; Greig 1989).

There are several cases where it is quite clear that a

*Fig. 9.85. Unlined cess-pit revealed during excavations on Flaxengate (F 72). The scale is 2m long (photo and copyright, City of Lincoln Archaeology Unit).*

stone-lined pit, attached to, or immediately adjacent to, a building acted as the collecting point for garderobe chutes within the building. Examples are known from both the Lower City and Wigford (Fig. 9.86; F 72, H 83, Z 86, SMG 82). These pits would have had to be emptied at regular intervals, and therefore only contained their latest contents when excavated. Sometimes they include deposits of household rubbish, including assemblages of well-preserved pottery but there is no way of telling whether this was typical of the pit in its normal use or simply what happened when the system was abandoned. A group of wicker-lined pits from Flaxengate (F 72), backfilled in the mid or late 12th century, are probably the earliest examples of pits intended to remain open for some time, rather than to be backfilled with cess or rubbish shortly after construction. Their location, in a line at what would have been the back of a property fronting onto Grantham Street, does not help to determine their function. If they were all open at one time we could suggest that they had some industrial function. They could even be pits for flax-retting, given the later name for the street in which they were found ('Flaxengate' is first recorded as a place-name in 1685 – Cameron 1985, 66). On the other hand, if the pits were sequential, they may have been dug to be backfilled with cess or rubbish, in succession to their unlined predecessors. They are, however, at the upper end of the size range for earlier rubbish and cess-pits.

As in previous centuries, a large number of pits seem to have been dug and backfilled without leaving any obvious evidence of their function. Those at Hungate (H 83) were excavated using the single context planning method which makes it possible to see that they must have had fills with a high organic content which consolidated after burial, leading to the sinking of any overlying deposits into the top of the pit, followed, sometimes, by the spreading of

*Fig. 9.86. Stone-lined cess-pit revealed during excavations on a site in St Mark's parish, Wigford (Z 86). The scale is 1m long (photo and copyright, City of Lincoln Archaeology Unit).*

makeup into the hollow thus formed. These pits cease at the end of the 12th century, but in this case only because the area was then covered by a large stone building. In the Bail, there is a contrast between the ordered pitting found on the tenement immediately north of the Mint Wall (WB 80) and that found to the north-west of St Clement-in-the-Bail, where it is possible that lime burning or some other industrial process may have been carried out (W 73). We may be justified in saying that roughly square or rectangular pits, particularly when occurring as inter-cutting groups, are evidence for domestic refuse disposal. Such a conclusion allows us to make provisional comments about settlement in parts of the city where structures have yet to be recovered by excavation. Consequently we can suggest that, because such pits occur at two other sites in the north-west corner of the Bail (WB 76, CL 85), they may be evidence for intensive domestic occupation in this part of the city between the later 11th and 12th centuries, probably fronting onto West Bight, and prior to the possible later medieval lime-burning here.

### Supply routes and victualling by water and land
#### Supply routes
Medieval Lincoln was connected to the surrounding countryside and to the wider world, by water and road, and it was these connections which made it a viable urban community (Fig. 9.87). Water transport would have been possible via the Witham to the North Sea. We have seen that bridges and the Stamp End causeway meant that boats coming from Boston may not have reached the walled city, but this route might not have been suitable for the sea-going vessels of the 14th century anyway, and it is clear that many goods destined for the city were unloaded further down the Witham at Dogdyke and, perhaps, at Short Ferry. Access to the Trent and, from there, the Humber estuary and the North Sea, on the other hand, depended on the condition of the Fossdyke. It has been suggested above that a Roman date for the Fossdyke's construction is unlikely and our study of medieval pottery supply (p. 116 and 241 above) has suggested that it may have first come into use in the late 10th century, when the quantity of Torksey ware found in the city suddenly increases. It would never have been possible to take anything larger than a small barge further south than Brayford Pool, up the Witham, and such vessels would have to negotiate the bridge carrying the Fosse Way at Bracebridge. Even so, small craft clearly did use the upper Witham as part of local supply networks and study of 10th- and 11th-century sculpted gravestones from the Ancaster region suggested that this was one of the main arteries for the distribution of these quarries' products (Everson and Stocker 1999, 44). In 1265 the citizens complained that the boats bringing turf and faggots and many other things with which to supply

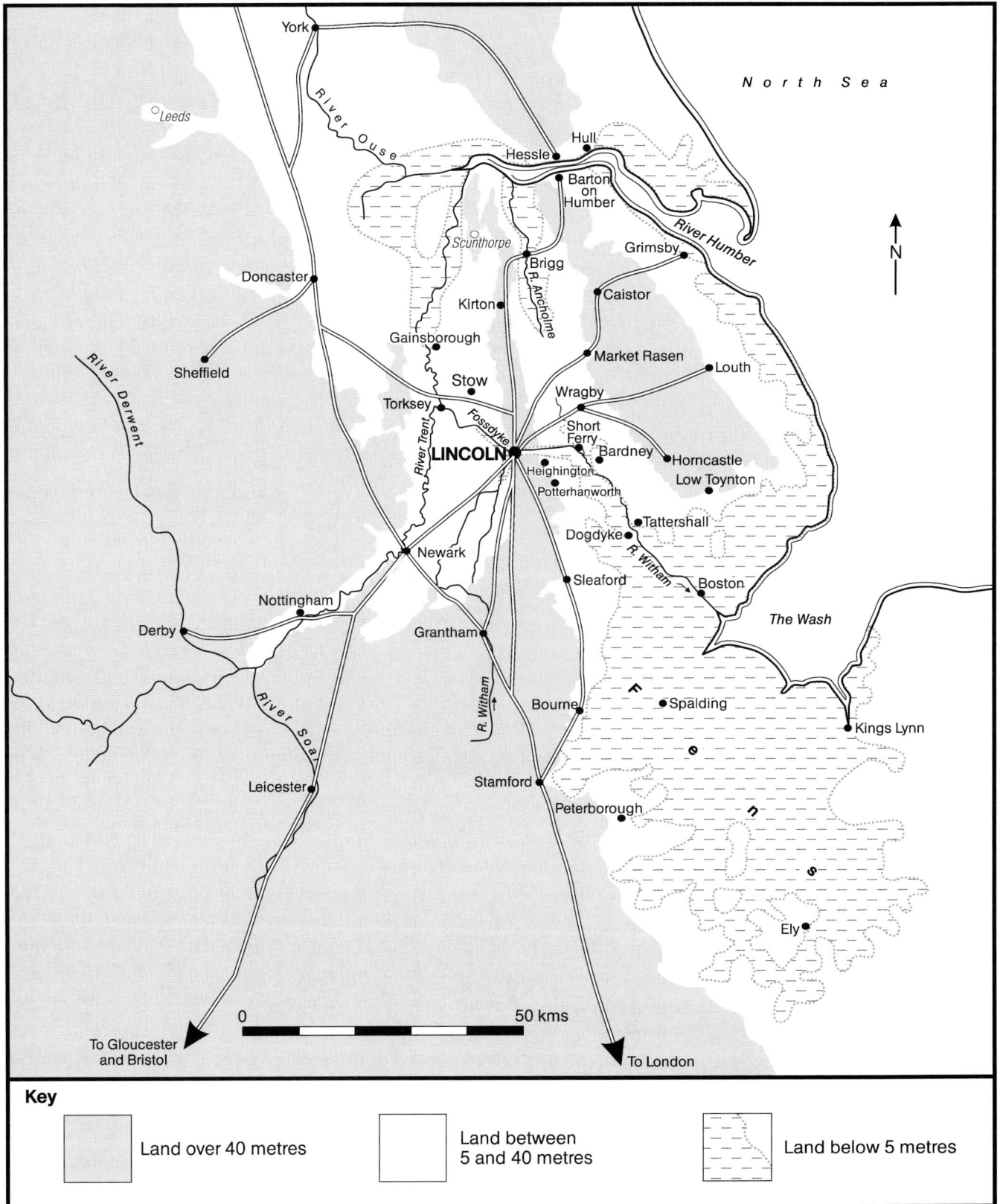

Fig. 9.87. *Lincoln's main communication routes in the medieval period (drawn by Dave Watt, copyright English Heritage).*

the city down river from the south had been ob-structed by the canons of St Katherine's Priory (Hill 1948, 347).

Within 10 km of Lincoln all known roads led into

the city, some reaching as far as the gates, others joining before they reach them. The road system can be divided into three types of route: the long-distance national routeways (Ermine Street north and south of the city, Fosse Way south of the city), roads which linked the city with its province (Wragby Road, Nettleham Road, Greetwellgate), and short-distance access routes to the surrounding fields, meadows, pasture and woodland.

Overland connections with London, Nottingham Leicester and York were all by means of long-distance route-ways, essentially of Roman origin. Most of these roads were probably in use from the 9th century onwards, but, equally, most are absent from documents until the later Middle Ages. The settlements of Kesteven were also reached by way of these long-distance routes, but some of the roads linking the Anglo-Scandinavian city with Lindsey were of intermediate length, and these routes all lead to and from the east gate of the Bail. A glance at the map of the city shows that, of the six streets which fan out from here (Nettleham Road, Wragby Road/Langworthgate, Greetwellgate, *Wainwellgate*, Pottergate and *Boune Lane*), there is evidence for the Roman origins of only two. These two, Nettleham and Wragby Roads, were clearly routes of importance into the surrounding Lindsey countryside; leading to Market Rasen, Caistor and Grimsby and Wragby, Horncastle and Louth respectively. Although there is no direct evidence for its being a Roman road beyond the Greetwell Villa, Greetwell Road, similarly, led to a medieval route along the north side of the River Witham towards Fiskerton and, eventually, to Bardney, Tattershall and Boston. All of these roads would have had the status of 'King's highway' in the later medieval period, as they probably did from the late 9th century.

By the late Middle Ages, major routeways were habitually known by the name of the place at the end of the route. Thus, we know of roads to Stow (*Stowgate*, which ran east–west across Low Field and is probably represented today by Carholme Road or West Parade), Greetwell and Langworth, all recorded in the early 13th century (Cameron 1985, 70, 77, 103). Similarly Ermine Street north of the city was sometimes called *Humber Street* (from 1237 – *Ibid.*, 74). It may be significant that all of these streets were to the north of the Witham gap, but there is no real evidence to suggest that Lincoln drew its supplies exclusively from Lindsey. Neither the documentary evidence, in the form of toponyms of the city's 13th-century inhabitants, nor artefactual evidence, mainly pottery, would support that view. It is therefore, presumably, just coincidence that there was no *Sleafordgate* or *Newarkgate* in Lincoln. Gates through the walls, however, were not just provided for the major long distance routeways. In the Lower City, the roads leaving the Clasketgate gate cannot be traced further than a few hundred metres and presumably existed primarily to give access to the Upper City (via *Holgate* and Pottergate), and to *Butwerk* and the Monks Abbey. *Midhergate* the putative 'middle street' in Newland, gave access only to the suburb of Newland and to the town fields beyond. Whilst the most northerly of the three New-

land roads, later known as *Clay Lane* or *Wong Lane* (and now marked by West Parade), probably gave access to Burton and the long distance trackway which linked the settlements along the spring-line to the north-east. The Upper City west postern gate gave access to the *Westcastle* suburb and thence to *Cliffgate* leading north-west down the hillside, in a similar direction to the modern Long Leys Road. It was heading overland, presumably to Torksey across the valley of the river Till, although it too may have gone no further than the city fields.

*Cereals and other plants – supply and consumption*
Both Von Thünen's central place theory (1875) and medieval practice in the hinterland of London (Campbell *et al.* 1992; 1993; Galloway *et al.* 1991; 1996) suggest that the bulk of cereals and cereal products used would have been obtained close to Lincoln – as was demonstrated by the surviving records for the supply of foodstuffs for the Parliament held in Lincoln in 1301 (Platts 1985, 103–8) (Fig. 9.88). Wheat was obtained from a large number of manors, both north and south of the city. Mostly, these were located on the limestone uplands of the Lincolnshire limestone and the chalk wolds. Oats were obtained mainly from the fens and the lower Trent valley. Malt was exclusively supplied from sources north of the Witham but was obtained from a range of environments.

The citizens of Lincoln had rights in the three great fields of the city, which lay on the limestone hilltop (Figs. 9.3, 9.89) and on the river terraces of the Till and the Witham north of the city. The three open fields (*North Field, East Field* and *Low Field*), containing about 1,800 acres, were enclosed in 1803 by Act of Parliament (Hill 1948, 331ff). Some ridge and furrow has been recorded in these areas by early aerial photography, and a study of the pattern of earthworks on the modern West Common is underway (English Heritage forthcoming). Land in these fields was allocated only to those citizens who lived north of the river; citizens living in Wigford had no rights in these common fields and, although they acquired rights of pasturage in rural extensions of the Wigford parishes to the south and east (in the *Cow Paddle* and on South Common), it seems they were never allocated any arable. This contrast between Wigford and the remainder of the city is of some importance, and may suggest not only that the total population of Wigford in the medieval period was not high. It probably also suggests that inhabitants here, whilst they might have a cow or two, did not have the obligation of much field work, either on their own behalf, or on behalf of their Lords. Wigford, then, may have been dominated by 'free' burgesses in a way that is not apparent in the city to the north.

Hill (*Ibid.*, 334) believed that the interests of the citizen's beasts (many seem to have owned one or two cattle) usually took precedence over the interests of the citizen 'husbandmen' who owned land in the

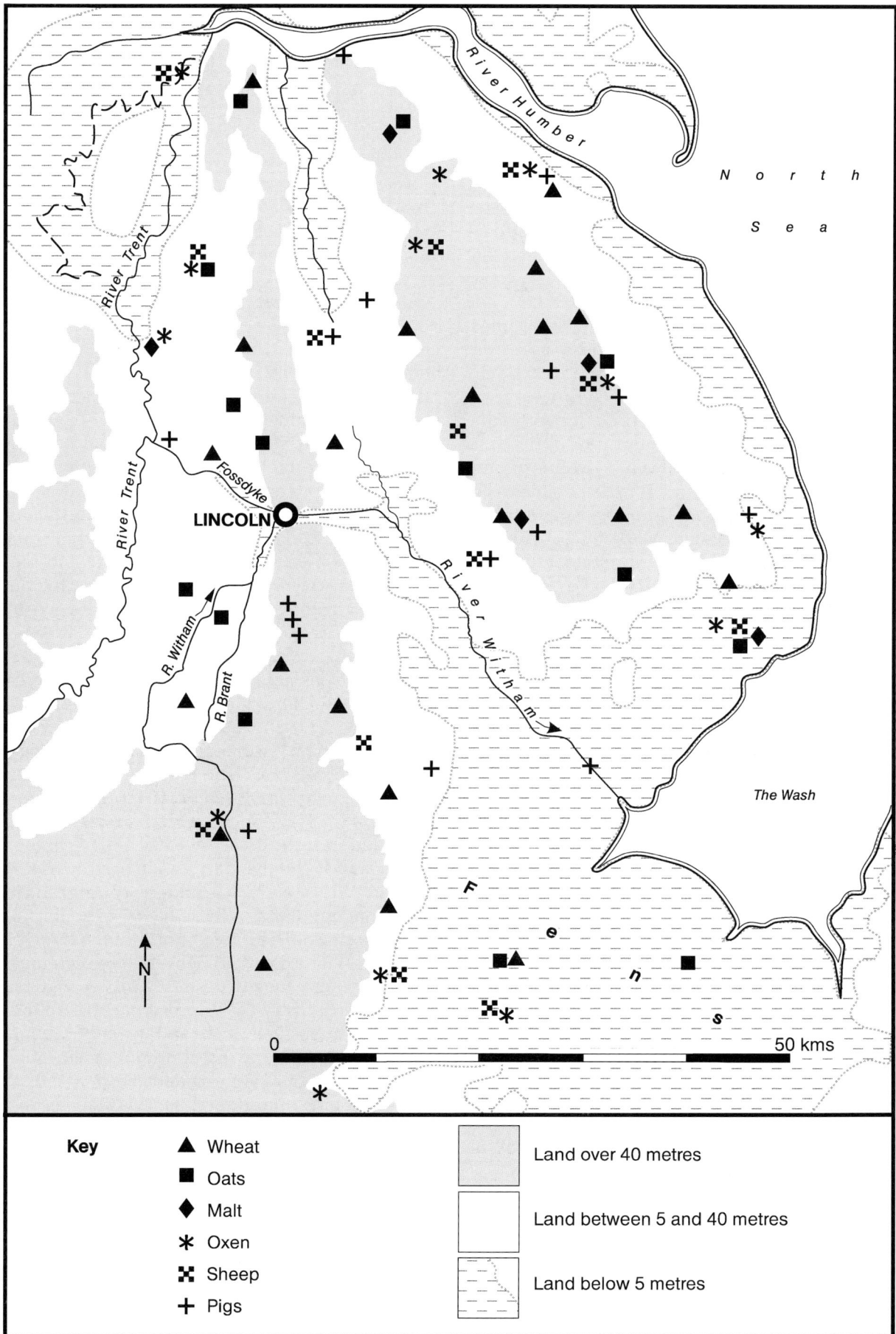

*Fig. 9.88. The origins of foodstuffs arriving in Lincoln to supply the parliament held there in 1301 (source, Platts 1985, figs 37 & 38 – drawn by Dave Watt, copyright English Heritage).*

*Fig. 9.89. View of the Upper City from the north-west by S H Grimm c.1784, showing the south eastern part of North Field – apparently under grass. Note the enormous scale of the Castle earthworks, especially when compared to the Bail rampart to the north, which seems to have been completely removed (although see also Fig. 9.10). Note also the county gallows, north of the line of Westgate (photo and copyright, British Library).*

fields (who were much fewer in number). Even if the husbandmen had been given a free hand, however, it is unlikely that Lincoln's three fields could have supplied more than a fraction of the city's cereal requirements and presumably, from very early in its history, the city formed a market for the surplus produce of surrounding estates. Wheat was mainly obtained from the limestone uplands, both to the north and south, whereas oats were obtained from the silt fenlands and barley from sites on the lower slopes, adjacent to fen and marshland (Platts 1985, 110). There is also documentary evidence for the production of rye, beans and peas (*Ibid.*). Analysis of carbonised and mineralised seeds recovered from soil samples by V Straker (1979) and L Moffett (1994) has demonstrated that the standard range of cereals (oats, bread wheat, club wheat, spelt, hulled barley and rye) was present between the 9th and 14th centuries, whilst the absence of chaff shows that the cereals arrived in the city already threshed. Threshing therefore took place at source, in suburban farms like those which are known to have lined the green at Newport, or in the settlements of more remote suppliers.

Quern stones, on the other hand, were a vital item of household equipment and there must have been great demand for suitable stone; one which would produce flour with as little contamination from the rock itself as possible. Fragments of over 40 querns have been recovered from 9th- to 12th-century levels, although it is possible that many of these may be of Roman date. Quern stones found in Lincoln are made from three main stone types; Millstone Grit, or similar Coal Measure sandstones, Niedermendig Lava and un-sourced sandstones. Two of these (one of Millstone

Grit and the other of Niedermendig Lava) were identified by Roe (1996) as being of Roman type whilst four were identified as being of Anglo-Scandinavian type (including a possible Niedermendig Lava mill stone from Michaelgate – MCH 84). There is a strong bias amongst these finds towards the Lower City; this is not simply due to the size of the Flaxengate assemblage since the same predominance is present even if that site is excluded. Only three of the finds were from the Upper City and six from Wigford. Chronologically, the sequence appears to be Niedermendig Lava followed by Millstone Grit and then a variety of sandstones. We must be aware, however, that the ubiquity of imported stones amongst the residual Roman material on most sites in Lincoln means that we cannot rely too heavily on such conclusions. The stones could have been imported by the Romans as building material centuries before they were re-used by the Anglo-Scandinavian population as querns. Analysis of similar finds from London suggested that the main period of use of hand querns was in the 10th and 11th centuries, after which time most grain would have arrived in the settlement already milled (Pritchard 1991, 162–4). Lincoln shows less sign of this pattern, either because hand milling continued longer or, more probably, because of the high quantities of residual material in later medieval and later levels.

Although references exist to windmills along the hill scarp to the north-west of *Westcastle* suburb from the early 16th century (Hill 1948, 336–7), there were probably mills in this favourable location from much earlier in the medieval period (Fig. 9.90). This is perhaps the most likely location for the windmill 'in Lincoln suburb' owned in 1326 by William Cause,

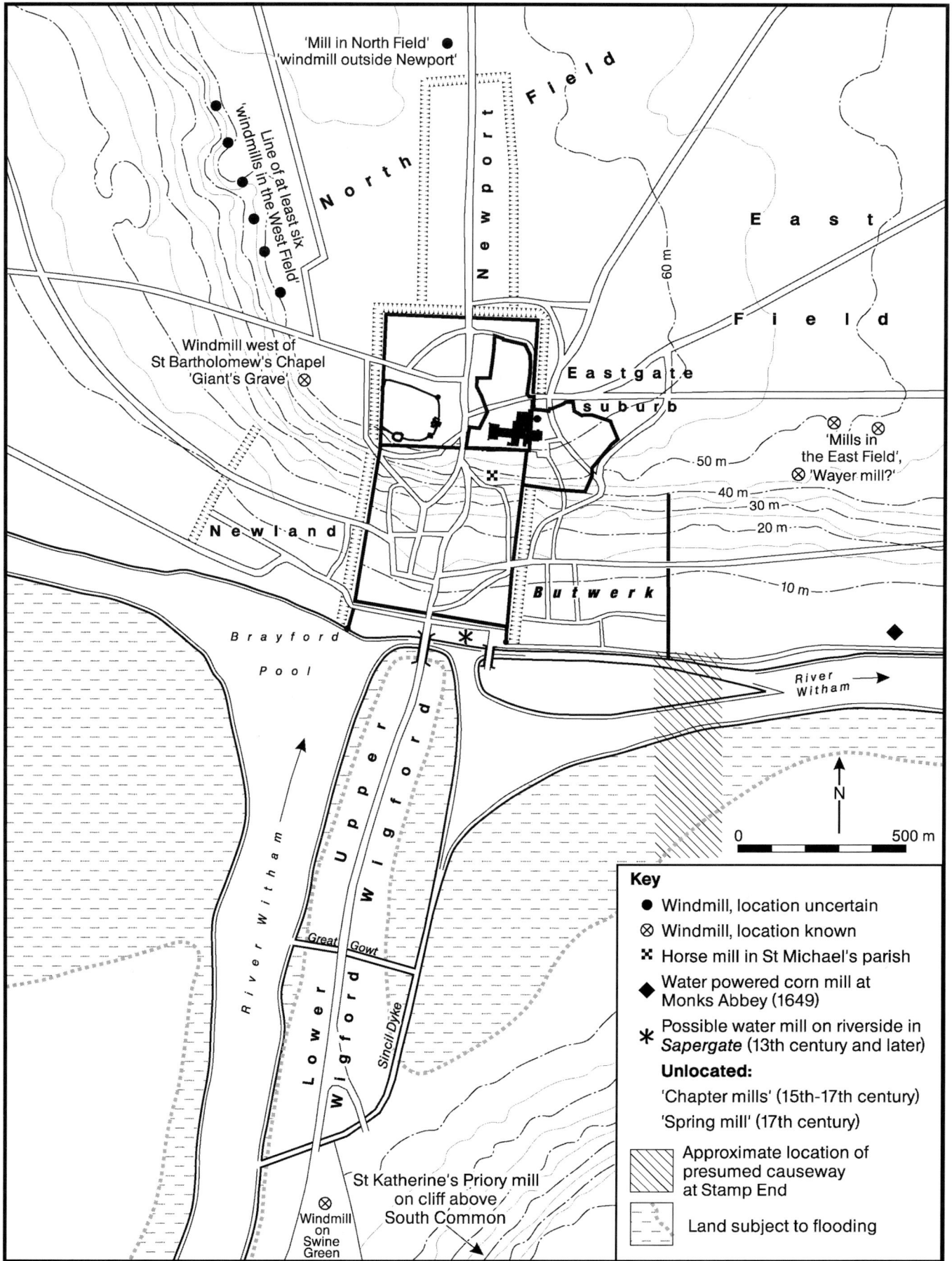

*Fig. 9.90. Documented medieval corn mills (sources, Cameron 1985, Hill 1948 – drawn by Dave Watt, copyright English Heritage).*

mayor in 1301 (*Ibid.*, 214). Further windmills existed by 1455 in the East Field (Lincolnshire Archives Office, Lincoln City Charters 6/54), and both these and the mills in the North Field are shown on Speed's map of *c*.1610 (Fig. 9.91). By 1265 the canons of St Katherine's Priory had also raised a windmill on the South Common. It was probably on the land between the road up Cross O'Cliff hill and the road to Bracebridge, possibly on the hill slope, or near its crest. In 1284–5 they sought leave to build what might be a second mill in the centre of the green outside their gate (*Ibid.*, 347). This may have been the same mill for which, in 1447 the Council claimed a rent of 11/– (*Ibid.*, 349).

There must have been, also, some water-mills in the city, and water-mills and horse-mills were brought into use in 1555 when there was no wind (*Ibid.*, 337). A mill of some sort (which – given its location may have been driven by water) was held by Barlings Abbey on the east side of *Briggate* (i.e. High Street) at *Sapergate* in the early 13th century. Grain to feed the mills, and also, probably, flour was sold at the Corn Market (*mercatum bladi*) at the foot of Steep Hill (first recorded 1310 – Cameron 1985, 22). Ovens which might have been used in the production of malt or for brewing are uncommon, if known at all, at this period, whilst the evidence for bread ovens has been discussed above (p. 257 – see also p. 292–4 below).

*Meat – supply and consumption*
Two major analyses of the animal bones from Lincoln have been published (O'Connor 1982; Dobney *et al.* 1996). The former report deals with the entire post-Roman assemblage from a single site (Flaxengate – F

72), whereas the latter is a selective study of material sampled from sites across the city and chosen to cover all periods. Even so, the difficulty of drawing firm conclusions is very real. In the first case, almost all the deposits on the site were heavily contaminated with residual Roman material, presumably including animal bone, whereas in the second case, the low numbers of identifiable bones recorded limits the conclusions that can be drawn. Figures for the consumption of the major domestic mammals show an increased presence of sheep in the Anglo-Scandinavian and Norman periods at the expense of cattle. The frequency of sheep is in fact higher in the later part of this period than at any time later. In terms of the meat that could be obtained from the carcass, however, cattle always formed between 80% and 90% of the total. Metrical data suggest that the cattle were of similar size to those used in the Roman and Early Modern Eras, but that the kill-off pattern was different. Roman cattle were much more likely to be killed as adults, whereas both late Saxon and Early Modern cattle were as likely to live until old age. This suggests that they only entered the food chain after having been used for other purposes, most probably traction.

Cattle can be raised on low-lying wet pasture, as well as on drier lighter soils, and it is likely that those supplied to Lincoln were reared on a variety of terrains in the surrounding countryside, from the Trent valley through the claylands of central Lindsey to the fens. Again this seems to be confirmed by the accounts for the 1301 Lincoln Parliament (Platts 1985, 103–8) (Fig. 9.88). These records distinguish between animals brought in on the hoof and dead. Surprisingly perhaps,

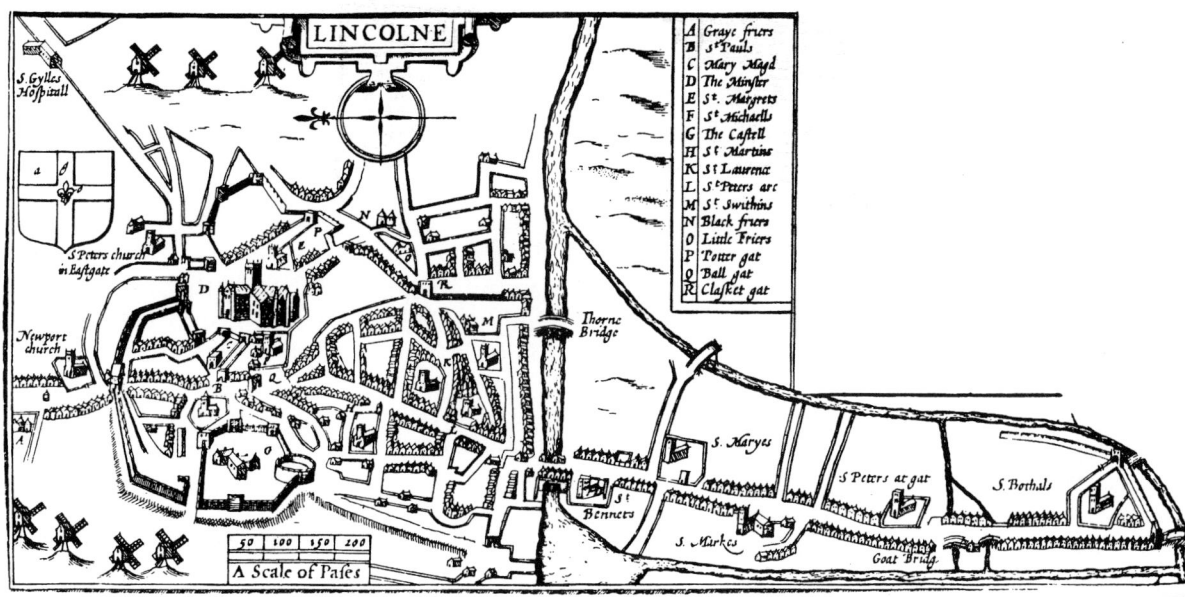

*Fig. 9.91. Lincoln in 1610 by John Speed (Speed 1611). Note the lines of windmills to the north-west and east of the Upper City. North is to the left.*

most of the meat was already butchered. Some may have been carried by boat, for example from the fens, but the majority came from sources with no easy water connection with the city and must have been carried on wagons or carts from all parts of the county. Even so, it is likely, given the predominance of their bones in the sampled Lincoln assemblages, that cattle would have been an important stimulus to the maintenance and development of roads into the city. Road such as those leading west through the Newland suburb, and east from Clasketgate gate, led to the rich pasture lands on the terraces above the river, and it was on these pastures that many citizens would graze their beasts. The South Common, *Bargate Closes* and *Cow Paddle*, to the south and south-east, were similarly used. By the 16th and 17th centuries, the commoners also grazed their cattle on *The Holmes Common*, a chain of islands north of Boultham parish, west of the main channel of the Witham, west of Wigford and east of Swanpool. It is likely that these pastures were also used earlier (Hill 1948, 338).

Sheep too were mostly kept till maturity, living longer than their later medieval successors, and they were also of similar size to those of the Roman period. O'Connor (1983) demonstrated that, between the 9th and the 12th centuries, the quantity of sheep consumed in Lincoln would have taken up the entire surplus of an area of about 20 miles in radius. Since such an area could not be entirely devoted to rearing sheep for Lincoln, the actual routes of supply must have been much longer, probably encompassing much of the county and Nottinghamshire. Unlike cattle, sheep cannot be reared on low-lying wet inland pasture, because of their susceptibility to liver fluke (although where the land is salty – as in the Lincolnshire Marshes – this is not a constraint, as the salt inhibits the snail that plays a vital role in the fluke's life cycle). The sheep marketed in Lincoln, therefore, probably came from pasture on the Lincolnshire limestone, from the Wolds or the Marshes, but not from either the peat fens or the central Lindsey vale – a distribution also confirmed by the records of the 1301 Parliament (Platts 1985, 103–8) (Fig. 9.88). What little evidence there is from the archaeological record of the 13th and 14th centuries confirms the increasing consumption of mutton during this period, which has been noted elsewhere (Dobney *et al.*1996, 40–42). No doubt this is a reflection of the dramatic development of the wool industry, which grew to dominate the county's agriculture in the later Middle Ages. St Katherine's Priory was one of the most important sheep-rearing monastic houses in the county (Owen 1971, 66) and in 1447 they struck a bargain with the Council over their rights to bring a large flock of their sheep to graze on South Common at shearing time (Hill 1948, 350).

The only other domesticates to be found in any quantity in Lincoln excavations are pig, dog and chicken, all presumably bred and reared in the city, but present in too small quantities in the sample for any study of their size or age at death. Pigs were herded by the tenants of St Mary's Abbey York on their estate east of the city in 1392 (*Ibid.*, 339) and from 1447, labourers of St Katherine's Priory were to drive their pig herd from the Priory to Canwick fields without interruption (*Ibid.*, 350). By 1511 the canons of St Katherine struck an agreement with the Council which suggests that their pigs were grazing on the South Common itself (*Ibid.*, 351).

Wild animals seem to have formed a very small part of the Lincoln diet in all periods, although, in the absence of a rigorous sieving policy on the sites excavated to date, it is not possible to evaluate the role of fish in the diet. However, their small contribution to the total meat weight represented by animal bones does not mean that they were necessarily unimportant. Fishing was certainly a major industry in the Brayford Pool (*Ibid.*, 338), as it was in the Witham more generally (White 1984b), but, with its wider network of maritime contacts, sea fish could have been brought in quite easily from both Wash and Humber (Fig. 9.87). The fish market was at the top of the hill (in St Michael-on-the-Mount parish) after 1549 and is first recorded in 1271 (Cameron 1985, 23). The fish bones excavated from Flaxengate were studied by Wilkinson (1982, 44–6) and revealed a typical un-sieved assemblage, dominated by the bones of large marine fish such as cod, haddock, salmon, flatfish, ling, shark and herring with only the larger freshwater fish represented (pike and roach). Studies carried out on fish bones from sites where sieving was routine show, during the period between the 9th and the 13th centuries, a replacement of freshwater fish, primarily eel, by marine fish. Furthermore, amongst the marine fish, there is an increasing predominance of large deep-sea fish, caught in the north Atlantic or Baltic and traded south. There is every reason to believe that this pattern would also have been found in Lincoln, but it remains to be demonstrated through excavation.

Documentary sources indicate the supply and sale of poultry at the poultry market, located at the north end of *Micklegate*, (probably on the modern Steep Hill) and first recorded in 1336, (Cameron 1985, 33). O'Connor identified 24 species of wild birds amongst the excavated assemblage at Flaxengate (F 72), of which all but six might have been eaten. Furthermore, two of these, the peregrine falcon and the goshawk, were used in hunting (1982, 44). The ecological niche of many birds has changed since the Anglo-Scandinavian period but the majority of the species found at Flaxengate are likely to have been caught in the river valleys, fens or coastal marshes.

### Commerce, crafts and industry

From its (re)foundation in the late 9th century through to the 14th century, Lincoln was an important industrial and commercial centre. The earliest stratified late 9th-century deposits at Flaxengate (F 72), predating evidence for the occupation of the site itself, have produced evidence for pottery manufacture, the working of antler and non-ferrous metalworking, whilst the first evidence for bone working and iron smithing is only slightly later. By the early years of the 10th century Lincoln also had its own mint and by the end of the century had a large compliment of moneyers, making it one of the most productive mints in England (Mossop 1970). Cloth working was also important in the 10th and 11th centuries and by the 13th century the preparation and marketing of cloth dominated the internal economy of the city (Hill 1948, 321–2; Bischoff 1975).

### Stone working

Stone working must always have been one of the major industries in medieval Lincoln but surprisingly little archaeological evidence for it has been gathered. This is partly due, perhaps, to the fact that many medieval quarries were themselves quarried away in the post-medieval and later periods and partly because the quarries are inaccessible, having been backfilled or built-over. Probably, the earliest quarries were those exploiting the Lincolnshire Limestone exposure along the Lincoln Edge and to the north and south of the Witham gap (Fig. 9.92). However, there is no archaeological evidence to show that this exposure was still being worked in the medieval period. It has been suggested, however, that it was the source of the stone used in the 10th and 11th century for grave-covers and grave-markers (Everson and Stocker 1999 *passim*). A petrological study of these stones by Worssam indicates that both the Upper Lincolnshire Limestone and two distinct formations within the Lower Lincolnshire Limestone were utilised (Worssam 1999, 18–19). In the mid or later 10th century, worked stone, attributed to a Lincoln industry, had also utilised reused Roman blocks, indicated in one case by the presence of a 'lewis hole' (Everson and Stocker 1999, 197–8). Such re-use of Roman stone was still being practised in the mid 11th century, as in the case of the reused Roman inscription found in the footings of St Mark's church (SM 76) (Stocker and Everson 1990).

By the late medieval period, quarries existed to the east of the Upper City as indicated by *-pit* place-names in documents such as the 1455 agreement between the Council and St Mary's Abbey, York (Lincolnshire Archives Office, Lincoln City Charters 6/54), but it is likely that they were established much earlier. Exca-

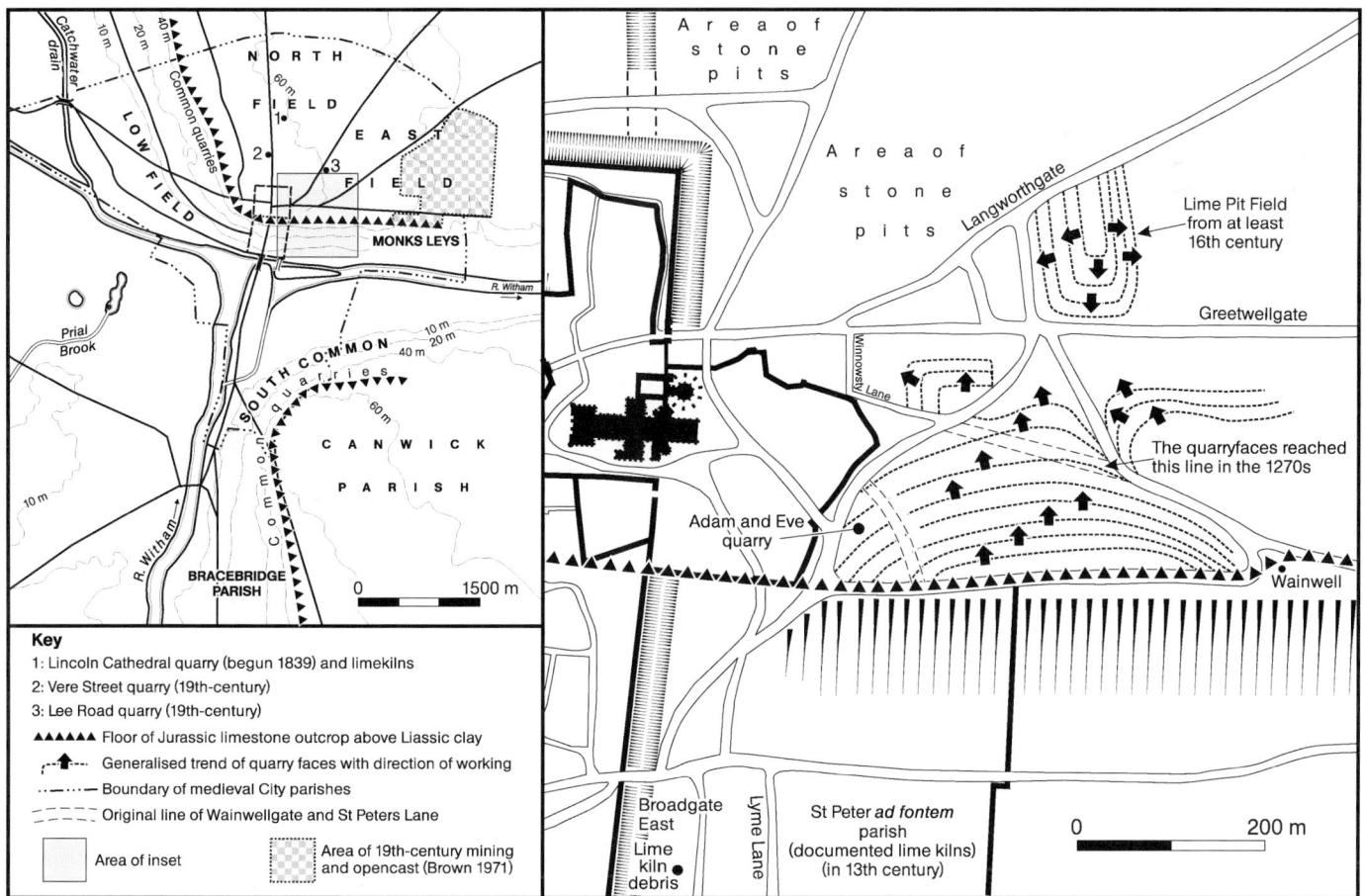

*Fig. 9.92. Medieval and later quarries in and around the city. The inset (right) shows the area of quarrying, on an industrial scale, east of the Close (drawn by Dave Watt, copyright English Heritage).*

vations in the grounds of buildings fronting onto Pottergate, within the Close, have revealed evidence for backfilled quarry pits. These presumably pre-date the layout of these properties, which were in existence by the late 12th century (Jones *et al.* 1984, 74–95) and could either belong to the Roman period or to the period between the 10th and 12th centuries. There is some indication in the documentary records for the Eastgate suburb for the proximity of quarries behind the line of settlement at the west end of Greetwellgate, west of Wragby Road (summarised in note form by Joan Varley and deposited in the Lincolnshire Archives Office). Excavations within the suburb at Langworthgate revealed extensive quarry pits, probably of medieval date (LG 89; LG 90). But the main area of quarrying was between Lindum Terrace (perhaps known as *Wintergate*) and Wragby Road (Fig. 9.92 inset). Adit mines extending westwards from working faces associated with these quarries were investigated by remote TV recording in 1987–89 (WC 87), although they appear to be of recent date (RAZ 11.41.2). Much of the land on which these quarries stood was owned by the Dean and Chapter until relatively recently, but it has recently been suggested by Everson and Stocker that the main stone quarries in 10th-century Lincoln may have been owned by the Bishop. The distribution of stone sculpture of probable Lincoln origin indicates a widespread trade in this stone in Lindsey from the 10th century (Fig. 9.93), but it is intriguing that the distribution does not extend into Kesteven. Many churches in the vicinity show that the quarries around Lincoln remained a source of good-quality stone, primarily used for architectural details, into and after the 14th century.

*Pottery import and manufacture*

It seems that pottery was being produced in Lincoln from very early in the Anglo-Scandinavian occupation of the city (Figs. 9.94 and 9.95). The earliest Anglo-Scandinavian levels excavated at Flaxengate produced abundant sherds of Lincoln Gritty ware (LG), some of which appear to be wasters whilst a similar high concentration, also with probable wasters, was found in a rubbish pit on the east side of Flaxengate (Coppack 1973). Shell-tempered wares, almost certainly of Lincoln origin, were found in the same deposits and at a slightly later date, in the early to mid 10th century, pottery was being produced just inside Clasketgate gate at Silver Street (Miles *et al.* 1989). It is thought that this production ceased in the late 10th century, although the site then apparently lay empty for a considerable time. The earliest evidence for occupation over the site of the pottery kiln is associated with 11th- or 12th-century pottery (LIN 73b). From the middle of the 10th century, almost certainly overlapping with the *floruit* of the Silver Street potters, pottery was being produced outside the *Werkdyke*, at the southern end of the eponymous Pottergate (TC 93; TCA 94). A kiln was discovered in this area during refurbishment of the Sessions House

(SES 97) and wasters from this site (though probably later than the kiln itself) indicate that production here continued into the mid 11th century.

Pottery production outside the *Werkdyke* seems to have ceased during the 11th century, perhaps as a result of the development of *Butwerk* into an economically more diverse suburb, and there is no archaeological evidence for pottery production north of the Witham in the 12th century. The small proportion of Lincoln's pottery supplied by the city's own industry in the 12th century suggests that it may have been provided by a single potter or workshop. A pottery kiln of early 13th-century date producing glazed jugs was recently excavated within the Lower City, on the steep hillside at Gibraltar Hill (MGC 00). The site seems to have been situated there to exploit the Jurassic clay, probably because this was marginal land.

South of the river, it is likely that potteries began operation in Wigford during the 12th century, since this is the date of the earliest tilery, located at the south end of the suburb. Archaeological evidence for this industry found to date is in the form of both wasters and kilns, but it is of later 13th-century and later date (ON 362; Z 86; ZE 87; Young *et al.* 1988). There is evidence for production from one site, east of the High Street in the 14th century (ZE 87) and a second site producing wasters was reported in the 19th century at Central Station (ILN 1848), to the north-east. It is possible, however, that this find was actually from the St Mark's Station site, and so was connected to the Z 87 site. Two further sites on the west side of the High Street have produced wasters of similar date (ON 362; Z 86). All these sites are in the central part of the Wigford suburb, and it may be that several tenements were engaged in pottery manufacture. Nevertheless, in a sample of 1650 named individuals from the *Warden's Accounts* of the 1290s (Bischoff forthcoming), only one potter was present, suggesting that, even at its peak, the industry was not important numerically.

The pottery of late 9th- to mid 12th-century Lincoln can be divided into 65 separate groups, some represented by thousands of sherds and others by single examples (Young and Vince 2003) and we have already used a number of the ceramic groups in this *Assessment* for dating purposes (Figs. 9.2, 9.48). Some of the more complete products of the city's industry are shown in Fig. 9.95. After the initial cataloguing of all the pottery from the 1972–87 excavations selected assemblages were chosen for study to provide a sequence through the period, ignoring for this purpose the geographical or social context of the site or assemblage. Each selected assemblage was re-examined and the identifications refined. Wares which could be demonstrated to be intrusive or residual were excluded from further study and the data used within the medieval pottery corpus to give an idea of the relative proportions and date ranges of the groups. All but a handful of sherds could be assigned to a broad source: regional imports; locally-produced

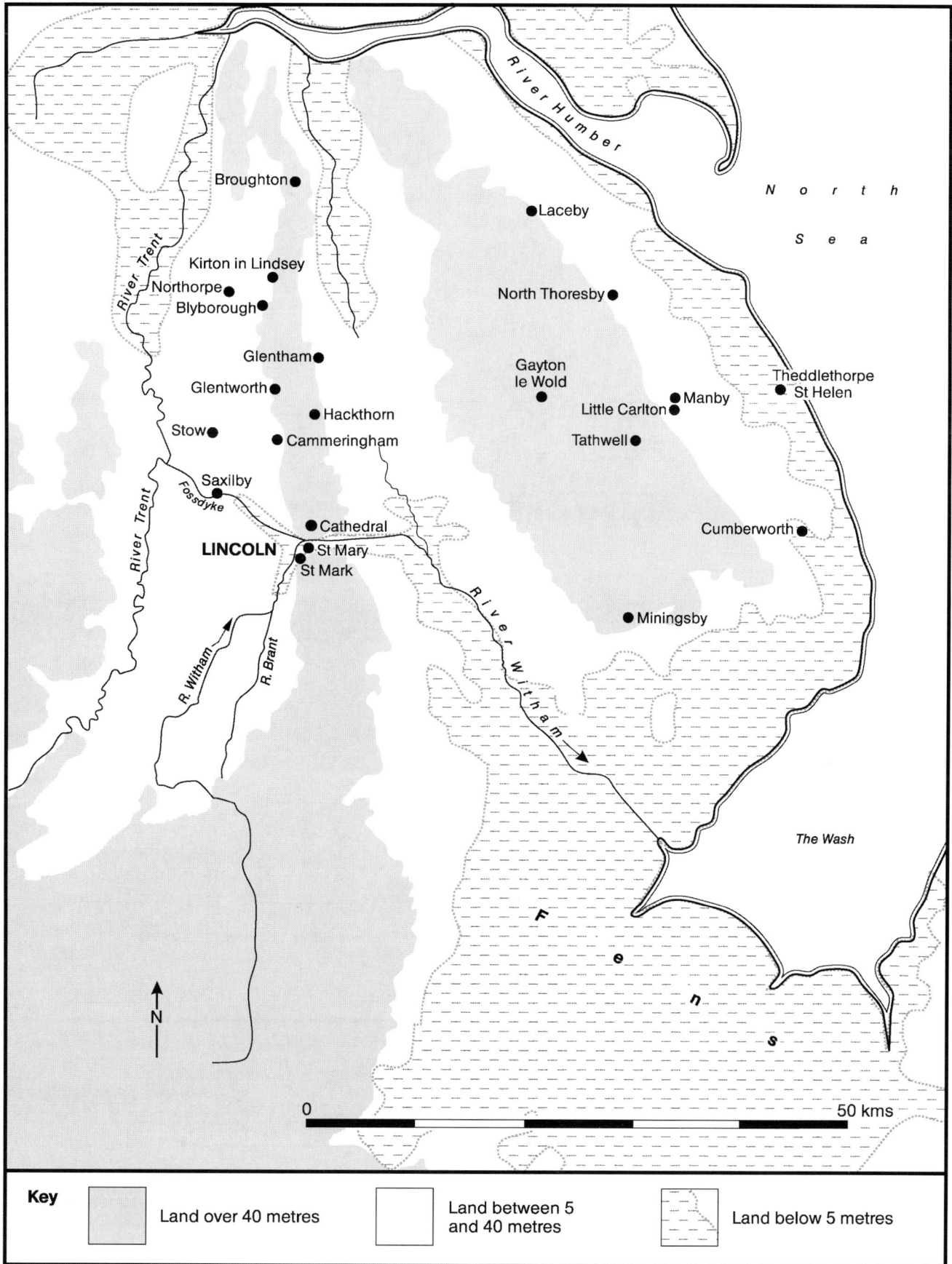

*Fig. 9.93. Complete distribution of grave-markers and grave-covers produced at the Lincoln quarries in the late 10th and early 11th centuries. The distribution is confined to Lindsey, even though the quarry source lies in the extreme south-west of the distribution pattern (source, Everson and Stocker 1999 figs. 15 & 16 – drawn by Dave Watt, copyright English Heritage).*

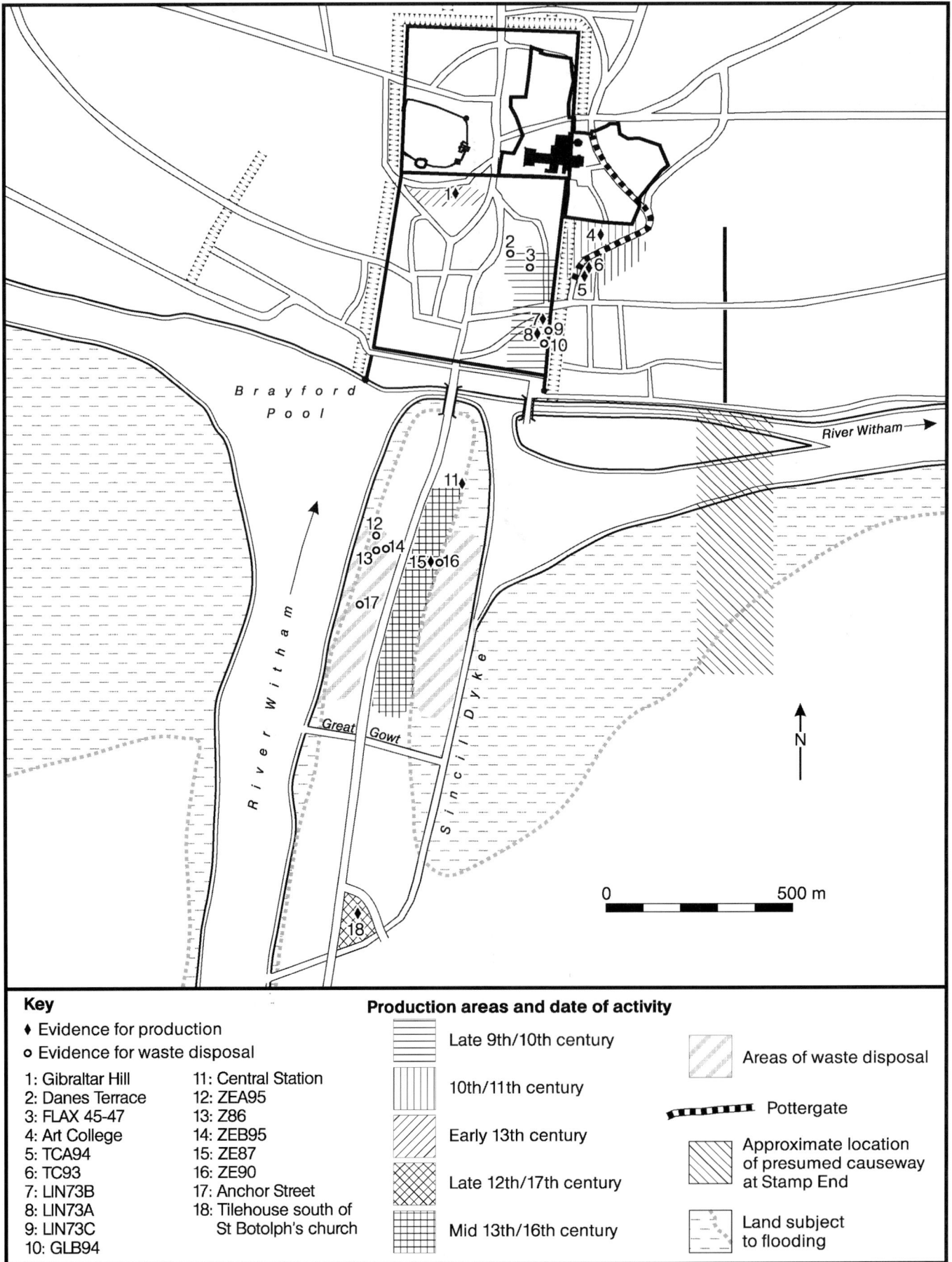

**Key**

♦ Evidence for production
○ Evidence for waste disposal

1: Gibraltar Hill
2: Danes Terrace
3: FLAX 45-47
4: Art College
5: TCA94
6: TC93
7: LIN73B
8: LIN73A
9: LIN73C
10: GLB94

11: Central Station
12: ZEA95
13: Z86
14: ZEB95
15: ZE87
16: ZE90
17: Anchor Street
18: Tilehouse south of
    St Botolph's church

**Production areas and date of activity**

Late 9th/10th century

10th/11th century

Early 13th century

Late 12th/17th century

Mid 13th/16th century

Areas of waste disposal

Pottergate

Approximate location
of presumed causeway
at Stamp End

Land subject
to flooding

*Fig. 9.94. Known pottery production sites in Lincoln, from the late 9th to the 16th centuries (source, Vince and Young forthcoming, drawn by Dave Watt, copyright English Heritage).*

a)

b)

c)

d)

*Fig. 9.95. Assemblages of pottery found in Lincoln of a) 10th century date, b) 11th century date, c) 12th century date and d) late 13th to mid 14th century date. The fluctuations in the proportion of Lincoln-made pottery are clearly shown as a) contains only Lincoln produced pottery. In b) only the Lincoln product is in the back row, left (SNLS), and in c) only two vessels are of Lincoln manufacture (back row centre and front row third from left). Finally, at the end of this Era, in d) the products are once again all produced in Lincoln. (photos and copyright City of Lincoln Archaeology Unit).*

wares (i.e. within 10km or so of Lincoln); Lincoln wares (i.e. where there is either kiln or waster evidence for production) and continental imports. For this purpose, Torksey ware (TORK) was taken to be a regional import, although given Torksey's status as a *suburbium* of Lincoln in the *Domesday Book*, this may give a misleading impression of the amount of regional pottery trade.

The general picture presented by our analysis is clear (Fig. 9.96a). Until the beginning of the 11th century the vast majority of the pottery used in Lincoln was produced in the city. After this date local wares and regional imports took an increasing proportion of the market. Imports from further afield are consistently unimportant in numerical terms although they too show a rise in the 11th century. This pattern is found elsewhere, for example in London, although there, apparently, the 10th-century ware was not local

but imported from the Oxford area. Nevertheless, the sudden increase in the number and location of pottery sources used is closely paralleled. As is the case at Lincoln, at London too imports from further afield were remarkably rare during the 10th century but became more common in the 11th century. At London, however, the earlier part of this pattern, with a relatively high quantity of imports in the very earliest levels (i.e. the late 9th or early 10th century), is missing, probably because little material of this date had been excavated (Vince and Jenner 1991).

The source of regional imports into Lincoln is shown in Fig. 9.96b. Wares of Yorkshire origin are very common in the 10th century, as are Norfolk (Thetford-type) wares. The latter can be divided into two groups, one probably from the Grimston kilns close to Kings Lynn and the other, which probably accounts for most of the earlier finds, from an unknown source. The East

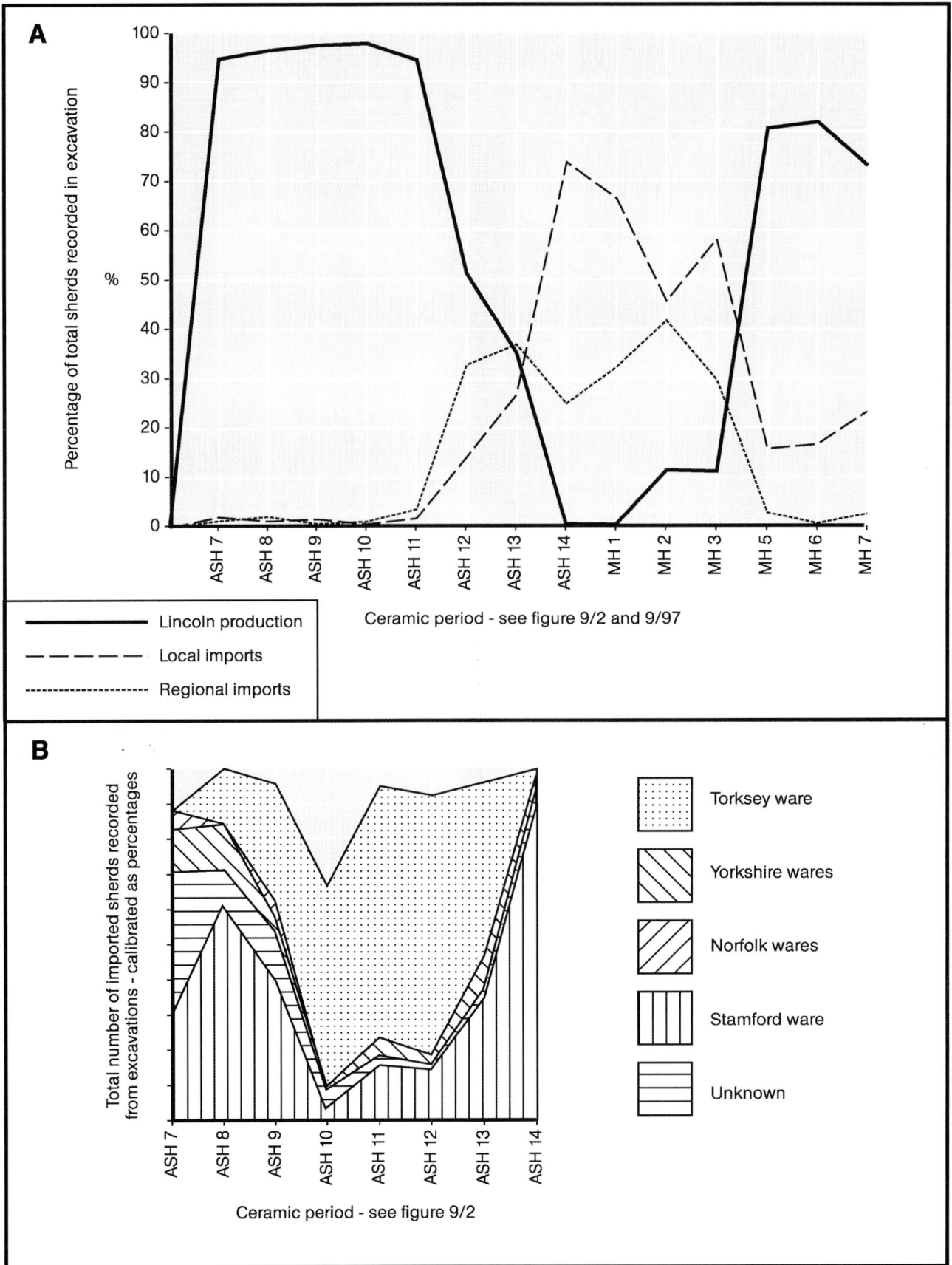

*Fig. 9.96A and B. A) Graph illustrating the rise and fall in the output of Lincoln pottery kilns, relative to imports, over time. The dates of the ceramic periods (ASH and MH) can be obtained from Figs. 9.2 and 9.97. B) Graph illustrating the relative quantities of selected pottery imports into Lincoln (expressed as a percentage of the total numbers of imports) in the period between the 9th and the 13th centuries (source, Vince and Young forthcoming, drawn by Dave Watt, copyright English Heritage).*

Midlands (Nottingham, Leicester and Newark) supplied only a small amount of pottery to Lincoln (too small a percentage to show on the graph). The only apparent surge (in horizon ASH 10) is probably a reflection of the very small quantity of regional imports from this horizon, due mainly to the near absence of Stamford wares. Stamford Ware exhibits a 'bimodal curve', being common in the early 10th century and then declining only to recover during the 11th and early 12th centuries – by which time they account for over 90% of the regional imports. Torksey wares, treated separately here, occupy a position between the two Stamford peaks. In both cases the majority of sherds found come from cooking and storage vessels and it is quite likely that the two wares were in competition. However, whether it was a temporary problem with supply from Stamford which allowed the Torksey potters to step into the Lincoln market or an increase in production at Torksey which kept out the Stamford wares is not possible to determine without similar data from other towns. An intriguing possibility is that the arrival of Torksey ware in Lincoln is linked to improvements in water transport. If as we have suggested (p. 240–1 above), a dam or weir at Stamp End was reconstructed during this period, utilising a much earlier structure, then this would have raised the water level within the Brayford Pool, allowing the canalisation of the Till and facilitating the construction of the short canal at Saxilby to create the Fossdyke to Torksey. Certainly, the final decline of Torksey wares in Lincoln is a true reflection of production, since there is no evidence that pottery production continued at Torksey into the 12th century, whereas there is known to have been pottery production in Torksey in the late 9th century, which is not represented on any scale in Lincoln (there is none in the selected ASH7 assemblage).

Sherds imported into Lincoln from further afield come from two main areas: the Rhineland and the Meuse valley (incorporating a series of wares whose parallels are in northern France). It is likely that both groups were exported to Lincoln via ports in the Rhine and Meuse deltas. Lincoln is unusual in its range of late 9th- or early 10th-century imports from such areas and this may be partly because such wares are not commonly recognised. It is likely, however, that the trade or contact that these vessels represent was uncommon and limited in extent.

Evidence for the export of Lincoln-made pottery has been gathered by Jane Young and the author as part of the East Midlands Anglo-Saxon Pottery Project (Vince and Young 1991; Vince 1994). An initial survey of finds of the main Lincoln ware (LKT) by Young shows that it supplied the entire province of Lindsey and was traded south of the Witham as well. However, in the south of the county, and in the fens, it was in competition with the Stamford potteries. LKT and other Lincoln wares have also been found outside the county to the north (for example at York, Beverley and Wharram Percy), west (at rural settlements in the

Sheffield area) and south-west (at Repton – Vince and Young forthcoming). Nottingham, Northampton and Leicester, which might have been thought to be within Lincoln's hinterland at this time (given that Lincoln wares were travelling as far as York), have not produced any such evidence. 10th-century wares are uncommon at these three sites, however, and their 11th-century assemblages contain Stamford wares and Torksey-type wares, the latter possibly being from Torksey itself and therefore evidence for trade with the Lincoln area.

The supply of pottery to the city between the 12th and 14th centuries can also be studied through analysis of stratified assemblages from the 1972–87 excavations. For this period, pottery can be divided into five horizons whose approximate calendar date ranges are shown in Fig. 9.97. At the beginning of the period, in the central part of the 12th century, only a small quantity of Lincoln's pottery was being made in the city – this was the start of the Lincoln glazed ware industry. Most, however, was being obtained from local sources, which have yet to be precisely located (ware types LFS, LOCC, LEMS). This state of affairs remained fairly constant until the early 13th century, when the Lincoln glazed ware industry began to expand, and by the middle of this century over three-quarters of the pottery used in the city was also produced here. As a consequence of this, less and less pottery was brought into the city from the surrounding countryside. Of this pottery of local manufacture, most came from Potterhanworth (Healey 1974; 1988), to the south-east of the city, whilst only a small quantity was obtained from kilns at Toynton All Saints (Healey 1984; Field 1996).

A similar picture is obtained by looking at pottery from sources outside Lincoln's immediate hinterland (Figs. 9.98 and 9.99). At the beginning of the period sizeable quantities of pottery were obtained from Stamford and Nottingham, amounting to 39% of all pottery used in ceramic period MH2 and 23% of that in MH3. With the growth of the Lincoln industry, however, the quantity of regional imports in the early 13th century falls to 9% and from the mid 13th century onwards never amounted to more than 5% of all pottery used in the city. Stamford and Nottingham remained major sources of non-local pottery in ceramic period MH4, although pottery from Beverley, Scarborough

| Horizon | Date range |
|---|---|
| MH2 | Mid 12th century |
| MH3 | Mid/Late 12th century |
| MH4 | Early to Mid 13th century |
| MH5 | Mid to late 13th century |
| MH6 | Late 13th to early/mid 14th century |
| MH7 | Early/mid to late 14th century |

*Fig. 9.97. List of date-ranges of Lincoln ceramic horizons between the 12th and 14th centuries (source, Vince and Young forthcoming).*

made in every subsequent period. Most of the hammer-scale was found embedded in the corrosion products of unidentifiable objects, but it was also found on nails, particularly of the late 11th and early 12th centuries, as well as on a variety of other objects (a buckle plate, a disc, a horse shoe, a key, a needle, a stud and wire). One such object was apparently an unfinished triangular hooked tag, showing that it was undergoing a manufacturing process when discarded or lost. Twenty-four such objects have been found in Lincoln excavations, all but five from the Flaxengate excavation (F 72) and it seems that they must have been a speciality of a smith working at that site. The output of smiths on this site can be presented in tabular form (Fig. 9.100). No other site excavated in Lincoln has produced both the size of assemblages and the chronological precision to add greatly to the picture gathered from Flaxengate. It is clear, however, that the Flaxengate site was not exceptional and that manufacturing of metal and other goods took place on most sites in the Lower City and Wigford.

From the later 12th century onwards, the archaeological evidence for metalworking becomes more scarce. This is almost certainly, in part, a reflection of the movement from short-lived timber buildings, whose repair or rebuilding gave plentiful opportunities for the deposition of metalworking evidence, to long-lived stone buildings. Another reason for this lack of archaeological evidence, however, might be the concentration of smiths and other metalworkers in certain parts of the town which have so-far not been investigated archaeologically. This certainly seems to be the case for the lower part of High Street within the Lower City. Documentary evidence shows that the owners of several of the properties on either side of the street in the parishes of St Peter-at-Pleas and St Peter-at-Arches were involved in metalworking. These include goldsmiths and lorimers and it is likely that the metalworking practised in this area was at the higher end of the spectrum of skills and was not routine re-shoeing of horses and production of nails and other household fittings. Lorimers were probably also associated with a forge mentioned in documents referring to *Briggate*, that part of the High Street between Stonebow and the High Bridge, on its western side. One John the Ironmonger was bailiff in 1310 (Hill 1948, 384, 401), but John may have sold ironwork imported into the city rather than indigenous products.

### Non-ferrous metalworking

Non-ferrous metalworking may have also been carried out from the late 9th century, although our understanding is potentially disabled by the presence of residual Roman metalworking debris in the early Anglo-Scandinavian levels on the Flaxengate site (F 72). Crucibles, however, can often be dated by their fabric. Both Stamford ware (code STCRUC) and unsourced Anglo-Scandinavian crucibles (code LSCRUC) occur in small numbers in the earliest levels, although their heyday came in the 10th and earlier 11th centuries (Fig. 9.103). Heating trays, used in the preparation of leaded glass jewellery (like those illustrated in Fig. 9.101, were made in three fabrics, all used for domestic vessels as well (ware types ELSW, LSH and LKT). They first occur on the site in early 10th century or later levels and are of fabrics which probably went out of use at the end of the 10th century. Only 37 out of 428 well-stratified crucibles from Flaxengate were not

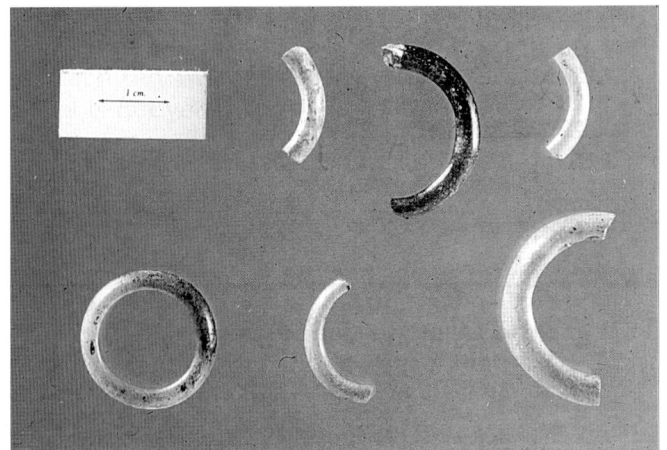

*Fig. 9.101. A selection of leaded glass rings from excavations at Flaxengate (F 72). These were probably manufactured on the site (photo and copyright, City of Lincoln Archaeology Unit).*

| Artifact date | Type not known | Buckle plate | Disc | Horse shoe | Key | Nail | Needle | Stud piece | Waste | Wire | Grand Total |
|---|---|---|---|---|---|---|---|---|---|---|---|
| Early 10th | 4 | 1 | 0 | 0 | 0 | 1 | 0 | 0 | 1 | 0 | 7 |
| Mid 10th | 13 | 0 | 0 | 0 | 0 | 1 | 0 | 0 | 0 | 0 | 14 |
| Late 10th/early 11th | 3 | 0 | 0 | 0 | 1 | 0 | 0 | 0 | 0 | 0 | 4 |
| Mid 11th | 34 | 0 | 1 | 1 | 0 | 4 | 1 | 0 | 0 | 1 | 42 |
| Late 11th /early 12th | 18 | 0 | 0 | 0 | 0 | 10 | 0 | 1 | 0 | 0 | 29 |
| Mid 12th | 0 | 0 | 0 | 0 | 0 | 1 | 0 | 0 | 0 | 0 | 1 |
| Grand Total | 72 | 1 | 1 | 1 | 1 | 17 | 1 | 1 | 1 | 1 | 97 |

*Fig. 9.100. Different products of the ironsmiths at Flaxengate (F 72) (source, City of Lincoln Archaeological Unit).*

demonstrably of Anglo-Scandinavian date and only two of these are in Roman fabrics (fabric types 'Unspecified Roman' and NVCC). The other crucibles are all items whose fabric could not be identified for one reason or another.

Anglo-Scandinavian crucibles of the LSCRUC type from Flaxengate were used for a variety of purposes and traces of a number of alloys have been found as a result of 'XRF analysis' carried out by Justine Bayley of the English Heritage Ancient Monuments Laboratory (Fig. 9.102 and 9.103). Much the most frequently used alloys were brass, bronze, copper and silver with brass. Stamford Ware crucibles were used for the same range of alloys but with a much higher proportion used for working silver, and silver working crucibles were present in small numbers from the late 9th century onwards. In the Upper City the only crucibles of late 9th- to mid 12th-century date came from St Paul-in-the-Bail, where over 80 fragments were found, mostly in late 10th- to mid 11th-century contexts, associated with the cellared structure at the east end of the site. The overwhelming majority of these were of Stamford Ware, a confirmation of the evidence from Flaxengate that this industry had a virtual monopoly in the supply of metalworking crucibles in the 11th and 12th centuries.

There is much less evidence for non-ferrous metalworking in Lincoln between the 12th and 14th centuries than in the Anglo-Scandinavian period. We remain uncertain whether this is due to a reduced output of metal goods, or to a shift in the location of workshops, or it may simply be related to the lack of appropriate archaeological deposits. Evidence for copper-alloy working of 13th- or 14th-century date has been found at Danes Terrace, in the form of waste re-used as makeup (DT 76), and at St Mark's Station (in a row of lean-to workshops using the south wall of the White Friars precinct as their north wall – Z 86). Documentary sources are slightly more informative and indicate a variety of metalworking trades present in the city in the 13th and 14th centuries. In 1293 and 1297 there are records of smiths, shearmen, shear-grinders, plumbers, locksmiths, lead-beaters, farriers and goldsmiths in the

*Warden's Accounts* (Bischoff forthcoming). Between 1200 and 1300 it has been calculated that there were at least seventeen goldsmiths working in the city (*Ibid.* 1975, 77). A group of late 12th- and 13th-century references suggest that metal-workers (or at least their shops) were located in *Mikelgate* (i.e. High Street) in the parishes of St Peter-at-Arches and St Peter-at-Pleas (Hill 1948, 154–6), but none of these has been investigated through excavation.

### The mint

Coins with the Lincoln mint signature occur from the early 10th century onwards, indicating that a mint was established in the city during its period of Viking rule (Mossop 1970). No real clue as to the location of this early mint, or its output, can be gained from the excavated evidence. The mint clearly continued to function in the early years of English rule, prior to the general inclusion of mintmarks on the coinage, introduced by Edgar in 973, and from that point onwards a series of moneyers is known, spanning the late 10th, 11th and 12th centuries. A single coin die has been found, on the Flaxengate excavation (F 72 – Blackburn and Mann 1995) (Fig. 9.104). It is dated to the early 11th century. Exactly how the die came to be discarded on the site is unclear. As we have seen, there is evidence for silver working at Flaxengate and it is possible that some of the crucibles found were used by a moneyer. At Winchester in the early Norman period it appears that the mint was a well-defined area in the High Street (to the north of the Cathedral), situated close to the commercial centre of the town. It seems that the Lincoln mint in the 13th century may have been in a similarly closely defined zone. Known moneyers and other mint officials held land in the south-west quarter of the Lower City, around the area later known as Mint Street, close to the High Street in St Peter-at-Arches and St Peter-at-Pleas parishes, where we have already noted a concentration of goldsmiths and where one of the shops housed a seal-cutter (Hill 1948, 154–6). It is possible that the nucleation of minting in the central south-western quarter of the Lower City took place

| Presumed date of use | Brass | Bronze | Copper | Silver | ND | Used | Grand Total |
|---|---|---|---|---|---|---|---|
| Late 9th | 3 | 0 | 0 | 2 | 0 | 0 | 5 |
| Late 9th–10th | 0 | 0 | 0 | 1 | 0 | 1 | 2 |
| Early 10th | 6 | 1 | 0 | 27 | 4 | 28 | 66 |
| Mid 10th | 3 | 0 | 1 | 4 | 2 | 6 | 16 |
| Late 10th–11th | 18 | 0 | 1 | 16 | 2 | 22 | 59 |
| Mid 11th | 88 | 3 | 0 | 13 | 4 | 38 | 146 |
| Late 11th–12th | 5 | 0 | 0 | 0 | 0 | 5 | 10 |
| Early 12th | 0 | 0 | 0 | 0 | 1 | 1 | 2 |
| Mid 12th | 2 | 0 | 0 | 0 | 0 | 2 | 4 |
| Grand Total | 134 | 4 | 3 | 63 | 13 | 105 | 322 |

*Fig. 9.102. Types of metal worked in crucibles found in excavations at Flaxengate (F 72) (ND = type of metal not recovered) (source, English Heritage Ancient Monuments Laboratory).*

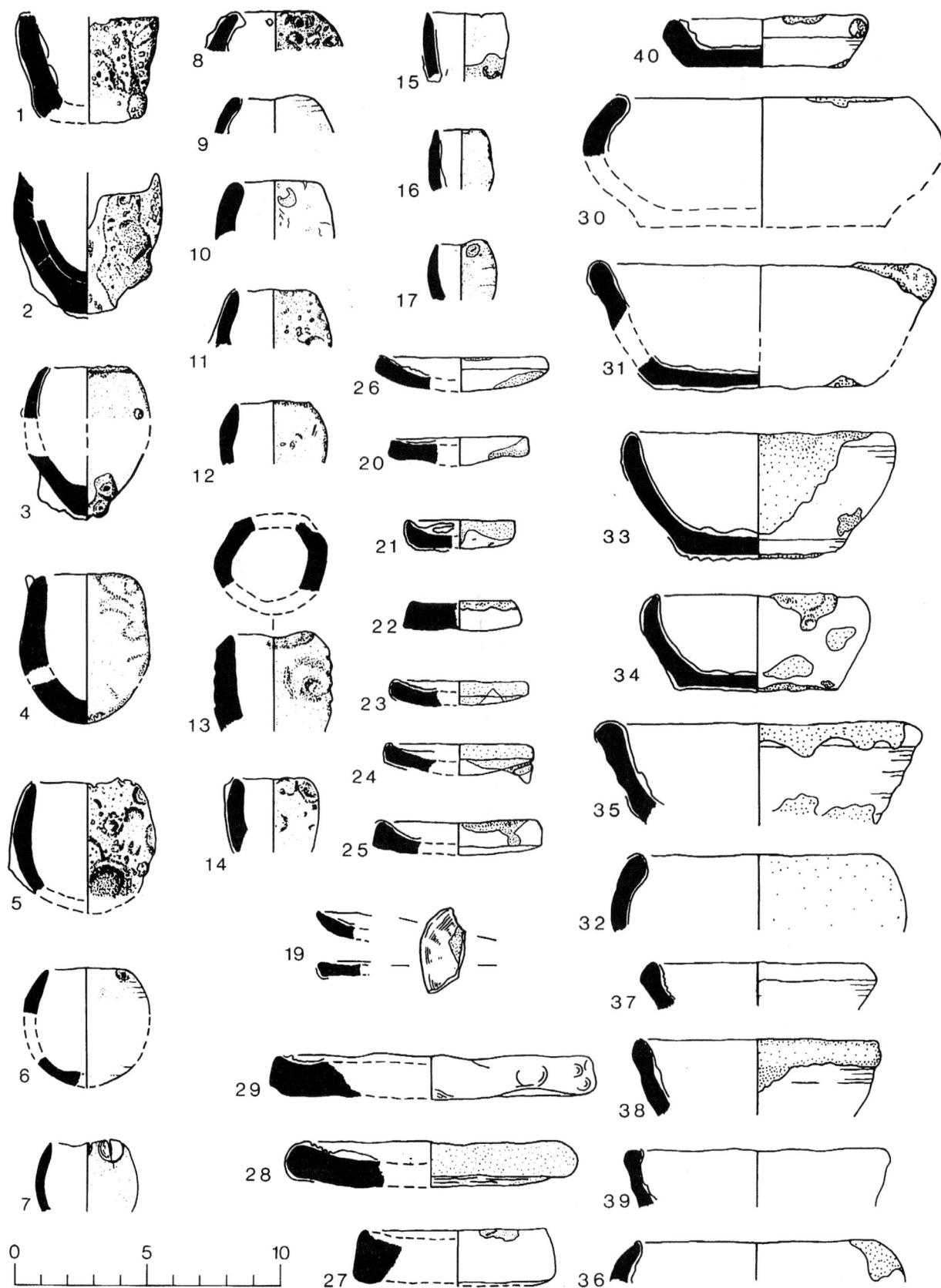

Fig. 9.103. Group of crucibles and heating tray fragments (of wares produced in Lincoln and Stamford) from excavations at Flaxengate (F 72) (source, Adams Gilmour 1988, Fig. 7, copyright City of Lincoln Archaeology Unit).

*Fig. 9.104. Coin die from excavations at Flaxengate (F 72) (photo and copyright, City of Lincoln Archaeology Unit).*

earlier, in the early Norman period. Even so, the role of moneyer was clearly one requiring both status and personal capital and the location of property held by a moneyer cannot be taken as firm evidence that minting took place on the site.

### Antler-working

Off-cuts of antler have been found at a number of sites in Lincoln (Fig. 9.105 and 9.107). In many cases the waste can be dated to the Anglo-Scandinavian period but there may be later pieces present too. A piece from the well at St Paul-in-the-Bail (SP 84), for example, was found in a post-medieval period context (Egan forthcoming). The finds are concentrated at sites in the southeast quarter of the Lower City, the waterfront, *Butwerk* and Wigford, with a single piece (a blank from comb manufacture, identified by I Riddler) from outside the west gate of the Upper City (CY 89). Fragments of unfinished comb were also recovered from the St Mark's Station site west of the High Street in Wigford (Z 86), Silver Street (LIN 73f) and Flaxengate (F 72).

Combs made of antler, bone or horn are common finds on Lincoln sites of this period (Figs. 9.106, 9.108 and 9.109). They can be dated by their style and archaeological context from the beginning of the Anglo-Scandinavian settlement to the late 11th or early 12th century, after which antler becomes much less common, being replaced mainly by bone combs (Mann 1982, 45). There is evidence that some of these combs, at least, were made in the town (see, for example, a composite comb in which the teeth had not been cut on some of the plates – Fig. 9.108). The bone connecting plates from horn combs are also common finds (Fig. 9.109), although the horn itself does not survive. Figs. 9.105 and 9.107 show the distribution of bone and antler

finds – some of which are of specifically Viking style and others are of more heterodox late Saxon types. The find sites of both bone and antler combs are concentrated in the Lower City and this pattern is unlikely to have a purely chronological explanation.

*The wool and cloth industries, spinning, weaving and dyeing*
The spinning of yarn was carried out as a domestic duty in Anglo-Scandinavian and Anglo-Norman society and there is thus little documentary evidence for it. Archaeologically, spinning is identified by spindle whorls, which are common finds from Lincoln excavations. Some of these spindle-whorls can be typologically dated to the Anglo-Scandinavian period whereas others can only be dated by their context. Spindle-whorls have been found on seven sites, in the Lower City, Wigford and *Butwerk* (Figs. 9.110 and 9.111). A single example from Flaxengate (F 72) has parallels on Viking sites, whereas the remainder are more typical of those found on other English sites of late 9th-century or later date. Unfortunately, apart from the distinctive asymmetrical whorls of Anglo-Scandinavian type, there is little to distinguish whorls of one period from those of another. Excluding probable Roman and Anglo-Scandinavian whorls there are 101 examples from the 1972–87 excavations of which 51 were made of stone, 46 of bone, five of re-used potsherds and one each of lead and shale.

Archaeological evidence for weaving has been found even more rarely, and is confined to recovery of smooth bone 'thread-pickers', or 'pin-beaters'. The smooth profile and size of these implements agrees well with their suggested use in compacting and making even the weft on a warp-weighted loom (Fig. 9.112). These finds have a similar distribution to the spindle-whorls, although extending that distribution northwards to Steep Hill (Figs. 9.110 and 9.113). On this evidence, it would seem that weaving took place throughout the entire 10th-century settlement. Interestingly, there are few, if any, loom weights from Lincoln. This suggests that the loom used, whilst being a vertical one requiring pin-beaters, did not use clay weights. This is in sharp contrast with the evidence for the middle Saxon period in Lincolnshire, when such weights were commonly used, and it suggests that the Scandinavian settlement of the county was accompanied by the introduction of a different loom type.

The weaving of cloth had become an important industry for Lincoln in the 12th century, and by the 13th century it was of paramount importance to the city's economy (Bischoff 1975). Prior to the later 13th century, a large proportion of the wool brought into the city was converted into a luxury fine cloth, called *scarlet*, for which the city was internationally famed (*Ibid.*, 121–4). Lincoln cloths were produced in back rooms and workshops all over the city, but Paul Bischoff demonstrates that there was a distinct cloth-weavers quarter in the south-west quarter of the Lower City, in the parishes of St Mary *Crackpole* and

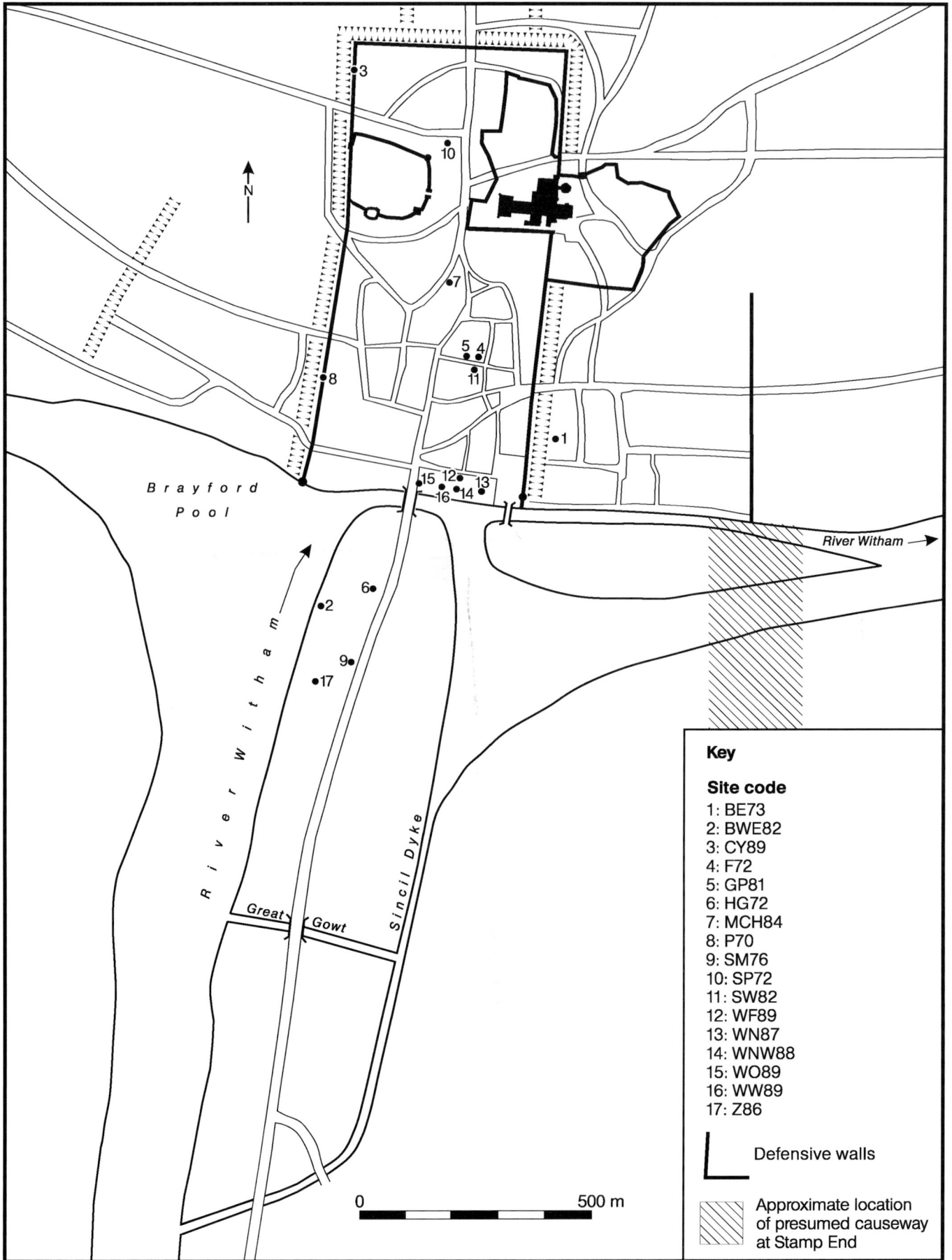

**Key**

**Site code**
1: BE73
2: BWE82
3: CY89
4: F72
5: GP81
6: HG72
7: MCH84
8: P70
9: SM76
10: SP72
11: SW82
12: WF89
13: WN87
14: WNW88
15: WO89
16: WW89
17: Z86

└ Defensive walls

▨ Approximate location of presumed causeway at Stamp End

*Fig. 9.105. Distribution of worked antler finds of Anglo-Scandinavian and medieval date from excavations in Lincoln. See also Fig. 9.107 (drawn by Dave Watt, copyright English Heritage).*

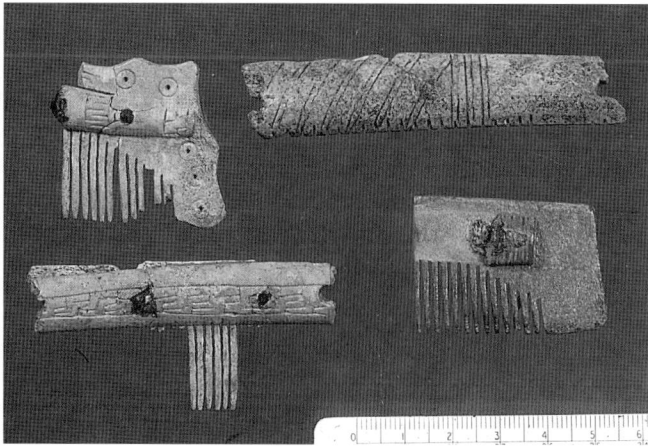

Fig. 9.106. Selection of comb fragments made from worked antler, from excavations at Flaxengate (F 72) (photo and copyright, City of Lincoln Archaeology Unit).

| Site code | Antler finds |
|-----------|--------------|
| BE 73 | 5 |
| BWE 82 | 1 |
| CY 89 | 1 |
| F 72 | 52 |
| GP 81 | 2 |
| HG 72 | 2 |
| MCH 84 | 5 |
| P 70 | 1 |
| SM 76 | 2 |
| SP 72 | 3 |
| SW 82 | 1 |
| WF 89 | 4 |
| WN 87 | 2 |
| WNW 88 | 5 |
| WO 89 | 19 |
| WW 89 | 2 |
| Z 86 | 2 |

Fig. 9.107. List of numbers of worked antler finds from excavations in Lincoln. See also Fig. 9.105 (source, City of Lincoln Archaeological Unit).

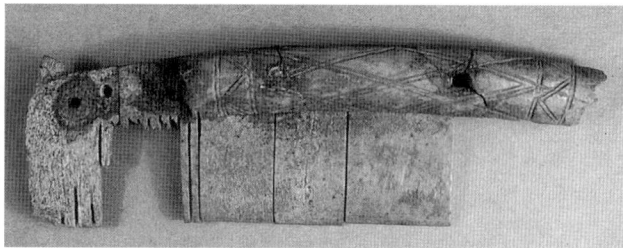

Fig. 9.108. Antler comb fragment of Anglo-Scandinavian date found in excavations in Saltergate in 1973 (LIN 73). The teeth have been only partially cut, i.e. the comb was not finished (photo and copyright, City of Lincoln Archaeology Unit).

Fig. 9.109. Bone connecting plates of antler (from Anglo-Scandinavian combs) from excavations at Flaxengate (F 72) (photo and copyright, City of Lincoln Archaeology Unit).

All Saints Hungate (1975, 66–9). The cloth production cycle also involved other traders, however, often employing women workers. The wool had to be prepared for spinning, then spun (and it is estimated that six spinners were needed to keep a single loom supplied), but practically no archaeological evidence for spinning of 12th or 13th century date has been recovered. Partly, this is because the south-western part of the Lower City has seen comparatively little archaeological investigation. Partly, also, it is because, by the later 12th century the looms used would have been constructed entirely from wood, and would leave no archaeological evidence for their existence, unless fragments were included in anaerobic deposits. Following weaving, the cloth would be fulled, dyed and sheared. Although Lincoln was most famous for its *scarlet*, it also produced *green* (a medium quality cloth) *murrey* (a cheaper, reddish coloured cloth, dyed using

madder and woad) and *russet*, *perse* and the un-dyed *blanquet* (Ibid, 125–6). The colours of all the Lincoln cloths would have been produced by the city's dyers, and it was said that the high quality *scarlet* (which made it sought-after all over Europe) was produced by the combination of high-quality dye (*granum* – made from crushed insects and imported from the Mediterranean) and Lincoln's distinctive 'hard' water supply (Ibid., 122, 144–7). We have some excavated evidence for the dyeing of yarn, in the form of sherds of ceramic vessels with traces of dye on their interiors. A variety of wares were utilised, mainly the local shell-tempered fabrics (ware types LKT and LFS) but including some late 11th- or early 12th-century types. The finds were concentrated in the Lower City – there is only one dubious find from Holmes Grain Warehouse in Wigford (HG 72) and two from Broadgate East in *Butwerk* (BE 73), but it is argued here that the

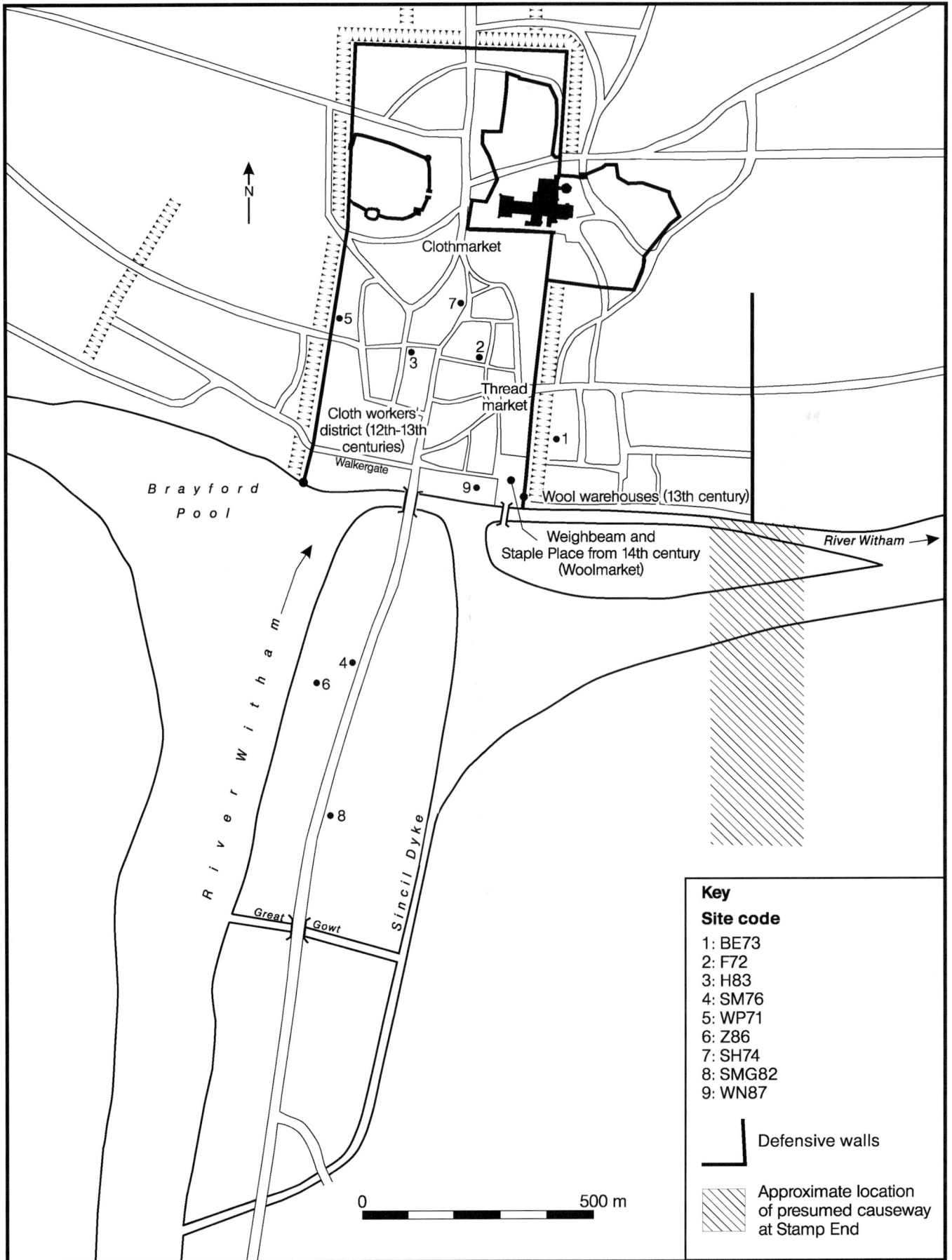

Fig. 9.110. Distribution of finds related to weaving from excavations mapped against other evidence for cloth-working and marketing. See also Figs. 9.111 and 9.113 (drawn by Dave Watt, copyright English Heritage).

| Site code | Period | Ceramic | Lead | Stone |
|-----------|--------|---------|------|-------|
| BE 73 | Late Saxon | | | 3 |
| F 72 | Late Saxon | 4 | | 1 |
| F 72 | Viking | 1 | | |
| H 83 | Late Saxon | | 1 | 5 |
| SM 76 | Medieval | | | 1 |
| WP 71 | Late Saxon | 1 | | |
| Z 86 | Medieval | 1 | | |

*Fig. 9.111. Locations and materials of spindle whorls found in excavations. See also Fig. 9.110 (source, City of Lincoln Archaeological Unit).*

| Site Code | Period | Bone |
|-----------|--------|------|
| BE 73 | Late Saxon | 1 |
| F 72 | Late Saxon | 4 |
| SH 74 | Late Saxon | 1 |
| SMG 82 | Late Saxon | 1 |
| WN 87 | Late Saxon | 1 |

*Fig. 9.113. Excavated finds of thread-pickers and pin-beaters. See also Fig. 9.110 (source, City of Lincoln Archaeological Unit).*

*Fig. 9.112. A selection of thread-pickers and pin-beaters from excavations in Lincoln (photo and copyright, City of Lincoln Archaeology Unit).*

street of the dyers (*Walkergate*) lay along the line of the southern city wall west of High Street, right in the centre of the cloth production area. No analysis of the residues in the excavated pots has taken place but they are thought from visual inspection to be madder.

Lincoln paid the largest sum, nationally, in the list of English towns who were taxed by the Crown in 1202 according to the numbers of cloths sold (*Ibid.* 120–1), and in 1348 an enquiry into the Lincoln cloth industry by the Royal Exchequer found that in the reign of Henry II there had been over 200 spinners in the city (Hill 1948, 326). During the heyday of cloth production in the 12th and 13th centuries, only a small proportion of the city's cloth output was sold in Lincoln itself – most of it went for sale to the great fairs at Stamford, St Ives, Boston, St Giles Winchester and Northampton, where the Lincoln cloth merchants

had a permanent allocation of rows of stalls (Bischoff 1975, 164–9). The small percentage of Lincoln's output intended for indigenous consumption was sold at two markets in the city – at the *Clothmarket* outside the south gate of the Upper City in the parish of St Michael-on-the-Mount (Hill 1948, 154; Cameron 1985, 22–3), which seems to have been distinct from the market for yarn at *Clewmarket* in the parish of Holy Trinity Clasketgate (*Ibid.* 1985, 21), and at Newport Fair between 17th and 29th June (Bischoff 1975, 162).

Lincoln was producing, then, a large number of cloths for the international market from the 12th century onwards. The earliest record of the purchase of cloths at Lincoln is in 1182 (Hill 1948, 325). It has been estimated that at its height, in the early 13th century, the cloth trade in Lincoln employed 40% of the total population of the city – perhaps two thousand workers (Bischoff 1975, 176). However, the cloth industry totally collapsed and all but disappeared in the final quarter of the 13th century (*Ibid.*, 277–87) and, between 1321 and 1331 there had been no weavers at all within the city and between 1331 and 1345 there were only a few spinners (Hill 1948, 326). After its implosion, clearly, the numbers involved in the industry fell away rapidly and, although the *Warden's Accounts*, for 1293 and 1297 mention a number of individuals concerned with the production of cloth (presumably for sale in the city's own markets), such workers are far outnumbered (by a ratio of over 2.7 to 1) by those producing clothes (Bischoff forthcoming) (Fig. 9.114). It seems clear that, by the mid 14th century, any cloth production in the city must have been largely for domestic consumption.

Lincoln's pre-eminence in the cloth trade meant that it automatically became an important centre of the wool industry also. The famous Aaron the Jew was involved in both the wool and the cloth trades, for example, when he died in c.1185 (*Ibid.*; Hill 1948 220). Wool produced in the county was brought to the city for quality inspection, weighing and packaging, before being exported. The trade was of fundamental importance to the city, not just because it was the staple commodity supporting the cloth industry, but also because the Council had been granted a tax on each sack of wool weighed at Lincoln, called *tronage*. The Council claimed in 1327 that it had received this tax 'since time immemorial' (Hill 1948, 245). The city's merchant oligarchy tried to hang on to their position in the wool trade, as the centre where the producer met the buyer, even once the cloth industry which had stimulated it vanished from the city after c.1300. Unfortunately, however, Lincoln was locked in a symbiotic relationship with Boston; a town which held many advantages compared with Lincoln. Its enormous international market (St Botolph's Fair) and its easy access to the sea for large ships would always tend to draw trade away from Lincoln. In 1326 national reforms in the marketing of wool, aimed at maximising the King's tax-share, resulted in the designation of Lincoln as one of eight 'staple towns', where inspection packaging and weighing had to take place by law. This was merely official recognition of an activity which had been undertaken in Lincoln for several generations already (Bischoff 1975, 271). In 1369, however, this important concession was transferred to Boston and, although the city's merchants simply transferred their operations down-river or to Hull, it meant that the city itself lost its legal status in the trade. In fact Paul Bischoff has shown that the loss of the Staple was not really of great significance in itself, except in so far as it represented official recognition that Lincoln had lost its place as a centre for international trade. The fact that it was transferred to Boston showed where the economic power had been relocated.

The archaeology of Lincoln's trade in wool is very rare. By 1354 the weighing equipment, along with warehouses offices etc. was on the north side of the Witham at *Staple Place* near Thorn bridge (Hill 1948, 160), but Paul Bischoff has collected evidence that the north bank of the river between Staple Place and Stamp End was lined with warehouses by the 13th century and probably for a century before that (1975, 200). Certainly the Hundred Roll jurors describe the whole river bank between Thorngate and *Calvecroft* as a storage area for wool (*Ibid.*, 200), and no doubt it was the Prior of Barlings' desire to obtain a good warehouse near the wharves at Stamp End which prompted him to try and obtain the Sack Friars' property in 1307 to store the Abbey's wool. The gift of the key to the warehouse in which the wool was stored was the symbol of the deal being struck, according to the *Constitutions* of the wool market drawn up in the late 13th century (*Ibid.*, 269–70). Most of the Lincoln wool merchants whose residences are known, lived in the few parishes around the water-side. Walter de Kelby, one of the greatest of 14th-century Lincoln's wool merchants, lived in St Benedict's parish and had shops and houses in St Peter-at-Arches, St Martin's and Holy Cross parishes (Hill 1948, 248–50), but it is not clear that these shops had anything to do with the wool trade.

*Other trades and crafts*
We have little documentary information about the leatherworkers of medieval Lincoln, although the parchment-market (*forum pelli*) was located at the

| Occupation | 1293 | 1297 |
|---|---|---|
| *Clothing Production* | | |
| Pinstress | 1 | |
| Seamstress | 2 | |
| Hatter | 1 | |
| Girdler | 5 | 1 |
| Glover | 6 | 2 |
| Tailor | 8 | 8 |
| *Cloth Production* | | |
| Lacemaker | 1 | 1 |
| Teaser | 1 | |
| Weaver | 1 | |
| Woadseller | 1 | 2 |
| Yarnmonger | 1 | |
| Fuller | 3 | 1 |

*Fig. 9.114. Numbers of workers in various occupations associated with the cloth industry from the Lincoln Warden's Accounts for 1293 and 1297 (source, Dr Paul Bischoff).*

| Artifact type | Site code | Context | Number of items |
|---|---|---|---|
| Strap | LIN 73F | 107 | 1 |
| Shoe | LT 72 | DO | 1 |
| Shoe | WN 87 | 83 | 1 |
| Shoe | WN 87 | 99 | 2 |
| Shoe | WNW 88 | 219 | 4 |
| Shoe | WNW 88 | 277 | 6 |
| Shoe | WNW 88 | 303 | 2 |
| Shoe | WNW 88 | 304 | 6 |
| Shoe | WNW 88 | 309 | 6 |
| Shoe | WNW 88 | 313 | 8 |
| Shoe | WNW 88 | 314 | 10 |
| Shoe | WNW 88 | 317 | 2 |
| Shoe | WO 89 | 526 | 2 |
| – | WO 89 | 535 | 10 |
| Shoe | WO 89 | 543 | 1 |
| Shoe | WW 89 | + | 2 |

*Fig. 9.115. Finds of Anglo-Scandinavian leather artefacts from city excavations between 1972–1987. See also Fig. 9.116 (source, City of Lincoln Archaeological Unit).*

junction of Hungate and Michaelgate, on the slope of the hill (Fig. 9.83d) (Cameron 1985, 39, 88). Leather off-cuts and other waste have been found in association with datable Anglo-Scandinavian leatherwork at several excavation sites on the waterfront south of the Lower City (WN 87; WNW 88; WO 89) (Figs. 9.115 and 9.116) indicating that much of this leatherwork is not domestic waste, but recycled material discarded by shoemakers after reusable pieces had been removed. The location of the finds is mainly determined by the survival of anaerobic deposits of this period used for rubbish disposal. Nevertheless, the absence of finds from the Wigford suburb, for example from sites such as St Benedict's Square (SB 85) or Brayford Wharf East (BWE 82), where anaerobic conditions were encountered, may indicate that shoemaking was concentrated in the Lower City (Fig. 9.116). In addition to the finds

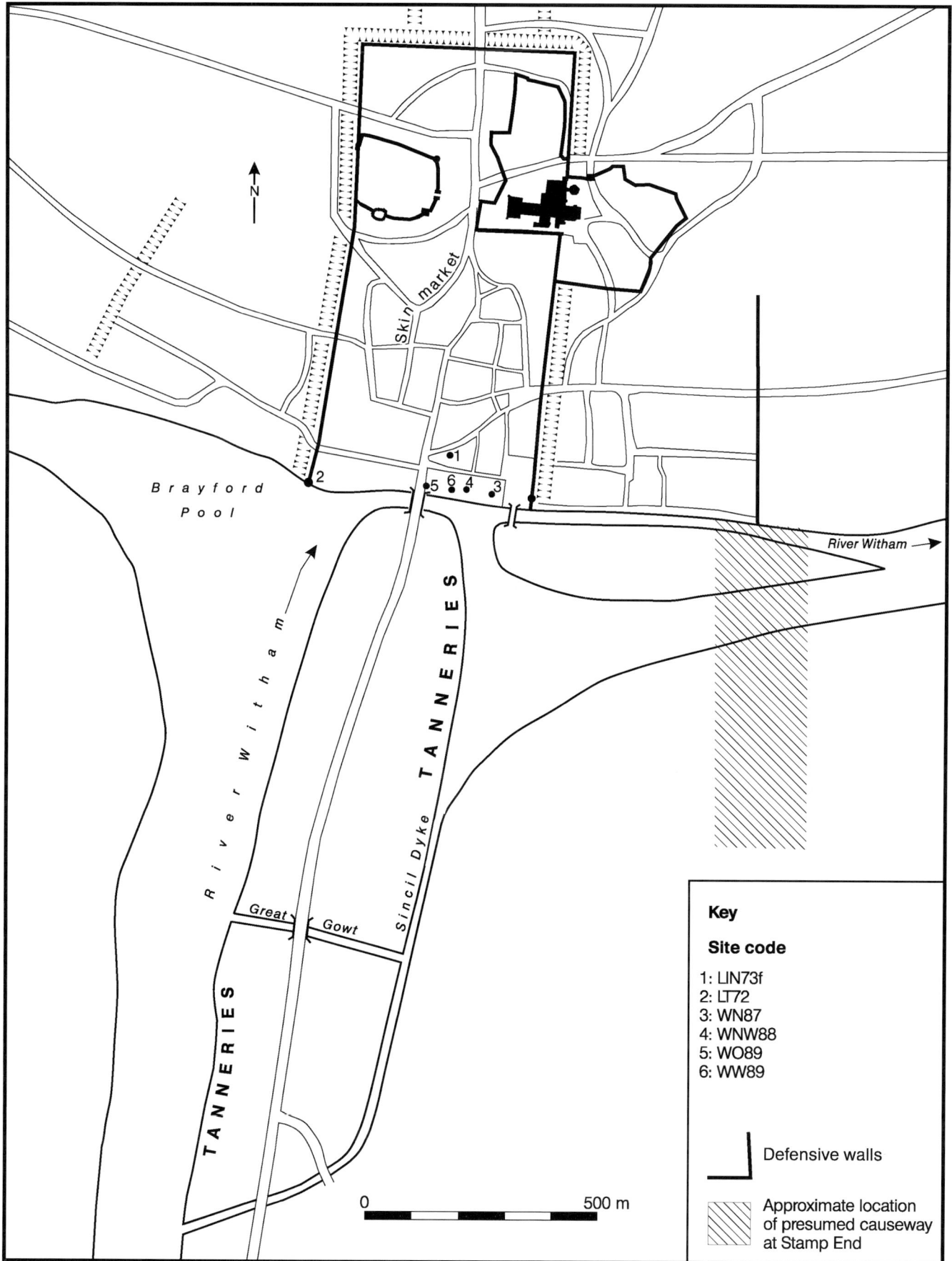

*Fig. 9.116. Distribution of evidence for medieval leather working from excavations mapped against medieval and early-modern tanners and tanneries known from documentary sources. See also Fig. 9.115 (drawn by Dave Watt, copyright English Heritage).*

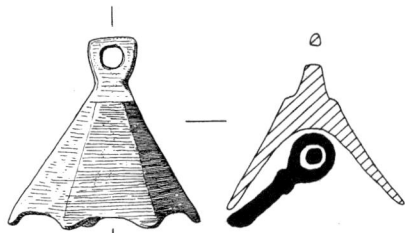

*Fig. 9.122. Miniature Anglo-Scandinavian bell from excavations at St Mark's Station (Z 86). This a typical find of the Anglo-Scandinavian period in north-west Europe and seven examples have been recovered from Lincoln (drawing and copyright, City of Lincoln Archaeology Unit).*

all, seven bells of this type have been found in Lincoln, on four sites; two in Wigford, one just outside the Lower City and one inside it (HG 72; Z 86; P 70; F 72). Seven bone tuning pegs, may be evidence for musical instruments, especially as six came from a single site – Danes Terrace in the centre of the Lower City (DT 74). Unfortunately they are not closely datable. A single such peg was also found somewhat further south, at Flaxengate (F 72).

### Physical anthropology

Despite the partial excavation of two Anglo-Scandinavian and medieval cemeteries at St Paul-in-the-Bail and St Mark's churches (SM 76; SP 72), and the examination of parts of St Bartholomew's church and hospital and St Peter Stanthaket, it is not possible to say anything much about the physical anthropology of the Anglo-Scandinavian or early Norman population and only a very little about the later medieval population. Regrettably, in the first two cases, the human remains were reburied before an adequate study was undertaken. In the third case, St Bartholomew (LH 84), it was not possible to separate burials of 12th-century date from those dating from the use of the cemetery as an over-spill from the Canon's graveyard in the Close. Associated pottery, in fact, suggests that most of the burials excavated here are of later medieval date. Burials of the High Medieval Era from the Whitefriars site (Z 86) have been studied, but provide only a small and undoubtedly atypical sample (Steane *et al.* 2001, 203). Despite this, a report on these remains has been prepared (Boylston and Roberts 1994) and as further burials are discovered and studied in future it should be possible to augment its findings.

# B. The High Medieval Era – The archaeological agenda. An introduction to the Research Agenda Zone entries (on CD-Rom)

## *David Stocker*

### Introduction

The High Medieval Era, between *c.*850 and *c.*1350, has been the most intensively investigated of all periods in Lincoln's archaeology. The terminal dates of this Era might be open to question and, before we consider its components, we should summarise the discussion which led to this date-bracket being selected. There can be little doubt that the city of the early and mid 10th century was greatly different from that of a hundred years earlier. In the early 9th century, the visitor would have found the area of Roman ruins, largely deserted, with a very sparse resident population, if any at all – outside any hypothetical monasteries. Many of those he or she did meet might have been seasonal residents or, perhaps, undertaking short-

term tasks on behalf of their social superiors. By the early 10th century, however, ruins had been levelled and the ground occupied by a population of perhaps one or two thousand people, who were mostly engaged in manufacturing, commerce and trade and lived permanently on the site. This new population rapidly became recognisably urban and so the town was re-founded. The new town of Lincoln prospered and the fact that it attracted a castle and a cathedral in the 11th century, as well as the attention of the warring armies of the Anarchy in the 12th, demonstrates that it was a place of national importance. Indeed Anglo-Norman Lincoln was one of the very largest and most prosperous cities in England and it had commercial contacts right across Europe.

Although this great prosperity lasted well into the 13th century, evidently it could not be sustained. By the 14th century the city was exhibiting all the signs of serious decline. Most English cities underwent 'late medieval decline' (Dobson 1990) but in Lincoln, this decline seems to have been earlier in its onset, more rapid, and more profound in its effects, than it was in other places. The evidence for the spectacular collapse of Lincoln's economy in the decades around 1300 (due to fundamental changes in the structure of the European cloth trade) has been collected and analysed by Paul Bischoff in his important (but still unpublished) thesis (Bischoff 1975). Exactly what brought about this dramatic reversal in the city's fortunes forms an important consideration in framing many of the RAZs which follow, but here we need to note that, having started in the final quarter of the 13th century, the decline was well underway by 1350 and by 1400 the town had changed out of all recognition. By the start of the 15th century, the town had lost more than half its population, large parts of it were de-populated and the basis of its economy had dwindled from the supply of international markets to the supply of regional and local ones. In fact the 15th-century town was much more similar to the modest market town of *c*.1700 than to the booming mercantile city of *c*.1200. As one might expect, the city's material culture reflects this economic dislocation precisely. The gross patterns in the archaeological evidence, discussed for the first time in this *Assessment*, associate sites dating from after *c*.1350, not with those of 1250, but rather with those of 1550 or 1650. In Lincoln, then, our archaeological High Medieval Era is judged to have ended somewhat early, in the first half of the 14th century, and our Early Modern Era to have started correspondingly early also.

## Economic Infrastructure

Many of the issues to be tackled in our archaeological research agendas for the period between 850 and 1350 are, fundamentally, about the competition for power in the city between its various groups of citizens. The interests of the initial re-founders of the city may have been primarily commercial, or at least, it seems that commerce quickly became the dominant factor in city life in the High Medieval Era. After all Dr Vince has shown us that there is evidence for manufacturing and trade on the Flaxengate site (F 72) for a generation or so before there is evidence for domestic occupation. Trade and commerce were evidently the factors, which transformed the city between 850 and 950 AD and it was also changes in the pattern of trade and commerce which brought the Era to an end between 1250 and 1350. Accordingly a preliminary group of 21 RAZs has been identified, aimed at exploring the chronology and character of the city's markets and commercial infrastructure. These can be accessed on the CD-Rom.

9.1 Stamp End causeway
9.2 City docks 1) wharves along Waterside North east of the wall and the *Blackdyke*
9.3 City docks 2) northern waterside between the walls
9.4 Wigford western shoreline
9.5 Wigford eastern shoreline – *La Gulle, Old Eye* and *Thorngate*
9.12 Roads
   9.12.1 Long distance roads
   9.12.2 Intermediate distance roads
   9.12.3 Local roads
   9.13.1 Bracebridge bridge
   9.13.2 Bishop's Bridges
9.14 Gowts Bridges
9.15 High Bridge and ford market
9.16 Newport market
9.17 Eastgate Market
9.18 *Beggarsholme* market in *Butwerk*
9.19 Newland market
9.20 Lower Wigford market
9.21 Market place on Castle Hill
9.22 The High Market of the Lower City and other Lower City markets
9.23.1 The *Clewmarket*
9.23.2 The *Maltmarket*

Most of these RAZ categories speak from themselves, but it may be helpful to explain some of the thinking behind some of groupings. One of the most important new perceptions arising from the *Assessment* process, for example, is the dominance of market places in the development of the plan of the city. Dr Vince suggests (above) that the first markets, within the walls, were originally accommodated within the existing street pattern, often utilising road junctions, and did not have purpose-made market places. However, following the re-design of the street layout in the 11th century identified by Dr Vince, it may be that the markets for staples migrated towards designated open spaces on the upper hill side (RAZ 9.22) where they can be located in the later medieval period through documentary sources. Such manipulations of the market areas may represent early acts of planning – evidence, perhaps, for early civic authority? They are evidence, certainly, for negotiations between different categories of power-holders in the city at this date. This is an issue that can be approached through the archaeological record, as evidence for the laying-out of markets will be revealed in sensitive future projects combining excavation with topographical analysis. Many of the markets outside the walls, on the other hand, seem to have dictated the plans of the suburbs that surrounded them – Newport, Eastgate, Lower Wigford (RAZs 9.16, 9.17, 9.20). These markets are probably good evidence that the suburbs were themselves founded around the markets and therefore a date for the layout of the market may indicate the date at which the suburb was first established. But, compared with the (earlier?) markets within the city walls, it is not clear that there was much negotiation between power-holders in the suburbs. In such cases it may be that a single power-holder (perhaps a feudal lord) organised his tenants into a pattern on the ground – one that would bring maximum profit. By comparison Newland market place (RAZ 9.19) is unusual in being clearly inserted into a pre-existing street-pattern. Although not the *raison d'être* for the suburb, the imposition of the market place after the street pattern had become established must speak either of a largely depopulated suburb or of an effective structure for communal decision-making.

As an archaeological resource, roadways are frequently ignored, but the *Assessment* has shown that they are potentially a rich source of information. The network of roads leading into the city today (and perhaps aiming originally for the various markets), was established in this High Medieval Era and Dr Vince shows us that these roads can be classified under three headings. The major long-distance routes have been distinguished as they pass through the town, except where they coincide with market places, and the archaeology of these can perhaps tell us the most about Lincoln's long-distance trade (RAZ 9.12.1). The archaeology of the 'intermediate' roads (RAZ 9.12.2), which linked the city with other towns in the region, can tell us about a different scale of trading network and (to some extent) about the supply of the city's population. The archaeology of 'local' roads (RAZ 9.12.3), like those which lead to the city's own fields, provide complementary information about victualling. There were, of course, many more minor roads in the settlement, between the houses, but the research questions asked of such streets should be indistinguishable from those asked of the houses and settlement zones which flank them. Consequently these minor roads are not given distinctive RAZs entries but form a part of the settlement RAZs by which they are surrounded.

## Housing the people

The new population supplying and servicing the new markets of Lincoln in the High Medieval Era needed to live somewhere, but in the present state of knowledge we can only divide the housing stock of the medieval city into fourteen RAZs based on geographical areas (rather than into the socio-economic areas which become possible in later periods). This should not imply, however, that we can't explore important issues surrounding the competing power relationships between different orders in the city. Comparisons between the different properties in each RAZ will be revealing, and may lead to the definition of further distinct groupings of housing-types, whilst comparison between the housing in different areas of the city will be even more enlightening – throwing into sharp contrast the differences between the social orders. The housing RAZs are:

9.24 Houses in the Bail (and the Close within St Mary Magdalene's parish)
9.25 Houses in the Lower City
9.26 Houses in Newport
9.27 Housing in *Westcastle*
9.28 Housing in Eastgate suburb (and the Close within St Margaret Pottergate Parish)
9.29 Housing in *Butwerk* suburb
9.30 Housing in *Thorngate* suburb
9.31 Housing in Newland suburb
9.32 *Willingthorpe*
    9.32.1 *Willingthorpe* Manor
    9.32.2 The Bishop's Garden, *Willingthorpe*
9.33 Housing in Upper Wigford (north of Great Gowt)
9.34 Housing in Lower Wigford (south of Great Gowt)
9.35 The Bishop's Palace

## Victualling and supply

The population living within the city and servicing the markets required supplies of food, drink and raw materials and it has proved straightforward to identify eleven RAZs that offer an understanding of the changing character of such supplies. The research agendas put forward in these RAZs are aimed, primarily, at understanding their role in the wider city economy, although in many there is interesting information to be gathered about the development of the technologies of rural agriculture and industry. The two outlying villages now within the District boundary (Boultham and Bracebridge) deserve more detailed research as independent settlement sites in their own right. For the present, however, these two RAZs concentrate on their economic and social relationships with the city.

9.6 Woodlands and wood-pasture to the south-west
9.7 Wetlands
9.8 Common pasture
    9.8.1 Enclosures west of Newland
    9.8.2 Un-enclosed pasture west of Newland
    9.8.3 Bracebridge pasture
    9.8.4 South Common
    9.8.5 Common pasture east of *Butwerk*.
9.9 The City's arable fields
    9.9.1 Lincoln common fields
    9.9.2 Fields of the parishes of Nettleham and Greetwell
9.10 Bracebridge
9.11 Boultham

## Industrial areas and activities

Many of the city's markets were supplied with goods manufactured within the city, and another satisfactory result of the *Assessment* process has been the definition of 11 dedicated industrial areas within the city. These are as follows:

9.36 The cloth production area
9.37 The mint and jewellery quarter
9.38 *Baxtergate*, the bakers' street
9.39 Pottery production sites in the Lower City
9.40.1 Pottery production area north of Monk's Road
9.40.2 Tile-house in St Botolph's parish
9.41 Quarries
    9.41.1 'Common' diggings in cliff faces north-west and south of city
    9.41.2 Quarries in the cliff face east of the city
    9.41.3 Stonepits north-east of Upper City
9.42 Windmills west of Bradegate
9.43 Windmills west of Battle Place
9.44 Windmills in East Field

With the exception of some of the pottery-production sites, these manufacturing quarters and areas have not been investigated hitherto with the aim of understanding their industries holistically. Whilst producing the RAZ texts, it has become clear that we should rethink our approach to such zones to ensure that future excavations and other research in these areas recover complete industrial systems and not simply isolated components. Furthermore, that process of understanding will also require investigation of the interactions between the industrial workers and their masters and between both workers and masters and their industrial quarter. Although we can say, at present, where some of the manufacturing took place, we have no idea whether the workers or the masters lived alongside the industrial plants to which they owed their livelihoods.

Lincoln stone was an important raw material for the city, and this was as true in the Anglo-Scandinavian and Norman periods as it had been in the Roman period. One of the many revealing aspects of the *Assessment* process has been quite how extensively the natural resources of the city – its deposits of freestone, ironstone and clay – have been exploited. Although both stone and clay were certainly quarried extensively in the Roman Era (RAZ 7.4, 7.5 and 7.14), the scale of this exploitation must have been small compared with enormous quarries which had developed (particularly just to the east of the city) by the 13th century (RAZ 9.41.2). Furthermore we can postulate that the city's quarries were of two types – those on common land (to which we should presume that many citizens had access) and those that were pri-

vately owned (in the case of the largest stone quarries, by the Church). The distinctions between the presumed exploitation of some of these resources 'in common' (RAZ 9.41.1 and 9.41.3) can be contrasted, to great effect, with the presumed exploitation by private owners (RAZ 9.41.2). The contrast offers yet another area in which future archaeological work can explore the power relations within the city, this time between those with common rights (theoretically safeguarded by the City Council) and those with capital.

Yet, although we can say quite a lot about Lincoln's stone and pottery industries, we are woefully ignorant of the archaeology of Lincoln's most important trade in the High Medieval Era – cloth manufacture. Considering how fundamental cloth manufacture was for both the rise of the city's economy to international importance and for its collapse at the end of this Era, this is a serious lacuna. It is particularly inexplicable as the deeper archaeological deposits in the primary area involved (north of the river and west of the High Street within the walled city) may be waterlogged (RAZ 9.36). These are amongst Lincoln's most valuable archaeological deposits and research work here is an urgent priority. Here too, we can expect to recover important information about power relationships. The mere fact that the cloth-workers eventually became largely confined to a single area suggests the influence of powerful interests manipulating the city's property market over time. By plotting the way in which small-scale production scattered across the city was brought together in a single area, future archaeological research can reveal a great deal about the changing balance of social power within the city.

## Administration and defence

Lincoln in the High Medieval Era was also a centre of government, both of the city itself and of the county and, consequently, a number of its institutions represent negotiations over power relationships in a more straightforward manner. The Stonebow, the seat of city government, and its predecessor on the Greyfriars site are discussed within RAZs 9.50.1 and 9.53.4, but the archaeology of six RAZs based on the city's boundary crosses can also help address issues of the city's own legal jurisdiction:

9.45.1 Cross on Cross O'Cliff Hill
9.45.2 *Broken Cross* at *Westcastle*
9.45.3 *Mile Cross* on Nettleham Road
9.45.4 *Humber Cross* on Ermine Street
9.45.5 *Stub Cross* on Greetwellgate
9.45.6 *Nettleham Mere* and contiguous features

To this group of RAZs concerned with administration and government we should add those concerned with the defence of the city – as defence and the administration of government are usually intimately connected, and the protection of the vassal (be it an individual or a corporation) was a principal responsibility laid on the feudal lord. As the 'county town', Lincoln also accommodated the local representatives of national government as well, of course, and the archaeology of the principal seat of this second power in the city, Lincoln Castle (RAZs 9.47 and 9.48), has much to tell us both about the exercise of power itself and about its waxing and waning through time. Additionally, county government had its own site for judicial activities, including execution, at *Battle Place* (RAZ 9.46) and, because the city duplicated such facilities, there is the long-term prospect of being able to compare the archaeologies of city and county justice. The Castle itself, of course, is a famous example of the monument type, which is itself under intense scrutiny at present (Johnson 2002). Increasingly the archaeological debate on medieval defensive structures has been between those who see castles and town walls as primarily of interest for military technology and those who wish to explore more subtle symbolic aspects of the same features, which illuminate social and political aspirations of those who built them. Lincoln's defences (both the Castle and other structures) are well suited to explorations of these questions and they are developed in this group of ten RAZs:

9.47   Upper City defences
9.48   Lincoln Castle from the mid 12th century
9.49   *Thorngate Castle*
9.50.1 Lower City defences
9.50.2 Close Wall
9.51   Suburb boundaries
    9.51.1 Newport boundaries
    9.51.2 *Butwerk* boundaries
    9.51.3 Newland boundaries
    9.51.4 Boundary of Upper Wigford (Great and Little Gowts)
    9.51.5 Boundary of Lower Wigford (The Sincil Dyke)

One view of the very origin of the new town of the late 9th century would stress the role of the foundation as a (perhaps fortified) base for Viking raiding parties. From the start, military considerations in Lincoln may have been in conflict with commercial interests, and it is this tension which we see reflected in the development of the various city walls. Whilst they may have proved suitable for the early Anglo-Scandinavian town, the ancient walls bequeathed to the medieval period by the Romans were simply too constrictive. Both the Upper City defences (RAZ 9.47) and those of the Lower City (RAZ 9.50) proved inadequate and had to be extended piecemeal. In each case we can learn something about the community pressing for the extension by a careful study of the expanded defensive line. This is most evident in the new Close Wall (RAZ 9.50.2)

which dates from the end of the High Medieval Era, and which is well documented, but the *Assessment* has also revealed the importance of the suburban boundaries, which may have had some defensive capacity and which were little known before this work started. These have been defined in five RAZs (9.51.1–5), and in each case careful archaeological study of the new defensive line will tell us much about the community around which the defensive boundary was extended, and also about the political and/or economic power of that community within the city as a whole. Our new understanding of the number and character of these suburban defences must encourage us, surely, to look for similar structures in other cities.

The 12th-century and later Castle (RAZ 9.48) has its own research design in the form of a conservation plan (Hayfield 2000) to which the RAZ defers. There was, in fact, a second castle in Lincoln, which is known from only a few documents – *Thorngate Castle* (RAZ 9.49). Although no archaeological work has been done here yet, the site offers the possibility of developing some of the issues discussed by judicious comparison with Lincoln Castle.

## The Church

The Church had recognised the importance of Lincoln in the religious life of its region in the Early Medieval Era, before the town's re-foundation, but during the High Medieval Era it invested in the settlement in an overwhelming way. The establishment of the Cathedral in the city in the 1070s was, perhaps, the principal marker of this investment, but many other institutions were founded here also. The question to be asked in our *Assessment*, of course, is whether this church interest was new, and resulted from the commercial success of the re-founded city, or whether it was merely the latest phase of recognition of the long-term significance of the city in religious life in the locality, which we have seen extended back to the Bronze Age. We need to understand, especially, the status of the pre-Viking churches in the settlement and whether the establishment of the commercial town enriched them or (conversely) encouraged the growth of different types of religious institution. By contrast, towards 1300 we should be interested in the extent to which ecclesiastical influence in the city fell away with the waning commercial and military significance of the city. Documentary history suggests that the dominance of the Church over the city continued despite the economic woes of the city at large and, by 1350, it was much the most important interest group within the town, but the archaeology may add complexity to this simple account.

The church in the medieval town has become a topic of great interest to archaeologists in recent decades, and there have been many case studies of individual towns and of the phenomenon of the urban church more generally. In this discussion of urban churches, Lincoln has usually figured prominently and, consequently, future work in Lincoln must seek to advance the broader national agenda as well the narrow interests of the city itself. Amongst the many recent surveys of the urban church at the national level, two stand out as being of particular value in the establishment of research agendas for the Lincoln church sites in the High Medieval Era – Morris 1989 (especially chapter 5) and Blair and Pyrah 1996. Both studies emphasise the interrelationship between the church and the community in which its sits, and that this interrelationship is as important for towns as it is for rural churches. The idea is that, of all its structures, the church is most likely to reflect the growth and development of the community. If excavations can only occur once in each parish, such studies seem to say, it should take place on the church site. Both Morris and Blair and Pyrah point out the importance of understanding the origins of each church site, and this issue is of particular relevance for towns because, for certain types of town, it seems that the establishment of a multiplicity of churches is one of the key indicators of urbanism.

Of course, the research agendas for many of the parish church sites will be similar. For each, for example, we are very interested in establishing the character of the foundation (was it proprietory or was it communal?) – a debate which is central to our overarching theme of understanding the balance of power relationships within the city. Furthermore a surprising number of the parish churches seem to be closely associated with the foundation of markets (having markets in their graveyards or being apparently founded to service an existing market) showing that the medieval church was not distinct from commerce, but was actively promoting it. The plans of churches and their architectural development will not only cast some light on different aspects of social relationships and negotiations in the surrounding parish (a subject which has recently been put on a secure footing by Pam Graves – 2000), but they will be important in their own right for architectural history more widely. Finally, the city's graveyards represent an extremely important resource of paleopathological information. Study of these remains is clearly the way to understand more about the life-styles of the citizens through time.

These issues have been taken up in individual research agendas for each of the 47 medieval parish churches. The bridge chapel of St Thomas is discussed in RAZ 9.15.

9.60 The parish churches
    9.60.1   St John Newport
    9.60.2   St Nicholas Newport
    9.60.3   St Bartholomew *Westcastle*
    9.60.4   St Peter Eastgate
    9.60.5   St Margaret Pottergate
    9.60.6   St Leonard
    9.60.7   St Giles

    9.60.8   Holy Trinity Greestone Stairs
    9.60.9   St Rumbold
    9.60.10  St Bavon
    9.60.11  St Augustine
    9.60.12  St Peter *ad fontem*
    9.60.13  St Clement-in-*Butwerk*
    9.60.14  St Stephen-in-Newland
    9.60.15  St Faith-in-Newland
    9.60.16  Holy Cross Wigford
    9.60.17  Holy Innocents
    9.60.18  Holy Trinity Wigford
    9.60.19  St Andrew Wigford
    9.60.20  St Benedict
    9.60.21  St Botolph
    9.60.22  St Edward Wigford
    9.60.23  St John the Evangelist Wigford
    9.60.24  St Margaret Wigford
    9.60.25  St Mark
    9.60.26  St Mary-le-Wigford
    9.60.27  St Michael Wigford
    9.60.28  St Peter-at-Gowts
    9.60.29  St Paul-in-the-Bail
    9.60.30  All Saints-in-the-Bail
    9.60.31  St Clement-in-the-Bail
    9.60.32  St Mary Magdalene
    9.60.33  St Michael-on-the-Mount
    9.60.34  St John-the-Poor
    9.60.35  St Andrew-under-Palace
    9.60.36  St Peter Stanthaket
    9.60.37  St Cuthbert
    9.60.38  St Martin
    9.60.39  St Lawrence
    9.60.40  St George
    9.60.41  Holy Trinity Clasketgate
    9.60.42  St Mary *Crackpole*
    9.60.43  All Saints Hungate
    9.60.44  St Peter-at-Pleas and St Peter-at-Arches
    9.60.45  St Swithin
    9.60.46  St Edmund.

As one would expect of a major medieval city, church investment in Lincoln was not confined to the parish churches and many monasteries and hospitals were founded during the High Medieval Era, including the Cathedral itself. A total of sixteen discrete RAZs have been identified:

9.52 The Cathedral
9.53 The friaries
    9.53.1 Augustinian Friary
    9.53.2 Dominican Friary
    9.53.3 Carmelite Friary
    9.53.4 Franciscan Friary
    9.53.5 Friary of the Sack and the Kyme chantry
9.54 St Katherine's Priory and St Sepulchre's Hospital
9.55 Monks' Abbey (Benedictine priory of St Mary Magdalene)

The Cathedral, probably (re-)established in Lincoln in 1073, is such a major and complex site that it requires its own free-standing research agenda, now available in the form of a model conservation plan (Gibbs 2001). RAZ 9.52 defers to the discussions of research priorities set out there and the complex and important research issues surrounding the Cathedral are not taken any further in this *Assessment*. The four friaries of the major orders in Lincoln (RAZs 9.53.1–4) represent a valuable group of such sites nationally, and in addition, Lincoln has a relatively rare example of the Friary of the Sack (RAZ 9.53.5). In all five cases, of course, the churches and other claustral buildings will be of interest from the architectural point of view, and plans need to be recovered. But we already know a great deal about fraternal plans (e.g. Butler 1984) and attention should now be turning to more complex aspects of the archaeology of friaries. One of the new avenues requiring exploration is the study of burial populations at friaries, and we badly need a fully excavated graveyard to provide a proper sample. Because they were patronised by all degrees of medieval society, a complete friary burial population may provide us with a microcosm of the city's sociology, in both life and death. As, typically, *all* of the various power groupings within a city are represented within friary graveyards, comparisons between the various mortuary behaviours on display will be especially revealing. In Lincoln, such a study may be best targeted at the Austin Friary in Newport (RAZ 9.53.1), which seems to be almost completely undisturbed.

Of the monastic houses and hospitals, each of which has its own distinctive research agenda, the Benedictine Priory of St Mary Magdalene, usually known as Monks Abbey (RAZ 9.55.1 and 9.55.2), is a rather unusual institution about whose archaeology surprisingly little is known. It has already been singled out in the Early Medieval Era as a potential early church site of great interest (RAZ 8.1.3), and the manner in which it developed during the High Medieval Era, into a very small, but apparently valuable, cell of St Mary's Abbey at York, has much to tell us about the ecclesiastical and commercial relations between the two cities. Certainly, the house occupied a pivotal role in the commerce of Lincoln itself, being associated with what is presumed to have been an early fair at *Beggarsholme* (RAZ 9.18) and, subsequently, having an imperfectly understood role *viz-a-viz* the Witham docks, which lay along its southern boundary (RAZ 9.2). If our understanding of the Prehistoric ritual importance of the Stamp End causeway is correct (RAZ 5.2), however, Monks' Abbey, which owned the bridgehead, represented Lincoln's continuity with a pre-Christian past as well as a possible early Christian one – a continuity which has recently been suggested for a number of other medieval monastic sites in the Witham Valley (Stocker and Everson 2003).

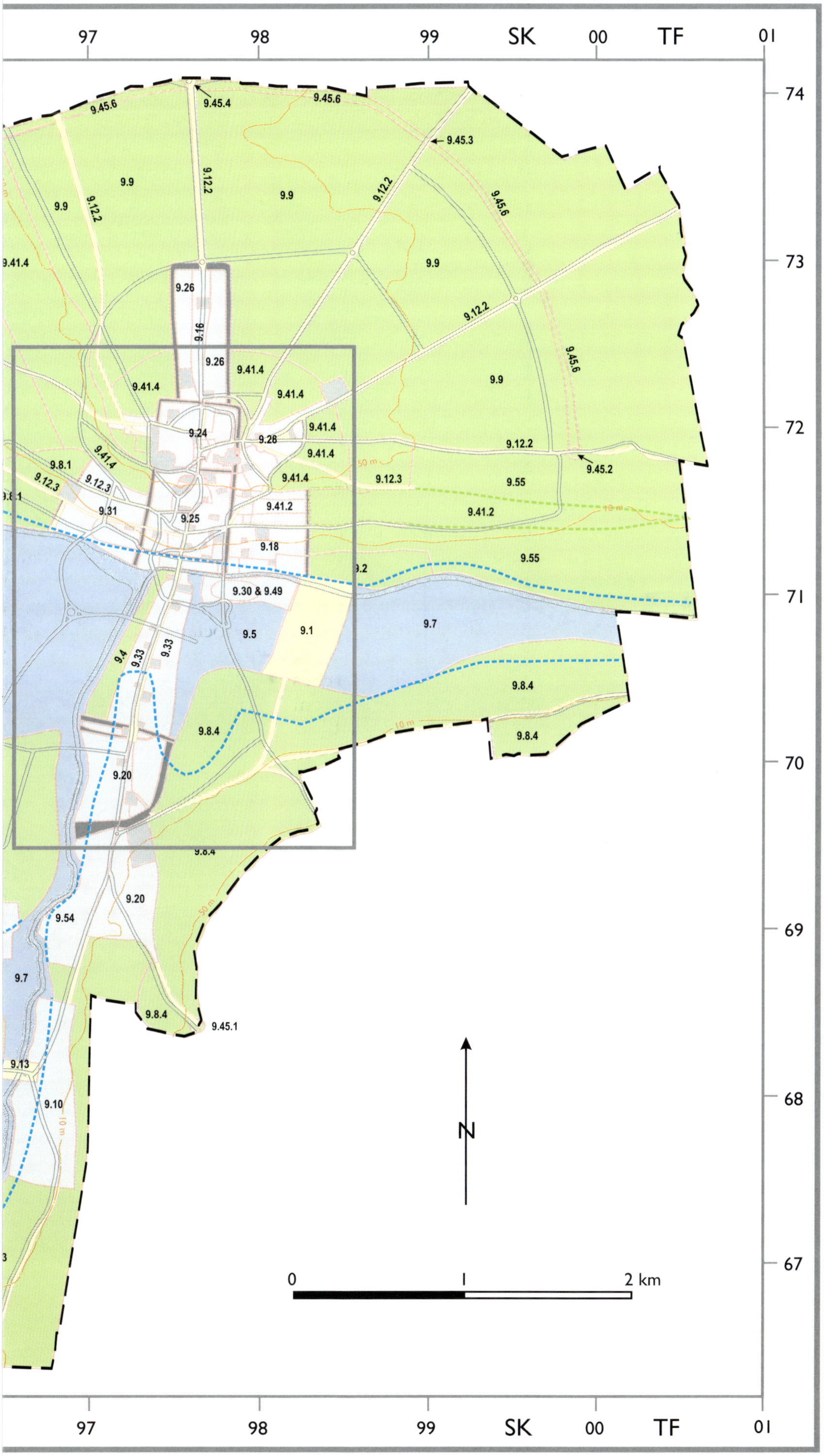

*Map 5. Research Agenda Zone locations for the High Medieval Era – See CD-Rom for details (drawn by Dave Watt, copyright English Heritage and Lincoln City Council).*

*...genda Zone locations for the High Medieval Era – See CD-Rom*
*...Watt, copyright English Heritage and Lincoln City Council).*

# 10. Lincoln in the Early Modern Era (*c.1350–c.1750*)

# A. Archaeological account

## Alan Vince

## Late medieval Lincoln (*c.1350–c.1550*)

### Introduction

In the late medieval period Lincoln underwent a dramatic transformation. Several important changes were underway before the middle of the 14th century, of which the most important for the archaeology of the city was undoubtedly the collapse of the cloth industry in the generation between *c*.1275 and *c*.1300. It has been argued, by Paul Bischoff (1975), that this collapse was ultimately responsible for checking the growth of the city at a time when other towns in the region were still expanding. A variety of factors probably combined to remove Lincoln's status as the economic hub of the East Midlands, which it had clearly retained from the 9th to the 13th centuries. Apart from the collapse of the indigenous cloth industry, the rise of competing ports such as Hull, Grimsby and Boston, and the inadequacy of the city's own waterways played an important part. It also seems likely that the Black Death had a large impact on the city's population and economy (Fig. 9.6), and the dramatic fall in population between the end of the 13th century and the middle of the 14th century has provided another useful indicator that Lincoln was entering another Era – that of the early modern city. Lincoln was to become a quieter place than it had been during the years of its prosperity, filling up for market days with people who lived outside the town. Gaps now appeared in the street-frontages, where the urban population used to live. The Early Modern Era can be divided itself into two sections by another cataclysmic event, as far as Lincoln was concerned, the dissolution of the monasteries. Both the collapse of the cloth industry and the Dissolution had consequences which are reflected in the city's

archaeology, although unlike a fire or major piece of civil engineering there is no precise marker in the ground to say 'this layer is earlier than 1348' or 'that layer dates to the Dissolution'.

The bubonic plague spread rapidly through England in 1349, as through the rest of Europe, and its immediate effect can be seen throughout the city when looking at wills recorded in the *Burwarmote Book* (Lincolnshire Archives Office, D&C Ms. 169). In several cases it seems that whole streets were depopulated. For example, between 1317 and 1369, 24 wills were proved in St Peter-at-Arches parish, averaging between zero and two wills in any one year, except that is for 1349, when nine wills were proved. It is clear from Paul Bischoff's work (1975) discussed above (p. 291 above), however, that the city was already in steep decline by this date and the drastic loss of population in 1349 might not have had such a lasting effect on the city were it not for the fact that it was already reeling from the collapse of the cloth industry. The Black Death, then, has to be set alongside the long-term changes in the region's economy which we have considered in the last chapter, from indigenous production of cloth from East Midlands wool, to wool export in-the-raw.

One of the clearest consequences of the decline of population brought about by extinction of Lincoln's manufacturing base and the subsequent withering of its commerce was a marked contraction in the area of land the city occupied. It seems clear that the whole of *Westcastle* suburb and significant parts of the suburbs of Newport, Eastgate, *Butwerk* and Newland reverted to pasture and closes. Even within the walled city there was considerable depopulation, with not just individual properties, but whole districts being described as waste, especially in the western part of the Lower City. In 1428 the collectors of a subsidy in the city (excluding the Bail) reported that there were no inhabitants at all in three parishes and fewer than ten inhabitants in ten more (Hill 1948, 287) (Fig. 10.1). The collapsing population numbers brought about a concomitant decline in numbers of parish churches, several of which were demolished during this period (see below). The decline was dramatic. The population graph (Fig. 9.6) shows that numbers tumbled in the first half of the 14th century, but declined much more slowly after that, reaching a nadir, apparently, in the mid 15th century (there were, apparently, fewer – perhaps many fewer – than 2000 inhabitants in 1445–6 – Hill 1948, 272). But from the mid 14th century to the mid 18th century, though very small, the population seems to have been quite stable at around 2,500 inhabitants. This compares, for example with Boston's population of about 3,500 in the mid 18th century (Thompson 1856, 98).

But Lincoln did not die. It would be more correct to say that its character in the later medieval period was merely radically different to what went before; its people evidently adapted to a new role in county and national society. It still retained considerable strengths as an urban centre. Most notably, the Dean and Chapter steadily increased their control of large stretches of the city, through the acquisition of land. The precinct was formalised into a walled Close at the same time that the cloth industry was collapsing (licences were granted in 1285, 1316 and 1318 – Hill 1948, 121), but the Close houses, within, continued develop and to be aggrandised through the 14th and 15th centuries (Jones *et al.* 1984; 1987; 1990). Furthermore the influence of the Cathedral ensured a degree of prosperity for traders of all sorts in the Bail, which also acquired three large 'courtyard' inns ('The Angel', 'The Antelope' and 'The White Hart') to provide temporary accommodation for those with business at the Cathedral.

Nor were the Dean and Chapter the only investors in the city. Lincoln as a whole developed as an elite centre where the surrounding aristocracy congregated for what later became 'The Season'. The social elite of the High Medieval Era had shared the Lower City and suburbs with artisans and shopkeepers, now it seems they became dominant in the townscape. During the later medieval period we see the continued growth of their urban residences downhill into imposing courts, often through the agglomeration of tenements into large contiguous holdings. We have already seen a good example of this in the *Sancto Laudo* estate, situated to the north of Guildhall Street and south of Mint Lane, which was subsequently bequeathed to the Cathedral (ed. Major 1958, 182, RA2373 – p. 217–8 above). There does not seem to have been a preference amongst the elite for any particular area within the city. Grand houses were built in the Bail (both inside and outside the Close Wall), the Lower City, Wigford, Newport, Eastgate, Newland and *Butwerk*. Only *Westcastle* was

not affected, probably because it had been almost completely taken over as an adjunct of the Castle, where judicial and other ceremonial functions were mounted (*Battle Place* and the county gallows) and where the Dean and Chapter's overflow cemetery had superseded St Bartholomew's parish churchyard.

## Defences

There is little, if any, evidence for substantial investment in the defences of Lincoln during the later medieval period. By the end of the 14th century, the Close Wall, the city wall and the defences of the Castle had reached their final form and the later medieval period merely saw their upkeep. In the case of the Close Wall, responsibility for its upkeep was transferred from the Dean and Chapter to individual lessees.

Previously, a wall built on top of the foundations of the south wall of the Roman city at Saltergate has been interpreted as part of a medieval refurbishment of the city's defences (LIN 73dii). However, there is little doubt that this was, in fact, the back wall of a domestic building fronting onto Saltergate (Fig. 10.2). Consequently the mention of encroachment of buildings over this stretch of the city wall in Edward II's charter of 1315 (ed. de Birch 1906, 3, No.16; Hill 1948, 242 and n.) probably reflects the disappearance of the wall at this point. With the exception of the disappearance of the south wall of the Lower City, apparently in the late 13th century (p. 183 and 217–8 above), the line of the remainder of the city's defences survived through the late medieval and Tudor periods. Only the stretch of extended city wall and terminal tower on the south-east corner of the circuit was encroached upon during this period. It was leased by the Council to a private individual in 1378 along with a length of the city ditch, although the Council retained the option of repossessing the property in time of war (Hill 1948, 157–8). Nevertheless the matter was thought sufficiently sensitive for the Crown for the lease to be entered in the Patent Rolls (*CPR* 1381–5, 302). However, on balance, the fact that late medieval access to *Butwerk* was through the gate to the south of this stretch of wall, rather than by continuing east along the line of Saltergate, suggests that the Lower City's east wall remained a barrier. There is excavated evidence from the south-west corner of the Lower City for the continued maintenance of the city ditch on this side during the later medieval period, although it was eventually allowed to silt up, and was used as a dumping place for cobbler's waste during the Tudor period (LT 72).

Documentary and pictorial evidence shows that the main city gates continued to be maintained during the late medieval period and some were given alternative uses (Clasketgate gate became the city gaol, for example). However, it was probably during the 14th and 15th centuries that the gates outside the Newland

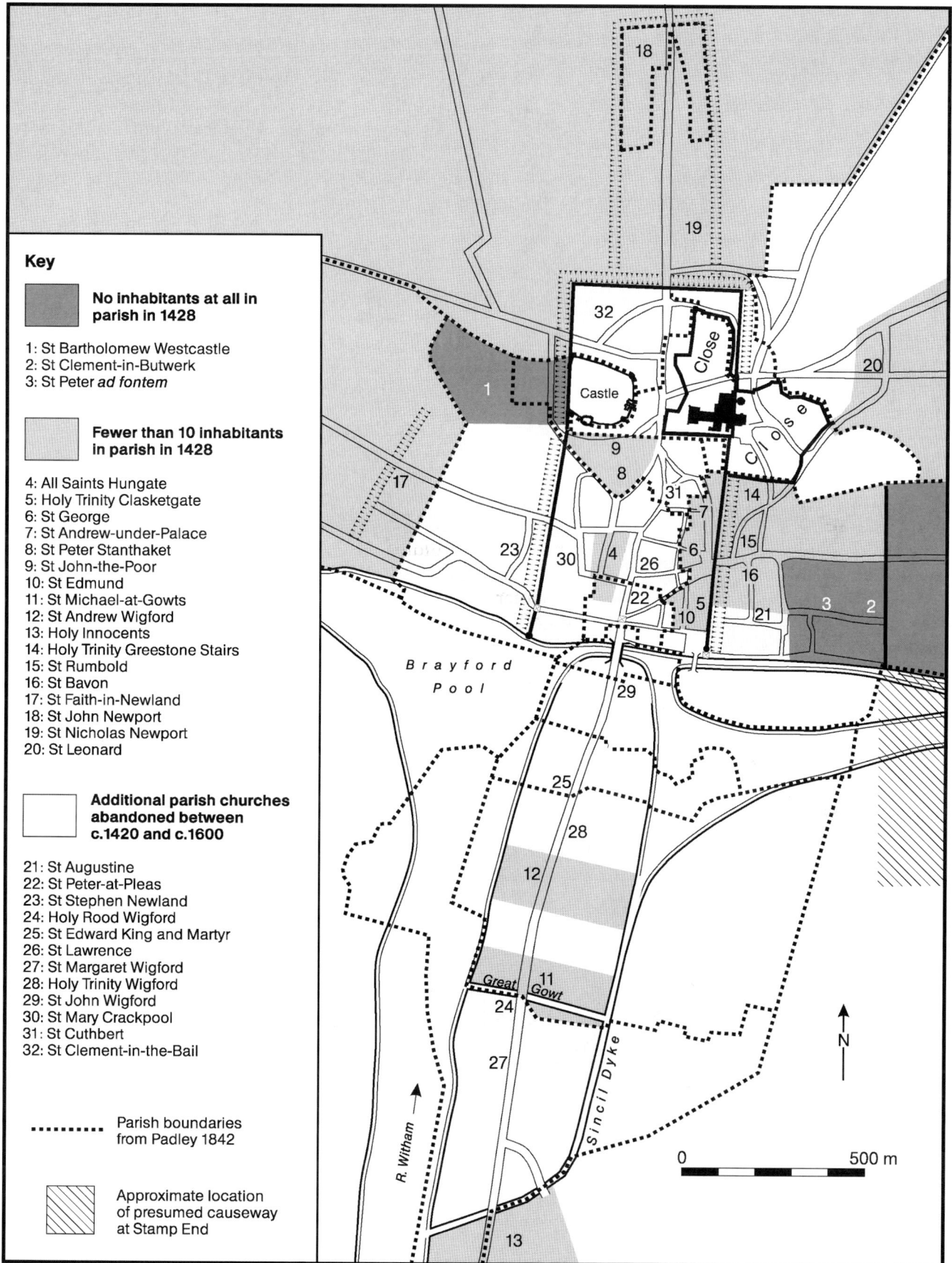

**Key**

No inhabitants at all in parish in 1428

1: St Bartholomew Westcastle
2: St Clement-in-Butwerk
3: St Peter *ad fontem*

Fewer than 10 inhabitants in parish in 1428

4: All Saints Hungate
5: Holy Trinity Clasketgate
6: St George
7: St Andrew-under-Palace
8: St Peter Stanthaket
9: St John-the-Poor
10: St Edmund
11: St Michael-at-Gowts
12: St Andrew Wigford
13: Holy Innocents
14: Holy Trinity Greestone Stairs
15: St Rumbold
16: St Bavon
17: St Faith-in-Newland
18: St John Newport
19: St Nicholas Newport
20: St Leonard

Additional parish churches abandoned between c.1420 and c.1600

21: St Augustine
22: St Peter-at-Pleas
23: St Stephen Newland
24: Holy Rood Wigford
25: St Edward King and Martyr
26: St Lawrence
27: St Margaret Wigford
28: Holy Trinity Wigford
29: St John Wigford
30: St Mary Crackpool
31: St Cuthbert
32: St Clement-in-the-Bail

........... Parish boundaries from Padley 1842

Approximate location of presumed causeway at Stamp End

Castle
Close
Close
Brayford Pool
R. Witham
Sincil Dyke
Great Gowt
N
0          500 m

Fig. 10.1. Depopulation in the city in the 15th and 16th centuries. The most specific evidence is provided by the Subsidy Collectors Accounts for 1428 (Hill 1948, 287), but several other ecclesiastical sources show that the intensively occupied area of the city shrank to The Close and the High Street on either side of the Witham crossing (drawn by Dave Watt, copyright English Heritage).

*Fig. 10.2. Medieval encroachment over the line of the southern city wall revealed in excavations at Saltergate in 1973 (LIN 73d). The view is taken from the west, looking east along Saltergate. The thick foundation relates to the Roman south wall of the lower city, whilst the narrower walls on top represent medieval domestic buildings facing Saltergate (photo and copyright, English Heritage).*

and *Butwerk* suburbs were lost, following their partial depopulation. We have no positive evidence for the existence of a gate at the north end of the Newport suburb, but such a gate is extremely likely, and this too would have been lost during this period. Although Clasketgate Gate was repaired in the late 16th or early 17th centuries (see the finials and other architectural details in the Buck sketch – Fig. 9.24), the only gate which we know to have been enhanced was the Stonebow (Figs. 9.25 and 10.3). There is documentary evidence for the demolition of the earlier building in 1390 and also for a long interval before the construction of the present structure in 1520 (Stocker 1997b). By this time, if not much earlier, the gate had lost any semblance of a defensive role and the new gate is actually more of a processional archway. The fact that this gate was rebuilt indicates the continuing symbolic importance of the Stonebow as the seat of city government and as a symbolic entrance to Lincoln.

### The extent of settlement

The best evidence for the extent of occupation within the late medieval city comes from documentary sources and is summarised by Hill (1948, 287). The collectors of the 1428 subsidy recorded that there were ten or fewer inhabitants in seventeen parishes and none at all in St Bartholomew, St Peter *ad fontem* or St Clement-in-*Butwerk* (Figs. 10.1 and 10.6). The map of these depopulated parishes shows clearly that the eastern and northern parts of the *Butwerk* suburb, the Newport suburb and the western parts of the New-

*Fig. 10.3. Stonebow from the south – a photograph taken in 1927 to commemorate the first double-decker bus route servicing the new working-class housing estate at St Giles. Co-incidentally it records the condition of the Stonebow's sculpture of c.1520 before heavy restoration (photo and copyright, Lincolnshire County Council, County Library Service, Local History Collection).*

land suburb had become more or less deserted. Parishes to the east and west of High Street, fronting onto the Brayford Pool and the Witham (St Stephen, St Mary *Crackpole*, St Swithin, and St Augustine) had evidently retained some population, and most of the parishes along the High Street, from St Michael-on-the-Mount south to St Botolph Wigford had also retained parishioners. The remainder of the Lower City was also largely depopulated, with almost all the parishes occupying the back-lands either side of High Street reporting fewer than 10 inhabitants. It is unfortunate that the Bail was not included within the account; as an undoubtedly prosperous area it would have provided a check on the validity of the figures elsewhere. The 1428 subsidy figures show that, effectively, the city's population in the early 15th century inhabited a cross-shaped settlement with properties lining the riverbank east–west and the main road at right angles to it. Although much of the remainder of the city area that had been occupied in the High Medieval Era continued to retain a few inhabitants, the population was sparsely scattered across large areas. In Newport suburb, which covered an area of about 10ha, for example, the total population in 1428 was fewer than twenty (i.e. there were fewer than two people per hectare). In *Butwerk*, outside the parish of St Augustine along the waterside, (a similar sized area to Newport) there were fewer than 30 parishioners. These are very small population figures, and represent occupation at rural, rather than urban, levels of density. The total population of Newland, for example, might have comprised no more than four or five households and that of *Butwerk* not many more.

Excavations at The Lawn (LH 84/LA 85/L 86) in *Westcastle* suburb produced evidence for intensive use of the cemetery of St Bartholomew in the late medieval period, but the documentary sources make it clear that these were not burials of parishioners but those of canons and others from the Close and Castle (ed. Foster 1933, 170–1, RA471). In April 1295 the Abbot of Selby Abbey, the holders of the advowson of the parish church, started negotiations which culminated, two years later, in the transfer of the advowson to the Dean and Chapter (ed. Foster 1933, 164–7, RA464–6). The hospital attached to the church in the 13th century, however, had been dissolved before c.1350 (Knowles and Hadcock 1953, 285). This area also continued to be used for the execution of justice through the late medieval period and appeals and executions took place here until the 19th century (Cameron 1985, 32). On the other side of the Upper City, excavations in the central and eastern parts of the Eastgate suburb (LG 89, WC 87) have produced late medieval pottery, even though the parish of St Leonard is one that had fewer than ten inhabitants in 1428. West of the Lower City, in Newland, the wide market street probably formed the focus for the small population living here, and late medieval occupation to the south, between

the street and Brayford Pool, has been demonstrated in excavations (BN 87). To the north of the street (in the area of the modern County Council offices), however, a large late medieval farm, known as *Cause Manor*, would have provided another centre of population, even though it would also have added to the rural atmosphere.

The focus of occupation in the Early Modern Era in *Butwerk* was the parish of St Augustine, which probably comprised the land north of the modern roads Waterside North and both sides of the modern St Rumbold Street. An unlocated mansion in this parish is known from a series of late 14th-century documents as *Godslove House* (*Ibid.*, 147). The college of chantry priests founded in the buildings of the Friars of the The Sack in 1358 (Hill 1948, 151) was relocated to the Cathedral by 1366 (Major 1974, 24) and its removal probably left this eastern part of the *Butwerk* suburb empty. Perhaps it was because of the new space available that the suburb was chosen as the location for St Hugh's Fair, put on a formal footing by the Royal charter of 1409, although this might have been a revival or a re-organisation of a much older institution (p. 232 above). The fair was (re) established in closes called *St Hugh's Crofts*, by 1455, which lay south and east of St Peter *ad fontem* church, and within that church's deserted parish (Lincolnshire Archives Office, Lincoln City Charters 6/54) (Fig. 9.66). By this date *St Hugh's Crofts* were divided into numerous *selions* or *styntes* ('shares' or 'allotments' – Cameron 1985, 187). It is possible that some of these were decayed tenements rather than arable *selions*, although the adjoining land to the east, *Baggerholm wong*, was arable. If this land (which was well inside the *Butwerk* suburb boundary) was regularly in arable, it not only dramatically demonstrates the disappearance of settlement, but it would also have restricted the times at which fairs could be held.

East of the *Butwerk* boundary, the prior of the Black Monks was in more or less constant dispute with the Council during the late 14th and 15th centuries over various rights in this part of the city. The boundaries of the monks' estates, *The Monks' Leys*, are given in two documents (one dated 1377 and the other 1455), which record attempts to agree on these rights (Lincolnshire Archives Office, Lincoln City Charters 6/54). One of these disputes was over the rights of citizens to land ships at *Blackdyke*, called *the Ryvall* in the earlier document, the important dock on the Witham, just below Stamp End. These documents also tell us of windmills along the cliff edge to the north, of extensive areas on top of the cliff and to either side of *Bagerholmegate* (modern Monks Road) which were under the plough, whilst the strip of land north of the river was mostly occupied by marsh, osier beds, willow trees and meadow. The Priory buildings themselves were enclosed with a wall and ditches, with its main gate opposite a lane leading to Greetwellgate (probably on the line of the modern Milman Road, known as *Love Lane* between the late 17th and late 19th centuries).

Following the collapse of St Peter *ad fontem* church its parish was united with the priory (Hill 1948, 287n).

The Wigford suburb also suffered some depopulation during the late medieval period, as witnessed by the reports of fewer than 10 parishioners in the parishes of St Andrew and St Michael-at-Gowts in 1428. However, these were both very small parishes indeed, and one reason for the decline in numbers in St Andrew's parish may have been the increasing size of the Sutton family's house (Hill 1948, 165–8). Indeed, at the Reformation, the family claimed that the parish church was their private chapel. The Suttons' large stone mansion, north of the church and west of the High Street, subsequently known as *John of Gaunt's Palace*, has been the subject of a recent detailed study (Stocker 1999) (Fig. 10.4). Other late medieval mansions are known to have existed in Upper Wigford, from the Great Gowt northwards to the Witham (Fig. 9.69 and 10.15), where *Scotch Hall* occupied a large plot immediately south of the river on the west side of High Bridge (*Ibid.*). Lower Wigford, from the Great Gowt to the Bar Gates, may have been somewhat different in character. There is little evidence for domestic occupation on the east side of St Botolph's Green whilst the properties on the west side seem to have retained their original long thin tenements into the 19th century, suggesting that there was no pressure here to amalgamate properties into large urban estates. There were minor industrial sites throughout the suburb, however. Tanners were situated on the west side of the street, for example. Tilers continued to operate both south of St Botolph's church and in St Mark's parish, whilst (also in St Mark's parish) the urban pottery industry excavated to the rear of tenements extending back from High Street at St Mark's Station East (ZE 87) also continued (p. 276 above). To the south of the Sincil Dyke the low number of parishioners in Holy Innocents parish in 1428 suggests that inmates of the major religious establishments of The Malandry, St Katherine's Priory and Holy Sepulchre probably accounted for most of the population in this area.

### The Church

Late medieval churches with wealthy patrons, even if few in number, would have supported one or more priests, new chapels, monuments, floors and windows as well as textiles. A guide as to the relative wealth of each parish church in the late 14th century is given by the Clerical Poll Tax of 1377 (McHardy 1992) (Fig. 10.5). Beneficed priests, vicars and rectors paid at the rate of 12d per person, un-beneficed priests, chaplains and clerks paid at the rate of 4d. From this we can see that the highest taxed churches were those clustering either side of the High Bridge: St Benedict, St Peter-at-Pleas, St Mary *Crackpole* and St Mary-le-Wigford. At the other end of the scale were churches which had only a single clerk: St John Newport and St Michael-at-Gowts (both churches with less than ten parishioners by 1428). Fifteen churches are not mentioned. Of these, the omission of several is explicable for administrative reasons – St Mary Magdalene would have been included within the figures given for the Cathedral, for example, whilst St Giles' ceased to be a parish church in the 13th century, although its fabric probably survived within St Giles' Hospital. We have seen how St Bartholomew's, similarly, had ceased to be a parish church at the end of the 13th century. Despite this, however, the church of St Bartholomew itself remained standing and two documents of the 1390s indicate that services were still held there, on St Bartholomew's day and vigil. The profits from these services were part of the endowment of the Cathedral choristers and they had sunk to below one mark in value. In 1391 this situation prompted the master, Sir Henry de Reepham, to obtain an indulgence from the Pope for anyone

*Fig. 10.4. 'John of Gaunt's Palace', Wigford, from the east by S and N Buck in 1724 (Oxford, Bodleian Library Ms, Gough Lincs. 15 f.48r–9v) (photo and copyright, Bodleian Library).*

| Church name | Rector | Vicar | Beneficed | Chaplain | Clerk | Not given | Grand total | Rank |
|---|---|---|---|---|---|---|---|---|
| St Benedict | | | 24 | 4 | 8 | 36 | 72 | 1 |
| St Peter-at-Pleas | 12 | | 12 | 12 | 4 | 4 | 44 | 2 |
| St Mary *Crackpole* | | 12 | 12 | | | 8 | 32 | 3 |
| St Mary-le-Wigford | | 12 | | | 4 | 16 | 32 | 4 |
| St Botolph | | | 12 | | | 8 | 20 | 5 |
| St Martin | | 12 | | | 4 | 4 | 20 | 5 |
| St Michael-on-the-Mount | | | | 12 | | 8 | 20 | 5 |
| St Peter Eastgate | | | 12 | 4 | | 4 | 20 | 5 |
| St Swithin | | | | 8 | | 12 | 20 | 5 |
| St Lawrence | | | 12 | 4 | | | 16 | 6 |
| St Margaret Wigford | | | | 8 | 4 | 4 | 16 | 6 |
| St Paul-in-the-Bail | 12 | | | | 4 | | 16 | 6 |
| St Peter-at-Arches | | | | 4 | 8 | 4 | 16 | 6 |
| Holy Cross Wigford | | 12 | | | | | 12 | 7 |
| St Andrew Wigford | | | | 8 | | 4 | 12 | 7 |
| St Cuthbert | | | | | 4 | 8 | 12 | 7 |
| St John Wigford | | | | | | 12 | 12 | 7 |
| St Mark | | | | 4 | | 8 | 12 | 7 |
| St Nicholas | | 12 | | | | | 12 | 7 |
| St Peter *ad Fontem* | 12 | | | | | | 12 | 7 |
| St Peter-at-Gowts | | | | 8 | | 4 | 12 | 7 |
| All Saints Hungate | | | | | 4 | 4 | 8 | 8 |
| Holy Trinity Wigford | | | | | 4 | 4 | 8 | 8 |
| St Augustine | | | | 8 | | | 8 | 8 |
| St Edmund | | | | | | 8 | 8 | 8 |
| St Margaret Pottergate | | | | 4 | | 4 | 8 | 8 |
| Holy Trinity Clasketgate | | | | | | 4 | 4 | 9 |
| St Bavon | | | | 4 | | | 4 | 9 |
| St Edmund | | | | | 4 | | 4 | 9 |
| St Edward Wigford | | | | 4 | | | 4 | 9 |
| St George | | | | | | 4 | 4 | 9 |
| St John Newport | | | | | 4 | | 4 | 9 |
| St Michael Wigford | | | | | 4 | | 4 | 9 |
| St Rumbold | | | | | | 4 | 4 | 9 |
| Grand Total | 36 | 60 | 84 | 92 | 60 | 192 | 524 | |

*Fig. 10.5. Amount paid in pence by the different orders of priests (including those whose status is not given) of Lincoln parishes in 1377, ranked in order of total payment (source, McHardy 1992).*

visiting the church (ed. Foster 1933, 176–8, RA479–80). The parish of All Saints-in-the-Bail had been combined with that of St Mary Magdalene when the Close Wall was constructed and the church was no longer used for services or burial. The structure itself was still standing in the 1490s and from 1496 it was used as a quarry for stone to repair or rebuild the large Close house called Deloraine Court in James Street (Jones *et al.* 1990, 70). The evident correlation between the high clerical poll tax in 1377 and population levels fifty years later (compare Figs. 10.1 and 10.5) suggests that many of the parish churches in the city gained much of their wealth through their parishioners, rather than always from a single rich patron. Such patrons certainly existed, however, as is shown by the Suttons' attempts to show that St Andrew Wigford was their private property (above).

A number of churches and their parishes ceased to function in the later Middle Ages (Fig. 10.6). We have already seen that some parishes, like St Peter *ad fontem*, were united with others in the Middle Ages. Other

such amalgamations include St Mary-le-Wigford, St Faith and St Andrew-under-Palace in 1263. It is possible that services continued to be held in all the churches in this united parish after this date. Amalgamation must have made difficulties for the few remaining parishioners in what had been St Faith's parish, because of its distance from the new parish church. This was less of a problem when St Michael-on-the-Mount parish grew to take in both St John-the-Poor and St Peter Stanthaket between 1428 and 1549. The new parish formed a contiguous block at the northern end of the Lower City.

The fate of St Stephen's, the remaining Newland church once St Faith had been amalgamated with St-Mary-le-Wigford, is less straightforward. The parish was not noted as having a low population in 1428, but there is no mention of any priest or clerk in the 1377 clerical poll tax, whereas the priests of St Mary *Crackpole*, which also lay in a decayed part of the city, paid 20d in tax, one of the four highest taxed churches in the city. This evidence might suggest that St

| Area/ Suburb | Church name | Number of parishioners in 1428 | Evidence for last use of church |
|---|---|---|---|
| Newland | St Faith-in-Newland | Less than 10 parishioners | Parish united with St Mary-le-Wigford in 1263. No subsequent mention of church in use |
| Extra Wigford | Holy Innocents | Less than 10 parishioners | United with the Malandry hospital – late 13th Century? |
| Bail | All Saints-in-the- Bail | Exempt from 1428 *Subsidy* | Parish united with St Mary Magdalene in 1317 |
| Bail | St Clement-in-the- Bail | Exempt from 1428 *Subsidy* | Mid-14th Century |
| *Butwerk* | St Clement-in- *Butwerk* | No parishioners | Mid-14th Century |
| Lower City | St John-the-Poor | Less than 10 parishioners | Parish united with St Michael-on-the-Mount before 1354. No subsequent mention of church in use |
| Lower City | St Andrew-under- Palace | Less than 10 parishioners | Parish united with St Mary-le-Wigford in 1263, but church continues as chapel until at least 1395 |
| Lower City | St Peter Stanthaket | Less than 10 parishioners | Parish united with St Michael-on-the-Mount. Church destroyed shortly before 1437 |
| *Butwerk* | Holy Trinity Greestone Stairs | Less than 10 parishioners | Disused by 1523 |
| Eastgate | St Leonard | Less than 10 parishioners | Disused by 1535 |

*Fig. 10.6. Known pre-Reformation losses from the parochial structure before the period of civic reform between 1530 and 1560. See also Fig. 10.1 (sources, Hill 1948; Stocker 1990).*

Stephen's parish had already been amalgamated with St Mary *Crackpole*. St Stephen's is mentioned in the Common Council minutes in 1516 but by 1546 these minutes record the church as 'now decayed' (Cameron 1985, 135; Stocker 1990). Furthermore, by the 19th century both of these parishes had been absorbed into the parish of St Martin. To confuse matters further, however, Cameron quotes Chris Johnson as saying that the endowment and churchyard of St Stephen were given to St Mary-le-Wigford, on the evidence of Terriers (1985, 135) whilst Hill quotes from the *City Minute Book* that in *c.*1541 the sheriff had been granted St Stephen-in-Newland in lieu of money in relief of their office (Hill 1956, 56). Presumably, the sheriffs were granted the land and buildings of the decayed church.

These general observations about the late medieval church in Lincoln can be augmented by three case studies where archaeological investigation has taken place – St Paul-in-the-Bail (SP 72), St Mark's (SM 76) and St Peter Stanthaket (SPM 83). The parish of St Paul-in-the-Bail came to include St Clement's parish, although the date of union is uncertain. St Clement's cemetery was a recognised landmark in 1425, but a deed of 1453 makes it clear that the church had gone by that date, although the parish was still regarded as distinct in 1457 (Jones *et al.* 1996, 127). By 1509, however, and perhaps much earlier, the whole of the Bail outside the Close was served by St Paul's church. The excavations at St Paul-in-the-Bail confirm that this church continued to be used throughout the late medieval period – but with little sign of investment in its fabric. Numerous generations of burials were inserted through the floors of church, where they can be dated to this period by their relationship to the early 14th-century rebuild, whilst antiquarian sketches of the church exterior (Fig. 9.78) and descriptions of

its interior suggest that the late medieval church was a patchwork of different phases (Fig. 9.42).

The church of St Mark in Wigford lay within a small parish in the medieval period, bounded by that of St Mary-le-Wigford on the north and the Carmelite friary and the parish of St Edward to the south. Despite its small size, the parish had a number of wealthy parishioners and a series of elite burials and patrons can be listed (Gilmour and Stocker 1986, 6–7). Yet, apart from a new south porch added in the 16th century, here too the fabric of the church in the 18th century seems to have been much as it had been in the 14th century, except for some re-fenestration and perhaps re-paving using plain Flemish tiles (*Ibid.*, fig 5).

The church of St Peter Stanthaket lay within what had been a prosperous area of the Lower City, with the skin market held immediately south of the church, at the northern end of Hungate, and the cloth market to the north, at the top of Michaelgate. Excavations on the east side of Michaelgate (MCH 84) in what may have been part of this parish revealed the backs of properties fronting onto Michaelgate (the medieval *Parchmingate,* Cameron 1985, 81) and confirm that the area was thriving during the 13th and early 14th centuries. However, the area became depopulated during the late 14th century, there is no mention of any clerk at the church in 1377, the parish, though still existing, had less than ten inhabitants in 1428 and by 1461 the church was demolished and the parish amalgamated with that of St Michael. The excavation of the west end of the church merely confirmed this evidence. Robbing of the church walls can be dated to the later 15th or 16th centuries, in broad agreement with the documentary evidence, whilst a collection of pottery from the 'graveyard soil' in the cemetery includes a scatter of late medieval and later pottery, indicating probably that the site lay open after the demolition of the church.

The lack of archaeological work on Lincoln's major monasteries means that we can say little about their development in the later medieval period beyond what can be understood from documentary sources. St Katherine's Priory remained by far the richest of these houses, dominating the south of the city. The minor excavations at Monks Abbey failed to discover any information about such matters (Stocker 1984a) and the investigations at St Bartholomew's (LH 84/LA 85/L 86) were not conducted with such questions in mind. However, the results from archaeological investigations at the Carmelite and Franciscan friaries show that they were flourishing institutions in the later medieval period (Z 86, LIN 73a–c, GL 91, GLA 94 and GLB 94; Stocker 1984b). At the Carmelite friary the extreme south-eastern part of the complex was revealed, which included a heavily buttressed building, presumably part of the friary church. The convent underwent a phase of reorganisation late in its history, which included the development of a small cemetery in this part of the precinct. This late reorganisation is probably related to the documented fire affecting the friary tower and other buildings in c.1490 (Hill 1948, 150 and n7).

## Streets and Buildings

A number of Lincoln's road names first occur in documents during the late medieval period (Fig. 10.7). Of these only three were '-street' names – *Finkle Street*, *Silver Street* and *Spital Street* – and none of these can be reliably identified. From its context in the 1455 agreement between the Council and the Black Monks (Lincolnshire Archives Office, Lincoln City Charters

6/54), it seems that *Finkle Street* was the modern Rosemary Lane (sometimes *Lyme Lane*), although another late medieval street name, *Spoute Lane*, also seems to refer to this lane. The name *Silver Street* did not refer to the modern Silver Street in the medieval period (though we have retained the modern name for the street in this *Assessment*). The modern street with this name was known as *New Street* between 1814 and 1843, whilst the medieval *Silver Street* may refer to a lost street in the Hungate district (Cameron 1985, 100). It may have been an alternative, late medieval, name for the modern Park Street, although this lane was known as *Aldusstigh* in the mid 14th century (*Ibid.*, 47). The name *Silver Street* might even refer to the *Silver Dyke*, another name for Sincil Dyke, and have been either a street leading to this dyke or along its bank (*Ibid.*, 38). Chris Johnson suggests that *Spital Street* was a name applied to Ermine Street (north of the city), and was therefore merely a renaming of an earlier street (*Ibid.*, 102).

The remaining new street name types all refer to small thoroughfares ('-lane', '-sty', '-alley' and '-row'). *Eel Row* in St Benedict's parish, which was probably the lane leading west from High Bridge, is probably the only one reflecting a specific trade or activity. Some were named from a landmark or destination (*Froskholm* – 'Frog Meadow' – in *Freskholme Lane*, a boundary path in *Lammersty*, St Mary-le-Wigford church in *St Mary Lane*, and a well or spring in *Spout Lane*). Others take their names from individuals (*Dowse Lane*, *Hawerby Lane* and *Sparrow Lane*). Incidentally, it is clear from the 1455 agreement between the Council and the Black Monks (Lincolnshire Archives Office, Lincoln City Charters 6/54) that *Sparrow Lane* then was the name for a part of Croft Street, running east–west, and not the north–south lane leading from Croft Street to the

| Street name | Parish/area | Earliest reference | Cameron 1985 Page no. | Comments |
|---|---|---|---|---|
| Woolstead | St Bavon | 1350 | 160 | |
| Spout Lane | St Bavon | 1350 | 102 | Another name for Rosemary Lane? |
| *Poor Alley* | | 1390 | 90 | Now Lucy Tower Street |
| *Hawerby Lane* | | 1395 | 71 | Next to the city prison |
| *Eel Row* | St Benedict | 1417 | 65 | |
| *Midlegate* | St Peter-at-Arches | 1450 | LAO/White Book LI/3/I f15v | Another name for High Street(mistake for Micklegate?) |
| *Persmith Lane* | St George | 1452 | 89 | |
| *Finkle St* | | 1455 | 65 | |
| *Fynkelstrete* | | 1455 | Hill 1948, 362 | Possibly Rosemary Lane |
| Sparrow Lane | | 1455 | 101 | |
| Stamp End | | 1455 | 102 | |
| St Mary Lane | | 1461 | 95 | Now St Mary's Street |
| Spital St | | 1509 | 102 | |
| Waterside | St Martin | 1519 | 44 | |
| *Bedehouse Lane* | | 1527 | 51 | |
| *Dowse Lane* | Bail | 1532 | 62 | |
| Cross O'Cliff Hill | | 1535 | 192 | |

*Fig. 10.7. Street-names with an origin in the late medieval period (sources, as shown).*

Witham which bears this name today. We have no archaeological evidence for the nature – surfacing, drainage, state of repair – of any late medieval lanes or streets.

The best evidence for the character of late medieval secular housing in Lincoln comes from the *Survey of Ancient Houses in Lincoln* (Jones *et al.* 1984; 1987; 1990; 1996). All the buildings described in detail by the *Survey* lay in the Close or the Bail, and may therefore be unrepresentative of many other parts of the city (see e.g. Plate 6.2). Nevertheless, they range from large complexes such as Atherstone Place in Eastgate to timber-framed halls, such as No 34 Bailgate, and shops, such as those on both sides of Steep Hill to the south of Castle Hill. The shops on the west side include Nos. 26–29 Steep Hill, a mid 14th-century timber-framed 'row' structure, which seems to have originally had a solar on the first floor but was divided into three shops at ground level. If the assessment we have made on the basis of plan-form analysis above is correct, this structure will represent a rebuilding of commercial properties, which had originally encroached on an earlier market place in the 12th century (p. 212 above).

Despite the wealth of evidence amassed by the *Survey*, it is not until the post-medieval period that we learn anything of the internal arrangements and probable functions of any of these buildings. As for their occupants, houses within the Close were usually assigned to a canon or official of the Cathedral, but we know little of the size of their households, or how much time such figures actually spent in residence. For properties in the Bail our knowledge is even more sketchy. Many tenements have no surviving documentation at all, even when the structure itself contains medieval work. Those that are documented usually provide a partial list of owners or tenants, at best, and only rarely any details of occupants. In some cases we know the occupation of the owner but, again, there is no certainty that this trade was carried out in the property.

At the top end of the scale of domestic building, the medieval Bishop's Palace seems to have reached its final form in the 15th century, with the work of Bishop Alnwick (1436–1449) (Coppack 2000). In 1541 Henry VIII visited Lincoln and stayed at the palace. We might therefore expect evidence for refurbishment, or even rebuilding, but no archaeological evidence of this visit has been recognised. Little is known of its use during the late 16th and early 17th centuries. It was attacked twice during the Civil War and subsequently abandoned. Rubbish deposits excavated in the kitchen and chapel courtyards, and a pit group from the chapel courtyard, dated to the period between 1726 and 1738, when the site was leased to Dr Nelthorpe (Chapman *et al.* 1975). Few of the finds from the various excavations at the Palace can be dated to the period before the Civil War, but neither have deposits associated with the damage caused during the War been recovered. Dr Coppack has suggested that this may be the result of

the Palace being kept clean except at times of alterations to ground level or fabric (1999).

## The waterfront

Despite the excavation of several sites north of the Witham between High Bridge and the *Werkdyke*, and an extensive watching brief carried out during the construction of the new Waterside Centre on Waterside North, we have no physical evidence for the nature of the late medieval waterfront. It is likely, nevertheless, that the north bank of the river consisted at this time of a more or less straight quayside along the modern line (p. 235–9 above). Furthermore, we can argue from the absence of any documentary evidence to the contrary, that access to any quayside along the north side of the river was only possible through the private tenements which fronted onto Saltergate or via the streets known as *Watergangsty* (Cameron 1985, 107) and the modern Thorngate. The latter may have led to a riverside street, *Thornbridgegate,* which ran eastwards through the extended city wall, over the *Werkdyke* and along the riverbank to Stamp End, along the line of the modern Waterside North. There is no evidence that the road alongside the river ran westwards to the High Bridge until *c.*1610, when a road on the line of Waterside North is shown on Speed's map (Fig. 9.91).

We know even less about land use and topography along the south side of the river in the late medieval period. Only one archaeological observation has been made, the 1982 watching brief carried out at Waterside South (WS 82). Interpretation of the various features observed in this sewer pipe trench has proved problematic, except at the east end, where it crossed the modern Sincil Street. Here, the boundaries of a watercourse running north–south were observed. In its initial phase the watercourse was a flat-bottomed ditch, but (in a second phase or subsequent phases) the watercourse was flanked by stone walls. During the excavation two of these walls were interpreted as forming east and west banks of a narrow channel 3.2m wide (Steane *et al.* 2001, 173–7), but subsequent analysis of the broader topography of the area in this *Assessment* has prompted us to reconsider this interpretation. The stone walls in question could equally represent the successive positions of the eastern shoreline of Upper Wigford, following episodes of land reclamation, with dumping of rubbish behind the walls (Fig. 10.15). 15th-century roof tile in the backfill behind the latest of these walls shows that the most easterly of the lines observed was not backfilled until, perhaps, the 16th century. On the other hand, peg tile from the construction levels of the earliest wall show that they may have been broadly contemporary with the first High Bridge in the mid 12th century. No observations closer to the modern southern river frontage have been made. However, to the west of High Bridge, north of St Benedict's church, *Scotch Hall,* which incorporated late 12th- or 13th-century masonry, seems to have run up to the line of the modern Witham Bank South.

There is no evidence for any substantial reclamation of the north Brayford shore after the middle of the 14th century, but the excavations at Lucy Tower Street and Brayford Wharf North do suggest that this area continued to be used and the river wall repaired when necessary (LT 72, BWN 75). On the eastern side of the pool too there is some evidence, from Dickinson's Mill (DM 72), for late medieval activity at the waterside. Unfortunately it was not clear whether this activity took place at the western end of properties fronting on to the High Street, or whether it related to a distinct range of buildings behind an active waterfront.

### Water supply and rubbish disposal

The only archaeological evidence for water supply during the late medieval and Tudor periods is for the continued existence, and presumed use, of the well at St Paul-in-the-Bail (SP 84). Since they are shown on post-medieval maps, the public wells at Newport (*Grantham Well*) and Eastgate (*Leadenwell*), both of which may have been provided originally by the Council to service the markets in those streets, were probably still in use, as, no doubt, was the well within the Exchequergate at the entrance to the Cathedral precinct. There has been even less archaeological evidence for waste disposal than for earlier periods. This lack of evidence is probably because many late medieval wells were simply re-dug in later periods, removing any evidence for their origin, whilst stone-lined cess- pits were used instead of the unlined or wattle-lined pits of earlier periods. These cess-pits were often incorporated into the structures of buildings and only produce finds dating from their disuse and abandonment. The site of one communal dunghill, or *laystall*, is known, but it is not documented until the 18th century (it was on the line of the western ditch of the Lower City, roughly on the site now occupied by City Hall).

### Supply routes and victualling

Since there are so few deposits of late medieval date from Lincoln excavations, little that can yet be said about the victualling of the city, at least not by using archaeological data. Nevertheless, there are several points worth making about the victualling of the city in the late medieval period, and it is a topic that can be effectively addressed using archaeological material.

### Meat – supply and consumption

The late medieval period saw a decline in the total exports of wool from England, and from Boston in particular, but there is no doubt that wool production remained an important part of Lincolnshire's rural economy (Platts 1985, 147–9). Monasteries like St Katherine's Priory seem to have played a prominent

role in this trade. A by-product of wool production was, of course, the availability of mature sheep, and therefore it is likely that mutton played a large part in the diet of the city at this period. It is also possible that the improvement of sheep breeds, both to select better fleece types and to increase the size of the animal, started in this period and in future we should be looking for datable samples of sheep bones to test this. The increasing use of the horse instead of the ox for traction during the late medieval period might be reflected in the size of horseshoes, of which there are a considerable number from the city, but evidence for horsemeat in the diet is rare and we can't say whether it formed a significant part of the diet. If this change were indeed to be reflected in the animal bone record, it would probably occur the form of changes in the 'age-at-death' and sex ratios. We might also expect a decline in the consumption of marine fish in the city as a result of the growth of coastal/estuarine ports such as Boston and Hull although there are plenty of documentary references to fishermen in this period. *Eel Row*, near the High Bridge, was first recorded in the early 15th century (Cameron 1985, 65), but of course the eels, although also marine fish, were probably caught in both the Witham and the Trent.

One of the features of late medieval Lincoln is the continuation of its role as a focus for the social elite, both ecclesiastical and secular. This might be reflected in the consumption of game. Perhaps the only excavated site where extravagant feasting might have taken place is St Mary's Guildhall (SMG 82) but unfortunately only small, unexceptional, assemblages were associated with the later medieval use of the hall (O'Connor 1991, 88–89, period 5). In a sample of 467 identifiable excavated bones from late medieval contexts in the city, Dobney *et al.* (1996) found three swan bones, the earliest occurrence of this species in their study, plus one buzzard bone. The buzzard might have been a wild bird hunting in the Wigford suburb area, but this species was sometimes used as a hawking bird (*Ibid.*, 52). This particular late medieval sample also produced the only example from their study of a curlew, a species eaten at feasts. However, the sample was much too small to see if such occurrences really were more common in the late medieval period, or whether there was a concentration of these wild birds in particular deposits or parts of the city.

### Supply and consumption of cereals and other plants

The part played by plants in the diet of late medieval Lincoln citizens is unknown. Bakers continued to be associated with the *Baxtergate* area between Stonebow and the High Bridge in this period, as well as in the Bail. They would have been supplied with flour from millers, whose mills we have already noted and who are recorded in documentary sources in both the Lower City and the Bail. It is possible that the millers recorded in *Baxtergate* simply held land there because of their association with the bakers, perhaps storing flour there for sale, but it is also possible that there might have been a water-mill on the west side of the High Bridge, in that area of the suburb within the parish of St Benedict. There is no evidence that the mill held by Barlings Abbey, at *Sapergate* (near the waterfront east of High Street) in the early 13th century survived into this period. The millers in the Bail would certainly have been using the windmills we have noted already, situated in East and North Fields (Fig. 9.90).

There are numerous references to gardens in the late medieval documentary sources and in some cases the status of their owners may suggest that they were ornamental, rather than primarily for horticulture. Such gardens were situated in the Bail, within the Lower City, and in the Newland, *Butwerk* and Wigford suburbs. Two gardens were noted in the 1455 agreement between the city and the Black Monks (Lincolnshire Archives Office, Lincoln City Charters 6/54), 'John Aleyn's garden' and 'a little garden called *Hempgarth'*. Both were located to the west of St Peter *ad fontem* churchyard, i.e. beyond the eastern fringe of the occupied area. The former may have been a pleasure garden, surrounded by a stone wall, whilst the name of the latter suggests it may have been used for growing hemp – and thus related to rope-making and the provisioning of ships on the Witham. Orchards are less frequently mentioned in Council deeds, and none have been noted in late medieval documents, but this is certainly not evidence that there were fewer orchards at this time than before or after. The orchard located just inside the west postern gate of the Bail was first so-called *c*.1180 and was next described as an orchard in a document of 1583 (ed. Major 1968, 200–1, RA2608; Lincolnshire Archives Office, LA Bij.3.18). There is no reason to suppose it was not an orchard throughout this period.

### Commerce, crafts and Industry

#### Pottery production and use

Throughout this period, the great majority of pottery used in the city was locally-made. The main centres of production were in the Wigford suburb, where we have noted that excavations on both sides of High Street in St Mark's parish demonstrated a long history of pottery and roof tile manufacture, beginning in the 13th century (p. 276 above). Waste from the later-medieval period of this industry has been found at the eastern end of the Magistrate's Court site (ZE 87) east of the High Street and to the west of the street, on the St Mark's Station site (Z 86). Late medieval pottery production was not limited to Wigford, however, and there is both documentary and archaeological evidence for pottery making in the Lower City and *Butwerk* during this period (Young and Vince forthcoming). It seems, however, that activity here was on a much smaller scale than in Wigford, and this evidence for two different economies of

production is interesting. The large-scale production in Upper Wigford took place in an area where pottery had been produced for several generations, and this contrasts dramatically with the pottery-making practised by individuals in the Lower City, and perhaps *Butwerk* (*Ibid.*). It seems probable that this second group of factories was less permanent in character, perhaps lasting only for the working life of the potter concerned. Pottery was not the only industry to be practised in the centre of the late medieval town, however, and there is evidence from Danes Terrace for non-ferrous metalworking (DT 74). It is unclear what exactly was being produced on the site but the finished items might well have been sold from a shop fronting onto The Strait.

The late medieval pottery sequence in Lincoln has been worked out by Jane Young (Fig. 10.8). The differences between the phases, and between the late medieval and the preceding 13th- and early 14th-century material, are slight. Nevertheless, it has been possible to divide the period into ceramic horizons based on the sequence of introduction of new forms, fabrics and decoration. This technique has been used primarily as an aid to dating stratigraphic sequences at excavations, but it can also be used to chart changes in the pottery supply of the city during the late medieval period. The products of these Lincoln industries were mainly glazed red earthenwares, with some vessels made in the coarse fabrics used for tiles (ware type TILE) although in the later 14th and 15th century (ceramic horizons MH 8–10), white-bodied finewares were also being produced (ware type LMF). Although the relative proportions of different Lincoln products varies from horizon to horizon, however, there is no evidence for a significant change in the proportion of pottery used in the city supplied from Lincoln kilns, which remains between 73% and 83% (Fig. 10.9). This finding shows that pottery use in Lincoln followed a similar pattern to use elsewhere in England.

Pottery from other Lincolnshire sources is tabulated in Fig. 10.10 (see also Fig. 9.99). It can be seen that most such imports found in the city come from Potterhanworth, a village on the western fen edge eight miles south-east of Lincoln (ware type POTT). The products of Potterhanworth were almost exclusively unglazed shell-tempered cooking pots and it is remarkable that this industry should have continued for so long without

| Ceramic Horizon | Date range |
|---|---|
| MH6 | Late 13th to early to mid-14th century |
| MH7 | Early to mid-14th to late 14th century |
| MH8 | Late 14th to early 15th century |
| MH9 | Early to mid-15th century |
| MH10 | Mid- to late 15th century |
| PMH1 | Early 16th century |

*Fig. 10.8. List of late medieval pottery horizons for Lincoln (source, Vince and Young forthcoming).*

any significant variation in the fabric or range of products. Other wares are found, mainly from the Toynton and Bolingbroke areas on the northern fen edge 30 miles to the east of Lincoln (ware types TOY, TOYII, TB) but, in the Lincoln assemblages collected so far these were insignificant in numerical terms. In the late 15th century, Bourne wares first occur, again in very small quantities (ware type BOU). Overall, then, there is an increase in the quantity of local pottery used at the start of the Early Modern Era, due entirely to the fact that the Potterhanworth industry began at the end of the 13th century, but there seems to be no significant change in the frequency of use of such wares from then on.

Non-local English wares from a number of sources have been found in late medieval Lincoln (Figs. 10.11 and 9.99). They come from two main areas; production sites in Yorkshire, whose products would have been obtained through waterborne transport (ware types BEVO, SCAR, YORK, BRANS, HUM) and wares produced in the Midlands, which may also have been traded by water, down the Trent from Nottingham (ware types MP, CIST, NOTG). These non-local wares never accounted for more than 5% of the pottery used in the city and are more common in the middle and later 15th century than earlier.

Imported pottery formed a small part of late medieval assemblages in Lincoln (Figs. 10.12 and 9.99). The wares came from three main areas; the Low Countries supplied glazed red earthenwares (ware types DUTR and DUTRT), the central Rhine valley supplied stoneware (ware type SIEG) and the Meuse valley also supplied stonewares (ware types RAER, LARA and LANG). All these wares were probably traded to Lincoln along the same trade routes, using

| Ware type | MH 6 | MH 7 | MH 8 | MH 9 | MH10 |
|---|---|---|---|---|---|
| LSW2 | 49.7% | 0.0% | 0.0% | 0.0% | 0.0% |
| LSW2/3 | 11.6% | 25.8% | 16.6% | 8.9% | 0.0% |
| LSW3 | 9.4% | 34.0% | 46.4% | 65.2% | 0.0% |
| LSWA | 7.8% | 13.2% | 7.0% | 1.3% | 6.5% |
| LSW1/2 | 4.2% | 0.0% | 0.0% | 0.0% | 0.0% |
| LSW | 0.2% | 0.0% | 0.3% | 5.7% | 1.3% |
| TILE | 0.1% | 0.0% | 0.2% | 0.0% | 0.2% |
| LLSW | 0.0% | 0.0% | 5.9% | 1.3% | 62.8% |
| L/LSW4 | 0.0% | 0.0% | 0.0% | 0.0% | 0.1% |
| LSW4 | 0.0% | 0.0% | 0.0% | 0.0% | 2.4% |
| LMF | 0.0% | 0.0% | 0.0% | 0.0% | 0.9% |

*Fig. 10.9. Percentages of different types of Lincoln-made pottery within the total assemblages of each of the late medieval ceramic horizons (see Fig. 10.8) (source, Vince and Young forthcoming).*

| Ware type | MH 6 | MH 7 | MH 8 | MH 9 | MH10 |
|---|---|---|---|---|---|
| Bourne (BOU) | 0.0% | 0.0% | 0.0% | 0.0% | 0.2% |
| Toynton All Saints (TOY) | 0.1% | 0.9% | 1.1% | 0.0% | 0.0% |
| Toynton All Saints (TOYII) | 0.0% | 0.0% | 0.0% | 0.0% | 0.2% |
| Toynton /Bolingbroke (TB) | 0.0% | 0.0% | 0.0% | 0.0% | 0.9% |
| Potterhanworth-type (POTT) | 14.4% | 20.9% | 17.4% | 16.5% | 15.0% |
| Medieval local fabrics (MEDLOC) | 1.1% | 2.5% | 1.1% | 0.0% | 1.5% |
| Late medieval local fabrics (LMLOC) | 0.0% | 0.0% | 0.5% | 0.6% | 1.1% |
| Total | 15.6% | 24.2% | 20.2% | 17.1% | 18.8% |

*Fig. 10.10. Percentages of 'local' pottery types in selected late medieval assemblages in each of the late medieval ceramic horizons (see Fig. 10.8) (source, Vince and Young forthcoming).*

| Ware type | MH 6 | MH 7 | MH 8 | MH 9 | MH10 |
|---|---|---|---|---|---|
| Beverley (BEVO) | 0.1% | 0.0% | 0.0% | 0.0% | 0.0% |
| Scarborough (SCAR) | 0.1% | 0.0% | 0.2% | 0.0% | 0.0% |
| York glazed ware (YORK) | 0.1% | 0.3% | 0.0% | 0.0% | 0.0% |
| Brandsby (BRANS) | 0.0% | 0.0% | 2.3% | 0.0% | 0.0% |
| Humberware (HUM) | 0.2% | 0.6% | 0.2% | 0.0% | 2.6% |
| Nottingham glazed ware (NOTG) | 0.3% | 0.9% | 0.0% | 0.0% | 0.0% |
| Cistercian-type ware (CIST) | 0.0% | 0.0% | 0.0% | 0.0% | 0.5% |
| Midland Purple-type (MP) | 0.0% | 0.0% | 0.0% | 0.0% | 0.3% |
| Medieval 'non-local' ware (MEDX) | 0.3% | 0.3% | 0.5% | 0.0% | 1.6% |
| Total | 1.0% | 2.1% | 3.2% | 0.0% | 5.0% |

*Fig. 10.11. Percentages of 'non-local' pottery types in selected late medieval assemblages in each of the late medieval ceramic horizons (see Fig. 10.8) (source, Vince and Young forthcoming).*

| Ware type | MH 6 | MH 7 | MH 8 | MH 9 | MH10 |
|---|---|---|---|---|---|
| Low Countries ware – DUTRT | 0.1% | 0.0% | 0.0% | 0.0% | 0.0% |
| Low Countries ware – DUTR | 0.1% | 0.0% | 0.0% | 0.0% | 0.3% |
| SAIM | 0.1% | 0.0% | 0.0% | 0.0% | 0.0% |
| Meuse Valley ware – LARA | 0.0% | 0.0% | 0.0% | 0.0% | 0.1% |
| ARCH | 0.0% | 0.0% | 0.1% | 0.0% | 0.0% |
| Siegburg (SIEG) | 0.0% | 0.0% | 0.0% | 0.0% | 0.3% |
| Raeren (RAER) | 0.0% | 0.0% | 0.0% | 0.0% | 0.4% |
| IMP | 0.0% | 0.6% | 0.0% | 0.0% | 0.1% |
| Langewehe (LANG) | 0.0% | 0.0% | 0.0% | 0.6% | 0.8% |
| Rouen (ROUEN) | 0.1% | 0.0% | 0.0% | 0.0% | 0.0% |
| Total | 0.3% | 0.6% | 0.2% | 0.6% | 2.0% |

*Fig. 10.12. Percentages of 'imported' pottery types in selected late medieval assemblages in each of the late medieval ceramic horizons (see Fig. 10.8) (source, Vince and Young forthcoming).*

the 15th and the 18th centuries to house the city's resident elite (Fig. 10.15 and Plate 6.4).

### Defences

We have little documentary or archaeological evidence for the state of the walls, gates and ditches of the city in the post-medieval period; however, some indication of the relative state of its fortifications may be provided by their fate in the Civil War. Lincoln changed hands several times in the early years of the war but it seems that the civic defences were never really tested. A show of strength was enough to force the surrender of the royalist forces in the Bail, Castle and Close in October 1643. Even so, the churches of St Nicholas and St Peter Eastgate were destroyed during this campaign. Hill suggests that they were demolished by Lord Willoughby, commander of the parliamentary forces, who was besieging the Royalists who were defending the Close (1956, 163).

By the following spring, however, Lord Manchester and Cromwell were besieging the Royalists who again held the city. The action started on 3rd May 1644 with an attack on the southern part of the city (at Great and Little Bargate), which fell to the Parliamentarians. The Royalists then withdrew to the Close and the Castle and were granted a day's relief because it was raining too hard for the attackers to ascend the hill. The following day, St Swithin's and St Bartholomew's churches were burnt. The Castle was attacked on the 6th using scaling ladders and the defenders fled, leaving about 50 dead. There were eight dead and 40 injured on the parliamentary side. About 650 men were taken prisoner, all their arms captured and, it seems, the Upper City was then pillaged. The army may have remained in Lincoln until early July. Clearly, the southern defences of the city, Sincil Dyke, the Bargates and any walling connecting the gates, did not cause the attackers any trouble; it was, rather, the steep nature of the hill and the slippery streets which hindered progress in the following days.

In 1648, Lincoln again saw action when a royalist force of 400 horse dragoons and 200 musketeers took the city. The parliamentary garrison at that time consisted of 30 men under the command of Captain Bee. They withdrew to the Bishop's Palace, which was stormed and set on fire, whilst the royalist forces raided the houses of known Parliamentarians and plundered the city (*Ibid.*, 162). Eventually Captain Bee surrendered. From the various accounts of the actions in Lincoln we can judge the state of the defences in Lincoln before and after the 1640s. It is clear that the Castle and the Close formed defensible circuits and, indeed, before the siege, the Royalists considered their 'upper works' (i.e. the Cathedral and the Castle) to be impregnable (*Ibid.*, 157). The Bail wall was almost certainly still intact, but the south side remained a potential weak point, especially where Drury Lane (shown on Speed's map of *c*.1610) crossed the line of the Roman south wall. On the north-east side it is likely that the wall survived, and in deeds concerning two closes in the north-west corner of the Bail, the King's wall is used as bounds from 1633 until the 1690s, when 'closes' replace the wall as boundaries (Lincolnshire Archives Office, CC27/152829). The Lower City, however, was almost entirely undefended, as can be inferred from Speed's map, where the western wall is shown as an earthwork. There is no sign of the Lucy Tower on Brayford (although we know that it survived as a structure until much later – Fig. 9.26) nor is there any sign of the equivalent tower at the south-east corner of the Lower City defences. The eastern wall is, however, shown surviving its entire length down to the Green Dragon.

After the Civil War, it seems that an attempt was made to repair the Close Wall, but probably more as a symbol of the Cathedral's separate identify rather than as a defensive structure, whereas the remaining defences were left to decline. There does not seem to have been any attempt to destroy the town defences after the Civil War, as happened elsewhere. Instead, the walls were allowed to decay, being gradually built up to and then built over. The laying out of the raised promenade at Besom Park along the western side of the Lower City in the 18th century, partially overlying the wall, took advantage of the height of the rampart and the lack of development in Newland to provide a recreational walk where the citizens could enjoy the views.

### Administration

In the post-medieval period Lincoln continued to be divided into three jurisdictions; the Bail, the Close and the City (which, however, still contained independent liberties like Hungate Manor and Beaumont Fee within it). The clearest expression of these divisions were the surviving internal barriers; the Bail was still defined by gates (if not by intact walls), and the medieval Close gates still divided it from both the Bail and the Lower City. Journeys through the Upper City would encounter gate after gate, all of which were capable of being shut. For example a journey from St Michael-on-the-Mount to St Peter Eastgate around 1690 would involve passing through the two gates on Steep Hill into the Bail, then passing through the two gates into the Close at the west end of Eastgate, out of the Close again via its east gate, on Eastgate, and finally though the east gate in the Bail wall. Briefly, during the Commonwealth, Close, Bail and the various liberties in the Lower City were all brought under the control of the Corporation (*Ibid.*, 164), and the liberty of Hungate Manor and of Beaumont Fee remained under Council control after the Restoration. These liberties were reflected in the survival of boundaries and the duplication of some administrative functions, like the provision of gallows (the City Council's gallows being on Canwick Hill

*B r a y f o r d*

*P o o l*

0    500 m

A ⊕  1

6

*River Witham →*

Channel between Wigford
and Thorngate filled in
between 1475 and 1610

L ▲    2

▲ C

3   ▲ D

7   ▲ E

**Upper Wigford**   8

F ▲

*T A N N E R I E S*

**Bargate Closes**

*drained in the 15th and 16th-centuries*

G ▲   ⊕ B

9

H ▲   4

*R i v e r   W i t h a m*

Great   10   Gowt

11

Little   Gowt

*The King's Dyke*

*(Sincil Dyke)*

12

**L o w e r
W i g f o r d**

N ↑

*T A N N E R I E S*

5

I ▲   Little
*   Bargate

Great
Bargate

J ▲

13

*S o u t h
C o m m o n*

Swine

Green

or

Lincoln Green

K ▲

*Newark Road
towards Leicester*

**Key**

• Elite secular buildings of
the High Medieval Era -
see figure 9/69

▪▪▪ Former monastic precincts

Approximate location
of presumed causeway
at Stamp End

Land subject to flooding

▦ Parish churches

**Parish churches still in operation
after the Reformation**
1: St Benedict
2: St Mary-le-Wigford
3: St Mark
4: St Peter-at-Gowts
5: St Botolph

**Parish churches lost in the late
Middle Ages and Reformation**
6: St John the Evangelist
7: St Edward King and Martyr
8: Holy Trinity Wigford
9: St Andrew Wigford
10: St Michael-at-Gowts
11: Holy Cross
12: St Margaret
13: Holy Innocents

⊕ **Nonconformist chapels**
A: Baptist Chapel 1701
B: Presbyterian Chapel 1672

▲ **New elite buildings of the
Early Modern era**
C: House known as 'Whitefriars'
D: Sibthorpe House
E: Marchmont House
F: Bromhead House
G: John of Gaunt's Palace
H: St Andrew's Row
I: The Reindeer
J: The Malandry
K: St Katherines Hall
L: 194 High Street
✳ Tile House

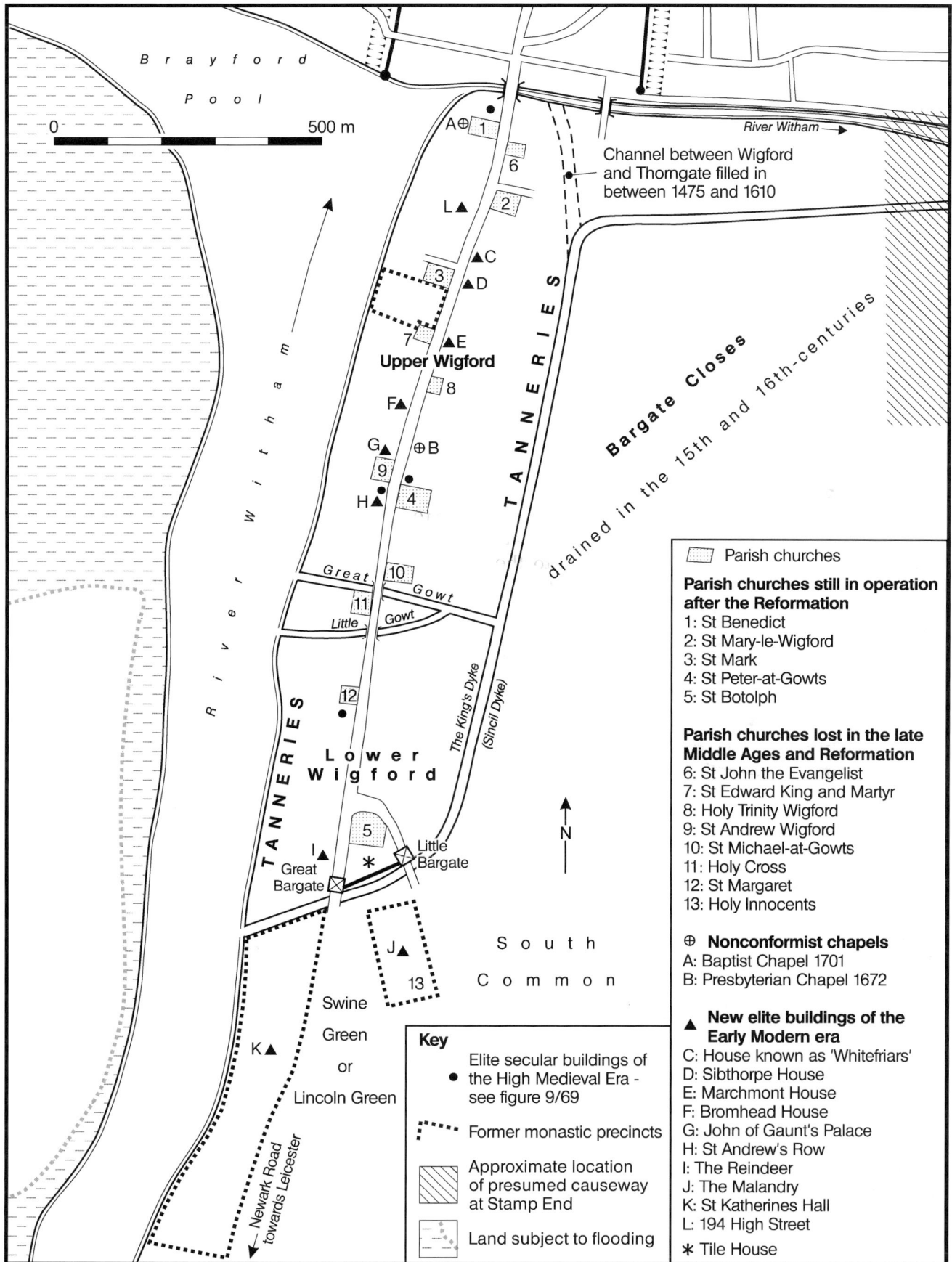

*Fig. 10.15. Reconstruction study of the Wigford area in the Early Modern Era, locating improvements in drainage and construction of new elite residences (drawn by Dave Watt, copyright English Heritage).*

whilst the sheriff's were outside the west postern of the Bail – Fig. 9.89).

The Common Council, which continued to provide government for the city, was based in the Guildhall, situated from 1520 in the chamber over the newly-rebuilt Stonebow (Stocker 1997b), which had the city gaol immediately to its east. The Council also had a pillory and stocks, probably both set up nearby (Hill 1956, 37–8). In addition to dispensing justice, the Common Council also regulated many aspects of town life, including the provision and checking of weights and measures (*Ibid.*, 82–3, 94–5). The County administration, on the other hand, retained the county gaol and the Shire Hall (essentially a court house) within the Castle bailey, and county justice was dispensed from there.

### The extent of settlement

The overall trend in the city's population is given in Figure 9.6, but in the Early Modern Era a series of surveys in the 17th and early 18th centuries gives us more detail and suggests a slight increase in population from *c.*3500 to *c.*4500 during the period. Such figures place Lincoln, still, as a modest market town in comparison with England more widely, and contending with Boston and even Stamford for the title of largest town in the county. The 17th- and 18th-century population information is detailed enough to permit a break-down of the trends by area of the city (Fig. 10.16). These data are discussed by Johnston (1991) and each data-set has its own problems of interpretation and incompleteness. Nevertheless, it is possible to guess at missing values for any parish by looking at earlier and/or later records and then to use these figures to look at variations in population density and even social structure within the city.

Luckily, all 13 post-medieval parishes are included in the *Protestation* of 1642, which recorded males over 18 years old. If this is compared with the 1662 Hearth Tax totals for dwellings in the same parishes we find that there are variations in the number of males to dwellings. In most parishes the ratio is between 1.3:1 and 1.9:1. These figures include parishes where most of the dwellings are likely to have been shops along the High Street, and which may also have been affected by a loss of domestic accommodation during the Civil War. In four parishes the ratio is between 2.3:1 and 2.5:1 adult males per dwelling: St Michael-on-the-Mount, St Mary-le-Wigford, St Swithin and St

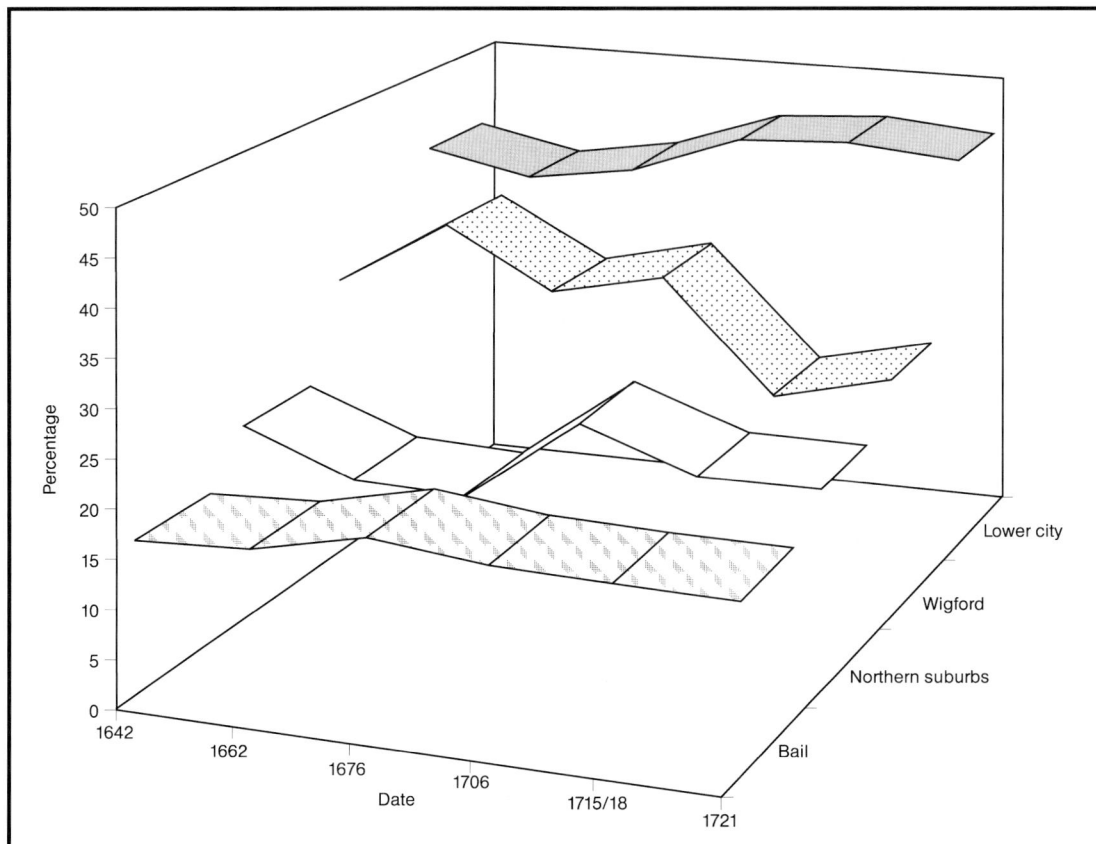

*Fig. 10.16. Graphs illustrating the relative trends in population in different parts of the city between 1642 and 1720 (drawn by Dave Watt, copyright English Heritage).*

Martin. This might be a result of the inclusion of a higher number of larger dwellings, containing perhaps two or more generations of the landowner's family and male servants, but the location of these parishes suggests that it is more likely to have been a reflection of multiple occupancy, i.e. lodgers. Finally, St Peter Eastgate and St Margaret Pottergate both have ratios of males per dwelling higher than three (3.5:1 and 3.2:1 respectively). The large average size of these households may be due to the presence of extended farming and clerical families as well as servants.

The Hearth Tax returns also give us some idea of the social topography, since there is a clear correlation between the number of hearths and status. In York, for example, dwellings with six or more hearths are taken to indicate a high status household (Hibberd 1983). In Lincoln in 1662, 43% of the houses in St Margaret Pottergate (i.e. the most prosperous part of the Close) had six or more hearths, including one house with as many as 20. On this evidence, the Close was by far the most prestigious area of the city, and there is a sharp contrast between the percentage of houses in St Margaret's parish with six or more hearths and the percentage of such properties per parish elsewhere in the city. There is also, as one might expect, a sharp contrast in the average number of hearths per house in parishes elsewhere in the city. In the city as a whole between 3.6% and 15% of houses in each parish had six or more hearths, compared with the 43% of houses in St Margaret's which enjoyed such facilities. From all this it seems quite clear that the Close did form a socially distinct area, devoid of lodgers, shops, cottages or other working-class housing. One further point worth making from the Hearth Tax data is that the percentage of 'small' houses (i.e. houses with only a single hearth) within the more 'ordinary' housing stock (i.e. houses with between one and five hearths) varies considerably from parish to parish. In St Mark's parish it is 52%, in St Swithin's it is 45% and it does not drop below 30% for any of the Wigford parishes except St Botolph's. At 4%, the low figure for the largely depopulated St Botolph's parish, at the southern end of Wigford is explained by the two very large houses, one large mansion with fifteen hearths and one of moderate size with seven hearths. The percentage of 'small houses' within the 'ordinary' housing stock is lowest in St Martin's parish, which has only 15% houses with a single hearth. These small dwellings were probably a mixture of High Street shops and labourers' cottages.

Population data for 1676 (Fig. 10.16) is derived from the total number of communicants and non-conformists over sixteen years old (ed. Johnston 1991, Table II). A comparison of these figures with those for 1642 shows that the ratio of men to women varies from 1.5:1 women to each man in St Botolph parish, to St Peter-at-Arches parish, which, with a ratio of 3:1, has more than twice as many women and young adults as men. These figures also show a trend for the

Wigford parishes to have more men than the Lower City parishes. They probably indicate that the Lower City housed more families with wives and children than Wigford, but it is also possible that there were female-only households in that part of town, plus a higher proportion of female and juvenile servants.

The survey undertaken by Bishop Wake in 1706 for the *Speculum Dioceseos* (ed. Cole 1913) has population totals which are suspiciously rounded to the nearest ten, and in some cases they are at such variance with the earlier or later records that they must be in error by as much as 200%! They are therefore not discussed further here. Instead, the two subsequent surveys in the *Speculum*, for 1715/18 and 1721 can be used, as they provide more believable figures (although four city parishes are omitted from the 1721 survey). Assuming the same level of accuracy for the two surveys, we can make a direct comparison of their totals. From them, we find that the populations of the Bail and Close, along with the north and western parts of the Lower City, were gently declining in the early 18th century, whereas the populations of the High Street parishes on either side of Stonebow (i.e. St Peter-at-Arches, St Mary-le-Wigford and St Mark) were slowly growing.

What we know of the locations of the dwellings in which the people recorded in these bald statistics lived makes it clear that, between *c.*1550 and *c.*1660, Lincoln's suburbs were very sparsely populated indeed, and open fields and farms came right up to the city walls in some areas. Indeed, even within the line of the defences, the north-west corner of the Bail was occupied by *Old Lincoln Field*, divided into 'crofts', 'pingles', 'orchards' and 'gardens' but with few or no houses (Fig. 9.89). Similarly, much of the western side of the Lower City was occupied by orchards, within the Beaumont Fee estate. Grimm's view of 1784, looking across the Lower City from Christ's Hospital Terrace shows a very rural scene, with only a few roofs showing above the trees (Fig. 10.17). The Eastgate suburb was included in the *Parliamentary Survey* of 1650, a detailed inventory of church property carried out by the Commonwealth government (Jones *et al.* 1984). The *Survey* describes buildings to the north of Langworthgate but they were few in number and often termed 'cottages', whereas 'fair residences' or 'mansions' were noted in the west of the suburb, including properties fronting onto Eastgate, north of St Peter's church (fronting onto Church Lane), and south of Greetwellgate. The *Parliamentary Survey*, together with unpublished tenement histories established by Joan Varley (in the Lincolnshire Archives Office), show that *c.*1650 the suburb included several waste plots that had previously been occupied. To the north of the Eastgate suburb green lanes and closes are shown on the 1803 Enclosure Award but it is not clear how many of these were once occupied. The Newport suburb seems to have been very sparsely occupied until the later

*Fig. 10.17. View over the Lower City from Christ's Hospital Terrace in c.1784 by S H Grimm. The building in the right-hand foreground is the Old Hospital of 1777 (by the notable architect John Carr of York) on the site now occupied by the former Theological College. The tower in the middle distance belongs to St Martin's church, built in 1740. It is a rural scene with more trees than houses, even though the Fossdyke had been re-open for a generation (photo, Usher Art Gallery, copyright British Library).*

18th century; nine houses were listed in the 1662 Hearth Tax in the parish of St Nicholas, one with a single hearth and two with six or more hearths. This distribution looks similar to that in St Peter Eastgate and in St Martin's parish and probably reflects similar semi-rural land-use with a few moderate-sized houses (perhaps farm-houses). A few 17th- and 18th-century references occur to *Newport Green*, indicating that by the post-medieval period this was not a metalled market place but a grassed space, presumably with the main metalled thoroughfare on its eastern side. Excavations at Bishop Grosseteste College (BGA 95) revealed no sign of activity over the sites of the medieval houses and much of the suburb must have reverted to closes and, on both sides of the main road, quarry pits. The mills along the cliff at Mill Road and in East Field continued in use during this period, and are shown on Speed's map of *c.*1610 (Fig. 9. 91).

Post-medieval activity in both the *Butwerk* and Newland suburbs was concentrated close to the city and the waterfront. To judge by the tithe map of 1842 and the enclosure award of 1803, substantial areas that had been occupied in the medieval period had reverted to pasture by the 18th century and were not occupied again until the expansion of settlement in the mid 19th century. The monastic buildings of the Black Monks were turned into an estate centre, but otherwise the area does not seem to have changed in character throughout this period. There is some indication that the cell's chapel was retained as a parochial church, serving the parish of 'St Peter-at-Wells and St Mary Magdalene' (Lincolnshire Archives Office, LD 57/1/

17), but by the 19th century, the former parish of St Peter had been absorbed into St Swithin's, although the Black Monks' estate was still separate and known as the *Monks' Liberty*. In 1585, the dock known as *Blackdyke* seems to have still been in operation, to judge by an agreement between the city and Robert Smith which covers similar ground to that of 1455 (Lincolnshire Archives Office, LD 57/1/17). By 1649 there was a 'water corn mill' within the capital messuage (Lincolnshire Archives Office, Lindsey Deposit 57/1/29) although this is only mentioned in one further document, in 1679 (Lincolnshire Archives Office, Lindsey Deposit 57/1/35). In the late 17th century part of the estate was leased to brick-makers, and is subsequently referred to as *Brick Kiln Close* (the plot lay on the hillside to the west of Milman Road – Lincolnshire Archives Office, Lindsey Deposit 57/1/42).

*Butwerk* itself ceased to exist as a separate suburb during this period. The city ditch, the *Werkdyke*, was back-filled from the Close Wall southwards to the Witham and Broadgate was laid-out over its line. This seems to have taken place in the late 16th century. The width of this street may suggest that it was intended to act as an additional market place. Despite this, there is no documentary evidence that markets were held in Broadgate itself. At the northern end of Broadgate the *Beast Market*, marked on the 1842 Padley map, was located on the site of St Rumbold's church-yard, extending over the probable line of the city ditch. The ancestry of this market is not known, and there is a 16th-century reference to St Rumbold *in the Swine Market*, which might suggest that the market originated in the street to the south of the churchyard (Cameron 1985, 42). Halfway down the street, the *Pig Market* was located at Unity Square in the 19th century but there is no evidence that this market was in existence before then. The *Sheep Market* was well-established off the southern end of Broadgate in the space south of the Greyfriary by 1623 (*Ibid.*, 37).

Following the Dissolution, the Newland suburb had no church of its own and was divided between St Martin and St Mary-le-Wigford. Newland Street West had ceased to be the main thoroughfare, being replaced by Carholme Road, whose course was diverted in the 18th century as a result of the construction of a racecourse on West Common. Much of the area was either occupied by open fields (such as *Short Leys*) and common land (*Carholme*) or with old enclosure. The 1803 enclosure map shows a rectilinear grid of crofts with green lanes running between them. At least one of these survives, as the back lane for properties fronting onto the south side of Alexandra Terrace. There appears to have been little change in the topography of the Newland settlement itself during the entire period from the 15th to the late 18th century and almost all developments in the suburb can be dated to subsequent periods. The only exception to this may be in the establishment of brick-works at the western end of the suburb and to the north of the West Common. Many such works are known from the late 18th or 19th century but (although not documented) some may have had their origins in the late 17th or early 18th century, by analogy with the *Butwerk* suburb. Between the Dissolution and the Industrial Revolution there had been various attempts to revitalise the Fossdyke, which had evidently become unusable in the later medieval period. One such attempt involved the construction of a wharf at the junction of the Fossdyke and the Brayford Pool at the end of the 16th century (quoted in Hockley 1992b). This seems to have involved the reclamation of one reach of the dyke, whose original line can be postulated. This initiative, like several others, seems to have failed.

## Church and chapel

The pattern of decline indicated by the collapse of Lincoln's medieval parochial structure in the 15th century was not really arrested by the Act of 1549 reducing the number of parish churches from around 40 to 13 (Fig. 10.1). The decay of the church fabrics continued and parishioners' numbers continued to decline. The physical decay was accelerated in some cases by damage caused during the Civil War (for example at St Botolph and St Benedict).

Between 1538 and 1540 Lincoln's four surviving friaries, St Katherine's Priory and St Mary Magdalene's Priory (Monks Abbey) were surrendered to the King. The religious houses in Lincoln seem to have suffered two contrasting fates. Some were converted into secular mansions, like the Granthams' house at St Katherine's

Priory. The Black Monks' estate (*Monks' Leys*) was purchased after the Dissolution by Richard Bevercotes and was acquired subsequently by the Sapcote family, who built a house from the ruins of the monastic buildings. Other monasteries seem to have been plundered by the King's agents and then left as ruins. This appears to have been the fate of the Austin Friary in Newport, which is shown as a ruin 70 years after the Dissolution on Speed's map of *c.*1610, and the Blackfriars in *Butwerk*, which was still a ruin in the early 18th century (Stocker 1990, 27–9). The two different types of fate experienced by former monastic sites are probably related to the location and character of the medieval complexes. The Black Monks' cell, for example, would probably have already contained many of the features to be expected in a mid 16th-century farm, as probably did St Katherine's Priory. The Greyfriary was the only one of the four friaries to be adapted for immediate reuse. Initially, it was let to Robert Monson, but by 1568 he had purchased it and endowed a free school, with assistance from the Council, who purchased the school in 1574 in return for the lease of the remainder of the friary land. The lower floor of the Greyfriars building became the home of *The Jersey School*, founded in 1594 to teach the crafts of knitting and spinning (Hill 1956, 92). The Greyfriars building survives and some recording took place in 1982 and in the mid 1990s when, unfortunately, little of the post-medieval history of the site was elucidated (Stocker 1984b; Jarvis 1996a; 1996b).

The Cathedral and Close survived the Reformation, although the Cathedral's many chantries were dissolved and a large amount of treasure was taken by the King (Hill 1956, 50). The Close continued to be a self-contained and enclosed part of the city and it was not until the Industrial Era that the Close gates were removed, as being a hindrance to traffic. The Civil War may, perhaps, have been a more damaging episode architecturally and topographically, and there was a programme of iconoclastic destruction in the Cathedral in September 1644, which brought about the defacing and destruction of many of the Cathedral church's monuments (Stocker 1985b, 143). Of these, the destruction of the Shrine of Little St Hugh, in the south choir aisle (Stocker 1986a) is worthy of note, as results of this iconoclasm have been detected in excavation. Parts of this monument were found in 1984 in the filling of the well at St Paul-in-the-Bail (SP 84) in a deposit which also contained other medieval and post-medieval church monuments (including a fragment of Cararra marble) and the lead cames from smashed stained-glass windows. It is thought that this well had been a public facility in the later medieval period and, if it had gone out of use in the mid 17th century, it may simply have been a convenient place to deposit debris from this defacing. However, it is also possible that there was some symbolic significance behind this remarkable deposit. Perhaps the well water had been accredited with supernatural

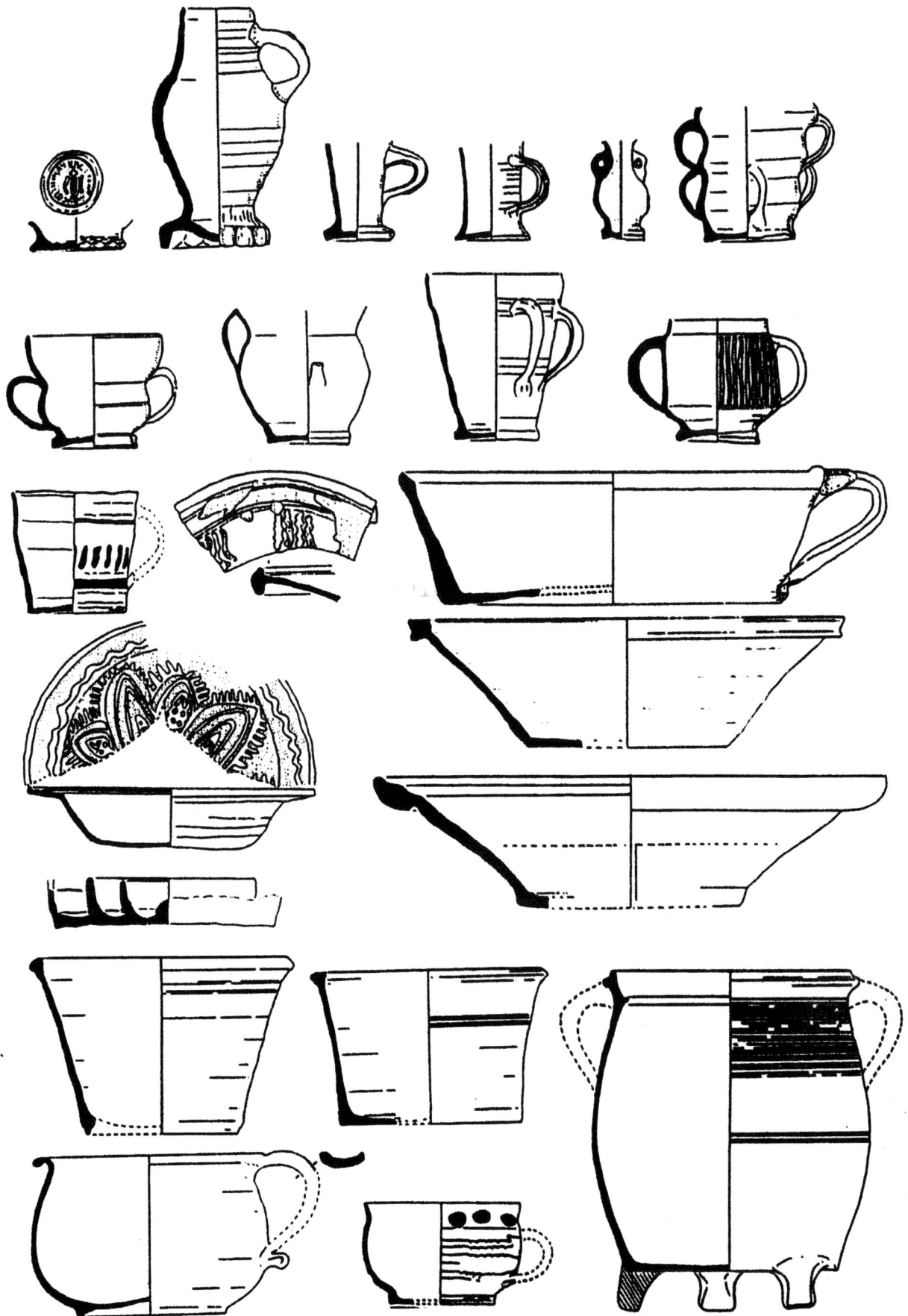

*Fig. 10.20. A selection of post-medieval pottery found in Lincoln. The forms are arranged in descending order of date from the top left to the bottom right. The earliest forms (top left) are from the late 15th or early 16th century whilst those in the bottom right are early or mid 18th-century in date (drawings and copyright Andrew White).*

## Defending the city

Like the city's economy, the defences of Lincoln were in poor shape for much of the Early Modern Era. The RAZs of the High Medieval Era have, once again, proved a valid and useful framework within which to construct a research agenda, although it seems we lack basic information about alterations made to the defences at these later dates. As is the case with so many other aspects of the city's archaeology in this long period of stasis, future work on the defences will focus on the impact of the collapse of the city's population and economy on structures which consumed so much labour and money. In fact there is an instructive contrast between the defences of the Castle (RAZ 10.48) and the Close (RAZ 10.50.2), both of which continued to be maintained by powerful institutions based outside the city itself, and the city walls – the responsibility of the citizens – which were simply allowed to disintegrate. Here also, then, we can suggest that research agendas relating to 'defence' structures in the Early Modern Era should concentrate on the competition between the different social and political groupings within the early modern city. The eleven RAZs dealing with the defensive structures in the Early Modern Era are:

10.47 Upper City Defences
10.48 Lincoln Castle from *c.1350–c.1750*
10.49 Thorngate Castle
    10.50.1 Lower City defences
    10.50.2 The Close Wall
    10.50.3 The Butts
10.51 Suburb boundaries
    10.51.1 Newport boundaries
    10.51.2 Butwerk boundaries
    10.51.3 Newland boundaries
    10.51.4 Boundary of Upper Wigford (Great and Little Gowts)
    10.51.5 Boundary of Lower Wigford (The Sincil Dyke)

## Church and chapel

In the introduction to the High Medieval Era we noted that archaeological study of the urban parish church can pay dividends well beyond our understanding of the church itself and we noted the value, particularly, of two recent volumes which present detailed research agendas for the subject (Morris 1989 and eds. Blair and Pyrah 1996). Both studies emphasise that the parish church is a barometer for the community in which it stands, and this is equally true of the Early Modern Era. In this Era, then, we should expect church archaeology to provide a very useful indicator of the shrinking of the city, both in its area and its population. But the barometer is not easily read. Relationships between the physical development of the church and its community are subtle and require careful assessment (cf. the methodology developed recently by Pam Graves – 2000). Early modern churches provided a theatre within which the competing interests of social groups within the parish and city were made clearly visible, particularly in the way in which space is distributed within each individual church. Churches, therefore, also tell us about intricate negotiations between social groups as well as about the size of their congregations. Furthermore their graveyards represent vital repositories of paleo-pathological information, which can tell us about the physical condition of the citizens in the early modern city. Did the city's economic decline have a deleterious effect on the health of its surviving citizens? Conversely, did the smaller population and the shift in the economy benefit the health of those who remained in the city?

As the commercial and the military significance of the city fell away in the late 13th century, the dominance of the church was waxing, and by 1350 it was much the most important interest group within the town. Throughout the period between 1350 and 1750 its only social and economic competitors were the Crown, who took little interest in the early modern city, the City Council, whose economic importance had been greatly reduced, and a few private individuals, who were rarely able to challenge the dominance of the clergy within the town. The large number of RAZs which represent the religious life of the city in the Early Modern Era reflect, to some extent therefore, the church's dominant position in the late Middle Ages, but they can be defined in such detail, also, because it is ecclesiastical records, rather than civic records, which have survived in great abundance.

Lincoln is fortunate to have several documentary surveys pointing to the economic state of churches across the city. In particular the *Subsidy Accounts* of 1428 provide a very clear picture of the decline of the parishes, with seventeen parishes having fewer than ten inhabitants, a further three having none at all and some parishes not even mentioned (which had, presumably, disappeared altogether), (Fig. 10.1; Hill 1948, 287). During the Reformation, the City Council mounted a campaign to liquidate the assets of the redundant churches and to skim off the profits for themselves. Their work was facilitated by an Act of Parliament in 1549 and, overall, the process of the sale of the redundant church sites and fabrics and their disposal to private individuals represents on the civic scale just as large a privatisation of urban space as the dissolution of the monasteries did on the national one.

Most of the RAZs defined for the parish churches of early modern Lincoln deal with questions posed by the contraction and closure of churches, matters which can be highly informative for the history of the city more widely. But several deal with attempts to 'privatise' church space by influential individuals, through the establishment of chantries (see also RAZ

10.53.5) and in at least one case (St Andrew Wigford – RAZ 10.60.19) by claiming that the parish church was actually a private chapel. Following the Reformation, of course, the churches which survived the 1549 Act will retain important information relating to the various doctrinal disputes and changes which characterised the national church in the 17th and 18th centuries. This period of church archaeology is not always dealt with as thoroughly as earlier periods, but its results can be equally revealing and several Lincoln churches offer the prospect of interesting case studies of these later periods (e.g. RAZ 10.60.33 or 10.60.45). The parish church RAZs for the Early Modern Era are as follows:

10.60 The parish churches

- 10.60.1 St John Newport
- 10.60.2 St Nicholas Newport
- 10.60.3 St Bartholomew *Westcastle*
- 10.60.4 St Peter Eastgate
- 10.60.5 St Margaret Pottergate
- 10.60.6 St Leonard
- 10.60.7 St Giles
- 10.60.8 Holy Trinity Greestone Stairs
- 10.60.9 St Rumbold
- 10.60.10 St Bavon
- 10.60.11 St Augustine
- 10.60.12 St Peter *ad fontem*
- 10.60.13 St Clement-in-*Butwerk*
- 10.60.14 St Stephen-in-Newland
- 10.60.15 St Faith-in-Newland
- 10.60.16 Holy Cross Wigford
- 10.60.17 Holy Innocents
- 10.60.18 Holy Trinity Wigford
- 10.60.19 St Andrew Wigford
- 10.60.20 St Benedict
- 10.60.21 St Botolph
- 10.60.22 St Edward Wigford
- 10.60.23 St John the Evangelist Wigford
- 10.60.24 St Margaret Wigford
- 10.60.25 St Mark
- 10.60.26 St Mary-le-Wigford
- 10.60.27 St Michael Wigford
- 10.60.28 St Peter-at-Gowts
- 10.60.29 St Paul-in-the-Bail
- 10.60.30 All Saints-in-the-Bail
- 10.60.31 St Clement-in-the-Bail
- 10.60.32 St Mary Magdalene
- 10.60.33 St Michael-on-the-Mount
- 10.60.34 St John-the-Poor
- 10.60.35 St Andrew-under-Palace
- 10.60.36 St Peter Stanthaket
- 10.60.37 St Cuthbert
- 10.60.38 St Martin
- 10.60.39 St Lawrence
- 10.60.40 St George
- 10.60.41 Holy Trinity Clasketgate
- 10.60.42 St Mary *Crackpole*
- 10.60.43 All Saints Hungate
- 10.60.44 St Peter-at-Pleas and St Peter-at-Arches
- 10.60.45 St Swithin
- 10.60.46 St Edmund

Lincoln's medieval friaries, monasteries and hospitals continued in religious use through the first two centuries of the Early Modern Era, of course, and all of these sites will retain many late medieval features of great interest. The RAZs all suggest that we take an interest in adaptations to the churches and other claustral buildings made during the final two centuries of their existence, which may cast light on the changing attitudes of the orders to their rules and to their relationship with the secular world. At the Dissolution, two institutions, the College of Vicars-Choral and the Cathedral itself, were re-founded along Protestant lines, but the remainder were handed over to private individuals or to the City Council. In the post-Dissolution period these sites retain considerable interest. Modern historical scholarship has tended to emphasise the vitality of early Tudor Catholicism (e.g. Duffy 1992) and their archaeology should cast light on the attitudes of the new secular owners to the old religion; was it deliberately denigrated or were its monuments treated with dignity and respect? In the case of the Carmelite Friary (RAZ 10.53.3) and St Mary's Conduit we may have rare evidence for the latter attitude, and we should expect more to be derived from future work. Little is known about the conversions of friaries for other uses in Lincoln or elsewhere and the chance should be taken to study this important aspect of early modern archaeology (Everson 1996). The dramatic conversions undergone by the former monastic sites after the Reformation represent the single most dramatic shift in the power balances between the different orders of Lincoln society and more must be done to understand this shift archaeologically. The RAZs for the greater churches are as follows:

- 10.52 The Cathedral
- 10.53 The friaries
    - 10.53.1 Augustinian Friary
    - 10.53.2 Dominican Friary
    - 10.53.3 Carmelite Friary
    - 10.53.4 Franciscan Friary
    - 10.53.5 Friary of the Sack and the Kyme chantry
- 10.54 St Katherine's Priory and St Sepulchre's Hospital
- 10.55 Monks' Abbey (the Benedictine priory of St Mary Magdalene)
- 10.56 The Malandry (the Hospital of the Holy Innocents)
- 10.57 St Bartholomew's and St Leonard's Hospitals
- 10.58 St Giles' Hospital

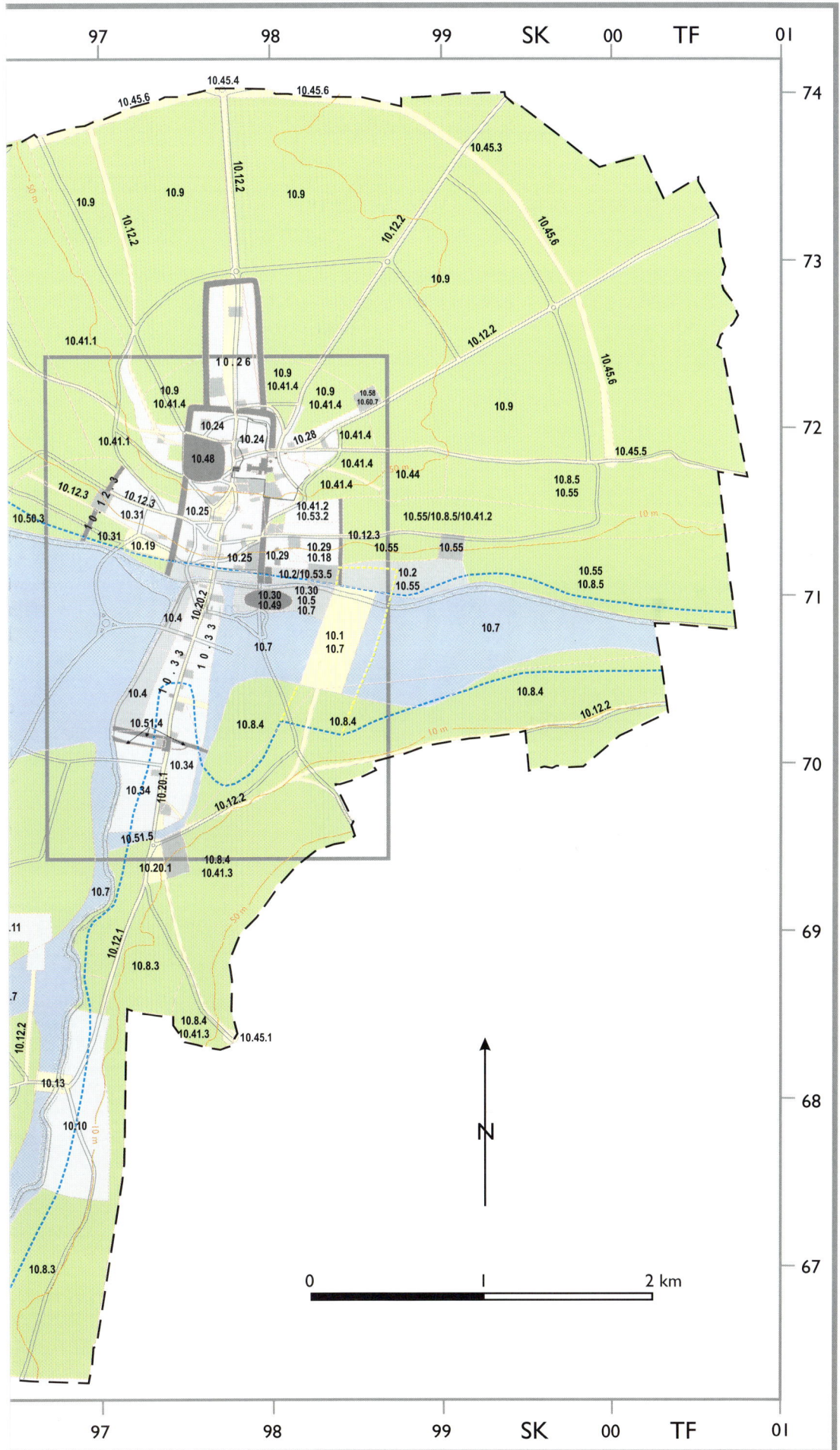

*Map 6. Research Agenda Zone locations for the Early Modern Era – See CD-Rom for details (drawn by Dave Watt, copyright English Heritage and Lincoln City Council).*

10.59   The College of the Vicars-Choral
10.61   St Mary Magdalene Hartsholme
10.62   Cathedral graveyard south-east of
         Angel Choir

Finally, Lincoln's Early Modern Era also saw the city become a centre for the growth of Dissent. Although some of the cathedral clergy participated influentially in doctrinal controversy, no one could suggest that Anglican Lincoln was a hot-bed of religious debate in the 17th and 18th centuries. Yet Lincoln has relatively early houses of Quakers (RAZ 10.63), Baptists (RAZ 10.64) and Presbyterians or Independents (RAZ 10.65). We have to ask why that should be. Given that Lincoln was hardly a great centre of population, with a large industrial working-class, there must have been some other impetus for the early Dissenters to open missions here. There was, as far as we know, no equivalent concentration of early Dissenting communities in Stamford or Boston. Was it the presence of the Cathedral itself? Is this concentration of early Dissent further evidence of Lincoln's long-term role as the region's principal religious centre?

## Education

Although in our definition of RAZs so far we have been stressing the economic powerlessness of early modern Lincoln, the Early Modern Era is also the period when the city's first schools become visible and, eventually, more independent of the church. The Cathedral school had existed long before *c*.1300 but it is only in the late Middle Ages that we are able to locate it on the ground and thus provide a simple research agenda (RAZ 10.67) The other three educational RAZs which we have managed to define, however, are new school foundations made after the Reformation as acts of philanthropy, either institutional – by the City Council (RAZ 10.66) – or private (RAZs 10.68 and 10.69). These RAZs establish a form of archaeological research agenda for these early schools that builds on the project work already completed (Stocker 1991), but realistically substantial progress in understanding the place of these schools within the early modern city will probably be led by analysis of surviving documentation.

# 11. Lincoln's Industrial Era (*c*.1750–*c*.1945)

## A. Archaeological account
### *David Stocker*

## Introduction

In the late 18th century, after at least four and a half centuries of stasis, once again Lincoln's character began to change. The economy picked up, the population started to increase and the town's fabric began to succumb to a 'great rebuilding' which would last until the First World War. Once again Lincoln became a major city in the realm and its contacts developed not just nationally but, for the first time since the 13th century, its manufactures were traded in European markets and beyond.

Obviously, our information and understanding for this important period of Lincoln's history is derived primarily from documentary history. As in earlier periods the main secondary source, to which everything else is referred, is Sir Francis Hill's monumental survey, especially *Georgian Lincoln* (1966) and *Victorian Lincoln* (1974). More recently John Herridge, working for English Heritage and Lincoln City Council, has produced his excellent report *The Industrial Archaeology of Lincoln* (Herridge 1999). This report has systematically collected together, for the first time, the evidence for much of Lincoln's industrial heritage and a considerable proportion of the information about the city's industrial sites set out below is taken from this source. Hill's and Herridge's studies are both drawn primarily from the city's documentary archives, which survive in enormous profusion for this period, as do the records of certain of the great Lincoln industrial concerns (e.g. Newman 1957 – on Ruston and Co.). Similarly the output of central government, increasingly regulatory in its role in this period, was so great that the account of the city's history from documentary sources has scarcely begun. More detailed biography, also, becomes a distinct possibility and Lincoln and Lincolnshire have their share of important auto-biographies and diaries, which cast light on the city's development from the individual's perspective (Hill 1966, x–xi; 1974, vii–viii). Finally, of course, newspapers become a vital source for understanding the sequence of contemporary events, and popular reactions to them. For the first seventy years of the period under consideration, Lincoln did not have its own newspaper, but relied on correspondents publishing in a variety of newspapers elsewhere, notably in the *Lincoln, Rutland and Stamford Mercury* (first published about 1712 in Stamford – Wright 1982, 19). It was not until 1828 that the first newspaper published in Lincoln, *The Lincoln Herald*, specialised in city affairs (Hill 1966, 292),

But what of archaeology? What role can archaeology play in a period when so much is already known from documentary sources? At least since the last War, and certainly since the 1970s, the answer to that question has been named 'industrial archaeology'. This discipline has developed largely to record and study the development of industry and technology, and it is only recently that it has attempted to place itself more firmly within theoretical and practical frameworks long established in archaeology of other periods (e.g. Palmer and Neaverson 1998, chapter 1). In Lincolnshire the work of recording industrial remains has been handled with skill and enthusiasm, not by the city's resident professional archaeologists, but by a group of dedicated amateurs of whom Catherine Wilson and Neil Wright have been particularly prominent. The Society for Lincolnshire History and Archaeology established an Industrial Archaeology Committee in 1964 and a journal called *Lincolnshire Industrial Archaeology* was published between 1966 and 1973. John Herridge's *Survey* (above) did not undertake systematic physical recording of individual structures, but it identified, for the first time, the wealth of such structures still surviving in the city, as well as pin-pointing the likely location of certain buried remains.

Even so, archaeological recording projects on structures of the Industrial Era have been few, and excavations of deposits of this period have been even fewer. This is all the more reprehensible when we remember that in *c.*1960 Lincoln was a more or less intact industrial settlement of the second half of the 19th century and there were few places in England where all aspects of the development of heavy engineering could be studied more effectively. Now, however, most of that inheritance of red-brick factories, warehouses and workshops has gone, without so much as a photograph being taken, and the physical detail of the settlement only exists on the early Ordnance Survey maps.

## Defences

The Industrial Era saw new fortifications built in many southern and eastern towns and cities in England, but Lincoln remained largely untouched by the military preparations against Napoleonic invasion. At the height of the invasion scare, in 1806, the military authorities decided to build a depot for storage of arms and ammunition on the corner of Carholme Road and Depot Street. Subsequently, during the Crimean War, plans were made for a much larger and more modern militia barracks on Burton Road, which survives intact and is a lesson to all interested in the great changes in military organisation which followed the Militia Act of 1852. These barracks became redundant themselves, when, in 1871, the militia was merged with the territorial regiments and by 1890 Lincoln had acquired the Sobraon Barracks, a complex with a 'keep' and a curtain wall further down Burton Road. It is very similar in its layout and design to many in county towns across England.

All three buildings (the Depot, the militia barracks and the Sobraon barracks) were intended to form individual links in the chain of national defence, of course, but we should not forget that they drew their recruits from the Lincoln community itself. Troops based in these establishments, for example, would have been used if the city suddenly needed defending. In the event, of course, the troops quartered here were called out, not infrequently during the 19th and early 20th century, 'in support of the Civil Power'. That is to say that they more often found themselves part of the police force, as in the riots of 1911 (Nurse 2001). Other buildings and structures specifically used by the military in training included the fine new Drill Hall in Broadgate, given to the City Council by Joseph Ruston in 1890 and the rifle butts complex on South Common, although both of these facilities were used by civilians as well as by the military.

During the two World Wars, however, Lincoln's role changed again. The city became an important centre for the manufacture of munitions, but this significance developed naturally out of the heavy engineering character of its industry in the second half of the 19th century and was in the hands of civilian engineers. This essentially civilian effort in the city included the development of the Tank, a development for which Lincoln is now world famous. Nevertheless there were active military bases in and around the city in both wars. Between 1915 and 1918 the Royal Flying Corps established what was called a 'reception aerodrome' on West Common, where machines built in the city were tested by military aviators and 'accepted' into their RFC squadrons. Similarly, in the 1939–45 war, like many other Lincolnshire fields, land inside the modern city boundary was taken for use as an RAF bomber base. This was RAF Skellingthorpe, which was built on pasture land in the south-west corner of the city's administrative area and which had a distinguished service history comparable with many other such Lincolnshire bases (Otter 1996, 210–218).

In 1940 there was, once again, a serious prospect of invasion and, as they were at most English cities, static defences were prepared by the Home Guard. The centre of the city was ringed with a continuous perimeter of wire, earthwork and other defences to create a defensive wall (Hurt 1991; Hurt and Barratt 1997) (Fig. 11.1). Only small parts of this perimeter have survived in the form of thickened and loop-holed walls, sockets in the pavements and other barriers, but it is notable how little of this defence relied on the defences of earlier ages. The way that this latest defensive circuit ignored all of the previous attempts, Roman, Anglo-Scandinavian and medieval, to ring the city shows just how much of a discontinuity there was between Lincoln in the 14th century and Lincoln in the 20th. The new defences bore no relationship to medieval defensive boundaries and nothing could illustrate more clearly both scale of the collapse of high-medieval Lincoln and the lack of continuity between the small market town of the early modern period and the industrial centre which developed in the 19th century.

## Extent of settlement

In the period between 1750 and 1945 the city underwent a second massive expansion; it grew even faster than it had between the 10th and the 12th centuries, and by the end of the period it was expanding well beyond the limits of the former medieval suburbs (Fig. 11.2). Traditionally the 're-birth' of Lincoln as a major urban centre is dated to the 18th September 1740, when the City Council granted a 999 year lease on the Fossdyke to Richard Ellison (the elder) of Thorne, a water engineer and merchant trading with the West Riding (ed. Birch 1906, 41, No.122). This is certainly an over-simplification, but the Ellison lease seemed to provide an excellent example of the type of dynamic capitalism,

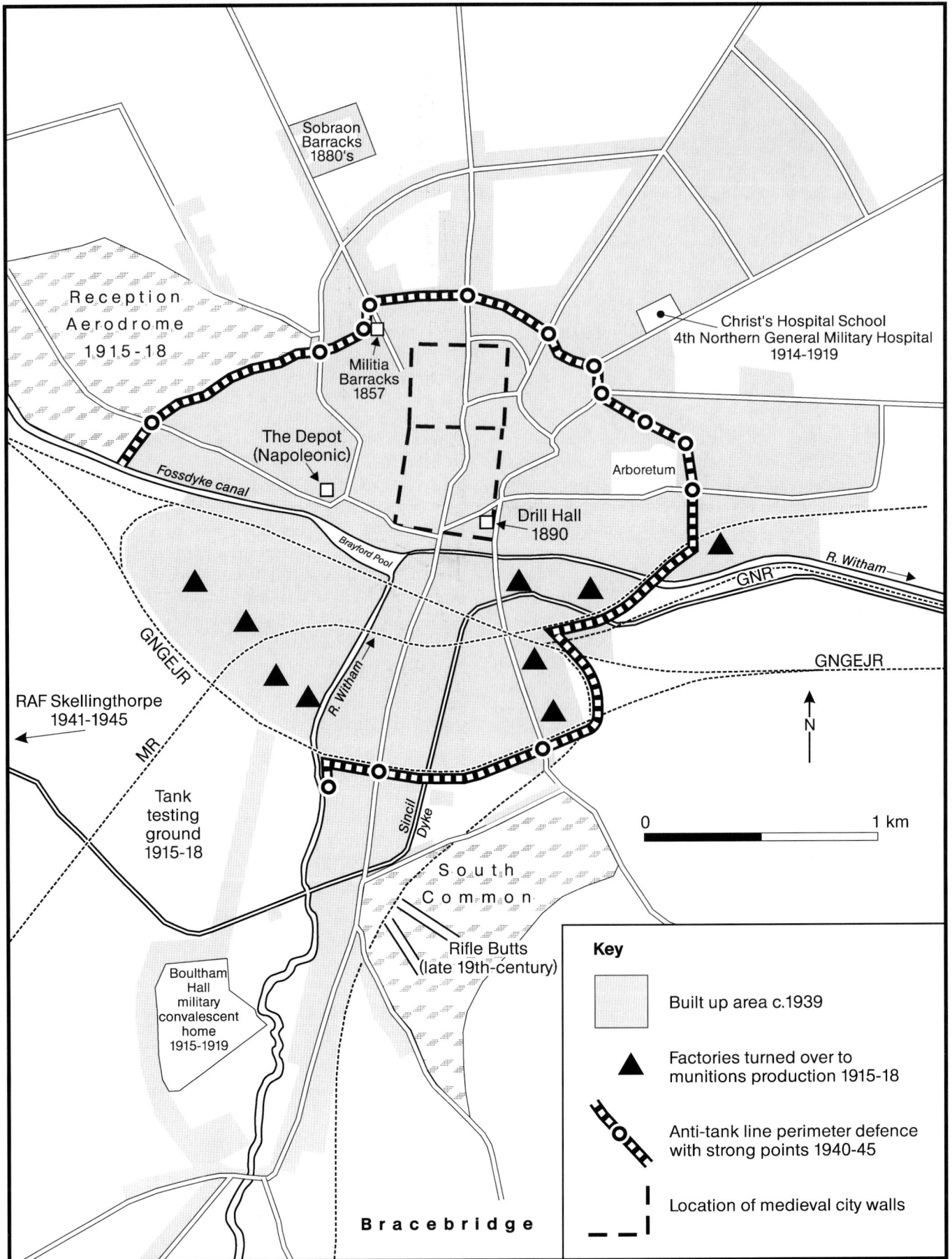

Sobraon
Barracks
1880's

Reception
Aerodrome
1915-18

Christ's Hospital School
4th Northern General Military Hospital
1914-1919

Militia
Barracks
1857

The Depot
(Napoleonic)

Fossdyke canal

Arboretum

Drill Hall
1890

Brayford Pool

R. Witham

GNR

GNGEJR

R. Witham

RAF Skellingthorpe
1941-1945

MR.

Tank
testing
ground
1915-18

Sincil
Dyke

South
Common

N

Rifle Butts
(late 19th-century)

0                    1 km

Boultham
Hall
military
convalescent
home
1915-1919

Bracebridge

**Key**

Built up area c.1939

Factories turned over to
munitions production 1915-18

Anti-tank line perimeter defence
with strong points 1940-45

Location of medieval city walls

*Fig. 11.1. Defence sites in Lincoln in the Industrial Era (sources, Hurt 1991; Hurt and Barratt 1997 and others – drawn by Dave Watt, copyright English Heritage).*

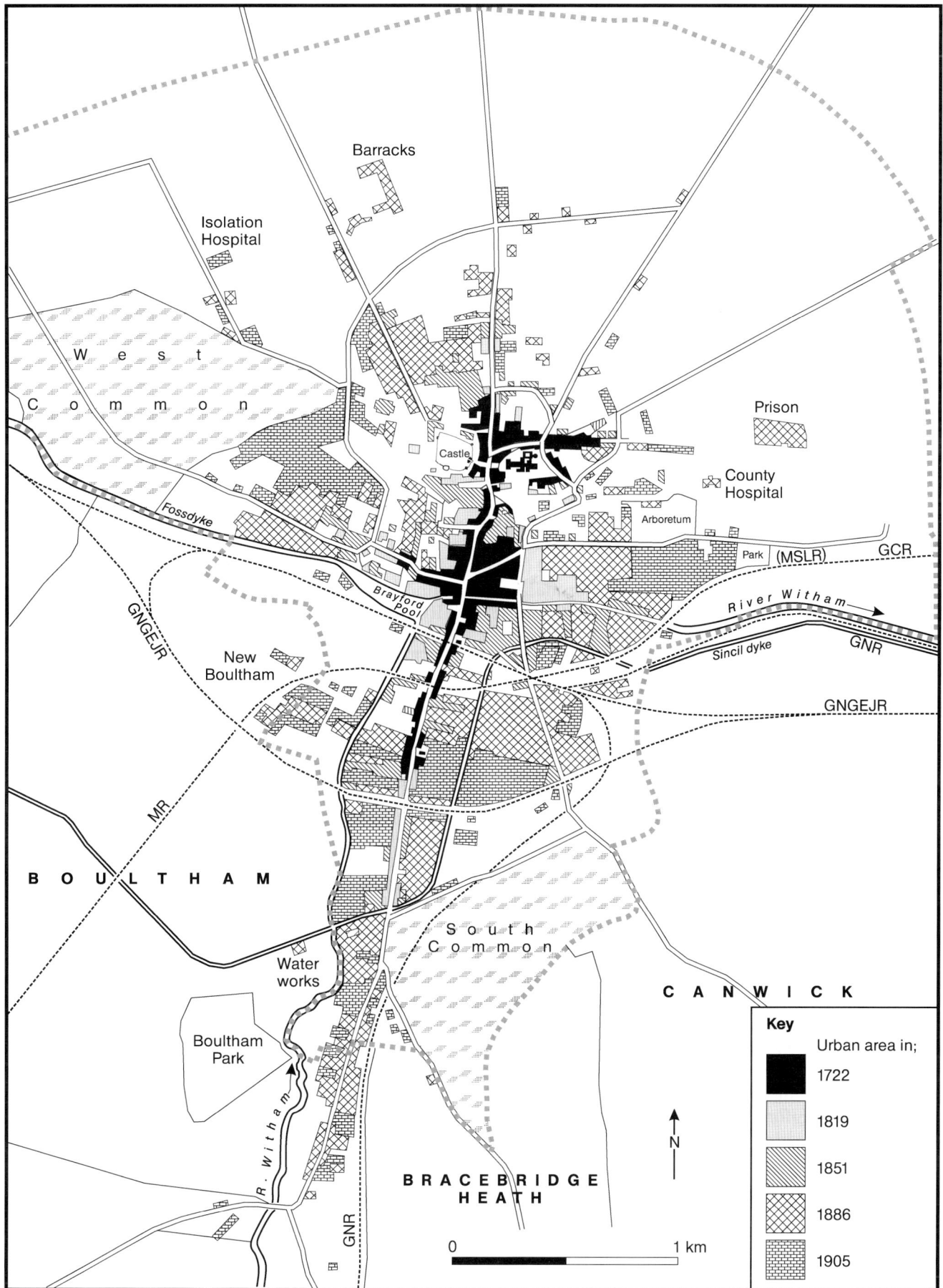

*Fig. 11.2. Growth of the built-up area of the city between 1722 and 1905 (source, Wright 1982, fig 20 – re-drawn by Dave Watt, copyright English Heritage).*

St Giles Estate
1920-1936

W e s t
C o m m o n

*Fossdyke canal*

Swanpool
Garden Suburb
1919-1925

*Brayford Pool*

*R. Witham*

GNGEJR

*Sincil Dyke*

GNGEJR

Planned

MR.

N

*R. Witham*

*Sincil Dyke*

Completed

S o u t h
C o m m o n

**B o u l t h a m**

Boultham
Park

0          1 km

Grainsby Close
'Pre-fab' Estate
c.1920

**B r a c e b r i d g e**

**Key**

Working/Lower Middle class
housing 1850-1945

▲   Principle factories and works

**N o r t h**

**H y k e h a m**

┘ ⌐   Location of Roman City walls

Chartist
settlement
Brant Road
c.1850

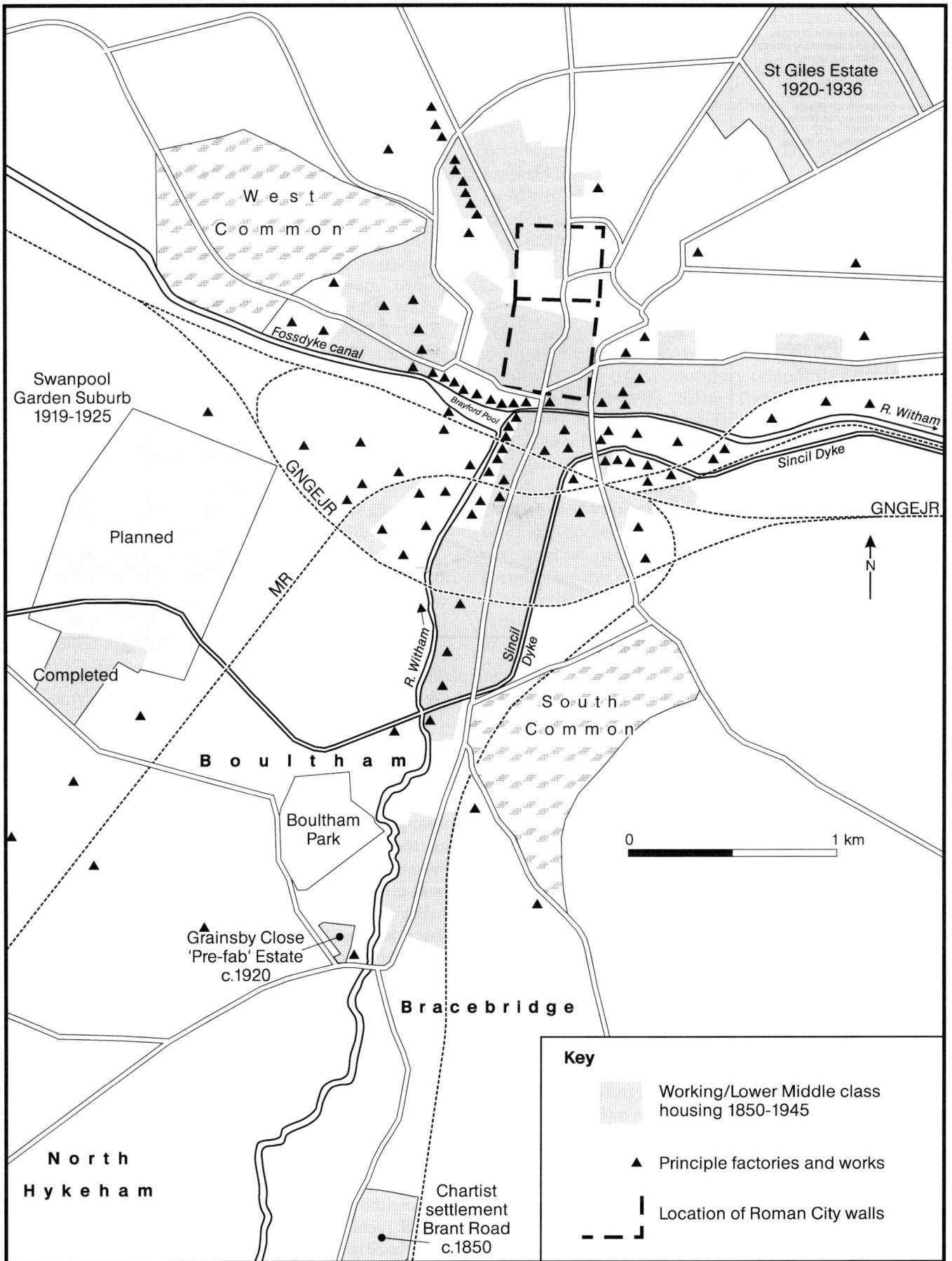

*Fig. 11.4. Main areas of workers' housing built 1850–1940, mapped in relation to the city's principal factories and works (drawn by Dave Watt, copyright English Heritage).*

Fig. 11.5. 'Big Wesley', the enormous Wesleyan Methodist chapel on Clasketgate from the south-east. It was built in 1836–7 under the Lincoln architect W A Nicholson and demolished in 1963 with only a minimal record (photo and copyright, Lincolnshire County Council, County Library Service, Local History Collection).

Fig. 11.6. The church of St Mark, as rebuilt in 1871–2 by the local architect William Watkins, from the north-east. The church was demolished in 1972, with minimal architectural recording, but the plan of this phase of the church was recorded during excavations in 1976 (SM 76; Fig. 9.73 – Gilmour and Stocker 1986) (photo and copyright, Lincolnshire Echo).

Fig. 11.7. The church of St Paul-in-the-Bail from the west, as rebuilt in 1877–8 under the architect Sir Arthur Blomfield. The church was demolished in 1971, with minimal architectural recording, but the site was excavated in 1972–9 (SP 72) (photo and copyright Lincolnshire County Library, Local History Collection).

England provision, however, was probably the demolition of the 'City Council's church' of St Peter-at-Arches in 1936 and its re-creation as the parish church of the new housing estate of St Giles. This transplantation shows, more dramatically than any academic study could, that the social planners of the 1930s thought it important that new estates like St Giles should have a sense of continuity with the past. It is unlikely, also, that the political symbolism of removing the City Council's church from its historic location outside the symbol of the ancient oligarchy, the Guildhall, and re-establishing it in an estate considered to exemplify the new democratic, even socialist, thinking would have been lost on contemporaries. Unfortunately no systematic archaeological or fabric recording was done when St Peter's was demolished and a great deal of crucial information on this critical site for the whole history of the city was lost during the subsequent re-development.

Throughout the Industrial period the Church of England was being threatened by the enormous rise in number of Dissenters in the city. On Sunday 14 March 1903 there were services held at a total of 34 Dissenting places of worship, compared with only 19 Church of England locations (Hill 1974, 313–6). The overwhelming majority of these Dissenting congregations were protestants (only a single Catholic church was in operation that day) and of these, the Methodists (with 17 places of worship) were in the majority, not only in numbers of chapels, but also in size of congregation. Next in size (of attendance) came the Congregationalists who held services at four chapels that day, and they were followed by the Salvation Army, who reported over 900 souls present. The Baptists, who only had three chapels in the city (Plate 7.4) were not large by comparison (with 703 attendances), whilst the Quakers, the longest-established of Lincoln's Dissenting communities, had a mere 76 people through the door.

The great majority of these Dissenting groups met in modest establishments with few architectural pretensions, but the large Wesleyan chapels in Clasketgate, Silver Street and High Street were distinguished and expensive buildings, aiming to match the best architecture of the established church (though, with the exception of St Catherine's South Common, they were in classical styles). Many of these notable churches and chapels have now been demolished (for example the *Big Wesley* of 1836 was demolished in 1963 and *Little Wesley* of 1873–5 was demolished in 1965), but few (if any) systematic records were made prior any of the demolitions.

## Streets and buildings

Commercial activity, of course, had been an everyday part of Lincoln's economic life long before the Industrial Revolution, and the markets of the Industrial Era continued, seamlessly, those of its predecessors. Produce continued to be sold along the High Street and The Strait, from the oat market at St Mary-le-Wigford northwards to old St Martin's. Livestock was traded on the east side of the city from Monks Road and Broadgate to St Swithin's Square. A large number of Lincoln's traders depended on the weekly influx of people that the markets attracted. The new, sheltered, Buttermarket was built in 1737 after demands from market traders, and a new Butchery and Shambles in Clasketgate followed in 1774. Most other commodities seem to have been traded largely in the open until the building of the 1879 Corn Exchange and Market, in which fruit, vegetables and fish were sold. Commercial dealing in corn took place in the huge upper hall, built to replace the inadequate Corn Exchange of 1847 immediately to the south. The present Central Market dates from 1938 and is an expansion of provision to the north of the 1879 Corn Exchange (Fig. 11.8). All of these new structures were impressive, having been designed by the most notable

of local architects in each generation, but no systematic recording has been undertaken during the various repairs and refurbishments they have undergone.

Within the city, passenger transport was still largely by horse, foot and, after 1860, bicycle, until the introduction in 1906 of the Corporation electric tram service from St Benedict's Square to Bracebridge via High Street and Newark Road. Since 1881, horse-drawn trams had been run on the same route by the Lincoln Tramways Company. The last tram ran in 1929, by which time Corporation motor buses had been operating for nine years, initially concentrating on the uphill parts of the city which could not be reached by tram. Private bus companies had begun to operate routes connecting Lincoln to other towns and villages from the beginning of the First World War. The Lincolnshire Road Car Company, established in Lincoln in 1922 as the Silver Queen company, became the leading operator in east and south Lincolnshire, later covering the whole county through the acquisition of smaller companies up to and after its nationalisation as part of the British Transport Commission in 1948 (White, 1989, 106–25).

As far as is known, no archaeology has yet been undertaken on any aspect of Lincoln's internal communications infrastructure, although in the late 1970s Catherine Wilson undertook an exemplary study of Lincoln-made street furniture types in Motherby Hill (Wilson 1980) (Fig. 11.9).

## Water supply and waste disposal

In 1760, the conduit and obelisk on High Bridge were erected to replace the conduit outside the Guildhall, although the supply system itself remained that fed from springs north of Monks Road and installed by the City Council in the 1540s (p. 325 above). Indeed, right into the 20th century, the conduit heads at Greyfriars, High Bridge and St Mary-le-Wigford remained important to the citizens of downhill Lincoln. The pipeline was extended further south from St Mary's to St Peter-at-Gowts in 1864 (where the faucet still survives) and further east to Baggeholme Road in 1869 (where an elaborate octagonal tower, now demolished, was built to contain the conduit head). There has been no systematic recording of this water supply system, although both the High Bridge and St Mary's Conduit have been the subject of intensive conservation programmes in the last 30 years and, in the latter case, some low level fabric recording was undertaken (Stocker 1990). Wells seem to have been scarce in the Lower City and Wigford but they continued in use in the Upper City throughout the 19th century; at least fifteen are marked on the 1888 Ordnance Survey map.

Lincoln's first pumped water-supply was established by the Lincoln Waterworks Company in 1848 by damming Prial Brook to the west of Boultham village

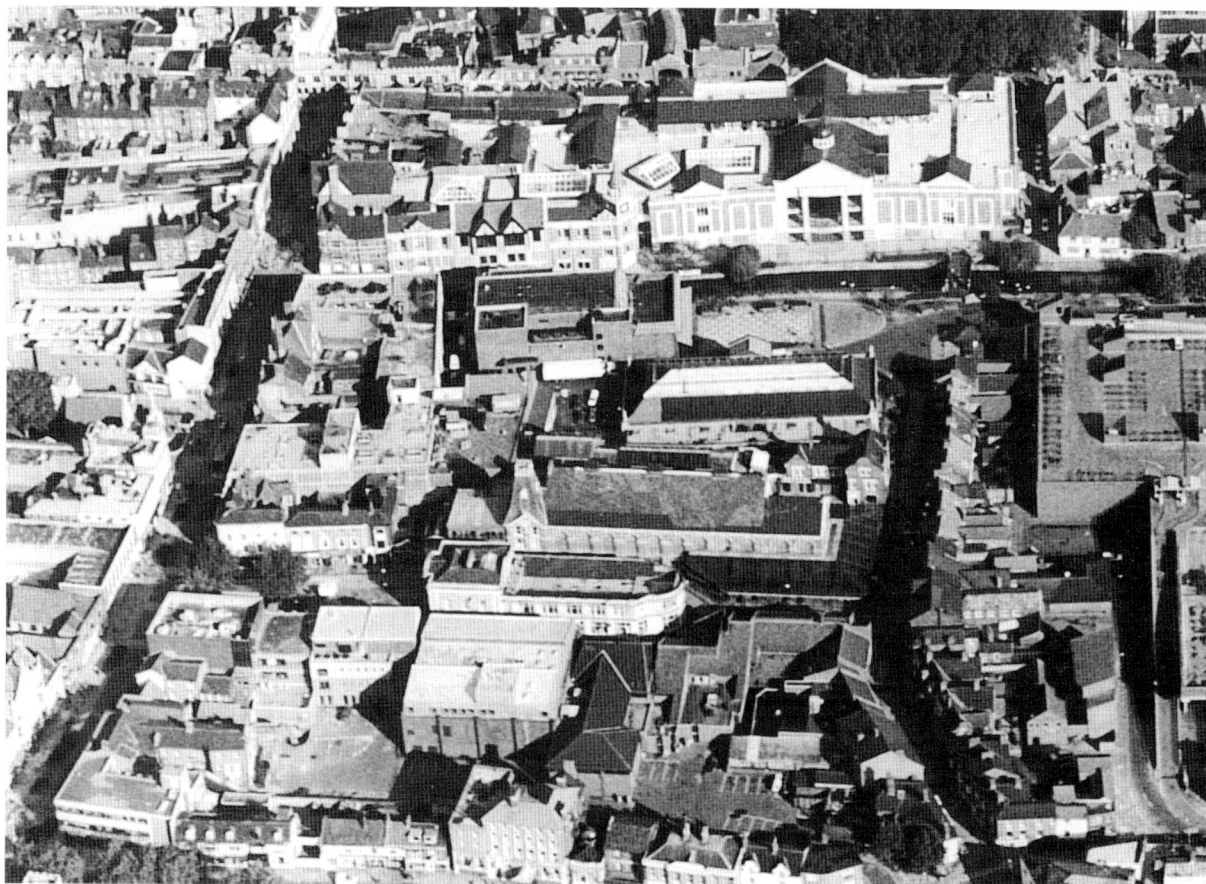

*Fig. 11.8. Lincoln's various Victorian and later market halls, built on and around the site of the medieval churchyard of St John Wigford, looking north. The southernmost building (facing west onto the open space of Cornhill) is the original Corn Exchange of 1847 (extended 1853). To the north is its replacement of 1879–80, with its distinctive tower at its south-west angle, whilst the roof to the north again is the covered Central Market of 1938, which incorporates the façade of the Buttermarket of 1737. Across the Witham, facing the Central Market is the enormous Waterside shopping complex of the 1990s (photo and copyright Lincolnshire Echo).*

to create a reservoir. Water was then carried by aqueduct to a waterworks at Altham Terrace where, following some basic treatment, it was pumped by steam engines, via cast-iron underground pipes, to open reservoirs at Chapel Lane and Bracebridge Heath (the latter outside city boundary). The system's capacity was rapidly exceeded and, with the lack of a proper sewage disposal system in the city, it became increasingly unhygienic. The Council took control of the whole system in 1872 but problems of public health continued, culminating in a serious typhoid epidemic in 1904/5. In the aftermath of the epidemic, a completely new supply was installed, with a borehole at Elkesley, Nottinghamshire, and, from 1911, water was pumped from Elkesley to water towers at Westgate (Fig. 11.10) and Bracebridge Heath.

Modern sewage treatment was slow in arriving in Lincoln and the Council's delay was a considerable scandal, which was taken up in Parliament (Hill 1974, 164–71). In 1876, however, the City Council finally accepted its responsibilities in this area with the opening of the Corporation Sewage Works in Great Northern Terrace and the Sewage Farm on Washingborough Road. Even so, it took until 1912 to connect the whole city to the sewage system. Circular filter beds replaced open fields before 1930 (Mills 2001). Both the waterworks site on Altham Terrace and the sewage treatment sites south-east of the city have been completely reconstructed since 1945 but no systematic recording has been undertaken.

## Supply routes

Improvements in transport infrastructure were vital to Lincoln's industrial growth. Without the improvements in canal transport, road transport and (especially) rail transport, Lincoln could not have become a major heavy-engineering centre by 1900. Without these connections it would have remained, presumably, a small cathedral city comparable with Chichester or Hereford. Before the establishment of the turnpike trusts in the middle of the 18th century and the subsequent investment in the roads, travel was

Fig. 11.9. Street furniture looking north along Motherby Hill. These products of the Lincoln foundry industry, still in situ in the 1970s, were the subject of a ground-breaking local recording project by C Wilson (Wilson 1980) (photo and copyright, Catherine Wilson).

Fig. 11.10. The new water tower on Westgate under construction in 1910–11 (photo and copyright, Lincolnshire County Council, County Library Service, Local History Collection).

slow and difficult. Lincolnshire farmers and graziers drove cattle and sheep, not only to local markets, but also as far afield as London. It was often impossible, especially during the winter, to make these journeys on what were no more than muddy tracks. Wagons carrying wool or grain were similarly hampered. Great improvements in overland transport were brought about by the establishment of turnpikes in the second half of the 18th century. From then on regular and predictable services could be organised and the rapid transport of small goods large distances across the country by carrier became possible. Lincoln was serviced by turnpikes to Wragby, Louth and Horncastle (trust founded in 1739), to Sleaford (via Canwick Hill – trust founded in 1756), to Brigg and Barton on Humber (trust founded in 1765) and to Newark (trust founded in 1777). Even so, the turnpikes had their limitations and could not cope with the transport of products in bulk.

Waterways were a much more efficient method of conveying bulky goods, but they too required improvement. Although of considerable technical in-

terest, the revitalisation of the Fossdyke in the 18th century has yet to be investigated archaeologically. We have already noted that the effect on the city of the Ellison's improvements on the Fossdyke following his acquisition of the lease in 1740 was seen almost immediately in the development of ancillary services around Brayford (Fig. 11.11). The warehouses, stores and food-processing buildings dependent on the Fossdyke continued in use into the 1960s and some survived in marginal uses until the 1980s, although many were demolished earlier. Only a little recording work was done on this major group of industrial buildings around Brayford Pool prior to their destruction.

At the beginning of the 18th century, the Witham between Lincoln and Boston was in a serious state of disrepair – with broken banks and regular flooding. Between 1762 and 1770 improvements were made, including a new lock at Stamp End (the subject of recording and study in 1976 – Wilson 1977), and the recutting of the channel through the fens to remove the meanders between Chapel Hill and Boston. The

*Fig. 11.11. 'Lincoln from the south-west, Early Evening'. A watercolour by Lincoln artist Peter de Wint, probably painted in 1820s or 30s (photo and copyright, Lincolnshire County Council, Usher Art Gallery cat No.73/12).*

shallow and narrow section at High Bridge was improved, it but continued to cause problems well into the 19th century. When the river was high there was insufficient headroom under the bridge, and until the channel was deepened following William Jessop's report of 1791, there was insufficient draught for even moderately laden vessels (Hill 1966, 134–5).

Furthermore, improvements to the river and canal system could not be undertaken without adjustment of the whole drainage network of the valley and improvement of the Witham below Lincoln was sometimes delayed by the conflicting interests of landowners whose fields needed drainage and protection from flooding, and those of boat owners who needed deep water for their vessels. The low-lying Witham around Lincoln had always been liable to flooding, and between 1804 and 1816, the 'Lincoln West Drainage Scheme', aimed to drain the lowlands on the west of the city to make the land more marketable for the owners, mainly Lord Monson. The engineer was Sir John Rennie. It involved the cutting of the Main, Catchwater and Prial Brook Drains and the raising of the banks of the Fossdyke. Problems persisted, however, through the 19th and 20th centuries,

with frequent flooding at Boultham, Bracebridge, Canwick Road and Waterside, where factory production was sometimes halted.

The first proposals to bring the railways to Lincoln had been made as early as the 1820s, and would have included the city on the main north – south route (Ruddock and Pearson 1985, 43–87). The city's location at the narrow and level breach in the limestone ridge appeared to many to be ideal, also, for an east – west route. This was achieved by the arrival of the Midland Railway and the Manchester, Sheffield and Lincolnshire Railway in 1846–8 (Fig. 11.12), but the main north–south line of the Great Northern Railway ran to the west, leaving Lincoln on a loop line from Boston. Despite this apparent disadvantage, the city was now connected to the rapidly expanding rail network, and agricultural and manufactured goods could be moved quickly to distant markets (Ruddock and Pearson, 1985, 220–1). Long distance carriage by road soon suffered a fall-off in commercial traffic, and although commercial water transport, mainly of agricultural produce, continued into the 20th century, the domination of the railways was irresistible. Within twenty-five years of their arrival, the small railway sheds and warehouses

*Fig. 11.12. Lincoln from the south-west in about 1860 showing the Midland Railway station (St Mark's) laid out on the (still undeveloped) carr-lands (Williams 1877, 585).*

close to the stations proved inadequate, resulting in the draining and development of the Ropewalk and West Holmes areas into major goods marshalling yards, along with East Yard and Pelham Street Junction. Companies in Carholme Road, Firth Road, New Boultham, Waterside South, Spa Road, Canwick Road and Newark Road all had private sidings to the main lines. Clayton and Shuttleworth's Dock Basin was progressively filled in during the century to accommodate sidings, yet a link with water transport was maintained with the Great Central Warehouse of 1907 on the Holmes at Ropewalk, with a dock on its north side which remained open until 1972. Until the expansion of the motorway network and the subsequent growth of the road haulage industry in the 1960s, rail continued to dominate the transport of goods, with Lincoln's yards playing a major role as a distribution centre.

The railways of Lincoln have been the subject of limited archaeological study (Betteridge 1985). In 1984, some excitement was generated by the discovery that some of the original stone sleeper blocks from the first railway line at St Marks had survived, although not *in situ* (Wall and Swift 1984). In the mid 1990s the great railway bridge across the Witham at Stamp End and its predecessors were the subject of a study by Barton and members of the Industrial Archaeology sub-Committee of the Society for Lincolnshire History and Archaeology (Barton 1998).

## Victualling the city and food-processing industries

### Meat and animal products

Because it had always been a centre for the sale, slaughtering and processing of sheep and cattle, Lincoln saw the growth of several important companies involved in animal processing during the Industrial Era. The great cattle market along Monks Road, in particular, provided meat for the slaughterhouses in the city, especially that in Clasketgate (though there were a number of others) and they, in their turn, supplied both butchers in the city and the developing tanning industry. No animal bone samples from archaeological deposits of the Industrial Era have been collected in Lincoln.

The first large 'industrial' tannery was established on the upper Witham in the early 19th century, by Thomas and Marmaduke Wetherell, and was in operation from the 1860s until at least 1928 (when it was known as Galsworthy's Tannery). It was conveniently located on the south side of the Midland Railway Station, with sidings into the works, and one of its buildings still survives. Johnson's skin yard (sometimes known as Shepherd's yard) on Sincil Dyke was in operation until the late 19th century, near modern Scorer Street, whilst to the west of the Witham, beyond Firth Road, a plant for leather processing and glue manufacture was founded in 1863 by Bernard Cannon, who took over an existing skin yard. Leather-working skills probably also underpinned allied businesses, like that founded by James Dawson in Unity Square to manufacture industrial belting, and they developed in symbiosis with the great engineering plants. The traction engines and threshing machines provided a convenient market for leather (for straps and belts of various kinds), whilst the glue was used in the extensive coachworks which were maintained by each of the major engineering concerns. Various leather products were made for military use during World War I, and James Dawson and Son Ltd still manufactures specialised belting along with ducting, hosing and other products using synthetic materials (Fig. 11.13). As well as skins, the bones were also used. Malam's Boneyard was established on Waterside South in the early 19th century, although it is not entirely clear what they manufactured and it seems to have merged with Doughty's bone mill and yard *c.*1850, which was between Sincil Street and High Street, where the Central Market now stands.

## Cereals, other foodstuffs and brewing

The line of windmills along the skyline north of the Castle remained a familiar sight to travellers from the west until the end of the 19th century. It has not been established how many of these were brick tower mills, like the surviving Ellis' Mill (built in 1798), but there was at least one example of a post mill, and one smock mill, of which early photographs have survived. Ellis' Mill has been the subject of a detailed recording programme undertaken during its repair and conservation (Fig. 11.14). There was investment in these traditional milling sites in the Industrial Era then, but by the end of the 19th century corn was being ground in increasingly large plants in the valley. It is known that the property bought by William Foster on Waterside North in 1846 contained a brick windmill (Lane 1997, 9) and by the end of the century there were new windmills in Gaunt Street, Mill Lane and Princess Street to the west of the High Street. The large windmill and its accompanying buildings on Princess Street, known as Le Tall's Mill, were the subject of a study prior to their conversion into flats (Tinley 1985) (Fig. 11.15). The construction of the steam-powered Seely's Mill at Brayford in 1839 marked the beginning of the end for wind power. The steam mills were sited on the waterways for ease of coal transport and water supply and some recording of Seely's Mill was undertaken prior to its demolition by Ian Beckwith (1968). In the 1840s a steam-powered flour mill was built in Princess Street, followed by the conversion of William Foster's

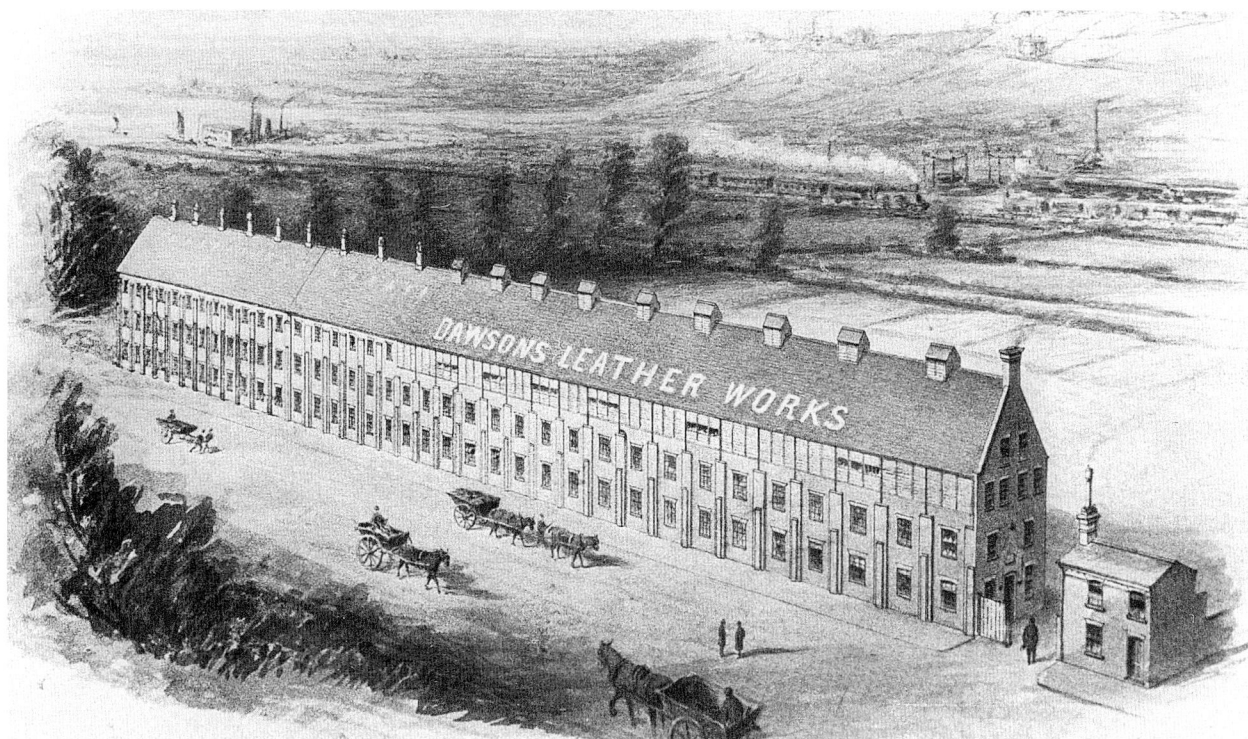

*Fig. 11.13. Dawson's new tannery in Beevor Street (depicted shortly after construction in 1886), one of the new industrial plants laid out on the carr-land following the expansion of the major foundries into this newly-developed area. The view is interesting, also, for its depiction of the 'West End' and the West Cliff Brickworks along the cliff edge (Fig. 11.23) beyond the line of windmills (photo and copyright, Lincolnshire County Council, County Library Service, Local History Collection).*

Fig. 11.15. Le Tall's Mill (now Crown Mill), Princess Street, Wigford, during re-construction at the end of the 19th century. The plant began as a large tower mill c.1835 and was subsequently (before c.1860) converted to run on steam power, once coal became available via the railway (photo and copyright Lincolnshire County Council, County Library Service, Local History Collection).

Fig. 11.14. Ellis' Mill, Mill Road. The last of the line of windmills which had stood along the cliff edge since the medieval period. This small tower mill was rebuilt in brick in 1784 and restored by the Lincoln Civic Trust in 1977 (Plate 7.2) (photo and copyright, D Stocker).

mill to steam in 1847. The excavation at Dickinson's Mill (DM 72) on the east side of Brayford, took its name from the large flour mill here perhaps dating from the 1840s and this building, at least, benefited from a basic level of recording prior to demolition (Chambers and Wilson 1972). There may have been an earlier steam mill on this site but, more certainly, William Rudgard's mill of the 1830s on the north wharf of Brayford was converted to steam power in 1856. Roller grinders replaced millstones in the late 19th century and some of the mills continued working into the 1960s, while others changed their use (Seely's Mill had become a grain warehouse owned by the Great Northern Railway by c.1900). Much of the produce of these great mills was sold outside Lincoln, however, to the industrial areas of the Northwest and the Midlands, via the Fossdyke and the railways; indeed Seely's Mill was served both by river and by a railway siding on its south side. The enormous 1884 Co-operative Flour Mill

on Waterside, a model installation in its day, continued to use barge transport for deliveries of grain until 1961, when it was demolished without records being made (Fig. 11.16).

Using this abundant supply of milled grain, Blaze Allot and Co. were already baking bread on an industrial scale in Monson Street in the 1860s, and Henry Kirke White set up his Steam Biscuit Works in Rosemary Lane in the 1880s. Windmills had been used in the county for crushing seed for oil and animal 'cake' since the 17th century (Wright 1982, 26–7), but it is not known if any contemporary Lincoln windmills were employed in this way. Doughty's, a well-known name in Lincoln milling, was established in Newport in 1791, and the firm may have been crushing seed for oil before moving to Waterside South in the 1850s. Here the surviving Doughty's Mill continued in operation through a succession of owners until 1985 and, fortunately, the building was the subject of a detailed study in 1998 (RCHME 1998) (Fig. 11.17). The large scale of Lincoln's milling attracted other types of food processing into the city, especially from the late 19th century. Pea-processing factories operated in Monson Street and Wigford Yard from the early 1900s, whilst Smith's Potato Crisps, now Walkers Snack Foods, opened their Newark Road factory in 1938. Confectionery was made by Poppleton's from 1880–1932 at their toffee factory at the east end of modern Beevor Street.

By the 18th century, barley had become one of Lincolnshire's major crops and Lincoln was an important producer of malt in the 18th and 19th centuries.

*Fig. 11.16. The Co-operative Flour Mill, Waterside North, from the south. The mill was built in 1886 and demolished, without record, in the 1960s (photo and copyright, Lincolnshire County Council, County Library Service, Local History Collection).*

*Fig. 11.17. Doughty's Mill, Waterside South. Being supplied by water, this mill was in operation before the arrival of the railways, but the surviving buildings were mostly built in 1863 and 1891. The building was the target of a recording project before its conversion to housing (RCHME 1988) (Plate 7.5) (photo and copyright, Lincolnshire County Council, County Library Service, Local History Collection).*

Although some malt was used in the city's own breweries, the majority was sold to the Midlands and Manchester. An account of 1836 reported that Lincoln had forty maltkilns and three quarters of their produce went to Manchester alone, a trade worth £40,000 a year (Hill 1974, 118). Even after the coming of the railways, the Fossdyke remained an important transport route for this commodity and, consequently, major maltings were situated on both Brayford Wharves, Waterside, Sincil Dyke, and the upper Witham from Brayford to Princess Street. The major Bass maltings complex, which survived until 2001 on Brayford Wharf North was the subject of a recording and research programme by Barlow (1984) (Fig. 11.18) before part of it was demolished. The remainder is currently still under threat. Further south, John Coupland's maltings in Lower Wigford were served by an artificially created inlet from the upper Witham, later filled in for the construction of Tealby Street and Henley Street *c*.1900. Thirty-one maltings, of which twelve were part of brewery sites, are recorded on the 1889 Ordnance Survey map. Most were probably purpose built, requiring extensive floor space, an exception being Dawber's maltings in the north range of the 12th-century St Mary's Guildhall, where malting had been taking place since at least the early 18th century. The St Mary's Guildhall maltings complex was the subject of detailed survey and excavation between 1982 and 1986 (Stocker 1991) (Fig. 11.19). The industry declined through the 19th century and the last major maltings (Thompson's Maltings immediately to the west of the GNR Honington Line in Milton Street) continued to operate until the Second World War.

Large-scale commercial brewing probably began in Lincoln *c*.1800. Many of the large brewers, such as Rudgard, Brook, Dawber and Winn, were also maltsters. Keyworth and Seely, and Rudgard had interests in malting and milling (Hill, 1974, 118). Bottled beer, ale and stout from Lincoln breweries were sold to national and international markets after the arrival of the railways in 1846, another example of the impact of the railways on the industrial development of the city. The same improved transport links, however, allowed competition from elsewhere into the city and local brewing declined steadily after the First World War. Hall's Crown Brewery on Norman Street was the only large brewery to survive into the 1930s.

Mineral water manufacturers and bottling companies enjoyed a period of success from the latter part of the 19th century, partly on the back of the city's successful brewing industry. J H Wright and Co.'s curiously named 'Botanical Brewery' occupied part of the former Dawber's Brewery on Carholme Road.

Fig. 11.18. *The germination floor of the former Bass, Ratcliffe and Gretton maltings on Brayford Wharf North. This structure was the subject of a detailed archaeological survey in 1983 (Barlow 1984). The western part has recently been demolished whilst the eastern is currently under threat (photo and copyright, Lincolnshire County Council, Museum of Lincolnshire Life).*

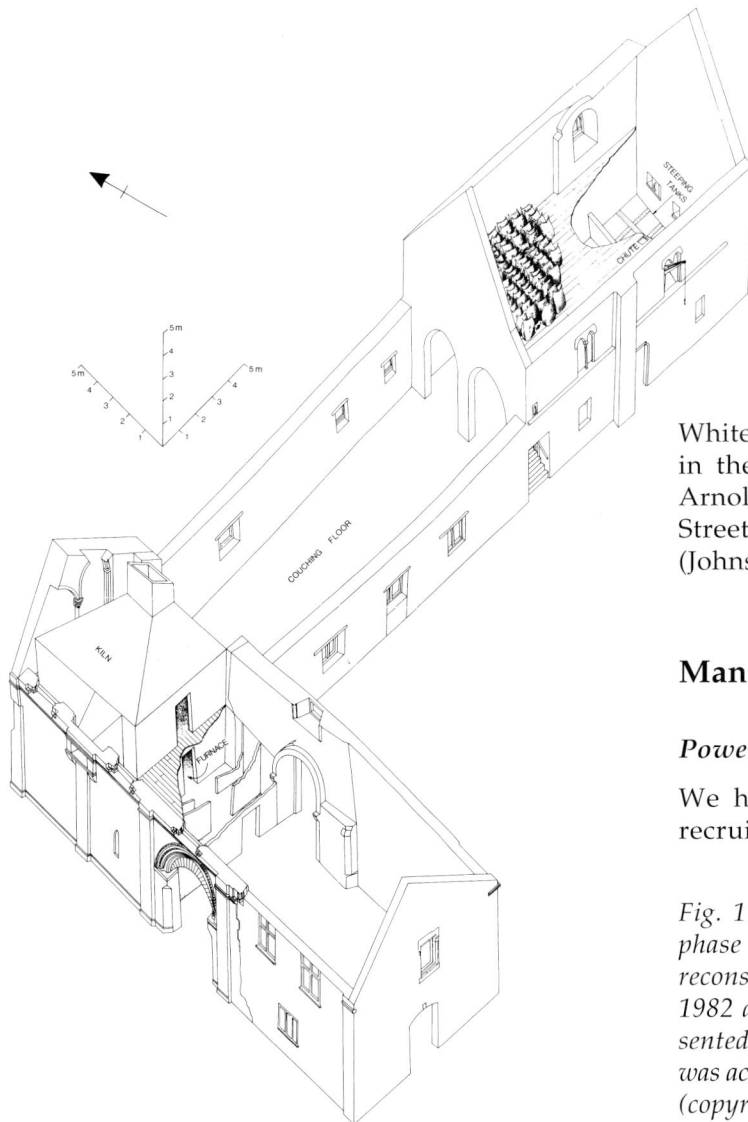

White's of Broadgate took over a business established in the 1860s and continued until 1961, and Frank Arnold's 1897 mineral water factory on St Rumbold Street is now part of Lincolnshire Archives Office (Johnson 1992).

## Manufacturing and allied industries

### Power supply

We have no real evidence that water-power was recruited on any scale by Lincoln industry in the

Fig. 11.19 (left). *Axonometric reconstruction of the final phase of malting at St Mary's Guildhall, Wigford, as reconstructed following archaeological recording between 1982 and 1986 (Stocker 1991). The kiln structures represented here probably date from after 1872, when the site was acquired by Dawber and Co, a well-known local brewery (copyright, City of Lincoln Archaeology Unit).*

earlier phases of the industrial revolution. The only major water powered mills of which we know are those in Bracebridge village (grinding corn) and the mill established at an uncertain date on Waterside North immediately west of High Bridge. We know very little about this mill, even though elements of its buildings still survive. It is likely that other mills (for both corn and other commodities) will have exploited the river in similar ways, by taking water off the main channel in bypass leats. The contribution of wind-power has already been discussed, and the topic of steam-power has been introduced. By the end of the 19th century, of course, Lincoln had become one of the main towns for the manufacture of mobile steam engines as well as of the components (such as boilers) for stationery ones. At one time or another engines were produced by all of the main engineering firms, but Ruston's, Clayton and Shuttleworth and Robey's were the best-known marques. Many Lincoln engines powered industrial machinery in Lincoln, as they did across the county, country and world.

Ironically, the large engineering plants of the 19th century increasingly used electricity to power the production of their mobile steam engines and several built their own generating stations or departments to supply electricity. Robey and Co. were the first, with a 3-engine, 100hp department on their Canwick Road site in the 1890s. Clayton and Shuttleworth's electric power station of 1914–16 was in a more favourable location in Spa Road, east of Stamp End, with railway sidings, room to expand and a faster river-flow for cooling water. The Corporation Electricity Works on Brayford Wharf North was not built until 1898 and despite increases in capacity and the construction of a

*Fig. 11.20. Interior of the City Electric Generation Station established on Brayford Wharf North in 1898. The building survives in a ruinous state and is currently under threat of demolition (photo and copyright, Lincolnshire County Council, County Library Service, Local History Collection).*

large rear building in 1913, it could not cope with the demand from industry (Fig. 11.20). It suffered from having no rail connection to bring in the large amounts of coal required to feed the turbines, relying instead on river barges. The Corporation struck a deal with Clayton's in 1919, who rebuilt their new power station to supply the city's needs – which it did until 1948, when the new St Swithin's Generating Station was completed on the same Spa Road site. Even so some large engineering companies continued to generate their own electricity; Ruston's owned two electricity stations by the 1920s.

Gas for street lighting was first supplied by the Lincoln Gas-Light and Coke Co. in 1829/30 from the Newland Gas Works between Waterside North and Carholme Road. The works used coal transported by canal to its wharf on Fossdyke. Another site was acquired across Carholme Road on the corner of Nelson Street, probably in the 1840s, where three replacement gas-holders were built by 1870. Gas continued to be produced here until 1932, but long before this, domestic and industrial demand had impelled a move to a larger site at Bracebridge. Bracebridge Gas Works had been in operation since 1876, but it was purchased by the Corporation in 1885 and totally reconstructed in 1932–3 and 1938–40, when demand rose considerably (Fig. 11.21). The Smith-Clayton Forge was a particularly heavy user of gas. The Bracebridge works were connected by railway siding to the Great Northern Railway (Honington Line), but there was no systematic recording of the plant when it was demolished in the early 1970s. The ruins of the important Newland Gas Works were the subject of a preliminary archaeological assessment in 1992 (RO 92 – Hockley 1992b). Clayton and Shuttleworth's Stamp End Works contained a two-holder gas works on the south side of Sincil Dyke in the 1880s, presumably for the production of their own gas. It is also known, from map evidence, that there were other private gas-holders at Hartsholme Hall and Monks Lane Stables.

### Extractive industry – stone and clay

Maps of the 19th century show several small limestone quarries, some disused, in the north-east part of the city in the areas near Greetwell Road, Wragby Road, Newport, Riseholme Road and Nettleham Road, where quarrying had been underway since the medieval period, if not earlier (p. 275–6 above and Fig. 9.92).

But these were all quite small-scale operations. Much more extensive ironstone quarrying and mining took place north of Monks Abbey, between Greetwell Road and Monks Road, from at least 1873–4, by the Mid Lincolnshire Ironstone Co. Their site was worked out by 1886, however, and activities were concentrated on the Greetwell Hollow quarry area, to the east, which continued production until 1939. During the lifetime of these quarries over four million tons were extracted manually and transported via narrow gauge

*Fig. 11.21. The new Lincoln Corporation Gas Works between the Newark Road (visible between the gas-holders) and the Grantham railway line (foreground), photographed in 1933. Gas production began here as early as 1875, but the site was greatly enlarged in 1932, 1938 and 1940. Most of it was demolished in 1972 without archaeological records being made (photo and copyright, Lincolnshire County Council, County Library Service, Local History Collection).*

horse-drawn tramway to Monks Abbey Sidings, to be taken via the Manchester, Sheffield and Lincolnshire Railway to steel works at Scunthorpe. Although they were sealed when exhausted, the stone mine adits, underground shafts and drifts are thought to remain (Brown 1971).

From a somewhat earlier date, stone quarried in Lincoln was being burnt to produce lime for the agricultural and building industries by several small concerns in the city. Five Lincoln lime burners are listed in an 1843 directory (Victor and Baker 1843). Open-cast limestone quarrying for hardcore has taken place east of modern Outer Circle Drive since the demise of the Greetwell Road mines and there remains one active 19th-century stone quarry within the city boundary, belonging to the Dean and Chapter of Lincoln Cathedral, east of Riseholme Road (Fig. 11.22).

Sand and gravel were extracted from the low-lying areas in the south-west part of the city, from Boultham Moor, and near the roads to Skellingthorpe and Doddington. There was a small sand pit on the Washingborough Road in the late 19th century. The railways needed large amounts of ballast and exploited the land to the west of Boultham Curve, and alongside the Midland Railway north of Doddington Road, where sidings were built.

We have seen that the local clays were used for brick-making in the Early Modern Era (RAZ 10.41), but brick remained a high status building material into the Industrial Era. Production had previously been in relatively small local kilns, sometimes established for a single job. There are, however, references to the city brick-maker and to brickyards in the Monks' Leys estate and in St Faith's parish in Newland in the early 18th century (Hill, 1956, 201, 211), which probably indicate production on a somewhat larger scale. The growth of

*Fig. 11.22. The Lincoln Cathedral Quarry. Although the quarries which provided the stone for its construction in the middle ages were much closer to the Cathedral itself (Fig. 9.92), this quarry off Ermine Street was opened in 1839 to provide stone for restoration work. The figure is Dr Peter Hill, Lincoln resident, Roman masonry expert and former Clerk of Cathedral Works (photo and copyright, D Stocker).*

Lincoln's population and industry from 1840–1900 created a large demand for cheap bricks for factories and housing which could not always be satisfied by Lincoln manufacturers, and imports were sometimes necessary (Hill, 1974, 124–5). Nineteenth-century maps record the locations of several brick-making sites, at West Parade close to West Common, Cross O' Cliff Hill, Greetwell Hollow and at Stamp End. John and Thomas Foster, owners of Foster's Brickyard in New-land, were also builders. The largest industrial brickworks within the city boundary, however, were probably the sites between Burton Road and Long Leys Road, belonging to the West Cliff Brick Works and the Albion Brick Works (Fig. 11.23). In 1889 the Lincoln Brick Company was formed from an amalgamation of two of the surviving Lincoln companies and two others at Waddington and Bracebridge. All the Lincoln brick-making sites had ceased production by c.1930, but manufacture continued at the Lincoln Brick Company's works at Bracebridge (just over the modern city boundary) until 1969 and at Waddington until the 1970s. Trade directories list brick and tile makers together, and further research would be necessary to establish the level of tile production. Only one of these major industrial sites has been the subject of modern archaeological study; the remains of the Cross O' Cliff Hill Brickworks have been surveyed by Stuart Squires (1992).

## Engineering and metal-working industries

Iron founding was the backbone of Lincoln's industrial prosperity in the second half of the 19th century (Fig. 11.3). The earliest foundry noted so far seems to have been Chambers' Foundry on Waterside South, which is first reported c.1813. By the time of Victor and Baker's 1843 *Directory*, three iron and brass founders are listed, along with five machine-makers and millwrights. It was from this modest skills base that the city's great engineering companies were to grow. The first business to develop into a national competitor was Clayton and Shuttleworth, who were based in the Stamp End Ironworks on Waterside South. When these premises were closed they were the subject of a preliminary survey by Catherine Wilson (1983) (Fig. 11.24). Clayton's neighbours to the west, Proctor and Burton were founded soon afterwards and (under the direction and ownership of Joseph Ruston from 1857) they were to out-perform the older firm (Fig. 11.25). Other foundries were soon established in the Waterside area, St Rumbold Street and Broadgate area, including the works of Robert Robey who first ventured into founding in 1854 in St Rumbold Street before moving to the large 'Globe Works' on Canwick Road later that same year (Fig. 11.26). Penney and Co. had a smaller works in Broadgate in 1854 and Richard Duckering had a similar establishment on Waterside North. The engineering companies founded in the 1840s and 50s (principally Foster's, Clayton and Shuttleworth, and Ruston and Proctor) were originally sited on Waterside North and South to utilise the Witham as a source of water and for transport of raw materials and products. But the railways, which arrived to the south of the works on Waterside South in the late 1840s, immediately took over the latter functions. This is no doubt why firms such as Foster's and Robey's, who had originally established themselves north of the river, expanded into new premises nearer the railway in the 1850s, It is also why firms like Clarke's Crank and

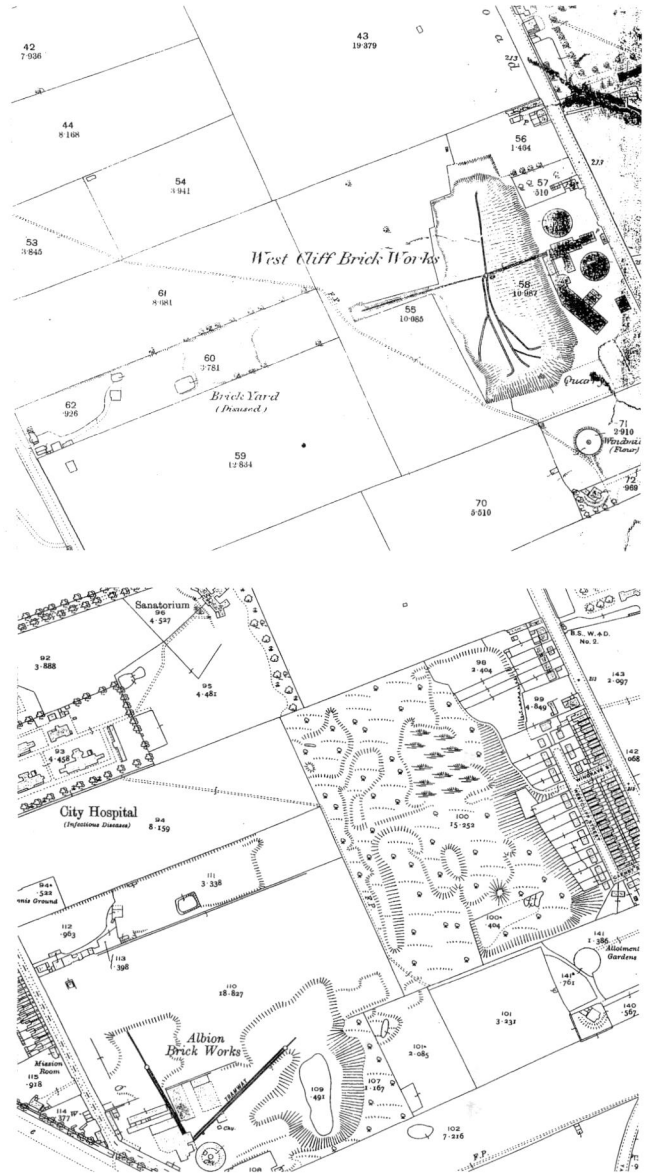

*Fig. 11.23. Plans of the large Albion and West Cliff brickworks complex between Long Leys Road and Burton Road, as depicted on the first edition Ordnance Survey map of 1889 (above) and on the third edition of 1930 (below). The West Cliff Brick Works seem to have been established on this large scale in 1860 and were demolished in 1911, whilst the Albion Works was constructed around 1900 and demolished about 1930. The circular structure at the Albion Works appears to be a circular 'Hoffman' kiln, and the circular structures at West Cliff Works could well be earlier examples of the same technology.*

Forge (founded in 1859) chose to build on land behind Ruston's, rather than anywhere near the river.

It was the transformation from heavy casting to precision engineering, however, that was to transform Lincoln's industrial economy. Clayton and Shuttleworth produced their first portable steam engine at their Stamp End Works in 1845 and, after success at the

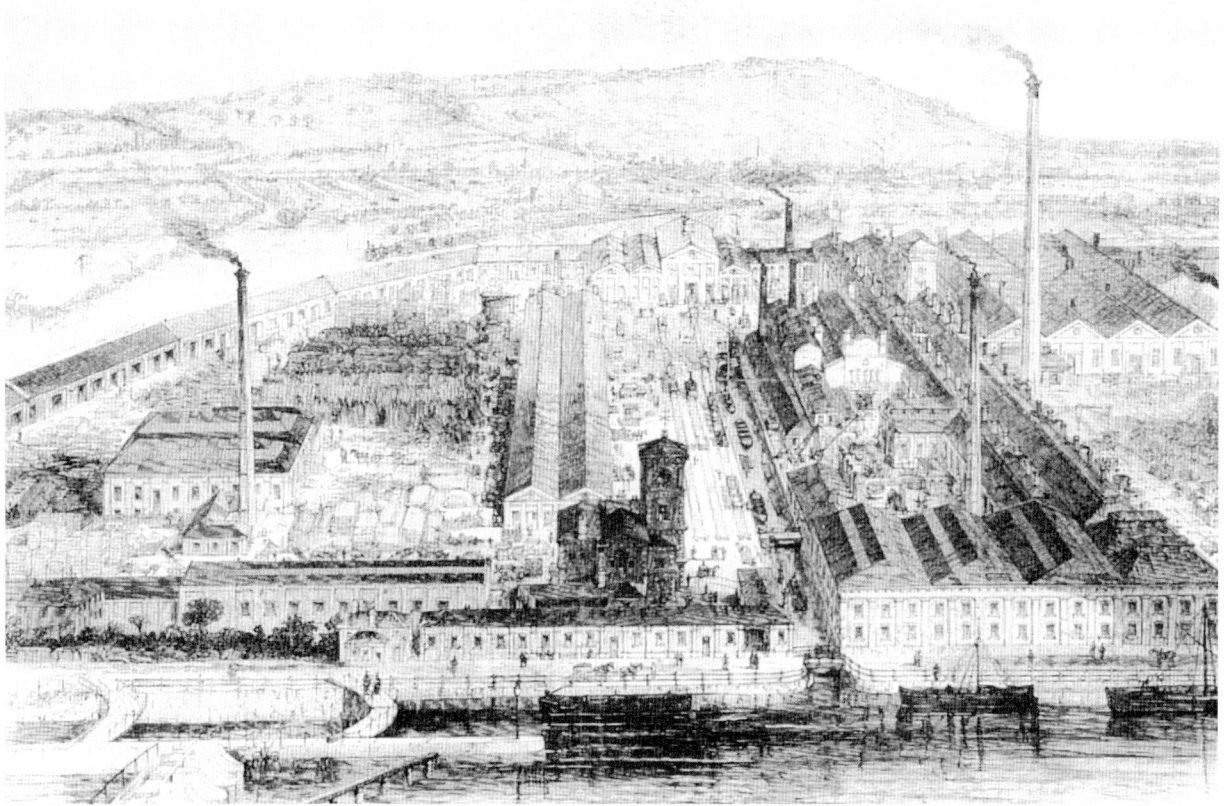

*Fig. 11.24. Panorama of Clayton & Shuttleworth's Stamp End Engineering Works on Waterside South, made in 1869. Founded on this site by 1842, Clayton's was the earliest of the large engineering concerns on which Lincoln's industrial revolution was based. South is at the top (see also Plate 8.1) (photo and copyright, Lincolnshire County Council, County Library Service, Local History Collection).*

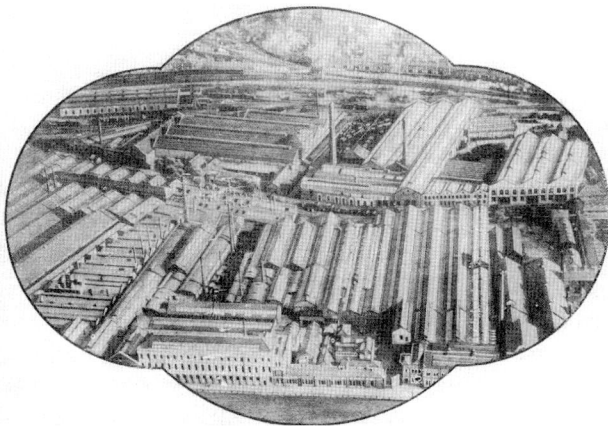

*Fig. 11.25. Enhanced aerial photograph of Ruston's Sheaf Iron Works on Waterside South in the 1930s. Ruston's became, perhaps, the most famous of all the Lincoln engineering firms. South is at the top (photo and copyright, Lincolnshire County Council, County Library Service, Local History Collection).*

Great Exhibition of 1851, expanded their production of steam engines and threshing machines to become the biggest such manufacturer in Britain (Fig. 11.27). By

1890 they had produced over 26,000 engines and 24,000 threshing machines. Like Clayton's, Ruston's and Robey's also specialised initially in the production of agricultural machinery: threshing machines, traction engines and portable steam engines. The years 1850 to 1880 witnessed a phenomenal growth in the demand for such products, not just across Britain but across Europe (particularly eastern Europe) and the World, and their manufacture transformed Lincoln from a county town into a major industrial centre. All of the major firms expanded and a second area of factories was opened west of Wigford, on the former carr lands south of the railway sidings that became known as New Boultham. The earliest plant in this area was the Ruston Sheaf Wood Works in Anchor Street in 1865, but they were soon followed by Foster's who transferred some of its operations to New Boultham (on the east side of modern Tritton Road), opening a wood-works on a 5-acre site in 1883 and moving there altogether in 1900. Having exhausted space on their Waterside South site, Ruston's eventually built their Boiler Works and Boultham Works on two sides of Foster's and, finally, the Spike Island Works on Beevor Street in 1915. The Ruston and Proctor Boiler Works on

*Fig. 11.26. Panorama (viewed from the west) of Robey's Globe Works on Canwick Road from a catalogue of 1898. The works was founded on this site in 1854, and although parts were demolished in 1986 without detailed archaeological record, important parts of the complex survive (photo and copyright, Lincolnshire County Council, County Library Service, Local History Collection).*

Firth Road were the subject of an archaeological study in 1984 (Betteridge 1985), but much of the remainder of this industrial landscape has gone since the 1960s without archaeological records being made. Clayton and Shuttleworth were able to expand eastwards from the Stamp End Works on both sides of the river (rather than join the other companies in New Boultham) and built, not only their electric power station (above), but also the Titanic Works, Abbey Works, and Tower Works between 1912 and 1916. All of these new heavy-engineering sites of the late Victorian and Edwardian period, at Waterside, Spa Road, New Boultham and Spike Island, were linked to the railway network by private sidings.

Towards the end of the 19th century, non-agri-cultural products began to be made. From the 1870s Ruston's were producing mechanical excavators, locomotives, traction engines, and steam-rollers. Foster's branched out into steam road vehicles in 1904. Robey's moved into mining and industrial engines, dynamos and gas and oil engines in the 1890s. The First World War saw the mobilisation of industry and Lincoln's factories rapidly adapted to the new de-mands, producing armaments, military vehicles, and

aircraft such as the Sopwith Camel (Figs. 11.1 and 11.28) and the Vickers Vimy bomber (at Clayton and Shuttle-worth's Abbey Works), and the 'Ruston biplane'. Foster and Co experimented with armoured fighting vehicles, resulting in the first military Tanks in 1916 (Lane 1997) (Fig. 11.29). After the war, however, the lucrative foreign markets for heavy agricultural engineering were lost, steam power was being overtaken by the internal combustion engine, and a decline ensued, with the city enduring high unemployment throughout the 1920s and 1930s. Despite continuing the production of railway rolling stock through a subsidiary, Clayton's never recovered from crippling losses incurred from heavy investment in pre-Revolutionary Russia. Its forge was sold to Thomas Smith's Stamping Works of Coventry in 1929, the enormous Titanic Works was sold to Clayton-Dewandre and the Stamp End Works to Babcock and Wilson in 1924. Ruston's joined with Hornsby's of Grantham in 1918 producing oil engines and locomotives, and went into partnership in the pro-duction of mechanical excavators with the American company Bucyrus-Erie in 1930 as Ruston-Bucyrus, and cut its ties with agriculture. Robey's went into tem-porary receivership in 1932, but through various

Fig. 11.27. *One example of the millions of machines built in Lincoln between the 1840s and the 1970s. This is a Clayton & Shuttleworth machine of about 1880, from a company advertisement (photo and copyright, Lincolnshire County Council, County Library Service, Local History Collection).*

Fig. 11.28. *A* Peters 2 *biplane being assembled in Robey's Globe Works in 1917 (photo and copyright, Lincolnshire County Council, County Library Service, Local History Collection).*

Fig. 11.29. *The* Hornet *tank built by Foster's at their Tritton Road Works. This example is being tested on the obstacle course built to the south of the factory in 1917 (the embankment of the 'avoiding line' can be seen in the background with the road bridge over Boultham Park Road) (photo and copyright, Lincolnshire County Council, County Library Service, Local History Collection).*

amalgamations, the works continued as a major employer into the 1980s.

Some of the companies that had started up at the same time as the engineering giants developed their own specialities and prospered well into the 20th century. J T B Porter's Gowts Bridge Works, of 1840, produced high quality ironwork, used for example in the construction of Doughty's Mill of 1891 (Fig. 11.17), the roof of the Drill Hall (1890) and the Montague Street Bridge. They were also gas engineers. Duckering made the ironwork for the Lincoln Corn Exchange in 1879 (Fig. 11.8), as well as a variety of agricultural machines, later specialising in kitchen ranges. These firms, together with Rainforth's and Foster's, supplied a variety of street furniture, such as street lamps, drain covers, handrail stanchions, pavement rain channels and street signs, examples of which are still in use (Fig. 11.9). John Cooke's Lindum Plough Works manufactured ploughs and agricultural vehicles until closure in 1937. After initial forays into steam-engine building, William Rainforth and Co. concentrated on agricultural implements, especially corn screens. They remained in their works on either side of Monks Road well into the 20th century, where they were conveniently placed for gatherings of farmers in the adjacent Cattle Market. Harrison's Lincoln Malleable Iron Works of St Mark's Street moved to North Hykeham and continued in business as part of Derby-based ironfounders, Ley's Malleable Castings.

*Wood-working industries.*

Timber for building and other purposes had been brought into the city for sale and use since time immemorial, and following the improvements of the 1740s, much of it now arrived via the Fossdyke and was stored in yards around Brayford Pool. Timber yards continued to have a presence here into the 20th century, and Hurst's Steam Sawmills were not founded until the 1890s. The biggest of the commercial saw mills was Newsum's, which began trading on the site which became the Drill Hall, Broadgate in 1856 and subsequently moved to land near the Pelham Street Crossing. Here it traded, as City Steam Mills, until 1918, with a short siding connecting it to the railway. It finally relocated to Carholme Road where it special-ised in pre-fabricated houses and precision joinery work, and where the rail link was maintained via a drawbridge over the Fossdyke to the Holmes marshal-ling yard. The company established timber plantations in the south-western parts of the modern District area, in Skellingthorpe and Boultham parishes, towards the end of the 19th century. In addition to these larger concerns working with timber, in the 19th century the city contained several smaller sawmills and yards, of which many were located off the lower High Street.

Timber was, of course, an essential material in the manufacture of agricultural implements, farm vehicles, coaches and the like. The large engineering companies were perhaps the largest users of timber, mainly for threshing machine bodies and other agricultural and transport vehicles and machines. Ruston's and Foster's both had separate wood-working factories, with extensive storage space, and part of Clayton's Stamp End site was also devoted to working timber. John Cooke's Lindum Plough Works south of Monks Road also produced a variety of timber-built carts and wagons from 1867 until its closure in 1937. The major engineering companies were not the only timber-workers in the industrial city, however. Lincoln had five coach-makers in 1843 (Victor and Baker 1843).

## Textile trades

We have seen that, by the 18th century, there was only a small amount of cloth being produced in Lincoln, and that exclusively for the local market. The in-dustrialised textile industry never became established in Lincoln. Sometimes it is said that this was because Lincoln lacked the water power which drove the Pennine textile mills, but water power was used in the city in the 18th and early 19th century, albeit on a small scale, and it is likely that more subtle factors, perhaps connected with the city's location on the transport networks, are more to blame. After all, we have already seen that the city was a focus for the collection of wool, and it was in order to ship fleeces to the West Riding that Ellison took the lease on Fossdyke in 1740. Ellison, evidently, thought it prudent to ship raw wool rather than to process it into cloth in the city and then ship the cloth.

We have also already seen that Benjamin Singleton and Co. (who joined with the brush maker Thomas

Flint in 1905) was an early producer of tarpaulins and waterproof covers for canal barges (p. 342 above). Later on the company found an even more lucrative market in providing tarpaulins, ropes and other textiles for the agricultural machinery and railway wagons produced by engineering companies like Clayton's, Ruston's and Foster's. A similar business was developed by Rainforth's at their rope-factory at the eastern end of Waterside South. William Rainforth, the company's founder, was originally a steam packet operator who also made barge sails and grain sacks. Singleton and Flint and Rainforth's were not the only producers of rope in Lincoln, however. The sites of 10 ropemakers are shown on the 1:500 scale Ordnance Survey maps of 1887–9 in various parts of the city. The essential requirements for such factories were simple; a supply route, for the sisal or other yarn (usually provided by the railway), and a long narrow piece of land for the twisting process.

The only attempt at large-scale textile production in Lincoln in the Industrial Era was made by W Patterson and Son when they founded their silk mill on Brayford Wharf East in 1878. It used steam power and had 200 female workers in the 1880s (Fig. 11.30). There was also a small textile factory on the corner of

*Fig. 11.30. Brayford Wharf East from the north about 1900. Amongst the tall buildings in the middle distance is Patterson's Silk Mill founded in 1871 and demolished in 1971 without archaeological record (photo and copyright, Lincolnshire County Council, County Library Service, Local History Collection).*

they were in previous times. Zoning in housing types has been a theme throughout the *Assessment* but, in the Industrial Era, the division between different types of housing appears particularly marked. Similarly the scale of Victorian industry meant that the large employers operated in dedicated industrial zones, where little else besides manufacture occurred (Fig. 11.3).

It is not just the distinctive character of the different zones which archaeology should seek to elucidate, of course, but the connections between them. Such connections might be physical (communications systems like railways, trams or buses) but they are also connections for the supply and dispatch of materials. The industrial factories, and other institutions needed to be well sited to prosper. They needed to have appropriate routes of supply for their raw materials, they needed power to convert such materials into products, and they also needed distribution routes through which the manufactures were sold.

The research agenda for the Industrial Era in Lincoln has been subdivided into a total of 158 RAZs, which have been grouped into the same blocks found useful in the High Medieval and Early Modern Eras (economic infrastructure, housing, industrial areas, victualling and supply, administration, defence, the church and education). These RAZs can be accessed via the CD-Rom. Finally, by way of introduction, a comment about the mapping of RAZs in the Industrial Era is necessary. In earlier Eras, the boundaries which apply to many research questions can only be plotted approximately but, in the Industrial Era, the enormously better documentation allows us to map many of the component boundaries precisely. In particular the first edition 1:500 scale map from the Ordnance Survey (surveyed and published 1887–9) provides boundaries for many of the components or groups of components for which we are proposing research agendas. Consequently in the boundaries of the component in many of the RAZ entries that follow, are derived from the boundaries mapped on this map.

## Economic infrastructure

The city's great industries, which fuelled the economic expansion characteristic of this Era, could not have existed without a well-founded transport infrastructure. Indeed, we have seen above that it was probably only the development of the transport network, and especially the coming of the railways, which enabled Lincoln to develop as a significant industrial centre in the first place. Archaeology is an excellent tool, of course, for discussing the radical changes in the city's commercial networks of the Industrial Era. Many of the research questions posed in the long list of 35 RAZs, which have been identified to deal with questions surrounding the development of the city's transport infrastructure, focus not only on the tech-

nology of the transport systems themselves, but on the impact the arrival of those systems had on manufactures and marketing in the city more widely. The transport infrastructure RAZs are as follows:

|        |                                              |
|--------|----------------------------------------------|
| 11.1   | Stamp End lock and causeway                  |
| 11.2.1 | Brayford's eastern waterside                 |
| 11.2.2 | Brayford's northern waterside                |
| 11.3.1 | Fossdyke, Brayford and Witham navigations    |
| 11.3.2 | Montague Street bridge                       |
| 11.3.3 | Footbridge at East Holmes Upper Witham       |
| 11.4.1 | Sincil Dyke                                   |
| 11.4.2 | Lincoln West Drainage Scheme and Gowts Drain |
| 11.4.3 | Pumping house Boultham Junction              |
| 11.4.4 | Pumping engine Pyewipe Junction              |
| 11.4.5 | Footbridge on Fossdyke over Main Drain       |
| 11.4.6 | Little Bargate Bridge                        |
| 11.5.1 | Stamp End dock and boat-building yard        |
| 11.5.2 | Brayford pool boat-building yard             |
| 11.6.1 | Long distance road routes                    |
| 11.6.2 | Bracebridge Bridge                           |
| 11.6.3 | Bargate toll bar and cottage                 |
| 11.6.4 | Gowts Bridge                                 |
| 11.6.5 | High Bridge and ford                         |
| 11.7.1 | Intermediate road routes                     |
| 11.7.2 | Toll bar at Canwick Road                     |
| 11.7.3 | Bridges at Bishop's Bridge                   |
| 11.7.4 | Victoria Bridge                              |
| 11.8.1 | Local road routes                            |
| 11.8.2 | Holmes Bridge                                |
| 11.8.3 | Firth Road bridge                            |
| 11.8.4 | Thorn Bridge, Melville Street                |
| 11.8.5 | St Mary's Bridge                             |
| 11.9   | Tram system                                  |
| 11.10  | Motor transport system                       |
| 11.10.1 | City Bus Garage, St Mark's Street           |
| 11.10.2 | Bus garage Burton Road                      |
| 11.10.3 | Motor engineers workshop, Scorer Street     |
| 11.10.4 | Motor garage and workshop Rudgard Lane, West Parade |
| 11.11  | Railway transport network                    |

During the discussions resulting in the Lincoln *Assessment* it soon became clear that the city has always been structured around its market places, which in addition to the transportation routes themselves, are the complementary part of the city's economic infrastructure. This perception is reflected in the numbers of RAZs identified for market sites in earlier Eras, alongside those for items of transport infrastructure. By the

Industrial Era, of course, we have more or less complete documentation for the city's markets, and this tells us that the great bulk of city production was sold in the industrial exchanges and marts of Europe and the Empire. As was the case with Lincoln cloths in the High Medieval Era, then, in the Industrial Era, few if any of the city's staple manufactures (heavy machinery of various types) were sold in the city itself. Lincoln's market was once again national and international. Lincoln was once again connected with national and international markets on a scale that had not been seen since *c.*1300. Consequently, although the Industrial Era included times of great economic prosperity for the city, ironically, relatively little impact of this is seen in the layout and structure of city's markets themselves. The city's market continued to be located in and near the High Street, where it had been relocated during the 16th century (RAZ 10.20.2, 10.22.9). The Industrial Era saw, however, a move away from the High Street itself into and around specialised buildings: The Cornhill, *The General Market* and *The Butchery*. This move into permanent quarters is an interesting manifestation of growing civic wealth and pride and deserves further investigation, which is recommended in several of the RAZs (see also Schmiechen and Carls 1999). But alongside the development of purpose-built structures for communal markets, an even more important factor driving trade off the streets themselves must have been the development of private shops, which, by *c.*1900 lined both sides of High Street in Upper Wigford as well as High Street north of the Stonebow and many subsidiary streets in the Lower City. Four RAZs have been identified which deal with this important aspect of the city's industrial archaeology:

11.21 Market Hill, the High Street from St Mary-le-Wigford to St Martin's parish
11.22 Market place at Castle Hill
11.23 Swine and beast market
11.24 The shambles, Clasketgate

## Housing the people

The Industrial Era was a time of dramatic physical expansion in Lincoln's traditional suburbs of Wigford, *Butwerk*, Newland and Newport, starting during the late 18th century and gaining speed during the 19th century (RAZs 11.25–27). By the early years of the 20th century almost every available space within the city's traditional suburbs had been developed. Expansion beyond the traditional limits started in the late 19th century and has continued, in fits and starts, up to the present day (RAZs 28–34). To the south of the city, the villages of Bracebridge, North Hykeham and Boultham have now been swallowed up within the suburbs of Lincoln, although local government boundaries still do not reflect this reality, and the 1974 City District boundary (which defines this *Assessment*) cuts ar-

bitrarily through modern suburban development to the south. To the north, however, the suburban expansion has been kept within the confines of the city's former open fields (the Enclosure Act was passed in 1803 – 43 George III Cap 120 – ed. Birch 1906, 63 No.511).

Lincoln saw two phases of great expansion of the housing stock for the lower orders of society. The first (represented by a single RAZ – 11.25) was a sudden increase in the number of modest cottages in the city in the century between about 1740 and 1840. This building boom was largely undertaken without planning and was achieved, often, merely by subdividing existing plots and properties to create cramped overcrowded dwellings and to maximise profits for landlords. It is no coincidence that this type of housing is very rare in the city today – what was not condemned in the 19th century was swept away by slum clearance in the 1920s and 30s. Even so the archaeological remains of this type of housing are of great interest (even though largely ignored hitherto) and the RAZ seeks to define a number of research questions which can help us understand the management of the expanding working population of the city before the coming of the railways and, along with them, Victorian social philanthropy.

First, however, came the 'false start' of the Chartists. In the late 1840s a small estate east of Brant Road, in the southern part of the District, became one of the Chartist Land Company's first colonies and, although these idealistic attempts to convert part of the working class into a 'free peasantry' are conventionally viewed as failures, the sites themselves are rich archaeological resources, allowing us to investigate many aspects of working class culture in the mid 19th century (RAZ 11.29.1). In fact, Lincoln has also retained large areas of good-quality working class housing erected by the new generations of more socially aware (and frequently Dissenting) capitalists. These houses represented a more realistic solution to working class deprivation than the Chartist colonies, and it is important that the value of these estates as archaeology is appreciated in future development work (RAZ 11.26). Such housing is the direct ancestor of the socially conscious housing schemes of the 20th century, of which there are several important examples in Lincoln. These schemes are not conventionally viewed in the city as heritage assets, but they are undoubtedly of great importance to Lincoln's history and development – hence the generation here of research agendas to explore them in future (RAZs 11.29.2, 11.30, 11.32).

Housing for the middle and upper classes of Victorian society is also well-represented in Lincoln, even though several of the key monuments have been demolished (e.g. Eastcliffe House and Monk's Manor). Here too important questions about the development of the city, and about the relationships between the social classes can be addressed through the archaeological record (RAZs 11.27, 11.28, 11.31). The complete list of RAZs aimed at exploring Industrial Era housing issues is as follows:

11.19.2 Bracebridge Hall
11.20    Boultham & Boultham Hall
11.25    Working class housing of late 18th and early 19th centuries in Newport, the Bail, Lower City and Wigford
11.26    Working class housing estates c.1850–1945 in Newport, Newland, Butwerk, Wigford and elsewhere
11.27    Housing in the Close and Eastgate
11.28    Newly built Victorian housing for the middle and upper classes c.1850–1918
11.29.1 Swanpool Garden Suburb
11.29.2 Chartist Colony in Brant Road
11.30    St Giles Estate
11.31    Middle class house building between the wars
11.32    'Prefabs' at Grainsby Close, Bracebridge
11.33    Bishop's Palace
11.34    Hartsholme Hall

## Feeding the city and the supply of staples

In an Era of more rapid and efficient communication, the supply of food and drink to the city could be organised in completely different ways. The vast bulk of such supplies came into the city through canals, along roads and, eventually, along the railways (see RAZs 11.1 – 11.11). Consequently it is quite clear that, in the Industrial Era, the agricultural area immediately around the city was no longer relied on to produce food and other supplies for the city itself. This was particularly true, of course, after the Enclosure Act of 1803. After that date, and the division of the city's hinterland into free-standing farms, the produce of the area surrounding the city went into a regional, or even national commodity market, being shipped towards wholesalers first by cart and canal and then by rail. This means that the research agendas for the areas around the city in this Era are much more closely related to the development of the agricultural and other industries regionally and nationally than they are to the development of the city itself. That does not mean, however, they are of less interest to us today. A great deal can be learnt about the industrialisation of farming and related industries in the 19th century through targeted research on individual sites and areas, and this has been recommended in the nine RAZs which follow:

11.12    Woodlands and wood-pasture to the south-west
11.13    The wetlands
11.14    Enclosed pasture and meadow east and west of the city
11.15.1 Un-enclosed pasture west of Newland, and West Common

11.15.2 Bracebridge pastures
11.16    South Common
11.17    City's arable fields
11.18    Open fields of parishes of Nettleham and Greetwell
11.19.1 Bracebridge village

## City Industries

Rather than devote a single RAZ to each manufacturing concern, a list of fifteen distinct industries has been allocated research agendas, and some of these RAZs are scattered in many different locations within the city. It was felt that exploring the minutiae of the development of each business was less important (and more easily achieved using documentary sources) than investigating the broader patterns in the development of the industry in the city as a whole. Similar approaches have been followed in much of the most influential writing on industrial archaeology in the past few decades (eg. Palmer and Neaverson 1998), and it underlies the approach adopted in English Heritage's MPP surveys of English Industry (Stocker 1995). Some of the Lincoln industries (such as quarrying and food-processing) developed out of small-scale industrial enterprises already active in the city, and it is extremely important that we understand this development. In the case of other industries, however, it is not really understood why they should become so successful in Lincoln particularly. The heavy engineering industry provides the most spectacular example of this second group – why should such an industry have been so successful in Lincoln, remote from the supply of the raw materials and, originally, with only a small skilled workforce? In addition to questions about their origins, in the case of each industry, the research agenda has been drawn up to ensure that its technological development is investigated in future work. In many cases, also, the RAZs propose investigations of the relationships between the industries and the social context in which they were set. The RAZs defined to deal with Lincoln's industries are:

11.35   Smithies
11.36   Heavy engineering works
11.37   Animal processing industries
11.38   Food processing industries & brewing industry
11.39   Textile industries
11.40   Wood processing industries
11.41   Quarries
       11.41.1 Clay quarries in the cliff face north-west and south of city
       11.41.2 Stone and clay quarries in the cliff face east of the city
       11.41.3 Quarries in the cliff face south of the city

11.41.4 Stonepits north and north-east
of the Upper City
11.41.5 The Cathedral Quarry,
Riseholme Road
11.41.6 Artificial stone manufacturers
11.41.7 Gravel quarries
11.42 Brick and tile manufacture
11.43 Chemical industries
11.44 Gas production industry
11.45 Electricity production industry
11.46 Water supply industry
11.47 Sewage industry
11.48 Laundry industry
11.49 Banking industry

## City and county administration

Documentary records for the administration of the industrial city are profuse and, in this part of the research agenda, we have to be particularly clear about the additional contribution that can be made by archaeology. We must aim to ensure that the archaeological information is consistent with the documentation, but also that the archaeological debate is taken into areas which are not accessible through documentary history. This group of zones includes a number which have developed out of the administrative structures and systems of earlier periods (RAZs 11.64, 11.65, 11.66, 11.67, 11.69). In each of these cases the challenge for archaeology is to explore the changes brought about by industrialisation on the structures within which these activities were housed (Plate 7.1). The 19th century also saw local and national administration take responsibility for a long list of additional functions, aimed at improving the lot of different groups within society. These new 'additional' functions ranged from health provision to recreation and their development was a fundamental aspect of Victorian culture. The 25 RAZs defined here are intended to provide a starting point for the archaeological exploration of these structures, sites and functions (RAZs 11.50 – 11.54, 11. 72, 11.73, 11.76 – 11.79):

11.50 Fire stations
11.51 Police stations
11.52 Hospitals
11.52.1 County Hospital, Drury Lane
11.52.2 County Hospital, Sewell Road
11.52.3 Isolation Hospitals around
West Common
11.52.4 Bromhead Nursing Home
11.53 Lunatic Asylum (The Lawn Hospital)
11.54 Dispensaries
11.64 The Stonebow
11.65 The Sessions House
11.66.1 New County Hall (assize court
in Castle)
11.66.2 The Judge's Lodgings

11.67 Prisons
11.68 The House of Industry, the Workhouse and the House of the Girl's Friendly Society
11.69 Gallows
11.70 Upper City (County) Assembly Rooms
11.71 Lower City (City) Assembly Rooms
11.72 City Library, Free School Lane
11.73 The Usher Gallery
11.74 Theatres and Cinemas
11.75 Private Clubs
11.76 Public Parks and Gardens
11.77 The Racecourse
11.78 Sports grounds
11.79 Swimming pools

## Education

In the same way that the organs of local and national administration took on responsibility for the provision of a wide range of public services in the industrial city, as it expanded, education (at least of the lower orders) also came to be seen as a largely public responsibility. Thus, compared with Eras that preceded it, the list of RAZs exploring educational structures in the Industrial Era is quite long and is dominated by buildings and sites under public, or semi-public, control. In the archaeology of educational structures, the dialogue between the different orders in society can be especially clearly heard, and although there has been very little archaeological work done on such sites and structures, they offer an important resource for future research. The nine RAZs defined with the aim of exploring the archaeology of education during the Industrial Era are as follows:

11.55 The Mechanics' Institute
11.56 School of Science and The Arts (The City School)
11.57 Lincoln Upper Grammar School (Upper Lindum Street site)
11.58 Girls' High School
11.59 Lincoln School (Wragby Road site)
11.60 Christ's Hospital (Bluecoats School), Christ's Hospital Terrace
11.61 Elementary Schools
11.62 Diocesan Training College (Bishop Grosseteste's College)
11.63 Theological College

## Defending the city

Defence remained an issue in Lincoln in the Industrial Era, albeit that most of the defence structures identified as RAZs were primarily aimed at external, rather than internal, enemies. However, although the RAF bomber base at Skellingthorpe (RAZ 11.86) was clearly not aimed at defending factions within the city from their own countrymen, some of the other installations were certainly designed (at least partly) to be secure against civil insurrection – the Depot and the Militia barracks (RAZs 11.81–83) for example. In addition to their value as evidence for military history, then, even the defence structures of the Industrial Era can be seen partly as evidence for the interplay of different power blocks within the city. Alongside their intrinsic research interest, the broader value of these sites as evidence for relationships between different groups in society, is taken up in many of the ten RAZs that follow:

11.80   The Close Wall
11.81   The Depot
11.82   The Militia barracks
11.83   The Sobraon barracks
11.84.1 Drill Hall, Broadgate
11.84.2 Rifle butts on South Common
11.85.1 Reception aerodrome on West
        Common 1915–18
11.85.2 Tank testing ground west of
        Boultham Park Road
11.86   Skellingthorpe airfield
11.87   Anti-Tank walls and perimeter
        defences 1939–45.

## Church and chapel

The church in the Industrial Era has not been greatly studied by archaeologists, although the period is included amongst the most important recent surveys of the urban church at the national level (Morris 1989 and eds. Blair and Pyrah 1996). Both studies emphasise the interrelationship between the church and the community in which it sits, as of all its structures, the church is likely to be that in which the growth and development of the community can be most easily read. Fourteen Lincoln parish churches were sufficiently robust communities to survive the long Early Modern Era (RAZs 11.91.1–16), and all were able to take advantage of the great revival in church-going which characterised the 19th century. But by this period, of course, the Anglican establishment was being seriously challenged by Dissenters of various types (RAZs 11.93–97). The archaeology of Dissent has not been extensively studied, despite the existence of a useful national research agenda (CBA 1985). Even though many key buildings have already been demolished, Lincoln still retains a valuable resource (both above and below ground) for the study of this aspect of religious history. Research agendas for sites associated with the Dissenters could have been established congregation by congregation (as they have been for the Anglican church) but it was felt that the benefits of studying each congregation individually

was outweighed by those gained when the sect was studied as a group.

The rapidly increasing population of later 19th-century Lincoln meant that there was greatly increased pressure on burial space in the cemeteries, and it was decreed that all cemeteries below hill should be closed by 1854, on health grounds (Mills 2001, 141). Although of recent date, these burial populations are of great paleopathological interest and some of the most interesting work within modern paleopathology has been done with populations like these (e.g. Molleson and Cox 1993). In particular, burial populations of this Era can tell us about the impact of the Industrial Revolution on the health of the population and about the environment more generally. The RAZs identified for the purposes of research (Plate 8.1) into the religious sites of the Industrial Era are as follows:

11.88  The Cathedral
11.89  The College of the Vicars-Choral
11.90  St Anne's Bedehouses
11.91  Anglican churches on ancient sites
       11.91.1  St Peter Eastgate
       11.91.2  St Margaret Pottergate
       11.91.3  St Benedict
       11.91.4  St Botolph
       11.91.5  St Mark
       11.91.6  St Mary-le-Wigford
       11.91.7  St Peter-at-Gowts
       11.91.8  St Paul-in-the-Bail
       11.91.9  St Mary Magdalene
       11.91.10 St Michael-on-the-Mount
       11.91.11 St Michael's Graveyard
                (formerly St Cuthbert)
       11.91.12 St Martin (original site)
       11.91.13 St Martin's Graveyard
                (formerly St Mary *Crackpole*)
       11.91.14 St Peter-at-Arches
       11.91.15 St Swithin old church
       11.91.16 St Nicholas, Newport
                (original site)
       11.91.17 All Saints, Bracebridge
       11.91.18 St Helen, Boultham
11.92  Anglican Churches on new sites
       11.92.1  All Saints, Monks Road
       11.92.2  St Andrew, Canwick Road
       11.92.3  St Faith, Charles Street West
       11.92.4  St Giles, Lamb Gardens
       11.92.5  St Martin, West Parade (new
                site)
       11.92.6  St Matthias, Burton Road
       11.92.7  St Nicholas, Newport (new
                site)
       11.92.8  St Swithin (new site)
       11.92.9  Holy Cross, Skellingthorpe
                Road
       11.92.10 St Matthew, Boultham Park
                Road

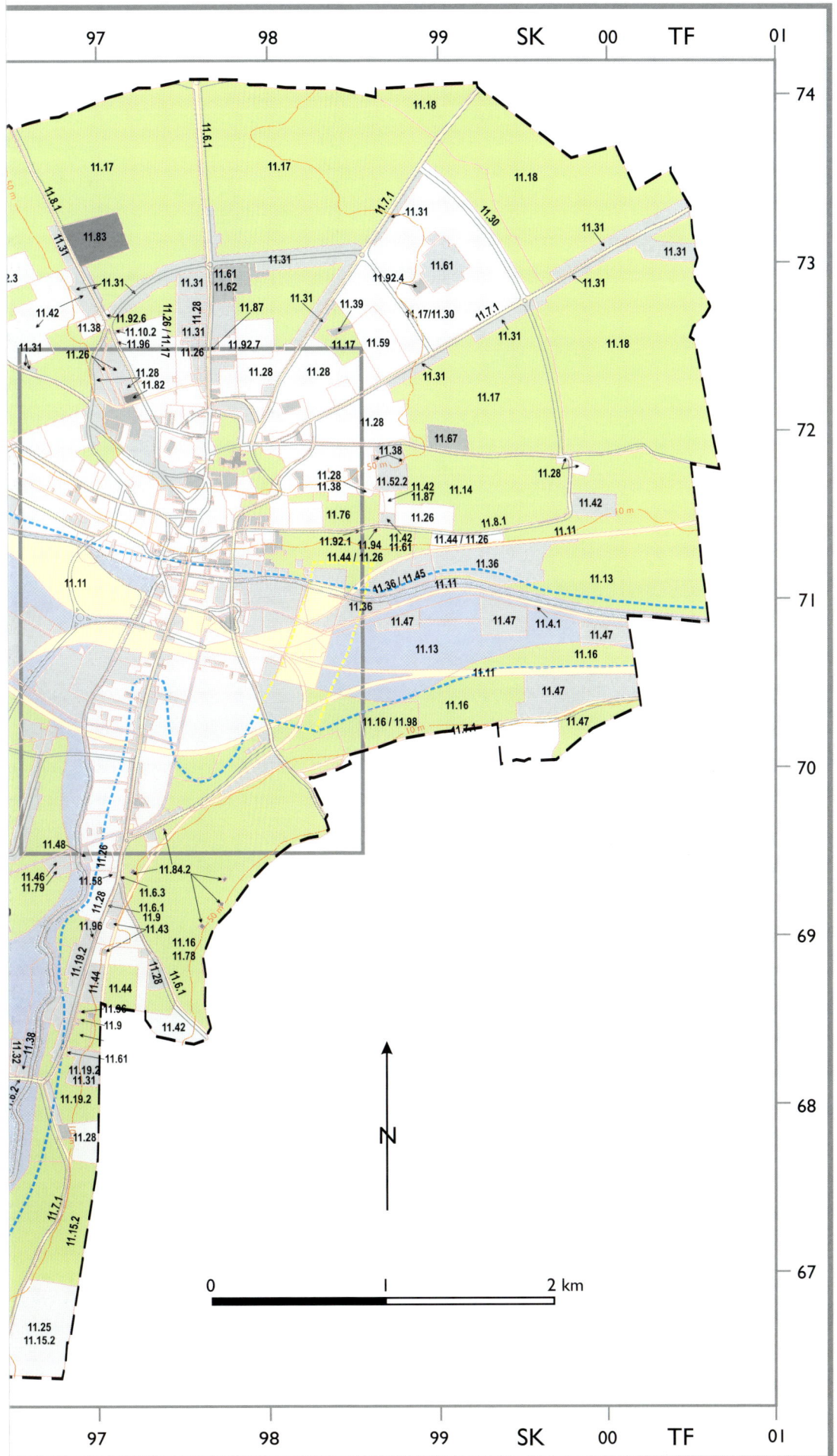

*Map 7. Research Agenda Zone locations for the Industrial Era – See CD-Rom for details (drawn by Dave Watt, copyright English Heritage and Lincoln City Council).*

72

71

70

N

1 km

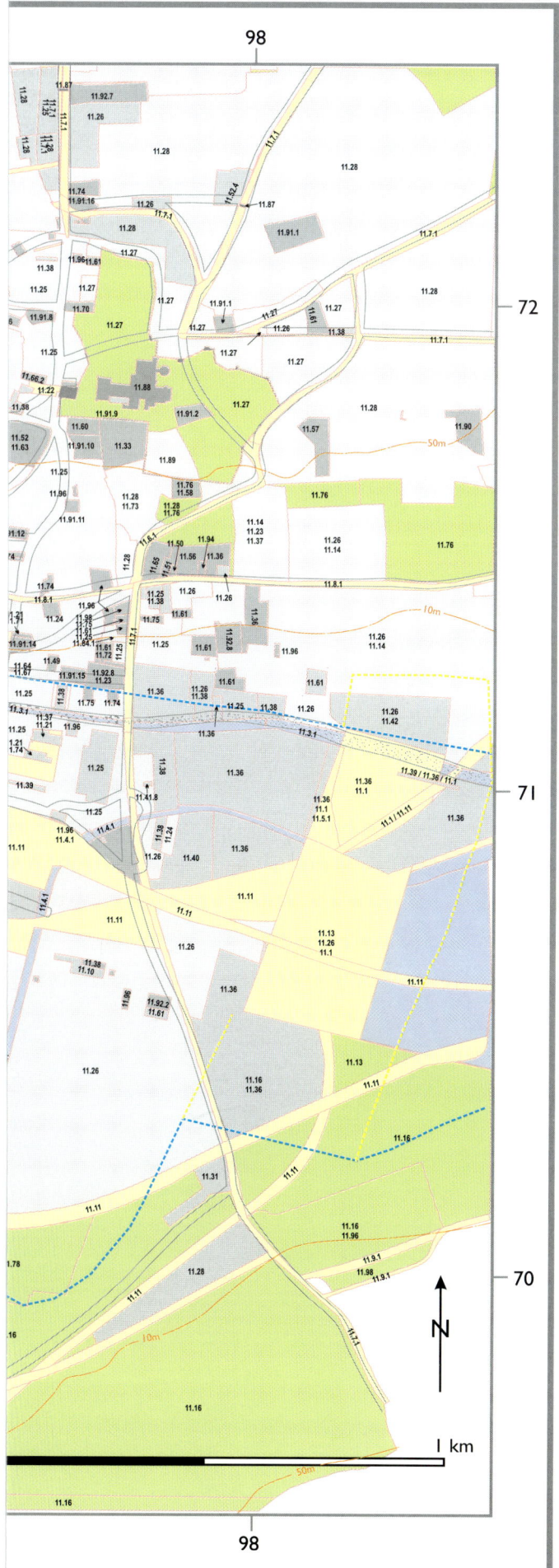

*Agenda Zone locations for the Industrial Era – See CD-Rom*
*Watt, copyright English Heritage and Lincoln City Council).*

# 12. Afterword

## David Stocker

## Assessing urban assessment

In this final section we should look briefly at the success, or otherwise, of the methodology evolved for this *Assessment* and especially for LARA. But before we look at Lincoln itself, we should recall Martin Carver's wise advice that 'each town creates its own version of its own history, and treads it underfoot' (1993, 1). Although archaeologists may find some of the work done in Lincoln valuable in preparing assessments of other towns, it is highly likely that the features of future assessments will vary from place to place. Eventually, when more comparable assessments have been completed, we will be able to compare variables across many towns. For example, it will be instructive, eventually, to compare Lincoln's RAZ list (Appendix 2) with similar lists from other cities. Presumably nothing will encapsulate the distinctiveness of Lincoln more succinctly than a comparison of its RAZ list with such lists from other English towns.

In Lincoln we took it as a fundamental tenet that the effective way to manage the urban archaeological resource was through a research agenda. To quote Carver again (and even more memorably), 'without a research purpose [archaeological] deposits remain mud' (*Ibid.*, 13). As explained in the paper reprinted here as Appendix I, LARA is primarily a research agenda, aimed at the practical management of Lincoln's urban archaeology. But because it is complete, both geographically and chronologically, it is also a 'characterisation' of the type English Heritage is now pioneering and recommending to Planning Authorities as an additional tool in the heritage-management tool-kit.

The members of the Lincoln assessment team were clear that, within the research agenda, Era divisions were absolutely necessary for the *Assessment* process, but deciding where the boundaries between some Eras should be drawn was very controversial. The Era boundaries we eventually chose are, of course, quite appropriate for Lincoln, but they would probably have been less so for York or Stamford. In particular, the decision to deal with the Roman *Colonia* Era as a unified whole rather than dividing the 2nd and 3rd centuries from the 4th century proved problematic; as was the decision to divide the High Medieval Era from the Early Modern Era at *c.*1350, rather than *c.*1300 (on the one hand) or *c.*1540 (on the other). In the event the validity of both of these decisions was demonstrated only once the RAZs had been created – and a number of RAZ texts have been written with such chronological overlaps in mind. As in so many projects, we found that an initial leap of faith was required at this early stage, which permitted work to proceed to the point where we could analyse the quality of our initial thinking.

Martin Carver also advised us that 'the research agenda is not a simple thing to be tacked together overnight by one person' it must be, instead, 'an open debate not a final statement' (*Ibid.*, 15). With the limited time and budget allowed, however, we were aware that we would not be able to conduct a wide-ranging consultation on the RAZ texts and, as a substitute, we evolved an internal 'brainstorming' technique through which they have all been sharpened. For this 'brainstorming', an initial draft of all the RAZ texts for a single Era was produced, and the team then debated each Era, RAZ by RAZ, taking a maximum of one Era per day. Some of the alterations which arose out of these 'brainstorming' sessions were merely corrections of fact, but many involved the introduction and interconnection of research themes and directions which would prove useful in generating the final account of the Era in question. This process has meant, of course, that Lincoln's research agenda is the product of the expertise and interests of the project team. Even though the team had been given the *imprimatur* of the Lincoln City Council Planning Office (via the city's archaeological 'curator', the City Archaeologist), we remain acutely aware that every one of the RAZ texts could, and should, be greatly improved. Ideally, the City Archaeologist would have called in expert advisors (and indeed the general public) to a much larger number of similar 'brainstormings' on each RAZ, or on groups of RAZs to ensure that the agenda proposed had the maximum support within the profession and outside.

Although comments on a number of RAZs were sought from external experts, we are aware that many could be improved further. And we hope that they will be, as an important aspect of LARA is its developmental character. LARA is viewed by the *Assessment* team as no more than a starting point, and we hope that each and every RAZ will be substantially revised in future by all who encounter it. We envisage that LARA will be regularly updated long into the future, and we recognise that, in fifty years' time, it is certain that most of our current research questions will have been replaced by others, which we cannot even imagine at present. This developmental aspect of LARA has been recognised not only in the provision made for updating whilst designing the computer system, and the administrative framework within which it operates, but also in the allocation of time within the City Archaeologist's future work programme for regular updating. At present it is envisaged that such updating will take place approximately once every five years, in line with the cyclical review of other aspects of Local Planning – but it may turn out to be a more continuous process than this implies.

We will have to wait to see whether revised versions of LARA will be published as books in future, and whether any such re-publication will be accompanied by discursive 'accounts' like those above. There will, however, always be a need for professionals in the city to communicate with the broader public and to explain advances in our understanding. LARA, of course, is designed to provide the framework for such communication. As we have already explained, the character of the large archaeological accounts in this volume has arisen from the amalgamation of the project aiming to synthesise the results of city excavations with the project to create an assessment of its archaeology suitable for use within the Planning structure. It remains to be seen what type of 'archaeological account' might be produced in Lincoln in future to accompany revised versions of LARA, but it seems likely that a free-ranging discussion of some type will be necessary.

Finally, then, we have to ask whether LARA fulfils the purpose set out for it. Does it, on the one hand, characterise Lincoln's archaeology in a useful and accessible form so that it can be used both by the Planning system and by the wider public? And is it, on the other hand, sufficiently rigorous as a research agenda to command professional support? To take the second question first, we have already given our reasons, and apologies, for the lack of professional validation for the RAZ texts, and we have explained that the City Archaeologist's intention is to begin the process of developing more informed research agendas through wider consultation – a process we see as continuing into the foreseeable future. Although we have found Martin Carver's advice on urban assessment invaluable in developing our thinking about

urban assessment, however, the reader will notice that we have made very little use of Lincoln's 'deposit model', which was created at the same time as the UAD. According to Carver, in order to manage the urban archaeological resource through the adoption of a research agenda (a process exemplified by LARA) we require not just the preparation of a detailed research agenda itself, but also a 'deposit model'. That is to say, in addition to using LARA to explain the issues we wish to address, we should also be making use of our documentation of deposit quality and location to predict precisely where we will attempt to address them (and, by implication, where we will do nothing). Whilst the *Assessment* team were agreed that the Lincoln 'deposit model' could provide useful information in very restricted areas, i.e. where there had been intensive recent excavation, it was felt that the limited numbers of data points available did not yet provide a sufficiently robust predictive tool to justify pre-selection of sites for research in the manner envisaged by Carver. We agreed it was far better to presume that some progress, however limited, could be made with our pre-defined research agenda on *every* development site – even if that progress consisted of nothing more than a desk-based exercise documenting the removal of relevant deposits during the course of earlier developments. At present, the policy in Lincoln is that site evaluations can be relied upon to establish the extent to which progress with the questions defined in LARA will be limited by the poor condition, or complete lack, of relevant archaeological deposits.

Even more important in some ways than LARA's professional credibility, however, is the question of whether it fulfils our ambition of supplying both the City Planning Service and the wider community with *useful* information about the city's archaeology. From the practical experience of using the system (for about a year at the time of writing) it seems that LARA provides just what the Lincoln Planners have been asking for from archaeologists. This success is mostly due to its complete coverage of the administrative area of the city. We have found that every development control decision can start now with a basic statement, derived from LARA, about the past history of the site through the seven Eras before it goes on its journey through officers and committee. This has meant that the heritage interest of the site is automatically at the root of the eventual decision, with all of the obvious benefits of information and integration that brings. Many writers on heritage management have commented that the problems caused by archaeology in the development process are not so much the costs involved, rather they relate to the delays and uncertainty that archaeological work can create in the developer's timetable if not raised sufficiently early in the planning process. Although it cannot eliminate delays, LARA does add greatly to the level of certainty about the archaeological component of development work. But more important than this, perhaps, is the intangible benefit of bringing the developer into the heritage-management process. We can now share the research agenda for the project with the developer from the start, asking her/him to use archaeological contractors to address certain worthwhile questions about the relationship of any site to our understanding of Lincoln, not just to dig a hole and report what they find. And it is not just the developer who can now be brought into this inclusive process. Plans are being made to give the local community more widely access to LARA (this book is only the start of that process). Now interested local people, school children, etc., can see the present state of knowledge in their part of the city, or in a topic which interests them. They can now undertake worthwhile research themselves, and play a useful role in the dialogue between our society and its past. In the long term this is the most important ambition of LARA, to bring an understanding of Lincoln's archaeology to the wider community.

## Assessing the archaeology of Lincoln

Although this book is an archaeological assessment of the city of Lincoln, we have also touched (of course) on some of the main themes in current debates about urbanism in Western Europe more generally. In particular, as the frameworks for the research agendas have developed, we have found ourselves dealing with the same nexus of economic, military and ritual motivations recognised in European urban archaeological research by Martin Carver in his influential *Arguments in Stone* (1993, chapter 2). Through the commentary that follows, these three threads weave in and out, and the *Assessment* process has enabled us to add significantly to our understanding of Lincoln's character as both an economic and military centre and as a ritual site.

As is the case with the history of so many British towns, previous writing on Lincoln has been weighed down by ideas of the city derived from 'Victorian' and 'Liberal' outlooks. We have been aware of Carver's injunction that we must 'escape the classical inheritance of urbanism as a concept' (*Ibid.*, 2), but, in doing so, we have found ourselves responding to previous explanations of the archaeology of Lincoln dominated by military and economic preoccupations. The motivation for the Roman base here was, it has been thought previously, primarily military. Explanations for the establishment of the *Colonia* have been expressed previously in both military and economic terms (i.e. the city has been thought of as a mechanism for infiltrating former legionaries into the native population, for providing a mobile reserve in case of rebellion and as a centre for tax-gathering and administration). The motivations underpinning the Anglo-Norman town (the foundation of the Cathedral and Castle) have been considered self-evidently economic and military, and explanations offered for

the City's industrial explosion after 1840 have also been related, primarily, to the agricultural economy. Even the motivation for the establishment of the Anglo-Scandinavian town (evidently an economic centre) has also been sought in a pattern of military 'burhs' established by the Viking 'Great Army'.

We have not found any of these economic and military explanations to be fundamentally unsound; clearly economic performance was a critical factor in the community's success, and there were times (the 4th century, the 10th – 12th centuries, the late 19th and early 20th centuries) when that economic performance was spectacular. Nor can the city's military role be doubted (in the 1st century, perhaps in the 9th, certainly in the 11th, 12th and early 13th centuries, and again in the 17th and 20th centuries). As we shall see, we think that the progress we have made in understanding the economic and military structure of the High Medieval Era has been considerable. But we have also found both that the city owed its origins to other factors besides the economic and the military, and that it was sustained by other impulses in the periods in between (as well as during) periods of economic success. Specifically, in Lincoln's case, the continuity has not been the city's role as an economic focus, or as a military strong point, but its role as a ritual centre (in its widest sense). This is the real discovery driven home by the *Assessment* – the fundamental characteristic of Lincoln as an urban place lies in its role as the regional centre for ritual performances, be they commercial, military, religious or educational.

Just as the city embarks on a new career educating tomorrow's citizens at its new university, we now suspect that the town owes its origins, not solely to the logic of a Roman military engineer, but to earlier rituals associated with passage; passage across a hitherto unsuspected causeway, to the east of the later settlement. This causeway, which occurs on so many reconstructions of Lincoln's topography in this volume, wags a reproving finger at the 'Rescue' archaeology years – and at this author amongst other archaeologists. Clearly if we were to have made great progress in understanding the city, this is where excavations should have taken place. Yet virtually no work at all has been undertaken within 500m of the suspected line (or lines) of the causeway; the 'Rescue' threats in this area simply did not arise, or were thought too remote from the 'historic core'. The *Assessment* has shown us the error of our old ways – it has suggested that this is where Lincoln began, where rites of passage across a sacred bog were performed. It was the ancient pre-urban focus, lurking down-stage like the rhinoceros in the sitting room, which the Romans tried to subvert or suppress with their own military establishment on the hill.

Or did the Romans try to assimilate the native gods associated with the river and its causeway into their own religious order? The evidence is not clear and we must explore the question in future work. Even before we start that work, however, we can at least say, on the strength of this *Assessment*, that the Romans were committed to extensive water-management schemes in Lincoln and, although many scholars would take this simply as further evidence for the Roman obsession with hygiene, it is already admitted that the *forum* well was important for ritual, rather than for utilitarian, purposes. But the Romans' concern for water in this city did not end with the *forum* well. Amongst the most prominent remains of the Roman city reported above are the remains of another colossal well, a water-storage tower, an aqueduct, a sewer system and a public fountain. Is this just what one should expect from Roman urbanism, or did water play a symbolic, as well as a utilitarian role in Roman Lincoln? And, if the attention paid to water management in Lincoln was exceptional amongst Roman towns, might that attention have owed its origins to the Romanisation of pre-Roman water deities resident in the city's pool? Hitherto, the predominance of the military agenda within Roman studies has meant that Roman Lincoln is routinely compared with Roman Gloucester, a comparable *Colonia*. The question raised by LARA is whether we should not also be comparing *Lindum Colonia* with *Aquae Sulis*, Roman Bath – a city whose *raison d'être* was also provided by a pre-Roman cult centre based on water spirits.

Roman Lincoln, however, can never have been merely a ritual centre – it clearly had a vibrant economy with a range of imports and exports exchanged in markets, including the *forum* itself. Mr Jones has provided exemplary reconstructions of these structures and set them, for the first time, in their international context. Relatively little work has been done on Roman Lincoln as a market centre, as yet, but this *Assessment* has asked a number of questions about the supply of the city's basic needs and suggested several research directions for the future.

Having failed to excavate any convincing evidence for settlement within the Roman walls between the 5th and the 9th centuries, the little information we have suggests that we should also be looking towards the causeway area east of the Lower City for that 'holy grail' of English urban archaeology – 'continuity'. Following this *Assessment* process, we now suspect that the northern end of the putative causeway was the location of both an unexplained (and possibly early) church site and of an unexplained (and possibly early) market site at *Baggerholme*. In our current state of ignorance, this is the best we can do with the city area in the pre-Viking period. If there ever was a major hall of the Kings of Lindsey (a *Villa Regalis*) 'at' Lincoln (as we must surely expect), then this is the only location we have found that might live up to the role. Such a site might, perhaps, have been something like Flixborough (ed. Loveluck forthcoming), a site in a topographical location not dissimilar to Monks Abbey. Viewed in this light, the former Roman walled city, with the intriguing archaeology at the churches of St

Paul-in-the-Bail and the two St Peters, might be seen as no more than a walled annex to a more important settlement site to the east – similar, perhaps, to the relationship between middle-Saxon Kingsholm and Gloucester, for example. In the final analysis, this is the most helpful thing that the *Assessment* process has been able to say about the famous St Paul-in-the-Bail site. Progress in understanding it, we believe, will only be made through efforts to see the site in its broader topographical context. Unfortunately the (admittedly limited) evidence of the finds from the river leave us unclear whether ritual deposition continued along the causeway in the Middle Saxon period – there are finds of both Roman and Viking date, but none in between. Can we presume that people were still crossing the river at or near this point, even though the Romans had constructed a second, altogether more substantial route at what we now call Wigford? Or is it more likely that the older causeway was impassable at this time? If it was, perhaps we can make the assumption that the place-name component -*wic* in Wigford, really does refer to an early entrepôt after all, but not one on the Wigford peninsula. As Dr Vince has now demonstrated that there was no *wic* in Wigford, perhaps the place-name Wigford refers to the ford that led to a *wic* on the *north* side of the river, near Stamp End?

Increasingly, traders attending our putative early market to the east of the city would be arriving by boat and another of the profound insights which has emerged through this *Assessment* is that the Witham frontage between the Roman walls was of relatively little commercial significance through most, if not all, of the city's life. Documentary history has given us little understanding of Lincoln's port installations, but our review of the archaeology makes it clear that medieval Lincoln had, in effect, had two ports – one below the causeway, in the area known in the late Middle Ages as *Blackdyke*, and one to the south and south-west of the walled city (along the western shore of Wigford and in Newland). The quays around *Blackdyke*, of course, were conveniently sited for our putative early market, under the walls of the Monks Abbey, but certainly from the 12th century (when the stone bridge at High Bridge was constructed) and perhaps since long before, boats arriving from the west could only reach as far as the Wigford 'hards'. But, apart from local traffic, shipping could not arrive at the city from the west at all, until the construction of the Fossdyke canal to the Trent and Torksey. Consequently, Dr Vince's demonstration that the pattern of pottery imports to the city strongly suggests that the Fossdyke was only opened towards the end of the 10th century must represent another major achievement of the *Assessment*. This discovery provides us with a very valuable *terminus post quem* in our sequence for the development of the Lower City. Furthermore, even though there are still counter arguments, it seems increasingly likely that the long-cherished myth that the canal was constructed by the Romans can no longer be sustained.

The re-occupation of the former Roman enclosure can be viewed, then, as a result of the increasing volume of trade. But this move, which we have shown undoubtedly occurred sometime between the end of the 9th century and the end of the 10th, could equally have been prompted by military, rather than commercial considerations, connected with the establishment of a Viking (or even an Edwardian or Edmundian) burh. If so, we might ask whether any move westwards from a putative Pre-Viking open market to reoccupy the former Roman enclosure was imposed from 'above' – speaking both socially and topographically? Another major outcome of the *Assessment* has been the revelation that the Upper City, the former Roman fortress, was not really urban at all until the 12th century. It seems to have been a reserved space, dominated by the halls of the aristocracy and by churches from at least the 10th to the 12th century. Oddly enough (but in common with many other aspects of the material culture), the Norman Conquest and the foundation of Lincoln Castle altered this situation very little, at least not immediately. The new castle, we can now demonstrate, consisted of little more than the appropriation of the existing Roman Upper City walls, the rebuilding of some gatehouses and the addition of a motte. After 1068 the enclosure continued to be dominated by the halls of the (new) aristocracy and by a group of privileged churches, just as it had been in the pre-Conquest period – albeit that one of the halls was now said to belong to the King and one of the churches was now promoted to episcopal rank. The major changes in the Upper City, its integration into the urban fabric and its connection with the booming commercial settlement climbing the hill towards its south gate, were not completed until the reign of Henry II, even though our evidence suggests that integration may have been an extended process.

The isolation of the Upper City from the remainder of the city through the 10th and 11th centuries is made crystal clear by the patterns of market places defined in the *Assessment* – many for the first time. The Upper City was nearly encircled by three of them; at the north, east and south gates. The two former both gave rise to suburbs, whilst the latter, on the steepest part of the hillside, provided the bridge between the bustling commercial town at the foot of the cliff and the Upper City. The dating of these satellite markets remains unclear (they are apparently undocumented in the historical record), although Dr Vince suspects that they are post- rather than pre-Conquest, on the basis of the pottery they have produced. Are they, then, foundations by the new Norman lords (perhaps those with halls in the Upper City enclosure), trying to maximise the income from their new estates? Not all were successful. The *Old High Market* (south of the south gate of the Upper City) came to play the role of the central internal market square, around which so

many later medieval planned towns revolved. But the Newport market was only kept going through City Council support and revival (for which there is a little documentary evidence) and that at Eastgate seems to have failed before it could be documented at all. Even though still used for festivals in the 18th century, it may have ceased to be active before the end of the 12th century. Or perhaps it was deliberately killed-off by the eastwards march of the Close?

In the period between the 10th and 12th centuries, then, the Upper City had its own independent *raison d'être*, as an enclave for the aristocracy and the church, whilst markets, where the population lived, were added around its periphery. However, the *Assessment* has revealed that important parts of the city downhill also owed their existence to the layout of great market places, of which the most spectacular was that which Dr Vince has identified in what we now call Lower Wigford. This huge funnel-shaped street, extending southwards from what we now suspect may have been an early entrance to the city across the Great Gowt, seems to have been about 1km long. It is inconceivable that such a huge space developed spontaneously, even though it is formed in the junction between converging roads. It must represent an act of planning by a single authority and, in this case, we have a *terminus ante quem* for its layout. The great market of Lower Wigford must have been established before the Sincil Dyke was cut across it, and (for various reasons to do with the foundation of the monasteries and hospitals to the south) the Dyke must itself have been cut before the end of the 11th century. The *Assessment* has also identified other, hitherto unknown, market spaces; the market (which we believe may have been inserted into the existing street pattern) at Newland, the *Maltmarket* space on Waterside North (which eventually became the wool market and housed the city weigh-beam), and the *Clewmarket* (the thread market), whose date of origin proved controversial within the *Assessment* team.

Lincoln in the 10th and 11th centuries, therefore, is now revealed as a patchwork of extensive suburbs, most of which are based on markets of one type or another; probably founded at different dates and servicing different clienteles. The suburbs were laid out around a central core in the Lower City and *Butwerk*, and here what evidence we have suggests that, initially (i.e. in the 10th and early 11th centuries), there was manufacturing, probably of artefacts to be sold in the new markets around the periphery (pottery, low-grade jewellery, clothing, leather). At this time, then, the Lower City of Lincoln seems to behave as an exemplary 'urban' focus. It is a permanent concentration of people who live, not by working the land, but by drawing in raw materials to be worked on and sold at the city's gates. As far as we can see, this whole process was owned, supervised and protected by the aristocracy, whose base, if not their actual residence, was in the Upper City – detached but visible.

Lincoln evolved, however, and by the 13th century

it had become a different style of urban centre. Although we have precious little archaeological evidence for it, it seems clear from Prof. Bischoff's work (1975) that manufacturing in the city became dominated by a single product (cloth) and that this was worked in a dedicated industrial quarter. Furthermore, the new dominant industry was not managed by the local aristocracy through their port-reeves (although, along with local monastic houses, they were investors in it), rather it was dominated by a group of merchants. These technocrats of their day oversaw production, and marketed their products, not in Lincoln, but in international fairs at towns like St Ives, Winchester, Northampton and Boston. At some stage then, probably in the late 11th or 12th century, Lincoln had pulled clear from the mass of English towns that were merely the administrative and market centres for their region, and joined a select handful of cities that participated directly in the international economy. In David Palliser's terms, Lincoln had risen from being an English 'Toytown or Trumpton' and joined the ranks of Europe's major urban and industrial centres (2000, 3). Unfortunately, we have relatively little new to say, either about the growth of the Lincoln cloth industry (or about its spectacular collapse) because, once again, the sites available for 'Rescue' archaeology were simply not in the right locations within the city. It is another major lacuna in our understanding of the development of urbanism in Lincoln and one that should be rectified through research-led investigation when circumstances permit.

The *Assessment* has, however, highlighted the continuity of a second major Lincoln industry, even if this has been based on topographical study rather than the results of excavation. Since the Roman period, Lincoln quarries had produced building stone and clay for pottery. The artefacts of the pottery industry have been intensively studied for many years, but the *Assessment* has pulled together the topographical evidence for its extent, in both the Roman and medieval periods. The contrast between the industries in these different periods is striking. The Roman industry was largely a rural one. The pots of the major 'Swanpool' industry were made a long way from Lindum's markets, probably with clay won during gravel extraction for construction purposes, and in an area where we suspect there would have been extensive charcoal burning to provide fuel for the kilns. By complete contrast, the Anglo-Saxon and medieval industries were established as close to their markets as possible, in *Butwerk* and Wigford, even if that meant building the kilns amongst the city's houses. Like the Roman potters of Swanpool, the Anglo-Saxon potters worked close to their clay diggings (this time in the cliff faces), but they had to import their fuel. Fuel would have been required for most of the other industries of medieval Lincoln and so, presumably, could have been purchased in the market place along with other raw materials.

By way of contrast with the detailed archaeological study of the city's pottery industry, and in spite of its importance, the stone quarrying industry of Roman and medieval Lincoln, remains virtually unknown. Once again none of the 'Rescue' opportunities has led to an exploration of this fundamental city industry, but at least maps, a preliminary estimate of date for the main quarry faces and a research agenda for the future have been produced through this *Assessment*. In fact, quarrying for both building stone and clay is one activity that seems to continue through Lincoln's dramatic economic reversal in the final quarter of the 13th century.

Although no sites which would cast direct light on the economic catastrophe that struck the city at this time have been excavated, almost all sites where deposits of the Early Modern Era have been investigated have produced indirect evidence for the impact of the city's economic collapse. In many cases, however, it is the stability that emerges once the contraction had occurred that is most striking about such sites. Frequently the pattern (and sometimes the fabric) of the buildings established by *c*.1250 lasted until the 18th or 19th century. Indeed this is the impression one gets from the writing of early tourists and even from the earliest photography; although rotting and collapsing, much of Lincoln's fabric did indeed belong to the High Medieval Era until it was swept away wholesale between 1850 and 1900 (Plate 6.3).

The *Assessment* process has shown us that the markets of the city were comprehensively re-organised during the Early Modern Era – and we now have the documentation to show that this was done, not by the will of individual magnates (as may have been the case with some earlier markets), but by the authority of the City Council. This is one of several signs that, as the shrunken town settled back into relative obscurity, the higher aristocracy lost interest and the community became dominated by the interests of a small resident oligarchy which held on to power. One of the most dramatic demonstrations of the power of the oligarchy within the early modern town was the Act of Union of Parishes in 1549. Here the City Council assumed responsibility for disposing of redundant churches in the city, and in the process made some of their number a large profit. This is a graphic example, drawn from documentary history, of the same process of consolidation of power in the hands of the oligarchy that we also see in the agglomeration of properties and in the construction of new elite dwellings. The changing relationships between groups holding power in the city is another of the ever-present themes that run through the LARA entries (and can be seen in the introductions to the RAZ texts for almost every Era).

The consolidation of parochial churches in 1549 and the transfer of church assets into private hands, of course, were aspects of the Reformation. In fact, although the Reformation and the Dissolution of the Monasteries must have been a severe psychological blow to a city so dominated by the church, the break in continuity seen in the archaeological record is not as dramatic as one might expect. Although adapted and shorn of their churches, former monastic properties continued in use, even though their new owners were secular lords. But the morale of the English church, the reason for Lincoln's medieval fame, had been damaged, and the collapse of the Cathedral's enormous central spire in 1548, at the height of Edward VI's attack on the Old Religion, seemed highly symbolic to contemporaries. Indeed when looking for vitality in religious affairs in Lincoln between the 16th and 18th centuries, we should probably not turn to the new Anglican church at all. One of the unexpected discoveries of the *Assessment* process was that Lincoln was something of a focus for the early Dissenters. It is not immediately obvious why early Dissenting communities (which were mostly rural in origin) should have chosen to set up urban chapels in Lincoln itself, under the noses of church and civil authorities. Was Lincoln acting once again, as it always had, as a location where the spiritual interests of the East Midlands were debated and represented? In an Era when Lincoln had lost its commercial role as anything other than a local market, can we see in the emergence of the Dissenters the fundamental character of the place re-asserting itself? Once again there has been no archaeological work on such issues to date, but these questions provide interesting material for our research agenda.

If it has failed to add greatly to our understanding of the archaeology of the Early Modern Era, the *Assessment* has at least pointed to two related conclusions about the moment at which the city emerged into the industrial age. First, the archaeological record does not really support the contention, frequently made on the basis of documentary evidence, that Lincoln's rise from its four centuries of slumber during the Early Modern Era was due to the injection of private enterprise when the City Council leased the Fossdyke to Richard Ellison I in 1740. There was some expansion of the city's population and the quantity of trade in agricultural produce passing through Lincoln certainly picked up. But, at best, in the archaeological record this phase amounts to an expansion of the city's existing economic hinterland. The city now exported perishable agricultural goods to the West Riding, as well as to the eastern Midlands, and there was a corresponding increase in the quantity and range of imported commodities (such as coal). Although somewhat larger in size, on the evidence of its material culture, however, Lincoln remained just another regional market town between 1740 and 1840, albeit one with a cathedral. The step-change came not with the arrival of the canals, but with that of the railways in 1846. The establishment of the great heavy engineering plants east and west of Wigford in the decades between 1840 and 1870 saw Lincoln return to a 'higher' rank of urbanism. As in the 12th and 13th centuries, once again a large percentage of Lincoln's population was involved in the large-scale

manufacture of a single type of commodity for an international (indeed global) market. This was not, however, an inevitable development. It was not the fate of all sleepy 18th-century cathedral cities to become great industrial manufacturers (Plate 8.1). Looked at dispassionately, indeed, it is not easy to understand why heavy engineering became established in Lincoln at all – after all, although it would have been quite possible technically and topographically, iron and steel were not actually made here. Archaeology could play an important role in addressing this fundamental question, but so far such questions have simply not been asked and no investigations have yet been undertaken with this research agenda in mind.

Finally, we have found that developing an understanding of the underlying topography of the city has been crucial to understanding the city's archaeology at all periods, including the modern. In Lincoln, we had assumed that we had a reasonable idea of how the physical topography of the city had developed before the *Assessment* began, but during the preparation of the Era maps it rapidly became clear how mistaken we were. Even the most penetrating of earlier studies had not resolved the topographical complexity of the valley floor, or even that of the 'upland' countryside immediately adjacent to the built-up area. But, although we have grappled with the problem in the Era maps (from which the maps printed in the volume are derived), our efforts have been ham-strung though a lack of basic information. In fact much relevant material for understanding the development of the city's topography may already exist in bore-hole records, but these are difficult to access and time has not yet been devoted to the problem. In this volume, we have put forward maps proposing a particular sequence of development for the wetland watercourses and islands on which Wigford, *Butwerk*, Newland and the Lower City are built. But we have to be honest and say that we could be making fundamental errors in our assumptions about them. At present the locations for some of the watercourses and islands are less certain, even, than the presence and location of the Stamp End Causeway, for which we at least have the evidence of artefacts.

Lincoln's archaeology, then, as revealed by the *Assessment*, displays many continuities across the centuries between prehistoric and modern times. This city's style of urbanism has been characterised by three distinct but inextricably interrelated strands; the economic, the military and the ritual. But although the city's role as a market and as a defensive base has risen to importance and fallen away again on more than one occasion, it is the ritual strand that has been a constant presence. As far as we know, the location was used for ritual purposes before it became an economic or a military centre and, whilst the city's fortunes as a market place and as a fortress have fluctuated (to say the least of it), the city has continued to be a centre of religious practice, even though the beliefs sponsored by those religions have themselves changed and developed. It was entirely appropriate then, that the novelist A S Byatt chose Lincoln as the setting for her fictional university in her 1990 master-piece *Possession*. To people who only know the city from its received image, Lincoln *sounds* like a place that should have had a university (i.e. the modern equivalent of a major ritual site) since earliest times, even if it only acquired one, finally, in 1996 (Plate 8.2). Having reviewed the whole span of the city's development now, it seems to us that it is Lincoln's role as the setting for regional rituals which has been constant through history; it is the ideologies which have changed, not the location. Lincoln, the 'City by the Pool', has always been known as a place of spiritual refreshment. Perhaps we can also say that, today, Lincoln continues to fulfil its destiny, whether we are thinking of the pilgrim at the Cathedral, the student at the University, the holidaymaker on the river or the visitor admiring its heritage.

# 13. Appendix 1
# Explaining LARA:
# the Lincoln Archaeological Research Assessment in its policy context

## David Stocker

## 1) Introduction

LARA, the Lincoln Archaeological Research Assessment, is an attempt both to summarise the archaeological debate on the City of Lincoln to date and to chart an agreed course for future work, which will continue that debate. It rides on the top of the collection, classification and analysis of archaeological data for the city achieved by the Urban Archaeological Database (UAD) and, in that respect, it can be seen as an extended 'discussion' similar to sections found at the end of site reports. But because LARA aims to assess the archaeological potential of the entire District Council area and to discuss the research agenda for areas which have never been investigated archaeologically, it is also legitimately described as a form of *characterisation* of the city from an archaeological perspective.

LARA also fits within a wider framework – the exercise has emerged from national English Heritage programmes of Urban Archaeological Assessment which themselves are rooted in developing concepts of both planning and archaeology. Urban Assessments (like all high level evaluation, assessment and characterisation work) are located right at the point at which academic debate meets the development planning and development control system and here, at this hinge, we need to bring together qualities and perceptions from both academic archaeology and planning skills and concerns. This is where academic archaeology meets the real world and it is therefore an indispensable step in 'informed conservation' in Lincoln.

### Archaeological Theory

We now live in a somewhat different theoretical environment from that in which some of us grew up. Thirty years ago archaeology was keen to define itself as a science, imitating the empirical method and insisting that all theorising had to based on extensive experimentation (i.e. excavation). We all thought that few conclusions could be drawn from archaeological data without extensive experimentation first. In this 1970s world, the most important task of the archaeologist working in the context of urban redevelopment was to identify where he thought there might be archaeology surviving and then argue for the funds to excavate before destruction to find out what the archaeology 'really' comprised.

This mind-set never dominated the whole of archaeology (it never really caught on in landscape archaeology for example), and it has lost ground steadily over the last three decades to more discursive approaches. Increasingly field archaeologists have been asked to do more than identify undifferentiated archaeology, which requires excavation before it can be discussed. It is no longer helpful for the archaeologist simply to point to an area where archaeology may exist and then ask for funding (either from a developer or from another funding agency) to find out what the archaeology consists of. Archaeologists are now expected, first, to attempt to predict what lies below the ground, to extrapolate from knowledge of similar sites and contexts, and to interpret and synthesise existing understanding far more broadly. Secondly, archaeological curators, funding bodies and indeed the general public, look for a pre-defined research framework within which an investigation can take place.

### Planning Theory

A major trend in Planning in the last ten years has been a shift away from the *ad hoc* decision-making that emerged during the 1980s back towards plan-led development more in keeping with some of the original aims of the Town and Country Planning Acts. Rather than making decisions on an *ad hoc* basis when the planning application is made, we are moving back towards a situation where planning negotiations should be conducted on the basis of agreed aims and objectives which have already been spelled out in the Local Plan, in advance, and given legitimacy through democratic consultation and political approval. The LARA methodology was developed to express ar-

A modified version of a paper given to various seminars on urban themes in Lincoln, London and Exeter (2000-2)

chaeological concerns in such a way that they could be easily deployed as part of planning negotiations conducted through plan-led development strategies. Put briefly, the archaeologists in Lincoln have spelt out, in an accessible way, what we want to achieve through future archaeological work, using plan-led planning strategies.

In the world of developer funding for archaeology that has been emerging for the past 15 years or so, we might also argue that the funders, usually developers, have a right to ask why they are being asked to pay for archaeology. It is sometimes clear why they are being made to pay for many other environmental and other subsidiary aspects of their development – in Lincoln, for example, that is all laid down in the Local Plan (and will be in its successors) – but the detailed reason why they are asked to pay for any particular piece of archaeology has often, in Lincoln, been left undefined. The broad reasons are defined clearly enough in national planning guidance (PPG16) (retrieval of evidence before destruction; destruction in effect being seen as pollution; hence the polluter pays) but in reference to specific development proposals detailed justification is unusual. Beyond the bald statement that 'archaeology' is present, there is rarely any explanation in the Local Plan, or in Supplementary Planning Guidance, available to the developer, to explain why he/she is required to pay for an excavation on a particular site, or how the community as a whole hopes to benefit from their investment.

## 2) The Present Position

### Current negotiating stances

Currently, most developer funded archaeological research is undertaken because the developer is told by national planning policy guidance that it is a requirement for obtaining planning permission. In practice this results in debates between the developer (or developer's consultant) and the curator being conducted with few visible rules. For the curator in most planning authorities it is not clear what would constitute a successful outcome – frequently it is nothing more than the mere presence of an archaeological phase in the development and the implementation of a written scheme of investigation. The curator has nothing against which to measure the success or failure of a planning condition imposed in this way. Worse still, for the developer, there is little positive to be taken away from the process. The less additional cost the archaeology brings the better, but nothing positive is offered by the planning authority to show that the developer's contribution might be valuable, might have a public benefit. At present the parameters for excavations set by some planning authorities are not expressed in terms of an increase in knowledge. Archaeological requirements are often indicated negatively, in terms of the preservation of unrecorded deposits, rather than positively, in terms of the gains in knowledge aimed at in dealing with deposits which are to be removed.

### Research Agendas or Frameworks

Partly this lack of defined aims and targets is because much of the archaeology profession has been too busy excavating individual sites to stand back and apply (or even to review) what they have learnt in a general sense. Excavation reports still focus on the presentation of excavated evidence rather than on the broader lessons for the city or region as a whole. And it is to try and rectify this that English Heritage has in recent years promoted programmes of research aiming to draw together conclusions from individual sites and surveys – the so called 'Research Frameworks Programme'. LARA should also be seen as a facet of this work, as well as an example of an Urban Assessment project and as an example of urban characterisation used as a way of helping to manage change.

## 3) Proposed Improvements in the Lincoln case?

### The Lincoln Urban Archaeological Database (UAD)

The work of pulling together the data on Lincoln's archaeology (the UAD completed six years ago) should be seen as part of this Research Frameworks process. This paper does not discuss the Lincoln UAD, but its construction should be recognised as the first step in a process of making the archaeological case. It can be conceptualised as the base of a pyramid (Fig. 13.1) – the material from which interpretation and ideas can be drawn, and on which policy and action can be built thereafter .

The next step in the pyramid towards making the archaeological case, is to make this data more readily comprehensible to the public. This is the purpose of LARA, a stepping stone from data (the UAD) towards policy (the Local Plan and/or its successors).

### From UAD to Local Plan : the role of LARA

*a) Characterisation*
Getting from the UAD to the Local Plan is not straightforward. Many authorities have simply referred to their databases (or similar documents) in their Local Plan, but this is a very limited response and in Lincoln it was felt to be inadequate. Although it helps to make this data publicly available in this way, the data on all UADs needs sophisticated interpretation before it can be understood. Furthermore it cannot be given the force of a Local Plan policy, (except in the most general terms – "Lincoln is a large archaeological site and we will ensure that archaeology is done"). No, we need an

Strategy - 'People'

Various professional
Assessments - 'Ideas'

Data - 'Things'

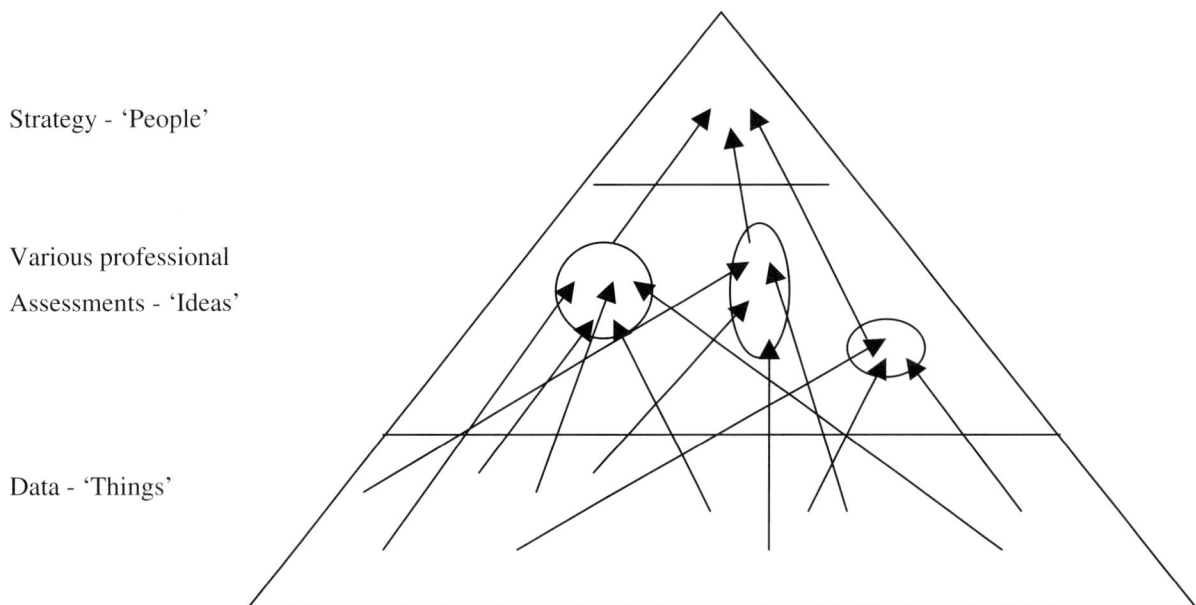

*Fig. 13.1. The hierarchy of tasks in holistic environmental planning.*

intermediate stage, where the data is interpreted more broadly, by professionals, and the current best guess as to the type of archaeology that will be found in any given spot, will be explained. In English Heritage this sort of work on an archaeological data-set is seen as one of the central elements of the process of characterisation. LARA , then, is also a characterisation of Lincoln.

In the abstract, then, we have clear aims for the archaeological assessment process and in LARA we have tried to put this theory into practice. The Lincoln methodology aims to characterise urban deposits in a way which is both acceptable professionally and which can also be used as the basis for Local Plan statements about our archaeological ambitions in every area of the city.

*b) Results*
LARA, then, is an attempt to express our understanding of the city's archaeology in a holistic, interconnected, way. Another way to describe LARA is to outline its beneficial results. Following the completion of LARA, rather than merely saying to the developer (or to the school teacher/pupil, or other interested party), that there is archaeology here and we want to excavate it. LARA says instead:

–   We have done a lot of previous work done in Lincoln, and the results of that work are summarised here in an easily accessible form, filtered through wider up-to-date interpretations of the past.
–   All this previous work allows us to see that any given part of the City Council Area has a specific archaeological character. LARA has defined this

character – and this is what we can now say/predict about the particular site in which you are interested.
–   Based on our current understanding we need you, in your contribution, to address a range of specific questions about the history of the city in your work on your particular patch – and LARA provides a list of them.

*Methodology*
So how are we going to characterise the archaeology of Lincoln? Well, for any meaningful characterisation we presumed that we should start by dividing up the city both geographically into character areas as in Historic Landscape Characterisation (Fairclough 2002). Furthermore, because Lincoln is a place with great time-depth (very well-known through 30 years of large scale excavation) it is possible to do this chronologically for several different periods of history. This process has created geographical and chronological units held on a simple GIS and relational database for each of seven broad periods into which we have broken up the history of the city. We have called these period Eras. 'Eras' are periods of time of markedly different lengths during which it seemed to the LARA team that there was a broad continuity in the city's material culture. Some of these Eras are highly debatable, of course, especially, perhaps, the way in which we have divided up the medieval and early modern periods. What is more, they will be different for different cities, but for Lincoln they are:

1–4)   Not assigned
5)       Prehistoric settlement in the immediate vicinity of Lincoln

6)   The Roman Military Era (*c.*43AD–*c.*90AD)
7)   The Roman Colonia Era (*c.*90AD–*c.*400)
8)   The Early Medieval Era (*c.*400–*c.*850)
9)   The High Medieval Era (*c.*850–*c.*1350)
10)  The Early Modern Era (*c.*1350–*c.*1750)
11)  The Industrial Era (*c.*1750–*c.*1945)

Within each Era, LARA seeks to identify sets of character areas, geographical components based on, but not defined by, buried archaeological structures, urban plan-form, building groups or past landscape and townscape. We were clear that we could not use the 'monuments' identified in the UAD as the basis for the geographical characterisation as there were far too few of them, they only covered a very small percentage of the District, and the boundaries of many of them were unknown. Consequently we devised a method for defining areas on the ground within which specified archaeological research questions could be addressed. We have therefore called LARA's geographical and chronological units RAZs, *Research Agenda Zones* and we have managed to define a total of some 550 across the entire District, from the Mesolithic to 1945.

Boundaries of these RAZs (which are always contiguous or overlapping – there is no 'white space', no unclassified areas) were decided through a small panel of Lincoln specialists considering which research questions should be asked within each Era at each point on the map. Texts were then generated and subject to further discussion and agreement. However, it is recognised that these individual research agendas represent the view of a limited group at a single moment in time and so, in the coming years, the City Archaeologist will seek views of many external specialists and continually improve the research agendas offered.

Some of the RAZs are single building complexes whilst others are large areas of land. For each of these RAZ components in each Era on the map there is a short text on the linked database. This means that for any given location in the District there will be a minimum of seven statements explaining, within each Era, what research questions archaeologists would like to see answered in future research at that point. Access via the GIS is very simple; you simply place the cursor at any point within the District boundary and it automatically provides the 7 (or more) database entries, the RAZ texts.

Each RAZ text has four parts:

–   a brief statement about the physical character of the component,
–   a statement about the relative archaeological significance of the component,
–   a statement about how we wish to explore it in future, and
–   a statement about how we have defined the boundary of the component – whether it is clearly defined or vague, whether it is known or guesswork.

In this way, then, we have encapsulated the archaeology of the city, and we have provided a clear statement of the research questions we wish to see addressed in future work. Although LARA's primary function is as an active GIS database, the complete RAZ texts and the maps, which go with them, can be abstracted and presented in hard copy to provide the City and the public with a comprehensive Research Agenda for any part of it at any given moment.

## 4) Using LARA

LARA was completed early in 2002 and is proving to be of enormous practical use. It structures the archaeological component within the daily development control process and has placed the archaeologists and heritage managers at the centre of the planning team.

Lincoln now has full documentation of our archaeological understanding in a format that allows our knowledge to be used within the Local Plan process, and as the basis for Supplementary Planning Guidance (SPG) in support of innovative Local Plan Policies. This sort of *characterisation* can be used in the same way that Conservation Area Statements can be used to conserve Conservation Areas, because the Council can judge any proposals against the characterisation statement and agree that it works towards the aims presented there, or not.

This is straying into a third stage of work, however. The drafting of holistic Local Plan Policies which encapsulate not just the Archaeological Research Assessment, but also those produced by other professional groupings (such as ecologists and townscape planners) was beyond LARA's brief. This is the uppermost stage in the pyramid shown in Fig. 13.1. However, LARA does ensure that the archaeological case is both well-organised and easily accessible when it needs to be combined with parallel assessments by these other interest groups in Plans for wider environmental management. Traditionally, we have called this tertiary phase the 'Strategy' phase and, in Lincoln we are currently drafting the specifications for such work aimed at bringing together the various professional assessments of the City into a single environmental plan.

## 5) Review of LARA

Finally it is important that we do not regard LARA as set in stone. It is merely a snapshot of the current state of archaeological understanding of the city. Next month, next year, new excavations and other discoveries will make aspects of the RAZ texts in each era obsolete. That is as it should be, and will be a sign of the success of the LARA approach. And coping with these continual changes should be no different from coping with change in any other aspect of Plan production. The Plan review cycles sweep up any new information in other professional fields and incorporate it into the revised documentation, and archaeology should simply be another part of that process. In each review cycle the Lincoln City Archaeologist will be faced with reconsidering LARA and redrafting it where appropriate.

Amongst all these other things, then, LARA is also a benchmarking exercise; providing the structure and the preliminary statement for a cyclical process that will provide Lincoln with a practical management tool for its archaeology into the foreseeable future.

# 14. Appendix 2
## Complete list of Research Agenda Zones (RAZs) for all Eras

7.10 BLANK
7.11 Housing areas
    7.11.1 Houses within the Upper City
    7.11.2 Suburban development north and west of the Upper City
    7.11.3 Suburban development east of the walled city
    7.11.4 Houses within the walled Lower City
    7.11.5 Houses within the southern suburb
7.12 The defences
7.13 Stamp End causeway
7.14 Area of *centuriation* to the north

*c) Sites and deposits illustrating largely 'public' and/or ritual motivation*

7.15 The *forum*
7.16 The baths
7.17 The aqueduct
7.18 The sewer system
7.19 Springs and pools on the hillside
7.20 Temple complexes in the Lower City
7.21 Possible temple complexes on islands in the lake
    7.21.1 The possible Wigford island temple
    7.21.2 Potential religious site on Hartsholme island
7.22 Upper Ermine Street
7.23 The Greetwell villa
7.24 Cemeteries
7.25 The late pre-Roman iron-age ditch system

# Chapter 8. The Early Medieval Era

8.1 Burial sites at St Paul's, the St Peters' and Greetwell villa
    8.1.1 St Paul-in-the-Bail
    8.1.2 The churches of St Peter and the Silver Street burial
    8.1.3 Greetwell villa estate and potential *wic*
8.2 Possible occupation site near Castle west gate
8.3 Reuse, abandonment and other treatments of Roman roads and other Roman monuments
    8.3.1 Central elements of former Roman city and Roman network
    8.3.2 Stamp End causeway
    8.3.3 Triple boundary ditch
    8.3.4 'Reserved' enclosure(s) defined by the Roman city walls
8.4 Land around city potentially usable for settlement and agriculture
8.5 Riparian deposits

# Chapter 9. The High Medieval Era

*Part 1) The market infrastructure*

*a) Water engineering and the port*
    9.1 Stamp End causeway
    9.2 City docks 1) wharves along Waterside North east of the wall and the *Blackdyke*
    9.3 City docks 2) Waterside North between the walls
    9.4 Wigford western shoreline
    9.5 Wigford eastern shoreline – *La Gulle, Old Eye* and *Thorngate*

*b) Victualling and agriculture in the vicinity*
    9.6 Woodlands and wood-pasture to the south-west
    9.7 Wetlands
    9.8 Common pasture
        9.8.1 Enclosures west of Newland
        9.8.2 Un-enclosed pasture west of Newland
        9.8.3 Bracebridge pasture
        9.8.4 South Common
        9.8.5 Common pasture east of *Butwerk*.
    9.9 The city's arable fields
        9.9.1 Lincoln city fields
        9.9.2 Fields of the parishes of Nettleham and Greetwell

*c) Rural Settlements in the vicinity*
    9.10 Bracebridge
    9.11 Boultham

*d) Road Networks*
    9.12 Roads
        9.12.1 Long distance roads
        9.12.2 Intermediate distance roads
        9.12.3 Local roads
    9.13.1 Bracebridge bridge
    9.13.2 Bishop's Bridges
    9.14 Gowts bridges
    9.15 High Bridge and ford

*e) Market Places*
    9.16 Newport market
    9.17 Eastgate market
    9.18 *Beggarsholme* market in *Butwerk*
    9.19 Newland market
    9.20 Lower Wigford market
    9.21 Market place on Castle Hill
    9.22 The High Market of the Lower City and other Lower City markets
    9.23.1 The *Clewmarket*
    9.23.2 The Malt market

*Part 2) The Living City*

*a) Housing*
    9.24 Houses in the Bail (and the Close within St Mary Magdalene's parish)

# Chapter 10. The Early Modern Era

*Part 1) The market infrastructure*

*a) Water engineering and the port*

*b) Victualling and agriculture in the vicinity*

*c) Rural Settlements in the vicinity*

*d) Road Networks*

*e) Market Places*

*Part 2) The Living City*

*f) Housing*

10.33 Housing in Upper Wigford (north of Great Gowt)

10.34 Housing in Lower Wigford (south of Great Gowt)

10.35 The Bishop's Palace

*g) Manufacturing and industrial plant*

10.36 BLANK

10.37 The mint and jewellery quarter

10.38 The bakers' street

10.39 Pottery production sites in Upper Wigford

10.40 Tilery in St Botolph's parish

10.41 Quarries

    10.41.1 Common quarries in the cliff faces north-west and south of city

    10.41.2 Quarries in the cliff face east of the city

    10.41.3 Stonepits north-east of the Upper City

10.42 Windmills west of *Bradegate*

10.43 Windmills west of *Battle Place*

10.44 Windmills in the East Field

*h) Administrative facilities*

10.45 Boundary markers

    10.45.1 Cross on Cross O'Cliff Hill

    10.45.2 *Broken Cross* at *Westcastle*

    10.45.3 *Mile Cross* on Nettleham Road

    10.45.4 *Humber Cross* on Ermine Street

    10.45.5 *Stub Cross* on Greetwellgate

    10.45.6 *Nettleham Mere* and contiguous features

10.46 Administrative buildings and sites

    10.46.1 *Battle Place*

    10.46.2 St Mary's Guildhall

    10.46.3 Upper City Assembly Rooms

    10.46.4 Lower City Assembly Rooms

**Part 3) Defending the City**

10.47 Upper City Defences

10.48 Lincoln Castle from *c*.1350–*c*.1750

10.49 *Thorngate Castle*

10.50.1 Lower City defences

10.50.2 The Close Wall

10.50.3 The Butts

10.51 Suburb boundaries

    10.51.1 Newport boundaries

    10.51.2 *Butwerk* boundaries

    10.51.3 Newland boundaries

    10.51.4 Boundary of Upper Wigford (Great and Little Gowts)

    10.51.5 Boundary of Lower Wigford (The Sincil Dyke)

**Part 4) Church and chapel**

10.52 The Cathedral

10.53 The friaries

    10.53.1 Augustinian Friary

    10.53.2 Dominican Friary

    10.53.3 Carmelite Friary

    10.53.4 Franciscan Friary

    10.53.5 Friary of the Sack and the Kyme chantry

10.54 St Katherine's Priory and St Sepulchre's Hospital

10.55 Monks' Abbey (the Benedictine priory of St Mary Magdalene)

10.56 The *Malandry* (the Hospital of the Holy Innocents)

10.57 St Bartholomew's and St Leonard's Hospitals

10.58 St Giles' Hospital

10.59 The College of the Vicars-Choral

10.60 The parish churches

    10.60.1 St John Newport

    10.60.2 St Nicholas Newport

    10.60.3 St Bartholomew *Westcastle*

    10.60.4 St Peter Eastgate

    10.60.5 St Margaret Pottergate

    10.60.6 St Leonard

    10.60.7 St Giles

    10.60.8 Holy Trinity Greestone Stairs

    10.60.9 St Rumbold

    10.60.10 St Bavon

    10.60.11 St Augustine

    10.60.12 St Peter *ad fontem*

    10.60.13 St Clement-in-*Butwerk*

    10.60.14 St Stephen-in-Newland

    10.60.15 St Faith-in-Newland and St Faith's brick kiln

    10.60.16 Holy Cross Wigford

    10.60.17 Holy Innocents

    10.60.18 Holy Trinity Wigford

    10.60.19 St Andrew Wigford

    10.60.20 St Benedict

    10.60.21 St Botolph

    10.60.22 St Edward Wigford

    10.60.23 St John the Evangelist Wigford

    10.60.24 St Margaret Wigford

    10.60.25 St Mark

    10.60.26 St Mary-le-Wigford

    10.60.27 St Michael Wigford

    10.60.28 St Peter-at-Gowts

    10.60.29 St Paul-in-the-Bail

    10.60.30 All Saints-in-the-Bail

    10.60.31 St Clement-in-the-Bail

    10.60.32 St Mary Magdalene

    10.60.33 St Michael-on-the-Mount

    10.60.34 St John-the-Poor

    10.60.35 St Andrew-under-Palace

    10.60.36 St Peter Stanthaket

    10.60.37 St Cuthbert

    10.60.38 St Martin

    10.60.39 St Lawrence

    10.60.40 St George

10.60.41 Holy Trinity Clasketgate
10.60.42 St Mary *Crackpole*
10.60.43 All Saints Hungate
10.60.44 St Peter-at-Pleas and St Peter-at-Arches
10.60.45 St Swithin
10.60.46 St Edmund
10.61 St Mary Magdalene Hartsholme
10.62 Cathedral graveyard south-east of Angel Choir
10.63 Quaker Meeting House
10.64 Baptist Chapel at Brayford Head
10.65 Presbyterian or Independent chapel in Upper Wigford
10.66 Free or Grammar School next to St Rumbold's churchyard
10.67 The Close School in College House
10.68 Christ's Hospital School (The Bluecoats School) 1 – St Mary's Guildhall
10.69 Christ's Hospital School (The Bluecoats School) 2 – Christ's Hospital Terrace

## Chapter 11. The Industrial Era

*Part 1) Infrastructure*

*a) Waterways*
11.1 Stamp End lock and causeway
11.2.1 Brayford's eastern waterside
11.2.2 Brayford's northern waterside
11.3.1 Fossdyke, Brayford and Witham navigations
11.3.2 Montague Street bridge
11.3.3 Footbridge at East Holmes Upper Witham
11.4.1 Sincil Dyke
11.4.2 Lincoln West Drainage Scheme and Gowts Drain
11.4.3 Pumping houses at Wellington Works and Boultham Junction
11.4.4 Pumping engine Pyewipe Junction
11.4.5 Footbridge on Fossdyke over Main Drain
11.4.6 Little Bargate bridge
11.5.1 Stamp End dock and boat-building yard
11.5.2 Brayford pool boat-building yard

*b) Road ways*
11.6.1 Long distance road routes
11.6.2 Bracebridge bridge
11.6.3 Bargate toll bar and cottage
11.6.4 Gowts Bridge
11.6.5 High Bridge and ford
11.7.1 Intermediate road routes
11.7.2 Toll bar at Canwick Road
11.7.3 Bridges at Bishop's Bridge
11.7.4 Victoria Bridge
11.8.1 Local road routes

11.8.2 Holmes bridge
11.8.3 Firth Road bridge
11.8.4 Thorn Bridge, Melville Street
11.8.5 St Mary's Bridge
11.9 Tram system
11.10 Motor transport system
11.10.1 City Bus Garage, St Mark's Street
11.10.2 Bus garage Burton Road
11.10.3 Motor engineers workshop, Scorer Street
11.10.4 Motor garage and workshop Rudgard Lane, West Parade

*c) Railways*
11.11 Railway transport network

*d) The rural setting*
11.12 Woodlands and wood-pasture to the south-west
11.13 The wetlands
11.14 Enclosed pasture and meadow east and west of the city
11.15.1 Un-enclosed pasture west of Newland, and West Common
11.15.2 Bracebridge pastures
11.16 South Common
11.17 City's arable fields
11.18 Open fields of parishes of Nettleham and Greetwell
11.19.1 Bracebridge village
11.19.2 Bracebridge Hall
11.20 Boultham & Boultham Hall

*e) Market Places*
11.21 Market Hill, the High Street from St Mary le Wigford to St Martin's parish
11.22 Market place at Castle Hill
11.23 Swine/beast market
11.24 The shambles, Clasketgate

*Part 2) The Living City*

*a) Housing*
11.25 Working class housing of late 18th and early 19th centuries in Newport, the Bail, Lower City and Wigford
11.26 Working class housing estates c.1850–1945 in Newport, Newland, *Butwerk*, Wigford and elsewhere
11.27 Housing in the Close and Eastgate
11.28 Newly built Victorian housing for the middle and upper classes c.1850–1918
11.29.1 Chartist Colony in Brant Road
11.29.2 Swanpool Garden Suburb
11.30 St Giles Estate
11.31 Middle class house building between the Wars
11.32 'Prefabs' at Grainsby Close, Bracebridge

11.33 Bishop's Palace
11.34 Hartsholme Hall

b) *Manufacturing Industry*
11.35 Smithies
11.36 Heavy engineering works
11.37 Animal processing industries
11.38 Food processing industries & brewing industry
11.39 Textile industries
11.40 Wood processing industries
11.41 Quarries
    11.41.1 Clay quarries in the cliff face north-west of city
    11.41.2 Stone and clay quarries in the cliff face east of the city
    11.41.3 Quarries in the cliff face south of the city
    11.41.4 Stonepits north and north-east of the Upper City
    11.41.5 The Cathedral quarry, Riseholme Road
    11.41.6 Artificial stone manufacturers
    11.41.7 Gravel quarries
11.42 Brick and tile manufacture
11.43 Chemical industries
11.44 Gas production industry
11.45 Electricity production industry

c) *Service industry*
11.46 Water supply industry
11.47 Sewage industry
11.48 Laundry industry
11.49 Banking industry
11.50 Fire stations
11.51 Police stations
11.52.1 County Hospital, Drury Lane
11.52.2 County Hospital, Sewell Road
11.52.3 Isolation Hospitals around West Common
11.52.4 Bromhead Nursing Home
11.53 Lunatic Asylum (the Lawn Hospital)
11.54 Dispensaries

d) *Education*
11.55 The Mechanics' Institute
11.56 School of Science and the Arts (the City School)
11.57 Lincoln Upper Grammar School (Upper Lindum Street site)
11.58 Girls' High School
11.59 Lincoln School (Wragby Road site)
11.60 Christ's Hospital (Bluecoats School) Christ's Hospital Terrace
11.61 Elementary Schools
11.62 Diocesan Training College (Bishop Grosseteste's College)
11.63 Theological College

e) *Judicial Functions*
11.64 The Stonebow
11.65 The Sessions House
11.66.1 New County Hall (assize court in Castle)
11.66.2 The Judge's Lodgings
11.67 Prisons
11.68 The House of Industry, the Workhouse and the House of the Girls' Friendly Society
11.69 Gallows

f) *Recreation*
11.70 Upper City (County) Assembly Rooms
11.71 Lower City (City) Assembly Rooms
11.72 City Library, Free School Lane
11.73 The Usher Gallery
11.74 Theatres and cinemas
11.75 Private clubs
11.76 Public Parks and Gardens
11.77 The Racecourse
11.78 Sports grounds
11.79 Swimming pools

**Part 3) Defending the City**
11.80 The Close Wall
11.81 The Depot
11.82 The Militia barracks
11.83 The Sobraon barracks
11.84.1 Drill Hall, Broadgate
11.84.2 Rifle butts on South Common
11.85.1 Reception aerodrome on West Common 1915–18
11.85.2 Tank testing ground west of Boultham Park Road
11.86 Skellingthorpe airfield (RAF)
11.87 Anti-Tank walls and perimeter defences 1939–45.

**Part 4) Church and chapel**
11.88 The Cathedral
11.89 The College of the Vicars-Choral
11.90 St Anne's Bedehouses
11.91 Anglican churches on ancient sites
    11.91.1 St Peter Eastgate
    11.91.2 St Margaret Pottergate
    11.91.3 St Benedict
    11.91.4 St Botolph
    11.91.5 St Mark
    11.91.6 St Mary-le-Wigford
    11.91.7 St Peter-at-Gowts
    11.91.8 St Paul-in-the-Bail
    11.91.9 St Mary Magdalene
    11.91.10 St Michael-on-the-Mount
    11.91.11 St Michael's graveyard (formerly St Cuthbert)
    11.91.12 St Martin (original site)

11.91.13 St Martin's graveyard (formerly St Mary *Crackpole*)
11.91.14 St Peter-at-Arches
11.91.15 St Swithin old church
11.91.16 St Nicholas Newport (original site)
11.91.17 All Saints Bracebridge
11.91.18 St Helen Boultham
11.92 Anglican Churches on new sites
11.92.1 All Saints Monks Road
11.92.2 St Andrew Canwick Road
11.92.3 St Faith Charles Street West
11.92.4 St Giles, Lamb Gardens
11.92.5 St Martin West Parade (new site)
11.92.6 St Matthias Burton Road
11.92.7 St Nicholas Newport (new site)
11.92.8 St Swithin (new site)
11.92.9 Holy Cross Skellingthorpe Road
11.92.10 St Matthew Boultham Park Road
11.93 Quaker Meeting House
11.94 Baptist Chapels at St Benedict's Square, Mint Street and Monks' Road
11.95 Presbyterian, Independent and Congregational chapels
11.96 Wesleyan and Methodist chapels
11.97 Salvation Army Citadel
11.98 Roman Catholic churches
11.99 Civic cemeteries

# 15. Bibliography

## 1) Abbreviations

CCR – Calendar of Close Rolls.
CIL – Corpus Inscriptionum Latinarum (Berlin).
CPR – Calendar of Patent Rolls.
CRR – Curia Regis Rolls.
HMC – 14th Report of the Historical Manuscripts Commission. Appendix Part VIII; The Manuscripts of Lincoln, Bury St Edmunds etc. London, 1895.
NMP – Air photographic plotting undertaken by the National Mapping Programme, English Heritage, Kemble Drive, Swindon.
SMR – Lincolnshire Sites and Monuments Record, Lincolnshire County Council, Planning Directorate, City Hall, Lincoln.

## 2) Published and Unpublished Sources

Abramson, P, Berg, D S and Fossick, M R, 1999, *Roman Castleford. Excavations 1974–85 Volume II. The Structural and Environmental Evidence*. Wakefield.

Adam, J P, 1994, *Roman Building Materials and Techniques*. London.

Addyman, P V and Whitwell, J B, 1970, 'Some Middle Saxon Pottery Types in Lincolnshire', *Antiquaries Journal* 50, 96–102.

Airs, M (ed.), 2000, *The Edwardian Great House*. Oxford.

Alarcão J and Étienne, R, 1977, *Fouilles de Conimbriga I: L'Architecture*. Paris.

Albone, J and Field, N, 2000, 'Archaeology in Lincolnshire 2000', *Lincolnshire History and Archaeology* 35, 40–56.

Allason-Jones, L and McKay, B, 1985, *Coventina's Well. A Shrine on Hadrian's Wall*, Chesters Museum.

Allison, P M, 1997, 'Roman Households: an archaeological perspective', *Roman Urbanism*, (ed. H Parkins). London, 112–146.

Ambler, R W, 1989, *Ranters, Revivalists and Reformers: Primitive Methodism and Rural Society South Lincolnshire 1817–1875*. Hull.

Ambler, R W, 2000, *Churches, Chapels and the Parish Communities of Lincolnshire 1660–1900*. The History of Lincolnshire 9. Lincoln.

Anderson, A C and Anderson, A S (eds. ), 1981, *Roman pottery research in Britain and north-western Europe*. British Archaeological Reports (British Series) 123. Oxford.

Anon. *c.*1933, *The Story of a Great Adventure*. Lincoln.

Armstrong, A, 1779, *Map of Lincolnshire*. Lincoln.

Ashton, M, 1980, 'The stratigraphy of the Lincolnshire Limestone Formation (Bajocian) in Lincolnshire and Rutland', *Proceedings of the Geological Association*, 91, 203–23.

Aspinall, P J, 1976, 'Speculative Builders and the Development of Cleethorpes 1850–1900', *Lincolnshire History and Archaeology* 11, 43–52.

Aspinall, P J, 1978, *The Building applications and the building industry in 19th century towns. The scope for statistical analysis*. Research Memorandum of the Centre for Urban and Regional Studies, University of Birmingham 68. Birmingham.

Aspinall, P J and Whitehand, J W R, 1980, 'Building Plans: a major source for urban studies', *Area* 12, 199–203.

Astill, G G, 1983, 'Economic change in later medieval England: an archaeological review', *Social relations and ideas: essays in honour of R H Hilton* (eds. T H Aston *et al.*). London, 217–47.

Atkinson, D, 1942, *Report on the excavations at Wroxeter (the Roman City of Viroconium) in the county of Salop, 1923–27*. Oxford.

Badie A, Sablayrolles R and Schenk J-L, 1994, *St Bertrand de Comminges. I : le Temple du forum et le Monument à Enceinte Circulaire*. Toulouse.

Baker, F L, 1957, *The History of Nettleham, Lincolnshire*. Gainsborough.

Baker, F T, 1936, 'Roman Pottery Kiln at Lincoln', *Lincolnshire Magazine* 3/7, 187–90.

Baker, F T, 1938, *Roman Lincoln*. Lincoln.

Baker, N, Dalwood H, Holt R, Mundy C and Taylor G, 1992, 'From Roman to medieval Worcester: development and planning in the Anglo-Saxon city', *Antiquity* 66, 65–74.

Ball, F and Ball, N, 1988, 'The Canterbury Try and Mitre Square: an appreciation of its proportions', *Antiquaries Journal* 68, 294–301.

Balty, J-Ch, 1994, 'Le Centre Civique des Villes Romaines et ses Espaces Politiques et Administratifs', *La Ciudad en el Mundo Romano*. Tarragona, 91–107.

Barker, P A, White R, Pretty K, Bird H and Corbishley M, 1997, *The Baths Basilica, Wroxeter. Excavations 1966–90*. English Heritage Archaeological Report 8. London.

Barley, M, 1964, 'The Medieval Borough of Torksey 1960–2', *Antiquaries Journal* 44, 164–87.

Barley, M, 1981, 'The Medieval Borough of Torksey 1963–8' *Antiquaries Journal* 61, 263–91.

Barley, M, 1989, 'Postscript', *Twentieth Century Lincolnshire*. The History of Lincolnshire 12 (ed. D Mills). Lincoln, 350–361.

Barlow, T, 1984, 'Maltings, Brayford Wharf North, Lincoln', *Lincolnshire History and Archaeology* 19, 114–117.

Barnes, T D, 1982, *The New Empire of Diocletian and Constantine*. Harvard.

Barnwell, P and Giles, C, 1997, *English Farmsteads*. London.

Barrett, J C, 1997, 'Theorising Roman Archaeology', *TRAC 96. Proceedings of the Sixth Annual Theoretical Roman Archaeology*

*Conference, Sheffield 1996* (eds. K Meadows, C Lemke and J Heron). Oxford, 1–7.

Barton, M J, 1998, 'Stamp End Railway Bridge, Lincoln', *Lincolnshire History and Archaeology* 33, 55–6.

Bassett, S R, 1989, 'Lincoln and the Anglo-Saxon see of Lindsey', *Anglo-Saxon England* 18, 1–32.

Bassett, S R, 1992, 'Churches and Towns in the West Midlands: the transition from British to Anglo-Saxon Control', *Pastoral Care before the Parish* (eds. J Blair and R Sharpe). Leicester, 13–40.

Bassett, S R (ed. ), 1989, *The Origins of the Anglo-Saxon Kingdoms.* Leicester.

Bateman, N C W, 1997, 'The London Amphitheatre: excavations 1987–96', *Britannia* 28, 51–86.

Bates, D, 1992, *Bishop Remigius of Lincoln 1067–1092.* Lincoln Cathedral Publications. Lincoln.

Batey, C, 1988, 'A Viking-Age Bell from Freswick Links, Caithness', *Medieval Archaeology* 32, 213–6.

Bean, G E, 1979, *Aegean Turkey* (2nd edition). London.

Beckwith, I, 1968, 'Brayford Wharf East', *Lincolnshire Industrial Archaeology Newsletter* 3/2, not paginated.

Beckwith, I, 1990, *The Book of Lincoln.* Buckingham.

Bedford, W, 1839, 'An Account of the Strata of Lincoln...', *Magazine of Natural History* (New Series) 3, 553–6.

Bedford, W, 1843, 'The Geology of Lincoln ...', *A selection of papers relative to the County of Lincoln read before the Lincolnshire Topographical Society 1841, 1842.* Lincoln, 15–28.

Bedon, R, Chevallier, R and Pinon P, 1988, *Architecture et Urbanisme en Gaule Romaine* (2 volumes). Paris.

Bell, T, 1998, 'Churches on Roman Buildings: Christian Associations and Roman Masonry in Anglo-Saxon England', *Medieval Archaeology* 42, 1–18.

Bennett, B, 1982, *The Catholic Church in Lincoln.* Lincoln.

Bennett, M and Field, F N, 1999, 'Archaeology in Lincolnshire 1999', *Lincolnshire History and Archaeology* 34, 24–37.

Benton, J and Sudell, T, 2001, *Memories of the Hartsholme Hall Estate.* Lincoln.

Beresford, G, 1987, *Goltho: The Development of an Early Medieval Manor c.850–1150.* English Heritage Archaeological Report 4. London.

Betteridge, S J, 1984, 'Industrial Archaeology Notes 1983', *Lincolnshire History and Archaeology* 19, 113–7.

Betteridge, S J, 1985a, 'Lincoln Railways', *Lincolnshire History and Archaeology* 20, 65.

Betteridge, S J, 1985b, 'Ruston and Proctor Boilerworks, Firth Road, Lincoln', *Lincolnshire History and Archaeology* 20, 65–6.

Biddle, M, 1968, 'Archaeology and the History of British Towns', *Antiquity* 42, 109–16.

Bidwell, P T, 1979, *The Legionary Bath-House and Basilica and Forum at Exeter.* Exeter Archaeological Report 1. Exeter.

Bidwell, P T, 1997, *Roman Forts in Britain.* London.

Bidwell, P and Holbrook, N, 1989, *Hadrian's Wall Bridges.* English Heritage Archaeological Report 9. London.

Bilson, J, 1911, 'The plan of the first cathedral church of Lincoln', *Archaeologia* 62, 543–64.

Birch, N C, 1999, *Stamford – An Industrial History.* Society for Lincolnshire Hisory and Archaeology. Lincoln.

Birch, W DeG, 1904, *List of Books belonging to the Mayor and Corporation ...* Lincoln.

Birch, W DeG (ed.), 1906, *Catalogue of the Royal Charters and other Documents belonging to the Corporation of Lincoln ...* Lincoln.

Bird, D G, 1996, 'The London Region in the Roman Period', *Interpreting Roman London. Papers in memory of Hugh Chapman* (eds. J Bird, M Hassall and H Sheldon). London, 217–232.

Birley, A R, 1979, *The People of Roman Britain.* London.

Bischoff, J P, 1975, 'Economic Changes in 13th Century Lincoln: Decline of an Urban Cloth Industry'. Unpublished PhD dissertation, Yale University.

Bischoff, J P, forthcoming, *The Lincoln City Warden's Accounts.* Lincoln Record Society Series. Lincoln.

Bishop, M C and Coulston, J C, 1993, *Roman Military Equipment.* London.

Bishop, M C and Freeman, P W M, 1993, 'Recent work at Osmanthorpe, Nottinghamshire', *Britannia* 24, 159–89.

Black, E W, 1996, 'Box Flue-Tiles in Britannia: the Spread of Roman Bathing in the First and Second Centuries', *Archaeological Journal* 153, 60–78.

Blackburn, M, Colyer, C and Dolley, M, 1983, *Early Medieval Coins from Lincoln and its Shire c.770–110.* Archaeology of Lincoln Series 6/1. London.

Blackburn, M and Mann, J E, 1995, 'A late Anglo-Saxon Coin Die from Flaxengate, Lincoln', *Lincoln Archaeology 1994–5.* Annual Report of City of Lincoln Archaeology Unit 7 (ed. M J Jones). Lincoln, 27–9.

Blagg, T F C, 1979, 'The use of Terra-cotta for Architectural Ornament in Italy and the Western Provinces', *Roman Brick and Tile* (ed. A McWhirr). British Archaeological Reports (International Series) 68. Oxford, 267–284.

Blagg, T F C, 1980, 'Roman civil and military architecture in the province of Britain: aspects of patronage, influence and craft organization', *World Archaeology* 12/1, 127–43.

Blagg, T F C, 1982a, 'Reconstructions of Roman decorated architecture: proportions, prescriptions and practice', *Structural Reconstruction. Approaches to the interpretation of the excavated remains of buildings* (ed. P J Drury). British Archaeological Reports (British Series) 100. Oxford, 131–161.

Blagg, T F C, 1982b, 'A Roman Relief-Carving of Three Female Figures, found at Lincoln', *Antiquaries Journal* 62, 125–126.

Blagg, T F C, 1983, 'The Re-use of Monumental Masonry in late Roman defensive walls', *Roman Urban Defences in the West* (eds. J Maloney and B Hobley). Council for British Archaeology Research Report 51. London, 130–35.

Blagg, T F C, 1984, 'An examination of the connexions between military and civilian architecture in Roman Britain', *Military and Civilian in Roman Britain* (eds. T F C Blagg and A C King). British Archaeological Reports (British Series) 136. Oxford, 249–265.

Blagg, T F C, 1990a, 'Architectural Munificence in Britain: the Evidence of Inscriptions', *Britannia* 21, 13–31.

Blagg, T F C, 1990b, 'The Temple at Bath in the context of classical temples in Western Europe', *Journal of Roman Archaeology* 3, 416–30.

Blagg, T F C, 1996, 'The External Decoration of Romano-British Buildings', *Architecture in Roman Britain* (eds. P Johnson and I Haynes). Council for British Archaeology Research Report 94. London, 9–18.

Blagg, T F C, 1999, 'Architectural stonework', *The Defences of the Lower City, Excavations at the Park and West Parade 1970–2 and a discussion of other sites excavated up to 1994* (ed. M J Jones). Archaeology of Lincoln 7/2 & Council for British Archaeology Research Report 114. York, 44–50.

Blagg, T F C, 2000, 'The Legionary Principia', *Roman Fortresses and their Legions* (ed. R Brewer). London & Cardiff, 139–48.

Blagg, T F C, 2002, *Roman Architectural Ornament in Britain.* British Archaeological Reports (British Series) 329. Oxford.

Blagg, T F C and Henig, M, 1986, 'Cupid or Adonis? A new Roman relief carving from Lincoln', *Antiquaries Journal* 66, 360–3.

Blagg, T F C and King A C (eds.), 1984, *Military and Civilian in Roman Britain.* British Archaeological Reports (British Series) 136. Oxford.

Blagg, T F C and Millett, M (eds.), 1990, *The Early Roman Empire in the West.* Oxford.

Blair, W J, 1992, 'Anglo-Saxon Minsters: a topographical review', *Pastoral Care before the Parish* (eds. J Blair and R Sharpe). Leicester, 226–66.

Blair, W J and Pyrah, C (eds.), 1996, *Church Archaeology. Research*

*Directions for the Future*. Council for British Archaeology Research Report 104. York.

Bland R, 1997, 'The changing patterns of hoards of precious-metal coins in the late empire', *Antiquité Tardive* 5, 29–55.

Bogaers, J E, 1977, 'Roman Tile-Stamps from Lincoln (Lindum) and the Legio V Alaudae', *Britannia* 8, 275–8.

Boghi, F and Boylston, A, 1996, 'The Medieval Cemetery of Pennell Street, Lincoln, Lincolnshire'. Unpublished report (SUS96), Calvin Wells Laboratory, University of Bradford.

Bögli, H, 1984, *Aventicum: Die Römerstadt und das Museum*. Archäologische Führer der Schweiz 20. Avenches.

Bonner, D, 1999, 'Appendix A: Flint Report', 'The Proposed Distict Centre, Nettleham Road' (ed. R Trimble). Unpublished Report (No 380) City of Lincoln Archaeological Unit. Lincoln.

Boon, G C, 1974, *Silchester: The Roman Town of Calleva*. Newton Abbott.

Boon, G C, 1988, 'Counterfeit Coins in Roman Britain', *Coins and the Archaeologist* (eds. P J Casey and R M Reece). London, 102–188.

Boutwood, Y, 'Prehistoric Linear Boundaries in Lincolnhsire and its Fringes', *Lincolnshire's Archaeology from the Air*. Occasional Papers in Lincolnshire History and Archaeology 11, (ed. R Bewley). Lincoln, 29–46.

Bowden, M (ed.), 2000, *Furness Iron. The Physical Remains of the Iron Industry and Related Woodland Industries of Furness and Southern Lakeland*. London.

Bowersock, G, 1996, 'The vanishing paradigm of the fall of Rome', *Bulletin of the American Academy of the Arts and Sciences* 149, 29–43.

Boylston, A and Roberts, C, 1994, 'Welton-Lincoln Trunk Main. Report on the Human Skeletal Remains'. Unpublished report, Calvin Wells Laboratory, University of Bradford.

Boylston, A and Roberts, C, 1995, 'Lincoln Excavations 1972–1987, Report on the Human Skeletal Remains', Unpublished report, Calvin Wells Laboratory, University of Bradford.

Bradley, R, 1971, 'A field survey of the Chichester entrenchments', *Excavations at Fishbourne 1*, Society of Antiquaries Research Report 26 (ed. B Cunliffe). London, 17–36.

Bradley, R, 1998, *The Passage of Arms. An archaeological analysis of prehistoric hoard and votive deposits* (2nd edition). Oxford.

Bradley, R, 2000, *An Archaeology of Natural Places*. London.

Brann, M and Donel, L, 1997, 'Close Wall, Lincoln: Archaeological Recording during Conservation Works'. Unpublished report, City of Lincoln Archaeology Unit (No 293), Lincoln.

Brann, M, forthcoming, *Survey work at the Bishop's Palace Lincoln*.

Brewer, R J(ed.), 2000, *Roman Fortresses and their Legions*. London & Cardiff.

Brigham, T, 1992, 'Basilica studies', *From Roman Basilica to Medieval Market. Archaeology in Action in the City of London* (ed. G Milne). London, 106–13.

Britton, J, 1812, *The Beauties of England: Lincolnshire*, London.

Brodie, A, Croom, J and Davies, J O, 2002, *English Prisons. An architectural history*. London.

Brodribb, G, 1987, *Roman Brick and Tile*. Gloucester.

Brooks, D A, 1986, 'A Review of the Evidence for Continuity in British Towns in the 5th and 6th centuries', *Oxford Journal of Archaeology* 5/1, 77–102.

Brooks, F W, 1934–5, 'The Hospital of the Holy Innocents without Lincoln', *Associated Architectural Societies Reports and Papers* 42, 157–188.

Brooks, R, 1986, *Lincolnshire Engines Worldwide*. Lincoln.

Brown, A (ed.), 1999, *The Rows of Chester. The Chester Rows Research Project*. English Heritage Archaeological Report 16. London.

Brown, A E (ed.), 1991, *Garden Archaeology*. Council for British Archaeology Research Report 78. London.

Brown, G B, 1925, *The Arts in Early England Volume 2 – Anglo-Saxon Architecture*. London.

Brown, I J, 1971, 'Gazetteer of Ironstone Mines in the East Midlands, Lincolnshire Section', *Lincolnshire Industrial Archaeology* 6/2 and 6/3, 46.

Brown, P R L, 1981, *The Cult of the Saints*. London & Chicago.

Brown, R A, 1959, 'A List of Castles, 1154–1216', *English History Review* 74, 249–80.

Bruce-Mitford, R, 1993, 'Late Celtic Hanging Bowls in Lincolnshire and South Humberside', *Pre-Viking Lindsey* (ed. A G Vince), Lincoln Archaeological Studies 1. Lincoln, 45–70.

Brühl, C L, 1988, 'Problems of the Continuity of Roman *Civitas* in Gaul', *The Rebirth of Towns in the West* (eds. R Hodges and B Hobley). Council for British Archaeology Research Report 68. London, 43–6.

Buckland, P C, 1976, *The Environmental Evidence from the Church Street Sewer System*. The Archaeology of York 14/1. London.

Buckland, P C, 1984, 'The 'Anglian' Tower and the use of Jurassic Limestone in York', *Archaeological Papers from York, Presented to M W Barley* (eds. P V Addyman and V E Black). York, 51–7.

Buckland, P C and Sadler, J P, 1985, 'Late Flandrian Alluviation in the Humberhead Levels', *East Midlands Geographer* 8, 239–251.

Burgess, S (ed.), 1990, *The Victorian Façade 1859–1918. William Watkins and Son Architects of Lincoln*. Lincoln.

Burnham, B, Collis J R, Dobinson, C, Haselgrove, C and Jones, M J, 2001, 'Themes for urban research, *c*. 100BC to AD200'. *Britons and Romans: Advancing an Archaeological Agenda*. Council for British Archaeology Research Report 125 (eds. S James and M Millett). York, 67–76.

Burnham, B and Wacher, J, 1990, *The 'Small Towns' of Roman Britain*. London.

Butler, H E (trans.), 1934, 'A Description of London by William Fitzstephen', *Norman London An Essay by F.M. Stenton*. Historical Association Pamphlet 93. London, 25–35.

Butler, L A S, 1984, 'The Houses of the Mendicant Orders in Britain: Recent Archaeological Work', *Archaeological Papers from York Presented to M.W. Barley*, (eds. P V Addyman and V E Black), York. 137–44.

Caffyn, L, 1986, *Workers' Housing in West Yorkshire, 1750–1920*. West Yorkshire Metropolitan County Council/RCHME Supplementary Series 9. London.

Caley, J, Ellis, H and Bandinel, B (eds.), 1817, *Monasticon Anglicanum ... by Sir William Dugdale* (6 volumes). London.

Calladine, A and Fricker, J, 1993, *East Cheshire Textile Mills*. London.

Cameron, A, 1993, *The Mediterranean World in Late Antiquity 395–600*. London.

Cameron, K, 1985, *The place-names of Lincolnshire, Part 1, The place-names of the City and County of Lincoln*. English Place-Name Society 58. Cambridge.

Campbell, M, 1991, 'Gold Silver and Precious Stones', *Medieval Industries* (eds. J Blair and N Ramsay). London & Rio Grande, 107–166.

Campbell, W A, 1971, *The Chemical Industry*. London.

Campbell, B M S, Galloway J A and Murphy, M, 1992, 'Rural land use in the metropolitan hinterland, 1270–1339: the evidence of inquisitiones post mortem', *Agricultural History Review* 40, 1–22.

Campbell, B M S, Galloway, J A, Keene, D and Murphy, M, 1993, *A Medieval Capital and its Grain supply: Agrarian production and distribution in the London Region c. 1300*. Historical Geography Research Series 30. London.

Carroll-Spillecke, M, 1993, 'Das Römische Militärlager Divitia in Köln-Deutz', *Kölner Jahrbuch* 26, 321–444.

Carrott, J, Hall, A, Issitt, M, Lancaster, S, Kenward, H and Milles, A, 1994, 'Evaluation of Biological Remains from deposits at the University College for Lincolnshire Site'. Unpublished report (94/21), Environmental Archaeology Unit, University of York.

Carrott, J, Issitt, M, Kenward, H, Large, F, McKenna, B and Skidmore, P, 1995, 'Insect and other invertebrate remains from excavations at four Waterside sites in Lincoln'. Unpublished report (95/10), Environmental Archaeology Unit, University of York.

Carver, M O H, 1993, *Arguments in Stone. Archaeological Research and the European Town in the First Millennium*. Oxbow Monograph 29. Oxford.

Carver, M O H (ed.), 1995, *Excavations at York Minster Volume I, From Roman fortress to Norman cathedral, by D Phillips and B Heywood*. London.

Carver, M O H, 1997, 'Town and anti-Town in the first millennium AD, Urbanism in Medieval Europe'. Unpublished pre-circulated paper from the *Medieval Europe, Brugge 1997* Conference, volume 1, 379–389.

CBA 1985, *Hallelujah! Recording chapels and meeting houses*. Council for British Archaeology Handbooks Series. London.

Chadderton, J (ed.), 2002, *The Legionary Fortress at Wroxeter. Excavations by Graham Webster 1955–85*. English Heritage Archaeological Report 19. London.

Chadwick, N, 1971, *The Celts*. Harmondsworth.

Chambers, J I and Wilson, C M, 1972, 'Dickenson's Mill, Lincoln', *Lincolnshire Industrial Archaeology* 7/2, 16–19.

Chapman, H, Coppack, G and Drewett, P, 1975, *Excavations at the Bishops Palace, Lincoln 1968–72*. Occasional Papers in Lincolnshire History and Archaeology 1. Lincoln.

Chapman, S D, 1971, *The History of Working Class Housing. A Symposium*. Newton Abbot.

Cherry, J, 1991a, 'Leather', *English Medieval Industries* (eds. J Blair and N Ramsay). London & Rio Grande, 295–318.

Cherry, J, 1991b, 'Pottery and Tile', *English Medieval Industries* (eds. J Blair and N Ramsay). London & Rio Grande, 189–209.

Chilver, G E F, 1941, *Cisalpine Gaul. Social and Economic History from 49BC to the Death of Trajan*. Oxford.

Chitwood, P, 1991, 'Lincoln's ancient docklands: the search continues', *Third International Conference of Waterfront Archaeology*. Council for British Archaeology Research Report 74 (eds. R L Good, R H Jones and M W Ponsford). London, 169–176.

Chowne, P, *et al.*, 1986, 'Excavations at an Iron Age Defended Enclosure at Tattershall Thorpe, Lincolnshire', *Procedings of the Prehistoric Society* 52, 159–88.

Christie N and Loseby S T (eds.), 1996, *Towns in Transition: Urban Evolution in Late Antiquity and the Early Middle Ages*. London.

Claridge, A, 1998, *Oxford Archaeological Guides – Rome*. Oxford.

Clark, D, 2000, 'The Shop Within? An Analysis of the Architectural Evidence for medieval Shops', *Architectural History* 43, 58–87.

Clarke, G, 1991, *The Cinemas of Lincoln*. Mercia Cinema Society publications. Wakefield.

Clarke, G, 2001, 'Lincoln's Cinemas in the Twentieth Century', *Aspects of Lincoln. Discovering Local History*, (ed. A Walker). Barnsley, 159–183.

Clarke, H and Ambrosiani, B, 1991, *Towns in the Viking Age*. Leicester.

Clarke, R H, 1955, *Steam Engine Builders of Lincolnshire*. Norwich.

Clauss, M, 2000, *The Roman Cult of Mithras* (translated R Gordon). Edinburgh.

Cleere, H, 1978, 'Roman Harbours in Britain south of Hadrian's Wall', *Roman Shipping and Trade: Britain and the Rhine Provinces*. Council for British Archaeology Research Report 24 (eds. J du P Taylor and H Cleere). London, 36–9.

Cocroft, W, 2000, *Dangerous Energy. The Archaeology of gunpowder and military explosives manufacture*. London.

Cole, R E G, 1897–8, 'Notes on the Ecclesiastical History of the Deanery of Graffoe to the close of the Fourteenth Century', *Associated Architectural Societies Report and Papers* 24, 381–448.

Cole, R E G, 1903–4, 'The Priory of St Katherine without Lincoln of the Order of St Gilbert of Sempringham', *Associated Architectural Societies Reports and Papers* 27, 264–336.

Cole, R E G (ed.), 1911, *Lincolnshire Church Notes made by Gervase Holles A.D.1634 to 1642*. Lincoln Record Society 1. Lincoln.

Cole, R E G (ed.), 1913, *Speculum Dioeceseos Lincolniensis sub episcopis W Wake et E Gibson, Part I AD 1705–1723*. Lincoln Record Society 4. Lincoln.

Coles, J, Orme B, May, J and Moore, C, 1979, 'Excavations of Late Bronze Age or Iron Age Date at Washingborough Fen', *Lincolnshire History and Archaeology* 14, 5–10.

Collingwood, R G and Richmond, I A, 1969, *The Archaeology of Roman Britain* (2nd edition). London.

Colsell, L (ed.), 1986, *Lincolnshire Built Engines by Richard Brooks and Martin Longdon*. Lincoln.

Colvin, H M, Allen-Brown, R and Taylor, A J, 1963, *The History of the King's Works Volume 2, The Middle Ages*. London.

Colyer, C, 1975, 'Excavations at Lincoln 1970–72: The Western Defences of the Lower Town. An Interim Report', *Antiquaries Journal* 55, 227–66.

Colyer, C and Jones, M J, 1979, 'Excavations at Lincoln, Second Interim report: Excavations in the Lower Town 1972–8', *Antiquaries Journal* 59, 50–91.

Conway, H, 1991, *People's Parks*. Cambridge.

Conzen, M R G, 1960, *Alnwick Northumberland: A Study in Town Plan Analysis*, Institute of British Geographers 27. London.

Conzen, M R G, 1968, 'The Use of Town Plans in the Study of Urban History', *The Study of Urban History* (ed. H J Dyos). London, 113–30.

Cookson, W D, 1843, 'On the Hospital of the Holy Innocents called Le Malandriu at Lincoln …', *Papers of the Lincolnshire Topographical Society 1841, 1842*, 29–48.

Cool, H E M and Philo, C, *Roman Castleford. Excavations 1974–85 Volume I, The Small Finds*. Wakefield.

Cooper, T (ed.), 2001, *The Journal of William Dowsing. Iconoclasm in East Anglia during the English Civil War*. Woodbridge.

Coppack, G C, 1973, 'The Excavation of a Roman and Medieval site at Flaxengate, Lincoln', *Lincolnshire History and Archaeology* 8, 73–114.

Coppack, G C, 1999, 'Conservation Plan for the Medieval Bishop's Palace at Lincoln'. Unpublished report, English Heritage. London.

Coppack, G C, 2000, *Medieval Bishop's Palace, Lincoln, Lincolnshire*. London.

Corney, M and Griffiths, N, forthcoming, A Catalogue of Late Roman Military Metalwork, *Britannia*.

Coulson, C, 1982, 'Hierarchism in conventual crenellation: an essay in the Sociology and Metaphysics of Medieval Fortification', *Medieval Archaeology* 26, 69–100.

Coupland, F and Taylor, G, 1995, 'Archaeology in Lincolnshire – Quarrington: Town Road' (eds. N Field and I George), *Lincolnshire History and Archaeology* 30, 48.

Courteault, P, 1921, 'An inscription recently found at Bordeaux', *Journal of Roman Studies* 11, 101–7.

Courtney, P, 2001, 'East Midlands Research Agenda' documentation. http://www.le.ac.uk/archaeology/pdf.

Cramp, R J, 1986, 'Anglo-Saxon and Italian sculpture', *Settimane di Studio del Centro Italiano di Studi sull' Alto Medioevo* 36, 125–142.

Cranstone, D, 2000, 'The Chemical Industry. Step 1 Report'. Unpublished report, English Heritage, London.

Crawford, B, 1999, 'The dedication to St Clement at Rodil, Harris', *Church, Chronicle and Learning in medieval and Early Renaissance Scotland* (ed. B. Crawford). Edinburgh, 109–122.

Cross, F L (ed.), 1957, *The Oxford Dictionary of the Christian Church*. London.

Crossley, D, 1994, 'The Iron and Steel Industries. Step 1 Report'. Unpublished report, English Heritage, London.

Crossley, D, forthcoming, 'The Engineering Industry. Step 1 Report'. Unpublished report, English Heritage, London.

Crummy, N, Crummy, P and Crossan, N, 1993, *Excavations of Roman and later cemeteries, churches and monastic sites in Colchester 1971–88*. Colchester Archaeological Report 9. Colchester.

Crummy, P, 1982, 'The origins of some major Romano-British towns', *Britannia* 13, 125–34.

Crummy, P, 1984, *Excavations at Lion Walk, Balkerne Lane and Middleborough, Colchester, Essex*. Colchester Archaeological Report 3. Colchester.

Crummy, P, 1985, 'Colchester: The mechanics of laying out a town', *Roman Urban Topography in Britain and the Western Empire*. Council for British Archaeology Research Report 59 (eds. F Grew and B Hobley). London, 78–85.

Crummy, P, 1988, 'Colchester', *Fortress into City* (ed. G Webster). London, 24–48.

Crummy, P, 1992, *Excavations at Culver Street, the Gilberd School and other sites in Colchester 1971–85*. Colchester Archaeological Report 6. Colchester.

Crummy, P, 1997, *City of Victory. The Story of Colchester – Britain's first Roman town*. Colchester.

Crummy, P, 1999, 'Colchester. Making towns out of fortresses and the first urban fortifications in Britain', *The Coloniae of Roman Britain: new studies and a review. Papers of the conference held at Gloucester on 5–6 July, 1997* (ed. H Hurst). Journal of Roman Archaeology Supplementary Series 36, 88–100.

Cummins, W A and Moore, C N, 1973, 'Petrological identification of stone impliments from Lincolnshire, Nottinghamshire and Rutland', *Proceedings of the Prehistoric Society* 39, 219–56.

Cunliffe, B W, 1988, *Greeks, Romans and Barbarians*. London.

Cunliffe, B W, 1991, *Iron Age Communities in Britain* (3rd edition). London.

Cunliffe, B W, 1995, *Iron Age Britain*. London.

Cunliffe, B W and Davenport P, 1985, 'The Temple of Sulis Minerva, Bath', *Antiquity* 40, 199–204.

Daff, T, 1981, 'The Establishment of Ironmaking at Scunthorpe', *An Industrial Island. A History of Scunthorpe* (ed. M E Armstrong). Scunthorpe, 31–8.

Dannell, G B and Wild, J P, 1987, *Longthorpe II: The Military Works-Depot: an Episode in Landscape History*. Britannia Monograph 8. London.

Darby, H C, *The Domesday Geography of Eastern England*. Cambridge.

Dark, K R, 1994, *Civitas to Kingdom. British Political Continuity 300–800*. Leicester.

Dark, K R (ed.), 1996, *External Contacts and the Economy of late Roman and Post Roman Britain*. Woodbridge.

Darley, G, 1975, *Villages of Vision*. London.

Darling, M, 1977, *A Group of Late Roman Pottery from Lincoln*. Archaeology of Lincoln 16/1. London.

Darling, M, 1981, 'Early red-slipped ware from Lincoln', *Roman pottery research in Britain and north-western Europe*. British Archaeological Reports (British Series) 123 (eds. A C Anderson and A S Anderson). Oxford, 397–415.

Darling, M, 1984, *Roman Pottery from the Upper Defences*. Archaeology of Lincoln 16/2. London.

Darling, M, 1988, 'Early Settlement at Lincoln – The Pottery', *Britannia* 19, 9–37.

Darling, M, 1998, 'Samian from the City of Lincoln', *Form and Fabric: Studies in Rome's material past in honour of B R Hartley* (ed. J Bird). Oxford, 169–177.

Darling, M and Jones, M J (eds.), 1988, 'Early Settlement at Lincoln', *Britannia* 19, 1–56.

Darling, M and Precious, B, forthcoming, *A Corpus of Roman Pottery from Lincoln*. Lincoln Archaeological Studies 6. Oxford.

Darling, M and Wood, K, 1981, 'Heighington Tile Kiln', *Antiquaries Journal* 61, 110–2.

Darvill, T and Gerrard, C, 1994, *Cirencester: town and landscape*. Cirencester.

Davey, P, 1971, 'Late Bronze Age Metalwork from Lincolnshire', *Proceedings of the Prehistoric Society* 37/1, 96–111.

Davey, P, 1973, 'Bronze Age Metalwork from Lincolnshire', *Archaeologia* 104, 51–127.

Davies, H, 2002, *Roads in Roman Britain*. Stroud.

Davies, J A, 1993, 'The study of coin finds from Romano-British towns', *Roman Towns: The Wheeler Inheritance. A Review of 50 Years' Research*. Council for British Archaeology Research Report 93 (ed. S Greep). London, 123–33.

Davies, J A, 1995, 'Roman Coins from Lincoln: an overview'. Unpublished report, Lincoln City Council. Lincoln.

Davies, J, 1996, 'Where Eagles Dare: the Iron Age of Norfolk', *Proceedings of Prehistoric Society* 62, 63–92.

Davies, J and Williamson, T, 1999, *Land of the Iceni. The Iron Age in Northern East Anglia*. Norwich.

Davies, S, 1989, *Quakerism in Lincolnshire*. Lincoln.

Davidson, H E, 1993, *The Lost Beliefs of Northern Europe*. London & New York.

Davison, D P, 1989, *The Barracks of the Roman Army from the 1st to the 3rd centuries AD*. British Archaeological Reports (International Series) 472. Oxford.

Dawes, J D, 1986, 'Human Bones from St. Mark's', *St. Mark's Church and Cemetery*. Archaeology of Lincoln 13/1(eds. B J J Gilmour and D A Stocker). London, 33–5.

Day, J, 1992, 'The Brass Industry. Step 1 Report'. Unpublished report, English Heritage, London.

DCMS 1999, 'Revised List of Buildings of Special Architectural or Historic Interest. City of Lincoln. County of Lincolnshire 17th list'. Unpublished report, DCMS, London.

Dean, L R, 1916, *A study of the cognomina of soldiers in the Roman legion*. Princeton.

Dearne, M J and Branigan, K, 1995, 'The Use of Coal in Roman Britain', *Antiquaries Journal* 75, 71–105.

Defoe, D, 1925–6, *A Tour through the Whole Island of Britain*. London.

Delaine, J, 1996, 'The Insula of the Paintings. A model for the economics of construction in Hadrianic Ostia', *Roman Ostia Revisited* (eds. A Gallina Zevi and A Claridge). Rome, 165–84.

De La Pryme, A, 1870, *The diary of Abraham De La Pryme, the Yorkshire antiquary* (ed. C Jackson). Publications of the Surtees society 54, for the year 1869. Durham, London &Edinburgh.

Dennison, E, 1998, 'MPP Monument Class Description. Decoy Ponds'. Unpublished report, English Heritage, London.

Dilke, O A W, 1971, *The Roman Land Surveyors*. Newton Abbott.

Dobinson, C S, 1998, *Monuments of War: the evaluation, recording and management of twentieth-century military sites*. London.

Dobinson, C S, Lake, J and Schofield, A J, 1997, 'Monuments of War; defining England's 20th-century defence heritage', *Antiquity* 71, 288–99.

Dobney, K, Jacques, S and Irving B, 1996, *Of Butchers and Breeds. Report on vertebrate remains from various sites in the city of Lincoln*. Lincoln Archaeological Studies 5. Lincoln.

Dobney, K, Kenward, H, Ottaway, P and Donel L, 1998, 'Down, but not out: biological evidence for complex economic organization in Lincoln in the late 4th century', *Antiquity* 72, 417–424.

Dobson, B, 1990, 'Urban decline in late medieval England', *The Medieval Town. A Reader in English Urban History 1200–1540* (eds. R Holt and G Rosser). London, 265–86.

Dolbey, G W, 1964, *The Architectural Expression of Methodism: The First Hundred Years*. London.

Dolley, M, 1975, 'The 1973 Viking-Age coin-find from Dunmore Cave', *Old Kilkenny Review* 1, 70–9.

Dolman, P, 1986, *Lincolnshire Windmills – A Contemporary Survey*. Lincoln.

Donel, L, 1991a, 'Lincoln Castle Banks', *Lincoln Archaeology 1990–1991*. City of Lincoln Archaeological Unit Annual Report 3 (ed. M J Jones). Lincoln, 9–12.

Donel, L, 1991b, 'Waterside North', *Lincoln Archaeology 1990–1991*. City of Lincoln Archaeological Unit Annual Report 3 (ed. M J Jones). Lincoln, 18–19.

Donel, L, 1992a, 'Lincoln Castle: Stability Survey; Archaeological Recording'. Unpublished report (No 13), City of Lincoln Archaeological Unit. Lincoln.

Donel, L, 1992b, 'Bracebridge Heath Kiln', *Lincoln Archaeology 1991–1992*. City of Lincoln Archaeological Unit Annual Report 4 (ed. M J Jones). Lincoln, 12.

Donel, L, 1993, 'Knights Place', *Lincoln Archaeology 1992–1993*. City of Lincoln Archaeological Unit Annual Report 5 (ed. M J Jones). Lincoln, 29–30.

Donel, L and Jarvis, M, 1990, 'Waterside North: Saltergate', *Lincoln Archaeology 1989–1990*. City of Lincoln Archaeological Unit Annual Report 2 (ed. M J Jones). Lincoln, 6–8.

Donel, L and Jones, M J, forthcoming, 'Archaeology at Lincoln Castle: Before and after 1068', *Lincoln Castle* (ed. P.Lindley). Lincoln

Dornier, A, 1987, 'Place-names in (-)wich: a preliminary linguistic survey', *Nomina* 11, 87–98.

Douet, J, 1995, 'The Water and Sewage Industries. Step 1 Report'. Unpublished report, English Heritage, London.

Douet, J, 1998, *British Barracks 1600–1914*. London.

Drinkall, G and Foreman, M (eds.), 1998, *The Anglo–Saxon Cemetery at Castledyke South, Barton-on-Humber*. Sheffield Excavation Reports 6. Sheffield.

Drury, M, 1888, 'Notes on the excavations for sewer works at Lincoln'. Unpublished Ms., Lincoln Central Library. Lincoln.

Drury, M, 1890, 'On a Concrete Causeway, supposed to be Roman, at Lincoln', *Journal of the British Archaeological Association* 46, 121–126.

Drury, P J (ed.), 1982, *Structural Reconstruction. Approaches to the interpretation of the excavated remains of buildings*. British Archaeological Reports (British Series) 100. Oxford.

Drury, P J, 1984, 'The Temple of Claudius at Colchester reconsidered', *Britannia* 15, 7–51.

Duffy, E, 1992, *The Stripping of the Altars. Traditional Religion in England c.1400–c.1580*. New Haven and London.

Duncan-Jones, R P, 1982, *The Economy of the Roman Empire: Quantitative Studies* (2nd edition). Cambridge.

Duval, N, 1977, 'La basilique de Zana (Diana Veteranorum): une nouvelle église à deux absides ou un monument à auges?', *Mélanges de l'École française de Rome, Antiquité* 89, 847–73.

Duval, N (ed.), 1989, *Actes du XI Congrès International d'Archéologie Chrétienne*. Paris & Rome.

Duval, N, Fontaine, J, Février, P-A, Picard, J-C and Barruol, G, 1991, *Naissance des Arts Chrétiens*. Paris.

Duval N and Caillet J-P, 1996, 'La Recherche sur les Églises doubles depuis 1936: historique et problématique', *Antiquité Tardive* 4, 22–37.

Duval, P M, 1961, *Paris Antique*. Paris.

Dyer, C, 1994, *Everyday Life in Medieval England*. London & Rio Grande.

Eagles, B N, 1979, *The Anglo-Saxon Settlement of Humberside*. British Archaeological Reports (British Series) 68. Oxford.

Eagles, B N, 1989, 'Lindsey', *The Origins of the Anglo-Saxon Kingdoms* (ed. S R Bassett). Leicester, 202–12.

Egan, G, forthcoming, 'Antler and bone', *Finds from the Well at St Paul-in-the-Bail*. Lincoln Archaeological Studies 9 (ed. J E Mann). Oxford.

Ekwall, E, 1930, 'How long did the Scandinavian language survive in England?', *Grammatical Miscellany offered to Otto Jespersen on his Seventieth Birthday* (eds. N Bergolm, A Brusendorff and C A Bodelsen). London & Copenhagen, 17–30.

Ekwall, E, 1960, *The Concise Oxford Dictionary of English Place-Names* (4th edition). Oxford.

Elliott, B, 1986, *Victorian Gardens*. London.

Elliott, H and Stocker, D A, 1986, *Lincoln Castle*, Lincoln.

Elvin, L, 1974, *Lincoln as it was*. Lincoln.

Elvin, L, 1976, *Lincoln as it was II*. Lincoln.

Elvin, L, 1979, *Lincoln as it was III*. Lincoln.

Elvin, L, 1981, *Lincoln as it was IV*. Lincoln.

Elsdon, S M, 1994, 'Late Bronze or Early Iron Age Pottery from Washingborough Fen', *Lincolnshire History and Archaeology* 29, 55–6.

Elsdon, S M, 1997, *Old Sleaford Revealed*. Oxbow Monograph 78. Oxford.

EMC 2001 – Early Medieval Coin Database, www-cm.fitzmuseum.cam.ac.uk/coins/emc/html

Engels, D, 1990, *Roman Corinth*. Chicago.

English Heritage, 1992, *Managing the Urban Archaeological Resource*. London.

English Heritage, 2000, *Power of Place. The future of the historic environment*. London.

English Heritage, forthcoming, 'Survey of the Commons of Lincoln'. Unpublished report, National Monuments Records Centre. Swindon.

Esmonde Cleary, A S, 1987, *Extra-Mural Areas of Romano-British Towns*. British Archaeological Reports (British Series) 169. Oxford.

Esmonde Cleary, A S, 1989, *The Ending of Roman Britain*. London.

Esmonde Cleary, A S, 1993, 'Late Roman Towns in Britain and their fate', *Pre-Viking Lindsey*. Lincoln Archaeological Studies 1 (ed. A G Vince). Lincoln, 6–13.

Esmonde Cleary, A S, 1998, 'The Origins of Towns in Roman Britain: the Contribution of Romans and Britons', *Los Origines de la Ciudad en el Mundo Romano* (ed. A Rodriguez Colmenero). Lugo, 35–54.

Esmonde Cleary, A S, 2000a, 'Putting the dead in their place: Burial location in Roman Britain', Pearce, J, Millett, M and Struck, M (eds.), *Burial Society and Context in the Roman World*. Oxford, 127–42.

Esmonde-Cleary A S, 2000b, 'Summing Up', *The Late Roman transition in the North*. British Archaeological Reports (British Series) 299 (eds. T Wilmott and P R Wilson). Oxford, 89–94.

Euzennat, M, 1994, '*Principia* militaires et forums civils', *La Ciudad en el Mundo Romano*. Tarragona, 197–203.

Evans, E, 1994, 'Military Architects and Building Design in Roman Britain', *Britannia* 25, 143–164.

Everson, P L, 1978a, 'Two Anglo-Saxon Cruciform Brooches', *Lincolnshire History and Archaeology* 13, 85–6.

Everson P L, 1978b, 'Aerial Reconnaissance in North Lincolnshire', *Lincolnshire History and Archaeology* 13, 82–3.

Everson, P L, 1979, 'Pre-Roman Linear Boundaries North of Lincoln', *Lincolnshire History and Archaeology* 14, 74–5.

Everson, P L, 1988, 'What's in a name? "Goltho", Goltho and Bullington', *Lincolnshire History and Archaeology* 23, 93–9.

Everson, P L, 1996, 'The After-Life of Monastic Houses: The Earthwork Evidence', *Lincolnshire People and Places: Essays in Memory of Terence R. Leach (1937–1994)* (ed. C Sturman). Lincoln, 13–17.

Everson, P L, 1998, '"Delightfully surrounded with woods and ponds": Field evidence for medieval gardens in England', *There by Design. Field Archaeology in Parks and Gardens* (eds. P Patterson). London, 32–8.

Everson, P L, 2000, 'Archaeological Research Agenda for Medieval Lincolnshire', http://www.le.ac.uk/archaeology/pdf.

Everson, P and Stocker D, 1999, *The Corpus of Anglo-Saxon Sculpture Volume V. Lincolnshire*. Oxford.

Everson, P L, Taylor, C C and Dunn C J, 1991, *Change and Continuity. Rural Settlement in North-west Lincolnshire*. London.

Everson, P L and Williamson, T, 1998, 'Gardens and designed Landscapes', *The Archaeology of Landscape. Studies presented* to *Christopher Taylor* (eds. P Everson and T Williamson). Manchester, 139–165.

Evison, V, 1996, 'Lincoln Glass Fragments'. Unpublished report, Lincoln City Council. Lincoln.

Exley, C L, 1970, *A History of the Torksey and Mansfield China Factories*. Lincoln.

Exley, C L and Williamson, D M, 1955–6, 'Some Notes on St Andrew's Hall Wigford', *Lincolnshire Architectural and Archaeological Society Reports and Papers* 6, 118–120.

Fairclough, G J, 2002, 'Cultural landscape and spatial planning: England's Historic Landscape Characterisation Programme', *Heritage of the North Sea Region: Conservation and Interpretation*. Papers presented at the Historic Environment of the North Sea InterReg IIC Conference, 29th –31st March 2001, South Shields (eds. L M Green and P T Bidwell). Shaftesbury, 123–49.

Fairclough, G, Lambrick, G and Hopkins, D, 2002, 'Historic Landscape Charaterisation in England and a Hampshire case study', *Europe's Cultural Landscape: archaeologists and the management of change*. Europae Archaeologiae Consilium Occasional Paper 2 (eds. G Fairclough, S Rippon and D Bull). Brussels, 69–84.

Faulkner, N, 1994, 'Later Roman Colchester', *Oxford Journal of Archaeology* 13/1, 93–120.

Faulkner, N, 1996, 'Verulamium: Interpreting Decline', *Archaeological Journal* 153, 79–103.

Faulkner, N, 1998, 'Urban Stratigraphy and Roman History', *Cirencester: The Roman Town Defences, Public Buildings and Shops*. Cirencester Excavations 5 (ed. N Holbrook). Cirencester, 371–88.

Faulkner, N, 2000, 'Change and decline in Late Romano-British Town', *Towns in Decline 100–1500* (ed. T R Slater). Aldershot, 25–50.

Fell, C, 1971, *Edward King and Martyr*. London.

Fell, C, 1978, 'Edward King and Martyr and the Anglo-Saxon Hagiographic Tradition', *Ethelred the Unready*. British Archaeological Reports (British Series) 59 (ed. D Hill). Oxford, 1–13.

Fellman, R, 1958, *Die Principia des Legionslagers Vindonissa und das Zentralgebäude der römischen Lager und Kastelle*. Zusammendruck aus Jber. Vind. 1956–7 & 1957–8. Brugg, 5–174.

Fellmann, R, nd., *Principia – Stabsgebäude*. Bonn.

Fenton, M, 1980, 'The Roman City Wall: building materials and methods', *The Defences of the Upper Roman Enclosure*. The Archaeology Lincoln 7/1 (ed. M J Jones). London, 37–47.

Fentress, E W B, 1979, *Numidia and the Roman Army*. British Archaeological Reports (International Series) 53. Oxford.

Février, P-A, 1969, 'Enceinte et Colonie (de Nimes à Vérone, Toulouse, et Tipasa)', *Hommage à Fernand Benoit Volume III*. Révue d'Etudes Ligures 35. Bordighera, 277–86.

Field, F N, 1980, 'Lincoln, Nettleham Glebe', *Lincolnshire History and Archaeology* 15, 77–78.

Field, F N, 1981, 'Cherry Willingham', *Lincolnshire History and Archaeology* 16, 70.

Field, F N, nd. (1982), *Fiskerton in the Iron Age*. Lincoln.

Field, F N, 1985, 'The Lincoln By-Pass', *Lincolnshire History and Archaeology* 20, 71–2.

Field, F N, 1986, 'An Iron Age timber causeway at Fiskerton, Lincolnshire', *Fenland Research* 3, 49–53.

Field, F N, 1996, 'Proposed Residential Development, Main Street, Toynton-All-Saints'. Unpublished report (No 213), Lindsey Archaeological Services, Lincoln.

Field, F N, forthcoming, 'Archaeological Investigations at Vicars' Court, Lincoln', *A History and Archaeology of the English Colleges of Vicars Choral* (eds. R A Hall and D Stocker). Oxford.

Field, F N and George I, 1998, 'Archaeology in Lincolnshire 1998' *Lincolnshire History and Archaeology* 33, 35–46.

Field, F N and Hurst, H, 1983, 'Roman Horncastle', *Lincolnshire History and Archaeology* 18, 47–88.

Field, F N *et al*. 2001, 'Excavations at Greetwell'. Unpublished report, Lindsey Archaeological Services, Lincoln.

Field, F N and Parker Pearson, M, 2003, *Excavations at Fiskerton*. Oxford.

Field, F N and White, A J (eds.), 1984, *A Prospect of Lincolnshire, being collected articles on the history & traditions of Lincolnshire in honour of Ethel H. Rudkin*. Lincoln.

Finberg, H P R, 1959, *Roman and Saxon Withington*. Occasional Papers of the Department of English Local History, Leicester University 8 (2nd edition). Leicester.

Finley, M I, 1981, 'The Ancient City: From Fustel de Coulanges to Max Weber and Beyond', *Economy and Society in Ancient Greece* (eds. M I Finley, B Shaw and R Saller). London, 305–327.

Finley, M I, 1985, *Ancient History: Evidence and Models*. London.

Fitzpatrick, A P, 1984, 'The Deposition of La Tene Iron Age Metalwork in Watery Contexts in Southern England', *Aspects of the Iron Age in Central Southern Britain* (eds. B Cunliffe and D Miles). Oxford, 178–90.

Fletcher, D, 2001, *The British Tanks 1915–1919*. Marlborough.

Foard, G, 2001, 'Medieval Woodland, Agriculture and Industry in Rockingham Forets, Northamptonshire', *Medieval Archaeology* 45, 41–95.

Foot, S, 1993, 'The Kingdom of Lindsey', *Pre-Viking Lindsey*. Lincoln Archaeological Studies 1 (ed. A G Vince). Lincoln, 128–40.

Foster, C W (ed.), 1914, *Lincoln Wills Volume 1. A.D. 1271 to 1526*. Lincoln Record Society 5. Lincoln.

Foster, C W (ed.), 1931, *The Registrum Antiquissimum of the Cathedral Church of Lincoln, I*. Lincoln Record Society 27. Lincoln.

Foster, C W (ed.), 1933, *The Registrum Antiquissimum of the Cathedral Church of Lincoln II*. Lincoln Record Society 28. Lincoln.

Foster, C W (ed.), 1935, *The Registrum Antiquissimum of the Cathedral Church of Lincoln III*. Lincoln Record Society 29. Lincoln.

Foster, C W and Longley, T (eds.), 1924, *The Lincolnshire Domesday and the Lindsey Survey*, Lincoln Record Society 19. Lincoln.

Foster, C W and Major K (eds.), 1937, *The Registrum Antiquissimum of the Cathedral Church of Lincoln IV*. Lincoln Record Society 32. Lincoln.

Foulds, T (ed.), 1994, *The Thurgarton Cartulary*. Stamford.

Fox, G E, 1892, 'Recent discoveries of Roman Remains in Lincoln', *Archaeologia* 53, 233–8.

Frend, W H C, 1992, 'Pagans, Christians and "the Barbarian Conspiracy" of AD 367 in Roman Britain', *Britannia* 23, 121–32.

Frere, S S, 1967, *Britannia: A History of Roman Britain* (1st edition). London.

Frere, S S, 1971, 'The Forum and Baths at Caistor by Norwich', *Britannia* 2, 1–20.

Frere, S S, 1979, 'Town Planning in the Western Provinces', *Beiheft zum Bericht Römische-germanischer Kommission* 58, 87–103.

Frere, S S, 1980, 'Hyginus and the First Cohort', *Britannia* 11, 51–60.

Frere, S S, 1983, *Verulamium Excavations 2*, Society of Antiquaries of London Research Report 41. London.

Frere, S S, 1987, *Britannia: A History of Roman Britain* (3rd edition). London.

Frere, S S and St Joseph J K, 1974, 'The Roman Fortress at Longthorpe', *Britannia* 5, 1–129.

Frere, S S and St Joseph J K, 1983, *Roman Britain from the Air*. London.

Fryer, J, 1973, 'The Harbour Installations of Roman Britain',

*Marine Archaeology*. Colston Papers 23 (ed. D J Blackman), 261–73.

Fryer, V, 1989, 'Finds from the Waterside', *Lincoln Archaeology 1988–1989*. City of Lincoln Archaeological Unit Annual Report 1 (ed. M J Jones). Lincoln, 8–11.

Fulford, M G, 1982, 'Town and Country in Roman Britain – a Parasitical Relationship?', *The Romano-British Countryside. Studies in Rural Settlement and Economy*. British Archaeological Reports (British Series) 103 (ed. D Miles). Oxford, 403–431.

Fulford, M G, 1985, 'Excavations on the sites of the Amphitheatre and Forum-Basilica at Silchester, Hampshire: an Interim Report', *Antiquaries Journal* 65, 39–81.

Fulford, M G, 1993, 'Silchester: the early development of a civitas capital', *Roman Towns: The Wheeler Inheritance: A Review of 50 Years' Research*. Council for British Archaeology Research Report 93 (ed. S Greep). London, 16–33.

Fulford, M G, 2000, 'The organisation of legionary supply: the Claudian invasion of Britain', *Roman Fortresses and their Legions* (ed. R Brewer). London & Cardiff, 41–50.

Fulford, M G and Timby, J, 2000, *Silchester: Excavations on the site of the Forum-Basilica, 1977, 1980–6*. Britannia Monograph 15. London.

Galinié, H, 1988, 'Reflections on early medieval Tours', *The Rebirth of Towns in the West AD 700–1050*. Council for British Archaeology Research Report 68 (eds. R Hodges and B Hobley). London, 57–62.

Galinié, H and Zadora-Rio, E (eds.), 1996, *Archéologie du cimetière chrétien*. Actes du deuxieme colloque A.R.C.H.E.A. Tours.

Galloway, J A and Murphy, M, 1991, 'Feeding the city: medieval London and its agrarian hinterland', *London Journal* 16, 3–14.

Galloway, J A, Keene, D and Murphy, M, 1996, 'Fuelling the city: production and distribution of firewood and fuel in London's region, 1290–1400', *Economic History Review* 49/3, 447–472.

Garnsey, P, 1970, *Social Status and Legal Privilege in the Roman Empire*. Oxford.

Garnsey P and Saller R, 1987, *The Roman Empire: Economy, Society and Culture*. London.

Garrigou Grandchamp, P *et al.*, 1997, *La Ville de Cluny et ses Maisons (XIe–XVe siècles)*. Paris.

Geake, H, 1999, 'When were Hanging Bowls Deposited in Anglo-Saxon Graves?', *Medieval Archaeology* 43, 1–18.

Gelling, M., 1987, 'English Place-Names derived from the compound wicham', *Place-name evidence for the Anglo-Saxon Invasion and Scandinavian Settlements* (eds. K Cameron and M Gelling)(2nd edition). Nottingham, 8–26.

Gem, R, 1993, 'The Episcopal Churches of Lindsey in the Early 9th Century', *Pre-Viking Lindsey*. Lincoln Archaeological Studies 1 (ed. A G Vince). Lincoln, 123–7.

Gibbons, A (ed.), 1888, *Early Lincoln Wills…*, Lincoln.

Gibbs, L, 2001, 'Lincoln Cathedral and Close Conservation Plan' (3 volumes). Unpublished report Dean and Chapter of Lincoln, 28 Eastgate, Lincoln.

Gilchrist, R, 1995, *Contemplation and Action. The Other Monasticism*. Leicester.

Gilchrist, R and Morris, R K, 1996, 'Continuity, reaction and rivival: church archaeology in England *c*.1600–1880', *Church Archaeology. Research directions for the future*. Council for British Archaeology Research Report 104. York, 112–126.

Gilmour, B J J, 1979, 'The Anglo-Saxon church of St Paul-in-the-Bail, Lincoln', *Medieval Archaeology*, 23, 214–17.

Gilmour B J J and Roffe D, 1999, 'Medieval and later occupation of the SW part of the Lower City', *The Defences of the Lower City. Excavations at the Park and West Parade 1970–2 and a discussion of other sites excavated up to 1994*. Archaeology of Lincoln 7/2 & Council for British Archaeology Research Report 114 (ed. M J Jones). York, 262–7.

Gilmour B J J and Stocker D A, 1986, *St. Mark's Church and Cemetery*. Archaeology of Lincoln 13/1. London.

Girling, M, 1979, 'Arthropod remains from Flaxengate, Lincoln'. Unpublished report, City of Lincoln Archaeological Unit. Lincoln.

Girouard, M, 1979, *The Victorian Country House*. New Haven & London.

Giuliani, C F, 1970, *Forma Italiae: Regio 1 – Volvmen Septimvm*. Rome.

Greenway, D E (ed. ), 1977, *John le Neve. Fasti Ecclesiae Anglicanae 1066–1300, III, Lincoln*. London.

Grenville, J, 1997, *Medieval Housing*. Leicester.

Going, C J, 1992, 'Economic "Long Waves" in the Roman period? A Reconnaissance of the Romano-British Ceramic Evidence', *Oxford Journal of Archaeology* 11/1, 93–117.

Gonzalez, J, 1986, 'The Lex Irnitana; a new Flavian Municipal Law', *Journal of Roman Studies* 76, 147–243.

Good, G L, Jones, R H and Ponsford, M W (eds.), 1991, *Waterfront Archaeology*. Council for British Archaeology Research Report 74. London.

Goodburn, D, 1991, 'New light on early ship- and boat-building in the London area', *Waterfront Archaeology*. Council for British Archaeology Research Report 74 (eds. G L Good, R H Jones and M W Ponsford). London, 105–15.

Goodchild, R G, 1946, 'The Origins of the Romano-British Forum', *Antiquity* 20, 70–77.

Gough, R (ed.), 1806, *Britannia … by William Camden* (4 volumes). London.

Grahame, M, 1997, 'Towards a Theory of Roman Urbanism: Beyond Economics and Ideal-Types', *TRAC 96: Proceedings of the Sixth Annual Theoretical Roman Archaeology Conference, Sheffield 1996* (eds. K Meadows, C Lemke and J Heron). Oxford, 151–162.

Graves, C P, 2000, *The Form and Fabric of Belief. An Archaeology of the Lay Experience of Religion in Medieval Norfolk and Devon*. British Archaeological Reports (British Series) 311. Oxford.

Green, M J, 1976, *The Religions of Civilian Roman Britain*. British Archaeological Reports (British Series) 24. Oxford.

Green, M J, 1983, *The Gods of Roman Britain*. Princes Risborough.

Green, M J, 1989, *Symbol and Image in Celtic Religious Art*. London.

Greep, S (ed.), 1993, *Roman Towns: The Wheeler Inheritance: A Review of 50 Years' Research*. Council for British Archaeology Research Report 93. London.

Greig, J, 1988, 'Plant Resources', *The Countryside of Medieval England* (ed. G Astill and A Grant). Oxford, 108–27.

Greig, J, 1989, 'Plant remains', *Lincoln Archaeology 1988–1989*. City of Lincoln Archaeological Unit Annual Report 1 (ed. M J Jones). Lincoln, 11–12.

Greig, J, 1991, 'Environmental Archaeology in Middle England – Research directions for projects funded by English Heritage'. Unpublished report, English Heritage, London.

Grew, F and Hobley, B (eds.), 1985, *Roman Urban Topography in Britain and the Western Empire*. Council for British Archaeology Research Report 59. London.

Grimes, W F, 1951, 'The Jurassic Way Across England', *Aspects of Archaeology in Britain and Beyond. Essays presented to O G S Crawford* (ed. W F Grimes). London, 144–71.

Gros, P, 1996, *L'Architecture Romaine: I, Les Monuments Publics*. Paris.

Haberey, W, 1971, *Die Römischen Wasserleitungen nach Köln*. Düsseldorf.

Hadfield, C, 1973, *British Canals: An Illustrated History* (4th edition). Newton Abbot.

Hadfield, C, 1986, *World Canals: Inland Navigation Past and Present*. London.

Hall, D, 1994, 'Ridge and furrow in the English Midlands', *The History of Soils and Field Systems* (eds. S Foster and T C Smout). Edinburgh, 94–100.

Hall, D and Coles J, 1994, *The Fenland Survey: an essay in landscape persistence*. London.

Hall, J, 1992, 'The Close Wall, Phase I'. Unpublished report (No 24), City of Lincoln Archaeological Unit. Lincoln.

Hall, J, 1993, 'The Close Wall, Phase II', Unpublished report (No 44), City Lincoln Archaeology Unit. Lincoln.

Hall, T et al., 1984, *Lincoln's Waterways 2*. Lincolnshire Education Aids Project. Lincoln.

Hallam, H E, 1965, *Settlement and Society. A Study of the early Agrarian History of South Lincolnshire*. Cambridge.

Halsall, G, 1996, 'Towns, Societies and Ideas: the not so strange case of late Roman and early Merovingian Metz', *Towns in Transition: Urban Evolution in Late Antiquity and the Early Middle Ages* (eds. N Christie and S T Loseby). London, 235–61.

Hamerow, H, 1993, *Excavations at Mucking, Volume 2: The Anglo-Saxon Settlement*. English Heritage Archaeological Report 21. London.

Hanson, W S, 1994, 'Dealing with Barbarians: The Romanization of Britain', *Building on the Past. Papers celebrating 150 years of the Royal Archaeological Institute* (ed. B Vyner). London, 149–63.

Hartley, B R, 1981, 'The Early Roman military occupation of Lincoln and Chester', *Roman pottery research in Britain and north-western Europe*. British Archaeological Reports (British Series) 123 (eds. A C Anderson and A S Anderson). Oxford, 239–47.

Hardy, E G, 1912, *Roman Laws and Charters*. Oxford.

Harries, J, 1992, 'Death and the dead in the late Roman West', *Death in Towns, Urban Responses to the Dying and the Dead, 100–1600* (ed. S R Bassett). Leicester, 56–67.

Harris, R B, 1994, 'The origins and development of English Medieval townhouses operating commercially on two stories'. Unpublished DPhil. thesis, University of Oxford.

Harris, W V, 1994, 'Child-Exposure in the Roman Empire', *Journal of Roman Studies* 84, 1–22.

Hassall, M W C, 1976, *Britain in the Notitia, in Aspects of the Notitia Dignitatum*. British Archaeological Reports (Supplementary Series) 15 (eds. R Goodburn and P Bartholomew). Oxford, 103–117.

Hassall, M W C, 1979, 'The Impact of Mediterranean Urbanism on Indigenous Nucleated Centres', *Invasion and Response*. British Archaeological Reports (British Series) 73 (eds. B Burnham and H Johnson). Oxford, 241–252.

Hassall, M W C, 2000, 'Pre-Hadrianic Legionary Dispositions in Britain', *Roman Fortresses and their Legions* (ed. R Brewer). London & Cardiff, 69–82.

Hassall, M W C and Hurst, H, 1999, 'Soldier and Civilian; a debate on the banks of the Severn', *The Coloniae of Roman Britain: new studies and a review. Papers of the conference held at Gloucester on 5–6 July, 1997* (ed. H Hurst). Journal of Roman Archaeology Supplementary Series 36, 181–9.

Hassall, M W C and Tomlin, R S O, 1977, 'Roman Britain in 1976: Inscriptions', *Britannia* 8, 426–9.

Hassall, M W C and Tomlin, R S O, 1979, 'Roman Britain in 1978: Inscriptions', *Britannia* 10, 339–56.

Hassall, M W C and Tomlin, R S O, 1982, 'Roman Britain in 1981: Inscriptions', *Britannia* 13, 396–422.

Haverfield, F, 1914, *The Romanisation of Britain*. Oxford.

Hawkes, J, forthcoming, 'Iuxta Morem Romanorum: Stone and Sculpture in Anglo-Saxon England'.

Hawkins, E, 1850, 'The Ancient Mint of Lincoln', *Memoirs illustrative of the history and Antiquities of the County and City of Lincoln communicated to the annual meeting of the Archaeological Institute of Great Britain and Ireland held at Lincoln, July 1848, ....* London, 49–57.

Hayes, P P, 1988, 'Roman to Saxon in the south Lincolnshire Fens', *Antiquity* 62, 235, 321–326.

Hayfield, C, 2000, 'Conservation Plan for Lincoln Castle'. Unpublished Report, Lincolnshire County Council, Lincoln.

Healey, R H, 1974, 'Archaeological Notes for 1973 – Pottery from Potterhanworth', *Lincolnshire History and Archaeology* 9, 30–33.

Healey, R H, 1984, 'Toynton All Saints: decorated jugs from the Roses kiln', *A Prospect of Lincolnshire* (eds. F N Field and A J White). Lincoln, 73–8.

Healey, R H 1988, 'Archaeology in Lincolnshire and South Humberside 1987 – Specialist potters at Potterhanworth', *Lincolnshire History and Archaeology* 23, 85–87.

Heighway, C M (ed.), 1970, *The Erosion of History. Archaeology and Planning in Towns. A Study of the historic towns affected by modern development in England Wales and Scotland*. London.

Heighway, C M and Bryant B, 1999, *The Golden Minster: The Anglo-Saxon Minster and Later Medieval Priory of St Oswald at Gloucester*. Council for British Archaeology Research report 117. York.

Heighway, C M, Garrodd, A P and Vince A G, 1979, 'Excavations at 1 Westgate St., Gloucester, 1975', *Medieval Archaeology* 23, 159–213.

Henderson, C G, 1988, 'Exeter', *Fortress into City* (ed. G Webster). London, 91–119.

Henderson, C G, 1991, 'Aspects of the planning of the Neronian fortress of legio II Augusta at Exeter', *Roman Frontier Studies 1989* (eds. V Maxfield and M Dobson). Exeter, 73–83.

Henderson, J forthcoming, 'The medieval and post-medieval vessel glass (finewares) from Lincoln excavations 1972–87', *Archaeological Journal*.

Henig, M, 1984, *Religion in Roman Britain*. London.

Henig, M, 1995, *The Art of Roman Britain*. London.

Herridge, J, 1999, 'The Industrial Archaeology of Lincoln. A report to Lincoln City Council on a Survey of Lincoln's Industrial Archaeology (1700–1945)'. Unpublished report (No 378) Lincoln City Council. Lincoln.

Hibberd, D, 1983, 'Data-linkage and the Hearth Tax. The case of seventeenth-century York', *The Hearth Tax: Problems and Possibilities* (ed. N Alldridge). Hull.

Higham, N J, 1992, *Rome, Britain and the Anglo-Saxons*. London.

Hill C, Millett M and Blagg T, 1980, *The Riverside Wall and Monumental Architecture in London*. London and Middlesex Archaeological Society Special Paper 3. London.

Hill, J W F, 1927–8, 'The Manor of Hungate or Beaumont Fee in the City of Lincoln', *Associated Architectural Societies Reports and Papers* 38/2, 175–208.

Hill, J W F, 1930, 'Lincoln Castle: the Constables and the Guard', *Associated Architectural Societies Reports and Papers* 40/1, 1–14.

Hill, J W F, 1948, *Medieval Lincoln*. Cambridge.

Hill, J W F, 1954. 'The Western Spires of Lincoln Minster', *Lincolnshire Architectural and Archaeological Society Reports and Papers* 5, 1–17.

Hill, J W F, 1956, *Tudor and Stuart Lincoln*. Cambridge.

Hill, J W F, 1966, *Georgian Lincoln*. Cambridge.

Hill, J W F, 1974, *Victorian Lincoln*. Cambridge.

Hill, J W F, 1979, *A Short History of Lincoln*. Lincoln.

Hill, K, 2001, 'The Middle Classes in Victorian Lincoln', *Aspects of Lincoln. Discovering Local History* (ed. A Walker). Barnsley, 88–100.

Hill, P, 1997, *Whithorn and St. Ninian: The Excavation of a Monastic Town, 1984–91*. Stroud.

Hill, P R (ed.) 2000, *Wigford: Historic Lincoln South of the River*. Survey of Lincoln Project Report 1. Lincoln.

Hingley, R, 1994, 'Britannia, origin myths and the British Empire', *TRAC 94: Proceedings of the Fourth Annual Theoretical Roman archaeology Conference, Durham 1994* (eds. S Cottam, D Dungworth, S Scott and J Taylor). Oxford, 11–23.

Hingley, R, 2000, *Roman Officers and English Gentlemen*. London & New York.

Hockley, J, 1992a, 'Proposed Skewbridge Area Plan Archaeological and Historical Study'. Unpublished report (No 1) City of Lincoln Archaeological Unit. Lincoln.

Hockley, J, 1992b, 'Proposed Ropewalk to Carholme Road Link – Archaeological and Historical Study'. Unpublished report (No 5) City of Lincoln Archaeological Unit. Lincoln.

Hockley, J, 1992c, 'Lincoln Eastern Bypass, Stage 1', Unpublished report (No 29), City of Lincoln Archaeological Unit, Lincoln.

Hodge, A T, 1992, *Roman Aqueducts and Water Supply*. London.

Hodges R and Hobley B, 1988 (eds.), *The Rebirth of Towns in the West AD 700–1050*. Council for British Archaeology Research Report 68. London.

Hodson, M B, 1982, *Lincoln Then and Now, Volume 1*. Lincoln.

Hoffman, B, 1995, 'The Quarters of Legionary Centurions of the Principate', *Britannia* 16, 107–153.

Holbrook, N, 1994, 'Corinium Dobunnorum: Roman Civitas Capital and Roman Provincial Capital', *Cirencester: Town and Landscape* (eds. T Darvill and C Gerrard). Cirencester, 57–86.

Holbrook, N (ed.), 1998, *Cirencester: The Roman Town Defences, Public Buildings and Shops*. Cirencester Excavations 5. Cirencester.

Hope, W St J, 1901, 'The Gilbertine Priory of Watton in the East Riding of Yorkshire', *Archaeological Journal* 58, 1–34.

Hopkins, K, 1983, *Death and Renewal*. Sociological Studies in Roman History 2. Cambridge.

Horsman, V, Milne, C and Milne, G, 1988, *Aspects of Saxo-Norman London I*. London and Middlesex Archaeological Society Special Paper 11. London.

Howlett, D R, 1994, *The Book of Letters of St. Patrick the Bishop*. Dublin.

Howlett, D R, 1997, *British Books in Biblical Style*. Dublin.

Hughes, M and Gaimster, D, 1999, 'Neutron activation analysis of maiolica from London, Norwich, the Low Countries and Italy', *Maolica in the North: the archaeology of tin-glazed earthenware in north-west Europe c.1500–1600*. British Museum Occasional paper 122 (ed. D Gaimster). London, 57–90.

Hurst, H, 1975, 'Excavations at Gloucester, Third Interim Report: Kingsholm 1966–75', *Antiquaries Journal* 55/2, 267–94.

Hurst, H, 1986, *Gloucester: The Roman and Later Defences*. Gloucester Archaeological Reports 2. Gloucester.

Hurst, H, 1988, 'Gloucester', *Fortress into City* (ed. G Webster). London, 48–73.

Hurst, H, 1999a, 'Topography and identity in *Glevum Colonia*', *The Coloniae of Roman Britain: new studies and a review. Papers of the conference held at Gloucester on 5–6 July, 1997* (ed. H Hurst). Journal of Roman Archaeology Supplementary Series 36, 113–35.

Hurst, H, 1999b, 'Civic space at *Glevum*', *The Coloniae of Roman Britain: new studies and a review. Papers of the conference held at Gloucester on 5–6 July, 1997* (ed. H Hurst). Journal of Roman Archaeology Supplementary Series 36, 152–60.

Hurst, H, 2000, 'The fortress-coloniae of Roman Britain', *Romanisation and the City: Creations, Transformations and Failures* (ed. E Fentress). Journal of Roman Archaeology Supplementary Series 38, 105–114.

Hurst, J, 1984, 'The development of medieval pottery research in Lincolnshire', *A Prospect of Lincolnshire, being collected articles on the history & traditions of Lincolnshire in honour of Ethel H. Rudkin* (eds. F N Field and A J White). Lincoln, 64–8.

Hurst, J., 1991, 'Medieval and Post-Medieval Pottery imported into Lincolnshire', *Land People and Landscapes. Essays on the history of the Lincolnshire region written in honour of Rex C. Russell* (eds. D Tyszka, K Miller and G Bryant). Lincoln, 49–65.

Hurst, J, Neal, D S and van Beuningen, H J E, 1986, *Pottery Produced and Traded in North-West Europe 1350–1650*. Rotterdam Papers 6. Rotterdam.

Hurt, F, 1991, *Lincoln during the War*. Lincoln.

Hurt, F and Barratt, J, 1997, *Lincoln War Diaries*. Lincoln.

Huskinson, J, 1994, *Corpus of Sculpture in the Roman World. Roman Sculpture from Eastern England*. London.

ICOMOS/TICCIH 1996, *The International Canal Monuments*. Occasional Papers for the World Heritage Convention. Paris.

Illingworth, C, 1810, *A Topographical Account of the Parish of Scampton in the County of Lincoln and of the Roman Antiquities lately discovered there; together with Anecdotes of the Family of Bolle*. Lincoln.

Illingworth, W (ed.), 1812–18, *The Rotuli Hundredorum*. Publications of the Record Commission. London.

ILN 1848, 'Excavations Recently Made – Chiefly for Railway Purposes in the Immediate Neighbourhood of Lincoln in the Collection of a Gentleman of the County', *Illustrated London News*, 8th April 1848.

Instone, E, 1995, 'The Iron and Steel Industries. Step 3 Report (Introduction)'. Unpublished report, English Heritage, London.

Isaac, B J, 1992, *The Limits of Empire: The Roman Army in the East* (revised edition). Oxford.

Isaac, P C G, 1980, 'Roman public health engineering', *Proceedings of the Institute of Civil Engineers* 68/1, 215–239.

James, S, 1984, 'Britain and the Late Roman Army', *Military and Civilian in Roman Britain*. British Archaeological Reports (British Series) 136 (eds. T F C Blagg and A C King). Oxford, 161–86.

James, S, and Millett, M, 2001, *Britons and Romans: Advancing an Archaeological Agenda*. Council for British Archaeology Research Report 125. York.

Janssen, W, 1988. 'The rebirth of towns in the Rhineland', *The Rebirth of Towns in the West AD 700–1050*. Council for British Archaeology Research Report 68 (eds. R Hodges and B Hobley). London, 47–51.

Jarvis, M 1996a, 'Central Library, Lincoln. Archaeological Excavation and Assessment' (2 volumes). Unpublished report (No 173), City of Lincoln Archaeological Unit. Lincoln.

Jarvis, M, 1996b, 'Greyfriars, Free School Lane, Lincoln. Archaeological Recording'. Unpublished report (No 266), City of Lincoln Archaeological Unit. Lincoln.

Jefferson, D, 2002, 'Possible Mine shaft – Adam and Eve Public House, Lincoln'. Unpublished report, Lincoln City Council, Lincoln.

Jennings, S and Young, J, 1986, 'The Pottery', *St. Mark's Church and Cemetery*. Archaeology of Lincoln 13/1 (eds. B J J Gilmour and D A Stocker). London, 35–40.

Johnson, A, 1983, *Roman Forts of the First and Second Centuries AD in Britain and the German Provinces*. London.

Johnson, A, 1997, 'Geophysical Survey of Greetwell Quarry area, Lincoln'. Unpublished report, Oxford Archaeotechnics, Lindsey Archaeological Services, Lincoln.

Johnson, C P C, 1992, *A Hive of Industry. An account of the St Rumbold Street area of Lincoln*. Lincoln.

Johnson, C P C and Vince, A G, 1992, 'The South Bail Gates of Lincoln', *Lincolnshire History and Archaeology* 27, 12–16.

Johnson, J S, 1983, *Late Roman Fortifications*. London.

Johnson, M, 1996, *The Archaeology of Capitalism*. London.

Johnson, M, 2002, *Behind the Castle Gate. From Medieval to Renaissance*. London & New York.

Johnston, J A (ed.), 1991, *Probate Inventories of Lincoln Citizens 1661–1714*. Lincoln Record Society 80. Lincoln.

Jones, D, 1973, *Chartism and the Chartists*. London.

Jones, D, 1988, 'Aerial Reconnaisance and Prehistoric and Romano-British Archaeology in Northern Lincolnshire – a sample study', *Lincolnshire History and Archaeology* 23, 5–30.

Jones, D, 1998, 'Long-Barrows and Neolithic Elongated Enclosures in Lincolnshire: an analysis of the photographic evidence', *Proceedings of the Prehistoric Society* 64, 83–114.

Jones, D and Whitwell, J B, 1991, 'Survey of the Roman fort and multi-period settlement complex at Kirmington on the Lincolnshire Wolds: a non-destructive approach', *Lincolnshire History and Archaeology* 26, 57–62.

Jones, G D B, 1962, 'Capena and the Ager Capenas', *Proceedings of the British School at Rome* 197, 116–208.

Jones, G D B and Mattingly, D J, 1990, *An Atlas of Roman Britain*. Oxford.

Jones, M E, 1996, *The End of Roman Britain*. Ithaca & London.

Jones, M J, 1975, *Roman Fort Defences to AD 117*. British Archaeological Reports (British Series) 21. Oxford.

Jones, M J, 1980, *The Defences of the Upper Roman Enclosure*. The Archaeology Lincoln 7/1. London.

Jones, M J, 1983, 'Coloniae in Britain', *Roman Urban Defences in the West*. Council for British Archaeology Research Report 51 (eds. J Maloney and B Hobley). London, 90–5.

Jones, M J, 1985, 'New Streets for Old: the topography of Roman Lincoln', *Roman Urban Topography in Britain and the Western Empire*. Council for British Archaeology Research Report 59 (eds. Grew, F and Hobley, B). London, 86–93.

Jones, M J, 1986, 'Archaeology in Lincoln', *Medieval Art and Architecture at Lincoln Cathedral*. Transactions of the British Archaeological Association Conference 1982 (eds. T Heslop and V Sekules). London, 1–8.

Jones, M J, 1988, 'Lincoln', *Fortress into City* (ed. G Webster). London, 145–66.

Jones, M J, 1991, 'Lincoln', *Britain in the Roman period: recent trends* (ed. R F J Jones). Sheffield, 69–73.

Jones, M J, 1992, 'Roman Lincoln', *Roman Lincolnshire* (by J B Whitwell). The History of Lincolnshire 2 (revised edition). Lincoln, xxvii – xxiv.

Jones, M J, 1993, 'The Latter Days of Roman Lincoln', *Pre-Viking Lindsey*. Lincoln Archaeological Studies 1 (ed. A G Vince). Lincoln, 14–28.

Jones, M J, 1994a, 'Theory, Practice and Research in an Urban Unit: a personal perspective', *Theoretical Roman Archaeology 1992* (ed. P Rush). Aldershot, 158–73.

Jones, M J, 1994b, 'St Paul in the Bail, Lincoln: Britain in Europe?', *Churches Built in Ancient Times* (ed. K S Painter). London, 325–347.

Jones, M J, 1996a, 'Review of J S Wacher, *The Towns of Roman Britain* (2nd edition)', *Britannia* 27, 487 9.

Jones, M J, 1996b, 'Early Church Groups in the British Isles', *Antiquité Tardive* 4, 211–215.

Jones, M J, 1998, 'Recent Discoveries in Britain and Ireland', *Acta XIV Congressus Archaeologiae Cristianae. Proceedings of the 13th International Congress of Christian Archaeology, Split/Pòrec* (eds. N Cambi and E Marin), 3, 395–420.

Jones, M J, 1999a, 'Roman Lincoln: Changing Perspectives', *The Coloniae of Roman Britain: new studies and a review. Papers of the conference held at Gloucester on 5–6 July, 1997* (ed. H Hurst). Journal of Roman Archaeology Supplementary Series 36, 101–112.

Jones, M J, 1999b, 'Lincoln and the British fora in context', *The Coloniae of Roman Britain: new studies and a review. Papers of the conference held at Gloucester on 5–6 July, 1997* (ed. H Hurst). Journal of Roman Archaeology Supplementary Series 36, 167–74.

Jones, M J, 2001, 'Early Christian Archaeology in Europe: Some Recent Research', *Archaeology of the Roman Empire: A tribute to the Life and Works of Professor Barri Jones*. British Archaeological Reports (International Series) 940 (ed. N Higham). Oxford, 319–33.

Jones, M J, 2002, *Roman Lincoln: Conquest Colony and Capital*. Stroud.

Jones, M J, 2003, 'Sources of effluence: water through Roman Lincoln', *The Archaeology of Roman Towns (Essays in honour of J S Wacher)* (ed. P R Wilson). Oxford. 111–127.

Jones, M J (ed.), 1981, 'Excavations at Lincoln. Third Interim Report: Sites outside the walled city 1972–1977', *Antiquaries Journal* 61, 83–114.

Jones, M J (ed.), 1999, *The Defences of the Lower City, Excavations at the Park and West Parade 1970–2 and a discussion of other sites excavated up to 1994, by Christina Colyer, Brian JJ Gilmour and Michael J Jones*. Archaeology of Lincoln 7/2 & Council for British Archaeology Research Report 114. York.

Jones, M J and Gilmour, B J J, 1980, 'Lincoln, principia and forum: a preliminary report', *Britannia* 11, 61–72.

Jones, M J and Wacher, J S, 1987, 'The Roman Period', *Urban Archaeology in Britain*. Council for British Archaeology Research Report 61 (eds. J Schofield and R H Leech). London, 27–45.

Jones, R F J, 1987, 'Burial Customs of Rome and the Provinces', *The Roman World* (ed. J Wacher). London & New York, 812–844.

Jones, R F J, 1993, 'Backwards and Forwards in Roman Burial', *Journal of Roman Archaeology* 6, 427–432.

Jones, R F J (ed.), 1991, *Britain in the Roman Period: Recent Trends*. Sheffield.

Jones, R H, 1980, *Medieval Houses at Flaxengate Lincoln*. Archaeology of Lincoln 11/1. London.

Jones, R H, 1981, 'Orchard Street', *Lincoln Archaeological Trust Eighth Annual Report 1979–80*, 15–17.

Jones, S, 1997. *The Archaeology of Ethnicity*. London.

Jones, S R, 1992a, 'Garmston House', *Lincoln Archaeology 1991–1992*. City of Lincoln Archaeological Unit Annual Report 4 (ed. M J Jones). Lincoln, 31–2.

Jones, S R, 1992b, 'The Norman House (46–7 Steep Hill)', *Lincoln Archaeology 1991–1992*. City of Lincoln Archaeological Unit Annual Report 4 (ed. M J Jones). Lincoln, 21–5.

Jones, S R, Major, K and Varley, J, (with Johnson C), 1984, *Survey of Ancient Houses I: Priorygate to Pottergate*. Lincoln Civic Trust, Lincoln.

Jones, S R, Major, K and Varley, J, 1987, *Survey of Ancient Houses II: Houses to the South and West of the Minster*. Lincoln Civic Trust, Lincoln.

Jones, S R, Major, K and Varley, J, 1990, *Survey of Ancient Houses III: Houses in Eastgate, Priorygate, and James Street*. Lincoln Civic Trust, Lincoln.

Jones, S R, Major, K, Varley, J and Johnson, C, 1996, *Survey of Ancient Houses IV: Houses in the Bail: Steep Hill, Castle Hill, and Bailgate*. Lincoln Civic Trust, Lincoln.

Kaye, D, Scorer, S and Robinson, D N, 1992, *Fowler of Louth. The Life and Works of James Fowler, Louth Architect 1828–1892*. Louth.

Keene, D, 1975, 'Suburban Growth', *The plans and topography of medieval towns in England and Wales*. Council for British Archaeology Research Report 14 (ed. M W Barley). London, 71–82.

Kemp, R, 1993, 'The Archaeology of 46–54 Fishergate', *Pottery from 46–54 Fishergate*. The Archaeology of York 16/6 (ed. E A Mainmain). York, 543–6.

Kemp, R, 1996, 'A Corpus of Medieval and later roof tile from Lincoln'. Unpublished report, City of Lincoln Archaeological Unit. Lincoln.

Kemp, R L and Gaves, P, 1996, *The Church and Gilbertine Priory of St Andrew Fishergate*, Archaeology of York 11/2. York.

Kennedy, D, 1984, 'Floating Road: a timber-rafted causeway at Scaftworth', *Popular Archaeology*, 5th March, 20–21.

Kenward, H, 1995, 'Insects from the Lincoln Waterfront, Waterside North: Saltergate', *Lincoln Archaeology 1994–1995*. City of Lincoln Archaeological Unit Annual Report 7 (ed. M J Jones). Lincoln, 39.

Keppie, L, 1983, *Colonisation and Veteran Settlement in Italy 47–14BC*. London.

Keppie, L, 1984. 'Colonisation and Veteran Settlement in Italy in the First Century AD', _Papers of British School at Rome_ 52, 77–114.

Keppie, L, 2000, 'Legio VIIII in Britain: the beginning and the end', _Roman Fortresses and their Legions_ (ed. R Brewer). London & Cardiff, 83–100.

King, A C, 1978, 'A comparative survey of bone assemblages from Roman sites in Britain', _Bulletin of the Institute of Archaeology_ 15, 207–232.

King, A C, 1991, 'Food Production and Consumption – Meat', _Britain in the Roman Period: Recent Trends_ (ed. R F J Jones). Sheffield, 15–20.

King, D J C, 1983, _Castellarium Anglicanum. An Index and Bibliography of the Castles in England, Wales and the Islands_ (2 volumes). London.

Knowles, D and Hadcock, R N, 1953, _Medieval Religious Houses England and Wales_. London.

Lake, J, Cox, J and Berry, E, 2001, _Diversity and Vitality. The Methodist and Nonconformist Chapels of Cornwall_. Truro.

Land Use Consultants, 1998, 'The Temple Gardens Lincoln'. Unpublished report, Lincoln City Council. Lincoln.

Lane, M R, 1997, _The Story of Wellington Foundry_. Lincoln.

Lane, T et al., 1993, _The Fenland Project Number 8: Lincolnshire Survey, the Northern Fen-Edge_. East Anglian Archaeology 66. Sleaford.

Laur-Belart, R, 1991, _Guide d'Augusta Raurica_. Basle.

Laurence, R, 1994, _Roman Pompeii: Space and Society_. Routledge.

Laurence, R and Wallace-Hadrill, A (eds.), 1997, _Domestic Space in the Roman World: Pompeii and Beyond_. Journal of Roman Archaeology, Supplementary Series 22. London.

Lavan, L, 1999, 'Late Antique Governors Palaces: a gazetter', _Antiquité Tardive_ 7, 135–64.

Leach, T R, 1971, _Robert Grantham of Dunholme, 1541–1618. An Elizabethan and His Charity_. Dunholme.

Leahy, K, 1984. 'Late Roman and Early Germanic Metalwork from Lincolnshire', _A Prospect of Lincolnshire being collected articles on the history & traditions of Lincolnshire in honour of Ethel H. Rudkin_ (eds. F N Field and A White). Lincoln, 23–32.

Leahy, K, 1993, 'The Anglo-Saxon Settlement of Lindsey', _Pre-Viking Lindsey_. Lincoln Archaeological Studies 1 (ed. A G Vince). Lincoln, 29–44.

Leahy, K, forthcoming, 'Middle Anglo-Saxon Lincolnshire – an Emerging Picture', _Markets in Early Medieval Europe_ (eds. T Pestell and K Ulmschneider). Macclesfield.

Leary, W, 1969, _Methodism in the City of Lincoln_. Lincoln.

Lee, F and Magilton J, 1989, 'The cemetery of the Hospital of St James and St Mary Magdalen, Chichester – A Case Study', _World Archaeology_ 21/1, 273–82.

Leeds, E T, 1936, _Early Anglo-Saxon Art and Archaeology; being the Rhind Lectures delivered in Edinburgh, 1935_. Oxford.

Leon, P, 1988, _Traianeum de Italica_. Seville.

Levick, B, 1967, _Roman Colonies in Southern Asia Minor_. Oxford.

Lewis, M J T, 1966, _Temples in Roman Britain_. Cambridge.

Lewis, M J T, 1984, 'Our debt to Roman Engineering: the water supply of Lincoln to the present day', _Industrial Archaeology Review_ 7/1, 57–73.

Lewis, M J T, 1995. 'A _Festuca_ from Chesters?', _Archaeologia Aeliana_, 5th Series, 23, 47–50.

Liebeschuetz, J H W G, 1992, 'The end of the ancient city', _The City in Late Antiquity_ (ed. J W Rich). London, 1–49.

Lindley, P (ed.), forthcoming, _Lincoln Castle_. Society for Lincolnshire History and Archaeology, Occasional Papers Series.

Ling, R, 1985, 'The Mechanics of the Building Trade', _Roman Urban Topography in Britain and the Western Empire_. Council for British Archaeology Research Report 59 (eds. F Grew and B Hobley). London, 14–27.

Ling, R, 1989, 'A Stranger in Town: finding the way in an ancient city', _Recent Archaeological Work at Manchester University: Studies in Honour of Lisa French_ (ed. D Woolliscroft). Manchester, 6–15.

Ling, R, 1990, 'Street Plaques at Pompeii', _Architecture and Architectural Sculpture in the Roman Empire_ (ed. M Henig). Oxford, 51–66.

Long, H C, 1993, _The Edwardian House_. Manchester.

Loseby, S, 1992, 'Bishops and cathedrals: order and diversity in the fifth-century urban landscape of southern Gaul', _Fifth Century Gaul: a crisis of identity?_ (eds. J Drinkwater and H Elton). Cambridge, 144–55.

Loveluck, C (ed.), forthcoming, _Flixborough: a High-Status Middle to Late Saxon Settlement in North Lincolnshire AD600–1000_.

Lowther, P et al., 1993, _The City of Durham: An Archaeological Survey_. Durham.

LUAU 1996a, 'The Quarrying Industry. Step 1 Report'. Unpublished Report, English Heritage, London.

LUAU 1996b, 'The Lime, Cement, and Plaster Industries. Step 1 Report'. Unpublished Report, English Heritage, London.

Ludlam, A J, 1995, _The Lincolnshire Loop Line (GNR) and the River Witham_. Headington.

Lugli, G, 1946, _Roma Antica: II Centro Monumentale_. Rome.

Lyons, N (ed.), 1983, _The Courts and Yards of Brigg_. Scunthorpe.

MacAvoy, F, forthcoming, _The Iron Age and Roman Settlement at Owmby, Lincolnshire_.

Mackreth, D F, 1987, 'Roman Public Buildings', _Urban Archaeology in Britain_. Council for British Archaeology Research Report 61 (eds. J Schofield and R H Leach). London, 133–147.

Macphail, R, 1989, 'Dark Earth', _Soils and Micromorphology in Archaeology_ (eds. M A Courty, P Goldberg and R Macphail). Cambridge, 261–8.

Macphail, R, 1994, 'The reworking of urban stratigraphy by human and natural processes', _Urban-Rural Connexions: Perspectives from Environmental Archaeology_ (eds. R Hall and H Kenward). Oxford, 13–43.

Magilton, J R, 1982, 'Monson Street', _Archaeology in Lincoln 1981–2_. Tenth Annual Report of the Lincoln Archaeological Trust. Lincoln, 17–19.

Magilton, J R, 1983, 'Excavation', _Archaeology in Lincoln 1982–3_. Eleventh Annual Report of the Lincoln Archaeological Trust. Lincoln, 10–18.

Magilton, J R and Stocker D A, 1982, 'St Mary's Guildhall', _Archaeology in Lincoln 1981–2_. Tenth Annual Report of the Lincoln Archaeological Trust. Lincoln, 8–16.

Mahany, C, Burchard, A and Simpson, G, 1982, _Excavations in Stamford Lincs., 1963–1969_, Society for Medieval Archaeology Monograph 9. London.

Major, K (ed.), 1940, _Registrum Antiquissimum of the Cathedral Church of Lincoln V_, Lincoln Record Society 34. Lincoln.

Major, K (ed.), 1950, _Registrum Antiquissimum of the Cathedral Church of Lincoln VI_, Lincoln Record Society 41. Lincoln.

Major, K (ed.), 1953, _Registrum Antiquissimum of the Cathedral Church of Lincoln VII_, Lincoln Record Society 46. Lincoln.

Major, K (ed.), 1958, _Registrum Antiquissimum of the Cathedral Church of Lincoln VIII_, Lincoln Record Society 51. Lincoln.

Major, K (ed.), 1968, _Registrum Antiquissimum of the Cathedral Church of Lincoln IX_, Lincoln Record Society 62. Lincoln.

Major, K (ed.), 1973, _Registrum Antiquissimum of the Cathedral Church of Lincoln X_, Lincoln Record Society 67. Lincoln.

Major, K, 1974, _Minster Yard_. Lincoln Minster Pamphlets (2nd series) 7. Lincoln.

Maltby, M, 1979, _Faunal Studies on Urban Sites: The animal bones from Exeter 1971–5_. Exeter Archaeological Reports 2. Sheffield.

Mann, J C, 1961, 'The Administration of Roman Britain', _Antiquity_ 35, 316–320.

Mann, J C, 1977, '*Duces* and *comites* in the 4th century', *The Saxon Shore*. Council for British Archaeology Research Report 18 (ed. D E Johnston). London, 11–15.

Mann, J C, 1985, 'Epigraphic Consciousness', *Journal of Roman Studies* 75, 204–6.

Mann, J C, 1987, 'A note on the so-called "Town Zone"', *Britannia* 18, 285–6.

Mann, J C, 1998, 'The creation of four provinces in Britain by Diocletian', *Britannia* 29, 339–41.

Mann, J E, 1981, 'An Ornamented Dagger Sheath', *Lincoln Archaeological Trust Ninth Annual Report 1980–81*, 25–6.

Mann, J E, 1982, *Early Medieval Finds from Flaxengate I: Objects of antler, bone, stone, horn, ivory, amber and jet*. Archaeology of Lincoln 14/1. London.

Mann, J E, 1986, 'Small Finds', *St Mark's Church and Cemetery*. Archaeology of Lincoln 13/1 (eds. B Gilmour and D Stocker). London, 41–3.

Mann, J E, 1988, 'Early Settlement in Lincoln – Other Finds', *Britannia* 19, 38–42.

Mann, J E, 1990, 'Finds from Saltergate', *Lincoln Archaeology 1989–1990*. City of Lincoln Archaeological Unit Annual Report 2 (ed. M J Jones). Lincoln, 8–9.

Mann, J E, 1999, 'Other Artefacts', *The Defences of the Lower City, Excavations at the Park and West Parade 1970–2 and a discussion of other sites excavated up to 1994, by Christina Colyer, Brian JJ Gilmour and Michael J Jones*. Archaeology of Lincoln 7/2 (ed. M J Jones) & Council for British Archaeology Research Report 114. York, 247–262.

Mann, J E, forthcoming, *Finds from the Well at St Paul-in-the-Bail*. Lincoln Archaeological Studies 9. Oxford.

Mann, J E and Reece R, 1983, *Roman Coins from Lincoln*, Archaeology of Lincoln 6/2. London.

Manning, W H, 1997, 'Ptolemy's Sources and Pre-Flavian Fortresses in Britain', *Roman Frontier Studies 1995. Proceedings of the 16th International Congress of Roman Frontier Studies*. Oxbow Monograph 91 (eds. Groenman-van Waateringe *et al.*). Oxford, 33–40.

Manning, W H and Scott, I R, 1989, *Report on the Excavations at Usk 1965–76: The Fortress Excavations 1972–74*. Cardiff.

Marsden, P, 1994, *Ships of the Port of London: first to eleventh centuries*. London.

Marsden, P and West, B, 1992, 'Population Change in Roman London', *Britannia* 23, 133–140.

Martin, A R, 1935, 'The Greyfriars of Lincoln', *Archaeological Journal* 92, 42–63.

Marvell, A G, 1996, 'Excavations at Usk', *Britannia* 27, 51–110.

Mason, D J P, 1985, *Excavations at Chester: 26–42 Lower Bridge Street 1974–6. The Dark Age and Anglo-Saxon Periods*. Grosvenor Museum Archaeological Excavation and Survey Reports 3. Chester.

Mason, D J P, 1988a, 'The Roman Site at Heronbridge, near Chester, Cheshire: Aspects of Civilian Settlement in the Vicinity of Legionary Fortresses in Britain and Beyond', *Archaeological Journal* 145, 123–157.

Mason, D J P, 1988b, '*Prata Legionis* in Britain', *Britannia* 19, 163–90.

Mason, D J P, 2001, *Roman Chester. City of the Eagles*. Stroud.

Mattingly, D J, 1997, 'Beyond belief? Drawing a line beneath the consumer city, Roman Urbanism', *Beyond the Consumer City* (ed. H M Parkins). London, 210–218.

Mattingly, D J (ed.), 1997, *Dialogues in Roman Imperialism*, Journal of Roman Archaeology Supplementary Series 23. Portsmouth Rhode Island.

Mawer, C F, 1995, *Evidence for Christianity in Roman Britain: the Small Finds*. British Archaeological Reports (British Series) 243. Oxford.

Maxfield, V, 1986, 'Pre-Flavian forts and their Garrisons', *Britannia* 17, 59–72.

Maxfield, V, 1989, 'Conquest and Aftermath', *Research on Roman Britain, 1960–89*. Britannia Monograph 11 (ed. M Todd). London, 19–30.

Maxfield, V and Dobson M (eds.), 1991, *Roman Frontier Studies 1989*. Exeter.

May, J, 1976, *Prehistoric Lincolnshire*. The History of Lincolnshire 1. Lincoln.

May, J, 1984, 'Major settlements of the late Iron Age in Lincolnshire', *A Prospect of Lincolnshire being collected articles on the history & traditions of Lincolnshire in honour of Ethel H. Rudkin*. Lincoln (eds. F N Field and A J White). Lincoln, 18–22.

May, J, 1988, 'Early Settlement in Lincoln – Iron Age Lincoln? The topographical and settlement evidence reviewed', *Britannia* 19, 50–55.

May, J, 1994, 'Coinage and the settlements of the *Corieltauvi* in East Midland Britain', *The British Numismatic Journal*, 64, 1–21.

May, J, 1996, *Dragonby. Report on Excavations at an Iron Age and Romano-British Settlement in North Lincolnshire* (2 volumes). Oxford.

Mays, S, 1997, *The Archaeology of Human Bones*. London.

Mayhew, S M, 1879, 'Recent Discoveries at Colonia Lindum', *Journal of the British Archaeological Association* 35, 308–316.

McDaid, M and Field, F N, 1996, 'Land Adjacent to Walnut House, Lilly's Road, Lincoln'. Unpublished report, Lindsey Archaeological Services, 25 West Parade, Lincoln.

McDaid, M, 1997, 'Land at Bunkers Hill, Greetwell, Lincoln'. Unpublished report (No 264), Lindsey Archaeological Services, 25 West Parade, Lincoln.

McGrail, S, 1978, *Logboats of England and Wales*. British Archaeological Reports (British Series) 51. Oxford.

McGrail, S, 1987, *Ancient Boats in NW Europe*. London.

McGrail, S, 1997, 'Roman-Celtic Boats and Ships: Characteristic Features', *Studies in Maritime Archaeology*. British Archaeological Reports (British Series) 256 (ed. S McGrail). Oxford, 223–8.

McHardy, A K (ed.), 1992, *Clerical Poll-Taxes of the Diocese of Lincoln 1377–1381*. Lincoln Record Society 81. Lincoln.

McInnes, J P, 1911, *History of Co-Operation in Lincoln 1861–1911*. Lincoln.

McKerrell Clough, T K and Cummins, W A (eds.), 1988, *Stone Axe Studies. Volume 2*. Council for British Archaeology Research Report 67. London.

McKinley, J, 2000, 'Phoenix rising: aspects of cremation in Roman Britain', *Burial Society and Context in the Roman World* (eds. J Pearce, M Millett and M Struck). Oxford, 38–44.

Mellor, M, 1994, *Medieval Ceramic Studies in England. A Review for English Heritage*. London.

Melton, B L, nd., *One Hundred and Fifty Years at the Lawn*. Lincoln.

Metzler, J, Millett, M, Roymans, N and Slofstra, J, 1995, *Integration in the Early Roman West, The role of Culture and Ideology*. Luxembourg.

Meyrick, S R. 1831, 'Description of two antient British Shields, preserved in the Armoury at Goodrich Court, Herefordshire …', *Archaeologia* 23, 92–7.

Miles, P, Young, J and Wacher, J, 1989, *A Late Saxon Kiln Site at Silver Street, Lincoln*. Archaeology of Lincoln 17/3. London.

Miles, D and Palmer, R, 1990, 'Thornhill and Claydon Pike', *Current Archaeology* 121, 19–23.

Miller, T, 1857, *Our Old Town*. London.

Millett, M, 1982, 'Distinguishing between the *Pes Monetalis* and the *Pes Drusianus*: some problems', *Britannia* 13, 315–320.

Millett, M, 1990, *The Romanisation of Britain*. Cambridge.

Millett, M, 1994a, 'An Early Christian Community at Colchester?', *Archaeological Journal* 151, 451–454.

Millett, M, 1994b, 'Evaluating Roman London', *Archaeological Journal* 151, 427–435.

Millett, M, 1995a, *Roman Britain*. London.

Millett, M, 1995b, 'Re-thinking religion in Romanization', *Integration in the Early Roman West, The role of Culture and Ideology* (eds. J Metzler, M Millett, N Roymans and J Slofstra). Luxembourg, 93–100.

Millett, M, 1999, 'Coloniae and Romano-British Studies', *The Coloniae of Roman Britain: new studies and a review. Papers of the conference held at Gloucester on 5–6 July, 1997* (ed. H Hurst). Journal of Roman Archaeology Supplementary Series 36, 191–6.

Mills, D R, 2001a, 'Introduction', *The Twentieth Century. What Heritage?* (eds. P Judson and C Lester). Lincoln, 3–5.

Mills, D R, 2001b, 'An "Edge-Land": The Development of the Witham Valley East of Canwick Road', *Aspects of Lincoln. Discovering Local History*, (ed. A Walker). Barnsley, 134–46.

Mills, D R (ed.), 1989, *Twentieth Century Lincolnshire*. The History of Lincolnshire 12. Lincoln.

Mills, J and Mills, D, 1997, 'Prehistoric Barrows in the Witham Valley at Canwick', *Lincolnshire Past and Present* 29, 3–5.

Mills, J and Mills, D, 1998a, 'A Case Study at Canwick of the Enduring Influence of Monastic Houses', *Lincolnshire History and Archaeology* 33, 47–54.

Mills, D and Mills, J, 1998b, *The New Lincoln School of Science and Art: who built it and who paid for it?* Lincoln.

Mills, J, Mills, D and Trott, M, 2001, 'New Light on Charles De Laet Waldo-Sibthorpe. 1783–1855', *Lincolnshire History and Archaeology* 36, 25–37.

Milne, G, 1985, 'Roman Waterfront Archaeology in London', *Conference on Waterfront Archaeology in Northern European Towns, Bergen 1983* (ed. A Herteig). Bergen, 31–45.

Milne, G, 1990, 'Maritime traffic between the Rhine and Roman Britain: a preliminary note', *Maritime Celt, Frisians and Saxons*. Council for British Archaeology Research Report 71 (ed. S McGrail). London, 82–4.

Milne, G, 1995, *Roman London*. London.

Milne, G (ed.), 1992, *From Roman Basilica to Medieval Market. Archaeology in Action in the City of London*. London.

Mócsy, A, 1974, *Pannonia and Upper Moesia*. London.

Moffett, L, 1993, 'Assessment of the charred plant remains from Lincoln backlog sites'. Unpublished report, City of Lincoln Archaeological Unit. Lincoln.

Moffett, L, 1994, 'Assessment of charred plant remains from Lincoln, lower city sites'. Unpublished report, City of Lincoln Archaeological Unit. Lincoln.

Molleson, T and Cox M (eds.), 1993, *The Spitalfields Project, 2: The anthropology, the middling sort*. Council for British Archaeology Research Report 86. York.

Moore, C N, 1979, 'Stone Axe studies from the East Midlands', *Stone Axe Studies: archaeological petrological, experimental and ethnographic*. Council for British Archaeology Research Report 67. London, 82–6.

Moore, D T, 1991, 'The Petrology and provenance of the Lincoln hones'. Unpublished report, City of Lincoln Archaeological Unit. Lincoln.

Morgan, G C and Jones, M J, 1999, 'Mortar Analysis', *The Defences of the Lower City, Excavations at the Park and West Parade 1970–2 and a discussion of other sites excavated up to 1994, by Christina Colyer, Brian JJ Gilmour and Michael J Jones*. Archaeology of Lincoln 7/2 (ed. M J Jones) & Council for British Archaeology Research Report 114. York, 205–6.

Morgan, P and Thorn, C (eds.), 1986, *Domesday Book: Lincolnshire*. History from the Sources (ed. J Morris) (2 volumes). Chichester.

Morris, I, 1992, *Death-Ritual and Social Structure in Classical Antiquity*. Cambridge.

Morris, R, 1989, *Churches in the Landscape*. London.

Morrison, K, 1999, *The Workhouse. A study of poor-law buildings in England*. London.

Mossop, H R, 1970, *The Lincoln Mint c 890–1279*. Newcastle upon Tyne.

Muthesius, S, 1982, *The English Terraced House*. New Haven & London.

Myres, J N L, 1946, 'Lincoln in the Fifth Century AD', *Archaeological Journal* 103, 85–8.

Myres, J N L, 1986, *The English Settlements*. Oxford.

Neal, D S and Cosh, S R, 2002, *A Corpus of Roman Mosaics of Britain I: Northern Britain*. London.

Newbery, C, 1978, 'Coade artifical stone: finds from the site of the Coade manufactory at Lambeth', *Collectanea Londiniensia. Studies in London archaeology and history presented to Ralph Merrifield*. London and Middlesex Archaeological Society Special Paper 2 (eds. J Bird, H Chapman and J Clark). London, 376–387.

Newman, B, 1957, *One Hundred Years of Good Company*. Lincoln.

Newton, F and Boyson, D, 2001, 'Buildings for Living', *The Twentieth Century – What Heritage?* (eds. P Judson and C Lester). Lincoln, 13–22.

Niblett, R, 2001, *Verulamium. The Roman City of St Albans*. Stroud.

Niblett, R and Thompson I, forthcoming, *St Albans Archaeological Assessment*.

Nowell, T, 2001, 'Remembering those in Lincoln's Prisons', *Aspects of Lincoln. Discovering Local History* (ed. A Walker). Barnsley, 27–35.

Nurse, P, 2001, *Devils let loose. The Story of the Lincoln Riots of 1911*. Grantham.

OAU 1998, 'Bridges. Step 1 Report'. Unpublished report, English Heritage, London.

Oleson, J P, 1984, *Greek and Roman mechanical water-lifting devices*. Toronto.

Oleson, J P, 1996, 'Water-lifting devices at Herculaneum and Pompeii in the context of Roman technology', *Cura Aquarum in Campania* (eds. N De Haan and M Jansen). Leuven, 67–77.

Olney, R J, 1979, *Rural Society and County Government in Nineteenth-Century Lincolnshire*. The History of Lincolnshire 10. Lincoln.

O'Connor, C, 1993, *Roman Bridges*. Cambridge.

O'Connor, T P, 1982, *Animal bones from Flaxengate c.870–1500*. The Archaeology of Lincoln 18/1. London.

O'Connor, T, 1983, 'Feeding Lincoln in the 11th Century – a Speculation', *Integrating the Subsistence Economy*. British Archaeological Reports (British Series) 181 (ed. M K Jones). Oxford, 327–30.

O'Connor, T, 1991, 'The Animal Bone', *St Mary's Guildhall Lincoln, The Survey and Excavation of a Medieval Building Complex*. The Archaeology of Lincoln 12/2 (ed. D Stocker). London, 88–91.

O'Neill, W, 1892, 'Account of Roman Remains in Lincoln', *Associated Architectural Societies Reports and Papers* 22, 66.

Ottaway, P, 1992, *Anglo-Scandinavian Ironwork from 16–22 Coppergate*. The Archaeology of York 17/6. London.

Ottaway, P, 1993, *Roman York*. London.

Otter, M, 1989, 'Lincoln Castle, West Gate', *Lincoln Archaeology 1988–1989*. City of Lincoln Archaeological Unit Annual Report 1 (ed. M J Jones). Lincoln, 13–16.

Otter, P, 1996, *Lincolnshire Airfields in the Second World War*. Newbury.

Ove Arup & Partners and York University with Bernard Thorpe 1991, *York Development and Archaeology Study*. Manchester.

Owen, A E B, 1988, 'Helen, Margaret and Andrew; Some Patterns of Church Dedication', *Lincolnshire History and Archaeology* 23, 73–5.

Owen, A E B, 1997, 'Louth Before Domesday', *Lincolnshire History and Archaeology* 32, 60–64.

Owen, D, 1971, *Church and Society in Medieval Lincolnshire*. The History of Lincolnshire 5, Lincoln.

Owen, D, 1984, 'The Norman Cathedral at Lincoln', *Anglo-Norman Studies* 6, 188–99.

Owen, D, 1994, 'Introduction: the English church in eastern England, 1066–110', *A History of Lincoln Minster* (ed. D Owen). Cambridge, 1–13.

Owen, D (ed.), 1994, *A History of Lincoln Minster*. Cambridge.

Pacey, R, 2002, *Lost Lincolnshire Country Houses Volume 5*. Burgh le Marsh.

Pacey, T E, nd., *To Fetch a Pail of Water. A Story of Water in Lincoln City*. Lincoln.

Padley, J S, 1851, *Selections from the Ancient Edifices of Lincolnshire*. Lincoln.

Page, W (ed.), 1906, *Victoria History of the Counties of England. Lincolnshire Volume II*. London.

Painter, K, 1999, 'The Water Newton silver: Votive or Liturgical', *Journal of the British Archaeological Association* 152, 1–23.

Palliser, D M(ed.), 2000, *The Cambridge Urban History of Britain I: c.600 – c.1540*. Cambridge.

Palmer, M and Neaverson, P, 1998, *Industrial Archaeology. Principles and Practice*. London.

Palmer-Brown, C, 1993, 'Significant New Dating Evidence for Linear Boundary Ditches', *Lincolnshire History and Archaeology* 28, 71–72.

Pantin, W A, 1961, 'Medieval Inns', *Studies in Building History. Essays in recognition of the work of B H St J O'Neil* (ed. E M Jope). London, 166–91.

Pantin, W A, 1962–3, 'Medieval English Town-house Plans', *Medieval Archaeology* 6–7, 202–39.

Pantin, W A, 1971, *Dernstall House, 33/34 The Strait, Lincoln, Historical Notes*. Lincoln.

Parker, J H, 1878, 'Notes on the discovery of a Roman porticus at Lincoln', *Archaeological Journal* 35, 396–8.

Parrissien, S (ed.), *Banking on Change. A Current Account of Britain's Historic Banks*. A report by the Georgian Group, The Victorian Society, The Thirties Society and The Ancient Monuments Society. London, 1992.

Pask, B M, 1997, *Newark the Bounty of Beer*. Nottingham.

Patrick, A, 1996, 'Establishing a Typology for the Buildings of the Floor Malting Industry', *Industrial Archaeology Review* 28/2, 180–200.

Patrick, A, 1998, 'The Malthouse, Wigford Yard, Off Brayford Wharf East, Lincoln'. Unpublished report, Lincoln City Council. Lincoln.

Peacock, D P S and Williams, D F, 1992, 'Imported Roman Marble from Lincoln'. Unpublished report (English Heritage Ceramic and Lithic Petrology Project), University of Southampton.

Pearce, J, 2000, 'Burial, society and context in the provincial Roman world', *Burial, Society and Context in the Roman World* (eds. J Pearce, M Millett and M Struck). Oxford, 1–12.

Pearce, J, Millett, M and Struck, M (eds.), 2000, *Burial, Society and Context in the Roman World*. Oxford.

Penrose, F C, 1878, 'Account of some Roman remains discovered at Lincoln', *Proceedings of Society of Antiquaries* 7/2, 433–43.

Perring, D, 1981, *Early Medieval Occupation at Flaxengate*. Archaeology of Lincoln 9/1. London.

Perring, D, 1991a, 'Spatial organisation and social change in Roman towns', *City and Country in the Ancient World*, (eds. J Rich and A Wallace-Hadrill). London, 273–293.

Perring, D, 1991b, *Roman London*. London.

Perring, D (ed.), 2002, *Town and country in England: Frameworks for Archaeological Research*. Council for British Archaeology Research Report 134. York.

Petch, D F, 1956, 'Archaeological Notes for the year 1956', *Reports and Papers of the Lincolnshire Architectural and Archaeological Society* 6, 61–71.

Petch, D F, 1960, 'Excavations at Lincoln 1955–58', *Archaeological Journal* 117, 40–70.

Petch, D F, 1962, 'A Roman Inscription, Nettleham', *Reports and Papers of the Lincolnshire Architectural and Archaeological Society* 9/2, 94–7.

Petch, D F, 1986, 'The Roman Public Baths at Lincoln'. Unpublished report, City of Lincoln Archaeological Unit. Lincoln.

Peterson, J W, 1993, 'A Computer-Aided Investigation of Ancient Cadastres'. Unpublished PhD thesis, University of East Anglia.

Petrikovits, H von, 1975, *Die Innenbauten römischer Legionslager während der Prinzipatszeit*. Opladen.

Pevsner, N and Harris, J, 1989, *The Buildings of England. Lincolnshire* (2nd edition ed. N Antram). Harmondsworth.

Philpott, R, 1991, *Burial Practices in Roman Britain. A survey of grave treatment and furnishing AD 43–410*. British Archaeological Reports (British Series) 219. Oxford.

Phythian Adams, C, 1996, *Land of the Cumbrians: A Study in British Provincial Origins AD 400–1120*. London.

Pietsch, M, 1993, 'Die Zentralgebäude des augusteischen Legionslagers von Marktbreit und die Principia von Haltern', *Germania* 71, 355–68.

Pietsch, M, Timpe, D and Wamser, L, 1991, 'Das augusteische Truppenlager Marktbreit', *Berichte der Römisch-Germanische Kommission* 72, 263–324.

Pitts, L F and St Joseph, J K, 1985, *Inchtuthil: The Roman Legionary Fortress*. Britannia Monograph Series 6, London.

Platts, G, 1985, *Land and People in Medieval Lincolnshire*. The History of Lincolnshire 4. Lincoln.

Polfer, M, 2000, 'Reconstructing funerary rituals: the evidence of *ustrina* and related archaeological structures', *Burial, Society and Context in the Roman World* (eds. J Pearce, M Millett and M Struck). Oxford, 30–7.

Posnansky, M, 1960, 'The Pleistocene Succession in the Middle Trent Basin', *Proceedings of the Geologists' Association* 71, 285–311.

Potter, T W, 1979, *The Changing Landscape of South Etruria*. London.

Potter, T W, 1981, 'Marshland and Drainage in the Classical World', *The Evolution of Marshland Landscapes* (ed. T Rowley). Oxford, 1–19.

Potter, T W, 1995, *Towns in Late Antiquity: Iol Caesarea and its Context*. Sheffield.

Potter, T W and Johns, C M, 1992, *Roman Britain*. London.

Poulter, A G, 1987, 'Townships and Villages', *The Roman World* (ed. J S Wacher). London & New York, 388‑411.

Pownall, J, 1792, 'Account of some Sepulchral Antiquities discovered at Lincoln', *Archaeologia* 10, 345–9.

Precht, G, 1986, *Colonia Ulpia Traiana: Die Römische Stadt*. Bonn.

Price, J, Cottam, S and Worrell S, forthcoming, *Roman Glass from Excavations in Lincoln*. Lincoln Archaeological Studies 8. Oxford.

Pritchard, F A, 1991, 'Small finds', *Aspects of Saxo-Norman London II: Finds and Environmental Evidence*, London and Middlesex Archaeological Society Special Paper 12 (ed. A G Vince). London, 120–279

Pryor, F M M, 1991, *Flag Fen Prehistoric Fenland Centre*. London.

Pryor, F M M, 2001a, The *Flag Fen Basin: Archaeology and environment of a Fenland landscape*. London.

Pryor, F M M, 2001b, *Seahenge. New Discoveries in Prehistoric Britain*. London.

Rackham, D J, 1998, 'Brayford Wharf East Bore Hole Investigations 1998'. Unpublished report, City of Lincoln Archaeoloigcal Unit. Lincoln.

Rackham, D J, 1999, 'Paleoenvironmental Results and Assessment, University of Lincolnshire and Humberside – Phase 3. Residential Accommodation, Lincoln Campus. Archaeological Evaluation and Sampling'. Unpublished Report (No 382), City of Lincoln Archaeological Unit, 7–17.

Rackham, O, 1986, *The History of the Countryside*. London.

Rainey, A, 1973, *Roman Mosaics in Britain*. Newton Abbott.

RCHME, 1997, 'The Sessions House and City Gaol, Lindum Road and Monks Road, Lincoln, Lincolnshire'. Unpublished report, National Monuments Records Centre. Swindon.

RCHME, 1998, 'Doughty's Oil Mill, Waterside South, Lincoln, Lincolnshire – Survey Report'. Unpublished report, National Monuments Records Centre. Swindon.

Reece, R M, 1980, 'Town and Country: the end of Roman Britain', *World Archaeology* 12/1, 77–93.

Reece, R M, 1987, *Coinage in Roman Britain*. London.

Reece, R, 1992, 'The end of the city in Roman Britain', *The City in Late Antiquity* (ed. J W Rich). London, 136–145.

Reece, R, 1993, 'Theory and Roman Archaeology', *Theoretical Roman Archaeology Conference: First Proceedings* (ed. E Scott). Aldershot, 29–38.

Reece, R, 1995, 'Models in Collision; East and West in Roman Britain', *Oxford Journal of Archaeology* 14, 113–5.

Reece, R, 1999, '*Colonia* in context: *Glevum* and the *civitas Dobunnorum*', *The Coloniae of Roman Britain: new studies and a review. Papers of the conference held at Gloucester on 5–6 July, 1997* (ed. H Hurst). Journal of Roman Archaeology Supplementary Series 36, 73–85.

Relf, J, 2001, 'Technical Education for Lincoln – "A Citizen's University"', *Aspects of Lincoln. Discovering Local History* (ed. A Walker). Barnsley, 115–133.

Renn, D, forthcoming, 'Cobb Hall Tower', *Lincoln Castle* (ed. P Lindley). Lincoln.

Reynolds, N M, 1975, 'Investigations in the Observatory Tower, Lincoln Castle', *Medieval Archaeology* 19, 201–5.

RIB 1965, *The Roman Inscriptions of Britain, Volume I, inscriptions on stone* (eds. R G Collingwood and R P Wright). Oxford.

Rich, J W (ed.), 1992, *The City in Late Antiquity*. London.

Richardson, H (ed.), 1998, *English Hospitals 1660–1948*. London.

Richardson, L, 1988, *Pompeii. An Architectural History*. Baltimore.

Richmond, I A, 1930, 'The First Years of Emerita Augusta', *Archaeological Journal* 87, 98–116.

Richmond, I A, 1946, 'The Roman City of Lincoln and the Four Coloniae of Roman Britain', *Archaeological Journal*, 103, 25–68.

Richmond, I A, 1966, 'Industry in Roman Briain', *The Civitas Capitals of Roman Britain* (ed. J S Wacher). Leicester, 76–86.

Richmond, I A, 1969, 'Roman Provincial Palaces', *Roman Art and Archaeology: Essays and Studies by Sir Ian Richmond* (ed. P Salway). London, 260–79.

Richmond, I A and Gillam, J P, 1950, 'Excavations on the Roman site at Corbridge 1946–1949', *Archaeologia Aeliana* 4th series 28, 152–72.

Riley, D N, 1977, 'Roman defended sites at Kirmington, S. Humberside and Farnsfield, Nottinghamshire, recently found from the air', *Britannia* 8, 189–192.

Riley, D N, Buckland P C and Wade J S, 1995, 'Aerial Reconnaissance and Excavation at Littleborough-on-Trent, Nottinghamshire', *Britannia* 26, 253–84.

Rivet, A L F and Smith, C, 1979, *The Place Names of Roman Britain*. London.

Roberts, B K and Wrathmell, S, 2000, *An Atlas of Rural Settlement in England*. London.

Robinson, D N, 1999, *Lincolnshire Bricks History and Gazetteer*. Heckington.

Robinson, N G, 1948, *Some Notes on the Steam Wagons of Clayton and Shuttleworth Ltd., Lincoln*. Newcastle-upon-Tyne.

Robson, J D, George, H and Heaven, F W, 1974, *Soils in Lincolnshire I*. Soil Survey Record 22. London.

Rodwell, W J, 1975, 'Milestones, civic territories and the Antonine itinerary', *Britannia* 6, 75–101.

Roe, F, 1996, 'Synthesis of Reports on Worked Stone'. Unpublished report, City of Lincoln Archaeological Unit. Lincoln.

Roffe, D, 2000, *Domesday. The Inquest and the Book*. Oxford.

Ross, A, 1968, 'Shafts, Pits, Wells: Sanctuaries of the Belgic Britons?'. *Studies in Ancient Europe: Essays presented to Stuart Piggott* (eds. J M Coles and D D A Simpson). Leicester, 255–85.

Ross, A and Feachem, F, 1976, 'Ritual Rubbish? – The Newstead Pits'. *To Illustrate the Monuments. Essays on Archaeology presented to Stuart Piggott* (ed. J V S Megaw). London, 230–7.

Rossi, F, 1995, *L'Area Sacra du Forum de Nyon et ses Abords. Fouilles 1988–1990*. Lausanne.

Roueché, C (ed.), 1989, *Aphrodisias in Late Antiquity*. London.

Ruddock, J G and Pearson, R E, 1985, *The Railway History of Lincoln* (2nd edition). Lincoln.

Ruddock, J G and Pearson, R E, 1989, *Clayton Wagons Ltd*. Lincoln.

Russell, E and Russell, R C, 1987, *Parliamentary Enclosure and New Landscapes in Lincolnshire*. Lincoln.

Salmon, E T, 1969, *Roman Colonisation under the Republic*. London.

Salway, P, 1981, *Roman Britain*. Oxford.

Salzman, L F, 1913, *English Industries of the Middle Ages*. London.

Samuel, M, 1989, 'The Fifteenth-century Garner at Leadenhall, London', *Antiquaries Journal* 69, 119–53.

Samuel, M, 1992, 'Reconstructing the Medieval Market at Leadenhall', *From Basilica to Medieval Market. Archaeology in Action in the City of London* (ed. G Milne). London, 114–125.

Sankey, D, 1998, 'Cathedrals, Granaries and Urban Vitality in Late Roman London', *Roman London, Recent Archaeological Work*. Journal of Roman Archaeology, Supplementary Series 24 (ed. B Watson). London, 78–82.

Saunders, J, 1834, *The History of the County of Lincoln ...* (2 volumes). London & Lincoln.

Sawyer, P H, 1981, 'Fairs and Markets in Early Medieval England', *Danish Medieval History: New Currents*, (eds. N Skyum-Nielsen and N Lund). Copenhagen, 153–168.

Sawyer, P H, 1998, *Anglo-Saxon Lincolnshire*. The History of Lincolnshire 3. Lincoln.

Schmiechen, J and Carls, K, 1999, *The British Market Hall. A Social and Architectural History*. New Haven.

Schnurbein, S von, 1974, *Die römischen Militäranlagen bei Haltern*. Münster.

Schnurbein, S von, 2000, 'Augustan Fortresses in Germany', *Roman Fortresses and their Legions* (ed. R Brewer). London & Cardiff, 29–40.

Schofield, J, 1994, *Medieval London Houses*. New Haven and London.

Schofield, J, 1997, 'Urban Housing in England, 1400–1600', *The Age of Transition. The Archaeology of English Culture 1400–1600*. Society for Medieval Archaeology Monograph 15 & Oxbow Monograph 98 (eds. D Gaimster and P Stamper). Oxford, 127–144.

Schofield, J and Leech, R H (eds.), 1987, *Urban Archaeology in Britain*. Council for British Archaeology Research Report 61. London.

Schofield, J and Vince, A G, 1994, *Medieval Towns*. Leicester.

Schiffer, M, 1985, 'Is There A Pompeii Premise?', *Journal of Anthropological Research* 41, 18–41.

Scott, E, 1993, 'Writing the Roman Empire', *Theoretical Roman Archaeology Conference: First Proceedings* (ed. E Scott). Aldershot, 5–22.

Scott, E (ed.), 1993, *Theoretical Roman Archaeology Conference: First Proceedings*. Aldershot.

Scott, I, 1985, 'First Century Military Daggers and the Manufacture and Supply of Weapons for the Roman Army', *The Production and Distribution of Roman Military Equipment*. British Archaeological Reports (International Series) 275 (ed. M C Bishop). Oxford, 160–207.

Scott, S, 1988, 'Early Settlement in Lincoln – Animal Bones', *Britannia* 19, 43–5.

Scott, S, 1989, 'The Early Days of Planning', *Twentieth Century Lincolnshire*. The History of Lincolnshire 12 (ed. D Mills). Lincoln, 181–211.

Scott, S, 1999, 'The animal bones from The Park, Lincoln', *The Defences of the Lower City, Excavations at the Park and West Parade 1970–2 and a discussion of other sites excavated up to 1994, by Christina Colyer, Brian JJ Gilmour and Michael J Jones*. Archaeology of Lincoln 7/2 & Council for British Archaeology Research Report 114 (ed. M J Jones). York, 236–46.

Scull, C, 1995, 'Approaches to Material Culture and Social Dynamics of the Migration Period in Eastern England', *Europe between Late Antiquity and the Middle Ages*. British Archaeological Reports (International Series) 617 (eds. J Bintliff and H Hamerow). Oxford, 71–83.

Sedgeley, J P, 1975, *The Roman Milestones of Britain: their petrography and probable origins*. British Archaeological Reports (British Series) 18. Oxford.

Sheldon, H, 2000, 'Roman Southwark', *London Under Ground: The archaeology of a city* (eds. I Haynes, H Sheldon and L Hannigan). Oxford, 121–50.

Shirley, E, 2001, *Building a Roman Legionary Fortress*. Stroud.

Shoesmith, R (ed.), 1980, *Excavations at Castle Green, Hereford*. Council for British Archaeology Research Report 36. London.

Simcoe, A, 1998, 'The Clay Industries. Step 1 Report'. Unpublished report, English Heritage, London.

Simmons, B B, 1979, 'The Lincolnshire Car Dyke', *Britannia* 10, 183–96.

Simmons, B B, 1980, 'Iron Age and Roman coasts around the Wash', *Archaeology and Coastal Change* (ed. F H Thompson), 56–73. London.

Simmons, B B, 1985, 'Fieldwork Techniques in the Lincolnshire Fens 1968–1978', *Archaeological Field Survey in Britain and Abroad* (eds. S Macready and F H Thompson ). London, 45–50.

Skeat, W W (ed.), 1868, *The Lay of Havelock the Dane*. London.

Smith, A, 1909a, *Roman Antiquities in the City and County Museum (Part 1)*. Lincoln City and County Museum Publications 3. Lincoln.

Smith, A, 1909b, *Roman Antiquities in the City and County Museum (Part 3)*. Lincoln City and County Museum Publications 7. Lincoln.

Smith, A, 1929, *A Catalogue of the Roman Inscribed Stones found in the City of Lincoln*. Lincoln.

Smith, D, 1984, 'Roman Mosaics in Britain: a synthesis', *Atti de III colloquio Internationale sul Mosaico Antico, Ravenna 1980* (ed. F Campanati). Ravenna, 357–80.

Smith, J T, 1997, *Roman Villas: A Study in Social Structure*. London.

Smith, N A F, 1976, 'Attitudes to Roman Engineering and the Question of the Inverted Siphon', *History of Technology* 1, 45–71.

Snell, A, 1984, 'Spring Hill', *Archaeology in Lincoln 1983–1984*. Twelfth and Final Annual Report of the Lincoln Archaeological Trust. Lincoln, 9–15.

Speed, J, 1611, *The Theatre of the Empire of Great Britain*. London.

Squires, S, 1992, 'Cross O'Cliff Brickworks, Lincoln', *Lincolnshire History and Archaeology* 27, 48–9.

Srawley, J H (ed.), 1966, *The Book of John de Schalby ....* Lincoln Minster Pamphlets 2. Lincoln.

Stanwell, R H and Baker, F T, 1938, 'The Newport Earthwork, Lincoln – excavations during July into August 1937', *The Lincolnshire Magazine* 3, 255–61.

Stark, A, 1810, *History of Lincoln ...,* Lincoln.

Steane, K, 1991, 'St. Paul in the Bail: a dated sequence?', *Lincoln Archaeology 1990–1991*. City of Lincoln Archaeological Unit Annual Report 3 (ed. M J Jones). Lincoln, 28–31.

Steane, K and Vince A, 1993, 'Post Roman Lincoln: Archaeological evidence for activity in Lincoln in the 5th–9th centuries', *Pre-Viking Lindsey*. Lincoln Archaeological Studies 1 (ed. A G Vince). Lincoln, 71–9.

Steane, K, Darling, M J, Mann, J, Vince A and Young J, 2001, *The Archaeology of Wigford and the Brayford Pool*. Lincoln Archaeological Studies 2. Oxford.

Steane, K, Darling, M J, Jones, M J, Mann, J, Vince A and Young J, 2003, *The Archaeology of the Upper City*. Lincoln Archaeological Studies 3. Oxford.

Steane, K and Jones, M J, *et al.*, forthcoming, *The Archaeology of the Lower City*. Lincoln Archaeological Studies 4. Oxford.

Stephens, P (ed.), 1993, *Newark. The Magic of Malt*. Nottingham.

Stephenson, J (ed.), 1858, *Simeon of Durham's History of the Kings of England*. London (reprinted 1987).

Stenton, D M (ed.), 1926, *The Earliest Lincolnshire Assize Rolls A.D. 1202–1209*. Lincoln Record Society 22. Lincoln.

Stenton, F M, 1934, *Norman London, an essay*. London.

Stephens, G R, 1985, 'Civic Aqueducts in Britain', *Britannia* 16, 197–208.

Stewart, I, 1967, 'The St Martin coins of Lincoln', *British Numismatic Journal* 36, 46–54.

Stocker, D, 1979, 'How does your garden grow ...?', *Interim, The Bulletin of York Archaeology* 4/4, 3–8.

Stocker, D, 1982, 'Lincoln, St Benedict's Church Tower', *Lincolnshire History and Archaeology* 17, 82–3.

Stocker, D, 1983, 'The West Gate of Lincoln Castle', *Archaeology in Lincoln 1982–3*. Eleventh Annual Report of the Lincoln Archaeological Trust. Lincoln, 18–27.

Stocker, D, 1984a, 'Recent Work at Monk's Abbey, Lincoln', *Lincolnshire History and Archaeology* 19, 103–5.

Stocker, D, 1984b, 'The Franciscan Friary at Lincoln: A Reassessment', *Archaeological Papers from York. Essays in honour of M.W. Barley* (eds. P V Addyman and V E Black). York, 137–44.

Stocker, D, 1985a, 'Excavations to the South of Lincoln Minster: An interim report', *Lincolnshire History and Archaeology* 20, 15–19.

Stocker, D, 1985b, 'The Tomb and Shrine of Bishop Grosseteste in Lincoln Cathedral', *England in the Thirteenth Century. Proceedings of the 1984 Harlaxton Symposium* (ed. W Ormrod). Nottingham, 143–8.

Stocker, D, 1986a, 'The Shrine of Little St Hugh', *Medieval Art and Architecture at Lincoln Cathedral*. Transactions of the British Archaeological Association Conference 1982 (eds. T Heslop and V Sekules). London, 109–117.

Stocker, D, 1986b, 'The excavated stonework', *St. Mark's Church and Cemetery*, Archaeology of Lincoln 13/1 (eds. B J J Gilmour and D A Stocker). London, 44 82.

Stocker, D, 1987, 'The Mystery of the Shrines of St Hugh', *St Hugh of Lincoln. Lectures delivered at Oxford and Lincoln to celebrate the eighth centenary of St Hugh's consecration as bishop of Lincoln* (ed. H Mayr-Harting). Oxford, 89–124.

Stocker, D, 1990, 'The Archaeology of the Reformation in Lincoln. A Case Study in the Redistribution of Building Materials in the Mid Sixteenth Century', *Lincolnshire History and Archaeology* 25, 18–32.

Stocker, D, 1991, *St. Mary's Guildhall, Lincoln. The Survey and Excavation of a Medieval Building Complex*. The Archaeology of Lincoln 12/1. London.

Stocker, D, 1993a, 'The Early Church in Lincolnshire. A study of the sites and their significance', *Pre-Viking Lindsey*. Lincoln Archaeological Studies 1 (ed. A G Vince). Lincoln, 101–22.

Stocker, D, 1993b, 'Introduction', *The City of Durham: An Archaeological Survey* (ed. P Lowther *et al.*). Durham, 28–30.

Stocker, D, 1995, 'Industrial archaeology and the Monuments Protection Programme in England', *Managing the Industrial Heritage* (eds. M Palmer and P Neaverson). Leicester Archaeology Monographs 2. Leicester.

Stocker, D, 1997a, ' "Also a Soldier..." Evidence for a Mithraeum in Lincoln?', *Lincolnshire History and Archaeology* 32, 21–24.

Stocker, D, 1997b, 'The Lincoln Stonebow and the Flattery of Princes', *Journal of the British Archaeological Association* 150, 96–105.

Stocker, D, 1999, '"A Very Goodly House Longging to Sutton …" A Reconstruction of 'John of Gaunt's Palace', *Lincolnshire History and Archaeology* 34, 5–15.

Stocker, D, 2000, 'Monuments and Merchants: irregularities in the distribution of stone sculpture in Lincolnshire and Yorkshire in the Tenth century', *Cultures in Contact. Scandinavian Settlement in England in the Ninth and Tenth Centuries* (eds. D Hadley and J Richards). Turnhout, 179–212.

Stocker, D, 2002, 'Salle et Hall dans les bâtiments urbains des douzième et treizième siècles', *La Maison Médiévale en Normandie et en Angleterre. Actes des Tables Rondes de Rouen (16 et 17 Octobre 1998) et Norwich (16 et 17 Avril 1999)* (eds. D Pitte and B Ayers). Rouen, 41–6.

Stocker, D, forthcoming a, 'The two early Castles of Lincoln', *Lincoln Castle* (ed. P Lindley). Lincoln.

Stocker, D, forthcoming b, 'Mobile meanings: An exploration of the symbolic value of re-used stone', *The Archaeology of Re-use* (eds. D Thackray, C Rosier and R Gilchrist).

Stocker, D, forthcoming c, 'The development of the College of the Vicars Choral of Lincoln Minster', *Cantate Domino. A History and Archaeology of the English Colleges of Vicars Choral* (eds. R A Hall and D Stocker). Oxford.

Stocker, D with Everson, P, 1990, 'Rubbish Recycled. A Study of the Re-Use of Stone in Lincolnshire', *Stone. Quarrying and Building in England AD43–1525* (ed. D Parsons). London and Chichester, 83–101.

Stocker, D and Everson P, 2001, 'Five Towns Funerals: decoding diversity in Danelaw stone sculpture', *Vikings and the Danelaw. Select Papers from the Proceedings of the Thirteenth Viking Congress, Nottingham and York, 21–30 August 1997* (eds. J Graham-Campbell, R Hall, J Jesch and D N Parsons). Oxford, 223–244.

Stocker, D and Everson, P, 2003, 'The Straight and Narrow Way. Fenland causeways and the conversion of the landscape in the Witham Valley, Lincolnshire', *The Cross Goes North. Processes of Conversion in Northern Europe, AD 300–1300* (ed. M Carver). Woodbridge, 271–88.

Stocker, D and Everson, P, forthcoming, *The Early Romanesque Tower in Lincolnshire. A Study in Architectural Symbolism.* Oxford.

Stocker, D and Vince, A G, 1997, 'The early Norman Castle at Lincoln and a re-evaluation of the original west tower of Lincoln Cathedral', *Medieval Archaeology* 41, 223–33.

Straker, V, 1979, 'Report on some seeds from Flaxengate, Lincoln from the 10th to 14th centuries AD'. Unpublished report, City of Lincoln Archaeological Unit. Lincoln.

Strickland, T J, 1996, 'Recent Research at the Chester legionary fortress: the curtain wall and the barrack veranda colonnades', *Architecture in Roman Britain.* Council for British Archaeology Research Report 94 (eds. P Johnson with I Haynes). York, 104–19.

Struck, M, 1995, 'Integration and continuity in funerary ideology', *Integration in the Early Roman West, The role of Culture and Ideology* (eds. J Metzler, M Millet, N Roymans and J Slofstra). Luxembourg, 139–150.

Struck, M, 2000, 'High status burials in Roman Britain (1st – 3rd centuries AD). The potential for interpetation', *Burial, Society and Context in the Roman World* (eds. J Pearce, M Millett and M Struck), Oxford, 85–96.

Stukeley, W, 1724, *Itinerarium Curiosum…* (1st edition). London.

Stukeley, W, 1776, *Itinerarium Curiosum…* (2nd edition). London.

Sullivan, R W, 1994, 'Saints Peter and Paul: Some Ironic Aspects of their Imaging', *Art History* 17/1, 59–80.

Swan, V, 1984, *The Pottery Kilns of Roman Britain.* London.

Swinnerton, H H and Kent, P E, 1949, *The Geology of Lincolnshire.* Lincolnshire Naturalists' Union, Natural History 1. Lincoln.

Sympson, E M, 1902, 'Old House in Corporation Street, Lincoln', *Lincolnshire Notes and Queries* 5/37, 65–6.

Sympson, E M, 1903, 'The Grey Friary Lincoln', *Lincolnshire Notes and Queries* 7/59, 193–202.

Sympson, E M, 1906, *Lincoln. A Historical and Topographical Account of the City.* Lincoln.

Sympson, T, 1737, '*Adversaria,* or Collections for a History of the City of Lincoln', Unpublished Ms., Bodleian Library, Gough Manuscripts, Lincoln 1. Oxford.

Taylor, C C, 1975, *Fields in the Landscape.* London.

Taylor, C C, 1979, *Roads and Tracks of Britain.* London.

Testini, P, Cantino Wataghin, G and Pani Ermini, L, 1989, 'La cattedrale in Italia', *Actes du XI Congrès International d'Archéologie Chrétienne* (ed. N Duval). Paris & Rome, 5–87.

Thacker, A, 1985, 'Kings, Saints and Monasteries in Pre-Viking Mercia', *Midland History* 6, 1–25.

Thomas, A C, 1985, *Christianity in Roman Britain to AD500* (revised edition). London.

Thomas, A C, 1994, *Shall These Mute Stones Speak? Post-Roman Inscriptions in Western Britain.* Cardiff.

Thomas, A C, 1998, *The Christian Celts: Messages and Images.* Stroud.

Thomas, C, Sloane, B and Phillpotts, C, 1997, *Excavations at the Priory and Hospital of St Mary Spital, London.* MOLAS Monograph 1. London.

Thompson, A H, 1907–8, 'Pre-Conquest church towers in North Lincolnshire', *Associated Architectural Societies Reports and Papers* 29, 43–70.

Thompson, A H, 1911, 'Registers of John Gynewell, Bishop of Lincoln, for the years 1347–1350', *Archaeological Journal* 68, 301–60.

Thompson, A H, 1913–14, 'Notes on the History of the Abbey of St Peter, St Paul and St Oswald, Bardney', *Associated Architectural Societies Reports and Papers* 32, 35–96, 351–402.

Thompson, F H, 1954a, 'Possible Roman quay found off St. Rumbold Street, Lincoln'. Unpublished report, Lincoln City and County Museum. Lincoln.

Thompson, F H, 1954b, 'The excavation of a Roman barrow at Riseholme, near Lincoln', *Antiquaries Journal* 34, 28–37.

Thompson, F H, 1955, *The Roman Aqueduct at Lincoln, Archaeological Journal* 111, 105–128.

Thompson, F H, 1956, 'Roman Lincoln, 1953', *Journal of Roman Studies* 46, 22–36.

Thompson, F H, 1960, 'The Deserted Medieval Village of Riseholme, near Lincoln', *Medieval Archaeology* 5, 95–108.

Thompson, F H, 1971, 'Some lost Roman bronzes from Lincoln', *Antiquaries Journal* 51/1, 100–103.

Thompson, F H and Whitwell, J B, 1973, 'The Gates of Roman Lincoln', *Archaeologia* 104, 129–207.

Thompson, P, 1856, *The History and Antiquities of Boston …* London.

Tiller, K, 1985, 'Charterville and the Chartist Land Company', *Oxoniensia* 50, 251–66.

Tinley, R, 1985, 'Le Tall's Mill, Lincoln', *Lincolnshire History and Archaeology* 46, 9–11.

Todd, M, 1965, 'Roman Stamped Tiles from Lincoln and their Origin', *Lincolnshire History and Archaeology* 1, 29–31.

Todd, M, 1981, *The Roman Town at Ancaster, Lincolnshire.* Exeter & Nottingham.

Todd, M, 1991, Peoples of Roman Britain. *The Coritani* (revised edition). London.

Todd, M, 1993, 'The cities of Roman Britain: after Wheeler', *Roman Towns: The Wheeler Inheritance. A Review of 50 Years' Research.* Council for British Archaeology Research Report 93 (ed. S Greep). London, 5–10.

Tomlin, R S O, 1983, 'Non Coritani Sed Corieltauvi', *Antiquaries Journal* 63, 353–5.

Tomlin, R S O, 1987, 'The Army of the Late Empire', *The Roman World* (ed. J S Wacher). London & New York, 107–133.

Toulmin Smith, L, 1910, *Leland's Itinerary of England and Wales* (reprinted 1964). Carbondale.

Toynbee, J M C, 1971, *Death and Burial in the Roman World*. London.

Trimble, R, 1994a, 'The New West Stand at Lincoln City Football Club, Sincil Bank'. Unpublished report (No 129), City of Lincoln Archaeological Unit. Lincoln.

Trimble R, 1994b, 'Kennington House'. Unpublished report (No 113), City of Lincoln Archaeological Unit. Lincoln.

Trimble, R, 1995, 'Watching brief at Lincoln City Football Ground', *Lincoln Archaeology 1994–1995*. City of Lincoln Archaeological Unit Annual Report 7. Lincoln, 16–17.

Trimble, R, 1997, 'Lincoln Eastern By-pass Stage 1 Evaluation. Interim Report'. Unpublished report (No 298), City of Lincoln Archaeological Unit. Lincoln.

Trimble, R, 1999b, 'The Proposed Distict Centre, Nettleham Road'. Unpublished report (No 380) City of Lincoln Archaeological Unit. Lincoln.

Trimble, R, 2000, 'Bunkers Hill, Lincoln. Archaeoloigcal evaluation'. Unpublished report (No 426) City of Lincoln Archaeological Unit. Lincoln.

Trimble, R, 2001, 'Bunkers Hill, Lincoln. Updated environmental assessment'. Unpublished report (No 456), City of Lincoln Archaeological Unit. Lincoln.

Trimble, R, 2002, 'Bunkers Hill, Lincoln (Area 5). Archaeological Excavation'. Unpublished report (No 476), City of Lincoln Archaeological Unit. Lincoln.

Trimble, R and Jarvis M, 1998, 'St Mark's Station, High Street, Lincoln'. Unpublished report (No 338), City of Lincoln Archaeological Unit. Lincoln.

Trollope, A and Trollope, E, 1860, 'Contributions to the History of Britain under the Romans. Roman inscriptions and sepulchral remains at Lincoln', *Archaeological Journal* 17, 1–21.

Trueman, M, 1994, 'The Electricty Industry. Step 1 Report'. Unpublished report, English Heritage, London.

Trueman, M, 1997, 'The Gas Industry. Step 1 Report'. Unpublished report, English Heritage, London.

Trueman, M, forthcoming, 'The Water and Sewage Industry. Step 3 Report'. Unpublished report, English Heritage, London.

Trunk, M, 1991, *Römische Tempel in den Rhein- und Westlichen Donau-provinzen*. Augst.

Turner, H L, 1971, *Town Defences in England and Wales An Architectural and documentary study 900–1500*. London.

Turner, J T, 1988, *'Nellie' The History of Churchill's Lincoln-built trenching machine*. Occasional Papers in Lincolnshire History and Archaeology 7. Lincoln.

Ulmschneider, K, 2000, *Markets, Minsters and Metal Detectors. The Archaeology of Middle Saxon Lincolnshire and Hampshire compared*. British Archaeological Reports (British Series) 307. Oxford.

Ussher, W A E, Jukes-Brown, A S and Stracher, A, 1888, *The Geology of the Country around Lincoln*. Memoirs of the Geological Survey 2. London.

Van de Noort, R and Ellis, S, (eds.)1997, *Wetland Heritage of the Humberhead Levels*. Hull.

Van de Noort, R and Ellis, S, (eds.)1998, *Wetland Heritage of the Ancholme and Lower Trent Valleys*. Hull.

Velay, P, 1992, *From Lutetia to Paris. The Island and the Two Banks*. Paris.

Venables, E, 1881, 'The dedications of the churches of Lincolnshire as illustrating the history of the county', *Archaeological Journal* 38, 365–90.

Venables, E, 1883, 'Notes on the portico of the Roman basilica in the Bail, Lincoln', *Archaeological Journal* 40, 317–9.

[Venables, E,] Precentor of Lincoln, 1883–4, 'The Vicars' Court, Lincoln, with the Architectural History of the College, and an account of the existing buildings', *Associated Architectural Societies Reports and Papers*, 17/2, 235–250.

Venables, E, 1884, 'Recent Roman Discoveries in Lincoln', *Archaeological Journal* 41, 317–20.

Venables, E, 1885–6, 'The recent discovery of the foundations of the apse of St Hugh's Cathedral at Lincoln', *Associated Architectural Societies Reports and Papers* 18/2, 85–96.

Venables, E, 1887–8a, 'The History and Description of St Swithin's Church, Lincoln', *Associated Architectural Societies Reports and Papers* 19/1, 22–32.

Venables, E, 1887–8b, 'A List and Brief Description of the Churches of Lincoln previous to the period of the Reformation', *Associated Architectural Societies Reports and Papers* 19/2, 326–354.

Venables, E, 1888, *Walks through the Streets of Lincoln. Two lectures delivered ... to the Young Men's Christian Association, on the Evenings of December 11th 1883 and December 11th 1885*. Lincoln.

Venables, E, 1891, 'Some Account of the Discovery of a Roman Villa in the Greetwell Fields near Lincoln', *Associated Architectural Societies Reports and Papers* 21, 48–52.

Venables, E, 1892, 'Some account of the Roman colonnade discovered in Bailgate, Lincoln', *Archaeological Journal* 49, 131–5.

Vergo, P, 1989, *The New Museology*, London.

Victor and Baker 1843, *The Lincoln Commercial Directory and Private Residence Guide*. Lincoln.

Vince, A G, 1990a, 'Dealing with 'Dark Earth': Practical proposals', *Lincoln Archaeology 1989–1990*. City of Lincoln Archaeological Unit Annual Report 2 (ed. M J Jones). Lincoln, 24–29.

Vince, A G, 1990b, *Saxon London: An Archaeological Investigation*. London.

Vince, A G, 1991, 'The Valencian Lustreware bowl', *St Mary's Guildhall Lincoln, The Survey and Excavation of a Medieval Building Complex*. The Archaeology of Lincoln 12/2 (ed. D Stocker). London, 88–91.

Vince, A G, 1993, 'People and places: integrating documents and archaeology in Lincoln', *Lincoln Archaeology 1992–1993*. City of Lincoln Archaeological Unit Annual Report 5 (ed. M J Jones). Lincoln, 4–5.

Vince, A G, 1994. 'The East Midlands Anglo-Saxon Pottery Project', *Lincoln Archaeology 1993–1994*. City of Lincoln Archaeological Unit Annual Report 6 (ed. M J Jones). Lincoln, 37.

Vince, A G, 1995, 'Approaches to Residuality in Urban Archaeology', *Interpreting Stratigraphy* 5, 9–14.

Vince, A G (ed.), 1993, *Pre-Viking Lindsey*, Lincoln Archaeological Studies 1. Lincoln.

Vince, A G and Jenner, M A, 1991, 'The Saxon and Early Medieval Pottery of London', *Aspects of Saxo-Norman London: 2, Finds and Environmental Evidence*. London Middlesex Archaeological Society Special Paper 12 (ed. A G Vince). London, 19–119.

Vince, A G and Jones, M J, *Lincoln's Buried Archaeological Heritage. A Guide to the Archive of the City of Lincoln Archaeological Unit*. Lincoln.

Vince, A G and Young, J, 1991, 'East Midlands Anglo-Saxon pottery project', *Lincoln Archaeology 1990–1991*. City of Lincoln Archaeological Unit Annual Report 3 (ed. M J Jones). Lincoln, 38.

Vince, A G and Young J, 1991–4, 'The East Midlands Anglo-Saxon Pottery Project'. Unpublished report, A G Vince Consultancy, 25 West Parade. Lincoln.

Vince, A G and Young, J, forthcoming, 'The Pottery from Excavations at Repton Church'. Unpublished report, Martin Biddle, Hertford College. Oxford.

Von Thünen, J H, 1875, *Der Isolierte Staat in Beziehung auf Landwirtschaft und Nationalekonomie* (3rd edition). Berlin.

Wacher, J S, 1975, *The Towns of Roman Britain* (1st edition). London.

Wacher, J S, 1979, 'Excavations at Lincoln, Second Interim report: Excavations in the Lower Town 1972–8 – Silver Street'. Eds. C Colyer and M J Jones, *Antiquaries Journal* 59, 81–4.

Wacher, J S, 1995, *The Towns of Roman Britain* (2nd edition). London.

Wacher, J S, 1998, 'The dating of town walls in Roman Britain', *Form and Fabric: Studies in Rome's material past in honour of B R Hartley* (ed. J Bird). Oxford, 41–50.

Wacher, J S, (ed.), 1987, *The Roman World*. London & New York.

Walker, J (ed.), 1991, 'Archaeology of the Fosse Way. Implications of the proposed dualling of the A46 between Newark and Lincoln'. Unpublished report, Trent and Peak Archaeological Trust, University of Nottingham.

Wall, T, and Swift, D, 1984, 'Stone Railway Sleepers at St Mark's Station, Lincoln', *Lincolnshire History and Archaeology* 19, 113.

Wallace-Hadrill, A, 1994, *Houses and Society in Pompeii and Herculaneum*. New Haven & London.

Waller, M, 1994, *The Fenland Project Number 9: Flandrian Environmental Change in Fenland*, East Anglian Archaeology 70. Sleaford.

Walthew, C V, 1975, 'The Town House and Villa House in Roman Britain', *Britannia* 6, 189–206.

Walthew, C V, 1983, 'Houses, Defences and Status: the towns of Roman Britain in the second half of the 2nd century AD', *Oxford Journal of Archaeology* 2/2, 213–4.

Walton, P, 1991, 'Textiles', *English Medieval Industries* (eds. J Blair and N Ramsay). London & Rio Grande, 319–354.

Walton Rogers, P, 1993, 'Textiles from the City of Lincoln 1972–1989'. Unpublished report, City of Lincoln Archaeological Unit. Lincoln.

Ward, A 1996, *The Lincolnshire Rising, 1536*, (2nd edition). Louth

Ward-Perkins, J B, 1970, 'From Republic to Empire: reflections on the early provincial architecture of the Roman West', *Journal of Roman Studies* 60, 1–19.

Ward-Perkins, J B, 1981, *Roman Imperial Architecture*. Harmondsworth.

Ward Perkins, B, 1996, 'Urban Continuity?', *Towns in Transition: Urban Evolution in Late Antiquity and the Early Middle Ages* (eds. N Christie and S T Loseby). London, 4–17.

Ward-Perkins, B, 1998, 'Cities', *The Cambridge Ancient History Volume 13* (eds. A Cameron and P Garnsey). Cambridge, 371–410.

Watson, B, 1992, 'The Norman fortress on Ludgate Hill in the City of London, England, recent excavations 1986–90', *Château Gaillard* 15, 335–45.

Watson, B, 1998, '"Dark Earth" and Urban Decline in Late Roman London', *Roman London, Recent Archaeological Work*. Journal of Roman Archeology, Supplementary Series 24 (ed. B Watson). London, 100–106.

Watson, B, (ed.) 1998, *Roman London, Recent Archaeological Work*. Journal of Roman Archaeology Supplementary Series 24. London.

Watts, D, 1989, 'Infant Burials and Romano-British Christianity', *Archaeological Journal* 146, 372–83.

Watts, D, 1991, *Christians and Pagans in Roman Britain*. London.

Watts, D, 1995, 'A Lead Tank Fragment from Brough, Nottinghamshire', *Britannia* 26, 318–322.

Webster, G, 1949, 'The Legionary Fortress at Lincoln', *Journal of Roman Studies* 39, 57–80.

Webster, G, 1960, 'A Romano-British Pottery Kiln at Swanpool, near Lincoln', *Antiquaries Journal* 27, 61–79.

Webster, G, 1979, 'Tiles as a Constructional Component in Buildings', *Roman Brick and Tile*. British Archaeological Reports (International Series) 68 (ed. A McWhirr). Oxford, 285–293.

Webster, G, 1980, *The Roman Invasion of Britain*. London.

Webster, G, 1981, *Rome Against Caratacus*. London.

Webster, G, 1985a, *The Roman Imperial Army* (3rd edition). London.

Webster, G, 1985b, 'Decorated Dagger Scabbards found in Britain', *The Production and Distribution of Roman Military Equipment*. British Archaeological Reports (International Series) 275 (ed. M Bishop). Oxford, 214 –9.

Webster, G, 1989, 'Deities and religious scenes on Romano-British pottery', *Journal of Roman Pottery Studies* 2, 1–28.

Webster, G (ed.), 1988, *Fortress into City*. London.

Webster, J and Cooper N (eds.), 1996, *Roman Imperialism: Postcolonial Perspectives*. Leicester Archaeological Monographs 3. Leicester.

Welfare, H and Swan, V, 1995, *Roman Camps in England*. London.

Wells, C M, 1972, *The German Policy of Augustus*. Oxford.

Westerdahl, C, 2002, 'Amphibian Transport Systems in North-western Europe: A survey of a medieval pattern of life', URL http://www.abc.se/~m10354/publ/amphibia.hbm.

Westlake, H F, 1919, *The Parish Guilds of Medieval England*. London.

White, A J, 1976, 'Archaeology in Lincolnshire and South Humberside 1975', *Lincolnshire History and Archaeology* 11, 55–64.

White, A J, 1977, 'Archaeology in Lincolnshire and South Humberside 1976', *Lincolnshire History and Archaeology* 12, 71–82.

White, A J, 1979a, *Antiquities from the River Witham. Part 1 Prehistoric and Roman*. Lincolnshire Museums Information Sheet, Archaeology Series No 12. Lincoln.

White, A J, 1979b, *Antiquities from the River Witham. Part 2 Anglo-Saxon and Viking*. Lincolnshire Museums Information Sheet, Archaeology Series No 13. Lincoln.

White, A J, 1979c, *Antiquities from the River Witham. Part 3 Medieval*. Lincolnshire Museums Information Sheet, Archaeology Series No 14. Lincoln.

White, A J, 1982, 'Roman Sculpture from Newland, Lincoln', *Lincolnshire History and Archaeology* 17, 80.

White, A J, 1984a, 'The Revd John Skinner's Tour to Lincolnshire, 1825', *Lincolnshire History and Archaeology* 19, 93–7.

White, A J, 1984b, 'Medieval Fisheries in the Witham and its Tributaries', *Lincolnshire History and Archaeology*" 19, 29–35.

White, A J, 1989, 'Post-Medieval pottery in Lincolnshire, 1450–1850'. Unpublished Phd thesis, Archaeology Department, University of Nottingham. Nottingham.

White, P R, 1989, 'Roads Replace Railways', *Twentieth Century Lincolnshire*. The History of Lincolnshire 12 (ed. D Mills). Lincoln, 103–133.

White, R H and van Leusen P M, 1997, 'Aspects of Romanization in the Wroxeter Hinterland', *TRAC 96. Proceedings of the Sixth Annual Theoretical Roman Archaeology Conference, Sheffield 1996* (eds. K Meadows, C Lemke and J Heron). Oxford, 133–143.

Whittaker, C R, 1995, 'Do theories of the ancient city matter?', *Urban Society in Roman Italy* (eds. T Cornell and K Lomas). London, 9–26.

Whittaker, C R, 1997, 'Imperialism and culture: the Roman initiative', *Dialogues in Roman Imperialism*. Journal of Roman Archaeology, Supplementary Series 23 (ed. D J Mattingly). London, 143–64.

Whitwell, J B, 1963, 'Archaeological Notes for 1962', *Lincolnshire Architectural and Archaeological Society Reports and Papers*, 10/1, 1–11.

Whitwell, J B, 1970, *Roman Lincolnshire*. History of Lincolnshire 2. Lincoln.

Whitwell, J B, 1980, 'East Bight, excavations 1964–66', *The Defences of the Upper Roman Enclosure*. The Archaeology Lincoln 7/1 (ed. M J Jones). London, 6–12.

Whitwell, J B, 1982, *The Coritani: Some Aspects of the Iron Age*

*Tribe and the Roman Civitas*, British Archaeological Reports (British Series) 99. Oxford.

Whitwell, J B, 1992, *Roman Lincolnshire*. History of Lincolnshire 2 (revised editon). Lincoln.

Whitwell, J B, 1995, 'Roman Small Towns in North Lincolnshire and South Humberside', *Roman Small Towns in Eastern England and Beyond* (ed. A E Brown). Oxford, 95–102.

Whitwell, J B and Wilson, C M, 1969, 'Archaeological Notes for 1968', *Lincolnshire History and Archaeology* 4, 99–119.

Wickstead, J, 2001, *C. Hodgson Fowler (1840–1910). Durham Architect and his Churches*. Durham.

Wightman, E M, 1985, *Gallia Belgica*. London.

Wilkes, J J, 1993, *Diocletian's Palace, Split: residence of a retired Roman Emperor*. Sheffield.

Wilkes, J J, 2000, 'The Danubian Region', *Roman Fortresses and their Legions* (ed. R Brewer). London & Cardiff. 101–20.

Wilkinson, K, Prosser L and Holbrook, N, 1995, 'The Origin, Development, Decline and Persistence of Cotswold Settlement, *c.*AD250–1200'. Unpublished report, Cotswold Archaeological Trust. Cirencester.

Wilkinson, M, 1982, 'Fish', *Animal bones from Flaxengate, Lincoln c.870–1500*. The Archaeology of Lincoln 18/1 (ed. T P O'Connor). London, 44–6.

Wilkinson, T J, 1986–7, 'The Palaeoenvironments of the Upper Witham Fen: a Preliminary View', *Fenland Research* 4, 52–6.

Wilkinson, T J, 1988, 'Early Settlement at Lincoln – The Soils', *Britannia* 19, 4–5.

Williams, D and Carreras, C, 1995, 'North African Amphorae in Roman Britain: a re-appraisal', *Britannia* 26, 231–52.

Williams, D and Vince A G, 1997, 'The characterization and interpretation of early to middle Saxon granitic tempered pottery in England', *Medieval Archaeology* 41, 214–220.

Williams, F S, 1877, *The Midland Railway: its rise and progress. A Narrative of Modern Enterprise* (3rd edition). London.

Williams, H, 1997, 'Ancient Landscapes of the Dead: The Reuse of Prehistoric and Roman Monuments as Early Anglo-Saxon Burial Sites', *Medieval Archaeology* 41, 1–32.

Williams, T D, 1993, *Public buildings in the south-west quarter of Roman London. The Archaeology of Roman London 3*. Council for British Archaeology Research Report 88. London.

Williamson, J, 1890, *A Guide Through Lincoln* (3rd edition). Lincoln.

Willis, S, 1996, 'The Romanization of pottery assemblages in the East and North East of England during the 1st Century AD: A Comparative Analysis', *Britannia* 27, 179–221.

Wilmott, T, 1997, *Birdoswald: Excavations of a Roman Fort on Hadrian's Wall and its Successor Settlements 1987–92*. English Heritage Archaeological Report 14. London.

Wilmott, T and Wilson, P R (eds.), 2000, *The Late Roman transition in the North*. British Archaeological Reports (British Series) 299. Oxford.

Wilson, C M, 1977, 'Fison's Factory Carholme Road, Lincoln', *Lincolnshire History and Archaeology* 12, 63.

Wilson, C M, 1977, 'Stamp End Lock', *Lincolnshire History and Archaeology* 12, 63.

Wilson, C M, 1980, 'Lincoln- Street Furniture of Motherby Hill', *Lincolnshire History and Archaeology* 15, 57–60.

Wilson C M, 1983, 'Stamp End Ironworks, Lincoln', *Lincolnshire History and Archaeology* 18, 116–7.

Winton, H, 1998, 'The Cropmark Evidence for Prehistoric and Roman Settlement in West Lincolnshire', *Lincolnshire's Archaeology from the Air*. Occasional Papers in Lincolnshire History and Archaeology 11 (ed. R Bewley). Lincoln, 47–68.

Wood, I N, 1987, 'The fall of the Western Empire and the end of Roman Britain', *Britannia* 18, 251–62.

Wood, I N, 1991, 'Internal crisis in fourth-century Britain', *Britannia* 22, 313–5.

Wood, J, forthcoming, 'The Sporting Heritage. Step 1 report'. Unpublished report, English Heritage, London.

Wood, K, 1981, 'The Roman Aqueduct at Lincoln: Recent Investigations', *Antiquaries Journal* 61, 107–10.

Wood, M, 1974, *Norman Domestic Architecture*. London.

Woolley, R M, 1913, *The Award of William Alnwick Bishop of Lincoln, AD 1439*. Cambridge.

Wordsworth, C and Bradshaw, H (eds.), 1892, *Statutes of Lincoln Cathedral ... Part 1*. Cambridge.

Wordsworth, C and Bradshaw, H (eds.), 1897, *Statutes of Lincoln Cathedral ... Part 2*. Cambridge.

Worssam, B C, 1999, 'Regional Geology', *The Corpus of Anglo-Saxon Stone Sculpture Volume V. Lincolnshire* (eds. P Everson and D Stocker). Oxford, 16–21.

Wragg, K, 1992, 'North-east Lincoln Mains Reinforcement'. Unpublished report (No 25), City of Lincoln Archaeological Unit. Lincoln.

Wragg, K, 1994, 'Site of Proposed University College of Lincolnshire, Brayford South, Lincoln'. Unpublished report (No 106), City of Lincoln Archaeological Unit. Lincoln.

Wragg, K, 1995a, 'Former St Mark's Station Site Lincoln. Sewer Installation'. Unpublished report (No 218), City of Lincoln Archaeological Unit. Lincoln.

Wragg, K, 1995b, 'Bishop Grosseteste College, Newport Lincoln'. Unpublished report (No 171), City of Lincoln Archaeological Unit. Lincoln.

Wragg, K, 1996, 'Principal's House, Bishop Grosseteste College, Newport, Lincoln'. Unpublished report (No 280), City of Lincoln Archaeological Unit. Lincoln.

Wragg, K, 1997a, 'Library Extension, Bishop Grosseteste College, Newport, Lincoln'. Unpublished report (No 262), City of Lincoln Archaeological Unit. Lincoln.

Wragg, K, 1997b, 'Land to the rear of 5 and 6 Eastgate: Archaeological Evaluation'. Unpublished report (No 300), City of Lincoln Archaeological Unit. Lincoln.

Wragg, K, 1998, 'Northern Subsidiary Sewer Scheme – Watching brief'. Unpublished report (No 340), City of Lincoln Archaeological Unit. Lincoln.

Wright, N, 1982, *Lincolnshire Towns and Industry 1700–1914*. The History of Lincolnshire 9. Lincoln.

Wright, N, 1983, *A Guide to the Industrial Archaeology of Lincolnshire and South Humberside*. London.

Wright, N, 1989, 'The Varied Fortunes of Heavy and Manufacturing Industry 1914 1987', *Twentieth Century Lincolnshire*. The History of Lincolnshire 12 (ed. D Mills). Lincoln, 74–102.

Wymer, J, 1999, *The Lower Paleolithic Occupation of Britain* (2 volumes.). Salisbury.

Yorke, B, 1999, 'Edward King and Martyr: A Saxon Murder Mystery', *Studies in the Early History of Shaftesbury Abbey* (ed. L Keen). Dorchester, 99–116.

Young, J, Hooper, J and Wilmott, A, 1988, 'Pottery from St Marks East', *Archaeology in Lincolnshire 1987–1988. Fourth Annual Report of the Trust for Lincolnshire Archaeology October 1988* (ed. E Nurser). Sleaford, 29–32.

Young, J and Vince, A G, 2003, *A Corpus of Anglo-Saxon and Medieval Pottery from Lincoln*. Lincoln Archaeological Studies 7. Oxford.

Yule, B, 1990, 'The 'dark earth' and late Roman London', *Antiquity* 64, 620–8.

Zebedee, D H J, 1962, *Lincoln Training College*. Lincoln.

Zienkiewicz, D J, 1986, *The Legionary Fortress Baths at Caerleon*. Gloucester.

# 16. Indexes

These indexes concentrate on the proper names of people and places. The first index deals with churches and parishes, buildings and businesses in the streets, suburbs and surroundings of Lincoln. The second index deals with people, past and present, and places outside Lincoln.

## Index One: Places in Lincoln (including Bracebridge, Boultham, Canwick, Greetwell, Nettleham, North Hykeham, Shellingthorpe)

*Boune Lane* 179, 221, 224–5, 232, 269
Bracebridge 187, 247–8, 267, 273, 297–8, 332–3, 342, 349, 355, 357, 364
Bracebridge Gas Works 355
Bracebridge Hall 248, 342
Bracebridge Heath 119, 347
*Bradegate* 220, 299, 334
*Brancegate* 252
Branston 247
Brant Road 365
Brayford 15, 25, 99–100, 184, 233, 238, 240, 244–5, 294, 312, 318, 326, 348, 351–3, 364
Brayford Head 100, 239, 242
Brayford island 35
Brayford North 228, 237, 239
Brayford Pool 15, 25–26, 40, 99–100, 116, 165, 167, 185, 187, 196, 204, 228, 235, 238–9, 241–2, 258, 267, 274, 281, 307, 323, 346, 348, 361, 364
*Brayford Street* 245
Brayford Wharf 16, 217, 237, 353
Brayford Wharf East 99, 240, 244, 292, 361
Brayford Wharf North 312, 352–5
*Brick Kiln Close* 322
*Briggate* 273, 284
Broadgate 48, 84, 87–8, 90, 93, 97, 186, 212, 232, 322–3, 331, 339, 346, 354, 357, 361, 368
Broadgate East 48, 86, 96–7, 194, 231, 233, 289
*Bromhead House* 317
Bromhead Nursing Home 367
Burgersh Chantry House 214
Burton Cliff 28
Burton Road 34, 152, 218, 220, 364
*Burtongate* 220
Burwarmote Court 169, 184
Bus Garage, Burton Road 364
Bus Station 100
*The Butchery* 346, 365
*Buttercross* 228
Buttermarket 346, 347
The Butts 335
*Butwerk* 156, 164, 167–8, 172, 183, 186–9, 194, 196, 198, 208–9, 218, 228, 230–4, 239, 241, 245, 249, 253, 261, 266, 269, 276, 287, 289, 297–8, 300, 303–4, 306–7, 314, 316, 322–3, 326, 330, 333, 335, 342, 365–6, 374–6

C & A store 100
*Calcroft* 241
*Calvecroft* 292
Canwick 20, 22, 25, 34, 121, 187, 242, 246–8
Canwick Heath Farm 20
Canwick Hill 220, 318, 334, 348
Canwick Road 349–50, 355, 357, 359, 364
*Carholme* 323
*Carholme Lane* 228
Carholme Road 188, 228, 230, 269, 323, 339, 350, 353, 355, 361, 362
Carline Road 230
Carmelite Friary 246, 301, 310, 311, 336
*Castello de Tornegat*, see Thorngate Castle
Castle 1, 62, 81, 159, 164–5, 166, 169–77, 179, 199, 201, 203, 207, 209–10, 212–3, 218, 220–1, 226, 253, 261, 266, 271, 300, 304, 307, 316, 318, 320, 335, 351, 367, 372, 374
Castle Hill 81, 169, 204, 212, 261, 263, 297, 312, 331, 365
Castle west gate 147, 174–5
Catchwater Drain 349
Cathedral 1, 4, 13, 17, 60, 62, 64–5, 79, 81, 144, 149, 159, 164–6, 169, 172, 176, 178–80, 182, 198–9, 201, 204, 207, 209–10, 212, 214, 221, 224–7, 235, 248, 253, 255, 301, 304, 307–8, 312, 317, 318, 323–4, 329, 330, 333, 336–7, 343, 356, 368, 372, 376
Cathedral Close 261

Cathedral Quarry 367
Cathedral School 182
Cathedral Street 194, 231
Cattle Market 360
*Cause Manor* 307
Causey Farm 332
Central Station 276
Central Library 183
Central Market 346–7, 351
Chambers' Foundry 357
Chancellor's garden 225
Chancery 254
chapels, see Congregational, Independent, Methodist, Presbyterian, etc.
Chapel Hill 348
Chapel Lane 43–4, 60, 147, 196, 199, 201, 204, 207, 210, 253
Chaplin Street 108, 132
Chapter House 224
Chartist Land Company 365–6
*Chiviotwall* 188
Christ's Hospital (Bluecoats School) 367
Christ's Hospital Terrace 179, 210, 260, 321–2, 367
churches, see under individual dedications
Church Lane 186, 220–1, 225, 227, 321
City Bus garage 364
City Hall 312
City Library 367
City School 367
City Steam Mills 361
Clarke's Crank & Forge 357
Clasketgate 28, 86, 90, 183–4, 194, 204, 207, 221, 230, 334, 343, 345–6, 350
Clasketgate gate 87, 183–4, 192, 232, 269, 274, 276, 304, 306
*Clay Lane* 228, 269
Clayton's (Claytons & Shuttleworth) 8, 342, 350, 355, 357–61
Clayton-Dewandre 359
*Clewmarket* 261, 263, 291, 297, 331–2, 374
*Cliffgate* 218, 220, 269
The Close 208–9, 211–12, 224–5, 232, 275–6, 296, 298, 304–5, 307, 310, 312, 316–8, 321, 323–5, 327, 330, 332, 335, 366, 374
Close Wall 169, 179, 182–3, 188, 212, 214, 224, 264, 300, 304, 309, 318, 322, 335, 368
*Clothmarket* 291
Co-op store 100
Co-operative Flour Mill 352–3
Cobb Hall 172–4, 177
*Coldbath* 266
College of the Vicars-Choral, see Vicars-Choral
Congregational chapels 369
Corn Exchange 346, 347
Corn Market 273
Cornhill 261, 347, 365
Corporation Electricity Works 355
Corporation Sewage Works 347
Cottesford Place 60–1, 80, 194, 196, 207, 214
County Hospital 367
*Cow Paddle* 269, 273
Croft Street 233–4
Cross O'Cliff Hill 272, 299, 334, 356
Cross O'Cliff Hill Brickworks 357
Crown Mill 352
*Cuckoo Pool* 17
Cuthberts Yard 44, 147, 152, 179

Danes Terrace 85, 192, 207, 253, 285, 295–6, 314
Danesgate 92, 192, 204, 214
Dawber & Co (brewers) 353–4
Deloraine Court 211, 309
The Depot 367
Depot Street 339

## Index Two:  People, and places outside Lincoln